CHAUCER

A TO Z

CHAUCER

A TO Z

The Essential Reference to His Life and Works

ROSALYN ROSSIGNOL

Facts On File, Inc.

Chaucer A to Z: The Essential Reference to His Life and Works

Copyright © 1999 by Rosalyn Rossignol

Facts On File, Inc.
11 Penn Plaza
New York NY 10001

Library of Congress Cataloging-in-Publication Data

Rossignol, Rosalyn.
Chaucer A to Z : the essential reference to his life and works / by Rosalyn Rossignol.
p.   cm.
Includes bibliographical references and index.
ISBN 0-8160-3296-3 (hc. : alk. paper)
1. Chaucer, Geoffrey, d. 1400–Encyclopedias.   2. Poets, English—
Middle English, 1100–1500—Biography—Encyclopedias.
3. Civilization, Medieval, in literature—Encyclopedias.   I. Title.
PR1903.R67   1999
821'.1—dc21   98-51842

Jacket design by Nora Wertz
Illustrations by Rich Rossignol

Printed in the United States of America

Hermitage VB 10 9 8 7 6 5 4 3 2 1

This book is printed on acid-free paper.

*T*his book is for my husband Paul and my son Richard.

Without them I never would have made it.

Contents

ACKNOWLEDGMENTS

Thanks are due, first of all, to Pam Wright, who literally found this project and talked me into doing it. I also greatly appreciate the support of Anne Baxter at Facts On File, whose gentle encouragement helped me through some of the most difficult hours. Bob Wolf was the best line editor an author could ask for. I also received tremendous support from Kevin Koch, my department chair at Loras College, who, when I was a newly employed assistant professor, helped me obtain release time to facilitate my work on this project. Another of my colleagues, Ray Wilson, assisted with the research on Chaucer scholars. Last but not least, I wish to thank my husband and family, whose patience and faith in me has been little short of miraculous.

INTRODUCTION

Popularly known as the Father of English Poetry, Geoffrey Chaucer has been praised and imitated by many writers of genius throughout the ages. William Shakespeare borrowed plots from Chaucer for two of his plays, *Troilus and Cressida* and *The Two Noble Kinsmen;* John Milton read him; Alexander Pope translated some of his work into the English of the 18th century; and William Blake created illustrations for *The Canterbury Tales.* Many notable artists have praised him, including Edmund Spenser, who called Chaucer the "well of English undefiled," and John Dryden, who, speaking of *The Canterbury Tales* in the preface to *Fables Ancient and Modern,* said, "Here is God's plenty." I, for one, have to agree with Spenser and Dryden. Chaucer has not only given us a wealth of intriguing characters and stories but also the language in which our literature is written, almost single-handedly rescuing English from literary obscurity. Following the conquest of England by William of Normandy in 1066, Anglo-Norman, a dialect of French, became the official language of the conquered nation. For the next three centuries, French dominated the court, schools and cultural life of England. By the second half of the 14th century, when Chaucer was growing to manhood, English had made great headway toward becoming once again the spoken language of all classes; literature, however, was still written primarily in French and Latin. Chaucer reversed this trend by bravely choosing to write poetry—even poetry intended for an audience of courtiers—in English. The success of his endeavors was so great that from that time forward English became, once again, the literary language of his native country.

For these gifts that he has given us, Chaucer deserves to be remembered and read—not only by students and scholars, but by all who enjoy great literature. It is my hope that this book, *Chaucer A to Z,* will enhance the experience of modern readers by providing important information about many features of the poet's life and work. In my comments on Chaucer's life and his texts I have tried to cover as much ground as possible without presenting an overwhelming amount of information or detail. Some of the interpretations offered are my own, derived from years of reading and graduate study; more derive from the work of two centuries of Chaucer scholars. I have mentioned these scholars whenever I took a specific idea from their writings, but have not provided the kind of detailed citations that would be found in studies intended primarily for an academic audience.

A NOTE ON THE ARRANGEMENT OF THE TEXT

For ease of reference, all entries are arranged alphabetically, hence the title *Chaucer A to Z*. Most entries on the literary texts are organized under two main headings: Summary and Commentary. When a name or term that appears within an entry appears in SMALL CAPITAL LETTERS, the term also has its own entry, where readers can find more detailed information on the topic.

A NOTE ON CITATIONS

All line citations are taken from *The Riverside Chaucer*, edited by Larry D. Benson (Houghton Mifflin, 1987), currently recognized as the standard critical edition of Chaucer's work. Translations from Middle to Modern English, unless otherwise indicated, are my own.

CHAUCER

A TO Z

abbreviato *Abbreviato* is a device derived from classical rhetoric that was commonly used by medieval writers as a way of indicating that some portions of a narrative—portions unimportant to the main point that the writer was trying to make—were being elided from his text. For example, in Chaucer's story of DIDO in *The LEGEND OF GOOD WOMEN,* when VENUS tells her son AENEAS how Dido became queen of Carthage, the narrator states that she "shortly tolde hym al the occasyoun / Why Dido cam into that regioun, / Of which as now me lesteth nat to ryme; / It nedeth nat, it were but los of tyme" (lines 994–97) [shortly told him all the reasons / Why Dido came into that region, / Of which matter I do not now wish to speak in rhyme; / It is not necessary, it would be a loss of time].

"ABC, An" One of the short poems attributed to Chaucer in the manuscripts, "An ABC," addressed to the Virgin Mary, is a close translation of a prayer from the medieval French poet Guillaume de Deguilleville's allegorical *Pèlerinaige de la Vie Humaine* ("Pilgrimage of Human Life"), first published in 1331. The poem comprises 23 stanzas, each beginning with a different letter of the alphabet, progressing from *A* to *Z;* there are no stanzas for the "modern" letters *j, u* and *w.* Each stanza contains a plea for assistance, usually in the form of mediation between the sinful narrator and God, so that the narrator may be forgiven and exempted from the punishment (condemnation to eternity in hell) he would deserve had Christ not died for his sins. Particular emphasis is laid on the Virgin's role as Christ's mother, and on the especially effective quality of her merciful intercession on behalf of sinful men. The poem is notable for its use of legal terminology, employing such words as *justyse* (judge, i.e., God), *assyse* (assize), *bille* (petition) and *aquitaunce* (acquittal) to describe the narrator's situation as if he were a plaintiff in a court of law. In addition to portraying himself as sinful, the narrator is also, like the speaker of 17th-century English poet John Donne's Holy Sonnets, characterized as one who flees from sin but cannot, without assistance, escape. Although the content of Chaucer's translation pretty faithfully preserves that of the French original, the English poet made some alterations in the work's structure to better accommodate his native tongue. While Deguilleville employed the standard eight-syllable line of French medieval verse, arranged in 12-line stanzas with only two rhymes per stanza, Chaucer reduced the stanzas to eight lines with a rhyme scheme of *ababbcbc.* His reduction in the number of words forced him to be more concise and, along with the additional rhyme, made it easier to render the poem in a language like English, which, because it lacks the standard inflectional endings of French, provides the writer with fewer choices from which to formulate rhymes. The poem survives in twelve manuscripts and a printed text, plus three fragments. In the surviving manuscripts it is titled "La priere de Nostre Dame" ("Prayer of Our Lady"). Its date of composition is unknown, but the poem is considered to be early, based on the heading in Speght's 1602 edition of Chaucer's work, which states that the translation was made at the request of BLANCHE, DUCHESS OF LANCASTER, as a prayer for her private use. In his recent biography of the poet, Derek PEARSALL suggests that it came out in the late 1370s, at a time when Chaucer had begun experimenting with iambic pentameter (a pattern of one weak stress followed by one strong stress, regularly repeated) in his verse. "An ABC" is the only thoroughly devotional work among Chaucer's short poems, although the Virgin is addressed elsewhere in Chaucer's work, in the "Invocation to Mary" of "The SECOND NUN'S TALE" and in the prologue of "The PRIORESS'S TALE."

Abigail (Abigayl) In the Old Testament of the Bible, Abigail was the wife of a wealthy sheep farmer named NABAL. When Nabal refused hospitality to a group of young men sent by King DAVID, David gathered his soldiers and rode toward Nabal's house, bent upon chastising the man for his insolence. Abigail, realizing what was likely to be the outcome of her husband's behavior, loaded donkeys with gifts of food and wine and met King David on the road. David accepted her peace offering and, when her husband died 10 days later, took Abigail as his wife. (*See* 1 Samuel 25:1–42). Abigail is alluded to twice in *The CANTERBURY TALES.* Both the old knight JANUARY of "The MERCHANT'S TALE" and Dame PRUDENCE of "The TALE OF MELIBEE" mention her as an example of a good wife because she saved her husband from the wrath of David.

Abradate (Habradates)   A king of Susa, the capitol of ancient Elam in western Iran. He reigned during the late fifth–early fourth century B.C. When he was killed in battle against the Egyptians, his wife, PANTHEA, killed herself with his dagger and fell across his body, mingling her blood with his before she died. The story appears in Saint JEROME's *Epistola adversus Jovinianum* (Letter against Jovinian). In Chaucer's "Franklin's Tale," Panthea is one of the virtuous wives whose example DORIGEN would like to follow when she is faced with the dilemma either of betraying her marriage vows or breaking her sworn promise to become the lover of the squire AURELIUS (lines 1414–18).

Abraham   A prominent figure in the Old Testament of the Bible, he was originally called Abram. God changed his name to Abraham, meaning "father of many," to signify that he would become the patriarch or father of the Jewish nation. He was married to his half-sister, SARAH. When Abraham reached the age of 85 and still had no children, he began to fear that he would not fulfill God's prophecy. His first child, a son by his wife's maid, Hagar, was born the following year and given the name Ishmael. His second, ISAAC, was conceived when Sarah was thought to be beyond childbearing age and born when Abraham was 100 years old. The story of Abraham's life is narrated in Genesis 11–25. Abraham is only mentioned once in Chaucer's work, in the Prologue to "The WIFE OF BATH'S TALE." The Wife gives his several marriages as an example to justify her own (lines 55–58).

Absalom (1)   A parish clerk and one of the principle characters in "The MILLER'S TALE," Absalom is introduced with a vivid, even flamboyant physical description. His curly golden hair fans across his shoulders. Together with his rosy complexion and gray eyes, these details suggest a medieval romance heroine rather than a hero. His dandyish character is emphasized by mention of his clothing: the red hose, white surplice and blue belt, and the shoes that have church windows carved into their leather. The comparison of his surplice to a blossom on a bough, and the information that he is squeamish about farting and fastidious in his speech, enhance the note of effeminacy. In addition to his position as parish clerk, Absalom also works as a barber, which in medieval times included bloodletting and administering other types of medical treatment. Absalom falls in love with ALISON (1), the young wife of the aged carpenter JOHN, and attempts to woo her with gifts and by serenading her with song. Alison, however, is in love with NICHOLAS, a young scholar who rents a room from her husband. Absalom is one of the key players in the poem's comic climax, where his squeamishness about bodily functions intensifies the hilarity of both of his visits to Alison's window, serving as coun-

terpoint to the sobriety of his revenge motive on the second visit.

Absalom (2)   The handsome and rebellious son of King DAVID whose life and tragic death are narrated in 2 Samuel 13–19:8. Chaucer mentions Absalom in the ballad that appears in the prologue to *The LEGEND OF GOOD WOMEN*, where reference is made to the beauty of his hair (line 249). Absalom is also referred to in "The PARSON'S TALE," where he appears in tandem with ACHITOFEL, King David's treacherous counselor, who turned against his lord to serve Absalom. Despite Absalom's rebellion, his father always sought to be reconciled with him. Absalom died when the mule he was riding ran beneath a low tree and his head was caught between two branches. Although he was still alive and the king had given orders not to harm him, Joab, one of David's followers, killed Absalom as he hung from the tree.

Academics   Name given to the followers of the Greek philosopher PLATO. LADY PHILOSOPHY refers to them in Book One, Prosa 1 of Chaucer's translation of *The Consolation of Philosophy* (*see* BOECE) when she reprimands the MUSES for seducing BOETHIUS away from the study of philosophy.

Achademycis   *See* ACADEMICS.

Achates   The armor-bearer and trusted friend of AENEAS who fled with him from TROY after the fall of that city in the TROJAN WAR. Achates is mentioned in this capacity in Chaucer's *HOUSE OF FAME* (line 226) and in the "Legend of Dido," which is the third narrative in *The LEGEND OF GOOD WOMEN*.

Achelous (Acheloys, Acheleous)   In classical mythology, Achelous was the river-god son of Oceanus and Tethys. He fought against HERCULES for the love of DEIANIRA and was beaten. When Achelous transformed himself into a bull, Hercules shamed him by breaking off one of his horns, thus bringing an end to the contest. The Naiads (water nymphs who presided over springs, streams, fountains and lakes) filled this horn with flowers and fruit, and it became identified with the horn of plenty. The battle between Achelous and Hercules is described briefly in *BOECE*, Book Four, Metrum 7, lines 43–45, and also, even more briefly, in the story of Hercules featured in "The MONK'S TALE." Both the MONK and LADY PHILOSOPHY, who relates the deeds of Hercules in the *Boece*, use his battle with Achelous to illustrate the hero's extraordinary strength and valor.

Achemenye   The empire of the Achemenides in Persia. In Chaucer's translation of BOETHIUS' *Consolation of Philosophy*, it is mentioned in Book 5, Metrum 1 as the country where the Tigris and Euphrates Rivers originate.

Achilles Son of Peleus and the sea nymph THETIS. When Achilles was a baby, Thetis dipped him in the river Styx so that he would be invulnerable, but she forgot about the heel by which she held him, an omission that eventually proved fatal. Achilles was the strongest soldier on the Greek side in the TROJAN WAR, but because of his anger toward AGAMEMNON, the commander in chief of the Greek forces, he refused to fight during a crucial period of the war, and the Greeks were nearly defeated. When he returned to the fighting he killed HECTOR, Troy's most valiant hero and King PRIAM's son. Achilles died shortly after when an arrow shot by PARIS, Priam's other son and the kidnapper of Helen (the event that caused the war), pierced his vulnerable heel. "The MAN OF LAW'S TALE" mentions his death as an example of one predetermined by fate and capable of being read in the stars. "The SQUIRE'S TALE" refers to Achilles' spear as a weapon which, like the sword given to King CAMBYUSKAN, could heal as well as harm (lines 236–40). CHAUNTICLEER, the noble rooster of "The NUN'S PRIEST'S TALE," and the BLACK KNIGHT of *The BOOK OF THE DUCHESS* both allude to Achilles' role as the slayer of Hector. His faithlessness to his lover, BRISEIS, is mentioned briefly in *The HOUSE OF FAME,* in the midst of a long catalogue of faithless men. Despite his considerable role in Shakespeare's play about TROILUS and CRISEYDE, Achilles appears only briefly in Chaucer's poem, although he functions significantly in the plot, slaying HECTOR (book 5, lines 1559–61) and Troilus (book 5, line 1806).

Achitophel (Achitofel) In the Old Testament of the Bible, Achitophel was the faithless counselor of King DAVID who betrayed his lord in order to serve David's rebellious son ABSALOM. When he fell out of favor with Absalom, Achitophel returned home, set his house in order, and hanged himself. Achitophel's role in Absalom's rebellion is narrated in 2 Samuel 15–17. The BLACK KNIGHT refers to Achitofel in *The BOOK OF THE DUCHESS* as an example of a great traitor (line 1,118). In "The PARSON'S TALE," Achitophel is an example of an evil adviser (line 638).

Actaeon (Attheon) The famous hunter who saw the goddess DIANA bathing. He was punished by being changed into a stag and torn apart by his own hounds. The narrator of "The KNIGHT'S TALE" spies his image painted on the wall of Diana's temple in ATHENS; EMILY, the maiden for whom two cousins, PALAMON and ARCITE, fight in this tale, also mentions him in her prayer to Diana to preserve her virginity. In asking that Diana preserve her "fro thy vengeaunce and thyn ire, / That Attheon aboughte cruelly" (lines 2302–03) [preserve me from your vengeance and your anger, / that Actaeon cruelly paid for], Emily reveals her view that marriage to either knight would be a kind of punishment.

Adam According to the Old Testament of the Bible, Adam was the first man, created by God to inhabit the Garden of Eden. His mate was EVE, whom God created to be a companion to him in the Garden. His disobedience to God by eating fruit from the Tree of Knowledge caused him and his descendants, the human race, to be dispelled from Paradise and to be subject to death. Adam's role in the Christian history of mankind is alluded to in many of Chaucer's works. "The PARSON'S TALE" tells the story of his creation and fall in detail as explanation of how sin came into the world (lines 320–35). Adam's story is the second of the EXEMPLUM-type tragedies narrated in "The MONK'S TALE." It follows the story of LUCIFER.

Adam Scriveyne The addressee of one of Chaucer's short poems, "CHAUCER'S WORDS UNTO ADAM, HIS OWNE SCRIVEYN." *Scriveyne* or *scrivein,* as it was variously spelled, is the Middle English word for scribe. In the seven-line poem addressed to his scribe, Chaucer rebukes him for the many mistakes he makes in transcribing Chaucer's work, and wishes that, if he doesn't mend his ways, he will develop an itching disease of the scalp to punish him for his negligence. Nothing is known about the identity of Adam, and it is possible that Chaucer could have chosen the name for its symbolic connotations, the biblical ADAM having been the originator of human error.

Admetus The King of Pherae, in Thessaly, who made APOLLO shepherd of his flocks when the god was banished to Earth and forced to serve among mortals in punishment for having killed the Cyclops. Because he treated the god with such kindness, Admetus won Apollo's lasting friendship. For this reason, when the FATES decided that it was Admetus' time to die, Apollo persuaded them to spare the man, provided he could find a volunteer who would die in his place. Unfortunately, his wife, ALCESTIS, was the only person who would agree to do this for him, and he was unable to prevent her from being taken to the underworld. HERCULES came by on the day of her funeral and, discovering what had happened, went down to HADES, conquered Death, and brought Alcestis back to her home. Although Alcestis is mentioned a number of times in Chaucer's work, Admetus' name occurs only once (as "Amete"), in *TROILUS AND CRISEYDE,* where it appears in a letter written by OËNONE from which PANDARUS quotes when he is trying to persuade TROILUS to take his advice on winning Criseyde's love (book 1, lines 659–65). In the letter, Oënone compares herself to Apollo, who, despite having discovered the art of medicine, was unable to cure himself when he fell in love with Admetus' daughter.

Adonis   A figure from classical myth, Adonis was the offspring of an incestuous union between Cinyrus, king of Cyprus, and his daughter Myrrha. Although himself a mortal, Adonis was beloved by two goddesses—VENUS, the goddess of love, and PERSEPHONE, the queen of Hades, the underworld or land of the dead. JUPITER resolved the conflict between the two goddesses by decreeing that Adonis should spend half the year with each. Accordingly, he spent the autumn and winter with Persephone in Hades; during the spring and summer he returned to the surface to be with Venus. In this respect his myth resembles that of Persephone, whose return to be with her mother, DEMETER, for the warmer half of the year also coincided with, and was considered to be the cause of, the coming of spring. Renowned for his great physical beauty, Adonis died while still in his youth, fatally gored by a boar during a hunting expedition. OVID tells his story in *METAMORPHOSES*, book 10. Two references to Adonis appear in Chaucer's work. In "The KNIGHT'S TALE," when PALAMON prays to Venus for victory in his battle with ARCITE, he asks her to help him for the sake of the love she felt for Adonis (lines 2224–26). In *TROILUS AND CRISEYDE*, TROILUS prays to her for inspiration and good luck on the night he comes to woo CRISEYDE, also asking this in the name of her love for Adonis (*Troilus*, book 3, lines 720–21).

Adoon (Adoun)   *See* ADONIS.

Adrastus   A legendary king of Argos and the leader of the group of chieftains who fought against the city-state of Thebes in the exploit that came to be known as the Seven Against Thebes. When the expedition failed, Adrastus escaped on his horse Arion. He then traveled to Athens, where he asked the noble THESEUS to help him persuade CREON, the ruler of Thebes, to let the defeated armies bury their dead. Theseus agreed to help him, and when Creon refused their request, Athens marched on Thebes. This story provides the backdrop for the beginning of Chaucer's "KNIGHT'S TALE" and his *ANELIDA AND ARCITE*, both of which were taken from the same source, BOCCACCIO's *TESEIDA* and the Latin poet STATIUS' *THEBAID*.

Adriane   *See* ARIADNE.

Aeëtes   In classical mythology, Aeetes was the offspring of the sun god Helios and Perse. He was king of Colchis when JASON came there in quest of the Golden Fleece. He agreed to let Jason attempt to attain the fleece, but demanded that the young man perform what he thought to be impossible tasks. These included yoking two fire-breathing bulls and using them to plow the field of Ares, which he then had to sow with dragon's teeth. Then he had to overcome the fully armed men who sprang from the sowing, and finally to conquer the sleepless dragon that guarded the tree on which the fleece was suspended. With the help of MEDEA, Aeëtes' sorceress daughter, Jason secured the fleece and stole away by night, taking Medea and Absyrtus, Aeëtes' son, with him. When Aeëtes pursued Jason's ship, Medea killed her brother, cut his body into pieces and threw them overboard, knowing that their father would pause to retrieve the pieces and give them a proper burial. Aeetes appears in *The LEGEND OF GOOD WOMEN* as one of the secondary characters in the story of how Jason wooed and then deserted Medea.

Aegeus   In classical mythology, Aegeus was one of the kings of Athens. After being married twice without having any children, he consulted the oracle at DELPHI. Not understanding the oracle's cryptic response, he proceeded to Troezen to get the advice of the wise King Pittheus. Pittheus gave Aegeus his daughter, Aethra, who had just been impregnated by Poseidon (NEPTUNE), the god of the sea. Aethra gave birth to THESEUS, who was recognized as Aegeus' son and heir. When Theseus grew up, he took on the responsibility of freeing Athens from the tribute it was required to pay each year to King MINOS of Crete. He promised his father that when he returned, he would hoist white sails on the ship to indicate his success. But he forgot his promise, and the ship returned with the same black sails with which it had sailed forth. Aegeus, watching from a rock in the harbor, despairingly hurled himself into the sea, which forever after was called the Aegean, after his name. In Chaucer's work, Aegeus appears as a minor character in "The KNIGHT'S TALE," where he is the only person able to comfort his son, Theseus, after the death of ARCITE (1). He does so by reminding Theseus that no man on Earth ultimately escapes death, and by comparing life to a pilgrimage (lines 2837–42). Aegeus is also mentioned briefly, again as the father of Theseus, in Chaucer's version of the life of ARIADNE that appears in *The LEGEND OF GOOD WOMEN* (lines 1944–47).

Aegidius, Saint   *See* GILES, SAINT.

Aegina   Aegina—Ennopye, as Chaucer calls it—is an island off the southeast coast of Greece. In the life of ARIADNE that Chaucer included in *The LEGEND OF GOOD WOMEN*, Ennopye is the island where THESEUS and Ariadne consummate their love as they sail back toward Athens following Theseus' successful encounter with the MINOTAUR.

Aegyptus   In classical mythology, Aegyptus was a king of Egypt. He fathered 50 sons, who married the 50 daughters of his brother DANAUS. All of his sons, with one exception, were slain by their wives on their wedding night. LYNCEUS, the son who was spared, was married to HYPERMNESTRA, whose tragic story Chaucer relates in *The LEGEND OF GOOD WOMEN*. In his version of the story, however, Chaucer reversed the names of the two fathers, giving Danaus sons and Aegyptus daughters, so that Aegyptus becomes Hypermnestra's father, who demanded that she poison her husband on the night following their nuptials. Because Hypermnestra disobeyed her father and helped her husband to escape, she was thrown into prison.

Aeneas A mythical hero of Troy and Rome. The offspring of VENUS and ANCHISES, he was cousin to HECTOR and thus a member of the royal line of Troy. He played a prominent part in the TROJAN WAR and became the leader of the Trojan survivors after Troy was taken by the Greeks. With a group of refugees, he set sail to find a place where they might settle, guided by oracles and prophecies from one country to another and watched over by his mother, Venus. In the course of his wanderings, he endured many trials and hardships, including the death of his father, Anchises, in Sicily. From there he was blown by a storm onto the coast of North Africa, where Queen DIDO of Carthage received and entertained him and his company. She fell in love with Aeneas; when he left her to continue his journey, she committed suicide. During the next phase of his adventures, Aeneas visited the underworld to speak with his father and learn the future of the state which it had been prophesied that he would found. Finally, arriving at the Tiber River in Italy, he learned by prophetic signs that he had reached the destination that the gods intended for him. He made peaceful overtures to the local king, LATINUS, who received him kindly, promising him the hand of his daughter LAVINIA. (Latinus had been informed, also by a prophecy, that his daughter should marry a stranger and that they would be the founders of a great race of people.) Another king, Turnus, claimed Lavinia for himself and led a war against Aeneas that ended in a duel between the two men. Turnus was killed; Aeneas then married Lavinia. He built a city, which he named Lavinium after her. There he reigned for the remainder of his life, after which he was granted immortality in heaven. The Roman poet VIRGIL (70–19 B.C.) brought together the various strands of legend related to Aeneas, and gave them the form they have possessed ever since, in his epic masterpiece, the *AENEID*. Through Aeneas the Romans traced their ancestry back to the Trojans; the Julian family, the Caesars, derived their name from Aeneas' son Iulus. In the *Aeneid*, Virgil portrays Aeneas as a just and pious man, devoted to his father and his son (both of whom he rescued from the burning city of Troy), faithful to his friends, peace-loving but a mighty warrior. In Chaucer's work he does not fare as well. In both *The HOUSE OF FAME* and *The LEGEND OF GOOD WOMEN*, as well as briefly in *The BOOK OF THE DUCHESS*, when Chaucer speaks of Aeneas it is in the context of his betrayal of Dido. In *TROILUS AND CRISEYDE*, Aeneas is also mentioned briefly as the friend of POLIPHETE, a man who had, in the past, harassed CRISEYDE with legal charges. No reference is made to his role as a soldier in the Trojan War, although according to Virgil, his fighting ability was second only to Hector's. In Chaucer's poem, that role is reserved for the hero TROILUS.

Aeneid An epic poem in Latin written sometime between 29 and 19 B.C. by VIRGIL. Composed in hexameters and left unfinished at the time of the poet's death, the *Aeneid* brings together the various strands of legend having to do with the Trojan hero AENEAS, making him the founder of Roman civilization. The work is organized into 12 books. In book 1, Aeneas, fleeing from the burning city of Troy, is cast by a storm onto the coast of North Africa where he is taken in by DIDO, the queen of Carthage. Books 2 and 3 contain Aeneas' account of the events, as he tells them to Dido, that have led him to her country. In book 4, Dido and Aeneas become lovers, but he abandons her when JUPITER urges him to set sail again so that he can fulfill his destiny. Dido then commits suicide. Book 5 recounts Aeneas' journey to Sicily, where he and his men engage in a series of competitions to commemorate the anniversary of the death of Aeneas' father, ANCHISES. Book 6 is the account of Aeneas' journey to the underworld and Elysium, where he speaks to his father and learns his destiny as the founder of Rome. Books 7 through 12 relate the fate of the Trojans as they reach the Tiber River and are received by Latinus, the local king. Other peoples living in the area resent the arrival of the Trojans and the projected marriage between Aeneas and Lavinia, Latinus' daughter. War breaks out, but the Trojans, with the help of the Etruscans, prevail. Chaucer summarizes the *Aeneid* in lines 151–382 of *The HOUSE OF FAME* to provide a context for Dido's lament, which is an important thematic component of his own poem about various kinds of fame, including reputation. In *The House of Fame*, Dido's suicide is largely a result of her having lost her reputation, and her knowledge that without it she cannot successfully rule her kingdom. The *Aeneid* is also mentioned in *The LEGEND OF GOOD WOMEN* as one of the sources Chaucer drew upon for the life of Dido that he includes in that work. In "The NUN'S PRIEST'S TALE," the lamentations of the barnyard hens when CHAUNTICLEER is seized by the fox are compared to the cries of the women of Troy when King PRIAM was slain (lines 3355–61), as described in the *Aeneid*.

Aeolus In classical mythology, the god of the winds. In his palace on the island of Aeolia, Aeolus kept the winds confined in a cave and compelled them to obedience. Those who desired the help of the winds would pray to Aeolus—as, for example, JUNO did when she desired him to create a storm that would endanger the life of AENEAS during his voyage from TROY after it had fallen to the Greeks. Chaucer refers to this incident in the summary of VIRGIL's AENEID that he includes in book 1 of The HOUSE OF FAME. In book 3 of the same poem, the goddess FAME sends for Aeolus to assist her in broadcasting throughout the world the various reputations that she awards to those who come to her court seeking fame. To fulfill that purpose, he brings two trumpets, Clere Laude (i.e., pure praise) and Sklaundre (slander), which he blows in accordance with her decision to award each petitioner either good fame or ill.

Aesculapius (Asclepius)   In classical mythology, the son of the god APOLLO and the legendary founder of medicine in ancient Greece. Aesculapius learned the art of healing from the centaur CHIRON and became a skilled physician, able even to restore life to the dead. So that PLUTO might not be deprived of the dead, Zeus killed Aesculapius with a thunderbolt. Apollo retaliated by attacking the Cyclops, the maker of the thunderbolt, and was in turn punished with having to serve time on Earth as a mortal. After a time, Zeus finally agreed to admit Aesculapius to the ranks of the gods. Aesculapius is mentioned in Chaucer's GENERAL PROLOGUE to The CANTERBURY TALES as one of the medical authorities whose teachings the DOCTOR OF PHYSIC had studied (line 429). Many medical books and treatises were attributed to Aesculapius in the Middle Ages.

Aeson   In classical mythology, the father of JASON. His half-brother, PELIAS, usurped Aeson's throne, but promised to restore it if Jason would bring him the Golden Fleece from the island of Colchis, a task that Jason promptly set out to accomplish. Before Jason's return, however, Pelias threatened to kill Aeson. Instead, he granted Aeson's request to be allowed to commit suicide by drinking the blood of a sacrificial offering. Another version of the story relates that Aeson was still living when Jason came back with MEDEA, and that Medea enabled him to regain his youth by boiling him in a mixture of magical ingredients. When Chaucer tells the story of Jason and Medea in The LEGEND OF GOOD WOMEN, Aeson surrenders his kingdom to Pelias after he has grown too old to govern (lines 1396–1405). This different version of the circumstances surrounding Pelias' rule appears in the medieval French version (*Ovide Moralisé*) of Ovid's METAMORPHOSES. Chaucer's version also omits the story of Aeson's rejuvenation.

Aesop   The legendary author of a collection of Greek fables. In ancient times various attempts were made to establish his identity as an actual person. Herodotus in the fifth century B.C. said that Aesop had been a slave living in the sixth century, and Plutarch, in the first century A.D. made him adviser to Croesus, the sixth-century king of Lydia. One tradition holds that he came from Thrace, while another that became popular in the Middle Ages traces his origins to Phrygia. The likelihood is that *Aesop* was actually just a name invented to attribute an author for fables centering on beasts. One of the earliest surviving editions of Aesop was compiled in the fourth century B.C. by the rhetorician Demetrius of Phaleron, but for the most part, until they were put into verse by the third-century poet Babrius, they were transmitted orally. They became known in western Europe through the 14th-century prose version compiled by the Byzantine scholar Maximus Planudes. A number of medieval authors adopted or were inspired by the works known as *Aesop's Fables*, including Chaucer, whose tale of CHAUNTICLEER and RUSSELL the fox (*see* "The NUN'S PRIEST'S TALE") is one of the finest surviving examples from the Middle Ages. Although it is uncertain exactly what source Chaucer drew upon for his fable, it bears a strong similarity to an Aesopian tale written in the 12th century by French author MARIE DE FRANCE, who, ironically, claimed to be translating from an English source. Another of Chaucer's works, *The PARLIAMENT OF FOWLS*, features animals (also birds) who talk and behave like people, but who belong to a different literary tradition, that of the debate poem, which commonly features animal antagonists. One of the earliest and most famous examples of this genre in English is the early 13th-century poem "The Owl and the Nightingale."

Affrican (Affrikan)   *See* SCIPIO AFRICANUS THE ELDER.

Affrike   *See* AFRICA.

Africa   Whenever Chaucer mentions Africa, he is referring to the northern coast of that continent, and specifically to Numidia (what is now eastern Algeria) and the ancient city-state of Carthage. Numidia was the setting for the meeting of King Massinissus and the Roman general Scipio Africanus the Younger, recounted in Macrobius' DREAM OF SCIPIO, a fifth-century Latin work that had considerable influence on Chaucer's early poetry. Carthage was the kingdom ruled by Queen DIDO, who fell in love with the Trojan hero AENEAS and then committed suicide when he abandoned her to pursue his destiny as the founder of Rome.

Against (Agayns) Jovinian   *See* JEROME, SAINT and JOVINIAN.

"Against Women Unconstant"   One of the poems that is not explicitly ascribed to Chaucer but about which there is little doubt of his authorship because of its similarity, in language, meter and subject matter to other short poems whose attribution to Chaucer is clear. Written in the French BALLADE form, it features three stanzas in RHYME ROYAL with a one-line refrain repeated at the end of each stanza. In keeping with the requirements of the form, Chaucer used the same three rhymes in all three stanzas without repeating any of the rhyme words (with the exception of the refrain). The subject of the poem is clearly identified by the title, which was supplied by W. W. SKEAT based on the heading in Stowe's 1561 edition, "A balade whiche Chaucer made ageynst women inconstaunt" [A ballade which Chaucer made against women inconstant]. The lover's complaint against his lady's inconstancy, or fickleness in love, was a commonplace of medieval lyric poetry. The comparison of the lady to a mirror which can take no permanent impression is interesting and also appears in "The MERCHANT'S TALE" to describe the women who pass through JANUARY's thoughts as he considers marriage (lines 1580–88). That image, however, as well as the others in this poem, was commonplace in such poetry of the medieval period. The poet's suggestion, in the repeated refrain, that the woman ought to dress all in green rather than in blue refers to the symbolic associations of these two colors. Blue, one of the colors in which the Virgin Mary is always depicted, was the color of fidelity, while green symbolized unfaithfulness (as well as, interestingly, fertility and the devil). The poem survives in three manuscripts and one early edition, Stowe's.

Agamemnon　In classical mythology, the son of the Mycenaean king Atreus. In his youth, Agamemnon and his brother, MENELAUS, were driven out of Mycenae by their uncle, Thyestes, who had murdered their father and usurped his throne. They went to Sparta, where Menelaus married Helen (HELEN OF TROY) and Agamemnon married her sister, CLYTEMNESTRA. Eventually Agamemnon returned to Mycenae, recovered his throne, and became the most powerful king in Greece. When Helen was abducted by PARIS (1), Agamemnon was made leader of the expedition against Troy. When the Greek ships had assembled to embark for Troy, they were delayed by a calm sent by Artemis, who was angry with Agamemnon for slaying a sacred stag. In order to appease the goddess, Agamemnon agreed to sacrifice his daughter, Iphigenia. The TROJAN WAR lasted 10 years. In the last year there arose a quarrel between Agamemnon and the warrior ACHILLES over the latter's captive (and lover), BRISEIS. The quarrel ended with Agamemnon taking Briseis and Achilles withdrawing from the battle. Later, Agamemnon returned Briseis to Achilles and urged him to return to the fight, but not until the death of Patroclus, beloved friend to Achilles, did Achilles do so. When

Agamemnon returned home at the end of the war he was murdered by his wife and her lover, Aegisthus. Agamemnon is mentioned briefly in Chaucer's TROILUS AND CRISEYDE as the leader of the Greek forces at Troy. In Chaucer's translation of BOETHIUS' CONSOLATION OF PHILOSOPHY, he is praised as the restorer of Menelaus' wife but criticized for the murder of his daughter.

Agaton (Agathon)　Presumably a writer, though his identity remains uncertain, Agaton is mentioned by Chaucer in Prologue F of The LEGEND OF GOOD WOMEN as the source of a legend recording the stellification of Queen ALCESTIS, who gave her life in exchange for her husband's (line 526). W. W. SKEAT identified Agaton with a Greek dramatist named Agatone, who is mentioned in DANTE's Purgatorio. The Latin author MACROBIUS, with whose work Chaucer was familiar, tells the story of Alcestis in his Saturnalia but does not mention her becoming a constellation.

Agenore's daughter　See EUROPA.

Aglauros (Aglawros)　In classical mythology, the sister of HERSE who was changed into stone by Hermes (MERCURY) because she attempted to stand in the way of the god's love for her sister. In TROILUS AND CRISEYDE, TROILUS mentions Aglauros when he appeals for Mercury's assistance in his attempts to woo CRISEYDE, reminding the god of his own passion for Herse (book 3, line 729).

Ahasuerus　A biblical character from the Old Testament. Ahasuerus was the king of Persia who married ESTHER. He was generally known for the vastness of his empire, his riches, his sensuality and love of feasting and his cruelty. The Book of Esther tells the story of how Ahasuerus banished his first queen because she refused to dance before a drunken audience at one of his feasts. Following a two-year search for a replacement, Ahasuerus chose Esther. She and her people were in Persia as a consequence of the fall of Jerusalem and the scattering of the Jews into captivity. One of Ahasuerus' advisors hated the Jews and persuaded Ahasuerus to order them to be wiped out, but before the plan could be carried out, Ahasuerus discovered that the Jew MORDECAI, Esther's guardian, had uncovered a plot to kill Ahasuerus and thus had saved his life. As a result of this revelation, Mordecai was raised to a position of honor in the kingdom, and the wicked advisor and his 10 sons were hanged on the gallows they had previously prepared for Mordecai. Historians generally agree that Ahasuerus is the same persons as Xerxes I (485–464 B.C.). Ahasuerus was murdered by a courtier and succeeded by his son, Artaxerxes Longimanus. He is mentioned briefly several times in Chaucer's work, twice in "The MERCHANT'S TALE" in connection with his wife, Esther, who is given as an example of wifely virtue. The aged JANUARY, who, after a long life of indulging his sensual appetite wishes to settle down with a young wife, includes Esther among a long list of women who served their husbands well, as part of his attempt to justify his own decision to marry (lines 1371–75). In "The TALE OF MELIBEE," MELIBEE'S wife, PRUDENCE, mentions Esther as an example of a woman who was able to give good counsel and to be a leader to her people (line 110). This is within the context of her efforts to persuade her husband to listen to her advice as he decides how to respond to those who broke into his house and attacked his family.

Alain de Lille   Known in Latin as Alanus de Insulis, Alain de Lille was born around 1128 in Lille, FLANDERS (now part of France) and lived until 1202. He was a theologian and poet (a not uncommon conjunction of professions in those days) so celebrated for the scope and variety of his learning that he became known by the epithet "the universal doctor." He studied and taught at Paris, lived for a time at Montpellier, and later joined the Cistercian monastic order at the abbey of Cîteaux. Alain wrote many theological treatises, including an argument against heresy and a collection of proverbs on moral conduct. The two works for which he received the most attention and which had the greatest literary influence in the medieval period were *De planctu Naturae* (The complaint of nature), a satire on human vices that especially targeted homosexuality, and *Anticlaudianus* (Chaucer calls it *Anteclaudian*), a lengthy allegory concerning the creation and perfection of the human soul that contains the curious image of the soul fastened to the body "with tiny little nails," ultimately derived from PLATO. Alain's conception of the goddess Natura (NATURE) in *De planctu Naturae* strongly influenced Chaucer's portrait of her in *The PARLIAMENT OF FOWLS*, where she presides over the mating ritual of the birds on Saint Valentine's Day. Alain's *Anticlaudianus* was one of the texts that provided medieval authors with a description of the heavens based on Ptolemaic astronomy (*see* PTOLEMY). Chaucer's narrator confirms the accuracy of Alain's model when he takes his heavenward journey in *The HOUSE OF FAME* (line 316).

Alan   One of the clerks of "The REEVE'S TALE." In Middle English, the word *clerk* denotes a church cleric or clerical scholar; i.e., one studying to be a cleric. Nevill Coghill's translation of *The CANTERBURY TALES* refers to Alan and JOHN THE CLERK as "biblical scholars" in the attempt to convey the latter sense. Alan and his fellow student are nearly indistinguishable. Neither one is described individually, and both of them, coming from the town of STROTHER in the north of England, speak with the same northern dialect. They are typical of their breed, Chaucer says, full of "mirth"

and "revelry." Their youthful high spirits in fact seem to provide the motive for their visit to SIMKIN the miller, where they hope to outwit his thievery by overseeing the grinding of their own grain. The tale takes some satiric jabs at the scholarly mentality, one of which is the ease with which the miller discovers their ruse and turns it to his own advantage, showing that, in the words of the miller, a scholar is not always the wisest man. The miller takes another shot at them when Alan and John ask him for lodging, saying that although his house is small, they can, by arguments of logic, change a space of 20 feet into one a mile wide. The only characteristic that distinguishes the two clerks from one another is that John seems to be the more cautious of the two, in contrast to Alan, who acts on impulse.

Alanus de Insulis   *See* ALAIN DE LILLE.

Alayn   *See* ALAN.

Albertano of Brescia   Thirteenth-century Italian author who wrote an influential treatise called *The Art of Speech and the Art of Silence,* which, among other things, instructed courtiers on how to deliver a diplomatic message. He also wrote the Latin *Liber Consolationis et Consilii,* which is the ultimate source of Chaucer's "TALE OF MELIBEE." Albertano's Latin work was first translated (and condensed) into French as *Le Livre de Melibée et de Dame Prudence* (The book of Melibee and Dame Prudence). Chaucer's version of the story is actually a fairly close translation of the French text. One noticeable omission that Chaucer made in adapting the work was to leave out a passage that speaks against having a boy as king. This helps date the tale's composition to sometime after 1376, when it was clear that the Black Prince's son Richard was going to accede to the throne as RICHARD II. Richard became king at the age of 10.

Albinus   *See* ALBYN.

Albion   An ancient name for Britain, probably derived from the Latin word for white, *albus,* and suggested by one of the island's geographical features, the white cliffs of Dover, which are sometimes visible from the coast of France. Chaucer uses the word once, in a short begging poem called "The COMPLAINT OF CHAUCER TO HIS PURSE."

Albon, Daun   Daun ("Sir") Albon is a name the Host (*see* Harry BAILLY) uses for the MONK in the prologue to "The MONK'S TALE" when he appears to be guessing at the man's first name. It is actually PIERS. The Host uses the correct name when he addresses the Monk in the prologue to "The NUN'S PRIEST'S TALE." Perhaps because Saint Alban was the first Christian martyr in Britain, his name became a generic one for monks in medieval literature.

Albyn Chaucer's version of the name of a Roman Consul referred to in BOETHIUS' *Consolation of Philosophy,* which Chaucer translated under the title *BOECE.* His actual name was probably Decius Albinus. In his attempts to tell LADY PHILOSOPHY why FORTUNE has turned against him, Boethius explains that he made himself an object of spite and vulnerable to attack by defending certain powerful Romans who had been accused of treachery and fraud against the government of THEODORIC, king of the OSTROGOTHS, who ruled in Italy from A.D. 493 to 526 after the capital of the Roman Empire had been moved to Constantinople. Albinus was one of the accused men whom Boethius risked his own reputation and life to defend.

Albyon *See* ALBION.

Alcathoe The hilltop fortress at Megara, an ancient district of the Greek city-state of Athens. The citadel was besieged by King MINOS of Crete when he attacked Athens following the death of his son ANDROGEUS. After having defeated all competitors in the Panathenaean games, Androgeus had been sent by the Athenian king, AEGEUS, against the Marathonian bull, and was killed. Minos won his war against the Athenians and imposed upon them the punishment of sending an annual tribute of seven young men and seven young women to be fed to the MINOTAUR in the labyrinth. Chaucer refers to the siege of Alcathoe at the beginning of the biography of ARIADNE that he includes in *The LEGEND OF GOOD WOMEN* (line 1902).

Alcebiades *See* ALCIBIADES.

Alceone *See* ALCYONE.

alchemy An ancient art or pseudoscience whose origins are murky but which may reach as far back as early Egypt or China. The principal aim of those who attempted to practice alchemy has generally been the same—to transmute base metals into gold by some kind of chemical reaction. Another goal that assumed some importance among practitioners was the discovery of an elixir that would restore a man's youth. Alchemy came to western Europe in the 12th and 13th centuries, mainly through the writings of Arabic scholars. The transmission of such knowledge was, however, intentionally rendered difficult by the use of symbolic languages and secret signs. In the Middle Ages and the Renaissance, swindlers who professed themselves alchemists would often use the promise that they were able to multiply gold to steal from people who were gullible enough to lend their gold so that it could be used in an "experiment." A similar scam is described by the narrator of Chaucer's "CANON'S YEOMAN'S TALE." Despite their failure to attain their ultimate aim, alchemists did contribute significantly to the future development of the science of chemistry by formulating the processes of distillation and sublimation and by inventing stills and furnaces.

Alcibiades Athenian politician and military commander of the fifth century B.C. who provoked the internal political conflicts that were the main causes of Athens' defeat by Sparta in the Peloponnesian War (431–404 B.C.). Strikingly handsome and intelligent, Alcibiades was as a young man attracted to the teachings of the philosopher SOCRATES, who was in turn impressed by Alcibiades' beauty and keen wit. The two men served together in the Athenian army, each courageously protecting the life of the other when he was wounded. As Alcibiades became increasingly involved in politics, however, he slowly abandoned the kind of intellectual integrity Socrates demanded in favor of political rewards. Although Alcibiades possessed great political and military abilities, his unscrupulous policy of self-interest made it impossible for the Athenians to trust him enough to fully exploit his talents. After the Athenian fleet was lost because it ignored his advice, Alcibiades took refuge in Phrygia with the Persian governor. However, the Spartans persuaded the Persian governor to have Alcibiades murdered. He was buried by his mistress at the risk of death. DORIGEN, the wife of ARVERAGUS in "The FRANKLIN'S TALE," alludes to the devotion of Alcibiades' mistress in her lament against the misfortune that has befallen her as a result of her rash promise to the squire AURELIUS (line 1439). She had promised to become his lover if he was able to move some rocks lining the shore on the coast of Brittany and thus make the return of her husband's ship less dangerous. When Aurelius accomplishes the feat, Dorigen compares her situation to other women whose faithfulness has been sorely tested and decides that she must commit suicide to preserve her honor. Like the biblical ABSALOM (2), Alcibiades became legendary for his beauty, and two of Chaucer's references to him are attributable to that. In *The BOOK OF THE DUCHESS,* the BLACK KNIGHT says that even if he possessed the beauty of Alcibiades (and the strength of Hercules, the wisdom of Minerva, etc.), he would still have loved the fair "White," the woman whose loss he mourns (line 1057). Alcibiades' beauty is also referred to in the *BOECE,* Chaucer's translation of BOETHIUS' *Consolation of Philosophy,* in which LADY PHILOSOPHY uses it to explain the superficial nature of physical beauty: "whoso lokide thanne in the entrayles of the body of Alcibiades, that was ful fair in the superfice withoute, it shulde seme ryght foul." (Book Three, Prosa 8, line 44) [whoever should look in the entrails of Alcibiades' body that was so beautiful on the outside, it should seem quite foul.

Alcione   *See* ALCYONE.

Alcmena   In classical mythology, the daughter of Electryon and Anaxo. Alcmena was married to Amphitryon, with whom she fled to Thebes after he accidentally killed her father. While her husband was absent from home, Alcmena was visited and impregnated by Zeus (*see* JUPITER) in the form of Amphitryon. As a result of this union she conceived HERCULES, whose birth the jealous HERA delayed for nine days. The night following the birth of Hercules, she delivered another child, Amphitryon's son Iphicles. CRISEYDE, in Chaucer's poem *TROILUS AND CRISEYDE*, alludes to Alcmena's tryst with Zeus at the conclusion of her first night spent with TROILUS. Perceiving the approach of the dawn which must separate them if they are to keep their love secret, she complains, "O nyght, allas, why nyltow over us hove / As longe as whan Almena lay by Jove?" (book 3, line 1427–28) [O night, alas, why will you not hover over us / As long as when Alcmena lay by Jove? (book 3, lines 1427–28]. Her complaint derives from a tradition of lyric dawn-songs, called "AUBES," or aubades, in European poetry.

Alcyone (Halcyone)   The daughter of AEOLUS and Enarete. When her husband CEYX failed to return as promised from a voyage to DELPHI, Alcyone said a prayer to JUNO, asking the queen of the gods to send her sleep and within that sleep a dream that would reveal her husband's fate. Juno sent MORPHEUS, the god of sleep, to animate the body of Ceyx, which then spoke to Alcyone while she was sleeping, telling her that he had been drowned and asking her to bury his body, which she might find washed up upon the shore. Overwhelmed with grief, Alcyone committed suicide by throwing herself into the sea, after which the gods took pity on the couple and changed them into sea birds. Since the wind-driven waves washed away their nests on the edge of the water, Zeus (*see* JUPITER) forbade the winds to blow during their breeding season, which lasted 14 days of winter. This is the origin of the term "halcyon days," which is sometimes used to describe a period of calm and peaceful happiness. In *The BOOK OF THE DUCHESS*, Chaucer's narrator reads the story of Alcyone in OVID's *Metamorphoses*. Suffering from sleeplessness which seems to have been brought on by lovesickness, the narrator decides to follow Alcyone's example in praying to Juno to send him to sleep, promising her a feather bed if she grants his request. Once asleep, he dreams of the BLACK KNIGHT, a man who, like Alcyone, is so overwhelmed by the loss of his mate that he seems on the verge of suicide.

Alcypiades   *See* ALCIBIADES.

Aldebaran   A reddish giant star in the constellation Taurus. One of the 15 brightest stars, it has an apparent visual magnitude of 0.86 with a diameter approximately 50 times that of our Sun. It is accompanied by a very faint red companion star. Aldebaran lies about 50 light-years from Earth and was once thought to be a member of the Hyades cluster, but in fact it is much closer. Its Arabic name means "the follower," and was probably chosen because it rises after the Pleiades cluster of stars. Aldebaran is one of the stars mentioned in Chaucer's *TREATISE ON THE ASTROLABE*.

Aldgate   One of six gates in the wall of the medieval City of London. On May 10, 1374, the mayor and aldermen of London leased a dwelling over Aldgate to Chaucer, rent-free, for life. Chaucer was in turn to keep the property in good repair and to allow entry for purposes of defense in time of war (the dwelling was actually built into the wall, and so formed part of the city's structural defenses). He was forbidden to sublet. This type of lease was not unusual, in that the city owned dwellings over other gates, which it sometimes leased to city officials. For example, Ralph STRODE, Chaucer's associate, had a similar apartment over Aldersgate. Chaucer probably attained the lease because of his family's longtime association with Adam de Bury, the mayor of the City whose name is on the lease, rather than, as some have suggested, through the influence of Alice PERRERS, EDWARD III's mistress, who owned some property near Aldgate.

Alecto   *See* ERINYES.

Alete   *See* ERINYES.

Alexander the Great   One of the most renowned military commanders in history, Alexander the Great was born in 356 B.C. at Pella in Macedonia, the son of PHILIP II of Macedon and Olympias. Educated by ARISTOTLE, he became king in 336 after his father was murdered. He led the Greek states in their war against DARIUS THE GREAT, king of Persia. After invading Persia and overcoming the Persian army, but without successfully subduing Darius, he conquered Egypt, where he founded the famous city of ALEXANDRIA, then returned to defeat Darius. Before his death in 323, he also conquered northern India. He died at the early age of 33, never having lost a battle in his entire career. He had significant influence on the development of eastern culture as he exported the ideas and ideals of Hellenistic Greece to those regions that he conquered. There are two versions of his death: according to one, he died of a fever contracted after swimming; in the other, he was poisoned. The brief biography of

Alexander included in Chaucer's "MONK'S TALE" (lines 2631–70) alludes to both. Alexander also receives brief mention in *The HOUSE OF FAME* and *The BOOK OF THE DUCHESS*.

Alexandria Seaport in Egypt, on the Mediterranean at the western end of the Nile delta. It was founded by, and took its name from, the renowned Greek military commander ALEXANDER THE GREAT, and became a center of Hellenistic culture. The city is mentioned several times in Chaucer's work. According to the GENERAL PROLOGUE to *The CANTERBURY TALES,* it is one of the places where the KNIGHT has been on military campaign. It is also mentioned in one of the minibiographies included in "The MONK'S TALE" as a city that was conquered by Petro, king of Cyprus (PIERRE DE LUSIGNAN). Its great size is alluded to in "The CANON'S YEOMAN'S TALE" when the yeoman says that the Canon he serves could "infect" an entire town, even one as large as Alexandria (or NINEVAH, ROME or TROY).

Aleyn (1) *See* ALAIN DE LILLE.

Aleyn (2) *See* ALAN.

Algarsif (Algarsyf) The eldest son of CAMBYUSKAN in "The SQUIRE'S TALE." Nothing more is said about him in the tale, with the exception of the final lines, in which the SQUIRE promises to tell the story of how Algarsif won his wife, THEODORA. The name apparently is derived from an Arabic star name.

Algeciras (Algazir) Located in the province of Cádiz, Spain, Algeciras is mentioned in the General Prologue to *The Canterbury Tales* as one of the places to which the KNIGHT (1) has traveled on his military campaigns (line 57).

Algus Arab mathematician who lived between 780 and 850 B.C. and who is primarily remembered for having invented Arabic numerals. Chaucer alludes to this fact in *The BOOK OF THE DUCHESS* when he has the narrator say that there were so many marvels in the forest he dreamed of that even the great mathematician Algus (Chaucer spells it *Argus*) would not have been able to count them all.

Alhabor The name assigned by Arab astronomers to the star more commonly known as SIRIUS, or the Dog Star, the brightest star in the night sky. Chaucer uses the name Alhabor to refer to the star in his *TREATISE ON THE ASTROLABE* (part 2, division 3, lines 41–49), where he describes its position in the heavens.

Alhazen Arab mathematician and physicist who was born around 965 in what is now Iraq. He made the first significant contributions to optical theory since the time of the famous Greek astronomer PTOLEMY. In his treatise on optics, translated into Latin in 1270, Alhazen published theories on refraction, reflection, binocular vision, focusing with lenses, parabolic and spherical mirrors, spherical aberration, atmospheric refraction and the apparent increase in size of planetary bodies near the earth's horizon. He was the first to offer an accurate explanation of vision, stating that light comes from the object seen to the eye. Alhazen is mentioned in the SQUIRE'S TALE when members of King CAMBYUSKAN's court are trying to figure out the design of the magic mirror that has been presented as a gift to the king's daughter, CANACEE (line 232). The mirror is supposed to be capable of foreseeing the future, but some people believe that its power arises from its optical design. Those who advance this theory support their opinion by referring to the authority of Alhazen, WITELO and ARISTOTLE, all of whom wrote scientific texts on the subject.

Alice (1) *See* ALISON (1).

Alice (2) *See* WIFE OF BATH.

Alisandre (Alisaundre) (1) *See* ALEXANDER THE GREAT.

Alisandre (Alisaundre) (2) *See* ALEXANDRIA.

Alison (1) The 18-year-old wife of JOHN THE CARPENTER in "The MILLER'S TALE." She is pursued by and falls in love with NICHOLAS, a young scholar who boards in her husband's house. The description of Alison is one of the most striking in all of Chaucer's poetry, playing off of the romance convention of providing a highly detailed portrait of the romantic heroine. This description departs from convention in its use of natural imagery. Alison's body is as slim and lithe as a weasle's, her apron as white as morning milk, her eyes as black as sloe berries. She is as pleasant to look upon as an early ripening pear tree and soft as the wool of a prize sheep. Her complexion shines more brightly than a newly forged gold coin. Alison is complicit in the trick which allows her to spend the night with Nicholas, her behavior fitting her description as a lusty young woman. She also possesses a lively sense of humor, which is displayed by her sudden inspiration to stick her bottom out the window when ABSALOM (1) requests a kiss. She is the only principle character in "The Miller's Tale" who is not punished for her misbehavior or stupidity.

Alison (2) *See* WIFE OF BATH.

Alison (3) As well as being the WIFE OF BATH's first name, *Alison,* or *Alys,* is also the name of her gossib (close friend), with whom she loves to walk about from house to house, hearing the latest gossip. (The word *gossip* actually derives from the Middle English *gossib*.) The name with its variants—Alice, Alys, Alisoun, etc.—was popular among members of the middle class during the time that Chaucer was writing, which perhaps explains why he chose to give it to several of his middle class characters, including the lovely young wife of "The MILLER'S TALE."

Alixandre Macedo   *See* ALEXANDER THE GREAT.

Alkaron   *See* KORAN.

Alla   Saxon king of Northumberland who weds CON-STANCE in "The MAN OF LAW'S TALE." Like most good-hearted pagans who come into contact with the virtuous and beautiful Constance, Alla is soon converted to Christianity. When he marries Constance, their brief period of happiness is interrupted by the machinations of his mother, DONEGILD, who disapproves of his bride, thinking her a "strange creature" because she is not of the same religious and cultural heritage. When Constance gives birth to a son while Alla is away from home, Donegild sends him a message saying that the child is a monster. When his reply asks that Constance and the child be kept safe until his return, she destroys that message and replaces it with forgery which orders that Constance and the child be cast out to sea in a rudderless ship. Upon learning what his mother has done, Alla kills her. His ensuing remorse leads him to make a pilgrimage to ROME, where he is reunited with his family, but again their happiness lasts only a brief time: Alla dies within a year of their return to Northumberland. The fact that he is reunited with his wife while acting in obedience to God's will contributes to the overall scheme of the tale, in which virtue is always (eventually) rewarded and sin always (rather more rapidly) punished. Alla is based on an actual historical figure, Aella, the Anglo-Saxon king of Deira in Northumbria (*see* NORTHUMBERLAND) who ruled from 559 to 588.

allegory   Literary term used to describe a story or visual image with a second meaning that is either partially or wholly hidden behind its literal or visible meaning. Allegory usually takes the form of personification in which abstract ideas or qualities are given human shape. Some examples of this in Chaucer's work would include the figures who inhabit the GARDEN OF LOVE in *The ROMAUNT OF THE ROSE*, such as the maiden named IDLENESS, who permits the lover to enter the garden, and MIRTH, who leads the dancing inside the garden. Allegory permeated the literature of the Middle Ages, in the realm of the secular and the sacred. It was a particularly important component in many of the dream visions written during the medieval period, including those of DANTE and William LANG-LAND as well as the *ROMAN DE LA ROSE*. Even though none of Chaucer's original works is pure allegory like the *Roman*, many of them feature one or more allegorical characters, such as the goddess FORTUNE in *The BOOK OF THE DUCHESS* (the BLACK KNIGHT states that he lost his queen by playing a game of chess against Fortune), the goddess FAME in *The HOUSE OF FAME*, and the goddess NATURE in *The PARLIAMENT OF FOWLS*. Philosophy takes the form of a wise lady in BOETHIUS' *Consolation of Philosophy*, translated by Chaucer, and Death appears twice in "The PARDONER'S TALE," first as a thief who has stolen one of the rioters' friends and then as a heap of gold coins. Some scholars have argued allegorical interpretations for other tales from the Canterbury group. Both "The CLERK'S TALE" of Patient GRISELDA and "The MAN OF LAW'S TALE" of CUS-TANCE may be read as an allegory of the soul's separation from and trial-ridden journey of return to God the Father. "The TALE OF MELIBEE" features such allegorical characters as MELIBEE's daughter SOPHIA ("wisdom") and his wife PRUDENCE, who are there to teach him the proper way to respond to an attack on his family. The five wounds sustained by Sophia in the attack suggest that she may be an allegorical representation of Christ, who, like Prudence, would advise Melibee to forgive his enemies and be reconciled with them. Finally, the animals featured in "The NUN'S PRIEST'S TALE," "The MANCIPLE'S TALE" and "The SQUIRE'S TALE" might be considered allegorical in that they are used to represent human behavior.

Allen, Judson B. (1932–1985)   Chaucerian scholar. While working on his doctoral dissertation at Johns Hopkins University, Judson B. Allen had the opportunity to study at Oxford University and made a discovery that led him to the work in which he would be involved for the next 20 years—the attempt to imaginatively realize the later Middle Ages. He became particularly interested in the question of the 14th century's uniqueness, pursuing this idea from as many different perspectives as possible. He coauthored (with his student Theresa Anne Moritz) *A Distinction of Stories: The Medieval Unity of Chaucer's Fair Chain of Narratives for Canterbury* (1981), a book that articulated the unity of Chaucer's poem in late medieval terms. Allen's most important book, *The Ethical Poetic of the Later Middle Ages* (1982), contributed greatly to our understanding of the relationship between ethics and aesthetics in medieval poetry, and to our knowledge of the degree to which contemporary literary theory informed medieval literary works.

Almachius   The Roman prefect who condemns CECILIA and her companions to death in "The SECOND NUN'S TALE."

Almageste Old French name given to the great astronomical treatise of the Greek astronomer PTOLEMY (Claudius Ptolomaios). The name is ultimately derived from the Arabic *al-majisjti,* where *al* is the article "the" and *majisti* represents the Greek word for "greatest." Ptolemy's work became such a definitive text in the field that the title was later applied loosely to other textbooks of astronomy. The *Almageste* (or perhaps the word is used generically here) is one of the textbooks possessed by the clerk NICHOLAS in "The MILLER'S TALE." The WIFE OF BATH claims to be quoting from the text in her prologue when she cautions her audience to be warned by her example in matters of love, saying, "Whoso that nyl be war by othere men, / By hym shul othere men corrected be." (lines 180–81) [He who will not be instructed by the example of others, / Shall be the example by which others will be instructed]. She quotes a second proverb, claiming the same source, later in her prologue when she says, "Of alle men his wysdom is the hyeste / That rekketh nevere who hath the world in honde." (lines 326–27) [Of all men, his wisdom is the greatest / Who never takes account of who controls the world—i.e., of what another man does]. Neither of these sayings was originally contained in Ptolemy's work, but they do appear in a collection of apothegms tacked on as a preface to Gerard of Cremona's Latin translation of the *Almageste.* The certainty with which the Wife attributes these remarks to the great astronomer may be intended to suggest that her knowledge of learned texts, a knowledge that she loves to display, is rather shallow.

Almena *See* ALCMENA.

Alnath According to Jacqueline de Weever's *Chaucer Name Dictionary, Alnath* is the name given by medieval star maps to the brightest star in the constellation Aries. The name may also refer to the first mansion, or house, of the moon. (In astrology, which in the Middle Ages was not considered a discipline distinct from astronomy, the heavens are divided into 12 parts by great circles through the north and south points of the horizon. Each of these parts is called a "house.") In modern astronomy, *Alnath* is the name given to the second brightest star in Taurus. The star is mentioned in "The FRANKLIN'S TALE," in which the magician from ORLEANS uses it to calculate the moon's position in order to perform the natural magic that will cause the rocks lying along the coast of BRITTANY to disappear (line 1281).

Alocen *See* ALHAZEN.

Alys (1) *See* ALISON (1).

Alys (2) *See* WIFE OF BATH.

Amazons In classical mythology, *Amazon* was the name given to a race of warrior virgins who in childhood had their right breasts cut off in order to streamline their bodies for the use of weapons. It was one of the 12 labors of HERCULES to obtain the girdle of their queen HIPPOLYTA, whom he killed. THESEUS also undertook an expedition against them and carried off Antiope, the sister of Hippolyta. The Amazons retaliated by invading Greece, but were defeated by Theseus in Athens. In another version of the story, Hippolyta was the one whom Theseus carried away and subsequently married. This is the version that Chaucer used in "The KNIGHT'S TALE," which opens with a description of how Theseus defeated the race of warrior women and took their leader as his wife.

Ambrose, Saint The son of a Roman nobleman, Ambrose was born in Trier, Germany, in 339. As an adult he was first a successful lawyer and then the governor of two cities, Aemilia and Liguria, in the Roman Empire. He became bishop of Milan, the capital of the province in which he governed, when the former bishop died, and he traveled to Milan to help ensure peace at the election of the bishop's successor. He spoke so eloquently to the crowd gathered there that they chose him, in spite of his reluctance, to be the next bishop. Despite his hesitation about assuming the post, he became an influential leader within the expanding church, encouraging the growth of monasticism and fighting hard against the resurgence of paganism and the popularity of heresies in the Western Empire. He also played an important role in politics within the empire, advising the emperors Gratian and Maximus and reproving the Eastern emperor Theodosius for ordering a massacre of thousands of men, women and children at Thessalonica as a reprisal for the death of a governor. Theodosius submitted to public penance, and as a result Ambrose is often pictured with the emblem of a scourge, symbolizing his power to bring the powerful to repentance. His other emblem is a hive of bees, suggestive of his eloquence and reminiscent of the tradition that when he was a baby a swarm of bees settled on him without doing him harm. Because Ambrose played an important role in the history of the church, he is considered (along with AUGUSTINE, JEROME and GREGORY THE GREAT) to be one of the four original doctors of the church. He is mentioned twice in Chaucer's work, both times in *The CANTERBURY TALES.* In her life of Saint CECILIA, the SECOND NUN notes that Ambrose wrote about the miracle of the crowns that were given to Cecilia and her husband in his preface to the canon of the Mass (lines 270–71). The last pilgrim to tell a tale on the journey to CANTERBURY, the PARSON, uses a definition of penitence taken from Ambrose's work to begin his own lengthy explanation of this sacrament (line 283).

Amete *See* ADMETUS.

Amphiaraus According to classical myth, Amphiaraus was the son of Oicles and HYPERMNESTRA. Gifted with prophecy, he took part in the Caledonian boar hunt and the expedition of JASON and the Argonauts when Jason went after the Golden Fleece. He is best known as one of the seven famous warriors who participated in the siege of THEBES aimed at helping POLYNICES, one of the sons of OEDIPUS, to take the Theban throne from his brother, ETEOCLES. Being a prophet, Amphiaraus foresaw disaster and at first opposed the expedition, but was convinced to support it by his wife, ERIPHYLE, who was bribed by Polynices with the gift of a magical necklace. Before leaving home, Amphiaraus made his two sons swear that if he was killed in the conflict, they would avenge his death by murdering their mother. Although he fought bravely at Thebes, the Seven were defeated, as he fled in his chariot the earth opened and swallowed him up. In the WIFE OF BATH's prologue (*see* "The WIFE OF BATH'S TALE"), the betrayal of Amphiaraus by his wife is one of the examples of wicked wives given by Alison's husband. His death following the siege of Thebes is mentioned twice in *TROILUS AND CRISEYDE* and briefly alluded to in the unfinished *ANELIDA AND ARCITE*.

Amphion (Amphioun) In classical mythology, Amphion was the son of Zeus (*see* JUPITER) and Antiope. Shortly after his birth on Mt. Cithaeron, he and his brother Zethus were abandoned by their mother, who was fleeing the wrath of her father, Nycteus. The two boys were raised by shepherds. On his deathbed, Nycteus made his brother Lycus swear to punish Antiope for the liaison that had resulted in her pregnancy. When Lycus found Antiope, he kept her as a slave for his wife. Eventually she escaped and went to Cithaeron to seek her sons' protection. At first they mistook her for a slave and were about to kill her on the orders of Lycus' wife, but when the shepherds told them the truth, they instead killed her aunt and uncle, who had enslaved their mother. After taking possession of Thebes, they set about fortifying it with a wall. Amphion played so beautifully on a lyre given to him by Hermes (MERCURY) that the stones moved into place of their own accord. Amphion later marred NIOBE. When their children were killed by APOLLO and Artemis (DIANA) because Niobe refused to honor the mother of that god and goddess, Amphion committed suicide. ARCITE and PALAMON, the two protagonists of "The KNIGHT'S TALE," are descended from Amphion (line 1546). In "The MERCHANT'S TALE," the music at JANUARY's wedding is compared to that which, in ancient times, had issued from Amphion's instrument (line 1716). The MANCIPLE's tale of Phoebus (APOLLO) and his CROW describes Apollo's musical ability as being twice that of Amphion of Thebes (line 116).

Amphiorax *See* AMPHIARAUS.

Anaxagoras Born around 500 B.C. in Anatolia, Anaxagoras was a Greek philosopher of nature remembered primarily for his cosmology and for his discovery of the true cause of eclipses. Around 480 B.C., Anaxagoras moved to Athens, which was then becoming the center of Greek culture. He brought with him the new practice of philosophy and the spirit of scientific inquiry. After living and studying in Athens for 30 years, he was prosecuted on a charge of impiety for asserting that the sun is an incandescent stone somewhat larger than the region of the Greek Peloponnesus. Although Pericles, who was the ruler of Athens at that time, managed to save his life, Anaxagoras was compelled to spend his last years in exile. In the *BOECE*, Chaucer's translation of the *Consolation of Philosophy*, Lady PHILOSOPHY mentions Anaxagoras among her examples of men who, like BOETHIUS, have suffered on her behalf. Boethius, like Anaxagoras, was exiled (Book one, Prosa 1, line 54).

Anchises In classical mythology, Anchises was the father of the famous Trojan hero AENEAS. The son of the king of the Dardanians, he was approached by Aphrodite (VENUS) as he attended his cattle on the slopes of Mt. Ida. The goddess appeared to him in the form of a mortal woman but later revealed her true identity, at the same time making him promise to keep their relationship a secret. Once, when wine had loosened his tongue, Anchises boasted of his affair with the goddess and was blasted by a thunderbolt. At the fall of Troy, Aeneas carried Anchises, now an old and helpless man, on his shoulders out of the city and took him along on his long wanderings in search of a place to settle. On all occasions of doubt, Aeneas turned to his father for advice, relying on his experience, judgment and wisdom. Before they reached their ultimate destination, Anchises died and was buried in Sicily. After landing in Italy, Aeneas descended into the underworld to consult his father about the future. Anchises is mentioned as the father of Aeneas in *The HOUSE OF FAME*, which summarizes part of Aeneas' adventures after he left Troy, and in *The LEGEND OF GOOD WOMEN* which contains a brief biography of DIDO, queen of Carthage, who fell in love with Aeneas.

Androgeus In classical mythology, Androgeus was the son of King MINOS of Crete. He attended school in Athens, where he also participated in the Panathenaean games. After Androgeus had defeated all other competitors in the games, AEGEUS, the king of Athens, sent him against the Marathonian bull, and Androgeus was killed. In revenge, his father waged a successful war against the Athenians and imposed a tribute on them that required that every year they send seven young men and seven young women to Crete, where they were sacrificed to the MINOTAUR in the labyrinth. Androgeus' death is mentioned at the opening of ARIADNE's biography in *The LEGEND OF GOOD WOMEN* because of its role in precipitating the journey of THESEUS to Crete, where he met Ariadne.

Andromache (Andromacha) In classical mythology, Andromache was the wife of HECTOR of Troy. The day before her husband was killed in the TROJAN WAR, she dreamed of his death and tried to persuade him not to attend the battle. On the following day, when he was slain and dragged through the dust by ACHILLES, she tried to hurl herself down from the wall but was prevented from doing so by her friends. Her son was also killed in the fall of Troy, and she was led away as a captive by Achilles' son, Neoptolemus, whom she later married. CHAUNTICLEER, the noble rooster who himself has a prophetic dream in "The NUN'S PRIEST'S TALE," cites Andromache's dream as support for his belief that one ought to heed such nocturnal warnings (line 3141). His wife, PERTELOTE, ridicules his concern, but it turns out that his dream was accurate.

Anelida A wholly fictional (as far as anyone knows) queen of ARMENIA who falls in love with, and is betrayed by, a false knight named ARCITE (2) in Chaucer's unfinished poem *ANELIDA AND ARCITE*. Her love complaint, contained within the poem, is Chaucer's most metrically and structurally sophisticated work, although the poem as a whole is one of his least successful.

Anelida and Arcite A short unfinished poem that treats subject matter that Chaucer later was to use more successfully in "The KNIGHT'S TALE" in *The CANTERBURY TALES*. The background sources of both works were the *THEBAID* of STATIUS and BOCCACCIO's *TESEIDA*, although the love affair between ANELIDA and ARCITE (2) is Chaucer's own invention. The form of the poem, with its combination of narrative and lyric love complaint, is French.

SUMMARY

The poem begins with a joint invocation to MARS (1), the god of war, and to POLYHYMNIA, the muse of sacred song, to assist the poet with his composition as he attempts to render in English the old Latin story of Queen Anelida and the false Arcite (2) before the passage of time puts it beyond all memory. The story itself opens with a Latin epigraph from STATIUS' *THEBAID* that announces that THESEUS, following the fierce battle with the Scythians, drew near to his native land in a laureled chariot, with the applause of happy people echoing to the heavens. Chaucer's first stanzas repeat and elaborate on this homecoming event, describing it in

greater detail and mentioning that Theseus has brought with him HIPPOLYTA, queen of the conquered AMAZONS and now his wife, and her sister, the fair EMILY. At the conclusion of that description, the narrator says he will now speak of Anelida and Arcite. First, he provides a brief summary of the war between GREECE and THEBES in order to explain how Anelida, queen of ARMENIA, came to be residing in the city of Thebes. (The relationship between the opening story of Theseus' triumphant return to ATHENS and the story of the two lovers who live in Thebes is never made clear in this unfinished poem.) Young, beautiful and steadfast, Queen Anelida has many admirers. Arcite, a young Theban knight who, we learn immediately, is deceitful in matters of the heart, uses his cunning to win the heart of Anelida, who loves him tenderly and honors him as if he were a king. While Anelida hides nothing from Arcite, even letting him read letters sent by other admirers before she burned them, Arcite is both untruthful and manipulative. Before long he grows tired of Anelida and begins to court another lady. To hide his own betrayal, he accuses Anelida of being unfaithful, making it appear to be her fault that he leaves her. The remainder of the poem describes Anelida's terrible suffering and narrates a plaintive letter she wrote to Arcite. The letter alternates between anger and condemnation of his behavior on the one hand and expressions of her continuing love and desire for his return on the other. The poem breaks off, unfinished, shortly after the conclusion of the complaint, saying that after completing her letter, Anelida fainted, and upon arising, went to the temple of MARS to perform a sacrifice.

COMMENTARY

Anelida and Arcite is generally considered to be Chaucer's first attempt to use material from Boccaccio's *Teseida*. What exists of the poem is divided into four parts: the Invocation, the Story, the Complaint of Anelida and the Story Continued. The Complaint, which relates Anelida's response to Arcite's betrayal, is considered structurally and metrically to be Chaucer's most complex surviving work, mimicking the form of the Pindaric Ode in its divisions into Proem, Strophe, Antistrophe and Conclusion. The content of the complaint is equally sophisticated, tracing with intense psychological realism the ebb and flow of emotions experienced by an abandoned lover who is unable to help herself because she cannot control the feelings or behavior of the man who has deserted her. Outside of the complaint, the poem is rather disappointing and even confusing, especially in the rough transition of scene from Theseus' triumphant reentry into Athens to Thebes, where the love story is set. As a solution to this puzzle, some readers have suggested that a stanza that would have effected the transition is missing. In theme, this poem is very similar to the brief biographies contained in Chaucer's *The LEGEND OF GOOD WOMEN*, each of which describes the life of a woman who was betrayed by the man she loved. The story of the deserted falcon in "The SQUIRE'S TALE" (one of *The CANTERBURY TALES*) has even more specific similarities to Anelida's situation. The opening description of Theseus' return to Athens with his queen Hippolyta and her sister Emily appears again in "The KNIGHT'S TALE." A knight named ARCITE (1) is also a character in the latter tale, but he is nothing like the Arcite of *Anelida and Arcite*. Although Chaucer does not mention the *Anelida* in lists of his own works, it is ascribed to him in three manuscripts and by John LYDGATE, so the evidence in favor of its authenticity is fairly strong. The date of the poem's composition is a lot less certain, although many scholars agree that it was probably composed sometime in the mid- to late 1370s (around the time of *The HOUSE OF FAME*).

Angelus ad virginem　Song sung by the clerk NICHOLAS in "The MILLER'S TALE." The Latin words mean "the angel to the Virgin (Mary)," and are actually the first three words of a song on the Annunciation. The mention of the song in the context of the MILLER's bawdy story has led some critics to suggest that the tale itself contains an extensive parody of the Annunciation, with Nicholas in the role of the angel Gabriel and JOHN THE CARPENTER in the role of Joseph the carpenter, whose unfaithful wife convinces him that the man she is cheating with is really an angel. This interpretation seems a bit of an exaggeration, especially considering that John's wife, ALISON (1), who has an affair with Nicholas, never makes any such claim about her lover. Still, Nicholas' sham spirituality and John's profession do give ironic potential to the song's use in this context.

Anglo-French　*See* ANGLO-NORMAN.

Anglo-Norman　Term denoting the French language as it was spoken and written in the British Isles from the Norman Conquest (1066) until the 14th century. A western dialect of French transplanted to Britain, it rapidly developed characteristics which distinguished it from the type of French spoken in the land of its origin. During the later medieval period, Anglo-Norman began to be replaced by continental French, which was studied by members of the nobility, some clergy and some members of the middle class (such as merchants). By the end of the 15th century, both Anglo-Norman and French virtually had been replaced by English, even in the realms of government and literature. Chaucer's decision to write in English was both a

result of, and a contributor to, this trend, but the French heritage of the Conquest also impacted his poetry. A substantial number of French-derived words and phrases that later became part of the English language are first recorded in his work.

Anglo-Norman Chronicle　A medieval "history" extending from the Creation to A.D. 1285. The word *history* is put in quotation marks here because, in the Middle Ages, fact and fiction were not distinctly separate categories, but rather existed at the two extremes of a single continuum. For that reason, fabulous stories such as those contained in Greek myths could be considered, and recorded, as history, alongside an event that happened during the reign of a contemporary king. Written by Nicholas TRIVET, who thrived around the end of the 13th century, the *Anglo-Norman Chronicle* is a perfect example of how the two came together. This chronicle is the source for Chaucer's story of Custance (CONSTANCE), which is related in "The MAN OF LAW'S TALE." The story of Constance demonstrates how fact and legend often came together in the same story. Constance was in fact Constantia, daughter of the Byzantine emperor Tiberius Constantinus. Maricius Flavius, who succeeded Tiberius as emperor, was historically Constantia's husband rather than her son, as he is recorded being in Trivet's (and Chaucer's) version.

Anne (Anna)　In VIRGIL's *AENEID*, Anne was the sister of Queen DIDO of Carthage. During AENEAS' stay in Carthage, Anne functioned as Dido's confidante, advising the queen to give in to her feelings for the wandering adventurer, since she felt no attraction to any of her other suitors. Following Anne's advice, the two soon became lovers, but shortly afterward Aeneas abandoned Dido to continue pursuing his destiny. After Dido's death, Anne traveled to Lavinium in ITALY and was hospitably received by Aeneas. Threatened by the jealousy of his wife, LAVINIA, and warned by Dido in a dream, Anne committed suicide by throwing herself into a river. In the *HOUSE OF FAME*, Dido blames Anne for the pain she suffers following Aeneas' departure (line 367). In *The LEGEND OF GOOD WOMEN*, Dido confesses her love for Aeneas to Anne and takes her advice (lines 1170–85).

Anne, Saint　The mother of the Virgin Mary. Although the Bible makes no mention of Anne and her husband, Joachim (also a saint), they have been honored by the Christian church since its early days. Anne is usually represented teaching her little daughter to read the Scriptures. Saint Anne is briefly mentioned in "The MAN OF LAW'S TALE," "The FRIAR'S TALE" and the Invocation to Mary contained in the prologue of "The SECOND NUN'S TALE."

Anne of Bohemia The sister of the duke of Luxembourg. When her brother was elected to succeed their father Charles IV as Holy Roman Emperor, she became a candidate in the search for a bride for King RICHARD II. The political goal of the match was to provide England with yet another ally against France. A marriage settlement was signed in May 1381 and Anne became queen of England on January 14, 1382. The pair were married in the chapel of the palace at Westminster, and she was then crowned by the archbishop of Canterbury. Richard had just turned 15; Anne was 16. There is some evidence that Chaucer's poem *The PARLIAMENT OF FOWLS* may have been written to celebrate either the engagement or the marriage itself. The marriage was not at first, however, looked upon very positively because of the high price that the English government had paid for the marriage agreement. But Anne's good nature and benevolence won the English people over nearly as quickly as she won Richard's heart, and she soon became known as "Good Queen Anne." Despite the fact that they had no children together to furnish Richard with an heir (something which, at this time, would have been considered the woman's fault), the king is said to have loved her deeply and, until her early death in 1394 at the age of 28, they were rarely separated. Although there is no evidence that Chaucer was intimately associated with either Richard or his queen, the poet specifically dedicated one version of *The LEGEND OF GOOD WOMEN* to her, with these lines appearing in the F prologue: "And whan this book ys maad, give it the quene, / On my byhalf, at Eltham or at Sheene." (lines 496–97) [And when this book is finished, give it to the queen, / At Eltham or at Sheen, on my behalf]. John LYDGATE in his work *The Fall of Princes* likewise noted that Chaucer wrote the *Legend* at the request of Queen Anne, which supports the authenticity of the dedication. The disappearance of these lines from the G version of the prologue may have occurred because Chaucer wanted to avoid any reference to Anne after her death. Richard was so stricken with grief when she died that he ordered the palace at Sheen completely demolished so that he would not be reminded of her.

Anselm, Saint Roman Catholic theologian, after his death named a saint of the church. Anselm was born in 1033 in the northern Italian town of Aosta. In 1093 he traveled to England and was appointed archbishop of Canterbury by William Rufus (son of William the Conqueror). Anselm reluctantly accepted the office but withdrew to Rome four years later when the king began to tyrannize over his authority. He returned to England at the accession of Henry I. Anselm wrote many theological and philosophical works and was the cornerstone of the Augustinian (*see* AUGUSTINE, SAINT) tradition in the Middle Ages, with its emphasis on faith in the search for reason. The PARSON of Chaucer's "PARSON'S TALE" quotes from the work of Anselm in describing what the anguish of the unredeemed will be like on Judgment Day (lines 169–70).

Antaeus In classical mythology, Antaeus was a giant who could not be conquered so long as he remained in contact with the earth from which he gained his strength (Gaea, the earth goddess, was his mother). HERCULES lifted and held him off the ground and was thus able to strangle him to death. This incident is mentioned as an episode in the life of Hercules in Chaucer's "MONK'S TALE." The same event is alluded to in Chaucer's translation of BOETHIUS' *Consolation of Philosophy*, where Hercules is given as an example of a man who, despite his great strength and abilities, was at last, like all men, overcome by death.

Anteclaudian *See* ALAIN DE LILLE.

Antecrist *See* ANTICHRIST.

Antenor In classical mythology, Antenor was the brother of HECUBA, queen of Troy. Antenor opposed the war with Greece and from the beginning advised returning HELEN to her husband, MENELAUS. When the Greeks first landed, Antenor saved their ambassadors from being treacherously killed by his countrymen, and in the last year of the war he protested the breaking of a truce by the Trojans and still proposed the voluntary return of Helen. The Greeks spared him at the sack of Troy, and he and his wife, a priestess of Athena (*see* PALLAS), were allowed to sail away. They eventually reached Italy, where they founded the city of Patavium (Padua). Antenor is a minor but pivotal character in Chaucer's *TROILUS AND CRISEYDE*. According to the sources Chaucer drew upon, Antenor betrayed his countrymen by sending the statue of Athena, on whose safety Troy depended, to ULYSSES. He was captured by the Greeks during one of the many battles of the war and then ransomed in exchange for CRISEYDE, whose father, CALKAS, had joined the Greek host earlier and now wanted his daughter with him. This exchange is the tragic event that causes TROILUS and Criseyde to become separated. Criseyde promises to find a way to leave the Greek camp and return to Troilus, but she never does. Antenor's treachery is also briefly mentioned by the BLACK KNIGHT in *The BOOK OF THE DUCHESS*.

Anteus *See* ANTAEUS.

Antheus *See* ANTAEUS.

Anthiocus *See* ANTIOCHUS.

Antichrist According to biblical tradition, the Antichrist is a false prophet and evil being who will set himself up against Christ and the people of God in the last days before the Second Coming. The term is used only in the writings of Saint JOHN in the New Testament. It refers to one who stands in opposition to all that Jesus Christ represents. John wrote that several antichrists, people who denied the deity of Christ, already existed in his day, but that the supreme Antichrist of history would appear at some time in the future. The PARSON of Chaucer's "PARSON'S TALE" refers to those who commit the sin of simony (the buying or selling of sacred or spiritual things such as the sacraments) as committing a sin that is exceeded in magnitude only by the great sin of LUCIFER and the Antichrist, the sin of pride (line 788).

Anticlaudianus   *See* ALAIN DE LILLE.

Antigone   The Antigone who appears in Chaucer's *TROILUS AND CRISEYDE* is CRISEYDE's niece, not the Antigone who was the daughter of OEDIPUS in the famous series of plays by SOPHOCLES. Chaucer's reasons for choosing the name are unknown. Her role in the *Troilus* is a minor one, but she does sing a song that makes Criseyde more receptive to the idea of receiving TROILUS as a suitor.

Antilochus   A figure from classical mythology, Antilochus distinguished himself in the TROJAN WAR for his bravery, intelligence and beauty. He was a special favorite of ACHILLES and brought him the news of PATROCLUS' death. He and Achilles were slain as Achilles was about to marry POLIXENA. The BLACK KNIGHT alludes to their deaths in Chaucer's elegiac poem *The BOOK OF THE DUCHESS* (line 1069).

Antiochus (1)   The man referred to simply as King Antiochus in "The MONK'S TALE" is Antiochus IV, who ruled in Syria from 175 to 164 B.C. Antiochus was surnamed Epiphanes (God manifest) but was called Epimanes (Madman) by his enemies. Enterprising and ambitious, he nevertheless had a tendency to cruelty that gained him considerable notoriety. His primary aim—to unify his empire by spreading Greek civilization and culture—brought him into direct conflict with the Jews. This conflict broke into open rebellion in 167 B.C. when he passed an edict outlawing certain features of Jewish ritual and requiring that all Jews participate in festivities honoring the Greek deities. The Jewish revolt, led by Judas Maccabeus, was successful. The Syrians were routed, and the ensuing cleansing of the Temple is now observed by the Jews as Hanukkah (the Feast of Lights). Following his defeat, Antiochus withdrew into Persia and died a madman. Accounts of the conflict between the Syrians and the Jews appear in the apocryphal book of 2 Maccabees. In the MONK's version of Antiochus' life, considerable emphasis is placed on how God punished Antiochus for his crimes against the Jews, afflicting him with terrible diseases and parasites that made his body rot. Stinking so horribly that none of his followers could stand to be near him, he died alone in the mountains (lines 2575–630).

Antiochus (2)   The king who, in the popular story of APPOLLONIUS of Tyre, committed incest with his daughter. The story is alluded to in the prologue to "The MAN OF LAW'S TALE" where the narrator, before commencing with his own tale, describes what kind of "cursed" story he is not going to deliver. Because the tragic story of Antiochus and his daughter was treated by John GOWER in his *CONFESSIO AMANTIS,* some scholars have viewed this reference as an oblique criticism of Gower's work. The *Confessio Amantis,* like *The CANTERBURY TALES,* is a collection of stories, though it differs in treating only a single theme—that of love.

Antoninus, Marus Aurelius   *See* CARACALLA.

Antonius   *See* ANTONY, MARC.

Antony, Marc   Roman general of the first century B.C. who served under Julius Caesar and later shared power with Caesar's grand-nephew Octavian and Marcus Aemilius Lepidus in the autocratic pact known as the Second Triumvirate. Following the civil war that effectively ended the Roman Republic, the triumvirs agreed to divide the rule of the empire. Antony took up the administration of the eastern provinces, which included Egypt, and this is when he first became involved with CLEOPATRA. He came into conflict with Octavian several times before the final break, which occurred when Antony formally divorced Octavia (his fourth wife and Octavian's sister) and bound himself irrevocably to Cleopatra and her cause. Octavian formally broke off all ties with Antony and declared war on Egypt. The defeat of the Egyptian fleet, Antony's death and Cleopatra's extravagant suicide are the details Chaucer emphasizes in the biography of Cleopatra that he includes in *The LEGEND OF GOOD WOMEN.* Antony's death is also depicted on the walls of the Temple of Mars in "The KNIGHT'S TALE" (line 2032).

Antonyus   *See* CARACALLA, MARUS AURELIUS ANTONINUS.

Antylegyus   *See* ANTILOCHUS.

Apelles   *See* APPELLES.

Apennines, the   Mountain range running the length of central ITALY. The Apennines form the western boundary of LOMBARDY, the region of northern Italy in which "The CLERK'S TALE" of patient GRISELDA is set. The CLERK mentions the mountains in the elaborate geographical description he includes in the introduction to his tale. That introduction is a direct translation of a passage from PETRARCH, whose *De obedientia ac fide uxoria mythologia* (Fable of wifely obedience and faithfulness) is the tale's source.

Apennyn   *See* APENNINES, THE.

Apius   The corrupt judge who wants to rape VIRGINIA in "The PHYSICIAN'S TALE." He gains access to the girl by bribing another man, CLAUDIUS, to swear in the court that Virginia is actually a slave girl who belongs to him and was stolen away by VIRGINIUS (actually the girl's father). Apius, presiding over the court, grants the man possession of Virginia, but her father thwarts the plan by beheading his daughter. Apius is hanged for his crime by a group of angry citizens.

Apollo (Phoebus)   In classical myth, Apollo is the god of music, poetry, prophecy and medicine, as well as the exemplar of masculine youth and beauty. The son of Zeus (JUPITER) and Leto, Apollo was one of the most popular gods in the Greek pantheon. His alternate name Phoebus means "brilliant" or "shining," and indicates his status as the god of Light and Truth. His shrine at DELPHI was arguably the most important of its day, and many people made pilgrimages there to consult the Delphic oracle, presided over by a priestess who received their questions and delivered her answers while sitting on a tripod stool over a chasm which emitted gaseous vapors. The answers often took the form of a riddle. Apollo was called Delian, after the island of Delos where he was born, and Pythian after his slaying of the serpent PYTHON (Phyton) which lived in the caves beneath PARNASSUS. He killed the serpent with his bow and arrows, with which he became so skilled as to be called the archer-god. One of the great loves of Apollo's life was a mortal woman named Coronis, who granted him her affection but also tried to deceive him by taking another lover. When the raven that he kept for a companion told him what she had done, Apollo punished the raven by turning its white feathers black, and he killed the woman. In remorse for the murder he did, however, rescue the child that was about to be born. AESCULAPIUS, the child of Coronis and Apollo, was raised and educated by CHIRON the centaur, under whose tutelage he came to possess an even greater knowledge of the healing arts than his father. The story of Apollo and Coronis is told in "The MANCIPLE'S TALE," although Coronis is not named but is merely referred to as Phoebus' wife. Chaucer alters the details of the narrative to point up the lesson that the MANCIPLE wishes to derive from his tale, which emphasizes the importance of guarded and considered speech. In *The HOUSE OF FAME*, MARSYAS was flayed for trying to play the pipes better than Apollo (lines 1229–32). Aurelias, in

"The FRANKLIN'S TALE" prays for Apollo's assistance (line 1031–43) and TROILUS curses him, in TROILUS AND CRISEYDE, when he is separated from his lover (book 5, lines 207–9 and 1853). Apollo is mentioned elsewhere in reference to the Sun.

Appelles   Artist who was supposed to have carved the fictional but elaborate tomb of Darius the Great (DARIUS [1]), the king of Persia. The tomb is mentioned in the WIFE OF BATH's prologue where she says that her fourth husband's tomb is not as elaborate as the one carved for Darius by Appelles because it would have been a waste to bury him at such expense. The comment reflects the bitterness she feels toward this husband, who, she felt, mistreated her because he had other lovers while they were married. An artist of the same name is mentioned in "The PHYSICIAN'S TALE." In describing the beauty of the tale's protagonist, VIRGINIA, the PHYSICIAN states that neither PIGMALION, Appelles nor Zanzis (ZEUXIS) could have created such a perfect creature. Although Appelles was the name of an actual painter who lived in Colophon and Ephesus during the fourth century B.C., and who was mentioned in CICERO's work, it seems more likely that Chaucer's sources were the *ROMAN DE LA ROSE* (where a pronouncement similar to the one in "The PHYSICIAN'S TALE" appears) and the *Alexandreis,* a medieval Latin epic by Gautier de Châtillon, which describes the fictional tomb of Darius and gives the sculptor's name as Appelles.

Appian Way   An ancient Roman paved highway that extended from Rome to Capua by Brundisium (Brindisi). It was about 350 miles long and was named for the Roman censor Appius Claudius Caecus, by whom it was begun around 312 B.C. In "The SECOND NUN'S TALE," CECILIA sends her fiance, VALERIAN, to the Appian Way (via Apia) to meet Pope URBAN, who is hiding out in a cave near the highway to escape the Roman persecution of Christians.

Appollonius   In the prologue to "The MAN OF LAW'S TALE," the narrator refers to the "cursed" story of "Tyro Appollonius," by which is meant the Greek romance popularly known as "Appollonius of Tyre." Written between the fifth and sixth centuries A.D. the story tells about King ANTIOCHUS, a villainous man who raped his daughter and then created a riddle for all of her suitors to answer. When Prince Appollonius of Tyre answered it correctly, the king set out to have him killed, but Appollonius escaped and embarked upon a series of adventures. When the SERGEANT OF THE LAW mentions this story, he says he is glad that the poet Chaucer has not written on such subjects. Chaucer's contemporary John GOWER tells a version of the story in his *CONFESSIO AMANTIS.*

Aquarius One of the 12 divisions of the zodiac, an imaginary belt in the heavens extending for about eight degrees on either side of the apparent path of the sun and including the paths of the moon and the principal planets. The zodiac is divided into 12 equal parts, or signs, each named for a different constellation. Aquarius is the 11th sign (*see* diagram under ASTROLOGY), which in Chaucer's day the Sun entered around January 12. In Chaucer's day, because the calendar was slightly different, the Sun entered Aquarius around January 13. The constellation of Aquarius appears in the sky between Capricorn and Pisces, near the celestial equator. When Chaucer uses astrological terms such as this, he most often employs them to indicate the approximate date of a narrative event or to show the passage of time. The sign Aquarius, however, is not mentioned in this capacity in any of Chaucer's imaginative work (unlike other signs), but only appears in his *TREATISE ON THE ASTROLABE*, where he describes the appearance and location of each of the 12 constellations and explains how to use them, in conjunction with the astrolabe instrument, to calculate the date.

Aquilo (Aquilon) The Roman name for BOREAS, the north wind. It is referred to by both its Roman and its Greek names in Chaucer's translation of BOETHIUS' *Consolation of Philosophy* where it is mentioned as the bringer of storms.

Arabia (Arabe, Arabye) Peninsula in Southwest Asia, between the Red Sea and the Persian Gulf. Although its northwestern border has fluctuated over the centuries, the name roughly indicated the same geographical area in Chaucer's time as it does today. King CAMBYUSKAN (the Mongolian conqueror Genghis Khan) in "The SQUIRE'S TALE" is referred to by his subjects as the king of India ("Inde") and Arabia ("Arabe"). Portions of both were contained in the Mongolian Empire. Arabia was also the home of the mythical phoenix, a bird that supposedly lived in the Arabian desert for 500 or 600 years and then consumed itself in fire, rising renewed from the ashes to start another life. There was only one phoenix at any time, and when the BLACK KNIGHT wants to describe the unique qualities of his lost queen in *The BOOK OF THE DUCHESS*, he compares her to the solitary bird.

Aragon Former kingdom in northeastern Spain which, from the 11th to the 15th centuries, gradually expanded to include Barcelona, Tortosa and Valencia as well as the Balearic Islands, Sardinia and Sicily. It was bordered on the west by the kingdoms of Navarre and Castile. Trumpet playing was a prominent feature of ceremonial life in late-13th-century Aragon, and Chaucer alludes to this in *The HOUSE OF FAME*, in which he mentions Aragonian clarion players among the musicians who are gathered in attendance on the goddess FAME (line 1248).

Arcadia (Arcadye) A pastoral district of the central Peloponnesus in ancient Greece. In Chaucer's translation of BOETHIUS' *Consolation of Philosophy*, the god MERCURY (1) is alluded to as the "Bird of Arcadia" because of his wings and because his legendary birthplace is a mountain in the region of Arcadia. The region was also famous as the home of the god PAN. The Roman poet VIRGIL, in his *Eclogues*, used the area to symbolize an ideal world of rural simplicity and tranquility.

Archemorus (Archymoris) In Greek mythology, Archemorus (also known as Opheltes) was the son of King Lycurgus of Nemea and Queen EURYDICE. HYPSIPYLE, formerly queen of Lemnos but now in service to Lycurgus, was his nurse. When the SEVEN AGAINST THEBES stopped in the Valley of Nemea to get water, Hypsipyle left the child unattended while she led the heroes to a spring. In her absence, he was killed by a snake that had been sent by JUPITER. The incident is referred to in *TROILUS AND CRISEYDE* during CASSANDRA's recitation of the events surrounding the siege of THEBES (book 5, line 1499).

Arcite (1) One of the main protagonists in "The KNIGHT'S TALE." A knight of THEBES, Arcite is a cousin of PALAMON and an enemy of Duke THESEUS of ATHENS. Arcite and Palamon are captured and imprisoned after Theseus attacks Thebes. While in prison, both fall in love with Theseus' sister, EMILY. Palamon sees her first and therefore feels he has the greater claim to her. Arcite disagrees, arguing that the law of love overwhelms such considerations. While Palamon remains in prison, Arcite, through the intervention of Duke PEROTHEUS of Thebes, is released on the condition that he never return to Athens. Finding that separation from Emily is an even greater torment than languishing in prison, Arcite determines to disguise himself as PHILOSTRATE, return to Athens and seek employment in Theseus' household so that he can at least watch his beloved from a distance. Eventually he secures a position as one of Emily's pages. He performs his duties so well that he attracts the attention of Theseus, who decides to reward his service by making him a squire. He remains in Theseus' court, pining for his beloved Emily, while his cousin Palamon finally escapes from prison. The two knights stumble across one another in the countryside near Athens. They start to fight there, but Theseus intervenes and the contest is postponed until a later date. The final battle takes the form of a tournament in Athens, with Theseus presiding. Arcite wins the tournament but is mortally wounded when he falls off his horse. Realizing that he is bound to die, he reconciles with Palamon and bequeathes to him

Emily's love. After a period of mourning, Palamon and Emily marry.

Although the two knights are very similar in characterization, Arcite stands out slightly as the more warrior-like of the two because of his alignment with MARS (1), the god of war, to whom he prays on the eve of the tournament. On the other hand, it is Palamon who escapes from prison and vows to return to Athens to claim his beloved at the head of an army. Arcite is content to sneak back into the city-state, assume an alias, and work as a servant in the household of his greatest enemy. This, and the fact that Palamon does first see and lay claim to Emily, has convinced some readers that Palamon is the worthier of the two knights. Others argue that Arcite is equally noble, citing his refusal to take advantage of Palamon's defenselessness when that knight confronts him in the Athenian countryside. Arcite's willingness to live as a servant just to be near the object of his affection also seems to soften his martial temperament, just as Palamon's vow to conquer Athens with an army suggests that his alignment with the goddess of love represents only one facet of his personality. All things considered, the knights are remarkably similar. Both evince a martial spirit and demonstrate passionate devotion to a lady; both take active, though different, means to acquire the lady; and both reflect philosophically on the situation in which they find themselves.

Arcite (2)   Theban knight who wins the love of Queen Anelida in Chaucer's unfinished poem ANELIDA AND ARCITE. Aside from his habitual deceitful behavior in matters of the heart, his character is scarcely developed. From what we do learn of him, however, he seems entirely unlike the faithful and passionate ARCITE (1) of Chaucer's "KNIGHT'S TALE," even though the two works derive from the same source, the THEBAID of STATIUS.

Arctour   *See* ARCTURUS.

Arcturus   A giant red star in the constellation Boötes, lying over the North Pole. The star is mentioned in the *BOECE,* Chaucer's translation of BOETHIUS' *Consolation of Philosophy,* when Boethius comments on how the divine intelligence causes all things in nature to proceed in an orderly fashion, just as the seeds that are sown under the star Arcturus grow tall when SIRIUS, the Dog Star, warms them with its heat. He wonders why this same sense of order and control does not govern the affairs of men.

Ardea   The capitol of the Rutuli tribe in Latium, Italy. The tribe went to war against AENEAS and his Trojan followers when Aeneas landed in Italy and claimed the hand of LAVINIA (the daughter of King Latinus), who had been promised in marriage to the king of the Rutulians. The town is mentioned in the biography of

Queen DIDO that appears in *The LEGEND OF GOOD WOMEN.*

Arge   *See* ARGOS.

Argeyes   *See* ARGIVES.

Argia   In classical mythology, Argia was the wife of POLYNICES, one of the two sons of OEDIPUS, ruler of Thebes. After Oedipus' banishment from Thebes, Polynices and his brother, ETEOCLES, agreed to an arrangement by which each of them would take turns governing the city. When Eteocles refused to surrender the throne at the end of his tenure, Polynices gathered a force of famous Greek heroes and invaded Thebes. The conflict that followed became known as the SEVEN AGAINST THEBES, so named because of the seven heroes who were leaders in the war against Eteocles. Chaucer mentions Argia's weeping during the burning of Thebes in the truncated version of this story that is related by CASSANDRA in book 5 of *TROILUS AND CRISEYDE* (book 5, line 1509).

Argives   The inhabitants of ARGOS, a Greek city in the Peloponnesus.

Argon   *See* ARGOS.

Argonautica   A first-century account of the classical Greek hero JASON's adventures with the Argonauts when he sailed out in search of the Golden Fleece. Chaucer refers to this version of the story, written by Roman author Valerius Flaccus, in the biographies of HYPSIPYLE and MEDEA that are included in *The LEGEND OF GOOD WOMEN.* Speaking to the reader, he says that if you want to know the names of the men who accompanied Jason on his adventure, you should consult the "Argonautycon" (line 1457).

Argonautycon   *See ARGONAUTICA.*

Argos   A city and its region in the northern Peloponnesus of GREECE. Ancient Argos dominated the Peloponnesus until the rise of Sparta. DIOMEDE, the man who woos CRISEYDE away from TROILUS in Chaucer's *TROILUS AND CRISEYDE,* is heir to the throne of Argos and to that of Calydon in Aetolia (modern Asia Minor). Her father, CALKAS, uses this information to convince Criseyde that she should receive Diomede's attentions more favorably. Argos is also the setting for the story of HYPERMNESTRA in *The LEGEND OF GOOD WOMEN.* Her father, DANAUS, was king of the city until he was killed by Hypermnestra's husband, LYNCEUS.

Argus (1)   Chaucer assigns this name to the builder of the ship *Argo,* on which the Greek hero JASON sailed when he set out to obtain the Golden Fleece. Thus, both the ship and the men who accompanied Jason on his adventure, the Argonauts, took their name from the ship's builder. Chaucer relates a brief version of Jason's adventures in the biography of HYPSIPYLE and MEDEA that he includes in *The LEGEND OF GOOD WOMEN*.

Argus (2)   *See* ALGUS.

Argus (3)   In classical mythology, Argus was the hundred-eyed, all-seeing guardian whom Hera (JUNO) entrusted with the keeping of Io, a maiden who was loved by Hera's husband, Zeus (JUPITER). Zeus had changed Io into a heifer in order to protect her from the jealousy of his wife. Hermes (MERCURY) was given the task of rescuing Io from her guardian, which he accomplished by playing on the syrinx and telling stories until all the eyes of Argus went to sleep, and then killing him. According to legend, Hera placed his eyes in the tail of the peacock. In "The KNIGHT'S TALE," Chaucer alludes to the incident involving Hermes when he describes how Mercury appeared to ARCITE in a dream, looking as he did when he visited Argus and put him to sleep. Mercury's ambiguous message, that ARCITE (1) should return to Athens where all of his woe will be brought to an end, together with the reference to Argus, provides a subtle hint of the misfortune that is to come (lines 1389–90). The WIFE OF BATH mentions Argus in her prologue when she says that her old husbands would not have been able to keep track of her even if they had made the many-eyed monster her guardian. The narrator of "The MERCHANT'S TALE" notes the fact that Argus was "blinded" (deceived) despite his many eyes to prepare the reader for the scene in which old JANUARY, having seen his wife having intercourse with another man, nonetheless doubts the evidence of his vision (line 2111). In *TROILUS AND CRISEYDE*, TROILUS refers to CRISEYDE's father, CALKAS, as Argus-eyed, claiming that he will be too watchful for her to slip away from the Greek camp and return to TROY (book 5, line 450).

Argyve (1)   *See* ARGIA.

Argyve (2)   CRISEYDE's mother in Chaucer's *TROILUS AND CRISEYDE*. It is uncertain why Chaucer chose this name, because this character is unnamed in all of the sources he is known to have drawn upon for his version of the story.

Ariadne   In classical mythology, Ariadne was the daughter of King MINOS and Queen PASIPHAE of Crete. She fell in love with THESEUS of Athens, who came to the island as one of a group of young people who were to be sacrificed to the MINOTAUR. She helped him escape from the labyrinth where the monster lived by

providing him with a ball of thread that he could unwind as he went in and then wind back up to find the way out. After killing the Minotaur, Theseus took Ariadne with him on the ship to Athens, promising marriage, but then abandoned her on the island of Naxos. BACCHUS found her, took pity on her desolation, and married her. The crown that he gave her for a wedding gift was placed among the stars. Ariadne is mentioned in the prologue of *The LEGEND OF GOOD WOMEN* as one in a list of faithful women. The story of her relationship with Theseus is the sixth "biography" to appear in *The Legend of Good Women* (lines 1886–2227). In the prologue to "The MAN OF LAW'S TALE," the narrator notes that Chaucer composed the "complaint" of Ariadne, presumably referring to the latter. She is also mentioned in *The HOUSE OF FAME*, where the narrator recalls the assistance she provided to Theseus, giving her credit for saving his life (line 407).

Aries   One of the 12 divisions of the zodiac, an imaginary belt in the heavens extending for about eight degrees on either side of the apparent path of the sun and including the paths of the moon and the principal planets. The zodiac is divided into 12 equal parts, or signs, each named for a different constellation. Aries is the first sign (*see* diagram under ASTROLOGY), which the sun enters around March 21. In Chaucer's day, because the calendar was slightly different, the sun entered Aries around March 12. The constellation of Aries, which is supposed to represent a ram, appears in the sky between Pisces and Taurus. When Chaucer uses astrological terms such as this, he most often employs them to indicate the approximate date of a narrative event or to show the passage of time. In "The SQUIRE'S TALE," he even uses it to describe the weather, when he notes that on King CAMBYUSKAN's birthday, March 15, "Phebus the sonne ful joly was and cleer, / For he was neigh his exaltacioun / In Martes face and in his mansioun / In Aries, the colerik hoote signe." (lines 48–51) [Phoebus the sun was quite jolly and clear, for he was near his exaltation (the position of its strongest influence) in the first ten degrees of Aries (Mars' face and his house), the choleric (hot and dry) sign]. (A slightly looser translation than usual is provided here to best convey the sense of the passage.) Rhetorically, this device elevates the style of the passage, and Chaucer typically makes use of it in two situations. Sometimes, as in this tale, it provides a way of noting the date of an event in terms that are in keeping with the noble theme and elevated sentiments of the work as a whole. On other occasions, as in "The NUN'S PRIEST'S TALE," his use of astrological terms in this manner has a comedic effect because of the contrast between the elevated style of the passage and the silliness of the plot and/or its characters. Chaucer's *TREATISE ON THE ASTROLABE* describes the appearance and location of each of the 12 constellations and explains how to use them, in conjunction with the astrolabe instrument, to calculate the date. Thus the information contained in the *Treatise on the Astrolabe,* for those capable of understanding it, provides an explanation of how the poet formulated these descriptions. Although *Aries* was the Greek name for the god of war, when Chaucer uses the term, he reserves it exclusively to denote the zodiacal sign. When he wants to indicate the god of war from classical mythology, Chaucer uses the Roman name MARS (1).

Arion   A quasi-mythical Greek poet born on the island of Lesbos in the seventh century B.C., Arion became quite wealthy serving as court poet to the ruler of Corinth, but when he tried to return home, the captain and crew of the ship in which he sailed demanded that he surrender his gold or his life. They allowed him to sing one last song before being thrown overboard, but his song so enchanted a dolphin that the animal saved his life and carried him to Lesbos. Arion's harp and the dolphin who rescued him were stellified—made into constellations, which are observed by the narrator of *The HOUSE OF FAME* as he is borne aloft into the heavens by the talking EAGLE who has been sent to carry him to FAME's palace (lines 1203–5).

Arionis harpe   *See* ARION.

Aristoclides   According to Saint JEROME's *Epistola adversus Jovinianum* (Letter against Jovinian), Aristoclides was the ruler of Orchomenos, who, after killing her father, desired the virgin Stymphalides. She fled to the temple of Diana, to whose statue she clung until she was stabbed to death. DORIGEN, in "The FRANKLIN'S TALE," mentions this episode as one of many examples of faithful women whose precedent she ought to follow when her marriage is threatened by the attentions of the squire AURELIUS (line 1387).

Aristotle   Greek philosopher of the fourth century B.C. who studied under PLATO and later set up a school just outside the city of Athens. Here he undertook scientific research into such subjects as music, physics, metaphysics, mathematics and astronomy in an attempt to increase humanity's understanding of the natural world. He wrote extensively on the subjects that he studied, and his written work, along with Plato's, had tremendous influence on the development of both pagan and Christian thought in the western world from the Middle Ages up until the present day. Although his writings came into western Europe by way of Rome, the study of his works declined and almost totally disappeared after the fall of the Roman Empire. For a time, knowledge of his writings was confined to the study of translations of two of his minor works and a number of commentaries made by

BOETHIUS. Boethius had studied the philosopher's work in great depth, and Aristotle's influence appears throughout Boethius' *Consolation of Philosophy,* which makes particular use of Aristotelian beliefs about the nature of the physical world. In the 12th and 13th centuries, as Aristotle's *Politics* and *Ethics* began to be rediscovered, his writings on man as a political and social animal, as well as some of his ideas about the nature of the universe (such as the absence of creation and the substitution of a "first mover" for a personal God), came into conflict with generally accepted Christian theology. Initially, his work was condemned by the church, but eventually, through the efforts of scholars and clergy like Robert Grosseteste and Thomas Aquinas, the task of reconciling Aristotelian and Augustinian philosophy began. Aristotle's writings were consistently a factor in molding the intellectual life of the Middle Ages. Their influence is clearly detectable in Chaucer's work, and not only in the *BOECE,* Chaucer's translation of the *Consolation of Philosophy.* The popularity of Aristotle's works in the university curriculum is reflected in the portrait of the CLERK who appears in the GENERAL PROLOGUE of *The CANTERBURY TALES* and who would rather own 20 books of Aristotle than fine garments or a fiddle or an elegant prayer book (line 295). In "The SQUIRE'S TALE," members of King CAMBYUSKAN's court use Aristotle's theories on optics in their attempts to explain the workings of the magical mirror that is presented to the king on his birthday (lines 232–35). Aristotle's conception of the physical universe makes its way into *The HOUSE OF FAME* as the basis for the theory of natural inclination, the idea that every natural object has a natural place that it tries to reach and in which it tries to remain. The EAGLE uses this theory to explain how sounds, which are composed of broken air, make their way into the atmosphere and ultimately to FAME's palace (lines 729–822).

Armenia   According to F. P. Magoun in *A Chaucer Gazetteer,* Armenia is the classical name of Hebrew Ararat, a country extending between the shore of Lake Van, the upper Euphrates River and Media. The country is mentioned once in Chaucer's work, as the home of Queen ANELIDA, the heroine of the unfinished *Anelida and Arcite.* How Anelida came to be in THEBES, where, according to the story, she is among those who are being held as hostages by CREON following the siege of Thebes, is never explained. Nor does the poem in its unfinished state give any clue as to why her identity as the queen of that city might be of significance within the context of the poem.

Armorica (Armorika)   During the Middle Ages, *Armorica* was the name by which the coastal regions of BRITTANY and Normandy were called. It is the setting for "The FRANKLIN'S TALE." The treacherous rocky Armorican coast functions as an important element of the tale's plot when DORIGEN, who is being pursued by an amorous squire named AURELIUS, finally accedes that she will become his lover if he can find a way to remove the rocks that make the seaward approach to Armorica so dangerous. In offering this as the condition of her love, she is ironically displaying consideration for her husband, whose return from a long voyage to England she anxiously anticipates. With the help of a scholar-magician who is able to make the rocks appear to vanish during an especially high tide, Aurelius accomplishes the feat. This poses a terrible dilemma for Dorigen, who must choose between keeping her word to the squire and preserving her marriage vows.

Arnaldus of Villanova A 13th-century Catalan physician, professor of medicine, religious reformer and writer. Although Arnald wrote on astrology and magic as well as medicine and theology, the popular belief that he authored an alchemical treatise called the *Rosarie* or *Rosarium philosophorum* ("Rosary of the Philosophers") cited in "The CANON'S YEOMAN'S TALE" is probably false. The CANON'S YEOMAN claims to quote from this text in the closing lines of his tale, which describes how a self-proclaimed alchemist cheats people out of their money. The quoted lines actually come from another alchemical text reputedly by the same author, entitled, *De lapide philosophorum* ("On the Philosophers' Stone"). The philosopher's stone was a legendary stone that was supposed to be capable of transmuting base metal into gold, which was the aim of the alchemist's practice.

Arnold of the Newe Toun *See* ARNALDUS OF VILLANOVA.

Arpies (Arpiis) *See* ERINYES.

Arras A city of the Artois region in northern France. During the Middle Ages the city was famed for its elaborate tapestries and other woven material. The allegorical figure of FRANCHISE in *The ROMAUNT OF THE ROSE* wears a garment fairer than any of Arras.

Arrius A man who, when his friend Latumyus complained that three of his wives had hanged themselves on the same tree, asked Latumyus for a sprig from that "blessed tree" to plant in his own garden. This anecdote, which ultimately derives from Latin author CICERO's *De oratore*, is one that the WIFE OF BATH's fifth husband, JANKIN (1), tells her. It is one of a series of the antifeminist stories that Jankin is so fond of and that lead to the crisis in their relationship.

Arsechieles *See* ARZACHEL.

Artemesia One of the women renowned for her chastity who DORIGEN in "The FRANKLIN'S TALE" remembers when she is faced with a crisis that tests her own faithfulness to her husband, ARVERAGUS (line 1415). According to legend, the Roman Artemesia built such an elaborate tomb for her husband, Mausolus, that to this day any elaborate tomb is called a mausoleum after him.

Arthemesie *See* ARTEMESIA.

Arthour, Kyng *See* ARTHUR, KING.

Arthur, King The most famous legendary figure in Britain's history and literature, King Arthur, his queen, GUINEVERE and his Knights of the Round Table were principal characters in an entire genre of literature that arose during Middle Ages, the chivalric (sometimes called Arthurian) romance. Gaining steadily in popularity from the 12th century onward, these stories typically describe the fairy-tale–like adventures of knights and other members of the feudal aristocracy as they participate in tournaments and battles, rescue maidens, come to the aid of kings and queens, defeat dragons and other mythical beasts, and, most importantly, ride out on noble and often seemingly impossible quests. Ideologically, romances are based upon the ideals of loyalty, honor and courtly love, and their plots often derive from some conflict or problem arising out of sexual attraction between a man and a woman. "The WIFE OF BATH'S TALE," which is set in Arthur's kingdom and features one of his knights, is no exception. The tale opens in Arthur's court, where a knight (KNIGHT [3]) has committed the crime of raping a young maiden. Arthur sentences the knight to death, but the queen begs that his life be spared, provided he can perform a deed that she will assign him. Arthur agrees; the knight is then given the task of going on a quest to discover what it is that women desire above all else. He must return and give the correct answer within one year. The knight searches for a long time in vain, and then finally encounters a loathsome old hag who offers to give him the correct answer. In exchange, he must promise to perform whatever task she requires once he has been pardoned. The knight's life is spared, but the hag requires that he marry her to fulfill his promise. On their wedding night, when the knight bemoans the fate that has married him to an ugly, ignoble and old woman, she lectures him on the nature of true nobility, and then gives him a choice: If he is willing to put up with her being unfaithful to him, she will transform herself into a beautiful young woman; otherwise, she will remain ugly and faithful. When the knight says she may decide what is best, thus giving her control over the situation, she tells him that she will be both beautiful and faithful. She is immediately transformed. In having

Arthur and his court function as a backdrop for the action rather than as the protagonists at the center of the action, this tale is typical of the French tradition in Arthurian romance.

Artois (Artoys) A region in northern France that was invaded by the English (who wished to claim it as their own) during the HUNDRED YEARS' WAR. It is mentioned in the GENERAL PROLOGUE to *The CANTERBURY TALES* as one of the places where the SQUIRE fought in his series of military campaigns.

Artour *See* ARTHUR, KING.

Arveragus A Breton knight and husband to DORIGEN in "The FRANKLIN'S TALE." The relationship between Arveragus and Dorigen is notable for the mutual love and respect which endures throughout their courtship and marriage, even when it is severely tested by the rash promise she makes to AURELIUS. Some scholars have seen in Arveragus the type of the ideal Christian husband; others have merely viewed him as an impossible ideal, perhaps even a caricature of the FRANKLIN as he is presented in the GENERAL PROLOGUE of *The CANTERBURY TALES*.

Arzachel Arzachel was the Latin name of an 11th-century Arab astronomer, Ibn al-Zarqali. Known for his excellent observations of the heavens, Arzachel also invented an improved astrolabe (an instrument for observing and mapping the heavens), which came to be known as Arzachel's sphere. Arzachel edited the Toledan Tables, a set of planetary tables based on observations he made at Toledo, Spain. Translated into Latin in the 12th century, the tables became a popular tool for astronomers until they were rendered obsolete by another set of tables made near the end of the 13th century. In "The FRANKLIN'S TALE," the magician whose natural magic causes the rocks lining the coast of BRITTANY to disappear beneath the waves uses the Toledan Tables to calculate the best time of year to perform his trick (lines 1273–74). Chaucer refers to the tables as "Arsechiele's Tables" in his *TREATISE ON THE ASTROLABE* (part 2, division 45, line 2).

Ascalaphus In classical mythology, Ascalaphus is a minor character who played a major role in the legend of CERES and her daughter PROSERPINE. When Proserpine was kidnapped by PLUTO, the god of the underworld, he agreed to let her return to the upper world provided she had eaten nothing during her sojourn in the land of the dead. It was Ascalaphus who told Pluto that she had eaten one seed from a pomegranate. For that reason, Pluto would only agree to let her spend a third of the year on the earth's surface; for the remainder of the year, she was required to return to

Hades, where she reigned as his queen. In response to this decision, Ceres, the goddess who governed the fruitfulness of the earth, caused the earth to become barren during the time that she must be separated from her daughter. To punish Ascalaphus for betraying her, Proserpine transformed him into an owl, and forever after the owls' cries have been interpreted as the harbinger of grief. In book five of *TROILUS AND CRISEYDE*, TROILUS alludes to this idea when he tells PANDARUS about his fear that CRISEYDE is not going to return from the Greek camp: "The owle ek, which that hette Escaphilo / Hath after me shright al thise nyghtes two." (book 5, lines 319–20) [The owl also, which is called Ascalaphus / Has shrieked at me throughout the last two nights].

Ascanius The son of AENEAS and CREUSA. At the fall of TROY, his father led him by the hand out of the burning city and took him along on the adventures that eventually ended with them settling in Italy. The war that Aeneas fought against the Latins and Rutulians in Italy began when Ascanius shot a pet stag owned by a peasant's daughter. Ascanius is mentioned as Aeneas' son in *The HOUSE OF FAME* and the portion of *The LEGEND OF GOOD WOMEN* that deals with Queen DIDO's life.

Asclepius *See* AESCULAPIUS.

Asia According to F. P. MAGOUN's *Chaucer Gazetteer*, Asia was originally likely to have been the name of a town in ancient LYDIA; or, it may have been the name of the country of Lydia. Use of the term to include all of Asia Minor originated with the late Romans. Chaucer mentions Asia in *The HOUSE OF FAME* when the narrator observes that the approach to FAME's throne is lined with heralds and pursuivants (heralds' assistants) displaying the arms of famous men from the three continents of Asia, Africa and Europe. The PRIORESS' tale of the young Christian martyr is also set in Asia ("Asye" is the Middle English spelling), though the country or city is unspecified.

Askanius *See* ASCANIUS.

Assuere *See* AHASUERUS.

Astrolabe, Treatise on the *See* TREATISE ON THE ASTROLABE.

astrology Astrology in general consists of the belief that events on Earth are influenced in a more or less predictable way by powers emanating from the stars and planets. The belief arose around 3000 B.C. in Mesopotamia, where there developed both the astronomical science of plotting the movements of the sun, moon and stars, and the astrological art of divination

Astrological table showing the order of the signs and their pictorial representations.

based upon these observations. The two branches, astronomy and astrology, were to remain virtually indistinguishable until the Renaissance and the rise of new scientific methods that promoted a more skeptical attitude.

When it first began to be practiced, astrology was concerned exclusively with public events, i.e., those affecting society as a whole, such as war, famine, plague and even the weather. Astrologers were employed by kings to report regularly on celestial omens, which they interpreted according to codified rules. Later, the scope of astrology extended to include predictions about the lives of individuals based on the positions of the stars at the moment of a person's birth.

Astrology spread to Europe by way of Greece. The Greeks built on existing Mesopotamian and Egyptian astrological lore by using their new understanding of geometrical principles to describe the movements of the planets. They also replaced the Mesopotamian deities who were equated with the planets with their own deities.

In the course of time, astrological theory began to be applied to medicine, an idea that still held sway during Chaucer's day and that obviously influenced the portrait of his DOCTOR OF PHYSIC in the GENERAL PROLOGUE to *The CANTERBURY TALES*. This physician, we are told, determines the time for his treatments and surgeries according to the most propitious arrangement of the stars and planets.

The attitude of the medieval Christian church toward astrology was problematical. Astrology was regularly con-

demned by church councils. Saint AUGUSTINE summed up the church's criticisms of astrology in his *City of God*, in which he reminded readers that the world is governed not by chance or fate but by divine providence, and that astrologers who predict a man's character from the stars do the work of demons by enslaving mankind's free will. Nevertheless, astrology continued to thrive, and some later theologians adopted a more tolerant attitude. Thomas Aquinas, for example, reconciled astrology with Christian beliefs by suggesting that the stars *influence* the bodily appetites, but that nothing prevents a man from withstanding those influences. In the later Middle Ages astrology was used on a wide scale to predict events. In 1337, for example, Geoffrey of Meaux foresaw famine and disaster following the appearance of a comet. The BLACK DEATH was likewise attributed to a malign planetary conjunction.

In much of Chaucer's work, imbued as it is with the influences of Greek and Roman mythology, astrological influences are alive and well and appear to function without conflict in a worldview that also embraces the idea of Christian providence. In his stories based on classical legends, like "The KNIGHT'S TALE," Chaucer could refer to the astrological influences governing the fate of ARCITE (1) and PALAMON without guilt; he was, after all, describing the lives of pagans. Yet he may have felt some discomfort with the practice of the art in his own day, as is suggested by a passage in his *TREATISE ON THE ASTROLABE* where, after he has gone on from astronomical information to the discussion of fortunate and unfortunate aspects of the stars, he suddenly does an about-face, saying that these are matters having to do with the rites of pagans in which he has no faith. Some of his contemporary characters, however, appear to be exempt from such scruples. The WIFE OF BATH uses astrology to explain why she had such difficulty getting along with her bookish husband, noting that the "children of Mercury" (i.e., scholars) love wisdom and science, while the "children of Venus," like herself, love having a good time and spending money. This, she says, is determined by the fact that the planet Mercury is powerless when it moves into the zodiacal sign of Pisces, where Venus is exalted (at her most powerful). She also describes her own personality with reference to astrology, noting that at the time of her birth the zodiacal sign of TAURUS, a house of Venus, was ascending, and the planet Mars was in it. The person born under these influences would display the somewhat martial character of aggression in love. A woman born under such a configuration was expected, in the Middle Ages, to be unchaste, as is noted in one of the Latin glosses to the ELLESMERE MANUSCRIPT.

Atalanta   There are two women named Atalanta in Greek mythology, both renowned for their fleetness of foot. The one mentioned in Chaucer's "KNIGHT'S

TALE," where her story is depicted on the walls of DIANA's temple, is the Arcadian Atalanta. According to legend, this Atalanta was a young woman who acquired great strength, speed and skill as a huntress as a result of having been nurtured by a bear after she was abandoned as an infant in the wilds of Greek ARCADIA. She participated in the great Calydonian boar hunt, wounded the boar and, when MELEAGER killed it, was given its head and hide as the victor's prize. Atalanta was sought by many suitors, but rejected all until one of them, Milanion, finally won her by defeating her in a race.

Athalante *See* ATALANTA.

Athalantes doughtres *See* ATLAS' DAUGHTERS.

Athalus *See* ATTALUS PHILOMETOR.

Athamante *See* ATHAMAS.

Athamas In classical mythology, Athamas was the son of AEOLUS, the wind god. He was king of Orchomenos in Boeotia and married a minor goddess named Nephele. When he abandoned her for another woman, Hera (JUNO), the queen of the gods, punished him with madness and killed one of the sons that he had by his second wife. In book four of *TROILUS AND CRISEYDE*, CRISEYDE swears that she will return to TROILUS or, if she does not, prays that she may be stricken with madness like Athamas and sent to dwell eternally in the pit of hell (book 4, line 1539).

Athenes (Athenys) *See* ATHENS.

Athens The ancient Greek city of Athens is mentioned often in Chaucer's work in relation to one or another mythological story that has the city as its setting. The Athenian court of THESEUS forms the background for the action of "The KNIGHT'S TALE," but students of classical history will be surprised to find that descriptions of the city, like those of TROY in *TROILUS AND CRISEYDE*, are more reminiscent of a northern European medieval city than a Mediterranean one. Greek soldiers, for example, are referred to as knights, and we find them engaging in a tournament. These and other medieval trappings that appear in the poems merely show Chaucer following what was conventional practice for the medieval poet writing about events taking place in another historical period and/or culture—to dress the story, and its characters, in contemporary clothing. This was not only a conscious effort to make the story familiar and meaningful to a medieval audience; it also reflected a lack of concern over what we would call historical and cultural accuracy.

Atiteris One of the minstrels observed in Fame's palace by the narrator of *The HOUSE OF FAME*. The name is probably a corruption of *Tityrus*, the name of the shepherd-singer in one of VIRGIL's *Eclogues*.

Atlas' daughters Chaucer uses this name to refer to the constellation of the Pleiades, which is named for the seven daughters of Atlas and Pleione. These seven women bore the names Taygete, Maia, Electra, ALCYONE, Sterope, Celaeno and Merope. They were hunting companions of Artemis (DIANA). One day, Pleione and her daughters encountered ORION in Boeotia; he, suddenly smitten with love, pursued them for five years. Zeus (JUPITER) rescued them from Orion by changing them into doves and then placing them among the stars. The EAGLE who bears Chaucer into the heavens in *The HOUSE OF FAME* urges him to use this opportunity to study the stars, and mentions the constellation of "Athalantes doughtres sevene" (line 1007) [Atlas' seven daughters] as one of those he ought to observe, but Chaucer declines, saying that he is too old for such an experience. The process of putting a person into the sky as a constellation, which often occurred in Greek mythology, is what Chaucer is referring to when he tells the eagle that he fears being stellified when he is carried up into the higher regions of the atmosphere.

Atropos In classical mythology, one of the three Fates, or goddesses of destiny. Clotho spins the thread of life for each human being, Lachesis determines the thread's length and Atropos cuts it off. Together, their function was to see that the fate assigned to each individual was carried out and that no mortal could escape or alter their decrees. Because birth and death were the two chief determining moments of fate, they were looked upon as goddesses of birth and death especially; but they might be invoked on any occasion of importance, such as a marriage. They were sometimes represented as ugly decrepit women, but more commonly as maidens of grave aspect, clad in long garments. TROILUS, in *TROILUS AND CRISEYDE*, calls upon Atropos to cut the thread of his life when he learns that his beloved CRISEYDE must leave TROY to join her father in the Greek camp (book 4, line 1208). Ironically, Criseyde later swears by Atropos when she promises that she will never be false to Troilus, calling upon the goddess to end her life if she should be.

Attaleia An independent principality in southern Anatolia that was attacked by Peter, king of Cyprus (*see* PIERRE DE LUSIGNAN), in August of 1361. Chaucer may have been thinking of this raid when he mentioned Attaleia ("Satalye") in the GENERAL PROLOGUE TO *THE CANTERBURY TALES* as one of the places where the KNIGHT (1) has been on military campaign (line 58).

Attalus Philometor (Attalus III)   The king of Pergamum who is thought by some to have invented the game of chess in the second century B.C. He is mentioned by the BLACK KNIGHT in *The BOOK OF THE DUCHESS* when the knight describes his game of chess against the goddess FORTUNE in which he lost his fair "White" queen (line 663). This is a metaphorical reference to the death of his wife, and Fortune is described as being a better player than Attalus, who invented the game.

Atthalante   *See* ATALANTA.

Atthenes   *See* ATHENS.

Attheon   *See* ACTAEON.

Attila (Attilla)   The king of the Huns, a fierce race of Asiatic people who invaded the Balkans in 441 and later advanced across the Danube, sweeping through Germany and France. In 451 Attila's progress was checked at Orleans by an alliance of imperial Roman and Visigothic forces. He suffered further defeat in a battle on the Catalaunian plains of Champagne. In 452 he turned his attentions to Italy, where he destroyed Aquileia and plundered Milan and Pavia. He was prevented from entering Rome, however, by the promise of tribute from the emperor Valentinian III. Legendary for his drunkenness, Attila is mentioned in "The PARDONER'S TALE" as an example of one who died in shame and dishonor after consuming too much alcohol (line 578). This is one of many cautionary examples given by the PARDONER, whose own morality is compromised by many of the excesses he warns others against.

Attrides   *See* AGAMEMNON.

Attropos   *See* ATROPOS.

aube (aubade)   A song or lyric poem lamenting the arrival of the dawn that must bring about the separation of two lovers. The form has no fixed metrical pattern, but is defined simply by its content. Very popular in France during the latter part of the medieval period, it was adopted in Germany by Wolfram von Eschenbach and in England by Chaucer. The most outstanding example in Chaucer's poetry appears in *TROILUS AND CRISEYDE*. On the morning following their first night together, the two lovers take turns chiding first the night, for leaving so soon, and then the day, for arriving so quickly. This aubade is derived from OVID's *Amores*, with the interesting variation that Chaucer has CRISEYDE express the sentiments usually given to the man, while Troilus voices those typically given to the woman. A parodic play on the convention of the dawn song appears in "The REEVE'S TALE" when one of the randy clerks bids farewell to MALKYN, the Miller's daughter: "Fare weel, Malyne, sweete wight! / The day is come; I may no lenger byde; / But everemo, wher so I go or ryde, / I is thyn awen clerk, swa have I seel!" (lines 30–34) [Farewell, Malkyn, sweet thing! / The day has come; I may no longer stay; / But forever more, wherever I go or ride, / I will be your own clerk, I swear!]. The clerk's attempts at using courtly language to speak to a woman of the lower class with whom he has had sex just to spite her father is a fine example of how Chaucer uses the high style of courtly literature to create a comic effect. The short astrological poem "The COMPLAINT OF MARS" also features two brief aubades as MARS and VENUS are separated by the approach of Phoebus APOLLO.

audience   Nowadays when we desire an evening's entertainment, we generally sit down in front of the TV, turn on the stereo, or perhaps go out to a movie, concert or a play. Or maybe we even pick up a book and read. If we read to anybody, it is usually our children. In Chaucer's day, however, reading aloud was one of the most popular forms of entertainment for literate adults, among the middle classes as well as the clergy and nobility. Indeed, one of the most famous surviving portraits of Chaucer pictures him reading his poem *TROILUS AND CRISEYDE* to a group of courtiers. During the early part of his career, and throughout most of it, Chaucer's audience was probably composed primarily of members of the court because, as a page to the countess of Ulster, and later as a member of the king's household, that was the milieu in which he lived and worked. A number of his poems are in fact believed to have been composed for specific occasions on which they were read aloud. *The BOOK OF THE DUCHESS*, for example, was probably written to commemorate the death of BLANCHE, duchess of Landcaster and wife to EDWARD III's brother JOHN OF GAUNT. In a lighter vein, *The PARLIAMENT OF FOWLS* may have been composed to celebrate the engagement of RICHARD II and ANNE OF BOHEMIA. These poems, and others that belong to the early and middle years of Chaucer's literary career, such as *The HOUSE OF FAME* and *TROILUS AND CRISEYDE*, reflect the tastes and concerns of the aristocracy. The works that are serious in tone and subject matter generally feature characters with whom members of this class could identify, while the comic works, like *The Parliament of Fowls*, gently poke fun at some aristocratic attitudes and preoccupations. In the latter part of his career, however, it seems likely that Chaucer's conception of his audience underwent some kind of transformation. When he began writing *The CANTERBURY TALES*, although he was still employed in the king's service, he was no longer closely associated with the court, and perhaps this led him to explore the possibility of writing for a larger audience. The characters in *The Canterbury Tales* are for the most part middle-class. The only two members of the nobility are the KNIGHT (1) and his son, the SQUIRE. And although the tales contained in the Canterbury collection include a couple of romances (a type of literature popular among the nobility), they also feature folk tales, BEAST FABLES, FABLIAUX, SAINTS' LIVES, wisdom literature, and a sermon, all of which would appeal to members of the middle class whose literacy level was rising fast at the end of the 14th century. The manner in which his books were read—i.e., whether silently and in private, or aloud and to an audience—was largely determined by the availability of books, which at this time still had to be copied out by hand. Because of the time and labor involved in creating or reproducing a book, they were naturally quite expensive, and this is one reason behind the practice of reading aloud. In that way more people were able to enjoy the same book.

Auffrike   *See* AFRICA.

Augustine, Saint   Born in Tagaste in northern Africa in 354, Augustine became one of the four great fathers of the Latin church. In his youth he studied rhetoric at a University in CARTHAGE and then taught rhetoric in Italy. According to his *Confessions,* which he wrote at the age of 45, he wasted his youth in dissolute living. Intellectually, he first embraced Neoplatonist and then Manichaean beliefs, but his search for truth eventually led him back to Christianity through the influence of Saint AMBROSE. He was baptized in 387, took up a monastic life for a short time, became a priest, and in 395 was consecrated bishop of Hippo in northern Africa. He died in 430 during the siege of Hippo by the Vandals.

Augustine's extensive writings include 500 sermons and 200 letters. They treat almost every aspect of Christian faith and morals, and much of what he wrote was aimed at defending orthodoxy against the pressures exerted by contemporary heretical groups such as the Donatists, Manichaeans and Pelagians. His distrust of sensory and material knowledge in favor of spiritual truth and revelation may have been a reaction against his earlier skepticism. In general, he believed that all truth was spiritual, that it derived from God who was truth incarnate, and that the acceptance of truth depended upon God's grace. He was in fact the first Christian theologian to express the doctrine of man's salvation by divine grace.

In his *City of God,* Augustine's best-known work, he presents the continuous struggle in history symbolically as a struggle between two cities—a city of those who do God's will and a city of unbelievers. He argued that although the two are intermingled and coexist here on Earth, they are fated to be completely and irrevocably separated at the end of time. This work also attempted to answer the criticisms of those who rejected Christianity because God had allowed Rome to fall, by attempting to show them the huge scale of the universe and God's plan for man, within which the fall of Rome was as a drop in the ocean.

Augustine's writings were known among most learned men in the Middle Ages, and references to them are scattered throughout Chaucer's work. The satiric portrait of the MONK in the GENERAL PROLOGUE TO *THE CANTERBURY TALES* notes that the worldly prelate has no desire to work with his hands and to labor as Augustine commanded. The reference is probably to a monastic rule used by Augustinian canons, though John GOWER also applies it to monks in the *Mirour de l'Omme.* In the "TALE OF MELIBEE," Dame PRUDENCE attributes to Augustine some of the advice she offers her husband on how to respond to the robbery that has troubled their family. In telling him that he should not place such a great value on material goods, she quotes Augustine as saying "The avaricious man is likned unto helle, / that the moore it swelweth the moore desir it hath to swelwe and devoure." (lines 1617–18) [The avaricious man is similar to hell / in that the more he swallows the more he desires to swallow and devour]. This particular quotation is not found in Augustine's works, but is similar to an idea expressed in the Bible in Proverbs 27:20. CHAUNTICLEER, the learned chicken of "The NUN'S PRIEST'S TALE," also appears to have read Augustine, and ironically his reading displays more accurate knowledge than that possessed by Dame Prudence. Chaunticleer mentions Augustine as he debates with his wife on the question of whether God's foreknowledge of an event has a compromising effect on the idea of free will. On a more serious note, Augustine's teachings are alluded to repeatedly in "The PARSON'S TALE," itself a sermon on penitence and the Seven Deadly Sins—pride, avarice, gluttony, ire, lechery, envy and sloth.

Augustus Caesar   Augustus Caesar, also called Caesar Augustus, was the grandnephew of JULIUS CAESAR and the first Roman emperor, ruling the empire from 27 B.C. to A.D. 14. He is mentioned once in Chaucer's work, in the *TREATISE ON THE ASTROLABE,* part one, section 10, where Chaucer is describing how the number of days in a month was decided for the Roman calendar. Listing the months by name, he notes that some of them were given Latin names reflecting their properties (like December, the 10th month of the Roman year), while some were named for Arabian statutes and some, like July (Latin *Julius*), were named for Roman leaders. He also states that Julius Caesar took two days out of February and put them in his month of July, while Augustus Caesar determined that August, the month named after him, must have 31 days. Chaucer errs in this passage by asserting that some of the months were given Arabic names; they are, in fact, all Roman. Also, Julius Caesar did not make the changes Chaucer attributes to him. Although he did give July 31 days, he took none from February. It was Augustus Caesar who took one day (not two) from February in order to give August as many days as July.

Aurelian (Aurelianus) The Roman emperor who ruled the empire from 270 to 275. Aurelian is mentioned once in Chaucer's work, in "The MONK'S TALE." The MONK does not actually tell one tale, but when invited to take his turn in the tale-telling contest he embarks upon a series of tragedies and can only be stopped by the Host's (*see* Harry BAILLY) forceful interruption. One of the tragedies relates the story of ZENO-BIA, the queen of PALMYRA in SYRIA. A noble and virtuous warrior queen, Zenobia and her husband, ODENATHUS, conquered many kingdoms in the Orient, but she was finally defeated by Aurelian, who attacked her at the head of the mighty Roman legion in the year 272. When he had overcome the queen and her armies, Aurelian paraded her in chains before his chariot (line 2351). Chaucer's story of Zenobia and her defeat by Aurelian is taken from BOCCACCIO's *De claris mulieribus*.

Aurelie *See* AURELIUS.

Aurelius The squire who is in love with DORIGEN, wife to ARVERAGUS, in "The FRANKLIN'S TALE." When we are introduced to Aurelius we find out that he has been in love with Dorigen for a long time but never had the courage to reveal his feelings. Arveragus' absence from home provides the motive and the opportunity for him to do so. Dorigen rebuffs his advances, affirming her devotion to her husband, but then teasingly promises to become Aurelius' lover if he can move or destroy some treacherous rocks along the coast of BRITTANY which pose a danger for incoming ships, including that of her husband's. Of all the lovesick young men who appear in Chaucer's poetry, Aurelius is perhaps the most appealing, because he, unlike any of the others, is able to overcome (or at least to redirect) his sexual urges when he understands the harm that will occur to the woman he desires.

Aurora (1) *Aurora* is the Roman name (and the name Chaucer uses) for the goddess of the dawn in classical mythology. From her couch in Oceanus in the Far East, she rose before the break of day to mount her golden chariot drawn by white horses. Her role was to herald the approach of the sun and to usher in the day. Representations show her with rosy fingers and gleaming white wings, clad in a saffron mantle. Captivated by the beauty of a mortal man, she carried him off in her chariot to live with her in the palace of the dawn. JUPITER, at her request, granted him immortality, but

because she had forgotten to ask for eternal youth, her lover grew extraordinarily old and was finally turned into a grasshopper. Her son, Memnon, supported King PRIAM in the TROJAN WAR. When he was killed by ACHILLES, she plunged into such inconsolable grief that she hid herself behind the clouds for a time of mourning. Forever after, in the early morning she shed tears for him which appear on Earth as dew. The goddess of the dawn is mentioned once in Chaucer's work where, interestingly enough, instead of shedding the dew, she is described as sending down the streams of morning heat that dry it up. The reference appears in the biography of THISBE that Chaucer included in *The LEGEND OF GOOD WOMEN* (line 774).

Aurora (2) The *Aurora* to which Chaucer refers in *The BOOK OF THE DUCHESS* is a 12th-century commentary on parts of the Bible by Peter of Riga. The BLACK KNIGHT, in the course of describing how he tried to woo the fair Lady WHITE with music, says that although he was not as good at making songs as was Lamech's son TUBAL, he did his best. He refers to Tubal as the first musician, who discovered the art while listening to his brother's hammer ringing against an anvil. The actual name of the biblical character of whom he speaks is Jubal, who in Genesis 4:21 is called the "father of all such as handle the harp and the organ." The ascription to Tubal with a *T* also occurs in the *Aurora*, which, according to the Black Knight, relates that the Greeks believe PYTHAGORAS invented music.

Auster *Auster* is the Roman name for Notus, the south wind. The troublesome nature of this wind, which was reputed to bring fog and sickness and to be harmful to plants and animals and dangerous to seafarers, is referred to several times in the *BOECE*, Chaucer's translation of BOETHIUS' *Consolation of Philosophy*. Boethius' references to the disturbances created by this wind suggest a parallel to his own misfortunes.

Austyn *See* AUGUSTINE, SAINT.

Averroës (Averrois) Spanish-Arab philosopher and physician of the 12th century. Later in life, when he served as a physician to the ruler of Morocco, Averroës was attacked by Muslim theologians for his rationalistic views. In his philosophical writings he denied personal immortality and creation, and he considered God to be simply a first agent or Prime Mover. Accused of heresy, he was imprisoned, and his books, except those concerned with science, were burned. His most influential surviving works are the commentaries he wrote on ARIS-TOTLE. It was probably his adherence to an Aristotelian worldview that made him unable to accept the fundamental doctrines of Islam and thus got him in trouble with the Muslims. In the latter part of the 13th century, his commentaries became important texts for those who wished to challenge the reconciliation between Aristotelian thought and Christianity that was taking place under the leadership of men like Albertus Magnus and Thomas AQUINAS. Averroës wrote on medicine as well as philosophy, and he is mentioned in Chaucer's GENERAL PROLOGUE TO *THE CANTERBURY TALES* as one of the medical authorities whose teachings the DOCTOR OF PHYSIC had studied (line 433).

Avicenna Arab physician and philosopher born near Bukhara in 980. His writings embraced every field of intellectual endeavor but exerted their greatest influence in the areas of medicine and philosophy. His enormous, encyclopedic *Canon of Medicine* was considered authoritative up until the end of the 19th century. Avicenna is mentioned in Chaucer's GENERAL PROLOGUE TO *THE CANTERBURY TALES* as one of the medical authorities whose teachings the DOCTOR OF PHYSIC had studied.

Avycen *See* AVICENNA.

Ayash *Ayash* is the modern name of Lyeys, a seaport near Antioch, in the medieval kingdom of Cilicia or Lesser ARMENIA. It is listed among those cities visited by Chaucer's KNIGHT during one of his military campaigns (line 58). Chaucer may have had in mind the successful campaign conducted by Peter of Cyprus (*see* PIERRE DE LUSIGNAN) against the city in 1367. The Cyprian army contained a number of English knights.

Babilan (Babiloigne; Babiloyne)   *See* BABYLON.

Babiloigne (Babiloyne)   *See* BABYLON.

Babylon   Ancient walled city, the capital of the Babylonian Empire, that was located between the Tigris and Euphrates Rivers. The city's origins are unknown. According to Babylonian tradition, it was built by the god Marduk. It must have been built some time before 2300 B.C. because it was destroyed about that time by an invading army. This makes Babylon one of the oldest cities of the ancient world. The city is mentioned twice in Chaucer's work. In *The LEGEND OF GOOD WOMEN* it is the home of THISBE, one of the ill-fated lovers in the popular classical legend of PYRAMUS AND THISBE, whose story resembles that of Shakespeare's Romeo and Juliet. Babylon was also the home of NEBUCHADNEZZAR, the king whose abbreviated biography appears in "The MONKS'S TALE." The greatest king of the Babylonian empire, Nebuchadnezzar enlarged the capital city to an area of six square miles and beautified it with magnificent buildings and the famous terraced hanging gardens, which he built for one of his wives. The city was famed for its beauty and opulence, and this is undoubtedly what the BLACK KNIGHT in Chaucer's *BOOK OF THE DUCHESS* is thinking of when he says that he would rather have his queen back than to possess all the riches of Babylon (line 1061).

Bacchus (Bacus)   In classical mythology, Bacchus, or Dionysus, was the Greek god of wine and, by extension, of nature's fertility as exemplified in the vine. He was the son of Zeus (JUPITER) and Semele. His worship spread rapidly from Thrace through Greece and the islands, and from there to Egypt and Asia and finally to the western Mediterranean. The intoxicating power of wine was considered to be symbolic of the intoxicating power of nature, and the rites associated with him were characterized by orgiastic revels, celebrated by women wandering in the woods and over the hills by night. Wildly uninhibited dancing accompanied the music of drum and flute. Sacrificial victims were torn apart and eaten raw. Milder celebrations of the deity emphasized his beneficent influence as the god of vegetable increase and the source of happiness and freedom from care, as well as the inspirer of music and song.

Bacchus' association with VENUS, the goddess of love, and the compatibility of wine and sexual enjoyment are mentioned twice in *The CANTERBURY TALES*, first at the marriage of JANUARY and MAY in "The MERCHANT'S TALE." Later, in "The PHYSICIAN'S TALE," the narrator states that wine had never passed over the lips of the chaste VIRGINIA because it was known to increase sexual desire. The god Bacchus likewise appears seated by the side of Venus in the garden of *The PARLIAMENT OF FOWLS*. In the prologue to "The MANCIPLE'S TALE," wine functions as a peacemaker when, after insulting the COOK, the MANCIPLE is able to speedily make amends by offering him a drink from his flask. The Host (*see* Harry BAILLY) responds by praising Bacchus for his ability to turn a serious matter into a jest (prologue; line 58). The *BOECE* twice alludes to Bacchus' association with the cultivation of the vine and wine-making.

Bailly, Harry   The innkeeper of the TABARD Inn, where the Canterbury pilgrims spend the night before departing on their pilgrimage to the shrine of St. THOMAS À BECKET at Canterbury cathedral. Referred to in the GENERAL PROLOGUE TO *THE CANTERBURY TALES* as the host of the inn, Bailly is described as a large man with big bright eyes who is bold in his speech, wise and manly. After the pilgrims have eaten supper, Bailly joins in their conversation and offers to reveal a plan that he pledges will help to shorten their journey by making it more enjoyable. The plan is for each of them to tell four stories—two on the way to the shrine and two on the return trip—as part of a storytelling contest. Bailly offers to accompany them both as guide and as judge for the storytelling contest. Upon their return, the winner will receive supper at the Tabard, which will be paid for by all the other pilgrims. Bailly also at this time establishes himself as a moderator among the pilgrims by suggesting that anyone who challenges his judgment regarding the tale-telling shall bear the expenses incurred by the rest of the company during the journey to CANTERBURY and back. We later see him fulfilling his role as moderator by suggesting the order in which the pilgrims participate in the contest (although his suggestions are not always followed), and by pronouncing judgment upon each pilgrim's performance (and sometimes, as in the case of the PARDONER, the MILLER and others, upon the pilgrim's character) in the prologues and epilogues to the various tales. The Host is one of the pilgrims thought to have been based on an actual person. A man named Henri Bayliff (such variations in the spelling of a person's name were common at this time) is listed in a government document as an "ostlyer," or innkeeper in SOUTHWARK in 1380–81. Chaucer is thought to have begun writing *The Canterbury Tales* around this time.

"Balade of Complaint, A" A short poem of doubtful authorship, sometimes attributed to Chaucer. Despite its title and its three stanzas, the work does not fit the French BALLADE form, which Chaucer was so fond of using for his short lyric poems, and its attribution to him by W. W. SKEAT, which is unsupported by any external evidence, appears one of the least justified. A typical lover's complaint in which the narrator addresses his lady, describing his lengthy service and the depth of his devotion in the hope of gaining some reward, the poem displays some debt to Chaucer but is far from attaining his typical level of expertise.

Baldeswelle *See* BAWDESWELL.

Baldwin, Ralph (1912–) Chaucerian scholar. Baldwin received his Ph.D. from Johns Hopkins. His book *The Unity of the Canterbury Tales* (1955; rptd. 1971) is a timeless study, the first to fully formulate the idea that the image of pilgrimage was the unifying theme of the Canterbury group. Focusing on the opening and closing portions of the work, Baldwin demonstrates how each contributes to this unity. The GENERAL PROLOGUE, with its images of springtime and rebirth, announces the pilgrimage and emphasizes its social and religious implications. The PARSON's sermon on penitence is read as a fitting conclusion to a journey that, by the end of the tales, clearly exhibits meanings on several different levels, one of them being the view of life as a pilgrimage ending in heaven. The PARSON's discussion of the Seven Deadly Sins looks backward to the sins of the different pilgrims, and forward to Chaucer's own confession in the RETRACTION with which the work closes.

Ball, John A vagrant English priest who, with Wat TYLER, was a leading force in the PEASANT'S REVOLT OF 1381. In the early stages of the revolt, before the mass of angry peasant's converged on London, Tyler and a band of his followers broke into the archbishop's prison in CANTERBURY where they liberated Ball, who was under arrest for propounding his radical ideas declaring that all men should be equal, that lordship should be abolished and that land should be taken away from the aristocracy and upper clergy and distributed among the poor. Ball provided the movement with an ideology, and, like many a successful dema-

gogue, he coined a slogan that achieved long-lasting fame: "When Adam delved and Eve span, / Who was then a gentleman?" The rebels proposed to make Ball the new archbishop of Canterbury; it is uncertain how this was reconciled with the idea of abolishing the hierarchy of the established church. For his part in the uprising, Ball was executed in the summer of 1381. Although Chaucer surely knew the role Ball played in the revolt, the only rebel leader mentioned in his poetry was Jack STRAW.

ballade One of the most popular of the artificial French verse forms in the Middle Ages. It should not be confused with the English term *ballad*, which is a type of poetry adapted for singing or recitation that typically takes the form of a dramatic narrative. The traditional ballade was characterized by a fairly rigid structure consisting of three seven- or eight-line stanzas rhyming *ababbcc* or *ababbcbc*, and an envoy (concluding half-stanza) of four lines rhyming *bcbc*. The last line of the first stanza forms a refrain that is repeated as the final line of the subsequent stanzas and of the envoy. Conventionally, the envoy opens with an address to a prince or a lord. Chaucer employed the ballade form for a number of his short poems, including "The COMPLAINT OF VENUS," "TO ROSEMOUNDE," "WOMANLY NOBLESSE," "FORTUNE," "TRUTH," "GENTILESSE," "LAK OF STEDFASTNESSE" and "The COMPLAINT OF CHAUCER TO HIS PURSE." It is a testimony to Chaucer's poetic genius that he was able to execute the rhyme scheme of the ballade form in these poems without ever repeating a rhyme word, except in the refrain.

Ballenus, Hermes *See* BELINOUS.

Balthasar *See* BELSHAZZAR.

Barberie (Barbary, Barbery) The word *Barberie* was used by writers of the medieval and Renaissance periods to refer to those parts of the world that were known to be pagan rather than Christian. According to F. P. MAGOUN's *Chaucer Gazetteer*, the word reflects an Old French adaptation of Latin *(terra) barbaria*, "foreign, barbarous country." Accordingly, the name should not be confused with the latter-day *Barbary* or *Barbary Coast*. The word appears once in "The FRANKLIN'S TALE" (line 1452).

Barnabo de Lumbardia *See* VISCONTI, BERNABO.

Basil, Saint (Basil the Great) One of the most celebrated of the Greek Fathers of the Catholic church. Born at Caesarea in Cappadocia (Asia Minor), he early distinguished himself as a student at Constantinople and at Athens. He was consecrated bishop of Caesarea in 370 and is famous for his defense of the Catholic faith before the Roman emperor Constantius. He left many writings, and the philosopher Erasmus considered him to be the finest orator of all time. In art, Saint Basil is represented standing near a fire with a dove perched on his arm. In the sermon that constitutes "The PARSON'S TALE," the narrator quotes Saint Basil's description of the fires of hell: "The brennynge of the fyr of this world shal God yeven in helle to hem that been dampned, / but the light and the cleernesse shal be yeven in heven to his children." (lines 220–21) [The burning aspect of this world's fire shall God give to those who are damned in hell, / but the light and the clearness of the fire shall be given to his children in heaven].

Basilie *See* BASIL, SAINT.

Basilius One of the men serving in the sixth-century court of THEODORIC, king of the Goths, who spoke out against BOETHIUS, causing him to be charged with crimes against the king and sent into exile. After making the allegations against Boethius, Basilius was also exiled. He is mentioned in Book One, Prosa 4 of the *BOECE* where Boethius tells LADY PHILOSOPHY how he came to be in the situation that she has found him in.

Bath (Bathe) City in southwestern England known for the hot springs of which, during their occupation of England, the Romans took advantage for constructing elaborate public baths. During the medieval period it was known as a clothmaking center. The WIFE OF BATH, who appears as one of the tale-tellers in *The CANTERBURY TALES*, is from "biside Bathe," beside Bath, which probably indicates that she lived in a village near the larger city. The Wife's profession is that of weaving cloth, which may be why Chaucer chose to have her come from the area surrounding a city known for its manufacture.

Baugh, Albert C. (1891–1981) Chaucerian scholar, educator, philologist and author. Baugh was best known for his writings on the English language and medieval literature and culture. This American scholar edited *A Literary History of England*, which includes a chapter on Chaucer's life and work. In 1963 he published an annotated edition of the poet's work entitled *The Major Poetry of Chaucer*, which offers critical texts of all Chaucer's major poems except the *ROMAUNT OF THE ROSE, ANELIDA AND ARCITE* and a few of the short lyrics. *The LEGEND OF GOOD WOMEN*, however, is only represented by version F of the Prologue and the life of CLEOPATRA. Additionally, *The CANTERBURY TALES* omits "The PARSON'S TALE" and "The TALE OF MELIBEE." Baugh also compiled an important bibliography of Chaucer criticism for the Goldentree Bibliography series. Revised and expanded in 1977, this volume contains 3,215 bibliographical entries on topics ranging from the poet's life and historical environment to his lost and apocryphal works. Entries for all the major and minor poetry and prose are included.

Baum, Paull (1886–1964) Baum, a professor of English at Duke University, made a number of important contributions to Chaucer scholarship, including *Chaucer: A Critical Appreciation* (1958) and *Chaucer's Verse* (1961). In *A Critical Interpretation*, Baum argues simultaneously for higher standards and for less "silliness" in Chaucer criticism, noting a trend to either eulogize the poet's work while studiously overlooking its faults, or to find complex and belabored hidden meanings within it. In *Chaucer's Verse*, Baum examines the "whole subject" of Chaucer's meters, to determine "what may have been his principles of versification and how clearly he followed them and to what effect." He concludes that it is a composite of the rhythm of contemporary spoken prose and the metrical forms the poet adopted. Of these components, the first is conjectural.

Bawdeswell A town in the county of NORFOLK, situated in the east of England, on the North Sea. It is mentioned in the GENERAL PROLOGUE to *The CANTERBURY TALES* as the home of the REEVE. Chaucer may have chosen this locale because of the popular belief that Norfolk people were crafty and treacherous. The Reeve's treachery lies in his mismanagement of his landlord's estate, where his duties include overseeing and maintaining pasture, fields and woods as well as collecting rents from tenant farmers. This Reeve has accumulated considerable wealth by cheating his master. There is some evidence that, in creating this portrait, Chaucer may have been thinking of an actual incident involving the estates of the earls of Pembroke, which lay in Norfolk. The reeve in charge of these estates was investigated for mismanagement in 1386–87.

Bayard The palfrey (horse) in "The REEVE'S TALE." Bayard belongs to the warden of SOLER HALL, a college at CAMBRIDGE (Cantebrigge) University. Two students, ALAN and JOHN THE CLERK, borrow him to take their grain to the local miller. While they oversee the grinding of their grain, SIMKIN, the miller, unties their horse so that he will have the opportunity to steal from them while they attempt to recapture the horse. When he is set free, the horse neighs a joyous "wehee" and gallops off to join a group of wild mares running in the fen. Paul RUGGIERS has suggested that the miller's action in setting free the horse's instinctive sexual energy also starts a chain reaction that will culminate in the release of the students' sexual energy as they give way to their instinctive desires with the miller's wife and daughter.

beast fable   A fable consists of a brief tale, either in prose or in verse, told to point out a moral. The most popular kind of fables are beast fables, featuring animals as characters to satirically illuminate the follies of humankind. The most famous of these are *Aesop's Fables,* and some of the material upon which Chaucer draws for "The NUN'S PRIEST'S TALE" has its ultimate source in the work attributed to AESOP. Other of Chaucer's works that contain elements of the beast fable are "The MANCIPLE'S TALE," which features a talking crow, and an earlier poem, *The PARLIAMENT OF FOWLS,* in which a group of birds engage in a love-debate.

Becket, Saint Thomas à   *See* THOMAS À BECKET, SAINT

Belial   *Belial* is an Old Testament term designating a godless or lawless person. It is also used as an alternative name for Satan. In "The PARSON'S TALE," where corrupt and licentious priests are spoken of as the "sons of Belial," the usage suggests both meanings.

Belinous   Belinous, or Hermes Ballenus, as Chaucer calls him, was a supposed disciple of HERMES TRISMEGISTUS ("thrice-great Hermes"), which was the Greek name given to Thoth, the Egyptian god of wisdom. A number of books on theology and magic written in the first centuries A.D. were attributed to this personage, though nothing is known about his life or that of his disciple, Belinous. It seems likely that the writers of these texts borrowed his name to give their works authority. Chaucer includes Belinous (but not Hermes Trismegistus) among the magicians he observes practicing their arts in FAME's palace in *The HOUSE OF FAME.*

Belle, the   A tavern in SOUTHWARK, a district of London south of the river Thames. In the GENERAL PROLOGUE to *The CANTERBURY TALES,* the narrator mentions the Belle (line 719) in order to specify the location of the TABARD Inn, where all the pilgrims gathered before embarking on their journey to CANTERBURY. He says that the Tabard is close to the Belle, suggesting that the Belle was, to some, better known than the Tabard.

Bellona   The Roman goddess of war, identified with the Greek goddess Enyo and looked upon as the wife or sister of MARS (1). She was represented with helmet, shield and spear. Chaucer mentions her in the invocation of this *ANELIDA AND ARCITE,* asking her and Mars to assist him in writing his poem ("song"). In the line where she is mentioned, Chaucer appears to use the name *Pallas* as an appositive for Bellona, thus exhibiting some confusion between PALLAS Athena, the goddess of wisdom who was also pictured in martial attire, and the goddess of war. They were in actuality two distinctly different goddesses. The mistake may have originated in the work of earlier authors, including the Italian BOCCACCIO, who sometimes confuse the two.

Belmarin (Banu Merin)   A powerful Berber dynasty that ruled what is now Morocco. Chaucer uses the name of the dynasty to refer to the country when he states, in the GENERAL PROLOGUE TO *THE CANTERBURY TALES,* that the KNIGHT (1) has campaigned in, among other places, Belmarye. The Knight's activity there may refer to attacks by Christian privateers on towns controlled by the dynasty. Interestingly, in "The KNIGHT'S TALE," he describes PALAMON's desire to kill ARCITE as being more fierce than a lion of Belmarye (line 57), so that the tale would seem to reflect the Knight's experience as well as simply retelling BOCCACCIO's *TESEIDA.*

Belmarye   *See* BELMARIN.

Belshazzar   The son of Nabonidus (and grandson of NEBUCHADNEZZAR) and the last king of the Neo-Babylonian Empire. According to the Old Testament book of Daniel, Belshazzar was fond of sensual pleasure. On one occasion he held a drunken banquet attended by his wives, concubines and a thousand of his lords, during which they all drank from the sacred vessels which his father (probably his grandfather) had taken from the Jewish Temple in Jerusalem, thus insulting the captive Jews and their God. According to the biblical story, the revelry was interrupted by the appearance of a hand writing upon the wall these words: "MENE, MENE TEKEL, UPHARSIN." Disturbed by this event, Belshazzar sent for DANIEL, a Jewish prophet, who interpreted the writing as a sign of doom for the Babylonian Empire. That very night, the soldiers of DARIUS THE MEDE (possibly another name for Cyrus the Persian) captured Babylon, and Belshazzar was killed. A version of this story, emphasizing the role of FORTUNE in Belshazzar's downfall, appears in Chaucer's "MONK'S TALE."

Benedict, Saint   Known as the Patriarch of the western monks, Saint Benedict was born at Norcia in central Italy in 480. In early youth he retired into a cave in the mountains near Rome, where he led a hermit's life. After three years of solitude, he built 12 monasteries for the numerous disciples who had gathered around him. In the year 529 he went to Monte Cassino, on the road to Naples, and there founded the great abbey of that name. The Rule written by Saint Benedict, in the course of a hundred years or so, was accepted by all western monks. It shows the way to religious perfection by the practice of humility, obedience, prayer, silence and retirement from the concerns of the world. Chaucer's satirical portrait of the MONK in the GENERAL PROLOGUE TO *THE CANTERBURY TALES* specifically notes that this member of the regular clergy sees no need for such a rule, which he considers outdated. The Monk violates the rule through his pride and worldliness.

Benedight   *See* BENEDICT, SAINT.

Beneit   *See* BENEDICT, SAINT.

Bennett, J(ack) A(rthur) W(alter) (1911–1981)   A New Zealand Chaucerian scholar who received a doctorate from Oxford University and who served as a professor at both Oxford and Cambridge, Bennett edited at *Medium Aevum* and wrote on a wide variety of medieval topics, notably on Langland and Gower. He edited "The KNIGHT'S TALE," wrote book-length interpretations of *The PARLIAMENT OF FOWLS* and *The HOUSE OF FAME*, and authored *Chaucer at Oxford and at Cambridge*, in which he studies not the Chaucerian scholarship at these universities, but rather "the roles that his clerks play in either place." Bennett explores the implications of the fact that Chaucer, a Londoner who served the king at court, "should include in *the dramatis personae of the Tales* no fewer than five academics" from Oxford or Cambridge.

Benoît de Sainte-Maure   A 12th-century French poet who was patronized by King Henry II of England, for whom he composed a verse history of the dukes of Normandy, Henry's ancestors. Benoît's most celebrated work is the *Roman de Troie* ("Book of Troy"), which told the story of the TROJAN WAR based on the writings of DARES PHRYGIUS and DICTYS CRETENSIS. The *Roman* was translated into Latin prose by Guido da Colonna, and thus served as a source for many subsequent writers, including BOCCACCIO, whose *FILOSTRATO* in turn became a source for Chaucer's TROILUS AND CRISEYDE. Chaucer also made considerable direct use of Benoît in *Troilus and Criseyde*, restoring some passages that Boccaccio had omitted, such as CRISEYDE's self-lacerating soliloquy that follows her jilting of TROILUS.

Benson, Larry D(ean)(1929–   )   Chaucerian scholar. A Berkeley Ph.D. who made his career at Harvard, Benson has produced studies of literary meaning derived from the interaction of the work and its tradition. After writing such a study of *Sir Gawain and the Green Knight*, Benson authored *The Literary Context of Chaucer's "Fabliaus"* and then turned his attention to Thomas Malory. In his book on the fabliaux, Benson's comment on the changes Chaucer made from his sources can be summed up by his comments on those in Chaucer's "Miller's Tale": "Chaucer's tale, for all its cruelties, is more humane" than the source he used. Not only does Chaucer mute the pain and injury, but he does not try to draw any "vengeful moral." Instead Chaucer, says Benson, "looks on with good-natured tol-

erance." Benson is probably most well known for serving as general editor for the third edition of the *Riverside Chaucer* (1987), recognized today as the authoritative scholarly edition of the poet's work.

Bere   *See* URSA.

Bernard   A Bernard is mentioned in Chaucer's GENERAL PROLOGUE TO *THE CANTERBURY TALES* as one of the medical authorities whose teachings the DOCTOR OF PHYSIC had studied (line 434). The name likely refers to Bernard of Gordon, who flourished around 1283–1309, teaching on the medical faculty at Montpellier in France. His most important work was the *Lilium medicinae*, which contains the earliest known reference to eyeglasses.

Bernard, Saint   Saint Bernard of Clairvaux was a 12th-century Cistercian monk who founded Clairvaux and other monasteries. He initially entered the monastery of Citeaux, together with 30 other noblemen of Burgundy whom he had, amazingly, persuaded to join him. His strong personality and tremendous zeal breathed new life into the Cistercian order and made it the most popular and influential of its day. Although dedicated to the monastic ideal of worshipping God in the seclusion of a monastery, Bernard lived a most active life, attending church councils, urging spiritual reform and ending a papal schism. The popularity of the cult of the Virgin and the flowering of mysticism in the centuries following his death are attributable to his influence. His eloquence in speaking and writing gained him the title "Mellifluous Doctor." The prologue of "The SECOND NUN'S TALE" alludes both to his eloquence and to his association with the Virgin by addressing Saint MARY as the flower of virgins of whom Bernard wrote so pleasingly. Bernard's writings are referred to repeatedly in the sermon that makes up "The PARSON'S TALE."

Berwick (Berwyk)   Although the town referred to as "Berwyk" in Chaucer's portrait of the PARDONER at first would seem to be the city of Berwick-on-Tweed, which lies at the edge of the river Tweed on the border between Scotland and England, the *Chaucer Gazetteer* argues against the certainty of this, noting that there are about 13 modern Berwicks distributed among the counties of Essex, Kent, Northumberland, Shropshire, Sussex, Worcestershire, Yorkshire, Norfolk, Suffolk, Oxfordshire and Lancashire. The narrator of the GENERAL PROLOGUE says that there was never another pardoner like this one, from Berwyk down to WARE. Whichever Berwick is correct, however, the town of Ware would still be at some distance from it, indicating that the Pardoner's jurisdiction extends over a considerable distance. The name *Berwick* comes from Old

English *bere-wic,* meaning "grain farm," which helps to explain its widespread usage.

Bethulia (Bethulie)   A city in the Babylonian Empire, occupied by the Israelites. According to the apocryphal book of Judith, this city was the setting for the story of JUDITH's beheading of HOLOFERNES. The city is mentioned twice in Chaucer's CANTERBURY TALES, once in "The TALE OF MELIBEE" and once in "The MONK'S TALE"; on both occasions the reference is to the story of Judith.

Bevis   *Bevis of Hampton* was a popular English metrical romance from the late 13th or early 14th century. Based on a 12th-century Anglo-Norman CHANSON DE GESTE entitled *Beuves de Hanstone,* the story tells of how Bevis' mother, the wife of Guy, earl of Southampton, has her husband murdered and marries the murderer. Bevis is sold into slavery in the East, where he converts Josian, the daughter of the king of Arabia, and then marries her. They have various adventures in the Middle East and in Europe, and eventually Bevis returns to England, where he kills his father's murderer. Chaucer mentions this romance hero in "The TALE OF SIR THOPAS," which is also a metrical romance written in TAIL-RHYME stanzas.

Bialacoil   In *The ROMAUNT OF THE ROSE, Bialacoil* is the Middle English version of the French name (*Bel Acueil*) for the allegorical figure who welcomes the Dreamer into the rose garden that is the geographical and symbolic center of the poem. The *Romaunt* is Chaucer's translation into Middle English of the famous French poem *Le ROMAN DE LA ROSE* by GUILLAUME DE LORRIS and JEAN DE MEUN. Chaucer only translated the poem up to line 1705, and Bialacoil does not appear until later, in an anonymous continuation known to scholars as Fragment B. Fragment B also breaks off unfinished and is picked up by another continuator in Fragment C, in which Bialacoil's name is accurately translated as "Fair Welcome."

Biblis   In OVID'S *METAMORPHOSES,* Biblis fell hopelessly in love with her brother Caunus. After he repulsed her and fled, she went mad. In *The PARLIAMENT OF FOWLS,* Biblis is one of the women whose story is depicted on a wall in the TEMPLE OF VENUS that is entirely dedicated to women who died for the sake of love; as a symbolic token the wall is also decorated with broken hunting bows to signify that these women no longer belong in the service of DIANA, the chaste goddess of the moon.

Bilia (Bilyea)   A Roman woman of the third century B.C., Bilia (or Bilyea) was famed for her chastity. She was married to the Roman general Dullius, who was notorious for his bad breath. Her patient tolerance of her husband's breath is evidently what earned Bilia her glowing reputation. In "The FRANKLIN'S TALE," Bilia is among the virtuous women whom DORIGEN recalls when resolving to remain faithful to her husband ARVERAGUS, despite her promise to become the lover of the squire AURELIUS, if he can remove the treacherous rocks lining the coast of BRITTANY (line 1455).

Black Death, the   Also known as the Plague (specifically, bubonic plague), the Black Death was an epidemic that visited England six times during Chaucer's lifetime. The bacterial disease was most commonly transmitted to humans by bites from infected fleas. Originating in the Near East, the plague traveled westward across the European continent, following the trade routes. The symptoms were a boil ("buboe"), usually on the thigh or upper arm, which started out the size of a chicken pox and grew to the size of a small orange. Victims also experienced headache, fever, chills, weakness, vomiting and excruciating muscle pain. The infection generally lasted three to four days and ended in death. One outbreak of the plague that occurred during 1348–49, when Chaucer was around six years old, wiped out between one-third to one-half of the English population. In some cases, entire villages were depopulated. Fortunately, Chaucer's family was living in Southampton instead of at their London home during the worst outbreak.

Medieval scientific and medical knowledge was far too primitive to understand the cause or suggest viable forms of treatment for plague. The standard regimen centered on bloodletting—opening a vein in the patient's arm and letting the blood flow into a bowl in order to remove "impurities" or any "excess blood." This procedure undoubtedly did more harm than good. Some people did manage to recover from the illness, but they were a distinct minority.

The Black Death is not mentioned specifically in any of Chaucer's poetry, but it does seem to lurk in the background or just beneath the surface. The widespread fear of death and the sense of helplessness that people often felt when faced with the threat of such a disease may have been one of the factors that led Chaucer to translate the sixth-century Roman author BOETHIUS' *Consolation of Philosophy* into English. Written by a condemned man while he awaited his fate in a prison cell, this work had as its basic message the idea that everyone ought to bear their misfortune in patience because everything that happens on Earth is part of God's universal and unalterable plan. Some people, of course, responded to the threat of the Plague by indulging themselves and "living it up" in a spirit of defiance. Likewise, a spirit of recklessness and risk-taking characterizes some of Chaucer's work, such as the silly, sexy FABLIAUX he included in *The CANTERBURY TALES,* the most well-known being "The MILLER'S TALE."

Black Knight   A central character in Chaucer's elegiac *BOOK OF THE DUCHESS*. Falling asleep after reading a story from OVID's *Metamorphoses,* Chaucer's narrator dreams of walking into a forest where he encounters a young knight, dressed entirely in black, sitting on the ground beneath a tree. Curiousity compels him to approach the man, who appears to be mourning. Coming up behind him, the narrator stands as still as he can, listening to the man speak some verses that reveal the source of his sorrow: His lady has died. When he has finished, the narrator decides to speak to the knight, to see if he can perhaps ease his pain. The rest of the poem consists of a dialogue between the two, whereby the knight gradually and indirectly, through metaphor and other figures of speech, reveals the whole story of his relationship with the lady, whom he refers to as "Fair White." The therapeutic value of the experience seems evident when, at the end of the poem, the knight leaves the narrator to return home, signaling a movement away from isolation and back into society. A series of noncomic puns near the end of the poem supports other evidence that the Black Knight may represent JOHN OF GAUNT, the brother of EDWARD III who played an influential part in the government of his grandnephew, RICHARD II. Gaunt lost his first wife, BLANCHE OF LANCASTER, when he was a young man, and it is believed that Chaucer composed *The Book of the Duchess* at Gaunt's request, to commemorate his wife's death. The puns referred to above play upon Blanche's name and the name of Gaunt's favorite residence: The knight is described riding away to a "long castle" (*Longcastel* was an alternative designation for Lancaster), with "walls white" (*blanche* is the French word for "white") on a "rich hill" (*Richmond* broken down into its components of *rich* and *mond,* i.e., "mound" or hill).

Blake, Norman (Francis) (1934–)   Chaucerian scholar. An Oxford-educated professor at the University of Sheffield, Blake has written on a variety of topics, from Viking sagas, to the medieval writer William Caxton, to *Middle English Religious Prose.* He edited Chaucer's *Canterbury Tales* for Edward Arnold, publishers.

Blanche of Lancaster   One of two daughters of the man who was England's richest and most powerful noble during Chaucer's lifetime, Henry, duke of Lancaster. Because Henry had no male heirs, his vast property holdings and other wealth would, at the time of his death, be divided between his two daughters, Blanche and Maud. This fact made both of them very attractive in the marriage market, and Blanche was eventually married to one of the most powerful men in the realm, the king's son JOHN OF GAUNT. Not very much is known about Blanche's life except that her relationship with her husband was, in a time when such relationships were the exception rather than the rule, a loving one. When she died, or perhaps on the anniversary of her death, her husband requested that Chaucer write a poem in honor of her memory. The result was the elegiac *BOOK OF THE DUCHESS,* one of the earliest of Chaucer's works to display his budding poetic genius. There is also some evidence, based on a note in Thomas SPEGHT's 1602 edition of Chaucer's work, that the "ABC" was written for the duchess, either at her request or that of her husband, who then presented it to her as a gift. Blanche died in 1368 of unknown causes. (Until recently, it was thought that she died a year later, during an outbreak of the PLAGUE.) At the time of her death, she was in her late 20s, but she had already borne five children, of whom three survived: two daughters, Philippa and Elizabeth, and a son, Henry of Bolingbroke, who would later seize the throne from RICHARD II to become HENRY IV, the first Lancastrian king.

Blee   At the beginning of the prologue to "The MANCIPLE'S TALE," we are told that the pilgrims are now approaching a little town with the charming name of BOBBE-UP-AND-DOWN, which is located near "the Blee." "The Blee" is Chaucer's quaint name for the Blean Forest, through which the pilgrims' road to CANTERBURY ran for a short distance. From the forest, the path led up a steep hill whose summit may have provided the pilgrims with their first glance of the cathedral towers.

Bobbe-up-and-down   Locality mentioned in the prologue to "The MANCIPLE'S TALE" to give the reader some idea of how far the pilgrims have traveled on the road to CANTERBURY. It is the last reference to a specific place along the pilgrim's highway, and has been frequently identified as the small village of Harbledown that stands two miles north of the cathedral city. Some scholars, including F. P. Magoun in the *Chaucer Gazetteer,* have argued that the name actually refers to "Up-and-Down-Field" in the parish of Thannington, which stands one mile southwest of Canterbury. Magoun notes that nowhere else does Chaucer take the kind of liberties in altering place-names that would be involved in changing Harbledown to Bobbe-up-and-down.

Boccaccio, Giovanni (1313–1375)   Italian author whose most famous work is the *DECAMERON.* The son of a Florentine merchant, Boccaccio was born in Paris and served as a clerk in a prominent banking house for some years. From about 1325 until 1340 he resided in Naples, where he began to study literature and wrote some of his early works. His point of view was greatly influenced during this time by his association with the

Angevin court. He moved to Florence in 1340, and from about 1350 onward was employed by the city as a diplomat. It was while living in Florence that he witnessed a devastating outbreak of the BLACK PLAGUE, which he describes in the introduction to the first day of the *Decameron.* Boccaccio's early literary efforts consisted primarily of love lyrics, the most successful of which were written in honor of his beloved Fiametta. In addition to the *Decameron,* which may have been a model for Chaucer's CANTERBURY TALES, his chief works include the *Filocolo,* a prose romance about two characters named Floris and Blanchefour; the *FILOSTRATO,* a poem that was the major source for Chaucer's *TROILUS AND CRISEYDE;* the *TESEIDA,* a poem about THESEUS, PALAMON and ARCITE (1), which Chaucer adapted for "The KNIGHT'S TALE"; and the *Ameto,* a combination of pastoral and allegory. Boccaccio also wrote a number of encyclopedic works in Latin. Chaucer used his *De claris mulieribus* (of virtuous women) as a source for the women's biographies in *The LEGEND OF GOOD WOMEN,* and the *De casibus virorum illustrium* (Concerning the misfortunes of famous men) provided Chaucer with examples of tragedy for "The MONK'S TALE."

Boece This, Chaucer's translation of BOETHIUS' *Consolation of Philosophy,* is, compared to his other works, a difficult text for the modern reader for a couple of reasons. First, being a philosophical text devoted to the articulation of ideas, it is much more abstract than anything else he wrote. Also, its views of the world and reality, although they underlie some basic ideas that still inform our thinking today, seem in many ways alien to a modern perspective unless, perhaps, that perspective is tempered or informed by some of the religious teachings that maintain a certain currency in contemporary Christian theology. For the same reasons, however, the *Boece* is a very important text for understanding the rest of Chaucer, because many of the ideas contained in it had considerable influence on his work. One of the most translated works in history, Boethius' book must have spoken meaningfully to many people throughout the Middle Ages. King Alfred the Great made the first English translation in the 890s and an edition or translation was subsequently produced approximately once every generation (30 years) until the beginning of the 18th century.

SUMMARY

The narrator, Boethius, has been imprisoned for allegedly plotting against THEODORIC, the Ostragothic King of Rome from 493–526. He is nearly overwhelmed by despair when the allegorical figure of LADY PHILOSOPHY arrives and initiates a debate with him. The debate's purpose is to provide the narrator with understanding and consolation.

Book One
The text opens with the Latin phrase *Incipit Liber Boecii de Consolacione Philosophie* [Here begins Boethius' *Book of the Consolation of Philosophy*]. Throughout the *Boece,* Latin rubrics and abbreviations such as "Metrum 1" and "Prosa 1" are used to demarcate individual sections of the work. The Latin phrase represents the first few words of the text from which Chaucer was translating; they reappear, in English, in the first line of that section. The words *Metrum* or *Prosa,* followed by a numeral, indicate whether the original Latin text of the portion which follows was in poetry (meter) or prose.

Metrum 1 Metrum 1 begins with the despairing word "Alas!" followed by a description of the narrator's state of mind, comparing his current woe with his previous happiness, a happiness that consisted of flourishing intellectual activity. Whereas in the past he had composed joyful verses, his mind is presently filled with dreary verses reflecting his wretchedness. The poetic muses who shared the glory of his youth remain with him, providing him with the words to write these dreary verses. Because of his recent suffering, the narrator continues, he has grown old before his time. His hair is prematurely gray and the slack skin trembles on his bones. Even Death, who pursued him when he enjoyed FORTUNE's favor, refuses to relieve his hardship now that Fortune has forsaken him.

Prosa 1 Prosa 1 describes the appearance of Lady Philosophy, although she is not identified by name until Prosa 3. She first appears to the narrator as he sits recording his woeful thoughts. Tall and stately, with burning eyes that see further than the eye of any mortal, she possesses great strength and vigor. Then, he notes that, in contrast to her initial appearance, she can shrink in stature until her height resembles that of common men, or, alternatively, that she is able to stretch herself upward until her head reaches the heavens or beyond, so that those who try to catch a glimpse of her do so in vain. Her clothes, which she made herself, are of fine and durable cloth, but their beauty has been eclipsed by age and neglect. A Greek letter Π, signifying the "active life," is embroidered into the hem of her garment, while the highest border (presumably near the neckline) features an embroidered *T,* signifying the "contemplative life." Between these two letters a series of steps extend like the rungs of a ladder, enabling men to climb from the lower position to the higher one. In some places the garment shows evidence that men have tried to cut the cloth and violently carry away whatever pieces they can get. In her right hand, the woman carries several small books; in her left hand, she bears a scepter.

When Lady Philosophy observes how the narrator is beset by the muses of poetry who hover about his bed, providing him with the words to describe his pain and despair, she glowers at them, demanding to know who has been responsible for allowing these "common strumpets of the theatre" to approach this sick man. She criticizes the muses for deepening his sorrow rather than relieving it, by pricking him with desire that is neither fruitful nor profitable but that, rather, encourages the destruction of the fruits of reason. She is particularly angry because they have been seducing and destroying the reason of a man who is dear to her because of his endeavors in the study of philosophy. She banishes the muses, stating her intention to heal him by recourse to her own, more useful, body of knowledge.

Blinded by his tears, the narrator is unable to recognize the woman standing before him as Lady Philosophy. He stands embarrassed and bewildered, waiting to discover what she plans to do with him.

Metrum 2   Metrum 2 begins with Lady Philosophy's lament on the state of the narrator's mind, which has lost its proper clearness, its former understanding of the universe derived from study and observation, and has been plunged into a darkness consisting of misunderstanding and ignorance.

Prosa 2–Metrum 3   Lady Philosophy announces that the time has come to leave off complaining and to administer medicine. She begins by reminding the narrator of his former status as one who has been nourished by the food and drink of philosophy and who thus should have been proof against those forces which have proved his undoing. When he fails to respond, she moves closer, pronounces that he has fallen into a lethargy (a kind of trance) and proceeds to wipe the tears from his eyes using the hem of her gown. This action restores their former strength.

Prosa 3   Prosa 3 recounts how the restoration of the narrator's sight is accompanied by the restoration of his mental faculties. Finally recognizing Lady Philosophy, he asks why she has come here to his place of exile. She responds that she would never forsake one like him who has suffered because of his service to her. She then recounts examples of others who have suffered on her account, including SOCRATES and ANAXAGORAS. She furthermore reminds him that the people who are the source of such persecution are wicked, and that no matter how strong or numerous they are, they ought to be despised. When Philosophy and those who serve her are attacked by such as these, they need to take refuge in the fortress of their leader (unnamed at this point), where they may be safe from the tumult and noise of those below who desire only trivial and useless things.

Metrum 4   Lady Philosophy characterizes the man who can withstand whatever Fortune brings. He is virtuous, sober-minded and impervious to the acts of fate. Neither the raging sea nor the threatening volcano nor the tumultuous storm is able to discomfit

him because he is possessed by neither hope nor fear; he is invulnerable to the emotional turmoil from which fear arises.

Prosa 4   Lady Philosophy continues speaking to the narrator, telling him that if he desires to be healed, he must first reveal his wound. Gathering his strength and courage, the narrator suggests that certain things should be obvious, based on the circumstances in which she has found him and how different they are from his former life. He then begins the narration that will delve into the particulars of how he came to be in the situation in which he finds himself. (His circumstances have yet to be specifically named; he is, in fact, in prison.) He recalls Philosophy's recommendations, taken from PLATO, that men who govern ought to study wisdom or that, alternatively, wise men ought to apply themselves to governing in order to provide for the general wellbeing and prevent the government of cities from falling into the hands of criminals. This is what, following her instructions, he had tried to do. Yet despite the fact that nothing other than the study of goodness and good intentions led him to take on a position of authority, he found himself engaged in great conflict with wicked men because of his constant efforts to defend the poor against those who, out of greed or other motives, would abuse and torment them. He specifically mentions resistance to two men, CONNIGASTE and TRYGWILLE, the latter of whom is the king's provost. He also mentions an instance in which he opposed the king, Theodoric, over an economic policy that would force people to buy grain from the king, at an inflated price, until all that grain had been sold. In all of the narrator's works he has labored for COMMON PROFIT, i.e., the good of all the people, even defending certain Roman consuls from those who would have stolen from them or falsely accused them of wrongdoing. And because of his own love of righteousness, he made no politically expedient alliances with members of King Theodoric's court simply for the sake of protecting himself. As a result, he has been vulnerable to, and a victim of, the accusations of wicked men—men who themselves have been condemned and exiled. Based on the testimony of these men, he has been accused of protecting the Senate by preventing his accusers from delivering letters which would have falsely accused the senators of wrongdoing against King Theodoric. Furthermore, the Senate that he was trying to protect has pronounced his actions felonious. He says he can understand how the criminals he has always worked against might desire his destruction, but he complains that he does not deserve such treatment by the Senate, which he has always defended. The reward of virtue, in his case, has been suffering. He also argues that no matter what he has been accused of, he should, by law, have been given the right to be present when his case was tried. Instead, he has been sent away from Rome and, without the possibility of defending himself from the charges against him, condemned to death. His tormentors have also, out of envy, attempted to destroy his character further by accusing him of sacrilege against God. And on top of everything else, many people, observing what has happened to him, mistake the actions of Fortune (*see* FORTUNE) for the judgment of God, believing that he has brought adversity upon himself by displeasing God. In closing, he says that affairs are now in such a state in Rome that criminals may act freely without fear of punishment, while the innocent are robbed of their security and any means of protecting themselves.

Metrum 5 Metrum 5 opens with the narrator's cry to God, who controls the workings of the universe, the movement of the planets and spheres, the division of day from night and of the seasons from one another so that all proceeds harmoniously, asking why He refuses to exercise his power to govern the behavior of men. Why does He allow Fortune to turn thing upside down, so that the innocent are punished rather than criminals, who are instead allowed to occupy positions of power and influence? The narrator concludes by asking God to extend his rule to govern the works of men so that they may no longer be tossed about and tormented in the sea of fortune.

Prosa 5 Prosa 5 begins Lady Philosophy's response to the narrator's complaint. First she pronounces that more serious than his physical exile from Rome is his spiritual exile from his true home, which is governed by God, not by any mortal being. While affirming the factual nature of what he has said regarding his persecution, she notes that she is more deeply concerned with the effect that his sorrow, anger and weeping have had upon his mind, causing it to grow feeble. Before stronger medicines can be applied, something must be done to ease his emotional turmoil.

Metrum 6 Metrum 6 appears to expand on the notion contained in the biblical Book of Ecclesiastes that to everything there is a proper season, assigned by God, and that He will not allow this order in the universe to be disrupted. Those who do attempt to disturb it will never achieve a good outcome.

Prosa 6 Lady Philosophy questions the narrator to get a firmer sense of how to provide him with a cure. After receiving his answers, she concludes that he feels exiled because he has forgotten his true nature, and that his belief that criminals possess might and are prosperous arises from a clouded understanding. He has forgotten who truly governs the world in his supposition that the mutations of Fortune are part of no plan or order. All of these misunderstandings

bring not only illness but death. Thus further discerning the causes of his distress, she announces that she will relieve him by bringing light to his darkened understanding.

Metrum 7 Lady Philosophy instructs the narrator to abjure four passions: joy, fear, hope and sorrow, because they obscure thought in the same way that clouds obscure the stars or that turbulence muddies the ocean waves.

Book Two
A Latin inscription notes the ending of the first book and the beginning of the second.

Prosa 1–Metrum 1 Prosa 1 of Book Two begins with Lady Philosophy explaining that, in the main, the narrator's distemper arises from his attitude toward Fortune. She reminds him that earlier, when he enjoyed good fortune, he despised and attacked her, fully aware, at that time, of her true nature. She expounds on the dual nature of Fortune, which is to bring sometimes prosperity, and, at other times, suffering and deprivation, all without apparent deserving by the recipient. Thus, the only profitable way to deal with Fortune is to endure both her gifts and her torments with patience. Trying to change her, to arrest the movement of her turning wheel (*see* WHEEL OF FORTUNE), is as futile as trying to alter the course of the winds. Metrum 1 illustrates the effects of Fortune's turning wheel, which enables her to cast down powerful kings and to raise up humble men. She is oblivious to human pain and laughs at human tears.

Prosa 2–Metrum 2 In Prosa 2, Philosophy assumes Fortune's voice in a debate with the narrator. Speaking as Fortune, she reminds him that her gifts to him and to all men are only temporary. He has no right to complain, since he enjoyed her gifts as well as deprivation. If those things that he complains of losing had truly belonged to him, he never could have lost them. She compares her actions to the changing of the seasons and to variations in the weather. Like the weather, it is her nature to change. This section concludes with a definition of tragedy as illustrating the deeds of Fortune. During Metrum 2, Philosophy continues to speak in the guise of Fortune, saying that even if the goddess of Plenty were to rain down her gifts upon the head of mankind, he would still weep and complain that it was not enough.

Prosa 3–Metrum 3 In Prosa 3, Philosophy ceases to speak as Fortune. She asks the narrator to respond and to say whether or not he can continue to defend his complaint against Fortune. He says that although Fortune's explanations were soothing to the mind when he heard them, his sorrow and pain still remain. Lady Philosophy affirms his response, saying that rather than being remedies for his sorrow, words such as these only nourish it and make it stronger. She goes on to remind him of specific honors, such as his wife's chastity, and occasions of happiness, such as his two sons being made Roman consuls on the same day. If he is unhappy because those times have passed, he should remember that the present time of woe will pass also. Metrum 3 contains more examples from nature of mutability. Thus, it follows naturally that the fortunes of men, who live in a mutable world, are mutable.

Prosa 4   The narrator finally acknowledges the truth of Philosophy's teachings. She notes that in his complaining he has forgotten that he still possesses many great things. Among these are his noble father-in-law, his faithful wife and his two sons who daily display the wit and wisdom of their father. The narrator again agrees with her assessment, but reminds her that these same examples also show what great honors and possessions he has lost. Philosophy upbraids his self-indulgence, bemoaning the fact that all men, no matter how happy or prosperous their lives, are never satisfied with what they have, but always want more. Many men, she tells the narrator, would consider themselves in heaven if they possessed the least part of what he owns. For this reason, he ought to remember that all mortal things are temporary and should be received and relinquished with equanimity. All people have the means to find bliss within themselves, through tranquility of the soul; therefore, they should not seek it in external, temporary delights. Tranquility of soul is something that Fortune may never take. It does not end with the death of the body, whereas all the gifts of Fortune are lost at that time.

Metrum 4   Metrum 4 uses a metaphor of house-building to advise those who desire to escape the instability of the world to build on a low and solid foundation, out of the storm's reach, rather than on a vulnerable mountaintop or on shifting sand.

Prosa 5   At the beginning of Prosa 5, Lady Philosophy announces that the time has come to proceed to the application of stronger medicine. She then embarks upon an analysis of Fortune's gifts, such as money, to determine their true worth. First, she proves that none of the narrator's possessions, whose loss is so painful to him now, ever properly belonged to him. She notes the irony of the fact that a man, who possesses divinity of soul, needs to possess household goods, which have no divinity, in order to feel complete. By becoming enslaved to a desire for such things, mankind debases his divine nature. Such is the condition of mankind, that only when it truly understands its own nature does its nobility surpass that of all other things; when it loses sight of that knowledge, it falls lower than all the beasts. Finally, riches and wealth often bring a man more harm than good by causing him to worry about losing them.

Metrum 5   Lady Philosophy eulogizes the first age of man wherein human beings lived in harmony off the fruits of the earth, before they had learned to do things like make wine, dye cloth, dig gold out of the earth and shed each other's blood out of greed and animosity.

Prosa 6–Metrum 6   Prosa 6 addresses the dignities and powers accruing to public office, which are not themselves inherently good but are dependent upon the virtues of the man who occupies the office. Furthermore, the power residing in such office extends only to superficial things; it cannot control another man's thought, nor does it provide protection from the vicissitudes of Fortune. Any dignities or power that a man may possess have in and of themselves no innate goodness or virtue; otherwise, they would never be possessed by wicked men. The same may be said of all Fortune's gifts. Metrum 6 uses NERO as an example of one who was blessed by Fortune, yet who performed great wickedness.

Prosa 7   The narrator responds to this part of Fortune's arguments by saying that he never coveted material things, but rather desired power in order to perform virtuous deeds so that men should remember his good government. Philosophy points out that this indicates a desire for glory or renown, which conflicts with perfect virtue. She deflates the meaningfulness of even this enterprise by reminding the narrator how insignificant the earth is when compared to the vastness of the heavens. Similarly, Fame, however long it lasts, amounts to nothing in the vastness of eternity. Finally, she reminds him that the glory of virtue, like Fortune's other gifts, cannot be retained after death when the soul cares nothing for the renown of this world.

Metrum 7   Metrum 7 is a meditation on the leveling power of death, which renders Fame meaningless. Those who achieve Fame suffer two deaths: that of the body, and that which occurs when renown fades into oblivion.

Prosa 8   Lady Philosophy states that lest the narrator should think that her hostility toward Fortune is uncompromising, she will discuss the benefits of Fortune's behavior. When Fortune treats a man favorably, she blinds him to the truth; but when she turns against him, she provides him with beneficial instruction showing him the frailty of worldly good and distinguishing his true friends from those who befriended him merely because of his good fortune.

Metrum 8   Metrum 8 celebrates love as the binding force of the universe, the force that preserves stability in the midst of change and enables contrary elements, such as the sea and the land, to exist together. If mankind only possessed the love that governs the physical universe, it would enjoy happiness.

Book Three
A Latin inscription notes the ending of the second book and the beginning of the third.

Prosa 1 Prosa 1 opens with the narrator's praises of Philosophy for enabling his recovery from despair. He now feels himself equipped to handle whatever new assaults Fortune makes on his well-being. He asks Philosophy to continue with his education and to reveal more of the remedies to which she had alluded earlier. Philosophy notes that she has saved this set of remedies for later because they are, at first, more biting or painful than the others; however, once put into practice, they will seem sweet. By following Philosophy's teaching, he will be led to true happiness. First, however, she will further explain the false goods or false causes of happiness so that, fully understanding them, he will be more able to repudiate them and to embrace true happiness.

Metrum 1 Philosophy uses examples from nature and the physical world to illustrate how the contrast between cloudy and clear, bitter and sweet, and so forth, may enhance the effect of the good part in each pair. In the same way, by first understanding the false goods, the narrator will more eagerly embrace the truth.

Prosa 2–Metrum 2 In Prosa 2, Philosophy defines true happiness as that complete good which, once obtained, leaves nothing more to be desired. It lacks nothing, but is a perfect state in which all other forms of goodness come together. While the desire for such happiness is planted naturally in the hearts of men, error often leads them to seek false goods (or goals) rather than true ones. Some seek riches, some honors and dignity, others power, and still others the renown of a glorious reputation, while there are some who hope to find happiness through sensuous delight. In conclusion, no matter how various men's goals are regarding happiness, all are really pursuing it as the end to their actions and desires. In Metrum 2, Philosophy uses various examples from nature to illustrate the law of natural inclination, whereby all things seek their proper place or path, just as the wild bird, well cared-for in a cage, always longs for the forest, or the green sapling, blown down by mighty strength, will spring back toward the sky if that force is removed.

Prosa 3 Philosophy notes that mankind also exhibits the force of natural inclination in its striving for happiness, but that many things mislead humanity in the course of the search. Riches, honors, power, reputation and sensual delight cannot be true goods because the possession of them is never sufficient. The narrator confirms that despite all he possessed, he still lacked perfect happiness.

Prosa 4–Metrum 7 Prosa 4 through Prosa 7 and Metrum 3 through Metrum 7 present a detailed argument showing how all the goods and objects of endeavor mentioned above (riches, honors, power, reputation and sensual delight) are incapable of providing mankind with true happiness. Therefore they are classified as false goods.

Prosa 8–Metrum 8 In Prosa 8, Philosophy states that not only does the attempt to achieve these false goods fail to bring ultimate fulfillment to the seeker, but that these goals may also cause harm to other people. For example, in order to get money, one has to take it from someone else; to get honors, one must subject oneself to those who bestow them. The seeking of power will cause other people to plot against you, while a famous reputation will destroy your security. Living a voluptuous life will cause others to despise you for being a slave to the body. In sum, these worldly goods are not paths which may bring mankind to true happiness. In Metrum 8, Philosophy bemoans the ignorance that blinds mankind and leads poor mortals to plunder the earth looking for that which has its dwelling in the heavens.

Prosa 9–Metrum 9 In Prosa 9, Philosophy announces that she will now examine the nature of true happiness. Here her conversation with the narrator is cast in the form of a dialogue, in which the narrator is given the author's name, Boece. However, instead of directly and positively defining true happiness, she once again begins by referring to the false goods previously discussed; but now she hints that sufficiency—the sense of complete fulfillment and the absence of lack—may be the key. Once more, the narrator finds himself in agreement with everything she says. Now they are finally ready to discuss the source of true happiness. In Metrum 9, Philosophy invokes God, the supreme governor of the universe, asking his assistance in the search for perfect truth.

Prosa 10 Having concluded that the sovereign good does exist and that it is the source of all other good, in Prosa 10 Philosophy proceeds to demonstrate the relationship between this sovereign or perfect good and God, in whom sovereign good resides. If perfect good did not reside in God, she reasons, He would not be the creator of all things; rather, there would have to be something antecedent to Him, and therefore more perfect than He, since perfect things are of earlier origin than imperfect things. Furthermore, since the perfect good is the source of true happiness, it follows that true happiness resides in and with God and is therefore identical to God.

Metrum 10 Lady Philosophy speaks to all mortals who have been held captive by the chains of earthly desire, inviting them to come to this source of true goodness, where they will find rest and security.

Prosa 11   Lady Philosophy explains the relationship of sovereign good to the concept of unity, pointing out that unity and good are the same because everything that exists does so only so long as it preserves its unity. The primary example of this truth is the relationship between the soul and the body. Providence has granted everything an instinct for self-preservation, which leads to the preservation of unity.

Metrum 11   Metrum 11 notes that he who seeks the truth should look inside himself, in the recesses of his mind, so that the light of truth may disperse the dark clouds of error. The seeds of truth that lie dormant in the mind may be awakened by the breath of learning.

Prosa 12   In keeping with the circuitous and repetitious structural pattern established by the progression of meaning in the text so far, Prosa 12 further explores several ideas that have already been introduced: that the world is governed by God, that God is all-sufficient, and that God is all-powerful or omnipotent. After providing further evidence of these truths, Philosophy then introduces the question of evil, which will be further explored in Book Four.

Metrum 12   Metrum 12 employs the story of ORPHEUS and EURYDICE as a parable to illustrate the dangers of fixing one's thoughts upon earthly things and thus losing touch with the sovereign good. Orpheus' inability to refrain from looking back to see if his wife was following him when they left Hades symbolizes the attachment to earthy things. The loss of his wife, which resulted from his attachment, represents the loss of sovereign good.

Book Four

A Latin inscription notes the ending of the third book and the beginning of the fourth.

Prosa 1   Prosa 1 begins with the narrator praising the enlightenment Philosophy has brought him thus far, but stating that he remains troubled by one thing: the fact that while God is the absolute ruler of all things and is equivalent to the sovereign good, evil nevertheless exists and is allowed to pass unpunished. Furthermore, while vice flourishes, virtue not only goes unrewarded but is cast down and trampled by the wicked. This troubles the narrator because such things should not be possible under the government of an omniscient and omnipotent God who wills nothing but what is for the best. Philosophy responds that the state of things would indeed be monstrous if what he describes were true, but it is not—it cannot be if all the previous conclusions that they have come to concerning God's management of the universe are true. She then announces her intention of proving to the narrator that under God's rule the good are always powerful, the wicked are always defeated and that happiness attends good men. In doing so she will show him the path by which he may return to his true country.

Metrum 1   Metrum 1 expands on the idea introduced by Philosophy at the end of Prosa 1 when she claims that she will provide the narrator's mind with the equipment (feathers) to rise from earth into the heavens, leaving the clouds behind and ultimately reaching heaven's outermost sphere (*see* PTOLEMAIC UNIVERSE), and then moving beyond even that to the region where God resides who is the source of light (and who governs the universe, etc.). If he does arrive in this place, the narrator will realize that this is his true home—where he was born and where he will choose to remain. If he should, from this perspective, decide to look down upon the earth, he will see that those tyrants who are now feared by all people will be exiled from those fair realms.

Prosa 2   Lady Philosophy sets out to prove the idea that the good are powerful and the bad, weak. First she returns to the already accepted premise that all men seek happiness. If this is true, then even evil or wicked men seek happiness. Since true happiness has been shown to be the same as true goodness (the sovereign good), which is equivalent to God, it follows that all men, even evil ones, seek the true good by simply seeking happiness. They turn away from the true course when they mistake partial or false goods for their goal. And since seeking partial or false goods can never lead to true happiness or sufficiency, evil men can never be as powerful as good men because they can never achieve their goal. If they willfully and knowingly desert the good in favor of evil, she goes on to say, they not only lose power, but they also cease to fully exist, just as a corpse, while it is still a man, may not be said to be a man in the full sense of the word. Things that exist preserve their rank, nature and their being. When they lose any of these essentials, they cease to be. Although the wicked may seem to have the power to act, they do not; such power is only an effect of weakness. They are able to do evil, but would not be able to if they retained the power of doing good.

Metrum 2   Lady Philosophy paints a picture of the proud and powerful king sitting on his throne whose external appearance is merely a mask for the inner turmoil of one who is himself tyrannized by lust, passion, grief and false hope. Ruled by these masters, the king himself is actually weak and feeble. Rather than controlling his actions, he is controlled by his passions.

Prosa 3   After recapitulating the idea that men who do evil may never truly prosper despite external appearances, Philosophy proceeds to elaborate on the way that evil diminishes a man, robbing him of his human nature—an idea that was introduced in Prosa 2. Some men, succumbing to evil, become like beasts. The man who succumbs to avarice is thus compared to a wolf; he who perpetrates fraud and trickery is likened to a fox; the man who rages with anger resembles a lion; and he who wallows in lust is like a filthy sow wallowing in the mire.

Metrum 3 Metrum 3 uses the story of ULYSSES' adventure on the island of the witch CIRCE as an illustration of the way that men may be turned into beasts. (When Ulysses and his men landed on Circe's island, the sailors—all except Ulysses—drank an enchanted wine and were transformed into swine. Their suffering was the greater because their souls remained those of men trapped in the bodies of animals.) Wickedness is even more destructive to men than is Circe's spell, because wickedness leaves the body intact but inflicts a deadly wound upon the soul.

Prosa 4 At the beginning of Prosa 4, the narrator concurs with the idea that wicked men are like beasts, but expresses the wish that they were also without the power to harm good people. Philosophy claims, once again, that they are actually without power, even though this belief runs contrary to popular opinion. She also raises the question of whether a wicked man who receives punishment suffers more than one who is not punished for his evil actions, arguing that he who does receive punishment is happier because the punishment of evil is a virtue and virtue is equivalent to happiness. Those who believe otherwise are blinded by error. Since their wicked deeds contribute primarily to their own suffering and oppression, those who have committed evil deserve pity rather than hatred. They ought to be brought to judgment as the sick are brought to a physician, so that by the medicine of chastisement they may be cured of their vices.

Metrum 4 Metrum 4 condemns war and strife among members of the human race as nonsensical, especially when considered alongside the many other perils that threaten mankind. Good men ought to be cherished and the wicked ought to be pitied and brought to correction.

Prosa 5–Metrum 5 In Prosa 5, the narrator says he understands the idea that happiness attends virtue while suffering follows vice, but that the operations of Fortune seem somehow exempt from this rule because she sometimes causes the worthy to suffer and the wicked to prosper. Philosophy responds by saying that this apparent injustice is merely a result of his ignorance regarding the manner in which God operates. Since God is a good governor and the supreme ruler of the universe, all things must necessarily proceed as they ought to. In Metrum 5, Philosophy gives examples of things that arouse fear and wonder in the hearts of ignorant men, such as the eclipse or dark phase of the moon, simply because they do not understand the cause. Fear and wonder cease when ignorance gives way to knowledge.

Prosa 6 In Prosa 6, the narrator asks Philosophy to explain the workings of the universe and how things which appear unjust are actually part of God's plan. Philosophy responds that although the subject is a difficult one for human comprehension, she will nevertheless try to enlighten him. The key elements of her explanation are Providence and Destiny. Providence is defined as the divine intelligence, proceeding from God, which creates the plan and order of the universe. Destiny is the force by which this plan is enacted. The closer something is to Providence (i.e., to the divine intelligence of God), the more immutable (or less subject to the force of Destiny) it is. Because all things have their origin in the Divine mind, the order of the universe and the way that events occur within it are as they should be. To someone who does not understand this order, the order of things appears confused, when in reality it is the human understanding of that order that is at fault. For example, the man who appears just or good to another man may appear otherwise in the eyes of Providence. If a good man suffers adversity, there may be a good reason for it. For example, some good men are allowed to suffer greatly so that their virtues may be exercised and strengthened by the practice of patience. The same principle applies to the destiny of the wicked. For example, some evil men are allowed to experience prosperity because poverty would prompt them to commit even greater enormities that those they are already guilty of. In sum, nothing occurs by chance in the realms of Providence and Destiny. Because God is the ruler of all things, all things are ordered and created for the best; therefore man should not question that order.

Metrum 6 Philosophy directs the narrator's attention to the great harmony and order that exist in the natural world, pointing out how the sun never invades the sphere of the moon and how the evening star regularly makes its appearance at sundown. For the same reasons, the seasons proceed in order from spring to summer to autumn to winter, these changes imparting life and growth to all inhabitants of the natural world. He who controls and directs these events is the world's Creator, and they are all motivated by the force of love.

Prosa 7–Metrum 7 Prosa 7 begins with Philosophy asking the narrator if he realizes the implication of what she has been explaining to him, which is that all fortune is good. (This returns their conversation to the narrator's original complaint, that he is suffering undeserved ill fortune.) For that reason, it is his obligation, she tells him, to embrace and do battle with whatever Fortune sends him—with adversity, so that it may not cause him to despair, and even with prosperity, lest it corrupt him. Metrum 7 gives several examples from classical literature of heroic men who embraced what Fortune sent to them and made the best of it. These men are AGAMEMNON, ULYSSES and HERCULES. It concludes with an exhortation for noble souls to follow the example of these men.

Book Five

A Latin inscription notes the ending of the fourth book and the beginning of the fifth.

Prosa 1   Prosa 1 opens with the narrator raising the question of chance. Can such a thing exist in the universe as it has been described by Philosophy? Philosophy replies that chance does not exist, because it is by definition an event that is not produced by any cause or chain of causes, and nothing of that nature can exist in a divinely ordered universe. An event that appears to occur by chance is in reality simply an unexpected outcome that can always be traced back to a cause or series of causes. And the causes that lead to the event ultimately proceed from Providence.

Metrum 1   Metrum 1 uses the path taken by the Tigris and Euphrates Rivers as an example of apparent chance that is really divinely determined. After springing from a single source, these rivers divide into two separate channels. If they were to reunite, they would cause many disasters, uprooting trees and destroying ships; thus, their continuing in their separate courses is an example of the work of Providence that appears to be chance occurrence.

Prosa 2   The narrator raises the difficult question of human free will and how it fits into a universe controlled by Providence and Destiny. Philosophy affirms the existence of free will, noting that those beings who seek to align themselves with divine thought have more freedom to act than those who do not. The wicked, who have allowed themselves to become enslaved to pernicious desires, are the least able to exercise free will. The eye of Providence watches over all and rewards each according to his merit.

Metrum 2   Metrum 2 is a hymn of praise to the omniscient power of God, a power that allows Him to see and know everything, including all present, past and future events.

Prosa 3   Prosa 3 resumes the discussion of free will, with the narrator noting that the idea of God's foreknowledge seems incompatible with man's free will. If God always already knows not only the works but also the plans and wills of men, then there can be no freedom of the will—no action or will other than that which Divine Providence has foreseen. If this was not

the case, then the prescience of God would not be infallible. The narrator goes on to say that he cannot accept the argument, put forth by some men, that something is not necessarily going to happen because God has foreseen it but rather that it is known to Divine Providence because it is going to happen. This, he argues, diminishes the force of God by putting his knowledge secondary to the event. Furthermore, if everything that happens is determined by Divine Providence, then it is useless to hope or to pray to God for anything.

Metrum 3   Metrum 3 sums up the position of mankind with relation to the question of Providence versus free will, contending that the mind of man, encumbered by its imprisonment in the body, is unable to fully understand the subtle way in which these two things are knit together. When a mortal nevertheless seeks to discover the answers to this and other similar questions, he is motivated by the memory of his soul's union with the divine. These intimations of immortality lead him to seek out greater truth.

Prosa 4   Prosa 4 returns to an analysis of the contradiction that the narrator perceives between the ideas of divine prescience and human free will. Philosophy offers an alternative view of the situation, proposing the idea that prescience can exist without being the necessitating cause of future events, that God can know what is going to happen without that knowledge having to determine what will happen. Part of the narrator's difficulty in understanding this idea derives from the limitations of human understanding. Philosophy thus takes the opportunity to explain how humans come to an understanding of something through perception (sense), imagination and reason.

Metrum 4–Prosa 5   Metrum 4 and Prosa 5 continue to explore the difficulty of answering this question of divine prescience versus human free will, given the limitations of human intelligence. If we could elevate ourselves to the level of divine intelligence, then we would perceive exactly how the prescience of God knows and understands all things, although they have no certain outcome.

Metrum 5   Metrum 5 is a celebration of the noble faculties of man which cause him, alone among the beasts, to heave himself aloft and, standing upright, to spurn the earth in favor of the heavens. Philosophy urges the narrator (and all earthly men) to take this figure as his example and to elevate his mind lest it should sink below its proper level.

Prosa 6   Lady Philosophy concludes her argument regarding divine prescience versus human free will by explaining the concept of God's eternal nature. God exists outside time or temporality, beholding past, present and future events simultaneously. His divine prescience therefore does not change the nature or outcome of things, but perceives those things as present which shall be produced in time. Thus, His prescience does not interfere with or limit human free will. This last section of the text closes with Philosophy's assurance that prayers are not in vain, but that when they are sincere they cannot be unsuccessful. Finally, she admonishes the narrator to resist vice, to honor and love virtue and to exalt his mind to God.

A Latin inscription notes the end of the Book of Boethius.

COMMENTARY

Chaucer's *Boece* was probably composed in the late 1370s or early 1380s. Its strongest influence on Chaucer's other work appears in his later efforts, particularly the narrative poem TROILUS AND CRISEYDE, which, some critics have argued, constitutes Chaucer's attempt to rectify an omission Boethius made when he neglected to include romantic love among the series of "false goods" pursued by humans in their quest for happiness. Both the despair TROILUS experiences when betrayed by his love and, more specifically, the spiritual awakening that occurs when his soul literally flies up into the seventh sphere are informed by the *Consolation,* and certain reflective passages, as noted in the summary of the *Troilus* contained in this book, are close to a direct translation of the Latin writer's work. The Boethian view of fortune influenced a number of *The* CANTERBURY TALES, most notably "The KNIGHT'S TALE," "The CLERK'S TALE," "The FRANKLIN'S TALE" and "The NUN'S PRIEST'S TALE." The latter has often been viewed as a philosophical corrective to "The MONK'S TALE," which exhibits an extremely negative view of human destiny controlled by the capricious goddess FORTUNE, practically ignoring the redeeming possibilities of human intelligence and free will. In the *Consolation,* intelligence and free will provide human beings with the keys that enable them to cope with and transcend fortune. The influence of Boethius also appears in some of Chaucer's lyric poems, including "THE FORMER AGE," "FORTUNE," "LAK OF STEDFAST-NESSE," and "TRUTH." "The Former Age" is actually a translation from the *Consolation,* Book Two, Metrum 5. When translating the work as a whole into what became known as the *Boece,* Chaucer had translated the meters, which were poetry in the Latin original, into prose, perhaps to better or more easily capture the sense of the words. The existence of "The Former Age" has prompted some scholars to suggest that Chaucer intended to create poetry translations for all of the meters which would perhaps eventually be used to replace the prose translations. Such an idea is, however, merely speculation.

Structurally, the work is divided into five books, each of which treats one or more aspects of the philosophical problem of man's existence in an apparently hostile world. At the heart of the matter lies a paradox: the regularity with which God governs the rest of the universe compared to the irregularity He permits in human affairs. An important example of this irregularity is the apparent prosperity of wicked men and the suffering of virtuous ones. Each book is also divided into sections, alternating longer passages of philosophical dialogue, designated *Prosa* (Prose), with shorter ones entitled *Metrum* (Meter). The proses generally consist of a dialogue between the narrator, sometimes referred to as "Boece," and Lady Philosophy, whose role is to enlighten him with responses to his questions and with further questions designed to arouse his own slumbering and bemused intelligence until it is able to perceive truth. The meters tend to be moments of reflection (on the argument thus far, to allow it to sink in), celebration (of some important insight gained thus far) or exhortation (to act upon an insight). They often employ concrete examples taken from classical mythology to illustrate the argument made in the previous prose section. For example, the fate of Ulysses' men on Circe's enchanted island is given to illustrate the way humans suffer when they let themselves be reduced to the level of beasts.

Many readers of Chaucer's *Boece* have speculated on the reasons why he chose to translate the text into Middle English. Some have argued, based on its pervasive influence in his later work, that he did it to provide himself with a convenient reference. Others feel that he did it simply because of his great admiration for the work and a desire to make it available to a wider audience. In the latter part of the 20th century it is easy to forget that the *Consolation of Philosophy* was for centuries one of the most influential books ever written in Latin. It was translated into Old High German, Italian, Spanish, Greek, French (by JEAN DE MEUN), Old English (by Alfred the Great) and early Modern English by Queen Elizabeth I, who felt it an important text for a monarch to know. Donald Howard, in his 1987 biography of Chaucer, speculates that Chaucer prepared his translation as an educational text for the young King RICHARD II.

It is also worth noting that Chaucer's translation has been faulted by some scholars for not adhering more closely to the classical text of Boethius, but in fact his version is a careful compilation rather than a strict translation, relying to some extent on the French translation of Jean de Meun and incorporating commentary by Nicholas TRIVET. Furthermore, the Latin text of Boethius that Chaucer used for his primary source would have been a Vulgate Latin version of the classical original that would not be expected to preserve the locutions of the original language. Specifically, Chaucer's Latin text was probably the version of the *Consolation* that typically accompanies Trivet's 14th-century commentary.

For Further Reading: For consideration of issues having to do with Chaucer's adaptation of BOETHIUS' text, see Bernard L. Jefferson's *Chaucer and the Consolation of Philosophy of Boethius* (1917, rptd. 1968). Perhaps due to the limited popularity of the text, very little has been written on Chaucer's *Boece* that would be of interest to the general reader. Those interested in the literary influence of the *Consolation* should consult Howard PATCH's *The Goddess Fortuna in Medieval Literature* (1927). C. S. Lewis provides a brief but notable critical reading of the *Consolation*, along with consideration of its influence on medieval literature, in *The Discarded Image* (1964, rptd. 1971).

Boetes   *Boetes* is the spelling Chaucer gives for the star Boötes, which is part of the constellation Arcturus. In the BOECE, LADY PHILOSOPHY mentions the movement of the star in the sky as an example of something that would arouse wonder and perhaps fear in the mind of someone who did not understand the laws governing the heavens. She is trying to convince the narrator that there may be things in the universe known to God that he (the narrator) does not understand. The *Boece* is Chaucer's translation of Boethius' *Consolation of Philosophy*.

Boethius   Anicius Manlius Severinus Boethius is best known to readers of Chaucer as the fifth-century Roman author of the *Consolation of Philosophy*, which Chaucer translated into Middle English under the title *BOECE*. The *Consolation* had considerable influence on many of Chaucer's own works, including *TROILUS AND CRISEYDE*, *The HOUSE OF FAME*, and several tales in *The CANTERBURY TALES*.

A member of the Roman aristocracy, Boethius served in the government of the Ostrogothic king THEODORIC, who ruled in Italy from A.D. 493 to 526, after the de facto fall of the Western Roman Empire. Reconciliation between the Roman aristocracy and the court of Theodoric was accomplished in part by diplomatic courtesy which included recognition of the Roman Senate and the appointment of Romans to almost all civilian posts. This partly explains how Boethius became, first a consul in Rome, and then a senior advisor and administrator (the Master of Offices) in Theodoric's court at Ravenna. In addition, Boethius had given Theodoric successful advice on how to deal with a famine. Despite his close working relationship with the king, however, Boethius maintained strong ties to the Senate, defending and protecting it whenever its power or reputation was threatened.

Boethius was charged with conspiracy against Theodoric after he supported a senator, Albinus, who had been denounced for conducting treasonable correspondence with the court of the Eastern Roman emperor Justin. In defending Albinus, Boethius found himself charged with writing letters advocating Roman liberty from Ostragothic rule. Furthermore, he was accused of using black magic to enhance his career—a charge that was liable, at that time, to be made against a philosopher who studied astronomy, which was one of Boethius' favorite disciplines. Perhaps the worst part of his downfall lay in the fact that the Roman Senate, whose champion he had been so often, did not come to his defense. Evidently some senators, especially those whose behavior he had criticized, resented his position in Theodoric's court and denounced him. After his arrest and imprisonment, he was tried in absentia by a Roman senatorial court at Ravenna. Unable to defend himself, he was sentenced to death. The events leading up to his imprisonment and sentencing are all discussed in his most famous work, the *Consolation of Philosophy*, where he meditates on and tries to make sense of his fall from good fortune.

As a writer, Boethius primarily devoted himself to a cultural tradition of translating Greek science and thought into Latin. He intended to translate all of ARISTOTLE and PLATO into Latin and to furnish the translations with commentaries, but achieved only part of his plan, translating a major part of Aristotle's *Organon* and none of Plato. His concern with the educational disciplines is reflected in his writings on arithmetic and music, two of the four members of the mathematics-based disciplines known as the quadrivium. (The other two were geometry and astronomy.) He may well have been the first person to use the word *quadrivium*, a concept that went on to become one of the basic building blocks of the medieval university curriculum. His concern with logic, reflected in his desire to translate Aristotle and Plato, comes across most powerfully in the *Consolation*, where he frequently refers to the arguments and examples of these writers to support his own logic-based analysis of his fate. The last thing that he is known to have written, the *Consolation* remains his most powerful work and the only one to receive much attention from modern readers.

Boghton under Blee   In *The CANTERBURY TALES*, "Boghton under Blee," or Boughton under the Blean Forest, is one of the villages through which Chaucer's pilgrims pass on the road to CANTERBURY. It is mentioned in the prologue to "The CANON'S YEOMAN'S TALE" as the village where the pilgrims are joined by the CANON'S YEOMAN, the only pilgrim to join the group en route. At this point they would be about five miles north of their destination. Chaucer occasionally uses such geographical markers to provide the tales with a sense of spatial and temporal reality.

Boitani, Piero (1947–) An Italian scholar who received his doctorate from Cambridge University, Boitani has taught Italian literature at Cambridge, English literature at a variety of Italian universities—notably at the University of Rome—and has chaired the program in Italian culture at the University of California, Berkeley. Boitani's dual background put him in an excellent position to write *Chaucer and Boccaccio.* He also wrote *Chaucer and the Imaginary World of Fame,* edited *The European Tragedy of Troilus* (1989) and co-edited *The Cambridge Chaucer Companion* (1986).

Bologna A commune in the north of Italy that lies at the foot of the Apennines. It is mentioned in "The CLERK'S TALE" to give readers a better idea of the location of PANICO. WALTER's sister, who receives and raises his children in secret after Walter takes them away from his wife, GRISELDA, is the duchess of Panico.

Boloigne (1) *See* BOULOGNE.

Boloigne (2) *See* BOLOGNA.

Book of the Duchess, The The Book of the Duchess is generally acknowledged to be the earliest of Chaucer's major poems. An elegiac poem, it commemorates and mourns the death of Blanche, duchess of Lancaster, who died in 1368 of unknown causes. (*See* BLANCHE OF LANCASTER.) At this time, Chaucer was an esquire in the household of the current king of England, EDWARD III. In this capacity, Chaucer would have come into contact with various members of the royal family, and this is doubtless how he met and became acquainted with the duchess and her husband, JOHN OF GAUNT, the duke of Lancaster. *The Book of the Duchess* is believed to have been written sometime between the duchess' death and 1372. It was probably read at one of the annual commemorations of her passing, which continued to be held for a number of years.

SUMMARY

Part One
An unnamed first-person narrator describes his sickness. Although he does not give it a name or mention a specific cause, the illness appears to be psychological rather than physical. The symptoms he notes—insomnia, a lack of interest in the world around him, the inability to feel joy and a pervasive feeling of "heaviness" or sorrow—all suggest depression. He hints at one possible cause when he says that he has been suffering for eight years, and that his cure lies within the power of only one "physician," which is most likely a reference to the healing power of the beloved, should she at last choose to return his affection. From this general description of his state of mind, the narrative progresses to a particular episode of insomnia when the narrator attempts to pass his sleepless hours by reading a book of tales, probably OVID's *Metamorphoses,* which contains a version of the story described below and was popular among medieval readers.

Part Two
The narrator next relates the story that he read, the tragedy of King SEYS and Queen ALCYONE. King Seys departs upon a sea voyage, leaving his wife behind. When weeks pass and she has not heard from him, Alcyone suspects that something may have gone wrong and prays to the goddess JUNO for news of her husband. Juno sends MORPHEUS, the god of sleep, to animate the drowned body of Seys, making it appear and speak to Alcyone in a dream in which he reveals his fate. Three days after learning of the king's death, Alcyone dies of overwhelming grief.

Part Three
When he has finished the tale, the narrator decides to try praying to Morpheus for sleep, naively promising to give the god a feather bed if he will come to the narrator's aid. Shortly after saying the prayer, he falls asleep. He dreams of waking in a chamber where the stained-glass windows depict scenes from the TROJAN WAR, and the walls are painted with scenes and text from the famous French allegory of love, *Le Roman de la Rose.* As he lies in bed, the narrator hears (still in his dream) sounds associated with hunting: horns, dogs barking, horses running and men shouting. Saddling his own horse, which awaits him in the chamber, he follows the sounds of the hunt until he comes upon a young puppy, who in turn leads him to a lone knight dressed all in black, sitting against a tree. Unaware of the narrator's approach, the BLACK KNIGHT begins to speak a tale of woe, recounting the recent death of his lady. The narrator waits until the knight has finished speaking, and then approaches to see if he can raise the knight's spirits. The rest of the poem consists of the knight recounting the story of how he met, fell in love with and married his lady. The narrator, pretending not to have overheard the knight's lament, periodically encourages the knight to continue speaking about his lady and what happened to cause him such grief. When he comes to relate the death of his lady, the knight initially speaks in metaphor, saying he played with FORTUNE at a game of chess and lost his queen. Finally, he speaks the true source of his pain, the death of his wife. At the same moment, the end of the hunt is sounded, and the knight, now referred to as "king," rides away to his home, a "long castle" on a "rich hill." The narrator, hearing the castle bell begin to strike, is awakened from his sleep and decides that his dream is worth recording.

COMMENTARY

During the time when Chaucer composed *The Book of the Duchess,* as a result of the Norman (French) Conquest in 1066 the literature of the English court was written primarily in French, even though the language spoken at court was a mixture of a dialect of French, ANGLO-NORMAN and Middle English. Chaucer was one of the first writers to compose for the court in English, but his early poems, including *The Book of the Duchess,* still show a strong French influence in vocabulary, style and structure. The poem's meter is a traditional four-stress, 18-syllable meter derived from French poetry. Like most verse of the time, it was undoubtedly written to be read aloud to a gathering of people. The printing press had yet to be invented, so each book had to be copied out by hand, which rendered it precious in both senses of the word—copies were rare and expensive. *The Book of the Duchess* survives in only three manuscripts, so it probably did not have a very wide circulation in Chaucer's day.

The poem is spoken by a first-person narrator and divided into three parts. The first part focuses on the lovesick narrator, describing his pain and sleeplessness. His insomnia leads him to read from a book of tales. The second part of the poem tells the story he chose to read, the tragedy of King Seys and Queen Alcyone. The third part recounts a dream he has after finally falling asleep. In this dream he meets a strange grieving Black Knight who eventually reveals the cause of his sorrow, his wife's death. One of literature's primary functions during the Middle Ages was to teach, both by doctrine and example, while simultaneously providing entertainment. Each part of *The Book of the Duchess* relates the predicament of someone who suffers from an excess of passionate grief, the kind of grief that results from lost or unrequited love, and at the same time illustrates the dangers of such excessive grief. The resolution of the knight's grief at the end of the poem is offered as a lesson to the reader as well as the narrator.

Dream poetry was a popular genre or type of literature in medieval Europe, particularly when the subject was love. Chaucer was to use this genre again when he composed *The HOUSE OF FAME* and *The PARLIAMENT OF FOWLS,* both of which deal with the subject of love. Detailed research has shown that Chaucer's immediate sources for his *Book of the Duchess* were several poems by the French writer Guillaume de Machaut. The names of these poems are "Le Jugement dou Roy de Behaingne" [The Judgement of the King of Bohemia], "Le Dit de la Fonteinne Amoureuse" [The Speech of the Fountain of Love], "Remede de Fortune" [The Remedy of Fortune] and "Le Dit dou Lyon" [The Sayings of the Lion]. A minor source, Jean FROISSART's "Le Paradys d'Amours" [The Paradise of Love] provided Chaucer with the opening lines of his poem.

Elements of all these poems are, like the ingredients of a recipe, lifted from their original context and recombined to make Chaucer's poem. The theme of the poem, that excessive passion may destroy a person's life, appears frequently in the literature of the period, and is related to medieval ideas regarding health and sickness (*see* HUMORS). According to the dictates of medieval medicine, the ideal way to maintain a state of health was to maintain one's emotional, intellectual and physical balance by not allowing any one emotion, intellectual interest or physical activity to consume an excessive amount of one's time and energy. But, of course, people in the 14th century, just like people today, found it much easier to preach and prescribe regarding such matters than to actually follow the recommended course of action. Chaucer's poem indirectly yet brilliantly addresses the question of what to do when one does become a victim of excessive grief. Simply stated, the answer seems to be, "look around you—there is always someone whose cause for grief is greater, whose suffering is more bitter. See if you can help that person. In doing so, you may help yourself." The narrator of the poem, pretending not to have overheard the knight's initial lament, prods him to tell the whole story leading up to his present emotional state. In recounting how he met, courted, and ultimately married his beloved wife, the knight seems to experience, along with the pain of recounting those events and his wife's loveliness, a kind of emotional catharsis that releases him from the paralysis of his grief. After listening to the Black Knight relate the story of losing his queen, the narrator understandably enough, seems to have forgotten his own grief.

Like much of Chaucer's work, *The Book of the Duchess* features references to stories and characters taken from classical (Greek and Roman) mythology. Scenes from the story of the Trojan War, for example, adorn the stained glass windows of the chamber the narrator dreams of waking up in. The Black Knight compares himself to TANTALUS, a famous figure of Greek mythology. He compares his queen to PENELOPE, the wife of Odysseus (*see* ULYSSES) in the Greek *Odyssey,* who was famed for her faithfulness to her husband. Chaucer also makes use of allusions to characters from the Bible, having the Black Knight, for example, refer to his queen as another ESTHER, the Old Testament model of wifely virtue. Allusions to the actual people that the poem commemorates also appear in the text of the poem. The knight's reference to his wife as "good fair White" (line 948) refers to Blanche, whose French name means "white" in English. The "long castel" ("castle") with white walls on a "ryche hil" ("rich hill") (lines 1318–19) to which the knight returns after leaving the narrator are puns on "Lancaster," the duchy Blanche brought to her husband when they married, and his favorite residence, Richmond, which at the time the poem was written was called Rychemont, or "rich hill."

For Further Reading: Readers interested in learning more about *The Book of the Duchess* should consider Bertrand Bronson's article "The *Book of the Duchess* Reopened" (*Publications of the Modern Language Association,* 1959), which initiated contemporary recognition of the poem as a consolation piece, analyzing the role of the narrator who leads the Black Knight through the grieving process to acceptance. A contrasting view is offered by James Neil Brown in "Narrative Focus and Function in the *Book of the Duchess*" (*Massachusetts Studies in English,* 1970), which describes the narrator of the poem as a socially naive "would-be courtier" who is trying to appear sophisticated in his exchange with the Black Knight. Brown argues that the contrast between this persona and the knight produces humor and ironically censures excessive grief. A good general assessment of *The Book of the Duchess* and its relationship to Chaucer's other early poetry may be found in Wolfgang CLEMEN's *Chaucer's Early Poetry* (trans. 1963). For a discussion of the historical context, see D. W. ROBERTSON, "The Historical Setting of Chaucer's *Book of the Duchess*" (in *Medieval Studies in Honor of Urban Tigner Holmes, Jr.,* 1966), and Edward Condren, "The Historical Context of the *Book of the Duchess*" (*Publications of the Modern Language Association,* 1971). Robertson's essay explores the difference between medieval and modern notions of grief and consolation; Condren's uncovers new historical evidence to establish a date for the poem's composition.

Book of the Lion, The   Mentioned among those works Chaucer claims as his own in the Retraction that follows *The CANTERBURY TALES, The Book of the Lion* is unknown and was presumably lost. It may have been a translation or adaptation of one of two French works, either the *Dit dou Lyon* [Word of the Lion] of GUILLAUME DE MACHAUT or Eustache DESCHAMPS' poem of the same name. Chaucer did borrow from these two writers on other occasions. Some scholars speculate even further afield by arguing that this lost poem may have been written in honor of Prince Lionel's marriage to Violante, daughter of Bernabo VISCONTI.

Bordeaux   Port city on the southwestern coast of France. In the Middle Ages, as today, the region surrounding the city was famous for its wine. Chaucer mentions the city in his portrait of the SHIPMAN that appears in the GENERAL PROLOGUE to *The CANTERBURY TALES*. Sailing back and forth between England and France on wine-laden ships, this man does not hesitate to steal a draught of the cargo while the cargo's owner is asleep. This along with other details shows the Shipman to be somewhat unscrupulous. Chaucer's PARDONER also alludes to Bordeaux as a wine-growing region in the ironic condemnation of drinking and other vices that appears at the beginning of his tale.

Boreas   In Greek mythology, Boreas was the name of the north wind, who, when he was not flying about in the atmosphere, shared a cave with the other wind gods on the island of Thrace. Although the subject of several legends, Boreas appears in Chaucer's work simply as a cold wind (one coming from the north) in the translation of BOETHIUS' *Consolation of Philosophy*.

Boughton-under-Blean   *See* BOGHTON UNDER BLEE.

Boulogne   A city on the North Atlantic coast of France, Boulogne (or as Chaucer spells it, Boloigne) is listed in the GENERAL PROLOGUE of *The CANTERBURY TALES* as one of the locations visited by the WIFE OF BATH on her peripatetic journeys to various sites associated with holy martyrs. A miraculous image of the Virgin Mary that had arrived in a rudderless vessel made this city a popular destination among pilgrims.

Bowden, Muriel   Bowden, a Ph.D. and professor at Columbia University, wrote *A Commentary on the General Prologue to The Canterbury Tales* (2nd ed. 1967) for both the general and specialist reader of Chaucer. This essential handbook to the GENERAL PROLOGUE examines the opening section of *The CANTERBURY TALES* in light of both medieval texts and modern scholarship, focusing primarily on its sources and background. Bowden gives meticulous attention to the portraits of the Canterbury pilgrims, and her examples from sermons, both orthodox and LOLLARD, show that Chaucer's style exhibits many features of 14th-century homiletic diction. While this book does address the issue of which portraits represent idealizations and which are written in the vein of satire, it does not consider their relationship to the genre of ESTATES SATIRE (as does Jill MANN's book, *Chaucer and Medieval Estates Satire,* 1973). Bowden's first book, *A Reader's Guide to Geoffrey Chaucer* (1964), grew from her interest in questions asked by students concerning Chaucer as a man, rather than as a poet, and also from her profound belief that no great artist is solely dependent upon his own genius. In this book, Bowden discusses the influence that 14th-century English life had upon Chaucer's writing, particularly in these areas: chivalry, religion, philosophy, science, everyday life and the literature he read.

Bradshaw Shift, the   The Bradshaw Shift, named after 19th-century British scholar Henry Bradshaw, who proposed the theory, represents one of the earliest attempts to establish an order for the different fragments of *The CANTERBURY TALES*. Bradshaw's theory postulated that Chaucer intended to put the references to places along the way to CANTERBURY in the correct geographical order. Finding ROCHESTER coming incorrectly after SITTINGBOURNE in the sequence presented by the ELLESMERE MANUSCRIPT, Bradshaw proposed moving Fragment VII (that containing "The SHIPMAN'S TALE," "The PRIORESS' TALE," "The TALE OF SIR THOPAS," "The TALE OF MELIBEE," "The MONK'S TALE," and "The NUN'S PRIEST'S TALE") to follow Fragment II (which contained "The MAN OF LAW'S TALE"). Other evidence and reasoning has shown that while this may have been the order Chaucer intended at one point in his composition and compilation of the tales, it was later superseded. The Bradshaw Shift was used by F. J. Furnivall in *The Six-Text Print of Chaucer's Canterbury Tales,* published by the Chaucer Society between 1868 and 1877. The *RIVERSIDE CHAUCER,* the edition currently favored as authoritative, presents the tales in the order established by the Ellesmere manuscript.

Bradwardine, Thomas An Oxford theologian of the 14th century who became archbishop of Canterbury. In his treatise *De cause Dei* he reaffirmed the orthodox doctrine of predestination and grace. CHAUNTICLEER, the learned rooster of "The NUN'S PRIEST'S TALE," mentions Bradwardine as one of the authorities whose work he has read on the question of predestination versus free will. Chaunticleer, like many thinkers of his day, was somewhat troubled by the idea that God's foreknowledge of all events might in some way limit humanity's ability to exercise choice. The dénouement of the tale offers an interesting and enlightening commentary on this doctrinal question, when the rooster, who believes that his doom has been foretold through a dream, exercises his wits to extricate himself from the situation that was prophesied.

Bradwardyn, Bishop *See* BRADWARDINE, THOMAS.

Breseyda *See* BRISEIS.

Bret (1) *See* BRETON.

Bret (2) *See* BRITON (2).

Breton An inhabitant of BRITTANY. Chaucer uses the term in the prologue to "The FRANKLIN'S TALE" when the FRANKLIN states that the story he is going to tell is one of those poetic romances known as BRETON LAYS. The WIFE OF BATH also alludes to this corpus of literature when she embarks upon her tale of King ARTHUR, of whom the "Britons (an alternative spelling of the word) speken greet honour" (line 1089).

Breton lays In English literature, Breton lays are short stories written in rhyme, like those of MARIE DE FRANCE. Their subject matter was the same as that of chivalric romances, i.e., the various adventures of noble knights and aristocratic ladies. The Breton lays written in English typically owe their identification to the fact either that the text itself claims to belong to the genre (as with Chaucer's "FRANKLIN'S TALE") or that the same story is told by Marie in French.

Brewer, D(erek) S(tanley) (1923–) British medievalist whose 1953 biography of Chaucer, simply titled *Chaucer,* continues to be an excellent introduction to the poet's life. Brewer has published more than 30 important book and articles on Chaucerian topics, many of them examining the relationship between the poet's work and his sources and also looking at the influence Chaucer had upon other writers such as John GOWER, Thomas HOCCLEVE, John LYDGATE, Robert HENRYSON and John Dryden. *Chaucer in His Time* (1973) and *Chaucer and His World* (1978) both provide a fascinating examination of the historical milieu in which he was writing. The latter is lavishly illustrated with manuscript illustrations, portraits, sculptures of important historical figures and photographs of such medieval artifacts as a pair of 14th-century leather shoes.

Briseis A Trojan woman who was taken captive by ACHILLES during the TROJAN WAR. Because AGAMEMNON took her away from him, Achilles withdrew from the fight, weakening the effort of the Greek troops. Finally, Agamemnon agreed to restore her so that Achilles would rejoin the struggle. The Man of Law, or SERGEANT OF THE LAW as he is called in the GENERAL PROLOGUE TO THE CANTERBURY TALES, mentions the story of Briseis as one that had been treated by the poet Chaucer (prologue to "The MAN OF LAWSTALE," line 71). Her story is only alluded to, however, in *The HOUSE OF FAME,* where Achilles' falseness to Briseis (he abandoned her after the war), is compared to AENEAS' treatment of Queen DIDO (line 389).

Britaigne (Britayne) (1) *See* BRITAIN.

Britaigne (Britayne) (2) *See* BRITTANY.

Britain Today the term Britain, or Great Britain, is used to refer to England, Scotland and Wales, all of which are united under the same government and occupy different parts of the same island. In Chaucer's time, Britain was simply another word for the Kingdom of England, which included Ireland, England and Wales, but not Scotland. Chaucer uses the term twice: once in "The FRANKLIN'S TALE" to refer to the place where ARVERAGUS is going to spend a year or two striving to win honor in tournaments and other chivalric exploits, and once in Fragment A of *The ROMAUNT OF THE ROSE* to refer to the nationality of the legendary King ARTHUR, whose brother is the escort of the allegorical figure Largesse.

Briton (Britoun) (1) *See* BRETON.

Briton (Britoun) (2) Briton is one of the names applied to the Celtic peoples who inhabited Britain before the invasions of the Romans in the first century A.D. Some Celts remained and were assimilated by their conquerors, but most migrated westward into Devon, Cornwall and Wales, as well as eventually into Scotland and Ireland; others left Britain entirely, emigrating to Armorica, or BRITTANY, on the western coast of France. Part of the adventures of CONSTANCE in "The MAN OF LAW'S TALE" take place in Northumberland in the far north of England during a time when some of its inhabitants were, according to the story, Christian Bretons. This means that they were among those Celts who converted to Christianity during the Roman occupation and who retained that faith after the Romans were gone.

Brittany Peninsula and former province of northwestern France between the English Channel and the Bay of Biscay. It is mentioned once in the GENERAL PROLOGUE to *The* CANTERBURY TALES, where we are informed that the SHIPMAN's knowledge of the waters he navigates is so thorough that he knows, among other things, the location of every creek or inlet in Brittany. Why he would need such minute knowledge of the coast brings up another question: Were all his voyages legitimate, or was he perhaps involved in some piracy which would have necessitated such knowledge? "The FRANKLIN'S TALE" is set in Brittany. The region's treacherous rocky coast functions as an important element of the tale's plot when DORIGEN, pursued by the amorous squire AURELIUS, finally consents to become his lover if he can find a way to remove the rocks that make the seaward approach to Armorica so dangerous. The situation is ironic in that by offering this as the condition of her love she is displaying concern for her husband, whose return from a soujourn in to England she anxiously anticipates.

Brixseyde *See* BRISEIS.

Brok A horse who appears in "The FRIAR'S TALE." Brok is drawing a cart that has become stuck in the mire and the man driving the cart yells and curses at him to encourage his pulling efforts. One of the man's curses commends the horse to the devil. This scene is observed by the tale's two main characters, one of whom is a summoner, the other a devil from hell. When the summoner asks why the devil doesn't fetch away the man's horse, the devil replies that the man's curse is not sincere. He does not really want the horse to go to hell; he just wants it to liberate his cart. Later, when an old woman who is being harassed by the summoner curses him to hell, the results are less benign.

Bromeholm In "The REEVE'S TALE," when the miller's wife wakes up to find that the student JOHN THE CLERK is lying on top of her, she believes that he is a demon and cries out beseeching the Holy Cross of Bromeholm to come to her aid. The reference is to a famous relic of NORFOLK, supposedly a piece of the original cross upon which Christ died. Known as the Rood of Bromeholm, it was thought to have been brought to Norfolk from Constantinople between 1205 and 1223. People made pilgrimages to visit the relic because of the miraculous powers attributed to it. It was considered able to free a person from demonic possession, which makes mention of it here particularly appropriate.

Bronson, Bertrand Harris (1902–1986) American Chaucerian scholar. After earning a Ph.D. from Yale, Bronson enjoyed a long career primarily at the University of California, Berkeley, mostly devoted to Samuel Johnson and 18th-century literature. However, several early works established his name in Chaucer studies. The first of these, "Chaucer's Art in Relation to his Audience" (in *Five Studies in Literature,* 1940) was one of the earliest attempts to examine this aspect of the poet's work. Then he published "*The Book of the Duchess* Reopened" (in *Publications of the Modern Language Association,* 1952), in which he argued against the current tendency to undervalue that early poem. During this period he also published articles on *The* HOUSE OF FAME and *The* PARLIAMENT OF FOWLS.

Bruges Town in the medieval country of FLANDERS (now a region in northwestern Belgium). An important port for the trade of wine and textiles with cities further north on the European coast, Bruges is appropriately a city frequently visited by the MERCHANT of "The SHIPMAN'S TALE," whose residence in just north of Paris. While the Merchant is on business in Bruges his wife gets herself into trouble with the sycophantic JOHN THE MONK. Bruges is also mentioned in "The Tale of Sir Thopas" as the city from whence came Sir Thopas' "hosen" (tights).

Brusendorff, Aage (b.1887) The first draft of Brusendorff's book *The Chaucer Tradition* was accepted as a doctoral thesis by the University of Copenhagen in March 1921. This Danish scholar's avowed interest in Chaucer studies has been to examine the way in which the knowledge of Chaucer's personality and writings was passed down by the first two generations of the 15th century, following Chaucer's death. This early tradition, Brusendorff argues, "offers the sole reliable basis for a true bibliographical canon of his works." *The Chaucer Tradition* consists of highly technical analysis of texts to establish dating, recover "lost works" and exclude "spurious texts."

Brutus Marcus Junius Brutus (whose name Chaucer spells "Brutes") was the Roman statesman and general of the first century B.C. who, after forming a close friendship with JULIUS CAESAR, conspired with other Roman senators to murder him. Their professed motive was to save the Roman republic from becoming a dictatorship ruled by a tyrant. When Brutus committed suicide during the civil war that followed the assassination, his wife, PORTIA, also took her own life. DORIGEN in "The FRANKLIN'S TALE" alludes to Portia's suicide when she is constructing a list of women famed for their faithfulness to their husbands. Dorigen uses these examples to boost her own resolve to remain faithful to her husband, ARVERAGUS, despite her promise to the squire AURELIUS that she would become his lover if he could accomplish the seemingly impossible feat of moving the huge rocks that line the coast of BRITTANY. Brutus is also mentioned in the brief biography of Julius Caesar that is included among the tragedies of "The MONK'S TALE." Referring to Brutus' role in the assassination conspiracy, the MONK suggests that Brutus' motive was envy of Caesar's power (line 2706). The name he is given here, Brutus Cassius, indicates that Chaucer believed two of the conspirators (another was named Cassius) to be one person. Chaucer was not the only medieval writer to make this mistake, which implies that it may have existed in some of the sources he drew upon. John LYDGATE repeats the error four times in his work.

Brutus Cassius *See* BRUTUS.

Bubonic Plague *See* BLACK DEATH.

Bukton The addressee of one of the short, epistolary poems attributed to Chaucer, "LENVOY DE CHAUCER À BUKTON." Like Chaucer, Bukton was probably a courtier.

Burdeux *See* BORDEAUX.

Burgundy (Burgoyne) Burgundy (Chaucer gives it the Old French spelling, "Burgoyne") is the name of a famous wine-growing region of southeastern France. From 1180 to 1453 it was a kingdom independent of France, governed by the dukes of Burgundy. Chaucer mentions Burgundy in his Middle English translation of the French *ROMAN DE LA ROSE* when he describes IDLENESS as possessing the fairest neck of any found in the regions lying between Burgundy and JERUSALEM. The word does not appear in the original text but was supplied by Chaucer in his translation (*The ROMAUNT OF THE ROSE*) to make the rhyme come out correctly.

Burnel the Ass A character in Nigel of Longchamps' late 12th-century satire, *Burnellus*. In "The NUN'S PRIEST'S TALE," RUSSELL the fox refers to this collection of comic beast fables in his attempts to flatter the rooster CHAUNTICLEER. Russell recalls a story about another rooster who revenged himself on a young man, who had kicked him, by refusing to crow on the morning that the man was to be ordained as a priest, thereby causing the man to oversleep and lose his livelihood. Russell claims that the wisdom of Chaunticleer's father (now deceased) far excelled the mere cleverness of the rooster mentioned in the story, and implies that he expects Chaunticleer's wisdom, along with his talent for singing, to excel even his father's. The unfortunate Chaunticleer falls for the fox's flattery and stretches out his neck to sing. In the next instant he finds himself being carried away, his neck clenched firmly between the fox's jaws. Ironically, Chaunticleer does turn out to be at least as clever as the rooster in the story, using his wits to extricate himself from this dilemma.

Burnley, (John) David (1941–) Chaucerian scholar at the University of Sheffield. Burnley has pursued an approach based on the concept that "the center of interest in a literary author should be his text," as he said in *Contemporary Authors*. In Chaucer studies, a number of Burnley's titles reflect this orientation: "Inflexion in Chaucer's Adjectives" (in the journal *Neuphilologische Mitteilungen*, 1982), *A Guide to Chaucer's Language* (1983), entries on Chaucer's Middle English in the *Year's Work in English Studies* for the years 1980–85, and, more recently, "The Sheffield Chaucer Textbase: Its Compilation and Uses" (in *Computer-Based Chaucer Studies*, 1993). Burnley believes that the text is best interpreted by detailed knowledge of the author's language in its historical context.

Burrow, John A(nthony) (1932–) An Oxford-educated professor at the University of Bristol, Burrow edited an important collection of scholarly articles entitled *Geoffrey Chaucer: A Critical Anthology* (1970). His most innovative contribution to Chaucer studies has been the book *Ricardian Poetry: Chaucer, Gower, Langland and the Gawain Poet* (1971), an examination of the four chief poets of the reign of King RICHARD II, which attempts to consider them as a group, finding in the midst of their apparent dissimilarities (in dialect, meter and subject matter) some common threads.

Busirus In classical mythology, Busirus was the son of NEPTUNE who ruled Egypt. All strangers who entered his country were sacrificed to JUPITER to bring an end to a period of drought. HERCULES put an end to this practice by killing Busirus and his son. The story of Hercules related in "The MONK'S TALE" states that Busirus' flesh was fed to his horses, but in OVID's *Metamorphoses* that fate is given to DIOMEDE, not Busirus. In the *BOECE*, Chaucer's translation of BOETHIUS' *Consolation of Philosophy*, LADY PHILOSOPHY notes that Busirus, who slew his guests, was in turn slain by a guest (Book Two, Prosa 6, line 67).

Cacus In classical mythology, Cacus was a giant who lived in a cave by the Tiber River. When HERCULES brought the cattle of Geryon to that place, Cacus stole some of them while Hercules was sleeping, dragging them backwards by their tails and hiding them in his cave. When Hercules awoke and found the cattle gone, he was at first misled by the direction of their footprints, which pointed away from the cave. As he was about to drive the rest of the herd away, a lowing sound issued from the cave, revealing Cacus' hiding place. After removing the stone that covered the cave's entrance, Hercules killed Cacus and recovered his cattle. The defeat of Cacus is mentioned along with Hercules' many other exploits in the brief biography of Hercules Chaucer includes in the "MONK'S TALE" (line 2107).

Cadmus In classical mythology, Cadmus (Chaucer's spelling is Cadme) was the legendary founder of THEBES. He was the son of Agenor and Telephassa of Phoenicia. When Zeus (JUPITER) carried off his sister EUROPA, Cadmus was sent to find the girl with orders that he must not return home without her. After a long fruitless search, Cadmus consulted the oracle at DELPHI and was told to follow a cow that he would find, and to build a city wherever she stopped. He was led into Boetia. Preparing to sacrifice the cow where she had halted, Cadmus went to a spring to get some water and was confronted by a huge serpent. Not knowing that the serpent was the offspring of Aries (MARS), he killed it with the assistance of Athena (PALLAS). On her advice he planted the serpent's teeth, which at once sprang up in the form of armed men, who then fought among themselves until all but five were dead. These five assisted Cadmus in building the Cadmea, which would become the citadel of Thebes. For having killed the serpent, Cadmus was forced to serve Aries for eight years, at the end of which time he became ruler of Thebes. Harmonia, the daughter of Aries and Aphrodite (VENUS), was given to him as a wife. Cadmus is credited with having introduced the Greek alphabet and, in general, with having been one of the founders of civilization. ARCITE (1) and PALAMON, the two Theban knights who are the chief protagonists of "The KNIGHT'S TALE," claim descent from the royal house of Cadmus.

Cain In the Bible, Cain is the name of the eldest son of ADAM and EVE, the first humans created by God, and the brother of ABEL. A farmer by occupation, Cain brought the fruits of the ground as a sacrifice to God. His brother, Abel, a shepherd, sacrificed a lamb from his flock. God accepted Abel's offering but rejected Cain's. Cain reacted to this event by killing his brother, thus committing the first murder. Cain is mentioned in "The PARSON'S TALE" during that portion of the tale (actually a sermon) that deals with shrift (confession and absolution by a priest) and penance. In order for shrift to be effective, the PARSON states, the person confessing must not despair of receiving the Lord's mercy, as Cain and JUDAS did (line 1015).

Calcas *See* CALKAS.

Caligula Roman emperor, also known as Gaius Caesar, who ruled from A.D. 37 to 41 and who was notorious for his cruelty and decadence. Book One, Prosa Four of the *BOECE* relates an anecdote wherein the narrator (BOETHIUS) recalls the words of JULIUS CANIUS, who was accused by Caligula of knowing and consenting to a conspiracy against the emperor. Canius responded by telling the emperor that if he were involved in such a thing, it would certainly not have come to the emperor's attention (i.e., he would have been clever enough to keep it from doing so).

Caliope *See* CALLIOPE.

Calipsa *See* CALYPSO.

Calistopee *See* CALLISTO.

Calkas A Trojan soothsayer and the father of CRISEYDE. Calkas plays an important role in Chaucer's longest single work, *TROILUS AND CRISEYDE,* which is set against the events of the TROJAN WAR. Believing that the Trojans are going to be defeated, Calkas decides to leave TROY and join the Greek camp. Initially he abandons his daughter, the widowed Criseyde, which forces her to become more and more dependent upon the support and protection of her uncle PANDARUS and other members of the Trojan nobility, including TROILUS. When she finally agrees to become Troilus' lover, it is at least partly because she needs his protection. But just as he had helped to bring the two lovers together, Calkas even more directly contributes to their breakup, arranging for the Greeks to offer a Trojan prisoner in exchange for his daughter, whom he now wishes to have with him. Although popular sentiment pressures Criseyde into going through with the exchange, she at first plans to slip away from the Greeks and rejoin Troilus; however, the encouragement she receives from her father to leave her past behind, in addition to her own fears about leaving the camp and traveling on her own, persuade her against going back to Troy.

Calliope (Callyope)   In classical mythology, Calliope is the muse of epic poetry, which means that she was believed to preside over the creation of such poetry and to determine the standards by which it was judged. Because of this, it became traditional for epic poets to invoke, or call upon, Calliope for inspiration and assistance in executing their writing. In *The HOUSE OF FAME*, Calliope and her eight sister-muses (although Calliope is the only one mentioned by name here) are gathered about the throne of the goddess FAME, whose praise they continually sing. In *TROILUS AND CRISEYDE*, Chaucer invokes both Calliope and VENUS in the opening lines of book 3, asking them to help him describe the great joy that TROILUS and CRISEYDE experience when they at last become lovers.

Callisto   In classical mythology, Callisto is a nymph from Arcadia who was an attendant to Artemis (DIANA). One of many women who attracted the jealousy of Hera (JUNO) after an affair with Zeus (JUPITER), Callisto was changed into a bear by the angry goddess and some years later encountered her son hunting in the forest. Not recognizing her, he pursued his mother and was on the point of killing her when Zeus changed her into the star called Arctos. Her son became the star Arcturus. Hera convinced Oceanus and Tethys never to allow Callisto to bathe in their waters; hence, the constellation of the Bear never sets. In "The KNIGHT'S TALE," Callisto's story is depicted on the walls of Diana's temple (line 2056). In this version of the story, her transformation is attributed to Diana's disappointment over Callisto's loss of chastity. Her story also appears on the walls of the TEMPLE OF VENUS in Chaucer's *PARLIAMENT OF FOWLS*. Again she is characterized as one of Diana's maidens who lost that status by falling in love (line 286).

Calydoigne (Calydoyne)   *See* CALYDON.

Calydon   A kingdom in Aetolia in western Greece, said to have been founded by Calydon, son of Aetolus. One of the rulers of Calydon was TYDEAUS, the father of DIOMEDE, an important character in Chaucer's *TROILUS AND CRISEYDE*. The fact that Diomede will inherit his father's throne is one of the reasons CRISEYDE decides to remain in the Greek camp and become Diomede's lover rather than return to TROY and TROILUS. Her motive is self-preservation as well as ambition. If she returns to Troy, it will be with the knowledge that the city is doomed, while if she stays in the Greek camp, herself being a Trojan, she will have no protector other than her father.

Calypso   In classical mythology, Calypso is a nymph who lived on the island of Ogygia where Odysseus (ULYSSES) was shipwrecked. She fell in love with the hero and offered him immortality if he would remain with her. Though he refused to do so, she kept him for seven years until commanded by Zeus (JUPITER) to release him. She then helped him build a raft, gave him provisions, and sent him on his way. Calypso is mentioned among the group of magicians and sorceresses who appear in FAME's palace in *The HOUSE OF FAME* (line 1272).

Calyxte   *See* CALLISTO.

Cambalo   The youngest son of CAMBYUSKAN in "The SQUIRE'S TALE." It is forecast that he will mediate the reunion of the lovesick falcon with her mate. Nothing more is said about him in the tale until the final lines, in which the SQUIRE promises to tell how Cambalo fought against two brothers in order to win CANACEE. It is possible, however, that the two brothers are Canacee's own and that this Cambalo bears the same name as Canacee's brother but is unrelated to her. The idea that incest may be implied comes from a tale of brother-sister incest that appears in John GOWER's *CONFESSIO AMANTIS*, a work that Chaucer knew, and upon which he drew in some of his other writing.

Cambises   *See* CAMBYSES.

Cambridge (Canterbregge)   University town situated on the river Cam in eastern England. In "The REEVE'S TALE," it is described as being not far from TRUMPINGTON. The two students who are determined that they will not be cheated by the corrupt miller in the tale attend SOLER HALL, more familiarly known as King's Hall, which was later merged into Trinity College. Cambridge University has existed since 1209.

Cambridge Companion to Chaucer, The   A volume of essays selected for the purpose of introducing students to a critical consideration of Chaucer's work. Edited by Piero BOITANI and Jill MANN and published in 1986, the collection focuses primarily on *The CANTERBURY TALES* (there are six essays on this work), with introductory chapters on the social and literary milieu in which the work was produced and on the literary influences of France and Italy. Another essay treats the early poems, *The BOOK OF THE DUCHESS, The HOUSE OF FAME,* and *The PARLIAMENT OF FOWLS,* and three are devoted to *TROILUS AND CRISEYDE.* The volume concludes with essays devoted to style and structure.

Cambyses (Cambises) Persian king who ruled from 529 to 522 B.C. Famous for his terrible temper and bloodthirstiness, Cambyses often appeared as a kind of symbol of those traits in popular literature up through the Renaissance. The corrupt and greedy FRIAR of "The SUMMONER'S TALE" uses the example of Cambyses to warn the ailing THOMAS (1) against the dangers of succumbing to anger (line 2043). The argument is part of the Friar's scheme to dupe Thomas out of money and, because succumbing to anger is the least of the poor man's problems, it is one of many ways the tale satirically illustrates the Friar's complete inability or unwillingness to properly minister to the needs of those whom he visits.

Cambyuskan The Mongol king of Sarray (Tsarev, present-day southern Russia) in "The SQUIRE'S TALE." The name "Cambyuskan" is probably the Latinized version of *Genghis Khan,* the Mongol emperor (1162?–1227) who ruled a portion of Russia stretching from the Black Sea to the Pacific. In this tale, the feast of Cambyuskan's nativity (his birthday) forms the occasion for the first part of the narrative, in which a messenger from the king of Arabia and India brings four magical gifts. Two of them, a bronze horse and an invincible sword, are for Cambyuskan; the other two, a magical ring and mirror, are presented to his daughter, CANACEE. The lengthy description of Cambyuskan with which the tale opens suggests that he is an example of a virtuous pagan, i.e., one who zealously upholds the laws of his own country. Specifically, he is loyal, wise, just, trustworthy, brave, strong, young and, in brief, lacking "noght that longeth to a kyng" (line 16). Despite these superlative qualities, Cambyuskan does not play much of a role in this tale, outside of what has already been mentioned here. The tale is unfinished, though, and the SQUIRE forecasts that he will speak of Cambyuskan's adventures in war. He is unable to do so because of the FRANKLIN's interruption.

Campaneus *See* CAPANEUS.

Campania (Campayne) Province in southern Italy, on the Tyrrhenian Sea. The narrator of the *BOECE,* in his attempt to explain to LADY PHILOSOPHY why he was exiled by King THEODORIC, lists all the occasions on which he challenged Theodoric's policies, including an instance when he opposed an economic policy that would force the people of Campania to buy grain from the king at an inflated price until all of it had been sold.

Cana The village in Galilee where Jesus (*see* JESUS CHRIST) performed his first miracle, turning water into wine at a wedding feast. The WIFE OF BATH refers to this miracle in her prologue in reference to the fact that she has been married five times. Evidently she has been reproved for marrying so many times by someone (probably a priest) who told her that since Christ only attended one wedding, by the same token she should only have been once to the altar. She is also able to use scripture to defend her multiple marriages, saying that she is merely obeying God's command to be fruitful and multiply. (Ironically, though, she seems to have no children, or at least she does not mention them.)

Canaan In the Bible, Canaan was the fourth son of HAM and the grandson of NOAH. Ham's descendants were dispersed into several distinct tribes, such as the Jebusites and the Zemarites. Eventually these people became collectively known as the Canaanites, pagan inhabitants of the land that God promised to ABRAHAM and his descendants. Under the leadership of Joshua, the Jewish people occupied the land of Canaan and divided it among the 12 tribes of the nation of Israel. In "The PARSON'S TALE" the name Canaan is mistakenly used to refer to Canaan's father, Ham, when the Parson states that slavery first came into the world when Noah prophesied that Ham should be a thrall (slave) to his brothers because of a grievous sin that he had committed. Ham's "sin" was that, after the Great Flood, he found his father, drunk and naked, asleep in his tent. Ham told his brothers, Shem and Japheth, who went into the tent and covered their father without looking at his body. Furious because his son had seen him naked, Noah placed a curse on Ham which supposedly doomed him and his descendants to be the slaves of his brothers, Shem and Japheth.

Canaanite woman In the Invocation to the Virgin Mary that appears at the beginning of "The SECOND NUN'S TALE," the nun compares herself to the Canaanite woman who approached Jesus in Matthew 15:22–28, asking Him to heal her daughter who was possessed by a devil. His apostles said that he should not help her, and Christ Himself at first appeared to agree, saying, "It is not meet to take the children's bread, and to cast it to dogs." When she continued to honor him and responded, "Truth, Lord: yet the dogs eat of the crumbs which fall from their master's table," he commended her faith and healed her daughter. In comparing herself to this woman, the nun displays humility but also the assumption that her request, which is for assistance in telling her tale, will be honored.

Canacee (1)   The daughter of CAMBYUSKAN in "The SQUIRE'S TALE." Canacee receives two marvelous gifts from the king of Arabia and India on the occasion of her father's birthday. One is a mirror that will enable her to foresee any adversity that might befall her father's kingdom. The other is a ring that will allow her to understand the language of birds and communicate with them in their own speech. The ring also has the property of revealing the healing properties of all plants. Canacee uses the ring to rescue a lovesick falcon. John GOWER's *CONFESSIO AMANTIS* contains the story of a young woman named Canacee, also a king's daughter, who falls in love with her brother and conceives a child by him. (*See* CANACEE [2].) It has been suggested that there may be a foreshadowing of such an incident in the life of Chaucer's Canacee, based on lines 667–69, where the SQUIRE promises to tell about her brother CAMBALO and how he "faught in lystes" with her other brothers "For Canacee er that he myghte hire wynne."

Canacee (2)   In classical mythology Canacee, the daughter of the Greek king AEOLUS, fell in love with and conceived a child by her brother Macareus. Macareus managed to escape his father's palace before the truth became known about their affair and Canacee's condition, leaving her to take the full brunt of their father's wrath. When the child was born, Aeolus had a sword sent to Canacee and commanded her to commit suicide by falling upon its point. After she had killed herself, the child was taken and abandoned in a forest. John GOWER included the story of Canacee and her brother in his *Confessio Amantis,* where he uses the story as a warning against the dangers of anger and melancholy. Interestingly, despite their incest, Canacee and her brother are portrayed very sympathetically, while her father, who had his daughter and the baby killed, is perceived as the wrongdoer. The unusual morality of Gower's treatment is alluded to in the prologue to "The MAN OF LAW'S TALE" where the SERGEANT OF THE LAW provides a list of Chaucer's works, noting that Chaucer would never have written such a wicked story as that of Canacee and her brother (line 78). Whether this comment may be taken to express Chaucer's opinion of Gower's work is open to debate but seems doubtful. Canacee is also referred to in the two versions (F and G) of the prologue to *The LEGEND OF GOOD WOMEN,* where she is listed as an example of a woman whose faithfulness to her lover, though great, pales beside that of Queen ALCESTIS, who agreed to die in her husband's place (prologue F, line 265; prologue G, line 219).

Cananee woman   *See* CANAANITE WOMAN.

Cancer   One of the 12 divisions of the zodiac, an imaginary belt in the heavens extending for about eight degrees on either side of the apparent path of the sun and including the paths of the moon and the principal planets. The zodiac is divided into 12 equal parts, or signs, each named for a different constellation. Cancer, or the Crab, is the fourth sign (*see* diagram under ASTROLOGY), which the Sun enters on or around June 22. In Chaucer's day, the Sun entered Cancer around June 12. The constellation of Cancer appears between Gemini and Leo in the sky. Chaucer usually employs such astrological terms to indicate the approximate date of a narrative event or to show the passage of time. In "The MERCHANT'S TALE," for example, he uses the following astrological description to note that four days have passed since the wedding of JANUARY and MAY: "The moone, that at noon was thilke day / That Januarie hath wedded fresshe May / In two of Tawr, was into Cancre glyden; / So longe hath Mayus in hir chambre abyden, / As custume is unto thise nobles alle" (lines 1885–89). [The moon, that at noon on the day that January and May married was in the second degree of Taurus, had now glided into the sign of Cancer; for this length of time May had kept to her chamber, as is customary among the class of nobles to which January belonged]. (A looser translation than usual is provided here to best convey the sense of the passage.) Rhetorically, the use of this device functions to elevate the style of the passage, and Chaucer typically makes use of it in two situations. Sometimes, as in "The KNIGHT'S TALE," it provides a way of noting the date of an event in terms that are in keeping with the noble theme and elevated sentiments of the work as a whole. On other occasions, as in "The NUN'S PRIEST'S TALE," his use of astrological terms can have a comedic effect because of the contrast between the elevated style of the passage and the silliness of the plot and/or its characters.

Cancre (Cancro)   *See* CANCER.

Candace   The Candace referred to in the short poem "AGAINST WOMEN UNCONSTANT" was a queen of India who in the fourth century B.C. supposedly tricked ALEXANDER THE GREAT into believing that she loved him, in order to attain power over him. The poem is addressed to a woman whom the narrator characterizes as fickle in the extreme, more unfaithful than DELILAH, CRISEYDE or Candace, all women who were famed for their betrayal of men who loved them. Candace of India is also mentioned in *The PARLIAMENT OF FOWLS,* where her story is depicted on the wall of the TEMPLE OF VENUS. In this instance, because she is pictured along with women who suffered adversity in love's service, the implication is that her feelings for Alexander were genuine.

Cane   *See* CANA.

Canius, Julius   *See* JULIUS CANIUS.

Canon (1)   A man who attempts to join the pilgrimage to CANTERBURY which serves as the framework for *The CANTERBURY TALES*. His arrival, riding as if the demons of hell are after him, comes late in the sequence of tales, and his somewhat demonic appearance suggests much about his character and motives. The CANON'S YEOMAN who accompanies him and who functions as his servant and helper initially brags about his master's abilities in the science of ALCHEMY, but when those abilities are challenged by the Host (*see* Harry BAILLY), the yeoman embarks upon a disparagement of the Canon that causes the man to flee in embarrassment. Once the man has gone, the yeoman speaks even more freely of the sordid life he has had in the Canon's service, a service that has deprived him of both worldly goods and health. It is not clear, however, whether the Canon for whom the yeoman worked has been consciously cheating those who contribute time and wealth to his enterprise, or whether he honestly believes that he will one day discover the secret for turning base metals into gold.

Canon (2)   One of the characters in "The CANON'S YEOMAN'S TALE." This canon practices ALCHEMY for the sole purpose of making money by cheating other people. The CANON'S YEOMAN depicts him plying his trade on a naive priest, first convincing the priest that he possesses a powder which, heated to the desired temperature, will turn quicksilver (mercury) into silver. After seeing the process demonstrated three times, the priest pays £40, a large sum in those days—the annual budget for an Oxford student was around £3—for the recipe. Some commentators have suggested that the Canon of the yeoman's tale is the same person as the Canon for whom the yeoman works, despite the yeoman's denial of that assumption. If they are one and the same person, the tale casts an even longer shadow of moral degeneracy over the characters of these two latecomers to the pilgrimage.

Canon's Yeoman   In *The CANTERBURY TALES*, one of two characters who join the pilgrimage en route. The CANON (1) and his yeoman appear riding their horses furiously in pursuit of the pilgrims who have just reached the village of BOGHTON UNDER BLEE, not far from their final destination. The narrator marvels at the appearance of the two men, noting the yeoman's discolored complexion which, the man explains, has come from staring too long into the fires kindled by his master, who is an alchemist (*see* ALCHEMY). The yeoman informs the Host that the two men wish to join the pilgrims, suggesting that the group may profit by such an acquaintance. When the Host presses him for more information, the yeoman hints that the Canon could,

through his craft, pave the path to CANTERBURY with silver and gold. The Host expresses skepticism, based on the poor ("sluttish" is his word) appearance of the Canon's apparel. Apparently overcome by the reasoning behind such an argument, the yeoman reveals that the Canon is actually a hoaxer who uses alchemy to trick people out of their money. At this point the Canon sidles closer to his servant to hear what the man is saying, discovers that he has been betrayed, and leaves the group. The yeoman, emboldened by his initial confession, now promises that he will never rejoin his master, and proceeds to tell "The CANON'S YEOMAN'S TALE," in which he purports to reveal the secrets of the alchemical trick.

"Canon's Yeoman's Tale, The"   The second of two tales in Fragment VIII (Group G) of *The CANTERBURY TALES*.

SUMMARY

At the village of BOGHTON UNDER BLEE (Boughton under the Blean Forest, about five miles from CANTERBURY), the pilgrims are overtaken by a man wearing a black cloak with a white ecclesiastical gown underneath and riding his horse so hard that it is covered with flecks of foamy sweat. This man, a church Canon (*see* CANON [1]), is accompanied by his yeoman, or manser-

Artist's rendering of the Canon's Yeoman, from the Ellesmere Manuscript of The Canterbury Tales. *The Canon's Yeoman is not described in the General Prologue because he joins the pilgrims after they are on the road.*

vant. The two explain in turn how the yeoman saw the pilgrims ride out from their previous night's lodging and alerted his master so that he could join their company. The yeoman turns out to be the more talkative of the two, so it is he who answers the Host's (*see* Harry BAILLY) questions, announcing that his master is an alchemist, a kind of cross between a chemist and a magician, who is able to turn base (nonprecious) metals into silver and gold. Responding to the Host's curiosity, the Yeoman rattles on, ultimately revealing too many details regarding his master's profession. The Canon, growing suspicious of their extended conversation, rides near and chastises his servant for revealing his secrets. When the yeoman defiantly continues talking, the Canon flees in embarrassment. The yeoman curses his former master, and then begins his tale with a promise to reveal all that he knows of the art of alchemy and how its practitioners deceive themselves and other people.

The yeoman has been with the Canon seven years, he says. He has lost everything he owned, including his health (his skin has been particularly affected from contact with chemicals and fire), and has decided to use his experience as a warning to others. As a preface to the tale he is about to tell, the yeoman presents a somewhat jumbled catalogue of various equipment and terminologies current in his master's profession, including the elusive "philosopher's stone," which was supposed to transmute base metals into gold or silver. He then gives an account of one of the methods whereby his master would attempt to "multiply" a small amount of money, making it grow into a larger sum. This is only a prelude to the actual tale the yeoman intends to tell of a canon (*see* CANON [2]) so full of deceit and falsehood that he could infect or pollute an entire town the size of ROME.

The yeoman's story then settles down to focus on one particular example of this man's corruption. This involves a somewhat naive chantry priest from London, from whom the canon borrows a mark, a coin equivalent to two-thirds of a pound. When the canon returns the money three days later as agreed, the priest commends him for promptly repaying his debt, remarking that others of his acquaintance have not been so conscientious. The canon pretends to be appalled by the very mention of such behavior and announces that in order to show his gratitude for the priest's kindness, he will show the priest his skills in "philosophie"—ALCHEMY. He asks the priest to send his serving man to fetch some quicksilver, or mercury, which the alchemist swears he will turn into silver right before the priest's eyes. As the canon begins heating the mercury in a crucible, he throws in a magical powder and calls for the priest's help in building up the fire. Then, pretending to assist him, the canon lays on top of the crucible a special piece of charcoal, one that secretly has been

hollowed out and filled with silver shavings secured with a wax seal. When the wax melts, the silver drops into the container. The mercury vaporizes, but the silver melts and the canon is able to pour it into a mold, from which he then extracts a silver ingot that appears to have been transmuted from the mercury. The priest excitedly congratulates and blesses the canon and begs the man to teach him his "noble craft." Thus encouraged, the canon offers to perform the feat a second time so that the priest may become more knowledgeable of his methods. The second trick is nearly the same as the first, except the silver filings are this time hidden within a hollow stick, with which the canon stirs the fire. The third time, the canon asks for a piece of copper, which he casts into the crucible and sprinkles with his powder. Then, when the mixture has been dumped into a basin of water to cool, he substitutes a silver ingot, which has been hidden in his sleeve, for the copper one, and invites the priest to fish it out. They take the silver to a goldsmith to assay its worth. Finding it to be genuine, the priest excitedly begs the canon for the recipe to the powder, which the canon agrees to sell him at the discounted cost of £40 as a special favor for a friend. The canon extracts the priest's promise that he will keep the recipe a secret, and the two part company. When the priest tries to use the recipe to duplicate the canon's results, he fails over and over again. Thus ends the tale of the canon alchemist and how he duped a gullible priest.

Now the yeoman enlarges upon his theme, extending the argument regarding the evils of alchemy to reflect upon the evils of money in general, asking his audience to consider how gold is a great cause of argument among people from all ranks of society. From there the perspective narrows once again, with a few final warnings against the temptations of alchemy, noting the paradox that attempts to multiply gold or silver typically result in their reduction through either theft or accident. The tale concludes with a final warning that includes an allusion to the First Fall of ADAM in Eden. The secrets of alchemy, the yeoman claims, are the secrets of God, who does not wish for man to achieve the philosopher's stone. And any man who seeks the contrary of God's will shall certainly not thrive.

COMMENTARY

Because the term is an unfamiliar one for many modern readers, any discussion of "The Canon's Yeoman's Tale" must begin with an explanation of alchemy. In brief, alchemy, or "philosophie," as it is sometimes termed, was a pseudoscience whose primary aim was to turn base metals (such as lead or mercury) into precious ones (specifically, gold or silver). It was based on ideas and theories about the nature of the physical world that originated in the ancient Middle East. Many of the alchemical treatises translated into Latin during the Middle Ages were originally written in Arabic. The alchemist's quest involved experimenting to find combinations of various different elements, such as ammonium chloride (Chaucer's "sal ammoniac"), arsenic sulphide ("orpyment"), copper acetate ("verdegrees") and borax ("boras"), which, upon being heated to an extremely high temperature, would burn off their impurities and combine together to make either gold or the philosopher's stone, which could itself then be used to turn base metals into gold. If the process proved successful, a series of four colors should have been observed within the vessel where the elements were heated. First, the oxidized materials would turn black, then white (the "albificacioun" mentioned by the Canon's Yeoman), yellow ("citrinacioun," from citrus, to indicate a lemon color), red ("rubificacioun") and finally gold. There were also attempts to make elixirs from the distillations of such experiments, in the belief that, just as the philosopher's stone would cause a base metal to achieve perfection by turning to gold, so would such an elixir, if given to a sick person to drink, promote perfect health and perhaps even immortality.

Considering the limitations of scientific understanding at the time these texts were written and translated, it is not surprising that their contents proved attractive to the people of their day, especially when we consider the continuing popularity of schemes to make money quickly and easily, and "miraculous" regimens to remain youthful.

Some readers express surprise that the characters involved with alchemy in the yeoman's tale, and in his life, are clerics, but in fact historical records show that most practitioners of the "art" were churchmen, mainly because it required fluency in Latin and a good education in order to understand the tremendously difficult texts. In accordance with the Yeoman's experience, there seem, historically, to have been primarily two distinct reasons why people practiced alchemy. Some people, like the yeoman's master, seem to have honestly believed, at least at first, that the aims of the practice were actually capable of being achieved, that base metals could indeed be transmuted into gold if only the correct combination and proportion of materials could be found. These individuals, according to the Yeoman's experience, were the self-deceived. Others, like the canon who bilks the priest of £40, merely practiced for the purpose of deceiving others and making money. Ironically, such practitioners did learn to "multiply," but not in the ways promised by the alchemical treatises. Such treatises were plentiful in Chaucer's day and are likely to have provided him with much of the information for the yeoman's prologue. Two of these treatises are mentioned at the end of the tale: the *Rosarie* of ARNALDUS OF VILLANOVA (Arnold of the Newe Toun)

and a "book Senior," which was a work translated from Arabic and known in Latin as the *Epistola solis ad lunam crescentem* (Letter of the Sun to the crescent Moon). As for the tale of the canon and priest, there is no known direct source, although a story by Ramón Lull (d. 1315) in which a swindler uses a somewhat similar trick to multiply some gold is one of the few plausible analogues.

Determining the tale's genre is even more problematic than finding its sources. Although it takes information from alchemical treatises, occasionally sounds like some of the condemnations of alchemy issued by the church and incorporates a tale which, aside from having no sexual dimension, resembles a FABLIAU, the way in which it combines these features grants it a total effect that seems much more complex than the sum of its parts. Perhaps the most intriguing question raised by the tale's themes and concerns relates to the reliability of the tale's narrator and, specifically, to whether we may trust his claim that the canon of his tale is not the same man as the Canon under whom he has served. The narrator calls the pilgrim's attention to this supposed fact twice, once at the beginning of the tale and once after he is some way into it. The adamant nature of his second notification calls attention to itself in such a way as to cast doubt upon his honesty. After all, if the canon of the tale is his master, the implication is that the yeoman himself has been involved in cheating people out of money while serving under that master. Considered in this light, the Canon's precipitous arrival among the pilgrims, along with the yeoman's initial praises of his master's abilities, suggests that the two men may have intended to practice their deception upon members of the group but were prevented from doing so by a combination of the Host's probing questions and the yeoman's loose tongue. Considering the latter's experience and poor health, he has probably been yearning for such an opportunity for some time.

The tale's most obvious theme is that alchemy, which is supposed to be a method of multiplying one's riches, paradoxically diminishes them instead. The details Chaucer uses to develop this theme relate it to two other tales in the Canterbury Group, "The PARDONER'S TALE" and "The SECOND NUN'S TALE." Like the protagonists of "The Pardoner's Tale," those who practice alchemy are motivated by greed, the lust for wealth. The death that awaits the three rioters at the end of that tale makes no actual appearance in the Canon's Yeoman's tale, but it is hinted at in the demise of the yeoman's health and by the blazing fires of the alchemical process which prefigure the fires of hell. When describing those who have been deceived by the alchemist, the yeoman often uses the term "bleynt" (blinded), which recalls the SECOND NUN's use of the same word to describe the spiritual state of nonbelievers. Fire also plays an important role in "The Second

Nun's Tale," there symbolizing the fires of lust to which CECILIA is immune, so much so that when she is placed into a cauldron over a blazing fire she does not even sweat. In contrast, the yeoman has been greatly affected by his proximity to the fires of the alchemical process; his complexion has turned a leaden shade of gray and his eyesight has literally become bleared. The ironies that emerge in the comparison of these two tales are further enhanced by those within the yeoman's tale, particularly his revelation that his complexion has gone through a process of turning from red to white to grayish-black, the opposite of the color process that was supposed to occur when the alchemical process was successful. Furthermore, not only has he gone from being financially well-endowed to a condition of poverty, but his health has diminished as well. He is so fragile, in fact, that merely speaking of the canon and his pursuits makes him feel ill, something he mentions several times. The character of both the canons in this tale affords comparison with another of *The CANTERBURY TALES*' ecclesiastical figures, the CLERK who tells the tale of patient GRISELDA. The canons, of course, are anything but patient in their greedy pursuit of wealth, and they offer a striking contrast to the poor Oxford scholar who is devoted to a pursuit of knowledge that disregards material wealth while maintaining a sense of moral virtue. Ironically, in dress they resemble each other, both wearing worn and tattered cloaks. The Clerk, however, seems to bear his poverty with patience and fortitude, while the canon feverishly seeks to escape his, through the quest for elusive riches.

From our own historical vantage point, we are able to see that the feverish pursuits of those who studied alchemy were not all in vain, that they were merely a prelude to the science of chemistry. Today it is indeed possible to manufacture precious substances in a laboratory, from gems like diamonds and emeralds, to disease-inhibiting pharmaceuticals. From this perspective it is useful to consider that Chaucer himself does not seem to be condemning scientific knowledge or the pursuit of the same (he did, after all, translate the *TREATISE ON THE ASTROLABE*), except in the case where such pursuit proved damaging to the human psyche or to human society, as alchemy for the sake of deceiving people clearly did. In contrast, in his *Inferno*, DANTE ALIGHIERI, whose work had demonstrable influence on Chaucer's, located alchemists with other practitioners of fraud in hell where they are endlessly tormented by a loathsome itch. This disease is the external symbol of their moral corruption, an infectious social disease with the potential to wreak destruction within the social body.

Canterbrigge   *See* CAMBRIDGE.

Canterbury   Cathedral city in the southeastern county of Kent, England, where the shrine of Saint THOMAS À BECKET is located. This shrine is the destination of the pilgrims who participate in the tale-telling contest that constitutes the framework of Chaucer's most famous work, *The CANTERBURY TALES*. Nowadays, Canterbury is the seat of the primate (highest official) of the Church of England, the archbishop of Canterbury. Saint Thomas occupied this office at the time of his martyrdom, but the Church of England had not yet split away from the Roman Catholic Church, so the archbishoprics in England were still accountable to higher officials in Rome. Chaucer may have chosen Thomas' shrine at Canterbury for this purpose because it was the most frequented place of pilgrimage in England from the end of the 12th century up until the English split with the Catholic Church in the 16th century, during the reign of King Henry VIII.

Canterbury Tales, The   Chaucer's most celebrated work. Put together near the end of his life (some of the tales were composed earlier in his career), *The Canterbury Tales* is also his longest work, extending to 17,000 lines of verse and prose. The work opens with a GENERAL PROLOGUE that describes the meeting of 31 pilgrims at the TABARD Inn in SOUTHWARK, a suburb of London on the south side of the river Thames. Vividly detailed portraits of 21 of the pilgrims form the body of this prologue, in which the narrator (later revealed to be "Chaucer") provides some hints about himself by the tone and manner of the descriptions. The group has gathered at the inn prior to embarking on a pilgrimage to the shrine of Saint THOMAS À BECKET at CANTERBURY. The narrator, who arrived at the inn separately, relates his decision to join the pilgrims and explains how the Host of the Tabard, Harry BAILLY, proposed a tale-telling contest to pass the time as they travel. The reward for the best set of tales is to be a dinner, paid for by the other pilgrims. The Host's instructions specify that each pilgrim should tell four stories, two on the way to the shrine, and two on the return. Only 24 stories are extant, however, which presents the possibility that Chaucer either did not finish the work before he died around 1400, or that he revised his intentions but neglected to revise the Host's instructions. As it is, the only traveler who performs twice is Chaucer, and that is because his first tale was not any good. The tales are often linked by narrative exchanges among the pilgrims, which are always lively and sometimes vociferous in nature, often reflecting cultural or social tensions. The absence of some links, and the varying order in which the tales appear in different manuscripts, further suggests that the work comes to us unfinished. It has nevertheless long been considered a literary masterpiece.

The stories of the *The Canterbury Tales* feature a broad spectrum of literary genres such as the BEAST FABLE, the chivalric romance, the FABLIAU (dirty story), the sermon and the saint's life. Often the tales seem highly appropriate to the teller, as with "The KNIGHT'S TALE" (a chivalric romance) and "The SECOND NUN'S TALE" (a saint's life). In other cases, as with "The REEVE'S TALE," the relationship between tale and teller depends upon the relationship between the teller and another of the pilgrims whom the teller wishes to insult. Sometimes the tale is an expression of the teller's ideas on a particular topic. The most famous of these is "The WIFE OF BATH'S TALE," which engenders a debate on marriage that is joined by the CLERK, the MERCHANT and the FRANKLIN. Chaucer's sources for *The Canterbury Tales* were many and varied, and are discussed at length under the individual entry for each tale. Some scholars believe that he got his idea for the framework from the Italian writer BOCCACCIO, whose *Decameron* also featured a group of storytelling travelers. Wherever he got the idea, the tales have enjoyed tremendous popularity and remained almost continuously in print since William Caxton's 1483 edition to the present, providing inspiration (and story material) for writers as famous as William Shakespeare, and leading many to agree with the 17th-century poet John Dryden who exclaimed that "here is God's plenty." The following brief synopses are given in the order that the tales appear in the ELLESMERE MANUSCRIPT and *The Riverside Chaucer.*

Just as the KNIGHT is the first pilgrim described in the General Prologue, so is "The Knight's Tale" the first to be related on the pilgrimage to Canterbury. The story, taken from Boccaccio's *TESEIDA*, tells of two prisoner knights, PALAMON and ARCITE (1), who fall in love with the sister-in-law of their captor, Duke THESEUS of Athens. Both of them eventually escape from prison and are given the opportunity to fight for EMILY's love, despite the fact that she does not want to marry either. Arcite, with the help of the god MARS (1), wins the tournament, but is thrown from his horse and killed immediately following. After a period of mourning, Emily is given to Palamon, and the two have a long and happy marriage. As mentioned above, "The Knight's Tale" belongs to the genre of chivalric romance (*see* CHIVALRY and COURTLY LOVE).

"The Knight's Tale" is followed by that of the drunken MILLER, who interrupts the Host's invitation to the MONK to tell the next story. "The MILLER'S TALE," a bawdy fabliau, narrates the attempts of two men, a student named NICHOLAS and a clerk named ABSALOM (1), to seduce ALISON (1), the wife of a naive old carpenter. One of them, Nicholas, is successful. Absalom ends up kissing her behind and being farted on by Nicholas.

The REEVE insists on telling the next tale because he believes that the Miller's was intended to insult him. The Reeve, like the cuckolded husband of "The Miller's Tale," is a carpenter by profession. In "The Reeve's Tale," two students, JOHN THE CLERK and ALAN decide to pre-

vent a corrupt miller named SIMKIN from stealing grain from their college when he grinds it into meal. At first the miller appears to outwit them by setting loose their horse and then stealing the grain while they try to catch it. Later, when they are forced to spend the night because it is too late to travel, they get their revenge by having sex with Simkins' wife and daughter.

The Reeve's performance is followed by "The COOK'S TALE." Like the Miller, the COOK appears to be drunk. This story of a rebellious young apprentice named PERKYN REVELOUR breaks off after only 58 lines, leaving little indication of how Chaucer intended to develop it.

"The MAN OF LAW'S TALE," which comes next, tells the story of CONSTANCE, the emperor of Rome's daughter whose marriage to the SULTAN OF SYRIA ends in tragedy because of her mother-in-law's hatred of the Christian faith. After her husband's murder, Constance is set adrift on the sea and eventually lands in northern England. Here she again suffers persecution because of her faith and is cast out to sea once more. At the end of the story, she is reunited with her father and her sufferings come to an end. Many scholars consider this story an allegory of the soul's journey away from and its final return to God, after suffering many hardships during the pilgrimage of life.

"The Wife of Bath's Tale" is the story of a knight-rapist who can only redeem himself and save his life by finding the correct answer to the following question: What do women desire more than anything else in the world? After traveling far and wide, he finally receives the answer from a loathsome hag he meets in the forest. She says that what women desire most is sovereignty over their husbands. The knight agrees that if her answer saves him, he will grant whatever she requests. As a result, he soon finds himself married to the hag. When she asks the young man whether he would rather have her beautiful and unfaithful, or ugly and faithful, he lets her decide (i.e., gives her sovereignty), and she grants him the best of both possibilities—beauty *and* faithfulness.

The next story, "The FRIAR'S TALE," tells how a summoner encounters a devil dressed as a yeoman. The two agree to share what they "earn" in the course of a day's work. When they come upon a carter who curses his horse, commending it to the devil, the summoner asks the devil why he did not take the animal. The devil answers that the man's curse was not heartfelt. But when the summoner is cursed by an old lady from whom he tries to extort money, the devil quickly carries him off to hell because her curse was sincere. The purpose of this tale is to insult the SUMMONER, who responds by telling a tale that makes fun of friars.

"The SUMMONER'S TALE" tells of a greedy friar who badgers a sick man for money to support his brotherhood. For his efforts, he receives the gift of a fart which he must divide among his brethren.

"The CLERK'S TALE" professes to be the translation of a story from PETRARCH, which also appears in Boccaccio's *Decameron*. It relates the events following the marriage of WALTER, the marquis of SALUZZO in northern Italy, to GRISELDA, a virtuous peasant girl. Although Walter married this woman for her wisdom and virtue, he feels the need to repeatedly test her obedience and devotion to him, which he does by taking away each of her children after they are born and by finally appearing to divorce her so that he may take another wife. Because Griselda never challenges or even seems to resent him despite the insults and injuries he offers to her, Walter ultimately relents, returns her children, and the two are reconciled. This tale provides a view of marriage that contrasts sharply with "The Wife of Bath's Tale."

"The MERCHANT'S TALE" is the MERCHANT's response to the Clerk's story of wifely obedience. Claiming to draw upon his own experience of how women really behave in marriage, the Merchant tells the story of the aged knight JANUARY, who, after refusing to marry throughout his youth, decides that he must now possess a young wife. His marriage to MAY is doomed to failure by the difference in their ages. She is pursued and soon falls for a young squire named DAMIAN, and the two lovers struggle to find the opportunity to consummate their passion. In the meantime, January loses his sight, which makes him more possessive; he tries to always have a hand on May. The lovers finally manage to rendezvous by climbing together into a pear tree while January sits below. January regains his sight and sees them having sex, but May is able to talk her way out of the situation.

"The SQUIRE'S TALE," which follows the Merchant's, tells of CAMBYUSKAN (Genghis Khan), whose birthday is graced by an array of magical gifts, including a ring for the king's daughter CANACEE (1), which enables her to understand the language of birds, and to speak to them in return. A female falcon tells Canacee the story of her betrayal by a male of her species, and the tale promises much more, far more than could be delivered in the space allotted to other tales, before it breaks off. "The Squire's Tale" remains unfinished.

The SQUIRE's performance is followed by "The FRANKLIN'S TALE." This is the story of a Breton knight, ARVERAGUS, and his wife, DORIGEN, whose happy marriage is disrupted by his two-year absence. During this time, Dorigen, whose devotion to her husband never comes into question, is ardently pursued by a squire named AURELIUS. She finally attempts to silence him by agreeing to become his lover if he can remove all the rocks lining the coast of BRITTANY. With the help of a magician, he succeeds, and Dorigen is faced with the dilemma of breaking her promise to him or betraying her marriage vows. Despite this complication, the story ends happily when Aurelius releases her from her promise. The mutual respect and devotion that Arveragus and Dorigen share offers another view of marriage.

One of the least popular of all *The Canterbury Tales*, "The PHYSICIAN'S TALE" narrates the life of the martyr VIRGINIA, who agrees to be killed by her father rather than submit to the lustful desire of the corrupt judge APIUS.

The physician's performance is followed by "The PARDONER'S TALE," in which three young rioters go out in search of Death, intending to kill him and thus put a stop to his ravages. They are distracted from their mission, however, when they find a large quantity of gold lying unattended in a field. They selfishly plot against each other to keep from having to divide the gold three ways, and as a result, they all end up dead. "The Pardoner's Tale" is considered one of the best Canterbury tales.

In "The SHIPMAN'S TALE," a merchant's wife borrows money from a corrupt monk (JOHN THE MONK). The monk, who poses as a family friend, borrows the sum from the merchant and then gives it to the man's wife (who is unaware of the money's source) in exchange for sexual favors. When the monk tells the merchant he has repaid the loan by giving the money to his wife, she is unable to deny receiving it, but claims to have believed it was a gift.

Disturbing to modern readers because of its apparent anti-Semitism, "The PRIORESS' TALE" is the story of a child murdered by Jews because he sings a hymn to the Virgin while passing through their neighborhood. His body, which was thrown into a latrine, is found because the Virgin miraculously enabled him to continue singing after his death. This tale belongs to the genre of miracles of the Virgin.

The pilgrim "Chaucer" tells the next story, "The TALE OF SIR THOPAS," whose subject matter and formal elements parody the kind of metrical romances that were popular in Chaucer's day. The tale breaks off when the Host interrupts its narrator, asking for something different.

Chaucer responds to this request with "The TALE OF MELIBEE," which relates the debate that takes place between MELIBEE and his wife, PRUDENCE, over how he should respond to the men who broke into his house and attacked his family. Both participants in the argument, but especially Prudence, draw upon the Bible, philosophy and other authoritative sources to support their point of view. This particular feature of the tale suggests that it belongs to the genre of wisdom literature, loosely defined as collections of wise sayings. Although not very popular among modern readers, this tale, and other members of its genre, were in high demand during Chaucer's day.

"The Tale of Melibee" is followed by "The MONK'S TALE," a collection of "tragedies," each one about someone who attains a high degree of success or felicity in life and then loses everything. The MONK's view of tragedy differs from classical or Renaissance ideas on the subject by emphasizing the role of fortune rather than that of character. The form of this tale is modeled on Boccaccio's *De casibus virorum illustrium* (On the fall of famous men).

"The NUN'S PRIEST'S TALE" follows the Monk's gloomy performance with a much more cheerful and optimistic story, a beast fable that tells how the rooster CHAUNTICLEER escaped the jaws of a wily fox who intended to eat him. The story's moral warns against succumbing to pride.

"The SECOND NUN'S TALE" follows that of the Nun's Priest. An example of the genre of the saint's life, it tells the story of Saint CECILIA, who converted her husband and several other people to Christianity before dying a martyr's death in ancient ROME.

The next narrative, "The CANON'S YEOMAN'S TALE," is related by a man who joins the pilgrims after they have already journeyed some distance along the road. The CANON (1) whom this yeoman serves is an alchemist (i.e., one who professes to turn base metals into precious ones). The purpose of the yeoman's story is to reveal how those claiming to be alchemists trick people out of their money.

"The MANCIPLE'S TALE" is a story derived from OVID's *Metamorphoses*. It tells how the god Phoebus (Apollo) had a pet crow who revealed that Phoebus' wife was unfaithful. The god killed his wife and then, stricken with horror and remorse, cursed the bird, depriving it of speech and turning its feathers black. The moral of this story is that one should exercise discretion in speech.

The last narrative is "The PARSON'S TALE," a long prose sermon describing the Seven Deadly Sins and defining true penitence.

In most manuscripts of *The Canterbury Tales,* "The Parson's Tale" leads straight into Chaucer's RETRACTION, in which the poet takes leave of his book and his life. Here he asks God's forgiveness for those things that he has written, including some of the foregoing tales, that contain elements of sin. Whether or not this document constitutes an actual record of a death bed confession is still under debate.

For Further Reading: So many good books have been written about *The Canterbury Tales* that it is difficult to know where to begin. One of the most readable explorations is Paul RUGGIERS' *The Art of the Canterbury Tales* (1965) which analyzes individual tales (except for those of the Physician, Monk, Manciple and Parson) under the headings of romance and comedy, describing how they depict various aspects of the human condition, and how they bring together different literary forms. Particularly interesting is Ruggiers' discussion of the narrator and his role in the poem. Another book that makes some important observations on the work as a whole is Ralph BALDWIN's *The Unity of the Canterbury Tales* (1955), the first study which pointed to pilgrimage as the unifying idea and central theme of *The Canterbury Tales.* An interpretive tale-by-tale reading is provided by Trevor WHITTOCK's *A Reading of the Canterbury Tales* (1968), which emphasizes the variety of world views represented in the work and notes how the recurrence of certain themes maintains a moral focus. The most thorough scholarly treatment of the General Prologue and each tale is Helen COOPER's contribution to *The Oxford Guides to Chaucer: The Canterbury Tales* (1989), which provides an excellent critical discussion of all the tales, including their probable dates of composition and their sources and analogues. For those interested in feminist theory, Carolyn Dinshaw's *Chaucer's Sexual Poetics* (1989) provides an enjoyable and enlightening read of "The Man of Law's Tale," "The Wife of Bath's Tale" and "The Clerk's Tale." Priscilla Martin's *Chaucer's Women: Nuns, Wives and Amazons* (1990) more fully discusses the role of women in a variety of Chaucer's texts, including *The Canterbury Tales.* Peggy Knapp's *Chaucer and the Social Contest* (1990) draws on recent literary theory, particularly on the writings of M. M. Bakhtin and Michel Foucault, to provide an interesting overview of the tales, which focuses on three areas of contention in the 14th century: the division of social duties into the three estates, the controversies surrounding religious reform efforts, and the roles of women.

Canticus Troili   Literally, "Troilus' Song," *Canticus Troili* is the Latin title given to a series of three songs composed by the hero of Chaucer's TROILUS AND CRISEYDE. The first appears early in book one when, after his first glimpse of the lovely widowed CRISEYDE at the temple of PALLAS Athena, he begins to fall in love. Because he has spent so much time taunting other men who have become victims of romance, TROILUS determines to keep his feelings secret. Following this resolution, he returns to the palace, where he lives and attempts to behave as he always has, making fun of those who are in love. He is unable, however, to keep up this pretense for very long and soon retires to his chamber, where he initially feels optimistic about the possibility of serving his lady and winning her love. With that in mind, he composes a song. In the text of the poem the song is headed by the rubric *Canticus Troili.* Its verses philosophically explore the paradoxes of love, particularly its sweet painfulness that leaves the lover longing for more of those things, such as the sight of his lady, that cause pain. The song is not taken from Chaucer's main source for the poem, BOCCACCIO's *FILOSTRATO,* but is a fairly close translation of PETRARCH's sonnet 88 ("In Vita"), number 132 in the Canzoniere, "S'amor non è." On the few occasions that

Chaucer deviates from this source, the variants seem due to his misunderstanding of the Italian.

The second *Canticus Troili* appears at the conclusion of book three, after Troilus and Criseyde have become lovers. In contrast to his earlier verses in praise of love, this time Troilus speaks of it as a force which binds together otherwise contrary or disruptive forces in nature, as well as the hearts of men and women, and thus keeps the universe functioning in an orderly fashion. As with the first song, Chaucer departs from his main source, this time substituting a song based on one of the metrical stanzas of BOETHIUS' *Consolation of Philosophy.* The third *Canticus Troili* appears in book five, after Criseyde has left TROY to join her father in the Greek camp. Even though Troilus at this point cannot be sure that his beloved will not come back—she has, after all, sworn many oaths that she will—he experiences a sense of foreboding that leaves him bereft of hope. In this mood, he composes another song, in which he personifies Criseyde as a guiding star and himself as a ship. Having lost her, he sails blindly through the darkness toward his death.

Considered together, the three "Songs of Troilus" seem to epitomize the three different moods governing the poem's narrative progression. The first song is anticipatory. Even though love causes him to suffer, Troilus welcomes the sensations of this unfamiliar emotion and eagerly looks forward to the days ahead. The mood of the second song is clearly celebratory, as Troilus relishes the fulfillment of emotional and physical consummation. Finally, the third song, even though the date upon which Criseyde promised to return has not yet passed, can only be described as elegiac, foreshadowing as it does the desolation he will experience as that date passes, a desolation that pursues him to the battlefield, where he is killed by the Greek ACHILLES.

Canyos In the BOECE, *Canyos* is the term Chaucer uses to refer to the followers of JULIUS CANIUS, one of the Roman philosophers mentioned by LADY PHILOSOPHY when she is giving the narrator examples of other people who have suffered on her behalf. The *Boece* is Chaucer's translation of BOETHIUS' *Consolation of Philosophy.*

Canyus *See* JULIUS CANIUS.

Capaneus According to classical mythology, Capaneus was one of the famous warriors who supported the cause of POLYNICES in his struggle to reclaim the throne of THEBES, a struggle that became known as the SEVEN AGAINST THEBES. While climbing the city's wall and boasting that not even Zeus himself could stop him, Capaneus was struck down by a thunderbolt. His wife Evadne threw herself into the flames of his funeral pyre. Evadne appears (she is not referred to by name,

but simply as "Capaneus' wife") in the beginning of "The KNIGHT'S TALE," where she accosts THESEUS as he passes along the outskirts of Thebes on the way home to Athens, asking him to force CREON, the ruler of Thebes, to let her and the other women whose kindred died in the battle bury their dead. The incident is important in that it establishes the events of "The KNIGHT'S TALE" along the continuum of stories that make up the mythical history of Greece. Capaneus' death at Thebes is alluded to twice more in Chaucer's work—once in the short, unfinished poem known as *ANELIDA AND ARCITE,* which is set in Thebes, and again in *TROILUS AND CRISEYDE* where CASSANDRA provides an extended summary of the siege against Thebes.

Cape Finisterre A promontory on the Atlantic coast of northwestern Spain. It is mentioned in the GENERAL PROLOGUE to *The CANTERBURY TALES* as one of the landmarks of the European coastline known to the SHIPMAN, who is an excellent navigator.

Capitolie Chaucer's Middle English version of the word *Capitol,* which he uses to refer to the Capitol in Rome where JULIUS CAESAR was assassinated. The incident is described in the brief biography of Caesar that appears in "The MONK'S TALE."

Capricorn One of the 12 divisions of the zodiac, an imaginary belt in the heavens extending for about eight degrees on either side of the apparent path of the sun and including the paths of the moon and the principal planets. The zodiac is divided into 12 equal parts, or signs, each named for a different constellation. Capricorn—the Goat or Sea Goat—is the 10th sign (*see* diagram under ASTROLOGY), which the sun enters on or around December 22. In Chaucer's day, the Sun entered Capricorn around December 12. The constellation of Capricorn appears in the sky between Sagittarius and Aquarius. Chaucer most often employs such astrological terms to indicate the approximate date of a narrative event or to show the passage of time. In "The FRANKLIN'S TALE," for example, he uses the following astrological description to note the time of year in which the MAGICIAN begins working on the illusion that will help AURELIUS win the love of DORIGEN: "Phebus wax old, and hewed lyk laton, / That in his hoote declynacion / Shoon as the burned gold with stremes brighte; / But now in Capricorn adoun he lighte, / Where as he shoon ful pale, I dar wel seyn" (lines 1245–49) [The sun grew old (reaching the end of the solar year) and turned the color of laton (a brasslike alloy, grayish-silver in color), the sun which had formerly, during the hot summer months, shone like burnished gold with bright streams of light; But now it has arrived in Capricorn, where it shines very pale, I dare well say]. (A looser translation than usual is provided here to best convey the sense of the passage.) Rhetorically, the use of this device functions to elevate the style of the passage, and Chaucer typically makes use of it in two situations. Sometimes, as in this tale, it provides a way of noting the date of an event in terms that are in keeping with the noble theme and elevated sentiments of the work as a whole. On other occasions, as in "The NUN'S PRIEST'S TALE," his use of astrological terms in this manner has a comedic effect, contrasting the elevated style of the passage with the silliness of the plot and/or its characters. Chaucer's TREATISE ON THE ASTROLABE describes the appearance and location of each of the 12 constellations and explains how to use them in conjunction with the astrolabe instrument to calculate the date. Thus, the information contained in *The Treatise on the Astrolabe,* for those capable of understanding it, provides an explanation of how the poet formulated these descriptions.

Caracalla, Marus Aurelius Antonius Roman emperor of the late second and early third centuries A.D. Caracalla's principal achievements were his colossal baths in Rome and his edict of 212 which gave Roman citizenship to all free inhabitants of the empire. His ruthless attitude in battle (he was responsible for a number of military massacres) led him to be regarded as one of the most bloodthirsty tyrants in Roman history. His murder of the Roman jurist Aemilius Papinianus is mentioned in the BOECE, Chaucer's translation of BOETHIUS' *Consolation of Philosophy.* Caracalla also killed his brother, Geta, while their mother struggled to protect him.

Caribdis *See* CHARYBDIS.

Carpenter, the One of a group of tradesmen mentioned, but not described individually, in the GENERAL PROLOGUE to *The CANTERBURY TALES.* The others in the Carpenter's group include a Weaver ("Webbe"), a Cloth Dyer ("Dyere") and a Tapestry Maker ("Tapycer"). These five men are all wearing the same type of uniform, indicating their membership in one of the medieval trade guilds, the forerunner of modern-day trade unions. The guilds set standards for the quality of the goods produced, regulated holidays and hours of work and fixed prices and wages to some extent. Certain details of Chaucer's portrait of the guildsmen, such as their silver- (rather than brass) mounted knives, might suggest either prosperity or pretentiousness, depending on whether one judges the portraits to contain elements of satire. Those scholars who argue against finding satire in their description note that Chaucer provided his guildsmen with none of the traditional mercantile vices such as fraud, usury and avarice. None of the guildsmen tells a tale on the pilgrimage to Canterbury, although a character in "The MILLER'S

TALE," JOHN, is a carpenter by profession. One of the other pilgrims, the REEVE, is also a carpenter, and the offense he takes at the MILLER's description of John leads him to present a satiric portrait of a miller in his own tale.

Carrenar *See* KARA-NOR.

Cartage (1) *See* CARTHAGE.

Cartage (2) The Cartage that is mentioned in the SHIPMAN's portrait in the GENERAL PROLOGUE to *The CANTERBURY TALES* is probably a mistaken or alternative spelling for Cartagena, a city on the southwestern coast of Spain. Elsewhere in Chaucer's work, *Cartage* is the author's Middle English spelling of "Carthage," the ancient city-state on the coast of North Africa. The context in which the city is mentioned here, in reference to the Shipman as the finest member of his profession to be found between the ports of HULL (on the river Humber in Yorkshire, England) and "Cartage," would suggest that Chaucer is referring to a contemporary city (contemporary with the pilgrims, that is), rather than one that was destroyed in 146 B.C., as was the African Carthage.

Cartegena *See* CARTHAGE (2).

Carthage Ancient city on the Mediterranean coast of North Africa, close to the modern-day city of Tunis. It was founded by the Phoenicians and destroyed by the Romans during the Punic Wars in 146 B.C. Carthage is mentioned numerous times in Chaucer's work, most significantly as the kingdom of DIDO, the queen of Carthage who fell in love with and was betrayed by AENEAS. The story must have been a favorite with Chaucer because he relates it in detail in two of his works—first in book one of *The HOUSE OF FAME* and later in the biography of Dido that appears in his LEGEND OF GOOD WOMEN—as well as alluding to it in other works, including *The BOOK OF THE DUCHESS* and *The PARLIAMENT OF FOWLS.*

Cassandra In classical mythology, Cassandra was the daughter of PRIAM and HECUBA, the king and queen of TROY, and sister to TROILUS, HECTOR, DEIPHEBUS and PARIS. Her beauty captured the attention of the god APOLLO, who gave her the gift of prophecy when she agreed to become his lover. However, when she changed her mind and refused to keep her promise, the god punished her by preventing anyone from believing her prophecies. During the fall of Troy, which she had foreseen, Cassandra sought refuge at the altar of PALLAS Athena. Ajax dragged her out of the sanctuary, but she was rescued by AGAMEMNON, who took her home with him as a slave. Agamemnon's wife

CLYTEMNESTRA and her lover Aegisthus murdered her and Agamemnon when they returned to Mycenae. Cassandra appears briefly as a character in book five of Chaucer's TROILUS AND CRISEYDE, where Troilus asks her to interpret a disturbing dream he has had. In the dream, he says, he was walking through a forest when he came upon CRISEYDE lying close in the embrace of a wild boar. When Cassandra tells him that the boar he saw holding Criseyde is the Greek warrior DIOMEDE, and that Criseyde has become Diomede's lover, he angrily refuses to believe her; but Cassandra's interpretation, like her prophecies, is correct. Cassandra is also mentioned briefly in Chaucer's early poem *The BOOK OF THE DUCHESS*. In trying to describe the grief that he feels over losing his wife, the BLACK KNIGHT exclaims that his sorrow exceeds even that of Cassandra, who witnessed the fall of Troy and the death of so many kinsmen (line 1246).

Cassiodorus Flavius Magnus Aurelius Cassiodorus was the learned secretary of King THEODORIC of the Ostrogoths, who conquered the Italian peninsular in A.D. 493. Theodoric allowed many members of the Roman aristocracy to hold positions in his government, and Cassiodorus, along with BOETHIUS, was among that number. Shortly after Theodoric died, Cassiodorus retired to a villa in Calabria, which he converted into a monastery where he spent the rest of his life (some 40 years) in study and prayer. While encouraging his monks to copy manuscripts written by the church fathers and by classical authors, he busied himself composing treatises on the SEVEN LIBERAL ARTS and in writing history and spiritual instructions. His *Institutiones Divinarum et Secularium Litterarum*, which was inspired by the work of Saint AUGUSTINE, advocated the union of Christian and classical studies in Christian education. Dame PRUDENCE, wife to the beleaguered MELIBEE in "The TALE OF MELIBEE," quotes numerous passages from the collection of instructions Cassiodorus wrote for his monks as she advises her husband not to take revenge against the men who have robbed them.

Cassius *See* BRUTUS.

Castor In classical mythology, Castor was the one of three children of Zeus (JUPITER) and Leda, with whom the god had intercourse in the form of a swan. The other children were POLLUX and Helen (*see* HELEN OF TROY). The two brothers, famous for their devotion to each other, were worshipped both as gods and as heroes. Both brothers took part in the Calydonian boar hunt and in the expedition of JASON and the ARGONAUTS. When Castor died, the heartbroken Pollux begged Zeus to kill him also, so that he might rejoin his brother. Instead, Zeus permitted both of them to spend alternate days in heaven and in the underworld. Because of this, they came to represent the principle of the ever-recurring change from light to darkness and from darkness to light. Castor and Pollux were eventually placed as stars in the heavens, where they became known as the constellation GEMINI, or the Twins. This constellation is mentioned in *The HOUSE OF FAME* by the eagle who is ferrying Chaucer through the air to FAME's palace. He wants to take the poet up into the region of the stars so that he can learn about them firsthand, but the poet refuses, saying that he is too old. The exchange reflects the poem's ongoing debate between the value of learning derived from direct experience versus learning derived from books. Chaucer says that knowledge of the stars is something he would rather learn from books.

Catallus *See* CATULLUS.

Catalonia (Cataloigne) Region in northeastern Spain, bounded to the east by the Mediterranean; to the north, by the Pyrenees; and to the west, by Aragon, with which, in Chaucer's day, it formed a joint kingdom. Trumpet playing was a prominent feature of ceremonial life in late 13th-century Catalonia; Chaucer alludes to this in *The HOUSE OF FAME*, where he mentions Catalonian clarion players among the musicians who are gathered in attendance on the goddess FAME.

Cato (Caton, Catoun) (1) *See* DIONYSIUS CATO.

Cato (2) *See* CATO THE CENSOR.

Cato (3) *See* CATO THE ORATOR.

Cato the Censor Cato the Censor, or Marcus Porcius Cato, also known as Cato the Elder, was a Roman statesman and orator born in 234 B.C. who, exhibiting unusual longevity for the time, lived to the age of 85. Considered the first Latin prose writer of importance, Cato the Censor was noted for his conservative and anti-Hellenic policies, in opposition to the ideals supported by the Scipio family (*see* SCIPIO AFRICANUS THE ELDER). Although Cato's influence on the growth of Latin literature was tremendous, the only work of his that survives in its entirety is a treatise on agriculture written around 160 B.C. In addition to an encyclopedia and a collection of maxims for his son, he also wrote the first Latin history of Rome, *Origines*, of which only a few fragments survive. Some traditions hold that the maxims were the source of the *Disticha Catonis*, a popular elementary school text during the medieval period (*see* DIONYSIUS CATO). LADY PHILOSOPHY evokes the spirit of Cato along with other great men of the past in her lament for the transitory nature of human fame which appears in Book Two, Metrum 7 of the *BOECE*.

Cato the Orator   Cato the Orator, or Marcus Porcius Cato, was also known as Cato the Younger to distinguish him from his great-grandfather CATO THE CENSOR. Born in 95 B.C., the younger Cato was a leader of the conservatives in the Roman Senate who tried to preserve the Roman republic against power seekers, in particular JULIUS CAESAR. In the *BOECE,* when LADY PHILOSOPHY quotes from the Roman poet LUCAN, saying that a victorious cause is one that has enjoyed the approval of the gods while a defeated one is one that was supported by Cato, she is undoubtedly referring to Cato's support of POMPEY, who opposed Caesar in the civil war that marked the beginning of the republic's demise. After Pompey's forces were defeated at Pharsalus, Cato led a small remnant of troops to Utica in Africa, where he committed suicide in 46 B.C. after learning of Caesar's decisive victory over the republican forces at Thapsus.

Catullus, Gaius Valerius   A Roman poet of the first century B.C. whose lyric poetry is generally considered the finest of ancient Rome. Twenty-five of his poems describe his love for a woman named Lesbia. Many other of his works find him expressing contempt and hatred for JULIUS CAESAR and other famous people of his era, so that the themes of his literary corpus might be said to range between the polarities of love and hatred, being heavily weighted at either end. The quality of his work has a similar range, from the sublime to the tedious, from the memorable to the imminently forgettable. Catullus is mentioned once in Chaucer's work, and that is in his translation of another author's text—BOETHIUS' *Consolation of Philosophy.* In the section of Book Three where LADY PHILOSOPHY is trying to convince the narrator that good fortune is not always truly good, she notes that receiving certain "dignities," such as being elected to high office, do not guarantee that one will win the respect of others or even be deserving of that respect. She mentions the Roman consul NONIUS, who was satirized by Catullus, as an example, recalling how Catullus referred to the consul as a "boch," or ulcer.

Caucasus   When the LOATHLY HAG in "The WIFE OF BATH'S TALE" is attempting to explain the indelible quality of true nobility to the young knight whom she has just married, she uses the following example: "Taak fyr and ber it in the derkeste hous / Bitwix this and the mount of Kaukasous, / And lat men shette the dores and go thenne; / Yet wole the fyr as faire lye and brenne / As twenty thousand men myghte it biholde; / His office natureel ay wol it holde, / Up peril of my lyf, til that it dye" (lines 1139–45) [Take some fire and bear it to the darkest house / Between here and the Caucasus mountains, / And let men shut the house up and depart; / Yet will the fire burn just as brightly / As

it would if twenty thousand men beheld it; / It will maintain its true nature always, / I swear on my life, until it dies]. The idea she is trying to impart is that true nobility, like elemental fire, does not need to be seen or broadcast in order to maintain its essence. The mountains to which she refers are located in southeastern Europe between the Black and the Caspian Seas, in the former U.S.S.R. This location was undoubtedly chosen for its remoteness.

Caunterbury   *See* CANTERBURY.

Caurus   The Roman name for the northwestern wind. The narrator of the *BOECE* mentions this wind in Book One, Metrum 3 when he compares the darkness of his mind to a stormy sky that has been stirred up by the wind named Caurus. What he needs, he says, is for a force such as the wind BOREAS (the north wind) to rush through and clear the clouds away so that he can see more clearly.

Caxton, William (ca. 1422–1491)   The first English printer. Born in the county of Kent Caxton had a successful career as a merchant and spent 30 years plying his trade in wool and other English goods in the Low Countries (the Netherlands, Belgium and Luxembourg) before he returned to England and set up a press at Westminster in 1476. Caxton printed about 100 books, a number of them his own translations from French, using eight different type fonts, the first of which he brought from Bruges. Around 1480, he began to use woodcut illustrations. His first edition of Chaucer, published in 1478, appears to be derived from a manuscript that has been lost; the second edition, dated 1484, features a prologue in which Caxton claims to have revised the text on the basis of a different manuscript supplied by a reader critical of the first edition. Both editions feature a series of woodcut illustrations and went on to become the basis of successive editions such as those of Wynkyn de Worde and William THYNNE.

Caym   *See* CAIN.

Cecile (Cecilie)   *See* CECILIA, SAINT.

Cecilia, Saint   The protagonist of "The SECOND NUN'S TALE," whose life was dedicated to serving God. Born a Roman citizen in the third century, Cecilia lived a quiet and virtuous life until she was betrothed to a pagan named VALERIAN. Having dedicated her virginity to God, she convinces Valerian that they should refrain from having sexual relations, telling him that the angel who watches over her would kill him if he made the attempt. The two are married but remain chaste. Valerian is baptized and becomes able to see the angel.

For the remainder of her life, and in the shadow of Roman persecution, Cecilia preaches the word of God, emphasizing the rational side of Christianity to encourage others to turn away from idolatry and superstition. The miracles associated with Cecilia feature the ability to perceive things, such as angels, that are hidden from ordinary sinners. For upholding her faith and refusing to perform a sacrifice to the Roman gods, Cecilia was sentenced to death and put into a cauldron with a great fire lit beneath it. When the heat and the flames did not harm her, the Roman prefect, ALMACHIUS, commanded that she be beheaded, which ultimately resulted in her martyrdom. Cecilia has traditionally been given the patronage of music because, according to the legend of her life, she sang to the Lord in her heart as the organs were playing during her wedding feast. Her patronage of roses recalls her martyrdom and the paradisal wreaths she and Valerian were given by the angel to signify their purity. Although Cecilia was a popular saint during the Middle Ages and the Renaissance, there is some doubt about her authenticity. No contemporary or near-contemporary writers mention her, including JEROME, AMBROSE, Damasus or Prudentius, all of whom were particularly interested in martyrs. The only real evidence for her existence, other than the late fifth-century legend that made her so popular, is that there was indeed a church founded by and named after a certain Roman matron named Cecilia, located in the Trastevere in Rome.

Cedasus   *See* SCEDASUS.

Cenelm, Saint   *See* KENELM, SAINT.

Cenobia (Cenobie)   *See* ZENOBIA.

Centauris (Centauros)   *See* CENTAURS.

Centaurs   In classical mythology, the Centaurs were creatures who were half man, half horse. They are mentioned twice in Chaucer's work, both times in association with the hero HERCULES. According to legend, when the centaur Pholus entertained Hercules in his cave on Mt. Pholoe, the aroma of the wine that they were drinking attracted other Centaurs, who attacked Hercules. Hercules beat them back, killing many with his poison arrows. This incident is mentioned in the biography of Hercules that appears in "The MONK'S TALE" and also in the *BOECE*, Chaucer's translation of BOETHIUS' *Consolation of Philosophy*.

Cenwulf's son   *See* KENELM, SAINT.

Cerberus   In classical mythology, Cerberus was the three-headed dog, with a mane and tail of snakes, who guarded the entrance to the underworld. Two stories in which Cerberus was overcome by visitors from above ground appear in Chaucer's work. When ORPHEUS went to Hades to rescue his wife EURYDICE, he charmed the dog with music. HERCULES overcame him with his bare hands, carried him up to Eurystheus and brought him back again as one of his 12 labors. The latter incident is mentioned in the biography of Hercules that appears in "The MONK'S TALE." In the *BOECE*, LADY PHILOSOPHY cites both of these stories as examples of heroes who achieved greatness by striving against daunting odds.

Cerces   *See* CIRCE.

Ceres   In classical mythology, Ceres was the Roman goddess of agriculture. She was identified with the Greek goddess Demeter so early in her history that the two can no longer be distinguished. Interestingly, the worship of Ceres in ROME was almost exclusively plebeian (i.e., working-class). Ceres appears in *The PARLIAMENT OF FOWLS* standing next to VENUS and BACCHUS in the Garden of Love. She also finds herself in company with the gods of wine and love when TROILUS curses them following CRISEYDE's departure from TROY in *TROILUS AND CRISEYDE*. The three are often grouped together in both art and literature because of a long-standing association among food, wine and love, an association that acknowledged the difficulty of feeling amorous on an empty stomach.

Cesar (1)   *See* JULIUS CAESAR.

Cesar (2)   *See* OCTAVIAN, GAIUS JULIUS CAESAR.

Cesar (3)   *See* CALIGULA.

Cesar Augustus   *See* AUGUSTUS CAESAR.

Cesiphus   *See* SISYPHUS.

Ceyx   In classical mythology, Ceyx, the husband of ALCYONE, was shipwrecked on a voyage to consult the oracle at DELPHI. Alcyone, who feared some kind of mishap when her husband failed to return by the promised date, found his body along the shore and tried to commit suicide by drowning herself. The gods, moved to pity by Alcyone's grief, changed the couple into birds and ordered the winds to be still for the 14 days of their breeding season in order that the waves not disturb their nests on the shore. In *The BOOK OF THE DUCHESS*, Chaucer's narrator reads OVID's story of Ceyx and Alcyone just before going to bed (lines 62–230). Suffering from sleeplessness that seems to have been brought on by lovesickness, the narrator dreams of a BLACK KNIGHT, a man so overwhelmed by the loss of his mate that he seems on the verge of suicide. The theme of love and loss forms the connecting link among the narrator, the story from Ovid and the narrator's dream.

Chaldea (Chaldeye) Chaldea was originally a small territory bordering the head of the Persian Gulf between the Arabian Desert and the Euphrates Delta—the southern portion of Babylonia. Later, after the reign of NEBUCHADNEZZAR II (King of Babylon from 605 to 562 B.C.), the term *Chaldea* came to cover practically all of Babylon. Chaucer refers to the country in the biography of Nebuchadnezzar that appears in "The MONK'S TALE," saying there was no scholar in all of Chaldea who could interpret Nebuchadnezzar's dreams better than DANIEL (line 2171).

chanson de geste This term, meaning "song of great deeds," was applied to the early French epic. The form originated in France in the early Middle Ages. The *Chanson de Roland,* a long poem that tells the adventures of the French hero Roland, dates from about 1100 and is the earliest and best surviving example. Chansons de geste originally reflected chivalric ideals and concentrated on fighting and adventure rather than on love; nevertheless, they supplied much of the material that went into the making of the later French and English medieval romances. The conventions of the chanson de geste had considerable influence on Chaucer's adaptation of BOCCACCIO's *TESEIDA,* "The KNIGHT'S TALE."

Chanticleer *See* CHAUNTICLEER.

Charybdis In classical mythology, Charybdis was the daughter of Poseidon (NEPTUNE) and Gaia, the earth goddess. Because she stole and ate some of HERCULES' cattle, Zeus (JUPITER) hurled her with his thunderbolt into the sea and under the huge rock that bears her name, on the Sicilian side of the narrows between Sicily and Italy. There she continued her practice of gluttony, three times a day swallowing a vast flood of water and spewing it forth again, thus causing a whirlpool dangerous to seagoing vessels. She sucked in the raft of Odysseus (ULYSSES) after his shipwreck, but the hero seized an overhanging fig tree and remained suspended until the raft came up again. In *TROILUS AND CRISEYDE,* TROILUS alludes to Charybdis in a song describing his despair after CRISEYDE has left TROY to join her father in the Greek camp. In an extended metaphor, the song compares Criseyde to the North Star and Troilus to a ship that has lost the star, which it needed to navigate the seas. Troilus predicts that his ship, wandering blindly, will be swallowed by the whirlpool of Charybdis. *See also* SCYLLA (book 5, line 644).

Chaucer, Agnes Geoffrey Chaucer's mother. A widow when she and John CHAUCER were married around 1340, she was previously married to a nobleman named Northwell. She came from a London family named Copton who were comparable in rank and wealth to the Chaucers, and she brought some property to the marriage. This came not only from her dowry but also from the portion she had inherited from her father, who had died when she was quite young; she was also an heir to the estate of her uncle Hamo, a coin-maker at the Tower of London, who had died with his son during an outbreak of the BLACK DEATH. Agnes and John lived together and raised their family in a house on Thames Street in the Vintry Ward, a district of London primarily populated by wine merchants. When John died in 1366, Agnes leased the house in Thames Street and the following July married Bartholomew Chappel, a London citizen who was also a vintner. She lived on for about 15 years, but nothing else is known about her relationship with her famous son.

Chaucer, biographies of Despite the popularity Chaucer's poetry enjoyed among his contemporaries, and the fact that, as a civil servant, his life was well documented, no significant biographies of Chaucer seem to have been written until the early years of the 20th century. Even then, much important research remained to be done before any biographical work could claim to be authoritative. This involved locating and gathering the contemporary information, much of which was published piecemeal until the appearance of *CHAUCER LIFE-RECORDS* in 1966. It was in fact the publication of this book, in addition to discoveries made by other scholars and published individually, that made possible the work of authors like Derek BREWER, Donald HOWARD and Derek PEARSALL, listed below. Ironically, the earliest major biography of the poet, by Emile Legouis, was originally published in French in 1910 as part of a series devoted to great foreign writers. It was translated into English in 1913. Some recent biographical studies include:

Brewer, Derek. *Chaucer.* 3rd rev. ed. London: Longman Press, 1973. This is a medium-length, very pleasant-to-read biography by an English scholar with excellent credentials.

Brewer, Derek. *Chaucer and His World.* New York: Dodd Mead, 1978. An account of Chaucer's life and times, embellished with beautiful color illustrations.

Chaucer Life-Records. Edited by Martin M. Crow and Clair C. Olson. Oxford: Clarendon Press, 1966. The book contains all contemporary records of Chaucer's life available at the time of publication, such as the transcript of the SCROPE-GROSVENOR TRIAL, which provides the best information we have about Chaucer's likely date of birth.

Chute, Marchette. *Geoffrey Chaucer of England*. New York: E. P. Dutton, 1946. This is a short, easy-to-read, but somewhat dated biography.

Gardner, John. *The Life and Times of Chaucer*. New York: Knopf, 1977. This is a very entertainingly written biography by a well-known modern novelist.

Howard, Donald. *Chaucer: His Life, His Works, His World*. New York: E. P. Dutton, 1987. One of the most recent and thorough biographies of Chaucer, Howard's book provides tremendous detail about the poet's life, his poetry and the times in which he lived. The book is learned without being stuffy, imaginative without crossing over into fiction.

Pearsall, Derek. *The Life of Geoffrey Chaucer*. Oxford: Blackwell, 1992. This critical biography represents a scrupulous and interesting interpretation of the facts surrounding Chaucer's life, without some of the fanciful embroidery and speculation found in other works of its kind. Its first appendix features illustrations of all existing portraits of the poet, along with commentary.

Chaucer, Elizabeth   Geoffrey and Philippa CHAUCER's eldest child is believed to have been Elizabeth Chaucer. The records concerning all of Chaucer's children are scanty, and all that is known of Elizabeth "Chausier," as her name is spelled in the records, is based on the report of her entering a convent, Barking Abbey, in 1381. If she was in her teens at the time that she joined the convent, she would have been born in the mid-1360s, shortly after Geoffrey and Philippa married. It is likely that she was named for Elizabeth, countess of Ulster, in whose service her parents became acquainted. JOHN OF GAUNT paid the substantial "dowry" for her admission to the convent, another fact that lends credence to the idea that Elizabeth was Geoffrey's daughter.

Chaucer, Geoffrey   The exact date of Chaucer's birth is unknown, but evidence derived from testimony he delivered in the famous SCROPE-GROSVENOR TRIAL suggests that he was born sometime between 1340 and 1345. Because he was born before it was fashionable, at least in the western world, to commemorate the lives of poets with biographical records, most of the information we have about Chaucer's life derives from the fact that he came from a family of fairly prosperous wine merchants and grew up to be a civil servant in the governments of King EDWARD III, RICHARD II and HENRY IV. Although Chaucer's father was from Ipswich, a river port in Suffolk, England, by the time Chaucer was born the family had moved to the Vintry (wine trading) Ward, or district, of London. His baptism was probably recorded in the parish registry at the church of St.

Martin in the Vintry, but those records would have perished with the church in the Great Fire of London in 1666.

The earliest document that gives evidence of the poet's existence is a page from the household accounts of Elizabeth, countess of Ulster, stating that on April 4, 1357, a total of seven shillings were paid for a tunic, some black and red hose and a pair of shoes for one "Galfrido Chaucer Londonie," i.e., Geoffrey Chaucer of London. Chaucer served Elizabeth as a page, and his duties in this capacity would have included serving at table and attending the countess at various ceremonies where he would function as one of her retinue. In Elizabeth's household he would also undoubtedly have continued the education that had begun in childhood, when he either attended one of the three London grammar schools near the family home in the Vintry or received instruction from a private tutor. Instruction in Latin (in which the Bible and most nonsecular literature was written), arithmetic, theology and possibly music would have been supplemented with French, etiquette and manners, dancing and other subjects pertinent to courtly society.

Following his service in the countess' household, Chaucer next appears as a soldier in the king's forces, serving under Prince Lionel, the husband of Countess Elizabeth. The series of conflicts between England and France that became known as the Hundred Years' War had recently begun. In September 1359, King Edward and his sons were invading France at the head of a considerable army. Edward's goal was to take the city of Reims and to be crowned king of France in Reims Cathedral, the traditional site of coronation for the kings of France. According to his testimony in the Scrope-Grosvenor case, Chaucer was among those soldiers positioned at the town of Réthel, near Reims, which Edward besieged in December 1359 and early January 1360. Chaucer was captured, but then ransomed shortly after for £16, a considerable sum at the time. The last recorded mention of Chaucer in service to Prince Lionel dates from peace negotiations at Calais in October 1360, when Chaucer was paid to transport letters from Calais to England.

The following six years of Chaucer's life are unaccounted for. The next document relating to his life is a safe-conduct paper for the period of February 22 to May 24, 1366, granted by Charles II of Navarre. It permitted "Geffroy de Chauserre" and three companions, their gear and horses, to travel through Navarre without being molested. No one knows the purpose of the journey, though it could have been diplomatic. Other important events that occurred in 1366 include the death of Chaucer's father, John Chaucer, and Chaucer's own marriage to Philippa Pan or "Paon" (*see* CHAUCER, PHILIPPA PAN), a woman who also had served in the household of the Countess Elizabeth but who

Carbon dating techniques suggest that the oak panel on which this portrait of Chaucer is painted may date as far back as circa 1400, and the pigment is one that was in use between 1400 and 1600. This information suggests that the portrait could be one of the earliest surviving representations of the poet. It is housed in the English Department Reading Room at the University of California, Los Angeles. Photograph by Tim Strawn, reproduced by permission of the Department of English, UCLA.

was by this time an attendant to Queen Philippa, the wife of Edward III. The marriage may in fact have been arranged by the queen. It is not known when Geoffrey Chaucer joined the royal household, but he is first recorded as a member on June 20, 1367, when he received a royal annuity, or annual wage, of 20 marks (about £13). His position is also uncertain. In one record he is described as "valettus," or valet; in another; he is referred to as an "esquier" or squire. In either position he would have been one of a group of about 40 young men in the king's service engaged for the purpose of performing various tasks, from making beds, bearing torches and setting up tables for meals, to traveling about England and the continent conducting business on the king's behalf.

Chaucer seems to have made a number of such journeys. On July 17, 1368, he is recorded as having passed over to the Continent by way of Dover and may

have been away from home for up to 106 days. He may, during that journey, have carried messages to Prince Lionel, who was in Milan, Italy. In the next two years he made at least one more journey to the continent, probably on matters concerning the war with France. Although Chaucer had undoubtedly begun writing before this time, his first major poem, *The BOOK OF THE DUCHESS,* belongs to this period. The work is a commemorative elegy for BLANCHE, duchess of Lancaster and wife of JOHN OF GAUNT, who died in September 1368. Gaunt's grant to Chaucer of a £10 lifetime annuity may have been to reward him for writing the poem.

There is some slight evidence that, during the period that he was in the king's service, Chaucer may have studied law at one of the Inns of Court, the London legal societies having the exclusive right to admit persons to practice law. The evidence comes from Thomas SPEGHT's 1598 edition of Chaucer, in which he states that "Master Buckley," who was at that time the keeper of records for the Inner Temple (one of the Inns of Court), testified to having seen a record "where Geffrye Chaucer was fined two shillings" for beating a Franciscan Friar in Fleet Street. In order to be fined by the society, Chaucer would have to have been a student there. Further evidence that Chaucer possessed some knowledge of the law derives from his work, specifically in his descriptions of the MANCIPLE and the SERGEANT OF THE LAW in the GENERAL PROLOGUE to *The CANTERBURY TALES.* The Manciple's job is to stock provisions for one of the Inns of Court, and the Sergeant of the Law belongs, as his title indicates, to the most prestigious and powerful rank of lawyers in existence at the time. Furthermore, Chaucer's later offices, as controller of the customs and clerk of the king's works, required that he keep records in Chancery hand, an international business hand with its own alphabet and writing method, and that he use French and Latin legal formulas, both of which were taught in the Inns of Court.

In comparison to the rest of his life, very little is known of Chaucer's married life, although many readers have attempted to infer certain things from his writings, a practice recent scholars often caution against. It is certain that Geoffrey and Philippa had at least two children: Thomas CHAUCER, born in the early years of their marriage, and Lewis CHAUCER, for whom *The TREATISE ON THE ASTROLABE* was written, in 1381. An Elizabeth CHAUCER, who became a nun, may have been their oldest child, but her parentage remains open to debate.

Chaucer's exposure to Italian literature and culture had a considerable impact on his later work, so his first recorded trip to Italy, in 1372–73, is an event of some significance. Probably chosen for his ability to speak Italian, Chaucer traveled as a diplomat, going first to

Genoa to negotiate the use of an English port by the Genoese merchant fleet, and then to Florence to discuss government loans. The visit to Florence has assumed particular importance among scholars because PETRARCH and BOCCACCIO were still alive and living in that region. Even if Chaucer did not meet them, he could hardly have avoided hearing a great deal about them and about DANTE, who, although he had died in exile 50 years earlier, was greatly revered in Florence. It is even possible that Chaucer obtained copies of some of these writers' works during this visit, copies that would have given him ready access later on when their work, particularly that of Boccaccio, became so influential upon his own.

The year following Chaucer's trip to Italy—1374— records him receiving a special gift from Edward III on the feast day of Saint George, England's patron saint. The gift consisted of a gallon pitcher of wine each day for life. Some scholars believe it to have been the reward for a poem presented to the king as part of the festivities. Chaucer also obtained a home in 1374 (until which time he would have occupied rooms in one of the king's residences). On May 10, the mayor and aldermen of London leased to Chaucer, rent-free for life, a dwelling over Aldgate, one of the six gates in the city wall. Chaucer's responsibilities were to keep the building in good repair and to allow entry for purposes of defense in time of war; he was not allowed to sublet. Such an arrangement was not unusual. Buildings owned by the city were often leased out, typically to city officials. In Chaucer's case, he was probably granted the lease because of his family's longstanding association with the mayor.

The year 1374 also saw Chaucer transferred to another position in Edward's government, that of controller (i.e., supervisor of tax collectors) for the export tax and for the subsidy (a heavier tax) on wool, sheepskins and leather, in the port of London. His position was an important one because wool was England's chief export. Taxes on the commodity helped to fund the king's wars and to pay the daily costs of government. Chaucer's annual salary for the position was £10, which was in addition to the lifetime annuity he had been granted earlier. In holding this post, Chaucer was following in the footsteps of his father and grandfather, who had both held offices in the customs service. Chaucer's performance must have been excellent, for in 1382 he was awarded the additional controllership of the petty customs, import and export duties on wine and other merchandise not assessed under the wool customs.

Chaucer's duties in the customs house did not, however, prevent him from being called upon by the king to perform further diplomatic duties abroad. Between 1376 and the end of 1377, he traveled to the Continent at least three times to participate in peace negotiations with France and to conduct other miscellaneous duties,

including the discussion of a possible marriage between Richard II and one of the French princesses. Edward III had died on June 21, 1377, and Richard's coronation was held shortly thereafter, even though he was only 10 years old at the time. Following the coronation, Richard confirmed and renewed Chaucer's offices and annuities.

Under Richard's government, Chaucer continued to serve as controller of the wool customs and to travel abroad on the king's business. In 1378 he went to Lombardy, Italy, on business having to do with the war in France. This was another opportunity for him to have contact with the work of the Italian authors mentioned above.

The year 1380 marks one of the most troubling episodes in Chaucer's biographical records, his being charged with rape by a woman named Cecilia CHAUMPAIGNE, the daughter of a London baker. The Latin term by which the charge was stated was *raptus,* which could have meant sexual rape, or possibly abduction; the same word was used to indicate both, and the surviving documents fail to specify the exact nature of his alleged crime. All that does in fact remain that directly involves Chaucer is a release given by Cecilia's father and mother, relieving Chaucer of the legal action that had been taken against him.

The following year, 1381, was when the great PEASANT'S REVOLT, also known as Jack Straw's Rebellion, occurred. On June 12 of that year a mass of disgruntled peasants, led by Wat TYLER, entered the city of London with the express intention of destroying traitors and rescuing King Richard from their clutches. Richard was 14 years old at the time, and ruled largely through the advice and consent of a group of noblemen, chief among whom was his uncle, JOHN OF GAUNT. These noblemen, it would later become obvious, were the "traitors" referred to in the peasants' proclamation. The anger at these men had several motives, the most immediate being a series of poll taxes imposed by Parliament between 1377 and 1381. The peasants gave vent to their feelings by executing those who were within reach, and looting and burning the residences of those who, like John of Gaunt, were not. There is no record of Chaucer's whereabouts during the rebellion, or of his response to it, but we do know that thousands of the rebels entered the city through Aldgate, the site of Chaucer's residence. A number of those who were murdered in the riots came from the Vintry Ward, where Chaucer still owned his father's house. The mob was finally brought under control and dispersed by King Richard with the assistance of some of the citizens of London. In short, Richard agreed to meet the rebels' demands, which included an end to serfdom and the elimination of class distinctions; in addition, all those who had participated in the revolt were granted pardon. Then came the order for the peasants to

Artist's rendering of Chaucer's portrait as it appears in the Ellesmere Manuscript of The Canterbury Tales.

return home peacefully, which, after a brief altercation, they did. Once they were gone, however, the promises that had been made were all nullified, and serfdom continued to be enforced. Four days after the conclusion of the revolt, Chaucer sold the family residence on Thames Street (in the Vintry) to a merchant named Henry Herbury.

During the decade 1374–84, while he was employed in the customs house and serving the king on missions to the Continent, Chaucer was also continuing to write. His work on *The HOUSE OF FAME* is usually assigned a date early in this period, shortly after his return from the first trip to Italy. *The PARLIAMENT OF FOWLS,* possibly written for the occasion of King Richard's engagement to Anne of Bohemia, was probably written around 1380–81, with work on the much longer *TROILUS AND CRISEYDE* beginning shortly after. The translation of BOETHIUS' *Consolation of Philosophy* was likely written close to the same time as the *Troilus,* based on the similarity of themes shared by the two works, although one is a philosophical treatise and the other a romance.

Some records show that when Chaucer went abroad on diplomatic business he was often given leave to

employ a deputy to perform his duties in the customs house. In 1385 he was granted permission to appoint a permanent deputy, and by 1388 records clearly indicate that he was living in Kent, a southeastern county with a significant coastline on the English Channel. On October 12, 1385, he was appointed to the position of justice of the peace in Kent, an office which at that time entailed a special responsibility because the French were threatening to invade the south coast. The year 1386 saw Chaucer's election as one of the two "knights of the shire" (members of the House of Commons) representing Kent in Parliament. In the same year he gave up his lease on the dwelling above Aldgate, which supports other evidence of his removal to a new residence in Kent. *Troilus and Criseyde* was probably completed and work on *The LEGEND OF GOOD WOMEN* begun.

Philippa, Chaucer's wife, disappears from the records after June of 1387 and is presumed to have died. Later that same year, Chaucer went to Calais on undisclosed business. This was the last recorded overseas journey that he made, an indication that he lost favor at court soon after. This change in his fortunes is further signified by the fate of three men with whom Chaucer had worked. In 1388, Sir Nicholas Brembre of the customs house, and Sir Simon Burley and Chief Justice Robert Tresilian, both members of the Kent peace commission to which Chaucer belonged, were executed through the influence of enemies of the king who had come to dominate Parliament at this time. Although Chaucer survived unharmed, he was twice sued for outstanding debts by John Churchman, collector of the customs at London.

Shortly after regaining power in May 1389, King Richard appointed Chaucer to his most prestigious and demanding office, that of clerk of the king's works. In this capacity he had responsibility for overseeing construction and repair at 10 royal residences and other holdings of the king. One was the Tower of London, which at that time served as a palace, fortress, prison, armory, mint and place of safekeeping for records. Other works he oversaw were Westminster Palace, the castle of Berkhamsted, and seven of Richard's other manors, including ELTHAM and SHEEN. He was also the overseer of hunting lodges in the royal forests, the mews (cages) where the king's falcons were kept at Charing Cross, various hunting preserves and gardens. Chaucer's wages in this position were two shillings a day, more than three and a half times his base salary at the customs house. Nevertheless, when he left the position in June 1391, an audit of his account showed that he was owed more than £87, which exceeded the total amount of his wages during the entire term that he was in office.

On June 22, 1391, Chaucer was appointed deputy forester of the royal forest at North Petherton in

Somerset. This was a large forest, and included villages, cultivated fields and pasture, as well as moor, marsh and wooded areas. Chaucer may have lived at Park House, a manor house within the precincts of the forest. His responsibilities are likely to have included overseeing the collection of fees for pasturing cattle, of tolls for traveling forest roads, and the prevention of illegal hunting (poaching). Two years later, Chaucer received a gift of £10 from King Richard "for good service." In the following year, 1393, Richard granted him an annuity of £20.

Little is known of Chaucer's life between 1394 and 1400, when the last records of his life appear. In 1397 the government entered another period of turbulence when Richard suddenly and belatedly decided to take revenge on the men who had in 1388 caused the exile or death of many of his friends. One of these men was John of Gaunt's son, Henry Bolingbroke. Henry was exiled in 1398, and when his father died the following year, Richard seized Gaunt's estates. Henry returned from exile to claim them, and then went even further, deposing Richard and claiming the crown for himself as Henry IV. Chaucer does not seem to have been greatly affected by Henry's accession, perhaps because of his longstanding connection with the Lancastrian branch of the royal family to which Henry belonged (both Chaucer and his wife had received annuities from Henry's father, and Chaucer had probably written *The Book of the Duchess* as an elegy to Henry's mother). After he became king, Henry renewed the grants Chaucer had received from Richard and granted him an additional 40 marks yearly for life. The concluding stanza of a late poem, "The COMPLAINT OF CHAUCER TO HIS PURSE," suggests, however, that the money was slow in coming.

Late in 1399 Chaucer moved back to London, taking a long-term lease on a house in the garden of Westminster Abbey. The site is now occupied by the Chapel of King Henry VII. The records show that he began to receive his annual payments from the royal exchequer again, but the last date of such a record is June 5, 1400. The exact date of the poet's death is uncertain. The inscription on his tomb in Westminster Abbey gives the date as October 25, 1400, but the tomb may have been erected as late as 1555. No other evidence remains to support the date given by the inscription. His burial in the abbey probably resulted from his being a tenant of the abbey and a member of the parish, and had nothing to do with his status as a poet. It is somewhat ironic, then, that Chaucer's tomb was destined to be the first one in the area now known as "Poet's Corner," and that he himself would become known as the "Father of English Poetry."

Chaucer: Glossary *See* DAVIS, NORMAN.

Chaucer, John Geoffrey CHAUCER's father, John, was a vintner, or wine merchant, by trade, although he had a

hand in a number of other mercantile ventures including the shipping of wheat to the European continent. Like his son, he was also employed for a time as a civil servant in the government of EDWARD III, serving first as deputy to the king's chief butler in the port of Southampton and, later, as a customs collector on exports of cloth and bedding. Belonging solidly to the middle class, the Chaucers possessed considerable wealth, including inherited lands and property, which gave them a somewhat higher social standing than those members of the merchant class whose wealth and property were newly acquired. In his biography of Geoffrey Chaucer, Donald HOWARD notes that Chaucer's father owned "buildings and land in London and Middlesex, a brewing establishment, twenty-odd shops outside the city wall of London at ALDGATE, ten and a half acres nearby, and various properties in Middlesex and Suffolk," an impressive catalogue of land and properties for someone outside the nobility. John Chaucer also seems to have had a brief career as a soldier. His name is recorded in a list of those who participated in an expedition against the Scots in 1327, and he took part in several skirmishes related to the political upheaval that followed the murder of Edward II in the same year. Eleven years later he served in the army of Edward III on the expedition to FLANDERS that signaled the start of the HUNDRED YEARS' WAR between England and France.

Chaucer, Katherine The only sibling of Geoffrey CHAUCER's of whom any record survives. The little evidence that exists suggests that she was close to Geoffrey in age, and that she married a young man named Simon Manning, who came from a prosperous family in Kent. Among the evidence of this sibling relationship is a legal document signed by Geoffrey when Katherine's husband was sued for debt and a record of Katherine inheriting some property in Greenwich the same year that John CHAUCER (their father) died.

Chaucer, Lewis Geoffrey Chaucer's second son. Little else is known of him aside from the fact that he was sent to school at Oxford at the age of 10 and that Chaucer's *TREATISE ON THE ASTROLABE* was written for him. There is also a record of him bearing arms, along with his brother Thomas, in 1403. Donald HOWARD's biography of Chaucer makes the interesting suggestion, based on the year that Lewis was born, 1381, that the child could have been an illegitimate son born to Cecilia CHAUMPAIGNE, the woman whom Chaucer was accused of raping. There is, however, no evidence beyond the coincidence of dates to support this idea.

Chaucer, Mary Geoffrey Chaucer's paternal grandmother. Mary Chaucer was married three times—to

John Heron, Robert Chaucer and Richard Chaucer, a relative of Robert's. Geoffrey's father, John CHAUCER, was the son of Robert. Robert died when John was an infant, so he was raised by his mother and her third husband.

Chaucer, Philippa Pan   Geoffrey Chaucer's wife. The exact date of their marriage is unknown, but a grant from the royal exchequer for a lifetime annuity to be paid to one Philippa Chaucer, who was at that time a damoiselle (lady-in-waiting) to EDWARD III's wife, suggests that they were probably married sometime that year. The annuity may have been a kind of wedding present, something that would help the couple set up their own household within the royal one. Chaucer himself is first recorded as a member of the king's household in 1367, when he received a similar annuity. Philippa Pan was the daughter of Sir Gilles de Roet, also known as "Paon," and she had served in the royal household since early youth, first as an attendant to Elizabeth, countess of Ulster (Edward III's daughter-in-law). When the countess died, Philippa entered the service of Edward's queen, also named Philippa. (*See* PHILIPPA OF HAINAULT.) Queen Philippa may well have arranged the marriage between Philippa Pan and Geoffrey Chaucer. The Chaucers appear to have had four children: Thomas, Lewis, Elizabeth and Agnes CHAUCER.

Chaucer, Richard   *See* CHAUCER, MARY.

Chaucer, Robert   *See* CHAUCER, MARY.

Chaucer, Thomas   Geoffrey and Philippa CHAUCER's eldest son. The exact date of his birth is unknown, but deducing from the date he entered military service, he was probably born around 1367. Because he served in the retinue of JOHN OF GAUNT and received many favors from that prince during his lifetime, as well as the fact that he adopted his mother's coat of arms rather than his father's, some scholars have speculated, even as early as the 16th century, that Thomas was Gaunt's bastard son fathered on Philippa in the early months of her marriage to Geoffrey. Although possible, there is no specific or concrete evidence for this theory. In his biography of Chaucer, Donald HOWARD suggests that Thomas chose his mother's coat of arms because it was more prestigious.

Chaucer Gazetteer   *See* MAGOUN, F. P.

Chaucer Life-Records   The long-awaited volume published in 1966 by the Oxford University Press and known as *Chaucer Life-Records* is exactly what its title implies—all of the existing records of the poet's life that John MANLY, Edith RICKERT and other devoted scholars were able to dig up. Edited by Martin Crow and Clair Olson, among many other topics the volume includes the following topics: "Chaucer's Parents and Their Home in the VINTRY"; "Chaucer's Service in the Ulster Household, 1357 Onwards"; "Chaucer's Capture in the Campaign of 1359–60"; "Chaucer's Journeys, 1366–98"; "Philippa CHAUCER, Wife of Geoffrey Chaucer"; "Chaucer's Service in the King's Household, June 1367 Onwards"; "Chaucer's Exchequer Annuity as Valettus and Esquire to EDWARD III, 1367–77"; "Chaucer as Controller in the Port of London, 1374–86"; "Chaucer's Connection with the House of Lancaster, 1374 Onwards"; "Deed of Release to Chaucer in Respect of the Raptus of Cecily CHAMPAIN, 1380"; "Chaucer's Deposition in the SCROPE-GROSVENOR CONTROVERSY, 1386"; "Chaucer's Children"; and "Chaucer's Death and Burial, 1400." The book is an indispensable resource to scholars engaged in biographical study of the poet.

Chaucernet   An Internet discussion group devoted to Chaucer studies. According to its Web page, its membership consists of "professors, graduate students, undergraduates and others from all over the world who either specialize in—or are merely interested in—Chaucer, his works and related topics." Internet users may join Chaucernet free of charge via e-mail. To do so, simply send to listserv@listserv.uic.edu a message reading "sub chaucer [user's name]." (Be sure not to put anything else in the message or on the subject line, or else it will not work.) Usually within a day or two, applicants will receive a reply from the listserve confirming membership in Chaucernet. Users will then begin receiving all of the queries and responses posted by other members of the group, and may send their own. When posting a message for all the other Chaucernet members to read, address it to chaucer@listserv.uic.edu, not to the listserv. For further information about the group, consult its Web page at http://dcwww.mediasvcs.smu.edu/chaucer/chaunet.index.html.

Chaucer Review   Begun in 1979, the *Chaucer Review: A Journal of Medieval Studies and Literary Criticism* is published by Penn State University Press. It features articles on Chaucer and related topics; some of the most renowned Chaucer scholars have (and still do) served on its editorial board. Since its inception, the review has published an annual unannotated listing of primarily American research, which includes works in progress as well as those already completed.

Chaucer's Language   The following discussion touches on some of the most obvious ways in which Chaucer's English is different from our own. Both explanations and examples are provided under each heading, but the list and the examples are far from exhaustive and do not take into account the difficulties presented by the convolutions of the poetic line (*see* CHAUCER'S LANGUAGE—VERSIFICATION).

Nouns

The noun in Chaucer presents few difficulties in interpretation, because it is formally and functionally nearly parallel to the noun in modern English. Inflectional endings are added to the base to distinguish number, but the complex inflectional system which in Old English indicated case and gender, as well as distinguishing weak from strong nouns, has largely disappeared.

Some nouns form their plural with *(e)n* instead of *(e)s*: *brethren, children, oxen, eyen, doghtren, foon, hosen, shoon, sustren.*

The possessive is usually indicated by adding *s* or *es*, but there is no apostrophe, so the reader must decide from context whether a noun is plural or possessive. A few nouns have no possessive ending. These are mainly nouns of relation descended from Old English. *Fader, suster, brother* are all examples: *Suster son* = Sister's son.

Pronouns (Unfamiliar forms are in bold print)

SUBJECT

Forms	1st person	2nd person	3rd person
singular	I, **Ich, Ik**	**thow, thou**	she, he, **hit**
plural	we	**ye**	**thei,** they

OBJECT AND PREPOSITIONAL

Forms	1st person	2nd person	3rd person
singular	me	**the(e)**	**hire,** him, **(h)it**
plural	us	**yow,** you	**hem**

POSSESSIVE

Forms	1st person	2nd person	3rd person
singular	my(n), **myne**	**thy(n)**	**hire;** his
plural	**oure**	**youre**	**hire, thair**

Relative Pronouns

Fourteenth-century English used a range of relative pronouns similar to that of Modern English. The spelling is slightly different sometimes (e.g., *whos* for *whose*) but they are usually recognizable from context. The commonest relative pronoun is probably *that*, which is used in place of *who*: "Palamon / That serveth yow." Finally, the reader should be aware that Chaucer sometimes omits the relative pronoun in circumstances that would seem unidiomatic in Modern English: "He sente after a cherl was in the town."

Demonstratives

Chaucer's language uses the demonstratives *that* and *this* (singular) and *tho* and *thise* (plural) in addition to a contracted phrase, *thilke* = "the like." These usages are

fairly straightforward once the reader learns to recognize the plural forms.

Adjectives

The final *e* inflexion is left over from Old English: *olde, leve, stronge, brode.*

Adverbs

The comparative endings *er* and *est* are the same as in Modern English, except they may be followed by final *e*: *fastere, faireste.*

The basic adverbial ending *ly* occurs in Chaucer (cf. *myrily, playnly*), but is probably less common than *liche* or *lyche: friendliche, friendlyche, rudeliche.*

Verbs

Verbs in the Germanic languages can be divided into two classes: the strong and the weak. In Chaucer's Middle English, as in Modern English, these are distinguishable only by the forms of the past tense and the past participle. In the strong verb, the past tense was formed by a change in the root vowel, and the past participle by the addition of the inflexional ending *e(n)*. Thus, in Chaucer's language we find the following strong verb forms:

Infinitive	Past Tense	Past Participle
knowe(n)	*knewe*	*knowe(n)*
take(n)	*toke*	*take(n)*
breke(n)	*broke*	*broke(n)*
stonde(n)	*stoode*	*stonde(n)*
speke(n)	*spake*	*spoke(n)*

Weak verbs form their past tense and past participles by the addition of *(e)d* or *t* as a suffix, usually appended to the stem of the infinitive, but sometimes to a special past form:

Infinitive	Past Tense	Past Participle
wedde(n)	*wedded*	*wedded*
daunce(n)	*daunced*	*daunced*
crepe(n)	*crepte*	*crept, cropen*

But (these are the "special forms" referred to above):

seke(n)	*soughte*	*sought*
werke(n)	*wroghte*	*wroght*
wende(n)	*wente*	*went*

The infinitive form by itself would be translated thus: *wedden* = "to wed," but it might also appear with the preposition *to: To wedden*, which would be translated the same.

Gynne (present tense) and *gan* (past), which are normally translated "begin" and "began," sometimes function periphrastically, indicating either past or present tense but not translated separately from the verb that follows. For example, *she gynneth wepe* = "she weeps," not "she begins to weep"; *she gan wepe* = "she wept," not "she began to weep." Readers should be alert when they encounter *gan*, which Chaucer uses very frequently in its periphrastic sense.

Negatives
A verb is usually negated by the use of the negating particle *ne*, which is often followed by the adverbs *no, noon, nat* or *noght*:

But wedded men ne knowe no mesure;

O Donegild, I ne have noon Englissh digne

Hise hors weere goode, but he ne was nat gay;

Ne studieth noght. Ley hond to, every man.

In Modern English these would be considered double negatives and nonidiomatic. In Middle English they are the norm rather than the exception.

With some verbs, the *ne* particle is prefixed to the verb form itself: *I not = I ne wot* = "I don't know." Other verbs with forms in which a preceding *ne* has coalesced with the stem of the verb are: *ben, wol, have,* and *wiste.* Some examples are given below:

"not to be"	"not to have"	"not to wish"	"not to know"
I nam			*I not*
thow nart		*thow nilt*	*nost(ow)*
he nys	*he nath*	*he nyl*	*he niste*
he nas	*he nadde*	*he nolde*	*he not*
it nere			

A list of common words that can be memorized for greater efficiency in reading:

ek, eek = "also"

wene, ich or ik, wot, wenest, wost = "to know," "I know," "you know," "he knows"

leve = "dear"

artow = "are you" (a contraction of *art tow*)

wiltow = "will you"

thynkestow = "do you think"

algate = "entirely," "surely," "continuously"

ich = "I"

ilke = "the same"

thilke = contraction of "the ilke"

swich = such

ay(e) = always, forever

fyn = end, goal

lette = hinder

soth = truth

niman, nam = to take

Chaucer's Language—Pronunciation   It is impossible to know exactly how Middle English was pronounced, simply because we do not possess any recordings of it. Therefore, an approximation (a very close approximation, we believe) has been created by linguists who study such matters by comparing related languages and by considering phonetic probability and the evolution of pronunciation. Their task is complicated by the fact that spelling was not regularized at the time in which Chaucer wrote, which means that a writer, or scribe, could spell a word any way he chose to, provided his choice could be interpreted by a reader. For example, Chaucer's name could be spelled *Chaucer, Chausier, Chauser* or *Chaussure*—and these are not the only possibilities.

One way in which Chaucerian English differs from modern English is in its accents. This is due primarily to the tremendous changes in the English language that resulted from the Norman Conquest in 1066 and the ensuing influx of French words into the English language (*see* ANGLO-NORMAN). This is one reason why, although the main stress of a Middle English word often falls on the same syllable as in modern English, there are some exceptions. For example, in words of native English descent (words from Anglo-Saxon), the stress tends to fall on the first syllable, unless it is a prefix. In those from French, such as *licour* (modern "liquor") and *servyse* (modern "service"), later syllables are often stressed. To complicate matters further, some words of French origin are stressed in more than one way, sometimes on the French pattern, but sometimes in accordance with the English pattern, depending on the how Chaucer needed the word to function in a line of verse.

As for individual sounds, linguists believe that the London English of Chaucer's time voiced vowel and consonant sounds as shown below. Whenever possible, pronunciation guide-words are given in English. This not possible when the sound has no counterpart in English (as in the case of the trilled "r"). The sample words and phrases are all taken from *The CANTERBURY TALES.* Italicized words are the ones to which the rule applies.

Short Vowels:

a as in "that"; for example, *Whan that April*

e (stressed) as in "men"; for example, *every*

e (unstressed) as in "*a*bout"; for example, *shoures*

i, y as in "hit"; for example, *inspired, knyght*

o as in "hog"; for example, *croppes, holpen*

u (sometimes written *o*) as in "full"; for example, *sonne*

Long Vowels:

a, aa as in "father"; for example, *maken, caas*

e, ee, ie as in "*a*te"; for example, *sweete, sleepen*

e, ee as in "c*a*re"; for example, *were, esed*

i,y as in "see"; for example, *inspired, shires*

o,oo as in "so"; for example, *soote, wolden*

o,oo as in "saw"; for example, *open, goon*

ou, ow, ogh as in "boon"; for example, *shoures, droghte*

u as in French "tu"; for example, *vertu, aventure*

Diphthongs

ai,ay,ei,ey are all approximately a combination of "a" and "i"; for example, *veyne, day, wey*

au,aw as in "mouse"; for example, *straunge, felaweshipe*

eu,ew as in "mew"; for example, *newe, trewe*

oi,oy as in "boy"; for example, *coy*

Consonants

With the following exceptions, pronunciation of consonants in Middle English is the same as Modern English:

cch as in "church"; for example, *recchelees*

g, gg as in "bridge"; for example, *corages, juggement*

gh (after a front vowel) as in German "ich"; for example, *nyght, knyght*

gh (after a back vowel) as in Scots "loch"; for example, *droghte*

h is silent in French loan-words; for example, *honoured*

r is trilled as in Scots; for example, *Aprill*

ssh as in "shall"; for example, *parisshe*

The 18th-century English poet Thomas Gray suggested that if the final *e* of words that appeared in Chaucer's verse were to be pronounced, it would make his verses scan (prove metrically regular). This turned out to be true. As a result, modern students are still taught to pronounce final *e* in Chaucer in each word that falls at the end of a line, and also those final *e*'s that appear within the line if it makes the line scan. Other evidence suggests, however, that there were several kinds of final *e*'s in Middle English, not all of them pronounced; so, the above rule may not be an exact indication of how the lines were originally intended to be spoken. One of

the best ways to get a sense of what it may have sounded like is to listen to one of the many professional recordings available, usually available in public and academic libraries.

Further information on pronunciation can be found in the introduction to the RIVERSIDE CHAUCER and in the book-length study *Chaucer's English,* by R. W. V. Elliott (1974).

Chaucer's Language—Versification   Chaucer's versification has enjoyed a fluctuating reputation over the past 500-odd years. From the 16th to the 18th centuries, when Middle English had evolved into Early Modern and then Modern English, his verse was generally considered to be rhythmical, but not metrically regular. Some modern scholars believe that this opinion, which arose from a misunderstanding of Middle English pronunciation, prevented Chaucer from being appreciated for his technical expertise as a poet. Prevailing critical opinion began to change near the end of the 18th century, after the publication in 1775 of Thomas TYRWHITT's *Essay on the Language and Versification of Chaucer* (volume four of his edition of *The CANTERBURY TALES*), which argued that the poet made extensive metrical use of inflectional (final) *e,* pronouncing the *e* at the end of words like *hadde* and *speche.* It had been discovered by Tyrwhitt (and others before him, but for some reason the idea had not caught on) that if inflectional *e* is pronounced where it should be, most of the metrical irregularities of Chaucer's verse vanish. This idea became widely accepted during the second half of the 19th century, and a series of editions of *The Canterbury Tales* were based on a metrically "normalized" text of the ELLESMERE MANUSCRIPT. The 1940 publication of John MANLY and Edith RICKERT's text heralded the advent of another theory. Manly and Rickert believed that the 19th-century editors and critics had gone too far in the direction of metrical regularization, creating an artificial metrically perfect text that was far from what the poet intended, even though the pronunciation of final *e* does play an important role in the rhythm of Chaucer's verse. Although this modified view is the most widely held today, a few scholars have also emerged who argue for a return to the original opinion, denying that Chaucer pronounced the final *e* either within the verse line or at the end of it. The argument between these two positions continues today, though. As A. C. Cawley points out in his notes to the Everyman edition of *The Canterbury Tales,* "A great many of Chaucer's verses can be read quite naturally with an iambic movement if final *e* is normally pronounced within the line, but elided before an initial vowel or a weak *h,* and slurred at the end of such words as *youre, hire, whiche, were.*" Furthermore, he suggests, "Chaucer is always varying the regular iambic-decasyllabic pattern, as the rhythms of natural speech dictate," so that "if we read

Chaucer's verse with natural stressing and with due regard for the elision or slurring of final *e,* we find that he gives us a strongly rhythmical movement of infinite variety, but one which is disciplined by the basic pattern of iambic verse."

Chaucer Society   One of many literary societies, including the Early English Text Society, founded by F. J. Furnivall for the purpose of collecting materials for the study of Chaucer. Established in 1868, the Chaucer Society was still in existence at the end of the 20th century.

Chaucer's Retraction   Chaucer's Retraction is a short piece of prose appearing at the conclusion of *The CAN-TERBURY TALES* in which Chaucer repents of writing those of his works which display vanity or are conducive of sin. Those he names are "the book of Troilus" (*TROILUS AND CRISEYDE*), "the book . . . of Fame (*The HOUSE OF FAME*), "the book of the XXV. Ladies" (*The LEG-END OF GOOD WOMEN*), "the book of the Duchesse" (*The BOOK OF THE DUCHESS*), "the book of Seint Valentynes day of the Parlement of Briddes" (*The PARLIAMENT OF FOWLS*), "the tales of Caunterbury, thilke that sownen into synne" (the Canterbury tales—those that tend toward sin), "the book of the Leoun" (*BOOK OF THE LION*), and many another book, song or "lecherous lay" that he may have forgotten about. For the virtuous works that he wrote, such as the *BOECE* and "othere bookes of legendes of seintes, and omelies, and morali-tee, and devocioun" (line 1087) [other books of saints' lives, homilies, and books of morality and devotion], Chaucer gives thanks to Christ and His Mother. The final lines—where he asks for grace to bewail his sins and to seek the salvation of his soul so that he may at the day of judgment be one of those that shall be saved—lend credence to the tradition that the piece is a deathbed confession, a tradition that appeared as early as the 15th century. Although Chaucer's authorship of the Retraction has been questioned by those who do not like to think that he would repudiate what we consider some of his greatest work, it is strongly supported by the Retraction's appearance in all manuscripts containing "The PARSON'S TALE" (the final tale of the Canterbury set) complete. There is furthermore a sense of continuity between the PARSON's performance and Chaucer's parting words. Responding to the Host's (*see* Harry BAILLY) request that he take a turn in the tale-telling contest, the Parson refuses to tell a fable, explaining that fiction is wretched falsehood, a use of language to mislead people. The tale that he then proceeds to tell is actually a sermon that outlines the Seven Deadly Sins and gives thorough instructions regarding penitence.

"Chaucer's Words Unto Adam, His Owne Scriveyn"   One of the short poems attributed to Chaucer in the manuscripts, "Chaucer's Words Unto Adam" consists of seven lines, in which the poet rebukes the young man who was apparently his scribe for making numerous errors in his transcription of Chaucer's work, which the poet then had to go back and correct. The *BOECE* and *TROILUS AND CRISEYDE* are specifically mentioned in the poet's expressed wish that if his careless scribe should have to write them out anew, he might develop "scalle," a scaly eruption of the scalp with which Chaucer's SUM-MONER was also afflicted. Because of the reference to *Troilus* and the use of the RHYME ROYAL stanza, it appears likely that Chaucer's poem to his scribe was composed around the middle of the 1380s. A stanza in book five of the *Troilus* also indicates that Chaucer was concerned over the accurate transmission of his text.

Chaumpaigne, Cecilia   The daughter of a London baker named William Chaumpaigne. Nothing is known of her acquaintance with Chaucer beyond what may be inferred from a legal document, dated May 4, 1380, in which William and his wife Agnes acknowledge a release to Geoffrey Chaucer of all legal procedures seeking redress for his alleged "raptus" of their daughter Cecilia. When it appeared in a legal document, the Latin word *raptus* could either mean sexual rape or kidnapping. What was meant in this particular case is not specified. Furthermore, what we do know of the situation is complicated by the following events. On June 30 of the same year, Robert Goodchild, a cutler, and John Grove, an armorer, both citizens of London, also granted Chaucer a general release from all actions of the law. The same day, Cecilia Chaumpaigne granted a similar release to Goodchild and Grove. Then, in a legal document dated several days later, John Grove agreed to pay Cecilia £10, a sum equivalent to Chaucer's annual salary as the controller of wool customs, due at Michaelmas (September 29, the feast day of the archangel Michael). Some scholars have suggested that Grove may have served as an intermediary in bringing about a settlement between Chaucer and Cecilia Chaumpaigne. It has likewise been suggested that Grove, because of his payment to the woman, was the principal in the case and Chaucer only an accessory. But it is possible that Chaucer also paid Cecilia, or her family, a sum of money and that the transaction was not recorded, or the record has been lost. Whatever happened, the records of this event have aroused concern among those who admire Chaucer's work and who do not want to believe that a man whose poetry displays such sensitivity could commit such a crime as rape.

Chaunticleer   The noble rooster who is the central protagonist of "THE NUN'S PRIEST'S TALE." Neville Coghill and J. R. R. Tolkien, who edited a 1959 edition of the tale, note that Chaucer's description of the rooster precisely follows Latin author GEOFFREY OF VIN-

SAUF's prescription for describing a beautiful woman, set down in his *Poetria nova*, the standard text on medieval poetics. Chaunticleer is certainly colorful, with a comb as red as coral and crenelated like a castle wall, a beak as black as jet, legs and toes the color of azure and feathers of burnished gold. As a character in a tale that is a hybrid of two forms, the BEAST FABLE and the beast epic, Chaunticleer speaks and behaves as if he is human—and a very well-read human at that, at least on the subject of dreams. He has seven "wives," the fairest one being called PERTELOTE. His tragicomic fall and rise most directly responds to the bleak view of human life offered in "The MONK'S TALE," but it has affinities with, or at least alludes to many other of *The CANTERBURY TALES*.

Cheapside   Referred to in Chaucer's work as simply "Chepe," Cheapside is a London street known in Chaucer's day for the prosperity of its merchants. That is why, in the GENERAL PROLOGUE to *The CANTERBURY TALES*, Chaucer's comparison of the Host (*see* Harry BAILLY) to a burgess of "Chepe" may be considered complimentary. A busy thoroughfare full of shops, it was also a popular location for processions and festivals. This feature of the district is alluded to in "The COOK'S TALE" when we are told that the tale's protagonist, PERKYN REVELOUR, manages to slip away from the cookshop where he works whenever there is a show to be seen in Chepe. The PARDONER mentions the street as a source of some Spanish white wine that he perceives as being particularly intoxicating (line 564); the Host likewise associates the district with wine when he states, in the prologue to "The MANCIPLE'S TALE," that he is so drowsy he would rather sleep than have a gallon of the best wine in Chepe (line 24).

Chepe   *See* CHEAPSIDE.

Chichevache   Chichevache, which in Old French literally means "lean cow," was a legendary cow who, in the Middle Ages, became proverbial because of the story of how she fed on patient wives and consequently had little to eat. Traditionally Chichevache was contrasted to Bicorne ("two-horned"), which fed on patient husbands and was always fat. The two horns would in this case allude to the horns associated with cuckoldry (having a wife who takes lovers outside marriage). Chaucer refers to Chichevache in the concluding stanzas of "The CLERK'S TALE," where he seems to speak directly to his readers, warning them that no man ought to test his wife's patience the way WALTER tested GRISELDA's, because he shall certainly fail. Speaking to the women in his audience, he exhorts them not to be like Griselda, lest Chichevache should eat them up (line 1188)!

childhood in the Middle Ages   Earlier in this century, some rather unscientific studies of childhood in the Middle Ages theorized that medieval children were treated very differently from children today or even in the last couple of centuries. Basing their opinions partly on the representations of children in art and partly on what they knew about certain circumstances, such as the high infant mortality rate, such writers concluded that children were (1) treated more or less as miniature adults, and (2) not greatly valued or cherished because of the likelihood that they might die before emerging from childhood. More recent research into primary sources such as household records, diaries and medical texts discloses a very different picture. Much of that research is brought together and synthesized in Frances and Joseph Gies' *Marriage and Family in the Middle Ages* (1987). For example, TROTULA, a 12th-century woman who practiced in the medical school at Salerno in Italy, wrote an important treatise on women's health, dealing with, among other things, the management of childbirth. Prescribed treatment for the newborn baby included instructions for tying the umbilical cord, bathing the child, clearing mucus from its lungs and throat and protecting the child from bright lights and loud noises during its first hours. She recommended that the newborn's senses be stimulated instead by "varied pictures, cloths of various colors, and pearls" and by "songs and gentle voices" (quoted in Gies, p. 198). Evidence like this indicates considerable concern over a child's welfare, starting in the first moments of life.

Although peasant women typically nursed their own children, women of the aristocracy and of the wealthy merchant class often employed wet nurses, who would supply the child with milk and, often, with the affection and attention that the parents may have been too busy to offer. Bartholomaeus Anglicus (Bartholomew the Englishman), a 13th-century Franciscan monk, described the nurse as taking the mother's place, bathing and changing its clothing, singing to it and chewing its food and generally sharing in the child's joys and sorrows. The role of the father with young children was typically that of disciplinarian, something that, until recently, had not changed very much since the Middle Ages. Whether or not a child attended school or received any kind of formal education depended on its class, gender and the wealth of its parents. Children of the nobility, female as well as male, were generally instructed by private tutors, sometimes within their own household, more often in another aristocratic household where the boys would also receive instruction in arms and the girls in needlework and other domestic arts. Both sexes were expected to learn certain rules of social behavior. Children of the urban middle class were often apprenticed into a trade as soon as they had learned to read and write, perhaps before. Peasant children usually joined their parents working in the fields as soon as they were old enough, but sometimes left home to become servants. There were some schools for young boys, housed in cathedrals, and ostensibly designed to train those who were destined to serve in the church. They were open to any whose parents could afford the tuition and board. The curriculum of these schools included Latin grammar, the Latin classics and philosophy. Instructors in one cathedral school, at Chartres, in France, devoted the morning to reading and interpreting Latin authors, the afternoon to grammar and the evening to philosophical discussion. Recitations of the previous days' lessons helped to improve retention of knowledge. Compositions imitating the authors they were studying helped students develop a good writing style. When students performed poorly, they were usually beaten, though corporal punishment was severely criticized and even condemned by some masters, including Saint ANSELM. Several of Chaucer's biographers believe that he attended such a cathedral school in London, perhaps the one not far from the family home in Thames Street, and there acquired the familiarity with the Latin classics displayed in his own work.

Children appear rarely in Chaucer's work. When they do, they are almost never personalized, but function merely as objects of pity, as in "The CLERK'S TALE," where GRISELDA is forced to give up her children in obedience to her husband's will, or in "The MAN OF LAW'S TALE," where CONSTANCE is cast adrift upon the sea with her infant son. The only child to be more particularly characterized appears in "The PRIORESS' TALE": the little boy who learned to sing the "alma redemptoris" and was murdered by Jews who were offended by his piety. There are no children accompanying their parents on the pilgrimage to CANTERBURY, except for the SQUIRE, and he would have been considered an adult by the standards of the Middle Ages. (He had already participated in military campaigns.) These facts do not suggest that Chaucer did not like children, but rather reflect the literary conventions of his day.

Chiron In classical mythology, Chiron was a CENTAUR (half man, half horse) renowned for his wisdom, justice and skill in the many arts taught him by APOLLO and Artemis (DIANA). He had many human friends and became the instructor of many of the great heroes of Greek myth. Chiron had a particularly close relationship with PELIUS, saving him from some other centaurs and helping win his wife, THETIS. Wounded accidentally by one of the poisoned arrows of HERCULES, Chiron endured such pain that he willingly gave up his immortality in order to escape it. Zeus (JUPITER) placed

Chiron among the stars as the constellation SAGITTARIUS, the Archer. By virtue of his ability to play the harp (taught him by Apollo), Chiron appears among the musicians gathered at FAME's palace in Chaucer's *HOUSE OF FAME* (line 1206).

chivalry Defined briefly, chivalry was the secular code of honor of the medieval European nobility. Chivalry flourished in western Europe between the mid-12th and the 16th centuries, and its rules applied primarily to the aristocratic fighting men who were called knights. The roots of the code reach back into the Dark Ages, when such early heroic epics of western European society as *Beowulf* were composed. The ideals promoted by the heroic code—bravery, loyalty and service to one's lord—were later softened by contact with the Christian church as its influence spread westward, and by the 12th century one of the defining characteristics of a knight was his Christian faith. Under the influence of the church, honor (especially in keeping one's word), virtue and courtesy were also enlisted as essential ingredients of knighthood.

The more organized medieval societies became, the more ceremony became an important feature of life. Chivalric ceremonies included the initiation of newly qualified knights, which concluded with the ritual dubbing, the giving of arms, which was often a part of initiation, and the adoption of distinguishing emblems and blazons, which became known as coats of arms and were passed down through generations within a single family. By Chaucer's day, a man had to rise to knighthood through several degrees conferred upon him by a man of higher political standing (usually a king or prince), beginning with that of page, graduating to squire, and finally to bachelor (the first degree of knighthood). Chaucer himself served as a page in the household of the king's brother Lionel, earl of Ulster.

During the Middle Ages, knighthood emerged as a feature of feudalism, the political, economic and social system in medieval Europe in which kings and other overlords granted land to certain of their followers in exchange for military and other services. These followers, commonly called "vassals," held various titles below that of their king (and the king himself could be the vassal of another king), one of which was "knight." The primary activity of a knight, his raison d'etre, was fighting. Knights often fought in wars and smaller military skirmishes either in the service of their own country or in that of an ally. The KNIGHT (1) who appears in the GENERAL PROLOGUE to *The CANTERBURY TALES* represents the ideal of this type of fighting man.

Knights also participated in tournaments. These were sporting events consisting of encounters, called jousts, in which knights on horseback tried to unseat each other with lances, the winner receiving a prize. In some cases, the fighting continued on foot after one of the combatants was knocked off his horse, providing he was still able to participate. The church disapproved strongly of tournaments, and casualties were often heavy, despite the protection of armor and strict rules of behavior; nevertheless, they continued to be popular into the early years of the Renaissance as training grounds for young warriors and as great spectacles in which seasoned fighting men could display their valor.

Among other things, the code of chivalry placed women on pedestals where they were to be worshipped and protected. This idea of service to women was at least partly the heritage of the French poets known as TROUBADOURS. Composing in Provençal during the 12th and early 13th centuries, in their verses these writers transferred sexual desire from the realm of degraded physical necessity to one of ennobling spirituality. When service to women became involved, the chivalric code became more complex. Knights were expected to serve ladies as well as their lords, performing deeds in their honor and often suffering great hardship (including the woman's refusal to reciprocate) on their account. The behavior that PALAMON and ARCITE exhibit toward Emily in "The KNIGHT'S TALE" is one example of this type of service, though Emily, unlike the heroines of many courtly romances, does not behave disdainfully toward either suitor.

Some scholars believe that chivalry played a crucial part in the slow but sure civilization of a military society that sprang from the rude and violent roots of tribal warfare, which constituted the heritage of European society at the beginning of the medieval period. Literature, both sacred and secular, was important not only in helping to formulate the ideas of chivalry, but also in reflecting and disseminating those ideas. Appearing on the scene at the beginning of the High Middle Ages, Chaucer's poetry would have typified this latter role. We can see the code of chivalry reflected throughout his work, from the lyric BALLADES he composed or translated early in his career, to his fullest expression of the code in the first Canterbury tale, "The Knight's Tale."

Chorus *See* CAURUS.

Christendom *Christendom* was a term of Old English origin that was used frequently in the later Middle Ages and Renaissance to designate those parts of the world where most of the inhabitants profess the Christian faith. When Chaucer uses the word in "The SECOND NUN'S TALE" of Saint CECILIA and in "The PARSON'S TALE," it indicates Christianity or the Christian faith. For example, the wicked Roman prefect ALMACHIUS threatens to condemn Cecilia and her companions to death if they will not renounce or deny their "Cristendom."

Christianity There was only one sanctioned form of Christianity in Chaucer's Europe, and that was Catholicism. From the beginning of the Middle Ages until the end of the 14th century, Christianity underwent many significant developments. Certain cardinal features, such as the belief in one God, the belief in the Trinity and the hope of salvation in a world to come, remained constant, but other elements were modified or eliminated, and different ones were substituted. The transformation began about 1050 and reached its zenith in the 13th century under the influence of such leaders at Saint Thomas Aquinas, Saint Francis of Assisi and Pope Innocent III. Some of the most significant developments were in matters of doctrine and religious attitudes. The religion of the early Middle Ages had been pessimistic, fatalistic and, theoretically at least, opposed to everything worldly. Man was considered to be inherently wicked and incapable of any good works except as the beneficiary of God's grace. God Himself was omnipotent, selecting for reasons of His own those human beings who would enter heaven, leaving the rest to follow the path to destruction. By the 13th century, quite different religious concepts had come to prevail. Life in this world was no longer held in contempt, but considered exceedingly important, not only in preparing for eternity but for its own sake as well. No longer was human nature regarded as totally depraved. Man could cooperate with God in achieving salvation. Instead of emphasizing the omnipotence of God, philosophers and theologians now stressed divine justice and mercy. The cult of the Virgin, which became popular beginning in the 12th century, further exercised a softening influence as sinners could pray to her to intercede with the Father on their behalf. (*See also* Saint BERNARD.)

The most inclusive statements of late medieval theology were contained in the *Summa theologica* of Saint Thomas Aquinas and in the pronouncements issued by church councils, especially the Fourth Lateran Council of 1215. New elements in this theology included the theory of the priesthood and the theory of the sacraments, which had never been formally codified before. It was now decided that the priest, by virtue of his ordination by a bishop and the latter's confirmation by the Pope, was the inheritor of a portion of the authority conferred by the Christ upon the apostle Peter (*see* Saint PETER).

By the end of the 12th century, the number of sacraments was fixed at seven: baptism, confirmation, penance, (*see* "The PARSON'S TALE" for complete explanation), the Eucharist, marriage, ordination and extreme unction (the last rite administered to the dying). The Catholic Church defined a sacrament as an instrument whereby divine grace was communicated to men. The sacramental theory as it came to be accepted during the last centuries of the Middle Ages included a number of separate doctrines. First, there was the doctrine that the sacraments were indispensable means of procuring God's grace, that no individual could be saved without them. Second, there was the principle that the sacraments were automatic in their effects. In other words, it was held that the efficacy of the sacraments did not depend upon the character of the priest who administered them. The priest might be a very unworthy or sinful man, but the sacraments in his hands would remain as unpolluted as if they were administered by a saint. Finally, at the Fourth Lateran Council, the doctrine of transubstantiation was made an integral part of the sacramental theory. This doctrine meant that the priest, at a given moment in the Eucharistic ceremony, actually cooperates with God in the performance of a miracle whereby the bread and wine of the sacrament are changed or transubstantiated into the body and blood of Christ.

The adoption of these two fundament theories, the theory of the priesthood and the theory of the sacraments, had potent effects in exalting the power of the clergy and in strengthening the formal elements in the Latin church. It also helped the church's systematic attempts to extend its moral authority over all of its lay members, whether of high or low degree. Two other effective methods of accomplishing this goal included excommunication and the requirement of oral confession. The effect of excommunication was to expel an individual from the church and to deprive him of all the privileges of a Christian, including salvation after death. Interestingly, despite the power of the church, some rulers did not take excommunication at all seriously. PEDRO OF CASTILE, when presented with a bull of excommunication by two of the pope's messengers, tore it in half and forced the messengers to eat it. The Fourth Lateran Council, in addition to being responsible for the doctrine of transubstantiation mentioned above, adopted the requirement that every individual member of the church must make an oral confession of his sins to a priest at least once a year, and then undergo the punishment imposed before becoming eligible to partake of the Eucharist. The result of this decree was to give the priest the authority of a moral guardian over every individual in his parish. Some parishioners escaped the potential tyranny of the system by offering their confessions to itinerant churchmen, such as Chaucer's FRIAR, who might offer them an easier penance in exchange for alms.

Ironically, as the church became more successful, it tended to become more worldly. To counteract this tendency, various reform movements were undertaken to eliminate corruption and worldliness from the church. Those involved in these efforts concentrated their attacks upon simony, which was defined as the buying and selling of church offices, any form of appointment to church office contrary to canon law and the investing of bishops and abbots with the symbols of their spiritual power by secular authorities. The sin of simony is defined and attacked as being the greatest of all sins in Chaucer's "Parson's Tale." Many of the other abuses that these reforms aimed at, such as the selling of pardons, absenteeism (when a priest left his parish to seek additional income elsewhere, often by accepting another ecclesiastical office) and defiance of the monastic rule are illustrated in *The CANTERBURY TALES* by Chaucer's portraits of the MONK, the FRIAR, the PARDONER and the SUMMONER. Chaucer depicts an ideal priest in the PARSON.

Although his writings illustrate a somewhat critical stance toward perceived abuses within the church, it is difficult to pin down Chaucer's personal attitude toward the Catholic faith. His work on the *BOECE*, as well as the strong philosophical vein that runs through *TROILUS AND CRISEYDE*, suggests that his personal faith had an intellectual edge to it, and we know from the evidence of "The Parson's Tale" that he was familiar with the writings of the church fathers, as well as with the Bible. Finally, in the famous Retraction at the end of *The Canterbury Tales*, Chaucer begs forgiveness for and revokes all his secular poetry. (*See* CHAUCER'S RETRACTION.) As the serious expression of a sober voice, this seems to manifest Chaucer's belief in an afterlife that has two options, salvation in heaven or damnation in hell.

Chrysippus *See* CRISIPPUS.

Chrysostom *See* JOHN CHRYSOSTOM, SAINT.

Cibella *See* CYBELE.

Cicero, Marcus Tullius Often referred to in English as "Tully," Marcus Tullius Cicero was a Roman statesman, lawyer, scholar and writer of the first century B.C. who tried to uphold republican principles in the final civil wars that destroyed the Roman republic. His writings include books of rhetoric, orations, philosophical and political treatises and letters. He is remembered today as the greatest Roman orator and the originator of what became known as Ciceronian rhetoric.

The son of a wealthy family, Cicero was born in 106 B.C. Educated in Rome and Greece, he quickly established a reputation as a brilliant lawyer, and in 63 B.C. he was elected consul. His oratorical powers helped to defuse the conspiracy of Cataline that same year, but some seven years later he found himself in the frustrating (for him) position of being forced to support the alliance of JULIUS CAESAR, CRASSUS and POMPEY. Unable to condone what he saw happening in Roman politics, Cicero abandoned public life in 56 B.C. He did not, however, abandon writing about politics as he saw it. Over the next few years, he completed the treatises *De oratore* ("On the Orator") and *De republica* ("On the State") and began the *De legibus* ("On Laws"). In 51 B.C. he left Rome to govern the province of Cilicia, in South Asia Minor, for one year. By the time he returned to ROME, Pompey and Caesar were each struggling for complete power. During this period Cicero continued to write, composing *De finibus bonorum et malorum* ("On the Different Conceptions of the Chief Good and Evil") and *De natura deorum* ("On the nature of Gods") and *De officiis* ("On [Moral] Duties"), among others. After Caesar's death, Cicero used his oratorical powers to try to persuade the Senate to declare war on Marc ANTONY, but in the meantime he made an enemy of Caesar's adopted son OCTAVIAN. The triumvirate of Octavian, Antony and Lepidus, formed in 43 B.C., had Cicero executed.

Cicero's writing had a considerable influence on Chaucer, who evidently knew much of his surviving work quite well. *The DREAM OF SCIPIO*, which was such an important source for some of Chaucer's dream vision poetry *(The BOOK OF THE DUCHESS, The PARLIAMENT OF FOWLS,* and *The HOUSE OF FAME)*, was the epilogue of Cicero's early work, *De republica.* It came down to Chaucer through the work of a fifth-century Latin writer, MACROBIUS, who expanded the work with an elaborate commentary. That Cicero was known and revered in the Middle Ages for his rhetorical powers is confirmed by one of Chaucer's pilgrims. The FRANKLIN, in the prologue to his tale, modestly states that the language of his performance must be "bare and plain" because he never learned to imitate Cicero's style (an exercise that was part of the "elementary" school curriculum in the type of cathedral school that Chaucer probably attended). Another of *The CANTERBURY TALES*, "The TALE OF MELIBEE," contains a generous sprinkling of quotations from a variety of Cicero's works, in particular *De officiis.* These quotations having to do with the performance of one's moral duty are employed by Dame PRUDENCE in the interest of dissuading her husband MELIBEE from taking revenge on the men who have assaulted and robbed his family.

Cilenios (Cilenius) *See* MERCURY.

Cimmerians In classical legend, the Cimmerians were a mythical people dwelling in the far west near Oceanus, the river that flowed in a circle around the edge of the world. The Cimmerians inhabited a land of mist and cloud and witnessed neither the rising nor the setting of the sun. Their land was the dwelling place of MORPHEUS, who slept in a cave near a stream that poured out from LETHE, the river of forgetfulness that flowed through Hades. The Cimmerians are mentioned in the Invocation to Morpheus that appears following the proem at the beginning of *The HOUSE OF FAME* (line 73).

Cipioun *See* SCIPIO AFRICANUS THE YOUNGER.

Cipre *See* CYPRUS.

Cipris *See* VENUS.

Circe In classical mythology, Circe was a sorceress who lived on the island of Aeaea. Upon landing on the shore of that island, Odysseus (ULYSSES) sent his men ahead to explore, and Circe transformed them into swine by giving them a magic potion to drink. One of them, however, escaped to warn Odysseus. After making himself immune to the spell by way of a root he received from Hermes (MERCURY), Odysseus went to Circe's palace, drank some of the potion without being transformed and forced the sorceress to restore the men to their natural form. Nevertheless, he became Circe's lover and remained with her for a year. The enchantments worked by Circe form part of the pictorial representations painted on the walls of Venus' temple in "The KNIGHT'S TALE." She likewise appears among other enchanters and magicians who gather in FAME's palace in *The HOUSE OF FAME.* In the BOECE, LADY PHILOSOPHY describes the transformation of Odysseus' men into different animals, pointing out that Circe's power over those men was negligible compared to the power of vice, because while Circe transformed their appearance, their hearts and minds remained human. Those who are corrupted by vice, though they look the same on the outside, are destroyed within.

Cirra In classical mythology, Cirra, like PARNASSUS and HELICON, was one of the homes of the MUSES. In the ancient world, Cirra was a town in Phocis on the Gulf of Crisa (modern Greek city of Amphissa, off the Gulf of Corinth). Chaucer mentions it in his invocation of POLYHYMNIA, the muse of song, at the beginning of the unfinished poem *ANELIDA AND ARCITE.*

Cirrea *See* CIRRA.

Cirus *See* CYRUS THE GREAT.

Cithe (Cithia) *See* SCYTHIA.

Citherea (Citheria) In classical mythology, *Citherea* is one of the names of the goddess VENUS. Chaucer uses the name three times, in "The KNIGHT'S TALE," in *The PARLIAMENT OF FOWLS* and in *TROILUS AND CRISEYDE,* and each time he speaks of or (as in the *Parliament)* to the goddess the context is complimentary. That the name *Citherea* was less familiar to a medieval audience than *Venus* is suggested by the fact that on two occasions he informs the reader that Citherea is really Venus.

Citheron (Citheroun) *See* MOUNT CITHAERON.

Civitate, De   *De Civitate* is the title Chaucer's PARSON uses to refer to Saint AUGUSTINE's influential work *The City of God*. For a description of the work, *see* the entry of Saint AUGUSTINE.

Clare, Saint (1193?–1253)   Saint Clare, a maiden of Assisi, Italy, became the first woman to embrace the life of utter poverty and unremitting austerity taught by Saint Francis, founder of the Franciscan Order. For 42 years she governed the first convent of Franciscan Sisters, insisting on the full observance of the Rule. The one favor she ever asked of the Holy See was that the convent might always remain without worldly goods of any kind. It is thus somewhat ironic that the EAGLE in Chaucer's *HOUSE OF FAME* should swear by her name as he describes FAME's palace, since that place and the people who strive to be represented there seem to be solely concerned with worldly achievements (line 1066).

Claudian   *See* CLAUDIANUS, CLAUDIUS.

Claudianus, Claudius   A Latin author of the late fourth century. An oriental Greek raised in Alexandria, Claudius Claudianus was in Rome from 395 to 404 and probably died in 408. Claudian achieved fame as a stylist and panegyrist. His unfinished poem, *De raptu Proserpinae* ("The Rape of Proserpine") was a part of the common school anthology known as the *Liber Catonianus* (which included the *Disticha Catonis; see* DIONYSUS CATO). The poem tells the story, derived from classical mythology, of how the god PLUTO abducted PROSERPINE, the daughter of CERES, the goddess of fertility and the harvest. When Ceres' grief caused the earth to become a wasteland, JUPITER ordered Pluto to restore Proserpine to her mother. Pluto agreed, but only after he had secretly given Proserpine a pomegranate seed so that, having eaten in the underworld, she would be obliged to return to him. But because the food she had eaten was so meager, she was only required to return for one third of the year; during the season that become known as winter, because of the earth's barrenness during that period. Chaucer alludes to Claudian's version of the story in the conclusion of "The MERCHANT'S TALE," where Pluto and Proserpine appear in the garden of the old knight JANUARY. The allusion appears to be included for those readers who would wish to know more about the story of Pluto and his lady. Chaucer refers to Claudian twice in an earlier poem, *The HOUSE OF FAME,* first mentioning him as an authority on the classical underworld, which was described in *De raptu Proserpinae,* and later including him as one of the poets whose statue-like forms line the approach to FAME's throne. Each of the poets lining this pathway bears on his shoulders the fame of some well-known person or event. The poet Claudian, we are

told, bears the fame of "helle," i.e., Hades, and of Pluto and Proserpine, the king and queen of that region.

Claudius (1)   The man who assists APIUS with his plot to rape VIRGINIA in "The PHYSICIAN'S TALE." Claudius falsely swears in court that Virginia is a slave belonging to him, who has been stolen by VIRGINIUS (in reality, Virginia's father). Claudius is punished for his crime by banishment from ROME.

Claudius (2)   *See* CLAUDIUS, MARCUS AURELIUS.

Claudius, Marcus Aurelius   Emperor of Rome from 268 to 270. Marcus Aurelius Claudius won the name Gothicus after his victory over the Goths at Naissus in 269 and was also known as Claudius Gothicus. Claudius Gothicus is mentioned in the brief biography of Queen ZENOBIA of PALMYRA that appears in Chaucer's "MONK'S TALE." In emphasizing Zenobia's fierce heroism, the MONK notes that both Claudius and GALLIENUS, emperor before him, anxiously treated with Zenobia to preserve the peace in the eastern portion of the empire because they did not want to meet her in battle. Because of this, she was able to expand her power into Egypt and seemed determine to make Palmyra the capital city of the Eastern Empire. She was defeated when the Emperor AURELIAN, Claudius' successor, finally captured Palmyra in 271.

Clemen, Wolfgang Herman (1909–)   Renowned German Shakespeare critic and scholar who has also contributed a book to Chaucer studies. Born in Bonn and educated at German universities and at Cambridge, serving brief stints in Great Britain and the United States, Clemen built his career at German institutions, culminating it at the University of Munich. *The Young Chaucer,* which he rewrote as *Chaucer's Early Poetry* (1964), includes chapters on *The BOOK OF THE DUCHESS, The HOUSE OF FAME* and *The PARLIAMENT OF FOWLS.* This book discourages the habit of reading Chaucer's early poetry as if its only value was as a transitional stage, a preliminary step toward *The CANTERBURY TALES.* Clemen nevertheless believes that studying the early poetry prepares us to approach Chaucer's masterpiece with a knowledge of the poet more important than either a knowledge of the stormy historical events surrounding his life, or of Chaucer's official record (which nowhere refers to him as a poet).

Clemence   In classical mythology, Clemence, or Clementia, was a Roman personification of Clemency (i.e., merciful forbearance), usually associated with emperor worship and first introduced at the time of the murder of JULIUS CAESAR. In "The KNIGHT'S TALE," the women who accost THESEUS on the way home from his war with the AMAZONS say that they have been living in the Temple of Clemence for two weeks, awaiting his arrival. Having a temple of Clemence appear in ancient Greece is of course an anachronism. Chaucer probably chose it because he had seen it mentioned in his sources and because the idea of clemency relates to what the women are seeking. Following the conflict known as the SEVEN AGAINST THEBES, CREON, the de facto ruler of Thebes, refused to allow relatives of the Greek soldiers who had been defeated to bury their dead. The women ask Theseus to intercede on their behalf and to persuade Creon to let them perform the customary funeral rites (which would be an act of clemency, since the dead were Creon's enemies). When Creon refuses, Theseus declares war on Thebes.

Cleo   *See* CLIO.

Cleopatra   Cleopatra—more specifically, Cleopatra VII—was the daughter and successor of King Ptolemy Auletes of Egypt. Cleopatra was born in 68 B.C. and died at the age of 38 when she committed suicide, according to Plutarch, by allowing herself to be bitten by an asp. Famous for her ambition and for her sexual charms, she had relationships with JULIUS CAESAR, who helped her defeat a rebellion, and after Caesar's death, with Marc ANTONY, with whom she attempted to challenge the rule of the Roman Empire in the eastern Mediterranean. Chaucer includes a brief version of Cleopatra's life in *The LEGEND OF GOOD WOMEN* (lines 580–705), in which he emphasizes her love for Antony and her despair when his fleet is defeated by OCTAVIAN. Chaucer's sympathetic treatment of her character is highly unusual for the time in which it was written. In the Middle Ages, when the civilization of Rome was considered superior to those of the Middle East and when women were routinely suspected of manipulating men for their own ends, Cleopatra became a symbol of uncontrolled sexual appetite coupled with unauthorized ambition. For this reason, some scholars feel that Chaucer's treatment of Cleopatra is ironic. It does, however, fit with the trend displayed elsewhere in the *Legend,* of ignoring the less flattering details of a woman's life in order to create a sympathetic portrait. Chaucer's story of MEDEA, whose murder of her own children goes unmentioned, is a case in point. Cleopatra is also mentioned in *The PARLIAMENT OF FOWLS* as one of Love's martyrs.

Clere Laude   In Chaucer's poem *The HOUSE OF FAME,* Clere Laude ("pure praise") is the name of a trumpet that the goddess FAME asks AEOLUS, the father of the winds, to blow whenever she decides to award one of her petitioners with good fame or reputation. The sound of this golden trumpet is described as being as loud as thunder. It reaches into every corner of the world and is accompanied by an odor of aromatic bal-

sam and roses. Fame does not base her rewards on desert, so some of those whose reputations are awarded Clere Laude have done nothing that would seem worthy of that prize. Aeolus also possesses a companion trumpet, Sklaundre ("slander"), which Fame instructs him to blow when she wishes to give someone a bad reputation. The two trumpets have counterparts in John GOWER's *Mirour de l'omme,* where they are called "Renomée" ("renown") and "Desfame" ("defamation"), but scholars are uncertain whether either author borrowed the idea from the other, or whether both got it from a common source.

Clerk, the   The portrait of the Clerk, or student, follows that of the MERCHANT in the GENERAL PROLOGUE TO *THE CANTERBURY TALES.* The two portraits contrast strikingly with one another, with the Merchant's wealth and materialism thrown into high relief by the student's poverty and devotion to enriching his mind rather than his pocketbook. He and his horse, who are both thin to the point of emaciation, provide concrete evidence of the Clerk's priorities, which lead him to spend all the money he can get on books rather than on clothing or other possessions. His threadbare cloak reminds us of those lines from the FRIAR's portrait

Artist's rendering of the Clerk of Oxford, from the Ellesmere Manuscript of The Canterbury Tales. *Although the book clutched in his hand testifies to the Clerk's preoccupation with learning, little else in this illustration corresponds to his description in the General Prologue. In particular, the man's thinness seems to have been transformed into corpulence.*

where that man is described as being "nat lyk a cloysterer / With a thredbare cope, as is a povre scoler, / But he was lyk a maister or a pope. / Of double worstede was his semycope" (lines 259–62) [not like a cloisterer with a threadbare cloak, such as that of a poor student, but he was like a master or a pope. His short cloak was of double worsted]. What we are told of the Clerk's character corresponds to his appearance. Diligently praying for the souls of those who provide him with the wherewithal to attend school, he speaks not a single word more than is necessary; when he must speak, his words are always consonant with moral virtue. The tale he tells, of the patient and virtuous GRISELDA, seems illustrative of the latter. The Clerk's field of study is logic, which was part of the basic university curriculum called the seven liberal arts. This curriculum was divided, apparently by BOETHIUS, into the trivium and the quadrivium. The former included grammar, rhetoric and logic, which were supposed to be the keys to knowledge, the subjects of the quadrivium were arithmetic, geometry, astronomy and music. The comment that this clerk has been engaged in the study of logic for a long time, in addition to the fact that he teaches, suggests that he has completed his undergraduate studies and is working toward the M.A. degree.

"Clerk's Tale, The"   The Clerk's tale of patient GRISELDA is one of several Canterbury tales that focus on the institution of marriage. The tale's themes appears to mirror the humble and serious demeanor of the narrator as he is described in the GENERAL PROLOGUE to the tales.

SUMMARY

In SALUZZO, a town of northern Italy, lives a marquis famed among his people for his good government. Under his rule, their lives are so comfortable and secure that they have only one complaint, which is that the marquise, whose name is WALTER, remains unmarried. His people fear that he may someday die, leaving them without an heir to carry on in the same benevolent tradition. Although he has never wished to marry, Walter acknowledges the cause of their concern and agrees to take a wife, on condition that he may freely choose the woman and that, whoever she may be, they promise to honor her and to treat her with the same respect that they would show to an emperor's daughter.

With these conditions met, Walter sets a date for his espousal and chooses a wife. Instead of selecting a woman from his own class, however, he decides to marry GRISELDA, the daughter of a poor peasant named JANICULA. Evidently, Walter has had his eye upon her for some time, taking note of her virtuous beauty and thinking to himself that if ever he should marry, she would be the one. When the day for the promised wedding arrives, Walter goes to the cottage where Griselda and her father live and asks Janicula for his daughter's hand in marriage. After receiving her father's consent, Walter speaks with Griselda, laying down certain conditions for the marriage, which are, in the main, that she must always do everything that he asks her to do, and that she must do it without complaining or questioning. Protesting her unworthiness to be his wife, Griselda agrees, promising upon her life never to disobey him either in thought or in deed. The two are married and Griselda proves such a kind and noble lady that the people find it hard to believe that she is Janicula's daughter. Furthermore, when Walter is absent from home, she successfully governs the land. There is no discord or ill feeling among her subjects that she is not able to apease and amend, and everything she does is for the common good of the people.

Before long, Griselda gives birth to a baby girl. Although a male would have been preferable (to serve as his father's heir), the pregnancy successfully carried to term at least suggests the likelihood that the couple will produce an heir in the future. Soon after the birth of his daughter, the marquis decides that he wants to test his wife's patience, to see if she will indeed live up to the promise she made on their wedding day. To this end, he goes one night to her chamber and, reminding her of that promise and of the poverty from which he raised her, tells her that he intends to take her daughter away. As an excuse for this deed, he lies to her, saying that the nobles he governs resent being subject to a poor man's daughter, and that they have resented it even more since her daughter was born. Therefore, to restore their faith in him, he wants to take her daughter away. He does not say what he intends to do with the child, and Griselda does not ask, though there is the suggestion that he means to have her killed. Griselda responds with complete humility: Both herself and her child are his property, for him to do with as he will, whether that be to save or "spill" (destroy).

When a man comes to take the child away, Griselda continues to behave stoically, kissing the child goodbye, giving it her blessing and asking only that if her daughter must be killed, the girl should be given a proper Christian burial. Walter does not have the child murdered, however, but secretly sends it to live with his sister, the countess of PANICO, near BOLOGNA. Meanwhile, Griselda behaves no differently than she ever has, but is always patient, kind and loving both to her husband and to his subjects, and she never mentions her daughter's name.

Four years pass, and Griselda gives birth to another child, this time a son. When the child is two years old, Walter decides to test his wife again. He has this child taken away as well. This time, the man who carries out Walter's command shows less regard for Griselda's feelings and refuses to answer when she requests that the child have a proper burial. Once again, Walter is not disappointed in Griselda's behavior. She never complains or reproaches him, nor is her demeanor toward him altered. This, the narrator reassures us, is not because Griselda does not love her children, but because she is such a steadfast wife and will not break her promise.

The people of the realm begin to speak against Walter, believing that he has murdered his own children. Nevertheless, he stubbornly persists in his scheme to test his wife.

The years pass. When his daughter has reached the age of 12, Walter secures a fake papal dispensation allowing him to annul his marriage to Griselda so that he may take another wife. Again, he gives the excuse of quelling the rancor and dissatisfaction of his people. Griselda's patience never falters; stripping herself of the clothes and jewels that Walter has given her, she asks only for a shift to hide her nakedness as she returns to her father's house—this in exchange for the dowry that cannot be returned, her maidenhood. Griselda's father receives her back into his home, fearing that she, like many another peasant girl, has simply served as a means to satisfy her lord's lust, only to be cast off when she no longer stirs his appetite. Preparations begin for Walter's new marriage. Because Griselda knows his taste and preferences better than anyone else, Walter asks her to come to the palace and make it ready for his bride. Griselda gladly submits to his will. Walter brings his 12-year-old daughter home to Saluzzo and presents her to the people and to Griselda as his new bride. When he asks Griselda what she thinks of the woman he has chosen, Griselda praises her beauty and expresses the wish that the couple may live in happiness and prosperity, but beseeches Walter not to torment his new bride. Overcome by her long-suffering humility, Walter finally decides that the testing of his wife has gone far enough. He reveals his satisfaction at her "wifely steadfastness" and takes her in his arms. Griselda is too stunned by this turn of events to understand what is going on, and when he goes on to reveal that the "bride" and her brother are actually their own two children, she faints. After she awakens, Griselda embraces her two children, giving thanks for this wonderful turn of events. Griselda is thus restored to her place as wife and mother and enjoys many good years living in prosperity with her family. Her daughter marries a worthy noble and her son succeeds her husband. The Clerk concludes his tale by marveling at Griselda's steadfast patience and remarking that the purpose of the story is not to suggest that wives ought to behave like Griselda, but to argue that every person should try to be as patient in the face of adversity. To this some manuscripts add a "lenvoy," or send-off, which speaks directly to women, exhorting them, in somewhat humorous terms, not to be humble or, worse still, put up with any abuse from their husbands.

COMMENTARY

The Clerk mentions that he has taken the tale from the work of PETRARCH, an Italian writer who was nearly contemporary with Chaucer. In fact, Petrarch's life was ending—he died in 1374—just around the time that Chaucer's literary career began. Petrarch's Latin story, *De obedientia ac fide uxoria mythologia* (A fable of wifely obedience and faithfulness) was itself a translation of the last tale in BOCCACCIO's DECAMERON. The story of Patient Griselda was a popular one during the Middle Ages. Boccaccio's version seems to be the earliest surviving written version of this form, but many key elements of the story reappear in folklore all over the world. One well-known version emphasizes the husband's wickedness even more; he is the robber bridegroom whom the brothers Grimm recorded in their collection of traditional German tales.

Although deciding which genre it belongs to has been one of the critical problems associated with "The Clerk's Tale," a number of scholars agree that it belongs most properly to the genre of the EXEMPLUM, i.e., a short tale used to illustrate a moral point, which here is the value of patience in adversity. Some have argued that the story belongs more specifically to the form of ALLEGORY, presenting, through the medium of human actors, a story of the soul's obedience to God. Walter's persistent testing and tempting of Griselda remind us of the temptations of Job in the Bible. It is also possible to read the tale from an ironic perspective, seeing it as a satirical commentary on the genre of the allegorical exemplum.

Certainly, to a modern sensibility, Walter's treatment of Griselda does seem harsh. Whether that would be the case in a society more hierarchically ordered is open to debate. According to the teachings of the church fathers, a woman was supposed to be obedient to her husband, just as the husband was supposed to be obedient to God. Saint PAUL wrote that the husband ought to be the head of a marriage just as Christ was head of the church. In practice, however, women often did not prove as malleable as Griselda, as the WIFE OF BATH demonstrates by telling us of her experience in marriage. Griselda's position is unusual in that she is married to a man to whom she owes not only the allegiance of a wife but also that of a servant, something to which both Griselda and Walter refer on those occasions when he approaches her with a "test" of her love and patience. The difference in their social status, which is further amplified by Walter's wealth compared to the poverty in which Griselda lived before her marriage, may perhaps have gone a long way toward ameliorating a medieval reader's censure of Walter's behavior. On the other hand, the Clerk himself condemns his behavior, as do the people under Walter's rule. Admittedly the people have different reasons for their condemnation, believing that Walter has murdered his own children, whereas the Clerk simply bemoans his "wicked" and self-serving behavior toward his wife.

Many readers have found Walter's behavior mysterious, even unfathomable. If he chose Griselda for her steadfastness and honesty, as he claims to have done, why does he need to test her, over and over again? The Clerk asks the same question, offering the explanation that "wedded men ne knowe no mesure," (i.e., no restraint) "when that they fynde a pacient creature" (lines 622–23). The text offers several additional clues to Walter's behavior. When he is first introduced as a man who is high born, noble, handsome, strong, young, full of honor and courtesy and discreet enough to govern his country, the last characteristic mentioned in this description suggests something of a falling off from the superlative quality of the foregoing terms. "Discreet enough" is hardly the language a poet as discriminating as Chaucer would choose to describe an excellent ruler.

A quick look at Chaucer's characterization of THE-SEUS in "The KNIGHT'S TALE" clearly illustrates this fact. The narrator goes on to describe Walter's one particular flaw, which is that he will not marry. This has become a cause of concern to the people whom he rules. They fear that he may die without an heir, and so leave them under the rule of a stranger. Thus they petition him to take a wife: "Boweth youre nekke under that blisful yok / Of soveraynetee, noght of servyse, / Which that men clepe spousaille or wedlok" (lines 113–15) [Bow your neck under that blissful yoke / Of sovereignty, not of servitude, / Which men call espousal or wedlock]. Although their language tries to paint a favorable picture of marriage, referring to it as a relationship of sovereignty, rather than a yoke of servitude, Walter sees it differently: "Ye wol . . . myn owene peple deere, / To that I nevere erst thoughte streyne me. / I me rejoysed of my liberte, / That seelde tyme is founde in mariage; / Ther I was free, I moot been in servage" (lines 143–47) [You wish . . . my own dear people, / What I never before thought to constrain myself to do. / I rejoiced in my liberty, / Which is seldom found in marriage; / Where I was free, now I must be in servitude]. The reason Walter has not married is because he does not want to lose his freedom. The very term that they attempt to disallow, "servyse," is the one he uses to epitomize his view of wedlock. Still, he agrees to their petition on one condition, that he may freely choose his bride, and that no matter whom he chooses, they will be content and treat her with due respect.

The Clerk says that Walter had been observing Griselda for some time, and that he chose her not because of her beauty (though she is beautiful), but because of her virtue, which in this case means goodness, though the hint at virginity is also appropriate. To choose a mate for such a reason is certainly praisewor-

thy, but the unfolding of the story suggests a darker motive in Walter's choice. Judged on his behavior alone, Walter is nothing more or less than a sadist. Shortly after the birth of their first child, we are told that "This markys in his herte longeth so / To tempte his wyf, hir sadnesse for to knowe, / That he ne myghte out of his herte throwe / This merveillous desir his wyf t'assaye; / Nedelees, God woot, he thoghte hire for t'affraye" (lines 451–55) [This marquis in his heart so desires / To tempt his wife, in order to know her steadfastness, / That he was unable to dispel from his heart / This wondrous desire to test his wife; / Unnecessarily, God knows, he intended to frighten her]. Although "sadness" in Middle English actually means "seriousness" or "steadfastness," the rest of this passage is quite damning, revealing Walter's obsession with frightening his wife for no apparent reason, other than the pleasure it gives him, which the text specifically refers to. After telling her that he means to take away her son, we are told that "forth he goth with drery [dreary] contenance, / But to his herte it was ful greet plesance [delight]" to see his wife "in pacience suffre al this array [treatment]" (lines 671–72, 670). To hide his cruelty from Griselda, he tells her that the people he governs resent her poor birth, which the reader knows to be a lie. Furthermore, each successive "test" is performed in a more abusive manner than the one before. When the sergeant acting on Walter's behalf comes to take away her son, he treats Griselda less sympathetically than when he took her daughter, brusquely refusing to answer her pleas to give the child's body a proper burial. And when Walter reveals his plan to annul his marriage to Griselda so that he can remarry someone of higher birth, he does so "in open audience," ruthlessly shaming her in public. Finally, he heartlessly requests that she return to the palace wearing her poor rags, to prepare it for the reception of his new wife. In the previous instances of his cruelty, Walter at least had an unselfish-seeming excuse, even if it was a lie; but in this, his motives are openly self-centered. He asks Griselda to decorate the castle and prepare for the banquet because she knows how he likes things done.

So what of Griselda's goodness and virtue? Can it possibly constitute virtue to sanction the behavior of a man like Walter? While it is true that he remains innocent of the darkest crime of which Griselda has reason to suspect him—that of murdering their children—he is extraordinarily guilty of the sin of pride, which in the period when Chaucer was writing ranked among the deadliest of the Seven Deadly Sins. And as far as she knows, he does order the children murdered. By accepting his will in such circumstances, Griselda becomes to a certain extent the accomplice of evil, even though the sin she commits is one of omission rather than commission. The Christian thing to do, in the Middle Ages as now, would be to protect the lives of her children, even if that meant that she must defy her husband.

All of these things work together to complicate any allegorical reading of the text, although it still seems possible to read it as an exemplum illustrating the value of perseverance in the face of evil-appearing circumstances. On top of this, or woven into the exemplary fabric of the tale, is what appears to be a strand of social commentary, offering a mildly satirical view of the respect accorded the nobility for no other reason than an accident of birth. Were it not for his position at birth, Walter would no doubt not possess the merit to achieve the respect he inherits along with his title; Griselda illustrates the opposite side of this coin. She makes such a marvelous lady that the people of Saluzzo cannot believe she is really the daughter of poor Janicula. In this way, "The Clerk's Tale" provides a concrete example of that dictum expressed by the loathly lady in "The WIFE OF BATH'S TALE," when she tells the recreant knight that true nobility is dependent on virtuous living rather than on status and wealth.

Ultimately, however, any reading of this text is going to depend, like any reading of any other text, on what the reader brings to the text in the way of his or her own intellectual, emotional and ideological baggage. That is why a feminist reader is likely to see the tale as sadistic male fantasy; why a reader coming to it from a traditional patriarchal point of view, like Harry BAILLY, can read it as an exemplum offering a passive and silent woman as the ideal model of womanly behavior; and why the Clerk himself, who sees the absurdity in Griselda's situation, feels the need to conclude his telling with an envoy that undermines the latter reading.

Clio In classical mythology, Clio was the muse of history. Clio and her sisters were goddesses who presided over the arts and sciences. Originally they were three in number, the so-called older muses, bearing the names Melete (meditation), Mneme (memory) and Aoide (song). Later their number grew to nine, and their names were Clio, Euterpe (muse of lyric poetry), Thalia (muse of comedy and pastoral poetry), Melpomene (muse of tragedy), Terpsichore (muse of dancing), Erato (muse of erotic poetry), POLYHYMNIA (muse of sacred song), CALLIOPE (muse of epic poetry) and URANIA (muse of astronomy). Their role was to assist humans in various creative acts and they are frequently invoked for that purpose in classical literature. Chaucer imitates that convention when the stories he tells, such as that of TROILUS and CRISEYDE, are drawn from the classical period. In the opening lines of *TROILUS AND CRISEYDE*, book two, he follows the example of the Latin author STATIUS in invoking the muse of history to assist him with this portion of the story in which the courtship of TROILUS and CRISEYDE begins.

Clitermystra *See* CLYTEMNESTRA.

Clytemnestra In classical mythology, Clytemnestra, or Clytaemnestra, was the wife of AGAMEMNON, with whom she had four children, including a daughter, Iphigenia. When the Greeks banded together to attack TROY following the abduction of King MENELAUS' wife, Helen (HELEN OF TROY), Agamemnon demanded that Clytemnestra bring Iphigenia to Aulis, where the Greek fleet had assembled but was unable to sail because they lacked a good wind. She obeyed, not knowing that her husband planned to sacrifice the girl to appease Artemis (DIANA) who had caused the wind to fail when a member of the Greek forces killed a stag sacred to her. During Agamemnon's absence, Clytemnestra became the mistress of his cousin Aegisthus, and when Agamemnon returned after the conclusion of the TROJAN WAR, she and her lover killed him. The story of Clytemnestra is one of the stories of evil women to which the WIFE OF BATH's fifth husband forces her to listen, until things come to a crisis and she forces him to burn his "book of wicked wives."

Coitu, De A treatise on sexual intercourse written by an 11th-century monk of Monte Cassino named Constantinus Africanus, or CONSTANTINE THE AFRICAN, who was considered one of the fathers of Western medicine. Chaucer mentions the book in "The MERCHANT'S TALE" as a possible source for one of the "letuaries" (medicinal mixtures) taken by the aged JANUARY on his wedding night to improve his sexual performance and enjoyment. The treatise was known to contain recipes for aphrodisiacs (line 1811).

Colatyn *See* COLLATINUS, LUCIUS TARQUINUS.

Colchis An ancient city in Asia Minor, at the eastern end of the Black Sea and just south of the Caucasus, to which JASON sailed to obtain the Golden Fleece. The city is mentioned in the version of Jason's adventures that appears in Chaucer's *LEGEND OF GOOD WOMEN*, under the double biography of Jason's two wives, HYPSIPYLE and MEDEA. Hypsipyle he married and abandoned on his way to Colchis; Medea was the daughter of the king of Colchis who used sorcery to help him secure the Fleece and then ran away with him.

Colcos *See* COLCHIS.

Collatinus, Lucius Tarquinus The cousin of TARQUINUS SEXTUS and the husband of LUCRECE, the virtuous Roman whose rape and martyrdom is described in Chaucer's *LEGEND OF GOOD WOMEN*. Collatinus sows the seeds of his wife's tragedy when he brags to Tarquin about her exceptional character, and then takes his cousin with him to spy on her as she laments her husband's absence. The two men are supposed to be employed at the siege of ARDEA, the capitol of the RUTULI tribe in Latium (modern Italy), but when there was a lull in the fighting, the men began talking about their wives to pass the time. This led to the fatal visit.

Colle (1) One of the dogs owned by the poor widow in "The NUN'S PRIEST'S TALE." It and two others join in the chase after RUSSELL, the sly fox who has seized the widow's rooster, CHAUNTICLEER.

Colle (2) "Colle tregetour" is mentioned as one of a group of magicians who appear in FAME's palace in Chaucer's early poem *The HOUSE OF FAME,* where he is described performing a trick whereby he made a windmill disappear underneath a walnut shell (line 1277). Although his identity remains uncertain, it has been suggested that he was an English necromancer named Colin T. who appears in a French manual of conversation composed around 1396. Since "Colle" was a variant of Colin, and "tregetour" means illusionist or sleight-of-hand artist, the hypothesis is not an unreasonable one.

Cologne German city on the Rhine River. It is mentioned in the GENERAL PROLOGUE to *The CANTERBURY TALES* as one of the pilgrimage sites visited by the WIFE OF BATH on her previous travels. At Cologne pilgrims visited the shrines of the three Magi (Wise Men), of Saint Ursula and of the Eleven Thousand Virgins said to have been massacred there.

Coloigne *See* COLOGNE.

Colossenses *See* COLOSSIANS.

Colossians In the portion of "The PARSON'S TALE" (actually a sermon) dealing with the sin of chiding (i.e., reproach), Chaucer paraphrases the words of Saint PAUL taken from his Epistle to the Colossians, chapter three: "O ye wommen, be ye subgetes to youre housbondes as bihoveth in God, and ye men loveth youre wyves" [Oh you women, be submissive to your husbands as God commanded, and you men, love your wives]. The discussion of chiding appears within a larger discussion of anger, which is one of the Seven Deadly Sins anatomized by the PARSON in his sermon of penitence.

Common Profit Common Profit is an idea that Chaucer derived from the *DREAM OF SCIPIO,* a fragment of CICERO's *Republic* that was translated with an extended commentary by the Latin writer Macrobius. In Cicero's work, the idea is defined as "all those who have preserved, aided or enlarged their country," but in Chaucer it has the more general meaning that every-

one should work together for the good of all mankind. In the climactic scene of the *Dream of Scipio,* young Scipio is taken by his grandfather high up into the heavens to observe the earth and to receive philosophical instruction on how best to live his life, which includes an exhortation to pursue Common Profit. Those who do not are doomed after death to whirl about earth in pain for many ages before they are forgiven. A good portion of the *Dream* is summarized in Chaucer's *PARLIAMENT OF FOWLS* and strongly influenced the concluding stanzas of *TROILUS AND CRISEYDE,* where TROILUS realizes the vanity of living in pursuit of wordly delights. The idea of common profit likewise informs "The CLERK'S TALE" and "The PARSON'S TALE," and the phrase also appeared in contemporary parliamentary proceedings.

"Complaint of Chaucer to His Purse, The" A short begging poem written in the French BALLADE form, with three stanzas of seven lines each (the most common ballade stanza was eight lines, but there were variations); a rhyme scheme of *ababbcc* with the same three rhymes repeated in all three stanzas; and a concluding envoy. It is testimony to Chaucer's poetic genius that he was able to execute the rhyme scheme of the ballade form without ever repeating a word, except in the one line refrain, "Beth hevy agen, or elles moot I dye" [Be heavy again, or else must I die], which formed the concluding line of each stanza. Typically, "complaint" poems feature a narrator describing his sad mood and appealing to some beloved lady to provide relief from his distress. In this poem, Chaucer appears to be playing off the conventions of the form, addressing his purse as if she were a beloved lady, but asking her to display some "heavy cheer" ("expression" and, by extension, "appearance" which would indicate that she had been replenished with coins) rather than the "light cheer" ordinarily requested by such plaintiffs. Another traditional image that he puns on is that of the yellow-haired beloved, when he asks that, before another day goes by, he may see "your colour lyk the sonne bryght / That of yelownesse hadde never pere" [your color like the bright sun / Whose yellowness is beyond compare]. The concluding envoy stanza, though it only appears in five of the 11 surviving manuscripts of the poem, is the strongest evidence we have for assigning the poem a date. It directs the narrator's complaint to the king ("conqueror" of Brutus' ALBION), and most likely represents Chaucer's efforts to have the annual pension that had been awarded to him by King RICHARD II renewed by Richard's successor, HENRY IV. If this is true, it must have been written sometime between September 30, 1399, when Henry was accepted as king, and February 16, 1400, when a document antedated to the day of Henry's coronation the previous year renewed the original annuity and increased it by an additional 40 marks.

Since Chaucer died later the same year, this could be the last poem that he wrote.

"Complaint of Mars, The" Poem that uniquely blends astronomy, mythology and human love. The actual movements of the planets Mars and Venus in the sky provide a metaphor for the progress of the relationship between god and goddess as it appears in classical myth.

SUMMARY

"The Complaint of Mars" is divided into three parts: an introductory "Proem," spoken by a bird on St. Valentine's Day; a "Story," told by the same narrator, which concerns the love of VENUS and MARS (1), and a "Complaint," spoken by Mars after he has been separated from his mistress.

The "Proem" sets the scene for a love poem with the bird narrator inviting his companions to join him in rejoicing to greet the rising sun on Valentine's Day, while simultaneously acknowledging that lovers who do not want to be discovered together will need to flee lest they be victims of gossip's wicked tongue. Yet they may at least take comfort in the knowledge that darkness will fall again. The bird goes on to say that in honor of Saint Valentine's Day he intended to sing the complaint that woeful Mars made upon departing from Venus on the morning that Phoebus (i.e., the Sun) discovered them with his fiery torches.

The "Story" briefly relates how Mars and Venus became lovers, translating the action of the mythological story into astronomical terms. The two planets move closer and closer to one another in the skies until they come into conjunction in the zodiacal sign of TAURUS, signified by the white bulls painted on the bed chamber where the two consummate their love. The sun, Phoebus APOLLO, is also moving toward Taurus, threatening to reveal their affair. Because Venus moves more rapidly through her orbit than Mars, Venus escapes to the next zodiacal sign, MERCURY (1). Slow-moving Mars is left behind, where he prepares to be overtaken and perhaps burned up by the fires of the sun. Although Mars dons his armor to prepare for the confrontation, his sorrow over being separated from Venus is so great that he can scarcely endure.

In contrast to the rest of the poem, the third part, the "Complaint" of Mars, is fairly conventional. It describes the sorrow suffered by the speaker, the excellence of his lady, and his greater sorrow that she may suffer without his being able to comfort her; it then questions the reason and motives of a god who constrains people to fall in love but denies them the means to satisfy their passion. Only in the final stanzas, in which he calls upon knights, whose patron he is, to have compassion on him, do we get a sense of the speaker's individuality.

The Complaint concludes with the request that all those who are in love remember and do some kind deed for Venus in this time of affliction.

COMMENTARY

The most interesting feature of Chaucer's "Complaint of Mars" is the way the "Story" portion of the poem combines astronomy and mythology into a relatively seamless whole so that the planets Venus and Mars become synonymous with the god and goddess. Their movements across the heavens provide a concrete physical correlative to the story of their love affair as it is recorded in OVID and elsewhere, although traditionally it was Venus' husband, VULCAN, and not Apollo, who discovered the lovers together. Chaucer's substitution doubtless arose from his desire to have the story reflect actual astronomical events for the year 1385. Incidentally, these events constitute the best evidence for providing the poem with a date of composition, although it is possible that the "Complaint" portion may have been composed at an earlier date and tacked on. Given the references to St. Valentine's Day in the beginning of the poem, some scholars believe that it, like The PARLIAMENT OF FOWLS, was an occasional poem composed for a St. Valentine's Day celebration. A few scholars have argued, based on some notes made by the manuscript copyist John SHIRLEY, that the poem symbolically represents a court scandal, hinting at a love affair between John Holland, Lord Huntingdon, and Isabella, duchess of York (the daughter of JOHN OF GAUNT). The dynamics of the poem's plot have caused some readers to point out similarities to *TROILUS AND CRISEYDE*. Like TROILUS, Mars is left behind, abandoned by a fearful woman who immediately throws herself into the arms of another lover (CRISEYDE takes DIOMEDE, Venus is received by Mercury). Both sets of lovers also seem to be caught in situations beyond their control, which raises the Boethian question of fate versus free will. "The Complaint of Mars" survives in eight manuscripts and in the early editions of Julian Notary (1499–1501) and William Thynne (1532).

Complaint of Nature, The *See* ALAIN DE LILLE.

"Complaint of Venus, The" One of the short poems attributed to Chaucer in the manuscripts. In a number of the manuscripts it follows "The COMPLAINT OF MARS," which it could be seen as responding to, although it does not specifically address the situation (the enforced separation of the planets Venus and Mars by their movements in their individual orbits) that forms the theme of that poem, nor does it allude in any way to the myths concerning the love affair of the Greek god and goddess.

SUMMARY AND COMMENTARY

"The Complaint of Venus" survives in eight manuscripts and two early printed editions. While "The Complaint of Mars" appears to be an original work, that of Venus is a translation/adaptation of three BALLADES by the French poet Oton de GRANDSON. The most significant change Chaucer made in adapting Grandson's work was to change the gender of the speaker from male to female.

The three ballades narrated by this female voice each develop a different idea, although the theme of love and the problem of jealousy help to bind the three parts together. Part One essentially praises the beloved's worthiness, the excellence that extends to every part of his being and causes him to be honored by all men. Part Two describes in great detail and with considerable emotion the misery inflicted by jealousy and how it robs the lover of any glad feeling. Part Three contrasts to Part Two by opening on a much calmer note as the narrator promises that, despite the torments of jealousy, she never wishes to be set free from love's snare. The last stanza then recalls the beloved's worthiness, reinforcing her decision to remain true and bringing the theme of the poem full circle. The poem concludes with an envoy, a conventionalized stanza of the ballade form which was typically addressed to a prince, patron or person of other importance. The speaker of the envoy is the poet rather than the narrator, and in this one Chaucer directs his comments rather nonspecifically to the plural "Princes," requesting that the work be given a favorable reception despite its imperfections, which he attributes to two things: his own age, which has dulled his spirits, and the difficulty of finding rhymes in English. (French was a far more suitable language for the composition of ballades because of its plenitude of similar-sounding inflectional endings.) Despite these difficulties, Chaucer succeeded admirably, strictly maintaining the same rhymes throughout each ballade and carrying one rhyme (on *-aunce*) through all three ballades and into the envoy itself. The purpose of the envoy could in fact be to call attention to the virtuosity of his performance.

The date of Chaucer's "Complaint of Venus" is, as with most of the other short poems, uncertain. In attempting to determine the approximate time of its composition, scholars have suggested that it probably followed shortly after that of "The Complaint of Mars," which was likely to have been written in 1385 or shortly thereafter. F. N. ROBINSON assigns it a later date based on the envoy's comment about the poet's age. A few scholars have argued, based on some notes made by the manuscript copyist John SHIRLEY, that the complaints of VENUS and MARS symbolically represent a court scandal, hinting at a love affair between John Holland, Lord Huntingdon, and Isabella, duchess of York (the daughter of JOHN OF GAUNT), but no historical evidence exists to corroborate this theory.

"Complaint to His Lady, A"   "A Complaint to His Lady" is actually a series of four fragments, or perhaps drafts, on the same theme—that of a lover who has served his lady for a long time without satisfaction or reward. As a result of that service, the lover suffers sleepless nights and ill health. In fragments one and two, the narrator describes his situation to an audience that may be described as a sympathetic but uninvolved third party. The third fragment is a description of the beloved's qualities in allegorical terms such as Beauty, Bounty (Generosity) and Sadness (Constancy), whereby the lover attempts to justify his devotion. The fourth and longest fragment is addressed directly to the lady. Here the lover argues the strength of his devotion, puzzling over the fact that the greater his love for her, the less attracted she is to him. This section closes with a final plea for some drop of pity to save his troubled heart from losing all hope. Considering the poem's fragmentary nature and thoroughly conventional language and sentiment, it is of little interest to most readers except, perhaps, as an experiment in versification. The first two fragments are written in RHYME ROYAL, the seven-line iambic pentameter stanza that Chaucer was to use for most of his major works. The third is in terza rima, a three-line stanza form with the rhyme scheme *aba bcb cdc*, etc., invented by the Italian poet DANTE ALIGHIERI. It represents the first known appearance of this Dantean verse form in English. The fourth fragment consists of nine stanzas and is the least polished of them all; the second of its nine stanzas has fewer lines and a different rhyme scheme than the rest. The poem survives in two manuscripts and in Stowe's 1561 edition of Chaucer's work. In one manuscript the poem is entitled "The Ballad of Pity" and treated as a continuation of "The COMPLAINT UNTO PITY." Although there is no concrete evidence by which to assign the poem a date of composition, the terza rima stanzas argue for placing it sometime after Chaucer's first trip to Italy in 1373, though it is possible that he knew Dante's work before visiting that country. The poem also bears certain similarities of language and sentiment to the unfinished ANELIDA AND ARCITE, whose nine-line stanza closely resembles the stanza used in fragment four of the "Complaint."

"Complaint Unto Pity, The"   One of the short poems attributed to Chaucer in the manuscripts, "The Complaint Unto Pity" is an allegorical lover's lament (see ALLEGORY). Like ANELIDA AND ARCITE, it is divided into a narrative plus a complaint. The narrative portion, which consists of eight stanzas, describes the lover's situation: how he has for a long time been in search of the allegorical figure of Pity so that he might tell her about his suffering in the service of Love. Finding Pity dead and buried "in a heart," surrounded by Beauty, Pleasure, Youth, Honesty and other allegorical figures associated with Love, he announces that his own hopes are dead as well. Nevertheless, he reveals the content of the "complaint" that he had written as a petition asking for Pity's help. This petition forms the second half (nine stanzas) of the poem. The complaint opens with words of praise directed to Pity and goes on to describe the deadly harm suffered by the narrator. As the poem develops, he explains that Cruelty, Pity's opposite, is responsible for his woe. So that men will not recognize her for who she is, Cruelty hides behind the mask of Beauty. Without the addition of Pity, the beloved's other qualities, such as Generosity, Gentleness and Courtesy, are meaningless. Furthermore, if Pity allows this state of affairs to continue, her renown will be quickly destroyed. For these reasons, the narrator says, she should have mercy upon him and come to his aid. The poem closes on a note of despair, with the narrator apparently giving up all hope that Pity will ever respond to his request; yet he vows that he will remain faithful anyway, weeping and mourning Pity's death with a sore heart.

"The Complaint Unto Pity" survives in nine manuscripts and was also printed in William Thynne's 1532 edition of Chaucer. Its use of allegory resembles that of the French ROMAN DE LA ROSE, of which Chaucer made a partial translation (*see* ROMAUNT OF THE ROSE). As with the other short poems, the date of composition is uncertain. Many scholars believe that it was written early in Chaucer's career because it is derivative (though no exact source has been found), displaying little of the innovation which was to characterize the poetry of Chaucer's mature period. His use of the RHYME ROYAL stanza, which became the stanza form for most of Chaucer's major works, suggests the alternative possibility of later composition (after The BOOK OF THE DUCHESS and The HOUSE OF FAME). Although it is not considered an important work of Chaucer's, "The Complaint Unto Pity" is well worth reading because it provides a glimpse of Chaucer doing what he so often and so comically elsewhere accuses himself of doing: writing love poetry. The situation of the narrator in the "Complaint" corresponds exactly to the persona of the unsuccessful love poet portrayed in *The Book of the Duchess, The House of Fame* and *The PARLIAMENT OF FOWLS*. Within these three poems, it is Chaucer's lack of success in the game of love that leads to the experience that provides the source for the poem.

"Complaynt d'Amours" The "Complaynt d'Amours," or "Love Complaint," is one of the short poems not attributed to Chaucer in the manuscripts but which W. W. SKEAT concluded was authentic because of its many echoes of Chaucer's language, its RHYME ROYAL rhyme scheme, and its appearance in manuscripts that do contain genuine pieces. The closing stanza furthermore states that the poem was written for the occasion of Saint Valentine's Day, when all the birds gather to choose their mates—an obvious reference to the situation Chaucer created in the plot of *The PARLIAMENT OF FOWLS*. In keeping with the conventions of the love complaints, this 13-stanza poem features a lovesick first-person narrator describing the suffering he endures as a result of unrequited love, suffering that is so extreme it will soon, he claims, bring about his death. It is addressed to the lady who causes his pain, although at one point he admits that by loving her against her will, he actually brings his grief upon himself. She, as is typical of the women to whom such poems are addressed, takes pleasure in his despair, responding to his lovelorn sighs with laughter. So although she is the epitome of beauty and goodness, she lacks the desirable quality of pity. In spite of that, the narrator vows that he will love her until death and asks that she accept this love complaint that he has written for her on the occasion of Saint Valentine's Day.

Concordances to Chaucer In 1991, a new computer-generated concordance entitled *A Complete Concordance to the Works of Geoffrey Chaucer* appeared, superseding the manually produced concordance of TATLOCK and Kennedy originally published in 1927. Edited by Akio Oizumi of Doshisha University in Kyoto, Japan, and programmed by Kunihiro Miki of Osaka University, this 10-volume reference work will be most useful to medieval scholars and linguists, including historians of the language. The basis for the concordance is *The RIVERSIDE CHAUCER*, now widely recognized as the standard scholarly edition of Chaucer. Each volume of the concordance contains a word index, a ranking word-frequency list and a reverse-word list. The concordance gives all occurrences of every word in the text, including "high-frequency" words.

Confessio Amantis The *Confessio Amantis* ("Lover's Confession") by John GOWER is a poem of some 33,000 octosyllabic lines featuring a series of 140 short narratives on the theme of love. These narratives are contained by a frame story, which features a lover (Amans) being instructed by Genius, the priest of VENUS. The exemplary stories, which are derived from classical literature, are organized under the headings of the Seven Deadly Sins and are the primary means by which Genius tutors his pupil. There are eight books, one for each of the sins plus one that gives an encyclopedic account of philosophy and morals. At the end, when the lover has been completely shriven of his sins and has a firm grasp of the ethics of love, his confessor announces that he is now too old for love and vanishes. After pondering Genius' abrupt departure, the poet realizes the truth in what he has been told and returns home. One of the unusual (for the time) features of this work, which has a parallel in Chaucer's poetry, is its extremely sympathetic attitude toward women, especially women who, according to the traditional legends about them, acted in ways that can only be interpreted as rebellion against male-domination. Gower's portrayal of MEDEA is one example. Several of the tales Gower tells correspond to stories in *The CANTERBURY TALES*. The story of Florent, for example, is very similar to "The WIFE OF BATH'S TALE"; that of Constance parallels "The MAN OF LAW'S TALE"; and Phebus and Cornide relates the same events as "The MANCIPLE'S TALE." Similarly, the story of PYRAMUS and THISBE is featured in Chaucer's *LEGEND OF GOOD WOMEN*, and the tale of CEYX and ALCYONE appears in *The BOOK OF THE DUCHESS*. It should be noted, however, that despite these correspondences between the two authors' work, there is little evidence that either of them used the other as a source. This has not prevented scholars from comparing the two, usually to Gower's disadvantage, despite the fact that the most accomplished stories in the *Confessio,* such as that of CANACEE (2) and Machaire, have no parallel in Chaucer's work.

Conigastus (Connigaste) Conigastus is a man mentioned in Book One of the *BOECE,* where the narrator (BOETHIUS) explains the reasons for his exile to LADY PHILOSOPHY. He refers to Conigastus as a powerful man who continually cheated and took property from the poor, who were unable to protect themselves from him. By defending the poor, Boethius says, he attracted the wrath of Conigastus and other powerful but unscrupulous men. Although a passing reference in CASSIODORUS confirms that Conigastus was an actual historical figure, nothing more is known about him.

Consolacione, Boece de *Boece de Consolacione* is the title by which Chaucer refers to his translation of BOETHIUS' *Consolation of Philosophy* in the Retraction that appears at the end of *The CANTERBURY TALES* (*see* CHAUCER'S RETRACTION). In modern editions of Chaucer's work, it is usually referred to simply as *BOECE*.

Constable of Northumberland A minor character in "The MAN OF LAW'S TALE." He finds CONSTANCE, whose ship has run aground on the sand in NORTHUMBERLAND, where this character is constable to ALLA, the Saxon king of that realm. The constable and his wife, HERMENGILD, take Constance into their home and eventually are both converted to Christianity by her. Because of his affection for her, the constable suffers greatly when he receives a message from Alla (actually forged by his mother, DONEGILD), commanding him to

cast Constance and her newborn baby out to sea in a rudderless ship.

Constance The heroine of "The MAN OF LAW'S TALE" and, like GRISELDA of "The CLERK'S TALE," one whose story may be read as an EXEMPLUM directing readers to believe that if their faith in God remains strong, things will eventually turn out all right even if they must meanwhile suffer tremendous hardship and deprivation. The daughter of the emperor of Rome, Constance is born in fortunate circumstances. A beautiful and virtuous young woman, she attracts the attentions of the pagan sultan of Syria, and her father marries her off to him, in the interests of forming a political alliance. In order to win her father's approval, the sultan was required to convert to Christianity, an act that enrages his mother, who promptly initiates an uprising against him. The sultan and Constance's Christian retainers are massacred, and Constance is cast adrift on the sea in a rudderless ship. After three years, she comes ashore in the north of England, where she endures more trials and tribulations. First she is falsely accused of murder. Then, after her innocence has been proven and she has married the king of the region, she again becomes the victim of her mother-in-law's wrath, which culminates in her once again being cast adrift upon the sea. Ultimately Constance's patient forbearance—her "constancy"—pays off and she is reunited with both her husband and her father. However, her husband only lives one year following their reunion, and the story concludes with her return to her father's house, where she lives happily and virtuously until her death. The fact that the story does not end until she is reunited with her father has been viewed as evidence for interpreting the story as an allegory representing the soul's journey away from and return to God the Father after a lifetime of tribulation. Chaucer's tale of Constance is based on a story in Nicholas TRIVET's *Anglo-Norman Chronicle,* a supposed history extending from the biblical Creation to 1285. John GOWER also tells the story in his *CONFESSIO AMANTIS.*

Constantine the African Constantine the African, referred to simply (and confusingly) as "Constantyn" by Chaucer, was a merchant, physician and scholar of the 11th century. Born in North Africa, he traveled widely in the Middle East as a merchant, and later became a monk, focusing his studies on medicine and philosophy. Constantine spent his last year at the monastery of Monte Cassino in Salerno, Italy, where he translated a number of Arabic works into Latin. The medical works that he translated gave western Europe its first general view of Greek medicine and helped to establish Salerno's reputation as a medical center. Constantine is mentioned in Chaucer's GENERAL PROLOGUE TO *THE CANTERBURY TALES* as one of the medical authorities whose teachings the DOCTOR OF PHISIC had studied. His work *De Coitu* (On coitus) is mentioned in "The MERCHANT'S TALE" as a source of recipes for the aphrodisiacs that the aged JANUARY has concocted, hoping to make his wedding night a memorable occasion.

Constantyn *See* CONSTANTINE THE AFRICAN.

continuatio A literary term derived from classical rhetoric. It denotes the pithy expression of a thought. Chaucer often combines continuatio with another rhetorical figure called OCCUPATIO, which denotes a condensing of the action. Here is an example from "The KNIGHT'S TALE." Following their glimpse of the lovely EMILY in the garden of THESEUS' palace, the two prisoner knights PALAMON and ARCITE (1) both vow to worship her for the rest of their lives. An argument breaks out between them over who has the most right to love her,

Artist's rendering of the Cook, from the Ellesmere Manuscript of The Canterbury Tales. *The Cook waves a meat hook in his left hand as a sign of his profession, in the other hand, he appears to carry his hat. Some observers believe that the square patch on his leg is a bandage covering the "mormal" mentioned in the description of him found in the General Prologue to* The Canterbury Tales.

which Chaucer concludes by saying, "Greet was the strif and long bitwix hem tweye, / If that I hadde leyser for to seye; / But to th'effect" (lines 1187–89) [Great was the strife, and long, between the two of them, / If I had the leisure to describe it; / But to the points].

Cook, the The Cook is one of the shortest of the detailed portraits in the GENERAL PROLOGUE TO *THE CANTERBURY TALES*. He is the only pilgrim who has been chosen to accompany the group to provide a specific service, and most of the lines describing him provide us with examples of his expertise in food preparation. The type of fare that is mentioned—stews, pies and ale—recalls what ordinarily would have been served in a tavern or an inn, though further information contained in the Cook's prologue indicates that he owns a shop out of which he sells his wares. The Cook's portrait in the General Prologue is fairly straightforward with the exception of one shocking, though understated, detail—the "mormal," or ulcer, on his shin. The narrator's insertion of this detail in the midst of describing the types of food the Cook can prepare is, to say the least, somewhat unappetizing. In addition, we later learn, through Harry BAILLY's remarks in the Cook's prologue, that the man is not above serving spoiled food in order to save money, thereby endangering the health of his clientele. Perhaps the ulcer on his shin is a symbolic reflection of this vice. The name that the Cook gives for himself in his prologue, "Hogge of Ware," and the fact that the Host addresses him as "Roger," have led some scholars to search for a real-life counterpart to the man, and several plausible candidates have been located. "The COOK'S TALE," concerning a riotous cook's apprentice named PERKIN REVELER is broken off after only 57 lines. It is long enough to show that it was likely to have belonged to the same genre (the FABLIAU) as the MILLER's and the REEVE's tales, but not long enough to reveal exactly what the plot may have been. A comment in the HENGWRT MANUSCRIPT suggests that Chaucer simply never finished the tale.

"Cook's Prologue and Tale, The" The Cook's unfinished tale follows that of the REEVE in the order established by ELLESMERE MANUSCRIPT.

SUMMARY

After responding gleefully to the REEVE's satirization of the MILLER in the previous tale, the COOK, Roger Hogge of WARE, offers to tell one of his own. Unlike the two previous tales, "The Cook's Tale" is not offered in requital to another story or to a perceived slight. However, when the Host, Harry Bailly, criticizes the manner in which Roger runs his business, selling pasties that have been warmed over many times and food that has been contaminated by flies, Roger promises that later in the tale-telling game he will deliver a story of a "hostileer" or innkeeper, to requite Harry for his remarks.

"The Cook's Tale" is the story of an apprentice cook named PERKYN REVELOUR, whose last name provides an apt representation of his behavior. The description of this young man at the beginning of the tale recalls the language used to describe the principals in "The MILLER'S TALE." He is merry as a goldfinch, brown as a berry and keeps his black locks of hair elegantly combed. He is as full of love as the hive is of honey, and takes advantage of every available opportunity, such as weddings and public festivals, to sing and dance. After this initial description, the portrait darkens as the narrator reveals Perkyn's fondness for drinking in the local tavern and gambling with dice. To support both of these habits, he steals from his master, the cook to whom he is apprenticed. For a time, the master attempts to reform the errant young man with rebukes, but even the occasional trip to NEWGATE Gaol (jail), the famous London debtors' prison, has no apparent effect upon his character. At last the master decides that it would be less costly to release the young man from his apprenticeship than to continue putting up with his behavior and risk the possibility that he will corrupt the master's other apprentices and servants. After losing his position at the cookshop, Perkyn Revelour moves in with another young rake whose habits are similar to his own, and whose wife, for the sake of appearances, runs a shop, although she maintains her livelihood by working as a prostitute. At this point the tale simply ends without any apparent resolution. It appears unclear, from what follows, whether or not it was interrupted or broken off.

COMMENTARY

At its beginning, "The Cook's Tale" appears to follow in the tradition of the two tales that come before, "The Miller's Tale" and "The REEVE'S TALE," both of which are FABLIAUX. Just as the comedy of "The Reeve's Tale" contrasts to the good-humored merriment of "The Miller's Tale" by providing a darker, more cynical view of human nature and human behavior, so does "The Cook's Tale" take that darkness and cynicism one step further. It is as if we see characters like SIMKIN the miller and NICHOLAS the clerk engaging in lying and cheating behavior that, abstracted from the background of comedy and the veneer of humanism provided by the artistry of the former tales, reveals the meanness and squalor of their motives.

"The Cook's Tale" is too short and undeveloped to trace its possible source. A number of theories have been advanced to account for the brevity of the tale and its abrupt ending. The HENGWRT MANUSCRIPT leaves the rest of the page blank except for a scribal note saying, "Of this cokes tale maked Chaucer na moore" [Of this cook's tale made Chaucer no more]. Since the poet was still working on The CANTERBURY TALES when he fell sick with the illness that would take his life, he may have intended to return to "The Cook's Tale" later. Certainly, the Cook's being called upon to tell a tale in the prologue to "The MANCIPLE'S TALE," which appears later in the series of Canterbury tales, with no mention of him having previously told one, suggests an inconsistency that has yet to be satisfactorily explained. On the other hand, in an article published in volume five of *Poetica,* Eric STANLEY has made a strong case for considering the tale to be complete as it is. As the basis of this interpretation, Stanley argues that the Cook reduces all to its lowest essentials. Seeing the two preceding tales as examples of what can befall a man who carelessly allows untrustworthy folk to share his dwelling (JOHN THE CARPENTER is undone by renting a room to the lascivious clerk Nicholas, and Simkin the miller suffers similarly when he allows two students to spend the night in his home), the Cook tells a story that offers an alternative to putting up with such a plague. When the apprentice becomes too much of an annoyance and an expense, the master simply throws him out, and that is all there is to it. Other readers have argued that the beginning of the tale is too specific in its description of Perkyn and the setting in CHEAPSIDE, a district of central LONDON, as well as in its introduction of the various forms of riotous behavior, for it to logically break off so suddenly. Finally, V. A. KOLVE has suggested yet another alternative, which is that the tale could have developed in a vein other than that of the fabliau. In *Chaucer and the Imagery of Narrative,* Kolve points out that other narrative possibilities abide in the existing fragment, such as that of a prodigal son story.

Cooper, Helen (1947–) English Chaucer scholar. The holder of a Ph.D. from Cambridge University, Helen Cooper began her career at Oxford and became editor for English at Medium Aevum in 1989. Although she is interested in other Medieval and Renaissance literature, her focus on Chaucer has led her to write *The Structure of the Canterbury Tales* (1983) and *The Oxford Guides to Chaucer: The Canterbury Tales* (1989). Helen Cooper told *Contemporary Authors:* "I was a confirmed medievalist by the age of about four, for reasons I am unable to recall." Nevertheless, she has written widely outside the area of medieval studies. In *Structure,* Cooper reviews various popular approaches—such as viewing the *Tales* as if the stories only exist to illustrate the psychology of the various pilgrims, or seeing the pilgrimage as primarily allegorical—pointing out the limitations inherent in each one. Taking a different view, she looks for a principle "rooted in the text" to account for both Chaucer's multiple variety and our sense that Chaucer knows exactly what he is doing and why. *The*

Oxford Guide is an excellent scholarly overview of the tales with discussion of their sources and analogues, and commentary. Cooper has also published several intriguing essays on Chaucer, including "The Girl with Two Lovers: Four Canterbury Tales" (in *Medieval Studies for J. A. W. Bennett*, 1981) and "The Shape-Shiftings of the Wife of Bath" (in *Chaucer Traditions: Studies in Honor of Derek Brewer*, 1990). "The Order of the Tales in the Ellesmere Manuscript," one of the most recent discussions of this topic, appears in *The Ellesmere Chaucer: Essays in Interpretation* (1995).

Coribantes   *See* CYBELE.

Corinth   Ancient city in the northeastern Peloponnesus of Greece, at the head of the Gulf of Corinth. (A modern city of the same name is located near the site of the original one.) In ancient times the city was noted for its luxury. Corinth is mentioned in "The PARDONER'S TALE" as the destination of the ambassador STILBOUN, who was sent by the kingdom of Sparta (Lacedaemon) to forge an alliance between the two. Upon his arrival, he found all the people engaged in gambling with dice. Without revealing the purpose of his errand, Stilboun returned home, telling his countrymen that he would never commit such a shameful deed as to negotiate an alliance with these people.

Corybantes   *See* CYBELE.

Corynne   In the final line of the Invocation that appears at the beginning of *ANELIDA AND ARCITE*, Chaucer announces that the material he draws upon to tell this story is from "Stace" (the poet STATIUS, author of the *Thebaid*), and "Corynne." The latter is thought to be a reference to the Theban poet Corinna, whose works have been lost but who is said to have defeated the great Pindar in a poetry competition. Where Chaucer may have gotten the idea to use Corinna as a source is uncertain, but he is known to have elsewhere invented a source (*see* LOLLIUS) when he so desired. His reasons for doing so are open to debate.

Corynthe   *See* CORINTH.

Costanza of Castile   The daughter of King PEDRO OF CASTILE. She and two of her sisters were given to EDWARD THE BLACK PRINCE as collateral to guarantee her father's war debt after Edward assisted Pedro in the war to regain his throne, which had been usurped by his illegitimate half-brother, Enrique de Trastamare. When the Black Prince returned to England to die, the women remained at Bordeaux, abandoned by their father as the price of his debt. The eldest entered a convent and died shortly after. The next eldest, Costanza, became heiress to the throne of Castile and

León, and the following year, 1371, was married to JOHN OF GAUNT at the age of 16; Gaunt was 31. When he brought his new wife to England to live, Philippa CHAUCER was assigned to her household. Costanza had two children by her marriage to Gaunt, one named Catalina, and a boy (named after his father) who died in infancy.

Count Ugolino of Pisa   *See* UGOLINO OF PISA.

courtesy   When the word *courtesy* (Middle English, *courtesie*) appears in Chaucer's work, it does not simply mean good manners. The concept of courtesy was really a part of the larger code of CHIVALRY, and involved an attitude of gracious humility and respectfulness that included self-respect and service to women.

courtly love   Courtly love, or *amour courtois*, as it was called in French, is the modern term given to a philosophy of love and a code of behavior which flourished in western Europe in the High Middle Ages. The exact origins of this philosophy cannot be traced with certainty, but several sources have been suggested, among them OVID's *Ars Amatoria* ("Art of Love"), Hispanic-Arabic love poetry and Platonic thought. Whatever the source, the feudal structure of society and the veneration of the Virgin Mary provided a fertile field for a doctrine of love that emphasized service and devotion to women. The ideas of courtly love were first given formal expression by 12th-century troubadours in the Provençal region of France, from whence they spread rapidly into Italy and northwards to fuse with Arthurian legends in such works as Chrétien de Troyes' romance of *Lancelot*. Because of the popularity enjoyed by French literature in England, the tradition easily made its way across the channel.

According to the system of courtly love, falling in love was typically accompanied by great emotional disturbances. The lover would experience bewilderment and helplessness, and would be tortured by mental and physical anguish that could lead to such symptoms as trembling, pallor, loss of appetite, sleeplessness and weeping. He (the lover who initiated the relationship was nearly always male) would agonize over his condition, engaging in endless self-questioning, reflecting on the nature of love and his own wretchedness. Once he had martialed enough courage to approach the lady with whom he was in love, several things might happen. First, she might agree to receive his attentions and bestow upon him some sign of favor (an object such as a sleeve was sometimes given that the knight might wear as a banner upon his helm), or she simply might agree to spend time with him in conversation. Once he had been accepted in this way, the knight would be inspired by his love to do great deeds. On the other hand, the lady might refuse to show any favor (usually referred to as "mercy"), in which case the knight might brand her a cruel and heartless specimen of her sex. But if the lady returned the knight's love too eagerly, she was condemned as being "of easy virtue." Thus while the lady might seem to be the dominant partner in such a relationship, she was just as rigidly bound by the conventions of prescribed behavior as was her lover. The code also included vows of secrecy (the relationship must not be revealed) and faithfulness; the breaking of either one could be considered a betrayal of the beloved.

The conventions of courtly love appear in a number of Chaucer's works. In *The BOOK OF THE DUCHESS*, the BLACK KNIGHT's wooing of his fair LADY WHITE is conducted according to its rules. In *The PARLIAMENT OF FOWLS*, the tercel eagles, representing the aristocracy of the birds who have gathered in the GARDEN OF LOVE to choose their mates, express a knowledge of the conventions in their wooing petitions. The noble eagles are contrasted to the lower birds, who want to dispense with the formalities and be on their way. In literature (and perhaps in life), courtly love sometimes involved a relationship between a married woman and an unmarried suitor, and this situation informs the plot of several of *The CANTERBURY TALES*. It is treated humorously in "The MILLER'S TALE" and "The MERCHANT'S TALE," while the potential serious effects are explored in "The FRANKLIN'S TALE" of DORIGEN and ARVERAGUS. By far, Chaucer's work that was most strongly and thoroughly influenced by the doctrine of courtly love was *TROILUS AND CRISEYDE*. TROILUS's behavior from the moment that he appears in the poem fits the pattern perfectly, from his initial scornful attitude toward other lovers to the intense suffering he experiences once he has been struck by CUPID's arrow. Readers who are puzzled by the secrecy with which Troilus and CRISEYDE wish to surround their relationship can find some explanation for that secrecy in the conventions of courtly love. Those conventions also help to explain Criseyde's reactions to Troilus' attentions and her fears regarding her reputation. (These matters are discussed in detail under the Commentary on *Troilus and Criseyde*.) For further information on the system of courtly love and its manifestation in medieval literature, including Chaucer's work, see C. S. LEWIS, *The Allegory of Love*.

Crassus, Marcus Licinius Marcus Licinius Crassus was a notoriously greedy Roman general of the first century B.C. who, when he was slain in battle by the Parthians, had molten gold poured into his mouth, signifying his avariciousness. He is mentioned disparagingly in *TROILUS AND CRISEYDE* as an example of greedy men who disdained love in favor of gold and other riches (book 3, line 1391).

Creiseyde *See* CRISEYDE.

Creon There were two Creons in Greek mythology, one the king of Corinth, the other the king of Thebes. The Creon mentioned most often in Chaucer's work is the latter. Creon of Thebes was the brother of Jocasta and therefore the uncle and brother-in-law of OEDIPUS, who unknowingly married his mother and became king of Thebes. Although Creon had succeeded Jocasta's first husband, he surrendered the throne in favor of Oedipus, who had freed Thebes from the domination of the Sphinx. When Oedipus left Thebes in disgrace after discovering that the woman to whom he was married was his mother, he made Creon the guardian of his children. Creon acted as regent for ETEOCLES and POLYNICES until they came of age and agreed to take turns acting as ruler. When Eteocles and Polynices killed each other in their struggle for sole possession of the Theban throne, Creon forbade anyone, on pain of death, to bury the bodies of Polynices or any of the other soldiers who had attacked the city. His refusal to authorize the proper burial rites attracted the attention of THESEUS, the ruler of ATHENS, on his way home from his battle with the AMAZONS. The resulting conflict between Theseus and Creon is described at the beginning of "The KNIGHT'S TALE." When Creon refuses Theseus' request to allow the burial of the dead, Theseus attacks and defeats the city, taking prisoner two Theban knights, PALAMON and ARCITE (1), who become the main protagonists of "The Knight's Tale." Creon's iron-handed rule of Thebes is also mentioned at the beginning of the unfinished poem *ANELIDA AND ARCITE*. Queen ANELIDA of ARMENIA is one of the people being held hostage in the city when she meets the knight ARCITE (2). The Creon who is mentioned as the father of JASON's third wife in *The LEGEND OF GOOD WOMEN* was the king of Corinth. When Jason abandoned MEDEA to marry CREUSA, Medea sent a poisoned garment to his new bride that burned her to death when she put it on. Her father was killed when he tried to respond to her cries for help.

Creseyde *See* CRISEYDE.

Cresus *See* CROESUS.

Crete Island in the eastern Mediterranean Sea. Typically, when the island is mentioned in Chaucer's work, it is in reference to the Greek hero THESEUS. By killing the MINOTAUR, which dwelt in the labyrinth beneath King Minos' palace, Theseus freed the city of ATHENS from paying Crete an annual tribute of seven young women and seven young men to be fed to the monster. Theseus' adventures in Crete are fairly thoroughly related in the story of ARIADNE that appears in Chaucer's *LEGEND OF GOOD WOMEN*. Crete is briefly mentioned in "The KNIGHT'S TALE," in which Theseus rides into battle against CREON, carrying a golden pennant

Creiseyde *See* CRISEYDE.

engraved with a representation of the Minotaur. PASIPHAE, the queen of Crete, is mentioned in "The WIFE OF BATH'S TALE" as one of the wicked women whom the WIFE's fifth husband likes to read about.

Creusa Although there are three women named Creusa in Greek mythology, the one most often referred to in Chaucer's work is the daughter of King PRIAM and Queen HECUBA of Troy, who married AENEAS. As Aeneas was leaving the burning city at the end of the TROJAN WAR, Creusa was lost in the darkness and confusion. Aeneas, going back to find her, met only her ghost, who prophesied his future and urged him to flee and to take care of their son, ASCANIUS. This Creusa is mentioned twice when Chaucer tells the story of Aeneas' adventures, first in *The HOUSE OF FAME* and later in *The LEGEND OF GOOD WOMEN*. Although she is not mentioned by name, a different Creusa, who was the daughter of CREON, king of Corinth, and who was to become the adventurer JASON's third wife, appears briefly at the end of MEDEA's story in *The Legend of Good Women*. Medea, who was Jason's second wife, grew angry with him for casting her aside and murdered Creusa by giving her a poisoned garment to wear on her wedding day.

Criseyde The principal female character in Chaucer's longest single work, *TROILUS AND CRISEYDE*, which tells the story of the love affair between the two people named in the title. At the opening of the story we learn that Criseyde is a beautiful and virtuous young widow living in TROY during the 11-year siege of that city that was known as the TROJAN WAR. She lives alone because her father CALKAS, who has foreseen the fall of Troy, recently left the city to join the Greek forces. One day she attends a religious service in the temple of PALLAS Athena, where her beauty wounds the eye and heart of TROILUS, a young warrior and son of the royal family who has previously scorned all thoughts of love. After some hesitation, with the assistance of Criseyde's uncle PANDARUS, Troilus sets out to woo Criseyde and eventually wins her, but they only enjoy their love a short time before tragedy strikes. Regretting his decision to leave his daughter behind when he left Troy, Calkas persuades the Greeks to ask for her in exchange for one of the Trojan prisoners taken in battle. The leaders on the Trojan side, under pressure from the people of Troy, agree to the exchange, leaving the lovers no choice but to comply with the decision or run away. Criseyde argues that they should comply, reassuring her companion that she will simply return to Troy as soon as she gets the chance. Troilus fears that something may happen to prevent her return, but he is unable to win her over, and so she departs. Once inside the Greek camp, Criseyde finds that it is not as easy to leave as she had hoped. Traveling alone among the tents of armed men

would be fraught with considerable danger; besides, she now believes her father's prediction that the city will be defeated and burned. In addition to these discouraging circumstances, she also begins to receive the attentions of a Greek warrior, DIOMEDE, who offers her his protection. Finally, instead of returning to Troy on the date that she had promised, she chooses to stay with the Greeks.

Criseyde's acceptance of Diomede's protection and the implication that she becomes his lover (Troilus sees him wearing a brooch that Troilus gave to Criseyde as a lover's token) have led many critics to pronounce her behavior utterly contemptible. Yet, a closer look at her character as it develops throughout the poem renders her decision not to return to Troilus understandable. From the very beginning, she is portrayed as a woman motivated by fear. She has been left alone in Troy by a father who is now accounted a traitor. She has previously been the victim of lawsuits, and her uncle Pandarus, in order to make her more dependent on Troilus' support, tells her that the man who had harassed her with a suit in the past is preparing to do so again. Finally, the importunity of Troilus, urged on by her uncle, makes it nearly impossible for her to refuse his advances without creating conflict between herself and other members of Troy's ruling family. On the other hand, by allying herself with Troilus, she gains their support, even though they do not know that she is his lover. She does seem to grow to love Troilus, but it is not with the same kind of intense infatuation; if deep, her love is also practical. Criseyde's arguments against their running away together are the best evidence of her common sense, especially when juxtaposed to Troilus' fanciful romanticism for which he would leave his title, power and family behind without a second thought. Idealistically, he may appear the more laudable for his willingness to do so, but his plan is not one that bodes well for their future, at least not as far as Criseyde is concerned. This dimension of Criseyde's character shows her to be a practical woman who deliberates carefully before acting. The circumstances in which she finds herself after her father's treasonable departure make her fear for her safety to such a degree that she is incapable, given her character, of acting other than she does.

These features of Criseyde's character are Chaucer's invention or the elaboration of incipient characteristics in the heroine of his source, BOCCACCIO's *FILOSTRATO*. If Chaucer's aim was to make her more sympathetic, however, he failed, or at least that appears to be the case from what little we know of his audience's response to the story. In the prologue to *The LEGEND OF GOOD WOMEN*, Chaucer claims to have taken on this project of writing about virtuous women in response to charges that he slandered women by creating such a character as Criseyde. A Scottish poet of the 15th century, Robert Henryson, wrote a sequel to the poem in which

Criseyde is punished for her infidelity by becoming infected with leprosy. Both of these responses suggest that Criseyde is a character more apt to be appreciated in a time when the moral standards for women's behavior are less repressive.

Crisippus   One of the authors included in the "Book of Wicked Wives" from which the WIFE OF BATH's fifth husband reads to her on a nightly basis until she forces him to throw it into the fire. This reference, compared to some of the other authors mentioned, is somewhat obscure, but probably alludes to an antifeminist writer mentioned by Saint JEROME in his *Epistola adversus Jovinianum* (Letter against Jovinian). Other scholars have suggested that Chaucer may have meant the Stoic philosopher Chrysippus, whose writing on marriage was quoted in a treatise by a later Stoic and could have been available for Chaucer to read.

Crisostom   *See* JOHN CHRYSOSTOM, SAINT.

Crist   *See* JESUS CHRIST.

Cristendom   *See* CHRISTENDOM.

Croesus   The last king of Lydia in the sixth century B.C. He conquered the Greek cities of Aeolia and Ionia (except Miletus), and invaded PERSIA, but was defeated by CYRUS THE GREAT. He became legendary for his great wealth. The story of his downfall, including the description of a famous prophetic dream he had shortly before his death, is told in "The MONK'S TALE" as one of the tragedies illustrating the role of FORTUNE in the demise of great men. The story of Croesus is the last one the MONK tells before he is interrupted by the KNIGHT. Although Croesus is mentioned as one of the people whose stories were painted on the walls of the TEMPLE OF VENUS in "The KNIGHT'S TALE," he was not a victim of love, and scholars have generally been puzzled by the reference to him in this context. J. A. W. BENNETT has suggested that Chaucer's inspiration here is ALAIN DE LILLE's *De planctu naturae* ("Complaint of Nature"), in which Croesus serves as an example of character traits changing to their opposites through love's power. CHAUNTICLEER, the learned rooster of "The NUN'S PRIEST'S TALE," uses Croesus' prophetic dream to justify his own belief in the power of dreams to foretell the future; the same dream is alluded to in the Invocation to *The HOUSE OF FAME*, where the narrator wishes that those readers who do not like his poem may suffer the same fate as Croesus (whose dream foretold that he would die by hanging, line 105).

crow   A bird belonging to, reverenced and ultimately punished by the god Phoebus (APOLLO) in "The MANCIPLE'S TALE." The story derives from OVID's story of Apollo and his raven in the *Metamorphoses*. At the beginning of the story, the crow, like Ovid's raven, has white feathers and is particularly beloved by Phoebus, who teaches it to speak. The bird is also able to sing more beautifully than a nightingale. But when the bird informs Phoebus that his wife has been having an affair with another man, the god flies into a rage and kills his wife. Later filled with remorse for his impulsive deed, he decides that the crow must have lied. As punishment, he curses the crow so that his feathers turn black, he loses his singing voice and no longer has the ability to speak. The emphasis given to the crow's ability to speak and the subsequent loss of that ability tie in with the MANCIPLE's overall message of the importance of guarding one's speech.

Crystyanytee   *See* CHRISTIANITY.

Cupid (Cupide, Cupido)   In classical mythology, Cupid, or Cupido, was the Roman name for the god of love. According to the earliest legends, he was one of the first beings to arise out of Chaos, and came to represent the principle of harmony and union active in forming the world and its inhabitants. A later tradition presents Cupid as the son of MARS (1) and VENUS, the goddess of love, to whom he is a constant companion. Although he was typically depicted as a child in Greek and Roman mythology, Cupid often appears a fully grown man in medieval illustrations of the god of love. The bow and arrows with which he is armed are used to pierce and inflame the hearts of his victims, inspiring them with irresistible passion for a beloved other. Cupid's golden wings provide him with speed of movement. The blindfold that he wears does not affect his aim, but causes him to proceed impulsively and irrationally, not caring for the consequences of his actions. Countless stories of his role in awakening the impulse to love appear in classical literature, and Chaucer mentions a number of the more famous ones in *The HOUSE OF FAME, The PARLIAMENT OF FOWLS* and "The KNIGHT'S TALE," all of which feature a TEMPLE OF VENUS adorned with paintings of those who were wounded by Cupid's arrows, often at the direction of his mother, Venus. Cupid himself is likewise represented in each temple, as a statue in "The Knight's Tale" and as a sentient being in the two dream visions. His presence as a life-like figure was probably inspired by his similar appearance in the French *ROMAN DE LA ROSE*, part of which Chaucer translated as *The Romaunt of the Rose*.

Curry, Walter C. (1887–1967)   Chaucer scholar who has also published many works on Shakespeare during a long career. Curry submitted *The Middle English Idea of Personal Beauty; As Found in the Metrical Romances and Legend* as his doctoral thesis at Stanford University in 1915. Many of his Chaucerian essays reveal Curry's interest in the raw material from which Chaucer constructed the pilgrims of *The CANTERBURY TALES*. In *Chaucer and the Medieval Sciences* (1926), Curry offers explanations based on medieval scientific theory for the appearance and behavior of the pilgrims. Much of this important book deals with the medieval pseudoscience of physiognomy—the idea that a person's physical features revealed important information about personality. An example of this would be the gap in the WIFE OF BATH's front teeth which, like her broad hips, would be interpreted as a sign of robust sexuality. The book also contains an important chapter on medieval dream lore that helps to illuminate the meaning of "The NUN'S PRIEST'S TALE" and the background of three dream-vision poems, *The BOOK OF THE DUCHESS*, *The HOUSE OF FAME* and *The PARLIAMENT OF FOWLS*.

curtesie   *See* COURTESY.

Custance   *See* CONSTANCE.

Cutberd, Seint   *See* CUTHBERT, SAINT.

Cuthbert, Saint   Saint Cuthbert was born at Melrose in Scotland on the river Tweed in the early seventh century. As a youth he tended his father's sheep until a vision of Saint Aidan ascending into heaven led him to embrace the monastic life. At Melrose Abbey he held the position of guestmaster (the brother in charge of all those who sought food and shelter at the abbey) and became known for his kindness to poor wayfarers. Although he later rose to great heights in the administration of the Catholic Church in England as bishop of Durham, it is his kindness to strangers that Chaucer commemorates, albeit in a somewhat irreverent context: In "The REEVE'S TALE," he is the saint whom the student John (John the Clerk) swears by when he asks the miller to let him and his companion, ALAN, spend the night at the miller's home. The miller agrees to the arrangement, with disastrous, if humorous, consequences.

Cybele   In classical mythology, Cybele was a fertility goddess. Her cult originated in ancient Phrygia but spread widely over Greece and was thence imported into Rome. She was considered the mother of all nature, representing the powers of fruitfulness and reproduction in humans, plants and animals. Her followers worshipped her with wild orgiastic rites: Surrounded by her attendants, the Corybantes, she would drive her lion-drawn cart through the forests to the accompaniment of ecstatic dancing and the music of flute, drum and cymbal. The rite culminated with the wounding and mutilation of the Corybantes, including self-castration. Cybele's symbols were the drum, the towered crown, the torch, the cymbals (tympanum), the flute, the horn, the lion, the oak and the pine. In Chaucer's prologue to *The LEGEND OF GOOD WOMEN*, he states that the goddess Cybele created the daisy (the flower that is honored in the prologue) in remembrance of Queen Alcestis and the courage that made her volunteer to die in her husband's place. Why Chaucer chose Cybele for this role is uncertain; there is no recognized tradition of her having created the daisy, although there is a similar story featuring CERES, the Roman goddess with whom Cybele was sometimes identified. The Corybantes and their rites are mentioned briefly in the *BOECE*, Chaucer's translation of BOETHIUS' *Consolation of Philosophy*, where their response to the dark phase of the moon is given as an example of superstitious behavior arising from ignorance.

Cymerie   *See* CIMMERIANS.

Cynthea (Cynthia)   *See* DIANA.

Cyprian   One of the men who became the enemy of BOETHIUS because Boethius defended ALBYN (probably Decius Albinus). In his attempts to tell LADY PHILOSOPHY why FORTUNE has turned against him, Boethius explains that he made himself an object of spite and vulnerable to attack by defending certain powerful Romans who had been accused of treachery and fraud against the government of THEODORIC, king of the Ostrogoths, who ruled in Italy from A.D. 493 to 526. Cyprian is also mentioned by CASSIODORUS in his *Epistles*.

Cypride   *See* VENUS.

Cyprus   Island (and former kingdom) at the eastern end of the Mediterranean, south of Anatolia (modern Turkey). The kingdom of Cyprus is mentioned once in Chaucer's work, in the brief biography of Pierre de Lusignan that appears in "The MONK'S TALE" as one of a series of tragedies designed to show the goddess FORTUNE's pervasive influence over great men. PIERRE DE LUSIGNAN was king of Cyprus during Chaucer's lifetime and was entertained by EDWARD III at the English court in 1366. Since Chaucer joined the royal household as an esquire to the king around this time, the two men may have come into contact with one another. This could explain why Chaucer included Pierre as one of only two contemporaries among the 17 portraits of "The Monk's Tale."

Cyrus the Great   The powerful king of Persia from 559 to 530 B.C. Within 20 years of becoming king, Cyrus had conquered the Medes, Lydians and Babylonians, making the Persians the dominant nation of the ancient world. The Old Testament of the Bible reports that following his conquest of

Babylonia (*see* BABYLON), Cyrus released the Jews from their long Babylonian Captivity. Respected as a wise and tolerant ruler, Cyrus was able to gain the goodwill of the varied ethnic and religious groups within his large empire, which extended from India to the western edge of Asia Minor (modern Turkey). Cyrus' reign ended with his death in battle in 530. He was succeeded by his son CAMBYSES II, who was known for his ill temper. Cyrus too, despite his overall reputation as a wise ruler, was remembered for certain instances of rash behavior, such as his destruction of the Gyndes riverbed in Babylon after one of his horses drowned in it. This incident is reported in "The SUMMONER'S TALE" as an example of the extremes to which excessive anger may lead a man. Cyrus' war against the Lydian king, CROESUS, is mentioned in the brief biography of Croesus that appears in "The MONK'S TALE." In this instance we are merely informed that Cyrus feared Croesus, who seemed to consider himself invincible but was of course ultimately defeated by Cyrus. As with all of the lives described in "The Monk's Tale," this one is meant to illustrate the revolving of FORTUNE's wheel as she raises one man up and causes another to fall. In the *BOECE,* too, the Lydian king's downfall and Cyrus' role in bringing it about are similarly viewed as an act of capricious Fortune.

D

Daedalus In classical mythology, Daedalus was an artist and inventor. Forced to flee Athens after throwing his nephew down off the Acropolis, Daedalus sought the protection of King MINOS in Crete. There he built the wooden cow which allowed PASIPHAE to have sex with the beautiful bull with which she had become infatuated, and also constructed the labyrinth in which her offspring the MINOTAUR was kept. Minos punished him for assisting Pasiphae by imprisoning him and his son ICARUS within the labyrinth, but Pasiphae helped them to escape. In order to get away from the island, Daedalus made wings of feathers and wax for himself and his son so that they could fly across the sea. Icarus flew so near the sun that his wings melted; he plunged into the water and drowned. Daedalus, however, succeeded in reaching Sicily. The king of Sicily offered him protection, and when Minos came after Daedalus, the king's daughter, who had fallen in love with the artist, killed Minos.

Daedalus is mentioned several times in Chaucer's work, first in *The BOOK OF THE DUCHESS*, where the BLACK KNIGHT claims that his sorrow over losing his fair LADY WHITE is so great that not even the marvelous devices of Daedalus (among other things) could distract him from it (line 570). In *The HOUSE OF FAME*, the narrator dreams that he is carried high up into the heavens by an EAGLE, who informs him that not even Daedalus or his son flew half so high (line 919). Later in the poem, when the narrator catches his first glimpse of the HOUSE OF RUMOR, he describes it as being more marvelous and intricate than the labyrinth Daedalus built for the Minotaur (line 1920). This labyrinth is part of the setting in Chaucer's story of ARIADNE, the daughter of King Minos who helped THESEUS defeat the Minotaur and escape from Crete. In Book Three of the *BOECE*, the labyrinth appears again as the narrator becomes so confused by LADY PHILOSOPHY's attempts to instruct him that he accuses her of trying to imprison him in a kind of mental labyrinth as complex as the one Daedalus constructed.

Dalida *See* DELILAH.

Damascene In the Bible, the inhabitants of the city of Damascus are called Damascenes. In the brief biography of ADAM, the first man, that appears in his "MONK'S TALE," Chaucer says that he was created in a "feeld of Damyssene" [field of Damascene]. The notion that the first human was made in a field where Damascus later stood occurs in BOCCACCIO's *De casibus* as well as in other medieval texts; where it originated is unknown.

Damascien Damascien is mentioned in Chaucer's GENERAL PROLOGUE to *The CANTERBURY TALES* as one of the medical authorities whose teachings the DOCTOR OF PHYSIC had studied (line 433). The name could refer to John of Damascus, an important Syrian theologian of the eighth century, but the name, or a variation of it, was also given to works by SERAPION the Elder.

Damasie, Saint *See* DAMASUS I, POPE.

Damasus I, Pope (Saint Damasus) Of Spanish extraction but born in fourth-century Rome, Damasus attended Pope Liberius in exile and succeeded him in 366, but had to struggle against an antipope, Ursinus, whose rebellion was finally crushed by the Emperor Valentinian. Saint Damasus held councils in Rome against the Arian and Apollinarian heresies. A cultured man, he was the patron of Saint JEROME, who under his direction produced an authoritative Latin text for Holy Scripture. Saint Damasus is remembered for having restored and beautified the tombs of the Holy Martyrs in Rome. His share in the development of the Roman Liturgy, mainly by the introduction of certain elements borrowed from the Eastern Rites, was considerable. Damasus is quoted in Chaucer's "PARSON'S TALE" as having said that the sin of simony (*see* CHRISTIANITY for a definition) was the greatest of all sins against God.

Dame Nature *See* NATURE, DAME.

Damian Primary character in "The MERCHANT'S TALE." Damian is the young squire and member of JANUARY's household who falls in love with January's young wife, MAY. Damian falls for May so suddenly and severely that he becomes physically ill from the excess of his emotions and must take to his bed. To relieve his passions, he writes May a letter confessing his love. When he receives confirmation that his feelings are returned and that he shall receive physical satisfaction at the earliest possible convenience, an instant cure is effected. The two lovers are finally united in a pear tree in January's enclosed garden.

Damyssene   *See* DAMASCENE.

Danao   *See* DANAUS.

Danaus   In classical mythology, Danaus was the twin brother of Aegyptus. He had 50 daughters (by different wives), whom he promised in marriage to the 50 sons of Aegyptus. These plans were disrupted, however, by the prophecy that he would be killed by one of his sons-in-law. To avoid the prophecy, Danaus fled to Argos, where he succeeded to the throne of Gelanor and achieved such power that the people called themselves Danaans after his name. He is credited with having been the inventor of wells, and of having built the citadel of Argos. When the sons of Aegyptus came to claim Danaus' daughters, he armed the women with daggers and ordered them to kill their husbands on their wedding night. All obeyed except HYPERMNESTRA, whose husband, Lynceus, escaped and later returned to kill her father. The story of Hypermnestra and the terrible decision she was forced to make on her wedding night, choosing between loyalty to her father and her husband's life, is related in Chaucer's *LEGEND OF GOOD WOMEN* (lines 2562–723). In his version of the story, however, Chaucer reversed the names of the two fathers, giving Danaus sons and Aegyptus daughters, so that Aegyptus becomes the father of Hypermnestra who demanded that she poison her husband on the night following their nuptials. Because Hypermnestra disobeyed her father and helped her husband to escape, she was thrown into prison.

Dane   *See* DAPHNE.

Daniel   In the Bible, Daniel was a Jewish prophet during the period known as the Babylonian Captivity of the Jews. He wrote the book in the Old Testament that bears his name. Daniel is thought of primarily as a biblical prophet and adviser to the Jews, but he also served as an adviser in the courts of foreign kings, remaining in governmental service through the reigns of the kings of BABYLON and into the reign of CYRUS THE GREAT, king of Persia, after the Persians became the dominant world power. Very little is known about Daniel's personal life. His family history is not mentioned, but he was probably from an upper-class family in Jerusalem, since it is unlikely that NEBUCHADNEZZAR, the king of Babylon who appointed Daniel as his adviser, would have selected someone from the lower classes for such a position. It is also unknown whether Daniel married or had a family. As a servant in Nebuchadnezzar's court, he may have been castrated and made into a eunuch, as was common in those days, but the text does not specify that this happened. Many of the most memorable stories of the Old Testament appear in the Book of Daniel. One is the story of Shadrach, Meshach and Abednego, the three Jewish men who refused to worship the gods of Babylon and were cast into a fiery furnace that King Nebuchadnezzar commanded to be heated seven times hotter than usual. When the three emerged unscathed, Nebuchadnezzar repented of his former anger and commanded that the god of the three men should be revered throughout the world. Another story, this one occurring in the reign of DARIUS of Persia, tells how Daniel was cast into a den of lions for daring to pray to his god during a period when making a request from any god or king other than Darius was prohibited. Daniel, like Shadrach, Meshach and Abednego, emerged from the ordeal unharmed, gaining new respect for the god of the Israelites. The story of Daniel and the lion's den is mentioned in "The MAN OF LAW'S TALE" as an example of the way in which God takes care of his own. CONSTANCE, the heroine of the tale, is similarly taken care of after she has been cast out to sea in a rudderless ship. Daniel's famed ability to interpret dreams, which caused him to be trusted above all other advisers to Nebuchadnezzar, is referred to in the brief biography of the Babylonian king that appears in Chaucer's "MONK'S TALE." The dream itself is mentioned in "The PARSON'S TALE." CHAUNTICLEER, the learned rooster of "The NUN'S PRIEST'S TALE," mentions Daniel's dream interpretations as evidence that dreams should be taken seriously. His wife, PERTELOTE, holds the opposite opinion. As it turns out, Chaunticleer is right.

Dante Alighieri   Dante Alighieri, often simply referred to as Dante, is considered by many to have been the most important Italian poet not just of his age but of all time. He was born in FLORENCE in 1265, but the circumstances of his early life are obscure. We know that in 1277 he was betrothed to his future wife, Gemma Donati, and that in 1289 he took part in military operations against Arezzo and Pisa. During this period of his life he fell in love with the girl who was to serve as the inspiration for his greatest work, the *Divina Commedia* (*Divine Comedy*), a tripartite allegory of encyclopedic breadth, chronicling the passage of the Christian soul from hell through purgatory to heaven. He calls her Beatrice in his poetry but her identity has been disputed. The generally accepted view is that she was Bice Portinari, who married Simone de' Bardi. When she died in 1290, Dante was devastated and sought consolation in the study of philosophy. Five years later he became active in the political life of Florence, an interest that was later to cost him his home. When a rival political faction gained control of the city, he was forced into exile. He eventually settled in Ravenna where he died in 1321.

Aside from the *Divine Comedy,* Dante's other surviving works include the *Vita nuova* (A new life), a collection of poems mostly about his love for Beatrice; the *Convivio,* or *Banquet,* an unfinished philosophical work; and the Latin treatise *De vulgari eloquentia* (On the eloquence of the common tongue), also unfinished, which consists of an inquiry into the form of vernacular language most suitable for poetry. Indeed, one of Dante's most important contributions to literature was his decision to compose his own poetry in the vernacular, which had hitherto been considered too ignoble for such uses. Another prose work, the *Monarchia,* is a Latin treatise on the universal empire and the relations between emperor and pope. Although he may have begun writing the *Divine Comedy* earlier in his life, it was not finished until shortly before his death.

Dante's work had considerable influence on Chaucer's practice of the craft of poetry, not least of all encouraging the English poet to use English, rather than Latin or French, to compose for a court audience. Chaucer's use of the dream vision in *The BOOK OF THE DUCHESS, The HOUSE OF FAME* and *The PARLIAMENT OF FOWLS* may also have been guided by Dante's use of that form in the *Divine Comedy.* Still, Chaucer does not often borrow wholesale from Dante the way he does from BOCCACCIO, taking plot and characters as well as translating specific passages. *The House of Fame,* where an eagle transports the narrator from a desert wasteland to Fame's palace is the exception, as scholars have pointed out the similarity between this episode and that part of the *Purgatorio* where Dante is similarly transported. Other passages from all three parts of the *Divine Comedy* (the *Inferno,* the *Purgatorio* and the *Paradiso*) find their way into this poem, suggesting that it may have been intended as some kind of a tribute to the Italian author, albeit a comic one. Some scholars, citing as further evidence the tripartite division of *The House of Fame* (which mimics the structure of Dante's poem), even go so far as to suggest that *The House of Fame* is a parody of the *Divine Comedy.* Others, discomfited by the idea that Chaucer would have attempted to parody such a serious and well-respected writer and his work, especially when his own career was far from established, disagree. Lines and passages, mostly from the *Divine Comedy* but occasionally from the *Convivio,* appear scattered throughout Chaucer's work, in *The Parliament of Fowls,* the "An ABC," *ANELIDA AND ARCITE, TROILUS AND CRISEYDE, The LEGEND OF GOOD WOMEN* and in a number of the Canterbury tales.

Danyel   *See* DANIEL.

Daphne   In classical mythology, Daphne was the daughter of the river god PENEUS in Thessaly. APOLLO, attracted by her beauty, pursued her. At the moment that she would have been captured, she prayed to DIANA and was turned into a laurel tree. In memory of her, Apollo adopted the laurel as one of his symbols. Daphne's story is depicted on the walls of Diana's temple in Chaucer's "KNIGHT'S TALE." On the night before the tournament that will decide which of the two knights, PALAMON or ARCITE (1), gets to marry EMILY, she prays at Diana's temple, asking that she not have to be married at all. Arcite wins the tournament, but immediately dies of a wound he received in the fighting. After a period of mourning, Emily marries Palamon. In *TROILUS AND CRISEYDE,* when TROILUS prays to Apollo to help him win the love of CRISEYDE, he asks him to do so in remembrance of his own love for Daphne (book 3, line 726). In these situations, the positions of Criseyde and Emily are both similar to Daphne's, but neither of the women escapes.

Dardanus, yate (gate) of   The gate of Dardanus was, according to GUIDO DELLE COLONNE, (one of Chaucer's sources for *TROILUS AND CRISEYDE*) the first of the city of TROY's six gates. In book two of the poem, TROILUS enters the city through this gate after triumphing in battle over the Greeks. His route through the city is chosen so that he may ride past CRISEYDE's window. Criseyde's uncle, PANDARUS, has suggested that such exposure to Troilus in his glory will help persuade his niece to accept the young warrior as her lover.

Dares Phrygius (Darius the Phrygian)   A Trojan priest mentioned by the Greek poet HOMER in the *Iliad.* He was supposed to have been the author of an account of the TROJAN WAR which is extant in a Latin prose version called *De excidio Troiae* (*Concerning the Fall of Troy*). Dating from the fifth century, this work and the history of TROY attributed to DICTYS CRETENSIS provided the most detailed accounts of the Trojan War available in western Europe during the medieval period. Everything written about Troy before the middle of the 17th century was to some extent dependent, either directly or indirectly, on the narratives of Dares and Dictys, and Chaucer's *TROILUS AND CRISEYDE* is no exception. Although Chaucer's direct source was BOCCACCIO's *FILOSTRATO,* the Italian poet drew upon the work of earlier writers whose ultimate sources were the classical accounts mentioned above.

Darius (Daryus) (1)   The Darius referred to in the WIFE OF BATH's prologue (*see* "WIFE OF BATH'S TALE") and noted for the elaborate design of his tomb is Darius III Codomannus, the king of PERSIA from 336 to 330 B.C. Darius III underestimated the strength of the army of ALEXANDER THE GREAT when the Macedonians invaded Persia. He was defeated in several major battles, and when he attempted to rally the eastern provinces of his empire, he was hunted down and assassinated by his own followers. These events brought the Persian Empire to an end and marked the beginning of the period of Greek dominance in the ancient world.

Darius (Daryus) (2) Darius the Mede is the name given to the successor of BELSHAZZAR, king of Babylon. In the Old Testament Book of Daniel, Darius is referred to as the "son of Ahasuerus, of the lineage of the Medes." According to the same source, he was the Persian king who made the prophet DANIEL a governor, or overseer, of several provincial leaders during the period known as the Babylonian Captivity of the Jews. Daniel's popularity with his subjects caused the other governors and the satraps under them to become jealous of Daniel and to plot against him. Darius then had Daniel thrown into the den of lions, but ultimately issued a decree that all in his kingdom must "tremble and fear before the God of Daniel." The only information that we have about Darius the Mede comes from the Bible. He is not mentioned by Greek historians or in any Persian literature, and Persian cuneiform inscriptions show that CYRUS THE GREAT (Cyrus II) was the successor of Belshazzar. One possible solution to this puzzle is suggested by the Greek translation of the Old Testament known as the Septuagint. In this work the king who defeats Belshazzar is called Cyrus, so it could be that Darius the Mede was simply an alternative title used to refer to Cyrus the Persian. Darius the Mede is referred to twice in Chaucer's "MONK'S TALE," first in the brief biography of Belshazzar as the man who overcame him, and later as one of the mighty kings who was in turn overcome by ALEXANDER THE GREAT. In the latter instance, Chaucer must be referring to a different Darius, Darius III Codomannus, the king of Persia from 336 to 330 B.C. who underestimated the strength of the army of Alexander when the Macedonians invaded Persia. (See DARIUS [1].) He was defeated by Alexander in several major battles. If Darius the Mede is the same person as Cyrus the Great, he would have lived about 200 years before Alexander the Great.

Dartmouth City on the southwestern coast of England in the county of Devon. It is mentioned in the GENERAL PROLOGUE TO *THE CANTERBURY TALES* as the home of the SHIPMAN, one of the Canterbury pilgrims. The *CHAUCER LIFE RECORDS* show that on November 11, 1373, Chaucer received a royal commission to go to Dartmouth, where he was to arrange for the restoration to its master of a Genoese merchant ship that had been seized by the port authorities. Some scholars believe that this episode influenced him to select the port city as the home of his Shipman.

Daunger One of the allegorical figures guarding the rose garden in the famous and influential French poem Le *ROMAN DE LA ROSE*. The word *daunger* was com-

monly used in medieval love poetry to mean "disdain." Within such poetry, a lady's "daunger" or disdain was one of the chief obstacles typically encountered by the lover who sought the lady's favor. In the *Roman,* Daunger, Shame, Dread and Wicked Tongue (malicious gossip) all try to prevent the lover from gaining access to the beautiful rose with which he has fallen in love. They are opposed by VENUS and BIALACOIL ("fair welcome"), who come to his aid and enable him to gain a kiss before Jealousy drives him out and imprisons the rose and Bialacoil in a strong fortress. Chaucer translated a portion of the *Roman* as *The Romaunt of the Rose,* but his translation breaks off before the episode described above. Chaucer's Middle English version was continued by two other writers. The three fragments are sometimes printed together and designated Fragment A, Fragment B, and Fragment C, as in the *RIVERSIDE CHAUCER* edited by Larry BENSON.

Daunte *See* DANTE.

David In the Old Testament, David was the second king of Israel. He was also the ancestor of Christ and the writer of numerous Psalms. The record of David's life is found in the first and second books of Samuel, the first book of Kings, and the first book of Chronicles. David's youth was spent in Bethlehem; he was the youngest son of Jesse, a respected man of the city. During this time he worked as the shepherd of his father's sheep, displaying great courage by killing a lion and a bear that attacked the flock. He also exhibited considerable musical talent in playing the harp. When King Saul, who had been forsaken by God and was troubled by an evil spirit, decided to choose a harpist whose music might soothe his spirits, he chose David. The young man's exposure to governmental affairs prepared him for his later service as Israel's king. David's first chance to show his heroism came during a Philistine invasion of the countryside surrounding Bethlehem, when the giant GOLIATH issued a challenge for a Hebrew warrior to meet him in single combat. Weighted with heavy armor, Goliath was equipped to engage in close-range combat. David's strategy was to fight him from a distance, using stones and a slingshot. David's defeat of the giant made him a hero among the Jews but also made an enemy of King Saul, who was already jealous of him. Saul's son JONATHAN, however, admired David for his bravery, and the two became lifelong friends. Although Saul had promised to reward the man who defeated Goliath, his jealousy and fear of David's popularity with the people eventually led the king to plot his death. During his flight from the king, David was twice given the opportunity to kill Saul while he was asleep, but he refused to do so.

After Saul died in a battle against the Philistines, the tribe of Judah, to which David belonged, elected him king of Judah. The rest of the tribes of Israel set up Ishbosheth, another of Saul's sons, as king. Two years later, when Ishbosheth was assassinated, David became king of the entire Jewish nation and began the work of reestablishing a united kingdom, creating a new capital at Jerusalem. David also reinvigorated the Jews' worship of God and began building a new temple of worship. Although he was considered a righteous and benevolent king, David is also remembered for his faults, one of the most notorious being his love affair with a woman named Bathsheba, which he attempted to cover up by having her husband killed in battle. David was also plagued by family tragedy. One of his sons, Amnon, raped and humiliated his half-sister, TAMAR. Another son, ABSALOM (2), rebelled against his father and tried to take away the kingdom by force.

David is mentioned several times in Chaucer's work. In "The MAN OF LAW'S TALE," the narrator refers to his battle with Goliath as an example of God intervening on behalf of a Christian confronted with a task that would seem to be beyond his strength. The heroine of the tale, CONSTANCE, endures a similar trial when she is cast adrift on the sea with her infant child. One of the Psalms of David is quoted in "The SUMMONER'S TALE" when the FRIAR, who is trying to get money from THOMAS, accuses the regular clergy of various abuses, including a certain irreverence toward Holy Writ. He describes them being fat as whales, waddling like swans and as full of wine as a bottle in the pantry. Their prayer, he says sarcastically, is full of great reverence, especially when they belch and say "*cor meum eructavit*" ("my heart has spoken"). These Latin words were the first of Psalm 45. Other of David's Psalms are quoted in a more serious context in "The TALE OF MELIBEE," where MELIBEE's wife uses them to convince her husband that he should not take revenge on the people who have robbed them and in "The PARSON'S TALE," which is a sermon on penitence and the Seven Deadly Sins.

David, Alfred (1929–) A Harvard Ph.D. who teaches at the University of Indiana, David has contributed both interpretation and scholarship to our understanding of Chaucer. In his interpretive effort, he has published *The Strumpet Muse: Art and Morals in Chaucer's Poetry* (1976) and a number of articles, including "Chaucerian Comedy and Criseyde" (in *Essays on Troilus and Criseyde*, 1979) and "Recycling Anelida and Arcite: Chaucer as a Source for Chaucer" (in *Studies in the Age of Chaucer*, 1984). A major scholarly contribution came in the form of his role as coeditor of the University of Oklahoma Press' *The Chaucer Varorium: V: The Minor Poets, Part I* (1982). More recently, he had written an article titled "The Ownership and Use of the Ellesmere Manuscript" (in *The Ellesmere Chaucer: Essays in Interpretation*, 1995), which traces the ownership of

this manuscript up to its present home at the Huntingdon Library in San Marino, California. The article also gives general consideration to the ways in which the ELLESMERE MANUSCRIPT has been used by scholars over the centuries.

Davis, Norman (1913–) Chaucer scholar, born in New Zealand. Davis won a Rhodes Scholarship in 1934. After stops in Lithuania and Bulgaria, as well as various institutions in Great Britain, he completed his career at Oxford. With wide-ranging interests in the medieval period, his major contribution to our understanding of Chaucer came when he authored the Oxford University Press' *A Chaucer Glossary* (1979).

Davit *See* DAVID.

Decameron The *Decameron* was the work of Giovanni BOCCACCIO, an Italian author who had tremendous influence on Chaucer, although Chaucer never mentions his debt to him. The most famous and enduring of Boccaccio's literary creations, the *Decameron* consists of a frame story in which seven young women, three young men and a small group of servants leave Florence and travel out into the Italian countryside to avoid an outbreak of the plague. To pass the time during their 10-days' journey, they entertain themselves by taking turns telling stories. Each person tells one story on each day, so that there are 100 tales in all. Like Chaucer's CANTERBURY TALES, these stories are recounted within the framework of the journey, and they also, like Chaucer's work, were drawn from many sources, including classical stories and FABLIAUX; for these reasons, and because of Chaucer's obvious debt to Boccaccio's work in "The KNIGHT'S TALE" and *TROILUS AND CRISEYDE*, many scholars believe that the *Decameron* directly inspired the framework apparatus of *The Canterbury Tales*. Some, however, believe that despite these similarities, the *Decameron* did not influence the structure of Chaucer's most famous work, at least not directly. There are, after all, notable differences between Boccaccio's conception and Chaucer's. Whereas Chaucer's pilgrims come from various disparate social classes, Boccaccio's storytellers represent one social class. (The servants do not participate.) Also, in Chaucer's work, the same person, Harry BAILLY, presides over the storytelling throughout, whereas in the *Decameron*, a new person is elected each day to perform this function, as well as determining other activities to be participated in by the group. Furthermore, the storytellers in Boccaccio's work are never particularized the way Chaucer's pilgrims are in the striking literary portraiture provided by the GENERAL PROLOGUE and then embroidered upon in the links between the tales. Finally, Chaucer's pilgrims recite their tales as they are traveling along the road, whereas Boccaccio's young aristocrats use storytelling as a means to pass the time at each place of lodging. Whether or not Chaucer ultimately got his idea for the framework of *The Canterbury Tales* from Boccaccio, we can at least be sure that the *Decameron* was the ultimate source for his "CLERK'S TALE," which relates the story of patient GRISELDA. Although Chaucer drew directly from PETRARCH's version of the story, Petrarch's debt to Boccaccio is clearly attested. Boccaccio's tale of Griselda was the final (the 100th) tale of the *Decameron*. Folktale elements of the story suggest that it probably existed earlier in oral form, but Boccaccio's is the earliest surviving written version. Another of the Canterbury tales that may have been inspired by Boccaccio's *Decameron* is "The SHIPMAN'S TALE," although the existence of other analogues makes the specifics of this relationship impossible to determine. The tales in Boccaccio's *Decameron* were probably written over a number of years in the early part of his literary career, but assembled in their final form between 1349 and 1351.

de casibus tragedy   The term *de casibus tragedy* derives from BOCCACCIO's *De casibus virorum illustrium* (Concerning the misfortunes of great men), in which tragedy is defined as the fall of a great man from prosperity to adversity. In composing his "MONK'S TALE," Chaucer borrowed both the idea and some of the examples Boccaccio gave, but whereas Boccaccio emphasizes the culpability of each protagonist in bringing about his own unhappiness, Chaucer stresses the role of FORTUNE in causing the tragedy. The idea of Fortune and its relationship to human destiny was also important in another of Chaucer's favorite works, the French *ROMAN DE LA ROSE,* where the allegorical figure of REASON warns the lover against Fortune's instability. The concept of tragedy was an unfamiliar one for medieval readers, for whom Aristotle's *Poetics* was not yet available. Such theoretical definitions of tragedy as did exist at this time were inconsistent with one another; a tale with an unhappy ending is the closest we can come to a general definition. For this reason, and because of Chaucer's influential position as a man of letters, his MONK's definition of tragedy became the "official" one until the widespread rediscovery of Aristotle's work in the early 17th century.

De casibus virorum illustrium   *See* DE CASIBUS TRAGEDY.

Decius Paulinus   A Roman consul in the fifth-century government of THEODORIC the Ostrogoth. When he fell into disfavor, and others in the government would have seized his property, BOETHIUS claims to have drawn "hym out of the jowes of hem that gapeden" (*BOECE,* Book One, Prosa 4, lines 96–97) [him (or possibly *them,* i.e., the riches) out of the jaws of those who gaped]. Paulinus was one of several people Boethius defended,

contributing to his own fall from favor, exile and eventual execution. The prosecution of Paulinus is mentioned by CASSIODORUS, who was at that time serving as Theodoric's chief secretary.

Decorat (Decoratus)   A Roman quaestor who supported the rule of THEODORIC, the Ostragothic king of Rome who forced BOETHIUS into exile and later had him executed. Decorat is mentioned in Book Three of the *BOECE,* when LADY PHILOSOPHY uses him as an example to explain how being elected or appointed to high public office does not necessarily increase the goodness or worthiness of the man who receives those honors. In doing so, she reminds the narrator that he himself refused to serve in the government with Decorat because he knew the man to be a lecherous scoundrel and an informer.

Decrees, Book of   The Book of Decrees probably refers to the compilation known as the *Corpus iuris canonici,* which consisted of the decretal collection (collection of papal decrees) made by Gratian in the 12th century, together with the decretals of Pope Gregory IX. Dame PRUDENCE, the wife of Melibee in Chaucer's "Tale of Melibee," quotes from the Book of Decrees when she says, "Seelden, or with gret peyne, been causes ybroght to good ende whanne they been baddely bigonne" (line 1404) [Seldom, or with great pains, are projects (or plans) brought to a good conclusion when they begin badly]. This and many other sayings adopted out of various texts are used by Prudence in her argument against getting revenge on those men who robbed Melibee and assaulted his wife and his daughter, SOPHIA.

Dedalus   *See* DAEDALUS.

Deeth of Blaunche the Duchesse   *See* BOOK OF THE DUCHESS, THE.

Deianira   In classical mythology, Deianira was the daughter of King Oeneus of Calydon and Queen Althea. HERCULES and the river god ACHELOUS both fell in love with her and fought to possess her. Hercules was victorious and became her husband. Once, when the two were on a journey together, Hercules employed a CENTAUR, NESSUS, to carry Deianira over a river while he himself swam across. Nessus fell in love with Hercules' wife and tried to carry her off, but Hercules felled him with a poisoned arrow. The dying Nessus gave Deianira his robe, which had been stained with the poisoned blood, telling her that it would serve to reawaken Hercules' love if ever he turned away from her. Later, when she became jealous of his attentions to another woman, Deianira sent the robe to Hercules on the occasion of a sacrifice. The poisoned robe did not kill him but caused him to be in such excruciating pain that he killed himself. When Deianira learned what had happened, she also committed suicide.

In Chaucer's work, Deianira first appears in *The HOUSE OF FAME*, which emphasizes Hercules' betrayal of his wife. She is later mentioned in the prologue to "The MAN OF LAW'S TALE" as one of the women whose story appears in Chaucer's *LEGEND OF GOOD WOMEN*, but no mention of her actually appears there. Evidence such as this lends credence to scholars who claim that the *Legend* was never finished. Deianira's role in her husband's death is one of the narratives that JANKIN (1), the WIFE OF BATH's fifth husband, likes to read to her from his Book of Wicked Wives, as mentioned in the prologue to "The WIFE OF BATH'S TALE." "The MONK'S TALE" also includes these events in its version of the life of Hercules.

Deiphebus   *See* DEIPHOBUS.

Deiphobus   In classical mythology, Deiphobus was the son of King PRIAM and Queen HECUBA of TROY. He was one of the leaders of the Trojans in the TROJAN WAR and the favorite of his brother HECTOR. After the death of PARIS, Deiphobus married Helen (HELEN OF TROY), the woman whom Paris had stolen away from her Greek husband, causing the Greeks to wage war against the city of Troy. When Troy was defeated, Helen led her original Greek husband, MENELAUS, to the room of Deiphobus and thus betrayed him; subsequently, he was mutilated and killed. Deiphobus is briefly mentioned in Chaucer's *HOUSE OF FAME* as one of those whom AENEAS sees when he visits his father in Hades. He plays a minor but significant role in the long poem *TROILUS AND CRISEYDE*, which is set in Troy during the Trojan War. CRISEYDE's uncle PANDARUS persuades Deiphobus to invite Criseyde to his house for dinner so that Pandarus can arrange an "accidental" meeting between his niece and Troilus, who, according to the poem, is Deiphobus' favorite brother. The meeting is designed to further insinuate the young knight into Criseyde's affections.

Delilah   According to the Bible (Judges 16), Delilah was the Philistine woman loved by SAMSON, the mightiest of Israel's judges. She betrayed Samson to the lords of the Philistines for 1,100 pieces of silver. Tricking Samson into believing that she loved him, Delilah convinced him to reveal the secret of his strength, which was his long hair. His hair was also the symbol of a sacred religious vow. While Samson slept at Delilah's home, a Philistine entered and cut his hair. Without his great strength, he was easily captured and imprisoned. Later, when he was exhibited blinded and in chains at a Philistine gathering in the temple of Dagon, his strength returned and he was able to pull down the temple pillars, causing it to collapse on top of himself and 3,000 observers. Chaucer tells the story of how Delilah robbed Samson of his strength in the brief biography of Samson that appears in "The MONK'S TALE." Although the overall purpose of the stories told by the MONK is to illustrate the vicissitudes of FORTUNE, in Samson's case he repeatedly remarks that men who tell their secrets to women will come to no good. The role played by Delilah in bringing about Samson's downfall is also mentioned in *The BOOK OF THE DUCHESS* and in the short poem "AGAINST WOMEN UNCONSTANT."

Delphi   Ancient Greek city in Phocis, on the slopes of Mount Parnassus, the mountain at whose summit the Greek gods were supposed to dwell. In ancient times the oracle of APOLLO was located there. People from all over the Greek world came to consult the oracle with questions of every kind, both personal and political. The exact oracular procedures are uncertain, but it is known that the Pythia (prophetess of Apollo) uttered the responses of the god. She carried out this function seated on a tripod, a bowl supported by three metal legs. Ancient pottery depicts Apollo himself seated upon the bowl. Her prophecies were transcribed into prose or verse by a priest or prophet stationed nearby, and then communicated to the inquirer. Some sources claim that the Pythia's inspiration came from the vaporous outpourings that issued from a chasm or cave, and depict the priestess seated on the tripod above such a cleft or opening. The petitioner who came to the temple with a question for the god had to go through certain prescribed ceremonies before he could receive an answer. First, he had to offer an expensive sacred cake upon the altar outside the temple. Once inside, he was required to sacrifice a sheep or goat. Then he could enter the innermost shrine of the temple, where a priest or prophet addressed his questions to the Pythia and interpreted her answers. In Chaucer's "FRANKLIN'S TALE," the squire AURELIUS, who falls in love with the married DORIGEN, prays to Apollo, promising that he will make a pilgrimage to Delphi (a considerable journey from the squire's homeland) if the god will move the rocks lying in the ocean off the coast of BRITTANY. The nature of his request is dictated by Dorigen's promise to become the squire's lover if he can accomplish this feat. When Apollo does not respond, Aurelius seeks the help of a magician. In book four of *TROILUS AND CRISEYDE*, it is revealed in an oblique manner that CRISEYDE's father, CALKAS, learned that TROY would lose the war by consulting the oracle at Delphi. Criseyde tells TROILUS that she will try to persuade Calkas that he may have misunderstood the oracle's pronouncements, to convince him that she may safely return to Troy.

Delphinus   Delphinus is the name Chaucer gives to the constellation more familiarly known as the Dolphin. It is one of the constellations mentioned by the EAGLE in *The HOUSE OF FAME,* as he carries Chaucer through the heavens to FAME's palace. At this point in their journey the eagle is trying to convince Chaucer to let himself be ferried up into the highest of the nine spheres, which is the home of the fixed stars. By so doing, the eagle argues, Chaucer could learn about the stars firsthand. Chaucer responds that there are certain things about which he would rather learn from books. The argument is related to the theme of knowledge based on experience versus knowledge derived from reading, a theme that surfaces throughout the poem.

Delphos   *See* DELPHI.

Delphyn   *See* DELPHINUS.

Demetrius   According to legend, Demetrius was a king of Sparta in the second century B.C. who was sent a set of dice by the king of Parthia. The gift was intended to show the Parthian ruler's lack of respect for a man who would engage in such games of chance. The narrator of "The PARDONER'S TALE" mentions this anecdote to illustrate the dangers of gambling (lines 621–26).

Democion's daughter   *See* DEMOTION'S DAUGHTER.

Demophon   In classical mythology, Demophon was a son of THESEUS, ruler of Athens, and PHAEDRA who fought bravely on the side of the Greeks in the TROJAN WAR, rescuing his grandmother, who had been taken to the city as a slave when HELEN OF TROY was kidnapped. On his return voyage to Athens, Demophon became shipwrecked on RHODOPE, where PHYLLIS, the queen of that country, entertained him and gave him money and supplies to repair his vessels. Demophon promised to marry her and sailed home to Athens to prepare for the wedding, but once there he forgot all about his vow. In despair over his betrayal, Phyllis hanged herself. Chaucer tells the story of Phyllis and Demophon in *The HOUSE OF FAME* (lines 388–96) and in *The LEGEND OF GOOD WOMEN* (lines 2394–2561). The tragic end of the love affair is also alluded to in *The BOOK OF THE DUCHESS* when the narrator tells the BLACK KNIGHT that if he commits suicide over the loss of his queen, he will surely be damned, just as Phyllis was for hanging herself.

Demotion's daughter   The daughter of Demotion, an Athenian aristocrat, is mentioned in "The FRANKLIN'S TALE" as a woman exemplary for her chastity. She committed suicide on learning that her betrothed had died; the alternative, marrying another man, seemed like bigamy to her. DORIGEN, the protagonist of "The Franklin's Tale," includes Demotion's daughter in a list of women famed for chastity that she uses to bolster her own resolve to remain faithful to her husband, ARVERA-GUS, rather than keep her rash promise to the squire AURELIUS.

Dempster, Germaine   Chaucer scholar. Germaine Dempster completed her work at the University of Liege and then received a grant for a two-year stay at Stanford University, where she wrote *Dramatic Irony in Chaucer* (1932); afterward, she became a professor at the University of Chicago. *Dramatic Irony* has a broader scope than its title may suggest. Dempster believes that key tactic in detecting irony is to identify how Chaucer changed the plots he inherited; hence the need to study Chaucer's sources. She points out that Chaucer offers relentless dramatic irony; the only question is whether it was intended or accidental. On this issue, Dempster asks that "no very strong proof" be required, considering that the better we come to know the poet, the less naive he appears. She expanded her work on sources by coediting, with W. F. Bryan, *Sources and Analogues of Chaucer's "Canterbury Tales"* (1941). This is a book with brief introductions for each tale, followed by its source(s) or analogue(s) in the original languages, with translations. Dempster's scholarship also exhibits a concern with textual matters. Her valuable contributions to Chaucer studies in this area include two articles in *Publications of the Modern Language Association:* "A Chapter in the Manuscript History of the Canterbury Tales: The Ancestor of Group d, the Origin of its Texts, Tale-order, and Spurious Links" (1948) and "The Fifteenth-Century Editors of the Canterbury Tales and the Problem of Tale Order" (1949). These essays explore the problem of establishing an order for *The CANTERBURY TALES* (a task Chaucer never completed), examining the development of various arrangements as recorded in the manuscripts. Along with an analysis of the relationships among the orders, Dempster suggests reasons for their influence on one another.

Denis, Saint (Saint Dionysius)   The sixth of the bishops of Vienne in France, Denis became known as the patron saint of that country. The corrupt monk (*see* JOHN THE MONK) of "The SHIPMAN'S TALE" swears by Saint Denis when he informs the merchant's wife that he and the merchant are not related, that he only calls the man his cousin in order to curry favor and thus have more opportunities to visit with her, whom he loves above all other women.

Denmark   Located in northwestern Europe, the country of Denmark occupies most of the peninsula of Jutland and several nearby islands in the North and Baltic Seas. In the 14th century, its holdings included a portion of southern Sweden. Denmark is mentioned only once in Chaucer, when the WIFE OF BATH says that she treats her husband as well as any wife between Denmark and India.

Depeford   *See* DEPTFORD.

De planctu Naturae   *See* ALAIN DE LILLE.

Deptford   A metropolitan borough of London, located about five miles south of the city. It is one of the towns the pilgrims pass by on their journey from London to the shrine of THOMAS À BECKET at Canterbury cathedral. The Host (*see* Harry BAILLY) calls attention to the town in the prologue to "The REEVE'S TALE" when he notes that they are approaching Deptford and that the time is half-way Prime (about 7:30 A.M.). This is one of a few geographical markers in the passages linking *The* CANTERBURY TALES that may have been intended to provide the pilgrimage framework with a stronger sense of realism, reinforcing the illusion that the pilgrims are actually journeying through time and space. F. P. MAGOUN disputes this idea in his *Chaucer Gazetteer:* "That the Knight and the Miller between them should have got through with three thousand odd lines of verse in such short order is merely part of the unrealism of the whole plan and should not be pressed or in any way rationalized here or elsewhere" (p. 60).

Dertemouthe   *See* DARTMOUTH.

Deschamps, Eustache   French poet whose reputation was well-established at the time Chaucer's was just becoming established. That is why Deschamps' recognition and praise of Chaucer's work in a poem written in 1385 was so significant. This poem is one of the first tributes to Chaucer's skill and, oddly enough, came at a time when France was preparing to invade England. Deschamps chiefly praises Chaucer's efforts at translating *Le* ROMAN DE LA ROSE and thus making it accessible to English readers. He also lauds the English poet's wisdom and learning as well as his literary style, which had been strongly influenced by French poets.

de Vere, Robert (1362–1392)   Robert de Vere, the ninth earl of Oxford, was one of King RICHARD II's closest friends, who were usually given the appellation of "favorite." The friendship between de Vere and the king aroused jealousy and hostility among other members of the nobility, particularly the young king's uncles. When de Vere claimed that he and his wife lacked the means to support their lifestyle, the king gave them various properties, one of which had belonged to the wife of Richard's uncle, THOMAS OF WOODSTOCK, the duke of Gloucester. Such favors turned other members of the nobility against de Vere. Richard made his friend a member of the privy council

and a knight of the Garter, and when the English colony in Ireland asked for the king's help in defending their settlement, he made de Vere the marquis of Dublin, promising him that captured lands not previously owned by the Crown would be his and his heirs' free of rent or service. Some of de Vere's detractors claimed that there was a homosexual relationship between the two men, a rumor that was supported by the fact that Richard sent a deputy to Ireland so that de Vere could remain at court. De Vere's greatest opponent in the king's Parliament was JOHN OF GAUNT, duke of Lancaster, and de Vere made several attempts to discredit and eliminate Lancaster, usually involving fabricated evidence that the duke was leading a conspiracy against the king's life. Finally tensions between the king's favorites and other factions of his government grew so intense that the duke of Gloucester, as constable of England and head of the High Court of Chivalry in England, summoned five of the men to appear before this court on charges of treason. All of the men except de Vere fled immediately. De Vere formed an army for his own defense but was defeated by Henry of Bolingbroke (later HENRY IV) at the head of an army supporting Gloucester's position. De Vere abandoned his troops and, after stopping in London to see Richard, was smuggled out of London and managed to escape to the Continent. He died several years later of a wound received during a boar hunt in France.

Deyscorides   *See* DIOSCORIDES.

Diana   In classical mythology, Diana was an ancient Italian goddess whom the Romans identified with the Greek Artemis. She was a goddess of light, of forest and mountain and of plants and animals not growing under the protection or fosterage of humans. She was also the goddess of fertility in women, presiding over childbirth under the name Lucina. The daughter of JUPITER and twin sister of APOLLO, Diana ranked as one of the greatest of the gods in the Roman pantheon. Like the Greek Artemis, she was commonly portrayed as a virgin huntress. Despite her patronage of childbirth, her chief characteristic was chastity, and maidens often prayed to her for that reason. She was known to severely punish violations of chastity in those who had vowed to serve her. Like her brother Apollo, Diana was a lover of music, song and dance, and just as he was the god of the sun, so was she the goddess of the moon. As a huntress, Diana was portrayed as clad in a short tunic extending from shoulders to knees; as the goddess of the moon, she would wear a long robe reaching to the ground with a veil and crescent on her head. Temples of the goddess Diana were a place where maidens who wished to preserve their virginity might take refuge, though to judge by the examples presented in Chaucer's work, such an action was rarely effective. In

Chaucer's "KNIGHT'S TALE," on the eve of combat between the two Theban knights, PALAMON and ARCITE (1), EMILY visits the temple of Diana to pray that the goddess will protect her virginity. The object of the knights' duel is to decide who will marry Emily, but she does not want to marry either one. Diana denies her petition and Emily is, after some delay caused by the champion's death, bestowed upon the survivor, Palamon. Another example appears in "The FRANKLIN'S TALE," when DORIGEN recalls the story of a maiden named STYMPHALIS who took refuge in Diana's temple when her father was slain. When she refused to come out and become his wife, she was murdered by her suitor. Diana's failure to protect maidens is brazenly exhibited in The PARLIAMENT OF FOWLS, where one wall of the TEMPLE OF VENUS is covered with broken bows, each one signifying an incidence of lost virginity. The bows, the narrator tells us, are hung there to spite Diana. Another aspect of the goddess, which receives brief emphasis in Chaucer's work, is her anger. Twice in "The Knight's Tale" we are reminded of the story of ACTAEON, the young man who saw Diana bathing. He was punished by being changed into a stag and torn apart by his own hounds. In TROILUS AND CRISEYDE, TROILUS' sister CASSANDRA tells him the story of the great Caledonian boar that Diana had sent to punish the Greeks for refusing to sacrifice to her. The boar wreaked havoc by devouring all their grain and destroying their vineyards. Finally, Diana is sometimes simply invoked (perhaps by one of her other names, Cinthia, Latona or Lucina), such as when CRISEYDE swears by the goddess of the moon that she will always remain faithful to Troilus. Such an oath is of course ironic, since the moon does not remain constant but waxes and wanes.

Dianira *See* DEIANIRA.

Dictis Cretensis *See* DICTYS CRETENSIS.

Dictys Cretensis (Dictys the Cretan) The supposed author of a diary of the TROJAN WAR. The language of the original text is uncertain, but it comes down to us in a Latin version. The preface, written in the fourth century by Lucius Septimius, claims that Dictys translated the work from a Greek version prepared for the emperor NERO from a Phoenician original. Dictys claims to have been present at the siege of TROY as a companion of the Cretan Idomeneus. This work and the history of Troy attributed to DARES Phrygius provided the most detailed accounts of the Trojan War available in western Europe during the medieval period. Everything written about Troy before the middle of the 17th century was to some extent dependent, either directly or indirectly, on the narratives of Dares and Dictys, and Chaucer's *TROILUS AND CRISEYDE* is no exception. Although Chaucer's direct source was BOC-

CACCIO's *FILOSTRATO,* the Italian poet drew upon the work of earlier writers whose ultimate sources were the classical accounts mentioned above. Dictys is referred to by the name of Tytus in *The HOUSE OF FAME,* where he is mentioned as one of the poets lining the approach to FAME's throne. Along with HOMER, Dares, GUIDO DELLE COLONNE and others, he helps to perpetuate the fame of Troy.

Didalus *See* DAEDALUS.

Dido The daughter of King Belus of Tyre, Dido was the legendary queen and founder of the great city of CARTHAGE in northern Africa. Her name means "wanderer" and perhaps derives from the fact that she came to Carthage as a result of a self-imposed exile from her homeland of Phoenicia. When her brother, Pygmalion, murdered her husband in order to gain possession of his rich treasures, her husband's ghost appeared to Dido in a dream, warning her against Pygmalion's treachery. Dido took the treasure and escaped to Africa, where she used her wealth to buy the land that became the basis for the city of Carthage. Dido was wooed by a neighboring king named IARBUS but refused him on the grounds that she would never marry again. However, she later fell in love with the Trojan AENEAS, who landed in northern Africa after his escape from TROY at the conclusion of the TROJAN WAR. When Aeneas deserted Dido to fulfill his destiny as the founder of the Roman race, she committed suicide, stabbing herself with Aeneas' sword on her funeral pyre.

The story of their love appears twice in Chaucer's poetry. In *The HOUSE OF FAME,* it forms a focus of book one, where Chaucer tells the story in a manner that is very sympathetic toward the queen. Emphasizing the despair she feels over not only losing Aeneas, but her reputation as well, he shows how essential this quality was for one who would rule. In this way, the story exhibits one facet of the poem's theme, the manifestations and uses of fame. The story is also notable for its condemnation of the behavior of Aeneas, who, in classical sources, is portrayed simply as a hero fulfilling his destiny. In *The LEGEND OF GOOD WOMEN,* Chaucer again tells the story from a point of view that highlights the queen's suffering and Aeneas' betrayal. Interestingly, in this story, the narrator even more vehemently censures Aeneas' behavior, offering him as an example of the kind of man who is particularly dangerous to women, one who appears virtuous, true and honorable, but whose treatment of his lover ultimately destroyed her, despite the fact that she had taken him in when he was a shipwrecked stranger in her land, showering him with gifts and then generously giving her love wholeheartedly. Dido is mentioned briefly in *The BOOK OF THE DUCHESS* when the narrator, playing devil's advocate with the BLACK KNIGHT, tells him that Dido was a fool for killing herself over a false lover (lines 731–34). In *The PARLIAMENT OF FOWLS,* she is mentioned as one of love's martyrs (line 289).

diet in the Middle Ages   Diet in the Middle Ages had at least two things in common with our eating habits today: Both the quality and the quantity of the food a person ate was determined by his or her income and social status. The diet of the peasantry, though much better than that of the urban poor, featured a lot of bread and grain products (such as gruel). Their most common drink was water, followed by beer or ale; their most common vegetables, onions, peas and beans, which could be preserved and prepared during the fall and winter when other vegetables were unavailable. Along with bread, peas and beans were the dietary staples of the peasantry; wealthier people ate them too, but spiced them with garlic and/or saffron, one of the most popular spices of the day.

As a member of the middle class serving in royal households, Chaucer would have had the benefit of sharing their food. This means that although his breakfast fare of bread and a little wine to wash it down varied little from the peasant's first meal of the day, the remainder of his daily consumption would be comparatively lavish, including meat, poultry, fish, vegetables, fruit, cheese, wines and various sweet desserts such as cake and pudding. At mealtime, servants set up trestle tables, which were spread with cloths. Cutlery included knives and spoons (but not forks), dishes for salt, silver cups and mazers (shallow, silver-rimmed wooden bowls for soup). The knives were used for carving and cutting the meat into small pieces, which was then eaten with the fingers. Roast meat or fish was served on a trencher, a thick slice of stale bread. Servants attended the diners with ewers (large water pitchers), basins and towels for washing.

Etiquette books suggest that good manners were important at the dining table. Such books advised diners not to drink with their mouths full and not to stuff their mouths or take overly large helpings. Considerable emphasis was laid upon keeping hands and nails clean, wiping the spoon and knife after each use and wiping the mouth before drinking. Dipping meat into the salt dish was likewise forbidden. Chaucer's portrait of the PRIORESS provides us with some hint of this etiquette in action when he notes that she was always careful not to let any morsel fall from her lips or to wet her fingers deeply in the sauce. And she wiped her upper lip so clean that not a speck of grease was seen floating in her cup after she drank.

Service at the table was marked by ceremony. There was a correct way to do everything, and part of a squire's training (which Chaucer would have experienced in the household of Elizabeth, countess of Ulster) included learning how to serve his lord and/or lady at meals. Dishes were to be presented in a certain order and in a prescribed manner. Carving the meat was another of the squire's tasks, and that too had to be done according to protocol.

The preparation of fresh or preserved meat was one of the supreme tests of medieval cookery, so it should come as no surprise that in the GENERAL PROLOGUE TO *THE CANTERBURY TALES* the COOK takes special pride in two meat dishes: blankmanger and mortrew. The former consisted of a paste made out of chicken blended with rice boiled in almond-flavored milk, seasoned with sugar, cooked until thick and garnished with fried almonds and anise. The latter, another pudding-like meat dish, was made of fish or meat that had been pounded and mixed with bread crumbs, stock and eggs. It was then cooked in boiling water to produce a kind of dumpling.

As stated above, the most common beverages were water, beer and ale. Milk was reserved almost exclusively for young children. The aristocracy and those of the middle class who could afford it drank considerable quantities of wine. In 14th-century England, most of the wine was imported from the Bordeaux region of France, and was drunk young in the absence of an effective technique for stoppering containers, which were typically casks or barrels. As a result, no attention was paid to vintage, and wine often soured before it could be consumed. Some of this sour wine was drunk anyway. Coming from a family of vintners, Chaucer would presumably have drunk wine with his meals, and there is one brief allusion to his fondness for drink in his poetry, when the EAGLE in *The HOUSE OF FAME* chides him for his lack of abstinence.

Chaucer's apocryphal reputation for being a gourmand has two explanations. First, in all but one of his existing portraits, he is depicted as being somewhat rotund. This image is supported by the reference to himself as a man "round of shape" in the poem "LENVOY DE CHAUCER À SCOGAN." In light of these bits of evidence, the suggestion has also been made that the FRANKLIN of the General Prologue, whose house "rains" food and drink, is actually a thinly disguised self-portrait of Chaucer. Since *The Canterbury Tales* is a naturalistic work of art, it seems only logical that its framework should contain references to the dietary habits of such pilgrims as the Prioress (mentioned above), the Franklin and the SUMMONER, who loves garlic, onions and leeks. The pilgrimage itself is framed by two meals. The first is the breakfast at which the Host (*see* Harry BAILLY) proposes that the pilgrims engage in a tale-telling contest to pass the time along their journey to CANTERBURY. However, the second meal, to be given as a prize to the contest's winner, exists only as a promise. When Chaucer completed *The Canterbury Tales,* his concerns, as evidenced by the Retraction, were no longer focused on earthly material things such as food. (*See* CHAUCER'S RETRACTION.)

Diogenes   Greek philosopher of the fourth century B.C. who founded the group of philosophers known as the Cynics. Diogenes won fame through his perpetual quest for an "honest" man. By "honest," he meant one who had adopted a natural life and repudiated everything conventional and artificial. The Cynics adopted as their principal goal the cultivation of self-sufficiency: every man should develop the ability to satisfy his own needs. Chaucer refers to Diogenes in the short poem "The FORMER AGE," which describes a time when humankind lived together peacefully in an Edenic paradise, cultivating such goals as those described by the Cynics. According to Diogenes, Chaucer says, such a paradise is maintained by the lack of possessions and wealth, these being things that draw the attention of tyrants and disrupt the peace.

Diomede   In classical mythology, Diomede was the son of Tydeus and the successor of ADRASTUS to the throne of Argos. He fought on the Greek side in the TROJAN WAR, leading 80 ships against Troy and distinguishing himself as the bravest of the Greeks, second only to Achilles as a warrior. With ULYSSES he went via an underground passage to the Acropolis of Troy and stole the Palladium, the image of PALLAS Athena that protected Troy from being defeated in battle. Diomede plays an important role in Chaucer's *TROILUS AND CRISEYDE* as the Greek warrior who wooed CRISEYDE's affections away from TROILUS. Diomede offers Criseyde his protection at a crucial moment, when she has been forced to join her father in the Greek camp outside Troy and fears for her safety. She is further influenced by the knowledge that Diomede will inherit the throne of Argos and become king of that region after the war is over. In contrast to Troilus, Diomede is bold and unselfconscious in his attempts to win Criseyde's love. He is able to perceive the relationship between Troilus and Criseyde by just seeing them together once, and uses that knowledge, along with other perceptions of her character, in a calculating and practical manner. Although these features make him seem like a manipulative opportunist, Chaucer softens the portrait by telling us that Criseyde did indeed love Diomede and was devastated when he returned to camp wounded from combat against Troilus.

Diomedes   In classical mythology, Diomedes was king of the Bistones in Thrace. He made a practice of feeding strangers to his horses. HERCULES, in the performance of one of his 12 labors, killed him and fed his body to the horses. Diomedes is mentioned in Book Four of the *BOECE* as an example of a powerful man who nevertheless was overcome by the turning of FORTUNE's wheel.

Dione   In classical mythology, Dione was the mother of Aphrodite (VENUS) by Zeus (JUPITER). Little is known of her other than her name which, interestingly, is the feminine form of the name Zeus (which in another form is Dios). At the end of book three of *TROILUS AND CRISEYDE,* the narrator praises Venus, calling her "doughter to Dyone" (line 1807), for helping him tell the story of Troilus' love.

Dionysius Cato   The supposed author of a collection of nearly 150 pithy sayings in Latin verse and prose composed around the third century A.D. by an unknown author or authors. The collection was generally referred to as *Disticha Catonis* ("Sayings of Cato"), and from the seventh century until the Renaissance, elementary school-age students memorized the maxims as their first training in Latin. By the late Middle Ages, the *Disticha Catonis* had been translated into most European vernaculars. There were similar collections of Latin maxims ascribed to other authors but sometimes referred to under the general heading of Cato's work. Such appears to be the case in Chaucer's "MILLER'S TALE" when the MILLER, speaking of JOHN THE CARPENTER, says that he was unaware of Cato's advice that a man ought to marry a woman equal to himself in class and age. The aged knight JANUARY, in "The MERCHANT'S TALE," quotes from the *Disticha Catonis* (among other texts) in attempting to justify his decision to take a wife. Considering the age of the wife whom he chooses, he seems to have missed, or chosen to ignore, the maxim quoted by the Miller, since January makes the same mistake as John, marrying a wife considerably younger than himself. As might be expected, the maxims of Cato appear frequently in Chaucer's "TALE OF MELIBEE," in which Dame PRUDENCE marshals all the wisdom literature has to offer in trying to dissuade her husband from hunting down and punishing the men who have robbed their family. Yet another reference to Cato (as "Catoun") appears in "The CANON'S YEOMAN'S TALE" where the CANON'S YEOMAN, speaking of his master, notes that a man who has a guilty conscience believes that all conversations have to do with him. The CANON (1) promptly confirms this assumption by guiltily riding away.

Dioscorides   Pedanius Dioscorides was a Greek physician and pharmacologist of the first century whose work *De materia medica* was the foremost classical source of modern botanical terminology and the leading pharmacological text until the end of the 15th century. Dioscorides is mentioned in Chaucer's GENERAL PROLOGUE to *The CANTERBURY TALES* as one of the medical authorities whose teachings the DOCTOR OF PHYSIC had studied.

Disticha Catonis   *See* DIONYSIUS CATO.

Dite   *See* DICTYS CRETENSIS.

Dives   The rich man in the parable of the rich man and the poor man (Lazarus) that appears in Luke

16:19–31. While Dives lived sumptuously attired and feeding on fine foods, the beggar Lazarus lay at the gate of the rich man's house, covered with sores, desiring to be fed with the crumbs that fell from Dives' table. When the beggar died, he was carried to heaven and rested in ABRAHAM's bosom. After the rich man died, finding himself in hell, he lifted up his eyes and could see a vision of Lazarus in Abraham's bosom. He cried out to Abraham, asking that Lazarus be allowed to drip water from his finger onto Dives' tongue to assuage his torment, but Abraham refused, reminding Dives of the positions the two men had occupied while they were still alive. The corrupt FRIAR of "The SUMMONER'S TALE" alludes to the story of Dives as he tries to coerce the ailing THOMAS into giving him some money (line 1877).

Doctor of Physic   The Doctor of Physic, or Physician, as he is called once the tale-telling contest has gotten under way, is one of the 22 pilgrims described in some detail in the GENERAL PROLOGUE TO *THE CANTERBURY*

Artist's rendering of the Doctor of Physic, from the Ellesmere Manuscript of The Canterbury Tales. *The doctor is depicted conducting an examination of what is probably urine to determine his patient's well-being.*

TALES. Like the SERGEANT OF THE LAW, he represents, and occupies, the highest attainable rank in his profession, one that could be attained only after more than 10 years of study and residency at a university. The superlative nature of the Physician's training and ability is abundantly in evidence at the beginning of his portrait. One example is the narrator's statement that this Doctor can speak with authority on both medicine ("physic") and surgery, which were considered two distinct professions in Chaucer's day, and only rarely practiced by the same person. This tone of unqualified praise and admiration does not, however, persist throughout the portrait. Some hints at satire appear when his mutually profitable relationship with the apothecary (pharmacist) and his belief in the medicinal property of gold (i.e., of making a profit) are mentioned. Citing these hints, Helen COOPER shrewdly points out that nearly every detail of his portrait primarily has to do with describing his knowledge and technique rather than with the results he achieves treating patients, something that is never specifically addressed. Like the FRIAR and the MONK, whose portraits are clearly satirical, he is inappropriately dressed for one of his rank and profession, another detail hinting at abuse or at least misplaced priorities. "The PHYSICIAN'S TALE," like "The MAN OF LAW'S TALE" about CONSTANCE, and "The CLERK'S TALE" concerning GRISELDA, is one of pathos involving a woman who is unjustly persecuted. "The Physician's Tale" stands apart from the other two, however, in having a tragic rather than a happy ending.

Dolphin   *See* DELPHINUS.

Domus Dedaly   This is the name Chaucer gives to the labyrinth that the mythological architect DAEDALUS constructed as a home for the MINOTAUR of Crete.

Donaldson, E(thelbert) Talbot (1910–1987)   A Yale Ph.D. who taught at Yale, Columbia and Indiana, Talbot Donaldson died on April 13, 1987, after spending some of his last hours in the hospital polishing his translation of the B-text of William LANGLAND's *PIERS PLOWMAN.* During his lifetime, Donaldson received every honor a medievalist might desire. He was a fellow of the Medieval Academy, a Corresponding Fellow of the British Academy, a Fellow of the American Academy of Arts and Sciences, the first president of the New Chaucer Society, president of the Medieval Academy, had two Guggenheim fellowships and won the Haskins Medal of the Medieval Academy (shared with George Kane) for the edition of the B-text of *Piers Plowman* (1975). He served on the editorial board of the *CHAUCER REVIEW* from its inception in 1966 until his death, and in addition to his non-Chaucer works, he published *Chaucer's Poetry: An Anthology for the Modern*

Reader (2nd edition, 1975), a text that remains popular in the classroom despite going in and out of print. The notes to this edition are especially helpful for students encountering Chaucer's English for the first time. In *Speaking of Chaucer* (1970), he says that "Chaucer often teaches himself, so that one is apt to find oneself in the classroom not at the lectern explicating the text but sitting with one's students as part of a delighted audience before whom the text unfolds itself." Several of Donaldson's more recent works show his interest in Shakespeare's treatment of Chaucerian themes and characters. He coedited the volume, *Chaucerian Shakespeare: Adaptation and Transformation* (1983) to which he contributed the essay, "Shakespeare's Taming of the Shrew and Chaucer's Wife of Bath: The Struggle for Marital Mastery." In 1985 he published a more personal meditation on how Chaucer influenced the dramatist, *The Swan at the Well: Shakespeare Reading Chaucer.*

Donegild The mother of King ALLA in "The MAN OF LAW'S TALE." She intensely dislikes her daughter-in-law, CONSTANCE, who is "so strange a creature" by virtue of her Christian, rather than pagan, heritage. When Constance gives birth to a son while Alla is away from home, Donegild contrives to send him a message saying that the child is a monster and its mother, therefore, must be an elf. Alla does not respond as she had hoped, but orders that the child and its mother be kept safe until his return. Donegild intervenes again, altering this message from the king so that it directs the constable in whose protection he left Constance to send his wife and child out to sea in a rudderless ship. When Alla reaches home and learns what his mother has done, he kills her. Later, repenting of that action, he makes a pilgrimage to ROME to take penance and is there reunited with his wife and son.

Dorigen The wife of the Breton knight ARVERAGUS in "The FRANKLIN'S TALE." The relationship between Dorigen and her husband is notable for the mutual love and respect they have for one another. That love is sorely tested, however, when Arveragus leaves home for two years. Dorigen, pining away for her absent husband, rashly promises her love (including sexual favors) to a young admirer, AURELIUS, if he can move or eliminate some threatening rocks that line the coast of BRITTANY and present a hazard for incoming ships. Dorigen's devotion to her husband is such that she never believes this feat can be accomplished; otherwise, she would not have made such a bargain. Psychologically her promise reveals that she is willing to consider anything if only it will ensure her husband's safe return. Dorigen's willingness to consider suicide and her unquestioning obedience to her husband's demand that she fulfill the terms of her agreement with

Aurelius have made her less than appealing to feminist readers, but to many within a medieval audience she would doubtless have appeared virtuous and heroic. The tale's happy ending affirms that both she and her husband have made the right decisions under stressful circumstances.

Dread One of the allegorical figures guarding the rose garden in the famous and influential French poem, *Le ROMAN DE LA ROSE*. In medieval love poetry, dread, or fear, is one of the chief obstacles typically encountered by the lover seeking to gain his lady's favor. In the *Roman*, DAUNGER, SHAME, Dread and WICKED TONGUE (malicious gossip) all try to prevent the lover from gaining access to the beautiful rose with which he has fallen in love. They are opposed by VENUS and BIALACOIL ("fair welcome"), who come to his aid and enable him to gain a kiss before JEALOUSY drives him out and imprisons the rose and Bialacoil in a strong fortress. Chaucer translated a portion of the *Roman* as *The ROMAUNT OF THE ROSE*, but his translation breaks off before the episode described above. Chaucer's Middle English version was continued by two other writers. The three fragments are sometimes printed together and designated Fragment A, Fragment B and Fragment C, as in the *RIVERSIDE CHAUCER*, edited by Larry BENSON.

Dream of Scipio The epilogue of M. Tullius CICERO's *Republic*, a work concerning political and moral philosophy, and arguing in favor of policy that would support the "common good" of all people. The *Republic* was unknown to medieval readers, except for this one portion which, along with an extensive commentary, had been preserved by the fifth-century Latin writer MACROBIUS. The *Dream* begins with the visit of SCIPIO AFRICANUS THE YOUNGER, a Roman general and statesman, to MASINISSA, king of Numidia, in 149 B.C. Scipio's adoptive grandfather, SCIPIO AFRICANUS THE ELDER had been one of Rome's most accomplished generals and was greatly admired by Masinissa. The two men, Masinissa and Scipio the Younger, sit up late into the night talking about Scipio's grandfather. The elder Scipio then appears to his grandson in a dream whose content is related in the rest of the work. Within that dream Scipio's grandfather takes him into the heavens and shows him CARTHAGE. (This is the prototype of many ascents to heaven in later literature, including those of DANTE and Chaucer.) By illustrating how small and insignificant Earth is in relation to the nine spheres (planets) with their heavenly harmony, he is able to warn his grandson against taking delight in worldly things, because at the end of time all worldly deeds will pass into oblivion. Those who are virtuous, however, and who further the common good will experience eternal joy after death. Those who are lawbreakers or who take delight only in the body will whirl about Earth in pain for many ages before they are forgiven.

Macrobius' "Commentary," which is more than 16 times longer than the *Dream,* uses passages from the *Dream* as the occasion for an elaborate exposition of neoplatonic doctrine. He also includes an encyclopedia on such subjects as arithmetic, astronomy, the music of the spheres, geography and dreams, which he divides and classifies as follows:

(1) The *somnium,* which shows us truths veiled in an allegorical form. A modern example would be a dream in which someone experiencing increasing financial difficulties dreamed of being lost in a desert with no food, water or shelter. This is the type of dream that Chaucer's narrators have in *The HOUSE OF FAME, The BOOK OF THE DUCHESS* and *The PARLIAMENT OF FOWLS.*

(2) The *visio,* which is a direct, literal revelation of the future. We would call it a prophetic or premonitory dream. Chaucer calls it an "avisioun." The rooster CHAUNTICLEER of "The NUN'S PRIEST'S TALE" has such a dream the night before he is attacked by RUSSELL the fox. In fact, when his wife, PERTELOTE, challenges his belief in the significance of his dream, Chaunticleer refers to Macrobius' commentary to affirm his position.

(3) The *oraculum,* a dream in which of one of the dreamer's parents or some other significant person appears to declare the future or give advice.

(4) The *insomnium,* which merely repeats working preoccupations, as if, for example, a ditch-digger goes to bed and dreams of digging ditches.

(5) The *visum,* which occurs when the dreamer is not yet fully asleep but sees shapes rushing through the mind. Nightmares belong to this class.

Scipio's dream, although referred to as a *somnium,* would appear to be a combination of types. In so far as someone appears in it to predict and warn, it is an *oraculum;* because it imparts what were considered to be literal truths about the celestial regions, it would also be a *visio;* in that its highest meaning is concealed, it could likewise be considered a *somnium.* Macrobius' commentary was not the only portion of his work that influenced Chaucer. In *The Parliament of Fowls,* Chaucer's narrator reads from and summarizes Scipio's dream, and when he (the narrator) goes to sleep, he is also visited by Scipio the Elder, who conducts him to the Garden of Love. In *The House of Fame,* the narrator has a dream in which an eagle carries him high above the Earth until it seems no bigger than a pin-prick, a vision that echoes the younger Scipio's experience of the world's smallness in comparison to the gigantic heavenly spheres. Finally, at the end of *TROILUS AND CRISEYDE,* when TROILUS dies he ascends, like the younger Scipio, into the highest celestial sphere where he perceives, looking down on Earth, the vanity and insignificance of human deeds, and especially of the kind of love that he has shared with CRISEYDE.

dream vision   The dream vision was a conventional narrative frame that was widely used in the Middle Ages. The narrator falls asleep and has a dream that becomes the main narrative of the poem. The dream is sometimes prefaced, as in Chaucer's work, with an introduction describing the circumstances that led up to the dream and influenced its content. Most dream visions of the medieval period are allegories like the famous French poem *Le ROMAN DE LA ROSE* and William LANGLAND'S *Vision of Piers the Plowman.* Chaucer employed the dream vision framework for four of his works: *The BOOK OF THE DUCHESS, The HOUSE OF FAME, The PARLIAMENT OF FOWLS, and The LEGEND OF GOOD WOMEN.* For a book-length study of the genre, see A. C. Spearing, *Medieval Dream Poetry.*

Drye Se   *See* GOBI DESERT.

Dun   The name given to the horse in the proverbial saying, "Dun is in the mire." Chaucer's Host (*see* Harry BAILLY) uses this expression in the prologue to "The MANCIPLE'S TALE" (line 5) to complain that things have come to a standstill. He is particularly annoyed with the COOK, who appears to have fallen asleep astride his horse. In the notes to the *RIVERSIDE CHAUCER,* V. J. Scattergood suggests that the saying derived from a rural game where players had to move an unwieldy object, supposedly imitating the freeing of a horse from the mud.

Dunmowe   Village near Chelmsford in Essex, England, where, until well into the 12th century, a side of bacon was annually offered to any married couple who had lived a year and a day without having an argument or repenting of their marriage. The WIFE OF BATH refers to this custom when she says that her first three husbands never had the bacon of Dunmowe fetched for them. She is alluding to the fact that those marriages, which saw her paired with men much older than herself, were filled with quarreling and strife.

Dunstan, Saint   One of the most famous saints of Anglo-Saxon England, Saint Dunstan was born about 925 and educated at Glastonbury Abbey, where, after spending some time at the court of King Athelstan, he returned to become a monk. In the monastery he lived a very devout life, dividing his time between prayer, study and manual labor. He was appointed abbot at Glastonbury under King Edmund, but after rebuking Edmund's successor for leading a sinful life, Dunstan was forced into exile for one year. He returned during the reign of Edgar, to whom he became a chief adviser. Edgar appointed him bishop of Worcester in 957 and archbishop of Canterbury in 961. Through his "Canons," Dunstan did much to restore ecclesiastical discipline in England. When he died in 988, Dunstan was buried at Canterbury cathedral. In "The FRIAR'S TALE," Dunstan is mentioned by the devil, who explains to the corrupt summoner how devils such as himself sometimes serve the purposes of God and men in the course of pursuing their accustomed objective—to steal men's souls. Saint Dunstan's power over devils and other ministers of Satan was commonly illustrated in lives of the saint with which Chaucer would have been familiar.

Dyane *See* DIANA.

Dyer, the (Dyere) One of a group of tradesmen mentioned, but not described individually, in the GENERAL PROLOGUE to *The CANTERBURY TALES.* His title indicates that he is engaged in the profession of dying cloth. The others in his group include a Haberdasher, Carpenter, Weaver ("Webbe") and a Tapestry Maker ("Tapycer").

These five men are all wearing the same type of uniform, which indicates their membership in one of the medieval trade guilds, the forerunner of modern-day trade unions. The guilds set standards for the quality of the goods produced, regulated holidays and hours of work, and fixed prices and wages to some extent. Certain details of Chaucer's portrait of the guildsmen, such as their silver- (rather than brass) mounted knives, might suggest either prosperity or pretentiousness, depending upon whether one judges the portraits to contain elements of satire. Those scholars who argue against finding satire in their description note that Chaucer provided his guildsmen with none of the traditional mercantile vices such as fraud, usury and avarice. None of the five guildsmen tells a tale on the pilgrimage to CANTERBURY.

Dyone *See* DIONE.

E

Eacides Chiron *See* CHIRON.

Eagle, the A character in Chaucer's early poem *The HOUSE OF FAME*. The poem is a DREAM VISION that describes the narrator's movement through a somewhat unreal landscape. First he visits a TEMPLE OF VENUS, where he sees VENUS and reads the story of queen DIDO depicted on the temple walls. When he leaves the temple, he finds himself standing in a desert wasteland. Far off in the distance he observes an eagle, who appears to be flying toward him. The eagle approaches and, to the narrator's surprise and dismay, scoops him up in his talons, carrying him up into the atmosphere. Citing the Italian writer DANTE ALIGHIERI's obvious influence elsewhere in the poem, most scholars believe that the eagle was inspired by a similar bird in Dante's *Divine Comedy*, one who ferried the poet Dante from purgatory to paradise. Chaucer's eagle does more than just transport his cargo, however; he also performs the function that the poet VIRGIL carried out in Dante's work, acting as the narrator's guide, explaining the purpose of his journey and pointing out various sights along the way. Although the eagle's instructions to Chaucer seem to be given in a serious mode, they have a humorous effect, especially when the two argue about whether it would be better for Chaucer to learn about the constellations from a book or by traveling up into the highest sphere of the heavens. The bird's attitude toward his traveling companion suggests that he views him at best as an intellectual inferior. He is highly critical of the poet's lack of a social life, describing his daily habit of returning home after he finishes his "reckonings" (referring to Chaucer's work in the Customs House), where he sits, "dumb as any stone," reading yet another book and living like a hermit. Despite his pedantic nature, the eagle does seem to be very intelligent, enlightening Chaucer on the principle of sound waves as he explains how speech that is spoken on Earth travels through the atmosphere to Fame's House. Anyway, it is unlikely that the portrait of the eagle was intended to be entirely comical, as medieval lore considered eagles to be noble birds. In *The PARLIAMENT OF FOWLS*, eagles are the most princely birds, and all the other bird who have gathered in Nature's presence to choose their mates must wait until matters have been settled among the eagles. Because of their excellent vision these birds of prey came to symbolize contemplation and philosophy, a life unclouded by passion and temptation.

Ebraecus, Flavius Josephus Jewish historian and a general of the Galilean Jewish army in the war against Rome (A.D. 66–70). The historical works of Josephus provide important background information for the New Testament of the Bible. They include information on agriculture, geography, politics, religion, social traditions and practices and insights into the characters of people such as HEROD (2) and PILATE. Chaucer refers to Josephus in *The HOUSE OF FAME*, where he is one of the poets lining the approach to the throne of the goddess FAME (line 1433). On his shoulders he bears the weight of Jewish history.

Ebrayk Josephus *See* EBRAECUS, FLAVIUS JOSEPHUS.

Ecclesiasticus One of the books of the Apocrypha, a group of books written during a time of turmoil in the history of the Jewish people, from about 200 B.C. to about A.D. 70. These books were excluded from some early Christian versions of the Old Testament, but continue to be included in those used by Roman Catholics. Ecclesiasticus, also called The Wisdom of Jesus, Son of Sirach, is a book of wisdom teachings; it is not the same as the Old Testament book of Ecclesiastes, which is thought to have been written by King SOLOMON. Ecclesiasticus covers many subjects, including faith in God as Creator and Sustainer of life, love of wisdom and ethical conduct, virtue and good deeds, the value of past traditions, proper behavior in eating and drinking, work and trading, study and teaching, poverty and wealth, and health and sickness. It was written by Jesus ben Eleazar ben Sira, a Jew living in Jerusalem around 190 B.C. Chaucer's WIFE OF BATH recalls that one of her fifth husband's prescriptions for ruling a wife came from Ecclesiasticus, which recommended that men keep a tight reign on their wives, not allowing them to wander about. This is a bane to the Wife of Bath who, in her previous marriages, has been accustomed to wander freely about the region in which she lives and to travel on pilgrimages to far-off destinations. (The fact that she is once again traveling as she relates the story foreshadows its ending.) Another possible reference to Ecclesiasticus appears in "The NUN'S PRIEST'S TALE," where the narrator (the NUN'S PRIEST) cautions the reader against falling victim to the snare of flattery, as the rooster CHAUNTICLEER is on the verge of doing. The dangers of flattery are a theme in several chapters of the apocryphal text. Since succumbing to flattery is also warned against in the Old Testament book of Ecclesiastes, the reference, which is rather vague, could be to that book also.

Echo In classical mythology, Echo was the beautiful nymph who by distracting Hera (JUNO), the queen of the gods, with continuous talk, kept her away from Zeus (JUPITER) while he was sporting with the nymphs. Hera punished Echo by preventing her from ever speaking again unless another spoke first, and from ever being silent if another did speak. Echo fell in love with NARCISSUS, but he did not return her love, and she grieved for him until she became nothing but a voice. Another story relates that Echo was loved by PAN, but instead of returning his love she pined for a Satyr who was unresponsive. Pan pursued her in vain, and finally he so annoyed the shepherds that they tore her into pieces. Echo is mentioned several times in Chaucer's work. He refers to her garrulous nature in the envoy to "The CLERK'S TALE," where he advises women not to be patient and quiet like GRISELDA, but to talk back to their husbands continually. AURELIUS, the squire who falls in love with DORIGEN in "The FRANKLIN'S TALE," compares his plight to that of Echo when she loved Narcissus, believing that he, like the nymph, will die unable to express his feelings. In an earlier poem, *The BOOK OF THE DUCHESS,* Chaucer uses Echo's love for NARCISSUS as an example of excessive passion as he tries to help the BLACK KNIGHT overcome his grief. In Chaucer's translation of the *ROMAN DE LA ROSE* (called *The ROMAUNT OF THE ROSE*), the narrator of that poem comes upon a magical spring named after the nymph while wandering about in the GARDEN OF LOVE. Looking into the spring, he sees a reflection of the beautiful rose with which he is destined to fall in love.

Eclympasteyr A minor classical deity, mentioned along with MORPHEUS, the god of sleep, in the description of Morpheus' cave that appears in *The BOOK OF THE DUCHESS.* The name does not derive from classical mythology, but it does appear in Jean FROISSART's *Paradys d'amours,* where Eclympasteyr is a son of Morpheus. The source of the name is uncertain, but it may have been invented by Froissart. In French, Froissart's native tongue, the root words of its two components, *enclin* and *postere,* together mean "supine."

Ecquo *See* ECHO.

Ector *See* HECTOR.

Ecuba *See* HECUBA.

Edippe (Edipus) *See* OEDIPUS.

editions of Chaucer's Work When the reference is made to "editions" of Chaucer's work, the term indicates a text that is printed rather than written out by hand like a manuscript. The editors who compile these editions have to choose what they believe to be the most authoritative texts, since most of Chaucer's work exists in multiple manuscripts whose language varies, and Chaucer, like other medieval poets, is not around to be consulted. The variations that occur from manuscript to manuscript may be the result of scribal error (the person who was copying the manuscript made a mistake), of the author's revisions, or even of changes by the scribe intended to improve the text. Sometimes it is possible for editors to determine whether the variation is a mistake or intentional; greater difficulties arise in deciding whether a "revision" was made by the author or by a well-intentioned scribe, or, when the dates of manuscripts are uncertain (as is usually the case with Chaucerian manuscripts), which is the original and which the revision.

These are just a few of the difficulties that Chaucer's editors have had to contend with, although more recent editors have at least been able to rely on a textual tradition established over centuries by scholars seeking an authoritative text—one that seems closest to what Chaucer intended. The discussion of editors and editions that follows is not exhaustive, but focuses on the most important milestones in a textual tradition that extends from the 14th century, when Chaucer composed, to today's readers and scholars.

The first printed edition of Chaucer was created by the first English printer, William CAXTON, who initially published *The CANTERBURY TALES* in 1478. When a reader informed him that the text was inferior to a manuscript version, Caxton dutifully attempted to correct his text, and went on to print a total of seven editions of Chaucer in his lifetime, suggesting the work's early popularity. The differences between the language of Caxton's texts and Chaucer's own Middle English can be explained by the tremendous changes in the pronunciation of English that occurred during the 15th century (Chaucer died around 1400), as well as the freedoms taken by the people who compiled the text before there was a systematic method for doing so. In addition to *The Canterbury Tales,* Caxton printed *The PARLIAMENT OF FOWLS, ANELIDA AND ARCITE, The HOUSE OF FAME, TROILUS AND CRISEYDE* and *The BOECE.*

Although there were several intervening editions printed by Wynkyn de Worde (Caxton's successor) and Pynson, the next important edition of Chaucer was published by William Thynne, an official in the household of Henry VIII, in 1532. With Thynne's work, we see the first serious attempt at establishing an authoritative text by collating various available manuscripts. William's son Francis claimed that his father owned 22 manuscripts of Chaucer's works, which he used to create his edition. Francis also reported that his father received a commission to search all the libraries of England for copies of Chaucer's work, for the purpose of correcting errors in the texts and adding to the Chaucer canon. Thynne was the first to print *The BOOK OF THE DUCHESS*, *The LEGEND OF GOOD WOMEN*, *The ROMAUNT OF THE ROSE* and *A TREATISE ON THE ASTROLABE*.

John Stow, a man best known for his work as a historian and antiquarian of the latter part of the 16th century, compiled an edition of Chaucer that was mainly derived from one put out by William Thynne, but with the addition of the short poems "GENTILESSE," "A COMPLAINT TO HIS LADY," "ADAM SCRIVEYNE," the "PROVERBS," thought to have come from Chaucer's pen and "AGAINST WOMEN UNCONSTANT."

Thomas SPEGHT, the next editor of Chaucer's work, actually began as an assistant on an edition begun by Stow and the English playwright Francis Beaumont. Although the text is very similar to that of Stow's earlier edition, Speght wrote an introduction to *The Canterbury Tales* and a "life" of Chaucer based upon information about Chaucer's parentage, his work, travels, etc. Speght was the first biographer to report that Chaucer's name appeared on the record of the Inner Temple at the INNS OF COURT (where all Englishmen who were preparing to be lawyers studied) and that he was fined two shillings for beating a Franciscan Friar in Fleet Street. Speght was the first editor to create a glossary, which emphasizes the rapid changes that were occurring in the language during the period. (A comparison of the text of the *Riverside Shakespeare* with that of the *Riverside Chaucer* will clarify this point.) Speght's second edition, published in 1602, included an explanation of Chaucer's metrics, an expanded glossary which included some etymologies and a revision of *The Canterbury Tales*.

John Urry, who edited the first edition of Chaucer to be published in the 18th century, died before that work was completed. Although it has been criticized as one of the worst editions of Chaucer ever produced, Urry, to his credit, was the first editor to include the entire accepted canon of Chaucer's works. Like Thynne, Urry put some effort into establishing an authoritative text by collating as many printed editions and manuscripts as he was able to get his hands on; his edition also included a biography and glossary, although these were created by others after Urry's death. On the other hand, Urry freely changed the text to bring Chaucer's verse into what he considered to be metrical regularity. These changes are what has caused the edition to be held in such low regard by modern scholars.

In the 1770s, Thomas Tyrwhitt, a scholar and editor who had an early career in politics, published an edition of *The Canterbury Tales* that signaled the beginning of serious scholarly attention to the editing process. Tyrwhitt was very careful to collate the 24 manuscripts to which he had access, and he displayed a sound ability to discern which ones were the best without ignoring valid alternate readings from inferior manuscripts. He was also the first to adopt an order for the tales based on the best manuscripts. His commentary is excellent, displaying a familiarity with the Italian writers BOCCACCIO and DANTE, as well as with the French poem that had such tremendous influence on Chaucer's work, the *ROMAN DE LA ROSE*.

Thomas Wright, an early 19th-century scholar and editor who made his living editing medieval English and Latin works, chose a single manuscript, Harley 7334, as the basis of his text, using collations from a small number of favored manuscripts to correct faulty passages. Wright's most important contribution was probably his commentary, some of which found its way into W. W. SKEAT's annotations later in the century.

Frederick J. Furnivall, founder of the Early English Text Society and the CHAUCER SOCIETY, has been called by some the midwife of 19th-century Chaucer scholarship. Furnivall was the first to recognize the superiority of the ELLESMERE and HENGWRT MANUSCRIPTS and, although he never edited an edition of the poet's work, he contributed greatly to Chaucer studies through his many manuscript transcriptions, including that of *Troilus and Criseyde;* these published transcriptions expedited the work of later scholars and furthered the task of establishing a canon of Chaucer's work. Among these transcriptions, his six-text parallel edition (a printed transcription of six of the best manuscripts) of *The Canterbury Tales,* together with the subsequent publication of two other manuscript transcriptions, was probably his most important legacy because it made it so easy for those who would edit the text in the future to compare manuscript variants.

Walter W. Skeat, arguably the greatest of the 19th-century editors of Old and Middle English literature, began his scholarly career as a mathematician. When Skeat returned to Christ's College in Cambridge as a lecturer, Furnivall invited him to edit the sprawling Old French romance *Lancelot of the Lake*. Skeat found the process interesting and did a good enough job to ultimately qualify as the editor of the Clarendon Chaucer, which, when it was published in 1895, was hailed as the best since Tyrwhitt's edition of 1775–78. Because he relied exclusively on Furnivall's six-text edition of the manuscripts and Harley 7334, his edition has since come to be considered too limited. He has also been criticized for metrical and orthographic emendations that had no basis in the manuscript tradition but which simply were done to regularize the text according to his own aesthetic principles. Nevertheless, Skeat's commentary, glossary and his work toward establishing the canon are all contributions whose importance is still recognized by Chaucer scholars today.

Robert K. ROOT, a scholar whose life spanned the transition from the 19th to the 20th centuries, focused on the problematic manuscript tradition of Chaucer's longest single work, *Troilus and Criseyde*. His edition of that poem, which he titled *The Book of Troilus,* represents the first modern critical edition of any Middle English poem. Because he chose to follow an unfounded theory of authorial revision in his collation of the available manuscripts, his edition is now recognized as unauthoritative, but his notes and commentary, which display extensive historical and literary knowledge, are invaluable to this day.

With the work of John M. MANLY and Edith RICKERT, we return to what is still considered Chaucer's greatest (and what has certainly been his most frequently edited) work, *The Canterbury Tales.* These two scholars devoted themselves to the monumental task of creating an edition of the tales that contains a detailed description of all the known manuscripts, a volume on the classification of the manuscripts, two volumes of text and four volumes recording manuscript variants. Their method of putting the manuscripts into genetically related groups and examining variants in order to eliminate scribal alterations aimed at recovering an archetype close to Chaucer's original intentions made this one of the most respected editions of the 20th century.

Fred N. ROBINSON's two editions of Chaucer's work, the first published by Houghton Mifflin in 1933, after 29 years of preparation, have been recognized as the authoritative editions of the 20th century, even though Robinson has been faulted for not strictly adhering to a "scientific" model of textual editing but sometimes depending upon subjective criteria for his decisions regarding emendations based on inferior manuscripts. His edition recognizes the authority of the Ellesmere and Hengwrt manuscripts, but uses Ellesmere as the primary basis of the text. It has proven invaluable for students and scholars alike, not only because of the intelligent job Robinson did in editing the text, but also because it contains all the works known to have been composed by Chaucer, in addition to some that were attributed to him but may not be genuine.

Robinson's second edition, which appeared in 1957, was adopted by Larry Benson, who expanded and enlarged the textual and critical apparatus of the text for Houghton Mifflin's 1987 edition—known as *The RIVERSIDE CHAUCER.* One reason for the outstanding quality of this edition was Benson's choice to delegate the tasks of writing introductions, explanatory and critical notes of various poems to different scholars according to their Chaucer specialties. Benson himself composed much of the general introduction; the criti-

cal apparatus for *The Canterbury Tales, The Parliament of Fowls* and *The Romaunt of the Rose;* and the excellent general bibliography. *The Riverside Chaucer* is currently the standard text for both students and scholars.

The Variorum Edition of the Works of Geoffrey Chaucer continues the tradition of scholarly collaboration. The ongoing project, begun in 1968, states as its goal the task of presenting "not a new critical text but a modestly emended or corrected Hengwrt text."

education in the Middle Ages   Whether one received a formal education in England in the 14th century depended on two things—gender and class. Because education was reserved primarily for males of the aristocracy or upper middle class, a majority of the populace was uneducated; many were illiterate. The chief supplier of education was the church, through its monasteries, cathedrals and parish schools modeled on the cathedral schools of northern France. Biographers of Chaucer believe that he may have attended a cathedral school located near his family home in London. The curriculum of such a school would have included instruction in Latin (in which the Bible and most nonsecular literature was written), arithmetic, theology and possibly music. Members of the nobility were typically educated by tutors, either in their own home or in the home of another member of their class to whom they had been entrusted for fosterage. For them, academic subjects would be augmented by tutelage in social skills and ceremony and the tremendously important, for the able-bodied male, skill of fighting.

Although he belonged to the middle class, Chaucer's education probably followed the aristocratic pattern. While we cannot be certain that he attended a cathedral school, it is certain that he received an education in manners and soldiering while in the household of the countess of Ulster and, later, in the service of Lionel, the duke of Clarence. Chaucer did not attend a university. These institutions, which developed in the 12th and 13th centuries, primarily received students who were intending to enter the church. The disciplines taught in the universities were divided notionally into the seven liberal arts, comprising grammar, rhetoric and dialectic (the Trivium); arithmetic, geometry, astronomy and music (the Quadrivium); and the higher subjects of theology, law and medicine.

One of the greatest differences between education in the Middle Ages and today relates to the method of learning. In classes, because of the rarity and expense of books, texts were reserved primarily for the teachers, who would read and explicate while the students busied themselves in writing and committing to memory. This emphasis on oral transmission permeated all levels of education and affected the method of study and exercise (i.e., disputation and dialogue), the structure of texts, and even the attitudes to the works that were studied.

Chaucer's knowledge of the educational practices of his day shows up in the portraits of various pilgrims who populate the GENERAL PROLOGUE OF *THE CANTERBURY TALES*. The CLERK represents the university student, the DOCTOR OF PHYSIC is one who has pursued the study of medicine and the SERGEANT OF THE LAW represents the highest level that could be attained in the legal profession. Chaucer himself is thought to have attended the Inner Court, one of the INNS OF COURT responsible for the education of English lawyers. A legal education would have served him well in the positions he held as an ambassador for EDWARD III and his heir, RICHARD II, and in his job as a controller in the Customs House.

Edward, Saint   Saint Edward of England, more popularly known as Edward the Confessor, was the son of Ethelred the Unready. Born around 1004 and brought up in exile on account of the Danish occupation of England, Edward was crowned king of England on the restoration of the Anglo-Saxon line in 1042. He was considered a just ruler and in all things considerate of the interests of his subjects, yet he made some enemies among the nobility because of his easy relations with the French Normans. He waged successful war against the Scots and the Welsh, while maintaining peace within the boundaries of his own kingdom. His remission of the tribute known as the danegeld (paid to the Danish king), the wise laws he enacted, and his protection of the interests of the church gained him lasting fame. When he died in January 1066, his body was entombed in Westminster Abbey, which he had restored during his reign. Saint Edward is mentioned once in Chaucer's work, in the prologue to "The MONK'S TALE" when the MONK, a bit over-zealous to perform in the tale-telling contest, announces that he will tell a tale, or two or three, one of them being the life of Saint Edward. Instead, he tells a series of tragedies relating the rise and fall of various famous men on FORTUNE's wheel.

Edward the Black Prince   Eldest son of EDWARD III and, by right of that relationship, Prince of Wales and heir to the throne of England. However, Edward died in 1376 before his father, and so it was his son Richard who succeeded to the crown (as RICHARD II). Known primarily for his exploits in battle, the Black Prince won an overwhelming victory over the French at Poitiers, which brought him enormous fame and popularity in England. As a governor, however, he demonstrated little talent, ruling as a tyrant rather than a statesman over the duchy of Aquitaine, which he had been granted by his father. Chaucer would not have known Edward personally, but may have come into contact with him during the time that he served in the household of Lionel, Edward's brother, or later as an esquire to King Edward. As a valettus or yeoman to Prince Lionel, Chaucer also evidently marched in the army division led by the prince of Wales during the siege of Reims in 1359.

Edward III   Although Edward III became king of England in 1327 when his father, Edward II, was deposed, the government was actually run by his mother, Queen Isabella, and her lover, Roger Mortimer. Several years later, 17-year-old Edward carried out a palace revolution in which Mortimer was seized and later condemned to death by Parliament. This dates the beginning of Edward's true reign, which was to last nearly half a century. Although the chroniclers of Edward's life and reign tended to praise him rather lavishly, modern historians have, until recently, tended to judge him rather harshly for putting the war with France (the Hundred Years' War) above all other concerns. To promote the war, he allowed powerful members of the nobility to have unprecedented influence in the government. He sacrificed the interests of the church, of sound administration and of the merchant class in political decisions favorable to the war effort. He also squandered the monetary resources of the government, leaving an empty exchequer for his successor, RICHARD II. On the positive side, Edward may simply have been trying to avoid the problems his father had from quarreling with the barons. Edward III cultivated the goodwill of these magnates and sought to reconcile old feuds and hostilities. He generously bestowed titles, honors and gifts of land. Perhaps most importantly, he waged a successful foreign war that kept the nobility occupied abroad and offered them the opportunity to gain renown and riches in the form of war booty and plunder. In this way, Edward was able to surround himself with a group of young and warlike barons who sympathized with him, admired him and remained loyal to him throughout his life. It has been suggested that Edward's relations with his barons were closer and happier than were those of any other medieval king in England. Edward is also remembered for promoting the cult of chivalry through the famous Order of the GARTER, which he created around 1348.

Edward and his queen, Philippa, had 12 children, three of whom died in infancy. Their first son, Edward, later known as EDWARD THE BLACK PRINCE, became a great warrior in the struggle against France, but died before he could inherit the crown. Two other sons, JOHN OF GAUNT and THOMAS OF WOODSTOCK, played a dominant role in the history of the realm. Chaucer served in the household of another son, Lionel, duke of Clarence, before he and his wife, also named Philippa, entered the king's household in the 1360s. Chaucer evidently served Edward as an esquire, traveling about the realm on the king's business and occasionally being asked to journey overseas as a kind of diplomat. In return for his service, Chaucer received lodging, food, clothing, daily wages and an annuity. In 1374, Edward appointed Chaucer to the office of controller of the export tax, or customs, on wool, sheepskins and leather, in the port of London, and of the subsidy, a heavier tax on the same merchandise. Chaucer continued to hold this important office after the king's death in 1377.

Egeus   *See* AEGEUS.

Egipcien Marie   *See* MARY THE EGYPTIAN, SAINT.

Egiste   *See* AEGYPTUS.

Eglantine, Madame   *See* PRIORESS.

Egyptian Mary   *See* MARY THE EGYPTIAN, SAINT.

Ekko   *See* ECHO.

Elcanor   Character mentioned in the opening lines of book two of *The HOUSE OF FAME* along with other figures, both real and legendary, who dreamed famous dreams. Three of these—ISAIAH, NEBUCHADNEZZAR and PHARAOH—are derived from the Bible. The identity of Elcanor, however, is uncertain. W. W. SKEAT suggests a character named Alcanor from the *AENEID* but he is not associated with any dream. John S. P. TATLOCK offers a more likely possibility when he suggests that Elcanor is derived from the Old French *Roman de Cassiodorus*, where Helcana, the heroine of the story, after changing her name to Helcanor, appears in her lover's dreams to convince him that he ought to marry. The only difficulty with this possibility is the fact that Helcanor's lover, not Helcanor herself, has the dream.

Eleatics (Eleaticis)   *See* PARMENIDES.

Eleyne   *See* HELEN OF TROY.

Eleyne, Saint   *See* HELEN, SAINT.

Eli   A judge and high priest in the biblical Book of Samuel. Although Eli was a deeply pious man who served God faithfully, he was unable to control his two sons, Phinehas and Hophni. These two men, both priests, took meat from sacrificial animals before they were dedicated to God. They also had sex with women who assembled at the tabernacle door. According to the biblical account, God punished Eli by allowing Hophni and Phinehas to be killed in battle against the Philistines. Upon hearing the news of their deaths, Eli fell backward and broke his neck. God's final judgment

against Eli and his descendants occurred when SOLOMON removed one of Eli's descendants, and put someone else in his place as high priest of the nation. In "The PARSON'S TALE," Chaucer refers to the sons of Eli as examples of evil priests, and he compares their wickedness to SATAN's.

Eliachim   In the apocryphal Book of Judith, Eliachim was a Jewish priest in the town of Bethulia who preached resistance against the army of HOLOFERNES, King NEBUCHADNEZZAR's general who was later beheaded by JUDITH. He is mentioned in the story of Holofernes' downfall that appears in Chaucer's "MONK'S TALE."

Elicon   *See* HELICON, MOUNT.

Eligius, Saint   The patron of goldsmiths and farriers (blacksmiths). For most of his life, Eligius served as goldsmith to King Clotar (Lothar) II, Merovingian king of France and father of Dabobert I. Clotar also commissioned him to make chalices, plaques and other artifacts for his court. In 640 Eligius resigned his position as master of the king's mint to become a priest and one year later, bishop of Noyon. He was a very successful preacher and founded three monasteries, one of them at Paris. His surviving homilies show a great concern over the revival of pagan practices, which was a perennial problem for the clergy in the early Middle Ages. Although only one ancient church was devoted to Eligius in England, his cult became so popular there that Chaucer's PRIORESS swears by his name, as we are told in the GENERAL PROLOGUE's description of her. Saint Eligius is also invoked (as Loy) by the carter of "The MONK'S TALE" when that man rescinds the previous curses he has laid upon his horses and blesses them, by God and Saint Loy, for drawing his cart out of a rut. The saint is associated with horses by extension of his patronage of farriers. There is a legend that relates how he once had to cut off the leg of a struggling horse in order to shoe it, but then restored the leg after he was done. Eligius' principle emblem is the horseshoe.

Elijah   In the Old Testament, Elijah was an influential prophet who lived during the ninth century B.C. He was instrumental in shaping Jewish history, and his ideas dominated Hebrew thinking for centuries after his lifetime. Elijah's most important contribution to Jewish history was his insistence that the religious practices of the Hebrew people must remain pure, that they must not be allowed to mingle with the worship of other gods, such as Baal and Asheroth. Because his views conflicted with those of Ahab, one of the kings of Israel during his lifetime, he often found himself the victim of hostility and persecution. For example, when King Ahab built a temple devoted to Baal worship, Elijah predicted that

God would send a drought to punish the people, and he was forced into exile for three years. Like MOSES, Elijah was sustained by God through miraculous means when he was forced to hide out in the desert. Ahab and his successor Ahaziah were punished for their defiance of God's wishes just as Elijah predicted they would be. At the end of his life, Elijah did not die but was carried bodily into heaven in a whirlwind. ELISHA, the only witness to this event, took up Elijah's mantle, which fell from Elijah as he ascended, and carried it throughout his ministry to demonstrate his continuation of Elijah's work. Elijah is mentioned three times in Chaucer's work. In "The SUMMONER'S TALE," the corrupt friar compares himself to Elijah (and a host of other holy men) as he tries to persuade the ailing THOMAS (1) to give him some money. The friar claims that his prayers are more effective because he, like Elijah when God spoke to him on Mount Horeb, practices fasting and contemplation. In actuality, these comparisons indicate the friar's sinfulness rather than his holiness because they either demonstrate pride (if he is telling the truth) or (what is more likely) indicate that he is a liar. Later in the tale, the friar claims that members of his order have more authority than those belonging to other religious institutions because the friars were originally founded by Elijah. This is based on an actual tradition of the Carmelites. Although the Carmelite order was established in 1209 or 1210, and endorsed by the papacy in 1226, the Carmelites stated that their founders were Elijah and his successor, Elisha. In *The HOUSE OF FAME*, when the narrator is seized by the EAGLE and flown high up into the heavens, he exclaims that he is not ENOCH, nor Elijah, nor ROMULUS nor GANYMEDE, all examples of characters who were taken up to heaven before death. Interestingly, while Enoch and Elijah are from the Bible, both Romulus and Ganymede appear in classical mythology. Such blending of pagan and Christian materials is typical of Chaucer.

Elise   *See* ELISHA.

Elisha   In the Old Testament of the Bible, Elisha was an early Hebrew prophet who succeeded and carried on the work of the prophet ELIJAH. Scholars have dated the period of his ministry from about 850 to 800 B.C. Unlike his predecessor, who was an outsider and a rebel, Elisha chose to work within the system, assuming his position as the rightful head of the official prophetic order in Israel and serving as a counselor to kings. He was also known for his willingness to mingle with and minister to people at every level of society, from the lowliest peasants to the wealthiest aristocrats. Elisha performed many miracles, twice as many as his forerunner. The first was his parting of the Jordan River shortly after he received Elijah's mantle (the symbol that he was to serve as Elijah's successor). His miracles

did not cease when his life ended: When a corpse was placed in Elisha's tomb, it came back to life as it touched the prophet's bones. During the medieval period, stories such as this helped to nourish a belief in the power of saints' relics, and help explain why so many people were eager to go on pilgrimages such as the one undertaken by Chaucer's pilgrims, who are on their way to visit the shrine of Saint THOMAS à BECKET in CANTERBURY. Elisha is mentioned once in Chaucer's work, in "The SUMMONER'S TALE" when the duplicitous friar tells poor ailing THOMAS (1) that friars are superior to other religious orders because they trace their descent from the prophets Elijah and Elisha. The Carmelites, a Franciscan order, did in fact make such a claim, even though their organization was not formally established until the first decade of the 13th century. Chaucer's reference to this claim in this context may indicate that he considered it to be facetious.

Elisium   *See* ELYSIUM.

Elisos   *See* ELYSIUM.

Ellesmere Manuscript   The Ellesmere manuscript of *The CANTERBURY TALES* is a lavishly illustrated manuscript produced early in the 15th century. Along with the HENGWRT MANUSCRIPT, it has come to be considered an authoritative text and is drawn upon heavily to produce standard editions of the *Tales*. Scholars use the Ellesmere text because it seems the most finished (it has the least number of problematical or "corrupt" lines), and because the order in which the tales appear makes the most sense based on deductions based on references to time and place that occur within the links between the tales. Interestingly, the Hengwrt manuscript was produced around the same time and seems likely to have been composed by the same scribe. Yet everything is unorganized and fragmented (one of the tales is even missing) in Hengwrt. The appearance of Hengwrt has led some scholars to believe that this is as close as Chaucer came to imposing an order on the tales, and that the scribe of Ellesmere was himself responsible for the more homogenized version. It is an interesting argument, but without the ability to consult either Chaucer or the scribe, the truth will probably remain hidden. One of the most interesting features of the Ellesmere manuscript is its illustrations. In addition to lavish scrollwork and other decorative features, its margins contain illustrations of all the pilgrims, including Chaucer, often reproducing the characteristics of the pilgrims as they are described in the GENERAL PROLOGUE. The portrait of Chaucer shown here is one of the earliest extant likenesses of the poet. In his recent biography of Chaucer, Derek PEARSALL suggests that the portrait's odd top-heaviness must derive from the scribe's attempt to adapt a three-quarter-length portrait such as that which appears in another manuscript, the Harley 4866. The Ellesmere manuscript is housed in the Huntington Library in San Marino, California, and all of its illustrations of the pilgrims are reproduced in Roger Sherman Loomis' book, *A Mirror of Chaucer's World*.

Elliott, Ralph W(arren) V(ictor) (1921–) Chaucer scholar born in Germany and educated in Scotland, Elliott has served as professor in several Australian universities. His interest is in the entire history of the English language, as he has published on a series of time periods from the age of Anglo-Saxon runes to Thomas Hardy. Along the way, he became interested in the 14th century and published *Chaucer's English* (1974). Elliott studies Chaucer's language from a developmental standpoint rather than as a static entity.

Eloi, Saint   *See* ELIGIUS, SAINT.

Elpheta   The wife of King CAMBYUSKAN and mother of CANACEE (1), CAMBALO and ALGARSIF in "The SQUIRE'S TALE." Elpheta is mentioned only briefly and not delineated as a character. Elpheta is also the name of a star in the constellation of SCORPIO. Chaucer may have derived the name from his readings in astronomy.

Eltham   One of Queen Anne's residences near London (*see* ANNE OF BOHEMIA). Chaucer makes reference to Eltham in the F version of his prologue to *The LEGEND OF GOOD WOMEN*, saying that when completed the book should be presented to the queen "at Eltham or at Sheene" on his behalf (line 497). Scholars have puzzled over the elimination of these lines from the G version of the prologue, speculating that Chaucer may have removed them after Anne's death to avoid any mention of the queen to her husband, King RICHARD II, who was so grief-stricken that he commanded her favorite residence at Sheen demolished so that it would not remind him of his loss. Some scholars believe that Queen ALCESTIS, who appears in the prologue and directs the poet to write the *Legend,* is meant to be an allegorical representation of Queen Anne.

Elye   *See* ELIJAH.

Elysium   In classical mythology, Elysium, or Elysian Fields, was the counterpart to Christian heaven, though its description more closely resembles that of the Garden of Eden. According to legend, Elysium was located far in the west on the banks of Oceanus, or in the Islands of the Blessed. Its inhabitants were never blasted by extremes of hot or cold weathers, but enjoyed a temperate climate where fruit trees produced three or four crops every year. The rulers of the land were Cronus and Rhadamanthus. In later tradi-

tion, Elysium came to be regarded as part of the underworld where those deemed worthy to experience everlasting happiness were assigned after death. This tradition is called upon in Chaucer's *TROILUS AND CRISEYDE* when CRISEYDE, hearing that she is to be given to the Greeks in exchange for ANTENOR, promises TROILUS that even if they are to be parted on Earth, their spirits will one day be reunited in Elysium.

Emelya   *See* EMILY.

Emetreus   Emetreus, king of Inde (INDIA), is a minor character in "The KNIGHT'S TALE." When THESEUS decides to hold a tournament where PALAMON and ARCITE (1), each supported by a fellowship of knights, will fight for the hand of his sister-in-law EMILY, Emetreus comes to ATHENS to fight on the side of Arcite. He is described in great detail, riding a bay-colored steed which is strapped in armor and covered with cloth of gold. His tunic is made of silk from TARSIA in Turkestan and is sewn with large white pearls. His mantle is adorned with many rubies. His curled yellow hair glitters like the Sun and his bright golden eyes shine out of a ruddy and freckled complexion. Around 25 years of age, he is already well bearded, and his voice has the strength of thunder. In spite of these qualities, Emetreus is soon knocked off his horse by Palamon and carried to the stake where those captured by Palamon or his supporters must remain until a winner has been determined. Emetreus does not appear in either of the sources Chaucer drew upon for the knight's tale. According to W. C. CURRY, his physiognomy is likely to have been inspired by representations of the god MARS, whose choleric temperament would have been mirrored in Emetreus' hair color, his ruddy complexion and the color of his eyes.

Emily (Emelye)   Emily (usually spelled *Emelye* in Chaucer's English) is the rather one dimensional heroine of "The KNIGHT'S TALE." She is the sister of Theseus, duke of ATHENS, and the woman with whom PALAMON and ARCITE (1) fall in love. Before setting eyes on Emily, the two knights, who are cousins, have sworn eternal affection and brotherhood. This motif of sworn brotherhood appears in several other tales in *The CANTERBURY TALES,* and often precedes some kind of betrayal or animosity between those who have sworn to be mutually loyal. Similarly, once their passion has been ignited by the sight of Emily, Palamon and Arcite become sworn enemies. Chaucer's description of Emily is true to type for the genre of chivalric romance. Specifically, she is "fairer . . . to sene / Than is the lylie upon his stalke grene, / And fressher than the May with floures newe — / For with the rose colour stroof hire hewe, / I noot which was the fyner of hem two" (lines 1035–39). [Fairer to look at / Than the lily upon its green stalk, / And fresher than the May with new flowers / For the color of her complexion rivaled that of the rose, / I don't know which was the finer of the two].

Palamon and Arcite worship Emily from afar for some time, without her even becoming aware of their devotion. We know very little else about this paragon of beauty, except that, on the eve of the day when Palamon and Arcite will engage in a contest to decide which of them gets to marry her, she prays to DIANA, goddess of chastity, to save her from having to marry at all. We are later told, when Arcite dies, that she had changed her mind and would like to have married him after all. She displays considerable grief at his funeral and mourns his death for several years afterward. When she is finally given to Palamon in marriage, to cement a treaty between Athens and THEBES, the two of them live happily ever after.

Emperor of Rome   The father of CONSTANCE in "The MAN OF LAW'S TALE." An actual historical figure who flourished in the latter part of the sixth century, his name, never mentioned in the tale, was Tiberius Constantinus and he was indeed a Byzantine emperor of ROME. He appears only peripherally in "The Man of Law's Tale"—at the beginning, when he agrees to wed his daughter to the pagan SULTAN OF SYRIA in exchange for that man receiving Christian baptism, and at the end, when he is reunited with his daughter after her many years of suffering and exile.

Eneas (Enee)   See AENEAS.

Eneyde (Eneydos)   See *AENEID*.

Engelond   A Middle English spelling of *England*, the country where Chaucer was born, lived and wrote his poetry. The name derives from one of the tribes, the Angles, who invaded England after the Roman occupation ended in the early part of the fifth century. The Anglo-Saxon conquest of the country was complete by around 450, and from that point forward the portion of the island from Hadrian's Wall to the southern coast came to be known as Angle-lond, which eventually became Engelond and, finally, England.

Englyssh   A Middle English spelling of *English*. Chaucer typically uses the word to refer to the English language, rather than as an adjective as in "an English village." Chaucer is known as the father of English poetry because he was the first author writing in English to create a style that was considered polished enough for the most sophisticated subject matter. Before Chaucer popularized English as a serious literary medium, French had been the preferred language of poetry in England, from the time of the Norman Conquest in 1066 until the end of the 14th century.

Ennok   See ENOCH.

Ennopye   See AEGINA.

Enoch   In the Old Testament, Enoch, the father of Methuselah, was "translated," or taken directly into heaven without experiencing death. In *The HOUSE OF FAME* Chaucer mentions Enoch to the EAGLE, who has scooped him up and seems to be flying higher and higher into the heavens. In noting that he is neither Enoch nor ELIJAH, Chaucer seems to be suggesting that he would be unworthy of such a fate, though his protests are ultimately derived from a desire to be set safely back on solid ground. The eagle responds that he need not worry and ultimately carries him to the region where FAME's palace stands in the air between heaven and earth, thus situated so that it can collect the emanations of sound that rise from the earth into the atmosphere, traveling like ripples through water.

"Envoy de Chaucer à Bukton"   See "LENVOY DE CHAUCER À BUKTON."

"Envoy de Chaucer à Scogan"   See "LENVOY DE CHAUCER À SCOGAN."

Eolus   See AEOLUS.

Ephesians   Ephesians, or The Epistle to the Ephesians, is one of four short epistles written by the apostle Paul (*see* PAUL, SAINT) while he was in prison; the others are Philippians, Colossians, and Philemon. Addressed to the Christians in Ephesus, a city on the western coast of Asia Minor, Ephesians describes Christ's position as the lord of the church, of the world and the entire created universe. Paul notes that although Christ has ascended into heaven His work is not over, rather, He is completing what he began in His earthly ministry by means of His extended body, the church. Chaucer's PARSON refers to Ephesians when he notes Paul's characterization of an avaricious man as the slave of idolatry (i.e., one who worships idols through the value he attaches to material goods).

Ephesios   See EPHESIANS.

Epicureans   Followers of the Greek philosopher EPICURUS. They are mentioned in the *BOECE*, Chaucer's translation of BOETHIUS' *Consolation of Philosophy*, by LADY PHILOSOPHY. She notes that following the philosopher SOCRATES' death, both the STOICS and the Epicureans claimed his ideas for their own. Lady Philosophy describes the subsequent twisting and wrenching of Socrates' meaning metaphorically, as the cutting and tearing of her own clothing that she had woven by hand.

Epicurus   A Greek philosopher who lived from 341 to 270 B.C., Epicurus counseled the doctrine of the enjoyment of virtue as the supreme good. During the Middle Ages, his name and philosophy became associated with the sins of self-indulgence and luxury. Chaucer's BOECE reflects this transformation when LADY PHILOSOPHY notes that Epicurus was overly concerned with the riches, honor, power, glory and delights of this world (Book Three, Prosa 2). Epicurus is mentioned again, in a lighter context, in the GENERAL PROLOGUE to *The CANTERBURY TALES*. The FRANKLIN, a man who takes great delight in good food and drink, which he graciously shares with others, is referred to as "Epicurus owene sone" (line 336) [Epicurus' own son].

"Episteles of Ovyde"   This is the title Chaucer gives to the Roman poet OVID's *Heroides*. The work is mentioned in the prologue to "The MAN OF LAW'S TALE" by the SERGEANT OF THE LAW, who proclaims that the poet Chaucer has told more love stories than appear in Ovid's Epistles, and then proceeds to name some of them. The *Heroides* is also mentioned in *The HOUSE OF FAME*, where readers who would seek to know more about the story of DIDO and AENEAS are directed to read about it in VIRGIL or the "Epistle of Ovyde." In version G of Chaucer's prologue of *The LEGEND OF GOOD WOMEN*, Queen ALCESTIS mentions Ovid's Epistles as a source of stories about virtuous and faithful women, directing Chaucer to create a collection of such stories to make amends for having translated the *ROMAN DE LA ROSE* and for having written *TROILUS AND CRISEYDE*, both of which portray women in very unfavorable terms. Scholars who have compared the text of the *Legend* with that of the *Heroides* believe that the latter served both as a model for Chaucer's poem and as a source for some of the minibiographies appearing therein.

Equatorie of the Planets   The *Equatorie of the Planets* is the most important work recently proposed for inclusion in Chaucer's canon. A Middle English translation of a Latin work ultimately based on an Arabian source, it describes the construction and use of an equatorium, an instrument for calculating the positions of the planets. Derek Price discovered it in a manuscript of astronomical tables in 1952. After comparing the word *Chaucer* with what may have been Chaucer's signature in a record dating from his work in the Customs House, Price concluded that the hand was the same and consequently, that the *Equatorie* was Chaucer's composition. Another study, by R. M. Wilson, showed that the language of the *Equatorie* was consistent with Chaucer's usage, in addition to which Chaucer himself, in the preface to *A TREATISE ON THE ASTROLABE*, had promised to compose third and fourth parts with information similar to that contained in the astronomical tables of the *Equatorie* manuscript. Fred ROBINSON, who edited what has come to be considered the most authoritative

20th-century edition of Chaucer's work, felt that this evidence was too circumstantial to constitute conclusive proof. For that reason, and because Price had published an edition of the text in 1955 complete with facsimile, transcription, translation, explanatory notes and full introductory and illustrative materials, Robinson did not include the text in his second edition. Larry BENSON, who based the 1987 *RIVERSIDE CHAUCER* on Robinson's text, made the same decision, for similar reasons.

Ercules   *See* HERCULES.

Erinyes, the   In classical mythology, Alecto, Tisiphone and Megaera were the names of the three Erinyes (or Furies, as they were called by the Romans). The daughters of Gaea, the Earth Mother, their role was to carry out the laws of vengeance. They were represented as winged maidens with snakes for hair, carrying torches, scourges and sickles. They punished without mercy those who violated natural family relationships, committed murder, perjured, violated the rules of hospitality or were guilty of excessive arrogance. Their method consisted of an eternal pursuit of the guilty, harassing him wherever he went and driving him into madness. Giving no consideration to the motives behind the crime that had been committed, they even pursued those, like OEDIPUS, who erred unintentionally. Their power extended into the underworld, where they often continued to torment their victims beyond the grave. From another point of view, the Erinyes were considered benevolent deities (hence their alternative name, Eumenides, or "the kindly ones") because they punished evildoers and safeguarded the good. Sacrifices to these goddesses consisted of water mixed with honey, milk, cake, black sheep and flowers. Chaucer mentions all three of the goddesses in the invocation to book four of *TROILUS AND CRISEYDE* when he asks for their help in describing the catastrophic denouement of the love affair between TROILUS and CRISEYDE.

Eriphilem   *See* ERIPHYLE.

Eriphyle   In classical mythology, Eriphyle was the sister of ADRASTUS, who gave her in marriage to AMPHIARAUS on the condition that if the husband and wife ever disagreed over anything, Amphiaraus would yield to his wife's judgment. When Adrastus organized the campaign of the SEVEN AGAINST THEBES to help POLYNICES in his effort to regain the throne of THEBES, Amphiaraus objected to the campaign because he foresaw that he would be killed. Eriphyle, bribed by Polynices with the famous necklace of Harmonia (a necklace made by Hephaestus [*see* VULCAN] that would destroy anyone who wore it), compelled Amphiaraus to participate in the war, but before leaving home,

Amphiaraus made his sons promise to avenge him by killing their mother when they grew up. Ten years later, Eriphyle was again bribed, this time to persuade her son Alcmaeon to join the expedition of the Epigoni against THEBES. Learning this, Alcmaeon, aided by his brother Amphilochus, murdered her. The story of Eriphyle's treachery appears in the *Book of Wicked Wives*, which the WIFE OF BATH's fifth husband likes to read to her.

Ermony   *See* ARMENIA.

Erro   *See* HERO.

Erudice   *See* EURYDICE.

Escaphilo   *See* ASCALAPHUS.

Esculapius   *See* AESCULAPIUS.

Eson   *See* AESON.

Esperus   *See* HESPERUS.

Essex   Essex is a county in the southeastern region of England, immediately to the northeast of London and bounded on its east by the North Sea. The name ultimately derives from the Saxons who, along with the Jutes and Angles, invaded and conquered the island in the fifth century. The former "kingdom" of Essex was ruled by the East Saxons. The county of Essex is mentioned in the prologue to "The WIFE OF BATH's TALE" when the WIFE OF BATH describes how often she quarreled with her first three husbands. Referring to an ancient custom whereby a side of bacon was annually offered to any married couple who had lived a year and a day without having an argument or repenting of their marriage, the Wife of Bath says that her first three husbands never had the bacon "in Essex at Dunmowe" (line 218) fetched for them.

estates satire   *See* Commentary under GENERAL PROLOGUE TO *THE CANTERBURY TALES*.

Esther (Ester)   In the Old Testament, Esther was the Jewish queen of the Persian King AHASUERUS. She was descended from a family that had been carried into captivity in about 600 B.C. and chose to stay in Persia rather than return to Jerusalem when the captivity ended. Esther was chosen by King Ahasuerus to replace his first wife, Vashti, who was banished from the kingdom when she refused to display herself to his guests following several days of drunken revelry. Esther served her people well when one of the king's advisors, a man named Haman, decided to revenge himself on the Jews because the prophet MORDECAI had refused to bow down to him. Haman persuaded the king to issue an edict permitting him to kill all the Jews and seize their property. Esther tactfully exposed Haman's plot and true character to the king, who rescinded the edict and granted the Jews the right to defend themselves. Haman was hanged on the same gallows that he had prepared for Mordecai. Jews still celebrate their deliverance from Haman's plot at the feast of Purim. Esther is mentioned several times in Chaucer's work as an example of a virtuous and faithful wife. JANUARY, the aged knight of "The MERCHANT'S TALE," uses her along with other examples of virtuous wives to justify his own decision to marry. Dame PRUDENCE mentions Esther's good advice to her husband as she tries to convince her own husband, MELIBEE, not to take revenge on the men who robbed and assaulted his family, in "The TALE OF MELIBEE." In *The BOOK OF THE DUCHESS*, the BLACK KNIGHT compares the goodness of his Lady WHITE to that of the biblical Esther, and in the prologue to *The LEGEND OF GOOD WOMEN*, the narrator notes that the meekness of Queen ALCESTIS outshines Esther's.

Estoryal Myrour   *Estoryal Myrour* (Historical mirror) is the title Chaucer gives to VINCENT OF BEAUVAIS' *Speculum historiale*, which Queen ALCESTIS refers to in the G version of the prologue to *The LEGEND OF GOOD WOMEN*. She mentions Vincent's work as a possible source for the stories of virtuous women that she wants Chaucer to write in order to make amends for having translated the *ROMAN DE LA ROSE* and for having made his own adaptation of BOCCACCIO's *FILOSTRATO*. Both of these works, in her opinion, detract from the reputation of her gender. Chaucer actually did use the *Speculum* as a source for his "legend" of CLEOPATRA.

Eteocles   In classical mythology, Eteocles was the son of King OEDIPUS of Thebes and Jocasta. He had a brother, POLYNICES and a sister, ANTIGONE. After it was discovered that Oedipus had committed the grievous error (albeit unknowingly) of marrying his mother, Eteocles and Polynices drove him out of Thebes and undertook to govern the city themselves, agreeing to rule alternately year by year. When Eteocles refused to be bound by that agreement, Polynices called upon ADRASTUS to help him organize an invasion of Thebes. In the conflict that followed, which became known as the SEVEN AGAINST THEBES, the brothers met in single combat and killed each other, fulfilling the curse that their father had laid upon them when they forced him to leave the city. CASSANDRA mentions Eteocles and Polynices in book five of *TROILUS AND CRISEYDE* as she recites the history of the Theban conflict to her brother TROILUS (lines 1485–1510).

Ethiocles   *See* ETEOCLES.

Etik   An unidentified source to which Chaucer refers in the F version of his prologue to *The LEGEND OF GOOD WOMEN:* "But I ne clepe nat innocence folye, / Ne fals pitee, for vertu is the mene, / As Etik seith; in swich maner I mene" (lines 164–66) [But I do not consider innocence folly, / Nor (do I call it) false pity, for virtue is the rule, / As Etik says; such is what I mean]. The passage appears within a description of the birds choosing their mates on the first day of May; in it Chaucer seems to be praising straightforward dealing in love, such as he sees among the birds, and perhaps indirectly criticizing humanity for undervaluing the same. W. W. SKEAT theorized that the "Etik" reference could be to ARISTO-TLE's *Ethics,* but also perhaps to an author, possibly the Roman poet Horace, who achieved fame for the odes he composed in the first century B.C.

Euclid/Euclide   Greek mathematician who authored an important work on geometry in the fourth century B.C. He is mentioned at the conclusion of "The SUM-MONER'S TALE" when the SUMMONER describes how the squire Jankyn (*see* JANKIN [2]) solved the problem of evenly dividing a fart among 13 friars. His solution is to have THOMAS (2), the originator of the fart, sit at the center of a cartwheel with 12 spokes, placing one friar at the end of each spoke and one in the middle, directly beneath Thomas. This way, when Thomas farts, the air and sound will travel down the spokes. The friar responsible for attracting this donation, by sitting directly beneath Thomas, will receive an even greater share than his brethren. For coming up with this ingenious solution, Jankyn is pronounced as good a mathematician as Euclid or the Egyptian PTOLEMY.

Eufrates   *See* EUPHRATES.

Euphrates   River in the ancient land of Mesopotamia (present-day Iraq). It flows from east-central Turkey through Syria and Iraq to join the Tigris. In Book Five of the *BOECE,* LADY PHILOSOPHY uses the paths taken by the Tigris and Euphrates Rivers as an example of apparent chance that is really divinely determined. After springing from a single source, these rivers divide into two separate channels. If they were to reunite, they would cause many disasters, uprooting trees and destroying ships; thus, their continuing in their course is an example of the work of Providence, although it appears to be chance occurrence.

Euripides   Greek playwright of the fifth century B.C. The youngest of the three great Attic tragedians, a group that included Sophocles and Aeschylus, Euripides did not win as much acclaim as the other two men. This was due mainly to the fact that his works seemed to question the morality of the legends upon which the religious beliefs of his countrymen were based. One of the strongest features of his work, and one that has doubtless led to its enduring popularity, lay in its presentation of ordinary human beings, especially women, with both passion and sympathy. Nineteen of his plays have survived, the most famous being *Medea.* His portrait of MEDEA had considerable influence on how she was portrayed in later literature, including OVID's *Heroides,* which Chaucer drew upon for his own portrait of Medea in *The LEGEND OF GOOD WOMEN.* In the *BOECE,* Chaucer's translation of BOETHIUS' *Consolation of Philosophy,* LADY PHILOSOPHY refers to Euripides' saying that "he that hath no children is weleful by infortune" (Book Three, Prosa 7, line 25) [he who has no children is happy through misfortune]. She mentions this in concluding her case that men wish for things that are not always in their best interests. The line is taken from Euripides' play *Andromache.*

Eurippe   *See* EURIPUS.

Euripus   A strait located between Euboea and Boeotia, which was famous for its strong and variable currents. In the *BOECE,* LADY PHILOSOPHY compares the turning of FORTUNE's wheel to the dangerous and unpredictable currents of the boiling Euripus (Book Two, Metrum 1, line 3).

Europa   Briefly mentioned as Aganore's daughter in prologue F to *The LEGEND OF GOOD WOMEN* (line 114), Europa was one of many women in Greek mythology to be kidnapped and ravished by Zeus (*see* JUPITER), the king of the gods. According to the legend, she was gathering flowers along the seashore one day when Zeus, having assumed the form of a beautiful bull, lay down at her feet. He appeared so gentle that Europa playfully climbed upon his back. Instantly he arose and plunged into the sea, carrying her with him. He took Europa to Crete, where she bore him three children, MINOS, Rhadamanthus and SARPEDON. Zeus then gave Europa as a wife to Asterius, king of Crete, who raised her children as his own. The lines in which she is mentioned are among many instances in Chaucer's work where he indicates the date by refering to astrological symbols. In this case, the reference to the sun rising in the breast of the beast that led away Agenore's daughter is a poetical way of saying that the sun is rising toward the middle sector of the sign of TAURUS the bull, which is a figurative way of saying that it is around May 1. The legend of Zeus and Europa also surfaces briefly in *TROILUS AND CRISEYDE,* when TROILUS calls upon Zeus in the name of his love for Europa to assist him in his attempts to woo CRISEYDE (bk. 3, line 722).

Europe   *See* EUROPA.

Eurus   In classical mythology, Eurus is the wind that blows from the southeast. It was typically associated with stormy weather, which may be why BOETHIUS chose to mention it in Book Two, Metrum 4 of his *Consolation of Philosophy* (translated by Chaucer as the *BOECE*) as a wind powerful enough to cast down even a stable and wary man who has prepared for its coming. He refers to Eurus again in Book Four as the wind that brought ULYSSES' ship to the island of CIRCE, who enchanted all his men and turned them into animals.

Eurydice   In classical mythology, Eurydice was the wife of the poet ORPHEUS. Shortly after her marriage the shepherd Aristaeus fell in love with her, and while fleeing from him she was fatally bitten by a serpent. Her heartbroken husband followed her into Hades, where his singing so charmed the gods of the underworld that they granted his request to take Eurydice back to the upper world. They imposed one condition—that he must pass through Hades without once looking back. Orpheus, followed by Eurydice, had nearly reached his destination when he looked back to make sure that his wife was coming and lost her forever. In book four, line 791 of *TROILUS AND CRISEYDE*, when the Trojans have agreed to turn CRISEYDE over to the Greeks in exchange for ANTENOR, Criseyde compares herself and TROILUS to Eurydice and Orpheus, who, forced apart in life, were reunited after death.

Eva   *See* EVE.

Evander   In classical mythology, Evander was the son of MERCURY and a prophetic Arcadian nymph. He led a group of people from Pallantion in ARCADIA to Italy, where they built a city on the spot that would later be the site of Rome. The Palatine hill derives its name from his former home. Evander taught the region's natives the arts of the Greeks, especially writing, music and the worship of PAN, HERCULES and others. When AENEAS arrived in Italy, Evander aided him against TURNUS by sending his son to fight for Aeneas. In the *BOECE*, Chaucer's translation of BOETHIUS' *Consolation of Philosophy*, LADY PHILOSOPHY notes that Hercules was able to avenge the wrath of Evander by killing the giant CACUS, who had stolen some of the cattle Hercules was supposed to be guarding. In this instance, Chaucer seems to have confused Evander with Eurystheus, the king of Mycenae who gave Hercules the 12 labors to perform.

Evangels, the   In "The MAN OF LAW'S TALE" the wicked knight swears upon the Evangels, or the Gospels of Matthew, Mark, Luke and John in the New Testament, when he accuses CONSTANCE of murdering HERMENGYLD. The knight's lie is revealed when a hand comes down from heaven and strikes him so hard that his neck is broken and he falls down dead.

Evaungiles   *See* EVANGELS, THE.

Eve   According to the Bible and Christian tradition, Eve was the first woman, created from one of ADAM's ribs to be his companion and helper. The story of Adam and Eve is related in GENESIS, the first book of the Bible. They are described as living together in innocence and happiness, without guilt and sin. However, Satan, in the form of a serpent, tempted Eve to eat from a tree whose fruit she had been forbidden, and she succumbed to the temptation and then offered the fruit to her husband. The result of their disobedience was the loss of innocence and the disturbing knowledge of sin and evil. This act of defiance also cost them their immortality; now they and their descendants would have to experience death. Eve's pain in childbirth and Adam's authority over her were additional punishments imposed upon her and her female descendants.

Eve is mentioned numerous times in *The CANTERBURY TALES*. In "The MAN OF LAW'S TALE," the narrator cites Satan's temptation of Eve as an example of how he uses women as instruments of destruction; the Sultaness of Syria, who murdered her son for marrying CONSTANCE, fits this pattern. Eve is also one of the wicked wives whose stories the WIFE OF BATH's fifth husband would read aloud before she rebelled and tore one of the pages from his book (*see* "The WIFE OF BATH'S TALE"). In "The MERCHANT'S TALE," the aged knight JANUARY uses God's decision to make a wife for Adam to justify his own decision to marry. The union that results is not quite as disastrous as that of Adam and Eve, but it does have its drawbacks when the young wife finds the attentions of a youthful squire more appealing that those of her ancient husband. Finally, "The PARSON'S TALE," which is actually a sermon on penitence, tells the complete story of Adam and Eve and their fall from innocence as it relates to original sin and how it has passed down to us, Adam's descendants.

exemplum   An exemplum (a Latin word whose plural is *exempla*) is a short tale illustrating a moral point. Exempla usually appear in sermons or other didactic works. Their popularity during the Middle Ages led to the creation of collections of exempla, classified according to their subject matter, which were used by preachers in preparing sermons. Because the entertaining narrative of some of these stories at times threatened to overshadow their moral implications, their use became controversial during the 14th century. John WYCLIFFE, the famous church reformer and translator of the Bible, protested against this tendency and omitted exempla from his own sermons. Exempla had a strong influence on medieval secular literature, as is illustrated by Chaucer's noteworthy use of the form in "The NUN'S PRIEST'S TALE" and "The PARDONER'S TALE." The former uses the story of a learned rooster named CHAUNTICLEER to illustrate the maxim that pride goeth before a fall, while the PARDONER's narrative of three men who go out in search of death and find a fortune in gold shows how the sin of avarice can have fatal results. (*See* BEAST FABLE.)

Exodus   Exodus, the second book of the Old Testament, deals with Israel's early years as a nation. Its name comes from the Greek word for "going out," referring to the Hebrew people, led by the prophet MOSES, going away from enslavement in Egypt to the "promised land." In "The PARSON'S TALE," which is actually a sermon on penitence, the PARSON notes that the first of the Ten Commandments, which appear in the Book of Exodus, states: "Thous shalt have no false goddes bifore me, ne thou shalt make to thee no grave thyng" (line 750) [You must have no false gods before me, nor shall you make any graven image for yourselves]. The passage is a paraphrase of Exodus 20: 3–4.

Ezechi   *See* HEZEKIAH.

Ezekiel (Ezechiel)   In the Old Testament, Ezekiel was a prophet whose family was carried away to Babylon during the period known as the Babylonian captivity of the Jews. He was about 25 years old at the time. Ezekiel prophesied to the captives who lived by the Chebar River at Tel Aviv, and he is the author of the Book of Ezekiel, which purports to contain prophetic messages received from God in a series of visions. Chaucer's PARSON quotes from Ezekiel 8:43 when he describes the shamefulness of sin as one reason men seek to perform acts of contrition or penitence. "The PARSON'S TALE" is actually a sermon describing true penitence.

fabliau The term *fabliau* (plural, *fabliaux*) refers to a genre that seems to have originated in medieval France. Flourishing in the 12th and 13th centuries, these bawdy and humorous stories typically featured middle-class characters involved in a plot dealing with some form of sexual misconduct or an obscene joke. The French fabliaux were usually written in octosyllabic couplets. The form was dispersed by the French jongleurs, professional musical entertainers who traveled around to the homes and castles of various noble families. Although fabliaux sometimes had ostensible "morals" attached to them, they lacked the serious intention of the fable or EXEMPLUM. The fabliaux was obviously one of Chaucer's favorite genres. He employed it over and over again in *The CANTERBURY TALES*. The tales told by the MILLER, REEVE, FRIAR, SUMMONER, MERCHANT, SHIPMAN and MANCIPLE are all fabliaux.

Fabricius, Gaius Luscinus A Roman general of the third century B.C. Gaius Luscinus Fabricius had a distinguished career as both a soldier and a diplomat, often combining the two functions, as he did in 280 when he was sent to treat for ransom and exchange of prisoners following the Roman defeat by Pyrrhus, the king of Epirus in Greece. When Fabricius refused to take any bribe from Pyrrhus, the latter was so impressed that he released his prisoners without ransom. Fabricius also served two terms as consul. He is mentioned once in the BOECE, Chaucer's translation of BOETHIUS' *Consolation of Philosophy*—in Book Two, Metrum 7, when LADY PHILOSOPHY asks Boethius to consider that those distinctions won during life are of little use to one dead and buried. Where, she asks him, is the good Fabricius now? Where is the noble BRUTUS or stern CATO? Their names may mean something now, but they will eventually, like everything else, be effaced by time.

Fairie (Fairye) Fairie (also spelled Fairye, Fayerye, and Faerie) was the name Chaucer and other medieval writers gave to the realm of the fairies. This was a place of magic and enchantment, where marvelous deeds were performed by both human and supernatural beings. Many of the adventures of King ARTHUR and his knights are associated with the realm of Fairie because enchantresses like Morgan le Fay and other magical figures appear in those stories.

One theory holds that legends of an enchanted land date back to the earliest known inhabitants of the British Isles, people who in Irish lore became known as the Sidhe. When later European settlers invaded, the Sidhe went underground (literally), living in barrows, springs and other enchanted places and coming out on moonlit nights to dance in the forest and perform various acts of mischief, usually aimed at vexing the descendants of their conquerors. Titania and Oberon in Shakespeare's play *A Midsummer Night's Dream* are examples of such figures. Fairies were sometimes suspected of kidnapping human children (for they, because of their magical powers, had long since ceased to be human) and replacing them with changelings who only appeared to be human.

Chaucer refers to this realm of Fairie in "The SQUIRE'S TALE," where an allusion is made to Sir GAWAIN, one of the legendary Arthur's knights, who is now considered to reside in this enchanted land; and in "The TALE OF SIR THOPAS," where the "hero" of the story, Sir THOPAS, falls in love with an elf queen of whom he has dreamed. He rides so far in pursuit of this queen that he actually enters the land of the fairies, where he encounters a giant named OLIPHAUNT. He does not, however, find the queen he is searching for, at least not before the tale is interrupted. Chaucer also uses the term *Fairie* to refer to the classical underworld as, for example, when he describes the god PLUTO as the "Kyng of Fayerye" in "The MERCHANT'S TALE."

Fair Welcome *See* BIALACOIL.

False-Seeming False-Seeming, or Fals-Semblant in the French text, is an allegorical figure who appears in JEAN DE MEUN's continuation of GUILLAUME DE LORRIS' *ROMAN DE LA ROSE*. The portion of the Middle English translation that Chaucer worked on does not include this character, but it is included in Fragment C, which was written by another, unknown, author. (*See ROMAUNT OF THE ROSE* for further discussion.) The character of False-Seeming functions primarily as the voice of social satire, revealing the hypocrisy of women, religion and the social order.

Fame Goddess who appears seated on her ruby throne dispensing reputations in book 3 of Chaucer's early poem, *The HOUSE OF FAME.* Fame is one of the most striking allegorical figures (*see* ALLEGORY) in all of Chaucer's poetry. When the narrator first glimpses her, she appears smaller than the length of a cubit (from the elbow to the top of the middle finger), but almost immediately she begins to stretch upward until her head touches the heavens while her feet remain on Earth. These and other physical details of the goddess' description are derived from VIRGIL'S *AENEID,* which features a similar goddess named Fama (often translated "Rumor"). Fame's body is covered with as many eyes as a bird has feathers, and as many ears and tongues as a beast has hairs. Her hair, the color of burnished gold, lies in waves and curls, and partridge's wings (a misreading of Virgil's *pernicibus alis,* i.e., "swift wings") adorn her feet. When people approach her throne to petition for good and enduring fame, the goddess responds rather capriciously, so that there seems to be little or no relationship between a person's deeds and their reputation. A person who has done good deeds and appears to deserve good fame, for example, may be awarded the opposite. On the other hand, some people who deserve good fame receive it. Thus there is no logic, not even poor logic, in her decisions. Her many eyes and ears suggest that very little escapes her sight and hearing, and the tongues allude to her function of spreading information. Chaucer parodies her varying height in the *BOECE* (his translation of BOETHIUS' *Consolation of Philosophy*) when he describes LADY PHILOSOPHY, who sometimes "constreyned and schronk hirselven lik to the comune mesure of men, and somtyme it semede that sche touchede the hevene with the heighte of here heved" (Book One, Prosa 1, lines 13–17) [contracted and shrunk herself to the common measure of men, and sometimes it seemed that she touched heaven with the height of her head]. Fame's capriciousness is surely related to that of FORTUNE, another goddess derived from Roman myth.

Fame, Book of   *See* HOUSE OF FAME, THE.

Fayerye   *See* FAIRIE.

Femenye   Femenye is the name Chaucer gives to the land of the AMAZONS in the account of THESEUS' expedition against that race of warrior women at the beginning of "The KNIGHT'S TALE." *Femenye* is an Old French form of the Latin *Femina,* which means "land of women." Early texts locate the Amazons' kingdom on the southern shore of the Black Sea. Chaucer's source, BOCCACCIO'S *TESEIDA,* places them in the region of Lake Maeotis, to which the name SCYTHIA was also applied.

Ferrara   A town in northern Italy through which the PO River flows. In the prologue to "The CLERK'S TALE" the CLERK follows PETRARCH, Chaucer's source, in

describing the geographical area that forms the setting for the tale of patient GRISELDA, the beautiful peasant girl who was chosen to be the wife of WALTER, the Marquis of SALUZZO.

Ferrare   *See* FERRARA.

Filostrato, Il   A dramatic poem by the Italian writer Giovanni BOCCACCIO, *Il Filostrato* was Chaucer's primary source for his longest single poem, *TROILUS AND CRISEYDE.* The title means "the one overcome by love," and Boccaccio claimed to have written it to reflect upon the ups and downs of his own love affair. Although the TROJAN WAR, which serves as the historical background to *Il Filostrato,* had been treated by many poets, beginning with HOMER, Boccaccio was the first to take a small episode, or group of episodes, from the great chronicles that narrated the whole story of the war, and to treat that episode in elaborate detail. This emphasis makes the poem ideal for Chaucer's interest in the personal and particular side of life rather than the martial and general. Yet while maintaining a tight focus on character, his adaptation is nothing less than a dramatic revision or re-envisioning. As Stephen Barney notes in his introduction to the poem in *The RIVERSIDE CHAUCER,* the English poet "radically transforms Boccaccio's poem, redistributing the weight given various parts of the story, adding long scenes, wholly reimagining the characters of Troilus, Criseyde, Pandarus, and inserting a number of rich dialogues, apostrophes, epic machinery, soliloquies, proverbs, and the like, which alter, especially under the influence of Boethius, the tone of the poem." As a result, Chaucer's poem is "at once funnier and graver, more learned and more light-hearted, tighter in organization and broader in implication, less original and less smoothly crafted, yet a fair companion to the works of those poets whom Chaucer names at the end: Virgil, Ovid, Homer, Lucan, and Statius."

Fisher, John H(urt) (1919–   )   Chaucer scholar. After completing a doctorate at the University of Pennsylvania, Fisher taught at a wide variety of universities. He edited *The Complete Poetry and Prose of Geoffrey Chaucer* (1977) for Holt Publishing and contributed a chapter on *TROILUS AND CRISEYDE* to Beryl Rowland's *Companion to Chaucer Studies* (1979). In *The Importance of Chaucer* (1992), Fisher points out that like all great writers, Chaucer is untranslatable; but he also remarks that "Chaucer's language is just close enough" so that most readers of modern English, with "a little effort," can experience "the raising of the hairs on the back of the neck that is the proof of perfect poetic expression." Fisher's interest in Chaucer's language is reflected in a series of other publications including "Chaucer's French: A Metalinguistic Theory" (in *Chaucer Yearbook,*

1992), "Chaucer and the Written Language" (in *The Popular Literature of Medieval England,* 1985) and "Chaucer's Last Revision of the Canterbury Tales" (in *Modern Language Review,* 1972). Fisher also edited annotated bibliographies of Chaucer criticism for *Studies in the Age of Chaucer* for the years 1977–80, and compiled *The Essential Chaucer: An Annotated Bibliography of Major Modern Studies* (1987), an excellent research source. His early book, *John Gower: Moral Philosopher and Friend of Chaucer* (1964) provides an insightful discussion of the relationship between the two 14th-century poets.

Fish Street   Now known as Fish Hill Street, Fish Street is a London street located just off Thames Street below London Bridge. The locale is mentioned at the beginning of "The PARDONER'S TALE" when the PARDONER warns his audience to beware of the moral dangers associated with drinking wine. He goes on to say that they should especially avoid those vintages for sale "in Fysshstrete or in Chepe" (line 564) [in Fish Street or in Cheapeside], because this wine is likely to have been diluted with a cheaper Spanish variety. The abrupt shift from a moral caution to a mercantile one ironically reveals the Pardoner's personal knowledge of that which he warns others against.

Flanders   In medieval times, Flanders was a country in northwestern Europe, on the North Sea. It included a part of northwestern France, the provinces of East and West Flanders in Belgium and a small portion of land now belonging to the Netherlands. The SQUIRE who is described in the GENERAL PROLOGUE to *The CANTERBURY TALES* has fought campaigns in Flanders and other parts of northern France, in contrast to his father whose campaigns took him to comparatively distant lands such as RUSSIA, GRANADA and MOROCCO. Flanders is also the setting for two of *The Canterbury Tales,* "The PARDONER'S TALE" of the three rioters who go in search of Death, and "The TALE OF SIR THOPAS," which parodies the type of romantic adventure stories that were so popular at the time. For "The Pardoner's Tale," Chaucer may have chosen the setting because of the Flemings' reputation for overindulgent consumption of alcohol. In the case of "The Tale of Sir Thopas," he probably selected Flanders because it was known primarily as a center of industry and trade, which makes it a rather comically inappropriate setting for knightly adventures of high seriousness.

Flegitoun   *See* PHLEGETHON.

Fleming   A native of FLANDERS. Chaucer refers to a Flemish saying in the prologue to "The COOK'S TALE." When the Host (*see* Harry BAILLY) chides the COOK for selling poor-quality wares in the food shop where he works, he tells the man not to be angry over a remark that is made in jest. The Cook responds, "Thou seist ful sooth . . . by my fey! / But 'sooth pley, quaad pley,' as the Flemyng seith" (lines 4356–57) [You say truly, . . . by my faith! / But 'true jest, bad jest,' as the Fleming says] and then goes on to warn that he will now tell the story of an innkeeper (the Host's profession), being sure that the Host has a good sense of humor and will not get angry. The adjective *quaad,* which means "bad," is something Chaucer may have picked up from his association with Flemish merchants in the Vintry district where his father's family lived and ran their wine business. A number of Flemish merchants were killed by rioting peasants during the PEASANTS' REVOLT OF 1381, an event Chaucer may have witnessed. He is thought to have been in London during the revolt, yet his poetry contains only one allusion to the event. It appears in "The NUN'S PRIEST'S TALE" when he describes the group of yelling people and dogs that are chasing after RUSSELL, the fox who grabbed the rooster CHAUNTICLEER by the throat and ran off to the woods. He says that Jack STRAW (one of the leaders of the revolt) and his followers were never half so loud, even when they killed any of the Flemings, as were these people in pursuit of the fox.

Flexippe   One of CRISEYDE's nieces in *TROILUS AND CRISEYDE.* The origin of the name is unknown. Flexippe is a minor character, appearing in one scene only, where Criseyde and three of her nieces (the other two are THARBE and ANTIGONE) walk in the garden of Criseyde's house. Antigone sings a song of love which stimulates Criseyde to start considering that perhaps having a lover shower her with attention would not be so bad (bk. 2, line 816).

Flora   In classical mythology, Flora was the Italian goddess of flowers and the fruitfulness of spring. Her festival, called the Floralia, was celebrated with games and dancing, dramatic productions of a sexually provocative character, and hunting games in the Roman Circus. In *The BOOK OF THE DUCHESS,* the landscape that the narrator enters within his dream is so beautiful that he imagines it to be the home of the goddess Flora (line 402). In version F of the prologue to *The LEGEND OF GOOD WOMEN,* the landscape encountered by the dreamer is similarly described as having been brought to fruition by the gentle breath of Flora and ZEPHYRUS, the west wind (line 171).

Florence   City in the region of TUSCANY in north-central Italy on the Arno River. The city is mentioned in "The WIFE OF BATH'S TALE" as the home of the poet DANTE ALIGHIERI. In 1372–73, Chaucer himself traveled to Florence in the service of King EDWARD III. A number of scholars believe that Chaucer may have met the poets PETRARCH and BOCCACCIO, who were living in the region, and perhaps have obtained copies of their work and of Dante's. All three Italian poets had a significant influence on Chaucer's later work.

Flymyng *See* FLEMING.

"Former Age, The" Lyric poem by Chaucer, describing an age when humankind lived together peacefully in an Edenic paradise.

SUMMARY

Surviving on fruits, nuts and grains offered by the earth's bounty, early humans lived together in caves and forests, where they were free from the tyranny of taxes and other ills that beset civilized human beings. They did not make war on each other, because they had no possessions that had to be guarded or that could be taken away. Nor did they have any weapons with which to fight. Devoid of all pride, envy and avarice, they lived together in humility with good faith serving as their ruler. The poem concludes with a lament that all of this has passed away to be replaced by a civilization where deceit, covetousness, treason, envy, manslaughter and murder hold sway.

COMMENTARY

"The Former Age" is one of four of Chaucer's shorter poems that distinctively shows the influence of the Roman writer BOETHIUS. Specifically, the poem appears to have been inspired by Book Two, Metrum 5 of the *Consolation of Philosophy*, where LADY PHILOSOPHY eulogizes the first age of man, an age when human beings lived in harmony off the fruits of the earth, before they had learned to do things like make wine, dye cloth, dig gold out of the earth and shed each other's blood out of greed and animosity. Many of these images are specifically recalled in Chaucer's poem. In one of the two surviving manuscripts, the poem is called "Aetas Prima" (i.e., the first age); in the other, "Chaucer upon the fyfte metur of the second book." The idea of a former golden age also figured in several other works that Chaucer commonly drew upon for his own poetry, the French ROMAN DE LA ROSE and OVID's *Metamorphoses*.

Fortune In classical mythology, Fortune (Latin: *Fortuna*) was the Roman goddess of chance who, like the Greek fates, dealt out men's destinies in a manner that often appeared illogical and capricious. In ancient Rome she was worshipped under many different names, corresponding to the various conceptions of her as favorable or unfavorable, as ephemeral or abiding. Whereas for the Romans it was possible, based on one's circumstances, to forget the negative side of the goddess, the medieval Christian writers who inherited the concept seem to have always tried to keep in mind that negative possibility, even in times of great good fortune. In medieval art, Fortune is often pictured as a blindfolded woman turning a wheel on which men rise and fall.

The goddess Fortune, and the concept of fortune, was important in a number of Chaucer's works. In *The BOOK OF THE DUCHESS*, the BLACK KNIGHT tells the narrator that he played a game of chess with Fortune (a personification of the concept) and lost his queen. What this really means, we later learn, is that she has died. The goddess FAME, in *The HOUSE OF FAME*, seems closely modeled on the goddess Fortune in the way that she indiscriminately dispenses good and bad reputations to people without considering whether they merit either. In the BOECE, Chaucer's translation of BOETHIUS' *Consolation of Philosophy*, Fortune is blamed for the predicament of the narrator (actually Boethius), who has been the victim of circumstance and ill-will among his compatriots in the court of THEODORIC, king of the Ostrogoths. The short poem "FORTUNE" describes how the goddess operates in the world of men and features a narrator who complains of her behavior. Fortune speaks in the poem and defends herself, saying she has granted him good experiences as well as bad, and exhorts him to trust in the wisdom of heaven (i.e., God), which rules over all, even Fortune. In *The CANTERBURY TALES*, the idea of Fortune appears most prominently in "The MONK'S TALE," which is a series of tragedies emphasizing the role of Fortune in causing the downfall of famous men and one woman. All in all, the concept of Fortune presented in Chaucer's work is a negative one, even though it, or she, is ultimately vindicated by the idea that Fortune operates within a Christian framework where God oversees the turning of Fortune's wheel.

"Fortune" A series of three linked BALLADES by Chaucer.

SUMMARY

Chaucer's "Fortune" begins with a complaint wherein the narrator describes the confusing and sometimes calamitous changes wrought by Fortune in the world. Nevertheless, the narrator concludes with a personal defiance of her powers in the tradition of SOCRATES. The second ballade consists of Fortune's response to the plaintiff's charges. She reminds him of the gifts she has bestowed upon him in the past, and points out that her apparent cruelty has a hidden benefit: Bereft of Fortune, he discovers who his true friends are. Finally, she concludes that the plaintiff must, like other men born under her variable reign, be content with his lot, which is determined by the revolution of Fortune's wheel. The third ballade contains one stanza spoken by the narrator, with two responding stanzas from Fortune. The narrator refuses to be mollified by Fortune's defense of herself, saying that he damns her teaching; it is adversity. In Fortune's final stanzas she suggests that the narrator's anger arises from the loss of his former good fortune. This time she justifies her behavior by comparing it to fluctuations in the natural world—the ebb and flow of the sea and changes in the weather. Like them, her mutability is a normal function of natural law, which is determined by God. The world is naturally changeable; the only stability is in heaven. The three poems conclude with an envoy addressed to the plural "Princes," in which the poet seems to be requesting advancement: "That to som beter estat he may atteyne" [That to some better rank he may attain].

COMMENTARY

In several of the 10 surviving manuscripts of this poem it is given the title "Balades de vilage [an error for "visage"] sanz peinture," a French phrase that means "Ballades on a face without painting." James I. WIMSATT suggests the meaning that Fortune is presented here without her usual application of cosmetics, but it could also mean that this is a portrait accomplished with words rather than paint. Like "THE FORMER AGE," "TRUTH" and "GENTILESSE," this poem contains strong echoes of the work of Roman philosopher and poet BOETHIUS. His *Consolation of Philosophy* also features a complaint against Fortune, a defense and a discussion of her significance, although it is LADY PHILOSOPHY rather than Fortune herself who points out the way that Fortune's operations are overseen by divine Providence. The plural "Princes" referred to in the envoy has been taken to refer to the dukes of Lancaster (JOHN OF GAUNT), York and Gloucester. According to this theory, Chaucer's request that either three of them, or two, should intercede on his behalf to his "best friend," is a reference to an ordinance that no royal gift or grant should be bestowed by RICHARD II without the consent of at least two of the three dukes. (The function of this ordinance was to curtail Richard's habit of giving extravagant gifts to those courtiers he favored, a practice which served to alienate him from certain members of the nobility.)

France France provides the setting for more of Chaucer's narratives than any other country except England. This is only natural, considering the proximity of the two countries, separated only by a narrow channel of the sea, and their shared history, which included mutual invading expeditions. Three hundred years before Chaucer was born, William the Conqueror, from the region of Normandy, conquered England and brought into the country a ruling nobility that continued to speak and write their native ANGLO-NORMAN dialect of French right up to Chaucer's day. In fact, by choosing to compose poetry in English for an audience

of members of the nobility, Chaucer was breaking new ground. Some of his tales that are set in France, like "The SHIPMAN'S TALE," reflect the fact that French literature provided numerous sources for him to draw upon. Despite this borrowing, during Chaucer's lifetime relations with France were troubled at best. Armed conflict with the French had entered a new phase as EDWARD III used war with France as a way to entertain his restless nobles and to supply them with new wealth in the form of plunder. At least one French poet, Eustache DESCHAMPS, is on record for his appreciation of Chaucer's verse.

Franchise, Dame An allegorical character who attends the god of Love in Chaucer's ROMAUNT OF THE ROSE, which is a translation of the French ROMAN DE LA ROSE. Her name means nobility of character or generosity of spirit and she is very beautiful. Her outstanding characteristic is the empathy she displays for any man who falls in love with her, feeling it to be her responsibility to assuage any harm he may come to on her behalf. Most of the allegorical figures featured in this poem function to either encourage the advances of the lover, like Dame Franchise, or to discourage him, like DAUNGER.

Frank, Robert Worth (1914–) Chaucer scholar. Frank earned a Ph.D. at Yale and taught at a variety of institutions before settling at Pennsylvania State University. His largest contribution to Chaucer studies is *Chaucer and "The Legend of Good Women"* (1972), the first full-length assessment of the poem, published by Harvard University Press. Frank says that he wrote this book because it is impossible to make an honest assessment of Chaucer's development as an artist without studying The LEGEND OF GOOD WOMEN, which he sees as innovative in genre, theme, technique and verse form. Frank also penned several valuable articles on other Chaucer topics. "A Reading of Chaucer's Reeve's Tale" (*Chaucer Review,* 1967) shows how the animal imagery in this tale helps to set the moral tone of the tale, of which the theme is unbridled passion. Images discussed include the runaway horse, the peacock, magpie and pig; the latter three were used by the church fathers to represent the passions of pride, wrath and lust, respectively. Another article, "Miracles of the Virgin, Medieval Anti-Semitism, and the Prioress' Tale" (in *The Wisdom of Poetry: Essays in Early English Literature in Honor of Morton W. Bloomfield,* 1982), illustrates that anti-Semitism was typical in medieval tales of the Virgin, and traces the roots of this convention within social, doctrinal and literary history.

Franklin, the The Franklin's portrait follows that of the SERGEANT OF THE LAW in the GENERAL PROLOGUE TO *THE CANTERBURY TALES.* The title *franklin* basically signi-

Artist's rendering of the Franklin, from the Ellesmere Manuscript of The Canterbury Tales. *The Franklin here is white-bearded, matching his description in the General Prologue.*

fies that this man is a landowner, "an early example," Larry Benson notes, "of the English country squire." Although he is labeled an Epicurean, i.e., one devoted to pursuing the delights and pleasures associated with the senses, there is nothing negative or satirical about his portrait. The provisions in his generously stocked pantry and wine cellar are not, for example, enjoyed in isolation; indeed, the Franklin has the reputation of being a veritable saint of hospitality (hence the reference to Saint Julian) in the region where he lives. A substantial portion of his description is devoted to the various dishes that seasonally furnish his table. The fact that he owns a "table dormant" that stands ready to receive food and drink at any hour, rather than the collapsible trestle variety that could be removed between meals and that was more typical of the average medieval household of someone belonging to his rank, underlines his constant readiness to serve as host. He has a beard that is either as white as a daisy or as the sun ("day's eye"), depending upon how one translates the Middle English *dayesye*. His sanguine complexion, according to medieval medical theory of the four bodily HUMORS, indicates a jovial and generous-minded personality as well as good physical condition. The Franklin's good-natured optimism is reflected by his tale of DORIGEN and ARVERAGUS, which shows the rewards of love and constancy in marriage. (*See* entry

for the set of tales known as the MARRIAGE GROUP.) It is not at all unusual that a man of the Franklin's position should serve in the offices mentioned at the conclusion of his portrait, as presiding officer at court sessions and as member of Parliament, sheriff ("shirreve") and auditor ("contour") for the shire in which he lived.

"Franklin's Tale, The" "The Franklin's Tale" follows the SQUIRE's interrupted performance in THE CANTER-BURY TALES. This romantic story of a Breton Knight and his faithful wife presents one of the most positive views of marriage encountered in Chaucer's work.

SUMMARY

In ARMORICA (see also BRITTANY) a knight named ARVERAGUS is in love with a lady named DORIGEN. He does many great deeds in her service until at last she takes pity on him and grants her love in return. Deciding to marry, they swear mutual faith and obedience. In addition, despite his socially sanctioned position of mastery over his wife, Arveragus promises never to exercise his authority over Dorigen against her will. She, in turn, pledges humility and fidelity. Thus begins an ideal marriage, which the narrator takes a moment to praise as such, noting that mutual obedience is the only key to a long and happy relationship. Arveragus takes his wife home to KAYRUDD, in Brittany, where they live in bliss and prosperity for more than a year. Then Arveragus decides to go to England to win honor in tournaments. He intends to be gone for two years.

During her husband's absence, Dorigen misses him sorely. She mourns him so deeply, in fact, that her friends begin to worry that she may die of grief, and they busy themselves at the task of cheering her up. Eventually their efforts pay off, and Dorigen is somewhat comforted. To further lift her spirits, her companions urge her to come outside and walk on the high cliffs above the sea. But Dorigen becomes dispirited again, seeing ships and barges come and go, but none bearing her husband home again. She becomes particularly upset by the sight of some treacherous black rocks standing in the sea and making the approach to land dangerous for incoming ships. Falling to her knees, she says a prayer, arguing that the rocks serve no good purpose and asking that they be destroyed.

Realizing that the view of the sea does little to calm Dorigen's mind, her friends take her to different places. One of these is a beautiful garden where, one day after a picnic, her friends decide to sing and dance for entertainment. Dorigen sits apart from the merriment, thinking about her husband. Among those dancing is a handsome squire named AURELIUS. Unbeknownst to Dorigen, this young man has for a long time been infatuated with her, but he has despaired of finding an opportunity to confess his love. This particular outing provides him with the opportunity. Before they part, he tells Dorigen how he feels about her and, following the familiar formula of courtly love, asks her to have mercy on him, or else she will cause him to die. Initially Dorigen tells him in no uncertain terms that she will never betray her husband; but she then teasingly agrees to grant his desire on one condition; that he remove all the rocks that make the coast of Brittany treacherous for ships. She adds that she knows this will never happen. Aurelius leaves her, promising to die a sudden and horrible death.

That night Aurelius, still burning in the fires of his desire, prays to APOLLO for help, asking the god to work a kind of natural miracle—causing the tide to remain at its highest, and thus covering the rocks along the coast for a period of two years. After the prayer, he falls down in a trance. He is found by his brother, who puts him to bed.

Meanwhile, Arveragus returns home. He and Dorigen are reunited in bliss and spend their days celebrating his return. Wretched Aurelius remains in bed, sick with love, for two years. His brother, who is a scholar, knows the cause of his illness but keeps it a secret, always trying to think of a solution or cure. Finally he remembers an episode from his days as a student in France, when he came across a book of "natural magic" that gave information about how to create illusions. With that in mind, he rouses his brother from bed and returns with him to ORLEANS, the city where he studied. Once there, they immediately make the acquaintance of a young scholar-magician who promises he can create the illusion they desire. For this assistance, Aurelius promises to pay £1000.

The two brothers return home and the magician keeps his promise. Aurelius visits Dorigen, reminding her of her vow and directing her attention to the sea below the cliffs where the black rocks are no longer visible. Realizing that she must lose her honor no matter what she does—whether she chooses to be unfaithful to her husband or to break her promise to Aurelius—Dorigen thinks over her situation, calling to mind examples of many women who chose death rather than becoming victims of a man's lechery. She decides to follow their example and commit suicide, but keeps putting it off until her husband comes home and asks why she is so upset. When she tells him what has happened, he says that she ought to keep her promise, because her "trouthe" (sworn promise) is a bond that she must keep in spite of the consequences. Then Arveragus breaks down and weeps, commanding his wife that she must never, on penalty of death, tell any person about this misadventure or give any sign that she is upset or depressed.

Dorigen goes to meet Aurelius at the appointed place (a garden), but instead runs into him on the street. When he asks where she is going, she says to the garden, where her husband has commanded her to go to keep her promise. Aurelius is so moved by her lamentation, and by the determination of her husband that she should not break her promise, that his own behavior seems to him degraded in comparison to their nobility, and he decides to release her from her bond. Dorigen returns home to tell her husband of their good fortune, and they live blissfully together for the rest of their lives, never again angry at each other. Aurelius, still obliged to the magician who created the illusion, visits him to determine a means of payment. When the magician finds out what has happened and why, he decides to release the squire from his debt, determining that a scholar ought to be able to do a courteous deed just as well as a squire and a knight. The Franklin closes his tale with a question, asking the company of pilgrims, Who, among the characters in his story, was the most generous?

COMMENTARY

The genre of "The Franklin's Tale" is self-declared. When the Franklin opens his prologue with the words, "Thise olde gentil Britouns in hir dayes / Of diverse aventures maden layes, / Rymeyed in hir firste Briton tonge, / Whiche layes with hir instrumentz they songe" (lines 709–12) [These old noble Britons in their day / Of various adventures made lays, / Rhymed in their original Briton language, / Which they sang to the accompaniment of music], he is giving the definition of a Breton lay. This genre originated, so far as we know, in Brittany, a peninsula of Northwest France that lies between the Bay of Biscay and the English Channel. When the Angles, Saxons and Jutes invaded Britain in the fifth and sixth centuries, many of the island's Celtic inhabitants fled to this area and eventually settled there permanently. Their British heritage is what gave the region its name of Brittany (Bretagne in French) and themselves the appellation of Bretons. Other medieval examples of the genre are the lays of MARIE DE FRANCE and the Middle English poem *Sir Orfeo*. Marie is thought to be the originator of the form.

There appears to be no indisputable surviving source for "The Franklin's Tale," though it does bear strong similarities to a tale in the *Filocolo* of the Italian writer BOCCACCIO. The plot situation of Boccaccio's tale is as follows: A wife makes a rash promise to have sex with an admirer because she believes he can never grant her desire, to make a garden bloom in January. With the help of a magician, he does, and the husband insists that his wife fulfill her part of the bargain. The admirer, overcome by the husband's generosity, releases her, and is likewise released from his own debt by the magician. What Chaucer adds to the basic plot found here is a stronger sense of character motivation, which in turn makes the characters both more believable and more sympathetic, despite the tale's idealism.

Although they do not serve as direct sources, some of Chaucer's favorite texts also appear to have influenced "The Franklin's Tale." Dorigen's questions about the existence of the treacherous rocks in a world designed by a benevolent God echo BOETHIUS' questions about the function of evil in his *Consolation of Philosophy*. The argument for equal partnership in marriage recalls a similar argument in the ROMAN DE LA ROSE. Chaucer's admiration for these works is shown both by the frequent allusions to them in his poetry and by his translations of them. (*See* commentary under ROMAUNT OF THE ROSE and BOECE for more information.) Dorigen's long complaint, where she recalls examples of wives and other women who have preferred death to violation of chastity, comes from another familiar source, Saint JEROME's *Epistola adversus Jovinianum* (Letter against Jovinian).

Although the Franklin does not explicitly offer his tale as a response or challenge to a previous pilgrim's efforts, it does repeat themes that have appeared before, such as the theme of sovereignty in marriage which is featured in "The WIFE OF BATH'S TALE" and "The CLERK'S TALE." The WIFE's tale, along with her prologue, argues that it is best to give the wife sovereignty over her husband in marriage. The CLERK's tale argues, in allegorical form, for trusting in the husband's right to the same, viewing that right as an extension of the divine order of things: The husband's position as head of the family mirrors God's as head of the church. Since "The Franklin's Tale" addresses the same issue, that of sovereignty in marriage, and appears last in the series, its position alone, as the last word on the subject, would seem to give it a certain amount of authority over the other two. Looking at the outcomes of the three tales, however, we see that they all have happy endings. By scratching a bit beyond the surface of the two previous tales, we can discern that both have an ending which restores or creates a kind of balance that was lacking at their outset. WALTER, for example, repents of his cruel behavior and finally recognizes GRISELDA as his true equal. The KNIGHT (3) who committed rape, the most aggressive act possible of mastery against a woman, submits to his wife's sovereignty and is rewarded with a wife who is both beautiful *and* faithful, instead of one or the other. Considered in this light, it appears that all three tales argue for a kind of balance of power between the two parties of a marriage, if that marriage is to be a happy one.

Another important theme that informs both "The Wife of Bath's Tale" and "The Franklin's Tale" is that of *gentilesse,* which might be defined as consistently behaving with goodness and generosity. The idea of *gentilesse* was problematic at the time when Chaucer was writing because members of the nobility were, simply by virtue of their birth, considered to be "gentle." That they did not always behave in such a manner is liberally illustrated by historical examples as well as examples in Chaucer's work which, upon several occasions, debates the definition of true gentility. In the Wife's tale, when the young knight-rapist complains to his loathly wife that she comes from low or ignoble parents, she catechises him on the true nature of gentilesse, which is not something that can be handed down from one ancestor to another, but is a virtue that comes from God. The Franklin has already shown, in his interruption of the SQUIRE's recital, that he is concerned with gentility, particularly with that which seems to be lacking in his own offspring, and it is chiefly on the basis of that virtue that he praises the Squire and his tale-telling efforts. While some critics have seen the Franklin's praise as self-serving, as cynical evidence of his social-climbing efforts, there seems little evidence of such an attitude toward the man in the remainder of Chaucer's characterization of him or in the tale that he is given to tell. The gentilesse displayed by Arveragus is nothing less than absolute faith in a benign Providence. When Dorigen reveals the details of her dilemma, he says "It may be wel, paraventure, yet to day" (line 1473) and urges his wife to keep her promise. The fact that the Franklin has created a character like Arveragus, whose gentilesse obviously functions as the centerpiece of the tale, suggests that the Franklin's gentilesse is not superficial but rather expresses an idealistic yearning toward perfection in a postlapsarian world.

In many respects, this tale as a whole serves to point out and emphasize one very basic tenet of Christian morality: that if one behaves as one ought according to the laws of God, things will somehow turn out for the best, even though it may be difficult to imagine such an outcome, given the circumstances. The tale also illustrates the contagiousness of Christian charity—how one person's decision to act honestly and faithfully can create a chain reaction of similar decisions by those who are affected. Specifically, Dorigen upholds her faith to her husband, who in turn behaves charitably toward her, and the squire, beneficiary of their actions, finds himself unable to profit from their good faith and love for one another. The scholar-magician, considering all these examples of people behaving charitably toward one another, feels obliged to meet the standard that has been set, and to prove that a scholar need not be outdone by a knight or a squire in the realm of noble deeds.

In plot, "The Franklin's Tale" most closely resembles that told by the MERCHANT. Both feature a squire in love with the wife of a knight, and a garden in which that love is to be consummated. In "The MERCHANT'S TALE," however, the wife, MAY, is not in love with her husband, JANUARY, but is all too eager to give solace to the lovesick squire. This, along with the many naturalistic details pointing to January's advanced age and the inappropriate burning fires of his lust, makes the tale a FABLIAU rather than a romance, distancing it from the concerns of the Franklin's story, and simultaneously illustrating a marriage in which the proper balance or harmony can never be established because of the difference in ages between old January and his young wife, May.

Chaucer's use of the garden as the setting for illicit love reflects a tradition in the literature of courtly love that, to some degree at least, arose from the influence of JEAN DE MEUN's use of the garden as the site of seduction in the *Roman de la Rose*. Within this tradition, gardens are, for those unwilling to engage in sexual intrigue, dangerous places. When Dorigen makes her rash promise to Aurelius, she is in a garden—the same garden to which she is returning at the end of the tale to fulfill that promise. The fact that Aurelius meets her on the street, instead of in the garden, helps to explain why, within the conventions of courtly love, she gets away with her virtue intact. Alone with her, surrounded by the beauties of nature, it might have been more difficult for the lustful squire to release his lady from her vow.

One final feature of "The Franklin's Tale" that seems to deserve comment is the way the plot depends upon what the narrator calls "natural magic." When the magician consults his astrological tables to discover the best time to create his illusion, he is, to some extent, depending on the alignment of the moon and the planets in their houses in order to determine when the highest tide of the year will occur, so that his "magic" will be aided by nature. During the Middle Ages, the term *natural magic* was inseparable from such scientific knowledge as circulated among human beings at this time, and self-proclaimed wizards would sometimes use their knowledge of astronomy (not yet distinguished from astrology) and other natural phenomena to give people the illusion that they possessed great powers, as does Mark Twain's Connecticut Yankee when he "creates" a solar eclipse over King Arthur's court.

French, Robert D. (1881–1954) A professor of English at Yale University, French authored one of the earliest student guides to Chaucer, *The Chaucer Handbook* (2nd ed., 1947). French felt that those who teach the poet have an obligation to inform students of the materials made available by scholarship, without which no understanding of Chaucer's genius can be complete. The goal of his handbook was to bring together in a concise form the widely scattered and sometimes otherwise inaccessible results of that scholarship.

Friar, the Huberd the Friar is the third clerical figure to be described in the GENERAL PROLOGUE to *The CAN-*

Artist's rendering of the Friar, from the Ellesmere Manuscript of The Canterbury Tales. *The Friar is tonsured and wears the appropriate robe. His horse seems rather small for his body.*

TERBURY TALES. The PRIORESS and the MONK, both of whom rank higher in the ecclesiastical hierarchy, are described before him. The order in which these clerical pilgrims appear mirrors their rank, showing a progression from highest to lowest. The Prioress is the mother superior of her convent, the Monk is an important member of a wealthy order and the Friar belongs to one of the four mendicant orders (the Carmelites, Augustinians, Dominicans and Franciscans) whose members took vows of poverty and supported themselves by begging, and whose founding mission was to relieve the suffering of the diseased and the outcast. From this description of what the Friar was supposed to be, it is easy to see that Chaucer's portrait of Huberd is one of the most satirical and damning ones to appear in the General Prologue. Rather than poverty and service to others, Huberd's chief concerns are maintaining a lively social life and making money. Although he makes his own living by begging and receiving voluntary donations, he scorns the company of other beggars and of lepers, preferring that of rich franklins (*see* the FRANKLIN), well-victualed innkeepers and fair wives. One reason for his popularity, it seems, is his license to hear confession. To enable him to compete successfully with parish priests in this capacity, the Friar has adopted the tactic of giving an easy penance to those from whom he anticipates receiving a substantial gift ("a good pitaunce"). The Friar's greed is lampooned by "The SUMMONER'S TALE," which, ironically, is itself a response to the Friar's depiction of an avaricious summoner. Perhaps the rivalry between these two men mirrors the competition among members of their professions for the limited resources of the average citizen. Another abuse hinted at in the portrait of Huberd is that of engaging in sexual activity. First, we are told that he "hadde maad ful many a mariage / Of yonge wommen at his owene cost" (lines 212–13) [had made many a marriage / Of young women at his own expense]. Although providing the dowry for a young woman whose family was unable to do so was a recognized charitable activity, the Friar's failure to exhibit any other type of charity, in addition to other details of the Friar's description, suggests that these lines refer to his efforts to find husbands for victims of his own seduction. The Friar's white neck, according to the medieval "science" of PHYSIOGNOMY, indicates a lecherous nature, which is further hinted in the references to his wanton ("wantowne") and merry nature. His skill in singing and making ballads likewise recalls the portrait of the SQUIRE, a young man devoted to the service of love. Despite these criticisms, the portrait is on its surface that of a man who leads a pleasant and enjoyable life: In the final lines of his portrait, we see a man who can romp ("rage") like a puppy ("whelp"), who is particularly successful in achieving reconciliations and ending quarrels and whose eyes "twynkled in his heed aryght / As doon the sterres in the frosty nyght" (lines 267–68) [twinkled in his head exactly like the stars on a frosty night].

"Friar's Tale, The"   This tale of a corrupt summoner sparks a bitter rivalry between the FRIAR and the SUMMONER, who feels that the story's insults are aimed at him.

SUMMARY

The Friar begins his tale with a commendation of "The WIFE OF BATH'S TALE" and a promise that his own will be about a summoner of whom "may no good be sayd." The Host interrupts, asking him to proceed with his tale and leave off comments directed toward those present. The SUMMONER responds, saying that the Friar should say whatever he wants; when the Summoner's turn comes, he will get his revenge.

"The Friar's Tale" tells about a summoner who abuses his office by false accusation and entrapment. A member of the laity employed by the church, the summoner's duties consisted mainly of carrying summonses from the episcopal court to an individual who had been charged in that court for certain offenses, and, in cases

where the accused was unable to travel to court, collecting a fine. According to Chaucer's tale, these offenses might be sexual ones such as fornication, adultery, prostitution and pandering, or others like slander, the robbing of the church (which included not paying a tithe of one's income to the church), the violation of legal contracts such as a marriage contract and/or the failure to observe any of the sacraments such as confession and communion. Because the summoner could collect the fine himself, and because attending the archdiocesan court often required travel and thus posed a hardship for many people, a summoner could, if he were so inclined, easily practice extortion, either through false accusation or by collecting a fine considerably higher than the amount he was required to turn over to the court. The summoner described by the Friar is particularly given to such abuses of his office. As the tale opens, he is on his way to visit an old widow whom he intends to bribe or trick out of some money. En route, he encounters a yeoman dressed in green and carrying a bow. They greet one another, and when the summoner says he is on his way to collect a "rente" that is owed to his lord, the yeoman asks if he is a "bailly" (i.e., bailiff), someone employed by a landowner to collect rent from tenants. Ashamed to admit his true profession, the summoner answers in the affirmative, to which the yeoman exclaims that he is a bailiff, too. Following this exchange, the two men become sworn brothers and decide to travel together for a time. Many of the details of their conversation are rich with irony, which only becomes apparent later when the yeoman reveals his true identity as a devil from hell. Yet even when he does so, the summoner reveals his own true nature by being intrigued rather than offended or frightened, and by maintaining that the oath of brotherhood still stands: "I am a yeman, knowen is ful wyde; / My trouthe wol I holde, as in this cas; / For though thou were the devel Sathanas, / My trouthe wol I holde to my brother / As I am sworn." (lines 1524–28) [I am a yeoman, this is widely known; / My word will I keep, as in this case; / For even if you were the devil, Satan, / My word shall I hold to my brother / As I am sworn]. To cement their bond, they agree to share out whatever goods they receive in the practice of their professions. Soon they come upon a carter, who curses his horse, commending it to the devil. When the summoner asks the devil why he does not take the horse, the devil replies that it is because the curse did not come from the heart. This observation is immediately illustrated by the carter's praise and blessing of the horse when it ceases stalling. Later they visit the poor old woman from whom the summoner hopes to extort some money. When she asks for a written copy of the indictment and permission to address the court through a representative, the summoner denies her request saying, "the foule feend me fecche /

If I th'excuse" (lines 1610–11) [the foul fiend fetch me / If I excuse you]. The old woman adds her own wish that he would go to the devil unless he should repent of what he has said. When the summoner refuses, the devil carries him off to hell, because the woman's curse was from the heart.

COMMENTARY

"The Friar's Tale" is a gem of irony and satire, its hard glittering surface giving no quarter to the man or to the profession it lambasts. The portrait of the Friar in the GENERAL PROLOGUE of The CANTERBURY TALES hints that he possesses considerable wit and learning, both of which are subtly projected in his story of the summoner who loses his soul to the devil. The genre of this tale is not as clearly defined as that of some of the other Canterbury tales, but it seems to derive from a traditional folktale formula which features, at its climactic moment, the delivery of a heartfelt curse. Structurally, it is divided into two parts. The first describes the abusive practices of the summoner, who gets money from members of the parish in which he serves by a combination of perjury, entrapment, blackmail and extortion. The Friar concludes his devastating portrait of this man with this pithy summary of his character: "He was, if I shal yeven hym his laude, / a theef, and eek a somnour, and a baude" (lines 1353–54) [He was, if I shall give him his due, / a thief, and also a summoner, and a pimp]. Situating his titulary profession between the other two suggests that there likewise exists a qualitative equivalency among all three, that being a summoner is no better or worse than being a thief or a pimp.

The second part is the tale itself, in which the summoner meets a demon disguised as a yeoman. The tale immediately launches into a pervasive and delicious irony. Both the summoner and the demon lie about their professions, each claiming to be a bailiff, an officer of justice under a sheriff, whose duty it is to execute writs and processes of law, a civil function that corresponds somewhat to the summoner's function in the ecclesiastical courts. The ironic aspect of this lie is that the summoner is indeed like the demon, both in profession and in character. Whereas the demon's job is to summon souls who have sinned against God, the summoner's is to bring to judgment those who have committed crimes against God's church. Furthermore, the summoner, like the devil, is an agent of evil, albeit in the social rather than the theological realm. The demon's disguise as a yeoman dressed in green and carrying a bow and arrows suggests that he is a hunter, and some scholars, like D. W. ROBERTSON, have seen in these details of his appearance hints at his true identity. In medieval iconography, the color green is commonly associated with denizens of the supernatural and the devil is often depicted as a hunter of souls. Recognition

of these details does add a degree of richness to the text, but the summoner's failure to recognize the demon's identity based on them does not seem very significant when, anyway, soon after their coming together, the demon openly admits his infernal nature.

The irony of the tale deepens considerably when the summoner, despite a number of indications that he will soon become the prey that the demon is in quest of, repeatedly misses the point. Perhaps, as Paul RUGGIERS has suggested, the man is blinded by the demon's pledge of brotherhood, by his seductive cordiality, and cannot imagine that he will turn against him; or, his blindness could simply be of the allegorical variety, showing that he is literally so blinded by sin that he is unable to perceive truth, even when it is delivered straightforwardly to him. The climax of the tale is prepared for by the episode in which the demon and his companion observe a carter who curses his horses for stalling in the road, yet they are not taken away by the demon because, as he explains, the curse was not sincere. When the summoner finds himself on the receiving end of such a curse, the inevitable outcome is visible to the reader long before it triggers the summoner's awareness. Chaucer intensifies the irony, and thus gives it a decidedly comic tone, by first having the summoner condemn himself when he tells the old woman from whom he is trying to extort money, "Nay thanne . . . the foule feend me fecche / If I th'excuse." (lines 1610–11) But of course, his condemnation of himself is not a sincere wish, although it does state what *is* going to happen if he does not excuse her of the fine he wishes to collect. When he threatens her further, accusing her of adultery, she exclaims, "Ne nevere I nas but of my body trewe! / Unto the devel blak and rough of hewe / Yeve I thy body . . . !" (lines 1621–23.) [Never was I anything but chaste in body! / Unto the devil black and rough in appearance / I commend your body!]. As readers, we fully expect him to be whisked peremptorily away to hell; but no, the meticulous demon (at this point showing himself to be more scrupulous than the summoner), has to make sure. So he asks her, "'Now, Mabely, myn owene mooder deere, / Is this youre wyl in ernest that ye seye?'" (lines 1626–27) ["Now, Mabel, my own dear old lady, / Is this your will in earnest that you speak?"]. Mabely, patient soul that she must be, answers yes, that is indeed her intention, unless "he wol hym repente" (line 1629) [he wishes to repent], giving him yet another chance to redeem himself. The summoner, blinded by greed, immediately retorts, "Nay, olde stot, that is nat myn entente, / . . . for to repente me / For any thyng that I have had of thee. / I wolde I hadde thy smok and every clooth!" (lines 1630–33) [Nay, old cow, that is not my intention, / . . . for to repent / For anything that I have gotten from you. / I wish I had your smock and every bit of cloth!]. The demon now steps in to collect his due, as cordial as ever, asking the summoner not to be angry, and exhibiting the last bite of his (or the Friar's) ironic wit when he says, "Thou shalt with me to helle yet tonyght" (line 1636) [You shall go with me to hell yet tonight], in perfect parody of Christ's promise to the repentant thief.

Frideswide, Saint   Eighth-century Anglo-Saxon abbess and a saint of the church. From childhood, she chose for herself the maxim, "Whatsoever is not God is nothing." Frideswide entered a religious order upon the death of her mother and afterward was put in charge of the monastery of St. Mary at OXFORD, which had been founded by her father. According to legend, Frideswide was delivered by prayer from the sexual advances of Algar, a Mercian prince. She died before the end of the eighth century, was later canonized, and also came to be honored as the patroness of the city and of the University of Oxford. In Chaucer's "MILLER'S TALE," JOHN THE CARPENTER calls upon Saint Frideswide for help when he breaks into the room of his lodger, NICHOLAS, and finds him apparently swooning. John believes Nicholas has lost his mind through too much study and calls upon Saint Frideswide not only because she is the saint of the town in which he lives, but also because she had a great reputation for healing.

Frisia (Frise)   Frisia, or Friesland, which in medieval times was a country, now forms part of the Netherlands. In a short poem, the "LENVOY DE CHAUCER À BUKTON," Chaucer tells his friend who is about to be married that it would be better for him to be taken prisoner in Frisia (Chaucer gives it the French spelling, *Frise*) than to marry. He may have chosen Frisia, rather than some other country, simply because it helped complete his rhyme, but, as Donald Howard points out in his biography of Chaucer, the Frieslanders had recently refused to ransom their own countrymen who were prisoners in England, and had killed their English prisoners. Thus,

being captured in Frisia meant death, a rather extreme alternative to marriage.

Froissart, Jean   French chronicler and poet from the region of Hainault who traveled widely in western Europe during the latter part of the 14th century, collecting material for his elaborate histories. He became the secretary to EDWARD III's queen, Philippa, in 1360, and accompanied EDWARD THE BLACK PRINCE to Spain when England agreed to back the claims of the deposed King Pedro (Pedro the Cruel) to the throne of Castile (*see* PEDRO OF CASTILE). In 1368 he joined Lionel, duke of Clarence, on his magnificent expedition to MILAN when the duke traveled there to be married to Violante Visconti. Froissart's writings about the occasion provide a detailed portrait of the expedition's grandeur (for example, Lionel was accompanied by 457 men and 1,280 horses). Froissart's chronicles provide historians and biographers of the period with a wealth of material, though consideration has to be taken of his propensity for embellishment and exaggeration. Froissart's poetry had some influence on Chaucer's work, his "Dittie de la Flour de la Margherite" (Poem on the marguerite flower) providing a number of lines adopted by Chaucer in *The LEGEND OF GOOD WOMEN* to describe the daisy with which the dreamer-narrator falls in love. *Marguerite* was another name for daisy. Froissart's *Paradys d'Amours* similarly provided a number of lines for *The BOOK OF THE DUCHESS*.

Frydeswyde, Saint   *See* FRIDESWIDE, SAINT.

Furies, the   *See* ERINYES.

Fynystere   *See* CAPE FINISTERRE.

Fyssh   *See* PISCES.

Fysshstrete   *See* FISH STREET.

G

Gabriel In the Bible, Gabriel is an archangel who acts as the messenger of God, appearing to DANIEL, Zacharias and the Virgin Mary (*see* MARY, SAINT). All of his messages were interpreted as foretelling the coming of Christ as the messiah. His appearance to Mary, when he tells her that she has been chosen to be the mother of God's son, is alluded to in Chaucer's "ABC," a poem of praise addressed to the Virgin.

Gaddesden *See* JOHN OF GADDESDEN.

Gaius Cesar *See* CALIGULA.

Galatea (Galathee) The heroine of the *Pamphilles de amore*, also known as the *Liber de Amore*, a 13th-century work attributed to the poet Pamphilus Maurelianus. It consists of a series of dialogues between two lovers named PAMPHILUS and Galatea. The secrecy surrounding their relationship is alluded to in Chaucer's "FRANKLIN'S TALE" when the FRANKLIN says that AURELIUS' brother, the only other person who knew about his love for the married DORIGEN, was as discreet concerning the matter as Pamphilus was regarding his love for Galatea.

Galatia *See* MILETUS.

Galaxye One of the names Chaucer uses to refer to the astronomical formation known as the MILKY WAY. He refers to it by this name in *The HOUSE OF FAME* when the EAGLE who has picked him up and proceeds to carry him high into the earth's atmosphere directs his attention to the formation and other sights that may be seen from this new vantage point. Chaucer also refers to the Milky Way by this name in *The PARLIAMENT OF FOWLS* when he describes a similar journey into the heavens taken by SCIPIO AFRICANUS THE YOUNGER in the *DREAM OF SCIPIO*, a text that influenced several of Chaucer's early poems.

Galen A second-century physician of Pergamum and Alexandria in Egypt. Credited with being the founder of experimental physiology, he was considered, after HIPPOCRATES, to be the most accomplished physician of the ancient world. Galen studied medicine in several cities of the eastern Mediterranean, including Alexandria. In 164 he moved to Rome, where he attended both the emperor Marcus Aurelius and his son, Commodus. His voluminous medical works constituted a comprehensive corpus of ancient medical lore and were accepted as authoritative during the Middle Ages. Galen is mentioned in Chaucer's GENERAL PROLOGUE TO *THE CANTERBURY TALES* as one of the medical authorities whose teachings the DOCTOR OF PHYSIC had studied. He is also referred to by the BLACK KNIGHT in *The BOOK OF THE DUCHESS*, who says he is so sick (from the loss of his queen) that he could not even be healed by such a master as Galen.

Galgopheye In "The KNIGHT'S TALE," Chaucer compares ARCITE's fierceness in battle to that of a tiger in the "vale of Galgopheye" whose little cub has been stolen from her. There is no known geographical region bearing this name; it may be a distortion of *Gargaphia,* the Latin name of a valley near Plataea in Boeotia which was considered sacred to DIANA because ACTAEON was slain there.

Galice (Galicia) In Chaucer's day, Galicia was the name of a province in northwestern Spain that was part of the kingdom of Castile. It is both remote and mountainous; nevertheless, during the medieval period, thousands of pilgrims—the WIFE OF BATH among them—came each year to visit the famous shrine of SAINT JAMES AT COMPOSTELLA. The Wife's visit to the shrine of Saint James is mentioned along with other popular pilgrimage destinations in her portrait in the GENERAL PROLOGUE to *The CANTERBURY TALES* (line 466).

Galien (1) *See* GALEN.

Galien (2) *See* GALLIENUS, PUBLICUS LICINIUS EGNATIUS.

Galilee The northernmost of the three Roman provinces of Palestine during the time of Jesus; the others were Samaria and Judea. Galilee extended from the base of Mount Harmon in the north to the Carmel and Gilboa ranges in the south. The Mediterranean Sea and the Jordan River formed its western and eastern boundaries, respectively. The wedding where Christ performed the first miracle, that of turning water into wine, took place in Cana, a city of Galilee. The WIFE OF BATH refers to this wedding and its location in the prologue to her tale when she tries to support her opinion that marriage is equal in worth to celibacy. Christ's attendance at a wedding and his performance of a miracle at the occasion was seen by the Wife as evidence in favor of her position.

Gallienus, Publicus Licinius Egnatius The son of the Roman emperor Valerian, Publicus Licinius Egnatius Gallienus himself ruled as emperor from 260 to 268. During his reign the major cities of Greece were sacked by the Goths. His own generals turned against him, and the succeeding period became known as the Reign of the Thirty Tyrants. The empire also suffered from frequent outbreaks of plague. Gallienus is mentioned in "The MONK'S TALE" as a commander who did not dare to face the warrior-queen ZENOBIA in battle, out of fear that she would put his troops to a rout or even slay him with her own hands.

Gallus, Sulpicius Sulpicius Gallus, referred to by Chaucer as Symplicius Gallus, was a distinguished Roman orator who became praetor (a magistrate ranking below a consul) in 169 B.C. and consul in 166. He was said to have repudiated his wife because he saw her on a public street with her head uncovered. In the prologue to "The WIFE OF BATH'S TALE," the Wife relates that when she ignored her fifth husband's demand that she stop walking about the town gossiping with her neighbors, he told her the story of Symplicius Gallus (lines 642–46), perhaps as a kind of threat.

Ganelon The count of Mayence in the Merovingian Empire, Ganelon was one of Charlemagne's paladins who, because he was jealous of Charlemagne's power and influence, planned the ambush at Roncesvalles in which Roland, Charlemagne's most famous knight, was killed. Roland's death was attributed to the treachery of Ganelon, whose punishment was to be torn to pieces by wild horses. Chaucer alludes to Ganelon's treachery in *The BOOK OF THE DUCHESS*, "The SHIPMAN'S TALE," "The MONK'S TALE" and "The NUN'S PRIEST'S TALE," where RUSSELL the fox is referred to as a false Ganelon for winning the confidence of the rooster CHAUNTICLEER and then seizing him by the neck.

Ganymede In classical mythology, Ganymede was the most beautiful of mortal men. While tending the flocks of his father, Ganymede was carried off by the eagle of Zeus, (*see* JUPITER) or by Zeus himself in the form of an eagle, to dwell among the gods and to act as their cupbearer. His father received a pair of divine horses as compensation for losing his son. Chaucer mentions Ganymede in *The HOUSE OF FAME* when, like Ganymede, he is ferried into the sky by an eagle. As if to recall the eagle, or himself, to reality, he exclaims, "what thing may this sygnifye? / I neyther am Ennok, ne Elye, / Ne Romulus, ne Ganymede . . . ." (lines 587–89) [What is the meaning of this? / I am not Enoch, nor am I Elijah, / or Romulus, or Ganymede . . .]. The mention of these figures from the Bible and legend adds to the comedy of the piece by the implied comparison between their noble journeys—their destinations are heaven and immortality—and Chaucer's relatively silly one—his destination is the palace of FAME, where the capricious goddess of that name illogically dispenses good and bad reputations.

Garden of Love The Garden of Love forms the setting for much of Chaucer's poem, *The PARLIAMENT OF FOWLS*, in which a narrator falls asleep and dreams that he enters a beautiful garden through a double-doored gate. One side of the gate invites the dreamer with words that promise relief of suffering and sorrow, followed by a blissful experience. The other side paradoxically warns that those who enter here will suffer great hardship in a place where trees never bear fruit. These inscriptions refer to the double nature of romantic love—its ability to bring both pain and happiness. Once inside, it appears that the favorable inscription is the accurate one, for the garden teems with verdant life. Sitting beneath the trees and among the many fragrant flowers are a number of allegorical figures, such as Beauty, Youth, Flattery and Desire, all of whom suggest the poem's indebtedness to the great French allegorical dream vision that influenced Chaucer's work in so many ways, the *ROMAN DE LA ROSE*. Readers who compare the two texts cannot fail to see the garden of the *Roman* reflected in Chaucer's garden, a similarity whose thematic importance is reflected in the garden's function as a place where the birds have come to choose their mates on Saint Valentine's Day. Chaucer's Middle English translation of the *Roman* (*The ROMAUNT OF THE ROSE*) interestingly breaks off once the geography of the garden and the central conflict of the poem, the dreamer's desire to possess a rose with which he has fallen in love, have been established, perhaps suggesting that these parts of the poem were of greatest interest to him. The garden is the literary descendant of the classical *locus amoenus* (pleasant place) and appears in abbreviated form in Chaucer's "MERCHANT'S TALE," where the aged knight, JANUARY, has a walled garden where he likes to make love to his young wife, MAY.

Garter, Order of the The Order of the Garter was created by King EDWARD III around 1348. Inspired by the ideals of King ARTHUR and his knights of the Round Table, the order was (and remains today) an exclusive society of 26 knights, including the sovereign. Its members were bound to fidelity and friendship toward each other in a brotherhood of honor. The order had its own chapel, herald, feasts and tournaments; membership in it was a mark of high distinction. There is a legendary story about the manner in which the order acquired its motto. It was said that Edward III had a mistress at Calais, whose dropped garter he recovered from a dance floor with the gallant remark *"Honi soit qui mal y pense,"* (Evil be to him who thinks ill of it). This phrase became the order's motto.

Gatesden   *See* JOHN OF GADDESDEN.

Gaudentius (Gaudencius)   One of three men who came forward to support the charge that was made against BOETHIUS of plotting against THEODORIC, the Ostragothic king of Rome in whose government Boethius served. The role he played in bringing about Boethius' banishment is referred to in Book One, Prosa 4 of the *BOECE,* Chaucer's translation of Boethius' *Consolation of Philosophy.*

Gaufred   *See* GEOFFREY OF VINSAUF.

Gaufride   *See* GEOFFREY OF MONMOUTH.

Gaunt   *See* GHENT.

Gaunt, John of   *See* JOHN OF GAUNT.

Gawain   A character from Arthurian romance, alluded to in "The SQUIRE'S TALE." A strange knight who enters the court of King CAMBYUSKAN bearing gifts from the king of Arabia and India is compared to Sir Gawain as possessing high reverence and courtesy (lines 89–97). The fact that this knight is a stranger and enters on a magical horse has suggested to some readers that he may echo the famous Green Knight of the 14th-century Alliterative Revival poem, *Sir Gawain and the Green Knight,* but others have pointed out that there exists no other evidence that Chaucer had read or knew of that poem. In the context of Arthurian romance, Gawain was often considered the epitome of chivalric courtesy.

Gawle, folk of   *See* MILETUS.

Gaza (Gazan)   In the Bible, Gaza was one of the major cities of the Philistines. Situated on the great caravan route between Mesopotamia and Egypt, at the junction of the trade route from Arabia, it was the southernmost city of Canaan. Its location made Gaza an ideal rest stop and a commercial center for merchants and travelers. In the Old Testament Book of Judges, Gaza is the scene of a rather dramatic performance by the biblical hero, SAMPSON, when he wrenches loose the city gates and carries them high up onto a hill to show the Philistines what great strength he possesses. This story is related in the brief biography of Sampson that appears in Chaucer's "MONK'S TALE" (lines 2015–94).

Geffrey   Geffrey, or Geoffrey, was Chaucer's first name. He refers to himself by his first name in several poems in which he himself acts as narrator, most notably in *The HOUSE OF FAME* where the EAGLE who carries him on a heavenward journey to Fame's palace calls him by his Christian name, and again in *The CANTERBURY TALES* where, as one of the pilgrims, he is called by name to participate in the tale-telling contest. Ironically, the tales that Chaucer, or Geffrey, tells, are not terribly good. One of them, "The TALE OF SIR THOPAS," is so bad that the Host interrupts him and makes him start again. This raises some question about whether the Geffrey who participates in the pilgrimage, and the "Geffrey Chaucer" mentioned in the prologue to "The MAN OF LAW'S TALE" as a notable poet of the day, should be considered to be the same. Obviously, on a literal level, they are. But in another sense, the narrator persona that Chaucer invents and inserts into his poetry is a fictional creation, an idea that is supported by the frequency with which Chaucer makes that narrator appear dimwitted or foolish, whether it is by having him tell a silly story like "The Tale of Sir Thopas," or by having the eagle in *The House of Fame* tease him about his bad luck in love.

Gemini   One of the 12 divisions of the zodiac, an imaginary belt in the heavens extending for about eight degrees on either side of the apparent path of the sun and including the paths of the moon and the principal planets. The zodiac is divided into 12 equal parts, or signs, each named for a different constellation. Gemini is the third sign (*see* diagram under ASTROLOGY), which in Chaucer's day, the Sun entered May 12. The constellation of Gemini, which is supposed to represent twins sitting together, appears between CANCER and TAURUS in the sky. Chaucer most often employs astrological terms such as this to indicate the approximate date of a narrative event or to show the passage of time. Occasionally, he uses them to call attention to planetary influences. His only mention of the zodiacal sign Gemini outside of his *TREATISE OF THE ASTROLABE* occurs in "The MERCHANT'S TALE," where he is describing the weather on the day when the aged knight, JANUARY, takes his young wife, MAY, into his enclosed garden to make love to her. It was a warm day, with the sun in Gemini and declining toward Cancer, which means that it was nearing the end of June.

Genelloun (Genyloun)   *See* GANELON.

General Prologue to *The Canterbury Tales*   The General Prologue of *The CANTERBURY TALES,* probably the best-known work of medieval English literature, is dominated by descriptions of the 29 pilgrims who, along with the narrator, are traveling to Canterbury to visit the shrine of Saint THOMAS À BECKET. At the end of the prologue, they agree to participate in a tale-telling contest, thus establishing the framework for the rest of this literary masterpiece.

SUMMARY

The poem begins with some of the most famous lines in English literature:

> Whan that Aprill with his shoures soote
> The droghte of March hath perced to the roote,
> And bathed every veyne in swich licour
> Of which vertu engendred is the flour;
> Whan Zephirus eek with his sweete breeth
> Inspired hath in every holt and heeth
> The tendre croppes, and the yonge sonne
> Hath in the Ram his half cours yronne,
> And smale foweles maken melodye,
> That slepen al the nyght with open ye
> (So priketh hem nature in hir corages),
> Thanne longen folk to goon on pilgrimages,
> And palmeres for to seken straunge strondes,
> To ferne halwes, kowthe in sondry londes;
> And specially from every shires ende
> Of Engelond to Caunterbury they wende,
> The hooly blisful martir for to seke,
> That hem hath holpen whan that they were seeke.
>
> (lines 1–18)

The lines maintain their power even in translation: "When April with its sweet showers the drought of March has pierced to the root, and bathed each vein of every leaf with such liquor, of which sweetness is engendered the flower; When Zephyr with his sweet breath has inspired in every grove and field the tender crops, and the young sun has run half his course in Aries, and small birds that sleep all the night with open eyes make melody (as nature urges them in their hearts), then people long to go on pilgrimages, and palmers long to seek foreign shores, distant shrines known in many lands; and especially, from even the farthest shires in England, they go to Canterbury to seek the holy blissful martyr who has helped them when they were sick."

At this point, the narrator moves from the general to the specific, saying that one day, in a season such as he has just described, he was in SOUTHWARK, staying at an inn called the TABARD and getting himself ready to go on pilgrimage to CANTERBURY. That night there lodged at the inn a group of 29 other pilgrims. The group was made up of various and sundry sorts of people who had met by chance and decided to travel together, since they all had the same destination. After speaking with each one of them, the narrator decided to join their company. But before he tells any more of what happened following his decision, he is going to describe his fellow travelers in terms of each one's circumstances, profession, social rank and attire.

The KNIGHT is described as a worthy man who practices CHIVALRY and displays the qualities of fidelity, good reputation, generosity and refined manners. He has spent much of his adult life fighting for his lord (a king or baron) in various wars, both in Christian lands and in pagan ones. He fought valiantly in Alisaundre (ALEXANDRIA), Pruce (PRUSSIA), Lettow (LITHUANIA), Ruce (RUSSIA), Gernade (GRANADA), Algezir (ALGECIRAS, in Spain), Belmarye (MOROCCO), Lyeys (AYASH, Turkey), Satalye (ATALIA, Turkey), in the Mediterranean and at Tramyssene (TLEMCEN, near Morocco). Even though this Knight is very brave, the epitome of nobility, he is also prudent, humble and kind. He rides a good horse, but is not richly attired. His tunic is made of fustian, a kind of coarse cloth, and his habergeon (coat of mail) is stained, probably with rust, because he has come straight from his most recent expedition to join the pilgrimage.

The Knight is accompanied by his son, a young squire. The SQUIRE is described as a lover and a lively

Artist's rendering of the Squire, from the Ellesmere Manuscript of The Canterbury Tales. *The Squire has curly hair and wears a short gown, in agreement with the description of him that appears in the General Prologue.*

"bachelor," which means that he has attained the first degree of knighthood. Much emphasis is laid on his appearance. His hair falls about his head in curly locks. He is of medium height and displays marvelous agility as well as great strength. His tunic, in contrast to his father's, is embroidered with red and white flowers. His gown is short, but its sleeves are long and wide. Several cavalry expeditions, in FLANDERS, ARTOIS and PICARDY (in and around France) form the sum of his experience in battle. His other accomplishments, for which he hopes to win the affection of his lady, are flute playing, singing, writing poetry, jousting, dancing and drawing. Yet he is also courteous, humble and willing to serve, as evidenced by his carving at his father's table.

A YEOMAN, employed as the Knight's serving man, forms the third member of the Knight's group. This Yeoman wears a green coat and hood and is accoutred with a mighty bow, a sheaf of peacock arrows, and a bracer to protect his arm from the bowstring. Short-haired and dark-complected, he is wise in "wood-craft," which means that he knows all the procedures and ceremonies related to hunting. He also wears a sword and buckler (a small shield) on one side and, on the other, a small sharp dagger with an ornamented handle. A Saint Christopher medallion hangs about his neck. He carries a hunting horn with a green baldric (strap). All of these characteristics considered together suggest to the narrator that he is a forester, i.e., gamekeeper, for the Knight.

The description of the Yeoman is followed by one of a PRIORESS. The characteristics and accomplishments of this noble lady do little to remind us that she is the superior of a convent. She sings and speaks French with a certain elegance (although her accent is that of an English convent school). Much is made of her irreproachable table manners, of how she never lets a morsel drop carelessly from her lips, takes great care not to dip her fingers too deeply in her sauce, and always carefully wipes her mouth. She is pleasant and amiable, and so tenderhearted that she weeps quite easily, even, for example, over a mouse caught in a trap. Fond of animals, she keeps several small hounds, feeding them with roasted meat, milk and fine white ("wastel") bread. The description of her face, apart from the nun's wimple that hides her hair, suggests that she could easily pass for the heroine in a medieval romance. Her nose is well-shaped, her eyes as gray as glass, her mouth small, soft and red, and she has a broad, fair forehead. She wears an elegant cloak and, wound about her arm, a bracelet of beads, possibly a rosary, which bears a golden brooch engraved with a crowned _A,_ followed by the words _Amor vincit omnia_ (Love conquers all).

A SECOND NUN rides with the Prioress and serves as her chaplain. Neither she nor the three priests mentioned here, who also accompany the Prioress, are

described; rather, the prologue advances quickly to tell of the next pilgrim, the MONK.

The overall impression imparted by the Monk's portrait is of a self-possessed and masterful man who, like the Prioress, is more enamored of worldy pursuits than he is intent upon devoting his life to God. He is described as an "outrider," which means that he has the task of riding out to visit and supervise activities on the estates belonging to his monastery, which would be devoted to livestock and crop farming. In keeping with his virile and expansive personality, he loves to hunt and keeps a number of valuable horses and greyhounds to aid him in that enterprise. He evidently belongs to the Benedictine Order, founded by Saint BENEDICT in 529, but not surprisingly, pays little heed to the rules of his order that discourage his two favorite pastimes, hunting and spending time away from the monastery. Of the Monk's dress we are given three telling details: The sleeves of his cassock are "purfiled," or trimmed at the cuff, with "grys," an expensive gray fur; the hood he wears on his head is fastened with an elaborate gold brooch called a love-knot; and his boots are soft and pliant. His bald head and face shine as if they have been anointed with oil, and his prominent eyes glow like a furnace. His body is fat, but in good condition, and he loves roasted swan more than any other meat.

The Monk is followed by a FRIAR, a limiter, which means that he possesses a license to beg within certain geographical limits. The description of his character at first sounds contradictory. He is wanton and merry, yet "a full solemn man"; but as the description progresses, we see that the solemnity merely functions as an official mask for the frisky opportunist underneath. This Friar excells in gossip and flattery, characteristics that, along with his authority to hear confession as he travels from town to town, ensure his popularity with those men and women who prefer the Friar's light and easy penance over the stricter demands of their parish priest. The Friar's sexual activity is hinted at in the statement that he has paid the marriage dowry of a number of young women, a duty that would normally have fallen to their fathers. Other features of his character similarly diminish our sense of this man's true devotion to his profession. In every town he knows the innkeepers and bartenders much better than the beggars or lepers whose acquaintance he considers neither respectable nor profitable. On the other hand, among those who possess money and power, he is both courteous and eager to be of service. He is such a successful beggar himself that even the poorest of widows cannot resist giving him at least a farthing. The Friar's earnings far exceed what he actually needs to sustain him, and his profit is reflected in his dress, which is much more magnificent than what would typically be worn by someone of his profession. Physically, this man is as strong as a "champioun" (professional fighter), yet his neck is as white as a lily and his eyes twinkle like the stars on a frosty night. He plays the harp and has a good singing voice, yet lisps when he speaks, by way of affectation. His name is Huberd, more recognizable in modern English as Hubert.

The description of the Friar is followed by that of the MERCHANT. The Merchant parts his beard in the middle and wears it in a forked style. The existing portraits of Chaucer show him sporting a beard groomed in a similar fashion. The Merchant's head is crowned by a flemish hat made of beaver skin, a material considered sufficiently elegant to have been worn by members of the nobility. His parti-colored clothing is interpreted by the artist of the ELLESMERE MANUSCRIPT as a red gown with blue and white flowers. Solemn and serious of speech, he frequently mentions the profit he makes in trade, a fault which formed part of the stereotype of the merchant in medieval estates satire. The comment that he uses his wits so well that no man knew he was in debt provides further evidence of the Merchant's business acumen, while at the same time suggesting the importance of a dignified demeanor to the success of his endeavors. The portrait concludes with the narrator's admission that he has never learned the Merchant's name, another detail that points to the guarded nature of the man's character, the discreet brand of secrecy so important to his profession.

The CLERK of Oxford also bears the marks of estates satire. Like any stereotypical university student, he is quite poor; the condition of his finances is revealed by his threadbare clothing and emaciated appearance. The value that he puts on learning is shown by the suggestion that he would rather buy books, which were very expensive at the time, than spend his money on any type of material comfort or entertainment. The comment that even though he is a philosopher, yet he has little gold in his coffer, is punning off the double meaning of the word *philosopher,* which could indicate one who studies ideas, like Aristotle, or one who studies ALCHEMY, the pseudoscience of transmuting base metal into gold. Like the Merchant, the Clerk is sober and serious in his speech, and as glad to teach as he is to learn.

The SERGEANT OF THE LAW appears next in the lineup. This man's title indicates that he has reached the highest order in his profession. He is characterized as prudent and wise, discreet and dignified. The reference to the Sergeant's having often been at the "Parvys" means that he followed common practice in giving client consultations at the parvis, or portico, of St. Paul's Cathedral in LONDON. As a judge, the Sergeant has served at a court of assizes. Originally these courts, which were held in the various counties, were used to decide disputes over land tenure. By the 14th century, however, judges in assize courts heard all civil cases originating in the counties where they had jurisdiction.

The Sergeant evidently makes a good deal of money in his profession, for his interest in property extends to his buying a great deal of it for his own possession. Some sarcasm appends to his portrait in the narrator's comment that "Nowher so bisy a man as he ther nas, / And yet he semed bisier than he was" (lines 321–22), which suggests a person who practices some degree of deception in presenting himself to the world. Still, he is an expert in his field, knows every statute from memory and can write up a flawless legal document. Furthermore, he dresses simply, in a motley tunic gathered at the waist by a silk belt.

A description of the FRANKLIN, whose title means "landowner," follows that of the Sergeant. The Franklin is an early version of the English country squire. He has held the office of sheriff ("shirreve") and member of Parliament for his shire. The comment about his presiding at judicial sessions as "lord" and "sire" suggests that he was also a justice of the peace. But by far the primary emphasis in this portrait lies on the Franklin's hospitality and his indulgence in Epicurean delights. His bread and ale are always of a high quality, and nowhere, the narrator tells us, was there a man better stocked with wine ("envyned"). His house is never without savory pies stuffed with meat, fish or fowl, and all of his provisions are so plenteous that his house apparently snowed ("snewed") food and drink. Additionally, the food offered on the Franklin's table varies with the changing seasons. His possession of a "table dormant," one which remained standing throughout the day instead of being dismantled and put aside between meals, adds to the sense of Epicurean graciousness which is the dominant impression of this man's portrait. Chaucer reveals only two details of the Franklin's physical appearance: He has a beard as white as a daisy (the same type of flower held by the white-bearded Chaucer in one of his most famous portraits); and his complexion is sanguine, which, according to the medieval theory of the four HUMORS, means that the man has a hearty and cheerful demeanor, is generous in spirit and has a good digestion. The sanguine temperament is dominated by blood, suggested, perhaps, by the ruddy complexion that usually accompanies it.

The portrait of the Franklin is followed by reference to a group of five guildsmen, none of whom is described individually. They are mentioned only by their professions of HABERDASHER, CARPENTER, WEAVER ("webbe"), DYER and TAPESTRY MAKER ("tapycer"). All of them wear the same type of livery, a uniform which by its appearance would identify the trade guild to which they belonged. Trade guilds, the medieval equivalent of modern trade unions, were established to uphold standards of production and to protect their members from competition. The prestige of the particular guild to which these men belong is indicated by the appearance of their uniforms, which are described as "fressh and newe," and by their accessories, the knives mounted in silver rather than brass, their expensive belts ("girdles") and money pouches.

The pilgrims are also accompanied by a COOK, whose name is later given as Roger Hogge of Ware, and who was apparently modeled upon an actual person of the same name and profession. He is accomplished in the basic culinary skills that would be appropriate for an innkeeper, such as the various ways of cooking meat and of making stews and meat pies. He can also recognize a London ale by its taste and make a delicious "blankmanger," a thick stew of chopped chicken or fish boiled with rice. All of these characteristics are startlingly contrasted with the comment that he has a "mormal," a kind of ulcerous, foul-smelling sore, on one of his shins.

The SHIPMAN, whose description follows that of the Cook, makes his home in Dartmouth, on the southwestern coast of England, a convenient location considering his occupation. He rides upon a "rouncy," or carthorse, and wears a tunic of coarse woolen cloth ("faldyng"). A dagger attached to a rope hangs about his neck and he sports a deep tan. Together with his choice of a mount these things suggest a roguish temperament that is underscored by the lines where the Shipman is described as having stolen wine during its shipment from the French region of BORDEAUX. The remainder of this man's portrait describes his expertise as a sailor, especially in the area of navigation. The ship upon which he sails is called the *MAUDELAYNE*.

The DOCTOR OF PHYSIC, or Physician, is the medieval equivalent of the modern-day physician. His title indicates that he possessed the most advanced training available at the time. The fact that he is knowledgeable in both physic (diagnosis and treatment) and surgery also indicates extensive training, since most medical practitioners of the time practiced in only one of these areas. The initial emphasis given to the doctor's knowledge of astronomy may strike the modern reader as peculiar, but a number of medieval medical texts stress the importance of planetary influences on physical and emotional health. This attitude reflects the fact that medieval science did not yet distinguish between astronomy and ASTROLOGY, or was just beginning to do so. The statement that this doctor kept his patient "in houres by his magyk natureel," and that he knew the cause of "everich maladye, / Were it of hoot, or coold, or moyste, or drye" (lines 416, 419–20) refers to another branch of medieval medical theory, that of the bodily humors. According to this theory, an individual's temperament and physical composition were thought to be determined by the four humors of the body (sanguine, phlegmatic, choleric and melancholic), corresponding to four bodily fluids (blood, phlegm, yellow bile and black bile), which in turn corresponded to four elements: air (hot and moist), water (cold and

moist), fire (hot and dry) and earth (cold and dry). Ideally, the humors and their related fluids would exist in a balanced state within the human body. If disease occurred, it could indicate an imbalance that would have to be corrected in order for health to be restored. Because each humor was considered to have a period of dominance during a certain six-hour period of each day, the timing of treatment was critical and had to be based upon whichever of the humors was involved in causing the disease. The doctor's relationship with apothecaries, the medieval equivalent of the pharmacist, is a mutually beneficial one in which each helps the other to make a profit. The doctor's reading includes works by GALEN, HIPPOCRATES and various other textual authorities. In keeping with the advice offered by some of these authorities, he takes care of his own health by eating a moderate diet that is both nourishing and digestible. An odd little detail is thrown in at this point, informing us that the doctor's "studie was but litel on the Bible," and alluding to the somewhat conventional (even at this point in history) association of science, particularly medical science, with atheism. Like many of the others in the General Prologue, this portrait includes a description of the doctor's apparel, though we learn little aside from its colors (*sangwyn* = red and *pers* = blue) and the fact that his clothing is lined with taffeta and sandal, two varieties of silk. Despite his rich attire, however, the doctor is careful about his spending. The last two lines—"For gold in phisik is a cordial, / Therefore he lovede gold in special" (lines 443–45)—refer both to the ancient use of small amounts of gold taken orally for medicinal purposes and to the Physician's love of money.

The Physician's portrait is followed by that of the WIFE OF BATH. In Chaucer's English, the word *wife* could also be used to simply mean "woman." Given the Wife of Bath's many marriages, in addition to the somewhat ironic fact that all the other pilgrims in the General Prologue are named with reference to their professions, its use here would seem to indicate that in her case *wife* should be granted the meaning it would have for a modern reader. The first detail given about the wife is that she suffers from hearing loss, which the narrator sympathetically (and perhaps ironically) pronounces "scathe," i.e., a pity. Aside from the profession of being a wife, she also engages in weaving. Her skill in the occupation surpasses the weavers of Ypres and Ghent, famous Belgian cloth-making centers in the 14th century. Her desire always to be the first in her church's congregation to present her offering, and the anger she has been known to display when such a privilege was denied suggests that she is proud. Since she has a reputation as a fine weaver, it comes as little surprise that the Wife has a fondness for adorning her head with fine linen kerchiefs, but the narrator's willingness to swear that on a Sunday their accumulated

Artist's rendering of the Wife of Bath, from the Ellesmere Manuscript of The Canterbury Tales. *In keeping with her description in the General Prologue, the Wife wears a wide-brimmed hat and spurs with rowels. Unlike the Prioress and the Second Nun, she rides astride.*

weight was 10 pounds, like her need to be first at the offering, hints at inordinate pride. Her scarlet stockings, bold face and ruddy complexion suggest a certain flamboyance in her personality, which is borne out by the remainder of her portrait. Her gapped teeth and broad hips point to a mature sexuality, while her fondness for talking and laughing reveal her highly sociable nature. A veteran of five marriages, she is also well-traveled, having been on pilgrimages to places such as Rome and Boulogne, and three times to Jerusalem. For this pilgrimage to Canterbury, she rides upon an "amblere," a kind of walking horse, wearing a hat as broad as a shield ("a bokeler or a targe"). The concluding lines of the Wife's portrait, "Of remedies of love she knew per chaunce, / For she koude of that art the olde daunce" (lines 475–76), again refer to her experienced sexuality, "the old dance" being a euphemism for sexual intercourse.

The description of the PARSON appears next in the General Prologue, although his tale appears last in the tale-telling contest, followed only by CHAUCER'S RETRACTION. The portrait embarks with a series of contrasts, announcing that although the Parson is poor in worldly goods, he is rich in spirit and in the performance of good works. The narrator praises the man's knowledge and his teaching ability, as well as his admirable patience and generosity. For example, instead of excommunicating his parishioners when they do not pay their tithes, he would distribute money from his own income and from the church offering to those who were in need. His parish, located in the country, is large, with the houses located at great distances from one another; nevertheless, and in spite of bad weather, the parson manages to visit those who are sick or in trouble, walking from place to place. By these means he provides a noble example to his flock, reflecting his belief that if a priest behaves wrongly, what might a layperson do? The Parson's goodness is further highlighted by contrasting him to the type of priest who would desert his parish to go off to London where he might seek yet another appointment and so collect an additional benefice, only occasionally returning to his own parish to make sure those left in charge were collecting tithes. Throughout the description, the Parson is compared to a shepherd caring for his flock and, by extension, to Christ in his role as the Good Shepherd. The portrait concludes with further reference to the superlative qualities of this priest, his combination of humility and a firm sense of right and wrong. These qualities not only allow him to lead by example, but also to apply rebuke, when necessary, to those of high as well as low estate.

The Parson is accompanied by his brother, a PLOWMAN. The Plowman is a paid farm laborer who works for hire and who apparently possesses some property. He is far from being a materialist, however, and would rather, if it lay within his might, thresh and make ditches and plow for every poor man, for Christ's sake. Living in peace and charity, he loves God first, his neighbor second (according to the Biblical injunction) and always pays his tithes. In accordance with his occupation, he wears a tabard—the loose, sleeveless outer garment of a workman—and rides a mare.

The MILLER's portrait emphasizes this man's size and strength. Stout, big-boned and well-muscled, he excels at the sport of wrestling. This hint of his brutishness is confirmed by the statement that there exists no door that he cannot either heave off its hinges or, failing that, break by ramming it with his head. The sword and buckler with which he is armed give further indication of his violent nature. The Miller's beard is thick and red, his mouth as large as a furnace, his nostrils black and wide. The top of his nose is garnished by a wart that sprouts a tuft of hairs. The references to him as a "janglere" and a "goliardeys" reveal that he enjoys telling dirty stories, just like the one he tells on the pilgrimage. In addition to the above characteristics, we are told that he cheats his customers who bring him grain to be milled. The Miller is dressed in a white coat with a blue hood, just as he is illustrated in the Ellesmere manuscript. He is skilled at playing the bagpipe and carries one of these instruments with him on the pilgrimage. In medieval symbology, the bagpipe was associated with passion and drunkeness; some critics point out its similarity to the male sexual organs, which suits "The MILLER'S TALE's" preoccupation with bawdy sex.

The next portrait is that of the MANCIPLE, whose occupation consisted of purchasing supplies, including food and drink, for one of the temples of the INNS OF COURT, medieval London's centrally located school of law. Each temple corresponded to a kind of individual college within the larger institution. Chaucer's use of the adjective *gentil* to describe the Manciple seems ironic, given the later revelation that he deceives those 30 experts of the law in whose service he is employed. He is nevertheless a shrewd businessman, always waiting and watching for the best deal.

The Manciple is followed by the REEVE, another man whose occupation is unfamiliar, at least in name, to modern readers. In Chaucer's day, *reeve* was the title given to a man who managed an estate or farm. Like the Manciple, the Reeve is very skilled in his occupation, and he also uses his skill to cheat his employer, the 20-year-old owner of the estate he manages. As a result, he has amassed so much wealth, the narrator tells us, that he is more able than his lord to purchase land. Physically, the Reeve is slender, with long stick-like legs. He wears his beard as closely shaven as he can get it, and shaves his head in a style similar to a monk's tonsure. According to medieval theory regarding the bodily humors, his choleric temperament indicates a rash temper and an inclination to lechery. As a young man, the Reeve learned the trade of carpentry, a fact that forms the basis of later conflict between the Miller and himself and which determines the type of tale the Reeve chooses to tell. The Reeve's horse is dappled gray and named "Scot," which is also the name of a horse in "The FRIAR'S TALE." The Reeve's attire consists of a long outer coat of dark blue ("pers"), and by his side he wears a rusty sword. The estate he manages, and upon which he has his own house, is near a town called Baldeswelle, modern BAWDESWELL, in the county of Norfolk. We are told that the Reeve rides at the very end of the train of pilgrims, perhaps unable to break the habit of shrewd watchfulness he employs while at work on his master's estate.

The Reeve's description is followed by that of the SUMMONER, a minor nonclerical official of the ecclesiastical courts. His job required that he deliver summonses for people to appear before a particular court, and he also acted as an usher while the courts were in session. The "crimes" for which a person could be summoned to an ecclesiastical court are ironically mirrored in the Summoner's habits—his drunkenness, lechery, greed and probable homosexuality. Physically, he is characterized by a fire-red and pimply complexion, swollen eyelids and patchy hair-loss in both his eyebrows and his beard, all of which suggest some form of inflammatory skin disease. Furthermore, the disease is resistant to all types of medical treatment. The "quyksilver" (mercury), "lytarge" (lead monoxide), "brymstoon" (sulphur), "boras" (borax), "ceruce" (white lead) and "oil of tartre" (cream of tartar) mentioned here were all used in medicine at the time. We are also given information about the Summoner's diet; his fondness for garlic, onions, leeks and strong red wine would, according to medieval medical theory, be one reason why he has such terrible eruptions on his skin. Drinking until he reaches a state of drunkenness, the Summoner begins to speak in Latin that he has learned the same way a parrot learns to mimic the speech of its master, by listening to it continuously (as he attended court sessions) without knowing what it means. The narrator's reference to him as a "gentil harlot and a kynde" is ironic and perhaps should be taken to mean that the Summoner excels at harlotry, i.e., sinful behavior, by his very nature. As might be guessed by the description of him thus far, the Summoner is revealed to be a man easily bribed. For a quart of wine, for example, he will overlook the crime of unlawful fornication. His attitude toward the ecclesiastical courts is further disclosed by the narrator's comment that, regarding any likable fellow he meets, the Summoner will discourage him from fearing excommunication as long as he keeps money, and not his soul, inside his purse. The narrator, however, is anxious to distance himself from such an attitude, and follows this revelation with the statement of his own belief that excommunication will cause damnation. The only details given of the Summoner's apparel refer to a large garland, or wreath, that he wears upon his head, and a round loaf of bread that he carries like a buckler, or small shield, both suggesting an irreverent or at least a festive attitude to the pilgrimage.

In companionship with the Summoner rides the PARDONER, who is employed by the Hospital of St. Mary Rouncesval, located in the London district of Charing Cross. He has just returned from Rome, where he traveled on business related to his profession. A pardoner was a churchman empowered to transmit, in exchange for alms, i.e., payment, something called an indulgence, a formal document granting the recipient (the payor) forgiveness for sin. To raise money for various projects, religious institutions, which included hospitals at this time, would often hire pardoners as professional fundraisers. A pardoner hired under such an agreement would, after paying a fee to the proper church officials, travel around a specified area, offering indulgences to those willing to pay for them. While the paying of alms was considered an important part of penance, the system presented considerable opportunities for abuse, and Chaucer's Pardoner takes advantage of those opportunities. Pardoners usually made their sales pitch in parish churches; part of their success thus depended upon their ability to deliver a good sermon. This Pardoner, the narrator tells us, is an accomplished preacher and possesses an excellent voice for singing offertories, hymns inviting people to present alms. He also possesses a collection of fake relics, such as the pillow case that he tries to pass off as Saint Mary's veil or the pig bones that he sells as saints' remains. According to the medieval "science" of PHYSIOGNOMY, the Pardoner's stringy yellow hair indicates a personality that is deceitful, sharp-witted and greedy for material gain. His wearing it long suggests a contempt for church regulations which dictated that clerics wear their hair short. The man's glaring eyes show that he is a glutton and a drunkard, one who generally leads a dissolute life. All of these characteristics appear in the portrait of the Pardoner that emerges in the prologue to his tale. Finally, the song he sings with the Summoner, "Com hider, love, to me!" along with the Pardoner's physical description and the narrator's belief that he is either "a geldyng or a mare," points to the possibility of a homosexual relationship between these two men.

The description of the Pardoner concludes Chaucer's portraits of the pilgrims who have assembled at the Tabard Inn in Southwark prior to embarking on their journey. Now, Chaucer promises, he will tell us how the group passed the night, and afterward the story of the journey itself. At this point he issues one in his series of disclaimers, asking the reader's pardon if anything that he says in quoting the speech of the other pilgrims should give offense. He excuses himself by claiming that anyone who claims to report a man's words should do so accurately, to the best of his ability; otherwise his words will be untrue. Following these words of caution, the narrator describes the Host of the Tabard who presided over their evening meal. He is a large man with bright eyes, bold of speech, wise and yet merry. After the pilgrims have finished their meal, he addresses them all together, speaking of his desire to furnish them with a pleasant pastime while on the road to Canterbury. The pilgrims accept his advice, which is that each pilgrim, during the course of their journey, shall tell four tales, two on the way down to the shrine and two on the way back to London. The pilgrim who gives the best performance shall then be rewarded with supper at the Tabard, which would be paid for by all the other participants. In addition, the Host states, he will join the pilgrimage to be their guide and to judge the tale-telling contests. If anyone gainsays his judg-

ment, that person will have to pay all traveling expenses incurred on the road. All the pilgrims agree to these terms, swearing an oath to adhere to his rules and conditions. The wine is fetched, everyone drinks and then goes to bed.

In the morning, after being awakened and gathered together by the Host, who has already assumed his role as leader of the group, the pilgrims depart. They have traveled a short distance outside of London, to a brook called the Watering of St. Thomas, when the Host proposes that the tale-telling contest begin. The first teller will be determined by the drawing of "cuts" or straws. The Knight, drawing the shortest, is chosen.

COMMENTARY

The General Prologue serves two purposes: It introduces each of the pilgrims (with the exception of the late-arriving CANON'S YEOMAN) and sets forth the story of how the tales came to be written. The narrator of the prologue, who has taken upon himself the task of providing a faithful record of the pilgrims and their tales, does not at this point name or describe himself, beyond making the modest claim that his wit is limited. Later, in the rubric which introduces the prologue to "The TALE OF SIR THOPAS," we discover that he is Chaucer, although the ineptitude with which he tells that tale advises against taking his naming of himself literally.

Like each tale in the collection it introduces, the prologue belongs to a recognized genre of the medieval period, estates satire. The aim of this genre was to provide an analysis of society by describing types of the various people who made up that society. This is why the pilgrims are referred to by their profession instead of their proper names. The purpose of the analysis provided by estates satire was to illustrate hierarchical divisions as well as the social function and morality of each character type. Generally speaking, medieval English society could be divided up into three estates: those who fight (such as the Knight), those who pray (such as the Parson) and those who labor (such as the Plowman). Every pilgrim in *The Canterbury Tales* falls into one or the other of these categories. The "satire" component of estates satire resided in the genre's method of enumerating the various abuses that each character type was prey to. Its aim was entertainment and instruction toward proper behavior. But while most estates satire takes the form of invective, Chaucer's employment of the genre shows a less clear-cut intention. Generally, he replaces straightforward criticism with a type of irony that employs the naive superlative. Described by a narrator who seems to want to like everyone he meets, all of the pilgrims are pronounced the very best of their kind. In the Parson's and Knight's cases, this is probably true; in the Monk's case, it would seem to be meant ironically, but there is no direct indication of that within the prologue. Essentially, we are given a great deal of information about each pilgrim, yet we are ultimately left to decide for ourselves, on the basis of their variations and our own knowledge, how to judge them, so that our response to the pilgrims becomes a measure of our own values rather than of simple agreement or disagreement with those of the author.

The structure of the General Prologue is somewhat haphazard. Chaucer himself apologizes that he has not described the people in an order determined by their social rank. Nevertheless, he does begin his description of the pilgrims with the Knight, the highest ranking member of the first estate. After describing this man's entourage, he moves on to describe the highest ranking ecclesiastics, the Prioress and the Monk. The Friar, whose portrait follows that of the Monk, is probably so placed because friars and monks were frequently grouped together in estates satire. The Merchant, Clerk, Sergeant of Law and the Franklin may be grouped together because they belong to the middle class and would have been considered more or less social equals. The logic behind the rest of the groupings is less obvious, although the Parson and Plowman appear together because they are brothers, and the Summoner and Pardoner because they are friends.

Although there were many examples of estates satire in existence that Chaucer could have consulted as sources for his text, he seems to have drawn primarily upon one of the most popular, the A-text of William LANGLAND's *Vision of Piers the Plowman* (*see* PIERS PLOWMAN). This version of Langland's work opens with a prologue that features a spring setting followed by descriptions of various people working, or not working, in a "field of folk" that is an allegorical representation of late-14th-century England. Many of Langland's descriptions here and later in the A-text, such as an idealized plowman, a thriving merchant, a friar who dresses in fine apparel and a corrupt pardoner, provide analogues to 16 of Chaucer's pilgrims.

Some of the themes laid out by the General Prologue are crucial to remember while reading the tales that follow. The most obvious of these is the theme of contest which manifests on so many levels. Most obviously, the pilgrims have pledged to engage themselves in a storytelling contest, the winner to be determined by the Host, who proposed the contest and designed its rules. Other kinds of contest appear in the rivalries which surface between various pilgrims, such as the Miller and Knight; the Reeve and the Miller; the Friar and the Summoner; and the Monk and the Knight. Some of these rivalries exhibit antagonism between various professions; others, such as that of the Knight and the Monk, suggest profound philosophical differences. Another important theme is the theme of pilgrimage, which during our reading of the tales, tends to become submerged beneath our involvement with each individual narrative. It should, however, be kept in mind, because Chaucer intended the pilgrimage to Canterbury to serve as a metaphor for the journey of each individual through life. Strong hints of the poem's cosmic dimension appear in the beginning of the General Prologue. Its very first lines refer to the coming of spring and its associations with rebirth, which along with the return of health after sickness, provides the spiritual and emotional impetus for embarking on a pilgrimage whose goal is to give thanks for renewed health. In this way, Chaucer forges a link between the temporal and the spiritual at the outset; while the tellers are telling their tales, it submerses and runs quietly like an underground stream, always present but never obtrusively so, and then resurfaces at the end, with the Parson's sermon and CHAUCER'S RETRACTION, to remind us of the ultimate goal of life's pilgrimage, which is heaven.

For Further Reading: Still one of the most accessible and informative discussions of the General Prologue, Muriel BOWDEN's *A Commentary on the General Prologue to the Canterbury Tales* (2nd ed., 1967) explains the many details of the prologue with reference to medieval sources, providing essential information on imagery and allusions that appear in the text. This book also provides a survey of modern scholarship in the first half of the 20th century. Those readers who would like to know more about estates satire, the genre that most heavily influenced the portraits in the prologue, should consult Jill MANN's *Chaucer and Medieval Estates Satire: The Literature of Social Classes and the General Prologue to the Canterbury Tales* (1973). Anyone interested in astrology might want to consider William Spencer's article "Are Chaucer's Pilgrims Keyed to the Zodiac?" (*Chaucer Review*, 1970), which suggests that each pilgrim in the General Prologue is associated with one of the planets and signs of the zodiac, citing details of the sketches that, according to medieval astrological theory, support this idea.

Genesis The first book of the Bible and one of five books (collectively known as the Pentateuch) supposedly authored by the Hebrew prophet MOSES. The word *genesis* means "origin, source, creation or coming into being." Genesis describes many important beginnings, such as the Creation, the Fall of man (the beginning of history) and the founding and early years of the ancient nation of Israel. Other noteworthy stories contained in this book are those involving NOAH and the Great Flood, ABRAHAM and ISAAC, JACOB and Esau, and JOSEPH and his brothers who sold him into slavery. "The PARSON'S TALE," which is actually a sermon, quotes from the Book of Genesis, chapter 9, during the portion of the sermon dealing with avarice: "Sooth is that the condicioun of thraldom and the first cause of thraldom is for synne" (line 755) [It is true that the condition of slavery and the first cause of slavery is sin]. The point that he is trying to make here related to the theme of greed is that since all men, by virtue of their sinful nature, are slaves, no man has the right unlawfully to take away another man's goods simply because he occupies a position of authority over that man.

gentilesse   A Middle English word derived from French which appeared frequently in courtly or chivalric literature, *gentilesse* originally meant "nobility of birth or rank." During Chaucer's day, it was evolving to include the idea of nobility of character. The two ideas appear at odds with one another in "The WIFE OF BATH'S TALE," in which a knight of noble birth rapes a young woman. The disparate connotations, however, are reconciled by the LOATHLY HAG who teaches the knight the "true" meaning of gentility or "gentilesse," which, she says, does not come from one's ancestors, but from God, and must be earned by each individual through the performance of good and honorable deeds. This same idea, that gentility does not automatically pass down from one's ancestors, is expressed even more explicitly in the short poem "GENTILESSE."

"Gentilesse"   One of the short poems attributed to Chaucer in the manuscripts, "Gentilesse" offers moral instruction that echoes the doctrine expressed by the LOATHLY HAG in "The WIFE OF BATH'S TALE"—that true nobility arises from virtue and is the gift of God, and is not something one inherits from one's ancestors. The "first stock" (i.e., "ancestor") referred to in the first lines of stanzas one and two has been variously interpreted as God (the Father of virtue) or Adam, before he committed sin. The poem has no specific source, but the ideas it contains reflect those expressed by LADY PHILOSOPHY in Book Three, Prosa 6 and Metrum 6 of BOETHIUS' *Consolation of Philosophy,* a work that Chaucer translated from Latin into English as *BOECE,* and one that strongly influenced his later work. The idea was also an important one in the work of another Italian poet, DANTE ALIGHIERI, and in the French *ROMAN DE LA ROSE.* Like many of the shorter poems Chaucer wrote, "Gentilesse" is composed in the French BALLADE form with three stanzas of seven lines each (the most common ballade stanza was eight lines, but there were variations), and a rhyme scheme of *ababbcc,* with the same three rhymes repeated in all three stanzas. It is testimony to Chaucer's poetic genius that he was able to execute the rhyme scheme of the ballade form without ever repeating a word, except in the one-line refrain that concludes each stanza. "Gentilesse" survives in 11 manuscripts and in two early editions by William Caxton (1477–78) and William Thynne (1532) (*see* EDITIONS OF CHAUCER'S WORKS), suggesting that, like the ballade "TRUTH," it was a popular poem in its day. In

the manuscripts it is typically titled "Moral balade of Chaucer"; the current title was suggested by W. W. SKEAT and adopted by later editors. As with many of the shorter poems, the date of composition is uncertain, though the influence of Boethius, as well as the poem's craftsmanship, suggests that it belongs to the mature period of Chaucer's literary career.

Genylon-Olyver   *See* GANELON.

Geoffrey of Monmouth   A cleric who taught at Oxford University between 1129 and 1151, Geoffrey of Monmouth was the first writer to create a "biography" of Britain's most famous legendary monarch, King ARTHUR. Geoffrey wrote in Latin, like most clerics of his day, and the first work he presented to the public was a series of mysterious "Prophecies of Merlin." His *Historia Regum Britanniae* (History of the Kings of Britain) was one of the most influential books of the Middle Ages. Geoffrey began his history by expanding on a Welsh legend found in the work of an earlier writer named Nennius, according to whom the island of Britain was colonized in the late 12th century B.C. by a party of Trojans under the leadership of Brutus, the great-grandson of the Trojan hero AENEAS. From thence, Geoffrey traces the imagined British monarchy through a series of kings, including the Lear made famous by Shakespeare, until he comes to Arthur. Chaucer alludes to Geoffrey's work in *The HOUSE OF FAME* when he states that Geoffrey's form (a kind of statue created from his speech and writing) appeared in FAME's palace, where it helped to support the great legend of TROY. Chaucer does not mention the Arthurian material—which, given Chaucer's clear preference for classical literature, is not too surprising.

Geoffrey of Vinsauf   A famous 12th-century rhetorician who is believed to have been born in England of Norman French parents. His surname, Vinsauf, is French for "safe wine" and may have derived from a treatise on conserving wines that was attributed to him. He wrote two influential handbooks on rhetoric, both of which became part of the curriculum of medieval education. One of them, the *Poetria Nova* ("New Poetry"), provides flamboyant illustrations of the rules it propounds, the most famous of which was a lamentation on the death of King Richard I. In "The NUN'S PRIEST'S TALE," Chaucer first recalls this lamentation of Geoffrey's (lines 3347–54), and then parodies it with his own extended lament comparing the grief of the hens over the rooster CHAUNTICLEER's capture to that experienced by the Trojan women when TROY fell to the Greeks at the end of the TROJAN WAR.

Gerland   One of the dogs owned by the poor widow in "The NUN'S PRIEST'S TALE." It and two others join in the chase after RUSSELL, the sly fox who has seized the widow's rooster, CHAUNTICLEER.

Germanicus   Germanicus Julius Caesar was the nephew and adopted son of the Roman emperor Tiberius and the father of the notorious CALIGULA, also a Roman emperor. Chaucer refers to Caligula as Gaius Caesar in the BOECE, his translation of BOETHIUS' *Consolation of Philosophy*. Boethius mentions an example of Caligula's paranoia to suggest a parallel to his own situation when he was accused of treason by officials in the government of THEODORIC, the Ostragothic king of Rome under whom Boethius served as a consul. Why the relationship between Germanicus and Caligula should be important in this context is uncertain, but Caligula (i.e., Gaius Caesar) is referred to here as Germanicus' son.

Germayne   *See* GERMANICUS.

Gernade   *See* GRANADA.

Gerounde (Geronde)   *See* GIRONDE.

Gervaise   A blacksmith and minor character in "The MILLER'S TALE," Gervaise provides ABSALOM (1) with the hot coulter which he uses to burn NICHOLAS on the "tout," or bottom.

Ghent   City in northwestern Belgium. In the Middle Ages it was part of the country of FLANDERS (Belgium did not exist at that time) and was a famous clothmaking center. Chaucer alludes to this fact in the GENERAL PROLOGUE to *The CANTERBURY TALES* when he notes that the WIFE OF BATH's skills as a weaver surpass those of YPRES and of Ghent. Ypres was also located in Flanders.

Gibraltar   A small peninsula at the southern tip of Spain, extending into the Mediterranean. It consists mostly of a rocky hill (the Rock of Gibraltar) more than 1,000 feet high. When CONSTANCE, the heroine of "The MAN OF LAW'S TALE," is put in a boat and cast adrift at the instigation of DONEGILD, her jealous mother-in-law, she sails down the coast of Britain and through the Strait of Gibraltar into the Mediterranean Sea. Eventually she is rescued by a Roman senator who takes her to ROME, where she is reunited with her husband and her father.

Gilbertus Anglicus   An English physician of the 13th century who wrote the *Compendium medicinae*. Gilbertus Anglicus is mentioned in Chaucer's GENERAL PROLOGUE to *The CANTERBURY TALES* as one of the medical authorities whose teachings the DOCTOR OF PHYSIC had studied.

Gilbertyn   *See* GILBERTUS ANGLICUS.

Giles, Saint   One of the most popular medieval saints, Giles was the patron of breast-feeding, the physically disabled, beggars and blacksmiths. There is some uncertainty about his origins, but he was born in the early seventh century and founded a monastery in Provence at a place which came to bear the name Saint-Gilles. According to his legend, Giles began his Christian life as a hermit and took his nourishment from the milk of a hind—hence his patronage of breast-feeding. One day when a local Visigothic king was out hunting, he shot at the hind but instead wounded Giles, with whom the animal had taken refuge. The saint was crippled as a result, and this seems to be the source for his patronage of the physically disabled.

The prayers of Saint Giles were considered to be so efficacious that it was unnecessary for the penitent who sought his intercession to make auricular confession. In England, 162 ancient churches were dedicated to Saint Giles. The two most famous were in London (St. Giles, Cripplegate) and Edinburgh. Giles is artistically represented either as a simple abbot with his staff of office or in a scene featuring one of the incidents of his life such as his shielding the hind. His emblems are the hind and the arrow.

Chaucer's work contains two references to Saint Giles. In "The CANON'S YEOMAN'S TALE," the canon who extorts money from the gullible priest swears by Saint Giles when he professes sympathy for the priest, who sweats profusely while tending the alchemical fire (line 1185). An oath to this saint seems appropriate in the circumstances because Giles was the patron of blacksmiths, who likewise endure great heat while working at the forge. The dreamer-narrator of *The HOUSE OF FAME* invokes Giles when he describes the Palace of Love, which appeared to be made entirely of beryl, a very hard, lustrous gem of which emerald and aquamarine are two varieties (line 1183). In this case, the decision to call upon Giles in support of his description perhaps indicates some fear of being judged insane.

Gille   A maidservant in "The MILLER TALE." She is such a minor character that she does not actually even appear in the action but is only referred to by NICHOLAS, a young student who lodges with JOHN THE CARPENTER and his lovely young wife, ALISON (1). When Nicholas warns John that they need to prepare themselves for the coming of a great flood, and that they must tell no one else of their plans, he says that the need for secrecy is so great, they cannot save anyone else, not even John's two servants, of whom Gille is one.

Gironde   In "The FRANKLIN'S TALE," DORIGEN challenges the amorous squire AURELIUS to remove all the rocks that line the coast of BRITTANY between "Gerounde" and the mouth of the river SEINE, in northern France (line 1222). According to F. P. Magoun's *CHAUCER GAZETTEER*, Gerounde in this case refers to the Gironde, an estuary or arm of the sea originating at the juncture of the Garonne and Dordogne Rivers, which feed into the Bay of Biscay just north of BORDEAUX. Thus, the Seine would be the northern limit and the Gironde the southern limit of the specified territory.

Glascurion   A British harper who appears among other harpers in FAME's palace in Chaucer's *HOUSE OF FAME*. He is probably the same person as the Welsh hero Glasgerion, who appeared in a well-known ballad. According to the ballad, Glasgerion, aside from achieving fame playing the harp, was a king's son who had won the favor of the daughter of the king of Normandy. Glasgerion's page found a way to take his place in an assignation with Glasgerion's lady, but the young woman, who had been fooled by the substitution, committed suicide when she learned the truth. Glasgerion responded by cutting off the page's head and then killing himself.

Gloucester, duke of   *See* THOMAS OF WOODSTOCK.

Gobi Desert   A great desert plateau in East Asia, chiefly in Mongolia, comprising about 500,000 square miles. Situated across a main trade route between China and Europe, the Gobi Desert was known to medieval Europeans because it was included in Marco Polo's description of the region. In Chaucer's *BOOK OF THE DUCHESS*, the desert is mentioned by the BLACK KNIGHT, who refers to it as the "Dry Sea" (line 1028). In keeping with his habit of using metaphors or other figures of speech to communicate, the Black Knight, in praising the character of the fair LADY WHITE, says that she would never lead a knight on by sending him away on quests to distant regions. One of the regions he mentions, which is considerably distant from England, is the Gobi Desert.

God of Love   *See* CUPID.

goliards   In the GENERAL PROLOGUE to *The CANTERBURY TALES*, Chaucer describes the MILLER as "janglere and a goliardeys," indicating that he is a man who likes to tell dirty stories. The term "goliardeys" alludes to the Goliardic school of medieval poetry, which typically celebrated sexual love and drinking (alcohol). The movement got its name from a group of wandering scholars in France, Germany and England in the 12th and 13th centuries who were the first to compose groups of such poems. Some goliardic lyrics also contain satire against the clergy, a characteristic that may play a role in several of Chaucer's FABLIAUX featuring corrupt members of the clergy, such as "The SUMMONER'S TALE" and "The SHIPMAN'S TALE." The most famous examples of

goliardic verse are found in the *Carmina Burana,* a 13th-century collection of Latin and German poems that was rediscovered in the 19th century. The name *Goliard* may be derived from the biblical GOLIATH, the symbol of lawlessness and evil, or from the Latin word *gula,* on account of the Goliards' supposed gluttony. The Miller's physical appearance suggests that the latter characteristic could apply to him as well.

Goliath (Golias)   In the Bible, Goliath was a Philistine giant. According to the Book of Samuel, Goliath was at least nine and a half feet tall, and perhaps as tall as 11 feet. He is also reported to have worn magnificent armor, which included a bronze coat of mail, bronze greaves, a bronze javelin, a spear with an iron head and a huge sword. Goliath challenged King Saul's army to find one man willing to engage in single combat with him. The outcome of the ongoing war between the Jews and the Philistines would then be determined by the winner. DAVID, who was at that time a young man, accepted the challenge and killed Goliath with a single stone from his sling. The stone struck the giant in the middle of his forehead. David went on to become Israel's next king. In "The MAN OF LAW'S TALE," this incredible feat of David's is given as an example of how ordinary people may overcome great obstacles through the grace of God. The heroine of "The Man of Law's Tale," CONSTANCE, also has to overcome great odds when she is cast adrift on the ocean with an infant son.

Goodelief   In *The CANTERBURY TALES*, Goodelief is the wife of Harry BAILLY, the Host who proposes the tale-telling contest as a way of pleasantly passing the time on the way to CANTERBURY. Goodelief (whose name means "good love") does not physically accompany her husband on the pilgrimage, but she does appear in spirit on at least one occasion. After hearing the pilgrim Chaucer's "TALE OF MELIBEE," in which PRUDENCE, MELIBEE's wife, advises him to be patient in his dealings with the men who have robbed him, the Host exclaims that he wishes his wife had heard this tale. She, he continues, has so little patience that when she hears him beating the servants, she brings him a club and exhorts him to break every bone! Although Goodelief was a popular woman's name in the 14th century, Chaucer's use of it here is obviously intended to be ironic.

Gootland   *See* GOTLAND.

Goths   The Goths referred to in the *BOECE*, Chaucer's translation of BOETHIUS' *Consolation of Philosophy,* are actually Ostrogoths, or Eastern Goths. The Goths were one of many Germanic tribes or nations that began to spread from their homelands in northern Europe down into the more southerly regions, starting in about the second century A.D. The Goths originally came from Sweden. By 526, their conquest of the Italian peninsula was complete and THEODORIC, the man in whose government Boethius served, was the reigning Gothic king of Rome.

Gotland An island in the Baltic Sea off the southeast coast of Sweden. In the portrait of the SHIPMAN that appears in the GENERAL PROLOGUE to *The CANTERBURY TALES,* Chaucer says that the man knew every harbor from Gotland to Cape Finistere in Spain, suggesting that he has had extensive experience sailing in the waters extending from the Baltic to the coast of northwestern Spain.

Gower, John An author and contemporary (roughly) of Chaucer's, John Gower probably receives a good bit less attention for his work than he otherwise would have, had Chaucer's work never come into existence. Born around 1330, Gower came from a family belonging to the gentry and wealthy enough for Gower to study law at the INNS OF COURT in London. He seems never to have practiced that profession, however, but instead devoted most of his intellectual energy to writing. The fact that he composed works in Latin and ANGLO-NORMAN (a dialect of French) as well as in English testifies to the extent of his classical education; it also reflects the fact that, up until Chaucer popularized literature in his native English, much of the literature that was read by the nobility in England was composed in French or Latin. The French *ROMAN DE LA ROSE,* for example, was a popular text among members of the English court. The same text was partially translated into English by Chaucer. Records of the time suggest that Chaucer and Gower were friends. Chaucer's *TROILUS AND CRISEYDE* was dedicated to Gower and Ralph STRODE, and the first version of Gower's *CONFESSIO AMANTIS* featured a tribute to Chaucer. That this tribute does not appear in a later version has been interpreted by some readers as evidence that the relationship between the two men was not always amiable. On the other hand, it is possible that Gower removed his tribute to Chaucer for political reasons similar to those that led him to excise the praises of King RICHARD II, which originally appeared in the conclusion, after Richard's style of governing had become unpopular with the powerful members of the nobility.

Gower's principle works are the Anglo-Norman *Mirour de l'Omme;* the Latin *Vox Clamantis;* and the *Confessio Amantis,* which, despite its Latin title, was written in English. The *Mirour de l'Omme* (Mirror of man) is an allegorical poem about the fall of man, with extensive anatomization of his virtues and vices. The *Vox Clamantis* features an apocalyptic theme imposed on the subjects of politics and kingship and reflects upon the PEASANT'S REVOLT OF 1381 and other domestic political events. The *Confessio Amantis* (Lover's confession) is a poem of some 33,000 octosyllabic lines featuring a series of 140 short narratives on the theme of love. These narratives are contained by a frame story that features a lover (Amans) being instructed by Genius, the priest of VENUS. The exemplary (*see* EXEMPLUM) stories, which are derived from classical literature, are organized under the headings of the Seven Deadly Sins and are the primary means by which Genius tutors his pupil.

Granada During the 14th century, Granada was a Moorish kingdom in southern Spain. In the GENERAL PROLOGUE to *The CANTERBURY TALES,* Granada is listed as one of the many locations where the KNIGHT has been on campaign. Most of his military campaigns have involved fighting against pagan (usually Muslim) occupiers of formerly Christian lands, and this one is no exception. The Moors were a Muslim people of Arab and Berber descent, originating in northwestern Africa, who invaded and occupied Spain in the eighth century.

Graunson   *See* OTON DE GRANDSON.

Gray, Douglas (1930–) Douglas Gray is an Australian scholar who did his graduate work at Oxford, taught in Australia and returned to Oxford as a professor of Medieval English Literature. In an interview with *Contemporary Authors,* Gray described his career as "trying to find out more about" medieval literature and "trying to make it more comprehensible to modern readers." He edited the volume on *Middle English Literature* for the *Oxford History of English Literature* (1986) and has written on a wide range of topics concerning Anglo-Saxon and Middle English. His articles on Chaucer include "Some Chaucerian Themes in Scottish Writers" (in *Chaucer Traditions: Studies in Honour of Derek Brewer,* 1990), "Chaucer and Gentilesse" (in *One Hundred Years of English Studies at Dutch Universities,* 1987) and "Chaucer and 'Pite'" (in *J. R. R. Tolkien, Scholar and Storyteller: Essays in Memoriam,* 1979). He also assisted Norman DAVIS with *A Chaucer Glossary* (1979).

Great Schism, the The split in the Roman Catholic Church known as the Great Schism grew out of a quarrel between King Philip IV of France and Pope Boniface VIII at the beginning of the 14th century. When Boniface died, Philip's own candidate was elected to the papacy, and the papal capital was transferred to Avignon in the Rhone valley, where it remained for nearly 70 years, a period that became known as the Babylonian Captivity. Not surprisingly, the popes who ruled from Avignon were unable to escape the charge of subservience to French interests. In 1378, an effort to restore the papacy to its original capital led to the election of two popes, Clement VII at Avignon, and Urban VI at Rome, each proclaiming himself the rightful successor of the apostle Peter. The resulting split was not healed until the Council of Constance in 1417. The English supported the Italian pope against the French one, and this understandably had a negative effect on English diplomacy in France and brought negotiations over a royal marriage between Richard II and the French king's daughter to a standstill. Chaucer made diplomatic journeys to France and Italy during this period and may have been involved in marriage negotiations on the king's behalf in both countries.

Great (Grete) Sea   Chaucer refers to the Mediterranean Sea as the Great Sea twice in his poetry, first in the story of Seys and ALCYONE that is included in *The BOOK OF THE DUCHESS* and later in his description of the KNIGHT's campaigns that appears in the GENERAL PROLOGUE TO *THE CANTERBURY TALES*.

Greece   When Chaucer refers to Greece it is always within the context of the ancient world as the home of those men and women of classical legend, such as JASON and MEDEA, who appear in his work. Ancient Greece encompassed an area extending from southern Macedonia across the Gulf of Corinth to include the area known as the Peloponnesus, a peninsula extending into the Ionian Sea and farther south to Crete. Its western boundaries lay across the Aegean Sea along the coastal strip of western Asia Minor. The four main groups of peoples in ancient Greece, named for their association with a specific location, were the Ionians, Dorians, Aeolians and Arcadians. The country of Greece provides the setting for "The KNIGHT'S TALE," most notably, and for a number of the stories related in the *The LEGEND OF GOOD WOMEN*. In *TROILUS AND CRISEYDE*, DIOMEDE says that he would rather serve Criseyde than be king of 12 Greeces (book 5, line 924).

Greece (Grece), Sea of   In "The MAN OF LAW'S TALE," Chaucer refers to the Mediterranean Sea as the Sea of Greece. It is where CONSTANCE, the heroine of the tale, sails each time her persecutors cast her adrift.

Greenwich   A town not far from London on the south side of the Thames, through which the Canterbury pilgrims passed on their journey to visit the shrine of Saint THOMAS À BECKET. In the prologue to "The REEVE'S TALE," the Host (*see* Harry BAILLY) uses the town as a geographical marker to call attention to the passage of time as he urges the REEVE to stop complaining about the MILLER's performance and to get on with his own story.

Gregory, Saint (Pope Gregory the Great)   A Roman born around 540 to patrician parents, early in his life Gregory gave up a political career to take religious orders. In 590, after serving seven years as papal legate to Constantinople, Gregory was elected pope. Gregory's achievements include the reform of church discipline, both among the secular clergy and in religious houses; successful dealing with those old heresies that were still active at the time; and the sending of Saint AUGUSTINE as the first missionary to the Anglo-Saxons in England. He is also credited with saving Rome from oppression by the Lombards, a Germanic people who were establishing a presence in Italy. His kindness to the poor became and has remained proverbial. Dame PRUDENCE claims to be quoting from Gregory in "The TALE OF MELIBEE" when she advises her husband to exhibit patience in his dealings with the men who assaulted and robbed his family (line 1497), although the passage has not been located in Gregory's work. "The PARSON'S TALE," which is actually a sermon on penitence, features a number of quotes from Gregory's *Morals*.

Grenewych   *See* GREENWICH.

Grete Sele   *See* GREAT SEA.

Grisel   The name Grisel appears in a problematic line of the short poem "LENVOY DE CHAUCER À SCOGAN." The poem consists of a kind of playful complaint directed to the Scogan mentioned in the title, who has apparently sinned against the god of love (CUPID) by ceasing to woo his lady when she refuses to be easily won. At the end of a stanza wherein the poet states his fear that the god of love will revenge himself on all men who are gray and round of shape (like Chaucer and Scogan) for Scogan's crime, he says, "But wel I wot, thow wolt answere and saye, / 'Lo, olde Grisel lyst to ryme and playe!'" (lines 34–35) [But well I know that you will answer and say, / Look at how old Grisel likes to rhyme and play]. If the Middle English interpretation is given to the word, it means "old man." In Old French, however, *Grisel* denoted an old gray horse. Either way, the speaker's projected statement obviously refers to Chaucer, and seems to express his belief that Scogan will find his poem amusing rather than serious.

Griselda   The heroine of "The CLERK'S TALE," Griselda is a young Italian peasant woman who arrests the attention of WALTER, the marquis of SALUZZO. When his people insist that Walter marry so that he can provide them with an heir, Walter chooses Griselda to be his bride. His choice is remarkable because, during the medieval period in Europe, for a variety of complex social, economic and political reasons, people very rarely married outside their social class. Walter violates this tradition because Griselda has impressed him as being a woman who possesses wisdom as well as beauty. Why he could not find a woman with similar qualities from within the nobility is hinted at in the explanation that Griselda's poverty and the hard work it necessitated helped to make her wise beyond her years. Nothing that she does either before or after the marriage suggests that Walter's original opinion of her was in error; nevertheless he feels compelled to test her love, first by taking away her children, then by having their marriage annulled so that he can marry someone of his own class and finally by asking her to return to his house as a servant to oversee preparations for the wedding banquet. Griselda bears all of these insults with patience and fortitude, earning herself the sobriquet "Patient Griselda," which still has currency today to describe a long-suffering wife. Ultimately, Walter's need to test Griselda's patient obedience is banished by her amazing steadfastness. He reveals that all of the hardships have been nothing more than a trial of her goodness and restores her to her position as his wife, simultaneously reuniting her with her children, whom she had thought to be dead.

Guido delle Colonne   Thirteenth-century Sicilian author who wrote the *Historia Destructionis Troiae* (History of the destruction of Troy), which was actually a prose version of BENOIT DE SAINTE-MAURE's famous poem, the *Roman de Troie* (Book of Troy). The Italian writer BOCCACCIO used Guido's version of the Troy story as the main source for his poem, *Il Filostrato*, which in turn was the main source of Chaucer's TROILUS AND CRISEYDE. In her *Commentary on the General Prologue to the Canterbury Tales*, Muriel BOWDEN has shown that Chaucer also drew directly on Guido's work. The famous opening of the GENERAL PROLOGUE, with its memorable evocation of spring, corresponds very closely to a passage in the *Historia*.

Guillaume de Lorris   Thirteenth-century French poet who began the influential allegorical work known as the *ROMAN DE LA ROSE*. He took his name from the small village of Lorris on the Loire River above Orléans in the north of France. Little is known about his origin or career aside from what can be inferred from the text of the *Roman*. He may have been born around 1212 and died about 1237. His works suggest that he was well-read in the Latin classics and that he particularly enjoyed OVID. He began work on the poem around 1230, intending to present it (or so he said) as a gift to his beloved. The aim of the work, which was initially 4058 lines long, was to expound "the whole art of love." To accomplish this he employed a dream-vision framework featuring a narrator who tells of a marvelous dream in which he entered a Garden of Love and encountered allegorical figures symbolic of various mental and physical aspects of romantic love that affect human behavior. For some reason (probably because he died), Guillaume failed to complete the project, but

the dream vision, as Guillaume formulated it, soon became the dominant genre of the literature of courtly love, and Chaucer was to use it in four of his major works: *The BOOK OF THE DUCHESS*, *The PARLIAMENT OF FOWLS*, *The HOUSE OF FAME* and *The LEGEND OF GOOD WOMEN*. Guillaume's poem was eventually completed by another French writer, JEAN DE MEUN, whose treatment of the subject of love is more distanced, philosophical and, occasionally, satirical. De Meun's continuation of Guillaume's poem expands the tone and scope of the work to include lust, friendship and even divine love.

Guillaume de Machaut   A very important French musician and poet of the 14th century. Although he achieved wide fame and is primarily remembered for his musical compositions, he contributed significantly to the development of such artificial verse forms as the BALLADE and the rondeau, both of which became popular among English poets. Machaut's work had its strongest influence on Chaucer in the author's early elegiac poem, *The BOOK OF THE DUCHESS*, which drew upon a poem called the *Jugement dou Roy de Behaingne* (Judgment of the King of Bohemia). This poem features a narrator who, as he walks in the meadows one spring morning, overhears a lady and a knight lamenting their various woes. The lady suffers because her lover has died; the knight because his beloved has betrayed him. The two argue about which has the greater cause for sorrow and eventually appear before the king of Bohemia, whose court of love is designed to decide disputes such as this. The king's verdict is that infidelity, rather than bereavement, merits the greater grief. Scholars have suggested that the dreamer's questions to the BLACK KNIGHT in *The Book of the Duchess* force him to declare that his relationship with the queen for whom he grieves was a perfect one, destroyed only by her death, and thus identical to that of the Lady in Machaut's poem. Confronted by this realization, he pulls himself together and leaves off mourning, returning to the society from which he has exiled himself.

Guydo de Columpnis   *See* GUIDO DELLE COLONNE.

Guy of Warwick   A popular English metrical romance dating from about 1300, *Guy of Warwick* seems to have been based on an ANGLO-NORMAN original. Guy is the son of Siward, earl of Warwick, and the story tells of the deeds he performs in order to win the hand of the beautiful Fenice. He rescues the daughter of the German emperor, fights the Saracens and slays their sultan. When he returns to England he is honorably received by King Athelstan (an actual historical figure), and marries Fenice. Then he goes adventuring in the Holy Land, where he performs more heroic deeds. When he returns to England he fights the Danish giant

Colbrand, kills the Dun Cow of Dunsmore and defeats a dragon in Northumberland. After these adventures he becomes a hermit. His wife, Fenice, feeds him but does not recognize him until, shortly before his death, he sends her his ring. This romance is unusual because it blends the genre of SAINTS' LIVES with that of a chivalric adventure story. Chaucer mentions Guy of Warwick in his "TALE OF SIR THOPAS" as an example of heroes to whom his own THOPAS may be compared.

Gysen The river Chaucer refers to as the Gysen in "The SUMMONER'S TALE" is actually the Gyndes, a tributary of the Tigris, located in the ancient kingdom of BABYLON. The river is mentioned in "The Summoner's Tale" when the corrupt monk, John (*see* JOHN THE MONK), warns THOMAS (1) against excessive anger by citing the example of Cyrus the Elder (*see* CYRUS THE GREAT), the Persian ruler who destroyed the bed of the Gyndes River when a horse of his was drowned in it (line 2080). The monk's admonitions to the sick man, who is justifiably angry because he realizes that John just wants to get money from him, only serve to increase the man's rage. Ultimately, Thomas scores a comically appropriate revenge by rewarding the monk's efforts with the gift of a fart.

H

Haberdasher, the   One of a group of tradesmen mentioned, but not described individually, in the GENERAL PROLOGUE to *The CANTERBURY TALES*. His title indicates that he is a dealer in hats or other small wares. The others in his group include a CARPENTER, WEAVER ("Webbe"), DYER of cloth ("Dyere") and a TAPESTRY MAKER ("Tapycer"). These five men are all wearing the same type of uniform, which indicates their membership in one of the medieval trade guilds, the forerunner of modern-day trade unions. The guilds set standards for the quality of the goods produced, regulated holidays and hours of work, and fixed prices and wages to some extent. Certain details of Chaucer's portrait of the guildsmen, such as their silver- (rather than brass) mounted knives, might suggest either prosperity or pretentiousness, depending upon whether or not one judges the portraits to contain elements of satire. Those scholars who argue against finding satire in their description note that Chaucer provided his guildsmen with none of the traditional mercantile vices such as fraud, usury and avarice. None of the guildsmen tells a tale on the pilgrimage to CANTERBURY.

Habradates   *See* ABRADATE.

Hailes Abbey   At the beginning of "The PARDONER'S TALE," the narrator warns against various kinds of sin, ironically revealing his own too intimate knowledge of the activities he admonishes others to avoid. One of those activities is swearing, which, he notes, often accompanies gambling. After reminding his audience of the Second Commandment against taking the Lord's name in vain, he gives examples of several oaths, one of which is, "By the blood of Crist that is in Hayles," (line 652). This "Hayles" is Hailes Abbey in Gloucestershire. The abbey, which was founded in 1246, in Chaucer's day possessed a vial that was supposed to contain the blood of Christ, a substance visible only to the eyes of those possessing a clean conscience. This idea mirrors the PARDONER's announcement regarding his own relics—that only those who are free from sin will be able to approach them and make an offering. This is one of the tricks he uses to manipulate his audience into giving him money.

Haly   The "Haly" mentioned in the GENERAL PROLOGUE to *The CANTERBURY TALES* as one of the medical authorities whose work the DOCTOR OF PHYSIC has studied is probably Haly Abbas (Ali ibn Abbas), a Persian who toward the end of the 10th century wrote a book on medical theory and practice known in the west as the Royal Book. Haly's work enjoyed wide circulation and prestige as a medical text in the medieval universities. The reference may alternatively be to Haly Eben Rodan (Ali ibn Ridwan), an Egyptian who wrote influential commentaries on GALEN and HIPPOCRATES in the 11th century.

Ham   *See* CANAAN.

Hanna, Ralph III (1942–)   American specialist in Middle English literature. After receiving a Ph.D. from Yale University, Ralph Hanna became a professor of English at the University of California–Riverside, where he has continued to teach and conduct research on Chaucer and other Middle English topics. For the academic year 1997–98, he also served as university lecturer in paleography (manuscript study) at Oxford University. Although Hanna completed the important work of editing, with Traugott Lawler, the text of the *BOECE* (Chaucer's translation of BOETHIUS' *Consolation of Philosophy*) for *The RIVERSIDE CHAUCER* (1987), he stated in an interview that he primarily does "Chaucer by accident," in accordance with his main interest in the Middle English "literature of learnedness." In the classroom and in his research, Hanna uses Chaucer to show how much modern apprehension of medieval texts has been conditioned by various editorial choices and assumptions. Hanna's interest in medieval texts and their transmission is reflected in much of his published work on Chaucer, including "(The) Editing (of) the Ellesmere Text" (in *The Ellesmere Chaucer: Essays in Interpretation*, 1995), "The Manuscripts and Transmission of Chaucer's Troilus" (in *The Idea of Medieval Literature: New Essays on Chaucer and Medieval Culture*, 1992), and "The Hengwrt Manuscript and the Canon of *The Canterbury Tales*" (in *English Manuscript Studies, 1100–1700*, 1989). Hanna's most recent work, which explores the text transmission issue more fully, is the book-length *Pursuing History: Middle English Manuscripts and Their Texts,* published by Stanford University Press in 1996.

Hannibal (Hanybal)   Famed Carthaginian general of the late third and early second century B.C. who was an extremely successful military strategist in the second Punic War (220–216 B. C.). He suffered his only defeat at the hands of the Roman general SCIPIO at Zama in 202 B.C. To escape capture by the Romans, Hannibal fled to ANTIOCHUS of Syria, then to CRETE and finally to the court of Prusias, king of Bithynia. There he ended his life by taking poison. As a result of his defeat, CARTHAGE was forced to surrender all her possessions except the capital city and its surrounding territory in Africa to Rome, and to pay a large indemnity. Hannibal's military tactics have been copied by generals throughout history, up to the present day. The narrator of "The MAN OF LAW'S TALE" says that when CONSTACE left ROME after marrying the SULTAN OF SYRIA, there was as much weeping as when Hannibal conquered the city.

Harpies   *See* ERINYES.

Hasdrubal's wife   Hasdrubal was king of CARTHAGE in the second century B.C. He was killed when the Romans invaded and burned the city during the third Punic War in 146. His wife and her two sons burned themselves in despair. Hasdrubal's wife's willingness to sacrifice her life rather than face dishonor is recalled by DORIGEN (lines 1399–404) in "The FRANKLIN'S TALE" when she is called upon to honor her promise to become the lover of the squire AURELIUS if he could remove some rocks from the coast of BRITTANY. She frivolously made the rash promise, thinking he could never accomplish such a feat. When he does, Dorigen is caught in a double bind because she must either renege on her promise or dishonor her husband. In "The NUN'S PRIEST'S TALE," PERTELOTE shrieks louder than Hasdrubal's wife when she sees RUSSELL the Fox seize the rooster CHAUNTICLEER by the neck and run off (lines 3362–65).

Hayles   *See* HAILES ABBEY.

Hector (Ector)   Brother to PARIS and TROILUS, son of King PRIAM and Queen HECUBA of TROY. Hector was the leader of the Trojans and one of the greatest warriors in the TROJAN WAR. He is represented in HOMER's *Iliad* not only as a brave and passionate soldier, but also as a devoted and tender son, husband and father. His killing of Patroclus, who wore the Achilles' armor into battle to fool the Trojans, was the deed that finally drew ACHILLES back into the battle, leading to Hector's downfall. When the rest of the Trojan troops had retreated inside the city walls to escape Achilles' rage, Hector alone remained outside to meet him. But when face to face with the Greek, Hector also became afraid and fled. Achilles chased him three times around the city walls before Hector turned to confront him and was fatally wounded by Achilles' spear. Achilles tied Hector's body by the feet to his chariot and dragged it through the dirt into his camp, determined to let it be eaten by dogs. Hector's father, Priam, finally persuaded him to restore the body to the Trojans, who took it back to the city and burned it in a funeral pyre after many days of mourning. In "The MAN OF LAW'S TALE" and "The NUN'S PRIEST'S TALE," Hector's death is given as an example of doom foretold, while his heroism is alluded to in "The KNIGHT'S TALE" and *The BOOK OF THE DUCHESS*. He plays a slightly larger role in Chaucer's *TROILUS AND CRISEYDE,* in which his role as the de facto governor of Troy is emphasized. When CRISEYDE is afraid of being cast out of Troy because of her father's treachery in leaving the city to join the Greek force, Hector offers her protection, which enables her to remain safely in her home.

Hecuba   In classical mythology, Hecuba was the queen of TROY and the wife of King PRIAM. Together the pair had many children who achieved fame in classical legend, including HECTOR, PARIS and CASSANDRA. Their youngest son, TROILUS, is one of the main characters in Chaucer's *TROILUS AND CRISEYDE,* a love story set against the backdrop of the TROJAN WAR. The cause of that war was Paris' kidnapping of Helen (HELEN OF TROY), the wife of MENELAUS, king of Lacedaemon, or Sparta. When Hecuba was pregnant with Paris, she dreamed that she bore a flaming torch which set fire to Troy and destroyed the city. So, when Paris was born, his parents exposed him on Mount Ida, hoping to save the city, but he was rescued and nurtured by a shepherd who raised the boy as his son. When he returned to Troy as an adult, his parents acknowledged him and received him into their family. After losing her husband at the fall of Troy, Hecuba was given to ULYSSES, whom of all the Greeks she is said to have hated the most. For these and other woes, she was said to have suffered more than any other mortal, and her name became proverbial for sorrow and suffering. Hecuba is mentioned only once in Chaucer's work, in book five of *Troilus and Criseyde,* where she is referred to as Troilus' mother. This reference does not appear in Chaucer's source, BOCCACCIO's *FILOSTRATO.*

Helen, Saint   Saint Helen was the mother of the Roman emperor Constantine, who became the first Christian emperor. After Helen became a Christian following the peace of the church in 313, she spent the rest of her life in the East and in Rome, where she died about 328, having passed her days in works of piety and charity. She is primarily remembered for having discovered the cross on which Christ was crucified, and for helping to recover and rebuild some of the holy places of Jerusalem. Saint Helen is mentioned once in

Chaucer's work, in the epilogue to "The PARDONER'S TALE." When the PARDONER concludes his performance by inviting the pilgrims to kiss the relics he carries with him (relics whose falsity he has already admitted), the Host Harry BAILLY, responds quite angrily, swearing by Saint Helen that he would rather castrate the Pardoner than kiss any relics of his (lines 951–53). Ironically, the relics associated with Helen, which included pieces of the True Cross, were some of the most famous in the history of saintly relics.

Helen of Troy   In classical mythology, Helen of Troy was the daughter of Zeus (JUPITER) and Leda, whom the god impregnated by assuming the form of a swan. The most beautiful woman in the world, Helen was kidnapped early in her life by THESEUS and Pirithous, but her brothers, CASTOR and Pollux, succeeded in rescuing her before any harm was done. While living with her mother and her foster-father, Tyndareus, Helen was wooed by the foremost heroes of the Greeks. After securing their promise that they would support the claim of the one that she chose, she decided to marry MENELAUS, the king of Sparta. The marriage was soon disrupted, however, by the arrival of PARIS, son of the king of Troy, who had been promised the possession of the most beautiful woman in the world by the goddess VENUS. After enjoying the hospitality of Menelaus and his queen, Paris committed an unspeakable breach of etiquette and abducted his host's wife. The Greeks' campaign to get her back became known as the TROJAN WAR.

Helen is briefly mentioned a number of times in Chaucer's work. For example, in *The PARLIAMENT OF FOWLS*, she is among those listed as love's martyrs (line 291). In "The MERCHANT'S TALE," the lustful old knight JANUARY will embrace his new young wife even more vehemently than Paris did Helen. Helen appears as a character in Chaucer's longest single work, *TROILUS AND CRISEYDE*, which takes place during the Trojan War. In this work she attends a dinner at the house of Deiphobus, one of TROILUS' brothers, and supports CRISEYDE's plea for protection by members of the royal family, protection from a man who, according to information she has received from her uncle, plans to pursue legal action against her.

Helicon, Mount   In classical mythology, Mount Helicon was the home of the Muses, those goddesses who presided over the arts and sciences, lending inspiration to those who practiced in those fields. The actual mountain is located in Boetia, a province of Greece located northwest of Attica. Chaucer mentions Mount Helicon as the Muses' home in *The HOUSE OF FAME*, *ANELIDA AND ARCITE* and *TROILUS AND CRISEYDE*.

Helie   *See* ELI.

Heloise (Helowys)   Born in Paris in 1101, Heloise was the niece of a canon of the cathedral of Paris. She was tutored by the famous scholar Peter Abelard, with whom she fell in love. After she gave birth to a son, the two were secretly married, although Heloise objected to the state of matrimony. Heloise then entered the convent at Argenteuil, where she later became abbess, and Abelard became a monk at the Abbey of St. Denis. Heloise's arguments against marriage, which appear in her letters to Abelard, form part of the Book of Wicked Wives that JANKIN (1), the WIFE OF BATH's fifth husband, likes to read aloud from (see prologue to "The WIFE OF BATH'S TALE," line 677).

Hemonydes   *See* MAEON.

Hengwrt Manuscript   The Hengwrt Manuscript (MS Peniarth 392D of the National Library of Wales in Aberystwyth) is recognized as one of the two most authoritative manuscripts of Chaucer's CANTERBURY TALES; the other, produced by the same copyist, is the ELLESMERE MANUSCRIPT. The reputation of the Hengwrt Manuscript rests primarily on the age—it was made within three or four years of Chaucer's death—and on the condition of the text, which, although its arrangement is somewhat jumbled, is substantially free of scribal and other types of errors. Some of the links (prologues and epilogues to the tales) are missing and the arrangement of the tales seems only "superficially plausible," in the words of Derek PEARSALL. These things, in addition to the different types of ink used and the spaces in the text, which seem to have been left for the insertion of material that was immediately unavailable, all suggest that the collection was put together in great haste. The Hengwrt Manuscript is thought to have been the first complete copy of Chaucer's greatest masterpiece.

Henry IV (1366–1413)   Henry IV was the grandson of King EDWARD III and the son of JOHN OF GAUNT. Gaunt ruled England as regent during the minority of RICHARD II. With the support of the nobility and commons, and by right of his own nearness in blood to the king, Henry usurped the crown from Richard during a particularly troubled period in the latter's reign. Henry came to the throne in 1399, late in Chaucer's career; this change in the government seems to have interrupted the payment of Chaucer's annuities and salaries (granted by Richard) from the royal exchequer. Although the date of letters patent confirming Chaucer's annuity suggests that they were issued on the day of Henry's coronation, other evidence suggests that they were actually issued around February 16, 1400, four months later. Perhaps this is why the final stanza of the begging poem, "COMPLAINT OF CHAUCER TO HIS PURSE," directs the narrator's request for a healthier looking purse to the king. Since Chaucer is thought to have died this same year, the "Complaint" could be the last poem that he wrote.

Henryson, Robert (?1414–?1506) A Scottish poet who, some critics believe, was strongly influenced by Chaucer. Very little is known about Henryson's life, but there is evidence that he attended Glasgow University and worked as a schoolmaster in Dumfermline. Like Chaucer, Henryson was interested in mythological themes and beast fables, and made use of them in his poetry. Among his most enduring works are "The Tale of Orpheus and Erudices His Quene," a retelling of the ORPHEUS and EURYDICE myth, and "The Testament of Cresseid," an alternative ending to Chaucer's TROILUS AND CRISEYDE. Whereas Chaucer's version of the story leaves the reader in some doubt regarding CRISEYDE's ultimate fate once she abandons TROILUS, Henryson narrates her own eventual abandonment by the Greek prince DIOMEDE, following which she contracts leprosy (believed to be a venereal disease in the Middle Ages). Troilus, in Henryson's version, does not die in battle. He and Criseyde encounter each other once more, after she has become a leper and lost both her beauty and her youth. The "testament" referred to in the title is Criseyde's last will and testament. Written after her encounter with Troilus, the document expresses remorse for her actions. In the final stanza of the poem, the narrator suggests that Criseyde's demise should stand as a warning to "worthy women" against the folly of such behavior. Most of Henryson's poems conclude with a moral lesson. Henryson claims that he discovered this alternative ending to the tragedy in "ane uther quair" (another book), but no such source has ever surfaced; it is most likely his own invention. Henryson's debt to Chaucer appears not only in his subject matter, but also in his use of the RHYME ROYAL stanza, a frame narrator, and the DREAM VISION form.

Hercules (Ercules) In classical mythology, Hercules (Greek *Heracles*) was the son of Alcmene and Zeus (JUPITER), who visited her in the guise of her husband, Amphitryon, while he was away at war. The most powerful of all Greek heroes, Hercules exhibited his physical prowess before the age of one by strangling to death two snakes. The snakes had been sent by Hera (JUNO), Zeus' wife, who hated Hercules because he was the offspring of her husband's infidelity. Later, when Hercules was married to Megara and had three sons, Hera caused him to go temporarily insane and kill his family. As penance for this crime, he performed the 12 labors of Hercules, the most famous of which was his getting the golden apples from Hesperides. Although he was not the wisest of the Greek heroes, he always displayed loyalty and devotion to his friends, as when he fought PLUTO to bring Alcestis, the wife of his friend ADMETUS,

back from Hades. That was his second visit to the underworld; on the first he had rescued THESEUS, the king of ATHENS, from the Chair of Forgetfulness. Hercules was so strong he could not be killed by human means. When a poisonous shirt mistakenly given him by his wife caused him unendurable pain, he commanded his friends to build a great funeral pyre on a mountaintop, then lay down on it and demanded that it be lit. Thus, he took his life. After his death he was reconciled to Hera, married her daughter Hebe, and lived with the gods on Mount Olympus. Many of his adventures, including the 12 labors, are summarized in *BOECE*, Book Four, Metrum 7, and in "The MONK'S TALE" (2095–2142). The story of HYPSIPYLE in *The LEGEND OF GOOD WOMEN* relates the part he played in JASON's seduction of that woman, daughter of the king of Lemnos. Hercules is also mentioned briefly in a number of *The CANTERBURY TALES*, mostly with reference to his great strength or to his many difficulties in love.

Heremianus The son of Queen ZENOBIA of PALMYRA and her husband, Odenathus. The story of Zenobia's rise and fall is told in Chaucer's MONK'S TALE (lines 2247–74). Following the Italian writer BOCCACCIO's version of the story, Chaucer supplies the detail that Zenobia dressed her two sons after the manner of kings (lines 2343–45).

Herenus *See* ERINYES.

Hereos, Lover's Malady of In "The KNIGHT'S TALE," we are told that ARCITE (1), one of two captive knights in love with EMILY, suffers from the "loveris maladye of Hereos" (1373–74). Hereos, or "heroic love" was a mental illness recognized and discussed by medieval medical texts. It was thought that in its most extreme form, this lovesickness could lead to physical disease and death. Arcite is not the only Chaucerian character to suffer from this crippling obsession. In the same tale, his cousin PALAMON is similarly afflicted, as is the squire AURELIUS in "The FRANKLIN'S TALE" and Damian in "The MERCHANT'S TALE." The BLACK KNIGHT in the early *BOOK OF THE DUCHESS* suffers so intensely it appears that he could die, but by far the most extended suffering for love is exhibited by Chaucer's TROILUS, whose "double sorrow" (the pain he endured before he won CRISEYDE's love and the grief he experienced after losing her) forms the dominant theme of Chaucer's longest poem, *TROILUS AND CRISEYDE*.

Hermano *See* HEREMIANUS.

Hermengild (Hermengyld) A minor character in "The MAN OF LAW'S TALE." Hermengild is the wife of the constable who finds CONSTANCE's ship washed ashore in Northumbria. She and her husband take Constance into their home and are eventually both converted to Christianity by her. When the advances of a knight (*see* KNIGHT [2]) whom Satan causes to lust after Constance are rebuffed by that lady, the knight murders Hermengild while the two women are asleep and then puts the knife in Constance's bed. The affection shared by the two women is, however, so well known that the knight who performed the murder is the only person willing to accuse Constance. By divine intervention, he is shown to be guilty of the crime and executed.

Hermes Ballenus   *See* BELINOUS.

Hermes Trismegistus   The supposed author of various books on the subjects of theology, magic and mysticism written in the early centuries A.D. Together they were called *Corpus Hermeticum* ("Works of Hermes"). The name Hermes Trismegistus comes from the Greek god Hermes (*see* MERCURY), who had a long association with magic and astronomy. *Trismegistus* means "thrice-great," and the two names together signified the Greek name for Thoth, the Egyptian god of wisdom. The works attributed to Hermes Trismegistus contain no alchemical formulas (*see* ALCHEMY), but their alleged author was claimed by Greek alchemists as the founder of their art. This fact is noted by the CANON'S YEOMAN, who refers to him as "philosophy's father." In the Middle Ages, "philosophy" was a euphemism for alchemy—hence the term "philosopher's stone" to refer to the sought-after substance that would transmute base metal into gold. "The CANON'S YEOMAN'S TALE" tells the story of a notorious alchemist who cheated many people out of their life's savings by promising to increase their money through magical means.

Hermione   In classical mythology, Hermione was the only daughter of Helen (HELEN OF TROY) and MENELAUS. Before the outbreak of the TROJAN WAR she had been betrothed to Orestes, the son of AGAMEMNON, but after his return from the war, her father gave her to PYRRHUS, the son of ACHILLES. After Pyrrhus was murdered at DELPHI, possibly by Orestes, she married Orestes. In the prologue to "The MAN OF LAW'S TALE," the SERGEANT OF THE LAW mentions Hermione as one of the women whose story appears in Chaucer's "Seintes Legende of Cupide" ("Saint's Legend of Cupid," i.e., *The LEGEND OF GOOD WOMEN*). The fact that her story does not appear in the collection adds credence to the idea that the work is incomplete and that Chaucer perhaps intended to return to it at some later date.

Hermus   A river in Asia Minor. Hermus (now Sarabat) is mentioned along with several other rivers in Book Three, Metrum 10 of the BOECE (Chaucer's translation of BOETHIUS' *Consolation of Philosophy*) when LADY PHILOSOPHY informs the narrator that all of the riches that could be brought to him by various rivers would only cloud his mind, rather than clearing it, by encouraging an attachment to worldly goods. The image of the river's running water causing the mind to be troubled rather than cleared plays ingeniously on the common symbolic association between running water and cleanliness or clarity, illustrating the point that, in man's limited perception, things are not always what they seem to be.

Hermyon   *See* HERMIONE.

Hero   In classical mythology, Hero was a priestess of Aphrodite (VENUS) at Sestos in Thrace. She was loved by LEANDER, a youth who lived in the city of Abydos on the other side of the Hellespont, a strait joining the Sea of Marmara and the Aegean Sea. Every night, guided by the light she set out for him, Leander would swim the Hellespont to visit Hero in her tower by the sea, returning to Abydos at dawn. One night, during a raging storm, he was drowned. When Hero came upon his corpse, which had washed up on shore during the night, she threw herself into the water, committing suicide. The story of Hero and Leander is mentioned in the BALLADE praising Queen Alcestis that Chaucer included in the prologue to *The LEGEND OF GOOD WOMEN*. Hero is not one of the women whose stories appear in the *Legend*, a fact that renders somewhat confusing the SERGEANT OF LAW's claim (made in the prologue to "The MAN OF LAW'S TALE") that the story of Hero and her lover can be found in Chaucer's "Seintes Legende of Cupide" (an alternate title for the *Legend*).

Herod (Herode) (1)   In "The MILLER'S TALE" Chaucer says that ABSALOM (1), who is hopelessly in love with the beautiful young ALISON (1), does many things to try to win her love, one of which is to play Herod "upon a scaffold hye." The Herod here referred to is undoubtedly Herod the Great, who was king of Judea at the time of Christ's birth. According to the gospel of MATTHEW, when Herod heard that three kings from the East had come seeking the newborn King of the Jews, he tried to eliminate Jesus by having all male infants in the Bethlehem region put to death. This may reflect his earlier policy of slaughtering all male infants who could possibly have been considered legal heirs to the throne. Although Herod was in some ways a good ruler, bringing stability to the region and respecting the Jews' right to their own culture and worship, he was periodically subject to bouts of paranoia (as evidenced by the above policy), which became more frequent in his later years and ultimately caused him to kill two of his own children. Herod's slaughter of innocents was commonly enacted in the biblical plays known as mystery plays, which were produced by English trade guilds in York, Coventry and other medieval cities. In playing the part of Herod, who typically appeared as a ranting madman, Absalom would have proved a figure more capable of arousing Alison's amusement than her admiration.

Herod (Herode) (2)   Herod Antipas was one of Herod the Great's sons (see HEROD [1]), after his father's death, he became tetrarch (regional ruler) over Galilee and Perea. Herod Antipas is primarily remembered for his part in the murder of JOHN THE BAPTIST at the request of his niece, Salome, and for his role in the judgment of Christ when he was condemned to death. The former is mentioned in "The PARDONER'S TALE" when the PARDONER gives examples of the harm that comes from drunkenness, alluding to the idea that Herod was drunk when he ordered the prophet beheaded. The part Herod played in the Crucifixion is hinted at in "The PRIORESS' TALE" when she refers to the Jews who murdered the little Christian boy as "new Herods," pointing to their antagonism toward Christianity (line 574). (*See also* JEWS, CHAUCER'S PORTRAYAL OF.)

Heroides   See OVID.

Herry Bailly   See BAILLY, HARRY.

Herse   In classical mythology, Herse was one of three sisters to whom Athena (PALLAS) gave a chest containing the infant Erichthonius with orders not to open it. When they disobeyed and opened the chest anyway, Erichthonius appeared to be a serpent, causing them to go mad and hurl themselves down from the Acropolis. Herse captured the attention of Hermes (MERCURY), who tried to convince her sister, AGLAUROS, to help him woo her. Aglauros asked Hermes for gold as payment, an act which further angered Athena, who was already mad because of her earlier disobedience. As punishment, Athena filled Aglauros with envy, so that she tried to prevent Hermes from going in to Herse. He retaliated by turning her into a rock. When Herse and Hermes finally got together, they produced a son named Cephalus. Herse is mentioned in book three of *TROILUS AND CRISEYDE* when the lovesick TROILUS prays to Mercury to give him the courage to enter CRISEYDE's bedroom. He calls upon the god in the name of his love for Herse.

Herynes   See ERINYES.

Hesperus   In classical mythology, Hesperus was the evening star, king of the western land, and, according to one version, father of the Hesperides who guarded the golden apples presented by Gaea, or Mother Earth, to Hera (JUNO), the queen of the gods, as a wedding present. Chaucer uses this name when he describes the movements of the evening star in the *BOECE*, his translation into Middle English of BOETHIUS' *Consolation of Philosophy*.

Hester   See ESTHER.

Hezekiah   In the Old Testament Hezekiah was the 13th king of Judah. His story is recorded in the Book of Isaiah. Hezekiah's father had allowed the kingdom to indulge in the worship of pagan gods and idols, but when Hezekiah inherited the throne he initiated reforms designed to do away with these practices. One of his first actions was to reopen the Temple, ordering the priests and Levites to sanctify themselves for service and to cleanse the Temple. Hezekiah's reformation reached beyond Jerusalem to include the cleansing of the entire land through the destruction of pagan temples, altars and images. Hezekiah is also remembered for his successful rebellion against Sennacherib, an Assyrian king who was trying to consolidate Jerusalem within the boundaries of his kingdom. Hezekiah's words to God, "I wol remembre me alle the yeres of my lif in bitternesse of myn herte" [I will remember all the years of my life with bitterness in my heart] are recorded twice in Chaucer's "PARSON'S TALE" (lines 135 and 983), where "bitterness of heart" (extreme and heartfelt sorrow) is described as one of the conditions that must be met for confession of one's sins to be effective.

Hierse   See HERSE.

Hippocrates   A physician in ancient Greece, Hippocrates is traditionally regarded as the father of medicine. Very little trustworthy information about the life of Hippocrates exists, but he appears to have traveled widely in Greece and Asia Minor practicing his art and teaching pupils, and he presumably taught at the medical school on his native island of Cos quite frequently. From shortly after the fifth century B.C., when he supposedly lived and practiced, Hippocrates' works, and some of those erroneously attributed to him, came to be considered authoritative medical texts and were stored in the great library at Alexandria, where they were edited and copied. Hippocrates is mentioned in the GENERAL PROLOGUE to *The CANTERBURY TALES* as one of the medical authorities whose teachings the DOCTOR OF PHYSIC had studied. In *The BOOK OF THE DUCHESS* the BLACK KNIGHT's grief cannot be cured, even by a healer like Hippocrates.

Hippolyta (Ipolita)   Queen of the AMAZONS and wife to Duke THESEUS of ATHENS in "The KNIGHT'S TALE." For one with such an illustrious mythological past, Hippolyta does not play a very large role in this tale. Her most consequential act is to convince Theseus not to kill ARCITE (1) and PALAMON when he encounters them fighting in the countryside near Athens. Behaving in such a way, Hippolyta illustrates the softening influence of the feminine temperament on the male aggression of the king. This ability to inspire mercy was an important feature of the feminine ethos in the Middle Ages and represents one reason why the Virgin Mary and her intercessions on behalf of humankind became an important addition to the Christian pantheon. Aside from that, she functions primarily as a companion to EMILY, Theseus' sister and the heroine of this chivalric romance. Her political heritage as queen of a race of women who refused to accept the yoke of marriage and servitude to men serves to enhance the reputation of Theseus, who was able to defeat her in battle and subsequently persuade her to be his wife. In Chaucer's main source for this tale, BOCCACCIO'S TESEIDA, Hippolyta and her troops repent of their former ways before their suppressed "feminine" qualities reemerge. Chaucer omits this information from his version of the story.

Hippomedon   In classical mythology, Hippomedon was the son of Aristomachus and one of the SEVEN AGAINST THEBES who fought with POLYNICES in his attempt to take the throne of THEBES back from his brother ETEOCLES. He is mentioned in the unfinished poem ANELIDA AND ARCITE and in book five of TROILUS AND CRISEYDE as one of the heroes who lost their lives on the tragic expedition against Thebes.

Hoccleve, Thomas (?1369–1426)   One of the most significant English poets of the 15th century. Hoccleve was employed as a scribe in the office of the Privy Seal, and a substantial part of his writings tells the story of his life and work, with particular focus on events leading up to a mental breakdown and his subsequent recovery from that illness, which he believes to have been caused by too much study. Works dealing with this topic are "La Male Regle de Thomas Hoccleve" ("The Mis-Rule of Thomas Hoccleve") and two shorter poems, "The Complaint" and "The Dialogue with a Friend." Traditionally, Hoccleve has been regarded a substandard imitator of Chaucer, but an examination of his work on its own merits suggests otherwise. Chaucer's use of himself as a narrator in his poetry and the self-referential remarks he makes may well have influenced Hoccleve's decision to write autobiographically, but Hoccleve's autobiographical work is much more intensely personal than Chaucer's. Although he was some 20 years younger than Chaucer, Hoccleve seems to have known him and had his picture set in manuscripts of his moral work, *The Regement of Princes,* along with a tribute of praise to the man he recognized as his master. He offers the portrait with the explanation that it is included for the benefit of those readers who do not know, or remember, what the poet looked like. (The manuscript was printed in the early 1410s; Chaucer died around 1400.) Because Hoccleve knew Chaucer, and because the manuscript with Chaucer's portrait would have been seen by others who did remember what the poet looked like, it is considered one of the most authoritative portraits of him.

Hoccleve Portrait   *See* HOCCLEVE, THOMAS.

Hogge   The name Hogge, or Hodge, was in Middle English the diminutive of "Roger," which is the name Chaucer gives to the COOK, one of the pilgrims who participates (or in his case, tries to participate) in the tale-telling contest that provides the framework for *The CANTERBURY TALES.* In the prologue to "The COOK'S TALE," Roger refers to himself as "Hogge of Ware" (line 4336), the latter denoting a town in Hertfordshire, some 30 miles from London, probably the Cook's birthplace. The idea that the Cook's portrait was inspired by a real person has led scholars to look for evidence of the same. Edith RICKERT discovered a contemporary of Chaucer's named Roger Knight de Ware of London, who was a cook by profession and who may have been a petty criminal if he is the same Roger de Ware, Cook, who is on record for breaking curfew.

Holdernesse   A marshy peninsula and grain-growing district east of HULL, in the county of YORKSHIRE. It is the setting for "The SUMMONER'S TALE," about a corrupt friar who manipulates people into giving him money by convincing them that it is going toward a good purpose. John MANLY believed that a jurisdictional dispute (an argument over who had the rights to serve the people in a particular geographical area) between the friars at Beverley (the principal town of the district) and the clergy of the cathedral led Chaucer to choose this location as the setting for this tale, in which the question of which members of the clergy should receive THOMAS' (1) tithe is debated.

Holofernes   According to the apocryphal Book of Judith, Holofernes was a general serving under NEBUCHADNEZZAR, king of the Babylonian Empire from 605 to 562 B.C. The story of his decapitation by JUDITH is related in "The MONK'S TALE" (lines 2551–30). (The entry for Judith notes each occasion the story is referred to in Chaucer's work.)

Homer   The supposed author of two early Greek epics, the *Odyssey* and the *Iliad.* Nothing is known for certain of Homer's birth or life, aside from the fact that he was writing (or perhaps compiling, pulling together earlier works) in the eighth century B.C. In the 14th century, Homer's works had not yet been translated out of Greek and into a language that Chaucer could read; thus, they were primarily known to him and to other western readers through descriptions (such as those in BOETHIUS' *Consolation of Philosophy,* which Chaucer translated) and small excerpts. Nevertheless, evidence from Chaucer's work suggests that he knew Homer's reputation among the ancients and was aware of the subject matter of at least one of his epic poems. In Chaucer's early work, *The HOUSE OF FAME,* Homer's likeness adorns the approach to FAME's throne. Standing upon a pillar of iron (a metal associated with MARS, the god of war), he is one of those poets upon whose shoulders rests the fame of the great legend of TROY and the TROJAN WAR. Later, at the beginning of *TROILUS AND CRISEYDE* where Chaucer introduces his subject, he notes that this same war will serve as a backdrop to the love story he is about to tell. For readers who want to read more about the battles and other martial events, he directs them to turn to Homer, or to DARES and DICTYS. These allusions to Homer's work point to the *Illiad*, which tells the story of the Trojan War from the Greek perspective. In "The MERCHANT'S TALE," there appears a reference to the faithfulness of PENELOPE, Odysseus' (ULYSSES) wife in the *Odyssey*, which suggests that Chaucer also knew of this work's existence.

Horaste In *TROILUS AND CRISEYDE*, a man with whom Pandarus accuses CRISEYDE of being in love. The purely fictitious accusation is made with the intention of justifying TROILUS' great misery and encouraging Criseyde to have pity on him. Criseyde had previously agreed to allow Troilus to woo her, but appeared unwilling to let their relationship progress any further. Pandarus, although he is Criseyde's uncle, has sworn to help his friend Troilus, and will use many varieties of trickery and deceit to weaken his niece's resolve to remain a chaste widow. The name Horaste does not appear in Chaucer's source, BOCCACCIO's *FILOSTRATO*. In "Some Observations on the Language of Chaucer's *Troilus*" (*Proceedings of Chaucer Society*, 1894) G. L. KITTREDGE suggests that he took his inspiration from a name made famous by Greek tragedy, Orestes, which was spelled *Horrestes* in GUIDO DELLE COLONNE's work.

Horeb Mount Horeb, called the "mountain of God" in the biblical Book of Exodus, is where the prophet MOSES heard God speaking in a burning bush and also where he received the Ten Commandments. It is also where the prophet ELIJAH went when he would speak with God. Both Elijah's experience and Moses' are alluded to in "The SUMMONER'S TALE" when the friar who is trying to bilk poor sick THOMAS (1) out of some money suggests that he, like the two prophets, lives a life of denial, dedicated to God's service, which in turn makes God more ready to respond to his prayers. The tale also mentions the mountain's other name, Sinai.

Horne Child An English metrical romance of the early 14th century. Like "The TALE OF SIR THOPAS," in which it is mentioned, *Horne Child* is written in TAIL-RHYME. The story tells of Prince Horn, who flees from his homeland in the north of England, accompanied by his tutor and some friends. He falls in love with Rimnild, the daughter of a southern king, and when her father discovers their romance, Horn again must take flight, this time into Wales and then Ireland. Ultimately he

returns to England, takes revenge on the people who betrayed him and marries Rimnild.

Host, the *See* BAILLY, HARRY.

House of Daedalus *See* DAEDALUS.

House of Fame, The This early dream-vision poem dealing with the theme of fame, or reputation, draws upon VIRGIL's *AENEID* and DANTE ALIGHIERI's *Divina Commedia*, and uniquely blends serious and comic themes.

SUMMARY

The Proem or prologue of *The House of Fame* begins with a discussion of the various types, causes and effects of dreams as they were known to medieval readers. The narrator admits that the scantness of his own knowledge prevents him from commenting further, and this general introduction of the subject concludes with the announcement of the narrator's intention to describe a particularly remarkable dream that he had on the 10th day of December. The Invocation, which follows, first addresses MORPHEUS, the god of sleep (and of dreams), asking him to assist the narrator in his attempts to describe the aforementioned dream. A second prayer is addressed to "he that mover ys of al" (i.e., the Christian God), asking his blessing on those who listen to the narrator's words, but cursing those who scorn to listen or who misjudge his work.

The Story begins by describing how the narrator fell asleep and began to dream that he was inside a temple made of glass, dedicated to the goddess VENUS. Inside the temple he finds many golden statues adorned with jewels and sitting on pedestals. In addition, the walls of the temple are decorated with paintings representing the goddess of love; her blind son, CUPID; and her husband, VULCAN. On one wall, inscribed on a tablet of brass he finds the first words of VIRGIL's *Aeneid*, translated into Middle English: "I wol now synge, yif I kan, / The armes and also the man / That first cam, thurgh his destinee, / Fugityf of Troy contree, / In Itayle, with full moche pyne / Unto the strondes of Lavyne" (lines 143–48). This inscription is followed by a series of engravings or paintings that depict the story of AENEAS' escape from TROY during its destruction by the Greeks. He mentions the betrayal of the Greek Synon, who convinced the Trojans to accept their gift of the Trojan horse; the deaths of PRIAM and Polytes; and the tragic loss of Aeneas' father, wife and two sons.

Chaucer's version of these events is very similar to that found in book one of the *Aeneid*, except that Chaucer augments the role played by the goddess Venus, who was Aeneas' mother, in saving his life. JUNO, the wife of JUPITER and traditionally a despiser of the Trojan nation, does not want Aeneas to escape and sends a storm to endanger his ship. He does manage to land safely, though, in CARTHAGE, on the northern coast of Africa. DIDO, the queen of that city, falls in love with him almost immediately. Aeneas takes advantage of the opportunities provided by her affection, and pretends to requite her passion, but readily deserts her when MERCURY, relaying a message from Jupiter, advises him to sail for Italy.

A large part of the poem is at this point devoted to a lament uttered by Dido when she finds herself abandoned by her lover. She bemoans his false promises, and thus a relationship between book one and the rest of *The House of Fame* is established by introducing the theme of reputation. Her own reputation, Dido believes, has been destroyed by her behavior toward Aeneas and by his subsequent betrayal. The queen's perception that her honor has been destroyed, combined with her longing for Aeneas, leads to her suicide. The conclusion of her story is followed by a catalogue of other women who were betrayed by their lovers, including PHYLLIS (betrayed by DEMOPHON), BRESEYDA (by ARCHILLES), OENONE (by PARIS), HYPSIPYLE (by JASON), MEDEA (also by Jason), DEIANIRA (by Hercules) and ARIADNE (by THESEUS).

Following this digression, the narrator returns to the adventures of Aeneas to mention his storm-tossed voyage, his journey into Hades to visit his father, Anchises, and finally, a brief summary of his arrival in Italy, where he established himself and married LAVINIA, the daughter of King LATINUS. Applauding the happy conclusion of Aeneas' story, the narrator returns to a consideration of his surroundings, wondering who made the marvelous temple and what country it is in. Hoping to discover some answer to these questions, he locates a door and goes outside, where he finds himself in a large field of sand which reminds him of the Libyan desert. Nonplussed by his surroundings, fearing that he may be having a hallucination, he prays to Christ to come to his aid. At the same time he becomes aware of a huge EAGLE soaring in the sky above him. The eagle begins to descend, and book one ends on a note of suspense.

Book two opens with another Proem, in which the narrator asks for the assistance of Cipris (Venus) in putting his dream, the product of his mind, down in writing. The dream narrative resumes with a description of the eagle's swift swoop to the earth, where it seizes the narrator in its talons and carries him aloft into the sky. Astonished and frightened, the narrator loses consciousness but is awakened when the eagle speaks to him in a human voice, commanding him to wake up. When he does, the eagle tells him not to be afraid, that the experience he is having has been sent for his benefit. Initially unable to accept the bird's reassurance, he wonders if he is going to die, or if, perhaps, Jove (the name Chaucer sometimes uses for Jupiter)

intends to "stellify" him, turning him into a constellation. The eagle, reading his mind, denies that he is to suffer such a fate and explains that Jove has arranged this adventure for the narrator to reward him for his long-suffering service to Venus and CUPID, the gods of love. Jove has taken particular pity on him because, despite his own lack of success in love's endeavors, he has continued to compose books, songs and ditties in honor of Love and his servants. The narrator has also aroused the god's pity by his isolation from society, the result of his preference for staying home and reading rather than going out to seek company and recreation. These explanations poke fun at the narrator by characterizing him as someone of small wit who sits reading "dumb as any stone" until his mind is dazed.

To reward him for his devotion and enable him to have some experience other than that provided by books, the narrator will be transported to a place called the House of Fame, where he will hear news of love in all its varied manifestations. When the narrator expresses skepticism regarding FAME's ability to gather such information by way of gossip or spies, the eagle embarks upon a lengthy explanation of how these tidings of love are transmitted to their destination. The House of Fame, he explains, is situated between heaven, the earth and the sea, so that whatever is spoken in any of these three places travels by Natural Inclination, a kind of medieval homing instinct, until it reaches the House. Next, addressing his listener as "GEFFREY," the eagle explains various medieval theories of sound, its characterization as broken air and its trajectory resembling that of ripples in water, traveling away from their source. At the conclusion of this explanation the eagle directs the narrator's attention to the manner in which these difficult concepts have been explained, employing simple language rather than making use of specialized, obscure terms or elaborate rhetorical devices. The narrator agrees that difficult ideas are best expressed in straightforward language. The eagle then promises that, before nightfall, the authority of what he has been describing will be confirmed by the narrator's experience.

They continue to sail above the earth, and now the eagle directs the narrator's attention to the scene below them, suggesting that if the narrator will name a place he recognizes, the eagle will be able to tell him how far away he now is from that place. When the narrator looks down he sees valleys, fields, rivers, towns and other features of the terrestrial landscape, but before long the earth is the size of a pinpoint and he can recognize nothing. The eagle next directs his gaze upward into the air where he observes various spirits of the air and the Milky Way, which was created by PHAETON when he stole his father APOLLO's chariot and drove the sun so recklessly that he burned both the earth and the air.

Now the eagle has flown so high that when the narrator looks down he sees clouds, mists, wind and storms. Amazed at such a sight, he praises the might and nobility of God and also thinks about BOETHIUS, who wrote that a thought may fly higher than a cloud. His mind travels further and further along this philosophical tangent until the eagle interrupts, asking if he would like to learn about the stars. The narrator answers no, saying that he is too old; furthermore, that is one subject he may just as easily read about in books written by those who are experts on the topic. In sum, he wishes to avoid directly probing the secrets of the stars, because if he were to look at them from this proximity, their brightness would destroy his eyesight. The eagle agrees that this may be true.

As they begin their final approach toward the House of Fame, the eagle directs the narrator's attention to the sounds issuing from it which to the narrator's ears seem like the beating of the sea against hollow rocks or the rumbling that thunder makes after its initial booming sound. He is frightened by the sound, but the eagle tells him not to worry: it will not bite him.

When they arrive, the eagle sets him down in a street and directs him to go and find the adventure that awaits him. Before following this directive, the narrator seeks some reassurance that the voices he hears have come here as the eagle described, and that there are no persons living in the house and making all this noise. The eagle confirms the accuracy of his previous description, but then goes on to inform the narrator that when speech enters the House of Fame it assumes the likeness of the person by whom it was spoken, so that it does appear to be a living person. With that, the eagle bids the narrator farewell, asking God's blessing upon him and promising to wait for him. Book two comes to a close.

At the beginning of book three, the narrator requests the assistance of Apollo, the god of "science and lyght." His main concern here, he explains, is not to show mastery of the art of poetry, but to accurately translate the experience of his dream into language.

"Geffrey" resumes his narration of the dream, describing the rock of ice upon which Fame's house is situated and noting that such a perch is a feeble foundation upon which to build and unlikely to bring glory to its builder. Drawing closer he observes that the ice is engraved with the names of famous people. Because it is melting, however, he finds it difficult to decipher them, which leads him to reflect on the saying, "What may ever laste?" The melting, he soon discovers, is caused by the heat of the sun. When he walks around to the north side of the ice, he finds that the names carved there, protected by the shade of the palace above, are still fresh and easy to read. These names belong to famous people who lived long ago, yet they are as fresh as if they had just been carved. Climbing to

the top of the hill, he reaches the House of Fame, which he pronounces a marvelous castle. After initially announcing his inability to describe it, he proceeds to do exactly that, saying that it is constructed entirely of beryl, adorned with gargoyles, pinnacles and numerous windows. The outer walls have many niches where minstrels and other storytellers stand. ORPHEUS is there with Orion (ARIAN) and the Centaur CHIRON, along with a famous Welsh bard named GLASCURION. These are chief among what appears to the narrator as a great crowd of storytellers and song-makers ("many thousand times twelve"), who have come bearing their instruments.

The musicians are followed by a group whose members attempt to manipulate Fame through the use or simulation of supernatural powers. They include witches, wizards, enchanters and sleight-of-hand artists. Among their ranks the narrator observes Medea, CIRCE, CALYPSO and SIMON MAGUS. Weary of describing people, he turns his attention back to the palace itself, musing upon its walls made of beryl and the way that they mirror and magnify everything that passes before them. He approaches the castle gate, which also seems to reflect the operations of Fame, built as much by hazard as it is by careful planning. Once inside the gate he encounters a press of people, some of them crowned like kings, who clamor for gifts to be bestowed by any who have come seeking reputation. Beyond them he spies a group of heralds and pursuivants (heralds' assistants), of whom there are so many, he says, that he could never describe them all.

The walls, floor and roof inside the palace are plated with gold a foot thick and richly adorned with precious jewels. The goddess Fame sits in a ruby throne mounted on a high dais or platform. Although she is feminine, she was not formed by Nature, the narrator states, having never before seen anything like her. At first glance, she appears smaller than the length of a cubit (the distance from the elbow to the top of the middle finger); but immediately after this, her body seems to extend from the earth into heaven. Her body is covered with eyes, ears and tongues, and on her feet grow partridges' wings. Like the walls of her palace, she is adorned with gold and jewels and surrounded by the melodious singing of the nine Muses. On her shoulders, Fame bears the arms and the names of Hercules and Alexander, who both have exalted reputations.

The approach to the goddess is lined on either side with pillars made of different kinds of metal. On top of each pillar stands a famous poet or storyteller who immortalized the deeds of famous people. Here the narrator finds Josephus the Hebrew, who wrote *The History of the Jews;* Statius, who chronicled the siege and fall of Thebes; HOMER, the Greek poet; DARES and DICTYS, who wrote of the TROJAN WAR; and others, including LOLLIUS, a supposed authority on the Trojan War whom Chaucer appears to have invented. The classical Roman poets Virgil and OVID also appear in this gallery of famous poets. The narrator's observations are interrupted by the influx of a great crowd of those who have come to petition Fame for various favors. She is approached by nine groups in all, and her response to the petitioners exhibits nothing so much as the capricious or arbitrary nature of fame and its acquisition. Some who ask for a good reputation based on their good deeds, she denies; others who ask for the same are granted their desire. Some who seek for good reputation are given a foul one, while others, who have lived wicked lives, are granted good fame. The same goes for two groups of idlers: one she rewards; the other she chastises for wasting their lives. Finally a group that asks for no fame, claiming to have performed good works for their own sake, is denied its request, while another has that same request granted.

The effects of Fame's decisions are made concrete with the assistance of EOLUS, the god of wind, who blows one of his two trumpets at the announcement of each verdict, unless the verdict is one of no fame. If a petitioner is granted good fame, Eolus blows his trumpet called "Clere Laude" (i.e., perfect praise); if the petitioner receives a verdict of ill fame, Eolus blows the trumpet called Sklaundre (slander). When each trumpet is blown both the sound that issues from it and the wind, either sweet or foul smelling, travel throughout the world.

In the midst of these observations, the narrator is approached by someone who inquires his name, asking whether he has come there to acquire fame. He answers in the negative, claiming that he would rather keep his experience and his thoughts to himself. When the being, which itself must be an embodied sound if the eagle's words hold true, persists in asking what he is doing there at Fame's house, the narrator replies that he has come to hear some new tidings, to gather some new material regarding love or other pleasing things, and reiterates the eagle's promise that he would hear tidings of that nature, a promise that has heretofore been unfulfilled. Hearing this, the being offers to guide him to another place where he will be able to hear the kind of tidings he originally wanted to. Leaving the castle, the narrator looks down into a valley, where he sees a marvelous house made of variously colored twigs woven together to resemble some kind of huge basket. It does not stand still but whirls about at a dizzying pace, making a variety of creaking and squeaking noises. It has many entrances, allowing sounds to travel in and out, and it is constantly filled with whispering and gossip concerning wars, peace, marriages, rest, labor, voyages, death, life, love, hate, accord, strife, praise, learning, success, building, health, sickness, fair weather, storms, famine, plenty, good or bad government, fire and various acci-

dents and so on. The house, which is shaped like a cage, is 60 miles long and, despite the fragile material of which it is constructed, built to last. Spying the eagle perched nearby, the narrator asks permission to see inside this House of Rumor, where he may perhaps learn something of interest. The eagle readily grants his request and flies him in through a window. Once inside, he finds himself unable to perceive the whirling motion that he observed from outside. The house is extremely crowded with what appear to be people exchanging new tidings, some speaking in a whisper, some loudly. Listening to their speech, the narrator discovers that the rumors increase in size as they are passed along. Some of the tidings fly up and out of the windows, heading for the House of Fame, where they hope to achieve more permanent status. Sometimes a true tiding and a false one try to fly out at the same time and are united forever.

Among the beings in the House of Rumor, the narrator observes shipmen, pilgrims, pardoners and couriers, all of whom, because they travel from place to place, serve as a source of news. As he rushes about gathering information, the narrator's attention is diverted to a corner of the hall where men speak of love tidings. A great noise issues from that direction and all of the other occupants of the hall begin to rush toward it, climbing on top of each other and shouting, "What thing is that?" At last he observes a man approaching. He cannot name the man but says that he appears to be one of great authority, and here the poem breaks off, evidently unfinished.

COMMENTARY

Like *The BOOK OF THE DUCHESS* and *The PARLIAMENT OF FOWLS*, both of which were also written early in Chaucer's literary career, *The House of Fame* is a DREAM VISION. It additionally incorporates the literary pattern of the allegorical journey, which was a popular feature of medieval poetry in the centuries leading up to Chaucer's. Chaucer's narrator himself alludes to "Marcian" (the work of MARTIANUS CAPELLA) and "Anteclaudian" (ALAIN DE LILLE's *Anticlaudianus*) as previous models of such heavenward journeys, and as he looks down upon the earth from the vantage point provided by the eagle's flight, his perception of the Earth as a "prikke" or pinpoint recalls CICERO's *Somnium Scipionis*, which also employs a dream vision as the vehicle for a journey up through the heavenly spheres. DANTE's *Divine Comedy* is the most famous example of the combination of these two features, and the eagle that transports the narrator from the Temple of Love to the House of Fame almost certainly derives from the eagle that carries Dante aloft in the *Purgatorio*, book nine. The primary and most obvious difference between these analogues and Chaucer's text is in tone, which in the analogues inclines to be philosophical and serious, while Chaucer's is philosophically comical. This is not to say that Chaucer's poem is an attempt to satirize or parody the other texts. It may simply be a lighthearted look at some of the same issues raised by those texts, a kind of mock-heroic focus on the temporal and the trivial in contrast to the lofty and eternal, a humorous look at what might actually be the concerns and preoccupations of a man less heroic than Dante who finds himself in the midst of a similar adventure.

Yet, in spite of its obvious relationship to other texts that were well known among intellectuals in Chaucer's time, *The House of Fame* is, at least for a modern reader, Chaucer's most puzzling work, and not only because it appears to be unfinished. Scholars wrestling with interpretation of the poem have suggested that its chief concerns are 1) defining the way that poetry is created, and 2) examining the operations of the capricious goddess Fame. The poem is divided into three parts called books. Each book, after a brief prologue, narrates a portion of a single dream. The dream itself and the journey the narrator takes within the dream provide the poem with its structural unity. Thematic unity is more difficult to discern, primarily because the theme of fame, introduced in book one, is abandoned, or at least suspended throughout book two, and not picked up again until book three. Furthermore, there appears to be some discrepancy between what the narrator is promised he will derive from the dream, the "tidings of love" mentioned by the eagle, and what he actually hears and sees, which has little to do with love, even when it appears in Love's temple. The story of Dido and Aeneas that is inscribed on the temple walls in book one does describe their love affair, but it focuses on Aeneas' abandonment of Dido, something Aeneas does in order to achieve more personal fame, an action that in turn deprives Dido of her reputation. At this point, the narrator does not realize that the dream has been sent to give him material to write about; but if his primary interest is in tidings of love, it would seem that his exit from the TEMPLE OF VENUS is somewhat premature.

The transition from the Temple of Venus to the House of Fame forms the subject matter of book two. This is where the fantastical heavenward journey, complete with its references to medieval science and its philosophical meditations, drives the focus of the narrative away from the theme of fame. Book two also addresses the issue of literary authority, which some scholars view as the central concern of the poem as a whole. After informing the narrator that the adventure he is having has been sent by Jove to reward him for his previously unrewarded service to the god of love (service that primarily took the form of writing love poetry), the eagle goes on to say that the purpose of the experience is to distract the narrator from his present worries and to provide him with new material to write about. The eagle's criticism of the narrator's preference for spending his free time reading rather than socializing hints that his previous writing has depended too heavily on knowledge acquired from books, and that it needs to be tempered by knowledge that comes from experience. The value of experiential proof is illustrated by the eagle's promise that everything he has told the narrator about the nature of speech and the manner in which it travels through the air to Fame's palace will be demonstrated by what the narrator observes once he arrives at his destination. The narrator does not dispute this suggestion, nor does he wish to avoid the impending adventure, but when the eagle offers to show him the stellar constellations so that he will be able to confirm what he has read about them in books, the narrator declines this opportunity, claiming that he does not require such proof, believing what he has read about them just as firmly as if he had seen it with his own eyes.

Book two closes with their arrival outside Fame's palace and the narrative thread is picked up when "Geffrey," as the eagle has called him, begins to describe the inhabitants of, and visitors to, the palace. Its permanent residents are the goddess Fame and a gallery of embodied sounds uttered by those who have contributed to the fame of others. Once he has entered the palace, the narrator observes the approach of various groups of petitioners who have come to ask the goddess Fame to grant them, variously, good fame, bad fame or no fame. The thematic focus of this book resides in the capricious quality of her responses, which have nothing to do with merit or desert. To an alert and rational observer, such a phenomenon would seem to empirically ratify the importance of firsthand observation, particularly coupled with the narrator's experience in the House of Rumor, where he sees further evidence of the way information is distorted as it passes from one individual to another. This lesson, however, appears to be lost on him as he, like everyone else in rumor's house, eagerly directs his attention to the approaching "man of great authority." The poem breaks off, leaving us with a sense of suspended resolution, but there does exist a superb irony in the fact that despite the narrator's conscious preference for authoritative *texts* over new and potentially challenging *experiences*, he nevertheless ends up writing about an experience—a dream that he has had. The final irony resides in how thoroughly the dream itself is derived from authoritative texts which it simultaneously subverts by way of its mock-heroic tone.

The reference to Chaucer by his first name in this poem, and the poet's use of a similar narrative persona in *The Book of the Duchess, The Parliament of Fowls* and the prologue to *The LEGEND OF GOOD WOMEN*, and in the introductions to "The TALE OF SIR THOPAS" and "The

TALE OF MELIBEE," has led scholars to speculate about the degree to which this (muddle-headed, pudgy, unlucky-in-love) persona corresponds to Chaucer the man. While most reputable full-length portraits (those featured in the ELLESMERE MANUSCRIPT and an early manuscript of HOCCLEVE's *Regement of Princes*) do suggest a certain portliness, the quality of his poetry and his successful professional life seem proof enough that he was not muddle-headed. As for his romantic life, nothing exists which might shed light on his relationship with his wife or other lovers.

For Further Reading: The most thorough discussion of *The House of Fame* is still J. A. W. BENNETT's book, *Chaucer's "Book of Fame": An Exposition of the House of Fame* (1968), which explicates the poem through identification of the allusions, imagery and echoes of earlier texts, such as Virgil's *Aeneid*. Bennett argues that the narrator's search for new poetic material is perhaps resolved when he enters the House of Rumor and encounters the "ceaseless movement and miscellanity of the ordinary life," which became the subject matter of Chaucer's later poetry. In *Chaucer and the Imaginary World of Fame* (1984), Piero BOITANI offers an interesting consideration of the poem in another context, that of the Western idea of fame, examining how that idea was expressed in various ancient and medieval texts. Boitani's analysis shows how Chaucer's poem borrows many images from this literary tradition. Readers who are puzzled by the poem's ending should read Donald Fry's "The Ending of the *House of Fame*" (in *Chaucer at Albany,* 1975), which argues that Chaucer ended the poem with the enigmatic "man of great authority" as a way to poke fun at various forms of traditionalism, especially literary forms.

House of Rumor The House of Rumor is a strange architectural construction that appears in Chaucer's early poem *The HOUSE OF FAME*. The counterpart to the beautiful and stately palace of FAME, the House of Rumor appears to be made out of yellow, red, green and white twigs all woven together in a fantastic manner to form a cage that is 60 miles long. It has as many entrances as a tree has leaves in summer and a thousand holes in the roof to release the sounds that come from within. The house does not stand still but whirls about as swift as thought, creaking, sighing and groaning, while a cacophony of voices issues from inside, voices ranging in sound from a whisper to a shout, all speaking at once on various subjects of gossip such as wars, marriages, work, deaths, love affairs, arguments, changes in government, etc. This description is to some small extent indebted to OVID's account of Fame's dwelling in his *Metamorphoses,* but there is no precedent in classical literature for a whirling house of twigs. Whirling houses were, however, fairly common in romance literature and in folktale. On a more realistic

note, it is unfortunately true that wicker was sometimes the only building material available to peasants, and Chaucer may have been drawing on experience as well as literature for his description of this nightmarish dwelling.

Howard, Donald R(oy) (1927–) American Chaucer scholar. During a career that included a Ph.D. from the University of Florida and led to Stanford, Howard edited *The Canterbury Tales: A Selection* (1969) and composed a variety of critical articles and books on Chaucer's poetry, including several essays focusing on TROILUS AND CRISEYDE. In his most important book, *The Idea of the "Canterbury Tales"* (1976), Howard suggests that Chaucer was the first literary artist who felt that a book could "present us with an idea of the world against which to measure our idea of ourselves, and so teach us who we are." Howard believes that the work is unfinished, not because it fails to follow the Host's plan, or because Chaucer died before he could finish it, but because the poet created a literary idea whose possibilities were inexhaustible. Howard also composed one of the most recent—and readable—Chaucer biographies, *Chaucer: His Life, His Works, His World* (1987). In the opening of this book, he notes the following peculiarity: Nowhere in the many records of Geoffrey Chaucer as a public and court figure does there exist any indication that this Geoffrey Chaucer is the same one who became famous even during his own lifetime as a poet, writer, translator and scholar.

Huberd *Huberd* is the name Chaucer gives to the FRIAR who appears in the GENERAL PROLOGUE TO *THE CANTERBURY TALES*. He is the only pilgrim other than the PRIORESS whose personal name is given in the prologue. *Huberd* was not a common name for an English friar in the 14th century, so the name has aroused some speculation as to Chaucer's reasons for choosing it. Muriel BOWDEN suggests that the description of the friar was based on that of a real person, a friar actually named Huberd (or Hubert, a variation of the name). Charles MUSCATINE argues that it derives from *Hubert,* the name of the kite in a French beast epic, the *Roman de Renart.* The latter was obviously known to Chaucer, as he drew upon it as a source for his "NUN'S PRIEST'S TALE," concerning a rooster named CHAUNTICLEER who is outwitted and nearly eaten by a fox named RUSSELL.

Hugelyn of Pyze *See* UGOLINO OF PISA.

Hugh of Lincoln Hugh of Lincoln was a child who was supposed to have been crucified by a Jew named Copin or Joppin in the English city of Lincoln in the year 1255, after having been starved and tortured. The body is said to have been discovered in a well where the murderer had stowed it after the boy died. It was reputed to have caused several miracles. The Jews who were accused of involvement in the murder were executed. The story was a popular theme in medieval poetry, and Chaucer draws upon it for "The PRIORESS' TALE" (in The CANTERBURY TALES), which also tells the story of a little Christian boy murdered by Jews. Chaucer's debt to the legend of Hugh is alluded to at the end of the tale, where the fate of the child in the PRIORESS' story is compared to that of the martyr of Lincoln.

Hull (Hulle)   A town officially known as Kingston-upon-Hull, on the River Humber in northeastern England in what was formerly part of the county of Yorkshire. It is mentioned in the portrait of the SHIPMAN that appears in the GENERAL PROLOGUE TO THE CANTERBURY TALES. In attempting to impart some idea of how superlative the Shipman's knowledge of ships and navigation is, Chaucer says there was not another like him to be found between Hull and CARTHAGE, the latter city having been located on the northern coast of Africa.

humanism   What we typically think of as "humanism" was the philosophical movement that accompanied the Italian Renaissance, which was only just beginning at the end of the 14th century. It would not spread into England for another hundred or so years. Nevertheless, there were some remarkable changes in the society and culture of medieval man that began in the 12th century with the sudden growth of towns, the founding of universities, and the expansion of trade. The latter, along with the Crusades, brought western European countries into contact with the learning and literature of faraway lands. People began to be interested once again in the disciplines of science and philosophy. Paper was introduced late in the 12th century, a development that made books more readily available and more affordable (in the past they had to be written on parchment, which was made of dried animal skin). All of these changes evinced a growing interest in the affairs of the world and a broadening of consciousness regarding the boundaries of what was considered "the world." With the benefits of better health, possibly the result of better nutrition, people began to be less focused on the hereafter and more focused on the here and now. As a result, a belief in the dignity of human nature began to take root, a belief that expressed itself in human determination to understand the laws of nature and to understand humanity's place in the universal order. This new awareness replaced a previous attitude which saw life as a mere trial to be endured on the way to heaven, and which scorned, or perhaps did not have leisure for, the delights of this world. In many ways, Chaucer's work represents a transitional view, reflecting a delight in the sights and sounds of the world and a desire to drink in all the knowledge, both from books and from experience, that was available to the poet, while at the same time revealing an awareness, albeit intermittently expressed, of the judgment that is to come after death. This fact is ironically most evident in Chaucer's most forward-looking work, The CANTERBURY TALES, which, although it elevates some of the most ribald stories of the age by casting them in poetry and inserting them within a social framework where they are enlarged by their surroundings, ends with a sermon, "The PARSON'S TALE," and a retraction (see CHAUCER'S RETRACTION) wherein the poet asks God's forgiveness for having written tales that "sownen into synne" (line 1085) [tend toward, or are conducive to sin].

humors   In the Middle Ages, an individual's body was thought to be composed of four "elements": earth, water, air and fire. These "elements" corresponded to four bodily fluids: blood, phlegm, yellow bile and black bile. The goal of medieval medicine was to keep these properties in balance, although it was believed that in each individual one humor tended to dominate. A sanguine person, whose humor was dominated by blood, would be ruddy in complexion, of good will and without malice, joyous and laughing, would enjoy a good digestion and be generous with both his possessions and his time. The FRANKLIN is an example of the sanguine personality. A phlegmatic person, like the CLERK, is slow-moving, thoughtful, serious and chaste. The choleric personality, evidencing an abundance of yellow bile, is thin, has a quick, hot temper and a strong libido ("is desirous of the company of women more than him needeth," according to the Secreta Secretorum, a medieval medical textbook). Chaucer's REEVE is described as a "sclendre, colerik man" (line 587 in the general prologue) [slender, choleric man]. The melancholic temperament, dominated by black bile, is thoughtful, deliberative, overly imaginative and somewhat sad or depressed. The MONK, who tells a series of tragedies for his tale, would seem to fit in this category. Not only did the humors influence a person's character, but they were also thought to be involved in the generation of disease when their balance was too greatly disturbed.

Hundred Years' War   A war between England and France that began in 1337 and did not conclude until 1453. The primary cause of the war was the longstanding conflict between the English and French Crowns over territory in France. At the beginning of the 14th century, English monarchs still held portions of two provinces in southwestern France, as vassals of the French Crown. The French kings resented the presence of a foreign power on their soil, despite the vassal (subordinate) status of the English. They also feared

The looting of a house during wartime. From British Library Ms. Royal 20 C VII f 41v. Reproduced by permission of the British Library.

that the English might make an alliance with FLANDERS against France because of English interest in the wool trade, which was centered in Flanders. As the dates show, the war actually covered more than a century, yet the fighting was by no means continuous. At the beginning, during the reign of EDWARD III, the English armies were generally victorious. They were better organized, better disciplined and better equipped than the French, who furthermore were divided by internal discord. Chaucer's brief military experience, when he accompanied Lionel, duke of Clarence, to fight in Burgundy and saw Edward III's first son, EDWARD THE BLACK PRINCE, gain fame as a soldier and leader of troops, was one of the campaigns of this war.

Huwe, Sir Sir Huwe is not a character, but rather a name that the FRIAR uses in his tale, along with the name Sir Robert, much as a modern writer would use the names "Tom, Dick or Harry." Speaking of the evil summoner who is the principle character in his tale, the Friar says, "He hadde eek wenches at his retenue, / That, wheither that sir Robert or sir Huwe, / Or Jakke, or Rauf, or whose that it were / That lay by hem, they tolde it in his ere" (lines 1355–58) [He also had women who were his followers, / Who, whether Sir Robert or Sir Hugh, / Or Jack, or Rafe, who whoever it was / That lay with them, they told it in his ear].

Hydra, the In classical mythology, the Hydra was a monster—a water serpent who inhabited the Lernaean marsh. It had nine heads, of which the middle one was immortal. When someone approached the Hydra in battle and succeeded in cutting off one of its heads, another one would immediately grow back. HERCULES, assisted by Iolaus, succeeded in killing it as one of his 12 labors. In the *BOECE,* LADY PHILOSOPHY uses the Hydra's ability to grow new heads as a metaphor when she explains how every time she dispels one of the narrator's doubts about the nature of the universe and the hidden causes of things, another will spring up to take its place.

Hymen In classical mythology, Hymen is the god of marriage and fruitfulness. He was thought to be the offspring of either VENUS and Dionysus or of Phoebus Apollo and one of the nine Muses. Hymen is mentioned several times in Chaucer's work, always in association with a marriage. In "The MERCHANT'S TALE," the narrator describes the happiness of the aged knight JANUARY on his wedding knight with great relish, adding that Hymen himself had never seen a merrier husband (line 1730). TROILUS, the hero of *TROILUS AND CRISEYDE,* addresses the god in one of his hymns praising love and giving thanks for his union with CRISEYDE which, ironically, is not sanctified by the bonds of marriage (book 3, line 1258). At the beginning of the story of PHILOMELA that appears in *The LEGEND OF GOOD WOMEN,* Chaucer notes that neither JUNO, the queen of the gods who also presided over marriage, nor Hymen, was present at PROCNE's wedding to TEREUS (line 2250). Later in the story, Tereus rapes Procne's sister, Philomela.

Hypermnestra   In classical mythology, Hypermnestra was one of the 50 daughters of DANAUS. She married her cousin Lynceus (Chaucer calls him "Lyno"), and was the only one of her father's daughters who did not murder her husband on their wedding night. Danaus had commanded all of his daughters to kill their spouses because of a prophecy that he would die at the hands of a son-in-law. When Hypermnestra helped her husband to escape, Danaus imprisoned his daughter for her disobedience, but the prophecy came true nevertheless, and Lynceus later killed Danaus. The story of Hypermnestra is the last to appear in Chaucer's unfinished *LEGEND OF GOOD WOMEN* (lines 2562–2723). It is faithful to the legend of the woman and her lover, except that Chaucer makes Hypermnestra the daughter of AEGYPTUS (the father of Lynceus), and refers to Lynceus as Danaus' son. As with the other women whose lives are described in the *Legend,* Hypermnestra is portrayed as a victim of the callous men in her life— not only her father, but also Lynceus who after she saved his life ran away without her, leaving her to face her father's anger alone.

Hypsipyle   In classical mythology, Hypsipyle, the daughter of King Toas, became queen of Lemnos, one of the Greek islands in the Aegean Sea. Because the women of the island had offended VENUS by neglecting her rites, the goddess caused their husbands to all take mistresses. The women became enraged and killed all the men on the island in revenge. Hypsipyle rescued her father by smuggling him down to the sea and putting him in a boat. When the adventurer JASON and his crew of Argonauts landed on Lemnos, Hypsipyle entertained them and fell in love with Jason, who promised to marry her. (Chaucer says that they were married.) After he remained in Lemnos long enough to father two children, Jason abandoned Hypsipyle to sail to COLCHIS, home to the Golden Fleece, the goal of his voyage. Chaucer tells his version of the story of Hypsipyle in *The LEGEND OF GOOD WOMEN* (lines 1467–1579). She is also mentioned in his *HOUSE OF FAME* among the women who suffered betrayal by men (line 400), and in "The MAN OF LAW'S TALE," where the narrator notes that Chaucer has told the story of Hypsipyle's complaint (line 67).

I

Iarbus In VIRGIL's *Aeneid,* Iarbus was king of the Gaetuli in northern Africa who fell in love with DIDO when she established her city of CARTHAGE north of his own kingdom. Dido turned down Iarbus' proposals of marriage and fell in love with the adventurer AENEAS. The heartache Iarbus felt over Dido's choice is mentioned in *The LEGEND OF GOOD WOMEN* (lines 1244–57). When Aeneas deserts her, Dido fears that the kings who live in the surrounding region (presumably including Iarbus) will destroy her (lines 1316–18).

Ibn-Serabi *See* SERAPION.

Icarus In classical mythology, Icarus was the son of the great architect DAEDALUS. He and his father escaped from King MINOS of Crete by flying away on wings that Daedalus fashioned out of feathers and wax. Icarus ignored his father's warning and flew so high that the sun melted the wax; he then fell into the sea and drowned. By the later Middle Ages, Icarus had become proverbial as an over-reacher. Chaucer refers to his disastrous flight in *The HOUSE OF FAME* when the EAGLE who is transporting the narrator through the air to FAME's palace informs him that they are flying even higher than Daedalus and Icarus. The reference is perhaps an ironic allusion to those writers who wish to rise high in the realm of fame, who are, like Icarus, over-reachers, attempting to climb higher than their own powers allow.

Idleness One of the allegorical figures in *The ROMAUNT OF THE ROSE,* Chaucer's translation of the famous French poem *ROMAN DE LA ROSE.* The poem is a DREAM VISION in which the narrator, after falling asleep, finds himself on the outskirts of a beautiful garden, which a high stone wall prevents him from entering. Eventually he locates a gate in the wall and knocks upon it, summoning a young maiden with blond hair, gray eyes and a pale complexion, all of which are conventional marks of beauty in the Middle Ages. The woman's name is Idleness and her only duty, she informs the narrator, is to keep herself beautifully dressed and coifed, and pleasantly entertained. She welcomes the narrator into the garden, where he is invited to observe the lord of the garden, MIRTH, who is celebrating the arrival of spring with a group of his followers.

Idra (Idre) *See* HYDRA.

Ikarus *See* ICARUS.

Il Filostrato *See FILOSTRATO, IL.*

Ilion (Illium, Ilyoun) Ilion (Latin, *Ilium*) was a name used by classical poets for the ancient city of TROY. Chaucer uses this name for the city in *The HOUSE OF FAME, The LEGEND OF GOOD WOMEN* and twice in *The CANTERBURY TALES.*

India (Inde) In Chaucer's day, the most significant realms on either side of India were China to the east and Arabia to the west. What knowledge Chaucer and his contemporaries in western Europe had of the region came primarily from traders who traveled the routes established by Marco Polo in the 13th century, bringing back silks and spices from the Far East. When Chaucer mentions India in his poetry, it always carries connotations of the exotic and mystical. One of the men who comes to fight on ARCITE (1)'s side in "The KNIGHT'S TALE" is EMETREUS, the king of India, whose somewhat outlandish appearance (his eyes are lemon-colored) is a sign of his origin. Similarly, in "The SQUIRE'S TALE." King CAMBYUSKAN's very unusual birthday presents are said to have been sent by the king of Arabia and India. They include a magic mirror that warns of coming adversity, a ring that enables the wearer to understand the speech of birds and the healing abilities of different plants and a sword that makes wounds that can only be healed by another stroke of the same sword. The exotic tiger was known to be a part of the fauna of India; hence, in the closing stanza of "The CLERK'S TALE," Chaucer admonishes women not to be as meek as GRISELDA in response to their husbands demands, but rather "egre as is a tygre yond in Ynde" (line 1199) [bold as is a tiger over in India].

Indus The great river that flows through southeast Asia from Tibet through Kashmir and Pakistan into the Arabian Sea. It is mentioned along with several other rivers in Book Three of the *BOECE* (Chaucer's translation of BOETHIUS' *Consolation of Philosophy*) when LADY PHILOSOPHY informs the narrator that all of the riches that could be brought to him by various rivers would only cloud his mind rather than clear it, by encouraging an attachment to worldly goods. The image of the rivers' running water causing the mind to be troubled rather than cleared plays ingeniously on the common symbolic association between running water and cleanliness or clarity, to illustrate the point that, in man's limited perception, things are not always what they seem to be.

Innocent III   *See* OF THE WRETCHED ENGENDERING OF MANKIND.

Inns of Court   The Inns of Court, which in the 18th and 19th centuries became famous as the school for the education of English lawyers, located in central London, originated as clubs that merely provided chambers for lawyers. Chaucer's biographer Donald HOWARD believes that they later took on the secondary function of providing legal training for the king's esquires, and still later became finishing schools for the gentry. The theory that Chaucer attended the Inns of Court is based primarily on the hints that he had legal training, hints provided both by his life and his work. The eminent Chaucer scholar Edith RICKERT believed that Chaucer's mission to Italy to negotiate the establishment of a seaport in England for Genoese citizens and merchants was the sort of assignment that would have been entrusted only to one with a sound knowledge of English law. Furthermore, one of the pilgrims in The CANTERBURY TALES, the SERGEANT OF THE LAW, is a lawyer of the highest rank. Both Chaucer's portrait of that individual and of the MANCIPLE, who in the GENERAL PROLOGUE is credited with outwitting the more highly educated lawyers for whom he works, have been considered by scholars as proof of Chaucer's intimacy with the Inns of Court. Then there is the evidence provided by Thomas SPEGHT, a Renaissance editor of Chaucer's work who, in his 1598 biography of the poet, noted that there was a record at the Inner Temple (one of the Inns of Court) of Chaucer being fined two shillings for beating a Franciscan friar on the street. This record has since been lost; but if it did exist at one time, it means that Chaucer must have resided, and thus been a student, at the Inner Temple when the incident occurred.

Iole   In classical mythology, Iole was the daughter of the king of Oechalia who promised to give Iole to HERCULES if the hero could defeat him in an archery competition. Although Hercules won the contest, the king refused to keep the bargain. In revenge, Hercules later returned to Oechalia, killed the king and his sons and took Iole captive. Iole indirectly caused the death of Hercules, because it was through jealousy over her that DEIANIRA sent him the poisoned garment which caused

him so much pain that he committed suicide. Hercules' betrayal of Deianira for Iole is mentioned in The HOUSE OF FAME as one of many examples of how men betray or mistreat the women who love them (line 403).

Ipomedon   *See* HIPPOMEDON.

Isaac   The only son of ABRAHAM, patriarch of the Jews, and SARAH. God asked Abraham to sacrifice Isaac in order to prove his willingness to submit to God's will. When he had built an altar, laid his son on top of it and was about to slaughter him, God stopped Abraham and provided a ram to be sacrificed instead. Abraham's obedience to God in this instance is often given as an example of absolute faith in God. Isaac married REBECCA, and together they had two sons, JACOB and Esau. Isaac is alluded to in "The TALE OF MELIBEE" and Chaucer's "ABC" to the Virgin.

Isaiah   A famous prophet in the Old Testament of the Bible. He wrote the Book of Isaiah and predicted the coming of the Messiah. Born in the holy city of Jerusalem, Isaiah spent his early years as an official of King Uzziah of Judah. When Uzziah died, Isaiah had a prophetic vision of God in the Temple, a vision that led to his own ministry as prophet. The book that is attributed to him both claims to prophesy the future of the Jewish nation, and specifically, God's intention to bring imminent judgment upon His people, to be followed by an outpouring of God's mercy and grace to the faithful remnant. The destruction of Jerusalem by the Babylonians in 587–586 B.C. (about 100 years after Isaiah's ministry ended) and the ensuing deportation of the people to BABYLON was considered the fulfillment of this prophecy. Excerpts from the Book of Isaiah are featured in Chaucer's "PARSON'S TALE" (lines 198–210; line 281). His visions and the prophecies that arose from them are alluded to in The HOUSE OF FAME when the narrator prefaces the record of his own dream vision with his belief that not one of history's illustrious dream interpreters, including Isaiah, would be able to unravel its meaning.

Isaude (Isawde; Iseult)   *See* ISOLDE.

Isidore of Seville   Isidore, archbishop of Seville in Spain who lived from 570 to 636, was a writer of encyclopedic works of knowledge that became quite popular in the later Middle Ages. His 20-volume *Origines* (also known as *Etymologiae*) argues that the natures of all things can be derived etymologically from their names. His words regarding the proper performance of penance are recorded in Chaucer's "PARSON'S TALE," which is itself a sermon on the subject of penitence.

Isiphile   *See* HYPSIPYLE.

Isis   In Egyptian mythology, Isis was the wife and sister of Osiris, the god who personified the growth of vegetation and the life-giving powers of the Nile River. According to legend, Osiris had once been a benevolent ruler of Egypt who taught his people agriculture and other practical arts and gave them laws. But he was treacherously slain by his wicked brother Set, and his body cut into pieces. His wife Isis went in search of the pieces, put them together, and miraculously restored his body to life. The risen god regained his kingdom and continued his rule for a time, but eventually descended to the netherworld to serve as judge of the dead. Just as Osiris was regarded as the father of Egyptian civilization, Isis was regarded as its mother. Her cult actually outlasted that of her husband and, during the Hellenistic Age, threatened to become dominant throughout the Near East. In *The HOUSE OF FAME,* one of the people who approaches FAME's throne claims to have burned the temple of Isis in Athens simply in order to get a name for himself (lines 1842–56). W. W. SKEAT suggests that Chaucer got the idea for this anecdote from the story of a man who was caught attempting to burn down the temple of DIANA at Ephesus.

Isolde   In Arthurian romance, Isolde is the daughter of King Anguish of Ireland. She meets Tristan and nurses him back to health after his battle with Morholt, her father's brother-in-law and fighting champion. She begins to fall in love with him during this time, but he returns to his home in Cornwall before anything further develops between them. The next time they meet, Tristan has been sent by his uncle Mark, the king of Cornwall, to woo Isolde as a bride for that uncle. As the two of them sail together back to Cornwall, they accidentally drink a love potion that was intended to be drunk by Isolde and Mark on their wedding night. Isolde goes through with the marriage, but she and Tristan cannot escape their passion for each other, and the romances that narrate their adventures generally tell of the series of deceptions they must practice in order to be together. In one version of the story, Tristan is finally murdered by King Mark out of revenge. In another, he receives a poisoned wound while assisting his brother-in-law, and dies of despair when he is tricked into thinking that Isolde refuses to come and heal him. Isolde is mentioned three times in Chaucer's work: once, briefly, by the Goddess FAME in *The HOUSE OF FAME;* once in *The PARLIAMENT OF FOWLS,* where she is listed as one of the lovers whose story is depicted on the wall in the TEMPLE OF VENUS; and once in the F prologue to *The LEGEND OF GOOD WOMEN,* where her beauty is invoked as a standard of comparison in the narrator's hymn of praise to Queen ALCESTIS.

Isope   *See* AESOP.

Israel   When Israel is mentioned in Chaucer's work, the reference may be to a geographical area, or it may be to the ancient nation of Jewish people. Geographically, Israel was the ancient kingdom north of Judah and south of SYRIA, bounded by the Mediterranean Sea in the west and the Syrian desert in the east. The "promised land" God gave to His people in the Old Testament, CANAAN, was located within the area known as Israel. The word is used in its geographical sense in *The LEGEND OF GOOD WOMEN,* when the narrator recalls Christ's words about the virtue of women, and that he could not find any faith greater than that of women throughout the wide land of Israel; likewise, in the brief biography of SAMSON that appears in "The MONK'S TALE," where we are told that Samson was at one time governor of Israel. About 100 lines later, in the biography of NEBUCHADNEZZAR, the word is used in its other sense, as the MONK states that King Nebuchadnezzar, the "faireste children of the blood roial / Of Israel he leet do gelde anoon, / and maked ech of hem to been his thral" (lines 2151–53) [fairest children of the royal blood / Of Israel he had castrated immediately, / and made each of them his slave], recalling a rather grim moment in the history of the Jewish people.

Italy   The country of Italy and its literature were to have a profound influence on Chaucer's work. Although he may have accompanied Lionel, the duke of Clarence, to Milan in 1366 for the Duke's wedding to Violante Visconti, the first record of Chaucer in Italy is of a journey made in 1372, when he was employed as an esquire of the king's chamber. His mission was to negotiate the establishment of a special seaport in England for the use of Genoese merchants. He was probably chosen for the mission because of his fluency in Italian, a language he may have picked up as a boy by associating with the Italian merchants with whom his father, a vintner, did business. The dawning of the 14th century was the dawning of the Renaissance in Italy, a movement in art and literature that did not blossom in England, a cultural backwater by comparison, until the 16th century. Experiencing for the first time Italy's culture and sophistication, Chaucer must have been amazed at what he found there, but perhaps he was most amazed by the attitude toward poets and poetry. Here the poet had much higher status than in England; the best poets were also considered philosophers and cultural historians, who played an important role in keeping the wisdom of the past, and especially the classical past, alive. VIRGIL was the great patriarch of Italian poetry; DANTE ALIGHIERI, who died in 1321, PETRARCH and BOCCACCIO were the inheritors of the tradition who did not stint in their devotion to it. Chaucer could not have helped being influenced by the respect accorded to poetry and its practitioners in Italy, and perhaps it gave him a new sense of himself and the role he was to have in shaping English literature. Most significantly for Chaucer, the poetry of Italy was composed in the vernacular of the people rather than in Latin, the formal language of the country. This use of the Italian vernacular has been credited with having a strong influence on Chaucer's determination to compose his own verse exclusively in English, the vernacular of his own country, rather than in French, which had been the dominant language of the English court and of its poets since the Norman Conquest in 1066. Some scholars have also suggested that Chaucer acquired copies of the works of Boccaccio and Petrarch on this first trip, which included a stop in Florence, the most progressive of the Italian states, both politically and culturally. Others believe that he acquired these works on a second trip, in 1378, when he seems to have been involved in marriage negotiations for King RICHARD II. "The CLERKS' TALE," about patient GRISELDA, and passages in the long poem *TROILUS AND CRISEYDE* are taken from the work of Petrarch. Chaucer draws even more heavily on Boccaccio, whose *FILOSTRATO* and *TESEIDA* were, respectively, the main sources for *TROILUS AND CRISEYDE* and "The KNIGHT's TALE." Selected passages from these and other works show up elsewhere, especially in *The HOUSE OF FAME* and *The LEGEND OF GOOD WOMEN*. Strangely enough, although Chaucer gives credit to Petrarch for "The Clerk's Tale," nowhere does he acknowledge his debt to Boccaccio.

Iulo (Iulus)   *See* ASCANIUS.

Ives, Saint   There are three possible candidates for the Saint Ives who is mentioned twice in *The CANTERBURY TALES*. The first is an Ivo of Persian nationality who came to England at the end of the sixth century and lived in Huntingdonshire. Miracles performed at his tomb bore witness to his sanctity. The town of St. Ives in Huntingdonshire takes its name from him. The second Ivo was a Breton saint and the patron of lawyers. Born near Treguier in 1253, he studied at Paris and Orleans, and all his life practiced law in his native city. His gratuitous services to the oppressed and needy earned him the title of "advocate of the poor." He treated orphans and widows as his most important clients. This Ivo died in 1303 and was canonized in 1347. The third candidate, Ivo of Chartres, was a canon in France during the 12th century. Distinguished by his learning, piety and zeal in God's service, Ivo reluctantly received consecration at Rome as bishop of Chartres from Pope Urban II. His episcopate was chiefly notable for the long war he waged against abuses in church discipline and for his strenuous upholding of the rights of the Holy See against the usurpation of monarchs. In "The SUMMONER'S TALE," the corrupt friar who is trying to bilk poor sick THOMAS (1) out of some money swears by Saint Ives that if Thomas does not behave charitably to the friars, he will not thrive (line 1943). In "The SHIPMAN'S TALE," the Merchant who is duped out of his money by another member of the clergy, a clever monk named John, also swears by Saint Ives as he tries to explain to his wife the difficulties of his profession.

Ixion   In classical mythology, Ixion was the king of the Lapiths. When he was married, he tried to get out of paying the bridal gifts he had promised by murdering his father-in-law, whom he threw into a fiery pit. Zeus (JUPITER) decided to purify him of this crime and took him up into heaven where he was granted immortality and received at the table of the gods. When he tried to seduce Zeus' consort, Hera (JUNO), the god fashioned a cloud resembling her, and by this, Ixion became the father of the CENTAURS. He was punished for his presumption in the underworld by being bound hand and foot to a fiery wheel that was forever turning. In *TROILUS AND CRISEYDE*, after TROILUS has been abandoned by CRISEYDE he is described as wallowing and turning in his bed like Ixion on his wheel (book 5, line 212). The ability of the musician ORPHEUS to ease Ixion's torment is mentioned in Book Three, Metrum 12 of the *BOECE*, Chaucer's translation of BOETHIUS' *Consolation of Philosophy*.

J

Jack Straw The leader of a party of insurgents from the county of Essex in the PEASANTS' REVOLT OF 1381. He is supposed to have led an especially brutal attack on Flemish merchants in the Vintry, the neighborhood where Chaucer spent much of his childhood. According to accepted calculations of Chaucer's birthdate (the exact day is unknown), the poet would have been around 36 years old at this time. No records tell us whether Chaucer was in residence or not when the horde of rebels entered the city through the ALDGATE, but his London residence was an apartment directly over that gate, leased to him for life by the mayor of London. Chaucer's only reference to the event appears years later in "The NUN'S PRIEST'S TALE," when he describes the noise that the widow and her neighbors make chasing the fox as being louder than the shouts of Jack Straw and his mob (lines 3394–97).

Jack Straw's Rebellion *See* PEASANTS' REVOLT OF 1381.

Jacob In the Bible, Jacob was one of the twin sons of ISAAC and REBECCA; his twin brother was Esau. Jacob became the favorite son of his mother, who assisted him in tricking Esau, the firstborn by a matter of seconds, out of his birthright and the blessing of his father, which accrued to that position. When Esau threatened to kill him, Rebecca sent Jacob to stay with her brother Laban. During his sojourn with Laban, Jacob fell in love with Laban's daughter Rachel, and he served Laban seven years for her hand in marriage. When Laban tricked Jacob into marrying his other daughter, Leah, Jacob served seven more years and finally won Rachel. The fact that Jacob was a bigamist is mentioned by Chaucer's WIFE OF BATH as evidence to justify her own multiple marriages, which, however, were successive rather than simultaneous. In "The MERCHANT'S TALE" (lines 1362–65) and "The TALE OF MELIBEE" (line 1097), the story of how Rebecca helped Jacob take Esau's birthright is given as evidence of the good help that women often provide to men, evidence to challenge the prevailing view of the antifeminist writers. Ironically, the story is related as evidence to support the notion that husbands ought to listen to their wives' counsel, yet while Rebecca is certainly helping her son, she is simultaneously helping him deceive her husband. Jacob's service to his father-in-law, Laban, is men-

tioned in "The PARSON'S TALE" as evidence of God's beneficence toward Laban, and as an example of the idea that God rewards those who serve Him well (line 443).

Jaconites (Jaconitos) According to GUIDO DELLE COLONNE, Chaucer's source for the story of JASON and MEDEA that he included in *The LEGEND OF GOOD WOMEN*, Jaconites was the capital city of COLCHIS, where Jason met Medea and captured the Golden Fleece. Other sources state that, historically, the chief town was one called Dioscuros.

Jakke Straw *See* JACK STRAW.

James, Saint (1) Saint James the Apostle, also known as James the son of Zebedee, was one of the original 12 apostles of Christ. James and his brother John are frequently associated with two other brothers, Peter and Andrew. The four were fishermen on the Sea of Galilee. Their call to follow Jesus is the first recorded event after the beginning of Jesus' public ministry. James and his brother were nicknamed "Sons of Thunder" by Jesus, evidently as testimony to their spirited natures. On one occasion, when a Samaritan village refused to accept Jesus, the two asked Him to call down fire in revenge. James was killed by Herod Agrippa I, the grandson of Herod the Great (*see* HEROD [1]), around A.D. 43. He was the first of the 12 apostles to be put to death and the only one whose martyrdom is mentioned in the New Testament. Words attributed to Saint James are quoted in "The TALE OF MELIBEE" and in "The PARSON'S TALE."

James, Saint (2) *See* JAMES OF COMPOSTELLA, SAINT.

James of Compostella, Saint The shrine of Saint James of Compostella in GALICIA, Spain, is one of many celebrated places of pilgrimage visited by the WIFE OF BATH, who loves to travel (GENERAL PROLOGUE, line 466). According to medieval legend, the body of James the Apostle was miraculously transported to Galicia in a rudderless boat. The legend achieved such popularity that the shrine at Compostella became, with Jerusalem and Rome, one of the three most important destinations of pilgrimages in the Middle Ages.

Janekyn *See* JANKIN (2).

Janicula The father of GRISELDA in "The CLERK'S TALE." Notable as being the poorest man in his village, Janicula agrees to give his only daughter, Griselda, in marriage to WALTER, the wealthy marquis of SALUZZO in northern Italy. When Walter sends Griselda back to her father following approximately 19 years of marriage, Janicula, who has always suspected Walter's motives, believes that he has simply grown tired of Griselda and feels that, because of her heritage as the daughter of a poor peasant, he can cast her off and marry another. One of the most moving scenes in the tale describes Janicula's meeting with his daughter upon her homecoming. Hearing that she comes wearing nothing but a smock (the medieval equivalent of a slip), he goes out to meet her carrying her old coat to put over her. But, for some reason which we are not told, the old coat no longer fits. Symbolically, this detail serves to remind us of the way that Griselda outgrew her former status as she adapted so naturally to her position as Walter's wife.

Jankin (1) Fifth and last husband to the WIFE OF BATH, one of the pilgrims who tells a tale in *The CANTERBURY TALES*. Jankin is the only one of the Wife's husbands whose name is revealed, and she claims to love him the best, even though he has, in the past, treated her badly, beating her and making her listen while he read from a book of the life stories of wicked women. One night she became so angry with him over the book that she tore three pages from it and threw them into a fire. A fight erupted in which he struck her unconscious (or at least, she pretended to be unconscious). This scared him so much that, as soon as she was better, he promised to abide by her wishes forever after, putting the governance of their property and himself into her hands, even to the extent of burning the offending book. And this is why, the Wife believes, they now get along so splendidly.

Jankin (2) A minor character in "The SUMMONER'S TALE." Jankin is a page who serves at table for the lord from whom JOHN THE FRIAR seeks redress when he has been insulted by THOMAS (1). Specifically, Thomas insulted the friar by presenting him with a fart instead of a donation of money. The lord of the village is more interested by the problem of dividing the fart into 13 parts so that it can be shared by all the friars in John's monastery than he is in the insulting nature of the bequest. Jankin solves the problem by suggesting the use of a cartwheel that has 12 spokes, turned on its side. Thomas, the bestower of the "gift," should sit at the hub of the wheel, with the 12 members of John's order positioned at the end of each spoke and John himself directly beneath the hub. That way, when Thomas farts,

each friar would receive an equal portion, except for John, who, as the chief recipient of Thomas' good wishes, would receive a slightly greater portion.

January The aged husband of MAY in "The MERCHANT'S TALE." His name recalls the month and the season of winter, which was associated with age and death, just as his wife's name recalls the spring, a time of birth and blossoming youth. January's character is notable for two features in particular. The first is his talkativeness, which stands in contrast to May's reticence and Damian's near muteness (he only speaks once, and that is in a whisper). January's fondness for his own speech is important because it provides the primary mechanism by which Chaucer constructs his second notable feature, his self-delusion. January uses language to deceive himself. For example, to convince himself that his reasons for desiring a wife are noble, he delivers a kind of encomium on the virtues of marriage that is completely undermined by the concupiscence revealed through his thoughts and behavior. In this regard we should recall that, in addition to its seasonal connotation, the name *January* has the same Latin root as the name of the Roman god JANUS, who had two faces and was the guardian of gates and portals, a feature that resonates symbolically with January's failed efforts to guard both the entry to his garden and access to his wife.

Janus The Roman god of doorways, entrances and gates, both of private and public places. He was also recognized as the god of all beginnings, particularly of units of time such as days, months and years. His chief festival was celebrated on the first day of each new year, in the month named after him, when people gave each other sweets so that the year to come might bring only what was pleasant. Janus was usually represented as having two bearded heads placed back to back so that he might look in two directions at the same time. This symbolized his function as the god of coming and going, which led to him being considered a god overseeing traffic on land and on sea. In "The FRANKLIN'S TALE," Chaucer alludes to Janus sitting by the fire to indicate the coming of the month of January and the passage of time as the squire AURELIUS pines away out of love for DORIGEN. In book two of *TROILUS AND CRISEYDE*, the narrator invokes Janus as the god of entrances to guide PANDARUS' steps as he approaches his niece's palace, where he is going to begin the process of wooing her for TROILUS.

Jason In classical mythology, Jason was the son of King AESON of Iolcus. When his father's throne was usurped by Jason's uncle, Pelias, Jason was put in the care of a CENTAUR, CHIRON. Once he was grown, he went to Iolcus to demand that his father's kingdom be restored to its rightful ruler. Pelias, figuring out who he was, stalled for time by agreeing to give up the kingdom if Jason could first bring him the famous Golden Fleece from the kingdom of AEETES in Colchis. Jason accepted the challenge and organized the Argonautic expedition, in which many of the most renowned heroes of Greece participated under his leadership.

After a series of adventures, including a love affair with HYPSIPYLE, the queen of Lemnos, Jason and his Argonauts arrived in Colchis, where Jason demanded the Golden Fleece. He was told that he might have it, provided he could accomplish certain seemingly impossible tasks. These included yoking two brazen-footed fire-breathing bulls, plowing the field of Ares and sowing it with dragon's teeth, overcoming the fully armed men that sprang from the sowing, and conquering the sleepless dragon that guarded the tree on which the fleece hung suspended. Jason succeeded in accomplishing these feats through the aid of MEDEA, the sorceress daughter of Aeetes, who had fallen in love with him.

Once he had attained the Golden Fleece, Jason took Medea and her brother and stole away from the island in the middle of the night. Aeetes pursued them but had to stop along the way to gather pieces of the body of his son. Medea had slain her brother and thrown his dismembered body overboard to delay her father's pursuit. Jason and Medea were married on their way home. When they finally reached Iolcus, the couple learned that Pelias had killed Jason's father to secure his claim to the throne. Medea avenged the murder by convincing Pelias' daughters that if they cut their father to pieces and boiled him in a cauldron, they would restore his youth. For this murder, Jason and Medea were driven out of Iolcus and went to Corinth. After living there for 10 years, Jason abandoned Medea in order to marry Glauce, or CREUSA, the daughter of King Creon. Medea foiled his purposes by sending Glauce a poisoned gown as a wedding gift, which destroyed her when she tried it on. Medea also killed the children that she and Jason had together and fled to Athens. According to one version of the legend, Jason died when part of his ship, the *Argo,* collapsed and crushed him after he had set it up as a memorial to his adventures. Another story relates that he committed suicide.

When Jason appears in Chaucer's work it is nearly always as a representative of the type of man who takes advantage of women by winning their love and then abandoning them. Oddly enough, despite the rather horrible nature of some of the deeds committed by Medea, Chaucer's attitude toward her shows more sympathy than his treatment of Jason. Jason's betrayal of Hypsipyle and Medea is treated at length in *The LEGEND OF GOOD WOMEN* (lines 1368–1679). There are also references to it in the introduction to "The MAN OF LAW'S TALE" (lines 72–74), in "The SQUIRE'S TALE" (lines 549–51), in *The BOOK OF THE DUCHESS* (line 727) and in *The HOUSE OF FAME* (line 401).

Jealousy An allegorical figure who appears in Fragment B of the Middle English translation of the French *ROMAN DE LA ROSE* that was begun by Chaucer and continued by two other anonymous poets. When the dreamer-narrator approaches the garden where grows the rose with which he has fallen in love, BIALACOIL (Fair Welcome) permits him to enter. He is challenged by DAUNGER (Disdain), SHAME, DREAD and WICKED TONGUE (Malicious Gossip), all enemies to love who try to prevent his access to his beloved. Finally, VENUS comes to his aid and he is able to kiss the rose, but Jealousy interrupts his bliss, driving him out of the garden while imprisoning Bialacoil and the rosebud in an impenetrable fortress.

Jean de Meun Jean de Meun was the continuator of the *ROMAN DE LA ROSE,* the important French allegorical DREAM VISION begun by GUILLAUME DE LORRIS. Jean de Meun was probably born not long after Guillaume died (around 1237) in the village of Meung on the Loire River below Orléans, not far from the birthplace of Guillaume de Lorris. He attended the University of Paris, studying the seven liberal arts, which during the medieval period were divided into the *trivium* (grammar, rhetoric and logic) and the *quadrivium* (arithmetic, geometry, astronomy and music). He was also interested in law and medicine, as well as philosophy and theology. In addition to writing a continuation of the *Roman,* his literary accomplishments include translating BOETHIUS' *Consolation of Philosophy* from Latin into French (Chaucer used this translation to assist him with his own), the *Life and Letters of Peter Abélard and Héloise,* and the *Military Art* of Vegetius, a fourth-century Latin writer who taught medieval soldiers how to besiege a castle and other strategies of war. Jean's relationship to the University of Paris remains uncertain. Some documents refer to him as Master Jean de Meun, which suggests that he had attained a Master of Arts degree, and he may very well have been a teaching master. The portrait of him which appears in manuscripts of the *Roman* shows him wearing the biretta appropriate to that rank. The portion of the *Roman* written by Guillaume de Lorris is a celebration as well as an anatomization of romantic courtly love in the allegorical mode (*see* ALLEGORY). Jean de Meun's continuation reflects a different poetic sentiment, which might even be termed antithetical to the idea of courtly love, or at least to its idealization. As a scholar with a decidedly philosophical bent of mind, Jean was equally interested in analyzing love, but in conducting such a task, he brought to bear a vast armory of scholastic learning and clerical bias which would lead him to take a much more cynical view of romantic love, which he seems to equate with lust, arguing that divine love and friendship are the more positive and desirable manifestations of the love impulse. Although Chaucer's work was more influenced by Guillaume de Lorris' portion of the *Roman* than it was by Jean de Meun's, the game of chess in *The BOOK OF THE DUCHESS* and the character of the WIFE OF BATH in *The CANTERBURY TALES* both strongly suggest a debt to the poem's continuator.

Jephthah   In the Old Testament of the Bible, Jephthah was the ninth judge of Israel, who led an army that saved the Israelites from being invaded by the Ammonites. On the eve of battle, Jephthah made a rash promise to God, vowing that if the Israelites were victorious, he would offer up as sacrifice the first thing that should come out of his house to meet him on his return. When Jephthah reached his home, his daughter, an only child, came running out to welcome him. Although Jephthah tore his clothing in recognition of the horrible act he had vowed to perform, the text seems to indicate that he kept his promise and sacrificed his daughter. Nevertheless, the Bible praises him as one of Israel's greatest judges. The story of Jephthah and his daughter is mentioned in "The PHYSICIAN'S TALE" when VIRGINIA, whose father is going to kill her to keep her from being dishonored by the false Roman judge APIUS, asks for some time to lament before her death, noting that Jephthah allowed this to his daughter (line 240). Ironically, Jephthah's daughter requested the time to bewail her wasted virginity; Virginia, on the other hand, is dying because she wants to preserve her maidenhood.

Jeremiah   In the Old Testament of the Bible, Jeremiah was the major prophet during the decline and fall of the southern kingdom of Judah. He wrote the Old Testament Book of Jeremiah. Jeremiah's ministry was to be one of tearing down and uprooting; from the very beginning, he was destined to be a prophet of doom, and sure enough, the end of his life saw the devastation of the nation of Israel, with the destruction of the capital city of Jerusalem in 587–586 B.C. and the deportation of most of its citizens to Babylon. Jeremiah is often called "the weeping prophet" because he cried openly over the sins and vices of his nation, which refused to heed his dire warnings and mocked his proclamations. Jeremiah, along with some other Jewish citizens, remained in Jerusalem after its fall, until the people of Jerusalem revolted against Babylonian rule and he was forced to flee to Egypt for safety. He continued his preaching in exile, but nothing is known of how his life ended. References to the Book of Jeremiah appear in "The PARSON'S TALE," which, appropriately enough, is a sermon on sin and penitence. A comment that the prophet made about swearing, and how it should never

be done except when swearing an oath in a case of judgment, is mentioned in the first part of "The PARDONER'S TALE" (line 635), where the PARDONER warns against the evils of idle swearing.

Jerome, Saint   A leading church father and author of the *Vulgate* (from the Latin word for "common") Bible. Jerome, who died around 419 or 420, was born and grew up in Aquileia, a town in northeastern Italy near the Adriatic Sea. After spending some time with an ascetic group in that city, he went on pilgrimage to Jerusalem and then went to live as a hermit in the Syrian desert. After a couple of years he moved to Constantinople and then to Rome, where he served as secretary to Pope Damasus. While in Rome he directed the spiritual instruction of a group of noble widows and virgins, some of whom followed him to Bethlehem, where he relocated shortly after the pope's death. The last 20 years of his life he spent in a monastery that one of these women had built for him. His most celebrated work, the *Vulgate,* a Latin translation of the Bible, was undertaken at the direction of Pope Damasus. The simple Latin prose style that he chose to use made the text available to a much larger audience than it would have been had he chosen to write in a high classical style, of which he was quite capable. Jerome's writings also included historical, hagiographical and biographical works as well as treatises on moral exegetical and dogmatic subjects. His militant nature is evident in the writings he leveled against the leading heresies of his day, Arianism, Pelagianism and Origenism. In this vein he also wrote an epistolary letter entitled *Epistola adversus Jovinianum* (Letter against Jovinian), in which he condemns the views of an unorthodox monk (Jovinian) who denied that virginity was necessarily superior to marriage. His views, derived from Christian asceticism, became an important source of antifeminist thought in the medieval period. As such, it is no surprise to find it listed among the works bound together in the Book of Wicked Wives, which the WIFE OF BATH's fifth husband reads to her from each night. Sayings attributed to Jerome are quoted in "The TALE OF MELIBEE" and "The PARSON'S TALE." The latter makes particular use of Jerome when describing the attitude one ought to maintain toward sin and judgment.

Jerusalem   Jerusalem was the sacred city and well-known capital of Judea during biblical times. The aim of the first great Crusade—the only crusade to achieve more than minimal success—had been to free Jerusalem from occupation by the Muslim Turks, and from the 12th century on it became an increasingly popular destination for pilgrims traveling from Europe to see the place where Christ lived and conducted his ministry. In the GENERAL PROLOGUE TO *THE CANTERBURY TALES,* it is mentioned as one of the locations that the WIFE OF BATH, who seems to go on pilgrimages to indulge her love of travel, has visited. The Wife herself alludes to the trip in the prologue to her tale when she says that her fourth husband died when she came back from Jerusalem. In "The MONK'S TALE," the Babylonian king NEBUCHADNEZZAR's two victories over Jerusalem (described in the Old Testament of the Bible) are mentioned in the brief biography of Nebuchadnezzar (lines 2147 and 2196). The second of those victories is alluded to in the MONK's story of Nebuchadnezzar's successor, BELSHAZZAR (line 2596). Belshazzar drunkenly proposed to his officers that they should profane the vessels of the Holy Temple of Jerusalem—vessels captured by his father—by drinking wine out of them, for which he was duly punished. Later in the same tale, we are told of the Seleucid king ANTIOCHUS' (1) attempts to suppress Judaism in Jerusalem and his intention to hammer the city when his attempts at suppression failed. This time God protected the city by striking Antiochus down. The most notable mention of the city of Jerusalem in Chaucer's work appears in the prologue to "The PARSON'S TALE." Here the PARSON prefaces his sermon on penitence with a reminder that life itself is a pilgrimage to "Jerusalem celestial" (line 51). He is referring to the idea expressed in the New Testament Book of Revelation that, after the Second Coming of Christ, the Savior will establish a new, celestial Jerusalem where all those who follow Him will live in perfect bliss forever.

Jesus, son of Sirach (Jesus ben Eleazar ben Sira) Author of the apocryphal Book of ECCLESIASTICUS, a book that offered advice on various topics touching religious practice and secular behavior. The author's antifeminist attitude toward women causes him to be quoted by the WIFE OF BATH's fifth husband and by the god PLUTO as he and his wife Proserpina sit in the garden of the aged knight JANUARY in Chaucer's "MERCHANT'S TALE." Dame PRUDENCE of "The TALE OF MELIBEE" employs several passages from Ecclesiasticus as she tries to dissuade her husband from taking revenge against the men who have robbed and assaulted his family. She cites the following quotation to argue that the bitterness he feels toward these men will sour his character: "A man that is joyous and glad in herte, it hym conserveth florissynge in his age; but soothly sorweful herte maketh his bones drye" (line 994) [A man who is joyful and glad at heart will flourish as he grows old; but truly a sorrowful heart will make his bones dry].

Jesus Christ (Jesu Christ; Jhesus) Jesus Christ, the human-divine son of God who was born of the Virgin Mary and who, according to Christian doctrine, died on the cross for the sins of humanity, is mentioned sev-

eral times in *The CANTERBURY TALES.* In the description of the PARDONER in the GENERAL PROLOGUE, the narrator states that a sail belonging to Saint Peter before Christ called him to become a disciple appears among the Pardoner's holy relics. Later, in the conclusion to the General Prologue, the narrator explains that he intends to relate each tale that was told along the way to CANTERBURY, and to relay each one just exactly as it was told, pointing out that Christ himself spoke on many topics in the Holy Bible. The suggestion that what he is doing somehow parallels Christ's teachings seems ironic, even though the satire of *The Canterbury Tales* could be considered essentially moral. All other references to Christ occur in "The PARSON'S TALE," a sermon on the subject of penance where Christ's words as they are recorded in the Bible are used to support the PARSON's arguments.

Jewerye Chaucer uses this term to designate the Jewish nation generally in *The HOUSE OF FAME* and a Jewish community in the anti-Semitic "PRIORESS' TALE." (*See* also JEWS, PORTRAYAL OF IN CHAUCER.)

Jews, portrayal of in Chaucer The only work of Chaucer's to feature Jews as characters is the "PRIORESS' TALE" where a group of Jews murder a little Christian boy. The tale is set in an unspecified city of ASIA whose ruler has allowed Jews to practice "foul usure and lucre of vileynye" (line 491) [foul usury and shameful profiting]. The child is attacked while walking through a Jewish neighborhood on his way home from school. As he walks he sings a holy song that he is trying to learn in honor of the Virgin Mary. His singing infuriates the Jews, who seize him and cut his throat. They attempt to hide his body in a latrine, but his mother manages to find him because God miraculously enables him to continue singing. The perpetrators of this terrible crime are seized and executed. The blatant anti-Semitism of this tale has always troubled Chaucer scholars. Those who are reluctant to believe that the poet could have harbored such views argue that the tale expresses the views of its teller, the PRIORESS, rather than those of its author, and that Chaucer is using the tale to criticize her morality rather than revealing his own. Others believe that Chaucer could easily have held such an opinion himself. The Jews had been expelled from England in 1290 and were reviled and despised throughout Europe for their refusal to acknowledge Christ's divinity. They were envied when they achieved prosperity and were often made scapegoats when things were not going well for other citizens. For example, in 14th-century Germany, around 2,000 Jews in the town of Strasbourg were burned because they were believed in some way responsible for outbreaks of the plague. Those who agreed to be baptized were spared.

Jhesus (filius) Syrak   *See* JESUS, SON OF SIRACH.

Joab   In the Old Testament of the Bible, Joab was the name of a general who fought under King DAVID. When David led an army to capture Jerusalem, he announced that whoever led the first attack against the city would become his chief and captain. Joab led the assault, and when the city was captured, David made him a general. Although he was a leader in several other successful military campaigns, Joab's character was stained when he helped David achieve the death of Uriah the Hittite so that David could possess Uriah's wife, Bathsheba. When ABSALOM (2), David's illegitimate but well-beloved son, led a revolt against his father, Joab remained loyal to David. Soon afterward, however, David gave command of the army to Amasa, Joab's cousin. Joab vented his jealousy by killing Amasa. Later, when Joab championed the cause of a rival for the king's throne against David's choice for his own successor, David had him killed. As David's general, one of Joab's duties in battle would have been to blow the trumpets to set on the charge of soldiers at the beginning of a battle, or, alternatively, to signal the battle's end. Chaucer alludes to the din that would have been made when he carried out this duty in "The MERCHANT'S TALE," when the loud music at the feast following the wedding of JANUARY and MAY is compared to the trumpeting of Joab (line 1719). Similarly, Joab and his trumpet appear with other musicians and minstrels in FAME' *The HOUSE OF FAME* (line 1245).

Job   In the Old Testament of the Bible, Job was a prosperous man who, as the result of a wager made between God and Satan, lost everything he owned, despite his reputation for being a blameless man who respected God and shunned evil. When Satan suggested that Job would remain righteous only for as long as it was financially convenient for him to do so, God agreed to let Satan test Job's faith. In the course of this testing, Job lost his livestock, his servants and his children. His prosperity was replaced by poverty. When Job remained faithful in spite of these ills, Satan afflicted him with painful boils, from the soles of his feet to the crown of his head. But when his wife told him to curse God and die, Job refused. When Job's faith proved unshakeable, his suffering finally ended and he became even more prosperous than he had been before. In the Bible and throughout history, Job has been considered a model of spiritual integrity, of one who triumphs through faith in the face of overwhelming adversity. The WIFE OF BATH refers to Job in her prologue when she describes how she used to tease and nag her old husbands, telling them they ought to exhibit some of Job's patience if they are going to talk about it all the time—which they presumably do in reference to the deceits she practices upon them (line 436). Job is also mentioned in "The

FRIAR'S TALE" when the devil explains to the evil summoner how God sometimes permits devils to torment His faithful followers, but only to a certain extent, harming the body but not the soul, just as Satan did with Job (line 1491). More to the point, in "The CLERK'S TALE," Job's patience is compared to that of the tale's heroine, GRISELDA, whose faith and obedience to her husband are sorely tested when he takes away her children, allowing her to think they are to be murdered (line 932). Although Job is not mentioned in "The MAN OF LAW'S TALE," the heroine, CONSTANCE, is similarly tested by terrible vicissitudes of fortune. In "The TALE OF MELIBEE," Dame PRUDENCE reminds her husband of Job's patience as she tries to persuade him against taking revenge on the men who robbed his home and assaulted his family. Finally, in "The PARSON'S TALE," Job's suffering is mentioned several times (for example, in lines 134 and 176) as the PARSON delivers his sermon on sin and penitence.

Joce   *See* JUDOCUS, SAINT.

Johan, Saint   *See* JOHN, SAINT.

John, Saint   Saint John, or John the Apostle, was one of Jesus' original 12 disciples. Before being called to follow Christ, John was a fisherman on the Sea of Galilee, along with his father, Zebedee, and brother, JAMES, who would also become a disciple. Of all the apostles, James and John, along with Peter, came to have the most intimate relationship with Jesus. Following their Lord's ascension, John continued in a position of leadership among the other disciples. Together with Peter, he bore witness before the Sanhedrin (the highest court of justice in Judea at the time) to his faith in Jesus Christ. As with the other disciples, John later became the subject of various stories in church tradition. TERTULLIAN said that he ended up in Rome, where he was plunged, unhurt, into boiling oil. A later tradition believed that both James and John were martyred. The dominant tradition, however, held that the apostle John moved to Ephesus in Asia Minor, and that from there he was banished to the island of Patmos. Although five books of the New Testament, including the Gospel of John, John 1, 2 and 3, and Revelation, have been attributed to John the Apostle, it seems likely that the first four were written by a companion of his, John the Elder, while Revelation was written by the evangelist himself. The writings attributed to John are mentioned numerous times in "The PARSON'S TALE" (*see* lines 216, 349, 564 and 687, for examples), itself a sermon on penitence. At the end of "The FRIAR'S TALE," the FRIAR says that if he had the time, he would draw upon descriptions of hell taken from the texts of Christ, PAUL and John so that his audience would understand the torments suffered by the evil summoner whose soul was snatched away to hell at his tale's conclusion (lines 1646–52). In "The PRIORESS' TALE," (lines 479–585), the PRIORESS imagines seeing the child martyr of her tale among the Holy Innocents described by Saint John in Revelation.

John Chrysostom, Saint   A Syrian born in Antioch in 344, John Chrysostom renounced the certain prospect of a distinguished public career to take holy orders. After leading the life of an ascetic for some time, he was ordained as a priest and became the right hand man of the then bishop of Antioch. His abilities eventually raised him to the bishopric of Constantinople, the eastern capital of the Roman Empire, where he successfully activated extensive reform. This action made him popular with the church, but it also created enemies in the court of the emperor Arcadius. These demanded Chrysostom's banishment, which was enforced in defiance of the pope's strenuous support for his cause. The saint died in exile in 407. John's surname, Chrysostom, which means "golden-mouthed," came from his marvelous and persuasive eloquence. The writings he left behind include a revised Greek liturgy, full commentaries on the Bible, a treatise on the priesthood and many homilies. Chaucer quotes from a sermon that was attributed to Chrysostom at the beginning of "The PARSON'S TALE," where the PARSON is defining the meaning of penitence (line 109). According to Saint John, penitence requires that people humbly welcome every hardship that is imposed upon them through penance. They must also be contrite in their hearts and make a full confession ("shrift of mouth").

John of Gaddesden   Referred to as "Gatesden" in the GENERAL PROLOGUE to *The CANTERBURY TALES* (line 434), John of Gaddesden was a Fellow of Merton College at Oxford in the 14th century and author of the medical text *Rosa anglica*. He is listed in the General Prologue as one of the medical authorities whose teachings the DOCTOR OF PHYSIC had studied.

John of Gaunt   The third son of King EDWARD III and Queen PHILIPPA. He was the most influential of Edward's sons during the last years of his father's reign, and served on the council which advised the new king, RICHARD II, his nephew, after Edward's death. He probably became friends with Chaucer when Chaucser served as a civil servant in the household of Edward, and Chaucer's poem, *The BOOK OF THE DUCHESS,* is known to have been written as a memorial to Gaunt's first wife, BLANCHE OF LANCASTER, who died of the plague around 1369. John of Gaunt's son, Henry Bolingbroke, became the first Lancastrian king of England (as Henry IV) when Richard II was deposed because of his unpopularity with the nobility and his ineffectuality as a ruler.

John the Baptist   In the New Testament of the Bible, John the Baptist was a moral reformer and preacher of messianic hope. He is commonly considered the harbinger of Christ. King HEROD (2) arrested John because he spoke out against Herod's immoral marriage to Herodias, the wife of his brother Philip. Herod may also have feared that John's popularity would lead to a revolt. John was executed at the request of Salome, Herodias' daughter. Salome danced before King Herod, who, greatly pleased with her performance, offered to give her anything she wanted. At her mother's urging, Salome asked for John the Baptist's head on a platter. In "The PARDONER'S TALE," the PARDONER mentions this incident as an example of a bad decision that was made under the influence of too much wine.

John the Carpenter   The somewhat dull-witted husband of lovely young ALISON (1) in the bawdy "MILLER'S TALE." After taking in a lodger, a young clerk named NICHOLAS, John is tricked into believing that Nicholas' study of the heavens has revealed that a second NOAH's flood is on the way. Following Nicholas' instructions, John constructs three wooden tubs to hang up in the roofbeams of his house. Their plan is that when the water rises high enough, they will cut the ropes by which the tubs are suspended and float to safety. On the night of the predicted flood, John, Alison and Nicholas each go to bed in one of the three tubs. But after John has fallen asleep, Alison and Nicholas climb down and hop into bed together, which is what they planned to do all along. Further developments then cause John to believe that the flood has indeed come. In his confusion, he cuts the ropes holding up his tub and crashes to the floor. Nicholas and Alison tell all the neighbors who are awakened by the noise that John has gone mad. John's betrayal by his wife, who is a good deal younger than he, is at least partly accountable to his age. Such May-December marriages were common in the Middle Ages, when a woman's (and sometimes a man's) marriage was customarily arranged by her parents for reasons other than love, usually having to do with the exchange of property. The WIFE OF BATH has been a party to three such marriages and often deceived her old husbands with younger men. JANUARY in "The MERCHANT'S TALE" is, like John, the victim of such deceit. The fact that John is a carpenter by profession is offensive to the REEVE (himself a carpenter), who responds to the MILLER's performance by telling another bawdy story in which a miller is the target of ridicule.

John the Clerk   One of the clerks of "The REEVE'S TALE." In Middle English, the word *clerk* denotes a church cleric or clerical scholar—i.e., one studying to be a cleric. Neville Coghill's translation of *The CANTER-*

BURY TALES refers to ALAN and John as "biblical scholars" in the attempt to convey the latter sense. Alan and his fellow student are nearly indistinguishable. Neither one is described individually, and both of them, coming from the town of STROTHER in the north of England, speak with the same northern dialect although currently enrolled at one of the colleges of Cambridge University. They are typical of their breed, Chaucer says, full of "mirth" and "revelry." Their youthful high spirits in fact seem to provide the motive for their visit to SIMKIN the miller, where they hope to outwit his thievery by overseeing the grinding of their own grain. The tale takes some satiric jabs at the scholarly mentality, especially in the ease with which the miller discovers their ruse and turns it to his own advantage, showing that, in the words of the miller, a scholar is not always the wisest man. The miller takes another shot at them when Alan and John ask him for lodging, saying that although his house is small, they can, by arguments of logic, change a space of 20 feet into one a mile wide. The only characteristic which distinguishes the two clerks from one another is that John seems to be the more cautious of the two. When they discover their horse loose in the fens, John rebukes his companion for not having lodged the animal in the barn. And when Alan reveals his plan to "swyve" (Middle English slang for "copulate with") the miller's daughter, John cautions him against such behavior, reminding him of the miller's reputation for violence. Also, rather than simply jumping on top of the woman he intends to have sex with, as did his companion, John creates a ruse by moving the baby's cradle, causing her to imagine John's bed as her own and thus to climb into it. All of this behavior considered together argues that John is a somewhat cautious young man, in contrast to Alan, who acts on impulse.

John the Friar   The friar in "The SUMMONER'S TALE." As a member of a mendicant religious order, the friar depends upon alms (i.e., the proceeds of begging) rather than personal or communal property. John is also referred to as a limiter, which means that he was licensed to beg within a specific geographical area. The tale tells the story of one particular episode of begging that resulted in John's receiving a worthless and insulting gift from a man named THOMAS (1), who had contributed money to various friars all his life and feels that he has never seen any good come of it.

John the Monk   Primary character in "The SHIPMAN'S TALE." John is the sensualist monk who claims kinship with the busy merchant whose wife he seduces in exchange for a "loan" of 100 francs. John raises the sum by borrowing it from the merchant and then repaying this borrowed money to the wife, letting her believe that it is his own money. She spends the night with him while her husband is on a business trip. John encounters the merchant before he returns home and tells him that the borrowed money has been repaid to his wife in his absence. When her husband asks her for the money, she claims, truthfully, that she thought the money was intended for her, as a gift for the hospitality the monk has received in their house (without specifying, of course, the full nature of that hospitality). John is just one example of Chaucer's clerical satire that appears throughout The CANTERBURY TALES.

Jonah (Jonas)   In the Old Testament, Jonah was a prophet who was swallowed by a great fish for disobeying God's command to preach repentance to the Assyrian city of Nineveh. In "The MAN OF LAW'S TALE," God's protection of Jonah during his sojourn inside the great fish is compared to His protection of CONSTANCE, the tale's heroine, during all the trials that she is forced to endure (line 486).

Jonathan   In the Old Testament, Jonathan was the oldest son of King Saul and a close friend of DAVID. Jonathan's loyalty to David was proven time after time as he warned David of his father's threats of vengeance and encouraged David in times of danger. The proverbial nature of their friendship is alluded to in the prologue to The LEGEND OF GOOD WOMEN, version F, when the narrator sings a BALLADE in which he mentions various types of human paragons, concluding that none are a match for Queen ALCESTIS, to whom his song is dedicated (line 251).

Joseph   In the Old Testament, Joseph was the 11th and favorite son of JACOB, and the first child by Jacob's favorite wife, RACHEL. Out of jealousy, Joseph's older brothers sold him into slavery in Egypt. There Joseph was sold to Potiphar, an officer of the ruling Pharaoh. His good conduct soon earned him the highest position in Potiphar's household, but when Potiphar's wife attempted to seduce Joseph and he refused, she accused him of the crime anyway and Joseph was sent to prison. However, news of Joseph's ability to interpret dreams reached Pharaoh, who had Joseph removed from prison and ordered him to interpret his (Pharaoh's) own troubling dreams. Joseph saw these dreams as a warning of impending famine, whereupon Pharaoh rewarded Joseph by giving him an important position in his government. When his brothers later came to Egypt to buy grain during the famine that Joseph had predicted, he tested them to see if they had repented. When their response showed that they had, he forgave them and asked them to move to Egypt where he could better provide the family with food and other essentials as long as the famine continued.

Because of his response to Potiphar's wife, Joseph is mentioned in "The PARSON'S TALE" as an example of one who obeyed the commandments of God by resisting the sin of lechery (line 443). The narrator of *The BOOK OF THE DUCHESS* compares his own dream—the one that is to be the subject of his poem—to Pharaoh's, saying that his dream is so marvelous he doubts that even someone as skilled as Joseph would be able to interpret its meaning (line 282). The narrator of *The HOUSE OF FAME* expresses a similar idea (line 516). In "The NUN'S PRIEST'S TALE" the rooster CHAUNTICLEER cites Pharaoh's dream as evidence that dreams can contain accurate warnings about the future (line 3133). Chaunticleer's dream of being attacked by a fox does come true by the tale's end.

Joseph, Saint In the New Testament of the Bible, Joseph was the spouse of Mary, the Virgin Mother of Christ, and thus Christ's foster father. Nothing is known of his life outside of those details reported in the Gospels, the most familiar of which is his profession as a carpenter. Joseph's role as Christ's foster father is mentioned briefly in "The PARSON'S TALE" (line 286).

Josephus, Ebrayk *See* EBRAECUS, FLAVIUS JOSEPHUS.

Jousting *See* CHIVALRY.

Jove *See* JUPITER.

Jovinian A fourth-century monk who suffered condemnation at Rome for his views concerning virginity, which he denied was a higher or more sanctified state than matrimony. Jovinian also attacked the belief in the perpetual virginity of Mary. These views drew attacks from both Saint JEROME and Saint AUGUSTINE.

Jubal *See* AURORA (2).

Jubaltre *See* GIBRALTAR.

Judas In the New Testament of the Bible, Judas, also called Judas Iscariot, was the 12th apostle and the one who betrayed Christ to the Romans, who arrested Christ prior to the Crucifixion. Judas was paid 30 pieces of silver for his deed. In some versions of the story, the realization of its enormity caused him to commit suicide. According to the gospel of John (John 12:6), Judas was the keeper of the apostles' money—a kind of treasurer for the group—and stole from them. This is alluded to in "The FRIAR'S TALE" when the FRIAR compares the main character of his tale, a corrupt summoner, to Judas, because the summoner steals out of the fines he collects for the ecclesiastical court for which he works (line 1350). Judas' more serious crime is mentioned in "The CANON'S YEOMAN'S TALE" when the CANON'S YEOMAN says that just as Judas' guilt did not contaminate the other apostles, so should the cor-

ruption of one canon (i.e., his boss) not be taken to indicate the moral state of the remainder (lines 1003–07). Judas' envy of MARY MAGDALENE, who anointed Christ's head with precious ointment, is given as an example of the sin of envy in "The PARSON'S TALE" (line 502). In another part of his sermon, the PARSON uses Judas as an example of the evils of flattery, comparing those who indulge in flattery to Judas' betrayal of Christ with a kiss (line 616). The latter notion would seem also to apply to "The NUN'S PRIEST'S TALE," whose narrator refers to the fox as a "newe Scariot" (line 3227) [new Iscariot] because he used flattery to trick the rooster CHAUTICLEER.

Judas Maccabeus In the Apocrypha, Judas Maccabeus was one of a family of Jewish heroes who helped deliver the Jews from persecution by the Syrian king ANTIOCHUS (1) Epiphanes. Considered one of the Nine Worthies by medieval scholars, Judas Maccabeus established a long line of priest-kings that lasted until supplanted by HEROD (2) in 40 B.C. The fact that he was able to overcome a large army with his own significantly smaller host is mentioned by Dame PRUDENCE in "The TALE OF MELIBEE" as she advises her husband against thinking that he will vanquish the men who robbed him just because he has more people fighting on his side (lines 1658–59).

Judges, Book of A book of the Old Testament that covers the chaotic 300-year period between Joshua's death and the beginning of a centralized government under King Saul. The story of SAMSON that appears in the Book of Judges is the basis of one of the brief biographies in "The MONK'S TALE" (lines 2015–94).

Judicum *See* JUDGES, BOOK OF.

Judith According to the Apocrypha that bears her name, Judith was a wise and brave Jewish woman dedicated to preserving the law of MOSES. During the reign of the Assyrian king NEBUCHADNEZZAR, one of his generals, Holofernes, was preparing to destroy the Jewish inhabitants of the city of BETHULIA. The people prayed to God to help them within five days, after which they would have to surrender. Judith went to the enemy camp, beheaded Holofernes, and brought his head back to the city. Terrified, the Assyrian army dispersed and the Jews were saved.

The story of Judith is mentioned several times in Chaucer's work. In "The MAN OF LAW'S TALE," she is given as an example of a woman whom God sustained through a difficult ordeal, just as he sustained CONSTANCE, the heroine of the Man of Law's story (line 939). JANUARY, the aged knight of "The MERCHANT'S TALE," uses Judith as an example of wise womanhood in his attempts to justify his decision to take a wife (line

1366). In "The TALE OF MELIBEE" PRUDENCE, the wife of MELIBEE, gives Judith as an example of a woman who was able to offer wise counsel to her people when trying to convince her husband to listen to her own advice (line 1099). Finally, the story of Judith and Holofernes is related in detail in "The MONK'S TALE," which uses Holofernes to exemplify how a man may suddenly fall out of grace with FORTUNE (lines 2551–74).

Judocus, Saint   Judocus was a seventh-century hermit who began life as the brother of King Judicael of BRITTANY. When Judicael abdicated, Judocus assumed the throne for several months but then left Brittany to make a pilgrimage to Rome, after which he retired to a hermitage in France, where he served God for many years. He died around A.D. 668. His tomb, famous for miracles, was at St. Josse-sur-Mer, near Montreuil, France. The WIFE OF BATH swears by Saint Judocus ("Joce" in Middle English) in her prologue when she explains how she responded to the infidelities of her fourth husband (line 483). The Wife would perhaps be familiar with the saint because her fondness for pilgrimages has led her to sites like the tomb of Judocus.

Juerie   *See* JEWERYE.

Jues   *See* JEWS, PORTRAYAL OF IN CHAUCER.

Julian, Saint   A seventh-century archbishop of Toledo in Spain who presided over the Spanish church in the time of the Visigothic kings, from A.D. 680 to 690, Julian was so greatly admired for his charity and kindness that he later became known as the patron saint of hospitality and accommodation. In the GENERAL PROLOGUE of *The CANTERBURY TALES*, Chaucer compares the FRANKIN, who is a gracious and liberal host, to Saint Julian (line 340). In *The HOUSE OF FAME*, the EAGLE swears by Saint Julian when he wants to call Chaucer's attention to FAME's palace (line 1022).

Julius Caesar   An exceptionally capable and ambitious Roman general and statesman who was dictator of the Roman Empire from 49 to 44 B.C., Julius Caesar was murdered in the capitol by a conspiracy of fellow senators whose ostensible purpose was to save the Roman republic from becoming a dictatorship. An abbreviated version of his rise and fall appears in Chaucer's "MONK'S TALE" as one of the tragedies of FORTUNE of which the MONK is so fond. The Monk refers to Caesar as the emperor of Rome, in keeping with a medieval tradition which regarded him as the first of the emperors. Interestingly, the story of Caesar's murder is depicted on the walls of the Temple of Mars in "The KNIGHT'S TALE" (line 2031), even though the KNIGHT's story of Palamon and ARCITE is set in the court of THESEUS in ancient Athens

and would therefore be considered older. In *The HOUSE OF FAME*, Julius Caesar is mentioned as one of the men whose fame rests on the shoulders of the Roman poet LUCAN (line 1502). The *TREATISE ON THE ASTROLABE* notes that the month of July was named for him and mistakenly claims that Caesar took two days out of the month of February in order to increase the number of days in July to 31 (part 1, paragragh 10). While he did in fact increase the number of days in July, it was not at February's expense.

Julius Canius   A Roman philosopher of the first century A.D. whom the emperor CALIGULA condemned to death for his beliefs. In the BOECE, Chaucer's translation of BOETHIUS' *Consolation of Philosophy*, he is mentioned by LADY PHILOSOPHY when she is giving the narrator examples of other people who have suffered on her behalf (Book 1, Prosa 4, lines 180–83). All the men she refers to were martyrs, a fact that chillingly foreshadows what actually did happen to Boethius.

Juno   In classical mythology, Juno was a Roman goddess and consort to the chief of the gods, JUPITER. Originally a goddess of light, she came to be known as a goddess of beginnings in general, and of birth in particular. Later she was additionally regarded as the special patron of women. Like the Greek goddess Hera, whose counterpart she was, Juno presided over the rite of marriage. Juno frequently involved herself in human affairs, as often as not to wreak vengeance for one of her husband's many sexual liaisons. Her anger against the city of Thebes, considered to be the cause of its destruction in "The KNIGHT'S TALE" and in the unfinished *ANELIDA AND ARCITE*, was brought on by Jupiter's affairs with two Theban women. The goddess' hatred for another group of people, the Trojans, is mentioned in *The HOUSE OF FAME* when the narrator observes the story of AENEAS and his escape from TROY on the walls of the TEMPLE OF VENUS (lines 198–218). In *TROILUS AND CRISEYDE*, PANDARUS believes that Juno will look out for the two lovers, obviously unaware of her antipathy toward the Trojan people (book 4, lines 1116–20). Juno's role as the protectress of women is invoked in *The BOOK OF THE DUCHESS* when Queen ALCYONE prays to the goddess for information about her husband, who has failed to return from a sea voyage (lines 108–10). Juno responds by sending MORPHEUS, the god of sleep, to animate her dead husband's body so that it can appear to her in a dream and inform her of his fate.

Jupiter (Jove)   The chief of the Roman gods, identified by the Romans with the Greek god Zeus. His consort was the queen of the gods, JUNO. Originally a sky god, he was worshipped as the controller of weather who could send lightning, thunder and rain. More than any other deity, he was considered the protector of the state, watching over its welfare, defending it and giving victory to its armies. He was also the god of destiny, knowing and controlling the future and, perhaps most significantly, the upholder of right, justice, virtue and the laws of nations. The myths of Jupiter are the same as those related of Zeus.

The god is mentioned numerous times in Chaucer's poetry. In *The HOUSE OF FAME,* the EAGLE who is ferrying the narrator to FAME's palace informs him that the experience he is about to have is the gift of Jupiter, sent as a reward for the narrator's heretofore unrewarded service to CUPID, the god of love (lines 612–26). In *TROILUS AND CRISEYDE* Jupiter is invoked numerous times, as in book three when TROILUS asks Jove to help him gain Criseyde's love (lines 722–25) and at the end of book four when CRISEYDE swears by him, promising to return to Troy within 10 nights (lines 1681–87). Jupiter is also mentioned a number of times in "The KNIGHT'S TALE," most notably in the scene which describes the gods arguing over whether PALAMON or ARCITE (1) should win the battle for EMILY's hand in marriage (lines 2238–2478). Interestingly, despite Jove's status as chief among the gods, it is SATURN who decides the victor. Jupiter is also mentioned briefly in

several of the biographies that appear in *The LEGEND OF GOOD WOMEN.*

Justinus Minor character in "The MERCHANT'S TALE." Justinus is the brother of JANUARY, the aged knight who wishes to marry a young woman. Justinus advises against the marriage, using antifeminist rhetoric to justify his position. Nevertheless, when January's mind is made up, Justinus aids in the negotiations and arrangements for the marriage. His name derives from the Latin *justitia* and suggests the truthfulness of his warnings against the marriage.

Juvenal Decimus Junius Juvenalis, more commonly known as Juvenal, was a famous Roman satirist whose work continued to be popular during the Middle Ages. He did most of his writing during the reigns of the emperors Trajan and Hadrian, from A.D. 98 to 128. Chaucer not only borrows excerpts from Juvenal, which appear in *TROILUS AND CRISEYDE* (book four, lines 197–201), the *BOECE* (Book Four, Metrum 5, lines 11 ff.) and the GENERAL PROLOGUE TO *THE CANTERBURY TALES* (line 626 ff.), but the WIFE OF BATH quotes the Roman author's comments on the blessed state of the poor man who doesn't have to fear thieves (lines 1192–94).

Kakus *See* CACUS.

Kara-Nor (Carrenar)   Lake located on the east side of the Gobi Desert in Central Asia. Its name means "Black Lake." Lying on a main trade route between China and Europe, the area was known to medieval Europeans through Marco Polo's description of the region. In Chaucer's *BOOK OF THE DUCHESS,* the lake is mentioned by the BLACK KNIGHT. In keeping with his habit of communicating through metaphors or other figures of speech, the Black Knight praises the character of the fair LADY WHITE by saying that she would never lead a knight on by sending him away on quests to distant regions. One of the regions he mentions, which is considerably distant from England, is that of Kara-Nor (line 1029).

Karibdous *See* CHARYBDIS.

Kaukasous *See* CAUCASUS.

Kayrudd   The town in BRITTANY where ARVERAGUS and DORIGEN, the two central characters of "The FRANKLIN'S TALE," live. The name would seem to be derived from the Welsh *Caer-rhudd,* which means "red house." Although there are several villages in Brittany with the name Kerru, which could be a modernization of the name Chaucer uses, none lies along the coast as described in the tale. The coastal setting is significant because Dorigen promises to become the lover of the squire AURELIUS if he can remove the rocks which line the coast and thus facilitate her husband's return voyage.

Kean, Patricia M.   Kean, who teaches at Oxford University, wrote *Chaucer and The Making of English Poetry* in two separately titled volumes: *Love Vision and Debate* (1972) and *The Art of Narrative* (1972). Kean sees Chaucer as the first poet writing in English to confront two problems: (1) finding verse forms appropriate to large scale works and (2) integrating subject matter from philosophy, morals and the "newe science" "into narrative structures" to give the whole "a new brilliance and a new depth of meaning." Kean's solutions to these problems, more than her borrowings from the prosodic traditions of other languages, established Chaucer as the "maker" of English poetry.

Kenelm, Saint   Saint Kenelm began his life as a prince of Mercia, one of the kingdoms of Anglo-Saxon England, in the ninth century. When he was seven years old, he succeeded to the throne on the death of his father, King Kenulph. Shortly after his coronation, his sister Cynefrith caused him to be murdered in the forest of Clent. According to legend, just before his death Kenelm dreamed that he climbed a beautiful tree which was cut down beneath him by his attendant, whereupon his soul flew to heaven in the form of a little bird. In medieval England, Kenelm was universally venerated as a saint and martyr. CHAUNTICLEER, the learned rooster of "The NUN'S PRIEST'S TALE," refers to Kenelm's dream as evidence for his own belief in dreams' prophetic nature (lines 3110–12).

Kent   County in southeastern England, with a coastline along the English Channel. The town of CANTERBURY, with its great cathedral and shrine of St. THOMAS À BECKET, is located in the county of Kent. In *The HOUSE OF FAME* and "The MILLER'S TALE," the narrators swear, or have one of the characters swear, "by Saint Thomas of Kent," which was a popular way of referring to the saint in the 14th century.

Kenulphus Son *See* KENELM, SAINT.

King Antiochus *See* ANTIOCHUS.

King Peter of Cyprus *See* PIERRE DE LUSIGNAN.

King Peter of Spain *See* PEDRO OF CASTILE.

Kings, Book of   When Chaucer refers to the Book of Kings, he is actually referring to the biblical books we know as 1 and 2 Samuel, because in the Vulgate (Latin) version of the Bible that he used, 1 and 2 Samuel were called 1 and 2 Kings. The books we know as 1 and 2 Kings were entitled 3 and 4 Kings. Chaucer mentions the First Book of Kings (i.e., 1 Samuel) in "The PARSON'S TALE" when the narrator makes reference to the sons of ELI as an example of corruption in the priesthood. He compares wicked priests to fallen angels, saying that they are angels of light transformed into angels of darkness, children of God who have become sons of BELIAL (line 897). Modern readers may find this story in 1 Samuel 2. In "The TALE OF MELIBEE," Dame PRUDENCE recalls a passage from the Second Book of Kings (2 Samuel 11:25) when she advises her husband against taking up arms against those men who have robbed him and assaulted his family. She says, "The dedes of battailles been aventurouse and nothyng certeyne, / for as lightly is oon hurt with a spere as another" (lines 1167–68) [The outcomes of battles are chancy and uncertain, / for as easily is one man hurt with a spear as another]. In 2 Samuel, these words are attributed to DAVID when he learns from JOAB that Uriah the Hittite has been killed in battle. Ironically, David is attempting to rationalize the man's death (an attitude quite contrary to the spirit in which the words are quoted by Prudence), and commands Joab to continue the fighting.

Kings, Second Book of   *See* KINGS, BOOK OF.

Kittredge, George Lyman (1860–1941)   Harvard profesor and scholar of Old and Middle English language and literature. Kittredge developed an interest in early New England history and published extensively on its folklore, in addition to his seminal works on Chaucer and other early English authors. His work ranges from the immensely technical *Observations on the Language of Chaucer's "Troilus"* (1894) to the gracious, popularly written *Chaucer and His Poetry* (1915), where he propounds his theory that there is a debate on marriage taking place between the tellers of "The WIFE OF BATH'S TALE," "The CLERK'S TALE," "The MERCHANT'S TALE" and "The FRANKLIN'S TALE." After Kittredge's study, these four tales became popularly known as the "MARRIAGE GROUP." Some of Kittredge's essays laid the groundwork for the work of later scholars who would research the relationships between Chaucer and his sources.

Knight, the (1)   The first pilgrim to be described in the GENERAL PROLOGUE to *The CANTERBURY TALES,* the Knight is also invited to tell the first tale. Because he and his son are the only two members of the nobility taking part in the pilgrimage, some readers have argued that his position is determined by social rank: He is the highest-ranking layman in the group. Like the PARSON and the PLOWMAN, the Knight is considered to be one of the ideal portraits featured in the General Prologue. As such he functions as a kind of paragon against which the virtues and failings of the other pilgrims may be measured. Much of the Knight's portrait is given to describing his military career, with particular emphasis on naming individual campaigns. The fact that all of them belonged to the series of holy wars known as the Crusades further enhances the nobility of his profession. Ostensibly, crusaders were not merely

Artist's rendering of the Knight, from the Ellesmere Manuscript of The Canterbury Tales. *The coat of mail (habergeon) mentioned in the General Prologue is missing, and the Knight's mount has a strange brand on its flank.*

fighting for land and power, but for the conversion of heathen lands and people to Christianity. Another way in which the Knight's portrait contrasts to those of the other pilgrims is in its focus on moral attributes rather than on physical appearance. At the beginning of the description, we are told that he is a worthy man who loves "trouthe and honour, fredom and curteisie" (fidelity, good reputation, generosity and courteous behavior) as well as prowess in arms. Although we are eventually presented with a few details such as his rust-stained tunic of fustian and his plainly attired horse, instead of being left to determine for ourselves how to interpret these items, we are informed that he is wise as well as worthy, as humble in demeanor as a maiden, and that he has never performed any "vileynye" (rude behavior) to any man.

In spite of these indications that Chaucer did not intend the Knight's portrait to be satiric, at least one reader, Terry Jones (of Monty Python fame) makes an interesting argument for viewing it as just that in his book on the subject, *Chaucer's Knight: The Portrait of a Medieval Mercenary* (1980). Such a view is significantly challenged, however, by historical evidence for the high regard in which the Crusades were held during the late 14th century (*see* Maurice Keen's essay in *English Court Culture in the Later Middle Ages*, edited by V. J. Scattergood and J. W. Sherborne). The tale that the Knight tells is a chivalric romance recounting the story of two noble knights, PALAMON AND ARCITE, and their rivalry for the love of EMILY, the sister-in-law of THESEUS, duke of Athens. *See also* CHIVALRY.

Knight (2)   A minor character in the "The MAN OF LAW'S TALE," this Northumbrian knight is inspired by Satan to lust after CONSTANCE, the pure, noble and long-suffering heroine of this tale. Consumed with frustrated desire and rage, he murders HERMENGILD, the wife of the couple with whom Constance lives, places the bloody knife in the hands of the sleeping Constance and then swears an oath that Constance committed the deed. At that very moment, a hand appears which strikes him down, while a voice from the heavens proclaims the woman's innocence. King ALLA, whom Constance later marries, condemns the man to death.

Knight (3)   An unnamed knight of King ARTHUR's court plays a major role in "The WIFE OF BATH'S TALE." After raping a young woman, this knight is condemned to death by the king, but then spared when the queen pleads on his behalf. His release is conditional, however; to earn his freedom, he must find the correct answer to the question: What is it that women desire most? He is given a year and a day to complete his quest. One year later, as he makes his way back to the court without a definite answer, he encounters a LOATHLY HAG in the woods. She promises to give him the correct answer if he will fulfill her request once his task is complete. The knight agrees and learns that what women desire most is sovereignty (i.e., the upper hand) in marriage. When he reports his answer to the queen, all the women in the court accept its validity and the knight gains his freedom—until the hag decides to collect on his promise. She requests that he marry her, and the knight follows through. But when he refuses to embrace his wife on their wedding night, the lady demands an explanation. She is old, ugly and poor, he says, attempting to justify his actions. The lady responds with a well-reasoned explanation of why none of these features is necessarily bad in a wife, and concludes by asking if he would rather have her beautiful and possibly unfaithful, or ugly and faithful. When the knight leaves the decision up to her, thus granting her the sovereignty that all women desire, she rewards him by instantly becoming beautiful and promising to remain faithful.

Although a number of readers see the Wife of Bath's tale as pro-feminist in its message, others are bothered by the serious nature of the knight's crime (rape) and his ultimate punishment (a happy marriage with a beautiful wife). One should, however, keep in mind that the knight has learned to behave in a way diametrically opposed to the position taken by any rapist, by trusting a woman and willingly relinquishing power to her.

"Knight's Tale, The"   The KNIGHT (1) is the first pilgrim to participate in the tale-telling contest on the road to CANTERBURY.

SUMMARY

"The Knight's Tale" is, appropriately, the story of two young warriors, PALAMON ARCITE (1). The setting is the city of ATHENS in ancient Greece.

Part One

The tale opens with a brief description of how THESEUS, duke of Athens, won his battle with the AMAZONS, mighty women warriors of SCYTHIA. Following the battle, Theseus took HIPPOLYTA, the queen of the Amazons, to be his wife. On his way home from this battle, Theseus encounters a group of women who are in mourning because CREON, the ruler of THEBES, has refused to allow the burial of their relatives who had been killed in a conflict with THEBES. Theseus attacks Creon, and in the ensuing battle Palamon and Arcite, two cousins fighting for Creon, are taken prisoner. Theseus brings them back to Athens and puts them in prison with a perpetual (i.e., life) sentence. Their prison is actually a well-fortified tower within Theseus' fortress, attached to the wall that surrounds a garden where Theseus' sister, the beautiful EMILY, frequently walks for recreation. Palamon, the first to set eyes on the lovely Emily, falls in love with her immediately. Arcite, who is sleeping, awakens and asks Palamon why he is so agitated. When Palamon tells him the reason— that he has been smitten by love—Arcite looks out the window, sees Emily, and also falls in love with her. From this point onward, the brotherly love the two cousins once shared turns into mortal hatred.

Part Two

After a time, Arcite, through the intercession of a Theban noble, is released from prison on the condition that he leave Athens and never return. Unable to bear his freedom away from Emily, he finally decides to disguise himself as a laborer and to seek a position as a servant in Theseus' household. He calls himself

PHILOSTRATE, a name that means "overthrown by love." Because he is young and strong he easily finds employment, and it is not long before he secures a position as a page of the chamber, or personal servant, to his beloved Emily. Arcite/Philostrate does so well in this position that, in recognition of his merit, Theseus promotes him to the post of squire in his own household.

Seven years pass, during which Arcite serves Theseus and Palamon languishes in prison. Finally, formulating a plan to escape to Thebes and come back with an army to fight Theseus, Palamon escapes from prison. He travels by night and takes cover during the day. Meanwhile, Arcite, who is now the chief squire of Theseus' court, rides out to enjoy the warm weather and to celebrate the coming of May by gathering flowers and greenery in the forest. At first his mood is cheerful and gay; but it soon turns gloomy as he thinks of Emily and speaks aloud of how his love for her has brought him so low that he serves as a squire to his greatest enemy. Unfortunately for him, Palamon has taken cover nearby and overhears every word. His anger ignited by what he sees as treachery on Arcite's part, Palamon leaps out of the bushes and confronts his cousin, swearing to kill him with his bare hands. Arcite, however, is not only in much better physical condition than Palamon, but he also has a sword, which he immediately draws to protect himself. Swearing to love Emily in spite of Palamon's threats, Arcite challenges him to a duel on the following day— a duel that will decide, by its outcome, which of them has the "right" to Emily's love. Palamon accepts the challenge. That night Arcite brings him food, drink and bedding; the next day he returns with armor and weapons. The two help each other into their armor, and the battle begins.

The two knights fight like animals. The narrator compares Palamon to a "wood" (mad) lion and Arcite to a cruel tiger. Theseus, who has chosen this morning to hunt out in the countryside surrounding Athens, chances upon the two knights and interrupts their struggle. He demands to know who they are and why they are fighting without a judge or other attendants. Palamon reveals the truth of the matter—who they are and why they are fighting, and says that they both deserve to die. Theseus agrees and proceeds to condemn them, but Hippolita and Emily, who are with him, beg for mercy. Theseus reconsiders, then decides to be merciful, and agrees to let them go if they will both swear friendship to him and his country, which they readily do. Theseus then suggests, since it would be impossible for Emily to marry both of them, that they participate in a tournament. The one who wins will marry Emily. The two knights accept this proposition and hurry home to Thebes to prepare for the contest.

Part Three
Part three begins with a lengthy description of how Theseus prepares for the upcoming tournament by constructing a huge stone amphitheater. The structure has three gates, facing east, west and north; each gate is surmounted by an altar and oratory. The eastward-facing gate features an altar to VENUS, the goddess of love; the west gate honors MARS (1), the god of war; and the northgate is dedicated to DIANA, the goddess of chastity. Chaucer provides an extended tableau-like description of each temple. The images portrayed in these descriptions emphasize the intensity of the passions involved in human love and hate. In the Temple of Venus, lovers are depicted tossing and turning with insomnia, crying out in frustration, and suffering the "fiery strokes" of desire. The Temple of Mars is painted with images of death and destruction: men killing one another in battle and in private conflict; buildings burning; and the personifications of Madness, Misfortune and Outrage. Diana's temple, on the other hand, features scenes taken from mythology that are in some way associated with the theme of chastity, such as the story of DAPHNE and Phoebus APOLLO and that of ACTAEON.

On the agreed upon date, Arcite and Palamon return to Athens, each bringing 100 knights to participate in the tournament. On the eve of the event, Palamon visits the Temple of Venus, where he prays for victory. When he makes his sacrifice, there is a delay, but the statue of the goddess finally gives him a sign which he takes to mean that his request will be granted. The next morning, Emily makes her way to the temple of Diana, where she prays that she might remain chaste and unmarried. The goddess appears and speaks to her, telling her that she must marry one of the knights, but not specifying which. Arcite prays for victory at the Temple of Mars. Following his prayer, the statue of Mars begins to shake, and Arcite hears a low murmur that says "Victory!" He takes this as a sign of his own success. Following this series of prayers, Chaucer changes the scene to listen in on a conversation between the pagan gods. Venus and Mars are arguing over whether Palamon or Arcite should win. JUPITER is trying to bring an end to their struggle when Saturn intervenes on Venus' behalf and grants the victory to Palamon.

Part Four
Duke Theseus, who had originally ordained that the tournament would be decided when one of the knights was either beaten or slain, modifies that decision, placing certain restrictions on the type of weapons that can be used so that neither of the contestants, nor any of their followers, is likely to be mortally wounded. Those who are overcome on either side, he continues, shall be taken to a holding area, where they will remain until either Palamon or Arcite is captured or slain. Those

who have come to view the tournament praise Theseus for his nobility. Palamon and his followers enter at the gate of Venus; Arcite and his men, at the gate of Mars. Theseus gives the sign for the contest to begin. The description of the battle is fairly brief, and concludes when Palamon, despite his courage and skill, is brought to the holding area on Arcite's side. Arcite's victory, however, is short-lived. A Fury (see ERINYES), a supernatural agent of retribution sent by SATURN, springs out of the ground and startles Arcite's horse. The horse shies and throws his rider, who is mortally injured in the fall. Strenuous attempts are made to heal the knight, and he regains consciousness long enough to make amends with his cousin and to suggest to Emily that, if she ever will be a wife, she should marry Palamon. There is a long description of the funeral rites that are held for Arcite, after which Palamon and the other Thebans depart for home.

An unspecified number of years pass. During that time the leaders of Athens decide to form alliances with certain countries, including Thebes. Theseus sends for Palamon, hoping to forge a political alliance by offering him Emily in marriage. When Palamon arrives in Athens, Theseus brings him together with Emily and delivers a long speech that is a meditation on the inevitability of change, describing the transitory nature of life as something ordained by Providence. Theseus advises the couple to cease mourning for Arcite, who cannot show them any gratitude for their devotion, and to marry, thereby making "of sorwes two / O parfit joye" (lines 3071–72) [of two sorrows / One perfect joy]. They eargerly take his advice, are soon married, and like two lovers in a fairy tale, live happily ever after.

COMMENTARY

"The Knight's Tale" is the first to be told on the pilgrimage to CANTERBURY, and provided we have read the General Prologue to the tales, we have a vivid image of the tale's teller. Chaucer's portrait of the Knight, unlike some of his others, seems completely lacking in satire or even the lightest shading of irony. The Knight's description shows us that he is an experienced soldier, a noble and serious man. The story he tells is a loose adaptation of the Italian writer BOCCACCIO's Il TESEIDA delle nozze d'Emelia (The story of Theseus concerning the nuptials of Emily), which was composed around 1339–41. Chaucer also draws upon another work that treats the same subject, STATIUS' Thebaid, and he may have used the Roman de Thèbes. The tale's philosophical dimension is derived from BOETHIUS' Consolation of Philosophy, which Chaucer was probably in the process of translating (as the BOECE) during the same period that he wrote The Canterbury Tales.

Chaucer's main source, the Teseida, is a poem of close to 10,000 lines. The fact that "The Knight's Tale" contains only some 3,108 lines gives an immediate idea of how much of his source Chaucer elided in writing his version. The most significant effect of the changes he made was to turn what was an epic of 12 books into a four-part chivalric romance, though some scholars have argued that it is more of a tragedy than a romance, with its philosophical meditations on Providence and the necessity of fate. Certainly it does have tragic elements, painting through the rapid alterations in Arcite's destiny a striking example of the medieval notion of Fortune's ever-turning wheel.

The historical setting of the poem is classical Greece, of which both Athens and Thebes were city-states. To students who have studied Greek civilization, it may come as a surprise to hear Greek soldiers referred to as knights and to find them engaging in a tournament. These and other medieval trappings that appear in the poem merely show Chaucer following what was conventional practice for the medieval poet writing about events taking place in another historical period and/or culture—to dress the story, and its characters, in contemporary clothing. This was not only a conscious effort to make the story familiar and meaningful to a medieval audience; it also reflected a lack of concern over what we would call historical and cultural accuracy. As an academic discipline, history did not even exist in the universities of medieval Europe, and very little was actually known about other times and cultures except what was portrayed in accounts that a modern reader would consider fictional or mythical. Fact and fiction were not even distinctly separate categories, but, rather, existed at the two extremes of a single continuum. One salient feature of Greek civilization does survive in the medieval poem, and that is the role played by the pagan gods. Venus, Mars and Saturn intervene to determine the outcome of events, yet their actions are placed within a larger framework of Christian Providence. Duke Theseus describes and explains this framework at the end of the poem in his speech about the Prime Mover and the divine order of the universe.

"The Knight's Tale" is a chivalric romance, a type of literature that was popular among the aristocracy of western Europe during the Middle Ages. This type of literature typically celebrated the adventures of knights who exhibited an idealized code of behavior that combined loyalty, honor and service to ladies. The genre's emphasis on love and courtly manners sets it apart from the CHANSON DE GESTE and other types of literature that featured knights and their military exploits. The main themes of "The Knight's Tale"—nobility, love, suffering, valor and courtesy—were typical themes of this genre. In plot it differs somewhat from the majority of chivalric romances because the two male competitors, Palamon and Arcite, are both portrayed favorably. In the typical romance, one of them would be portrayed less favorably, or even as a villain, like King Mark in the romance of TRISTRAM and ISOLDE. But the fact that Palamon and Arcite, who are, after all, cousins, so closely resemble one another, makes it difficult to favor one of them over the other. This, along with other sources of tension in the poem, undercuts the very ethos that the poem appears to celebrate, that of the aristocratic way of life.

Chaucer develops this tension in a number of ways. One is by having the narrator, and sometimes even the knights themselves, display ambivalence toward their own motives and behavior. At the end of their first argument over who has the better "right" to love Emily, Arcite exclaims, "We stryve as dide the houndes for the boon; / They foughte al day, and yet hir part was noon. / Ther cam a kyte, whil that they were so wrothe, / And baar awey the boon bitwixe hem bothe." (lines 1177–80) [We strive like the hounds did for a bone; They fought all day, and still had no part of it. / There came a kite, while they were so angry, / And it bore away the bone between them both]. When the two men finally come to blows in the woods outside Athens, they are both in their fury compared to wild animals, Palamon to a "wood leon" [mad lion] and Arcite to a "crueel tigre" [cruel tiger]. These descriptions of animalistic behavior form a sharp contrast to the knights's nobility and virtues referred to elsewhere.

Another feature of the poem that deflates the elevation of its subject matter is the author's often abrupt switch from elegant language and beautiful imagery to language that is plain and blunt and even ironic, such as the description of Arcite's fluctuating emotional state as he roams the woods on May Day: "Into a studie he fil sodeynely, / As doon thise loveres in hir queynte geres, / Now in the crope, now doun in the breres, Now up, now doun, as boket in a well." (lines 1530–33) [Into a kind of trance he suddenly fell, / As is the quaint custom of these lovers, / Now up in the leaves, now down in the briars, / Now up, now down, like a bucket in a well]. It is difficult to maintain a mental image of the knight as a noble lover when he is compared to a bucket in a well. Similarly, the high seriousness of their struggle for Emily's affection rapidly descends to the level of comedy when Theseus reminds us that Emily has not even been aware of their devotion for some time: "And yet they wenen for to been ful wyse / That serven love, for aught that may bifalle. / But this is yet the beste game of alle, / That she for whom they han this jolitee / Kan hem therfore as muche thank as me. / She woot namoore of al this hoote fare, / By God, than woot a cokkow or an hare!" (lines 1804–10) [And yet they expect to be completely wise, / Those that serve love, despite whatever may happen. / But this is yet the best joke of all, / That she for whom they have this passion / Owes them as much thanks as she owes me. / She knows no more of all this tempestuous activity, / By God, than knows a cuckoo or a hare"].

The description of Arcite's death is another puzzling passage, when the struggle to save him culminates with these abrupt, rather dismissive lines: "Hym gayneth neither, for to gete his lif, / Vomyt upward, ne dounward laxatif. / Al is tobrosten thilke regioun; / Nature hath now no dominacioun. / And certeinly, ther Nature wol nat wirche, / Fare wel phisik! Go ber the man to chirche! / This al and som, that Arcita moot dye. . . ." (lines 2755–61) [To keep his life, neither benefits him, / Vomiting upward, nor a laxative which makes things go in the opposite direction. / All is destroyed in this region (of the body); / Nature now has no control there. / And certainly, where Nature will not be effective, / No use in trying medicine! Go, take the man to church! / This is the long and short of it, that Arcite must die. . .].

Throughout the poem, Chaucer alternates passages of great stateliness and beauty with lines similar to those quoted above, so that ultimately the poem exists in a kind of stylistic limbo, making it difficult to decide what our attitude to it should be. Ought we to take it seriously or ironically? Or should we attempt, as Donald HOWARD does, to reconcile these two extremes? In his excellent book, *The Idea of the Canterbury Tales*, Howard offers this solution to the hermeneutic dilemma that "The Knight's Tale" poses: "I think Chaucer is satirizing not the Knight himself but the knightly mentality, including its literary tastes, and that he is satirizing it with delicate irony—is satirizing something for which he had respect" (p. 234).

Yet it seems something more than respect, even a kind of empathy, that shines through in the great power of some of the serious passages, such as the description of the Temples of Mars and Venus, which, far from trivializing the passions that are represented by the images in each of the temples, suggests their power and inevitability in shaping the course of human events. Arcite's dying speech, in which he reconciles with Palamon and bequeaths Emily's love to him, and the description of Arcite's funeral, display nobility and pathos and pull the reader in, destroying the objectivity and emotional distance created by the ironic and satiric lines.

The ending works similarly. First we are told that Theseus' motives for recalling Palamon to Athens are entirely political: "Ther was a parlement / At Atthenes, upon certein pointz and caas; / Among the whiche pointz yspoken was, / To have with certein contrees alliaunce, / And have fully of Thebans obeisaunce" (lines 2970–74) [There was a parliament / At Athens, to discuss certain points and cases; / Among the points put forward was, / To have an alliance with certain countries, / And securely have the homage of the Thebans]. In order to expedite this obeisance, and to thus have the leadership of Thebes swear loyalty and obedience to Athens, Theseus is only too willing to offer his sister in marriage. But none of this is mentioned when he brings Palamon and Emily together and delivers a long and serious speech about the order of the universe as it was designed and set in motion by the "Firste Moevere" (Primum Mobile). The speech is a direct borrowing of ideas from the philosopher Boethius, whose work Chaucer translated, and it ultimately suggests that change (including death) is a necessary feature of the universe, and that the two people who are left behind should stop mourning over what they cannot change and make the best of what is left to them—i.e., that they should marry. All of which is a very circumspect way of suggesting that they do what is also best for Theseus, though it perhaps takes a somewhat jaded and cynical eye to discern the duke's motive throughout his extended and very moving speech. Furthermore, once Palamon and Emily are married, their life together is described in terms of unmitigated bliss: "For now is Palamon in alle wele, / Lyvynge is blisse, in richesse, and in heele, / And Emelye hym loveth so tendrely, / And he hire serveth so gentilly, / that nevere was ther no word hem bitwene / Of jalousie or any oother teene." (lines 3101–06) [For now is Palamon entirely happy and prosperous, / Living in bliss, with wealth and good health, / And Emily loves him so tenderly / And he serves her so courteously, / That never was there any harsh word between them / Of jealousy or any other grief].

On the other hand, the possibility of irony surfaces again when one reflects upon what it is that Palamon and Emily have to reconcile themselves to. The Boethian idea of resignation to one's fate was after all conceptualized by a man who was condemned to life in prison, and eventually to death. The mental picture of Palamon and Emily, who still "grucchen" or complain about Arcite's welfare even though he has now been dead for several years, having to be persuaded to resign themselves to wedded bliss, seems to a modern reader slightly reminiscent of Br'er Rabbit resigning himself to being thrown into the briar patch. Nevertheless, there is no real indication within the poem that their behavior, either their extended mourning for Arcite or their final willingness to be married, stems from any hidden or ignoble motives. The final effect of this is to suggest, both on the part of narrator and on the behalf of his characters, the kind of naiveté or innocence portrayed without qualification by other chivalric romances, but which Chaucer, as a member of the gentry and as one attached to the court as a civil servant, would have seen with a kind of double vision that enabled him to portray simultaneously an idealistic and a practical vision of those who professed to live by the chivalric code of honor. Although the noble and chivalric elements of the tale seem in their bulk to outweigh the passages that display an ironic tone, the tale's context offers a further qualification. It is immediately followed (and "quited" or answered) by the MILLER's bawdy FABLIAU which in many ways parodies the situation and sentiment of "The Knight's Tale."

Yet it is testimony to the poem's complexity that, despite all of its unresolved tensions between the noble and the base, the serious and the comedic, the problem it presents—the question of destiny versus the role played by man's free will—still comes across powerfully and lingers in the reader's mind long after other impressions have faded.

Kolve, V. A. (1934–) The recipient of multiple awards for outstanding teaching and scholarship, Kolve taught at Stanford and the University of Virginia before joining the faculty of the University of California–Los Angeles. Although he has written widely on a variety of medieval topics, his most important work in Chaucer studies is *Chaucer and the Imagery of Narrative: The First Five Canterbury Tales* (1984). As indicated by its title, this book provides an iconographic reading of "The KNIGHT'S TALE," "The MILLER'S TALE," "The REEVE'S TALE," "The COOK'S TALE" and "The MAN OF LAW'S TALE." Supporting his reading with many illustrations from medieval art, Kolve theorizes that Chaucer built these and other tales around central narrative images, such as the "rudderless" boat in "The Man of Law's Tale," at least partly because medieval memory depended so heavily upon the visual. Kolve's interest in this area also appears in an article, "From Cleopatra to Alceste: An Iconographic Study of *The Legend of Good Women*" (in *Signs and Symbols in Chaucer's Poetry*, 1981). Here Kolve argues that the tale of Cleopatra, which opens the *Legend*, provides a paradigm for the main theme of the collection, which is fruitless pagan tragedy. Although the poem in its unfinished state indicates a respect for the pagan past and for women, Kolve believes that if Chaucer had completed the work, he would have transcended this idea in a tale of ALCESTIS, who, because she was willing to die in place of her husband—and was then returned to life because of her generosity—can be read as an icon of Christian resurrection. With Olson Glendenning, Kolve also edited the Norton critical edition *Chaucer: The Canterbury Tales* (1989).

Koran The Koran, or Qur'an, is the name of the sacred book of the Muslims. It consists of revelations delivered orally by Muhammad at Mecca and Medina in the seventh century A.D., and initially committed to memory by professional remembrancers. The verses were eventually written down and were translated into Latin by Robert of Chester and Hermann the Dalmatian in 1143. Like the Bible, the Koran emphasizes God as the absolute creator and sustainer of a universe whose order reflects his infinite power, wisdom and authority. God provides guidance for mankind through His revealed Word, and mankind will be judged by the standard of that guidance on Judgment Day. The stern justice of God is tempered, however, by mercy and compassion.

Despite these similarities to biblically inspired religion, Chaucer's one reference to the Koran reflects the medieval western European view of Muslims as anti-Christian pagans. In "The MAN OF LAW'S TALE" the wicked SULTANESS OF SYRIA, in trying to turn her counselors against her son, says that he has abandoned the holy laws of the Koran since he married the Christian Constance (line 332).

Kynges, Book of *See* KINGS, BOOK OF.

Kynges, Seconde Book of *See* KINGS, BOOK OF.

Laban In the Bible, Laban was the father-in-law of JACOB. After leaving home to escape the wrath of his brother Esau, Jacob encountered a beautiful young woman named RACHEL at a well in Haran. Her father, who was also Jacob's uncle, promised her to his nephew in return for seven years of labor. After the time was up and Jacob had fulfilled his portion of the bargain, Laban tricked him by giving him his older daughter, Leah, and forcing him to work seven more years for Rachel (*see* Genesis 29). The work that Jacob did for Laban is mentioned in "The PARSON'S TALE" as an example of God's beneficence toward Laban and, more generally, as an indication of how God rewards those who keep his laws (line 443).

Laborinth (Laboryntus; labyrinth) *See* DAEDALUS.

Lacedaemon (Lacedomye; Lacidomye) *Lacedaemon* is another name for the region in the southern Peloponnesus of Greece that is more commonly known as Sparta. The region is mentioned in "The FRANKLIN'S TALE" when DORIGEN recalls, among many other stories of chaste women, how a group of 50 virgins from Lacedaemon chose to die rather than be raped by a group of invaders from MESSENE. The story is taken from Saint JEROME's *Epistola adversus Jovinianum* (Letter against Jovinian). In "The PARDONER'S TALE," the narrator draws upon Lacedaemon's reputation for sobriety when he tells the story of a Spartan ambassador, STILBOUN, who travels to CORINTH, a city known in the ancient world for its loose morality, to forge an alliance, but changes his mind because he finds so many of the Corinthians engaged in gambling (line 605). The anecdote forms part of the PARDONER's disquisition on the tavern vices of gambling, gluttony and swearing.

Lachesis In classical mythology, Lachesis was one of the Fates, the three goddesses who collectively determined the length of a person's life. Clotho spun the thread of life, Lachesis determined its length and Atropos cut it off when it was time for death. The daughters of Zeus and Themis, these goddesses made sure that the fate assigned to each individual was carried out, and no mortal could escape or alter their decrees. The narrator's reference to Lachesis and her sisters at the beginning of book 5 of *TROILUS AND CRISEYDE* indicates that his story is winding to a close and that the death of TROILUS, whose thread is running out, is not far off (line 7).

"Lack of Steadfastness" *See* "LAK OF STEDFASTNESSE."

Ladies, Book of the XXV The Book of the XXV Ladies is one of the titles by which Chaucer refers to what modern editors call *The LEGEND OF GOOD WOMEN*. He refers to the work by this title in the Retraction (*see* CHAUCER'S RETRACTION) that follows *The CANTERBURY TALES*, listing it among those works that he asks God to forgive him for writing because they seem too caught up in worldly vanities. It is thought that the Retraction was written when Chaucer was ill and approaching death, which helps to account for this remarkable change in attitude. His reference to the ladies as being 25 in number has led to the speculation that he had intended to include more women's biographies in the work and was perhaps unable, at the time, to remember how many he had already completed. This is supported by the fact that the last biography, that of HYPERMNESTRA, breaks off before the end. There is also the remote possibility that he had completed others, but that they did not find their way into the existing manuscripts of the poem. This could be why the MAN OF LAW, in the prologue to his tale, states that the work (which he calls the "Saint's Legend of Cupid") included the stories of DEIANIRA, HERMIONE, HERO, HELEN OF TROY, BRISEIS, LAODAMIA and PENELOPE (lines 62–75).

Ladomya *See* LAODAMIA.

Lady Philosophy An allegorical figure who plays a major role in the BOECE, Chaucer's Middle English translation of BOETHIUS' *Consolation of Philosophy*. The work begins with the narrator (Boethius) in exile, lamenting the current state of his life and misfortunes. In the midst of his complaint, a beautiful yet ancient woman with a piercing gaze appears. As he looks at the woman, her size mysteriously alters. Sometimes her height appears to extend into the heavens; sometimes she is no taller than other human beings. Her clothes are finely made, but dark and dusty in appearance. The lower hem of her garment is embroidered with the Greek letter π, and the upper border features the letter θ. Between the two letters there are steps like a ladder so that men might climb from the lower letter to the higher one. But instead of using her peaceably, men have violently torn here garments and carried pieces away. In her right hand, Philosophy carries her books, and in her left hand, her scepter. Her first action is to banish the Muses who have been keeping Boethius company, accusing them of increasing his sorrow with their sweet-seeming venom. The rest of the *Boece* (and of the *Consolation of Philosophy*) consists of a dialogue between Lady Philosophy and Boethius wherein she instructs him so that he may better understand and thus cope with his suffering, rather than spending the remainder of his life groaning and complaining over the bitterness of his fate.

Lady White   In *The BOOK OF THE DUCHESS*, Lady White is the allegorical white queen whom the BLACK KNIGHT claims to have lost when he played a game of chess with FORTUNE. As the poem progresses, the Knight reveals that Lady White was not a mere playing piece but a very beautiful, kind and loving woman whom he wooed, won, and then lost to death. Lady White probably represents Blanche (the French word for "white"), the duchess of Lancaster (*see* BLANCHE OF LANCASTER) and wife to JOHN OF GAUNT, who is represented in the poem by the Black Knight. This elegiac poem is thought to have been written to commemorate Blanche's death, which occurred in 1367.

Laius   In classical mythology, Laius was the king of Thebes who fathered OEDIPUS. Since an oracle had foretold that Laius would be killed by his own son, when Oedipus was born, Laius ordered a slave to pierce his feet and leave him exposed on Mount Citheron. Oedipus did not perish, but was saved by a shepherd and grew up as the son of King Polybus of Corinth. After leaving Corinth to avoid fulfilling the prophecy that he would kill his father (whom he thought to be Polybus), Oedipus met Laius on the road and killed him in a fight that arose when neither man was willing to yield the road to the other. He proceeded on to Thebes, where he solved the riddle of the Sphinx and, without knowing who she was, married his mother, Jocasta, and thus became the next king of Thebes. The story of Laius and his son are mentioned in book 2 of *TROILUS AND CRISEYDE* when CRISEYDE tells her uncle PANDARUS that she has been reading the "Romance of Thebes" of which it was a part (line 101).

"Lak of Stedfastnesse" ("Lack of Steadfastness")
One of Chaucer's shorter poems, written in the French BALLADE form. It has three stanzas of seven lines each (the most common ballade stanza was eight lines, but there were variations), a rhyme scheme of *ababbcc* with the same three rhymes repeated in all three stanzas and

a concluding envoy (a conventionalized stanza appearing at the close and usually addressed to a prince or some other important person). Each of the three ballade stanzas concludes with the same one-line refrain; aside from this, no other rhyme-word is repeated throughout the poem or in any of Chaucer's ballades, a feat attesting to his considerable skill working in this sophisticated artificial verse form. The poem's theme, lamentation over the moral decay of society, was a familiar one in Chaucer's day and took its most compelling form in William LANGLAND's visionary poem, *PIERS PLOWMAN*, also written in the 14th century. Because the idea was commonplace, it is impossible to point to any particular source or inspiration for Chaucer's poem, but the poem does contain many interesting parallels to the prologue of John GOWER's *CONFESSIO AMANTIS* which expresses similar concern over moral and political corruption in the realm of England. Among the many forms of immoral behavior referred to in Chaucer's poem are deceitful words and deeds, bribery (the willingness to to anything for "mede"), dissension, covetousness, conspiracy and fickleness, all of which result, the poet claims, from a lack of steadfastness. The concluding envoy, addressed to King RICHARD II, exhorts the king to take action against these crimes by enduring nothing that should be punished and wielding a "sword of castigation." The final lines, "Dred God, do law, love trouthe and worthinesse, / And wed thy folk agein to stedfastnesse" (lines 27–28) [Fear God, obey the law, love truth and worthiness, / And join your people again to steadfastness] suggest further that Richard ought himself to be a good example to his people. The poem survives in 14 manuscripts and one early printed edition. In John SHIRLEY's manuscript, the poem is called "Balade Royal made by our laureal poete then in hees laste yeeres" [Royal ballade made by our poet laureate in his last years]. This and the comment in MS Marley 7333 that Chaucer sent the poem to Richard who was then residing at Windsor Castle have been used to assign the poem an approximate date of 1397–99.

Lameadoun   *See* LAOMEDON.

Lamech   In the Old Testament, Lamech was a son of Methushael (Methuselah) and a descendant of CAIN. He is the first man mentioned in the Bible as having two wives, Adah and Zillah. The WIFE OF BATH uses Lamech as an example of someone who married more than once in the attempt to justify her own multiple marriages, which, however, were successive rather than simultaneous (prologue to "The WIFE OF BATH'S TALE," line 54). Lamech's bigamy is considered in a less positive light in "The SQUIRE'S TALE," when the falcon who has been betrayed by her lover complains to CANACEE of her mate's infidelity (line 550), and in the unfinished *ANELIDA AND ARCITE*, where the Armenian queen, ANELIDA, finds herself in similar circumstances after granting her love to the Theban knight ARCITE (2) (line 150). In both instances, the unfaithful lovers are compared to Lamech.

Lamedon *See* LAOMEDON.

Lamek (Lameth) *See* LAMECH.

Lamuel *See* LEMUEL.

Lancelot Lancelot, or Lancelot du Lac, was an important figure in Arthurian Romance. A French knight in the English court of King ARTHUR, he first appeared in the 12th-century work of French poet Chrétien de Troyes, *Le Chevalier de la Charrette* ("The Knight of the Cart"); this romance focuses on the adulterous love affair of Lancelot and Guinevere, emphasizing the intensity of his devotion to the queen to such a degree that the effect is sometimes comical (perhaps intentionally so). He is best known to modern audiences through modern adaptations of the Arthurian saga which focus on the love triangle of King Arthur, Guinevere and Lancelot. In adaptations that follow the traditional story line, the relationship of these three people is staged against a background of Arthur's struggle to hold together a kingdom constantly threatened by both internal and external strife. The pathos of the story derives from the fact that in addition to being the queen's lover, Lancelot was also the king's best friend and his most valued knight, two things that led the king to ignore hints that the man was betraying him by sleeping with his wife. Ultimately, despite the French knight's love for his king and the king's desire to overlook his wife's infidelity, the two are forced into battle by other knights who are jealous of Lancelot or who have other personal reasons for wanting to destroy him. Ultimately Lancelot and Arthur are reconciled, and the knight spends his last years as a hermit. Lancelot is mentioned only once in Chaucer's work, in the unfinished (or more specifically, interrupted) "SQUIRE'S TALE," when the SQUIRE attempts to describe the festive dancing that accompanied King CAMBYUSKAN's birthday celebration. Finding himself at a loss for words, he exclaims that only someone such as Lancelot would be able to accurately portray the subtle flirting and other sly behavior that went on (line 287). His choice of Lancelot obviously relates to the knight's involvement in a covert love affair.

Lancelot du Lac, book of When the NUN'S PRIEST pauses in the midst of his tale to announce that the story he tells, of the rooster CHAUNTICLEER, his "wife" PERTELOTE and RUSSELL the fox, is as true as the "book of Launcelot de Lake" (line 3212), he is either knowingly or unknowingly confirming that it is a fiction.

The "book" he refers to is probably part of the Vulgate Cycle, a 13th-century French prose romance that told the entire story of LANCELOT's life, from his birth to the fall of the Arthurian fellowship and Lancelot's death.

Langland, William Fourteenth-century English poet who wrote the important social satire, the *Vision of Piers Plowman* (*see* PIERS PLOWMAN). Very little is known of Langland's life or even of his identity, beyond the likelihood that he resided in London and also spent some time in the area of the Malvern Hills in the West Midlands which forms the setting for his poem. It also seems probable, considering the content of his poetry, that he was a monastic. Chaucer drew upon the character descriptions presented in Langland's poem for his portraits of the pilgrims in the GENERAL PROLOGUE TO *THE CANTERBURY TALES*.

Language—Pronunciation *See* CHAUCER'S LANGUAGE —PRONUNCIATION.

Language—Versification *See* CHAUCER'S LANGUAGE— VERSIFICATION.

Laodamia In classical mythology, Laodamia was the wife of PROTESILAUS, one of the Greeks who went to fight in the TROJAN WAR and was killed when the ships landed, before the battle ever began. Laodamia responded to his death by committing suicide. In Saint JEROME's *Epistola adversus Jovinianum* (Letter against Jovinian) she is mentioned as a faithful wife. In the prologue to "The MAN OF LAW'S TALE," the SERGEANT OF THE LAW states that Chaucer included the story of Laodamia in the "Saint's Legend of Cupid" (another title for *The LEGEND OF GOOD WOMEN*), but it does not in fact appear in that work, though she is mentioned as one of love's martyrs in the prologue (version F, line 263). In "The FRANKLIN'S TALE," DORIGEN thinks of Laodamia's virtue as she faces the choice of being faithful to her husband or keeping her promise to become the lover of the squire AURELIUS (line 1445).

Laodomya *See* LAODAMIA.

Laomedon (Lameadoun) In classical mythology, Laomedon was the father of PRIAM, the king of TROY during the TROJAN WAR. According to legend, Zeus (JUPITER), the king of the gods, punished Phoebus APOLLO and Poseidon (NEPTUNE) for attempting to dethrone him by forcing them to serve Laomedon for wages. They built the walls of Troy for the king, but when Laomedon refused to pay the agreed-upon price, Apollo sent a plague and Poseidon a sea monster to destroy his people. As the only means of appeasing Poseidon, Laomedon chained his daughter Hesione to a rock as food for the monster. HERCULES rescued her in exchange for Laomedon's promise that he would give Hercules some horses. When Laomedon again failed to keep his word, Hercules destroyed the city of Troy, killed Laomedon and all his sons except Priam and took Hesione captive. In *The BOOK OF THE DUCHESS,* the narrator falls asleep and dreams that he wakes up in a chamber decorated with the history of Troy, including the story of King Laomedon. The story has a more immediate relevance to the action in *TROILUS AND CRISEYDE* when CRISEYDE's father, CALKAS, predicts that Troy will fall because Phoebus (Apollo) and Neptune are still angry over Laomedon's failure to pay them.

Lapidarius (Lapidaire) An 11th-century treatise on gemstones and their supposed properties of healing and other characteristics. Chaucer refers to it in *The HOUSE OF FAME* when describing the walls inside FAME's palace, which are encrusted with gems such as those found in the *Lapidaire,* as numerous as the grasses growing in a meadow (line 1352).

Latinus (Latyne) According to VIRGIL's *AENEID,* Latinus was the King of Latium (the future site of Rome). When the Trojan AENEAS arrived in Latium, Latinus believed him to be the stranger to whom an oracle had commanded him to marry his daughter, LAVINIA. For that reason, Latinus welcomed Aeneas and offered him Lavinia's hand. But Turnus, a native prince who also wanted to marry Lavinia, stirred up hostility against Aeneas which led to war. When the war ended with the death of Turnus, Aeneas and Latinus carried out their agreement and united their people under joint rule. Another version of the story relates that the war against Turnus took place after Aeneas and Latinus had amalgamated their people, and that Latinus was killed in battle. The story of Latinus and Aeneas is engraved on the wall of the glass temple that Chaucer visits in book one of *The HOUSE OF FAME* (line 453).

Latona *See* DIANA.

Latumeus A character who appears in one of the anecdotes related in the prologue to "The WIFE OF BATH'S TALE." Complaining of how her fifth husband would offend her by reading from his Book of Wicked Wives, an anthology of stories denigrating women, the Wife relates that in one of the stories a man named Latumeus told his friend Arrius that in his garden he had a tree from which three of his wives had hanged themselves. Latumeus speaks in sorrow but his friend responds by asking for a sprig of "that blessed tree" to plant in his own garden (line 757). Analogues to this story appear in several medieval texts, possible sources for Chaucer's version. The ultimate source is the Roman poet CICERO's *De oratore.*

Laude *See* CLERE LAUDE.

Launcelot *See* LANCELOT.

Launcelot du Lake, Book of *See* LANCELOT DU LAC, BOOK OF.

Lavinia (Lavina) According to VIRGIL's *AENEID,* Lavinia was the daughter of LATINUS and princess of Latium, an ancient region in southern Italy. She was betrothed to TURNUS, the ruler of a neighboring kingdom. When her father revoked his promise to Turnus in order to marry Lavinia to AENEAS, a war ensued. Lavinia was ultimately wed to Aeneas and, according to legend, their heirs became the founders of Roman civilization. In *The BOOK OF THE DUCHESS* (line 331), Lavinia's story is depicted on panels of glass in a room where the dreamer/narrator "wakes up" (in fact, he is still dreaming). Aeneas' marriage to Lavinia is mentioned in *The HOUSE OF FAME* (line 458) and *The LEGEND OF GOOD WOMEN* (lines 1325–31).

Lavinium An ancient city in Italy where AENEAS landed after fleeing from TROY following the TROJAN WAR. According to the Roman poet VIRGIL, Italy, or Latium, as it was called in ancient times, was the country in which Aeneas was destined to found the nation that would build the great Roman Empire. In book 1 of *The HOUSE OF FAME* Lavinium is mentioned in the story of Aeneas engraved on the walls of a glass temple (line 148).

Layus *See* LAIUS.

Lazar (Lazarus) The beggar in Jesus' parable about a rich man and a poor man (not to be confused with the LAZARUS whom Jesus reportedly raised from the dead). The rich man despised the beggar, paying no attention to his requests when he passed by him each day. However, after his death, Lazar was carried by angels to heaven, where he found comfort. The rich man, on the other hand, found himself consigned to hell and eternal torment. This parable, found in Luke 16:19–31, is alluded to in "The SUMMONER'S TALE" (line 987) by the corrupt FRIAR (2), who uses it to try to frighten THOMAS (1) into giving him some money.

Lazarus In the Gospel of John, Lazarus is the brother of Martha and Mary of Bethany, two of Jesus' closest followers. His death and subsequent resurrection through Jesus' intervention was considered one of most important miracles of Jesus' ministry (John 12:1–44). Because of the publicity surrounding this event, the chief priest of Bethany plotted to kill Lazarus. The tears that Jesus shed when he learned of Lazarus' death are mentioned in "The TALE OF MELIBEE." When Dame PRU-

DENCE demands that MELIBEE stop crying over the harm that has come to his family through the robbers who stole his property and assaulted his daughter, Melibee responds that weeping is nothing to be ashamed of; witness the example of Jesus when he discovered the death of his friend Lazarus (lines 985–86).

Leander   *See* HERO.

Legend of Good Women, The   Subtitled *The Saints' Legend of Cupid, The Legend of Good Women* is the last of Chaucer's DREAM VISION poems.

THE PROLOGUE

The prologue exists in two forms, which scholars have designated F and G. The two are very similar in content, with two notable exceptions. In the G version, Chaucer eliminated much of the love poetry that (somewhat absurdly) features the daisy as its object, although the flower retains its importance as a symbol of faithful womanhood and continues to be a favorite flower of the narrator. Overall, this renders the tone of the prologue less comical. A feature of version G that does not appear in F is CUPID's specific instructions regarding books the narrator might have consulted if he wanted to tell stories of famous women who were faithful in love, rather than those, like CRISEYDE, who betrayed their lovers. For various reasons, most scholars agree that G is a revision of F. Stylistically, G is somewhat more polished; it is also better organized and more unified. Because both versions contain nearly the same information, the summary included below is based on F, with additional material from G mentioned in parentheses.

SUMMARY

The Legend of Good Women (with "legend" taking the medieval meaning of "life," as in "biography") opens with a thoughtful meditation on one of Chaucer's favorite issues of debate—the value of knowledge gained from experience versus that of knowledge derived from books. Noting the popular idea that there is joy in heaven and suffering in hell, the (unnamed) narrator admits that no one makes this statement from direct experience. On the other hand, he acknowledges that people ought not discount something just because they have no personal experience of it, and concludes with the idea that there is much useful and true information to be found in old books. He himself, although he modestly claims to possess little knowledge, is so fond of reading that he can rarely be dragged away from his studies, except on certain holidays, especially that of May Day (May 1), when the birds sing and the flowers spring up. He is particularly fond of a certain flower, the red and white daisy, and praises

it in terms that sound as if he is praising the beauty of an admired woman, one with whom he is infatuated. Fearing that he lacks the ability to properly or sufficiently praise the lovely flower, he asks assistance from those who are more accomplished writers than he is, saying that he performs his task in honor of love, which he persistently and comically relates to his feelings for the daisy.

It is in fact his desire to witness the unfolding of this flower on this May morning that has taken him away from his studies and out into the world of nature, where he observes the birds singing songs of love and welcome to the summer. Alluding to the earlier *PARLIAMENT OF FOWLS,* he recalls how the birds chose their mates on Saint Valentine's Day. After spending the entire day contemplating the lovely daisy, the narrator finally makes his way home at sundown and, a couple of hours later, goes to bed. Once he has fallen asleep, he dreams that he has gone back to the meadow to visit the flower he loves so dearly. While there, he sees the god of love (Cupid) walking hand in hand with a queen. The queen is dressed in a green gown and wears on her head a golden net surrounded by a coronet of white petals carved from a single pearl. Her appearance reminds him of the daisy. The god of love wears a robe of silk embroidered with green branches and red rose petals. His golden hair is crowned with the Sun, and in his hand he holds two fiery darts, the proverbial arrows used by Cupid to wound the hearts of those whom he would cause to fall in love. Cupid's back sports wings like those of an angel, and, the narrator notes, although Cupid is reputed to be blind, he appears to be glaring in the narrator's direction. The queen who accompanies him is so beautiful that she inspires the narrator to compose a ballad in her honor. Following the ballad, the narrator further explains his devotion to the queen, describing how she was able to save him from the wrath of the god of love. In the midst of his dream, as he is standing in the meadow observing the queen and Cupid, they are approached by 19 ladies in royal dress who are all true lovers. Kneeling down before the daisy, they all speak at once, saluting the flower as the symbol of faithful womanhood. Joined by the god of love and the queen, they seat themselves on the grass and all are silent until Cupid notices a stranger (the narrator) kneeling alongside the group. He soon recognizes the man as the translator of the *ROMAN DE LA ROSE* and the author of *TROILUS AND CRISEYDE.* Because these works are critical of romantic love and of women, Cupid believes that the narrator is a traitor and promises severe punishment for his crimes against love. (In version G, Cupid discourses at length on the way that many women have remained faithful throughout their lives and suffered great pain on behalf of love, reminding the narrator of the various books wherein he could have found such stories.)

When Cupid has finished haranguing the narrator, the queen intervenes on the narrator's behalf, offering various reasons why his alleged crime may not be as serious as the god initially interprets it to be. Perhaps, she suggests, he was writing at the command of someone else, and the works in question do not express the narrator's true opinion or beliefs. Alternatively, he may also be sorry for what he has done and deserve forgiveness. At any rate, she continues, the god should be merciful and not behave like a tyrant, punishing the man before he has even had a chance to explain or defend himself. She further reminds her companion that the man kneeling before him has also written some things in praise and honor of love. Although he is not a very accomplished author, she says, offering the conventional comical appraisal of Chaucer's talents, he did write *The HOUSE OF FAME*, the Death of Blanche the Duchess (*The BOOK OF THE DUCHESS*), *The Parliament of Fowls,* and the story of the love of PALAMON and ARCITE (1) of Thebes (an early version of "The KNIGHT'S TALE"), as well as many ballads and other hymns to celebrate love's holidays. Having offered this defense of the narrator's character, the queen reveals her identity as Alcestis, queen of THRACE, and offers a plan which will allow the narrator to make amends for what he wrote in the *Romaunt of the Rose* and the *Troilus*. The plan is for him to write a book about women who, unlike CRISEYDE (or at least his portrait of her) have proven faithful in love for the duration of their lives. The god of love graciously approves this course of action. After thanking the queen for her efforts on his behalf, the narrator begins to defend his work on the *Romaunt* and the *Troilus,* saying that his intention was not to slander love, but to further faithfulness in love by exposing those who practice falsehood and treachery in its name. The queen silences his argument, saying that he must not attempt to get into a dispute with the god of love. Further instructions are issued by both the queen and Cupid regarding what he is to put in his projected book, including Cupid's recommendation that he stick to narrating the essential events of each woman's life since he has so many stories to tell. Finally the two mythological figures depart, and the narrator straightaway begins work on his book.

THE LEGENDS (LIVES)

Cleopatra

This short biography of CLEOPATRA relates how she became the queen of Egypt after the death of her husband, PTOLEMY XII. At about the same time, a Roman senator, Marc ANTONY, left ROME bound for Egypt at the head of an army; his mission was to bring more nations into the Roman Empire. Instead of completing his task, however, Antony becomes the lover of Queen Cleopatra, despite the fact that he is married to

Caesar's sister. Enraged by Antony's behavior, Caesar's son Octavian leads an army in pursuit of the renegade general. Antony and Cleopatra muster their troops and, taking ship, go out to meet their attackers. On separate ships, they become separated during the battle, the description of which is one of the more interesting passages in the *Legend*. When it becomes evident that Octavian is to be the victor, Antony commits suicide. Cleopatra returns home and constructs a magnificent monument for Antony's remains, and then also commits suicide because of her vow that she would always be with him, always feeling what he felt. Her method of suicide is to have a large pit dug next to Antony's shrine, which she then fills with poisonous serpents, and into which she throws herself. The narrative concludes with a commendation of Cleopatra's great faithfulness in love.

Thisbe

The legend of PYRAMUS and THISBE, though not as famous as that of Antony and Cleopatra, is known to modern audiences because of its appearance in Shakespeare's *A Midsummer Night's Dream,* where it forms the subject of the play within a play put on by the mechanicals (Bottom and Company) for the court of Duke THESEUS of Athens. In Chaucer's version, the story is set in the ancient city of BABYLON. Pyramus and Thisbe are the children of two lords whose properties adjoin. They meet and fall in love and would like to be married, but both of their fathers forbid it. Unable to deny their love, the two young people frequently slip away to converse through a crack in the wall that separates the two estates. One night, they plan to run away together. Each is to leave home alone; they will rendezvous the following night by the tomb of King NINUS. Thisbe reaches the appointed place ahead of Pyramus. As she settles down to wait, a lioness approaches to drink from a spring beside the tomb. Thisbe flees and takes refuge in a cave, not realizing that she dropped her wimpled headdress near the tomb. The lioness, whose mouth is bloody from a recent kill, attacks the headdress, leaving it torn and covered with blood.

After the beast has reentered the nearby forest, Pyramus approaches the tomb for his rendezvous with Thisbe, but instead of his lover he finds the bloodied headdress, which he recognizes as belonging to her. Believing that she has been killed, and that it is his fault because he arrived later than she for their appointment, he stabs himself to death with his sword. Thisbe returns from the cave just in time to witness his final struggle with death and turns the sword upon herself, determined that if she cannot be with him in life, she will follow him into death. In concluding the story, the narrator notes that Pyramus is one of the few men he has come across in his reading who has proven to be true in love, but his last sentence is reserved for praise of Thisbe, who dared to do as much as a man for her love.

Dido

The story of DIDO begins with the narrator's announcement that he's going to rely upon VIRGIL and OVID for his version of the life of this famous queen of CARTHAGE. The narrative begins, however, with AENEAS' escape from Troy in the midst of its destruction by the Greeks at the climax of the TROJAN WAR. After landing his ship upon the coast of Libya, Aeneas and his companion ACHATES encounter Aeneas' mother, the goddess VENUS, disguised as a huntress. Venus directs them to go to Carthage, where Dido rules as queen.

When they arrive in the city, Aeneas goes to a temple, where he sees Dido performing her devotions. He also sees the story of Troy's destruction painted on the temple walls. Venus has made him invisible, so at first he observes the queen without being seen. While he is watching her, some of his companions, from whom he had become separated during their voyage from Troy, come into the temple to seek aid and comfort from the queen. Aeneas becomes visible, is reunited with his comrades, and Dido takes all of them to her royal palace, where she provides them with all they need, and more. She showers Aeneas with such fine gifts as horses, jewels and sacks of gold. For his part, Aeneas returns to his ship, where he gathers clothes, brooches, rings and other rich things to present to the queen. He also brings with him his son, ASCANIUS.

The more time Aeneas and Dido spend together, the more they become attracted to each other. Dido soon finds herself so inflamed with desire that she cannot sleep, and she confides in her sister, ANNE, that she wants to marry Aeneas. The following morning, Dido arranges a hunting expedition. Aeneas and his men accompany the queen on the hunt, during which a storm arises. Dido and Aeneas take refuge from the weather inside a cave. Aeneas declares his love for the queen and promises to be faithful to her forever; she, in return, agrees to be his wife for as long as she lives. Following the incident, wicked rumors about Aeneas' behavior with the queen arise.

At this point, the narrator interrupts the story with some advice to women, warning them against trusting men and condemning men generally for various types of betrayal typically practiced upon women. Aeneas is offered as an example of this type of man, one who appeared so virtuous, true and honorable, but whose treatment of his lover ultimately destroyed the woman who not only loved him but who had taken him in when he was a shipwrecked stranger in her land, giving him power over her body and her country. With his desire for the queen eventually sated, Aeneas secretly begins to prepare his ships, planning to slip away in the night. When Dido becomes suspicious, he tells her that his father's spirit and the god MERCURY have both visited him in his sleep, telling him that he must fulfill his destiny to conquer Italy. Dido is devastated by this revelation of his plans. Throwing herself at his feet, she begs him at least to marry her before he goes so that she may die an honorable woman. She also tells him that she is pregnant with his child. None of these arguments changes his mind, however, and he shortly deserts her just as he had planned, leaving behind his sword and a garment of some kind. When Dido awakens to find him gone, she kisses the cloth many times and then commands her sister to make a pyre. While that is being done, she writes Aeneas a letter—not one that she expects will bring him back, but simply to remind him of what she has lost through loving him. That done, she stabs herself with his sword and then casts her body on the burning pyre.

Hypsipyle and Medea

The stories of HYPSIPYLE and MEDEA are grouped together because both women were betrayed by the same man, JASON of Thessaly. Hypsipyle's story, similarly to Dido's, begins with the history of the man who betrayed her, noting that he was the son of King PELIAS of Thessaly. Pelias had a brother named Eson (AESON), to whom, when he felt he had grown too old and weak to rule, he bequeathed his kingdom. During Eson's reign, Jason grew to manhood. He became so popular with the lords of the country that Eson began to fear that Jason would soon attempt to supplant him as king. For that reason, Eson devised a scheme to send Jason on a quest to retrieve the famous Golden Fleece from the island of COLCHIS where it was guarded by a dragon and two fire-spitting brass bulls.

Chaucer relates how Jason accepts the adventure and soon departs on the ship *Argos*, taking along a company of men that includes HERCULES. On its way to Colchis, their ship lands first on the island of Lemnos, where Jason and his crew are welcomed by Hypsipyle, the queen of the island, who opens her home in hospitality to the strangers. While lodging with her, Jason and Hercules come up with a plan whereby Hercules, whom she has taken into her confidence, will speak of Jason's character and qualities in such a way that she will not be able to help falling in love with him. The result is that Jason and the queen are soon married. We are told little about the marriage except that it provides Jason with "substaunce" (i.e., income) for "purveyaunce" (provisions), so that, after he paused long enough to father two children, he can continue on his mission to Colchis. When Jason deserts her, Hypsipyle, like Dido, composes a letter to her husband, reproving him for his betrayal. Despite what he has done, she remains a faithful wife for the rest of her life and dies out of sorrow over his loss.

The story of Medea opens with Jason's arrival at Colchis. After presenting himself to King AEËTES, Jason secures permission to try to capture the Golden Fleece. His bravery, along with other outstanding qualities of his character, arouse the interest of the king's daughter, the wise and beautiful Medea, and FORTUNE causes her to fall in love with him. For this reason she offers her supernatural powers to assist him with his adventure, provided he will agree to marry her. With her help Jason attains the fleece and she returns to Thessaly with him, neglecting to say good-bye to her father. She bears two children, and then finds herself deserted as Jason goes off on another adventure and takes up with another woman. The tale concludes with yet another letter, wherein the betrayed Medea complains of what she has suffered at the hands of her lover. No mention is made of the infamous revenge she took against him.

Lucrece

This is the story of LUCRECE's rape by Tarquin (see TARQUINIUS), the son of the last king of Rome. During an idle period in the Roman siege of Ardea, a soldier named COLLATINUS praises the beauty and goodness of his wife and offers to take Tarquin, who is also participating in the siege, to see her. They make their way to Collatinus' house and sneak inside, where they observe his wife asking the servants for news of the siege and weeping because she misses her husband's company. In the midst of this display of wifely chastity and virtue, Collatinus reveals himself and they enjoy a brief reunion. After returning to camp, Tarquin finds himself unable to stop thinking about the beautiful Lucrece. Obsessed with the idea that she must be his lover, he sneaks into her house one night and rapes her. When she begs for mercy, he is so cruel that he threatens to kill a stableboy and place him in the bed with her so that she may be accused of adultery, thus losing not only her life but also her reputation. At this point, Lucrece faints; she does not awaken until her attacker has gone. Dressing herself in mourning, she summons her friends, telling them what has happened and that she cannot bear the harm that will come to her husband's reputation as a result. Although they reassure her that she is not to blame for what occurred, she is unable to overcome her shame and stabs herself to death. The entire city of Rome mourns her loss, and Tarquin and all his kin are banished for his crime.

Ariadne

The story of ARIADNE's betrayal by THESEUS begins with a brief history of how the ancient city-state of Athens became obligated to supply a yearly tribute of young men and women to be sacrificed to the MINOTAUR of CRETE. In the past, the cities of Athens and Crete had enjoyed peaceful relations until ANDROGEUS, King MINOS' son, was murdered while attending school in Athens. Minos attacked and defeated Athens, the out-

come of which was the agreed-upon tribute arrangement mentioned above. The sacrificial victims were chosen by lot, and it chanced that one year Theseus, the son of the Athenian king EGEUS, was chosen. So Theseus was sent to Crete and cast into a prison, where he awaited his fate.

Fortunately, the prison just happened to be near the bedchamber of Minos' two daughters, Ariadne and PHAEDRA, who thus were able to overhear the young man's woeful lamentations. Moved to pity by his cries, Ariadne formulates a plan that will enable him to defeat the Minotaur and escape from the labyrinth where the monster lives. The plan includes providing him with a weapon, such as a sword, with which to attack the monster; with balls of wax and tow (unspun flax) to throw into its gaping mouth (these to lessen his hunger and encumber his teeth); and with a ball of twine that Theseus can unroll as he makes his way into the labyrinth so that he can follow its trail back out when the monster is defeated.

Bringing the jailer into their confidence and promising that he will be rewarded for helping them, Ariadne and Phaedra visit Theseus and present him with the plan. He gratefully accepts their assistance and humbly offers to spend the rest of his life serving Ariadne as a page, provided he may be disguised so that no one else in her father's court will recognize him. He also promises to reward the jailer by sending him to Athens and making him one of the greatest men of that country. Ariadne responds that it is not appropriate for a man as noble as Theseus to serve as her page; he should instead make her his wife and return to his own land and an honorable position. Her sister, Phaedra, must also come lest she be punished for her part in planning the escape. Theseus eagerly agrees to these terms, now swearing to Ariadne that he has been in love with her since before he even left his own country and has been devoted to serving her for seven years.

The day of the sacrifice arrives, and Theseus is cast into the labyrinth to face the monster. Following Ariadne's advice and using the tools she has provided him, he kills the Minotaur and escapes.

Theseus, Ariadne, Phaedra and the jailer then set sail for Athens. They land on the island of Oenopia (AEGINA), where Theseus has a friend who provides them with shelter. During their stay they feast, dance and sing in celebration of their escape, and Theseus treats Ariadne as his wife. (The implication is that they are already sharing a bed.) Continuing on their way to Athens, they make one further stop on an unnamed, uninhabited (except for wild beasts) island where Theseus, getting up in the middle of the night, takes Phaedra and the rest of his crew and embarks for Athens, leaving the sleeping Ariadne behind. His motive for doing so, the narrator states, is that he finds Phaedra more beautiful than her sister. When

Ariadne awakes and discovers everyone gone, she runs to the shore, where she sees Theseus' ship already out at sea even though the moon is still shining. Thinking at first that he left her behind by mistake, she climbs up onto a high rock and ties her kerchief to a long pole which she waves back and forth, hoping to get his attention. When the ship continues to sail away, she falls down in despair, pitifully kissing the footprints left by her lover on the beach. The narrator leaves her here, directing those who would know more of her story or of her complaint against her false lover to read the story in Ovid.

Philomela

The story of PHILOMELA, her sister PROCNE and their betrayal by Procne's husband TEREUS begins with the narrator's evaluation of Tereus' character, which was so foul, he claims, that it makes his eyes grow painful to read it. At the wedding of Tereus, king of Thrace, and Procne, daughter of King Pandion of Athens, neither JUNO, queen of of the gods, nor HYMEN, the Greek god of marriage, were in attendance; but the Furies (*see* ERINYES), demonic ministers of revenge and punishment in the Greek pantheon, were. Following this ill-omened beginning, the two live together for five years, after which Procne, homesick for her sister, begs her husband to bring Philomela to Thrace for a visit. Tereus agrees and sails to Athens, where his heart becomes ignited with desire for the beautiful Philomela the moment he sees her.

After successfully negotiating with her father, promising to take good care of her and to send Pandion's other daughter, Procne, back to Athens to visit in return, Tereus and Philomela set sail for Thrace. When they arrive, instead of taking her to the court he leads her to a dark cave inside a forest where, despite her attempts to resist him, he rapes her. Then, to silence her cries and to make sure she may never tell anyone what has happened, he cuts out her tongue. Finally, he imprisons her in a castle, where he can use her whenever and however he wants. He then returns home to his wife. To explain her sister's absence, Tereus tearfully informs Procne that when he got to Athens he found her sister dead.

During her imprisonment in the castle, Philomela, deprived of tools with which to write, contrives another way to tell the story of her victimization by Tereus: She weaves it all into a tapestry which, when it is finished, she manages to convey to her sister. Learning the secret of Philomela's fate, Procne hurries to find her and the two rush, weeping, into each other's arms. The narrator leaves them here, reminding us that Philomela never did anything to deserve such treatment, and noting that women must always be wary of men who, even if they do not behave as evilly as Tereus, are unlikely to remain true for very long.

Phyllis

The story of PHYLLIS, queen of Thrace, and her betrayal by DEMOPHON, the son of Theseus of Athens, is in its outline very similar to the story of Theseus and Ariadne. Although he is not a captive, Demophon finds himself, like his father, helplessly stranded in a strange land where he is dependent upon the goodwill of a woman to save his life and to assist him in returning home. In return for her assistance, Demophon promises to marry Phyllis. He makes use of her and her resources to regain his health and otherwise prepare for the journey back to Athens. By the time he takes his leave of her, saying that he only wants to go ahead to make arrangements for their wedding, he has achieved the status of lord of that land and receives the obeisance given him as if it is his due. He sets sail, his ships full of provisions from the queen's stores, and returns to Athens. Although he had promised to return within a month, Phyllis waits until four have passed before she concludes that he is not coming and like many of the other women whose stories are told in the *Legend,* writes him a letter condemning his behavior and yet partially blaming herself for too readily granting her love. After vowing to Demophon that he will soon see her body floating in the harbor of Athens, Phyllis hangs herself. In conclusion, the narrator offers this story as yet another example of the way in which men are likely to betray women, and urging them to trust, in love, no man other than himself.

Hypermnestra

The tale of HYPERMNESTRA's betrayal by her husband LYNCEUS begins with a brief explanation of her lineage, including the fact that she and Lynceus were cousins, their fathers, DANAUS and AEGYPTUS, being brothers. The narrator assures us, however, that there was no law barring such a marriage in ancient Greece. Coming from families with many children, Hypermnestra and Lynceus are each their father's favorite child. Hypermnestra in particular is described in exemplary terms, her nativity overseen by VENUS, who gave her great beauty; by JUPITER, who granted her a good conscience, faithfulness and dread of shame; and by the FATES, who determined that she would be compassionate, sober and wise. The influence of MARS (1) was so weak at the time of her birth that he was unable to make her cruel, but the negative influence of SATURN was sufficient to determine that she would die in prison.

After Hypermnestra and Lynceus are married, Aegyptus visits his daughter privately and demands that she must do as he instructs her or else never leave his palace alive. Not knowing what else to do, Hypermnestra fearfully agrees, as long as what he asks will not lead to her own destruction. Her father then reveals that he has had a dream which predicted that her husband would cause his death. Unable to think of any other way to keep himself secure from such a threat, Aegyptus commands his daughter to drug her husband on their wedding night and, when he is asleep, to cut his throat. Left with a knife and a cask of drugged wine, Hypermnestra initially considers carrying out her father's request, but then decides that it is completely against her nature. Realizing that she would rather die herself than kill her husband, she awakens him and urges him to escape. He leaps from the chamber and runs away, abandoning his wife. Unable to effect her own escape, Hypermnestra is left to confront the wrath of her father, who throws her in prison. The story seems near the end but breaks off with no conclusion.

COMMENTARY

Despite the likelihood that it was written during Chaucer's "mature" period, when he also wrote *Troilus and Criseyde* and *The CANTERBURY TALES, The Legend of Good Women* possesses little of the popular appeal of those two works, at least for modern readers. There is evidence, however, of its popularity among Chaucer's contemporaries, judging from the number of surviving manuscripts. Certainly some parts of the work—especially the prologues—contain memorable poetry. Since it is the first work in which Chaucer used the decasyllabic (10-syllable) couplet that he was to employ for most of *The Canterbury Tales,* some readers have offered the explanation that he wrote the *Legend* as a kind of practice piece or warm-up for what was to be, for him, a much more important undertaking. The word *legend* in the work's title means "life" or "biography," and indeed Chaucer derived the form of the brief biographies he includes in the poem from the popular medieval genre, the lives of the saints. There is perhaps some irony in the fact that the genre on which he modeled this work was devoted to describing the lives of people who were martyrs for God, while the women Chaucer describes were all martyrs to secular, romantic love, something that was frequently criticized by the Christian church in Chaucer's day. Women themselves were often specifically targeted in such criticism, which had by this time developed into a tradition known as antifeminism. Some readers have felt that Chaucer created the *Legend* with the same motive that (they feel) he had for creating a character like the WIFE OF BATH—as a critique of the antifeminist perspective which inevitably depicted women as the guilty prevaricators, tempters and abusers in their relationships with men.

The sources upon which Chaucer drew for the individual biographies of the women in his *Legend* are varied, but most of them come from classical literature. Ovid's *Heroides* evidently served, along with the genre of the saint's life, both as a model for the work as a whole and as a source for some of the lives. Specifically, the epistolary character of the *Heroides* led Chaucer to include letters, written by his abandoned heroines, commenting on their experience. Chaucer also frequently drew upon another of the Roman poet's works, the *Metamorphoses.* A number of critics have noted that many of the women whose biographies appear in Chaucer's *Legend* are also featured in John GOWER'S *CONFESSIO AMANTIS,* but it is generally agreed that the two works were composed independently of one another. While it is possible that one version of the stories did predate and influence the other, it has been impossible for anyone to prove conclusively the seniority of either. Generally, Gower's versions of the stories are more developed and therefore more interesting; one of the major criticisms of this work of Chaucer's has been the relative flatness of the individual narratives, which are in some cases difficult to distinguish one from the other. The legend of Phyllis and Demophon, for example, is like a repeat of the story of Theseus and Ariadne, something that the narrator willingly acknowledges in order to point out how a bad tree produces bad fruit (Theseus is Demophon's father); nevertheless, in reading the stories, one cannot help but wish the characters and their actions were more colorfully and individually drawn.

There is one part of the poem that displays both color and individuality—the prologue. It comes in two versions (both are printed in *The RIVERSIDE CHAUCER*), and the F version, although usually considered an earlier, unrevised version of G, is without a doubt the most interesting of the two. In it we once again encounter the Chaucerian narrator of the early dream visions, *The House of Fame* and *The Parliament of Fowls,* who, himself unable and unfit to be a lover, strives to serve the god of love by writing poetry in his honor. The naïveté and emotionalism of this narrator are two of his most appealing and comical traits, and they appear again in version F of the *Legend*'s prologue where the narrator appears literally to have become infatuated with a flower. Most of this material has been deleted from G. The prologue is furthermore, like the poems mentioned above, a dream vision and it is Chaucer's last.

Chaucer's possible reason for writing the poem is also mentioned in the prologue, where reference is made to his authorship of *Troilus and Criseyde* and to his translation of the *Roman de la Rose,* both of which are criticized by Cupid and Queen Alcestis as being derogatory toward love and toward the female gender. Whether or not he was actually criticized for his portrayal of a faithless woman in the *Troilus* or for his rendition of JEAN DE MEUN's misogynist satire on romantic love is questionable, but there certainly existed a precedent for bringing an author or fictional character up on charges of heresy against the doctrine of love, a practice that originated in the French Courts of Love of Eleanor of Aquitaine and her daughter Marie de

Champagne. The accusation of the narrator and the defense that is made for him in Chaucer's poem are actually very similar and probably indebted to a French poem, GUILLAUME DE MACHAUT's *Jugement dou Roy de Behaingne*. This poem also formed the source for another of Chaucer's works, *The Book of the Duchess*.

On the factual side, there is testimony from another English poet and contemporary of Chaucer's, John LYDGATE, who in his work *The Fall of Princes* noted that Chaucer wrote the *Legend* at the request of Queen ANNE OF BOHEMIA, the wife of King RICHARD II. This supports the dedication that appears in version F of the prologue but was deleted from version G.

As mentioned previously, Chaucer's *Legend of Good Women* has not enjoyed much popularity in recent times. Although its authenticity as part of the Chaucer canon has never been doubted, up until recently it has received little attention, even from Chaucerian scholars, and it is rarely taught in Chaucer courses. Many critical studies of Chaucer's work do not even discuss the poem, and those that do usually treat it negatively. This is beginning to change, however, with the development of feminist scholarship which has naturally interested itself in a collection of stories about women written by one of the greatest poets of the English language.

For Further Reading: See Robert W. Frank, Jr., *Chaucer and the Legend of Good Women* (1972), for a thorough consideration of narrative technique and a defense of the poem's critical status. Frank is one who sees the *Legend* as in part a preparation for *The Canterbury Tales.* Robert O. Payne's *The Key of Remembrance: A Study of Chaucer's Poetics* (1963) contains a good analysis of the prologue. More recently, Lisa Kiser, in *Telling Classical Tales: Chaucer and the Legend of Good Women* (1983), analyzes Chaucer's use of his source material. Kiser believes that the short biographies parody the practice of distorting classical stories in order to point a moral. A very strong feminist reading of the *Legend* appears in Sheila Delany's *The Naked Text: Chaucer's Legend of Good Women* (1994). Delany's introduction also briefly summarizes the poem's critical reputation from the time of its writing up to the present, pointing out its use in the early 17th century as a text supporting the idea that the abuse of married women by their husbands should be outlawed. A shorter but equally interesting feminist perspective on the poem may be found in Caroline Dinshaw's *Chaucer's Sexual Poetics* (1989). Dinshaw reads the poem as a reaction to the "threat of disorder and unfulfillment that the feminine poses in *Troilus and Criseyde*," a reaction that provides "unproblematic fables of faithful women repeated over and over." A more conservative (in goals and methodology) recent book-length treatment of the *Legend* that seeks to reconcile the apparent contradictions of the work and of its critical heritage is Donald Rowe's *Through Nature to Eternity: Chaucer's Legend of Good Women* (1988).

Lemnos (Lemnon)   An island in the Aegean Sea. According to classical legend, Lemnos was the home of the princess HYPSIPYLE, who succumbed to the charms of the adventurer JASON as he sailed the Aegean on his quest for the Golden Fleece. Chaucer tells his version of this story in *The LEGEND OF GOOD WOMEN* (lines 1368–1679).

Lemuel   In the Old Testament, Lemuel is a king of Massa. Proverbs 31 records the advice given to him by his mother to avoid drinking wine, which encourages princes to forget the law and perverts their judgment. The PARDONER alludes to her advice at the beginning of his tale when he warns his listeners against the vices of gluttony (which includes excessive drinking), gambling and swearing.

Lenne, Frere N.   *See* NICHOLAS OF LYNN.

Lent(e)   In the liturgical calendar of the Catholic Church (and, in modern times, of other denominations also), Lent is a 40-day period of penitence and fasting observed between Ash Wednesday (when Christians go to confession and receive the mark of ashes on the forehead to signify their sinfulness) and Easter Sunday. In the prologue to "The WIFE OF BATH'S TALE," the Wife recalls that it was in the season of Lent that she confessed her love to the clerk JANKIN (1), telling him that if she should become a widow, she would marry him. The Wife appears to be using the reference simply to recall when the event occurred, but her behavior, which would be considered immoral by medieval standards, appears all the more outrageous in that context, especially when she notes that her husband was away from home all during Lent that year.

"Lenvoy de Chaucer à Bukton"   Rendered in English, the title of this short epistolary poem would be "Letter from Chaucer to Bukton." Like his poem addressed to SCOGAN and the short one to ADAM SCRIVEYNE, it is humorous in intent and written in response to a particular occasion—in this case, Bukton's impending marriage. After saying in the first stanza that he dares not speak of the woe that is in marriage lest he himself should fall into such foolishness, the narrator spends the remainder of the poem doing exactly that, comparing marriage to a prison, metaphorically referring to it as the "chain of Satan." Repeating the apostle PAUL's dictum that it is better to marry than to burn, he advises his friend to seek advice from Holy Scripture; if that does not convince him of his folly, experience soon will. The concluding stanza seems to mitigate the sentiment of the preceding ones somewhat when the poet tells his friend, "If thow be siker, put the nat in drede" (line 28) [If you're sure (about what you're doing), don't worry], but he also suggests that Bukton might want to consider reading "The WIFE OF BATH'S TALE" (in *The* CANTERBURY TALES). The Wife's tale takes as its theme the very same "woe that is in marriage," suggesting that the only way for a man to have peace within that institution is to surrender control of the relationship to the woman. According to the Textual Notes in the Riverside edition of Chaucer's work (*The RIVERSIDE CHAUCER*), "Lenvoy de Chaucer à Bukton" survives in two manuscripts and two early printed editions, though this is contradicted by the explanatory notes, which state that only one manuscript and one early edition survive. The identity of the addressee, Bukton, is unknown, but two possibilities have been suggested. One is Sir Robert Bukton of Suffolk, who was a squire of Queen Anne (*see* ANNE OF BOHEMIA) and later of King RICHARD II. The other, Sir Peter Bukton of Holderness in Yorkshire, was steward to the future King HENRY IV (JOHN OF GAUNT's son) and, after Henry's coronation, guardian to his son, Thomas of Lancaster. Chaucer's long-standing association with the court could have brought him into contact with either man. Like most of the short poems attributed to Chaucer, this poem's date of composition is uncertain, but the reference to "The Wife of Bath's Tale" would seem to suggest that it belongs to the latter part of Chaucer's career.

"Lenvoy de Chaucer à Scogan"   The title of this short poem translates into English as "Letter from Chaucer to Scogan," and it represents one of the first examples, in English, of light epistolary verse. The poem opens with an allusion to some great, unspecified catastrophe that has had such widespread ramifications that even the gods up in heaven weep and wail, and the narrator says that he is almost dead of fear. The second stanza reveals that it is SCOGAN, the poem's addressee, whose offense has caused these terrible events. The third stanza accuses Scogan of pride and recklessness which led him to commit blasphemy, and, finally, comically reveals the exact nature of his deed, which was to give up his lady because she would not take pity on his distress. Then, to add insult to injury, the offending Scogan evidently committed his decision to paper. Because of what his friend has done, the narrator now fears that CUPID, the god of love, will be avenged on all those who, like Scogan and the narrator, are gray-haired and "rounde of shap" (line 31) (i.e., "chubby"). Fearful of the consequences, in the final stanza before the concluding envoy the narrator protests that he will write no more poetry, though ironically that is exactly what he is doing at the moment. The "stremes hed of grace" (lines 43–44) [stream's head of grace] referred to in the envoy has been taken to mean the head of the Thames at Windsor Castle, the chief residence of King RICHARD II during the latter part of Chaucer's career. The image of Scogan kneeling at the stream's head while Chaucer lies as "dul as ded" (line 45) [dazed as a dead man] at the other end suggests that Scogan may have greater access to the king's favor at the time of the poem's composition. If the reference is to Windsor, it (along with Chaucer's reference to himself as gray-haired and overweight) suggests that the poem may be dated to the latter part of Chaucer's career. The poem survives in three manuscripts and two early printed editions.

Leo   One of the 12 divisions of the zodiac, an imaginary belt in the heavens extending for about eight degrees on either side of the apparent path of the Sun and including the paths of the Moon and the principal planets. The zodiac is divided into 12 equal parts, or signs, each named for a different constellation. Leo is the fifth sign (*see* diagram under ASTROLOGY), which, in Chaucer's day, the Sun entered about July 12. The constellation of Leo, which is supposed to represent a lion, appears between CANCER and VIRGO in the sky. Chaucer uses such astrological terms to indicate the approximate date of a narrative event or to show the passage of time. For example, in book 4 of *TROILUS AND CRISEYDE*, CRISEYDE promises TROILUS that she will return from the Greek camp "Er Phebus suster, Lucina the sheene, / The Leoun passe out of the Ariete" (lines 1591–92) [Before Phoebus' sister, Lucina the bright, / Should pass out of Aries and into the sign of Leo]. The astrological influence of Leo on behavior is alluded to in "The KNIGHT'S TALE." In the scene where the gods on Mount Olympus debate who should win the battle between PALAMON and ARCITE (1) for the love of EMILY, SATURN notes that he (i.e., his planet) is currently in the sign of Leo, and that is one of the reasons why he is intent on performing "vengeance and pleyn correccioun" (line 2461) [vengeance and unadorned correction]. Such behavior concurs with the view of Leo expressed in Ptolemaic astrology, which considered the sign to increase the negative tendencies of all bad things.

Leon (Leoun)   *See* LEO.

Leonard, Saint   One of the most popular saints of the later Middle Ages. Although he reputedly lived during the sixth century, no record of him exists earlier than the 11th. Around 1025 a life of him was written which claimed that he was a member of the Frankish nobility who was converted to Christianity by Saint Remigius. Leonard's godfather was Clovis, founder of the Frankish monarchy. After he had become a Christian, Clovis offered Leonard a bishopric, which he refused in favor of becoming first a monk and later a hermit.

Legend has it that one day while Clovis and his wife were out hunting in the forest near Leonard's cell, the queen went into labor. Leonard safely delivered the child, and as a result became a patron of pregnant women. In return for this deed, Clovis gave Leonard as much land as he could ride a donkey over in one night. Leonard used the land to found the abbey of Noblac, later renamed Saint Léonard, near Limoges. Leonard also came to be considered the patron of captives and prisoners of war. When Bohemond, the crusading prince of Antioch, escaped from a Muslim prison in 1103, he made a pilgrimage to Noblac and made an offering at the saint's shrine out of gratitude for his release. In England, 177 churches are dedicated to him in token of his once great popularity among the English people. Chaucer's London home was approximately two miles from Saint Leonard's nunnery of STRATFORD ATTE BOWE, where the fictional PRIORESS of *The CANTERBURY TALES* is said to have gone to school (GENERAL PROLOGUE, line 125). In *The HOUSE OF FAME,* the narrator, himself a gently self-mocking caricature of Chaucer, recounts that, on the night of the dream which forms the subject of his poem, he fell asleep very quickly, feeling as weary as a man who has gone on a two mile pilgrimage to the Shrine of Saint Leonard, to pray that the saint might ease his burden (line 117). What kind of burden he may be alluding to is difficult to say, though some commentators have argued that Chaucer may have been thinking of the ROMAN DE LA ROSE, in which the saint is invoked by those who find themselves prisoners of an unhappy marriage. It is also possible, of course, that the reference may have no bearing on Chaucer's life at all beyond the poet's desire for a specific detail that would accommodate his rhyme while conveying the idea of someone who grows tired after a relatively short walk.

Leoun, Book of the *See* BOOK OF THE LION.

Lepe A wine-growing district in Spain, Lepe is referred to in "The PARDONER'S TALE." Cautioning the other pilgrims to avoid drinking too much wine, the PARDONER tells them especially to avoid the white wine of Lepe because of its intoxifying potency (line 563–70). This and other detailed information about the quality of wines in London reveals that the Pardoner's knowledge of what he condemns is perhaps a little too intimate, suggesting his own indulgence in the vice of drunkenness.

Lete *See* LETHE.

Lethe In classical mythology, Lethe was the river of forgetfulness in the underworld (Hades). Those who had died would drink from it upon their arrival in Hades, or, less often, upon their departure from Hades

to live again on Earth. One branch of Lethe flowed by the cave of MORPHEUS, the god of sleep. It is mentioned in *The HOUSE OF FAME* in the narrator's invocation of Morpheus, who "duelleth in a cave of stoon / Upon a strem that cometh fro Lete" (lines 70–71) [dwells in a cave of stone / Beside a stream that comes from Lethe].

Lettow *See* LITHUANIA.

Lewis, C(live) S(taples) (1898–1963) A Cambridge don born in Belfast, Northern Ireland, and educated at Oxford, Lewis won wide acclaim as a Christian apologist and writer of science fiction, children's fantasy and scholarly criticism of Renaissance literature. His wide-ranging career crossed Chaucer's path in his first scholarly work, *The Allegory of Love* (1936), in which he asserted that "the Canterbury Tales are glorious reading but they have always been sterile." It was, rather, the earlier Chaucer whom contemporaries admired and whom two centuries of English poets imitated. From Chaucer's time through Lewis' own day, Lewis claims, nothing resembling an imitation of *The CANTERBURY TALES* has been written by any English poet. He believes that "If Chaucer's Tales have had any influence, it is to be sought in our prose rather than in our verse." Worse, reading Chaucer's earlier poetry in the light of his last, unique work leads to misunderstanding of the earlier. Lewis also wrote *The Discarded Image* (1964), a book that reconstructs the world view of the later medieval period, illuminating the influence of many of the authors that Chaucer used as sources or, like ALAIN DE LILLE, simply alluded to.

Libeaus Desconsus This term is a corruption of the phrase *le bel inconnu,* which means "the fair unknown." It is the title of a 14th-century English metrical romance written in tail-rhyme stanzas, like Chaucer's "TALE OF SIR THOPAS," in which it is mentioned. The authorship of many medieval romances remains unknown, but this one is believed to have been composed by Thomas Chester, a contemporary of Chaucer who also wrote the popular *Sir Launfal. Libeaus Desconsus* tells the story of Gingelein, the illegitimate son of Sir GAWAIN. He asks King ARTHUR to make him a knight, but because his name and parentage are unknown, he is knighted simply as "Li Beaus Desconsus." His many adventures center around rescuing the imprisoned Lady of Sinadoune. In Chaucer's "Sir Thopas," the knight's name is given as "Sir Lybeux." The most well-known surviving version of this story is found in Thomas Malory's *Morte D'Arthur* in "The Tale of Sir Gareth of Orkney." In this version the fair unknown is Gawain's younger brother rather than his son.

Libra One of the 12 divisions of the zodiac, an imaginary belt in the heavens extending for about eight degrees on either side of the apparent path of the Sun and including the paths of the Moon and the principal planets. The zodiac is divided into 12 equal parts, or signs, each named for a different constellation. Libra is the seventh sign (*see* diagram under ASTROLOGY), which, in Chaucer's day, the Sun entered on September 12. The constellation of Libra, which is supposed to represent a balance scale, appears between VIRGO and SCORPIO in the sky. Chaucer usually uses such astrological terms to indicate the approximate date of a narrative event or to show the passage of time. The only time he mentions Libra in his poetry, however, seems to be for symbolic purposes as well. The reference appears in line 11 of the prologue to "The PARSONS'S TALE," the last tale in *The CANTERBURY TALES.* Commenting that the Sun has fallen quite low in the sky (indicating that it is late afternoon), Chaucer additionally notes that the sign in which the Moon has its exaltation (its strongest influence), Libra, has begun to rise (i.e., its constellation was coming over the horizon and rising into the sky). W. W. SKEAT points out, however, that the Moon is exalted in Taurus rather than in Libra. Because the first of the three "faces" of Libra was the Moon, there is the possibility, Skeat suggests, that Chaucer confused the terms "exaltation" and "face." Chauncy Wood, in *Chaucer and the Country of the Stars* (1990), argues that Chaucer mentions Libra as a symbolic allusion to divine justice, foreshadowing the theme and tenor of the sermon that follows in "The Parson's Tale."

Libya   Today, Libya is a country in northern Africa between Algeria and Egypt, with coastline along the Mediterranean Sea. In the 14th century the name was used to denote all of northern Africa west of Egypt, also known at this time simply as Africa. In book one of *The HOUSE OF FAME* in the story of DIDO in *The LEGEND OF GOOD WOMEN,* Chaucer, says that Libya is where the Trojan adventurer AENEAS landed following his escape from the burning city of TROY, and his adventures in that region are related. At the end of book one of *The House of Fame,* the narrator finds himself in a field of sand that reminds him of the Libyan desert (line 488). Various reasons for this allusion to Libya have been suggested which attempt to trace it to another literary source, but the fact that the narrator has just been reading the story of Aeneas and Dido on the walls of a temple that he was exploring seems reason enough for him to be reminded of the region where the two lovers met.

Lignano, Giovanni da   Referred to as Lynyan in the prologue to "The CLERK'S TALE," Giovanni da Lignano was a 14th-century Italian scientist, professor of canon law and papal emissary. The CLERK compares him to the poet PETRARCH, saying that Lignano illuminated Italy with philosophy just as Petrarch did it with poetry

(line 34). Lignano wrote on law, ethics, theology and astronomy. In his will he left an endowment to assist impoverished Milanese youth studying at Bologna, where he taught. This partiality to poor young scholars may be what earns him the praises of the Clerk, who is himself in a position to appreciate such assistance.

Limote   In *The HOUSE OF FAME,* among the magicians who congregate in FAME's palace is one called "Limote" (line 1274), whom W. W. SKEAT believes to be the sorcerer mentioned in the New Testament book of Acts 13:8. When the proconsul (deputy) of the island of Cyprus asked to hear the word of God from the missionaries Saul and Barnabus, Limote (here called "Elymas") tried to prevent the proconsul's conversion. He was miraculously blinded for his interference.

Lincoln   City in northeastern England. The county of Lincolnshire, where it is situated, is bounded to the east by the North Sea. Lincoln was the home of the famous child martyr HUGH OF LINCOLN, whose memory is invoked at the conclusion of "The PRIORESS' TALE" (line 648), which tells the story of a similar child martyr.

Lithuania (Lettow)   The GENERAL PROLOGUE TO *THE CANTERBURY TALES* informs us that Lithuania ("Lettow") is one of the many exotic (for an audience of medieval Englishmen and women) places that the KNIGHT has visited on military campaign (line 54). In Chaucer's day, Lithuania would have constituted a large area south of present-day Latvia, including part of the Ukraine to the Black Sea. In *The RIVERSIDE CHAUCER* Vincent DiMarco notes that the country's sovereign had been converted to Christianity in 1386, an event that, theoretically, should have brought an end to crusading campaigns (which were ostensibly directed at pagan countries).

Livia   In the "WIFE OF BATH"'S PROLOGUE, the Wife describes a Book of Wicked Wives from which her fifth husband reads to her. The book is an anthology of stories, from history, literature and the Bible, about women who have behaved in ways that many would consider unflattering to the female gender. One of these women, the Roman matron Livia Drusilla ("Lyvia"), plotted with her lover to poison her husband (lines 747–50).

Livy (59 B.C.–A.D. 17)   Livy, or Titus Livius, was a famous Roman historian who enjoyed the patronage and friendship of AUGUSTUS CAESAR. His great history of Rome, *Ab Urbe Condito* ("Regarding the Condition of the City") was used by Chaucer as a source for portions of *The PARLIAMENT OF FOWLS, The BOOK OF THE DUCHESS, The LEGEND OF GOOD WOMEN* and the *BOECE.* Livy is mentioned (as "Titus") as a source in *The Book of the Duchess* (line 1084), *The Legend of Good Women* (lines 1683 and 1873) and "The PHYSICIAN'S TALE" (line 1), but textual evidence suggests that, for the story of the Roman martyr VIRGINIA, that appears in the Physician's narrative, Chaucer actually drew upon the French *ROMAN DE LA ROSE* for his version.

Loathly Hag Primary character in "The WIFE OF BATH'S TALE." A young KNIGHT (3) who has committed rape and been sentenced to either find out what it is that women desire most, or die, meets this woman in a forest. When she discovers his predicament, she offers to tell him the answer, if he will first promise to do whatever she asks, provided the answer proves correct. The knight agrees, and they return to King ARTHUR's court together. She tells the knight that what women desire most is sovereignty over their husbands and lovers. In return for giving him the correct answer, she asks that he marry her. On their wedding night, when he is unable to embrace her because of her low birth, age and ugliness, she lectures him on the nature of true gentility, and then asks if he would rather her to be beautiful and unfaithful or old, ugly and faithful. He leaves it to her to decide which alternative will be the most pleasing and honorable for them both. His choice is rewarded by her swearing that she will henceforth be both young and beautiful, *and* faithful, because he allowed her to make the decision. The loathly hag or lady is a stock character in medieval romance. Outside of this tale, she is most familiar to readers from her important role in the 14th-century Alliterative Revival poem, *Sir Gawain and the Green Knight,* where she represents one incarnation of the enchantress Morgan le Fay, who is trying to find a way to frighten Queen Guinevere to death. The most vivid description of a loathly lady appears in John GOWER's "Tale of Florent" from the *CONFESSIO AMANTIS.* There she is described as having a low nose, a high forehead, small and deep-set eyes, wrinkled cheeks that hang down slack to her chin, shrunken lips, gray hair, black skin, a short neck, bowed shoulders and a large body. Chaucer simply tells us that she is the foulest human being one might imagine.

Lollard Term that refers to followers of John Wycliffe, an Oxford professor who, at the end of the 14th century, launched an attack upon the Catholic Church, denouncing the immorality of the clergy and the temporal power of the church. He likewise insisted on the supreme authority of the Scriptures as the source of belief and denied transubstantiation (the idea that the bread and wine of the Mass were actually transmuted into Christ's body and blood at the moment of consecration).

The word *Lollard,* derived from the Dutch *lollaert,* means "mumbler." It constituted a derogatory reference to the Wycliffites' method of prayer. The word was conveniently confused with an already existing Middle English word, *lollere,* according to the *Middle English Dictionary,* which meant "a lazy vagabond, fraudulent beggar."

In the epilogue to "The MAN OF LAW'S TALE," the Host hints that the PARSON must be a Lollard because he objects to the Host's swearing (line 1173). Presumably he does so because the Lollards raised special objections to the taking of oaths. This does not, however, mean that the country parson is a Wycliffite, for many people who favored a stricter morality than was currently popular were accused of Lollardy. Furthermore, "The PARSON'S TALE" exhibits none of the marks of Wycliffe's teachings.

Lollere *See* LOLLARD.

Lollius A fictitious Latin poet, whose work Chaucer claimed was the source for his *TROILUS AND CRISEYDE* (book 1, line 394). The absence of such a work and comparison of Chaucer's poem with other treatments of the story have led scholars to conclude that BOCCACCIO's *FILOSTRATO* was actually his primary source. Interestingly, Chaucer also mentions Lollius in *The HOUSE OF FAME* as one of the poets whose images lead to FAME's throne (line 1468). Along with STATIUS and other "real" poets, he is there to help ensure the lasting fame of the TROJAN WAR.

Lombards People from the region of LOMBARDY in Italy. The merchant in "The SHIPMAN'S TALE" conducts business with some Italian bankers from Lombardy who have offices in PARIS (2) and BRUGES.

Lombardy A region in northern Italy, east of the Apennine Mountains. The city of SALUZZO, the setting for "The CLERK'S TALE," is located there. The geographical description of Lombardy that appears in the prologue to "The Clerk's Tale" (lines 43–51) is derived from the *prohemium* (prologue) of PETRARCH's *De obedientia ac fide uxoria mythologia* ("A fable of wifely obedience and faithfulness"), which is the source of the tale that follows. In "The SQUIRE'S TALE," the SQUIRE alludes to the region's reputation for producing fine horses by describing the brass horse presented to King CAMBYUSKAN on his birthday as well-proportioned and strong "Right as it were a steede of Lumbardye" (line 193) [just as if it were a steed of Lombardy]. Chaucer traveled to the area at least twice for diplomatic purposes. (*See* VISCONTI, BERNABO.)

London (Londoun) London was the bustling capitol city and center of commerce in England during Chaucer's day. It had a population of about 50,000, which made it by far the largest city in the country. It had become the country's chief wool exporting port early in the 14th century and had taken control of the French-dominated wine trade in the 1320s. By the latter part of the 14th century, the city's prosperity had reached a level never seen before. Already in 1340 it was five times richer than the city of Bristol, its main trading competitor. On the other hand, London was still small compared with other European cities such as Paris, Genoa and Florence, whose populations may have reached as high as 100,000 each.

London was the intellectual and cultural center of England, boasting numerous schools and libraries, though in these areas it also suffered in comparison to continental cities where the influence of the Italian Renaissance was already in full flower. It was in many ways a city of contrasts. Most of its streets were unpaved and littered with animal dung and other refuse. Some even had great ditches running down the center that functioned as sewers, carrying garbage as well as human and animal waste toward the Thames River, which functioned as a giant sewage line leading out to the sea. On the other hand, one could also find sumptuous town houses and palaces (like the Savoy, belonging to JOHN OF GAUNT), public buildings and churches adorning the city streets. On holy days and other festivals, the streets were adorned by magnificent pageants and processions. Those processions often featured the king and other members of the nobility, who appeared with great pomp and display as they embarked upon and returned from journeys both peaceful and martial.

During the medieval period, the city was surrounded by great stone walls which, beginning in the period of Roman occupation had been built and gradually expanded as a fortification. Most of the city's inhabitants still lived within the square mile enclosed by these walls (although its growing population had forced some outside). The house that Chaucer moved into after he and Philippa (*see* Philippa CHAUCER) were married was located above the Aldgate, one of the city's seven main gates. The house that he had grown up in was located on Thames Street, near the river, a location that was important for the family's business in the wine trade.

South of the city, just over the Thames River, lay the bustling borough of SOUTHWARK where the TABARD Inn was located. This was where Chaucer's pilgrims gathered and spent the night before embarking on their journey to Canterbury. Most of the pilgrims are from areas outside of London, ranging as far to the west as DARTMOUTH and BATH, and northeastward into the county of NORFOLK, but the COOK, who is distinguished by his ability to recognize a draught of London ale (General Prologue, line 382), is from the city, along with, perhaps, the five guildsmen—the HABERDASHER, CARPENTER, WEAVER, DYER and TAPESTRY MAKER. The WIFE OF BATH's husband is away on business in London when she flirts with JANKIN (1) and suggests that he

should be her next husband, and in "The MILLER'S TALE," the gullible JOHN THE CARPENTER sends his servants to the city (line 3632) in anticipation of the great flood that his lodger NICHOLAS has predicted. Apart from the pilgrims already mentioned, the only character in *The CANTERBURY TALES* who lives in London is the priest who was duped by the treacherous CANON (2) of "The CANON'S YEOMAN'S TALE" (line 1012).

Longinus (Longius)   In Christian tradition, the Roman centurion who pierced the side of Christ during the Crucifixion. The legend is referred to in the X stanza of Chaucer's "ABC" to the Virgin Mary, where the narrator praises the sacrifice Christ made on the Cross (line 163).

Looth   *See* LOT.

Loreyne   *See* LORRAINE.

Lorraine   A region in northeastern France, near the German border. It is mentioned only once in Chaucer's work, in his translation of the *ROMAN DE LA ROSE*. The narrator notes that the minstrels who play and sing in the garden of MIRTH sing songs from Lorraine, where their "notes bee / Full swetter than in this contre" (lines 767–68) [notes are / Much sweeter than in this country].

Lorris, Guillaume de   *See* GUILLAUME DE LORRIS.

Lot   In the Old Testament, Lot is ABRAHAM's nephew who settled near the town of Sodom. When two angels were sent to warn him of the wicked city's impending destruction by God, he and his family fled. His wife, however, did not obey the angels' command to resist looking back at the city and was turned into a pillar of salt. Following his escape from Sodom, Lot lived in a cave with his two daughters, who served him wine and enticed him into incest. At the beginning of "The PARDONER'S TALE," the PARDONER uses the story of Lot and his daughters to warn the other pilgrims about the dangers of drunkeness (line 485).

Lowes, John (1867–1945)   Although most famous for *The Road to Xanadu*, a study of Coleridge's "Rime of the Ancient Mariner," Lowes was a prolific Chaucer scholar whose keenest interest seems to have been the relationship between Chaucer's work and its sources. In "Chaucer and Dante" (*Modern Philology*, 1915), he argues for a strong Dantean influence on Chaucer's reading of BOCCACCIO. "The Franklin's Tale, Teseide, and the Filocolo" (*Modern Philology*, 1918) discusses the relationship between two of Boccaccio's works and Chaucer's "FRANKLIN'S TALE," pointing out that, despite Chaucer's claim that the tale comes from a BRETON LAY, its primary source is the *Filocolo*. "Chaucer and the Miroir de Mariage" (*Modern Philology*, 1910–11) discusses the poet's use of that French text in the prologue to "The WIFE OF BATH'S TALE." "Illustrations of Chaucer Drawn Chiefly from Deschamps" (*Romanic Review*) and "The Chaucerian 'Merciles Beaute' and Three Poems of Deschamps" (*Modern Language Review*, 1910) illustrate Chaucer's debt to the French poet Eustache DESCHAMPS, who was Chaucer's contemporary. "Chaucer's Boethius and Jean de Meun" (*Romanic Review*, 1917) points out Chaucer's dependence on JEAN DE MEUN's French translation of BOETHIUS' *Consolation of Philosophy* in creating his own Middle English version, the *BOECE*. Other essays examine the influence of Alanus de Insulis (ALAIN DE LILLE) and Macrobius. In his book-length study *The Art of Geoffrey Chaucer* (1936), Lowes theorizes about the general influence that the French sources and French literature had upon Chaucer as a poet, arguing that he brought an element of realism to overly allegorized, intellectualized continental forms.

Lowys *Lowys* is the spelling given to the name of Chaucer's son Lewis in the *TREATISE ON THE ASTROLABE*, which work Chaucer claims to have written for him. (*See* CHAUCER, LEWIS.)

Loy, Saint *See* ELIGIUS.

Luc *See* LUKE, SAINT.

Lucan The writer whom Chaucer refers to as Lucan was the first-century Roman poet Marcus Annaeus Lucanus. The grandson of the rhetorician Seneca and the nephew of SENECA the philosopher, Lucan was favored by the emperor NERO early in his career. Nero, however, grew jealous of Lucan's poetic ability. Lucan joined a conspiracy against the emperor and when it failed was ordered to commit suicide. Lines from Chaucer's *LEGEND OF GOOD WOMEN*, *PARLIAMENT OF FOWLS*, *TROILUS AND CRISEYDE*, the *BOECE* and "The MAN OF LAW'S TALE" can be traced to Lucan's *Pharsalia*, whose theme was the civil wars of Julius CAESAR and POMPEY. Chaucer mentions the Roman poet's work in *The HOUSE OF FAME*, the *Boece*, *Troilus and Criseyde*, "The Man of Law's Tale," and "The MONK'S TALE." In the latter, the MONK recommends that readers who want to know more about Caesar consult Lucan's *Pharsalia*, (line 2719). In *The House of Fame*, Lucan is one of the poets lining the approach to FAME's throne (line 499). He stands on a pillar of iron, the metal associated with MARS (1) and with war, bearing the fame of Julius Caesar and Pompey. Near the end of *Troilus and Criseyde*, Lucan is one of the poets whose steps Chaucer sends his book to "kiss," implying an indebtedness to the classical tradition represented by VIRGIL, HOMER, OVID, STATIUS and Lucan (book 5, line 1792).

Lucifer (Sathan; Sathanas) *Lucifer* is one of the names Chaucer uses for the angel who, in the Old Testament, defied God and was cast out of heaven into hell; from there he proceeded to continue his war against his former master by tempting the first man and woman, ADAM and EVE, to eat fruit from a forbidden tree. When they did, they lost their immortality and the right to live in the paradise of Eden which God had created expressly for them. The stories of Lucifer's rebellion and of Adam's fall from grace form the first two brief biographies of "The MONK'S TALE," which is a series of mini-biographies of people whose lives illustrate the MONK's theory of tragedy as a fall from fortune. Lucifer was also the name of the Morning Star. This is the sense in which the name is used in the *BOECE*, Chaucer's translation of BOETHIUS' *Consolation of Philosophy*.

Lucilia (Lucia) The wife of the Roman poet Lucretius who, according to legend, accidentally poisoned her husband with a potion that she had hoped would make him more amorous. Her story is one of those included in the Book of Wicked Wives from which the WIFE OF BATH's fifth husband, JANKIN (1), used to read to her. Her anger over these stories led to a great fight between the Wife and her husband, which concluded with him burning the book and giving her the respect and the trust that she craved.

Lucina *See* DIANA.

Lucrece (Lucresse; Lucretia) A Roman of the late sixth century B.C., Lucrece was the daughter of a consul and wife to Tarquinus COLLATINUS, an army officer. When Collatinus boasted of his wife's beauty and fidelity to his comrades in battle, and took his cousin, Sextus Tarquinus (*see* TARQUINIUS) to see her for himself, the latter was overcome by uncontrollable desire for the woman as the men observed her without revealing their presence. Later he secretly returned to the house alone and raped Lucrece, threatening to kill her if she tried to resist. The next day, she sent for her father and husband, and told them what Tarquin had done. Although they forgave her (!), she committed suicide because she was unable to live with the humiliation of what had happened. In "The FRANKLIN'S TALE," Lucrece is one of the women whose virtue DORIGEN would like to imitate when she is faced with the choice between breaking her promise to AURELIUS or betraying her marriage vows. Lucrece is likewise mentioned as an example of a virtuous wife in the introduction to "The MAN OF LAW'S TALE" (line 63), and in *The BOOK OF THE DUCHESS* (line 1082), where the BLACK KNIGHT compares her goodness to that of his deceased wife. In *The LEGEND OF GOOD WOMEN*, the narrator says that although Lucrece was exceptional, ALCESTIS (who died in her husband's place) is more virtuous (prologue F, line

257). The complete story of Lucrece's rape is also related in *The Legend of Good Women* (lines 1680–1885).

Lucye   *See* LUCILIA.

Luke, Saint   An evangelist of the first century A.D. and disciple of Saint PAUL, Luke wrote both the New Testament book of Acts (the Acts of the Apostles), as well as the Gospel of his own name which provides us with one version of the life of Christ. By tradition a Greek physician, Luke's version of Christ's life emphasizes the Savior's compassion for all people. Luke gives more attention than any other evangelist to the women who came into contact with Christ. He also penned some of the most memorable of the Bible's parables, such as those of the Good Samaritan and the Prodigal Son. The latter is mentioned by Chaucer's PARSON in the penitential treatise which constitutes the last of *The CANTERBURY TALES* (line 700). The Parson also refers to Christ's parable of the lost sheep whose return is celebrated (line 701), affirming that "likewise joy shall be in heaven over one sinner that repenteth, more than over ninety and nine just persons, which need no repentance" (Luke 15:7), and to the thief hanging on the cross next to Him (line 702), who begs to be remembered and to whom the Lord answers, "Today shalt thou be with me in paradise" (Luke 23:43); both of these episodes illustrate the Savior's compassion. In Acts, Luke shows himself not only concerned with spreading the word of God, but also with making links between sacred and secular history. Many of his details have been affirmed by archeological discoveries. When Luke is represented pictorially with other evangelists, his symbol is an ox, in reference to the sacrifice described at the beginning of his Gospel. When he is represented alone, he is usually pictured as an evangelist engaged in writing. He is the patron of artists as well as physicians because of an apocryphal tradition that he painted the Virgin Mary's portrait.

Lumbardes   *See* LOMBARDS.

Lumbardye   *See* LOMBARDY.

Lumiansky, R(obert) M(ayer) (1913–1987)   An educator at Tulane, Duke and the University of Pennsylvania, Lumiansky ended his career at New York University. He is best known for *The "Canterbury Tales" of Geoffrey Chaucer* (1948), a modern English prose translation that included the GENERAL PROLOGUE and "The Nun's Priest's Tale" in Middle English for the sake of comparison. Lumiansky also published *Geoffrey Chaucer's "Troilus and Criseyde"* (1952), another prose translation. Lumiansky's explicative writings include a number of essays and the book-length study *Of Soundry Folk: The Dramatic Principle in "The Canterbury Tales"*

(1955; rptd. 1980), in which he argues that Chaucer goes beyond merely suiting the tale to the teller on the basis of his or her profession. Chaucer does this, but adds external and internal motivation based on psychology and relationships with other pilgrims. Thus, he creates a situation of "extended self-revelation of which the teller is not fully aware." Lumiansky is also the author of a number of articles on Chaucer, including "Chaucer's *Parlement of Foules:* A Philosophical Interpretation" (in *Chaucer Review,* 1970), which provides a survey of criticism on the poem and then offers a new interpretation: that the poem is a unified expression of Chaucer's search for a way of reconciling true and false happiness.

luna   The Latin word for "moon." In "The CANON'S YEOMAN'S TALE," the CANON'S YEOMAN reveals that, in ALCHEMY, *luna* is the word they use to designate the metal silver (line 826).

Lybeux, Sir   Sir Lybeux (from the French *Lybeaus Desconus,* "the Fair Unknown"), was the hero of a Middle English romance by Thomas Chester, a contemporary of Chaucer's. The unknown knight is actually a son of Sir GAWAIN named Guinglain and has no other literary existence outside that tale. Chaucer mentions Sir Lybeux as one of the heroes of romance who are nothing in comparison to his own Sir THOPAS (line 890). The comparison, like Chaucer's praise of the bumbling Thopas, is ironic.

Lybye   *See* LIBYA.

Lycurgus   In classical mythology, there are two kings named Lycurgus. One was a king of Thrace who, because he mistreated Dionysus (BACCHUS), was blinded or (according to another story) caused to go mad and kill his own son as punishment. In "The KNIGHT'S TALE," Chaucer confuses this Lycurgus with another Greek king of the same name, Lycurgus of Nemea, father of the child Opheltes who was killed by a serpent because of the negligence of his nurse, HYPSIPYLE. Lycurgus appears in the tale as a supporter of the knight PALAMON in the tournament that has been organized to determine who will win the love of EMILY. Chaucer gives him a striking physical appearance, with shaggy eyebrows, eyes that glow yellow and red, and long dark hair as black as a raven. He arrives in ATHENS wearing a bearskin and riding in a gold chariot drawn by four white bulls (lines 2128–54). Chaucer also makes Lycurgus the father of PHYLLIS in *The LEGEND OF GOOD WOMEN* (line 2425), which tells the story of her tragic love affair with DEMOPHON, although the exact identity of her father remains in question.

Lyde   *See* LYDIA.

Lydgate, John   English poet who wrote primarily in the first decade of the 15th century and whose work was strongly influenced by Chaucer's poetry. Several of his works are clearly attributable to the older poet's influence. For example, his *Complaint of the Black Knight* is modeled on *The BOOK OF THE DUCHESS; The Temple of Glass* is indebted to *The HOUSE OF FAME;* and *The Flower of Courtesy,* like *The PARLIAMENT OF FOWLS,* is a Valentine's Day poem. Lydgate also treated the ever-popular medieval themes of the TROJAN WAR in his *Troy Book,* and the story of the SEVEN AGAINST THEBES in *The Siege of Thebes.* These themes appear in Chaucer's *TROILUS AND CRISEYDE* and are alluded to in many of his other works. Like Chaucer, Lydgate had another career besides that of writer. He took holy orders and was admitted to the monastery of Bury St. Edmunds in about 1385, served as abbot of another religious house for a short time around 1420, and shortly after returned to Bury, where he spent the rest of his life. Some of his short poetry is quite fine, and certainly the 18th-century literary critic Joseph Ritson's famous comment that he was nothing more than a "voluminous, prosaick and drivelling monk" is undeservedly harsh.

Lydia   In the ancient world, Lydia was the name of a large territory in western Asia Minor, roughly corresponding to the present-day Turkish province of Saruehan. Rich in natural resources, it was famed for its production of figs, grain, grapes and olives. CROESUS, whose story is narrated in "The MONK'S TALE," was a king of Lydia.

Lyeys   *See* AYASH.

Lygurge   *See* LYCURGUS.

Lynceus   *See* HYPERMNESTRA.

Lyncoln   *See* LINCOLN.

Lynn, Nicholas of   *See* NICHOLAS OF LYNN.

Lyno   *See* HYPERMNESTRA.

Lynyan   *See* LIGNANO, GIOVANNI DA.

Lyvia   *See* LIVIA.

Mabely The old woman in "The FRIAR'S TALE" who curses the wicked summoner and, literally, sends him to the devil (line 1626). The reason for her anger is that he has falsely accused her of committing sins, such as adultery, which would require her to either appear in an ecclesiastical court or to pay a fine. He contrives the accusation in the hope that she will be intimidated into giving him the money, which he will then pocket rather than turning over to any authority.

Maccabees, Books of The books of Maccabees belong to the Apocrypha, a collection of books written during a time of great turmoil in the history of the Jewish people, from around 200 B.C. to about A.D. 100. The first book of Maccabees tells about the struggle of the Jews in Judea under the leadership of one family, the Hasmoneans, from about 175 to 135 B.C. Judas Maccabeus was the family's most famous leader. The second book of Maccabees describes the events that occurred in Judea from 191 to 162 B.C., in a sense serving as a prologue to the first book. Second Maccabees 9 is the original source of the story of King ANTIOCHUS (1) of Syria, which is narrated in "The MONK'S TALE" (lines 2575–2630).

Macchabee (1) *See* MACABEES, BOOKS OF.

Macchabee (2) *See* JUDAS MACCABEUS.

Macedo *See* ALEXANDER THE GREAT.

Macedonia (Macedoyne; Macidoyne) An ancient kingdom in southeastern Europe, in the southern Balkan Peninsula. It is now a region divided among Greece, Yugoslavia and Bulgaria. The region is mentioned several times in Chaucer's poetry. In *The BOOK OF THE DUCHESS*, the BLACK KNIGHT exclaims that he would rather have his lady back than possess all the riches of BABYLON, CARTHAGE, Macedonia, ROME or NINEVAH. All of these places were famed for their wealth in the ancient world. The soldier who tried to rape SCEDASUS, whose story is alluded to in "The FRANKLIN'S TALE," is from Macedonia (lines 1428–36), and of course ALEXANDER THE GREAT, whose biography is related briefly in "The MONK'S TALE," was the son of PHILIP of Macedon (line 2656).

Macedonian, the *See* ALEXANDER THE GREAT.

Machaut, Guillaume de *See* GUILLAUME DE MACHAUT.

Macrobius (Macrobeus; Macrobye) *See DREAM OF SCIPIO.*

Madrian In the prologue to "The MONK'S TALE," the Host (*see* Harry BAILLY) swears by the "corpus" (body) of "Madrian" that he would rather have his wife hear the previous story, "The TALE OF MELIBEE," than have a whole barrel of ale. The nature of his oath would suggest that he is referring to a saint named Madrian, but there is no such saint of that name. The name could be a scribal error for Hadrian or Adrian, who later came to be known as the patron saint of brewers, or it could simply be one of the Host's occasional malapropisms. As Susan Cavanaugh points out in the notes to *The RIVERSIDE CHAUCER*, the man has trouble with any oaths beginning "corpus."

Maeon In classical mythology, Maeon was the grandson of CREON of THEBES. After OEDIPUS had been driven out of Thebes by his two sons, POLYNICES and ETEOCLES, they made an agreement to rule Thebes in alternate years; but when Eteocles' turn was up, he refused to yield to his brother. Polynices persuaded his father-in-law, ADRASTUS, to help him launch an invasion of Thebes to recapture the throne. Because seven famous Greek heroes (including Polynices) were recruited to fight on his behalf, the expedition became known as the SEVEN AGAINST THEBES. Maeon, who supported Eteocles, was one of 50 men sent out of the city to ambush TYDEUS, who was one of the famous Seven. Tydeus killed 49 of the men and sent Maeon back to Eteocles. Maeon (whom Chaucer calls "Hemonydes") is mentioned in *TROILUS AND CRISEYDE* when TROILUS' sister CASSANDRA recites the history of Thebes prefatory to telling her brother that DIOMEDE, the son of Tydeus, is CRISEYDE's new lover (bk. 5, line 1492).

Magdelene (Magdeleyne) *See* MARY MAGDELENE, SAINT.

Magician Minor character in "The FRANKLIN'S TALE." The magician is a young scholar from ORLEANS in France who offers to assist AURELIUS in his quest to win the love of DORIGEN, who is married to the Breton knight ARVERAGUS. Dorigen has promised Aurelius that if he can remove some treacherous black rocks that line the coast of BRITTANY and that thus imperil her husband's homecoming from England, she will be his lover. The magician uses "natural magic," based on astronomical calculations, to help create the illusion that the rocks have disappeared. When he learns that Aurelius released Dorigen from her vow, however, the magician cancels the debt that Aurelius owed him for performing the trick.

Magoun, Francis P. (1895–1979)   A Harvard Ph.D. with further study at Trinity College, Cambridge University, Magoun went on to become a professor at his alma mater and a fellow of the Medieval Academy. His published works include translations and philological studies of various medieval texts and, rather surprisingly, a *History of Football from the Beginnings to 1871.* His most lasting contribution to Chaucer studies was the *Chaucer Gazetteer* (1961), which lists and discusses all geographical names and names of geographical origin, or with geographical associations, in Chaucer's work.

Mahoun   *See* MOHAMMED.

Maius   *See* MAY.

Makomete   *See* MOHAMMED.

Malkyn (1)   The daughter of the miller, SIMKIN, in "THE REEVE'S TALE." She is the granddaughter of the local parson. (The parson's illegitimate daughter is Malkyn's mother.) Malkyn really only figures in the beginning and end of the tale; during the interim, where the action focuses on the students, JOHN THE CLERK and ALAN and their interaction with Simkin, she disappears, only reappearing when her father sends her to town to buy victuals and ale for dinner. Her physical description, like that of her father, bespeaks a certain grossness that exists incongruously alongside traits of beauty. For example, she is tall and fat, with a pug nose, but has eyes as gray as glass. She has broad buttocks, but her breasts are high and round like those of a romance heroine. Her hair is described as "fair," which in Middle English suggests beauty rather than blondness. In the eyes of her grandfather, the church parson, she is considered beautiful; based on that assumption, he has made her his heir, hoping to marry her to a member of the nobility. The fact that she remains unmarried at the age of 20 suggests that he hopes in vain. Incidentally, the frequency with which church clerics fathered offspring during the medieval period is attested to by a corresponding frequency of official church edicts issued against such

practices. In his notes to the text of "The REEVE'S TALE," Larry BENSON mentions that there exists an actual record of a parson of TRUMPINGTON (the small town in which the miller lives) who in 1342 was succeeded in office by his son. The self-serving attitude of this supposed servant of God is succinctly portrayed by Chaucer's comment about how he wishes to keep his property in his family yet does not care if he should bankrupt the church.

Even though Malkyn is past the age of prime marriageability, she does not seem to deserve the fate that is in store for her, which is to be "swyved" (Middle English slang for sexual intercourse) thrice, by one of the students in revenge for her father's thievery. She makes the best of the situation, however, by imagining that the young man is her true lover. Alan encourages this sentiment, at least for the moment, when he says his farewell, promising that wherever he shall go, he will belong to her alone. In exchange for his promise, she tells him where to find the cake that was made with stolen grain, and bids him a tearful farewell.

Malkyn (2)   The neighbor or serving maid in "The NUN'S PRIEST'S TALE" who, wielding a distaff (a staff upon which wool, flax or other material would be wound for spinning into thread) as a weapon, joins in the chase after RUSSELL, the sly fox who has seized the poor widow's rooster, CHAUNTICLEER. The chase of the fox was a stock scene in medieval art and poetry.

Malle   *Malle,* a diminutive of the name *Malkyn,* is the name given to the sheep owned by the poor widow of "The NUN'S PRIEST'S TALE," who also owns the rooster CHAUNTICLEER, the main protagonist of the tale.

Malone, Kemp (1889–1971)   Philologist, editor and Shakespeare scholar. Malone taught at Johns Hopkins University from 1926 to 1956. He contributed a variety of essays and a book-length study, *Chapters on Chaucer* (1951), to an understanding of the poet. The book's introduction explains that it was generally written for "readers who have some acquaintance with Chaucer's writings but are not professional Chaucerians." In his chapters on the Canterbury pilgrims, Malone argues that with the sole exception of the PARDONER and his tale, readers must resist the temptation to read the tales as "pieces of indirect self-characterization." The complete failure of the two tales that Chaucer puts into his own mouth, the mouth of the greatest taleteller of them all, should warn us that we cannot judge the teller by his or her literary performance. Malone also published an annotated edition of Chaucer's poetry, *The Works of Chaucer,* for Johns Hopkins Press in 1953, and produced a phonographic recording of "The NUN'S PRIEST'S TALE" to illustrate the proper pronunciation (based on linguistic evidence) of Chaucer's

Middle English (*see* CHAUCER'S LANGUAGE—PRO-NUNCIATION).

Malyne *See* MALKYN.

Manciple, the   The Manciple's portrait follows that of the MILLER in the GENERAL PROLOGUE TO *THE CANTERBURY TALES,* and like the Miller, the Manciple is a cheat. The title of his profession, along with information provided in his description, indicates that he is a kind of purchasing agent for one of the "temples," or schools, of the great London law school known as the INNS OF COURT. His duties consist of buying provisions for the temple, and he is such a shrewd businessman that he always comes out ahead. He is so shrewd, in fact, that he is able to swindle the men for whom he works, something that leads the narrator to marvel upon the man's ability to do so in spite of his relative lack of education (compared to that of the lawyers). We are given no physical description of the Manciple's features or of his clothing—a strong contrast to the portrait of the Miller, whose red hair, huge mouth, wide nostrils, blue hood and white cloak are very striking visual details. We do get a more personal glimpse of the Manciple's personality, however, in the prologue to his tale when he criticizes the COOK's drunkenness; but when the Host (*see* Harry BAILLY) tells him to be careful lest the Cook should start examining the Manciple's failings, the man quickly backs off, displaying a strong reluctance that he himself should be the object of scrutiny. "The MERCHANT'S TALE," concerning Phoebus APOLLO and his CROW, is intended to function as a moral fable stressing the importance of discretion in speech. The ironic nature of the Manciple's interpretation of the story is discussed in the Commentary section of the following entry on the tale itself.

Artist's rendering of the Manciple, from the Ellesmere Manuscript of The Canterbury Tales. *The Manciple is mentioned in the General Prologue to the tales, but Chaucer does not provide any description of his physical features or attire, so the artist was free to use his own creativity in this portrait. The item he holds in his hand may be a gourd filled with wine drawn from the pouch hanging at his waist.*

"Manciple's Tale, The"   "The Manciple's Tale" is based on a story in OVID's *Metamorphoses* that, in recounting the god Phoebus Apollo's life on Earth, explains how crows came to have black feathers.

SUMMARY

Near the town of BOBBE-UP-AND-DOWN (probably Harbledown, about two miles from CANTERBURY), the Host, Harry BAILLY, begins to poke fun at the COOK, who is so drunk or sleepy that he can hardly stay astride his horse. For penance, the Host continues, the Cook must tell a tale. The Cook responds that he would rather sleep than have a gallon of the best wine in CHEAPSIDE. The MANCIPLE chimes in this time, saying that he, for one, will gladly excuse the Cook from telling a tale, considering how badly his breath stinks. The Cook takes a swing at him and falls off his horse. It takes several people and a great deal of effort to remount him. The Host then invites the Manciple to take his turn in the tale-telling game, but warns him that he ought to be careful how he speaks to the Cook, lest that man should, when he is sober, get back at the Manciple by revealing some of his shady business dealings. Taking heed of the warning, the Manciple makes amends with the Cook by offering him some wine. The Cook drinks deeply and thanks the Manciple, sending the Host into spasms of laughter. He comments upon the wonderful effects of good drink, blesses BACCHUS, the god of wine, and invites the Manciple to begin his tale.

The Manciple begins by recalling that when Phoebus lived on Earth, he was the most accomplished knight in all the world. He slew the serpent Phyton (PYTHON) and performed many other noble deeds with his bow and arrows. He was also a great musician, able to play a variety of instruments and possessing a beautiful singing voice. Phoebus kept a white crow as a pet and taught it to speak. It was also able to sing, in a voice more beautiful than any nightingale. Phoebus also had a wife whom he loved more than anything else in the world, and of whom he was very jealous and possessive. Having introduced the wife, the Manciple departs briefly from the train of his narrative to offer some reflections on the futility of trying to guard a wife's chastity, comparing a wife who is kept well-guarded to a bird in a cage, a cat kept in the house or a she-wolf in heat; he then denies that these examples refer to women. He returns to his story, but only for nine lines, after which he digresses again to comment on the deceptive nature of language, and specifically, on how a poor woman who becomes a man's lover is called his "wench" or "lemman," while a wealthy woman who does the same thing is called the man's "lady."

This said, the Manciple returns to the main narrative. Despite Phoebus' efforts, his wife took a lover, who visited her while her husband was away. When Phoebus returned, the crow revealed the wife's adultery. Overwhelmed with jealousy and rage, Phoebus killed his wife, then broke all his musical instruments and his bow and arrows. Later, realizing the enormity of what he had done, he blamed the crow for driving him mad with false [sic] accusations. He cursed the crow, pronouncing that never again would it be able to speak or to sing, and henceforth all crows would have feathers of black to symbolize its treason. The Manciple concludes his tale with a rather drawn-out moral which stresses the importance of discretion in speech.

COMMENTARY

The Manciple's tale of the crow is ultimately derived from Ovid's *Metamorphoses,* though a number of intermediate versions by GUILLAUME DE MACHAUT, John GOWER and the anonymous authors of *Ovide moralisé* and *The Seven Sages of Rome* tell the same story, with minor variations. None, however, seems to have changed it as much as Chaucer. In Ovid, the bird is a raven; Chaucer changes it to a crow. Regardless of any reasons he may have had for so doing, this alteration immediately lowers the tone of the story toward the comedic. Chaucer also makes the woman Phoebus' wife instead of his mistress, as she is in the original, and omits the detail that she is pregnant. Her pregnancy, Phoebus' desperate attempts to save her and his success in saving the unborn child are all important features of Ovid's story, adding tremendously to its pathos. Their disappearance from Chaucer's version, along with his decision not to give the wife a name, preserves the emotional monotone of the story, which never strikes more than a single note at a time—first jealousy, then rage, then regret. The avowed message of the tale is similarly uncomplicated. It belongs to the genre of the EXEMPLUM, i.e., a fictional story with a moral point. Writers of the later Middle Ages often drew upon classical mythology to create such works, simply revising the story so that it was able to support some kind of Christian "moralitee," which would be explicitly attached to the end of the story. The "moralitee" of "The Manciple's Tale" is that it is unwise to speak too much. Although he purports to teach the same lesson that RUSSELL the fox learns in "The NUN'S PRIEST'S TALE," the Manciple utilizes 45 lines to do it, while the NUN'S PRIEST requires only three lines. The fact that he uses so many words to tell his audience not to talk overmuch creates an ironic contrast between the form of his language and its meaning. This irony is further illustrated by his commentary on the deceptive or misleading qualities of language given in the example of the poor woman whose lover calls her a "wench" and the noble lady who is referred to as her lover's "lady." In reality there is no difference at all in their behavior. There also seems to be a certain irony in the fact that the crow is punished not for telling a lie or for literal prolixity such as that displayed by the Manciple, but for telling the truth, for "talking too much," in the same sense meant by television gangsters when referring to someone who has turned informant. Thus, the ultimate irony of the tale is that the "moralitee" is not really moral at all, at least not in the sense that morality is usually defined, but is rather a recommendation to behave in an expedient or politic manner, to speak the truth only when the truth is sure to be appreciated. The crow, for failing to lie or to refrain from speaking, is deprived of the ability to speak, as well as losing his lovely singing voice and his beautiful snowy white color.

Critical reception of "The Manciple's Tale" has varied greatly over the years. Some readers dismiss it out of hand, pointing to its fractured structure, poorly developed plot and characterization and its rhetorical padding. Others have asserted that these apparent weaknesses are actually Chaucer's way of revealing the inconsistencies and weaknesses of the Manciple's character; they are the vehicles that carry the story's ironies. The charge that tale and prologue are only very loosely connected, another criticism to which the tale has often been subjected, seems easily refuted. Consider the Manciple's decision to make amends to the Cook, which he does only out of the fear that he has spoken too freely, and so may have given the Cook cause to speak with equal forthrightness about the Manciple's behavior which, in his business dealings at least, seems a trifle shady. His choice of a tale that warns against the dangers of loose speech displays an intellect that aspires to be shrewd and cunning, even if it does not actually achieve that effect. Its failings in that area underscore the inadequacy of such superficially applied philosophy.

It should also be noted that "The Manciple's Tale" once again addresses the question of the reliability and trustworthiness of women within the institution of marriage. Phoebus' wife falls into the category of the unfaithful wife, but it is hard to make any judgment about her behavior because we know so little else about her other than those two facts: that she is married to Phoebus and that she takes a lover. MAY's betrayal of the aged JANUARY in "The MERCHANT'S TALE" and DORIGEN's steadfast faithfulness in "The FRANKLIN'S TALE" provoke much stronger emotional responses because the reader knows so much more about the characters involved. Similarly, the antifeminist examples of the caged bird, housebound cat, and she-wolf in heat, which are derived from the ROMAN DE LA ROSE rather than from Ovid, carry a lot less weight than they might, and not only because they are poorly incorporated into the body of the tale. Phoebus' wife, the woman whose nature they are supposed to illustrate (despite the Manciple's silly disavowal of their application to women) is a mere cardboard character, so unlifelike that her death means less than the crow's deprivations.

It is possible, however, that "The Manciple's Tale" was composed near the end of the period during which *The Canterbury Tales* were written, and that Chaucer died before he was able to make final revisions to the manuscript. If so, it is, as some have argued, merely a rough draft of what could have been a much better tale. We do not have that tale, however, and the one that we do have seems to work very well thematically in the order to which it is typically assigned, appearing immediately before "The PARSON'S TALE," which is the last in the Canterbury group. The Parson's prologue begins with a movement away from fiction that specifically denounces the use of that mode as a vehicle for transmitting truth, a pronouncement that follows easily from a performance like the Manciple's, where fiction is little more than distortion in the service of deception.

Manes In classical mythology, Manes were spirits of the dead, worshipped by the Romans as gods. They were not individualized, but functioned collectively as the souls of the ancestors of a family, interested in the welfare of the family. Sacrifices of milk, oil, honey, wine and the blood of sacrificial animals were offered to them at the graves of the dead, which were adorned with wreaths of roses, violets and lilies. In *TROILUS AND CRISEYDE*, the warrior DIOMEDE tells CRISEYDE that the Greeks will destroy the city of TROY and its inhabitants so utterly that they will terrify the Manes (bk. 5, line 892), presumably because of the number of Trojans who will suddenly appear in the underworld after having died in battle.

Manly, John Mathews (1865–1940) One of the most influential Chaucer scholars of the early 20th century,

John Manly is primarily remembered for his coeditorship, with Edith RICKERT, of *The Text of the Canterbury Tales: Studied on the Basis of All Known Manuscripts* (1940), an eight-volume compilation of all known manuscripts, published by the University of Chicago Press. Most of Manly's explications of Chaucer's text appear in the form of short articles focused on historical problems such as Chaucer's life (as with "Chaucer as Controller" published in the *Times Literary Supplement*, June 9, 1927), or the possible identity of various pilgrims from *The CANTERBURY TALES*. He also published articles on Chaucer's style and on the meaning of particular words, as well as more general explorations of meaning in a text, such as his "What is Chaucer's *House of Fame*" in *Anniversary Papers of G. L. Kittredge* (1913). His concern with historical matters is also reflected in the book-length study *Some New Light on Chaucer* (1926), which includes chapters on Chaucer's education and career, his family, and possible sources for the portraits of the Host (*see* Harry BAILLY), the REEVE, the MILLER and various other of the Canterbury pilgrims.

Mann, Jill (1943–) Professor of Medieval and Renaissance English at Girton College of Cambridge University, Mann writes primarily on topics having to do with the work of Geoffrey Chaucer and Thomas Malory. Her most important publications on Chaucer are *Chaucer and Medieval Estates Satire* (1973), which looks at Chaucer's use of the genre of ESTATES SATIRE in the GENERAL PROLOGUE to *The CANTERBURY TALES*, and *Geoffrey Chaucer* (1991), a feminist reading of Chaucer's work that examines his relatively positive representation of women in comparison with other medieval texts and traditions. With Piero BOITANI, Mann edited *The CAMBRIDGE COMPANION TO CHAUCER* (1986), which contains her essay entitled "Chance and Destiny in *Troilus and Criseyde* and the *Knight's Tale*."

Man of Law, the   *See* SERGEANT OF THE LAW.

"Man of Law's Tale, The"   The Man of Law's story may be compared to the biblical story of Job.

SUMMARY

Following "The COOK'S TALE," the Host, Harry BAILLY, calculates the hour and the day to be 10 A.M. on the 18th of April—something he would not in actuality have been able to do without consulting astronomical instruments and tables. Concluding that one quarter of the day has already passed, he delivers a meditation on the nature of time as something that, once gone, can never be recovered, and he admonishes the pilgrims to seize the moment. In particular, he calls upon the Man of Law (*see* SERGEANT OF THE LAW) to tell the next tale. The Man of Law assents to his request, but first delivers a lengthy disclaimer, saying he cannot think of any tales that have not already been told by the poet Chaucer. This he follows by a catalogue of Chaucer's work, ending with a description of The LEGEND OF GOOD WOMEN. Here his mind evidently starts to work associatively, for The Legend of Good Women reminds him of a similar work by one of Chaucer's contemporaries, the CONFESSIO AMANTIS of John GOWER, which he does not mention by name, but rather refers to two of the tales that were a part of Gower's work, the stories of CANACEE and APPOLLONIUS of Tyre; Chaucer, he says, would never have written these because they feature incestuous relationships. What all of this has to do with the story he is about to relate is not very clear, except in the sense that his tale of CONSTANCE (Custance, in Chaucer's English) features a heroine of extraordinary virtue who contrasts vividly to all the women mentioned in the prologue, even the ones Chaucer wrote about in his Legend of Good Women.

The tale itself begins with the story of three Syrian "chapmen," i.e., merchants, who travel to ROME. While sojourning in that city, they see and hear stories of Constance, the daughter of the Roman emperor, who is as virtuous as she is beautiful, young but not immature and the mirror of courtesy. After returning to their own country, they describe her so movingly to the SULTAN OF SYRIA that he falls in love with her. He is so smitten, in fact, that he is sure he must either have her or die. Persuaded by his counselors, who look into the matter, that the only way to satisfy his desire lies within the bounds of holy matrimony, the sultan agrees to forswear his own Muslim faith and to be baptized as a Christian. The emperor of Rome sees this as an excellent opportunity to convert a pagan ruler, so the two parties quickly come to an agreement. Constance is not consulted, but her reaction makes it clear that she does not wish to leave her family and friends to travel to a strange land with a husband whom she has never met. With a brief meditation on the idea that women are born "to thraldom and penance, / And to be under mannes governance" (lines 286–87) [to servitude and penitence, / And to be subordinate to men], she bids her family farewell and, with a retinue of lords, ladies, bishops and knights, takes ship for SYRIA. Meanwhile, the sultan's mother has decided to take revenge on her son for abjuring his faith. Gathering her counselors together, she and they plot a welcome dinner which actually turns out to be a massacre of the sultan and all the Christians who came with Constance from Rome— all, that is, except Constance, whom they cast adrift on the ocean. Her ship is well-stocked with food and contains all the treasure that the lady brought with her, but they give her no crew.

Praying to God to keep her safe, Constance survives more than three years drifting in the ocean, until she finally comes aground in NORTHUMBERLAND, a region in the northeast of England. She is found by the constable of a local castle. He and his wife, HERMENGILD, are, along with most of the people living in that country, pagan Saxons. They take Constance into their home, where she works diligently to earn her keep and soon wins their affection. Before long she converts Hermengild, and shortly afterward, her husband, to Christianity.

Satan, angered by Constance's good deeds, causes a young KNIGHT (2) who lives in the nearby town to be overcome with lust for the maiden. When she rebuffs his advances, the knight waits until the constable is away, then sneaks into his house in the middle of the night, murders Hermengild, and places the bloody knife by Constance's side. Finding his wife dead and evidence pointing to Constance's guilt, the constable turns to the ruler of the region, King ALLA, for advice. Since everyone else who lives in the constable's house swears that Constance loved Hermengild and would never do such a thing, the king asks the one man who bears witness against her (the man who himself committed the murder) to swear on a holy book that he is telling the truth. When he does so, a hand appears out of the air and smites him on the neck so forcefully that he falls down and his eyes burst out of their sockets. At the same time a voice is heard declaring Constance's innocence. So amazed are they by this miraculous event that the king and many of those present are converted to Christianity. The wicked knight is slain, and soon after Constance and King Alla are married.

Peace does not last for long, though, as once again Constance finds herself the target of a mother-in-law's enmity. When Constance gives birth to a baby boy while her husband is away, the king's mother, DONEGILD, intercepts the messenger who is sent to bear the tidings to Alla and replaces the original message with one of her own. The false message reports that Constance has given birth to a monster, and that Constance must be an elf. Dismayed by the news, the king nevertheless responds with a letter directing that his child and wife remain where they are to await his homecoming. Again, Donegild intercepts the message and replaces it with one of her own, which directs that Constance and her child should be set adrift upon the ocean. The constable is appointed to carry out the task. Again, Constance is supplied with food for her journey and cast adrift without a crew. The king arrives home shortly thereafter. Discovering his wife is gone and that his mother engineered the plot to get rid of her, Alla kills his mother.

Constance and her son, MAURICIUS, drift upon the sea for five years before they approach land. We are not told the name of the first place they come to, only that it is a "hethen," i.e., pagan, land. Many people living in a castle on the shore come out to stare at the ship and its occupants, but no one approaches, until, one night, the steward of the castle boards the ship and attempts to rape Constance. She struggles with him and he falls overboard as the ship sets off once again. The ship sails through the Strait of Gibraltar, drifting aimlessly until finally the Virgin Mary intervenes and brings Constance's trials to an end.

As her ship drifts in the Mediterranean, it is discovered by the ship of a Roman senator—the very same senator who had been sent by Constance's father, the emperor of Rome, to wreak vengeance upon the Syrians who massacred their sultan and Constance's retainers. The senator does not recognize her, nor does she reveal her identity. Nevertheless, he takes her home and presents her to his wife, who is actually her aunt, though this woman also does not recognize Constance.

Meanwhile, King Alla repents of having slain his mother and makes a pilgrimage to Rome to receive penance from the pope. The senator, with whom Constance is living, is invited to dine with Alla, and Constance persuades him to take along Mauricius. When Alla sees the child, who looks exactly like Constance, he asks to see its mother, and goes home with the senator. Constance is afraid of Alla at first, not having known that her banishment from his kingdom was ordered by his mother. The tears Alla sheds upon seeing her suggest his innocence, which he soon proclaims aloud. The two are then reunited, and shortly afterward Alla invites her father, the emperor of Rome, to dine so that he may at last be reunited with his daughter. The child, Mauricius, stays with his grandfather and becomes the next emperor of Rome. Constance and Alla return to England. One year later Alla dies, and Constance, her adventures finally at an end, returns to Rome, where she lives virtuously and happily until her death.

The tale is followed by an epilogue that does not appear in all manuscripts of The CANTERBURY TALES but which has been accepted as genuine by most scholars. The epilogue primarily consists of the Host praising "The Man of Law's Tale" and asking the parish priest to tell such another one. The priest, otherwise known as the PARSON, criticizes the Host for swearing, whereupon the host suggests that the priest must be a LOLLARD because of his apparent prudishness. The Host continues to prod the Parson for a tale, but is interrupted by the SHIPMAN, who announces that he does not want to hear any preaching and says he will now tell his own tale.

COMMENTARY

The order in which The Canterbury Tales appear in most editions of Chaucer's work has "The Man of Law's Tale" coming fourth in a series beginning with "The KNIGHT'S TALE," followed by "The MILLER'S TALE," "The REEVE'S TALE," and "The Cook's Tale." "The Man of Law's Tale" marks a wide departure from the tone and character of the three tales preceding it, all of which deal with middle- to lower-class characters in situations ranging from low comedy to moral squalor. This tale, on the other hand, is closely akin in both style and meaning to "The CLERK'S TALE," concerning patient GRISELDA. Both can be read as allegorical renderings of the soul's separation from and journey of return to God the Father, based on the ancient Christian idea that the soul originally derives from, or is created by, its heavenly Father. The trials and tribulations that the female characters must endure are symbolic of the suffering to which the soul must submit during its sojourn on Earth. The heroine's name, Constance, signifies "constancy," and indeed, patience and steadfastness are her primary qualities. Otherwise, except for her role in converting Hermengild and her constable husband, Constance is basically passive, like the rudderless ships that carry her forth to her destiny. The battles fought and victories won are fought and won by God, Christ and the Virgin Mary. Her enemies, two male and two female, are all pagans, goaded into action against her by Satan. Reduced to its essence, her life is simply a battlefield for these opposing forces of good and evil, with her soul going as the prize to the winner.

Chaucer's main source for this tale was Nicholas TRIVET's ANGLO-NORMAN CHRONICLE. Written around 1334 by a Dominican friar for one of King Edward I's daughters, this chronicle was supposed to be a history of the world; but like all histories written during the Middle Ages, it was a collage of extracts from other manuscripts, no doubt containing elements of fact which were, however, well-diluted with legend and myth. For example, Constance was in fact Constantia, daughter of the Byzantine emperor Tiberius Constantinus (d. 582), and Mauricius Flavius, who succeeded Tiberius as emperor, was historically Constantia's husband rather than her son. John Gower also wrote about Constance in his Confessio Amantis, alluded to in the introduction to "The Man of Law's Tale," and there is some evidence that Chaucer drew directly upon this work for several passages. The most notable parallel between Chaucer's version and Gower's is the scene relating Constance's words to her son when they are forced to take ship in Northumberland. Trivet's depiction of this scene is comparatively abrupt and exhibits none of the pathos belonging to the former. In fact, all of the most substantial amplifications Chaucer worked upon his source seem to have had as their goal making the character of Constance more interesting, believable and, perhaps, pitiable. The tale itself is so full of miraculous events that it is difficult to believe that it could have been read as history, at least in the sense that we understand the meaning of the term. It does at times read more like one of the fabulous SAINTS' LIVES that were popular during Chaucer's day, although those works of literature were also reputed to recount the actual lives of historical persons.

The introduction and epilogue of this tale present some problems for editors and readers, the most notable of which is perhaps the Shipman's interruption of the Host in the epilogue. The Shipman's words suggest that he will be the teller of the next tale, yet in the most reliable copies of existing manuscripts of *The Canterbury Tales,* "The WIFE OF BATH'S TALE" appears next; hence, this is the order preserved by most editors many of whom argue from the evidence that Chaucer died before finishing this his last work, leaving the sequence of the tales and a number of other problems unresolved. The most problematic feature of the introduction is the Man of Law's promise that he will speak a tale in prose, when the tale itself turns out to be in RHYME ROYAL. This could be yet another indicator that the work as a whole was unfinished and in a state of flux when Chaucer fell sick and died.

Mantuan (Mantoan) This term for a resident of the Italian city of Mantua is used in reference to the Roman poet VIRGIL in *The LEGEND OF GOOD WOMEN.*

Map, Walter (d. ca. 1208) A Welsh archdeacon at Oxford during the reign of Henry II. Between 1181 and 1192, Map wrote a satirical miscellany called *De Nugis Curialium* ("Courtiers' Trifles"), which contains the antifeminist work attacking marriage that is attributed to Valerius in the prologue to "The WIFE OF BATH'S TALE" (line 671).

Marc Antony *See* ANTONY, MARC.

Marcia *See* MARSYAS.

Marcia Cato (Catoun) Marcia Cato was the wife of a Roman, Cato Uticensis (Cato the Younger), who, unwillingly divorced from her husband, returned to him when they had grown old. She is mentioned in the prologue to *The LEGEND OF GOOD WOMEN* (version F, line 252) as an example of a perfectly faithful spouse who must nevertheless bow to the greater perferction of Queen ALCESTIS, who offered to die in her husband's place.

Marcian *See* MARTIANUS CAPELLA.

Marcus Tulyus *See* CICERO, MARCUS TULLIUS.

Mardochee *See* MORDECAI.

Marie, Egyptian *See* MARY THE EGYPTIAN, SAINT.

Marie, Saint *See* MARY, SAINT.

Marie de France A 12th-century French poet who wrote 12 *Lais,* each one a Celtic story told in ANGLO-NORMAN couplets. Although she was born in France, she appears to have done most or all of her writing in England. She also wrote a collection of AESOP's fables, which she called *Isopet* and claimed to have translated from English. Her fable, "Del cok e del gupil" ("Concerning the Cock and the Fox") was one of the primary sources of Chaucer's "NUN'S PRIEST'S TALE."

Mark, Saint The author of the New Testament Gospel of Mark. The WIFE OF BATH attributes Christ's miracle of the loaves and fishes, when he fed five thousand people with only five loaves and two fish, to Mark (line 145) but it actually appears in the Gospel of John (*see* JOHN, SAINT). Mark is mentioned in the prologue to "The TALE OF MELIBEE" as one of the biblical authors who tells the story of Christ's passion (line 951).

Marmarica (Marmoryke) In ancient geography, Marmarica was a region on the north coast of Africa between Egypt and Cyrenaica in eastern Libya. It is referred to in the BOECE, Chaucer's translation of BOETHIUS' *Consolation of Philosophy,* in Book Four, Metrum 3, when LADY PHILOSOPHY describes how the sailors accompanying ULYSSES were changed into beasts by the sorceress. One of them, she says, was transformed into a lion like those found in Marmarica, a place where lions might reasonably have been expected to appear in the sixth century, when Boethius lived.

Marriage Group The "Marriage Group" is the name George Lyman KITTREDGE gave to a series of four of *The CANTERBURY TALES* that all treat the subject of marriage. The group includes "The WIFE OF BATH'S TALE," "The CLERK'S TALE," "The MERCHANT'S TALE" and "The FRANKLIN'S TALE." Kittredge believed that the last of these, "The Franklin's Tale," represented Chaucer's vision of the ideal marriage, guided by mutual love, respect, trust and honor. "The Wife of Bath's Tale" also, however, seems to argue for mutuality. Even though the WIFE OF BATH pursues dominance over her husbands both in life and within her tale, her ultimate goal is to find someone who respects her and is worthy of her own respect. "The Clerk's Tale," to a medieval audience accustomed to seeing stereotypical representations of either ideal womanhood or its opposite (and nothing in between), depicts a perfectly patient, faithful, long-suffering—not to mention beautiful and wise—woman who obeys her husband in absolutely everything. "The Merchant's Tale" features another stereotype, the lovely young woman married to an ugly, jealous old man and destined to seek a lover with whom she has more in common.

Kittredge felt that these tales responded to each other; more specifically that the CLERK's and MER-

CHANT's tales, both of which follow the Wife's performance, are intended as a corrective or challenge to her view. The Clerk, for example, believes that there was once an ideal of wifely conduct, but that it exists no more; while the Merchant believes that women are sly and deceitful, and that men can only be happy in marriage through willful blindness to their wives' treachery. The position of "The Franklin's Tale" as the last in the group of four helps to affirm its position as an illustration of what may be achieved when the partners in a marriage possess true love and the best intentions. Of course, to a large degree, the view of marriage expressed in each tale primarily reflects the personality and larger belief system of the teller. The Wife affirms the happy ending of her fifth marriage by mirroring that ending in her tale. The Clerk obviously has no experience of women outside of books, and that is clear from the content of his tale. The Merchant's negative experiences with his own marriage are specifically mentioned in the prologue to his tale, and then reflected in the tale's content. The Franklin does not comment on marriage outside of the story he tells, but his personality is so equable and merry, and his tale so positive and optimistic, that it is certain he has never suffered because of his matrimonial state.

Marrok, Strayte of　*See* GIBRALTAR.

Mars (1)　In classical mythology, Mars originally was a Roman god of fertility. He gradually came to be identified with the Greek god Aries, and hence functioned primarily as a god of war. In the ancient legends, Mars and Athena (PALLAS Athena), the goddess of wisdom, are usually arrayed against each other, as in the TROJAN WAR, in which Athena supported the Greeks and Mars fought for the Trojans. Through Athena's aid, DIOMEDE succeeded in wounding Mars and forcing him to leave the battle. The god's dealings with female goddesses were not always hostile, however. He and VENUS, the goddess of love, were lovers. The story of how they were once caught by Helios, the sun god, who revealed their treachery to VULCAN, Venus' husband, is the subject of Chaucer's "COMPLAINT OF MARS." Mars also makes brief appearances in *The HOUSE OF FAME, ANELIDA AND ARCITE,* and *The LEGEND OF GOOD WOMEN.* The popular view of Mars in the Middle Ages was as a god who exulted in the noise and tumult and slaughter of battle. He was not typically concerned over the wisdom or justice of a particular side, or about the reasons over which wars were fought. Perhaps this helps explain why ARCITE (1), who prays to Mars for assistance in battle in "The KNIGHT'S TALE" (lines 2373–2420), is allowed to win the fight but loses his life in an accident shortly afterward. Brutal and pitiless, Mars was attended in battle by lesser deities representing Fear, Terror, Strife, Tumult and Destruction. He is pictured sometimes on foot, sometimes in a chariot drawn by two to four fiery steeds. Gigantic in stature, muscular and with a thundering voice, he made an imposing figure in his plumed helmet, armed with shield and spear. This is how he appears in the tableau-like description of the god's statue which stands in the temple of Mars at one end of the jousting field where PALAMON and ARCITE (1) are to fight for the love of EMILY (lines 2041–50).

Mars (2)　The planet Mars is mentioned several times in Chaucer's poetry in association with its astrological significance (i.e., the influence it was likely to shed on events that occurred during its periods of ascendancy). For example, in "The MAN OF LAW'S TALE," the configuration of the planets in the heavens and especially the dominant influence of Mars is what dooms the marriage of CONSTANCE to the SULTAN OF SYRIA (lines 301–05). This negative influence would be the result of Mars' cruel and warlike nature (*see* MARS [1]). Mars is also one of the planets whose position in the heavens and other characteristics are discussed in Chaucer's *TREATISE ON THE ASTROLABE.*

Marsyas　In classical mythology, Marsyas was a Satyr who played the flute so well that he challenged Phoebus APOLLO to a contest. The god accepted on the condition that the winner might do as he pleased with the loser. When the Muses, acting as judges, awarded the victory to Apollo, he reacted rather harshly, binding Marsyas to a tree and skinning him alive. In *The HOUSE OF FAME,* Chaucer mentions seeing Marsyas standing among the minstrels who are gathered in FAME's palace (line 1229), strangely referring to him by the feminine pronouns "she" and "her" and not mentioning the word *Satyr,* although Chaucer does allude to her (his) death by flaying.

Marte　*See* MARS.

Martianus Capella　Fifth-century Roman author who wrote *De Nuptiis Mercurii et Philogiae* (*On the Marriage of Mercury and Philology*) to introduce his son to the Seven Liberal Arts. The work contained an extended discussion of astronomy, including the description of a flight through the heavens to which Chaucer alludes during his flight to FAME's palace in *The HOUSE OF FAME* (line 985). Martian's work is also mentioned in "The MERCHANT'S TALE" when the narrator refers to the *De Nuptiis* and makes the comical remark that even such a poet as Martianus would be hard pressed to describe the marriage between the old knight JANUARY and the young MAY, (line 1732) who might be said to represent Age and Youth, respectively.

Martin of Tours, Saint　Born around 315 in what became the country of Hungary, Martin became a cavalry officer in the army of Emperor Constantine, and when stationed at Amiens, France, gave half his cloak to a freezing beggar. Christ appeared to him wearing the same garment, inspiring Martin to be baptized. He became a conscientious objector, left the army and lived as a hermit before deciding to serve God more actively by preaching against the Arian heresy and founding the first monastery in Gaul. He was made bishop of Tours by demand of its people. As bishop, Martin defied the authority of the church by preaching against the death penalty. Because he died on the pagan feast day of Vinalia, when new wine was customarily tasted, he is considered the patron of new wine and drunkards, as well as of beggars, innkeepers, harvests, horses, soldiers and tailors. The corrupt monk of "The SHIPMAN'S TALE," Sir John (see JOHN THE MONK) swears by Saint Martin when he informs the merchant's wife that her husband is not her cousin. Martin was the first saint who was not also a martyr. His feast day is November 11.

Mary, Saint   In the New Testament, Mary was the mother of Jesus. Little is known of her background other than that she was the daughter of Joachim and Anna, and descended from the line of DAVID. When Mary was engaged to marry JOSEPH, a carpenter, the angel Gabriel appeared to her and announced that God had chosen her to bear the Messiah. Although it is obvious that she was present during the childhood of Jesus, nothing is known of what role she played between His infancy and the 12th year of His life, when He left his parents to stay behind at the temple so that He might begin preparing Himself for His ministry on Earth. Mary was present at her Son's first miracle, the turning of water into wine for the wedding at CANA. Except for a few brief instances, the Scriptures do not mention Mary again until she stands at the foot of the cross on which her Son was crucified. During the medieval period in Europe, Mary (customarily referred to as "the Virgin Mary" or simply as "the Virgin") gained immense importance as a saint and intermediary between Christians and their God. Much devotional literature had her as its subject or object. Chaucer's "ABC" to the Virgin is an example of this. Also, in the prologue to "The PRIORESS' TALE," the PRIORESS asks for the saint's assistance in telling her tale of a little boy who was martyred for his own devotion to the holy Mother (line 537). Mary's role as intermediary is somewhat rhetorically invoked by the narrator of "The MAN OF LAW'S TALE" on several occasions when the tale's heroine, CONSTANCE, is found to be in dire straits (lines 641, 841, 920).

Mary the Egyptian, Saint   Saint Mary the Egyptian was a prostitute in fifth-century Alexandria who repented of her sins while on pilgrimage to Jerusalem. Following her conversion, she lived in the desert for 47 years, subsisting on weeds and grasses, having taken only two and a half loaves of bread into the desert with her. She is mentioned in "The MAN OF LAW'S TALE" as an example of another woman for whom Christ provided food, just as he fed the faithful CONSTANCE during the three years that she drifted on the sea after being put into a rudderless boat and set adrift by the wicked SULTANESS OF SYRIA.

Mary Magdelene, Saint   Mary Magdalene appears in the New Testament. She was a woman from whom, according to Scripture, Christ cast out seven devils. After Christ healed her of this affliction, she became one of His followers. "The PARSON'S TALE" mentions Mary Magdelene twice in the examples the PARSON gives to illustrate the sin of envy. The first refers to an episode from John 12:4–6, in which Mary anointed Christ's head with precious ointment, arousing the envy of JUDAS, who said the oil should have been sold and the money distributed to the poor. The second example, from Luke 7:39, mentions her weeping at Christ's feet and then washing and anointing them (line 947), which aroused the disdain of Simon the Pharisee, who berated Christ for allowing a sinful woman to do this. Christ rebuked him, saying that Mary showed Him more respect than the Pharisee, who never offered Him water to wash even when He was a guest in his house.

Masinissa (Massynisse)   The king of Massylian, or eastern Numidia, from around 238 to 149 B.C. He played host to SCIPIO AFRICANUS THE YOUNGER during the third Punic War when Scipio is said to have had the famous dream about his grandfather that appears in the DREAM OF SCIPIO. Chaucer mentions Masinissa when he relates this episode in the first part of The PARLIAMENT OF FOWLS (line 37).

Matthew, Saint (Mathew, Saint)   Evangelist and author of the first Gospel, which bears his own name. A contemporary of Christ and one of the 12 apostles, Matthew originally, before his call to follow the Lord, was a Jewish man named Levi who worked as a tax collector for the Romans. The new name that he took after his conversion means "gift of Yahweh." He continued to be associated with his original occupation, however, as the patron of bankers and accountants. Martyred in either Ethiopia or Persia, as an apostle he usually is pictured with one of the supposed implements of his martyrdom, a spear, sword or halberd. His traditional emblem as an evangelist is a man, because his genealogy of Christ emphasized His human family tree. Other representations show Matthew writing at a desk while an angel keeps watch, or holding a money bag or box in token of his former profession. He is sometimes portrayed wearing glasses, perhaps to help him read his account books. Matthew's prohibition against swearing is alluded to in "The PARDONER'S TALE" as part of the list of sins to be guarded against (lines 633–34) with which the narrator prefaces his tale of the three rioters. The PARSON refers to the Gospel of Matthew a number of times in the sermon that constitutes his tale, again mentioning the warning against swearing (lines 587–89), along with other prescriptions for Christian behavior.

Maudelayne The vessel on which the SHIPMAN of the GENERAL PROLOGUE to *The CANTERBURY TALES* sails. Larry BENSON's notes in *THE RIVERSIDE CHAUCER*, based on the research of several scholars, point to evidence that a ship called the *Maudelayne* sailed out of Dartmouth, and that in 1391 its captain, Piers Risselden, was involved with a famous pirate in the capture of three foreign ships carrying wine. The General Prologue was probably composed before this date, but the suggestion that Chaucer drew upon this incident is intriguing. In his portrait of the Shipman, Chaucer refers to the *Maudelayne* as a "barge," which, if he is using the word precisely, would indicate a single-masted vessel steered by oars and lacking a deck, but possessing fore- and after-castles, about 80 feet long and 20 feet wide.

Maure *See* MAURUS, SAINT.

Mauricius In "The MAN OF LAW'S TALE," Mauricius is the son of CONSTANCE and King ALLA of Northumberland. He becomes the heir of Constance's father, the emperor of Rome. Historically, he was Constance's husband, Mauricius Flavius Tiberius (ca. 539–602) rather than her son, but he did succeed the Emperor Tiberius Constantinus (d. 582). In "The Man of Law's Tale," the first five years of Mauricius' life are spent in exile with his mother. His resemblance to her captures King Alla's attention during the king's visit to Rome and leads to the reunion of their family.

Maurus, Saint The first disciple of Saint BENEDICT of Nursia. Maurus was with him as a monk at Subiaco in Italy, where Saint Benedict founded the Benedictine Order, and afterward at Monte Cassino. According to tradition, around 528 Maurus was sent by Benedict into France to found monasteries in that country. He is said to have established the great abbey of Glanfeuil on the Loire River. In the years before his death he resigned his position there and lived a hermit's life. Chaucer alludes to the relationship between Benedict and Maurus when he notes in the GENERAL PROLOGUE TO *THE CANTERBURY TALES* that the Monk considers the Benedictine Rule—that established by Saint Benedict and Saint Maurus—to be too strict for his own worldly tastes (line 173).

Maximus The Roman officer who takes pity on VALERIAN and TIRBURTIUS (Tiburce) in "The SECOND NUN'S TALE." After taking the condemned men home to spend the night with him, Maximus listens to the wise preaching of CECILIA, who comes to visit her husband and brother-in-law, and is converted to Christianity. The following day, when Valerian and Tiburtius are beheaded, Maximus sees their souls fly up to heaven. Maximus becomes a preacher and converts many other people to Christianity, until ALMACHIUS finally has him beaten to death. Cecilia herself is arrested and ultimately martyred for her part in having the body of Maximus buried; she was later canonized.

May The young and nubile wife of JANUARY in "The MERCHANT'S TALE." May is based on a stock figure of the young and beautiful woman who marries an old, lecherous man. She is reminiscent of ALISON (1) in another FABLIAU, "The MILLER'S TALE," but is perhaps not as lively nor as lovingly described. Her marriage to January and subsequent willingness to take a younger lover has been criticized by some commentators as revealing her to be an opportunist. Since the marriages of young women in the Middle Ages were typically arranged by their fathers or other male guardians with little input from the woman involved, such a criticism seems unfounded. The fact that May is never heard to speak until the end of the tale, in contrast to January's garrulous speech, reinforces the sense that she has little control over what happens to her. The deceitful nature of what she says when she does speak (promising that she will never marry again should January die, and denying that she is having sex with DAMIAN) paradoxically shows that the only way she can exert control over her fate is by lying.

Mecene *See* MESSENE.

Medea In classical mythology, Medea was the daughter of AEËTES, king of COLCHIS. When the Greek adventurer JASON arrived in Colchis seeking the Golden Fleece, Medea fell in love with him and used magic to assist him in performing a series of difficult tasks imposed by her father. After Jason obtained the fleece, the two fled Colchis on board his ship. Medea delayed her father's pursuit by strewing the sea with the limbs of her slain brother. Jason married Medea, who continued to further his ambitions, first by killing his uncle PELIAS, who had usurped his father's throne in Iolcus. Later, when he tried to discard her in order to marry Glaucus, Medea murdered the bride with a poisoned robe sent as a wedding gift. She also killed the two children she had with Jason, and then escaped in a winged chariot to ATHENS. In Athens, Medea married King AEGEUS and bore him a son, but because she plotted against the life of THESEUS, Aegeus' son by a former marriage, she was forced to flee again. This time she returned to Colchis, killed her father's usurper and restored him to the throne. Chaucer mentions Medea a number of times in his poetry. In the prologue to "The MAN OF LAW'S TALE," the SERGEANT OF THE LAW says that Chaucer tells the story of Medea in the "Saint's Legend of Cupid" (another name for *The LEGEND OF GOOD WOMEN*), mentioning the murder of her children. Interestingly, although the story of Jason and Medea does appear in the *Legend* (lines 1580–1679), there is no reference to the children, probably because Chaucer's express intention in that work is to provide favorable portraits of women who suffered for love's sake. Accordingly, his version of the story emphasizes Medea's faithfulness and Jason's betrayal. In *The HOUSE OF FAME*, Medea is likewise referred to as a betrayed woman (line 401). Medea is also mentioned in "The KNIGHT'S TALE," where her enchantments are depicted on the wall of VENUS' temple (line 1944). Her image also appears on the stained glass window of the dreamer's room in *The BOOK OF THE DUCHESS* (lines 321–30). Later in the same poem, the dreamer tells the BLACK KNIGHT that if he kills himself, he will be as damned as Medea was for slaying her children (lines 725–26).

Medes   Medes is the name Chaucer gives to the people of Media, an ancient kingdom located in present day northwestern Iran. In the story of the Babylonian king BELSHAZZAR as related in "The MONK'S TALE," the biblical prophet DANIEL interprets some handwriting that appears on the palace walls to mean that Belshazzar's kingdom is going to be divided between the people of Media and the Persians.

Mediterranean Sea   The Mediterranean extends from Palestine to the Strait of Gibraltar and separates Europe from Africa. Chaucer commonly refers to this body of water as the "Great Sea" and the "Sea of Greece." It is mentioned in *The BOOK OF THE DUCHESS* (lines 67–69, 208), *The HOUSE OF FAME* (lines 238, 255) and, most often, in *The LEGEND OF GOOD WOMEN* (lines 950, 953, 958, 1048, 1188, 1278) because several of the women whose lives are related in this text lived in Greece. In "The MAN OF LAW'S TALE," CONSTANCE, the tale's heroine, sails across the Mediterranean when she is set adrift by her wicked mother-in-law, the SULTANESS OF SYRIA (line 464).

Megaera   *See* ERINYES.

Megera (Megaera)   *See* ERINYES.

Melan   *See* MILAN.

Meleager (Meleagre)   In classical mythology, Meleager was the son of Calydon and Althaea. When he was seven days old, the Fates announced that he would not outlast a piece of wood that at that moment was burning on the fire. His mother extinguished the fire, grabbed the piece of wood, and hid it away. When he was grown, Meleager proved to be one of the bravest of the Greek heroes. He took part in the expedition of JASON and the Argonauts and was the leader of the Calydonian boar hunt, in which many heroes joined to try to rid Calydonia of a wild boar that had been sent by DIANA to ravage the country. Meleager fell in love with ATALANTA, a woman who participated in the hunt and who gave the boar its first wound. When he had killed the animal, Meleager gave her the skin and killed his mother's brothers when they tried to take it away from Atalanta. Althaea was so enraged that she took the hidden piece of wood and threw it into the fire. When it was consumed, Meleager suddenly died. The story of this hunt and of the part that Meleager played is pictured on the walls of Diana's temple in "The KNIGHT'S TALE (line 2071). Meleager's appearance there is appropriate for two reasons. First, the adventure that led to his death had been instigated by Diana. Secondly, she was the goddess of virginity and Meleager died without consummating his love for Atalanta. The story of Meleager's role in the boar hunt also appears in CASSANDRA's narration of crucial events in Greek history in book five of *TROILUS AND CRISEYDE* (lines 1474–82).

Melibee   The protagonist of Chaucer's "TALE OF MELIBEE." Melibee is a young and fairly wealthy young man whose wife and daughter, PRUDENCE and SOPHIA, have been attacked and beaten during his absence from home. Although the etymology suggested for his name within the tale, *mel bibens,* or "a man that drynketh hony," is false, it suits the interpretation given it by Prudence, who argues that God has allowed Melibee to suffer misfortune because he has experienced so much wealth and worldly happiness (drunk honey) that he has forgotten God. Melibee wants to take revenge upon the men who attacked his family, and the tale consists of a debate between himself and his wife in which she uses wise sayings and arguments from biblical and classical authorities to convince him not to seek vengeance.

Menelaus   In classical mythology, Menelaus, the son of Atreus and brother of AGAMEMNON, became heir to the king of Sparta when he married the king's daughter, Helen (*see* HELEN OF TROY), the most beautiful woman in the world. The TROJAN WAR was essentially fought to help Menelaus get back his wife, abducted by PARIS (2). Nevertheless, despite his valor he was a minor character in most accounts of the war, a fact attested to by Chaucer's omitting him from *TROILUS AND CRISEYDE* and other treatments of the Trojan War, with the exception of the *BOECE,* Chaucer's translation of BOETHIUS'

Consolation of Philosophy (book four, metrum seven, line seven.)

Mercenrike   *See* MERCIA.

Merchant, the (1)   The Merchant's portrait follows that of the FRIAR in the GENERAL PROLOGUE to *The CANTERBURY TALES*. In contrast to many of the other descriptions of the pilgrims in the General Prologue, the Merchant's is very brief (only 14 lines, compared to the 62 devoted to the Friar) and the details used to describe him are very conventional, giving us little information about his character. His forked beard, his clothing and his elegant boots reveal nothing except that he has attained a level of wealth suitable to his profession. The idea that he delivers his opinions solemnly and that he readily reveals the amount of his profits suggests a certain amount of pride, something that is further hinted in the dignified ("estatly") manner in which he conducts his financial wheeling and dealing. His anxiety over the safety of the sea (presumably he is referring to the threat of piracy) between Middleburg in the Netherlands, and his mention of Orwell on the English coast, indicate that he was probably involved in the wool and cloth trade. The prologue to "The MERCHANT'S TALE" reveals a little more about his personal life, namely that he recently married and, so far, has not found the experience a pleasant one. The tale that he proceeds to tell constitutes an ironic treatment of marriage in which a wealthy old knight named JANUARY, after choosing a wife some 40 years younger than himself, anticipates a wedded life of uninterrupted bliss. It is offered in response to the idealistic representation of virtuous womanhood presented in "The CLERK'S TALE."

Merchant, the (2)   Primary character in "The SHIPMAN'S TALE." This busy and successful man is a financier who deals in international exchange, rather than one who buys and sells commodities. His most memorable characteristic is his preoccupation with business. This is illustrated by an early scene which reveals that he spends most of the day in his counting house, pausing only long enough to eat and counsel his wife in thrifty housekeeping. Despite his professional acumen, the merchant is completely taken in by the unscrupulous Sir JOHN THE MONK, who visits his house often in the guise of a dear friend to both the merchant and his wife. The monk is actually an opportunist, just waiting for the chance to take advantage of this relationship in some way that will be profitable to himself. This happens when the merchant's wife asks Sir John for a loan. The wiley monk borrows the money from her husband, but does not tell her where he got it. In exchange for the loan, he requires that she have sex with him. Then, when the merchant asks John to repay the money he has borrowed, he claims to have already done so—when he gave the borrowed sum to the merchant's wife. When the wife claims that John never said he was repaying a loan, and that she assumed the money was a gift for her, we do not really know whether the merchant suspects the truth.

Artist's rendering of the Merchant, from the Ellesmere Manuscript of The Canterbury Tales. *The Merchant lacks the distinguishing "forked beard" described in the General Prologue, but his gown does show blue and white flowers that represent "motley" and his cap is rolled in a style known as "Flaundrish."*

"Merchant's Tale, The"   "The Merchant's Tale" tells of the "woe that is in marriage" when an aging knight marries a young and beautiful woman.

SUMMARY

The prologue to this tale, issued in response to "The CLERK'S TALE," shows that the MERCHANT's experience of marriage has been nothing like that of WALTER and his patient GRISELDA. The merchant's wife is so ill-tempered, he claims, that even if the devil were to be married to her, she would overmatch him. He generalizes outward from his own experience to claim that "wedded men lyven in sorwe and care" (line 1228). A bit of a surprise comes at the end of this speech when the man reveals that he has been married for only two months.

The Host, Harry BAILLY, invites him to tell a tale of "wyves cursednesse" since he knows so much about it; the merchant agrees, but declines to speak any further about his personal experience.

"The Merchant's Tale" tells the story of an old knight named JANUARY, who, for the first 60 years of his life, merely followed where his sexual appetite led him in his desire for women. Now that his life is almost over, he decides he ought to take a wife and have some children. A long passage of 129 lines justifies this decision by praising the virtues of marriage, defying those learned men who have written against it and giving numerous examples of good wives.

When January calls his friends together to tell them of his decision, he reveals another facet of his plan: He intends to marry a young wife, one of no more than 20 years of age. He rationalizes this decision by saying that an older woman would be more difficult to rule, that a younger woman will more easily bear children. Furthermore, he remarks, the only thing about him that is old is his gray hair; his heart and limbs remain young like the evergreen.

His friends have various comments to make about his decision, some for it and some against it. His brother PLACEBO declares his full agreement with January's plan, but JUSTINUS, another brother, disagrees. His marriage, he claims, has brought him nothing but expense and a restriction of his freedom. He warns January that he will not be able to please his young wife sexually, a caution that gets repeated later on. Nothing can sway January from his decided course of action, though, and he soon busies himself to find a bride. It is not long before his choice settles on MAY, a young woman who, in her beauty, her womanly bearing, her seriousness and her lower station in life, somewhat disconcertingly reminds us of Griselda. The only trait Griselda has that is not mentioned here is virtue; why this is so becomes apparent as the tale unfolds.

There is one matter that preys on January's conscience, and which he discusses with his brothers before becoming betrothed: He is so certain that his married life will be one of absolute bliss that he is afraid he will lose the right to go to heaven when he dies, having already had his heaven on Earth. His brother Justinus snidely reassures him that God will likely take pity on him and cause his wife to make his married life a purgatory. This time, however, Justinus qualifies his promise that January will regret his decision to marry, saying that the marriage will not endanger his salvation, provided that he not please his wife too much in bed or give in to her desire for sex too frequently.

Justinus and Placebo negotiate the terms of the marriage, which includes the transfer of some property to May. Shortly thereafter, the marriage is celebrated. Now the emphasis of the narrative turns directly to sexual desire, making it clear that January's decision to marry

and his choice of a bride stem more from libido than any other considerations. Throughout the wedding feast, he voluptuously anticipates bedding his new wife and even contrives to hurry the festivities to a close so that he may do so. Paradoxically, though, prior to going to bed he tries to increase his desire by drinking various wines and a mixture of aphrodisiacs.

Once the couple have been ceremoniously put to bed, January apologizes for the offense he is about to do unto May, but then explains that, because they are married, nothing that they do can be considered sin. Then he "laboureth," we are told, until dawn. Meanwhile, a young squire named DAMIAN, who carved the meat at the wedding feast, has fallen head over heels in love with May. During the four days that May keeps to her chamber as was customary for new brides belonging to her husband's class, Damian's lovesickness develops to such a pitch that he can no longer rise from his bed. Overcome with longing, he finally vents his feelings by writing May a note professing his love. January's request that May should visit the ailing Damian provides him with an opportunity to give her the note, but he begs her not to reveal what he has done, for then he would be killed.

May reads his note in the privy and then returns to bed with her old husband. January asks her to remove her clothes so that he can have intercourse with her. She obeys, the narrator tells us, but whether it seemed to her paradise or hell he cannot tell. Before long May discovers that she has fallen in love with Damian and feels that she must relieve his suffering. She gives him a note to this effect, beseeching him to be healed, promising to meet him when the opportunity arises. Damian arises the next morning completely cured.

January, by way of adding pleasure and luxury to his existence, has an enclosed garden built and planted with flowers and trees. It is so beautiful that PLUTO and PROSERPINA often visit. The garden is kept locked for privacy, and one of the activities that January enjoys within its bounds, weather permitting, is having sex with May.

Life in general seems to be going very well for January, when suddenly FORTUNE turns against him and he goes blind. Now it becomes more difficult than ever to keep his wife under surveillance, and January, accordingly, becomes even more jealous and attentive. To guard against his wife committing adultery, he attempts to keep his hand upon her at all times. May, bursting with desire for young Damian, conceives a plan which will, despite January's precautions, allow the two of them to consummate their love. First she makes a wax impression of the key to January's garden so that Damian can make a duplicate. This accomplished, when the weather grows warm May entreats her husband to go with her into the garden. When he consents, she gives Damian a signal indicating that he should go before. Once all three of them are in the garden, January makes a fine speech to May beseeching her to remain faithful to him and promising to put all his property in her name in return. May readily agrees, saying that if she should ever break her marriage vows January ought to drown her. Then she signals Damian to climb into a pear tree.

The action is interrupted at this point by a dialogue between PLUTO and PROSERPINA, who are observing the three humans in the garden. Pluto delivers a speech full of the standard medieval antifeminist rhetoric, pointing to May's bad behavior. To punish her, he determines that he will restore January's sight when May has sex with Damian. Proserpina responds angrily to Pluto's charges against womankind, giving historical examples showing that men can be just as wicked. She decrees that if Pluto restores January's sight, she will grant May, and all women who come after her, the ability to talk her way out of the situation.

As an excuse to climb up into the pear tree with Damian, May announces a craving for pears, referring to herself in such a way as to suggest that she may be pregnant. January, unable to climb because of his blindness, consents to let her stand on his back to hoist herself into the tree's branches. At last Damian and May are united. He pulls up her smock and, in Chaucer's words, "in he throng," i.e., thrust. January immediately regains his sight, looks up at his wife, and sees her having sex with Damian. He cries out in surprise. May never loses her composure, but explains to him that she was directed to struggle with a man in a tree as a prescription to restore her husband's sight. When January protests that she was having sexual intercourse with that man, she further explains that having just recovered his vision, he must not have seen correctly. When he persists in accusing her, May turns the tables by becoming angry with him for not appreciating that she has eliminated his blindness. At last he believes her and the two of them are accorded once more.

COMMENTARY

There is some uncertainty surrounding the question of sources for "The Merchant's Tale." January's deliberation on the virtues of marriage echoes parts of Eustache DESCHAMPS' *Mirour de mariage,* although at least one scholar has argued that both Chaucer and Deschamps derived their works from a common source, the *Lamentationes* of Matheolus. Other influences on this portion of the text are the *Liber de amore Dei* ("Book of the Love of God") and the *Liber consolationis et consilii* of ALBERTANO OF BRESCIA, which Chaucer translated as his "TALE OF MELIBEE." Chaucer also draws upon a work that serves him elsewhere in his characters' debates on the topic of marriage, Saint JEROME's *Epistola adversus Jovinianum* (Letter against Jovinian).

The second part of the tale, which focuses on January's marriage and lovemaking, may, according to Larry BENSON's notes in *The RIVERSIDE CHAUCER,* be taken from Giovanni BOCCACCIO's *Ameto,* which describes an aged and impotent man who is married to a nubile young woman. The tale's ending borrows a common FABLIAU plot in which the blinded husband regains his sight just at the moment of his wife's sexual liaison with another man.

The blending of all these source materials makes it difficult to determine which genre, if any, the tale belongs to. Perhaps its closest kin, in terms of plot, is the fabliau. Other elements, like the use of characters belonging to the upper classes (January is a knight) and the tale's mixing of high and low style, complicate the text beyond definition. Some scholars have argued that Chaucer was using this tale as a vehicle for experiment in style. The tale also has a fair number of textual problems, the most notable example being the narrator's reference to other men as "secular" when he, a merchant, clearly could not be a member of the clergy. This may indicate that the tale was originally intended to belong to one of the clerical pilgrims, and that when it was ultimately given to the Merchant, these lines went unrevised.

Traditionally, there have been two approaches to reading "The Merchant's Tale." The earliest, put forth by George Lyman KITTREDGE and others, suggests that the tale is a reflection of the Merchant's character and the concerns of his own life, specifically the bitter experience of his marriage. More recent scholars argue against reading too much of the Merchant's bitterness into the tale, seeing it as a playful satire on marriage, targeting both men and women with its wit. Certainly the narrative's portrayal of January is less than sympathetic. His long argument on the virtues of marriage does little to mask the basis of his own decision, which has its foundation in greed and lust. No longer young, attractive or able to have sex with any woman he desires, he now determines to "buy" a young and beautiful woman, who, as his wife, will have to obey him in all things. His propensity to think of his future wife as property is revealed in the statement that "A wyf is Goddes yifte verraily; / Alle othere manere yiftes hardily, / As londes, rentes, pasture, or commune, / Or moebles—alle been yiftes of Fortune" (lines 1311–14) [A wife is truly God's gift; / All other kinds of gifts, such as land, income from rent, pasture, or the right to use land held in common, / Or personal property—all be the gifts of Fortune]. January's lust is portrayed over and over again in the text, first, and with some subtlety, in his comparison of a young woman to tasty victuals: "She shal nat passe twenty yeer, certayn; / Oold fissh and yong flessh wolde I have fayn. / Bet is . . . a pyk than a pykerel, / And bet than old boef is the tendre veel" (lines 1417–20) [She shall not be older than twenty, certainly; / Old fish and young flesh is what I would prefer. / A pike is better than a pickerel, / And tender veal is better than old beef]. January's use of the word "flesh" recalls biblical remonstrances against succumbing to the temptations of the same, where "flesh" is a euphemism for "sex."

January's eagerness to bed his new wife, and the voluptuous anticipation with which he contemplates the wedding night, show beyond a doubt that he is a representative of the *senex amans,* or aged lover, a figure who appears frequently in Chaucer's work and in medieval literature in general. In *The Canterbury Tales,* the figure appears in "The MILLER'S TALE," where the aged JOHN THE CARPENTER is married to young ALISON (1); in "The Tale of Melibee"; in "The WIFE OF BATH'S PROLOGUE," where the wife describes having been married to two old men; and in the REEVE's prologue, where the REEVE confesses to being afflicted by a sexual energy inappropriate to his age. In addition to January's lust, and as an extension, perhaps, of his view of his wife as property, is his desire to control her. He explains to his friends that he expects a young wife to be completely pliable to his will, like "warm wax" in his hands. When he goes blind and feels his control slipping because he cannot observe her every move, he nearly goes mad out of fear that she may deceive him. Finally his jealousy and possessiveness overcome him completely, and he desires that even if he should die, she may never love or marry again but should always be a widow. Chaucer combines these aspects of January's behavior with certain naturalistic physical details, such as the manner in which the slack skin around his neck jiggles when he sings and the way he wakes himself by coughing, to create a portrait of a man with whom the Merchant would hardly wish to identify, and with whom a young girl would hardly wish to make love.

May, on the other hand, seems more difficult to evaluate. Critics have in the past criticized her for marrying an old man and then committing adultery with a younger one, believing that the irony in the tale is aimed specifically at her and the gender that she represents, rather than at the situation she is in. But we do not know whether the marriage was of May's choosing. Like Griselda, who also married above her social station, May's marriage may well have been contracted by her father or some other male relative acting on her behalf. In the Middle Ages that certainly would have been more common, especially considering her youth, than for her to have entered the contract of her own volition. Further comparison between May and Griselda reveals more similarities. While May does not have to endure insults of the extreme type perpetrated by Walter against his wife, she does have to submit her will entirely to her husband's lust (will and sexual desire), which she does without objection until her own lust intervenes to disrupt the one-sided, apparent har-

mony of their marriage. The tale's conclusion in fact suggests that "The Merchant's Tale" can be read as a realist's response to the philosophical lessons of "The Clerk's Tale," showing how a real woman, put into Griselda's position, might respond. The WIFE OF BATH's personal experience, recounted in her prologue, lends additional support to this view. Another of the tales that, like the Clerk's, may be read as a contrast to the Merchant's is the KNIGHT (1)'s. Like "The Merchant's Tale," "The KNIGHT'S TALE" features an enclosed garden and a beautiful, but inaccessible, lady. Helen COOPER suggests that "The Knight's Tale" contains "in ideal form many of the courtly attributes and motifs that are debased in the Merchant's Tale," such as EMILY's association with the month of May and the incorporation of pagan gods who act upon and correspond to human characters (lines 212–13).

Merchant's Wife, the This character in "The SHIPMAN'S TALE" forms one half of traditional comic duo: the spendthrift wife married to a husband who is wealthy but tight with his money. Like most such wives, she finds a way to get around her husband's stinginess, borrowing money from their mutual friend, Sir JOHN THE MONK. She seems little dismayed by John's demand that they have sex in exchange for the loan, and is equally ready to repay her husband in the same coin. They have both been the victims of Sir John's wiliness when he borrowed money from her husband in order to loan it to her, without telling her where it came from. This trick enabled him both to reap the (sexual) benefits of giving her the money and to tell her husband that he repaid his debt.

Mercia A kingdom that, roughly, occupied the west midlands region of England during the Anglo-Saxon period (ca. 449–1066). Saint KENELM, whose dream of being murdered is related in "The NUN'S PRIEST'S TALE," was a king of Mercia before his death (line 3112).

"Merciless Beauty" One of the short poems probably written by Chaucer but not explicitly attributed to him in the manuscripts or by other forms of external evidence (such as comments by other poets or scribes). Along with a number of works that undoubtedly came from Chaucer's pen, the poem survives in a single manuscript. That, in addition to the Chaucerian style displayed by the poet in executing the roundel form, has led to its acceptance by most modern scholars as genuine.

The poem is divided into three parts, each comprised of three stanzas. The first stanza of each part states the refrain, which is then repeated at the end of the second and third stanzas. Each part has a different refrain. The theme of parts one and two is a traditional courtly one, the "lover's wound." The narrator has been wounded by looking into his lady's eyes and can only be healed if she will show him some pity. Otherwise, he will die. In part three, the theme takes a comic turn as the narrator boasts of how he has escaped from love's prison by becoming fat, and rather than bemoaning his loss, he celebrates his freedom: "Sin I fro Love escaped am so fat, / I never thenk to ben in his prison lene; / Sin I am free, I counte him not a bene" (lines 27–29) [Since I, being so fat, have escaped from Love, / I never anticipate being lean in his prison; / Since I am free, I consider him (Love) not worth a bean]. Thus the poem humorously concludes by rejecting the values of the courtly love tradition in favor of personal comfort. As with most of Chaucer's shorter poems, the date of the composition of "Merciless Beauty" is uncertain, but the reference to the poet's widening girth has led some to suggest that it may belong to the later period.

Mercury (Mercurius) (1)   In classical mythology, Mercury was the Roman god of trade, commerce and travel, and of luck and good gifts, who early on became identified with the Greek god Hermes. Taking on the attributes of the latter, he additionally became the deity of wind (from which he got his swiftness), of gymnastics, of eloquent speech and learning in general and of astronomy, and the promoter of the health and fertility of plants and animals. He also functioned as the messenger and herald of the gods and the bringer of sleep and dreams. Mercury was traditionally pictured wearing a low-brimmed hat with wings, and carrying a caduceus, a wand having two wings at the top and entwined by two serpents. His sandals were also winged. Mercury is mentioned frequently in Chaucer's poetry, most often appearing in his function as messenger, as he does in The HOUSE OF FAME when JUNO sends him to summon MORPHEUS (line 429). In "The KNIGHT'S TALE," he takes a more consequential role, speaking to ARCITE (1) in a dream and telling him to return to ATHENS, where he will find an end to all his woes (line 1385). The ambiguity of this promise is typical of this god, who was also known for playing tricks on people.

Mercury (Mercurius) (2)   The smallest planet in the solar system and the one nearest to the Sun, Mercury is named for the god MERCURY (1), whose attributes suggest the planet's astrological influences. The WIFE OF BATH notes the planets' influence on human affairs when she says those born under the sign of VENUS (like herself) and those born under MERCURY (like her husband, who is a cleric and scholar) often do not get along (line 697). Mercury is also among those planets whose position in the heavens and other characteristics are discussed in Chaucer's TREATISE ON THE ASTROLABE.

Messene (Messenia)   A region in the southwestern Peloponnesus of Greece. In "The FRANKLIN'S TALE," DORIGEN recalls how a group of 50 virgins from Lacedaemon chose to die rather than to allow themselves to be raped by a group of invaders from Messene (line 1379). Dorigen uses this, and many other examples of women who remained chaste despite tremendous pressure, in order to strengthen her own resolve against granting the squire AURELIUS the sexual favors she had rashly promised him.

Messenus   See MISENUS.

Metamorphoses   See OVID.

Metellius   According to Valerius Maximus, a first-century Roman writer, Egnatius Metellius was a Roman who beat his wife to death with a stick because she drank too much wine. The WIFE OF BATH alludes to this story in the prologue to her tale, saying that if she had been his wife, he would not have prevented her from drinking (line 460).

Methamorphosios   See OVID.

Meun, Jean de   See JEAN DE MEUN.

Micah   In the Old Testament, Micah was a prophet and the author of the eponymous Book of Micah. He was a younger contemporary of the great prophet ISAIAH. Micah was highly critical against those who falsely claimed to be prophets of the Lord, using their position to lead the Jewish people into false hopes (of escaping God's wrath and judgment) and further error. Little else is known about this prophet, except that his ministry took place around 750–687 B.C. His prophetic words about how, when faced with God's judgment, sons and daughters would rebel against their fathers and mothers, and related families against each other, are echoed in the portion of "The PARSON'S TALE" (actually a sermon) which discusses the torments of hell (line 201).

Michias   See MICAH.

Midas   In classical mythology, Midas was a king of Phrygia who is most commonly remembered for his ability to turn everything he touched into gold. When even his food and drink were affected by his magical touch, he prayed to Dionysus (BACCHUS) to take this gift away. On another occasion Midas acted as judge in a musical contest between APOLLO and PAN. When the king decided in favor of Pan, Apollo punished him by transforming his ears into those of an ass. By wearing a hat Midas concealed his humiliation from everyone save his barber who, not daring to tell anyone else the secret but unable to keep it to himself, whispered it into a hole in the ground. Some reeds that later grew out of the hole would whisper, whenever the wind blew, "Midas has asses' ears." When Chaucer's WIFE OF BATH recalls the story, she has Midas' wife play the role of the barber, using the tale to illustrate women's inability to keep a secret (lines 951–53). This version of the story is one she undoubtedly learned from her fifth husband Jankin (1), who used to read to her from a "Book of Wicked Wives." Midas is also mentioned in book 3 of *Troilus and Criseyde,* where the narrator pauses in his description of the lovers' joy to say that those who despise love should, like Midas, be granted asses' ears (line 1389).

Middle English Dictionary The *Middle English Dictionary* (MED), edited by Hans Kurath and a host of other scholars, and published by the University of Michigan Press, is a multivolume dictionary of Middle English from ca. 1000 to 1475. Entries are based on the Southeast Midlands dialect (that of London and surrounding areas). Citations provide variant and grammatical forms, parts of speech, etymology, meanings and illustrative quotations. The work was begun in 1952 and, when complete, will largely supersede the Middle English entries in the *Oxford English Dictionary* and Stratman's *Middle English Dictionary* (revised by Henry Bradly in 1891), currently the only complete Middle English dictionary in existence. Currently complete up through Volume T, fascicle 7, its accuracy and reliability make the MED an indispensable tool for scholars working with Chaucer's language and literature.

Middleburgh The town of Middleburgh was a Dutch port on the island of Walcheren. It is mentioned in the portrait of the MERCHANT that appears in the GENERAL PROLOGUE TO THE CANTERBURY TALES. There the Merchant is described as desiring that the sea be protected at all costs between Middleburgh and Orwell on the English coast. From 1384 to 1388 Middleburgh was a port through which wool was allowed to be exported. This information has been used to argue that wool is one of the staples in which the Merchant trades, and to suggest a possible date of composition for the Merchant's portrait.

Milan (Milayne) A city in northwestern Italy in the region of LOMBARDY. Bernabò VISCONTI was the lord of Milan whose niece, Violanta, married Chaucer's first patron, Lionel, duke of Clarence. The story of Bernabò's fall from power (he was assassinated) is related in Chaucer's "MONK'S TALE" (lines 2399–2406).

Miletus (Milesie) A city in ancient Ionia on the southwestern coast of Asia Minor. In "The FRANKLIN'S TALE," DORIGEN recalls the story of seven virgins of Miletus who, rather than allowing themselves to be raped by marauding soldiers, committed suicide (line 1409). These seven Milesian virgins form part of a catalogue of virtuous women whose example Dorigen would like to follow, even though she has promised to become the lover of the squire AURELIUS if he can remove the treacherous rocks from the coast of BRITTANY. The bargain ironically reveals Dorigen's love for her husband,

whose return voyage from England would be endangered by the rocks.

Milky Way The galaxy (composed of stars, gas and dust) to which our solar system belongs. It stretches in a broad, luminous band across the nighttime sky. In *The HOUSE OF FAME,* the EAGLE who ferries Chaucer through the atmosphere on the way to FAME's palace points out the Milky Way, calling it by the name of "Galaxie" and also mentioning its popular English name of "Watlynge Strete" (line 939) [Watling Street], alluding to the broad road running from London through Canterbury to Dover.

Miller, the The portrait of the Miller follows that of the PLOWMAN in the GENERAL PROLOGUE TO THE CANTERBURY TALES. The Miller is the first member of the third estate (the working class) to be overtly satirized,

Artist's rendering of the Miller, from the Ellesmere Manuscript of The Canterbury Tales. *The Miller is depicted playing the bagpipes that are described in the General Prologue. His mount is the least attractive of all those horses featured in the Ellesmere Manuscript. His thumbs literally are gilded to remind us of his thievery.*

and the details of his portrait indicate both physical and spiritual grossness. His short-shouldered, thick-set body is perfectly suited to his favorite sport, wrestling, and this, along with the one other example given to demonstrate his strength—that there was no door he could not either heave off its hinges or bash in by battering it with his head—suggests a man who is crude to the point of brutishness. He is also a thief, stealing from those who bring their grain to him for milling into flour, and tells stories full of "sin" and "harlotry" (obscenities). The three animals mentioned in his portrait—the ram, fox and sow—all correspond to these elements of his personality. The ram corresponds to the miller's strength; the fox, to the wiliness and cunning the Miller employs in stealing from his customers; and the sow, to the bestial quality of the lewd stories he tells. According to the medieval "science" of PHYSIOGNOMY, his red hair likewise hints at deceit and treachery. (Red hair, prominent moles and a huge mouth were conventionally associated with ugliness in medieval iconography.) The bagpipe that he carries and plays has been variously interpreted as a symbol of gluttony, lechery (because of its physical resemblance to the male genitalia) or drunkenness. "The MILLER'S TALE" is the second to be told on the pilgrimage to CANTERBURY. Although the Host (see Harry BAILLY) has invited the MONK to succeed the KNIGHT (1), who told the first one, the Miller drunkenly interrupts, announcing his intention to requite the Knight's telling. The story that he tells is a FABLIAU, a comic tale of adultery that in many ways functions as a subversive mirror of the Knight's depiction of romantic love.

"Miller's Tale, The"   The silly, sexy love triangle of "The Miller's Tale" offers a comic rebuttal to the high seriousness of the KNIGHT (1)'s chivalric romance.

SUMMARY

A well-to-do carpenter named John (see JOHN THE CARPENTER) who lives in OXFORD, is married to a pretty wife, ALISON (1), much younger than himself. NICHOLAS, a clever student, rents a room in John's house and takes a fancy to John's wife. One day, when John is out of town, Nicholas professes his love to Alison while simultaneously grabbing her crotch. Alison pushes him away, threatening to cry out for help. Nicholas lets her go, but pleads for her mercy so effectively that she promises to satisfy him when the opportunity arises, but warning him that they must be careful of her husband's jealousy. Nicholas tells her not to worry, then busies himself to come up with a plan that will allow them to sleep together without her husband's knowledge.

Meanwhile, another young man in the community has fallen in love with the nubile young Alison. He is a parish clerk, ABSALOM (1). Although accomplished in singing, dancing and playing a musical instrument called the cithern, he comes off as somewhat of a fool compared to the clever Nicholas. Stricken with love for Alison, Absalom serenades her beneath the window of her bedchamber and sends her a bevy of gifts, including wine, mead, ale, cakes and money. He also tries to impress her by playing the character of HEROD (1) in the town's cycle of mystery plays. But all is to no avail, for Alison is in love with Nicholas.

The next time John has to go out of town, Nicholas begins to work on his plan to trick the carpenter, a plan he partly reveals to Alison. Stocking his room with enough food and drink to last a couple of days, Nicholas locks himself in and does not come out or answer the door when John, now returned from his journey, sends his servant to see whether something is wrong. Together, John and the servant break down the door. They find Nicholas sitting stock still and staring into space. John shouts at Nicholas to wake up, then says a charm to dispel evil spirits. Nicholas appears to come out of his trance-like state and, after making John promise not to repeat anything that he says, tells the carpenter that he has seen signs in the heavens foretelling that on a certain day in the near future there will be a great storm that will flood the earth even worse than NOAH's flood. Nicholas goes on to say that if John will follow his instructions, the three of them—John, Alison and Nicholas—may be saved. He then directs John to purchase three wooden containers, each large enough for a person to fit into and to float in, and he tells John to furnish the containers with enough food and drink to last for a day, after which the waters will subside. John purchases the containers and suspends them from the roof with ropes exactly as Nicholas instructed him, putting the tub for his wife at a good distance from his own. The tubs are each furnished with food, with ladders for easy access and with an axe for cutting the ropes when the water rises enough for them to float.

On the eve of the day for which the flood has been predicted, John, Alison and Nicholas climb into their respective tubs. John soon falls asleep; Alison and Nicholas climb down from their tubs and into bed, where they engage in sexual relations. In the meantime, Absalom, thinking that John has gone out of town again, decides to go to Alison's window before dawn and make a full confession of his love. Unimpressed by his love-longing, Alison calls him a fool and tells him to go away. Absalom says he will, provided she gives him a kiss. Going to the open window, she calls him over. As Absalom reaches up to kiss her, Alison thrusts her bottom out of the window so that he kisses "hir naked ers" [her naked ass]. It is so dark that Absalom does not realize what is going on until he feels a patch of rough hair; he jumps back, thinking that he has felt a beard. Nicholas collapses in laughter.

Realizing now that he has been tricked, Absalom swears to get revenge. He makes his way to a blacksmith's forge where he borrows a hot coulter (a blade for attaching to a ploughshare). Carrying the hot steel by its cold handle, Absalom returns to Alison's window and says he has brought her a gold ring, which he will give her in exchange for another kiss. This time, Nicholas sticks his ass out the window. It is still dark, so Absalom, thinking that he is speaking to Alison, asks her to speak so that he knows where she is. Nicholas responds to this request with a resounding fart. Using the sound to locate his target, Absalom strikes Nicholas upon the ass with the hot iron.

Nicholas is burned so badly that he cries out, "Help! Water Water! Help!" awakening the carpenter. Believing that the flood has come upon them, John cuts the ropes that bind his tub to the roof and comes crashing down. Alison and Nicholas run out into the street, which is now filled with neighbors awakened by the fray. Alison and Nicholas inform them that the carpenter has gone mad, and assign to him all the responsibility for the plan to escape from the great flood. The neighbors believe the story and have a good laugh at John's expense. Eventually the entire town believes him to be mad.

COMMENTARY

"The Miller's Tale" belongs to the genre of the FABLIAU, or bawdy tale, which became very popular in France during the 12th and 13th centuries. The French fabliaux were usually written in octosyllabic (eight-syllable) couplets. By casting his own in rhyming pentameters, Chaucer worked a variation on the form, but stuck to the essential characteristics of the French stories in plot and characterization. One of the standard plots of the fabliau is the cuckolding of a dim-witted husband by a sly and lustful student. The stock characters tend to be members of the middle class, and the description of their behavior tends to be bluntly realistic and humorous. There is no immediate source for "The Miller's Tale"; however, three features of its plot are well-known medieval anecdotes. These are the fear of a second Noah's flood, the misdirected kiss and the branding with a hot iron. Although other fabliaux appear among *The CANTERBURY TALES*, "The Miller's Tale" is the best known and most often anthologized.

The poetry of "The Miller's Tale" deserves particular mention because it furnishes an excellent example of the serious artistry that permeates all Chaucer's work, but is less often considered in readings of his comedic tales. Stephen Knight's chapter on the tale in his book *The Poetry of the Canterbury Tales* provides an insightful discussion of Chaucer's language and style in "The Miller's Tale," pointing out how the lines used to describe Nicholas, fluent and filled with learned words,

reflect his character. John, the carpenter, is likewise described in language that is rugged and graced with terms befitting his trade, as in this description of him preparing for the predicted flood: "He gooth and geteth hym a knedyng trogh, / And after that a tubbe and a kymelyn, / And pryvely he sente hem to his in, / And heng hem in the roof in pryvetee. / His owene hand he made laddres thre, / To clymben by the ronges and the stalkes / Unto the tubbes hangynge in the balkes, / And hem vitailled, bothe trogh and tubbe, / With breed, and chese, and good ale in a jubbe, / Suffisynge right ynogh as for a day." (lines 3620–29) [He goes and gets him a kneading trough, / And after that a tub and another large container, / And in secrecy he had them brought to his house, / And in secrecy hung them in the rafters. / With his own hand he made three ladders, / To climb by the rungs and the uprights / Into the tubs hanging in the rafters, / And he stocked both trough and tub, / With bread, cheese, and good ale in a jug, / Sufficient for a day.].

The description of Alison, like that of a courtly lady in a medieval romance, is highly detailed and emphasizes her beauty; but the terms by which that beauty is depicted, such as the comparison of her shape to that of a weasel, create an earthy and tangible portrait rather than an ephemeral and idealized one. Some of the more conventional details of feminine beauty are in fact reserved for the portrait of Absalom, whose curled hair shines like gold and fans out beautifully across his shoulders. Absalom's foppishness is likewise suggested by his red hose and elaborately ornate shoes that feature the pattern of a church window carved into their surface.

"The Miller's Tale" is the second to be told on the pilgrimage to Canterbury. Although questions have been raised about the final order that Chaucer intended the tales to take, there is no doubt that the Miller's bawdy story of Alison, the carpenter's wife, and her two suitors was meant to follow and respond to the Knight's lofty and noble chivalric romance. When Harry BAILLY, the Host, invites the Monk to succeed the Knight in the tale-telling contest, the Miller drunkenly interrupts, insisting that he will now tell a tale to "quite" (requite, or pay back) the Knight's. His interruption constitutes a challenge to order and authority, and Bailly calls attention to it as such when he asks the Miller to be patient and let some "bettre" man tell the next tale. The Miller refuses to be reined in, however, and soon embarks on the tale that in many ways functions as a subversive mirror of the Knight's story. Both of the tales are about love, and both feature a love triangle where two young men vie for the affection of the same young woman. "The Miller's Tale" also contains some verbal echoes of the Knight's performance. First, one of the phrases used to describe ARCITE (1)'s lovesickness, "Allone, withouten any compaignye" [Alone without any company] is repeated verbatim to introduce Nicholas. Nicholas' declaration of love for Alison is couched in the familiar phrases of courtly wooing, when he exclaims that unless she returns his love, "For deerne love of thee, lemman, I spille" (line 3278) [For secret love of thee, dear heart, I die]. The fact that he speaks this courtly language while simultaneously grabbing her crotch further undermines the courtly values ordinarily incorporated in the use of such language. Indeed, all of these features reflect parodically on the lofty tone and elevated subject matter of the romance. In the typical romance, such as "The Knight's Tale," love is an idealized, even intellectualized, emotion, fraught with questions of great philosophical import like the mechanism of destinal order in the universe. In "The Miller's Tale," love is instinctual and basic, a matter of physical desire and the most expedient means of satisfying it. Peggy Knapp's *Chaucer and the Social Contest* provides a recent and interesting examination of the Miller's opposition to the Knight.

Minerva In classical mythology, Minerva was the Roman goddess of wisdom who was identified with the Greek goddess Athena (*see* PALLAS). She was also the patroness of arts and invention. Her myths are generally the same as those related to Athena. In *The BOOK OF THE DUCHESS*, the BLACK KNIGHT says that even had he possessed the wisdom of Minerva, he still would have loved the fair "White," his lady who has been stolen away by death. In *TROILUS AND CRISEYDE*, PANDARUS swears by Minerva (book 2, line 232) when he tells his niece, CRISEYDE, that she is the woman he most loves in all the world (except for his mistress). Such swearing is prefatory to his revealing that his friend TROILUS, whose suit Pandarus supports, is in love with her. Later (book 2, line 1062), Troilus prays to Minerva, asking her to assist his wit as he prepares to write a letter to Criseyde. In the story of Queen DIDO that appears in *The LEGEND OF GOOD WOMEN*, reference is made to the Trojan Horse, which, dedicated to Minerva, was used to destroy the city of TROY. Greek soldiers entered the city by concealing themselves in the horse, which was presented to the Trojans as a gift.

Minnis, Alastair J. British scholar who works out of the Centre for Medieval Studies at the University of York. In editing *Chaucer's "Boece" and the Medieval Tradition of Boethius* (1993), Minnis wishes "to place the *Boece* within the tradition" and "in the culture which made it possible." He coauthored *The Shorter Poems* volume in *The Oxford Guides to Chaucer* (1991). The volume provides background and commentary on Chaucer's work except for *TROILUS AND CRISEYDE* and *THE CANTERBURY TALES*, including broad cultural issues, matters concerning the text, sources, language and

other elements—all leading to critical interpretation and assessment. Minnis also wrote *Chaucer and Pagan Antiquity* (1982) and *Medieval Literary Theory and Criticism* (1991).

Minos In classical mythology, Minos, the legendary king of CRETE, was the son of Zeus (JUPITER) and EUROPA. When Poseidon (NEPTUNE) sent him a bull to sacrifice, Minos found the animal so beautiful that he substituted another and kept it for himself. As punishment, Poseidon caused Minos' wife, PASIPHAE, to fall passionately in love with the animal, by whom she became pregnant. The resulting offspring was a monster, half-man, half-bull, that was given the name of MINOTAUR and imprisoned in a labyrinth beneath the royal palace. When Minos' son ANDROGEUS was murdered while attending school in Athens, the king waged war against the Athenians and exacted a terrible tribute from them. Every nine years, seven young men and seven young women had to be sent to Crete to be fed to the Minotaur. The Minotaur was defeated and the tribute ended by the Athenian prince, THESEUS. After his death, Minos became a judge of the lower world. His decisions divided the good from the bad and sent each soul to its respective final resting place. Minos' role as a judge of the dead is alluded to in *TROILUS AND CRISEYDE*, (book 4, line 1188). The story of Minos' daughters, ARIADNE and PHAEDRA, who left Crete with Theseus after he killed the Minotaur, is related in *The LEGEND OF GOOD WOMEN*.

Minotaur In classical mythology, the Minotaur was the monstrous offspring of PASIPHAE, the queen of Crete who was inspired with desperate passion for a bull that the sea god Poseidon (NEPTUNE) had sent to her husband, King MINOS, to be used as a sacrifice. Pasiphae's attraction to the bull was Poseidon's way of punishing her husband. After Pasiphae conceived and gave birth to the MINOTAUR, Minos hired the famous builder DAEDALUS to construct a labyrinth beneath the royal palace as a place for the monster to live. When Minos' son ANDROGEUS was murdered in Athens, Minos began exacting tribute from the Athenians every nine years. The tribute consisted of seven young men and seven young women who were fed to the Minotaur. The Athenian prince THESEUS put an end to the tribute arrangement by killing the Minotaur. Theseus was assisted by Minos' daughters, ARIADNE and PHAEDRA, who fled with him after the monster's defeat. The story of their involvement with Theseus is related in *The LEGEND OF GOOD WOMEN*. Theseus is also a character in "The KNIGHT'S TALE," where he is described as riding home from battle carrying a banner embroidered with a picture of the Minotaur.

Mirra *See* MYRRAH.

Mirth In Chaucer's *ROMAUNT OF THE ROSE,* a partial translation of the immensely popular French *ROMAN DE LA ROSE,* Mirth is the male allegorical figure who possesses the Garden of Love. After being admitted to the garden by IDLENESS, the dreamer-narrator observes Mirth, who is tall and more attractive than any man the dreamer has ever seen. His face is as round as an apple, his complexion ruddy and white and all his features elegant and proportional. His hair is curly and bright, his shoulders broad and his waist narrow so that he almost appears to be a statue, except that he is very nimble and light-footed. His youth is attested to by his scant beard. His clothing is made of samite, a rich silk cloth, and his tunic is fashionably slashed to reveal the lining. On his head he wears a crown or garland of flowers that was fashioned by his beloved. Mirth is accompanied by his beloved, a beautiful woman who represents Gladness. He and his followers amuse themselves with singing and dancing, activities in which the narrator is happy to take part.

Misenus In classical mythology, Misenus was the trumpeter of HECTOR who went to Italy with AENEAS following the TROJAN WAR. Near Cumae, while Aeneas was absent, he challenged Triton to a contest and was drowned by the angry god. Misenus appears among the minstrels whom Chaucer observes in FAME's palace in *The HOUSE OF FAME.*

Mnestheus In the saga of the TROJAN WAR, Mnestheus was one of the Trojans who was taken prisoner when the Greeks captured ANTENOR. His fighting efforts are mentioned in *TROILUS AND CRISEYDE* (book 4, line 51). The capture of Antenor and the ensuing agreement between the Trojan and Greek forces to exchange him for CRISEYDE is what causes the two lovers, TROILUS and Criseyde, to be separated.

Mohammed Mohammed was the founder of the religion of Islam, which provided much of the driving force behind the development of Arabian civilization from the seventh century onward. He was born around 570 in the city of Mecca. Later in his life, after marriage to a wealthy widow gave him leisure for religious study and contemplation, he began to believe that the social and moral conditions in Saudi Arabia were badly in need of reform. His teachings were based on communications from the deity, Allah. The basic doctrines of Islamic religion as developed by Mohammed revolved around belief in one God, Allah, and in Mohammed as His Prophet. The Koran is the Islamic equivalent of the Christian Bible. In Chaucer's day, when religious tolerance was practically non-existent, practitioners of Islam were rarely treated sympathetically either in life or in literature. The Islamic SULTAN OF SYRIA who falls in love with CONSTANCE in "The MAN OF LAW'S TALE" is portrayed sympathetically because of his willingness to desert Mohammed (called "Makomete" and "Mahour" in the tale), and convert to Christianity to marry Constance. His mother, however, is the stereotypical evil "paynim" (pagan) who, resenting her son's conversion (lines 330–36), resorts to the drastic measure of murdering him and setting his new wife adrift on the ocean in a rudderless boat.

Moises *See* MOSES.

Monesteo *See* MNESTHEUS.

Monk, the One of the pilgrims described in the GENERAL PROLOGUE to *The CANTERBURY TALES.* The Monk's portrait follows that of the PRIORESS and her retinue, and precedes that of the FRIAR (1), with the result that all of the clergy belonging to fraternal orders are grouped together and arranged according to their status. The Prioress, as head of a convent, comes first; the Monk, a prominent member of a wealthy order, appears next; and the Friar, whose order was based on the idea of voluntary poverty and who supported himself by begging, is last. Like the Prioress, the Monk is an impressive specimen of humanity. The first details of his portrait refer to his handsome and manly appearance. His position as an "outridere"—i.e., one who takes care of the monastery's business requiring travel—and his fondness for hunting both add to our impression of his worldliness, a quality that he, in contrast to the Prioress, flaunts openly, declaring that the Benedictine Rule and other strictures placed upon men of his profession are unreasonable and outmoded. The apparent aggressiveness of his personality is further displayed in his physical description: "His heed was balled, that shoon as any glas, / And eek his face, as he hadde been enoynt. / He was a lord ful fat and in good poynt; / His eyen stepe, and rollynge in his heed, / That stemed as a forneys of a leed" (lines 198–202) [His head was bald, and shone like glass, / And also his face, as if he had been anointed. / He was a large man and in good physical condition; / His eyes were bright and rolling in his head, / Which steamed like a furnace under a cauldron]. Some of these traits could also indicate a strong sexual drive, a characteristic that may be further hinted at by the "curious pin" he uses to fasten his hood, which features a "love-knotte" at one end. The Host (*see* Harry BAILLY) hints further at this possibility when he addresses the Monk in the prologue to "The MONK'S TALE," expressing the opinion that the Monk's manly qualities would have made him a better lover and breeder than a churchman. The Monk patiently waits for the Host to finish and then, rather than responding to the man's suggestions, somewhat pompously announces that he will now tell a tale, or two, or three, and then perhaps a version of the Life of

Artist's rendering of the Monk, from the Ellesmere Manuscript of The Canterbury Tales. *The Monk is pictured wearing a black habit and a wide-brimmed hat that prevents us from seeing his shiny bald head. Although the horse is shown with the golden bells mentioned in the General Prologue, the Monk himself seems to lack the bravado of his verbal description, perhaps to mirror the melancholy of his tale.*

Saint EDWARD. But first he will tell a series of tragedies, which appear to be his favorite type of literature. (He says he has a hundred of them in his cell.) Another trait he seems to share with the Prioress is a fondness for fine clothing. He dresses like a wealthy gentleman, in a fur-lined tunic and supple leather boots. The Monk's tale follows the pilgrim Chaucer's "TALE OF MELIBEE."

"Monk's Tale, The" A series of brief biographies designed to illustrate the fickleness of FORTUNE.

SUMMARY

Prologue
The Host (*see* Harry BAILLY) responds to "The TALE OF MELIBEE" by exclaiming that he wishes his own wife,

GOODELIEF, would exhibit as much patience as MELIBEE's wife, PRUDENCE, instead of behaving like a shrew and urging him to violence and acts of vengeance. He invites the MONK to take his turn at the game of tale-telling, but not before delivering a few ribald comments regarding the Monk's appearance. In bearing, the Host notes, this monk is like an officer; he must be a man of some importance within his order. This observance leads him to further comments on the Monk's attractive physique, comments which come to a climax when the Host breaks into lamentation over the Monk's religious profession, with its accompanying vow of chastity. This is such a waste, the Host exclaims, considering the Monk's obvious value as breeding stock. The Monk waits until the Host has finished and then, without comment on what has been said, announces that he will tell a tale, or two, or three, beginning with the life of Saint EDWARD the Confessor or perhaps with some tragedies, which he defines as stories of people who experienced great prosperity followed by a descent into misery.

Tale
The tale begins with the Monk repeating his definition of tragedy, referring now to the role played by FORTUNE in bringing about both prosperity and adversity. This introduction is followed by a series of 16 "tragedies"' that recount, some briefly and some in great detail, the lives of various biblical and historical figures who experienced prosperity followed by adversity. They are listed and described briefly here in the order in which they appear.

1. LUCIFER—the fallen angel who became SATAN.

2. ADAM—the first man, who lived in Paradise until he committed the first sin.

3. SAMSON—Old Testament champion of the Israelites. A man of great physical strength, his power depended on his hair remaining unshorn. Samson revealed the secret of his strength to his lover, Delilah, who cut it off while he was sleeping and betrayed him to his enemies. When he was displayed by being chained between two pillars in a temple belonging to the Philistines, he avenged himself by pulling the pillars down and making the temple fall, killing himself and everyone inside.

4. HERCULES—classical hero who won fame by performing feats requiring great physical strength. Hercules was also betrayed by a woman, his lover DEIANIRA, who gave him a venomous shirt that burned his skin, causing him so much pain that he committed suicide.

5. Nabugodonosor (NEBUCHADNEZZAR)—a king of Babylon who twice conquered Jerusalem and took

captives from among the Israelites. One of these, DANIEL, was able to interpret the king's dreams. King Nebuchadnezzar was very proud and full of self-confidence during his prosperity, believing that not even God might deprive him of his high estate. But then one day he was suddenly stricken with madness and so completely deprived of reason that he began to live like a beast, eating hay and lying out in the rain. When he was an old man God restored his wits, and the king lived forever after in fear and respect of God's power and grace.

6. Balthasar (BELSHAZZAR)—King Nebuchadnezzar's son, who did not learn anything by his father's experience. Belshazzar worshipped idols and had so little respect for the God of the Israelites that he used their holy vessels to drink wine. While engaged in this activity, an arm appeared and wrote some words upon the wall which Belshazzar called upon Daniel to interpret. Daniel announced that it was a prophecy of Belshazzar's doom. The man was slain later that night.

7. Cenobia (ZENOBIA)—the queen of PALMYRA in Syria. From the beginning of her life, Zenobia fled the company of women, preferring to run in the woods, hunt and wrestle. She kept her virginity because she did not want to put herself under the power of any man. But at last her friends persuaded her to marry Odenake (ODENATHUS), the ruler of Palmyra. The two lived in joy and felicity, yet Zenobia was so chaste that she would never consent to have intercourse with her husband except for the purpose of having children. As queen, Zenobia was a great warrior, a wise ruler and a good mother to the two sons she had with Odenathus. Together, she and her husband conquered many kingdoms in the East, which they ruled together until Odenathus's death. After his death, she ruled alone, still making war and conquering other lands. Finally, however, she was overcome by the Roman emperor AURELIAN (Aurelianus), who made her march in chains before his chariot.

8. Petro Rege Ispannie—King PEDRO OF CASTILE in Spain was a contemporary of Chaucer's. He was murdered by his brother, who reigned after him.

9. Petro Rege de Cipro—PIERRE DE LUSIGNAN, the king of Cyprus, was also a contemporary of Chaucer's. He was slain out of envy by three of his own knights.

10. Barnabo de Lumbardia (Bernabò VISCONTI)—Lord of MILAN in Italy and another of Chaucer's contemporaries. His nephew, who was also his son-in-law, caused him to fall from power and to be imprisoned. He died soon after.

11. Hugelino Comite de Pize (UGOLINO OF PISA)—a nobleman of Pisa in Italy, falsely accused by the bishop of Pisa and put into prison, along with his four children. All died of starvation.

12. NERO—infamous Roman emperor. He performed various acts of violence, including slitting open his mother's womb to see where he had been conceived, and forcing SENECA, who had been his teacher when he was a youth, to commit suicide by slitting his wrists in a warm bath. Finally the Roman people all turned against him and he committed suicide to escape their wrath.

13. Oloferno (HOLOFERNES)—a captain under King Nebuchadnezzar who was famed for his skill in war. One night while he lay drunk in his tent he was beheaded by an Israelite woman named JUDITH. This version of the story, which differs from that found in the Book of Judges, appears in the apocryphal Book of Judith 1–16.

14. Rege Antiocho (King ANTIOCHUS [1])—Antiochus IV, king of Syria. His story is told in the apocryphal Book of Maccabees. The prideful King Antiochus hated the Jews so much that he warred upon them at every opportunity. When he had determined to attack Jerusalem, God smote him with an invisible wound that caused him tremendous pain in his gut. Still, he would not waver from his intention, until he became so ill that his flesh began to rot and stink. Finally he was deserted by his companions, who could no longer bear the smell of him, and he died alone on a mountainside.

15. Alexandro—ALEXANDER THE GREAT, son of Philip of Macedon, was one of the greatest conquerors who ever lived. He was also the flower of knighthood and greatly blessed by Fortune. According to the Monk's version of the story, he was poisoned to death by his followers.

16. Julio Cesare (JULIUS CAESAR)—the great Roman emperor who did the most to expand Rome's empire in western Europe. In recounting Caesar's conflict with Pompey the Great, the Monk digresses to lament the latter as another victim of Fortune. Caesar also lost favor with Fortune and was betrayed by BRUTUS Cassius, who plotted the attack in the capitol that cost Caesar his life. The name "Brutus Cassius" can be traced back to a probable scribal error in an early Latin version of the story in which the Latin et ("and") that originally appeared between the two names was dropped.

17. Cresus (CROESUS)—the proud king of Lydia whom CYRUS THE GREAT sentenced to be burned to death. When a storm put out the fire, Croesus escaped and rallied his troops to fight again. After a dream

in which JUPITER washed him and PHOEBUS dried him off, he became even more confident that he should win. His daughter, however, interpreted the dream to mean that he would hang on a gallows, where his body would be washed by the rain and dried by the sun. His daughter's prediction came true.

At this point, "The Monk's Tale" is interrupted by the KNIGHT (1), who calls for an end to the telling of such depressing tales. The Host agrees and asks the Monk to tell a different sort of story, one of hunting, perhaps. The Monk refuses, saying he no longer has any spirit for the game.

COMMENTARY

The subtitle of "The Monk's Tale," *De Casibus Virorum Illustrium,* provides a strong clue to its genealogy. Translated into English, the Latin phrase means, "concerning the misfortunes of great men," and it was the same title given by BOCCACCIO to an earlier, similar work. The most significant difference between Chaucer's tale and Boccaccio's lengthy work in prose has to do with the role played by Fortune. Although Boccaccio's work also tells the lives of men who fall from prosperity to adversity, it emphasizes the culpability of each protagonist in bringing about his fall, rather than putting the blame on an undiscriminating Fortune. The idea of Fortune and its relationship to human destiny came from another of Chaucer's favorite sources, the *ROMAN DE LA ROSE*, in which the allegorical figure of REASON warns the Lover against Fortune's instability. And although the concept of tragedy may be seen to function in Boccaccio's work, the Latin word *tragedia* never appears there, but it is used by BOETHIUS in his *Consolation of Philosophy*, from which Chaucer probably derived both the idea and the word. The concept itself was an unfamiliar one for medieval readers for whom Aristotle's *Poetics* were not yet available. Such theoretical definitions of tragedy as did exist at this time were inconsistent with one another; "a tale with an unhappy ending" is the closest we can come to a general definition. For this reason, and because of Chaucer's influential position as a man of letters, his Monk's definition of tragedy became the "official" one until the rediscovery of Aristotle's work in the early 17th century.

A couple of textual problems are presented by the manuscripts of "The Monk's Tale." First, the tragedy of Adam is omitted in several of the early manuscripts of *The CANTERBURY TALES*. Of slightly more interest is the uncertain order of the stanza groups. The three most authoritative manuscripts—the ELLESMERE, the HENGWRT and the Gg, place the four stanza groups having to do with contemporaries of Chaucer (Pedro of Castile, Pierre de Lusignan, Bernabò Visconti and Ugolino of Pisa) at the end of the tale so that, from beginning to end, it follows a roughly chronological order. Other manuscripts, which greatly outnumber the three mentioned above, feature the four contemporary stanza groups inserted between those having to do with Zenobia and with Nero. Despite the fact that it disrupts the tale's chronological order, the latter is the order favored by most editors, primarily because it allows the stanza group dealing with the life of King Croesus to appear in the final position. The last Croesus stanza repeats the Monk's definition of tragedy, thus giving the tale a kind of closure and effecting a smooth transition to the prologue of "The NUN'S PRIEST'S TALE," where the Host echoes the Monk's final line, "And covere hire (Fortune's) brighte face with a clowde" (line 2766). It seems much more logical for the Host to refer to a line that has just been uttered, rather than one spoken 100 lines earlier.

The metrical form, i.e., rhyme scheme and meter, of "The Monk's Tale" is the most complex of the tales in the Canterbury group. Each stanza has eight lines that rhyme *ababbcbc*. This structure also appears in Chaucer's "ABC" to the Virgin. Although the syntax of "The Monk's Tale" is somewhat sophisticated, in keeping with its elaborate rhyme scheme and meter, the tale's language tends toward the plain and simple. The use of specific details and sensational events of betrayal and murder certainly makes it more interesting to read than its immediate predecessor, "The Tale of Melibee," which is full of abstractions and repetition, but morally it rises no higher than the level of pulp fiction, rendering it in that category inferior to "Melibee." As a member of the clergy, the Monk's view of tragedy ought to provide a framework within which the series of tragedies described in the tale can be understood as occurring in a universe under the direction and control of the Christian God. Although God does play a role in some of the tragedies, the tale as a whole contains no mechanism to distinguish the fate of the innocent from the guilty. Examples of good and evil, pagan and Christian, are jumbled together in such a way as to suggest a kind of leveling which, theologically speaking, was antithetical to a medieval Christian view of the universe. In the Middle Ages, after all, the ability to distinguish good from evil was paramount, even though the innocent sometimes suffered and the guilty prospered. The lack of a comprehensible moral framework in a tale told by a clergyman gives it a darkly ironic twist and suggests that this tale, like others in the Canterbury group told by members of the clergy, serves as a vehicle for Chaucer's criticism of corruption in the church.

The inconsistency in the tale's moral framework is mirrored by inconsistencies of form among the tale's short narratives. The length of each tragedy varies from one eight-line stanza to 16 eight-line stanzas, so that there is tremendous variation in the scope and detail with which each life is portrayed. Some of the vignettes, like that of Zenobia, tell the character's life story from beginning to end, while others give only the scantiest, even cryptic, details of the protagonist's downfall. The overall effect is a lack of symmetry and balance in both form and in meaning. It is possible to read this artistic failure as a symptom of the Monk's moral degeneracy. Alternatively, since most of the shorter tragedies relate the lives of contemporary, or near contemporary figures, perhaps Chaucer merely felt less of a need to supply details that would already be familiar to his audience.

Monte Viso A mountain in northern Italy, Monte Viso is the highest of the Italian Alps. Referred to by the name "Mount Vesulus" in the prologue to "The CLERK'S TALE" (lines 47, 58), it is described there as the source of the PO River. The CLERK's geographical survey of northern Italy is translated from PETRARCH's proem, or introduction, to the Italian tale that served as Chaucer's source for "The Clerk's Tale."

moral Gower In the palinode that concludes Chaucer's *TROILUS AND CRISEYDE*, he dedicates that work to John GOWER, whom he refers to there as "moral Gower," perhaps basing this assessment on a personal relationship with the poet, or perhaps just as a reflection of the moral concerns expressed in Gower's work. Following this inscription, "moral" became Gower's epithet.

Mordecai In the Old Testament Book of ESTHER, Mordecai was the uncle who adopted Esther after the death of her parents. He was a resident of Susa, the Persian capital of the Babylonian Empire during the reign of King AHASUERUS. When two of the king's eunuchs conspired to assassinate Ahasuerus, Mordecai exposed the plot and earned the king's goodwill. After Esther became queen, Mordecai was able to use her influence to get rid of a powerful official who was plotting to kill all the Jews in the Persian Empire, and to secure a position for himself as an official who was second in power only to the king. The assistance Mordecai received from his niece is mentioned in "The MERCHANT'S TALE" by the aged knight JANUARY, who uses this and other examples of good women to bolster his argument in favor of marriage (line 1373).

Morocco Called "Belmarye" in the GENERAL PROLOGUE to *The CANTERBURY TALES*, Morocco in northern Africa is one of the places where the KNIGHT (1) has been on military campaign (line 2630). The name "Belmarye" (Benmarin, or Banu Merin) refers to the

name of the Muslim dynasty which ruled the area during the 14th century.

Morpheus In classical mythology, Morpheus was one of the myriad sons of the god of sleep. His particular territory was that of dreams. Morpheus had noiseless wings and appeared in human form, while his brother Phobetor appeared only in the form of animals, and another brother, Phantasus, borrowed the forms of inanimate objects. Morpheus lived in a cave inside a mountain from which flowed Lethe, the stream of forgetfulness. In *The BOOK OF THE DUCHESS*, JUNO sends Morpheus to animate the drowned body of King Ceix (line 136), who then appears in the dream of his wife, Alcyone, to inform her that he has died. The narrator of the poem, suffering from insomnia, prays to Morpheus for sleep, comically attempting to bribe the god with the gift of a feather bed. Interestingly, soon after uttering this prayer, he falls asleep (lines 238–75).

Moses In the Old Testament, Moses was the Hebrew prophet who led the Israelites out of bondage in Egypt. During their years of wandering in the wilderness, Moses served as their leader and received the Ten Commandments from God on Mount Sinai. The story of the release from bondage is narrated in the Book of Exodus. When Moses was born, Pharaoh, with an eye to preventing a possible revolt, had given orders demanding the execution of all male Hebrew children. Moses' mother saved his life by putting him in a waterproof basket in which he could float hidden among the reeds of the Nile. He was found by an Egyptian princess and came to be reared and educated as a prince in the Egyptian court. As a young man, Moses was forced to flee into exile after he killed an Egyptian for beating a Hebrew slave. He remained in exile for 40 years and then returned to Egypt to lead the Israelites into freedom. Although Moses served as their leader during 40 years of wandering in the wilderness, he was not allowed to enter the promised land of CANAAN because he committed an act of disobedience against God. In the *Chaucer Name Dictionary*, Jaqueline de Weever notes that during the Middle Ages, Moses was considered to be somewhat of a magician (probably because of his Egyptian education and the miracles he performed) and there was a legend that he possessed two magic rings. These rings are compared (in lines 247–51) to the one that CANACEE (1) receives in "The SQUIRE'S TALE." Canacee's ring allows her to understand the speech of the birds and to know at a glance the names and healing virtues of all the plants. In "The SUMMONER'S TALE," the friar, who is trying to wheedle money out of poor, sick THOMAS, argues that the prayers that he may make on Thomas' behalf (if Thomas gives him money, he implies) will be more effective because he, like Moses, engages in fasting to make himself ready to receive God's commandments (line 1885). In both the prologue to "The PRIORESS' TALE" (lines 467–68) and in the "ABC" (lines 89–93), the Virgin Mary (see MARY, SAINT) is compared to the burning bush through which God commanded Moses to return from exile and lead the Israelites out of Egypt. The fact that the bush burned without being consumed would be parallel to Mary's having conceived Christ without losing her virginity. "The PARSON'S TALE" quotes Moses' words from Deuteronomy 32:24, 33 when he describes what hell will be like for those sinners who fail to repent (line 195).

Mount Cithaeron   A mountain between THEBES and CORINTH where Bacchic revels were traditionally held. In classical mythology, the infant Oedipus was abandoned there after his father learned the prophecy that the child would grow up to kill his father and marry his mother. It was also the legendary home of the Furies (see ERINYES). In "The KNIGHT'S TALE," Chaucer refers to "Citheroun" as the dwelling of VENUS (line 1936), obviously misinterpreting a reference to the island of Cythera (where Greek mythology places Venus' home).

Moyses   See MOSES.

Muscatine, Charles (1920–   )   A Yale Ph.D. who built his career at Berkeley, Muscatine wrote extensively on Chaucer. His most influential work is *Chaucer and the French Tradition: A Study in Style and Meaning* (1957). This study examines the influence that the styles of French poetry had upon Chaucer's style, concentrating specifically on features of ALLEGORY, courtly romance and BEAST FABLE. Muscatine argues that Chaucer fused these traditions in his mature poetry, *TROILUS AND CRISEYDE* and *The CANTERBURY TALES,* through a combination of juxtaposition, blending and parody. The contrast between the various styles and tones creates tension between the ideal and everyday reality. *In Poetry and Crisis in the Age of Chaucer* (1972), which he edited, Muscatine authored an important chapter on Chaucer entitled, "Irony and Its Alternatives." Here he notes that while irony is Chaucer's "characteristic response to the fourteenth-century dilemma," there are other important ideas and attitudes in his poetry, such as idealism, heroism, realism and pathos, all of which may be linked to contemporary (14th-century) sensibilities. With Derek BREWER, Muscatine coedited the collection *Chaucer and Chaucerians* (1966), which provides critical responses to Chaucer's work from the time of near-contemporaries to the 20th century.

Myda   See MIDAS.

Mynerva (Mynerve)   See MINERVA.

Mynos   See MINOS.

Mynotaur   See MINOTAUR.

Myrrah   In classical mythology, Myrrah was the daughter of Cinyras, king of Cyprus. When her mother boasted that Myrrah was more beautiful than VENUS, the goddess punished her by causing Myrrah to fall in love with her father. By deceiving her father, she managed to lie with him and became pregnant with ADONIS. Upon discovering what she had done, Cinyras pursued her with a sword. In answer to her prayer for protection, the gods transformed her into a myrrh tree, the fragrant gum resin of which was considered to be her tears. In *TROILUS AND CRISEYDE,* the tears of TROILUS and CRISEYDE as they contemplate having to be separated are compared to those of Myrrah (book 4, line 1139).

mystery plays   Mystery plays were a popular form of drama in Europe from the 13th through the 16th century. Enacting events of the Bible from the Creation to Christ's Ascension, the plays were composed in cycles (a collection beginning with the Creation or some other early biblical event, and ending with an event from the latter part of Christ's life). They were performed by trade or religious guilds with each play in a cycle being performed by a different guild. For example, in the York Cycle, the *Killing of Abel* was presented by the Glover's Guild. It is believed that the plays were not staged in a theater but on wagons that progressed throughout the city, stopping from time to time for a performance. They were typically performed on the religious feast day of Corpus Christi. Although there is archival evidence that mystery plays were performed in many English towns, only four complete cycles survive, each named after the town where it originated and was performed: the York, Chester and Wakefield cycles, along with the *Ludus Coventriae* (also called N-town because its origin is uncertain). The cycles were immensely popular and characters from some of the plays find their way into other literature of the time, including Chaucer's poetry. "The MILLER'S TALE" in particular contains references to several popular plays. When NICHOLAS is trying to convince JOHN THE CARPENTER to get ready for a second great flood, he reminds him of the biblical story of the great flood and of how much trouble NOAH had getting his wife to come into the ark (lines 3534–39), a story that was commonly presented within the mystery cycles. Another character in this tale, ABSALOM (1), is said to be notable for the way that he plays the part of HEROD (1), who was typically portrayed as a ranting madman (line 3384). What cycle of plays he would be likely to have performed in is uncertain, since no text has survived for the town of OXFORD, where "The Miller's Tale" is set. Although these plays were not as influential as other types in influencing the development of Elizabethan drama, and were not performed for hundreds of years, a number have been revived in the 20th century, most notably in the city of York.

N

Nabal   *See* ABIGAIL.

Nabugodonosor   *See* NEBUCHADNEZZAR.

Narcissus   In classical mythology, Narcissus was the son of the river god Cephisus and the nymph Liriope. A beautiful young man who was loved and sought after by many, Narcissus became known for his indifference to affection. When he rejected the nymph ECHO, she pined away until she became nothing more than a voice. Nemesis, the goddess who chastised extravagant pride and the arrogance of unresponsive lovers, punished Narcissus by causing him to fall in love with his reflection in the water of a forest pool. Unable to satisfy his own longing, he stayed in that spot until he died. The flower that sprang up from the spot where he died bears his name. The narrator of *The* BOOK OF THE DUCHESS uses the story of Echo's death as a warning to the BLACK KNIGHT, who seems in danger of pining away for his lost LADY WHITE. The story of Narcissus appears depicted on the walls of Venus' temple in "The KNIGHT'S TALE" (line 1941). In "The FRANKLIN'S TALE," because he cannot tell DORIGEN of his love, the squire AURELIUS believes that he will pine away like Echo did for Narcissus (lines 951–52). The narrator of *The Book of the Duchess* warns the BLACK KNIGHT about the dangers of excessive love, giving Echo's death as an example (line 735–36).

Narice, country of   *See* NERITOS, MOUNT.

Naso   *See* OVID.

Nature, Dame   Dame Nature or simply Nature, is a goddess-like figure who appears in *The* PARLIAMENT OF FOWLS. She holds court in the Garden of Love where, on St. Valentine's Day, all the birds have congregated to choose their mates. She presides over the ritual, keeping order among the squabbling fowl and deciding the outcome of the dispute between three male eagles who have all chosen the same female (lines 309ff). The figure of Nature is derived from ALAIN DE LILLE's *De planctu Naturae* ("Complaint of Nature"), wherein she bemoans man's sins against nature that have led to his unfruitfulness. When Chaucer introduces her in his poem, he says that she appears just as Alain describes her in his "Pleynt of Kynde" (line 316). This same figure is invoked in "The PHYSICIAN'S TALE," when the narrator describes the martyr-heroine VIRGINIA, whom "Nature hath with sovereyn diligence / Yformed . . . in so great excellence" (lines 9–10) [Nature has with sovereign diligence / Formed . . . in such great excellence]. These lines are followed by Nature's own comments about the young girl's qualities and a meditation on Nature's place in the cosmos, in which she performs the services of a deputy ("vicaire general") to God, creating all earthly creatures in His honor (lines 11–28). Chaucer also presents the goddess Nature as the creator of beautiful women in ANELIDA AND ARCITE (line 80) and in *The BOOK OF THE DUCHESS* (line 871).

Nebuchadnezzar   A king of the Babylonian Empire from 605 to 562 B.C., Nebuchadnezzar captured JERUSALEM, destroyed the Temple, and carried the people of Judea into captivity in Babylon. The goal of Nebuchadnezzar's policy of transporting captured people to other parts of his empire was to provide him with slave labor for conducting extensive building projects, one of which, the famous hanging gardens of Babylon, was considered one of the seven wonders of the ancient world. After making an arrogant boast about all that he had achieved (*see* the Book of Daniel 4:30), Nebuchadnezzar was struck down at the height of his power. Driven out of office, he ended up living with the beasts of the field and eating grass, but God subsequently restored his sanity. The story of Nebuchadnezzar's reign is told in "The MONK'S TALE" (lines 2143–82), where it serves as an example of the MONK's theory of tragedy. A famous dream that he had is referred to in *The HOUSE OF FAME* (line 515) when the narrator brags that not even Nebuchadnezzar's dream was as marvelous as the one he is about to describe. Nebuchadnezzar's dream is also mentioned in "The PARSON'S TALE" (line 125), where it is interpreted in relation to the theme of penitence in the PARSON's sermon.

Nembrot   *See* NIMROD.

Neot, Saint   Neot was a monk who lived at Glastonbury Abbey in the ninth century. According to tradition, he was a counselor to the famous Saxon king, Alfred the Great. Later in his life he retired to a hermitage in Cornwall, where he gathered a small band of disciples. After death, his remains were supposedly translated to a place now called St. Neots, in Huntingdonshire, England. In "The MILLER'S TALE," the blacksmith GERVAISE swears by Saint Neot when he marvels that ABSALOM (1) is up and about so early (line 3771).

Neptune In classical mythology, Neptune was a Roman sea god who early became identified with the Greek god Poseidon. As the reigning deity of the sea, Neptune had power over storms and winds and was considered to be responsible for whether ships came safely into harbor or foundered in the deep. He had a palace in the depths of the sea, but rode over the sea's surface in a golden chariot drawn by swift horses with brazen hoofs and golden manes. He used his trident, a three-pronged spear, to make the earth quake and the rocks crack open. He was said to have created the horse by striking a rock, from which the animal sprang forth. He was typically represented as a strong, powerful figure with a beard and long curling hair. He was sometimes nude, sometimes clad in a long robe. Statues of him were placed in harbors. One of the myths about Neptune tells that he and Phoebus APOLLO helped Lamedon, the king of TROY and PRIAM's father, construct the city's protective walls. When Lamedon refused to pay them, the gods became angry. In *TROILUS AND CRISEYDE*, CRISEYDE's father, CALKAS, prophesies that the city will be defeated by the Greeks because of the gods' anger (book 4, lines 120–24). Neptune's position as god of the sea is mentioned in "The FRANKLIN'S TALE" (line 1047) and in *Troilus and Criseyde* (book 2, line 443). In the story of PHYLLIS and DEMOPHON that appears in *The LEGEND OF GOOD WOMEN*, Chaucer describes how Neptune's compassion caused Demophon, after fleeing from Troy, to be cast, nearly drowned, onto the shores of the land were Phyllis was queen.

Neritos, Mount A peak in the country of Ithaca which, according to classical legend, was the home of the famous Greek adventurer Odysseus (ULYSSES). In the *BOECE*, Book four, Metrum 3, Ulysses is referred to as "duc of the cuntre of Narice" [Duke of the country of Mount Neritos].

Nero Roman emperor (ruled 53–68) who was notorious for his cruelty and egocentricity. Nero was a student of the philosopher SENECA and appeared to show great promise, but seems to have been driven insane by the intoxication of power. He had his mother murdered, ordered Seneca to commit suicide, and was believed to have started the fire which caused Rome to burn. In the *BOECE*, Book Two, Metrum 6, LADY PHILOSOPHY describes the great destruction he caused. His love of

luxury and his banishment of Seneca are discussed in Book Three, Metrum 4 and Prosa 5. A version of the emperor's fall from power is related in "The MONK'S TALE" (lines 2463–50). In "The KNIGHT'S TALE," his death is depicted on the walls of Mars' temple (line 2032). He is likewise briefly mentioned in "The NUN'S PRIEST'S TALE" (lines 3369–73) when the narrator compares the cries of the chickens when CHAUNTICLEER is seized by the fox to the cries of the senators' wives when Nero set fire to Rome. This blend of high style (the classical simile) and low subject matter is a powerful source of the tale's humor.

Nessus In classical mythology, Nessus was a Centaur who lived by the River Evenus and would carry travelers across for a fee. When HERCULES employed him to carry his wife, DEIANIRA, across, Nessus was seized with a passion for the woman and attempted to carry her away. Hercules prevented his escape by shooting the Centaur with a poisoned arrow. As he died, Nessus gave Deianira some of his poisoned blood (or a robe stained with the blood), telling her that it would restore Hercules' love if he ever began to stray in his affections. When Deianira later tried to use the blood to that effect, it tortured Hercules so much that he committed suicide. This episode is mentioned in the life of Hercules that appears in "The MONK'S TALE" (lines 2119–26).

Newe Town (New Town) *See* ARNALDUS OF VILLANOVA.

Newgate Prison A notorious London prison where PERKYN REVELOUR, the principal character of "The COOK'S TALE," sometimes finds himself as a result of his riotous living.

Nicanor (1) In the apocryphal books of 1 and 2 Maccabees, Nicanor was one of the generals chosen by Lysias to accomplish the destruction of the Jews. His defeat by JUDAS MACCABEUS is mentioned in the story of King ANTIOCHUS (1) related in "The MONK'S TALE" (lines 2591–92).

Nicanor (2) An officer of ALEXANDER THE GREAT at the capture of Thebes (fourth century B.C.). A Theban maiden who killed herself out of love for him is included among a list of virtuous women who appear in the thoughts of DORIGEN, the female protagonist of "The FRANKLIN'S TALE," as she contemplates whether or not she is going to be able to remain faithful to her husband (line 1432).

Nicerates wife *See* NICERATUS' WIFE.

Niceratus' wife The woman referred to by this title in "The FRANKLIN'S TALE" was, according to tradition, the wife of a famous fifth-century Athenian general who was executed during a period known as the Reign of the Thirty Tyrants. Her suicide following her husband's death is one of many examples of woman's faithfulness that DORIGEN invokes as she ponders how she can remain faithful to her own husband, ARVERAGUS, after rashly promising to become the squire AURELIUS' lover (line 1437).

Nichanore   *See* NICANOR (1) AND (2).

Nicholas   A young scholar and one of the principle characters of "The MILLER'S TALE." He rents a room in the house of JOHN THE CARPENTER, who lives in OXFORD, and he is in love with John's young wife, ALISON (1), who soon falls in love with him. He is depicted as possessing a clever and sly intelligence that is somewhat masked by his air of meekness. As a scholar, he has studied the regular university curriculum of the Seven Liberal Arts, which included grammar, dialectic, rhetoric, arithmetic, music, geometry and astronomy, but his chief interest lies in predicting the weather through ASTROLOGY, which itself was not distinct or separate from the science of astronomy at this time in western Europe. Certain aspects of his characterization suggest that he may represent a debased version of the courtly lover, notably his musical ability, the perfuming of his room and himself with herbs and spices, and the language with which he attempts to woo Alison, which consists of phrases that sound as if they could have been lifted verbatim from a courtly romance. Chaucer refers to him 11 times as "hende Nicholas," and Larry BENSON suggests that the poet is playing upon the various meanings of the epithet, which he lists as "courteous," "gracious," "gentle," "nice" and possibly "handy, near at hand." He tricks John into providing an occasion for Alison and him to spend the night together by convincing the carpenter that another great flood, one even more destructive than NOAH's flood, is on its way.

Nicholas, Saint   Although there are several saints by the name of Nicholas, the one referred to in Chaucer's work was the fourth-century archbishop of Myra in Asia Minor. Because of the innocence of his own life (as an infant he fed from his mother's breast only twice weekly, once on Wednesdays and once on Fridays) and his devotion to children, he came to be regarded as their patron saint. In "The PRIORESS' TALE," the PRIORESS is reminded of Saint Nicholas by the holiness of the murdered Christian boy (line 514).

Nicholas of Lynn   A Carmelite friar and a lecturer in theology at Oxford University in the 14th century. He was also somewhat of an expert on astronomy and authored a popular treatise on the astrolabe and a 76-year calendar during the reign of King EDWARD III. In the prologue to his TREATISE ON THE ASTROLABE, Chaucer states that he has based the calculations for his tables of longitude and latitude and other tables on the work of "Frere N. Lenne" (Friar Nicholas of Lynn). He also used Nicholas' tables to calculate the position of the Sun in the sky as it is presented in the introduction to "The MAN OF LAW'S TALE," in "The NUN'S PRIEST'S TALE" and in the prologue to "The PARSON'S TALE."

Nimrod   In the Old Testament, Nimrod was the son of Cush and great grandson of NOAH. He was a fierce and aggressive warrior who became a mighty king. According to the Bible, the principal cities of his kingdom were Babel, Babylon, Erech, Accad and Calneh. His is traditionally regarded as the builder of the Tower of Babel and a man whose pride and ambition led him to attempt to overstep human boundaries. He was also considered the founder of cities. In "The FORMER AGE," Nimrod is given as an example of the corrupting influence of civilization on the earthly paradise that existed before men started staking out territory and waging war, mining metals out of the earth and otherwise sowing the seeds of destruction (line 58).

Ninevah   The city of Ninevah was the capital of ancient Assyria, located on the Tigris River opposite modern Mosul in northern Iraq. The biblical prophet JONAH, fleeing a divine command to preach repentance to Ninevah, was swallowed by a giant fish (or whale) and then spewed up on the city's shores. The city is mentioned in "The MAN OF LAW'S TALE" (line 486) when the narrator notes that He (God) who protected Jonah while he was in the fish's belly likewise watched over CONSTANCE, the tale's protagonist, as she drifted on the sea in a rudderless ship. The huge size of the ancient city is alluded to in "The CANON'S YEOMAN'S TALE" when the narrator says that his master, the CANON (1) who cheats people through his practice of ALCHEMY, could deceive a whole town, even one as large as Ninevah, ROME, ALEXANDRIA or TROY (line 974). The riches of the city are referred to by the BLACK KNIGHT in *The BOOK OF THE DUCHESS*, when he says that he would prefer the love of his fair LADY WHITE to all the wealth that was ever in BABYLON, CARTHAGE, MACEDONIA, Rome or Ninevah (line 1063).

Ninus   The ninth-century king of Assyria whose tomb is the assigned meeting place for the doomed lovers PYRAMUS and THISBE. Their story is related in Chaucer's *LEGEND OF GOOD WOMEN*, lines 706–923.

Niobe   In classical mythology, Niobe was the daughter of TANTALUS and the wife of AMPHION of Thebes. Proud of her seven sons and seven daughters, she boasted herself the superior of the goddess Latona, who had only two children, APOLLO and DIANA, and refused to participate in the worship of the goddess. In revenge, Latona sent her children to kill Niobe's. Amphion responded by taking his own life. Niobe wept inconsolably until JUPITER transformed her into a statue. In *TROILUS AND CRISEYDE*, PANDARUS compares the weeping TROILUS to Niobe as he tries to determine the cause of his friend's grief so that he may help him to find a remedy (book 1, lines 699–700).

Nisus In classical mythology, Nisus was a king of Megara. His authority and his life were magically protected by a lock of purple hair that grew upon his head. When King MINOS of Crete was besieging Megara, Nisus' daughter SCYLLA fell in love with him as she watched the battle from behind the city walls. Thinking to win his love by her action, she cut off the purple lock of hair. Instead of rewarding her for this service, Minos rejected Scylla, who, according to legend, either swam along behind the ship or was bound to the bottom of his ship and dragged through the water. For her sin against her father, she was changed into the bird known as ciris (lark), while Nisus was transformed into a bird of prey and her natural enemy. The story of Scylla's love and rejection by Minos is briefly told in Chaucer's *LEGEND OF GOOD WOMEN* at the beginning of the story of ARIADNE (line 1908).

Nisus' daughter *See* SCYLLA.

Noah According to the Old Testament, Noah remained faithful to God at a time when the world was so filled with sin and evil that God decided to destroy it with a great flood. To reward Noah's faithfulness, God forewarned him and commanded him to build a great ship, or ark, where he and his family and one pair of every kind of animal would be safe when the waters came. The ship took 120 years to build. When it was finally ready, Noah, his wife and their sons and daughters-in-law went into the ark and closed the door. The rain and floods lasted 40 days. After they had subsided, Noah's family went forth to repopulate the earth, having been given the same command that God originally gave to ADAM and EVE—to be fruitful and multiply. The rainbow was sent as promise that God would never again destroy the earth by water. The story of Noah's ark was a subject of the biblical MYSTERY PLAYS that were performed in many English towns each year on the feast of Corpus Christi. In the play about Noah, his struggle to get his wife to come into the boat was typically filled with hilarity. In "The MILLER'S TALE," NICHOLAS tricks JOHN THE CARPENTER into believing that God is going to send another flood (lines 3518 ff). Instead of building an ark, however, John and his household will escape by rigging up a series of tubs hung by ropes from the ceiling rafters. There will be three tubs: one for John, one for his wife, ALISON (1),

and one for Nicholas. The aim of the trick is to separate the jealous carpenter from his wife so that she and Nicholas can spend the night together. It is successful in that respect, but when the humiliated and angry ABSALOM (1) (Alison's other suitor, who is tricked into kissing her rear end) strikes Nicholas on the buttocks with a hot iron, Nicholas' cries for water make John think that the flood has come, so he cuts the ropes holding up his tub and comes crashing to the floor. All of his neighbors conclude that he is mad for believing that another flood was coming. "The PARSON'S TALE" also mentions Noah and his family (line 766), noting that "thraldom" or slavery was never known on Earth until Noah laid a curse on his son Ham, who, after finding his father drunk and naked, called his brothers to come and see. The curse stated that the sons of Ham would be the servants of the sons of Shem and Japheth.

Noe (Noes) *See* NOAH.

Nonius (Nonyus) A historical figure, Nonius was a Roman government official during the triumvirate of OCTAVIAN, Lepidus and ANTONY in the first century B.C. In the *BOECE*, LADY PHILOSOPHY uses him as an example of wicked men whose evil becomes the more obvious when they occupy a position of power (Book Three, Prosa 4).

Norfolk A county in eastern England, on the North Sea. The portrait of the REEVE that appears in the GENERAL PROLOGUE TO *THE CANTERBURY TALES* notes that the man lives near a town called "Baldeswelle" (BAWDESWELL) in Norfolk (line 619).

Northfolk *See* NORFOLK.

Northumberland (Northhumbreland) Today, Northumberland is the name of the northernmost county of England, bordering Scotland. When Chaucer uses the name in "The MAN OF LAW'S TALE," it does not, according to F. P. MAGOUN's *Chaucer Gazetteer*, refer to this region, but to a far earlier Anglian kingdom, Deira. According to Magoun, this ancient kingdom, sometime after King ALLA's death, joined with another named Bernicia to form the large kingdom of Northumbria (roughly approximating the modern counties of East and West Yorkshire and Lancashire). In "The MAN OF LAW'S TALE," Northumberland is where CONSTANCE, the heroine of the tale, comes ashore after drifting in a rudderless ship all the way from SYRIA (lines 508 ff). Alla, the pagan king of the region, is influenced by her example to convert to Christianity and to make her his queen.

Norton-Smith, John (1931–) An American who was educated at Oxford and made his career in Great

Britain as a university teacher and editor, Norton-Smith published *Geoffrey Chaucer* (1976) for Routledge and Kegan Paul, where he served as general editor of their "Medieval Authors Series." The purpose of this book was to discuss those aspects of Chaucer's art which are concerned with the problems of structure and form. Norton-Smith applies the structuralist method developed in R. S. Crane's *Language Criticism and The Structure of Poetry* (1953), which had been extended to medieval Latin literature by Erich Auerbach in *Literary Language and Its Public,* London (1965). Another essay dealing with form is "Chaucer's Epistolary Style" (in *Essays on Style and Language: Linguistic and Critical Approaches to Literary Style,* 1966), in which Norton-Smith argues that the *Satires* and *Odes* of the Roman poet Horace influenced the syntax, imagery, tone and structure of "LENVOY DE CHAUCER À SCOGAN" and "LENVOY DE CHAUCER À BUKTON." This article also discusses the verse epistles of *TROILUS AND CRISEYDE.* Norton-Smith is probably the only Chaucer scholar to argue against the critical view that *ANELIDA AND ARCITE* is an unfinished poem, which he does in "Chaucer's 'Anelida and Arcite'" (*Medieval Studies for J. A. W. Bennett,* 1981).

Note, Saint   *See* NEOT, SAINT.

Nothus   In classical mythology, Nothus was the south wind. The troublesome nature of this wind, which was reputed to bring fog and sickness, to harm plants and animals and to be dangerous to seafarers, is referred to several times in the *BOECE,* Chaucer's translation of BOETHIUS' *Consolation of Philosophy* (Book Two, Metrum 6, line 25; Book Three, Metrum 1, line 8). Boethius' references to the disturbances created by this wind suggest a parallel to his own misfortunes. Boethius also calls the wind by its Roman name, Auster (Book One, Metrum 7, line 3; Book Two, Metrum 3, line 11).

Nowelis Flood   *See* NOAH.

Nun's Priest, the   One of the pilgrims who engages in the tale-telling contest that provides the framework for *The CANTERBURY TALES.* The tale that he tells (*see* "NUN'S PRIEST'S TALE") is a BEAST FABLE about a rooster named CHAUNTICLEER who dreams that he is in danger and then, after a lengthy learned discussion with his wife, PERTELOTE, wherein they debate the significance of dreams, finds himself in the very situation that he had dreamed about. Although this tale, which constitutes a lively response to the MONK's dreary catalogue of tragedies, is one of the most admired of the Canterbury tales, very little is revealed about its teller. He is not described at all in the GENERAL PROLOGUE (all of the others, except the CANON'S YEOMAN, are) but only mentioned in passing as one of three priests accompanying

the PRIORESS. Some scholars have viewed the mild antifeminism of his tale (which is, after all, directed toward a hen rather than a woman) as a reflection on his position as subordinate to a woman. The care with which he disclaims ownership of the antifeminist rhetoric would seem to suggest that he is somewhat anxious about expressing such views.

"Nun's Priest's Tale, The"   The NUNS'S PRIEST's story of a witty rooster and the fox who nearly tricks him into becoming dinner has always been a favorite with readers.

SUMMARY

A poor widow lives simply and frugally in her small cottage with her two daughters. They own three pigs, three cows, a sheep, some chickens and a cock named CHAUNTICLEER, who has a wonderful voice for crowing. He instinctively knows the time of day and is able to crow every hour on the hour more accurately than a clock or abbey "orlogge" (timepiece). He is also very

Artist's rendering of the Nun's Priest, from the Ellesmere Manuscript of The Canterbury Tales. *The Nun's Priest is not described in the General Prologue. The illustrator portrays him as a rather small man with a pale, almost effeminate face.*

attractive, with a comb redder than fine coral, a black beak, azure legs and toes and gold feathers. The seven hens who share his domain are both his sisters and his "concubines." The most beautiful one, PERTELOTE, is described in courtly terms such as "fair," "courteous," "discreet" and "debonaire." Chaunticleer sings to her courtly songs such as "My lief is faren in londe," and loves her above all the other chickens.

One morning just at dawn, Chaunticleer begins groaning in his sleep. Pertelote, who sleeps next to him on the perch, asks him what is the matter. Awakened, he explains that he has had a dream that scared him half to death. In the dream he was roaming up and down the chicken yard when he saw an animal like a dog, yellowish-red in color, with black-tipped tail and ears. When he has finished telling her about his dream, Pertelote rebukes him for being a coward and tells him he should take no account of dreams. Pertelote believes that dreams are caused by overeating or indigestion, or by an imbalance in the bodily HUMORS. She explains her theory to Chaunticleer, adding a saying from Cato (DIONYSIUS CATO) which argues against taking dreams seriously, and then suggests that he try eating some of the laxative and digestive herbs from the garden.

When she has finished, Chaunticleer thanks her for sharing her knowledge but responds to her arguments by recounting several instances in which dreams were prophetic of things to come. First he tells the story of two friends who went on pilgrimage together. One of the towns they entered was so crowded with people that they were forced to take separate lodgings, one of them in an ox's stall, the other in a room at an inn. That night the one lodged at the inn dreamed that the other one cried out to him that he would be murdered in the ox's stall unless his friend came to help him. Awakened by fright, the man realized he had been dreaming and went back to sleep. He dreamed the same dream twice more. The third time, his friend appeared to him as a bloody corpse, asking that he go to the city's west gate in the morning where he would find his friend's body hidden in a cart full of dung. When morning came, the friend who slept at the inn went to find the other man but was told that he had awakened early and left town. His suspicions aroused, the man went to the west gate and found there a dung cart, just as the dream had predicted. He began to cry out that his friend had been murdered, and called upon the magistrates of the town. The cart was emptied, and, sure enough, there was his friend's body buried in the dung. Concluding this tale supporting the validity of dreams, Chaunticleer cannot resist the temptation to recall yet another applicable proverb, noting that whatever men do, murder will always be discovered.

The next story also has to do with traveling. Two men getting ready to sail over the sea have their voyages delayed by bad weather. Finally the wind begins to change, and they go to bed happy, confident that they can sail on the following day. That night one of them has a dream in which a man informs him that if he should depart on the following day, he will surely be drowned. He awakens and tells his companion about the dream, but the other man laughs at him, declaring that no dream is going to keep him from his business. So the first man, believing in dreams, decides to delay his trip for a day; the other sails the next morning. His ship goes down and he is drowned.

The third story Chaunticleer tells comes from the life of Saint KENELM, who dreamed that he would be murdered but took no heed of the warning and suffered the consequences. This example is followed by several more authoritative examples of the reliability of dreams, including MACROBIUS' DREAM OF SCIPIO and dreams attributed to the biblical DANIEL, King CROESUS and ANDROMACHE.

Concluding from these examples that he probably will suffer adversity, Chaunticleer asks his wife to leave the matter alone for now. He begins praising her beauty and other excellent qualities which lead him to defy all kinds of dreams. With those words, the rooster flies down from his perch, finds some food in the yard, embraces his Pertelote 20 times and copulates with her just as many. Now full of self-confidence, he struts proudly up and down the chicken yard looking as fierce as a grim lion and as royal as a prince in his hall. But suddenly his fortune changes.

In the midst of a long disquisition by the narrator, on traitors and on the dangers of taking counsel from a woman, we learn that a fox has broken through the hedges and is hiding among the cabbages, awaiting his chance to spring on Chaunticleer. Glancing at a butterfly among the cabbages, the rooster perceives the fox crouching there. He cries out and is about to flee when the fox speaks to him in very courtly terms, claiming to be his friend who has come into the yard only for the pleasure of hearing him sing. The fox continues in this vein, piling one flattering remark upon another until Chaunticleer is completely blinded by his own conceit. The fox suggests that Chaunticleer perform for him, recalling that when the rooster's father, also a friend to the fox, would crow, he would close his eyes and stand on tiptoe, with his neck stretched out long to make his voice as strong as possible. Eager to prove that he is his father's equal, Chaunticleer assumes the same stance and begins to crow. Sir RUSSELL, the fox, quickly seizes the cock by his throat and runs off with him toward the woods. This event is followed by another lament in the high style comparing Chaunticleer's fall to that of King RICHARD I. The hens add their voices to the chorus, crying louder than the ladies of TROY when King PRIAM was slain, crying like HASDRUBAL'S WIFE when the Romans killed her husband and burned CARTHAGE.

The old widow and her daughters, hearing the noise from the chicken yard, run outside and start to chase the fox. Joined by the dogs and their neighbors, they make such a fray that it sounds like a riot. Chaunticleer, riding along clutched in the fox's mouth, encourages his captor to turn around and curse those who follow him, telling them that he intends to eat the cock in spite of what they may do. They fox opens his mouth to answer; the cock flies out and alights high in a tree. When the fox apologizes for his rude behavior and begs Chaunticleer to come back down, the cock is smart enough to refuse and curses them both, himself for being overcome by flattery. The fox finishes the curse, asking God to send misfortune to anyone who chatters when he ought to keep silent.

The NUN'S PRIEST concludes his tale by saying that if anyone in his audience thinks it foolish, he ought to remember the moral (the "fruit") and forget the rest (the "chaff"), for all that is written is capable of teaching us something.

COMMENTARY

"The Nun's Priest's Tale" is a hybrid of two related genres, the BEAST FABLE and the beast epic. The central episode of the tale, beginning with Chaunticleer's crow to the Sun in TAURUS and ending with the moral to be drawn from the tale, bears considerable similarities to MARIE DE FRANCE's 12th-century beast fable, *Del cok e del gupil* ("Concerning the Cock and the Fox"), though Chaucer's source may have been another, less familiar version of the same story. Such stories were intended to be entertaining, while at the same time providing instruction on the subject of human morals and behavior. They were popular among itinerant preachers, particularly those belonging to the mendicant (begging) orders, who needed to make some money off their sermons. A beast epic, the *ROMAN DE RENART* ("Book of Reynard"), was probably Chaucer's major source for the description of the farm, Chaunticleer's dream, and his relationship with his favorite hen. This genre takes the fable's propensity for having animals behave like humans one step further by glorifying that behavior and creating the potential for comedy that succeeds so well in descriptions of Chaunticleer's heroism and the courtliness of his chickens. It is ironically the success of the mock-epic comedy that thwarts the customary function of the fable to teach us a serious lesson about human nature. If "The Nun's Priest's Tale" teaches anything, it can only be that we ought not take ourselves so seriously. It is, after all, pride and overconfidence that prove the undoing of both cock and fox, if we can even conclude that there has been an undoing since the tale closes with no one the loser, but rather two who have grown a bit wiser.

Although easily enjoyed for its own sake, "The Nun's Priest's Tale" is best considered as a response to "The MONK'S TALE," and specifically, to the MONK's view of tragedy. Within the series of stories related by that noble cleric, an assortment of individuals, regardless of their guilt or innocence, their intelligence or lack of the same, find themselves brought low by the machinations of a blind and indiscriminate, even capricious force called FORTUNE, from which there is no escape. The tale of the Nun's Priest takes this notion and turns it on its head. Despite the tale's ominous beginning, with a dream that seems to prophesy tragedy, and the apparent fulfillment of that dream when the fox seizes Chaunticleer by the neck, a bit of quick thinking on the rooster's part leads to a happy, if rather rambunctious and breathless, conclusion, exploding the idea of one inescapable outcome. There is even a slight suggestion that the dream as a prophetic device was entirely unnecessary. When Chaunticleer first sees the fox, even though he has never seen one before except in his dreams, he *instinctively* fears the animal and crows a warning to the other chickens. We may wonder if perhaps Chaucer, or the Nun's Priest, isn't trying to tell us something about our own human ability to recognize danger and evil if we keep our vision clear of emotions like pride. At any rate, the line of cause and effect, running between the rooster's pride and stupidity and its result (his ending up in the fox's mouth) is distinctly drawn and clearly refutes the Monk's idea of a blind and indiscriminate destinal force.

In the prologue to "The Nun's Priest's Tale," the Host, Harry BAILLY, calls for something merry, and the story of Chaunticleer admirably rises to the occasion in addition to serving as a critique of "The Monk's Tale." The latter is not, however, the only one of the Canterbury tales implicated in the rich and varied tapestry of this fable. As an epic its language echoes the heroic similes and chivalric epithets common to chivalric romance, the genre represented in the Canterbury group by "The KNIGHT'S TALE." Yet the use of such imagery to describe lustful chickens in a barnyard setting suggests an outlook and attitude more akin to that expressed by the MILLER. One of the exempla (*see* EXEMPLUM), Chaunticleer tells the story of the murdered man whose body was hidden in a dung cart, concludes with the moral "mordre wol out," recalling a secondary theme of "The PRIORESS' TALE" of the murdered child. And the warning against taking the advice of flatterers recalls PRUDENCE's advice to her husband in "The TALE OF MELIBEE." JANUARY, in "The MERCHANT'S TALE," follows the advice of the flatterer PLACEBO, rather than listening to the more honest opinion of JUSTINUS, and marries a wife who will never love him. The debate over the advisability of trusting women's counsel recalls similar debates in "The WIFE OF BATH'S TALE" and "The Tale of Melibee." On a smaller scale are such echoes as the lament of the Trojan women (first used in a simile in "The MAN OF LAW'S TALE"), and NERO's slaying of the Roman senators (previously mentioned in the Monk's life of Nero). For these reasons, "The Nun's Priest's Tale" has been called an epitome, or summing up, of *The Canterbury Tales* thus far.

Nynus   *See* NINUS.

Nynyve(e)   *See* NINEVAH.

Nyobe   *See* NIOBE.

Nysus   *See* NISUS.

Nysus doghter   *See* SCYLLA.

O

Occian In ancient times, the word *Occian* denoted the sea or waters surrounding the known world of Europe, Africa and Asia—in effect the Atlantic Ocean and the North Sea. It is mentioned in "The MAN OF LAW'S TALE" (line 505) to indicate that portion of the Atlantic Ocean between the Strait of Gibraltar and England, and in the *BOECE* (Book Four, Metrum 6, line 14).

occupatio A literary term derived from classical rhetoric (hence the Latin name). It denotes an author's refusal to describe or narrate something (event or otherwise) in such a way that the refusal itself actually has the effect of describing or narrating what the author intended to omit, although usually in abbreviated fashion. Chaucer uses the device frequently in longer works like "The KNIGHT'S TALE" and *The LEGEND OF GOOD WOMEN*. A good example appears at the beginning of "The Knight's Tale," when Chaucer refers to the battle between THESEUS and the AMAZONS: "And certes, if it nere to long to heere, / I wolde have toold yow fully the manere / How wonnen was the regne of Femenye / By Theseus and by his chivalrye; / And of the grete bataille for the nones / Bitwixen Atthenes and Amazones; / And how asseged was Ypolita, / The faire, hardy queene of Scithia; / And of the feste that was at hir weddynge, / And of the tempest at hir hoomcomynge; / But al that thyng I moot as now forbere" (lines 875–85). [And certainly, if it were not too long to hear, / I would have told you the whole story / Of how the kingdom of the Amazons was overcome / By Theseus and his knights; / And of the great battle on that occasion / Between Athens and the Amazons; / And how Hippolita was besieged, / The fair, courageous queen of Scythia; / And of the celebration there was at their wedding, / And of the storm that accompanied their homecoming; / But all those things I must now forgo telling]. The use of *occupatio* here allows Chaucer to condense his material so that he can advance quickly to the part of the story that concerns him most, the conflict between Theseus and CREON that sets the stage for his two knightly protagonists, ARCITE (1) and PALAMON.

Octavian, Gaius Julius Caesar Gaius Julius Caesar Octavian, known in his youth as Octavian, was the grandnephew of JULIUS CAESAR, and the first Roman emperor (called Augustus), serving in that office from 27 B.C. to A.D. 14. Before he became emperor, Octavian was part of a tripartite autocratic government which included Marc ANTONY and Marius Aemilius Lepidus. It was known as the second triumvirate, although the bulk of power was shared between Octavian and Antony. The two men cemented their alliance by Antony's marriage to Octavian's sister, Octavia, but conflict broke out when Antony became involved with CLEOPATRA and began putting the claims and rights of the Egyptian queen above those of Rome. When Antony finally divorced Octavia, her brother formally discarded all ties with Antony and declared war on Egypt. The civil war between Octavian and Marc Antony is described in the biography of Cleopatra that Chaucer included in his *LEGEND OF GOOD WOMEN* (lines 624–53).

octosyllabic couplet An octosyllabic couplet is an eight-syllable rhyming couplet (pair of lines). Chaucer used these couplets, which were derived from French verse, in such poems as *The BOOK OF THE DUCHESS*.

Octovyan *See* OCTAVIAN.

Odenathus (Odenake) Odenathus Septimus was the king of PALMYRA in the second half of the third century B.C. He became the husband of ZENOBIA, the warrior queen whose story is narrated in "The MONK'S TALE" (lines 2247–2374). Historically, Odenathus is remembered for having taken the side of the Romans against the Persians following the siege and fall of Antioch. After helping restore Roman rule in the Eastern Empire, Odenathus was assassinated by his son Herodes and his nephew. Following his death, Zenobia ruled Palmyra, serving as regent for her son Athenodorus.

Oedipus In classical mythology, Oedipus was the son of King LAIUS and Queen Jocasta of THEBES. Because of a prophecy that Laius would die at the hands of his son, the king ordered a servant to expose the child, with his feet pierced and bound, on the side of Mount Cithaeron. Instead, the servant gave him to a shepherd of King Polybus of Corinth, who carried him to the palace. There Polybus and his queen, having no children of their own, raised him as their son. When he was grown, Oedipus went to consult the oracle about the truth of a rumor that he was not really the son of Polybus and Periboea, but instead of receiving a direct answer to that question, was told that he would kill his father and marry his mother. In order to avoid this fate, Oedipus set out for Thebes instead of returning home. On the way he met Laius, and a quarrel sprang up because Oedipus would not yield the road. In the fight that followed, Oedipus killed his father without knowing his identity. He continued on his way to Thebes, where CREON, now ruling in Laius' place, had offered the kingdom and the hand of the widowed Jocasta to whomever should free the land of the Sphinx. Accomplishing this task, Oedipus became king and married Jocasta (without knowing that she was his mother), who bore him four children: ETEOCLES, POLYNICES, ANTIGONE and Ismene. Years later Thebes was visited by a plague, and the oracle commanded the expulsion of the murderer of Laius as the only means of relief. Discovering that he was guilty, Oedipus blinded himself and wandered out of Thebes as an exile, accompanied only by his faithful daughter, Antigone. He found refuge finally at Colonus in Attica. There he was befriended and purified by THESEUS and, having propitiated the Furies (ERINYES), died in peace. A variation of the story tells that Oedipus was driven out of Thebes by his sons, and that he laid upon them a curse that they would kill each other, a curse that was fulfilled during the siege of Thebes.

Oedipus' story is alluded to twice in Chaucer's work, both times in TROILUS AND CRISEYDE. On one occasion when PANDARUS visits his niece, CRISEYDE, he finds her with a group of her women, and she tells him that they have been reading a "romance of Thebes" (book 2, line 84) that tells the story of King Laius and Oedipus his son. Because the text from which they are reading is described as having 12 books, this is probably a reference to the authority Chaucer often turned to for the story of Thebes, the *Thebaid* of STATIUS. Later, in book 4 of the poem, TROILUS compares himself to Oedipus when he says that he will, like the Theban king, end his life in darkness (possibly suggesting that he will blind himself) and despair if he loses Criseyde (line 300).

Oenone In classical mythology, Oenone is the name of a nymph who lived with PARIS (1) on Mount Ida and bore him a son. When he deserted her to pursue the Greek beauty Helen (HELEN OF TROY), Oenone returned to her father, but not before extracting her lover's promise that, should he be wounded in the coming war (Oenone had the gift of prophecy), he would return to her. Remembering Oenone's skill in the healing arts, Paris did indeed seek her out after he was wounded by the arrow of PHILOCTETES. At first she refused to help, and sent him back to TROY. When her love overcame her jealousy, she followed, and finding him dead, committed suicide. Paris' betrayal of

Oenone is mentioned in *The HOUSE OF FAME* (line 399) where it is compared to AENEAS' betrayal of DIDO. In *TROILUS AND CRISEYDE,* PANDARUS tells TROILUS about a letter Oenone wrote to Paris, comparing her unrequited love to his own passion for some unnamed lady (lines 652–67).

Oenopia *See* AEGINA.

Oetes *See* AEËTES.

Of the Wretched Engendering of Mankind In version G of the prologue to Chaucer's *LEGEND OF GOOD WOMEN,* Chaucer alters the list of works that Queen Alceste offers in his defense when he is accused by the god of love (CUPID) of writing books that will turn people against love. Added to the list is a work Chaucer called "Of the Wreched Engendrynge of Mankynde, / As man may in Pope Innocent yfynde" (lines 414–15) [Of the Wretched Engendering of Mankind / As one may find it in the work of Pope Innocent]. The reference is to a text by Pope Innocent III that was called *De Miseria Humane Conditionis* ("On the Misery of the Human Condition"). Written in the early years of the 12th century, *De Contemptu Mundi,* as it was commonly known, describes the miseries of human life, in every possible variation, from the cradle to the grave. Chaucer's translation of this text does not survive, so we do not know what kinds of changes he may have made in adapting it to his own tastes, but the decision to spend a significant amount of time with such a gloomy work suggests a moral seriousness that is unparalleled elsewhere in his work, with the possible exception of "The PARSON'S TALE," a sermon on penitence which includes descriptions of the Seven Deadly Sins.

Oise A river that flows through northern France and empties into the Seine. In *The HOUSE OF FAME,* the noise issuing from the HOUSE OF RUMOR is described as being so loud that if the house had stood next to the Oise River, people would have been able to hear it easily as far away as ROME (line 1928).

Old Age One of the allegorical figures whose image is depicted on the walls of the Garden of Love in the *ROMAUNT OF THE ROSE* (Chaucer's translation of the French *ROMAN DE LA ROSE*). The walls of the garden are painted and carved with pictures of various allegorical figures, all of whom are female. Elde, or Old Age, is portrayed as shrunken, diseased and childishly dependent (lines 349–412).

Old Testament The Old Testament of the Bible is mentioned by name twice in Chaucer's work. In "The PARDONER'S TALE," the narrator preaches that all the great deeds and victories that were achieved in the Old

Testament were performed by those who were abstinent and engaged in prayer (lines 574–77). In "The NUN'S PRIEST'S TALE," the learned rooster CHAUNTICLEER advises his wife, PERTELOTE, to look in the Old Testament where she will find that the prophet DANIEL had faith in the meaning of dreams (lines 3127–29).

Oliphaunt   The three-headed giant encountered by THOPAS in Chaucer's "TALE OF SIR THOPAS." Thopas meets this creature after entering the region of the fairies in search of the elphen queen, with whom he hopes to have a love affair. The giant challenges him to fight, but because Thopas has left his armor at home, he flees, promising to return the next day and to slay the giant with his lance. We never know whether he does or not because the tale is interrupted by the Host (*see* Harry BAILLY).

Oliver   The Oliver whom Chaucer mentions in *The BOOK OF THE DUCHESS* and in "The MONK'S TALE" was one of the heroes of the Charlemagne legend who died with ROLAND in an ambush at Roncesvalles. The ambush had been set up by GANELON, Roland's stepfather, who thus earned notoriety as a traitor, while Oliver gained fame for his unwavering loyalty to his friend. The story is told in the 12th-century *Chanson de Roland* (*Song of Roland*). In "The Monk's Tale," Pedro of Castile's betrayal by his brother is compared to Ganelon's betrayal of Roland, while Oliver's faithfulness is offered as the virtuous alternative (lines 2387–90). In *The Book of the Duchess*, the BLACK KNIGHT tells Chaucer that if he repented of his love, he would be worse than Ganelon, who betrayed Roland and Oliver (lines 1116–23).

Oloferne (Olofernus)   *See* HOLOFERNES.

Olyver   *See* OLIVER.

Omer   *See* HOMER.

Opilio (Opilion)   In the BOECE, Chaucer's translation of BOETHIUS' *Consolation of Philosophy,* Opilio was one of the men who accused Boethius of conspiring against King THEODORIC (Book One, Prosa 4, line 114). As a result, Boethius, who had served as one of Theodoric's most trusted advisers, was exiled and later executed. *The Consolation of Philosophy* was written during his exile.

Orcades   *See* ORKNYES.

Order of the Garter   *See* GARTER, ORDER OF THE.

Oreb   *See* HOREB.

Orewelle   *See* ORWELL.

Origines upon the Maudelayn *Origines upon the Maudelayn* was the title Chaucer gave to a lost translation that he made of a famous Latin homily, *De Maria Magdalena,* attributed to the early Christian theologian and scholar Origen. The work is mentioned in the prologue to his *LEGEND OF GOOD WOMEN* (version F, line 428). The homily focuses on the grief of MARY MAGDELENE, who was inconsolable until Christ appeared to her in the garden. Queen ALCESTIS mentions the work in defense of Chaucer when he is accused by the god of love (CUPID) of slandering women.

Orion   *See* ARION.

Orion's Harp   In the sky the harp of Orion forms the constellation Lyra. This constellation is mentioned in *The HOUSE OF FAME* by the EAGLE who is ferrying Chaucer through the air to FAME's palace (line 1205). He wants to take the poet up into the region of the stars so that he can learn about them firsthand, but the poet refuses, saying that he is too old. The exchange reflects the poem's ongoing debate between the value of learning derived from direct experience versus learning derived from books. Chaucer says that knowledge of the stars is something he would rather learn from books.

Orkneys (Orkades)   The Orkneys are a set of islands north of Scotland. In Chaucer's *TROILUS AND CRISEYDE,* CRISEYDE reveals an anachronistic knowledge of northern European geography when she declares to the Greek DIOMEDE that the people of TROY are as worthy as any dwelling in the lands between "Orkades and Inde" (book 5, line 971) [the Orkneys and India]. The reference would be anachronistic because the civilization of ancient Troy had not, as far as we know, sailed beyond the boundaries of the Mediterranean Sea.

Orleans (Orliens)   A city in north-central France. A university was located there, and in the 14th century the city achieved fame as a center for astrological studies. In "The MERCHANT'S TALE," the brother of the squire AURELIUS attended the University of Orleans, pursuing a degree in law. Confronted with Aurelius' lovesickness, this brother recalls that as a student he had once seen a magic book that contained information about producing illusions. This prompts him to return to Orleans, where he hopes to find a practitioner of the magical arts who can assist Aurelius by making it appear that the treacherous rocks lining the coast of BRITTANY have vanished. DORIGEN, the object of Aurelius' infatuation, has said that if he can perform such a feat, she will become his lover.

Orpheus   In classical mythology, Orpheus was the son of Oeagrus and the Muse CALLIOPE. His skill in composing songs and playing the lyre were so great that wild beasts, and even trees and stones, were charmed by it. He accompanied the adventurer JASON on his argonautic expedition, where he encouraged the crew with his music. His singing also enabled him to win the love of the nymph EURYDICE, who became his bride. Immediately after the marriage, Eurydice was bitten by a snake while running across a meadow, trying to escape the advances of the shepherd Aristaeus. When she died, Orpheus was so devastated that he descended into the underworld to find her, using his music to charm CERBERUS, the three-headed dog who guarded the entrance to the realm of the dead. After Orpheus' singing threatened to put an end to all the suffering in Hades, PLUTO, the god of the underworld, agreed to restore Eurydice on one condition: that she walk behind Orpheus as he led her to the surface, and that he refrain from looking back until they had reached their destination. They had almost arrived at the exit when Orpheus, out of his deep love for his wife, turned to see if she were still following, and she immediately vanished. The story of Orpheus and Eurydice appears in the *BOECE* (Book 3, Metrum 12), where it is interpreted as a warning to all who would fix their affections on earthly things (just as Orpheus fixes his affection on the physical image of his wife) and in so doing lose sight of the higher good. The poet and his lady are also mentioned in *TROILUS AND CRISEYDE* when CRISEYDE tries to console TROILUS with the idea that they will one day be reunited, like Orpheus and Eurydice, in the Elysian fields (book 4, lines 785–91). All other references to Orpheus in Chaucer's work focus on his musical abilities. In *The BOOK OF THE DUCHESS,* for example, the BLACK KNIGHT claims that his grief over losing his lady is so great that not even Orpheus' music could soothe him (lines 567–69). Orpheus appears in *The HOUSE OF FAME* among the other musicians who congregate at Fame's palace, and in "The MERCHANT'S TALE," the narrator ambiguously notes that neither Orpheus nor AMPHION, another famous musician, ever made such a melody as that produced by the instruments at JANUARY's wedding (lines 1715–17).

Orwell   A harbor in eastern England, at the confluence of the Orwell and Stour Rivers, near present-day Harwich and directly opposite the Dutch port of MIDDLEBURG on the island of Walcheren. It is formally known as Orwell Haven. In the GENERAL PROLOGUE to *The CANTERBURY TALES,* Chaucer says that the MERCHANT would like to have the sea between these two ports protected (from threat of piracy) no matter what the cost (lines 276–77). The reference suggests that he may have been engaged in the wool trade.

Osewold   *See* REEVE, THE.

Osney (Oseney; Osenay)   In Chaucer's day, Osney was a village near the city of Oxford in England. The village was long ago swallowed up by the city's expansion. It is mentioned in "The MILLER'S TALE" as the place where JOHN THE CARPENTER goes on business, providing an opportunity for his wife, ALISON (1), and their lodger, NICHOLAS, to plan their infidelity (line 3274). One may wonder why the two fail to take advantage of his absence to accomplish their ends but instead work out an elaborate scheme to be executed upon his return. One possible explanation is that the household servants would have been present and could later tell John that his wife was unfaithful. The scheme that Nicholas comes up with does, after all, get the servants out of the way along with their master.

Ostrogoths   The Ostrogoths were a tribe originally coming out of central Asia that swept across and down through Europe to conquer the Italian peninsula in the fifth century. The philosopher BOETHIUS, whose *Consolation of Philosophy* Chaucer translated (*see* BOECE), was a Roman who served in the government of the Ostrogothic king THEODORIC. Accused of plotting against the king, Boethius was exiled and later executed.

Oswald   *See* REEVE, THE.

Oton de Grandson   A French poet of the 14th century whose triple BALLADE was the source of Chaucer's "COMPLAINT OF VENUS." Chaucer acknowledges that he is borrowing from Oton's work in the final line (82) of the poem.

Ovid (Ovide)   Ovid (full name Publius Ovidius Naso) was a first-century Roman writer of love elegies (*Amores*) who experimented with a variety of other forms, including the imaginary letter (*Heroides*), mock didactic verse (*Ars amatoria,* i.e., "The Art of Love" and *Remedia amoris,* "The Remedies of Love"), and the sprawling narrative consisting of a series of stories related thematically (the *Metamorphoses*). *His* Fasti ("Feasts") was a calendar of Roman festivals. Ovid also wrote several elegies, including *Tristia* ("Sorrow") and *Epistulae ex Ponto* ("Epistle from Ponto") after the emperor AUGUSTUS exiled him to the Black Sea region in A.D. 8 Ovid says he was being punished for a poem he had written, but the true reason has never been established.

Ovid's writing enjoyed considerable popularity until the coming of Christianity to Rome. The church's disapproval of his immorality kept his work out of circulation for about six centuries following the conversion of the emperor Constantine. Interest in his literary productions revived during the 11th century, when poets in the cathedral schools began using him as a model, making adaptations of his stories more palatable to a

Christian audience by interpreting them allegorically. A French work, the *Ovide Moralisé,* featured 15 books of the *Metamorphoses,* each one provided with a moral interpretation. This work served as the primary source for Chaucer's knowledge of the *Metamorphoses.* The Roman poet's influence on Chaucer is ubiquitous, providing him with a number of the stories that appear in *The LEGEND OF GOOD WOMEN:* the "legends" of HYPSIPYLE and MEDEA, and of ARIADNE, PHYLLIS, DIDO, LUCRECE and HYPERMNESTRA. Dido's story also appears in book 1 of *The HOUSE OF FAME,* and in book 3 the narrator sees Ovid's image lining the approach to FAME's throne (lines 1486–92).

Other references are as follows. In *The BOOK OF THE DUCHESS,* the BLACK KNIGHT experiences such despair over the loss of his LADY WHITE that not all the remedies for love (suggested in Ovid's *Remedia amoris*) can cure him (lines 567–68). At the end of *TROILUS AND CRISEYDE,* Chaucer sends his poem to kiss the footsteps of a series of great poets from antiquity, including Ovid (book 5, lines 1786–92). In the prologue to his tale (lines 53–55), the SERGEANT OF THE LAW states that Chaucer has written more stories about lovers than Ovid wrote in his "Episteles" (*Heroides*). The WIFE OF BATH claims to have gotten her story of King MIDAS from Ovid (lines 952–82), and the poet's *Ars amatoria* is one of the works included in her husband JANKIN (1)'s "Book of Wicked Wives" (*see* the Wife's Prologue, line 680). In "The MERCHANT'S TALE," the narrator ironically compares the situation of Ovid's PYRAMUS and THISBE (two tragic lovers who were forbidden to be together) to that of MAY and DAMIAN, who are having difficulty finding an occasion to commit adultery (lines 2125–31). In Chaucer's "TALE OF MELIBEE," Dame PRUDENCE twice considers the advice Ovid offers in *Remedia amoris* in counseling her husband on how to deal with the men who attacked his family and robbed his home (see lines 975–77, 1325 and 14).

Ovid's art (Ovydes art)   "Ovid's art" is the title the WIFE OF BATH uses when referring to the Latin poet OVID's *Ars amatoria* (*see* her Prologue, line 680). It is one of the works included in her husband's anthology of stories about wicked women.

Owst, Gerald R. (1894–1962)   Owst received his doctorate in Literature from Cambridge University, where, in the latter part of his life, he became a Fellow and Professor Emeritus. His work in medieval studies includes serving as secretary to the British Academy's Medieval Latin Dictionary Committee. In his book, *Literature and Pulpit in Medieval England* (1933; rev. ed. 1961) Owst takes issue with John MANLY's belief that Chaucer's Canterbury pilgrims represent particular individuals of the poet's acquaintance, pointing out how thoroughly representative and even commonplace many of them are in 14th-century sermons. He refers to preachers of Chaucer's era as "masters in the art of vivid Realism and incisive portraiture." Since Chaucer claims to know much of "homelies," it seems only logical that these literary works, largely neglected by modern readers, should be considered as a source for what earlier scholars have attributed to Chaucer's invention.

Oxford (Oxenford)   City in south-central England in the county of Oxfordshire. It is the site of England's oldest and one of its most prestigious institutions of higher learning, Oxford University. The CLERK who appears in the GENERAL PROLOGUE TO *THE CANTERBURY TALES* and who participates in the tale-telling contest studies at Oxford, as did the WIFE OF BATH's fifth husband, JANKIN (1). The city is also, somewhat ironically, the setting of "The MILLER'S TALE," which is one of the coarsest tales told during the pilgrimage. In the prologue to his *TREATISE ON THE ASTROLABE,* Chaucer notes that the instrument he has provided for his son Lewis CHAUCER was constructed according to the latitude of Oxford.

Oyse   *See* OISE.

Padua (Padowe)   City (now a commune) in northern Italy. Chaucer's CLERK claims to have learned the story he relates in "The CLERK'S TALE" from PETRARCH in Padua (line 27). Petrarch was at this time the archdeacon of Padua, and lived there from 1368 until his death in 1374.

Palamon   One of the main protagonists in "The KNIGHT'S TALE." A knight of THEBES, he is cousin to ARCITE (1) and enemy to Duke THESEUS of ATHENS. He and his cousin are captured and imprisoned after Theseus attacks Thebes. While in prison, he and Arcite both fall in love with Theseus' sister, EMILY. Palamon sees her first and therefore feels he has the greater claim to her. Arcite disagrees, and the two become sworn enemies. While Arcite is eventually set free to return to his native Thebes, Palamon remains in prison for seven more years before he escapes. His intention is to gather an army in Thebes and then to return and fight for Emily, but during his flight from Athens he encounters Arcite, who has disguised himself as PHILOSTRATE and become a squire in Duke Theseus' court. The two knights fight for the right to woo Emily, but are interrupted by Theseus, who separates them and postpones the fight for a later date. The final contest takes the form of a tournament. Arcite wins the contest, but is mortally wounded. After a period of mourning, Emily and Palamon are married.

As many scholars have pointed out, Palamon and Arcite are very similar to one another in a number of ways, including their bravery and skill in battle, their devotion to Emily and their steadfast assertion of will that nevertheless bows to accept fate's inevitability. On the other hand, Chaucer does make some alterations in the characterization of both knights when adapting them from their source, BOCCACCIO's *TESEIDA*. One significant change is to emphasize the singularity of Palamon's devotion to VENUS, instead of having both knights pray to Venus and MARS (1). The creation of a more direct and obvious alignment between Palamon and Venus on the one hand, and between Arcite and Mars on the other, increases the sense of inevitability which adheres to the outcome of events in this tale. Both knights' prayers are answered. Arcite prays for victory in battle and wins the battle. Palamon prays only for possession of his beloved and wins that possession. The *Teseida* does provide some physical description to distinguish the two knights from one another, but the little bit that Chaucer carries over into his tale only lets us know that one of them is bald while the other has a black beard and thick head of hair. In the *Teseida*, Arcite is the one with bushy hair.

Palamon and Arcite   *Palamon and Arcite,* or *The Love of Palamon and Arcite of Thebes,* seems to be the title Chaucer gave to an early, lost version of "The KNIGHT'S TALE." The only evidence for the poem's existence appears in the prologue to *The LEGEND OF GOOD WOMEN* (lines 420–21), where Queen ALCESTIS mentions it as one of the works Chaucer wrote that ought to earn him some credit with the god of love (CUPID). Some early scholars believed that this version might have been significantly different from the one that came to be included in *The CANTERBURY TALES,* but the current consensus is that Chaucer simply took a tale that he had already written and put in some minor revisions to reflect the character of the teller.

Palathia (Palatye)   A region on the southwest coast of Turkey near the site of ancient Miletus. In Chaucer's time it was an independent emirate ruled by a Seljuk Turk. It is mentioned in the GENERAL PROLOGUE to *The CANTERBURY TALES* as one of the places where the KNIGHT (1) has been on military campaign. Like his other campaigns, this one involves taking military action against pagan forces—"another hethen in Turkye" (line 66) [another heathen in Turkey].

Palinurus   In classical mythology, Palinurus was the man who piloted AENEAS' ship after the fall of TROY. As they sailed from Sicily to Italy, the god of sleep, obeying NEPTUNE's demand for one victim in exchange for allowing Aeneas to reach Italy safely, caused Palinurus to fall asleep and then hurled him overboard. He swam for four days, finally managing to reach land, only to be seized and killed by its inhabitants. Aeneas met and spoke with Palinurus, learning how he had died, when he ventured into the underworld. In *The HOUSE OF FAME,* the story of his meeting is depicted on a brass tablet in the TEMPLE OF VENUS (line 443).

Palladium (Palladion)   The Palladium was an ancient image of the goddess PALLAS Athena which stood in the city of TROY. It was said to have been given to the city by the gods at the time of the city's founding. According to legend, as long as the Palladium remained in Troy, the city could not be taken by invaders. This is why the Greek forces tried to get possession of it during the TROJAN WAR. The task was finally accomplished by ULYSSES and DIOMEDE, who raided the temple by way of an underground passage. In *TROILUS AND CRISEYDE,* Prince TROILUS catches his first glimpse of the beautiful widow CRISEYDE during a religious festival held in honor of the Palladium (book 1, lines 155–75).

Pallas (Pallas Athena)   The Greek goddess of wisdom and of war, who sprang fully grown and sheathed in armor from the head of her father, Zeus. As goddess of war she usually fought as a defender and protector, in contrast to the bloodthirsty and vengeful war god MARS (1). She showed special favor to a number of warrior-heroes, including DIOMEDE, ACHILLES, ULYSSES, HERCULES and JASON. She was also known as a protectress of cities, especially of Athens, which derived its name from her, and of Troy, where the famous image of the PALLADIUM protected the city from invasion. The goddess was typically represented helmeted and carrying a shield, with a goatskin thrown over her shoulders. Most references to her in Chaucer's work occur in *TROILUS AND CRISEYDE.* In book 2, for example, CRISEYDE cries out to Pallas for help when she understands that her uncle PANDARUS is trying to convince her to make TROILUS her lover (lines 425–27). VIRGINIA, the martyr-heroine of "The PHYSICIAN'S TALE," is said to be as wise as Pallas (line 49). In the short unfinished poem "ANELIDA AND ARCITE," the goddess is mistakenly identified with BELLONA, the Roman goddess of war who was also the sister of Mars (line 5).

Palmyra (Palymerie)   An ancient city in central SYRIA. ZENOBIA, whose story appears in "The MONK'S TALE" (lines 2247–2374), was the queen of Palmyra.

Pamphilus (Pamphilles)   The hero of a medieval Latin comedy, *Liber de Amore,* dealing with the theme of love. The work was attributed to the 13th-century author Pamphilus Maurlianus, and takes the form of a dialogue between the hero and his beloved, GALATEA. In "The FRANKLIN'S TALE," the narrator notes that the squire AURELIUS loves DORIGEN as secretly as Pamphilus loved Galatea (line 1110). In "The TALE OF MELIBEE," Dame PRUDENCE quotes from Pamphilus when she agrees with her husband that wealth is a positive feature of their lives (lines 1556–61). A number of lines from the *Liber de Amore* appear in Chaucer's *TROILUS AND CRISEYDE,* though there is no mention of their source in the poem.

Pan   In classical mythology, Pan was an Arcadian god of shepherds, herdsmen and hunters who came to be more generally considered a god of nature. He served as protector of flocks and herds, driving away wild animals that would harm them. Pan was represented as having a bearded human head with two short horns, the torso of a man and the legs and feet of a goat. When he attempted to woo the nymph Syrinx she jumped into a pond and was transformed into a reed. The god made a musical pipe out of reeds and named it after her. In *The BOOK OF THE DUCHESS,* the BLACK KNIGHT is described as being more distraught over losing his lady than the god Pan (lines 511–13). Presumably the reference is to Pan's loss of Syrinx.

Pandarus (Pandare)   In classical mythology, Pandarus was a favorite of the god APOLLO, who tutored him in archery. He was known for his skill as an archer in the TROJAN WAR, in which he fought against the Greeks. In Chaucer's *TROILUS AND CRISEYDE,* as CRISEYDE's uncle and TROILUS' friend, he plays an important role in bringing them together. Because of his apparent eagerness to have Troilus succeed in seducing his niece, his name entered our language as a common noun meaning "a procurer for sexual purposes." This role that he plays of go-between was the invention of BOCCACCIO, whose *FILOSTRATO* was the source of Chaucer's poem. In Boccaccio, however, Pandarus (called "Pandaro") is the cousin rather than the uncle of Criseyde, and presumably near the same age as the two lovers, which makes his behavior seem a little less sleazy than it does when he is older. In keeping with the morality of Chaucer's time, as her uncle, and particularly in the absence of her father, Pandarus ought to be acting as Criseyde's protector, placing that duty above his friendship to Troilus. Pandarus also appears playing the role of go-between in Shakespeare's play, *Troilus and Cressida,* where the darkness of his motives is even more strongly emphasized.

Pandion (Pandyon)   In classical mythology, Pandion was a king of ATHENS and the father of PROCNE and PHILOMELA, two sisters whose tragic story is narrated in Chaucer's *LEGEND OF GOOD WOMEN* (lines 2228–93). Procne married TEREUS of Thrace, who, overcome with a violent lust for Philomela, persuaded Pandion to let her come visit her sister. Pandion initially refused to part with Philomela, but finally agreed to let her go, asking in exchange that Tereus allow Procne to visit him at least once before he dies. However, instead of taking Philomela to her sister, Tereus led her to a dark cave, where he raped her and cut out her tongue in order to silence her. Chaucer's version of the story does not tell what happened to Pandion, but in legend he is said to have died of grief over the fate of his daughters.

Panik (Panico) In "The CLERK'S TALE," WALTER sends his young daughter and son to live with his sister, the countess of Panik, when he wants to test his wife's devotion by making her think that he has killed the children. In an article that appeared in the journal *Modern Language Notes* (1952), Derek PEARSALL identified Panik as Panico, a castle named after the family who lived there, located about 20 miles south of Bologna.

Papinian (Papynian) Papinian, or Aemilius Papinianus, was a Roman prefect of magistrates in the early third century. His murder at the hands of the emperor CARACALLA is mentioned in the *BOECE,* Chaucer's translation of BOETHIUS' *Consolation of Philosophy* (Book Three, Prosa 5, lines 49–52). It is one of LADY PHILOSOPHY's examples of great men executed by powerful, but corrupt, rulers.

Parables of Solomon The Parables of Solomon are a series of wise sayings that appear in the Old Testament Book of Proverbs. They begin in Proverbs 10:1 and continue through 20:27. Although they do not contain any of the antifeminist rhetoric found in other parts of Proverbs, the WIFE OF BATH says that they appear in her husband's anthology of antifeminist literature that she calls his "Book of Wicked Wives." The reference occurs in line 679 of the prologue to her tale. Ironically, Proverbs 31:10–31 contains the description of the perfect wife, who is in many ways the antithesis of Chaucer's "Wife".

Parcae (Parcas) In classical mythology, *Parcae* is the Latin name for the Fates, three goddesses whose function was to see that the destiny assigned to each member of the human race was carried out. The three were Clotho, who spun the thread of life; Lachesis, who determined its length; and Atropos, who cut it off. In Roman mythology, Parca was originally a goddess of birth, but early on she came to be identified with the Greek Fates, or Moerae, and split into three goddesses instead of one. In *TROILUS AND CRISEYDE,* the narrator invokes the "angry Parcas" at the beginning of book 5 to assist his telling of TROILUS' tragic end (line 3).

Pardoner, the The Pardoner's portrait follows that of the SUMMONER in the GENERAL PROLOGUE to *The CANTERBURY TALES.* The primary duty of this church official was to sell "indulgences," official church documents which were recognized as providing a substitute for the temporal punishment of sins. While contrition and confession were believed to remove the moral guilt of sin, the need for punishment would also need to be satisfied, either on Earth or in purgatory. Alternative ways of satisfying this requirement consisted of such things as giving alms or performing penitential acts which involved the voluntary undertaking of physical hardship or suffering.

Aside from the title of his profession, the first information we are given about this man is that his customary place of employment is ROUNCIVALE, a hospital located in Charing Cross, a neighborhood on the periphery of medieval LONDON. Larry BENSON's notes to *The RIVERSIDE CHAUCER* explain that this hospital was very active in the sale of indulgences to raise money. (All hospitals were at this time operated by the Catholic Church as charitable institutions.) Interestingly, this particular hospital's sale of indulgences had, by the time that Chaucer was writing *The Canterbury Tales,* twice been associated with fraud involving the fabrication of these documents.

After learning about his place of employment, we discover that the Pardoner is a friend and companion of the Summoner, with whom he sings what appears to be a love song. The Pardoner's physical description includes thin locks of straight yellow hair that hang down over his shoulders and staring eyes that are compared to those of a hare. His voice is high like the bleat of a goat and his chin is naturally hairless rather than recently shaven. All of these characteristics lead to the narrator's deduction that this man is either "a geldyng or a mare," i.e., either castrated or homosexual. His long hair and refusal to wear his hood both suggest defiance of the rules governing clerical attire.

Despite these characteristics, the narrator proceeds in typical fashion to state that, regarding his occupation, the Pardoner is exceptionally skilled. This remark does not, however, indicate that the narrator is naively taken in by the Pardoner's tricks and deceptions. When describing the man's relics, the narrator clearly shows his own understanding that the relics are fake, and the people who buy them are the Pardoner's "apes," or dupes. The narrator does, however, grudgingly admit that the man is also an excellent speaker when it comes to either reading a lesson or delivering a sermon, and that he is also an excellent singer, all talents that he cultivates because his ability to make a living depends upon them.

"The PARDONER'S TALE," one of the most finely crafted of *The Canterbury Tales,* excellently illustrates the Pardoner's storytelling talents while at the same time providing an example of a sermon on his favorite theme, *radix malorum est cupiditas* (Latin for "greed is the root of evil"). This tale of three rioters who go out seeking to slay Death, and are themselves slain by their own greed, constitutes the perfect ironic commentary on the Pardoner's practice of his profession, which is itself motivated entirely by greed.

"Pardoner's Tale, The" The story of three rioters who go in search of Death in order to destroy him, but become his victims instead.

SUMMARY

In the prologue to his tale, the PARDONER explains to the other pilgrims his technique for convincing people to give him money, which is to preach on the subject of greed as the root of all evil (*Radix malorum est Cupiditas*). He freely admits to showing people false relics (such as bits of bone supposed to have belonged to a famous saint) and other trickery to gain their trust. Furthermore, he is not at all ashamed to say he does not care a fig about the state of their souls, but only about their pocketbooks. He concludes his prologue with an exposé on his own numerous vices which include drinking and having a wench in every town. Finally, he promises that, once he has had a good drink of ale, he will tell a moral tale.

The Pardoner's tale begins with the introduction of a group of young people who live a riotous and sinful life of gluttony, drunkenness, gambling (dicing), swearing and lechery. Immediately following the introduction of this group, the Pardoner digresses to give

Artist's rendering of the Pardoner, from the Ellesmere Manuscript of The Canterbury Tales. *In this illustration, the artist paid careful attention to the details supplied by Chaucer in the* General Prologue. *His cap has a "vernicle" (a miniature copy of Saint Veronica's handkerchief, upon which Christ's features were miraculously imprinted) sewn in front, and his long yellow hair trails out beneath it. A satchel of pardons is slung around the horse's neck.*

examples of the various vices listed above and how they have brought calamity and ruin to the lives of other people, primarily characters from the Bible or from history. He also gives examples of people who have prospered by avoiding such behavior. When he returns to his tale, it focuses on three of the riotous revelers. One day while drinking in a tavern, these three men see a corpse carried through the street. Inquiring the identity of the dead man, they learn that he was one of their gang, who was slain the night before by a thief named Death. The bartender comments that Death has slain a great many people lately, which rouses the three rioters to action. Together they swear to find and to slay this fellow, Death.

Shortly after they set out in search of Death, the three men come upon an old man. The man complains of being unable to find a young man willing to trade "his youthe for myne age"; nor is Death willing to take his life, from which he is eager to be parted. When he attempts to pass by the three rioters, they refuse to let him go until he tells them where they can find Death, with whom he seems so conversant. He tells them to look beneath a tree in a nearby field and there they shall find him. Following his instructions, they find the tree and, beneath its shade, a huge heap of gold coins, which causes them to immediately forget their original errand. Because it would be dangerous to carry the gold through town during the day, one of the men decides they must draw straws to decide who will go into town for food and drink while the other two stay with the gold until nightfall, when they may safely carry it home. The youngest draws the short straw and goes off to town. As soon as he leaves, one of those remaining urges his companion to help him kill the man who has gone so that the two of them may divide the gold instead of having to split it three ways. The other man agrees, and they plan how they will commit the murder. Meanwhile, the youngest is likewise filled with fantasies regarding how nice it would be to enjoy the gold all by himself. With that in mind he visits an apothecary (pharmacist) to buy some poison, saying that he has a problem with vermin. Placing the poison in drinking bottles intended for his companions, he makes the rest of his purchases and returns to the field and the gold. The two others waste no time in killing him, but decide that they will eat and drink before they bury his body. The bottle they drink from happens to be one with poison, so it is not long before they join their former comrade.

The tale ends with a peroration from the Pardoner to avoid the sins of gluttony, lechery, gambling and avarice, sins to which he now adds that of murder. Then he invites members of his audience, in this case the pilgrims, to come forward and receive pardon (God's), which he (the Pardoner) will gladly give in exchange for money or other possessions such as jewelry, cutlery or wool. He also calls attention once more to his collection of holy relics, calling upon the Host (*see* Harry BAILLY), as the most sinful of the crew, to set an example by coming forward immediately to make an offering. The Host responds with considerable ire, saying that the Pardoner will next ask him to kiss his old stained undergarments as if they were the relic of a saint. But what he would like to do instead, the Host says, is to cut off the Pardoner's testicles and enshrine them in a pig's turd. The Pardoner is so furious at this attack that he cannot speak. The KNIGHT (1) intervenes with conciliatory words for both men and persuades them to kiss and make up.

COMMENTARY

The Pardoner's prologue, like the WIFE OF BATH's, takes the form of a confession. It was most likely modeled on, or at least inspired by, the confession of False Semblant (False Seeming) in the *ROMAN DE LA ROSE*, a work that Chaucer translated earlier in his career. The character of the Pardoner presented here also bears some similarity to the Vice character of medieval morality plays. What was striking about this character was his straightforward admission to the audience of his evil nature and intentions (typically to seduce the play's main character, representing the soul of man, into sin and damnation), which were kept hidden from the protagonist.

Because the Pardoner proposes to give the pilgrims an example of his preaching by way of his tale-telling, the genre of his tale is considered to be a sermon, although it does not strictly adhere to the characteristic structure of a medieval sermon. It does, however, have a clearly defined two-part structure whose parts correspond to the two central parts of a formal sermon. The first of these consists of an introduction stating the theme of his performance—the deadly tavern vices which include gambling ("hasardrye"), the swearing of false oaths, gluttony (which includes drunkenness) and lechery. This portion of the tale features some extremely inflated rhetoric, the product of a professional who excels at using language to play on people's emotions, particularly guilt and fear. Ironically, in the midst of this conscience-wrenching harangue, the detail with which the Pardoner describes the sins he cautions against gives him away, recalling his own sinfulness, which he so glibly admitted in his prologue. For example, in the middle of his cautionary words against the drinking of wine, "Now kepe yow fro the white and fro the rede," he continues, "And namely fro the white wyn of Lepe / That is to selle in Fysshestrete or in Chepe. / This wyn of Spaigne crepeth subtilly / In othere wynes, growynge faste by, / Of which ther ryseth swich fumositee / That whan a man hath dronken draughtes thre, . . ." (lines 562–68) [Now guard yourself from the white and from the red, / And

especially from the white wine of Lepe / That is for sale in Fish Street or in Cheapside. / This Spanish wine secretly finds its way / Into other wines, growing nearby, / From which there rise such vapors / That when a man has taken three drinks . . .]. His words betray familiarity with the effects of this wine that could only arise from personal experience. Likewise his pronouncements against swearing could serve as a tutorial for anyone interested in learning a few choice phrases to fling about.

The second part of the tale, the story of the three revelers, is written in a plain style with no ornamentation of any kind. Although it serves as an EXEMPLUM within the context of the sermon, it is based upon a common folktale that has analogues throughout Europe and Asia. Many of the analogues are quite similar, featuring three revelers, a quest for Death and an old man who gives them directions. Thus it is impossible to suggest that

Tavern Scene From British Library Ms. Add 27695 f 14r. Reproduced by permission of the British Library.

any of the surviving versions served as Chaucer's particular source, especially since Chaucer does not in this adaptation, in contrast to what he does elsewhere in the tales, individualize the characters by giving them names or in any other way making them more realistic. Yet, despite its lack of originality, Chaucer's version has been considered one of his most powerful narratives, primarily because of the context within which it is set as the tale told by the Pardoner. The reason that this tale suits the Pardoner so well is because of the way it plays off the man's occupation and those who buy his wares. The chief error made by the three rioters is a conceptual one: In believing that they can kill Death, they mistake something nonmaterial (an event) for something material. This is not to say that death does not affect the material body, but rather that the significance of death resides in what happens to the soul. In Christian terms, if the soul is saved, bodily death is of no consequence. Those who buy pardons, on the other hand, mistake something material (a piece of paper that says their sins are forgiven) for something nonmaterial (God's true forgiveness).

A similar tension, between the spiritual and the physical, is at work in the epilogue to the tale, imbedded within what seems to be, superficially, merely a scatological insult. When the Host attacks the Pardoner's invitation to make an offering to his relics, he says, "Thou woldest make me kisse thyn olde breech, / And swere it were a relyk of a seint, / Though it were with thy fundement depeint!" (lines 948–50) [You would like to make me kiss your old underwear, / And would swear it was the relic of a saint, / Though it were stained by your anus]. As Helen COOPER points out, one of the relics enshrined at Canterbury were the filthy breeches of Saint Thomas (see THOMAS À BECKET), which the saint had, during his lifetime, neglected to change over the years as a way of mortifying the flesh. Looking at this tale from the vantage point offered by history, it seems clear that its two primary themes—that of questioning the relationship between outward forms and inward spirituality, and that of the blatant corruption of some of the Catholic clergy—foreshadow the tensions that will explode in the 16th century with the Protestant Reformation. Interestingly, leading up to that period, it was the sale of pardons and the veneration of relics that aroused the most widespread pressure for reforms, both within the Catholic Church and from those like Martin Luther who broke with the church entirely.

Because the Pardoner has, in his prologue, admitted that the relics he carries are fakes and that his own motive is greed rather than any concern for the salvation of those to whom he preaches, many readers are surprised when, at the end of his tale, he invites the pilgrims to make offerings to his relics and to buy pardons. The Host's angry response suggests that no one is taken in by the Pardoner's invitation, so perhaps the epilogue's purpose is simply to illustrate the man's moral blindness, his inability to see or realize the evil that he does, an inability fostered by his own sinfulness. This same blindness explains why he can tell a tale showing how avarice kills while leading a life dominated by that very motive.

The relationship between tale and teller in "The Pardoner's Tale" leads to one final consideration: Should we trust, or believe in, or even listen to the tale of an untrustworthy teller? Chaucer draws so much attention to the Pardoner's vice of deception, both in the prologue, where the man admits his trickery and in the epilogue, where he attempts to practice it on the pilgrims, that it is impossible to read this tale without considering this question, which in Chaucer's day mirrored a more serious debate over whether a person could be absolved by a corrupt clergyman. It is worth noting that nowhere in his confessional prologue does the Pardoner say that the pardons he sells are not effective, even though he admits that he does not care at all about the spiritual well-being of those to whom he sells them. There is, however, a moment within the tale itself in which the Pardoner undoes himself, it seems, by revealing the inherent inadequacy of the pardons he has for sale. At the conclusion of the tale, in a flight of rhetorical fancy, he speaks a nougat of self-contradictory truth when he says, "Allas, mankynde, how may it bitide / That to thy creatour, which that thee wroghte / And with his precious herte-blood thee boghte, / Thou art so fals and so unkynde, allas?" (lines 900–03) [Alas, mankind, how can it be / That to your creator, who made you / And paid for you with his precious heart's blood, / You are so false and so unnatural, alas?]. Just as he cannot seem to help revealing his own sinfulness, he also cannot help revealing the true price of forgiveness, Christ's death on the Cross.

Paris (1)   In classical mythology, Paris was one of the sons of King PRIAM and HECUBA of TROY. Because of a prophecy that he would bring about the destruction of that famous city, his parents left him exposed in the Phrygian mountains. Found and raised by shepherds, he married the nymph OENONE, daughter of the river god Cibrenus. Paris was chosen by the goddesses JUNO, MINERVA and VENUS to determine which one was the fairest. Each of them offered him a bribe, but Venus' promise to help him win the most beautiful woman in the world won out. This incident, known as the "Judgment of Paris" is mentioned in *The HOUSE OF FAME* (lines 199–201), where Paris' failure to choose Juno is given as the reason for her animosity toward the city of Troy. In keeping with her promise, Venus assisted Paris in abducting Helen (HELEN OF TROY), the beautiful wife of MENELAUS, the king of Sparta, after he was hospitably entertained at that king's palace. Paris' betrayal of his host led to the TROJAN WAR, in which a gathering of the Greeks' mightiest warriors besieged Troy for 10 years before accomplishing the city's destruction.

Paris' abandonment of Oenone made him a popular example of a false lover. He is evoked for this reason in "The SQUIRE'S TALE" (lines 543–57), in which a female falcon compares her unfaithful lover to Paris. Similarly, in *The HOUSE OF FAME,* Paris' treatment of Oenone is compared to AENEAS' desertion of DIDO (line 399). In *The BOOK OF THE DUCHESS,* the story of Paris and Helen appears on the walls of the room that the dreamer-narrator wakes up in (lines 326–31), and in *The PARLIAMENT OF FOWLS,* it adorns the walls of the Temple of Venus (lines 288–94). The lovers are alluded to briefly in "The MERCHANT'S TALE" when the aged knight JANUARY imagines that on his wedding knight he is going to embrace his wife, the tender young MAY, more eagerly than Paris ever embraced Helen (lines 1753–54). Although Paris is responsible for the Trojan War that forms the setting of *TROILUS AND CRISEYDE* in addition to being one of TROILUS' brothers, he never directly appears as a character but is only mentioned by others, for example, PANDARUS tries to convince Troilus that if CRISEYDE does not return from the Greek camp, he can get another lover, just like Paris when he left Oenone for Helen (book 4, lines 596–609).

Paris (2)   Paris, the capital city of France, is mentioned several times in *The CANTERBURY TALES.* In the GENERAL PROLOGUE, the French spoken by the PRIORESS reveals that she learned it in an English school rather than in Paris (lines 125–26). In the WIFE OF BATH's prologue, she notes that HELOISE, the lover of Abelard, was the abbess of a priory not far from Paris (line 678). In "The SHIPMAN'S TALE," Paris is home to Sir JOHN THE MONK, who is a good friend of the merchant and visits the merchant and his wife in SEINT-DENYS, a town north of the city.

Parlement of Briddes   An alternate title for Chaucer's *PARLIAMENT OF FOWLS.*

Parliament of Fowls, The   The first recorded literary association between the saint and romantic love, this dream-vision poem tells what happens when a group of birds gathers to choose their mates on Saint Valentine's Day.

SUMMARY

The Parliament of Fowls begins with the narrator's reflections on love, its paradoxes and elusive nature, which, we quickly learn, are perceptions based on reading rather than experience. These general reflections lead him to recall a particular book he read not long ago, Tullius' *DREAM OF SCIPIO.* After briefly describing the length (seven chapters) and scope (of heaven, hell and Earth, and the souls that therein dwell) of the book, he embarks upon a more detailed summary of the text. The summary begins by telling about the Roman general Scipio (SCIPIO AFRICANUS THE YOUNGER) coming into Africa, where, after meeting Masinissa, king of Numidia, he had a dream in which his grandfather, Scipio "Affrycan" (SCIPIO AFRICANUS THE ELDER) appeared.

Within the dream, Scipio the elder takes his grandson on a heavenward journey leading him up through the various spheres of the Ptolemaic universe until they reach the final sphere, the Stellatum, where the fixed stars reside. From this vantage point, the elder Scipio directs his grandson's vision downward to gaze upon the Earth and tells him to meditate on the relative significance of its inhabitants and their various preoccupations. The Earth's small size in comparison with the rest of the universe reinforces his argument that his grandson should not become overly attached to worldly delights. He also instructs the young man on certain philosophical issues such as COMMON PROFIT, the idea that everyone should work together for the good of all mankind. Doing so is the means of ensuring oneself a place in heaven. On the other hand, breakers of the law, along with lecherous folk, are condemned to a kind of purgatory, where they whirl about the Earth in continual pain until they are at last forgiven and granted admission to the joys of heaven.

The daylight begins to fade while he is reading, so the narrator puts his book aside and gets ready for bed, consumed by a heavy thoughtfulness that has been provoked by his possession of a thing that he does not want and by his concomitant lack of something that he desires. Neither "thing" is defined or described, but Chaucer's use of this kind of elliptical phrase elsewhere in his poetry typically constitutes a reference to unrequited love. When the narrator finally falls asleep, he dreams that Scipio Affrycan appears at his bedside and begins to speak to him, commending his diligence in reading "myn olde bok," [my old book] and offering to reward him for his labors. Rising from his bed, the narrator accompanies Affrycan to a garden surrounded by a high wall made of green stone. They pause before a gate that has verses inscribed on either half. The inscription on one side is welcoming, announcing that men who enter this way are coming into a haven of solace, bliss and "dedly woundes cure" [deadly wounds' cure] where spring reigns eternal. The other gate speaks a warning, saying that disdain and sorrow wait on the other side in a garden where the trees are barren of both leaves and fruit. While the repeated phrase "Thorgh me men gon" [Through me men go] in these lines clearly echoes "Per me si vi," part of the inscription over the portal of hell in DANTE's *Inferno,* Chaucer's inscriptions refer to the two faces of love, which in their extremes may be either blissful or devastating.

Attracted by the first inscription and repelled by the second, the narrator finds himself unable to either leave or enter until his guide solves the problem by shoving him forward through the gates, reassuring him that the inscriptions do not apply to him, but only to those who are recognized as Love's servants. Affrycan goes on to suggest that even though he is not a lover, he can still learn something by observing, and so perhaps get new material for his writing.

Affrycan takes the narrator's hand and leads him around the garden, where he observes many different kinds of trees in full leaf, blossoming flowers, a river and a green meadow with streams full of small fish. Birds sing on every branch, rabbits play in the meadow, deer roam about and the air is always temperate, all of which suggests a kind of paradisal garden echoing the Garden of Eden.

CUPID, the god of love, rests beneath one of the trees with his bow and arrows ready to hand. He is accompanied by "Wille" (i.e., Desire) his daughter, who tempers his arrows by placing their heads in a spring. Other allegorical figures also rest nearby, including "Aray" (clothing), "Lust" (Desire), "Curteysie" (Courtesy), "Craft" (Deceit), "Delyt" (Delight) and others, who all play a part in the drama of romantic love. Next, the narrator spies a temple made of brass standing on pillars of jasper. A group of beautiful women in disheveled clothing dance perpetually before the temple and hundreds of pairs of white doves are perched upon the roof. Lady Peace and Dame Patience sit beside the temple door; "Byheste" (Promise) and "Art" (Craft or Skill) appear behind them, sometimes hovering inside the doorway and sometimes venturing out. Inside the temple the narrator discovers a strong wind made of sighs engendered by desire. It blows about making all of the temple's altars burn the brighter with renewed flame. He realizes that jealousy causes all the suffering that is endured there. PRIAPUS, the god of gardens and fertility who is typically represented with an erect phallus, VENUS, the goddess of Love, BACCHUS, the god of wine, and CERES, the goddess of agriculture and fecundity are found among the inhabitants of the temple. Venturing further into its depths, the narrator finds a wall hung with broken bows symbolizing love's scornful attitude toward DIANA, the goddess of chastity. The walls are painted with illustrations of people who suffered and died in the service of love, such as HERCULES, DIDO, HELEN, ISOLDE, TROILUS, PYRAMUS, CLEOPATRA and others.

As he leaves the temple and reenters the garden, the narrator comes to a glade upon a hill of flowers where he observes the goddess NATURE sitting before an audience of birds who are making a great deal of noise. Because it is Saint Valentine's Day, he explains, the birds have all come together to choose their mates with Nature's assistance. There are so many of them, in fact, that the narrator can hardly find a place to stand. The goddess, he goes on to explain, looks exactly as she is described by Aleyn (ALAIN DE LILLE) in his *Pleynt of Kynd* ("Complaint of Nature"). She commands every bird to take its place and the birds immediately obey, arranging themselves in a kind of hierarchical order. The birds of prey ("foules of ravyne") are perched in the highest branches, the birds that eat worms come next, the seed fowl below them on the grass and the waterfowl lowest of all in the dale or valley.

The narrator proceeds to describe different members of the various groups, touching briefly on certain of their characteristics. The birds of prey, for example, are represented by the royal eagle, the goshawk, the falcon and the hardy sparrowhawk. After giving several representatives of each class, he concludes that birds of every kind were gathered there to choose their mates. With her hand Nature holds a beautiful "formel" (female) eagle, about whom she begins to speak to the other birds, first reminding them why they have come and then announcing that the "tercel" (male) eagle, because he is the wisest and worthiest bird, shall have the first choice. The only requirement or condition that she makes regarding the birds' choices is that the female who is chosen must agree to the match. The tercel speaks, naming as his choice the female who sits on Nature's hand, and describing his devotion in very courtly terms. Upon hearing his words, the female eagle blushes but does not otherwise respond. Another male eagle, one of a lower rank, now speaks, claiming that he loves the female the best or at least as well as the first male, and that he has loved her longer; therefore, he has a better right to be rewarded with her love in return. His language, in keeping with his rank, is more boisterous and aggressive than his rival's. At this point a third male eagle comes forward, proposing himself as the proper mate for the lovely female. When he has finished making his own argument, which he bases upon the idea that the length of the lover's service is not as important as the intensity of his devotion (he possesses the latter but not the former), the lesser birds, who have been waiting for the eagles to finish so they can have their own turn, begin to raucously complain of the eagles' long-windedness. Nature interrupts their distempered chatter, proposing that each class of birds debate the issue of the eagle's mate among themselves and then choose one representative who shall present their group's solution to the problem at hand. All the birds agree to this proposal and, once again, the eagles have the first turn.

The birds of prey choose a male falcon to deliver their opinion. He first acknowledges the difficulty of making such a decision, but then offers the suggestion that the eagle who is the worthiest in knighthood, the highest in rank and the most nobly bred ought to be the most suitable choice, but that the female eagle should, after all, be the one who makes the final decision. The waterfowl, represented by the goose, delivers the next opinion, which is essentially the same as the falcon's but expressed in a comparatively succinct, and somewhat vulgar (according to some of the other birds) fashion: "I seye I rede hym, though he were my brother, / but she wol love hym, lat hym love another!" (lines 566–67) [I say I should advise him, even if he were my brother, / That unless she should love him, he should love another!].

The sparrowhawk criticizes the vulgarity of the goose, and all the noble birds have a laugh at her expense. Then it is the seed fowls' turn to speak. This group is represented by the turtledove, who expresses the opinion that a true lover will continue to love, even unto death, whether he is accepted or not. The duck breaks in to criticize the futility of such a philosophy and reasserts the practical nature of the goose's verdict. The duck is interrupted by the male falcon, who finds such a solution insulting and improper, suggesting that their class of birds have no idea of the true meaning of love.

The cuckoo speaks next, representing the birds that eat worms. Evidently growing impatient with the slow progress being made, he suggests letting the eagles wrangle over the question as long as they want, as long as he can have his mate and be gone. If the eagles cannot make up their minds, maybe the best solution is for them all to remain single. This verdict is likewise received with contempt by the birds of prey. The merlin now speaks on their behalf, pointing out the vulgarity and lewdness of the cuckoo's behavior. (The cuckoo was thought to lay its eggs in the nests of other birds.)

Having listened to the opinions of all the different groups, Nature now calls the birds to order and announces that the choice shall be left to the female eagle. For her own part, she says, she would advise the lady to choose the royal tercel (the first who spoke), who appears to be the noblest and the most worthy. At last the female eagle speaks, praising Nature and asking for a year's respite in which to consider the matter, after which time she will make her decision known. Nature grants her request, telling the male eagles to be of good heart and continue in service to their lady. This business concluded, she proceeds to pairing off the other birds, who are likewise mated in mutual consent.

The purpose for their gathering fulfilled, the birds begin their departure in an ecstasy of delight, embracing each other with their wings and winding their necks together. Their departure is accompanied by a roundel sung by a group of birds previously selected to provide music for the occasion. The poem includes the words of this hymn welcoming spring, and then concludes with the narrator's awakening at the end of the song. The narrator immediately searches for something else to read, in the hope that one day he will read something that will help him to fare better in his life.

COMMENTARY

According to current theories on the dating of Chaucer's works, *The Parliament of Fowls* was probably composed in the late 1370s or early 1380s, after *The HOUSE OF FAME* and before *TROILUS AND CRISEYDE*. It is the third poem in which he employs the device of the DREAM VISION. Previously, in *The BOOK OF THE DUCHESS* and *The House of Fame,* he had used this device as a vehicle to explore the theme of love and to consider experience and authority (previously written texts) as alternative sources for literary creation. While *The House of Fame* presents a more theoretical meditation upon these ideas, the *Parliament* plunges its readers into an experience that has become a text without self-consciously drawing attention to that fact. The result is a comparatively seamless artistic creation which many critics see as the culmination of Chaucer's experimentation with the dream vision formula. The poem also represents a step forward in Chaucer's developing mastery of the poetic line. The four-beat couplet that he employed in his earlier work has now been replaced by the seven-line RHYME ROYAL stanza, whose longer line and less obtrusive rhyme scheme offered the possibility of elegance as well as flexibility. Its similarity to ottava rima (Boccaccio's stanza) enabled Chaucer to smoothly translate selections from that author into his native English. Boccaccio's *Teseida* was Chaucer's source for the Garden of Love and its allegorical inhabitants, with the exception of the goddess Nature. She derives, as Chaucer informs us within the text of the poem, from the *Pleynt of Kynd* ("Complaint of Nature") of Alain de Lille. The allegorical garden of the *Roman de la Rose* may also have influenced this part of the poem, though there is little in the way of direct imitation.

Within the dream vision framework, Chaucer employs another genre, that of the debate poem. The discourse of the birds who gather in the garden to choose their mates bears some resemblance to the *demande d'amour,* the love debate of French literature, which typically posited a situation in which each of several suitors tries to present the best case for himself as the lady's choice. The speeches of the three tercel eagles in Chaucer's poem clearly recall this type of contest, with the difference that the participants are birds rather than humans. Wolfgang CLEMEN's commentary on the poem additionally points out that the fairy- or folktale theme of the contending lovers provides a suggestive parallel. Features of this motif that appear in Chaucer's *Parliament* include the judge who will decide which of the suitors deserves to win the lady, a "general public" in the debate and the postponement of the decision, which the judge eventually leaves up to the lady herself. The main difference between both of these possible influences and Chaucer's debate is the fact, already mentioned above, that the characters engaged in this discussion are birds rather than people.

This brings us to a consideration of one further possible generic influence, that of other literary "parleys" or parliaments of birds that appeared prior to the period in which Chaucer was writing and which were typically written by clerics. These writers employed the debate form as a vehicle for a kind of didactic discourse consisting of little more than the exchange of proverbial sayings. For his vivid and dramatic characterization of the birds, Chaucer seems to have drawn upon the BEAST FABLE tradition, wherein human behavior as well as human speech embodied in animal forms becomes the means for satiric commentary upon human society. Chaucer even more clearly employs the beast fable to this effect in "The NUN'S PRIESTS'S TALE" of *The CANTERBURY TALES*, where, interestingly enough, his chief protagonist is once again a bird.

I have already mentioned that this poem, like *The Book of the Duchess* and *The House of Fame,* treats the theme of love. It is the oldest surviving Valentine's Day poem and marks the first known association between Saint Valentine, whose life appears to provide no rationale for his choice as the saint of romantic love, and that theme. The poem may also have been composed to celebrate or commemorate a particular historic occasion, the engagement of King RICHARD II to ANNE OF BOHEMIA. The two were married in January of 1382, which corresponds favorably to the likely date of the poem's composition. Scholars who have researched this angle argue that the formel eagle represents Anne; the three tercels, three of her suitors: Richard (the royal tercel who speaks first), Friedrich of Meissen (the second tercel, who is of lesser rank but has served her longer), and the dauphin of France (the third tercel, who, like the dauphin, was unable to boast of his length of service). One year appears to have lapsed between Richard's courtship of Anne and their betrothal. This could be the year's "respite" referred to at the poem's end.

Most attempts at interpretation of the poem have concentrated on the debate portion and either ignored or slighted the material that the narrator summarizes at the poem's beginning when he describes the occasion leading up to his fabulous dream. He had been reading, he tells us, in a book called "Tullyus of the Drem of Scipioun." Tully, or Tullius, is actually the classical author more familiarly known to us as CICERO, and the "Dream of Scipio" was the final portion of his *Republic*. A version of this text, together with an extended commentary, had been preserved for the Middle Ages by MACROBIUS (ca. 400), whose work also provided Chaucer with the material on the classification of dreams that appears at the opening of *The House of Fame*. As mentioned in the summary above, it recounts the experience of the Roman general Scipio the Younger ("Scipioun"), who dreams that he meets his famous grandfather, Scipio the Elder ("Affrycan") upon his return to the home of his ancestry, Carthage, in northern Africa. Chaucer's version of this text describes the younger Scipio's dream, in which his grandfather carries him aloft into the region of the stars' abode. As they look down upon the great city of CARTHAGE, Affrycan instructs his descendent in a philosophical perspective (also described in the summary given above) that emphasizes the necessity of conducting one's life in a way that will be conducive to the public good (living according to the rule of "common profit"), and of resisting attachment to worldly pursuits and delights.

What has been so puzzling to many of the poem's readers is how this very serious and somber philosophical perspective relates to the lively gathering of birds in the Garden of Love. The idea that they are related at some level is suggested by the fact that they appear in the same poem, with the one (the reading material) leading to or inspiring the other (the dream). Furthermore, when the narrator falls asleep, he initially dreams that he is approached by the elder Scipio, who initiates a dream journey, acting as his guide. Instead of leading him up into the heavens, however, Affrycan directs the narrator to the gate of Love's garden, and when the narrator hesitates to enter, pushes him through. A further explicit connection between the book that he was reading and the dream comes from the information Affrycan gives him when the former explains that this dream has been sent by Venus ("Cytherea") to reward him for reading "myn olde bok" ("my old book").

The question remains, however, as to how the narrator's observations in the garden may relate to the philosophical content of that "old book." Regarding what the narrator observes in the Temple of Venus, there seem to be some definite connections. The "likerous folk" [lecherous people], described in the book as those who "after that they ben dede, / Shul whirle aboute th'erthe alwey in peyne," (lines 79–80) [after they are dead, / shall whirl about the earth always in pain] seem to have their counterpart in the "sykes hoote as fyr" that the narrator encounters in Love's temple. These sighs, engendered by desire, whirl like a hot wind throughout the temple, fanning the fire on every altar. And although the allegorical figures and deities who occupy the temple and its environs are presented impartially, the temple walls are filled with paintings depicting the sufferings of lovers, most of whose amorous relationships were tainted by lust. As for the remainder of the dream, which contains the debate of the birds who have come to the garden to be united with their mates, it would seem to offer a view of a very different kind of love, and one that would be more in keeping with Scipio's injunction to live in a way that promotes common profit. In Alain's "Complaint of Nature," the goddess Natura puts forth an argument pleading the cause of life and procreation that offers a corrective counterpoint to the ascetic element of *contemptus mundi* ("despise the world") in Scipio's philosophy, while at the same time admirably complementing his point about common profit. It was acceptable Christian doctrine, after all, to consider sex within marriage as both lawful and desirable as a means for carrying out God's command to be fruitful and multiply, thus providing Christian offspring who would continue God's work on Earth. The debate between the birds, which really boils down to a clash between two different conceptions of love—a courtly, idealistic and romantic one (represented by the eagles and other birds of prey), contrasted to a practical and expedient one (represented by the goose, the duck and the other waterfowl), would appear to illustrate the difficulty of putting into practice such an idea as common profit because of the fact that what appears to be in the best interest of one individual or social group may not be the same for another. Chaucer conveys this idea with exceptional aplomb by dramatizing the debate and having the birds speak for themselves, without himself taking sides in the matter. In this way, each point of view throws light upon the other so that the strengths and weaknesses of both are revealed with a gentle touch of satire. Because these strengths and weaknesses are related to social class, this portion of the poem appears to anticipate both the method and the intent of the portraits presented in the GENERAL PROLOGUE to *The CANTERBURY TALES.*

For Further Reading: Derek BREWER's introduction to *Geoffrey Chaucer: The Parlement of Foulys* (1972) provides a good discussion of topics useful for understanding the poem, including its occasion, literary tradition, sources and background, rhetoric, language, meter, manuscript tradition and themes. A longer study devoted primarily to interpretation is J. A. W. BENNETT's *The Parlement of Foules: An Interpretation* (2nd ed., 1965), which analyzes the poem as an exploration of Christian love infused with Neoplatonic thought and imagery. This book is particularly useful for identifying the sources of the poem's themes and images. It also examines the importance of love to Chaucer's conception of social and cosmic order. Readers who are interested in learning more about the historical context of the poem should consult Larry Benson's "The Occasion of the *Parliament of Fowls*" (in *The Wisdom of Poetry: Essays in Early English Poetry in Honor of Morton Bloomfield,* 1982), one of the most recent appraisal of evidence for the date and events surrounding the poem's composition.

Parmenides (Parmanydes) Greek philosopher of the fifth century B.C. who founded the Eleatic school of phi-

losophy, which held that the singular and unchangeable "Being" was the only reality and that plurality, change and motion were only illusory. He was the first to declare that the world was a sphere. In the *BOECE,* LADY PHILOSOPHY quotes Parmenides when she notes that the divine substance moves the world while the substance itself is still (Book Three, Prosa 12, lines 189–99).

Parnassus (Parnaso) Parnassus, or Mount Parnassus, is a mountain located in central Greece near the Gulf of Corinth. In ancient times, it was considered sacred to the god APOLLO and the Muses. In the prologue to "The FRANKLIN'S TALE," the FRANKLIN agrees to tell the next story but modestly states that he knows no fancy rhetoric, that he has never slept "on the Mount of Pernaso" (line 721) [on the mount of Parnassus]. In *The HOUSE OF FAME,* at the beginning of book 2, the narrator invokes the help of those who live on Mount Parnassus in describing a fabulous dream that he has had (line 521). A similar invocation appears at the beginning of the fragment *ANELIDA AND ARCITE* (line 16). At the end of the third book of *TROILUS AND CRISEYDE,* the narrator thanks the Muses of Parnassus for the assistance they have given him in describing TROILUS' struggle and his joys.

Parson, the The Parson's portrait follows that of the WIFE OF BATH in the GENERAL PROLOGUE to *The CANTERBURY TALES.* The Parson is undeniably the most admirable of the pilgrims. The details of his description reveal that he is the priest of a rural parish who displays great concern for the spiritual well-being of his parishioners. Although he is a learned man and an accomplished preacher, he teaches as much by example as by words, visiting members of his parish when they are sick or in trouble and fulfilling his duties in bad weather as well as good. Much of the information provided in his portrait focuses on what he does not do, such as excommunicating people for failing to give a tithe (10 percent) of their income to the church, or leaving his post vacant and traveling to London in hopes of securing a second income. These behaviors that he avoids would be characteristic of a corrupt priest. Despite the Parson's kindness and goodwill, he is not tolerant of obstinate sinners and, be they of high or low rank, he does not hesitate to issue a sharp rebuke when such is called for. Chaucer gives us no description of the Parson's clothing or physical features, which increases our sense of him as an ideal figure. His tale, which is a sermon on the subject of penitence is the last to be told on the pilgrimage to CANTERBURY. The PLOWMAN described in the General Prologue is his brother.

"Parson's Tale, The" Only two of the Canterbury tales are written in prose. One of them is "The TALE OF

MELIBEE"; "The Parson's Tale," a sermon on the topic of penitence, is the other. It is interesting that both tales address the theme of forgiveness.

SUMMARY

Prologue

By the time the MANCIPLE has ended his tale it is four o'clock in the afternoon. The Host, (*see* Harry BAILLY), self-appointed leader of the pilgrims, announces that only one more tale remains to be told and that is the PARSON's. He invites the Parson to tell a fable, but the man declines, reminding them of Saint PAUL's advice against telling fables or fictions. Instead, he will speak "a merry tale in prose" that shows them the path to spiritual pilgrimage with its ultimate destination in heaven. Thus will he conclude the game of tale-telling and bring the contest to an end.

Tale

Our Lord in heaven wishes that no man should perish but that all should enjoy eternal life. There are many paths or ways that lead people to salvation, but one of the noblest of these is penitence. Therefore everyone

The sin of Avarice From British Library Ms. Add 28162 f9v. Reproduced by permission of the British Library.

ought to learn as much as they can about penitence: what it is, from whence it comes, how it works, how many types there are, which things apertain to it and which things hinder it.

Penitence is defined with reference to the church fathers, Saint AMBROSE, Saint ISIDORE OF SEVILLE, Saint GREGORY and Saint AUGUSTINE, as serious regret for sins that have been committed, and the intention never to perform such deeds again. True penitence may be achieved through three actions. The first is contrition of heart; the second is the confession of sins to a priest or other qualified clergyman; and the third is satisfaction, meaning the prayers or other deeds offered in reparation for sin. (The latter to be imposed by the clergyman who heard the confession.)

The tale moves next to define each of the terms offered above. Contrition is defined as heavy and penetrating sorrow and it has six causes. The first cause that may bring a person to contrition is the remembrance of sin accompanied by shame and regret. The second cause is the knowledge that sin makes man a thrall, or slave. The third cause is fear of Judgment Day and the torments of hell. (The latter are described in great detail, with emphasis on the idea that everything that has been pleasant on Earth shall be turned into its opposite. For example, those who have enjoyed luxurious beds and soft sheets here in this life will find themselves lying on beds of maggots and covered with blankets of worms.) The fourth cause of contrition is the memory of the good things that a person might have done (missed opportunities), or the good works that have been accomplished but are of no account unless accompanied by penitence. The fifth cause of contrition is the memory of Christ's suffering. Here it is noted that every kind of sin is a reversal of the natural order of things. For example, a man's reason ought by right to have sovereignty over his body and sensual nature; sin perverts this order so that sensual desires gain the upper hand. Remembering the pain that Christ suffered on the cross should minimize the temptation of such pleasures. The sixth cause of contrition is the hope of three things: the forgiveness of sin, the gift of grace which will aid forgiveness and the promise of life in heaven. The section on contrition ends with some final notes regarding its nature, such as the requirement that it be universal; in other words, a contrite man cannot be sorry for just part of his misdeeds. Sinful thoughts are also considered here, with the recommendation that they be included as well.

In most manuscripts of the tale, the next part of the text is introduced with a Latin rubric, "Explicit prima pars Penitentie; Et sequitur secunda pars eiusdem" [Here ends the first part of penitence; and its second part follows]. The second part, or stage, of penitence is confession, the true admission of one's sins to a priest. Before embarking on a lengthy discussion of the different types of sin, which constitutes most of the remainder of the Parson's tale, he reminds his audience of how sin first came into the world with ADAM and EVE in Paradise. Because these two disobeyed God's commandment that they must not eat the fruit of a certain tree in Eden, they lost their immortality and became mortal. This mortal nature was in turn passed down to all their descendents, that is, all the people who have ever inhabited the Earth. Furthermore, because the sin that they committed involved concupiscence (strong desire) for something that was not rightfully theirs, so is the same concupiscence the cause of all our sin, making it impossible for a man to be immune to every temptation. Concupiscence, together with the temptations sent by the devil, leads to sinful thoughts which, unless they are immediately dispelled, often lead to sinful deeds. Sinful deeds fall into two basic categories: deadly (also called "mortal") and venial. Venial sins are less serious than deadly ones, but many of them together, the Parson warns, can add up and bring a man to damnation. Venial sin is defined generally as everything that a man does that is not pleasing to God or done for the love of God or for his sake, but for the love of worldly things. Deadly sin is sin that causes a man's heart to turn away from God, in the event that he loves some worldly thing, creature or deed more than he loves God.

Another Latin rubric concludes this section of the text and introduces the next: "Explicit secunda pars Penitentie. Sequitur de septem peccatis mortalibus et eorum dependenciis, circumstanciis, et speciebus" [Here ends the second part on Penitence. Now follows the section on the Seven Deadly Sins and their subdivisions, circumstances, and species]. The Seven Deadly Sins are defined as the "chieftains" of sin, with pride standing as the first of the group and the root of all the others.

Pride is divided into two types, internal and external. Internal pride consists of disobedience, boasting, hypocrisy, disdain, arrogance, haughtiness, impudence and insolence. The proud person may be hubristic, impatient, argumentative, presumptious, contumacious, irreverent and/or vainglorious. Each variety of pride is further defined, sometimes through example. The foregoing species of pride are internal, i.e., they exist within the heart and mind of man. External pride is that which attaches to the wearing of extravagant, lewd or any other type of clothing that draws attention to oneself. The remedy of pride is humility.

The next in the catalogue of Seven Deadly Sins is envy. Envy is defined as sorrow for another man's prosperity and/or joy of another's harm. Arising from malice, envy goes against all virtues and goodness. Envy is further defined through its different types and subdivisions. Love is the remedy of envy.

The third deadly sin is ire, or anger. Ire takes two forms: sudden, or venial, which springs up without the advice and consent of reason; and deadly, which arises from long consideration and the intention or desire to do vengeance. Ire engenders hate, war and eventually manslaughter if it goes unchecked. Swearing, often done in anger, is discussed here, as well as the less clearly related sins of lying, flattery and scorn. The remedies of ire are meekness and patience.

The fourth deadly sin is accidie, which means spiritual sloth or indifference. Under this heading the Parson also discusses the sin of wanhope, which is despair of God's mercy that grows out of the fear of having sinned too much to be forgiven. The remedy of these sins is strength, of which there are several different species or kinds. The first is magnanimity, which encourages those who possess it to undertake difficult tasks and to undertake them reasonably, with wisdom. The virtues of faith and hope also aid against the sin of accidie by helping men to accomplish good works. Finally, this sin may be guarded against by constancy, or stability of faith.

The fifth deadly sin is avarice, which is grouped together with "coveitise" (covetousness). The difference between the two is explained thus: Coveitise is the desire for things one does not have; avarice is the withholding or hoarding of things that one possesses but does not need. Avarice is one of the most serious sins because it leads to lying, theft and false oaths. He who is guilty of avarice is compared to the idolater who worships false gods; his goods to which he is so attached are his idols. The remedies of avarice are mercy and pity. If a man has mercy on his fellow beings, he will not wish to hoard his goods, but, rather, will use his excess wealth to help those less fortunate than he.

The sixth deadly sin is gluttony, which includes drunkenness as well as overeating. Being overly particular about food and spending too much time and care in its preparation are also prohibited. The remedy of gluttony is abstinence.

The seventh deadly sin is lechery, which is defined as any sexual act or desire outside of intercourse for the purpose of procreation within the bounds of lawful marriage. Lechery is particularly undesirable in women and creates a variety of societal problems such as the possibility of raising a bastard as one's own child and having that child inherit one's property, perhaps wrongfully disinheriting one's own offspring. In this section are included interdictions against various sexual liaisons including incestuous and homosexual ones. Chastity is the remedy of lechery. This concludes the part of the tale defining the Seven Deadly Sins.

The Parson's tale began with the intention of exhibiting the three requirements of penitence: namely, contrition, confession and satisfaction. After the first of these, contrition, was defined, the text took a kind of detour into describing the Seven Deadly Sins so that the sinner might know exactly what it is he needs to be contrite for. Having concluded this series of definitions, the tale returns to explicate the conditions of confession and satisfaction.

The section dealing with confession begins with a discussion of the circumstances surrounding sin, by which the Parson means the conditions under which sinful acts are committed. These facts must be included in confession because they help to determine the sinner's degree of culpability, which in turn will determine the nature and degree of satisfaction that must be performed. True confession furthermore requires that the sinner be truly sorry and full of shame for his sins, that he confess all of his sins, that he make a full confession as soon as possible after committing sin, that he make confession out of his own free will and that the confession be made to a lawful priest.

Satisfaction is defined as the action that must be taken by the penitent sinner in atonement for the sins that he has confessed. The terms of satisfaction are decided by the priest who hears confession, and they generally involve what the Parson terms "almesse" (the performing of charitable deeds) and "bodily peyne" (prayers, vigils, fasting and virtuous teaching). Charitable deeds are further defined as providing assistance to one's neighbors, either in the form of good counsel and comfort, or, if need be, in the form of food, clothing and lodging. Visiting those who are sick or in prison is another form of charity.

The section on "bodily peyne" focuses primarily on prayers, giving specific instructions for saying the *Pater noster* (Our Father, otherwise known as the Lord's Prayer), which may not only perform the function of satisfaction but also may prevent one from succumbing to further temptations. Fasting consists of avoiding worldly pleasures as well as abstaining from food. Virtuous teaching consists not only of speaking and writing, but of teaching by example, especially by behaving with patience and forbearance in the case of illness and loss. The wearing of clothing that mortifies the flesh, such as a hair shirt or chain mail next to the skin, and the whipping of one's own body, are also acceptable forms of "bodily peyne."

After a brief reconsideration of some points that have already been made regarding various obstacles to true penitence, the tale concludes in a grand rhetorical flourish with the reminder that the fruit, or reward, of penitence is, according to the word of Jesus Christ, the endless bliss of heaven.

COMMENTARY

The last tale in the Canterbury group, although it reads like a sermon, actually belongs to the genre of the penitential treatise. Such works became popular after a decision by the Lateran Council in 1215 that oral confession must be made at least once a year. Naturally, in order to make a good confession, people needed to know as much as possible about the sins of which they might have been guilty and about the spiritual and physical mechanics of penitence. Chaucer draws upon three existing penitential works (or perhaps upon later redactions of those works). They were the *Summa de poenitentia* (The chief points of penitence) of the Dominican Raymund of Pennaforte; the *Summa vitiorum* (The chief sins), written by the Dominican William Peraldus; and the anonymous *Summa virtutum de remediis anime* (The chief remedies of virtue for the soul). The definitions of contrition, confession and satisfaction come from the *Summa de poenitentia;* the material on the Seven Deadly Sins is taken primarily from the *Summa vitiorum;* and the remedial virtues inserted following the definition of each deadly sin derive from the *Summa virtutum.* A large number of quotations from the Bible and the church fathers help to flesh out the text and to give it the authority of which medieval writers were so fond. Of these sources, the New Testament appears to be quoted the most often.

Because its religious subject matter is not typically appealing to a majority of modern readers, and because it has more than its share of stylistic awkwardnesses and errors, "The Parson's Tale" rates as one of the least popular of the Canterbury group, among scholars as well as general readers. In fact, some editions of The CANTERBURY TALES, such as Nevill Coghill's translation for Penguin Classics and David Wright's for Oxford's World Classics, either leave the tale out or provide the prologue with only a summary of the tale. A few scholars have argued that the tale was written by someone other than Chaucer to conform to some of the specifications laid out by Chaucer in the prologue to the tale. This is in keeping with the idea that Chaucer died before he was able to compose something suitable for the Parson's performance. While Chaucer's death may indeed have prevented him from revising the text, most contemporary scholars agree that "The Parson's Tale" is his own work. There is a lot of evidence within the tale to relate it to other members of the Canterbury group, since it comments upon many of the same issues, such as the relationship of men and women in marriage ("The WIFE OF BATH'S PROLOGUE" and "The WIFE OF BATH'S TALE," "The MERCHANT'S TALE" and "The CLERK'S TALE"), the deadliness of coveitise ("The PARDONER'S TALE"), the fickleness of FORTUNE ("The KNIGHT'S TALE," "The NUN'S PRIEST'S TALE") and the rewards of steadfast patience and trust in God ("The MAN OF LAW'S TALE," "The FRANKLIN'S TALE"). It is possible to read the Parson's tale as a kind of call to penitence, aimed specifically at some of the pilgrims: at the WIFE OF BATH for her pride in clothing and desire for mastery over her husband, at the PARDONER for his lechery and greed, at the MILLER and the REEVE for their choleric tempers, at the MONK for his avarice and pride as well as for his flawed view of Providence and God's mercy.

The structure of "The Parson's Tale" is marked throughout with clear subject divisions that appear to serve as the kind of mnemonic device advocated in medieval treatises on rhetoric. As such, the structure of the narrative would not only enhance the clarity of its message but would also serve as a device to aid the memory of the speaker—in this case, Chaucer's Parson. After opening with a quotation from Scripture, the Parson announces that he is going to explicate the three parts of penitence: contrition, confession and satisfaction, thus forecasting the division of his tale into three main parts. These three parts are divided and subdivided many times in order that he may discuss such secondary topics as the six causes of contrition or, falling within the latter category, the seven reasons for despair in hell. The proliferating, sometimes confusing Chinese-box structure of the tale was a target of criticism until the discovery of other penitence handbooks with a similar structure.

The second major division of the treatise, dealing with confession, also contains the description of the Seven Deadly Sins, a recital that is both vivid and lengthy enough to make the reader altogether forget the place and function of what he is reading in the larger scheme of the work. The function of these vivid descriptions of sin is, as suggested above, to awaken within those listening to or reading the tale a desire to repent. Both in the prologue to his tale and in its opening lines, the Parson has clearly delineated his intention to raise the physical metaphor of pilgrimage to a spiritual level. In the prologue, he states: "And Jhesu, for his grace, wit me sende / To shewe yow the wey, in this viage, / Of thilke parfit glorious pilgrymage / That highte Jerusalem celestial" (lines 48–51) [And may Jesus, for his grace, give me the ability / To show you the path, in this journey, / Of that perfect, glorious pilgrimage / That is called celestial Jerusalem]. His tale likewise begins with a scriptural quotation from the prophet Jeremiah that uses the words "path" and "way" as metaphors for spiritual direction. There are many spiritual paths that lead people to Christ and glory, the Parson goes on to say, and one of the best is called penitence.

Chaucer facilitates the Parson's purpose by giving the prologue a setting less particularized than those mentioned in the two preceding tales. "The CANON'S YEOMAN'S TALE" commenced near the village of BOGHTOUN UNDER BLEE and the Host calls for the next teller when they have reached BOBBE-UP-AND-DOWN, a village two miles from Canterbury. By the time the MANCIPLE has concluded his performance we might expect that the pilgrims would be even closer to their destination, but the only indication of their position is that they are approaching the edge of a village, a "thropes

ende." The atmosphere of the prologue is otherwise created by an emphasis on the declining Sun and lengthening shadows of the late afternoon, which adds a sense of urgency to the telling, something referred to by the Host when he admonishes the Parson to hurry up and get started because "the sonne wole adoun" (line 70) [the sun is sinking]. Despite this admonition, in addition to the Host's request that the Parson "beth fructuous, and that in litel space" (line 71) [be fruitful, and brief in what you say], the Parson tells a longer tale than any of the other Canterbury pilgrims.

Chaucer the Pilgrim tells the only other prose tale in the Canterbury group, "The TALE OF MELIBEE," ostensibly because he is a failure at poetry. The Parson refuses poetry on similar grounds, saying, "I kan nat geeste 'rum, ram, ruf,' by lettre, / Ne, God woot, rym holde I but litel bettre" (lines 43–44) [I can't tell a tale with rum, ram, ruf, by letter, / And rhyme, God knows, I consider but little better]. The "rum, ram, ruf" refers to the popular alliterative poetry of the northeast, where *Sir Gawain and the Green Knight* was composed, and the Parson's attitude toward such uses of language, if not clear in line 43, is spelled out for us in line 44, where he announces that he doesn't hold poetry in much esteem. His response to the Host's invitation began with a refusal to tell a fable with the explanation that fiction is wretched falsehood, an attitude given credence by reference to Saint Paul's words to Timothy. For these reasons, and because the tale is preceded by "The MANCIPLE'S TALE," which questions the safety and reliability of language at all, "The Parson's Tale" has given some readers the impression that it represents a closing down of, or turning away from the possibilities of imaginative literature, a movement that culminates in the famous Retraction (*see* CHAUCER'S RETRACTION).

Parthenopaeus In classical legend, Parthenopaeus was distinguished for his beauty and for his skill with the bow. Against the prohibition of ATALANTA, who was his mother, he became one of the SEVEN AGAINST THEBES. He was killed in the siege of THEBES, but with his dying breath commanded that his hair be cut off and sent to his mother in place of his body. Parthenopaeus' role in the war with Thebes is mentioned in Chaucer's ANELIDA AND ARCITE (line 58) and in *TROILUS AND CRISEYDE* (bk. 5, line 1503).

Parthes *See* PARTHIANS.

Parthians The people of the ancient country of Parthia, which was located southeast of the Caspian Sea. To illustrate the lack of respect people have for gamblers, the narrator of "The PARDONER'S TALE" refers to a story in which the king of the Parthians sent the king of Sparta a set of gold dice as a sort of public insult (lines 621–26), pointing to the fact that the Spartan king engaged in dicing. In the BOECE, LADY PHILOSOPHY refers to the fact that Rome, as mighty a civilization as it once was, was unknown among the Parthians. Is it likely then that the fame of a single Roman such as BOETHIUS will ever reach such places? (Book Two, Metrum 7). Her statements are part of a larger discussion of the significance of worldly reputation.

Parthonope   See PARTHENOPAEUS.

Pasiphae   In classical mythology, Pasiphae was the wife of King MINOS of CRETE. Together they had eight children, several of whom are also mentioned in Chaucer's work: ANDROGEUS, ARIADNE and PHAEDRA. To show the gods' approval of Minos as the ruler of Crete, Poseidon, the sea god, sent the king a beautiful bull to sacrifice. The king decided to keep the animal and sacrifice another in its place. As punishment, Poseidon caused Pasiphae to be inspired with an uncontrollable love for the bull. The builder/engineer DAEDALUS contrived a means for her to have intercourse with the animal, which led to the conception of the MINOTAUR, a creature half-bull and half-man who was kept in a labyrinth (also built by Daedalus) beneath the royal palace. Pasiphae's lust for the bull is one of the stories of wicked women that the WIFE OF BATH's fifth husband forced her to listen to until she revolted and made him burn his book. The Wife mentions the legend in her prologue (lines 733–36), condemning Pasiphae's desire but pronouncing it too grisly to speak of.

Patch, Howard R. (1889–1963)   Patch taught at Smith College after receiving his Ph.D. from Harvard. In *On Rereading Chaucer* (1939) a book with no scholarly apparatus, Patch gracefully offers tentative observations regarding Chaucer's humor. Patch sees humor as something based on incongruities that stop just short of the disastrous. When the incongruity leads to disaster, tragic irony takes the place of comedy, as in *TROILUS AND CRISEYDE*. The book is punctuated with Patch's own sense of observant humor. He also edited *Selections From Chaucer* (1921) with William Neilson, president of Smith College and former professor of English at Harvard. In this book Patch and Neilson condense Chaucer by cutting scenes, such as the entire garden scene in *Troilus,* which contains ANTIGONE's love song, and all of TROILUS' conversation with his sister CASSANDRA. Thus, their edition would be the last in which any careful reader would choose to read Chaucer. Perhaps Patch's most significant contribution to Chaucer studies is his book, *The Goddess Fortuna in Medieval Literature* (1927), in which he traces the origins of the goddess back to pagan Rome, and examines her manifestation in a variety of medieval texts. FORTUNE makes frequent appearances in Chaucer's work and is the presiding deity of "The MONK'S TALE," which consists of a series of

brief tragedies, all describing the life of someone whom Fortune favored and then discarded. Patch also contributed a number of articles to Chaucer scholarship, including "Chaucer and the Common People" (*Journal of English and Germanic Philology* 1930), which examines the attitudes toward the lower classes in Chaucer's work, explaining the importance Chaucer granted the idea of COMMON PROFIT (which emphasized the good of society as a whole rather than individual gain).

Patmos (Pathmos)   A small, rocky island in the southeastern portion of the Aegean Sea. Saint JOHN the Apostle was banished there by the Roman government. During his exile, he wrote the Book of Revelation. This connection is the reason that the island is mentioned in "The PRIORESS' TALE" (line 583).

Patterson, Lee (1940–)   Chaucer scholar. The recipient of a Ph.D. from Yale University, Patterson taught at Johns Hopkins and Duke University before returning to his alma mater. Patterson wrote *Chaucer and the Subject of History* (1991), one of the earliest and lengthiest attempts by an American scholar to apply contemporary literary theory to the work of an English medieval poet. In the introduction to this book, Patterson explains the theoretical background of his study, particularly emphasizing the philosophical ramifications of Freudian and Marxist readings. His own approach is most closely allied to the theoretical approach known as New Historicism, and emphasizes the dialectical relationship between the (human) subject and history. This is evidenced by his interest in the social meaning of Chaucer's texts, i.e., what meanings emerge when they are read in relation to other forms of contemporary (14th-century) discourse. Typical of Patterson's conclusions is his judgment that *TROILUS AND CRISEYDE* can be read as a "representation of a society under siege," parallel to the disputed sovereignty, conspiratorial factionalism and disastrous militarism of England in the 1380s. At the same time, he acknowledges that the poem's meditations on history are "both too general and too profound to be contained by any narrowly partisan purpose." Patterson has also written a number of articles on Chaucer's poetry, which display similar interests. For example, "'For the Wyves Love of Bathe': Feminine Rhetoric and Poetic Resolution in the *Roman de la Rose* and the *Canterbury Tales*" (*Speculum* 1983) compares the formal and rhetorical aspects of the speeches of JEAN DE MEUN's La Vielle (an allegorical figure in the *Roman* which served as a model for the WIFE OF BATH) and Chaucer's Wife. This article shows how the wife appropriates masculine rhetoric for her feminine purposes.

Paul, Saint (Paul the Apostle)   Born in Tarsus several years following the death of Christ, Paul was a Jew with

Roman citizenship who, after receiving rabbinic training, devoted himself to persecuting Christians. After seeing a vision in which the Lord spoke to him as he traveled along the road to Damascus, Paul repented his former actions and became one of the most ardent supporters of the early church. His specific mission was to carry the Christian faith to the Gentiles, which he did in his travels throughout Asia Minor and Greece. His letters to different church communities that were in the process of establishing themselves form the basis of much of Christian doctrine. Paul was arrested in A.D. 59 and taken to Rome where he was imprisoned for five years and then executed. His letters to the early churches in Corinth, Thessalonika, Philippi, Galatia, Rome, Colossae, and to his fellow apostle, Philemon, were collected and published near the end of the first century, and became part of the New Testament of the Bible. Other epistles of the New Testament, such as the Letter to the Ephesians, are attributed to Paul, but were probably written by his followers. Paul's works are mentioned or alluded to many times in *The CANTERBURY TALES*. The WIFE OF BATH refers to his First Letter to the Corinthians when discussing the value of virginity versus marriage in the prologue to her tale (see especially lines 73–76, 77–79 and 100–04). There are other, scattered references in "The FRIAR'S TALE," "The PARDONER'S TALE," and "The SUMMONER'S TALE" (all told by pilgrims whose professions involve church affiliation), but most appear in "The PARSON'S TALE," wherein the PARSON makes ample use of examples from Paul's letters to illustrate his sermon on the subject of penitence.

"Paul's" (St. Paul's Cathedral)   Paul's is a kind of nickname for ST. PAUL'S CATHEDRAL in London. It is mentioned several times in *The CANTERBURY TALES*. In the GENERAL PROLOGUE, the PARSON is described as a man who stays at home and tends to the needs of those in his parish, rather than running off to London to obtain an appointment as a chantry priest at Saint Paul's Cathedral (lines 509–10). Chantry priests were employed by wealthy patrons for the purpose of saying prayers for their patron's soul after death. In "The MILLER'S TALE," the foppish clerk ABSALOM (1) has the design of a stained glass window from Saint Paul's Cathedral carved in the leather of his shoes (line 3318). In the prologue to "The NUN'S PRIEST'S TALE," the Host (*see* Harry BAILLY) compares the speech of the MONK, whose tale has just been interrupted by the KNIGHT, to the sound of Saint Paul's bell that "clappeth loud" (lines 2780–81). Both men are tired of listening to the Monk's tales of gloom and doom.

Paulus   Lucius Aemilius Paul was a Roman consul of the second century B.C. who was given the surname Macedonicus after he defeated Perseus, the last Macedonian king, and brought an end to Rome's conflict with that region. In the BOECE, Book Two, Prosa 2, LADY PHILOSOPHY, speaking as FORTUNE, describes how Paulus wept after capturing Perseus (lines 63–66).

Paulyn   *See* DECIUS PAULINUS.

Pavia (Pavye)   Pavia, in northwestern Italy in the region of Lombardy, is the birthplace of JANUARY, the aged knight whose marital misadventures form the subject of "The MERCHANT'S TALE." During Chaucer's day the city was famous for the vices of its citizens, one of them being lechery. There is a possibility that Chaucer chose this setting for the tale because the Lombards were active in international trade, which would have made them professional rivals of the MERCHANT who tells the tale. This would provide a rationale for his cynical depiction of the characters of January, DAMIAN and MAY.

Payne, Robert O. (1924–)   American Chaucer scholar. After receiving a Ph.D. from Johns Hopkins, Payne spent 13 years at the University of Cincinnati and eight at the University of Washington before moving to City University of New York. His book, *The Key of Remembrance: A Study of Chaucer's Poetics* (1963), has long been considered a seminal study of Chaucer's literary self-consciousness, illustrating how medieval poetic theory developed out of classical poetic and rhetorical traditions. Payne sees Chaucer's poetry as an ongoing exploraion of and experimentation with the poetic traditions he inherited, and illustrates this argument with examples from the DREAM VISION poems, *TROILUS AND CRISEYDE* and *The CANTERBURY TALES*. Payne's interest in Chaucer's narrative persona is more thoroughly developed in the essay "Late Medieval Images and Self-Images of the Poet: Chaucer, Gower, Lydgate, Henryson, Dunbar" (in *Vernacular Poetics in the Middle Ages,* 1984), where he describes the various kinds of personas that appear in the works of Chaucer and his near contemporaries. Here Payne supports the generally accepted idea that the personas these poets adopt within their works reflect their poetic purposes more than their individual personalities. *Geoffrey Chaucer* (1986) is Payne's contribution to the Twayne series, written for a reader who is not a beginner in the study of literature, he says, but who may be a beginner in the study of Chaucer and Medieval literature.

Pearsall, Derek (Albert) (1931–)   Scholar, writer and editor on a wide range of medieval topics. Educated at the University of Birmingham, Pearsall eventually became a professor at Harvard. His specific Chaucer work includes the Variorum edition of "The Nun's Priest Tale" (1984) and *The Canterbury Tales: A Critical Study* (1985), which begins with traditional matters such as dating of manuscripts, proceeds to a critical discussion of the tales and ends with a chapter entitled "Audience and Reception" emphasizing, in the manner of the German reader-response theorist Wolfgang Iser, the ways in which Chaucer's rhetorical choices are directed at eliciting specific responses from his readers. Pearsall's interest in Chaucer's audience is also evidenced by an earlier article, "'The *Troilus* Frontispiece and Chaucer's Audience" (in *Yale English Studies*, 1977), which discusses a famous manuscript illustration featuring Chaucer reading to a group of courtiers. Pearsall's essay, "The English Chaucerians" (in *Chaucer and Chaucerians: Critical Studies in English Literature,* 1966) surveys Chaucer's influence on 15th-century poetry, including the work of Thomas HOCCLEVE, John Clanvowe, Stephen Hawes, John Skelton and Alexander Barclay, among others. Pearsall's more recent work includes a critical biography of Chaucer entitled *The Life of Geoffrey Chaucer* (1992), which represents a scrupulous and interesting interpretation of the facts surrounding the poet's life without some of the fanciful embroidery and speculation found in other biographies. Its first appendix features illustrations of all existing portraits of the poet along with commentary.

Peasants' Revolt of 1381   The Peasants' Revolt of 1381 began on Wednesday, June 12, when a mass of disgruntled peasants, artisans, craftsmen, some clerics and yeomen led by Wat TYLER, entered the city of London with the express intention of destroying traitors and rescuing King RICHARD II from their clutches. King Richard, who was 14 years old at the time, ruled largely through the advice and consent of a group of noblemen, chief among whom was his uncle JOHN OF GAUNT. These noblemen, it would later become obvious, were the "traitors" referred to in the peasants' proclamation. The peasants' anger at these men had several motives, the most immediate being a series of poll taxes imposed by Parliament between 1377 and 1381. The purpose of these taxes was to shift part of the burden of taxation onto the peasantry, but because they were a flat tax of a shilling per person ("poll" meant "head"), they obviously affected the poorer citizens of England much more harshly than they did those who were better off. The peasants had other grievances as well; in addition to the elimination of the poll tax, their demands included the abolition of serfdom (the condition of peasants who were bound to work the land of a particular lord and thus not free to seek a different landlord or other employment). For some reason, the peasants did not blame the king for their plight, but, rather, believed that once they would be able to meet with him, he would take their side against his "evil counselors." The more radical ideas espoused by participants in the revolt were supplied by a renegade priest, John BALL, who argued for the equality of all men and the common ownership of property.

In the course of the revolt, several groups of peasants came into the city from the surrounding countryside in Kent and Essex. Once they were inside the city walls, their anger erupted into an orgy of violence against people and property. They burned the houses of lawyers and other government officials. Because they believed that foreigners unjustly competed with them for English wages, they attacked Flemish merchants, slaughtering them in the street outside the church of St. Martin's in the VINTRY, the church Chaucer attended when he was a child and lived in that parish. They broke open several prisons, releasing the prisoners and attacking their guards. Finally, they attacked and looted the Savoy, the palace of John of Gaunt, who had been the leading force behind the establishment of the poll taxes of 1379 and 1380. Gaunt was in favor of increasing taxation to finance his wars on the Continent, an activity which did not find much favor with members of the working classes, whose only fight was a constant battle to put food on the table. No doubt they would have attacked Gaunt himself had he been at home or otherwise accessible. To his great fortune, however, he was safely in Scotland. William Sudbury, the archbishop of Canterbury, and Robert Hales, the treasurer, also targets of the peoples' anger, were not as lucky. These men, along with one of the royal tax collectors, John Legge, and Gaunt's personal physician, William Appleton, whose only crime was his relationship with Gaunt, were seized and beheaded on Tower Hill.

As noted above, chief among the peasants' demands was an audience with King Richard, and after a couple of abortive attempts Richard finally arranged one with a group led by Wat Tyler, the man credited with instigating the revolt. They met at Smithfield, a suburb of London. Tyler's demands were basically the same ones the peasants had been proclaiming from the beginning of their uprising—an end to serfdom, the elimination of class distinctions among the citizens of England (with the king being the one exception to this rule) and the division of the church's estates among the people, among other demands. All of the terms were granted, in addition to which, those who had participated in the revolt were granted pardon. Then came the order for the peasants to return home peacefully; but before the rebels could respond, an altercation broke out between Tyler and one of the king's attendants. The mayor of London, possibly afraid that Tyler was going to attack the king, seized him and dragged him from his horse. Another of the king's attendants ran the downed man through with a sword. The peasants were about to transform into yet another violent mob when Richard rode out before them, proclaiming himself their new captain. They followed him away from the scene and he finally successfully persuaded

The Peasants' Revolt, as depicted in a 14th-century manuscript. John Ball is the man on horseback; Wat Tyler, wearing a black hat, is the leader of the group on the left. From British Library Ms. Royal 18 EI f 165v. Reproduced by permission of the British Library.

them to return to their homes. Once they were gone, however, the promises that had been made were all nullified and serfdom continued to be enforced.

Where was Chaucer when these events were taking place? Although records suggest that he was present in London (he was then employed as Controller of Customs, i.e., export taxes, on wool), we have no more precise indication of his whereabouts. He may have been at his home in ALDGATE, or he could have been barricaded in the Tower with other members of the court. The only remaining record of his response consists of several lines at the end of "The NUN'S PRIEST'S TALE," itself a rather lighthearted look at the issue of FORTUNE versus free will as these forces operate on and within human nature. The lines appear in his description of a widow and her neighbors pursuing a fox who

has seized her prize rooster, CHAUNTICLEER. The noise of the chase is commented upon thus: "Certes, he Jakke Straw and his meynee / Ne made nevere shoutes half so shrille / Whan that they wolden any Flemyng kille, / As thilke day was maad upon the fox" (lines 3394–97) [Indeed, Jack Straw and his followers never shouted half so shrilly / when they desired to kill any Fleming, / as was made this day in pursuit of the fox]. It is possible, of course, that the experience influenced his verse in less direct ways.

Pedmark   *See* PENMARCH.

Pedro of Castile   A contemporary of Chaucer's, King Pedro of CASTILE in Spain was one of two "moderns" who are included in the gallery of people presented in

"The MONK'S TALE" (lines 2391–98). King Pedro, known among his enemies as Pedro the Cruel, had been deposed by his illegitimate half-brother Enrique de Trastamare when EDWARD THE BLACK PRINCE led an army into Spain to recapture the throne for him. This was in 1367, one year after Chaucer is recorded as having traveled in Spain, where he may have been sent in an embassy to Pedro's court. England's involvement in Pedro's cause may be the reason why Chaucer included the king among those whose lives the MONK uses to illustrate his idea of tragedy. Although the English expedition was successful, Pedro did not enjoy his restoration for very long: He was assassinated by Enrique in 1369. Two years later, in 1371, JOHN OF GAUNT married Pedro's daughter Costanza and thereafter considered himself Pedro's rightful heir, assuming the title of King of Castile and León. After Costanza came to England, Chaucer's wife Philippa seems to have served in her household for two years, which may have given Chaucer another reason to memorialize Pedro in a favorable manner, referring to him as "O noble, O worthy Pedro, glorie of Spayne" (line 2391), while other of his contemporaries, including the pope who excommunicated him, considered him an unprincipled tyrant.

Pegasus (Pegasee)   In classical mythology, Pegasus was a winged horse who sprang from the body of Medusa (a hideous Gorgon) when she was beheaded by the Greek hero Perseus. He immediately flew up into the heavens, where PALLAS Athena caught and tamed him. In "The SQUIRE'S TALE," King CAMBYUSKAN receives as a birthday gift a magnificent brass horse that somehow seems to be alive. Speculating about what the horse will be able to do, some of the people present expect that it may, like Pegasus, be capable of flying (line 207).

Peleus (Pelleus)   *See* PELIAS.

Pelias   In classical mythology, Pelias was the son of the sea god Poseidon (NEPTUNE) and Tyro. He and his twin brother, Neleus, were exposed by their mother on a mountainside, but were found and brought up by herdsmen. In the meantime, Tyro married Cretheus, king of Iolcus, and had three other sons. One, AESON, succeeded his father to the throne of Iolcus. When Pelias and Neleus learned the identity of their parents, they attacked Aeson, driving him out of Iolcus, and Pelias took his place as king. An oracle warned Pelias to beware of a man with one shoe. After the passage of 20 years, JASON, the son of Aeson, showed up wearing the skin of a panther and one shoe, and demanded that his father be restored to his rightful place. Pelias agreed to his request provided Jason would obtain and bring to him the Golden Fleece. While Jason was gone in search of the fleece, Pelias killed Aeson. When Jason found

out what had happened, he had his sorceress wife, MEDEA, cook up a horrible revenge for his uncle. Promising to help them restore their father's youth, Medea persuaded the daughters of Pelias to cut their father into pieces and boil him in a cauldron. Jason and Medea were driven out of Iolcus by Pelias' son, Acastus. In Chaucer's *LEGEND OF GOOD WOMEN*, the story of HYPSIPYLE, who became Jason's wife and was later deserted by him, begins by recounting Pelias' usurpation of the throne of Iolcus and his initial encounter with Jason (lines 1396–1450).

Pemond   *See* PIEDMONT.

Penalopee   *See* PENELOPE.

Pene   *See* CARTHAGE.

Penelope   In classical mythology Penelope, the wife of Odysseus (ULYSSES), remained faithful to her husband for 20 years while he was away fighting the TROJAN WAR and then trying to find his way home. The events of these years are recounted in the Greek poet HOMER'S two famous epics, the *Iliad* and the *Odyssey*. Penelope's legendary fidelity caused her to be considered an exemplar of virtuous wifehood. As such she is mentioned in the prologue to *The LEGEND OF GOOD WOMEN* (version F, lines 252–53 and version G, lines 206–07), the introduction to "The MAN OF LAW'S TALE" (line 75), and the short, unfinished poem "ANELIDA AND ARCITE," where the fidelity of ANELIDA, the queen of ARMENIA, is described as comparable (line 82). In "The FRANKLIN'S TALE," Penelope is one of the women whose example DORIGEN wishes to emulate when she confronts the decision of whether to keep her promise to the squire AURELIUS or to remain faithful to her husband, ARVERAGUS (line 1443).

Peneus (Penneus)   In classical mythology, Peneus was a river god. He was the husband of CREUSA and father of DAPHNE, the nymph who was pursued by APOLLO and transformed into a laurel. He is mentioned in "The KNIGHT'S TALE" in the story of Daphne and Apollo as it is depicted on the walls of DIANA's temple (lines 2062–64).

Penmarch   In "The FRANKLIN'S TALE," the narrator states that after his marriage to DORIGEN, the knight ARVERAGUS takes her home to a place "nat fer fro Pedmark" (line 801) [not far from Penmarch] which is later given the more specific appellation of "KAYRUDD." Kayrudd had never been satisfactorily identified, but Penmarch is located in the southwestern corner of the Cape of Brittany. Although the shoreline of the area does feature dangerous rocks like those that appear in the tale, making Dorigen anxious about her husband's sea voyage home from England, it does not have high cliffs like those Chaucer describes. The cliffs must then be Chaucer's invention.

Pepin (Pepyn) In *The ROMAUNT OF THE ROSE,* Chaucer's partial translation of the French *ROMAN DE LA ROSE,* the dreamer-narrator of the poem describes the pine tree beneath which he discovers the well of NARCISSUS as being more beautiful than any growing "sithe the tyme of Kyng Pepyn" (line 1458) [since the time of King Pepin]. King Pepin, or Pepin the Short as he was sometimes called, was the son of Charles Martel and father of Charlemagne. He was elected king of the Franks in 751, bringing an end to the Merovingian dynasty of kings and establishing that which became known as the Carolingian after its most famous member, Carolus Magnus (Charlemagne). As the *Roman de la Rose* was composed in the early part of the 13th century, the pine tree in question would be, theoretically speaking, the fairest that has been seen in five centuries.

Perce *See* PERSIA.

Percival (Perceval) A character from Arthurian Romance. Percival's earliest known appearance is in an unfinished romance composed in the 12th century by French author Chrétien de Troyes. Chrétien's *Roman de Perceval* also introduced a famous motif in Arthurian literature, that of the Grail. In this romance, Percival is a naïve country bumpkin from Wales who falls in love with the idea of knighthood after seeing some armored men riding through lands belonging to his mother. Swearing to become a knight himself, he rides out in search of Arthur's court, is knighted by the king, and thereafter meets the mysterious Fisher King, a maimed king who can only be healed when Percival asks the proper question concerning the Grail. A Middle English version of the story, *Sir Perceval of Galles,* was composed around 1350 in the north of England. This romance employs TAILRHYME, the verse form that Chaucer uses in "The TALE OF SIR THOPAS." Toward the end of "Sir Thopas," the hero of that tale is described as drinking from a well in a forest just like "the knyght sire Percyvell" (line 916) [the knight Sir Percival]. It was common practice in romance tales to compare the deeds of one famous knight to another, but the focus was hardly on something as trivial as drinking from a well. This detail would seem to relate to Chaucer's intention of parodying the romance genre in writing "The Tale of Sir Thopas."

Percyens *See* PERSIANS.

Percyvell *See* PERCIVAL.

Perkyn Revelour The one and, really, only principle character of "The COOK'S TALE" (considered by some critics to be a fragment). Perkyn is an apprentice in a cookshop in CHEAPSIDE, a district of central LONDON. He is described as being fond of singing, dancing, drinking in taverns and gambling with dice. He steals from his master to pay his gambling debts, and is eventually dismissed from his apprenticeship as a result of this behavior.

Pernaso *See* PARNASSUS.

Perotheus Minor character, friend to Duke THESEUS and to ARCITE (1) in "The KNIGHT'S TALE." Perotheus uses his influence with Theseus to gain the release of Arcite from prison. The only condition of the release is that Arcite must never return to ATHENS. The friendship of Theseus and Perotheus was, according to accounts of their lives and adventures contained in Greek mythology, a long-standing relationship based on considerable mutual devotion. Chaucer conveys the depth of their friendship by mentioning that when one of them was dead, "His felawe wente and soughte hym doun in helle" (line 1200) [His friend went and sought him down in hell].

Perrers, Alice A contemporary of Chaucer's, Alice Perrers was King EDWARD III's mistress. After the death of Edward's queen, PHILIPPA, the influence of his mistress grew until she and William Latimer, the lord chamberlain, dominated the court. Their position was protected by JOHN OF GAUNT, the king's most influential son, and they misused their power to the extent of lining their own pockets with money from the royal exchequer. Mismanagement of Edward's wars in France, in addition to the corruption at court, eventually brought opposition from Parliament. In 1376, Sir Peter de la Mare, the speaker of the Commons, with behind-the-scenes support from certain members of the nobility, attacked the corrupt courtiers and brought charges before the House of Lords. Latimer and Richard Lyons, a powerful merchant, were condemned, and Alice Perrers was driven from the court. The incident is notable for being the first recorded use of impeachment. It was not long, however, before Latimer and Perrers were back at court, reasserting their influence over the king until his death in 1377. We do not know of any specific contact Chaucer may have had with the king's mistress, but it is reasonable to assume, as does Donald Howard in his biography of Chaucer, that they knew each other. John CHAUCER, the poet's father, is on record as standing surety for Richard Lyons in 1374, guaranteeing that Lyons would cause no harm to Perrers or prevent her traveling about on her own or the king's business. Chaucer's father probably knew Lyons because they were both vintners.

Perses *See* PERSIANS.

Persia Country—present-day Iran—located in southwest Asia between the Caspian Sea and the Persian Gulf. In "The MONK'S TALE," the narrator informs readers that ZENOBIA, the warrior queen of PALMYRA, is descended from the kings of Persia (line 2252).

Persians (Persiens) Inhabitants of the country of PERSIA (modern-day Iran). In "The SUMMONER'S TALE," the narrator mentions CYRUS THE GREAT, a notable ruler of the Persians, as an example of a wrathful man (line 2079). In "The MONK'S TALE," Balthasar (BELSHAZZAR) is told that because he offended God, his reign is going to end and his realm will be divided between the Medes (people of Media, now part of northern Iran) and the Persians (line 2235). Queen ZENOBIA, whose life story follows that of Balthasar, is descended from Persian kings (line 2252), and, according to the MONK, her story is told by Persian writers (although no known Persian account of Zenobia exists).

Pertelote The rooster CHAUNTICLEER's favorite wife in "The NUN'S PRIEST'S TALE." A courtly and beautiful chicken, Pertelote advises her husband to take no heed of his frightening dream about a beast attacking him. She delivers a lengthy dissertation on the causes of dreams, which in her opinion are caused by imbalances in the bodily HUMORS. Her prototype is probably a similar hen named Pinte who appears in one of the French beast-epic cycles about the adventures of a fox named REYNARD. Like the WIFE OF BATH, Pertelote claims that women desire their husbands to be "hardy, wise, and free [generous] / And secree [discreet]" (lines 2914–15). The argument that erupts between Pertelote and her husband links this tale to the debate over women's counsel that enlivens several other of *The CANTERBURY TALES.*

Peter, Saint (Petre) The apostle Peter, also known as Simon Peter, was one of the most prominent of Jesus' 12 disciples. His brother, Andrew, was also one of the 12. Like JAMES and JOHN, Peter and Andrew were fishermen on the Sea of Galilee when they were called to Christ's ministry. The Gospel of John states that the two had previously been disciples of JOHN THE BAPTIST. Peter was the first to be called, and his name appears at the head of every list of the disciples in the New Testament. He was with Christ on a number of important occasions, including his agony in Gethsemane and his transfiguration. Peter was the first apostle to witness the Resurrection, although before the Crucifixion he denied knowing Christ three times, fulfilling his Lord's prophecy that he would do so. Because Peter was the first apostle to recognize Christ as the promised Messiah, and because Christ referred to him as "the rock" upon which he would build his church, he is considered by the Catholic Church to have been the first pope. Peter is also significant in having been the first of Christ's followers to realize the importance of spreading Christianity among the Gentiles (non-Jews).

There are numerous references to Peter in Chaucer's work, most of them in *The CANTERBURY TALES.* In the GENERAL PROLOGUE, the PARDONER carries among his relics a piece of the sail that supposedly belonged to Saint Peter when he sailed as a fisherman on the Sea of Galilee (lines 696–98). In "The MILLER'S TALE," when NICHOLAS pretends to have fainted in his room after having a vision of a second Noah's flood, JOHN THE CARPENTER tries to arouse him, invoking the aid of Saint Peter's sister (line 3486). The corrupt friar who tries to get money from poor, sick THOMAS (1) in "The SUMMONER'S TALE," says that he is diligent in the study of the words of Saint Peter and Saint Paul, following, like Peter, Christ's command to fish for men's souls (lines 1819–21). In "The TALE OF MELIBEE," Dame PRUDENCE advises her husband that he ought to take heed of Peter's words on patience, advising him to be Christlike in refraining from cursing those who would curse him, and in beating those who beat him (lines 1501–04). The advice is in this case especially appropriate, since MELIBEE's family has been physically assaulted and he is anxious to take revenge on their assailants. The PARSON quotes from Peter a number of times in his sermon on penance, noting, for instance, that whoever commits sin becomes the slave of sin (line 141). Aside from the remaining quotations from Peter in "The PARSON'S TALE," and the examples given above, all other mentions of Peter's name in Chaucer's work occur when the characters use his name in an oath.

Peter Alfonce *See* PETRUS ALPHONSE.

Petrak (Frauncyes) *See* PETRARCH, FRANCES.

Petrarch, Frances (Francesco Petrarca) Regarded by many as the father of Italian humanism, Frances Petrarch was born in Arezzo in 1304. His family migrated to Avignon in France when his father was expelled from Florence as a result of political intrigue. According to reports, this is where, in 1327, he first saw Laura, the woman who inspired his love poetry, which was to influence and shape the poetry of so many who came after him, including Shakespeare. Petrarch remained in France until 1353, but he made extended visits to his homeland. On one of these, in 1341, he was named poet laureate in Rome. From 1353 until his death 21 years later he remained in Italy, but continued to travel widely. As the father of humanism in Italy, Petrarch played a key part in reviving the study of Latin and Greek literature, but for English writers he primarily provided inspiration to the early writers of sonnets such as Thomas Wyatt, Sir Philip Sidney and Henry Howard, the earl of Surrey. Today Petrarch is best known for his "Rome Sparse," a collection of Italian lyrics that includes the long series of poems in praise of Laura. Since Petrarch and Chaucer were alive at the same time, and Chaucer was known to have been on several extended diplomatic missions in Italy, scholars have speculated that the two may have met, but there is no evidence for such a meeting. In the prologue to "The CLERK'S TALE," the narrator claims Petrarch as the source for his story of patient GRISELDA. The reference is to his *De obedientia ac fide uxoria mythologia* ("A fable of wifely obedience and faithfulness"), which is actually a translation of one of the tales featured in BOCCACCIO's *Decameron*. In "The MONK'S TALE," the narrator claims that the source for his story of Queen ZENOBIA is Petrarch, but it is actually taken from Boccaccio's *De claris mulieribus* ("Of virtuous women").

Petro, King of Cipre   *See* PIERRE DE LUSIGNAN.

Petrus Alphonse   Petrus Alphonse is the Latin name of the physician and scholar Pedro Alphonso, who was born to Jewish parents in Aragon in 1062. His Jewish name was Moshe Sephardi. He took the name Pedro Alphonso in honor of his godfather, Alfonso VII of Castile, whose physician he was. The work for which he is remembered is primarily didactic, such as his *Contra Judaeos,* a polemic against Judaism and Islam, and his *Disciplina clericalis,* a collection of tales that was meant to function as a guidebook for clerics. In Chaucer's "TALE OF MELIBEE," Dame PRUDENCE quotes from the latter work when she advises her husband to take his time in getting revenge (line 1053) and refrain from making friends with his enemies (line 1189), and gives him various other pieces of advice on how to deal with the men who robbed him and assaulted his family.

Phaedra   In classical mythology, Phaedra was the daughter of King MINOS of CRETE and his wife, PASIPHAE. She was the sister of ARIADNE. According to legend, she became THESEUS' wife after the death of his first wife, Antiope. Phaedra fell in love with her stepson, Hippolytus and when he rejected her she falsely accused him of wanting to be her lover to her jealous husband. The sea god Poseidon sent a monster from the sea to frighten the horses of Hippolytus as he rode in his chariot, and the young man was killed in the wreck that followed. Phaedra committed suicide in remorse. In Chaucer's *LEGEND OF GOOD WOMEN,* Phaedra is the youngest sister of Ariadne. Theseus takes both of the women with him after defeating the MINOTAUR, but abandons Ariadne, whom he had promised to marry, because her sister is more beautiful (lines 2169–78). The story also appears, in an abbreviated version, in *The HOUSE OF FAME,* where the narrator compares

Theseus' desertion of Ariadne to AENEAS' betrayal of Queen DIDO (lines 405–26).

Phaeton   In classical mythology, Phaeton was the son of Helios (Phoebus APOLLO in Roman mythology) and the nymph Clymene. He grew up with his mother and her husband, Merops, the king of Ethiopia, believing himself to be the latter's son. But after learning the truth from his mother, Phaeton traveled to the palace of the sun and demanded the privilege of driving the sun's chariot for a single day. Helios granted his request, but gave him very specific instructions, including warnings about the dire consequences that could result from not following them. (According to one version, Phaeton did not have his father's permission to drive the chariot, but stole it with the aid of his sisters.) At first his journey went well, but Phaeton lost control of the fiery horses, strayed from the beaten track, and drove so near the earth that it was scorched. Zeus (JUPITER) struck Phaeton with a thunderbolt and hurled his body into the river Eridanus. In *The HOUSE OF FAME,* the EAGLE who ferries Chaucer into the heavens speaks of the legend that the MILKY WAY was created when Phaeton lost control of his father's horses as they sped through the atmosphere (lines 940–59). In book 5 of *TROILUS AND CRISEYDE,* TROILUS feels that the days dividing him from his reunion with CRISEYDE are so long that Phaeton must be driving his father's chariot again, upsetting the natural rhythm of time (lines 659–65).

Phanie (Phanye)   In classical mythology, Phanie was the daughter of King CROESUS of LYDIA. When her proud father dreamed that he was in a tree, being washed by JUPITER and receiving a towel from Phoebus (*see* APOLLO), he asks his daughter for an interpretation. She tells him that the tree signifies the gallows and the operations of the two gods the rain that will wash him and the sun that will dry him as he hangs there. The story is told in the brief biography of Croesus that appears in Chaucer's "MONK'S TALE" (lines 2742–56).

Pharaoh (Pharoa; Pharoo)   Pharaoh was the title given to the ancient hereditary kings of Egypt. The title was used in the Old Testament to refer to several Egyptian rulers who are not differentiated from each other by name, although clearly they are not one person. The Pharaoh referred to in Chaucer's poetry is probably Amenhotep IV, who ruled during the 18th dynasty in the 14th century B.C. He is believed to be the one whose dreams were interpreted by JOSEPH in the biblical Book of Genesis. In *The BOOK OF THE DUCHESS,* the poet claims to have had a dream so wonderful that not even Joseph, who served the Pharaoh of Egypt in such kind, could interpret it (lines 280–83). This sentiment is echoed in *The HOUSE OF FAME* (lines 515–16). In "The NUN'S PRIEST'S TALE," the learned rooster CHAUNTICLEER uses the story of Joseph and Pharaoh as evidence that dreams do indeed sometimes speak of the future (lines 3132–35), and the narrator of "The PARSON'S TALE" affirms that God blesses those sinners who repent just as he blessed Pharaoh (lines 441–42).

Phasipha   *See* PASIPHAE.

Phebus   *See* APOLLO.

Phebuseo   A Trojan hero who seems to have been invented by Chaucer for his poem *TROILUS AND CRISEYDE.* He is not mentioned in Chaucer's source for the poem, BOCCACCIO's *FILOSTRATO.* In Chaucer's poem, Phebuseo fights to save ANTENOR from the Greeks (book 4, lines 50–54). After Antenor is captured, the Greeks offer to release him in exchange for CRISEYDE.

Phedra   *See* PHAEDRA.

Pheton   *See* PHAETHON.

Phidon   According to Saint JEROME, Phidon was a prominent Athenian of the fifth century B.C. whose daughters were forced to dance naked over their father's corpse by the men who executed him. They drowned themselves in a well to preserve their virginity. In "The FRANKLIN'S TALE," DORIGEN places Phidon's daughters among the virtuous women that she wishes to emulate when tempted to betray her husband (lines 1369–78).

Philip (Philippe)   In the story of ALEXANDER THE GREAT that appears in "The MONK'S TALE," the narrator notes that Alexander is the son of Philip (line 2656). This refers to Philip II, king of MACEDONIA during the fourth century B.C. Because the Greek city-states to the south of his kingdom had been so weakened by wars among themselves, Philip was able during his lifetime to gain dominion over all of them save Sparta. Philip was murdered as the sequel to a family brawl. His son and successor, Alexander, expanded the Macedonian Empire into PERSIA, annexing the whole ancient Near Orient from the Nile to the Indus Rivers.

Philippa of Hainault   The queen of EDWARD III, Philippa was from Hainault, a small Flemish-speaking principality on the French border. The two were married in 1328 when she was 14 and Edward was 16 years old. Philippa was very popular with the English people, something that is reflected by the large number of female children given her name during the period. She also enjoyed a close relationship with her husband, often accompanying him on his travels and on military expeditions, even when she was pregnant. She was a great patron of the arts and of learning. Queen's College at Oxford University was founded with her money. She also became the patron of Jean FROISSART, a poet from her native land, appointing him her secretary. Froissart's *Chronicles,* written during Edward's reign, provide the most complete (if not the least biased) record of events for the time period. On the negative side, Philippa seems to have been a poor manager of money, accruing large debts about which there was some protest. She bore five sons who survived into adulthood, all having politically influential lives. EDWARD THE BLACK PRINCE was a famous warrior and the father of the next monarch, RICHARD II, whose disastrous reign saw the beginning of a long civil war between family factions. JOHN OF GAUNT, who became the duke of Lancaster through his marriage to the duchess BLANCHE, was father to Henry Bolingbroke, who would challenge Richard's fitness to rule and ultimately usurp the throne as HENRY IV. Philippa's youngest son, THOMAS OF WOODSTOCK, also antagonized Richard, and his murder was considered by some to have been carried out at Richard's instigation.

Chaucer began his career as a courtier during the reign of Edward, first serving as a page in the household of Elizabeth, countess of Ulster and wife to Philippa's second son, Lionel, duke of Clarence. In 1359, Chaucer accompanied Lionel on a military expedition to France, where he was captured and subsequently ransomed. Sometime in 1360 Chaucer joined the household staff of Queen Philippa and King Edward, serving as *valettus* to the king. Chaucer's marriage to Philippa Pan may have been arranged by Queen Philippa who, if Philippa Pan was Philippa Roet of Hainault, was the young woman's guardian. Queen Philippa died in 1369, just after the death of Prince Lionel.

Philippians (Philipenses)   In the New Testament, Philippians is one of the four shorter epistles, or letters, written by the apostle Paul while he was in prison in Rome. The title of the epistle is taken from the town of Philippi in MACEDONIA, where, according to tradition, Paul founded the first Christian church on European soil. Paul's letter to the Philippians is concerned primarily with exhortations to his fellow Christians to remain faithful and to work diligently toward establishing a stronger personal relationship with Christ, which will help them overcome differences among themselves. In "The PARSON'S TALE," Chaucer's PARSON quotes from Philippians to demonstrate the sinfulness of taking the name of Christ in vain by swearing (lines 598–99).

Philistines (Philistiens)   A tribal group mentioned in the Old Testament as occupiers of the land of

Palestine, also known as CANAAN. The Philistines are believed to have come to this area from the island of Crete in the MEDITERRANEAN SEA. During the early years of their occupation they maintained peaceful relations with the Jewish tribes living in the area. In the 12th century B.C., five cities—Ashdod, Ashkelon, Ekron, Gath and Gaza—came under the control of the Philistines, who shortly thereafter began to attack their Israelite neighbors. Their success in warfare was primarily attributable to two things: superior iron weaponry and a more centrally organized government and military. The biblical hero SAMSON once visited a Philistine "harlot" in Gaza, and, upon leaving the city, tore down its gate and carried it away in an apparent effort to intimidate the Philistines who were plotting to kill him. When he fell in love with DELILAH, the Philistines convinced her to help them capture him by enticing him into revealing the secret of his great strength. The story of Samson is related in Chaucer's "MONK'S TALE" (lines 2015–94), where his deeds to spite the Philistines are mentioned.

Philoctetes   In classical mythology, Philoctetes was the man who piloted the *Argo*, the ship used by the adventurer JASON when he and the Argonauts sailed out in search of the Golden Fleece. His role in the adventure is mentioned in the story of HYPSIPYLE that appears in Chaucer's *LEGEND OF GOOD WOMEN* (line 1459).

Philomela   In classical mythology, Philomela was the daughter of Pandion, king of Athens, and sister to PROCNE. Procne married TEREUS, king of Thrace, and after five years of separation from her family, convinced her husband to bring Philomela to Thrace for a visit. After successfully negotiating with her father, promising to take good care of her and to send Procne back to Athens to visit in return, Tereus with Philomela set sail for Thrace. When they arrived, unable to control his lust for her, Tereus led Philomela to a dark cave inside a forest, where he raped her. Then, to make sure she would never tell anyone what had happened, he cut out her tongue. Finally, he imprisoned her in a castle where he could use her whenever and however he wanted to, and returned home to his wife, saying that Philomela died back in Athens. During her imprisonment in the castle, deprived of tools with which to write, Philomela contrived another way to tell the story of her victimization by Tereus: She wove it into a tapestry, which she managed to convey to her sister. Learning the secret of Philomela's fate, Procne hurried to find her and the two plotted to take revenge against Tereus by killing his son Itys, cooking him into a stew, and serving him to his father. After discovering that he had eaten his son, Tereus pursued the women, but they escaped him by being transformed into birds, Philomela into a nightingale.

Chaucer tells the story of Philomela and her sister in *The LEGEND OF GOOD WOMEN* (lines 2228–2393), but he leaves out the part about their revenge against Tereus, presumably because his intention was to show the victimization of women by men. Naturally, he would not want to include material that might prejudice the readers' opinion against his protagonists. He treats the story of MEDEA, who also murdered her children, similarly. The appearance of several nightingales in *TROILUS AND CRISEYDE* would seem to allude to Philomela.

Philomene   *See* PHILOMELA.

Philosopher's Stone   *See* ALCHEMY.

Philostrate   The alias that ARCITE (1) adopts in "The KNIGHT'S TALE" when he returns to ATHENS to pursue his infatuation with EMILY. In Chaucer's main source for this poem, the *TESEIDA* of BOCCACCIO, Arcite assumes a different name, Penteo. Chaucer probably took the name Philostrate from Boccaccio's *Il FILOSTRATO*, the primary source of *TROILUS AND CRISEYDE*. The term means "army lover," but Chaucer may have taken it to mean "overcome by love."

Philotetes   *See* PHILOCTETES.

Phisic   *Phisic* is the title given to Aristotle's *Physics* in the *BOECE*, Chaucer's translation of BOETHIUS' *Consolation of Philosophy*. When Boethius asks LADY PHILOSOPHY to explain whether or not anything may occur by chance, or if all things are controlled by divine Providence, she answers that Aristotle's *Physics* provides an admirable solution to the question by explaining the mechanism by which seemingly chance events occur as a result of remote causes (Book Five, Prosa 1, lines 63 ff).

Phisiologus   *See* PHYSIOLOGUS.

Phitonissa   Phitonissa is the name Chaucer gives to the Witch of Endor who, in the Old Testament (1 Samuel:28), was consulted by King Saul before he led the Israelites in battle against the invading PHILISTINES. Saul asked for the witch's help because he received no response from God regarding the outcome of the impending battle. She raised the spirit of the prophet SAMUEL, who prophesied victory for the Philistines and the death of Saul and his sons. In the Vulgate Bible, the witch is referred to as a woman with a python, which would appear to be the source of the name Phitonissa. She is mentioned in "The FRIAR'S TALE" when the devil explains to the summoner that fiends like himself sometimes animate dead bodies and speak through them, just like the spirit of Samuel was animated by the Phitonissa when it spoke to Saul (lines 1507–10).

Phitoun   *See* PYTHON.

Phlegethon   In classical mythology, Phlegethon is a fiery river that flowed through the underworld. In *TROILUS AND CRISEYDE*, when TROILUS thanks PANDARUS for helping him woo CRISEYDE, he tells Pandarus that he has raised his soul from Phlegethon and carried it up into heaven.

Phoebus   *See* APOLLO.

Phyllis   In classical mythology, Phyllis was a Greek princess who ruled the kingdom of THRACE after the death of her father, Lycurgus. When DEMOPHON was shipwrecked on the shores of her country as he sailed home from the TROJAN WAR, she showed him generous hospitality, which included the means to continue his voyage. The two were married, but Demophon left for his home in ATHENS alone, promising to send for Phyllis when he had prepared a suitable reception. When he failed to return, Phyllis hanged herself and was transformed into an almond tree. Chaucer tells the story of Phyllis and Demophon in *The LEGEND OF GOOD WOMEN* (lines 2394–2561). He uses Phyllis as an example of women who are faithful in love but suffer betrayal by the men with whom they form alliances.

"Physician's Tale, The"   This story of the extreme measures a father takes to preserve his daughter's virginity may seem distasteful to modern readers.

SUMMARY

A Roman knight named VIRGINIUS has an only daughter, named VIRGINIA, who is outstanding in virtue and beauty. The narrator in particular makes much of her chastity and the diligence with which she guards it. One day shortly after her 14th birthday, she and her mother are walking through town on their way to a temple when a man named APIUS, a judge by profession, sees her and decides that he must possess her sexually. Realizing that she will never willingly submit to his desire, the judge decides to pursue his goal by other means. He bribes a man named CLAUDIUS (1) to appear in court and accuse Virginius of having stolen a slave woman from his own household, claiming that Virginia is the woman. Despite Virginius' objections, Apius rules in favor of Claudius and orders Virginius to surrender his daughter. When Virginius returns home, he tells his daughter what has transpired and explains that she must either die or be shamed. Without waiting for her response, he determines that she shall die. Virginia begs him for some time to consider her fate, but soon resolves that she ought to die rather than lose her chastity. She falls down in a faint and her father cuts off her head, which he then presents to the judge. Apius condemns her father to be hanged for what he has done, but a huge crowd of people flock to the knight's aid. Somehow they know that Apius is responsible for the tragedy, and Apius is condemned to be hanged instead of Virginius. The people also want to kill Claudius for his part in the plot, but because Virginius intercedes for him, Claudius is merely banished.

COMMENTARY

The immediate source for this tale, as for so much of Chaucer's work, is JEAN DE MEUN'S *ROMAN DE LA ROSE*, where the story of Virginia is told to illustrate the corruption of justice without love. Both Chaucer and Jean de Meun acknowledge that the tale originally comes from a historical chronicle written by the Roman author LIVY (59 B.C.–A.D. 17), though Chaucer probably possessed no personal knowledge of the original source. John GOWER also included this tale in his *CONFESSIO AMANTIS*.

"The Physician's Tale" is believed to have been written either when Chaucer first began composing *The CANTERBURY TALES*, or when he was writing the work that gives numerous examples of suffering and virtuous women, *The LEGEND OF GOOD WOMEN*. Most scholars give it a probable date of no earlier than 1386 because it is not mentioned in the prologue to *The Legend of Good Women* which contains a list of what Chaucer has written so far. And since Chaucer's text shows no familiarity with Gower's rendering of the tale published in 1390, it seems likely that Chaucer's version was written before this date.

The genre of the tale appears to be a hybrid of two forms, the moral exemplum and the historical tale. The events it relates are ultimately derived from a historical source (Livy's *Historia*), and they are used to point up a moral attached to the end of the story: that sin always gets its reward (i.e., punishment). The problem with this moral is that, in this story, goodness is punished also. Virginia dies because of her beauty and virtue just as surely as Apius dies for his sins. For this and other reasons, some scholars (BREWER, MUSCATINE and DONALDSON) have argued that the tale is rather poorly constructed, from the standpoint of both narrative structure and character motivation. Others (Middleton, McCall, ALLEN and Moritz) see the tale as one dealing with issues of moral complexity and the problems arising from the same. Examining the tale in the context of the other Canterbury tales appears to support the latter view.

Although the order of the tales in the different manuscripts varies somewhat (*see* Manuscripts under the main entry for *The Canterbury Tales*), and "The Physician's Tale" is one whose position in that order is less than certain, it nevertheless has considerable relevance to the tale which customarily precedes it, "The

FRANKLIN'S TALE," concerning DORIGEN and ARVERAGUS. Like "The Physician's Tale," "The Franklin's Tale" features a woman who must make the choice between shame and honor. Dorigen's promise to give her love to (i.e., have sex with) the squire AURELIUS if he can remove the rocks from the sea off the coast of BRITTANY is made in a lighthearted tone; and her response to his accomplishing the feat—she contemplates but then puts off suicide—renders the mood of the tale less urgent than that of Virginius and his daughter, and in fact helps to point up Virginius' fatal flaw. While Dorigen and her husband act and react with patience and trust in God's good grace, Virginius rushes home to behead his daughter as soon as he receives the corrupt judge's verdict. Only five lines later, a crowd of 1,000 people comes rushing to Virginius' aid, proving that his daughter's death was needless, if only her father had been as patient and willing to trust in Providence as were Dorigen and her husband Arveragus. Granted, the setting of "The Physician's Tale" is pre-Christian Rome; however, references to a Christian framework are numerous within the introductory verses where Virginia's virtue and beauty are described, and not without representation in the narrative portion of the tale (for example, upon her death Virginia says "Blissed be God that I shal dye a mayde!" (line 248) [May God be blessed that I shall die a virgin!]. Therefore it seems reasonable to conclude that Christian morality should be in operation.

Even within a Christian framework, it is still possible to read the relationship between the Franklin's and Physician's tales another way. For one thing, "The Physician's Tale" is offered as a history, a story of events that really happened, whereas "The Franklin's Tale" is a self-confessed romance, on top of which it is also somewhat naively idealistic. Perhaps Chaucer's "Physician's Tale" was simply intended as a realistic account of how human nature was likely to respond, at this point in history, to circumstances in which a woman's honor was threatened with sexual pollution. Or, to take a less cynical view, the tale of Virginia at least shows that the problem presented and happily resolved in "The Franklin's Tale" has more than one possible solution.

This tale also links up with a problem examined over and over again in various tales within the Canterbury group, that of the suffering of the innocent in a moral universe. Some other tales that grapple with this theme are "The SECOND NUN'S TALE," "The PRIORESS' TALE" and "The CLERK'S TALE." In the first two of these, however, Christian martyrdom is offered as justification and reward for that suffering, and in the latter, GRISELDA's fortitude ultimately wins WALTER's trust and repentance for the way he has treated her in the past. Virginia's death seems, in contrast, both pathetic and empty, as if a void has opened up and swallowed her, leaving no positive aftereffects, such as conversion or repentance or even the report of her bliss in heaven, to balance out the tragedy of her premature death on Earth.

Physics   *See* PHISIC.

Physiognomy   The medieval "science" of divining the character and mental qualities of individuals based on their physical features. In *Chaucer and the Medieval Sciences,* Walter Clyde CURRY draws on various medieval sources to show how Chaucer used theories of physiognomy in creating the pilgrims who are described in the GENERAL PROLOGUE TO *THE CANTERBURY TALES.* For example, the REEVE's pale complexion and slender legs are considered to be signs of a strong libido, a characteristic confirmed by his admission that his sexual appetite is unsuitably strong for his advanced age. Similarly, the short arms and broad shoulders of the MILLER indicate ignorance and a tendency to wicked behavior.

Physiologus   *Physiologus* was the name given to a Latin bestiary that contained approximately 50 descriptions of various real and imaginary animals, birds and stones. The descriptions were interpreted allegorically to illustrate Christian doctrine. The Greek original from which the work takes its name dates from sometime between the second and fourth centuries A.D. "Physiologus" may have been the name of the work's original author or compiler. In "The NUN'S PRIEST'S TALE," the narrator describes PERTELOTE and her sisters singing more merrily than the mermaids described in *Physiologus* (lines 3268–72).

Picardy   An old French province including what are now the departments of Somme, parts of Pas-de-Calais, Aisne and Oise in northern France. In the GENERAL PROLOGUE to *The CANTERBURY TALES,* Chaucer tells us that the SQUIRE has been on military campaigns to FLANDERS, ARTOIS and Picardy (line 86). The references indicate that the Squire's military experience has kept him fairly close to home, in contrast to his father, who has made forays into LITHUANIA, PRUSSIA and TURKEY.

Pictagoras (Pictigoras)   *See* PYTHAGORAS.

Piedmont   The Piedmont that is referred to in Chaucer's work is a region of northwestern Italy on the borders of Switzerland and France. The town of SALUZZO, which forms the setting of "The CLERK'S TALE," is located in the region of Piedmont. The area is described in the proem of "The Clerk's Tale" (lines 43–52).

Pierides   In the prologue to "The MAN OF LAW'S TALE," the narrator says that when giving his performance, he does not want to be compared to the Muses that men call "Pierides" (lines 91–92). The name is taken from the birthplace of these goddesses, Pieria. The SERGEANT OF THE LAW would appear to have confused them with the daughters of King Pierus, who challenged the Muses to a singing contest and, losing, were transformed into magpies.

Pierre de Lusignan Pierre de Lusignan, or "Petro, kyng of Cipre" (i.e., Cyprus), as Chaucer's MONK calls him, is one of three contemporaries whose "tragic" lives are recalled in "The MONK'S TALE." Besides these three, the MONK's exempla are from classical myth and the Bible or from ancient history. The stanza dedicated to King Pierre recalls his most famous military exploit, the capture of Alexandria in 1365, and laments his assassination by those who were jealous of his chivalric exploits. Pierre visited England in 1363 and was entertained by JOHN OF GAUNT, one of King EDWARD III's sons, at the Savoy Palace, where Chaucer, a page in the household of Lionel, duke of Clarence, may have caught a glimpse of him. It is also possible that Chaucer knew of him only through GUILLAUME DE MACHAUT's *Prise d'Alexandrie*, which celebrated his famous victory.

Piers, Daun Daun, or "Sir" Piers is the name of the MONK who appears in the GENERAL PROLOGUE to *The CANTERBURY TALES* and who participates in the tale-telling contest. His name is not mentioned until the KNIGHT (1) interrupts his performance, asking him to tell a different tale (line 2792).

Piers Alfonce *See* PETRUS ALPHONSE.

Piers Plowman Considered by many to be the greatest poem of the Alliterative Revival, which took place in the 14th century in England, *Piers Plowman* is a religious allegory by William LANGLAND. In a series of DREAM VISION, the poem traces the dreamer-narrator's search for answers to many important philosophical and religious questions, the most important of which seems to be, "How may I save my soul?" Langland's famous vision of the "Field of Folk" that appears in the poem's prologue features a description of 14th-century English society, focusing on its failure to live up to the ideals espoused by Christianity. Although Chaucer seems to have drawn upon the descriptions of the people in this portion of the poem for some of the pilgrims in the GENERAL PROLOGUE to his *CANTERBURY TALES*, the tone of the two works could not be further apart. While they both belong to the genre of ESTATES SATIRE, Chaucer's satire seems most of the time rather mild and almost playful, displaying a rather indulgent attitude toward its subject. Langland, on the other hand, expresses savage indignation in describing the corruption of those who

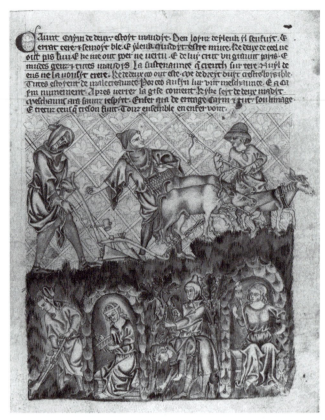

Peasants at work in the fields and at home From British Library Ms. Add 47682 f 6. Reproduced by permission of the British Library.

occupy positions of power and influence in both the secular and the clerical realms.

Pigmalion *See* PYGMALION.

pilgrimage During the medieval period, the concept of pilgrimage was primarily of a journey to a shrine or holy place. Despite this ostensible purpose, however, many people seem to have considered them in the same spirit in which we consider vacations. People went on pilgrimages both to places near their own homes and to faraway lands. Surprisingly large numbers, considering the expense and time involved, traveled to the holy city of Jerusalem, and numerous written accounts of these journeys still exist. Storytelling was known to be a popular way of passing the time on these journeys, so the frame that Chaucer created for his *CANTERBURY TALES* had its counterpart in reality. The journey that Chaucer's pilgrims take, to the shrine of Saint THOMAS À BECKET, would lead them along a familiar and well-traveled route leading southeastward from LONDON to the city of CANTERBURY, some 50-odd miles away. From a religious standpoint, every pilgrimage symbolically represented the course of human life, the journey of the soul from its earthly to its heavenly home. The conclusion of *The Canterbury Tales* reveals that this idea also plays an important role in our understanding of the literary work.

Piramus   *See* PYRAMUS.

Pirois (Piros)   *See* PYROIS.

Pirrus   *See* PYRRHUS.

Pisa   An Italian city in the region of TUSCANY on the Arno River. In the series of tragedies that make up "The MONK'S TALE," Chaucer tells the story of Count UGOLINO OF PISA, imprisoned along with his children by the bishop of Pisa (lines 2407–62). The story, based on an account in DANTE's *Inferno*, is considered to be the finest of those related by the MONK because of the pathos with which the plight of the count and his children is described.

Pisces   One of the 12 divisions of the zodiac, an imaginary belt in the heavens extending for about eight degrees on either side of the apparent path of the Sun and including the paths of the Moon and the principal planets. The zodiac is divided into 12 equal parts, or signs, each named for a different constellation. Pisces is the 12th sign (*see* diagram under ASTROLOGY), which, in Chaucer's day, the Sun entered on February 12. The constellation of Pisces, which is supposed to represent two linked fishes, each one swimming in the opposite direction, appears in the sky between Aquarius and Aries. Chaucer most often employs astrological terms such as this to indicate the approximate date of a narrative event or to show the passage of time. Occasionally, he uses them to call attention to planetary influences. In "The SQUIRE'S TALE," for example, when it is time for music and dancing to follow King CAMBYUSKAN's birthday feast, the narrator notes that VENUS is at her zenith—her position of greatest influence—in "the Fyssh" (i.e., Pisces); thus, the goddess of love presides over the dance in which the king's daughter, CANACEE, is partnered by the stranger knight who brought the exotic gifts that had been presented to her father and herself during the feast (line 273). The fact that Venus was considered to be exalted (to have special potency or power) in Pisces would seem to hint at the development of romance between Canacee and the knight, but the SQUIRE's performance goes off on so many tangents before it is interrupted by the FRANKLIN, that we never know.

Pize   *See* PISA.

Placebo   Minor character in "The MERCHANT'S TALE." Placebo is a kind of yes-man to his brother JANUARY, the aged knight who decides to marry a young woman. While January's other brother, JUSTINUS, advises against the marriage, Placebo, whose name derives from the Latin *placebo*, which means "I shall please," simply provides validation for every idea or course of action January decides upon. Placebo is the type of flatterer warned against in "The TALE OF MELIBEE" and "The PARSON'S TALE."

Plague   *See* BLACK DEATH.

Plato (Platon)   Greek philosopher of the fifth century B.C. He was born in Athens in 427 to noble parents. Although his real name was Aristocles, he was nicknamed Plato by one of his teachers because of his broad face and physical build. He became a pupil of the great philosopher SOCRATES at the age of 20 and remained so until Socrates' tragic death. The most distinguished of Socrates' pupils, he also drew upon other sources in formulating his ideas, including the teachings of PARMENIDES and the Pythagoreans. He was a prolific writer. Some of his most notable writings, all in dialogue form, are the *Apology*, the *Protagoras*, the *Phaedrus*, the *Timaeus* and the *Republic*.

Plato's philosophical ideas were similar to those of his master, Socrates. He disputed the theory of reality as chaos, substituting a view of the universe as ultimately spiritual and purposeful. He aimed to refute the Sophist ideas of relativism and skepticism, and to provide a foundation for ethics. In order to realize these aims, he developed his doctrine of Ideas, wherein he admitted the relativity and flux of the physical world but argued that this is only part of the picture. The other part, he believed, was a spiritual realm composed of eternal forms, or Ideas, which only the mind can conceive. Each of these Ideas was the pattern of some particular class of objects or relation between objects on Earth. For instance, there woud be Ideas of man, tree, color, beauty, justice, etc. These were not, moreover, invented by the mind of man, but were spiritual things that had always been in existence. Ruling over all Ideas was the Idea of the Good, the active cause (creator) and guiding purpose of the universe. Things we perceive in the physical world, things subject to change and decay, were only imperfect copies of these superior forms, Ideas.

Plato's ethical and religious beliefs were strongly influenced by his doctrine of Ideas. While believing that true virtue has its basis in knowledge, he admitted that knowledge derived from the senses is limited and even flawed. For that reason, he argued that true virtue consisted in the apprehension of the eternal Ideas of goodness and justice. The body he regarded as a hindrance to the mind, but he did not reject the appetites and emotions altogether, believing rather that they should simply be subordinated to reason and the intellect.

During the Middle Ages, the *Timaeus* was the most widely known of Plato's dialogues. A fourth-century Latin translation including commentary was made by Calcidius, and became the basis of medieval Platonism. Chaucer's work was influenced by Plato's ideas, both directly and indirectly. BOETHIUS' *Consolation of Philosophy*, which Chaucer translated into Middle English as the BOECE, is deeply indebted to Plato's philosophy, as the following examples (which are not exhaustive) show. In Book One, Prosa 4, LADY PHILOSOPHY states that Plato offers confirmation of her teachings and notes that nations would be much happier if their rulers studied wisdom (lines 26–30). This idea is taken from Plato's *Republic*. In Book Three, Prosa 9, Lady Philosophy reminds Boethius of Plato's injunction to ask for God's help, even in small matters (lines 189–94). This notion derives from the *Timaeus*, whose opening lines evidently served as the source for Metrum 9 of Book three, which is a hymn of praise to the divine creator of heaven and Earth whose Idea of the Good served as prototype for all created matter. Plato's doctrine of reincarnation of the eternal soul also appears in Book Three, Metrum 11 (lines 43–47). Of Chaucer's original works, *The HOUSE OF FAME* was the most strongly influenced by Plato. He is the ultimate authority for the idea that the air is populated with different kinds of spirits or demons ("eyryssh bestes"), which are pointed out to Chaucer by the EAGLE as he is ferried through the atmosphere to FAME's palace. In the same poem, Plato and ARISTOTLE are both given as sources for the idea of "natural inclination" which the eagle offers to explain how sound rises through the air to Fame's palace (lines 729–60), although Chaucer's direct sources for the information were probably Boethius and DANTE. A famous line from the *Timaeus*, "the wordes moote be cosyn to the dede" [the words must be cousin to the deed] is quoted in the GENERAL PROLOGUE to *The CANTERBURY TALES* (line 742) as Chaucer states his reasons for recording the tales as they were spoken. The phrase is echoed in "The MANCIPLE'S TALE": "the word moot cosyn be to the werkyng" (line 208) (same translation as above), as the MANCIPLE apologizes to his audience for using a word like "leman" (lover) in speaking of a woman who was unfaithful to her husband.

Pleiades *See* ATLAS' DAUGHTERS.

Pleyndamour This knight is mentioned in Chaucer's "TALE OF SIR THOPAS," together with several other heroes of popular English metrical romances such as GUY OF WARWICK. As of yet, however, there appears to be no existing romance featuring a hero of this name, aside from a brief episode in Thomas Malory's *Morte D'Arthur,* where a knight named Sir Playne de Amoris is overthrown by another knight named La Cote Male

Tayle. Most scholars believe that the name, which could be translated "Complaint concerning Love," was invented by Chaucer.

Pleynt of Kynd This is another title for ALAIN DE LILLE's *De planctu Naturae* (Complaint of Nature).

Plowman, the The Plowman's portrait follows that of his brother, the PARSON, in the GENERAL PROLOGUE TO *THE CANTERBURY TALES*. Like his brother, the Plowman is an admirable figure, selflessly devoted, in this case, to the ideal of hard work. Living in peace and perfect charity, loving God first and then his neighbor as much as himself, he displays a willingness to work for nothing if to do so were possible. Both his attire and his mount give further evidence of the Plowman's humility. He is dressed in a tabard—a loose, sleeveless tunic typically worn by workmen—and rides a mare. The Plowman does not participate in the pilgrims' tale-telling contest.

Pluto In classical mythology, Pluto, known to the Greeks as Hades, was the ruler of the underworld to which souls traveled after death. Because he lived beneath the earth, and despite the fact that he was feared because of his association with the dead, Pluto was also looked upon as the bestower of riches derived from the earth such as gold, silver and jewels. Pluto did not often leave the underworld, so there are not many myths about him. On one occasion when he did rise to the surface, VENUS ordered her son CUPID to shoot the god with one of his love-darts. The first maiden he saw after his heart was pierced was PROSERPINA, the daughter of Demeter (CERES), who was gathering lilies and violets in a meadow near Mount Aetna. Smitten with love for her, he carried her off to his realm beneath the earth and made her his queen.

In *The HOUSE OF FAME*, the image of the poet Claudian stands on a pillar of sulfur because in telling the story of Pluto and Proserpina, he "bar up al the fame of helle" (line 1510–11) [bore all the fame of hell]. In *TROILUS AND CRISEYDE*, Pandarus swears to look out for CRISEYDE's best interests by all the gods in heaven, or else, he says, let him be sent to hell with Pluto, just like TANTALUS (lines 590–93). In "The KNIGHT'S TALE," the goddess DIANA is depicted on the walls of her temple with her eyes cast down toward Pluto's dark region (lines 2081–82), and when EMILY prays to the goddess to preserve her virginity, she calls her "Queen of the regne of Pluto derk and lowe" (line 2299) [Queen of the realm of Pluto, dark and low]. Emily refers to her by this title because of Diana's traditional representation as one of a trio of related goddesses represented in the heavens by Luna, on Earth by Diana and in the underworld by Proserpina.

Pluto's most famous appearance in Chaucer's work is in "The MERCHANT'S TALE," in which the king of the underworld and his queen choose the enclosed garden of the aged knight JANUARY in which to frolic. The poet implies that they visit the place habitually (lines 2038–41), which makes it less surprising that they are there and participate in the tale's climax when January's young wife MAY is on the point of having sex with the young squire DAMIAN in a tree while her blind and jealous husband sits below. Pluto, angered by the deception, which he sees as further evidence of the treasons women practice on their husbands everyday, decides to restore the old man's sight. Proserpina, in retaliation, provides May with an explanation that will make her husband doubt the evidence of his vision (lines 2225–2319).

Po River in northern Italy that flows for some 400 miles from the Cottian Alps east into the Adriatic Sea. The river's source, a spring in MONTE VISO, and its course as it runs toward Emilia, then through FERRARA and finally Venice, where it empties into the sea, is part of the geographical description of the region of LOMBARDY with which the prologue to "The CLERK'S TALE" concludes (lines 46–50).

Poetria Nova *See* GEOFFREY OF VINSAUF.

Poets' Corner An area in the south transept of Westminster Abbey which contains the tombs of, or monuments dedicated to, Chaucer, Edmund Spenser, William Shakespeare, Ben Jonson, John Milton and many other distinguished poets and authors. Although Chaucer was initially buried at the entrance to St. Benedict's chapel in the abbey, in 1556 his remains were moved to a new tomb set against the east wall of the south transept and he became the first poet to be buried in what would come to be known, in the 17th century, as Poets' Corner.

Poilleys In "The SQUIRE'S TALE," the magical brass horse that the emperor CAMBYUSKAN receives for his birthday is so perfectly made that the people gathered for the celebration are reminded of the fine "Poilleys" (Apulian) steeds hailing from that region on the southeastern coast of Italy (line 195).

Poliphemus *See* POLYPHEMUS.

Poliphete A character mentioned in *TROILUS AND CRISEYDE* who was apparently invented by Chaucer. When PANDARUS wants to make his niece CRISEYDE feel threatened so that she is more vulnerable to TROILUS' advances, he tells her that her old enemy, a man named Poliphete, is about to involve her in a lawsuit (book 2, lines 1467–69). This episode, which does not appear in any of Chaucer's sources, makes Pandarus appear more onerous and Criseyde less blameworthy in the events that follow.

Polite(s) In VIRGIL's *Aeneid*, Polite is one of King PRIAM's sons. He was slain by PYRRHUS when the Greeks captured Troy. This incident is recorded on the walls of the TEMPLE OF VENUS in Chaucer's *HOUSE OF FAME* (lines 158–61). In *TROILUS AND CRISEYDE*, Polite is one of the Trojan princes who tries to defend ANTENOR, who is nevertheless taken prisoner by the Greeks (book 4, lines 50–56).

Polixena In classical mythology, Polixena was a daughter of King PRIAM and Queen HECUBA of TROY. The Greek warrior ACHILLES saw and fell in love with her during one of a series of peace talks that took place between the Greek forces and the Trojans during the TROJAN WAR. He offered to support an end to the war if Priam would agree to give him Polixena as a wife, but when he went to the temple of APOLLO in Troy to discuss the proposal with Hecuba and PARIS (1), he was ambushed and killed. After the war was over and the Greeks were returning home, the ghost of Achilles appeared and demanded the sacrifice of Polixena on his grave. The command was carried out by his son.

In *The BOOK OF THE DUCHESS*, the BLACK KNIGHT recalls that Achilles died because of his love for Polixena, hinting at his own plight (lines 1066–71). In *TROILUS AND CRISEYDE*, the narrator notes that CRISEYDE was fairer than Polixena when he describes the beginning of TROILUS' lovesick obsession for her (book 1, lines 454–55). Later, when he has enlisted the help of Criseyde's uncle, PANDARUS, in his quest to gain her love, Troilus promises to reward Pandarus by giving him Polixena or one of his other sisters (book 3, lines 409–13). In *The LEGEND OF GOOD WOMEN*, Polixena is mentioned as one of love's martyrs in the ballade that the narrator sings to honor Queen ALCESTIS (prologue F, line 258; prologue G, line 212).

Pollux *See* CASTOR.

Polydamus In classical mythology, Polydamus was a Trojan warrior born on the same night as HECTOR, whose close friend he was. Although he participated in the war against the Greeks, he was more valued as an adviser. In *TROILUS AND CRISEYDE*, Polydamus was one of the warriors who tried to prevent ANTENOR's capture (book 4, lines 50–56).

Polyhymnia In classical mythology, Polyhymnia was the muse of sacred poetry. She lived with her eight sisters on Mount Helicon. Chaucer invokes her assistance in the opening stanzas of the unfinished poem *ANELIDA AND ARCITE* (lines 15–20).

Polymnestor In BOCCACCIO's *FILOSTRATO*, Polymnestor was a king of Thrace who helped defend the city of TROY against the Greeks in the TROJAN WAR. He is mentioned in book four of *TROILUS AND CRISEYDE* as one of the heroes whose efforts to prevent the capture of ANTENOR (lines 50–56) lead to CRISEYDE being surrendered to the Greeks and thus separated from TROILUS.

Polymya *See* POLYHYMNIA.

Polymyte(s) *See* POLYNICES.

Polynestore *See* POLYMNESTOR.

Polynices In classical mythology, Polynices was the son of King OEDIPUS of THEBES and Queen Jocasta. He had a brother named ETEOCLES and a sister named Antigone. After it was discovered that Oedipus had committed (albeit unknowingly) the grievous error of marrying his mother, Eteocles and Polynices drove him out of Thebes and undertook to govern the city themselves, agreeing to rule alternately year by year. When Eteocles refused to be bound by that agreement, Polynices called upon ADRASTUS to help him organize an invasion of Thebes. In the conflict that followed, which became known as the SEVEN AGAINST THEBES, the brothers met in single combat and killed each other, fulfilling the curse that their father had laid upon them when they forced him to leave the city. CASSANDRA mentions Eteocles and Polynices in book 5 of *TROILUS AND CRISEYDE* as she recites the history of the Theban conflict to her brother TROILUS (lines 1485–1510).

Polyphemus In Homer's *Odyssey*, Polyphemus was one of the Cyclops, the wild, one-eyed giants who lived in caves near the sea and who provided for themselves by raising sheep and goats. Polyphemus was the strongest of the Cyclops and was able to hurl mountaintops into the sea as evidence of his might. When ULYSSES landed on his island, Polyphemus captured him and his companions and imprisoned them in his cave. Ulysses and his men escaped by putting out the giant's eye and then suspending themselves beneath the bellies of his sheep so that they could pass undetected through the cave's entrance when he released his flocks to pasture. This story of Ulysses' deception of the Cyclops is related in Book Four, Metrum 7 of the *BOECE* as an example of a man who overcomes the obstacles thrown in his way by hostile fate.

Pompeus (Pompe; Pompei; Pompeye) *See* POMPEY THE GREAT.

Pompey the Great Gnaeus Pompeius, or Pompey the Great, was one of three generals who formed the first triumvirate in the first century B.C. (The other two were JULIUS CAESAR and Marcus CRASSUS.) Pompey won fame as the conqueror of SYRIA and Palestine, while Caesar concentrated on attacking the Gauls, adding to the Roman state the territory of modern Belgium and France. In 52 B.C., after a series of riots in Rome, the Senate elected Pompey as sole consul. As a result, a deadly rivalry broke out between Caesar and Pompey. After being defeated at Pharsalus, Pompey fled to the eastern portion of the empire, hoping to gather enough troops to regain control of the Italian peninsula. He was ultimately defeated and soon afterward murdered at the instigation of the king of Egypt. In *The HOUSE OF FAME*, the image of the Roman poet LUCAN bears the fame of Caesar and Pompey on its shoulders (lines 1497–1502). In "The MAN OF LAW'S TALE," the narrator states his belief that the destiny of all men, including Pompey and Caesar, is written in the stars, even before they are born (lines 190–99). Pompey's conflict with Caesar is narrated in the story of Caesar's life that appears in "The MONK'S TALE" as an example of a tragedy of FORTUNE (lines 2671–2726).

Poo *See* PO.

Poperinghe (Poperyng) The town in FLANDERS where Chaucer's Sir THOPAS, the hero of "The TALE OF SIR THOPAS," was born. In the 14th century, the town (like so many in Flanders) was noted for its cloth and for its pears.

Porcia *See* PORTIA.

Portia The daughter of Cato Uticensis and wife of the Roman Marcus BRUTUS, close friend of JULIUS CAESAR who participated in his assassination. Like her husband, she was an ardent believer in the republican cause. She committed suicide in the wake of her husband's flight from Rome after Marc ANTONY vowed revenge against those who were part of the assassination plot. The Roman historian Plutarch reports that she killed herself by inhaling the fumes of a live coal. In "The FRANKLIN'S TALE," because of her devotion to her husband Portia is placed among the virtuous women whose example DORIGEN would like to follow (lines 1448–50).

Portugal (Portyngale) Country on the Iberian peninsula in southwestern Europe; it lies between Spain and the Atlantic Ocean. In the epilogue to "The NUN'S PRIEST'S TALE," the Host (*see* Harry BAILLY) praises the NUN'S PRIEST for his performance, and then goes on to praise the man's physical appearance, including his complexion, which needs no cosmetics such as "greyn of Portyngale" (a type of red dye derived from the dried bodies of an insect and imported from Portugal) to give it a ruddy glow (lines 3458–60).

Poul *See* PAUL, SAINT.

Poules   *See* SAINT PAUL'S CATHEDRAL.

Pratt, Robert A. (1907–1987)   Robert Pratt was distinguished by his interest in the books that Chaucer read, which led him to become the moving spirit behind the founding in 1945 of the Chaucer Library, the goal of which was to collect and preserve medieval manuscripts and texts by publishing them in modern editions. He also wrote many articles on the books known to and used by Chaucer, such as "Three Sources of the Nonnes Preestes Tale" (*Speculum,* 1972). Pratt's other important contributions to Chaucer scholarship include "The Order of *The Canterbury Tales*" (*Publications of the Modern Language Association,* 1951), an article that reopened the argument over Chaucer's intended order for the tales by defending the BRADSHAW SHIFT and stimulating further debate which continues to this day. His edition of *The Tales of Canterbury* (1974) provided materials for the text of *The CANTERBURY TALES* in the current *RIVERSIDE CHAUCER* (1987).

Priam (Priamus)   In classical mythology, Priam, the son of Laomedon, was king of TROY at the time of the TROJAN WAR. This conflict, wherein the chief warriors of Greece laid siege to the city of Troy, came about because one of Priam's sons, PARIS (1), had kidnapped Helen, the beautiful wife of the Greek king Menelaus. (*See* HELEN OF TROY.) Priam was too old to participate in the fighting, and although he presided over the councils of war, he usually left important decisions to others, including his eldest son, HECTOR. Known for his gentleness and piety, he was respected both by his own people and by many of the enemy soldiers. The many misfortunes suffered by his city and his family during the war caused him to be looked upon as a figure of pathos. When Troy fell to the Greeks, Priam first witnessed the death of his young son POLITES and was then slain by his son's attacker, PYRRHUS.

The narrator of *The BOOK OF THE DUCHESS* mentions Priam among the Trojan War heroes depicted on the glass of the room in his dream (line 328). In *The HOUSE OF FAME*, the fall of Troy and Priam's death are depicted on a tablet of brass in the TEMPLE OF VENUS, where these events serve as a prelude to the adventures of AENEAS. TROILUS, the hero of *TROILUS AND CRISEYDE*, was another of Priam's sons, and the king appears as a minor character in the poem. He makes his most significant appearance in book 4, when he sends an escort to bring Greek ambassadors to Troy (lines 139–40) and then during the meeting with them is petitioned by the Trojan people to let CRISEYDE be exchanged for the warrior ANTENOR, who was captured by the Greeks in battle (lines 183–95).

Priapus   In classical mythology, Priapus was the son of VENUS and BACCHUS. He was the god of the creative power of nature in the human, animal and plant worlds, and was considered the patron of horticulture or gardens. Physically, he was represented as an ugly little man with enormous genitals signifying his creative power. According to one legend, he was in love with a nymph who refused his advances. He tried to sneak up on her and take advantage of her while she was sleeping, but just as he was about to do so, an ass brayed, awaking the nymphs and the gods, who laughed at his condition of sexual excitement. Chaucer alludes to this story in *The PARLIAMENT OF FOWLS* when he describes Priapus in a similar state in the TEMPLE OF VENUS (lines 253–59). In "The MERCHANT'S TALE," the narrator says that Priapus could not have described a more beautiful garden than the one belonging to the aged knight JANUARY (lines 2034–37). The reference is doubly appropriate because this enclosed garden is where January likes to have intercourse with his wife when the weather is fine.

Priest   The "annueleer" or chantry priest of "The CANON'S YEOMAN'S TALE" who is deceived by the CANON (2), who claims to possess the secrets of alchemy, i.e., of turning base metals into precious ones. The priest is first taken in by the canon because of the apparent honesty he displays by repaying a loan on time. Unused to such behavior, the priest mistakenly uses it to gauge the verity of the canon's claim that he can transform quicksilver (mercury) into silver by the application of heat and a magical powder. After observing the transformation three times (he actually witnesses three tricks), the priest pays £40 for the powder's recipe, but after the canon's departure finds himself unable to duplicate the experiment.

Primum Mobile   Translated, this Middle English term means "first movable" or, alternatively, "first mover." It is a term related to structural descriptions of the Ptolemaic universe. Formulated by PTOLEMY, an astronomer of ancient Egypt, this theory of the universe put the earth at the center of our solar system. Surrounding the earth were a series of hollow and transparent spheres, each one larger than the one before. Each of the first seven spheres contained one luminous body. Closest to the earth was the Moon; then came MERCURY (2), Venus, the Sun, MARS (2), Jupiter and SATURN (2). The sphere beyond Saturn, where all the fixed stars resided, was called *Stellatum.* The Primum Mobile was the ninth sphere, beyond which existed a vast emptiness, a void of both time and space. God caused the Primum Mobile to rotate, and its movement caused the rotation of the Stellatum, which caused that of Saturn, and so on, down to the last moving sphere. This is the model of the universe that informs Chaucer's work. An understanding of its structure is especially important for works like *The HOUSE OF*

FAME, *The PARLIAMENT OF FOWLS*, and the conclusion of *TROILUS AND CRISEYDE* because portions of the action take place in the heavens. This model of the universe was brought into question by the 15th-century Italian astronomer Copernicus, who formulated the Copernican theory which put the Sun at the center.

Prioress, the   The Prioress is the fourth pilgrim to be described in the GENERAL PROLOGUE TO *THE CANTERBURY TALES*. Aside from her title and her ability to sing the divine service, little else in the portrait of this woman seems indicative of her profession. Most of the characteristics mentioned here derive from traditional formulas used to describe courtly heroines. They include physical features like her small mouth, her well-formed ("tretys") nose and her gray eyes, as well as behavioral characteristics such as her refined table manners, dignified demeanor and the tenderheartedness she displays toward small animals. Her name, Madame Eglentyne, means "briar rose," and has similar associations. All of these things together reflect the likelihood that she originally came from a noble family and joined the convent for economic reasons rather than religious fervor. (Because marrying off the eldest daughter was often very expensive for a noble family, the younger ones frequently went into religious ser-

Artist's rendering of the Prioress, from the Ellesmere Manuscript of The Canterbury Tales. *The Prioress rides sidesaddle and wears the habit of a Benedictine. Mirroring her description in the General Prologue, she has a broad forehead and a small mouth. The shadow of a wimple can just be detected.*

vice.) Unlike the portraits of the three pilgrims who precede her in the General Prologue, Chaucer's description of the Prioress does appear to contain some satire. Her mastery of French, one of the achievements that suggests refinement and nobility, is rendered less impressive by the narrator's statement that she speaks a provincial dialect rather than the Parisian variety spoken at court. The details of her physical description which make her sound like the heroine of a courtly romance are qualified by this hint about her size: "For hardily, she was nat undergrowe" (line 156) [For certainly, she was not undergrown], which by way of understatement politely suggests that she is overweight. Nuns were ordinarily forbidden to keep animals, which shows that either she had a special dispensation for her small hounds or she was breaking the rules. Her feeding of roasted meat and wastel bread to the dogs would also seem to be a violation of her order, since to do so suggests luxury and wastefulness. Finally, her preoccupation with her appearance, expressed by her pleated wimple and fine jewelry, and her swearing, all seem to further undermine the idea that she takes her profession seriously. While none of these attributes may impress a modern reader as serious flaws, the blatant anti-Semitism of the tale she tells does raise troubling questions about her character and about general attitudes toward the Jewish population in Europe at this time. The Prioress is accompanied by another nun, a chaplain and three priests. Although none of these individuals is described, the SECOND NUN and one of the priests (the NUN'S PRIEST) do participate in the tale-telling contest.

"Prioress' Tale, The"   The PRIORESS, whose love of small defenseless creatures is mentioned in the GENERAL PROLOGUE, tells the story of a little boy who is murdered because of his piety.

SUMMARY

The prologue of "The Prioress' Tale" is a song of praise in honor of the Virgin MARY which concludes with the prayerful request that the Virgin provide guidance and assistance to the PRIORESS as she commences to tell her tale.

The tale begins with the description of a Jewish ghetto that once lay within a Christian city in Asia. A street running from one end to the other is used as a thoroughfare. A Christian school for children stands at one end of the road. One of the children who attends this school is the seven-year-old son of a widow, who, tutored by his mother, exhibits great devotion to the Virgin Mary. One day at school he hears some of the older children singing a song of praise to Christ's mother. Determined that he too must learn this song, he persuades one of the older students to teach him the words and their meaning. Hoping to master the song before Christmas, he practices singing it every day as he walks to and from school, passing through the Jewish neighborhood. Satan causes the Jews to become infuriated by the boy's singing, and a group of them conspire to pay someone to cut his throat. After the boy is killed, they throw his body into a latrine or sewage pit. The poor widow waits all night for her child to come home, and in the morning goes out to search for him. When she enters the ghetto and asks the people who live there if any of them have seen her son, they tell her no. She keeps looking and eventually wanders near the place where his body has been hidden. As she searches there, the corpse of the little boy begins to sing the song he had been learning, the *Alma redemptoris*, so loudly that all the Christian people who are traveling on the thoroughfare come to see him. When they discover that his throat has been cut, they send for the magistrate of the town, who arrests the people responsible. The child is taken up and carried to a nearby abbey, where his mourning mother refuses to leave his side. Meanwhile, the Jews who killed him are sentenced to death and executed. Because the child is still singing, the abbot asks him how it is that he sings with a cut throat. The child explains that when he was injured the Virgin came and placed a seed upon his tongue, which enables him to keep on singing. She also told him not to be afraid, and that when the seed was removed she would come for him. The abbot removes the seed, the child ceases to sing, and everybody falls down weeping upon the pavement. The tale closes with the Prioress making an invocation to HUGH OF LIN-COLN, also slain by "cursed Jewes," to pray for God's mercy on her and her fellow travelers.

COMMENTARY

This tale belongs to a genre known as Miracles of the Virgin, which is a subdivision of the larger group known as Saints' Lives. The prologue, which has been praised as Chaucer's finest piece of devotional poetry, is made up of excerpts from the eighth Psalm, from the Little Office of the Blessed Virgin Mary, and from the Mass of the Holy Innocents, all woven together with superb artistry. Echoes of HEROD (1)'s slaughter of the innocents also appear in the text of the tale and provide an analogic link to events in the biblical past, relating the slaughter of this innocent child to a similar event in the life of Christ.

As with most of the Canterbury tales, despite this tale's general similarity to others belonging to the same genre, it bears certain marks of distinction which set it apart. One significant alteration that Chaucer made was to change the little boy's age from 10 (as it is in most of the analogues) to seven. The child's immaturity increases the tale's pathos and makes his achievement,

learning the *Alma redemptoris,* that much more remarkable. Chaucer's version is also the only surviving one in which a grain on the child's tongue allows him to continue singing. In other versions, the miracle is accomplished by such as a lily, a gem or another object symbolically associated with the Virgin. A variety of suggestions have been offered regarding the symbolic meaning of the grain. The best explanation seems to be that it derives from a commemoration of Saint Thomas sung during the second Vespers of the Feast of the Holy Innocents, where a seed is the symbol of both martyrdom and the soul winnowed from the body.

To a modern audience, the most troublesome aspect of "The Prioress' Tale" is its anti-Semitism. Modern scholars have tended to deal with this problem in one of two ways. Some have argued that Chaucer was using the tale as a vehicle to further extend the irony that characterizes the Prioress' portrait in the General Prologue. There she is described as an attractive and somewhat worldy woman, at least in the attention that she pays to her appearance and her table manners, which are described in minute detail. Her dress, jewelry and her name, Madame Eglantine, suggest that she comes from the nobility, and hint at elements of romance (she wears a golden brooch ambiguously engraved "*Amor vincit omnia,*" i.e., "love conquers all"). Her conscience is described as so charitable that she would weep if she saw a mouse caught in a trap. She also keeps small dogs as pets, which constitutes a minor violation of holy orders but further illustrates her fondness for smallness and innocence. This fondness carries over into her tale, but stands in ironic contrast to the callous ignorance she displays toward the Jews, who are depicted as depraved villains simply because of their ethnicity. On the other hand, when trying to determine Chaucer's attitude toward either the tale or the character of the Prioress, we must remember that anti-Semitism was as common and acceptable in 14th-century Europe as racism was in the American South before the Civil War. Although Jews were tolerated for their skill and utility in business matters, they continued to be scorned on the basis of their faith (which denied the divinity of Christ) and because they practiced usury, lending out money for interest, which was forbidden by the Bible, and thus was against Christian law. The tale itself is certainly equivocal in its treatment of the Jews and, if nothing else, reveals the Prioress to be a woman as naive and simpleminded as those whose lives and sufferings rouse her to pity.

As with other members of the Canterbury group, considering this tale in context provides some further clues to interpretation. At first glance, the story the Prioress tells would seem to have little relationship to the one preceding it, "The SHIPMAN'S TALE," which is a FABLIAU. But the latter tale does feature a monk as one of its principle characters, and that monk does engage in activities which are offensive to the Prioress, as she hints when she describes the abbot in her tale: "This abbot, which that was an hooly man, / As monkes been—or elles oghte be" (lines 642–43) [This abbot, who was a holy man, / As monks are—or else ought to be]. But the greatest contrast is not between the behavior of the clergy in the two tales, but between the respective general attitudes these tales display toward people who make a profit from dealing in money. Considered alone, the merchant who appears in "The Shipman's Tale" seems to be portrayed as a personable man, affectionate and generous to his friends, tolerant of his spendthrift wife. Compared to the monk who loans the wife money so he can have sex with her, and the wife who is willing to have sex with the monk just to get the money, the merchant comes across as morally upright, the most admirable of the trio. The fact that he makes a profit of 1,000 francs on the international exchange market (which falls outside the church's ban on taking interest) simply shows that he is an astute businessman. But when his profession is juxtaposed to that of the Jews who live in the Asian ghetto, a double standard suddenly appears, as if to remind us that although usury was forbidden by the Christian church, government officials were all too willing to take a share of the Jews' profits through taxation. In the notes to this text that appear in *The RIVERSIDE CHAUCER*, Larry Benson explains that the tale should not be considered in light of the realities of English life during the 14th century, because Jews had been banished from England since 1290; however, as a merchant, Chaucer would undoubtedly have had dealings with Jewish merchants on the Continent. His position in these circumstances would also have provided him with the opportunity to discern this double standard. If he reveals it with more subtlety than other criticisms of English and European society that appear in *The Canterbury Tales*, this could be due to the sensitive nature of the issue within his profession.

Procne   In classical mythology, Procne was the daughter of King PANDION of ATHENS who married TEREUS of THRACE. After their marriage, Tereus became inflamed with lust for his sister-in-law PHILOMELA, and raped her when she came to visit Procne in Thrace. To prevent her from telling anyone what had happened, he cut out Philomela's tongue and kept her hidden, telling Procne that she had died at home in Athens. Philomela finally managed to communicate what had happened by weaving it into a tapestry that she sent to her sister. Procne rescued her sister and then took revenge on her husband by killing Itys, her son by Tereus, and serving him as food to his father. When Tereus pursued the women with a sword, the gods transformed them all into birds. Procne became a swallow; Philomela, a nightingale; and Tereus, a hawk. Chaucer tells the story of Procne and Philomela in *The LEGEND OF GOOD WOMEN* (lines 2228–2393). He uses it as an example of how faithful women are betrayed by the men they love. Procne (spelled "Proigne") is also mentioned in *TROILUS AND CRISEYDE*, when PANDARUS hears a swallow singing the sorrowful story of her sister's fate outside his window (book 2, lines 64–65).

Proserpina (Proserpyne)   In classical mythology, Proserpina was the Roman name of the goddess called Persephone by the Greeks. She was the daughter of Zeus (JUPITER) and CERES, the goddess of grain and harvests. She was kidnapped by PLUTO, the god of the underworld, who carried her off to his realm of the dead where he made her his wife and queen. Ceres, stricken with grief, wandered throughout the earth for a long time seeking her lost daughter and causing the earth to become barren. Zeus finally intervened to restore Proserpina to her mother, but because the young woman had eaten part of a pomegranate while she was in the underworld, she was obliged to return there for one-third of each year. This myth was used by the ancients to explain the renewal of vegetation in the spring (when Proserpina was said to return to her mother) and its subsequent death in the winter (when she descended to Pluto). As queen of the underworld, Proserpina was considered a goddess of death, but as the daughter of Ceres she was a goddess of fertility and vegetation.

She appears several times in Chaucer's poetry. In *The HOUSE OF FAME*, she is mentioned in her capacity as queen of the underworld when the narrator describes the image of the poet Claudian (CLAUDIANUS) bearing up the fame of Pluto and Proserpina (lines 1507–12). The reference is to Claudian's popular Latin poem, *De raptu Proserpinae* ("The Rape of Proserpine"). In *TROILUS AND CRISEYDE*, TROILUS responds to PANDARUS' suggestion that he find another lover to replace CRISEYDE by saying that she will remain in his heart forever, even when he is dead and down in hell with Proserpina (book 4, lines 470–76). On a lighter note, Proserpina also appears in "The MERCHANT'S TALE," in which she and her husband frequent the enclosed garden where young MAY and the squire DAMIAN plan to deceive May's blind and jealous husband, JANUARY. Because January is so protective of May that he never takes his hands off her unless he has to, the young lovers decide that they will try to consummate their desire in a pear tree that grows in the garden. May will climb it, ostensibly to gather some fruit, and Damian will be waiting for her. When Proserpina and Pluto spy what is going on, Pluto vows to restore January's sight and thus reveal his wife's deception. Proserpina vows in exchange to grant May the ability to talk her way out of it, which she does with exceptional aplomb. The episode appears at the end of the tale (lines 2225–411).

Protesilaus In classical mythology, Protesilaus was one of the Greek warriors who fought against Troy in the TROJAN WAR. His death fulfilled the prophecy that the first of the warriors to set foot on Trojan soil would be the first to die. Even though they had only been married for one day before his departure for the war, when his wife LAODAMIA heard about his death she was inconsolable with grief. Her entreaties, joined with those of her husband, convinced the gods of the underworld to let him return to her for three hours. After his departure she made a wax image of him and gave it such lavish caresses that her father burned it. She committed suicide by throwing herself into the fire. In "The FRANKLIN'S TALE," Laodamia is one of the virtuous women whose example DORIGEN recalls when she is tempted to be unfaithful to her husband, ARVERAGUS, in order to fulfill the terms of a vow (lines 1445–47).

Protheselaus *See* PROTESILAUS.

"Proverbs" The shortest of the short poems attributed to Chaucer in the manuscripts, these aphoristic verses are there given the title "A Proverbe of Chaucer." The poem consists of only two stanzas, each containing four lines. The first stanza notes that although many clothes are unnecessary on a hot day, no man will cast away his "pilche" (outer fur garment), metaphorically referring to the difficulty of discarding unnecessary possessions or, possibly, outmoded ways of thinking. The second stanza describes how the person who attempts to embrace the whole world will be able to absorb or retain little of what he encompasses or experiences. Some editors have rejected the authenticity of these lines because of the irregular rhyme of *compas* (a noun) with *embrace* (a verb). In order for the rhyme to work, the final *e* of *embrace*, which would ordinarily be pronounced to indicate that it was functioning as an infinitive, would have to be silent. Also accepted as evidence that the lines were not penned by Chaucer is the transcriptionist John SHIRLEY's failure to attribute them to him.

Pruce *See* PRUSSIA.

Prudence The wife of MELIBEE in Chaucer's "TALE OF MELIBEE." Having been attacked and beaten by Melibee's enemies while he was away, Prudence uses wise sayings from biblical and classical authorities to persuade her husband against taking vengeance. Her name comes from the Latin word *prudentia,* which denotes wisdom and discretion.

Prussia In Chaucer's day, *Prussia* designated a kingdom in northern Europe on the Baltic Sea, more or less equivalent to the later East Prussia. In the latter part of the 14th century, it was under the control of the Teutonic Order, a military and religious order of German knights organized in 1191 for service in the Crusades. In the GENERAL PROLOGUE OF *THE CANTERBURY TALES,* the narrator notes that the KNIGHT (1) has received high honors in the Prussian court (lines 52–53). In *The BOOK OF THE DUCHESS,* the BLACK KNIGHT says of his lady that she was not one of those to send knights out on difficult quests to faraway lands such as Prussia (line 1025).

Pseustis One of the minstrels observed in the goddess FAME's palace by the narrator of *The HOUSE OF FAME* (line 1228). His name means "falsehood," and he appears in a well-known medieval textbook, the *Ecloga Theoduli,* as a shepherd who enters a poetic contest with Alithia, the daughter of Jove (JUPITER) and herself a personification of truth.

Ptholome(e) *See* PTOLEMY.

Ptolemy Ptolemy, or Claudius Ptolemaeus, was an Alexandrian mathematician of the second century who invented trigonometry and wrote on geography, optics and the theory of music. His most famous work was the *Mathematica syntaxis* ("The System of Mathematics"), popularly known as the ALMAGESTE, an Arabic-derived name that meant "the greatest [work]." It is a vast work on astronomy and mathematics which compiled all of the knowledge possessed on the subject of astronomy at the time. The work was written in Greek but later translated into Latin and Arabic. An abridged Latin translation of the 12th century, entitled *Tetrabiblios* ("Four Books"), was well-known during Chaucer's day and could be the source for much of the astronomical and astrological information that appears in his work (*see* ASTROLOGY). For references to Ptolemy's work in Chaucer's writings, see the entry on the *Almageste.*

Pycardie *See* PICARDY.

Pygmalion In classical mythology, Pygmalion was a king of Cyprus who made a statue of a maiden so beautiful that he fell in love with it. When he prayed to VENUS to give him a wife who looked like the statue, the goddess breathed life into the stone image. VIRGINIA, the martyr-heroine of "The PHYSICIAN'S TALE," is said by Dame NATURE to be more beautiful than any creature made by the hand of man, including that fashioned by the sculptor Pygmalion (line 14).

Pyramus In classical mythology, Pyramus was the ill-fated lover of THISBE. The two young people lived in ancient Babylon, on estates with adjoining properties. They fell in love but their parents forbade them to marry. Deciding to elope, the two arranged to slip away from their homes in the dark of night. They planned to meet at the tomb of King NINUS. Thisbe arrived first but a hungry lioness frightened her into taking refuge in a cave. She dropped her cloak, which the animal attacked with bloody claws. When Pyramus arrived and found the cloak but not Thisbe, he assumed the worst and stabbed himself. When Thisbe returned and found her lover dead, she also committed suicide. Pyramus is mentioned as one of the martyrs in the Temple of Venus in Chaucer's PARLIAMENT OF FOWLS (line 289). He is mentioned briefly in "The MERCHANT'S TALE," where the narrator remarks that in the case of MAY and DAMIAN love will find a way, just as it did for Pyramus and Thisbe (lines 2125–28). A complete version of the story of Pyramus and his lover is told in The LEGEND OF GOOD WOMEN (lines 706–923).

Pyrois In classical mythology, Pyrois was one of the four horses who drew the Sun's (APOLLO) chariot through the sky. The others were Eous, Aethon and Phlegon. In TROILUS AND CRISEYDE, when the two lovers spend their last night together, TROILUS greets the dawn by complaining that Pyrois and the other horses who pull the Sun's chariot have taken a shortcut to spite him (book 3, lines 1702–05).

Pyrrhus According to VIRGIL's *Aeneid,* Pyrrhus was another name for Neoptolemus, the son of ACHILLES who killed PRIAM when the Greeks won the TROJAN WAR. This story is related on the walls of the TEMPLE OF VENUS in *The HOUSE OF FAME* (lines 159–61). In "The MAN OF LAW's TALE, when the Roman emperor's daughter CONSTANCE marries the SULTAN OF SYRIA and has to go to his country, the narrator claims that the weeping accompanying her departure was more pitiful than that which was heard when Pyrrhus broke down the walls of Troy (lines 288–94). Similarly, in "The NUN'S PRIEST'S

TALE," we are informed that the ladies of Ilion (Troy) made no greater noise of lamentation when Pyrrhus killed their king, than did the chickens in the barnyard when a fox seized the noble rooster CHAUNTICLEER (lines 3355–61).

Pythagoras Greek philosopher and mathematician of the sixth century B.C. Among the main tenets of his philosophy were the belief in numbers as the ultimate elements in the universe and in the transmigration (reincarnation) of souls. Chaucer refers to Pythagoras on three occasions in his work; interestingly two of the references appear in *The BOOK OF THE DUCHESS* and may reflect some of the reading he was doing at the time of the poem's composition. The first reference is when the BLACK KNIGHT is attempts to explain how he lost his queen by playing chess against FORTUNE. He says he wishes he had known some of the strategies of Pythagoras (line 667). Perhaps then he could have played better and won the game. Later, when the knight relates how he attempted to woo the fair LADY WHITE with music, he mentions the tradition that Pythagoras was considered, among the Greeks, to be the father of music (line 1167). In the *BOECE,* Chaucer's translation of the *Consolation of Philosophy,* BOETHIUS mentions Pythagoras as one of the philosophers whose work has influenced his way of life.

Python In classical mythology, Python was a monstrous serpent who sprang up from the mud and stagnant water that remained after JUPITER sent a flood to destroy the human race. APOLLO destroyed him with his arrows. The slaying of Python is mentioned at the beginning of "The MANCIPLE'S TALE" (line 109), which relates the story of Apollo (Phoebus) and his crow.

Q

Quirinus (Quyryne) One of the appellations of the mythological figure ROMULUS, for whom Rome was named. He is referred to by this name in *TROILUS AND CRISEYDE,* book 4, when the narrator invokes MARS (1), the father of Quyryne (Quirinus) to assist him in telling the story of how TROILUS lost both his life and his love (line 25).

R

Rachel In the Old Testament, Rachel was the youngest daughter of LABAN and the second wife of JACOB. Rachel did not conceive any children during the early years of her marriage to Jacob, which caused her to become depressed, but finally she bore a son named JOSEPH, who became his father's favorite and who eventually was sold into slavery by his jealous brothers. Rachel died following the birth of her second son, whom she named Ben-Oni ("son of my sorrow"), but Jacob later renamed him Benjamin ("son of the right hand"). Although Rachel was Jacob's favorite wife, the line of David and ultimately the messianic line passed through Leah and her son Judah, not Rachel. Rachel weeping for her children became symbolic of sorrow and tragedy. Perhaps that is why the mother of the little Christian boy who is murdered (ironically by some Jews) in "The PRIORESS' TALE" is referred to as a "new Rachel," as she weeps inconsolably by her son's corpse.

Ralph *See* RAUF.

Ram *See* ARIES.

Rape of Proserpina, The *See* CLAUDIANUS, CLAUDIUS.

Raphael An archangel who figures in the apocryphal Book of Tobit, Raphael is mentioned in "The PARSON'S TALE." In the portion of his sermon having to do with the sin of lust, the PARSON recalls Raphael's condemnation of sexual relations between man and wife that are conducted solely for the purpose of pleasure (line 905).

Rauf *Rauf*, a Middle English spelling of *Ralph*, is the name given to one of the fornicators whose deeds with various "wenches" of the parish are confessed to the wicked summoner of "The FRIAR'S TALE" (lines 1355–58). The summoner uses the information to extort money from the men, whom he could otherwise force to appear in an ecclesiastical court to answer for their sins. That the women are described as being "at his retenue" [in his service] suggests that the men are being set up.

Raven In *The HOUSE OF FAME*, the EAGLE who ferries Chaucer through the heavens to FAME's palace asks him if he would not like to see the constellation known as the Raven (more commonly known to us as "Corvus") and other constellations that he has thus far only read about in books (lines 1000–10). The poet replies that, in this case, book knowledge is sufficient. He obviously feels some anxiety about being flown through the air in the grip of an eagle's talons.

Ravenna (Ravenne) A town in north-central Italy. For the greater part of his reign in Italy, THEODORIC the Ostrogoth made his home and held court in Ravenna. When he died he was interred there in a great mausoleum that he had erected as a burial place for himself and his successors. BOETHIUS, statesman and author of the *Consolation of Philosophy*, which Chaucer translated into Middle English as *BOECE*, was a Roman who served in Theodoric's government, dividing his time between his home in Rome and Theodoric's court at Ravenna until he was accused of plotting against the king, exiled and subsequently executed. The *Consolation of Philosophy* was written during his exile and represents his attempts to come to terms with his own situation and, more generally, with the role played by FORTUNE in shaping men's lives.

In Book One, Prosa 4, Boethius describes how his accusers, Basilius, OPILIO and GAUDENTIUS, had been commanded to leave the city of Ravenna because of crimes they had committed against the state. Then, on the day that their banishment went into effect, they accused Boethius, and their testimony was accepted as factual, leading to his exile (lines 110–39).

Razis *See* RHAZES.

Reader's Guide to Geoffrey Chaucer Although originally published in 1964, Muriel BOWDEN's *Reader's Guide* still provides a useful introduction to Chaucer's poetry and its contexts for undergraduates and general readers. Bowden addresses reader interest in Chaucer as a person as well as a literary genius, and her five chapters on *The CANTERBURY TALES* include information about the historical and cultural milieu in which his most popular work was produced. The *Guide* also features individual chapters on each of the DREAM VISION poems. The final, perhaps weakest, portion of the book treats Chaucer's longest single poem, *TROILUS AND CRISEYDE.*

Reason An allegorical figure who appears in Fragment B of the ROMAUNT OF THE ROSE, Chaucer's translation of the French ROMAN DE LA ROSE. When the dreamer-narrator of the poem finds himself estranged from his beloved rose and falls into despair, Reason intervenes, trying to convince him that his passion is both foolish and harmful.

Rebecca (Rebekka) In the Old Testament, Rebecca is the wife of ISAAC and the mother of JACOB, from whom the 12 tribes of Israel are descended. She enabled Jacob to secure his brother Esau's birthright by disguising him with animal skins before he approached his father to receive his blessing. Because Isaac was nearly blind, he attempted to identify his firstborn by touch, and when his hands felt the hairy animal skins, he assumed that he was speaking to Esau. Considering her role in deceiving her husband, it seems ironic that Rebecca appears as an example of wifely wisdom in "The MERCHANT'S TALE" (lines 1362–65) and "The TALE OF MELIBEE" (line 1098).

Red Sea (Rede See) The Red Sea lies between northeastern Africa and western Arabia. It is now connected with the Mediterranean Sea by the Suez Canal, but in Chaucer's day its only outlet was into the Indian Ocean, by way of the Gulf of Aden. In Book Three, Metrum 3 of the BOECE, LADY PHILOSOPHY discusses man's tendency to avarice, noting that even if a covetous man had so many jewels from the Red Sea that his neck was weighed down, he would still try to get more (line 5). A classical text that speaks of the jewels in the Red Sea was Pliny's *Natural History*.

Reeve, the The Reeve's portrait follows that of the MANCIPLE in the GENERAL PROLOGUE TO *THE CANTERBURY TALES*, although, according to the narrator, he rides at the very end of the procession. In contrast to the Manciple, about whose physical appearance we are given no information, his is a strikingly detailed portrait, beginning with the first line's characterization of him as "sclendre" (slender) and "choleric." The latter refers to his temperament and, according to the medieval theory of the bodily HUMORS, would indicate that he possesses a shrewd wit, a sharp tongue and a lecherous disposition. The shrewd wit is amply demonstrated by information given here about how he conducts himself in the practice of his profession. The title of reeve indicates that he acts as the manager of a manor or estate, overseeing the protection and maintenance of pasture, fields and woods belonging to the lord of the estate. In addition to overseeing all of the work done on the estate, he would also generally be responsible for collecting any rents (in goods or services) from those who lived on and farmed any portion of the estate. This particular reeve appears to excel in

Artist's rendering of the Reeve, from the Ellesmere Manuscript of The Canterbury Tales. *The Reeve is depicted as he is described in the General Prologue with long legs, a slender body, a clean-shaven face, and riding a dappled-gray horse.*

carrying out these duties, and particularly in discerning any cheating by those who work under him such as the herdsmen ("hierde") or individual farm managers ("baillif"). He himself, however, is not above practicing certain deceits upon the estate's owner who, at 20 years of age, would be a particularly vulnerable target. The Reeve's sharp tongue and lecherous disposition, characteristics suggested by his physical features, are not explicitly referred to in the General Prologue, but do surface later in both the prologue to his tale and the tale itself. In the prologue, he announces his intention to requite the MILLER for that man's insulting description of a carpenter (carpentry is one of the Reeve's skills), and also confesses his own "coltes tooth" which inspires him with a lustful appetite inappropriate to his age. The tale that follows tells of a swindling miller whose pride is brought low when both his wife and his daughter are tricked into having sex with two students.

"Reeve's Tale, The" "The Reeve's Tale" follows and responds to "The MILLER'S TALE," capitalizing on the Miller's reputation as a thief.

SUMMARY

At TRUMPINGTON, near CAMBRIDGE, there lives a miller named SIMKIN who owns the exclusive right to grind all the "corn" (the Middle English word for grain) in a given area. He takes advantage of his position by stealing grain from his customers, which is easily done, since they leave the grain with him for milling and then come back to pick it up later. The miller is married to the illegitimate daughter of a parson, and they have two children, a 20-year-old daughter and a six-month-old baby boy.

The plot of the story begins to take shape when the manciple of SOLER HALL (King's College) at Cambridge University, falls gravely ill with some form of dental disease. It was the manciple's responsibility to stock the college with provisions, including flour from milled grain, but because of his malady he is unable to fulfill that role. The crafty miller seizes this opportunity to steal from the college, taking 100 times more grain than he usually does. The warden, or master, of the college notices the theft and accuses the miller, who blusteringly swears that he has taken nothing. Angered over what has happened, and eager to get the best of the miller, two impoverished students named John (JOHN THE CLERK) and ALAN (Aleyn) ask permission to go to the mill and oversee the grinding of their own grain. The warden agrees to let them go. When they arrive at the mill, John and Alan pretend to be interested in the process of milling grain as an excuse to watch the proceedings, but the miller is not fooled. While they are busy making sure he does not have the opportunity to steal any of their grain, the miller slips outside and unties their horse, which quickly runs off to cavort with some wild mares.

When their grain has all been ground, the "meal" (flour) bagged up and made ready for travel, John and Alan discover that their horse, which actually belongs to the warden of their college, has escaped. They go running out to look for it, and Simkin quickly steals half a bushel of their flour. Giving it to his wife, he tells her to bake a cake with it. It takes the students all day to catch the horse, and they are exhausted by their efforts. They ask Simkin to let them spend the night, agreeing to pay him for food and lodging. Simkin replies that there is not much space, but says they are welcome to what there is. The students and the miller's family drink quite a bit of ale with their evening meal. Then they all retire to bed in one large chamber.

Simkin and his family fall asleep right away, but the two students are kept awake by the miller and his wife's noisy snoring. Alan decides to make the best of the situation and to copulate with the miller's daughter, which will grant him some revenge for the day's losses. Not wanting to be left out, John gets up and moves the baby's cradle, which lies at the foot of the wife's bed, to the end of his own bed. When the wife gets up in the night to relieve herself, she returns to the bed that has the cradle at its foot and climbs under the sheets with John. Both of the women enjoy themselves considerably. When Alan, who was sleeping with the daughter, attempts to return to his own bed, he encounters the cradle. This confuses him into thinking that his own bed is the miller's, so he goes to a different bed, which itself turns out to be the miller's. Climbing into bed he wakes up Simkin, whom he takes to be his friend John, boasting that he has "thries in this shorte nyght / Swyved the milleres doghter bolt upright" (lines 4265–66). [Three times in this short night / Screwed the miller's daughter flat on her back]. The miller seizes him by the throat. They fall to the floor fighting. The noise awakens the miller's wife, who jumps up, grabs a stick and attempts to whack Alan; however, mistaking her husband's bald head for a nightcap, she hits Simkin instead. The students complete the beating and then escape, taking their horse, their meal and the cake that was made with the stolen flour. The REEVE closes his version of this story by explaining its moral point, which is that he who does evil deeds should expect evil to be done unto him.

COMMENTARY

Like "The MILLER'S TALE," to which it responds, "The Reeve's Tale" is a FABLIAU, or bawdy story, featuring middle-class characters in a comic situation that includes sexual activity. As is not the case with "The Miller's Tale," sources may be found for every part of "The Reeve's Tale." The "cradle trick" with which the tale concludes is a very popular motif in the French fabliaux. The tale also bears some similarity to one of the stories in BOCCACCIO's DECAMERON. No one story, however, contains all the features of Chaucer's version combined in the same way or with such finesse.

The Reeve begins his tale by criticizing the one that has just been told, the Miller's tale, for its ribaldry. Furthermore, since the Reeve is both an old man and a carpenter by trade, he cannot help taking it as a personal affront that the Miller made an aged carpenter the butt of his joke. The Reeve vows to take revenge on the Miller through his own tale. So, as with the Miller's response to the KNIGHT (1), requital once again figures as the motive for the choice of story, though in this case the implied criticism has as its object the tale's teller rather than its meaning or subject. "The Reeve's Tale" does, however, parody some features of courtly romance to suggest a view of love in contrast to the idealized version of "The KNIGHT'S TALE." The most obvious and direct parody revolves around the character of MALKYN (Malyn), the miller's daughter. Her physical description bespeaks a certain grossness that exists incongruously alongside traits of beauty. For example, she is tall and fat, with a pug nose, but has eyes as gray as glass. She has broad buttocks, but her breasts are high and round like those of a romance heroine. When Alan leaves her bed, their parting recalls one of conventional features of courtly romance, the tearful parting of the knight and his lady at dawn.

Structurally, "The Reeve's Tale" is divided into two parts, constructed around two tricks. The motive of both tricks is, like the motive of the tale itself, revenge. In the first part two students, Alan and John, discover that the miller who grinds the grain for their college has stolen a large quantity of that grain. They decide that it will be fun to visit that miller with their own grain and to oversee its grinding, thus frustrating the miller's attempts to perform his customary thievery. However, the miller, Simkin, is not fooled by their pretended interest in the mechanics of milling flour. While they keep an eye on their grain, he unties their horse so that they have to spend all afternoon trying to catch it. And of course, he steals a sizeable portion of their flour as revenge for their attempt to get the better of him.

With the second trick, the students get their revenge on the miller. The tale's beginning relates that the miller is a proud and disdainful man with a querulous temper. His wife, the illegitimate daughter of the local parson, is also haughty and pretentious. We know little about the character of their 20-year-old daughter, except that the parson has made her his heir, hoping to bestow her on a member of the nobility, which again suggests a kind of unwarranted pride, since she is, after all, illegitimate. In the Middle Ages, this was a considerable social handicap. The two students deflate the miller's pride, and his wife's as well, when they take their own revenge by having sex with the wife and daughter.

Because they are both fabliaux, and because "The Reeve's Tale" follows and responds to "The Miller's Tale," the two are often compared. Most critics consider "The Miller's Tale" superior to its fellow, citing its more thorough and well-rounded characterization and the expansive and tolerant attitude toward human fallibility. Although it makes fun of the characters who seem to deserve to be duped for one reason or another, "The Miller's Tale" does so in a gently mocking manner with the stress on the merriment of the situation. The wit of "The Reeve's Tale" is, in comparison, a good deal more acerbic, which suits the Reeve's temperament. He is a bitter man, not just toward the Miller but toward the passage of time which has made him an old man, yet left him with the sexual appetite of youth. Whereas the pace of the Miller's story is slow and leisurely, that of the Reeve's is quick, emphasizing action rather than description, and arousing little of the reader's sympathy for any of the characters. Some of the action is itself rather brutal, especially the description of the students taking their "revenge," although the women's reactions suggest that they enjoy the sexual activity.

When we laugh at the humor of both these tales, it is good to remember that their comic action would stand against a different social and theological background for members of the medieval audience which would be most likely to hear the tales. Even if they did not adopt orthodox religious views, these members of the aristocracy and the middle classes were still aware of them and would have known that pride and lust took turns heading the list of the Seven Deadly Sins. Because Chaucer did not express his beliefs or opinions on these topics directly, and because the tales and characters who tell them range from the disreputable and even dissolute (like the Miller) to the "typical" middle-class bourgeois (like the WIFE OF BATH) to the humbly devout PARSON, it is impossible to know which of two prevailing theories about Chaucer's attitude toward sin is more accurate. One (popularized by D. W. ROBERTSON in his *Preface to Chaucer*) argues that Saint AUGUSTINE's view of sin dominated the interpretation of secular as well as religious art and literature, and that therefore, Chaucer did not "approve" of the base, instinct-driven behavior of characters in the fabliaux. Rather, Robinson believes, Chaucer was offering up their foolish antics as a satirical judgment of such behavior, behavior that lowers men to the realm of the beasts. Other readers have read Chaucer's bawdy tales in much the same spirit as they are offered by their tellers, as a challenge to or disruption of religious and social orthodoxy. Chaucer's famous "deathbed" Retraction (*see* CHAUCER'S RETRACTION) would seem to support the latter view, since in that work he asks God's (and the reading public's) forgiveness for those of the Canterbury tales that "sownen into" (i.e., tend toward or imitate) "synne" (line 1085).

In the final lines of the poem, the Reeve attaches a moral tag to his tale, saying "Lo, swich it is a millere to be fals! / And therfore this proverbe is seyd ful soothe, / 'Hym thar nat wene wel that yevele dooth.' / A gylour shal hymself bigyled be." (lines 4318–21) [Lo, see how it is for a miller to be false! / And therefore this proverb is said very truthfully, / 'He who does evil should not expect good. / A cheater shall himself be cheated].

This feature of the tale looks backward to the type of literature from which the fabliaux is thought to have descended, the fable and EXEMPLUM, which, after presenting a story ostensibly for entertainment, would offer a proverbial interpretation of the story for the reader's edification.

Regulus (Marcus Atilius Regulus)   A Roman consul in 257 and 256 B.C. During his consulship in 256, he defeated the Carthagenians during the first Punic War. In 255, however, he was defeated and captured by Xantippus and thus, as LADY PHILOSOPHY notes in the *BOECE,* obliged to submit to his enemies (Book Two, Prosa 6, line 70). Philosophy uses Regulus as an example of the vicissitudes that men suffer at the hands of FORTUNE.

Remedie of Love   *Remedie of Love* is the Middle English title Chaucer assigns to the Latin poet OVID's *Remedia amoris* in his "TALE OF MELIBEE." When her husband, MELIBEE, begins to weep following the attack on his home and family, Dame PRUDENCE remembers the advice Ovid gives in this work about how to comfort one who has suffered a loss (line 976).

Renart le Contrefait   *Renart le Contrefait* ("Reynard the Trickster") is the title of a French cycle of beast tales belonging to the epic tradition. The tales tell the adventures of a fox named Renart and of his deceitful interactions with other animals and humans. The sixth branch of the cycle, seems to have influenced Chaucer's treatment of the CHAUNTICLEER story in his "NUN'S PRIEST'S TALE." Specifically, in the French tale that tells of Renart's encounter with the rooster are to be found the hen's skepticism regarding the truthfulness of dreams, her denunciation of fear and cowardice, and an inflated and expanded narrative style, all of which are notable features of Chaucer's version.

Rennes   A city in northwestern France. In Chaucer's day a very fine kind of linen made in Rennes was used for sheets and pillowcases. A set of such pillow cases are offered to MORPHEUS and JUNO by the narrator of *The BOOK OF THE DUCHESS* if they will assist the narrator in overcoming his insomnia (lines 249–55).

Retraction   *See* CHAUCER'S RETRACTION.

Reynard   The *Roman de Renart* featuring Renard the fox was a popular medieval cycle of beast tales. One branch of the cycle included the story of Chaunticleer and the fox that, in MARIE DE FRANCE's version, became Chaucer's source for "The NUN'S PRIEST'S TALE," even though the fox in Chaucer's version is named RUSSELL. In the story of PHYLLIS that Chaucer included in his *LEGEND OF GOOD WOMEN*, he describes how DEMOPHON, the duke of ATHENS and son of THESEUS, behaved just like his father in betraying the woman who was in love with him. He is compared to Renard, who, as the son of a fox, behaves just as one would expect from a fox (lines 2448–51).

Reynes   *See* RENNES.

Rhazes   Rhazes, whose Arabic name was Abu Bakr Muhammad ibn-Zakaruya al-Razi, was born near Teheran in Persia in 865. He was a physician and scholar who composed an influential encyclopedia of health that was translated into Latin as the *Liber medici-*

nalis Almansoris ("Al-Mansur's Book of Medicine") in the late 12th century. His monograph on smallpox is the earliest description of that disease still in existence. Rhazes, spelled "Razis," is one of the medical authorities whose works have been studied by the DOCTOR OF PHYSIC as described in the GENERAL PROLOGUE TO *THE CANTERBURY TALES* (line 432).

Rhodogune   A daughter of the Persian king DARIUS (1). When her nurse suggested that she remarry after the death of her husband, she killed the woman. In "The FRANKLIN'S TALE," Rhodogune is one of the virtuous women whose example DORIGEN recalls follow when she is pressured to betray her husband to fulfill her rash vow to the squire AURELIUS (line 1456).

Rhodope   In OVID's *Heroides* Rhodope is the name given to the country surrounding the Rhodope mountain range in Thrace. DEMOPHON was shipwrecked on the shores of Rhodope as he attempted to sail home to Athens from the Trojan War. He was nursed back to health by Phyllis, the queen of that land, whom he promised to marry and then betrayed. The story of Demophon and Phyllis is narrated in *The LEGEND OF GOOD WOMEN* (lines 2394–2561).

Rhyme Royal   A seven-line iambic pentameter stanza rhyming *ababbcc*. Chaucer was the first English poet to use the Rhyme Royal stanza, which he employed for *The PARLIAMENT OF FOWLS*, "The MAN OF LAW'S TALE," "The CLERK'S TALE," "The PRIORESS' TALE," "The SECOND NUN'S TALE" and his longest single work, *TROILUS AND CRISEYDE*. Some other poets who have used the form are John LYDGATE, Thomas HOCCLEVE, William Dunbar, John Skelton, William Shakespeare and, in the 19th century, William Morris. The name of the stanza seems to have derived from its use in *The Kingis Quair* ("The King's Book"), a 15th-century poem attributed to King James I of Scotland.

Richard, Kynge   *See* RICHARD II.

Richard I   King of England from 1189 to 1199, Richard I played a greater part in affairs on the European continent than in England. This is hardly surprising, considering that he spent all but six months of his 10-year reign either defending his possessions on the Continent or waging the Third Crusade, which had been organized to recapture the cities of Acre and Jerusalem from the Muslims, who had conquered them in 1187 as part of their campaign against Christian forces in the area. He was nevertheless quite popular among his subjects, who revered him as a crusader, and feared by his enemies, who knew him as a man of strength and shrewdness. GEOFFREY OF VINSAUF wrote a famous lament on the death of King Richard that Chaucer praises and then parodies in his lament over the fate suffered by the noble rooster CHAUNTICLEER in "The NUN'S PRIEST'S TALE" (lines 3347–74).

Richard II (1367–1400) King of England from 1377 to 1399, Richard II was one of three kings to reign in England during Chaucer's lifetime. (The other two were Richard's grandfather, EDWARD III, and his cousin, HENRY IV.) Richard was 10 years old when he inherited the throne, his father, Edward the prince of Wales (EDWARD THE BLACK PRINCE), being already deceased. A council of regency was established to advise the young king and to rule in his name until he should come of age. The council was composed of some of the most powerful members of the English nobility, including the king's uncle, JOHN OF GAUNT, the eldest living son of Edward III.

Throughout his life, Richard struggled against the domination of these men. Regarding most of them as crude and brutal, he formed his own circle of friends and favorites, some of whom he elevated to prominent positions in his government. For example, he made Michael de la Pole, the son of a famous merchant, chancellor and invested him with the title of the earl of Suffolk. Richard's constant chafing against the rule of his uncles increased their frustration with the young king, and in 1386 they influenced Parliament to demand the impeachment and imprisonment of Suffolk. When the king continued to resist the advice of the older magnates, many of whom were his uncles, they took stronger measures to curb his independence. He finally appeared to accept their attempts to advise and control him, and a period of relative peace ensued, lasting from 1388 to 1397. In 1397, however, Richard lashed out at the people who had tried to dominate

King Richard II meets with the rebellious Kentishmen in the Peasants' Revolt of 1381. From British Library Ms. Royal 18 EII f 175.

him, and either banished or executed many of the most important nobles in his kingdom. From 1397 to 1399, he seems to have gone too far, trying to free himself from the control of Parliament. In 1399, when John of Gaunt died, Richard seized his uncle's estates, which should have descended to Gaunt's son, Henry Bolingbroke (later Henry IV), then living in exile. Infuriated by Richard's actions, Henry raised an army and came back to England to reclaim his inheritance. Meeting with little resistance, he went on to force Richard's abdication, afterward claiming the crown for himself.

Despite all of this political turmoil, Richard, who was himself a man of refined manners and cultivated tastes, made his court a center of artistic achievement. The most important literary development of his reign was the replacement of French by English as the language of the nobility. The movement toward the domination of English had begun before Richard's reign, to a large extent because of the wars with France and a resulting reaction against all aspects of French culture.

Chaucer established himself as a courtier and civil servant during the reign of Richard's grandfather, but most of his major poetry was written during Richard's reign, with Richard renewing those grants and annuities that had been made by King Edward III to the poet. The precise nature of Chaucer's contact with the young king is uncertain, but there is strong evidence that his poem, *The PARLIAMENT OF FOWLS,* was written in honor of Richard's marriage to ANNE OF BOHEMIA. Chaucer held various offices in Richard's government: In 1382 he was appointed Controller of the Petty Customs on wine and other merchandise in the port of London, in addition to the position he already held as controller of the King's Custom and Subsidy of Wools, Hides and Wool Fells. In 1385 he was appointed justice of the peace in Kent, and in 1389, shortly after Richard's proclamation of independence from his counselors, he was appointed Clerk of the King's Works, which made him responsible for the upkeep of certain of the king's buildings and lands. Despite the success Chaucer enjoyed under Richard, he cannot, however, have been too close to the king. If he had been, the ups and downs of his career would have more closely reflected the king's successes and failures, and his annuities and grants would not have been renewed, as they were, by the man who deposed Richard, Henry Bolingbroke.

Richesse   Richesse, or Riches, is one of the allegorical figures in the *ROMAUNT OF THE ROSE,* Chaucer's translation of the popular French DREAM VISION *Le ROMAN DE LA ROSE.* When the dreamer-narrator gains entry to the Garden of Mirth, he discovers a kind of festival taking place. The god of love, i.e., CUPID, dances in the garden, surrounded by various attendants, all of whom stand for qualities desirable or necessary for the game

of Love. The god dances with Beauty, who appears as a beautiful woman, and next to her stands Richesse (i.e., wealth). She is a lady of high status and great nobility whom nobody wishes to displease since she has such great power to either help or hinder the advancement of others. Richesse is wearing an extremely rich purple gown covered with gold embroidery and bordered with silk ribbons in which are woven the stories of dukes and kings. Her buttons are enameled with fine gold, and she wears a collar of jewels around her neck. A belt around her waist features two stones, each of which has powerful healing properties, and her head is crowned with a circlet of pure gold encrusted with rubies, sapphires, emeralds and a carbuncle (a red stone) that shines so that it provides light in the darkness and casts an eternal aura of brightness around her face. Richesse is accompanied by an unnamed young man whom she dotes upon and who adheres to her because of his attachment to material things (lines 1033–1142).

Rickert, Edith (1871–1938)   American scholar, one of the earliest women to make an outstanding contribution to Chaucer studies. Edith Rickert received her Ph.D. in 1899 from the University of Chicago, to which she returned as a professor in 1924. With John M. MANLY, Rickert coauthored *The Text of the Canterbury Tales, Studied on the Basis of all known Manuscripts* (1940) an edition of eight enormous volumes which is evaluated in *Editing Chaucer: The Great Tradition* (1984). This task was so enormous that, according to Manly's preface, it actually killed Edith Rickert. Manly describes Professor Rickert's determination to finish the task even through a near-fatal heart attack and her doctor's orders not to overwork. In addition, Rickert was, in Manly's words, a "stimulating and self-sacrificing teacher," which added significantly to her load. *The Text of the Canterbury Tales* is a relentless, detailed description of all extant manuscripts of the tales, the fullest source available for its textual materials. *Chaucer's World* (1948), a collection of materials Rickert had gathered while working the Chaucer edition, was edited by two of her students and published posthumously. The materials include 14th-century social records, translated and arranged under various subject categories including London life, training and education, entertainment, travel, war, religion and others. This book was the forerunner for the invaluable *CHAUCER LIFE RECORDS* (1966, edited by Martin Crow and Claire Olson), wherein were published the 493 records of Chaucer's life collected by Manly and Rickert from civil, ecclesiastical and private sources.

Rifeo   (Ripheus)   In BOCCACCIO'S *FILOSTRATO,* Chaucer's source for his *TROILUS AND CRISEYDE,* Rifeo is a Trojan hero taken prisoner by the Greeks during the TROJAN WAR. Chaucer makes him one of the warriors who tried to prevent ANTENOR's capture (book 4, lines 50–56). The Greeks later offered to release Antenor in exchange for CRISEYDE, whose father resided with the Greek host. The exchange caused the separation of the two lovers, leading to TROILUS' despair and death.

Ripheus *See* RIFEO.

Rising of 1381 *See* PEASANTS' REVOLT OF 1381.

Riverside Chaucer, The Published by Houghton Mifflin in 1987, *The Riverside Chaucer* is currently considered the authoritative edition of Chaucer's work. This means that the majority of scholarly books and articles written about any of Chaucer's poetry and/or prose would cite this edition for all quotations and other references, unless the nature of the work at hand called for referring to a different edition. As is announced in the preface to the text, it was originally intended to be a revision of F. N. ROBINSON's second edition of *The Works of Geoffrey Chaucer,* but the editors soon discovered that the study of Chaucer had expanded so greatly since 1957, when that edition appeared, as to require a completely new edition with new introductory materials, bibliography, explanatory notes, textual notes, glossary and index of proper names. The texts of the poetry and prose were also reedited, although they were still based on Robinson's text, which had been based on SKEAT's of 1894, which itself took the ELLESMERE MANUSCRIPT as its authority. Although *The Riverside Chaucer* was begun under the general editorship of Robert PRATT, Larry BENSON took over and completed the project with the assistance of many talented scholars.

Robbins, Rossell Hope (1912–1990) Born in England and educated at Cambridge University, Robbins emigrated to the U.S. and became a professor of English at SUNY–Albany. His interests were extremely broad, including not only Medieval and Renaissance scholarship, but also such diverse subjects as T. S. Eliot, witchcraft and demonology, and the history of jazz. Robbins edited *Chaucer at Albany* (1975), a collection of articles that looked at Middle English texts and their contexts; he also contributed to several volumes of Chaucer scholarship, including Beryl Rowland's *Companion to Chaucer Studies* (1979), for which he wrote "The Fabliaux," an essay asserting that Chaucer's irony is "essentially a modern discovery," and not something that would have been apparent to a 14th-century audience. He further believes that we should not "blind ourselves to the real indecency and immorality" of the FABLIAU. Robbins also wrote the entry on "The Chaucerian Apocrypha" for *The Manual of Writings in Middle English, 1050–1500* (1974), discussing those poems of uncertain authorship which have been, for

various reasons and at various times, attributed to Chaucer.

Robert, Sir One of the fornicators whose deeds with various "wenches" of the parish are confessed to the wicked summoner of "The FRIAR'S TALE" (lines 1355–58). The summoner uses the information to extort money from the men whom he could otherwise force to appear in an ecclesiastical court to answer for their sins. That the women are described as being "at his retenue" ("in his service") suggests that the men are being set up.

Robertson, D(urant) W(aite) Jr. (1914–) American Chaucer scholar. After receiving a Ph.D. from the University of North Carolina–Chapel Hill, Robertson taught in a variety of institutions before establishing himself at Princeton. Regarded by many as a leading scholar of medieval literature, Robertson based his career on the principle that critical evaluations of earlier literature "should be based firmly on knowledge gained from primary sources. If we cannot understand literary works in terms that would have been understood by their authors we shall not understand them at all." Accordingly, Robertson's *Preface to Chaucer* (1962) is a monumental work that attempts to prepare readers for Chaucer's poetry by providing them with a survey of the historical and cultural background to Chaucer's writing. Robertson followed the *Preface* with another work grounded in the same philosophy but with a narrower focus, *Chaucer's London* (1968), in which he continues his mission to point out that people in the Middle Ages were very different, that the world they lived in was very much unlike our own in ways that we must at least attempt to understand before we may truly appreciate the literature of the period. Robertson's work was extremely influential in the decade following its publication. In recent years, however, scholars have questioned his ideas regarding the uniformity of human experience during the period he describes, using historical records to show that there was much more variety and dissent than Robertson acknowledges.

Robinson, F(red) N(orris) (1871–1966) Chaucer scholar. A Harvard Ph.D. with additional graduate degrees from the University of Freiburg, Bowdoin College and Ohio State, Robinson primarily focused his scholarship on philology. Early in his career he devoted his attention to Celtic languages such as Gaelic (Old Irish) and Welsh. His extensive publications include texts, essays and translations, chiefly in the fields of Celtic philology, medieval literature and the history of religions. In 1933 he completed *The Works of Geoffrey Chaucer,* an edition of Chaucer's oevre based on the 1894 edition of W. W. SKEAT, featuring the most extensive set of explanatory notes and bibliography yet seen in an edition of Chaucer. A revised, second edition was published in 1957. (For further information, *see* EDITIONS OF CHAUCER'S WORK.) The text of the current *RIVERSIDE CHAUCER* is based on this edition.

Robyn (1)   Robyn, or Robin, is the name of the MILLER who is described in the GENERAL PROLOGUE TO *THE CANTERBURY TALES* (lines 545–66) and who tells the second tale along the road to CANTERBURY. Jill MANN, in *Chaucer and Medieval Estates Satire,* points out similarities between the portrait of the Miller and that of "Robyn the rybaudoure," a figure who appears in William LANGLAND's *Vision of Piers Plowman* and who perhaps provided Chaucer with the Miller's name.

Robyn (2)   JOHN THE CARPENTER's servant in "The MILLER'S TALE." When John's lodger, NICHOLAS, locks himself in his room and does not come out, John sends Robyn up to rouse him. When the young man is unable to wake him by knocking on the door and calling out to him, he peeps through a hole in the door. He sees Nicholas lying on the floor as if he is in a stupor, which he reports to his master, and then assists Nicholas in breaking down the door. The first name of the MILLER who tells this tale is also Robyn.

Robyn (3)   In book 5 of *TROILUS AND CRISEYDE,* when TROILUS expresses his certainty that CRISEYDE will return that evening from the Greek camp, PANDARUS agrees, but thinks to himself, "From haselwode, there joly Robyn pleyde, / Shal come al that thow abidest heere. / Ye, fare wel al the snow of ferne yere!" (lines 1174–76) [From the hazel wood, where jolly Robin played, / Shall come all that you wait for here. / Yes, farewell all the snows of yesteryear!]. His skeptical reply may refer to the popular figure of English legend commonly known as Robin Hood (such anachronisms are not uncommon in Chaucer's poetry), or the reference could simply be to a kind of rustic person who lives in the woods. Robin would be an appropriate name for such a person.

Rochele, the   "The Rochele" is Chaucer's way of referring to the French wine-growing region of La Rochelle, which is mentioned by the narrator of "The PARDONER'S TALE" as he describes the evils of drunkenness and the necessity of avoiding certain wines with which he, alas, seems all too familiar (lines 562–71).

Rochester   A town in Kent, on the river Medway, about 30 miles southeast of London, Rochester is one of the geographical markers used to indicate the progress of the pilgrims toward CANTERBURY and the shrine of Saint THOMAS À BECKET in *The CANTERBURY TALES.* According to F. P. MAGOUN's *Chaucer Gazetteer,* Rochester was a well-known overnight stopping place between SOUTHWARK and Canterbury, being the only such suitable place apart from Dartford and Ospringe. In the prologue to "The MONK'S TALE," the Host (*see* Harry BAILLY) notes that they draw near to Rochester (line 1926) as he asks the MONK to take his turn in the tale-telling contest in which they have all agreed to participate.

Rodogone   *See* RHODOGUNE.

Rodopeya (Rodopeye)   *See* RHODOPE.

Roger (1)   *See* COOK, THE.

Roger (2)   *See* RUGGIERI DEGLI UBALDINI.

Roland   The Roland mentioned by the BLACK KNIGHT in *The BOOK OF THE DUCHESS* (line 1123) is the hero of the famous French epic poem the *Chanson de Roland* (*The Song of Roland*). According to the poem, Roland was the nephew of Charlemagne and the commander of the rear guard of his army that, as it returned from a successful campaign in northern Spain, was ambushed by Saracens. The name of GANELON, Roland's stepfather who betrayed the French to their enemies, came to be synonymous with the idea of treachery. The Black Knight says that if he were to repent of loving his lady, he would be worse than Ganelon, who betrayed Roland and OLIVER, Roland's companion in arms.

Roman de la Rose, Le   A very influential allegorical poem composed by two French authors in the 13th century. GUILLAUME DE LORRIS began work on the poem around 1230 but left it unfinished at his death around 1237. JEAN DE MEUN, a scholastic who attended the University of Paris and who was born at about the time of Guillaume's death, continued and concluded the poem sometime around 1275. The story in Guillaume's part of the poem is a celebration as well as an analysis of courtly love embodied in a DREAM VISION. The first-person narrator, after falling asleep one night, dreams that he discovers an enclosed garden (the Garden of Love), wherein, after gaining admittance, he encounters allegorical figures personifying the various forces, both mental and physical, that affect human behavior in the realm of romantic love. After falling in love with a beautiful rosebud whose reflection he has seen in the well of NARCISSUS, the dreamer spends the remainder of Guillaume's portion of the narrative trying to possess the rose, but only succeeds, briefly and with the help of VENUS, in claiming a kiss. Jean de Meun's continuation of the poem reads much like a reaction against the sentiments expressed in Guillaume's portion. Whereas Guillaume's portrayal of romantic love is idealistic and emphasizes the lover's submission to and worship of his beloved, Jean's portrayal of that kind of love comes across as cynically satirical, especially within the antifeminist passages that portray the ways in which women deceive and trick men. But Jean's interest is not limited to romantic love; his intellect ranges over the subject from a more philosophical perspective, considering divine love and friendship as well as providing lengthy discussion of the many facets of sexual love. In fact, one of the most famous and controversial passages of the poem is Jean's description of the lover's penetration into the sacred precincts of the ivory tower where he seizes the rose, plucks the bud and spills a bit of seed at the center, which has the consequence of making the bud expand and enlarge into pregnancy.

In its time, the *Roman* was one of the most widely read and influential works of literature. There are more than 200 surviving manuscripts, and the work was put into print very soon after the introduction of the printing press in Europe, perhaps even as early as 1481. The dream vision, as it was formulated by Guillaume de Lorris, became the dominant genre of the literature of courtly love. Chaucer not only translated a portion of the work (*see* ROMAUNT OF THE ROSE), but also used it as a model for the dream-vision framework of four of his own works: *The BOOK OF THE DUCHESS, The PARLIAMENT OF FOWLS, The HOUSE OF FAME* and *The LEGEND OF GOOD WOMEN.*

Roman de Renart   The *Roman de Renart* ("Romance of Reynard") is an Old French beast epic which recounts the adventures of a fox named Renart (in English usually spelled *Reynard*), his clashes with his rival, a wolf named Isengrim, and various adventures wherein he figuratively represents the man who preys on society, is brought to justice, but then cleverly escapes. The beast epics are distinguished from BEAST FABLE primarily by their amorality. The focus of the stories was not on the lesson to be learned from Renart's predicament but on the fox's cunning and his ability to extricate himself from difficult situations. One episode from the *Roman de Renart* was the source for MARIE DE FRANCE's beast fable *Del cok e del gupil* ("About a Cock and a Fox"), which is thought by many scholars to have been the immediate source of Chaucer's "NUN'S PRIEST'S TALE." All three tell the story of a rooster named CHAUNTICLEER who dreams that he is going to be attacked by a strange animal that comes into the farmyard. After telling his dream to one of the chickens, he is tricked by the fox into making himself vulnerable. The fox seizes him and is running away to the woods when Chaunticleer tricks the fox into opening his mouth. Gaining his escape, the rooster flies into a tree, and each animal curses himself for his foolishness. Chaucer took this basic framework of the story and expanded it with anecdotes, moral applications, literary allusions and rhetorical flourishes, many of which serve to illu-minate the character of the rooster, Chaunticleer, and add the mock-heroic dimension from which arises most of the story's humor.

Roman de Troie   *See* BENOIT DE SAINT MAURE.

Romance (Romaunce, Romauns) of the Rose   *See* ROMAN DE LA ROSE, LE.

Romaunt of the Rose, The   Chaucer's (unfinished) translation of *Le ROMAN DE LA ROSE.*

SUMMARY

Chaucer's poem opens with a defense of the integrity and significance of dreams. To bolster his argument, the narrator briefly cites the example of MACROBIUS' *DREAM OF SCIPIO* ("Cipioun"). Following this brief introduction, he begins describing himself as a young man, 20 years of age and ripe for the experience of love. One night after going to sleep, he dreamed a fabulous dream which the god of love ("Love") has asked and commanded him to put down in rhyme. The book shall be called the Romance of the Rose, and it will contain everything about the art of love. He prays that the woman in whose honor it is written will receive it graciously, and claims that because of her worthiness she herself merits the title "Rose of every man."

The dream begins with the description of a May morning five or more years ago. (The implication is that he dreamed the dream during the month of May, and also that it was a May morning within the dream.) During the night, while asleep, he dreams that he has awakened early in the morning. After getting dressed, he decides to go out into the country to hear the birds sing. In the course of his walk, he comes upon a river, which he follows through a meadow until he reaches a garden enclosed by high walls. The walls are painted and carved with pictures of various allegorical figures, all of whom are female and all of whom are disfigured in accordance with the vice they represent.

The first figure is Hate. She is flanked on either side by Felony (crime) and Villainy (rudeness). Other figures represented there include Coveitise (covetousness); Avarice (who is as green as a leek); Envy (who is tormented by anyone's good fortune); Sorrow (who, like Hate, is also considerably angry), Elde (old age, who is realistically portrayed as shrunken, diseased and childishly dependent); Pope-Holy (hypocrisy); and Poverty, whose portrait is set in a niche away from the others to symbolize how poverty is ashamed and despised by all. Despite the discouraging appearance of these wall adornments, the narrator perceives that the garden enclosed by the walls is a place where he may enjoy such solace and amusement that he must find a way to get inside. The singing of the birds in the garden is so beautiful that he would rather be allowed to enter than to be given £100 (worth perhaps $1,000,000 in today's money).

Finally he becomes so desperate to get over the wall that he decides to walk around it until he finds the gate, reasoning that there must be one somewhere. At last he is successful and comes to a small locked wicket, which he knocks upon insistently until his summons is answered. The door is opened for him by a young maiden with blonde hair, gray eyes, a white complexion and other conventional marks of beauty. Her head is crowned by a garland made of roses and her tunic is made of green cloth from Ghent. Her only duty, in the month of May, is to keep herself beautifully dressed and merry. When the dreamer asks the maiden what her name is, she replies that it is Idleness and that men call her thus because she strives for nothing but joy, amusement and combing and braiding her hair. She volunteers further information, explaining that she is acquainted with MIRTH, the lord of the garden who imported the trees therein from Alexandria (in Egypt) and then had the surrounding wall built and adorned with the portraits that the dreamer has observed there. Mirth, she says, in company with a train of followers, often comes to the garden and in fact is there now, listening to the singing of the birds. The dreamer decides that he must see Mirth and enters the garden. Once he is inside, his heart is filled with gladness to find himself in such an earthly paradise. The singing of the birds is so beautiful he thinks it must be as fair as that of angels or mermaids. Reveling in their music, he is filled with a happiness that has no parallel in his previous experience. In gratitude to Idleness for providing him with this opportunity, he swears to be her friend.

Remembering his desire to see Mirth, the dreamer sets off down a narrow path hedged by mint and fennel. Very soon he discovers Mirth and his group of followers, who are entertaining themselves with singing and dancing. Chief among those singing is Gladness, who is Mirth's beloved. All of the company participate in the dance, including Mirth, who is accompanied and led about by two fair damsels. Another lady, whose name is Courtesy, observes the dreamer's approach and asks him why he has come. But without waiting for an answer, she invites him to join the dancing, which he does without hesitation.

Participating in their revels affords him the opportunity for even closer observation of Mirth and his followers, and he now offers descriptions of each of them. First is Mirth, tall and more attractive than any man the dreamer has ever seen. His face is as round as an apple, his complexion ruddy and white and all his features elegant and proportional. His hair is curly and bright, his shoulders broad and his waist narrow so that he almost appears to be a statue, except that he is very nimble and light-footed. His youth is attested to by his scant beard. His clothing is made of samite, a rich silk cloth, and his tunic is fashionably slashed to reveal the lining. On his head he wears a crown or garland of flowers that was fashioned by his beloved.

Gladness, who is Mirth's beloved, now dances with him. Her beauty is compared to that of a new rose, her skin so soft and tender that it could easily be torn by a small briar. Her forehead is wrinkle-free, her eyes gray, her hair a shining yellow. The garland she wears is made of embroidered gold and her samite gown is also gold-adorned. On the other side of Gladness stands the god of love (CUPID), who is dressed not in silk or any other cloth, but in a mysterious garment composed of flowers and leaves. He, like Mirth, also wears a crown of roses. The god of love is accompanied by a squire ("bachelor") named Sweet-Looking, whose primary function is to carry the god's bows and arrows. One of the bows is made of wood that is knotty, foul and black. The other is elegant, smooth and long, proportional and without blemish. Its surface is decorated with geometric designs and portraits of ladies and young men. In addition to the bows there are 10 arrows. Five of the arrows are excellently made and tipped with pure gold points, and each of them has a name. The first, and fairest, is called Beauty; the second, Simplicity; the third, Franchise (generosity of spirit); the fourth, Company (companionship); and the fifth, Fair-Semblaunt (Fair-Seeming). Fair-Semblaunt is the least hurtful arrow of all because, although it can make a large wound, the wound will nevertheless heal quickly. These arrows belong to the elegant, well-proportioned bow. The other fives arrows are described as being "black as the fiend of hell," and they belong to the foul, crooked bow. The first of these is called Pride; the second, Villainy; the third, Shame; the fourth, Wanhope (despair); and the last, New-Thought. The dreamer concludes this description by promising that he will explain the significance of each arrow before the end of his book.

Returning to the task of describing those who are dancing, he focuses next on a lady called Beauty, who, he says, is as bright and clear as the moonlight. Her skin is an tender as the dew of a flower and her expression as straightforward as that of a bird in a bower. Like those of the other beautiful females in the poem, her features are all proportional and elegant. Two additional characteristics, which distinguish her from the rest, are the length of her hair, which reaches to her heels, and the fact that she neither plucks her eyebrows nor wears cosmetics, of which she has no need. Beauty dances in the company of the god of love, and next to her stands RICHESSE (i.e., wealth), a lady of high status and great nobility whom nobody wants to displease, since she has such great power to either help or hinder the advancement of others. Unfortunately, her court is full of flatterers who try unjustly to influence her against people. Richesse is wearing an extremely rich purple gown covered with gold embroidery and bordered with silk ribbons in which are woven the stories of dukes and of kings. Her buttons are enameled with fine gold, and she wears a collar of jewels around her neck. A belt around her waist features two stones, each of which has powerful healing properties, and her head is crowned with a circlet of pure gold encrusted with rubies, sapphires, emeralds and a carbuncle (a kind of red stone) that shines so that it provides light in the darkness and casts an eternal aura of brightness around her face. Richesse is accompanied by an unnamed young man whom she dotes upon and who adheres to her because of his attachment to material things. Better than anything else he loves fine horses, keeping a great house, elegant clothes and plenty of gold and silver to spend.

The next figure to be described by the dreamer is Largesse (generosity), also a woman, whose greatest joy is the bestowal of gifts, which makes her the favorite of both rich and poor. Her beneficence is contrasted to the ill effects of Avarice, one of the vices pictured on the outside of the wall whose opposite she is. Just as she creates many friends for herself, so does Avarice, through her greed, create enemies. Largesse wears a gown of rich purple Saracen, a cloth imported from the East. Her face is well-formed and clear, and she wears the collar of her dress open because she has just given away, as a present, a gold brooch that she was wearing there. She is holding hands with a worthy knight, the brother of King ARTHUR of Britain who has come to the dance from a tournament where he performed great deeds of chivalry for the love of his lady.

Next to this knight dances Franchise (nobility of character, generosity of spirit), who in appearance is very similar to Beauty. Her own outstanding characteristic is the empathy she displays for any man who falls in love with her, feeling it to be her responsibility to assuage any harm he may come to on her behalf. Beside her dances another unnamed but attractive young man who is reckoned the son of the lord of Windsor. The next figure described is Courtesy, who earns everyone's praises by being neither proud nor a fool. She it was who invited the dreamer into the dance. Wise, prudent and virtuous, she is always fair of speech and never says ill of anyone. In contrast to the other women described thus far, Courtesy is dark-complexioned yet bright of face, and she has a pleasing shape. Courtesy is also accompanied by a knight well-known for his honor in battle.

Idleness, too, is present at the dance, but having already introduced her, the narrator does not describe her again. She is accompanied by Youth, a young girl not yet 12 years of age, who is wild, flighty and somewhat foolish but intends no harm. Youth too is accompanied by a young lover who strives to kiss her whenever he can. Like two young doves, neither of them is ashamed to be kissing in public.

Having now described all those who led the dance, the dreamer now desires to explore the garden further. The dance breaks up, and all of the dancers depart in pairs. The god of love, however, summons Sweet-Looking (who bears his bow and arrows), and taking his golden bow and one of the arrows, prepares to shoot. The dreamer is at this point unaware of the god of love's actions, and so he continues wandering up and down, intent on seeing every sight the garden has to offer.

Next he describes the garden itself. It is square in shape (as long as it is wide), and every tree bears fruit (offspring) except for the "hidous" (ugly) ones, of which there are two or three. Some of the trees that grow plentifully there are the pomegranate, nutmeg, almond, fig and date trees. Spices such as clove, cinnamon, cardamom and ginger abound as well. Among the fruit trees proper are peaches, apples, plums, pears and cherries, and the leaf trees include maple, ash, oak, plane, yew, poplar and linden trees. Nut trees and olives grow there too. The trees were planted at regular intervals from one another, the dreamer notes, and have grown tall and broad so that their interlocking branches shade the tender grass from the sun. Deer, squirrels and rabbits are observed playing among the trees. Water is provided by wells (free of frogs) and streams make a pleasant sound. The grass growing beside these streams and wells is as thick and soft as velvet, perfect for lying down upon with a lover.

Flowers grow plentifully in the garden, in winter as well as in summer. In contrast to his catalog of trees, the dreamer mentions only two by name, the violet and periwinkle. As he goes about these explorations, the dreamer is followed unawares by the god of love, just as a hunter follows a beast through the forest. The dreamer stops to rest beside a well beneath a pine tree. The stone border of the well is engraved with the words, "Here starf the fayre Narcisus" [Here perished the fair Narcissus].

The dreamer pauses in the narrative of his own experience to briefly tell the story of NARCISSUS, the beautiful young man who disdained the love of ECHO. After being rejected so cruelly by the object of her affections, and before dying of a broken heart, Echo prayed that he might suffer the same fate as she and pine away in unrequited love. The prayer was answered when Narcissus, hot and thirsty after a day of hunting, paused to drink at the aforementioned well and fell in love with his reflection in the water. Realizing that his desire could never be fulfilled, he lost his wits and died shortly after. At the conclusion of this story, the narrator offers it as an example of what may happen to ladies who are to blame for their lovers' demise.

Once he has realized that this well is the well of Narcissus, the dreamer begins to withdraw in fear, but then changes his mind and decides to peer into the water. The water is crystal clear and down at the very bottom of the well he can see two crystal stones. When the Sun shines down into the well, the crystal catches the light and refracts it into a hundred colors. The crystals also act as a mirror and are able to reflect everything in the garden for him who gazes into the well. This is the same mirror that Narcissus looked into and it has the property of making any man who looks at it fall in love. Because of this quality, the well is named the Well of Love. Himself falling prey to the well's charms, the dreamer finds himself mesmerized by the images reflected there. Now, though, he wishes he had never looked therein because he is caught in Love's snare.

Reflected in the mirror, among a thousand other things, he sees, enclosed by a hedge, a rosebush full of roses and is suddenly seized with a raging desire to see it. As he approaches the rosebush he smells the roses' perfume and is struck to the heart. He would like to pick one of the roses to carry with him, but is too afraid of displeasing the lord of the garden. Surveying the bush, he is especially attracted by the buds because they last longer than those that have already opened. From among these buds he chooses the fairest and brightest and sweetest smelling. . . .

Here Fragment A of the text breaks off. The English translation is continued in two more fragments (B and C) by other authors. None of the three fragments is certain to have been written by Chaucer, but most scholars have accepted Fragment A as his work based on studies of its style and language.

COMMENTARY

The French *Roman de la Rose* by GUILLAUME DE LORRIS and JEAN DE MEUN influenced Chaucer's own work more than any other literary text. He was to use the dream vision that had been created by Guillaume as the model for similar visions in a number of his own poems, including *The BOOK OF THE DUCHESS*, *The PARLIAMENT OF FOWLS*, *The HOUSE OF FAME* and *The LEGEND OF GOOD WOMEN*, all of which feature a dreamer-narrator reporting the content of a marvelous dream. *The Parliament of Fowls* even has a Garden of Love very like the one inhabited by Mirth and his allegorical companions. Given his evident admiration for the work and the fact that he translated BOETHIUS' *Consolation of Philosophy,* another work that had a strong influence on his own literary creations, it hardly seems surprising that Chaucer would undertake a translation of the French text. What is surprising, or at least frustrating, is that the Middle English text attributed to Chaucer in a 1532 edition published by William Thynne may not have been written by Chaucer at all. Scholars who have studied that text generally agree with a division

of the work (made by M. Kaluza in 1893) into three parts: fragments A, B, and C. The division is based on the idea that each part was written by a different author. The only part that most scholars currently accept as Chaucer's work is Fragment A (lines 1–1705), although *The RIVERSIDE CHAUCER* includes the translation in its entirety. Whether or not any part of this particular translation was composed by Chaucer, there is some external evidence that he did undertake such a project. In the prologue to *The Legend of Good Women,* the God of Love accuses Chaucer of heresy for translating the *Roman.* John LYDGATE, in *The Fall of Princes,* mentions that Chaucer had translated the work, and Eustache DESCHAMPS, the important French poet who was such a great admirer of Chaucer, also alludes to that idea. Interestingly, the work is not referred to in other catalogues of Chaucer's work, including CHAUCER'S RETRACTION. The date of Fragment A's composition is as uncertain as its authorship, but if it is Chaucer's, then based on choices the poet made regarding language and versification, it was likely written during the early phase of his career. As a translation, it is fairly faithful to the French original, but nevertheless makes thorough use of the English idiom and of imagery found in typical English metrical romances.

In terms of content, the material translated in Fragment A forms a satisfactory narrative unit, beginning with the dreamer's stated intention of relating his dream experience and ending with his choice of the most beautiful and sweet-smelling rosebud as the object of his devotion. Considering that this portion contains the elements of the poem having the greatest influence on Chaucer's own work, we may speculate as to whether he completed only the part that was most significant to him. Another obvious possibility is that he did complete a translation that has not survived.

The subject of the poem is love, and the portion translated in Fragment A attempts to represent allegorically the process of falling into romantic love. According to the vision presented here, certain prerequisites are needed to set the scene. First, there is the spring morning which stimulates romantic desire. Second, there is some kind of obstacle that must be overcome—in this case the wall surrounding the garden. The allegorical figures present in the garden indicate various physical and mental ingredients necessary for love's chemistry to be activated, such as Idleness, Mirth, Beauty and others. The dance which they invite the dreamer to join is a metaphorical representation of courtship. Interestingly, although the dreamer gladly participates in the dancing, he is still functioning as an observer. It is not until he wanders off alone and gazes into the well of Narcissus that he too becomes afflicted by the wound from Cupid's arrow and feels the passion that leads him irresistibly toward the lovely rose. In the continuation afforded by Fragment B, the dreamer swears allegiance to Love and is instructed in the rules of behavior for a lover. The God of Love warns him of what he may expect to suffer (because a man loves more tenderly the thing he has bought most dearly), but also promises him some solace in the form of Good-Hope, Sweet-Thinking, Sweet-Speech and SWEET-LOOKING, all of which will attend upon his relationship with his beloved. He then approaches the rose garden, which BIALACOIL (fair welcome) permits him to enter, but he is opposed by DAUNGER (disdain), SHAME, DREAD and WICKED TONGUE (malicious gossip). Although Venus comes to his aid and enables him to attain a kiss, JEAL-OUSY drives him out of the garden and imprisons the rosebud and Bialacoil in a strong fortress. The dreamer falls into despair and is approached by Reason, who tries to convince him that his passion is both foolish and harmful. Fragment B ends before the conclusion of Reason's discourse, and, without a break in the manuscript, Fragment C picks up the French text about 5,000 lines later, creating a somewhat confusing transition to the portion of the poem where the God of Love has called together a council of his barons to get their advice on conquering the castle where the rose has been imprisoned. Fragment C is taken from Jean de Meun's portion of the *Roman* and features a long speech by Fals-Semblant (false-seeming) revealing the hypocrisy of women, religion and the social order. The Middle English translation breaks off before the council concludes. In the French text the dreamer ultimately triumphs, winning full possession of his lovely rose.

For Further Reading: There is no better commentary on the *Roman de la Rose* and the tradition to which it belongs than C. S. LEWIS' *Allegory of Love* (1936). For a comparison of Chaucer's translation with the French original, see Caroline D. Eckhardt's "The Art of Translation in *The Romaunt of the Rose*" (*Studies in the Age of Chaucer,* 1984).

Rome The capital city of Italy and formerly the capital of the Roman republic, the Roman Empire and the papal states, Rome is mentioned in Chaucer's work more often than any other European capital. In the GENERAL PROLOGUE TO *THE CANTERBURY TALES,* the narrator mentions Rome among the many places that the WIFE OF BATH has been to on pilgrimage (line 465). The PARDONER, also in the General Prologue, is described as having come straight from the papal court in Rome to join the pilgrimage to CANTERBURY (line 671). The papal court is where he would obtain the pardons that he offers to sell to his traveling companions. Rome is the setting for part of "The MAN OF LAW'S TALE." The tale's heroine, CONSTANCE, is a

daughter of the Roman emperor, who agrees to marry her to the SULTAN OF SYRIA. After a long and eventful life, Constance returns to Rome, where she is reunited with her father and, after her second husband's death, spends the remainder of her life. In the prologue to "The WIFE OF BATH'S TALE," the WIFE OF BATH mentions that Saint JEROME was a cardinal in Rome (line 673) when she gives her catalogue of the writers whose works appeared in her husband's "Book of Wicked Wives." WALTER, the husband of GRISELDA in "The CLERK'S TALE," sends to friends of his in the papal court in Rome (line 737), asking them to counterfeit a dispensation for him to secure a divorce from his wife as part of his efforts to test Griselda's patience and fidelity. In "The SQUIRE'S TALE," members of CAMBYUSKAN's court marvel over the magic mirror that he receives as one of his birthday gifts, some of them noting the existence of a similar mirror in Rome (line 231). Rome is also the city where LUCRECE committed suicide after being raped by Tarquin (*see* TARQUINIUS); that story appears in Chaucer's *LEGEND OF GOOD WOMEN* (lines 1680–1885) and is mentioned in "The FRANKLIN'S TALE" as DORIGEN recalls various examples of virtuous women (lines 1405–08). In "The MONK'S TALE," Queen ZENOBIA and her husband conquer many cities that belonged to the empire of Rome (lines 2313–16) and are feared by several of its emperors, but at last the emperor AURELIAN defeats her and makes her walk before him wearing golden chains as he triumphantly enters the city (line 2357–64). Also in "The MONK'S TALE," NERO is the emperor who "Rome brende for his delicasie" (line 2479) [burned Rome for his pleasure], and Julius Caesar, another emperor, is assassinated in the capitol (lines 2695–10). In "The NUN'S PRIEST'S TALE," the barnyard hens shriek more loudly over CHAUNTICLEER's misfortune than did the wives of the Roman senators who were executed by Nero when he burned Rome (lines 3369–73). Rome is the setting for the life of Saint CECILIA, which forms the subject matter of "The SECOND NUN'S TALE"; and in "The CANON'S YEOMAN'S TALE," the narrator says that he knows of a canon whose trickery and deceits are clever enough to swindle a whole town, even one as large as Rome (lines 972–75). BOETHIUS was a native of the city of Rome, so it is mentioned numerous times in Chaucer's translation of Boethius' autobiographically inspired *Consolation of Philosophy*. In the story of CLEOPATRA that appears in *The LEGEND OF GOOD WOMEN,* ANTONY is referred to as a rebel against Rome (line 591). In *The BOOK OF THE DUCHESS,* the BLACK KNIGHT says he would still have loved his LADY WHITE, even if he possessed all the wealth of Rome (line 1063); and in *The HOUSE OF FAME,* the narrator finds in FAME's palace the images of all those clerks who wrote of Rome's mighty works (line 1504).

Romulus The legendary founder of Rome. He and his twin brother Remus were the offspring of the god MARS (1) and a mortal woman, Rhea Silvia, who was the daughter of Nimitor, the king of Alba Longa, the city built by AENEAS' son ASCANIUS and ruled by his descendants. When Numitor's brother, Amulius, took the throne away from him, he forced Rhea Silvia to become a vestal virgin so that she would not conceive any heirs to challenge his claim to the throne. When she bore twins as a result of her visitation by Mars, Amulius ordered that the boys be thrown into the Tiber River, but they were rescued by a she-wolf, an animal sacred to Mars, and then brought up by a royal herdsman. Romulus and his brother grew up to be formidable warriors. After deciding to found a city in the place where they had been rescued and brought up, rivalry between the two brothers over the exact site of the city led to the death of Remus, and Romulus founded the city of Rome on the Palatine Hill with himself as its sovereign. After a long and eventful reign, he vanished in a thunderstorm while reviewing his troops. The peculiar manner of his death is alluded to in *The HOUSE OF FAME*, when the narrator, fearing the reasons for which he is being carried aloft into the heavens by an EAGLE, exclaims that he is not Romulus (line 589) or any other personage from the Bible or mythology whose fate was to be carried alive into heaven.

Ronyan, Saint (Saint Ronyon) Two of the pilgrims in *The CANTERBURY TALES,* the Host, Harry BAILLY, and the PARDONER, swear by Saint Ronyon, both in the introduction to "The PARDONER'S TALE." Interestingly, there was no saint by that name. Some scholars have suggested that the name is simply an odd spelling of Ronan, a Celtic saint of the first century A.D. who was venerated in Brittany. The name could also be a variant pronunciation of Ninian, a Scottish saint of the fifth century. A Briton by birth, Ninian was educated in Rome and then sent as a missionary to the southern Picts of Scotland. Nothing in the legends surrounding the lives of either would suggest why they might be chosen for the context in which they appear.

Root, Robert K. (1877–1950) A Yale Ph.D. and Princeton professor, Root produced *The Book of Troilus and Criseyde* (1926), an edition of the poem with an elaborate introduction, notes, bibliography and index. In the mostly technical introduction, Root includes a section titled "Moral Import," in which he comments on the effect of the changes Chaucer made when he adapted BOCCACCIO'S *FILOSTRATO* (the primary source of *TROILUS AND CRISEYDE*): "Chaucer's narrative is not only more human, more real, more genuine in its passion; it is much wiser. In the code of courtly love which Boccaccio accepts without question, Chaucer sees inherent contradictions and fallacies." CRISEYDE becomes the "type of mutability, of the transitoriness and fallacy of earthly happiness." Dealing with "The MILLER'S TALE" in his book *The Poetry of Chaucer* (1906), Root feels the need to explain Chaucer's choice of this and other apparently immoral tales, arguing that he chose to insert these tales "not as works of art, nor even as a necessary part of a great artistic whole, but merely as a diverting interlude."

Rosarie (Rosarium philosophorum) *See* ARNALDUS OF VILLANOVA.

Rosemounde *See* "TO ROSEMOUNDE."

Rouchestre *See* ROCHESTER.

Rouncivale Rouncivale, or, more precisely, Saint Mary of Rouncesval, was the name of a hospital at Charing Cross in London. In the GENERAL PROLOGUE TO *THE CANTERBURY TALES* (line 670) we are told that the PARDONER is employed by this hospital which, in the latter part of the 14th century, was very active in the sale of pardons or indulgences, documents that granted remission of whatever punishment might still be due for a particular sin after the sinner had performed penance. The money was reportedly used for a building fund.

Rowland *See* ROLAND.

Rowland, Beryl (1928–) Born in Scotland, Rowland received a Ph.D. from the University of British Columbia and became a professor at York University in Canada. She wrote *Blind Beasts: Chaucer's Animal World* (1971), which demonstrates that the animal imagery in Chaucer's poetry represents human weakness, and that its effect depends upon the medieval conception of man as the only rational "animal." Drawing upon bestiaries and other iconographic works, she describes the vices with which individual beasts were traditionally associated, and then shows how, in his mature works, Chaucer composed sophisticated tapestries of animal imagery to enrich theme as well as characterization. In addition to this book, Rowland has edited and contributed to several collections, notably *Companion to Chaucer Studies* (rev. ed. 1979), which contains 22 bibliographic essays by eminent Chaucerians examining the history and dominant trends in Chaucer criticism from its beginnings. Rowland contributed the chapter "Chaucer's Imagery." Rowland also published an extremely interesting essay, "Chaucer's Blasphemous Churl: A New Interpretation of the Miller's Tale" (in *Chaucer and Middle English Studies in Honor of Rossel Hope Robbins,* 1974), in which she identifies a pattern of sacred allusions in the tale, arguing that their cumulative effect is a parody of the Annunciation, Christ's family, Noah's flood and the Trinity.

Ruce   *See* RUSSIA.

Rufus   The "Rufus" mentioned in the GENERAL PRO-LOGUE TO *THE CANTERBURY TALES* as one of the medical authorities whose work the DOCTOR OF PHYSIC has studied is probably Rufus of Ephesus, a Greek who wrote on medical topics during the first century B.C.

Ruggieri degli Ubaldini   Archbishop of PISA from 1278 to 1295. Chaucer refers to him as "Roger" in "The MONK'S TALE," in the story of how Count Ugolino of Pisa was accused by the archbishop and imprisoned, along with his children, in a tower where they were then starved to death (lines 2407–62). The story is considered one of the best of the short tragic tales featured in the MONK's performance.

Ruggiers, Paul G(eorge) (1918–)   Chaucer scholar. Ruggiers received his Ph.D. from Cornell University and joined the faculty at the University of Oklahoma. He is the general editor of *A Variorum Edition of the Works of Geoffrey Chaucer* (1979–), the aim of which is to present fresh texts from the best manuscripts, with variants from important manuscripts and editions up to the present time. Textual and explanatory notes summarize the scholarship and criticism up to around 1980. Ruggiers also edited *Editing Chaucer: The Great Tradition* (1984), which contains 12 essays on the major editors of the poet from the invention of printing to the first half of the 20th century. This is an excellent resource for readers interested in the transmission of Chaucer's text. Ruggiers' other work on Chaucer includes a chapter explaining the Italian influence on Chaucer's poetry for Beryl ROWLAND's *Companion to Chaucer Studies* (1979). His article titled "Notes Towards a Theory of Tragedy in Chaucer" (*Chaucer Review,* 1973) made the important observation, now widely accepted, that Chaucer's idea of tragedy must be understood in terms of fortune and providence, that tragedy is merely "one episode in the larger pattern of reconciliation of man to God." Ruggiers' book-length critical study *The Art of The Canterbury Tales* (1965) rests on the principle that the tales, as parts of a greater whole, represent more within the frame of the pilgrimage than they can

each represent individually, and that it is thus important to consider them within this relationship rather than in isolation. By analyzing the relation between the parts (the tales and tellers) and the whole (the framework of pilgrimage), and demonstrating how the framework provides dramatic unity, Ruggiers tries to offset the view that *The CANTERBURY TALES* is only a collection of poems and not a single work with an intended design.

Rupheo   *See* RIFEO.

Russell   The crafty fox in "The NUN'S PRIEST'S TALE" who tricks and runs off with the rooster CHAUNTICLEER. The character of Russell is based on a fox named REYNARD (or Renart), who forms the subject of several French beast epics. Reynard, however, was a red fox, whereas Russell is described as being a "col-fox," i.e., reddish-orange with black-tipped feet, ears and tail. Although Chaunticleer has never seen a fox before, except in his prophetic dream of the night before, the rooster instinctively knows that he is an animal to fear. The fox is able to trick the rooster by appealing to his vanity, and Chaunticleer escapes from the fox's mouth by appealing to his pride. Both of these incidents provide the tale with its moral tag: "Lo, swich it is for to be recchelees / And necligent, and trust on flaterye" (lines 3436–37) [Lo, such is the outcome when someone is heedless, and negligent, and trusts in flattery].

Russia (Russye)   In the description of the KNIGHT (1) that appears in the GENERAL PROLOGUE TO *THE CANTERBURY TALES,* Russia ("Ruce") is mentioned as one of the places the Knight has been on military campaign (line 54). In his notes on the Knight's portrait for *The RIVERSIDE CHAUCER,* Vincent DiMarco suggests that the reference may indicate the principalities of Pskov, on the Livonian frontier (north of LITHUANIA) and Novgorod, on the Volkhov frontier of the Grand Duchy of Moscow, also noting that in 1378 Pope Urban VI offered support to those aiding the crusade against the Russian Orthodox. Nearly all the Knight's campaigns involve the idea of defending the Christian faith against pagans or heretics.

S

Sagittarius (Sagittarie)   One of the 12 divisions of the zodiac, an imaginary belt in the heavens extending for about eight degrees on either side of the apparent path of the Sun and including the paths of the Moon and the principal planets. The zodiac is divided into 12 equal parts, or signs, each named for a different constellation. Sagittarius is the ninth sign (*see* diagram under ASTROLOGY), which, in Chaucer's day, the Sun entered around November 12. The constellation of Sagittarius, which is supposed to represent an archer, appears in the Southern Hemisphere near SCORPIO, where it is the largest portion of the MILKY WAY. Chaucer most often employs astrological terms to indicate the approximate date of a narrative event or to show the passage of time, but his only mention of the sign of Sagittarius is in his *TREATISE ON THE ASTROLABE*, where he notes that it is one of the 12 signs of the zodiac (part 1, division 8, line 4), and discusses its position in the sky and its relationship to the other signs (II.6.16, II.28.35, II.28.38).

Saint Paul's Cathedral   The Saint Paul's Cathedral in London that is mentioned several times in *The CANTERBURY TALES* was a medieval structure that was destroyed in the Great Fire of 1666. In the GENERAL PROLOGUE, the PARSON is described as a man who stays at home and tends to the needs of those in his parish, rather than running off to London to obtain an easy and lucrative appointment as a chantry priest at Saint Paul's Cathedral (lines 509–10). Chantry priests were employed by wealthy patrons for the purpose of saying prayers for their patron's soul after death. In "The MILLER'S TALE," the foppish clerk ABSALOM (1) has the design of a stained glass window from Saint Paul's Cathedral carved in the leather of his shoes (line 3318). In the prologue to "The NUN'S PRIEST'S TALE," the Host (*see* Harry BAILLY) compares the speech of the MONK, whose tale has just been interrupted by the KNIGHT (1), to the sound of Saint Paul's bell that "clappeth loud" (lines 2780–81). Both men are tired of listening to the Monk's tales of gloom and doom.

Saint's Legend of Cupid   The title Chaucer gives to his *LEGEND OF GOOD WOMEN* when it is described by the SERGEANT OF THE LAW in the prologue to his tale (lines 57–76). The Sergeant of the Law praises the work for its virtue and notes that it is a work Chaucer composed in his youth (line 57).

saints' lives   Fabulous stories that related the lives of various saints. Saints' lives were one of the most popular forms of literature in the early Middle Ages. One of the most famous compilations of this type of literature was the *Legenda Aurea*, or Golden Legend, by Jacobus de Voraigine, an Italian Dominican friar of the 13th century. Chaucer's *CANTERBURY TALES* contains one saint's life, "The SECOND NUN'S TALE," which narrates the story of Saint CECILIA. The *Legenda Aurea* was one of the tale's sources. Other members of the Canterbury group that display some features of the saints' lives are "The PRIORESS' TALE" (specifically belonging to the genre of Miracles of the Virgin MARY), "The PHYSICIAN'S TALE" (where VIRGINIA is a kind of martyr to her virginity) and "The MAN OF LAW'S TALE" (where CONSTANCE patiently suffers many trials similar to those suffered by the saints and is miraculously sustained by God).

Salamon (Salomon)   *See* SOLOMON.

Salter, Elizabeth (1925–1980)   British scholar. Salter attended the University of London, taught at Cambridge and eventually became a professor at the University of York. She is one of the foremost experts on LANGLAND's *Piers Plowman* but also wrote *Chaucer: The Knight's Tale and The Clerk's Tale* (1962). In this book Salter sets out to combat the danger of labeling Chaucer any one thing, such as a reformer or satirist, and then interpreting everything he wrote in the light of the label. Salter praises the range of Chaucer's attitudes toward his subjects, "by turns reverent, serious, admiring, skeptical, indignant, facetious and sorrowful." Salter also wrote several articles on *TROILUS AND CRISEYDE*.

Saluces   *See* SALUZZO.

Saluzzo   A region in northern Italy at the base of Mount Vesulus (MONTE VISO), Saluzzo is the setting for "The CLERK'S TALE." WALTER, who marries the tale's heroine GRISELDA, is the marquise of Saluzzo (lines 63–64). Although she is the daughter of a peasant, Griselda proves such a wise and noble consort to Walter that her fame spreads throughout Saluzzo and into other regions (lines 414–20).

Samaritan, the   The gospel of John in the New Testament tells the story of a woman whom Christ met at a well near the city of Samaria (John 4:7–18). In response to Christ's suggestion that she bring her husband to the well, the woman said that she had no husband. Christ responded that she answered truthfully, despite the fact that she had been married five times, for the fifth husband was not truly her husband (the implication being that all marriages beyond the first were immoral). The WIFE OF BATH ponders the meaning of this story in the prologue to her tale (lines 12–34), wondering why it is that SOLOMON, who also appeared in the Bible, was allowed to have so many wives without suffering reproof. The Wife, like the Samaritan woman, has been married five times and would like to believe that she has not committed sin by doing so. Her focus on gender bias in these examples is one of the features of her prologue that lends credence to the view of her as a protofeminist.

Samson (Sampson; Sampsoun)   A Biblical hero from the Old Testament who was known for his great strength. The events of his life are related in Judges: 13–16. Samson was born during a dark period in the history of the Israelites when they were suffering oppression and harassment from neighboring PHILISTINES. Samson was consecrated by his parents as a Nazirite (this word means "consecrated") and was supposed to live his life as an example to the people of Israel, bringing them back into a close relationship with God. As a sign of their vows, Nazirites were not supposed to cut their hair or shave. The purpose of leaving the hair long was to provide a visible marker of the person's dedication to God.

Samson's great strength aided him in his conflicts with the Philistines. On one occasion he killed a thousand Philistine soldiers with the jawbone of an ass (Judges 15:15). But his usefulness to the defense of Israel was compromised by his weakness for pagan women. He married a Philistine woman against his parents' wishes, and later in his life his lust for the Philistine DELILAH proved to be his undoing when he told her that his great strength was derived from his long hair. While Samson slept, she admitted Philistine soldiers, who cut off his hair, blinded him and took him prisoner. Enslaved by the Philistines, Samson was forced to work at grinding grain. However, when Samson was later chained between two pillars in the Temple of Dagon, put on display as a kind of battle trophy, God allowed his strength to return long enough for him to pull the pillars down, collapsing the temple walls and killing thousands of the enemy along with himself.

The story of Samson and his fall is narrated in "The MONK'S TALE" (lines 2015–94). In "The KNIGHT'S TALE," SATURN, the pagan god of calamities, claims responsibility for Samson's death (line 2466). In "The MAN OF LAW'S TALE," the narrator states that the fate of Samson, and of all men, was written in the stars before his birth (line 201). The story of Samson's downfall is one of the stories that the WIFE OF BATH's fifth husband likes to read to her from his "Book of Wicked Wives" ("WIFE OF BATH'S PROLOGUE," line 721). In "The PARDONER'S TALE," the narrator refers to the fact that, as a Nazirite, Samson would abstain from wine (line 555), even though the sound that drunken men make when they snore sounds like his name: "Sampsoun, Sampsoun!" (line 554). In *The BOOK OF THE DUCHESS*, the dreamer tells the BLACK KNIGHT that although ECHO died for NARCISSUS, and Samson for Delilah, there is no man alive who would die for the loss of a queen in a game of chess (lines 735–41).

Samuel   In the Old Testament, Samuel was one of the great Hebrew prophets who came after MOSES, and was the last judge or military leader of Israel. He led his people in their ongoing conflict with the PHILISTINES. During his time of service, the people of Israel began to demand that they, like surrounding nations, should have a king to lead them. Samuel reluctantly gave in to their wishes and, when he was an old man, anointed Saul as the first king of Israel. When Saul was rejected by God for disobeying divine orders, Samuel was sent to Bethlehem to anoint DAVID, who became a much more successful ruler. In "The FRIAR'S TALE," the devil mentions the story of Samuel's ghost speaking to Saul through the PHITONISSA (the Witch of Endor) as an example of how evil spirits can animate the bodies of mortals (lines 1506–10). The story appears in 1 Samuel 28:7–20.

Santippe   Santippe, spelled *Santippo* in BOCCACCIO's *FILOSTRATO*, which was Chaucer's primary source for his *TROILUS AND CRISEYDE*, is one of the Trojan heroes whose efforts to prevent the capture of ANTENOR by the Greeks are in vain (book 4, lines 50–56). Santippo, rendered as *Antipus, Anthiphus* and *Xantipus* in GUIDO DELLE COLONNE, and as *Antif* or *Xantif* in BENOIT DE SAINT MAURE—both earlier sources of the Troy story—was the king of Frisia and King PRIAM's ally.

Sapor   *See* SHAPUR.

Sarah   In the Old Testament, Sarah was the wife of ABRAHAM and the mother of ISAAC. God had promised Abraham that he would become the father of a great nation, but the couple remained childless until Sarah was 90 years old, when she gave birth to Isaac. Through their descendants, Abraham and Sarah came to be considered the father and mother of the Hebrew people. (*See* Genesis 12–23.) In the New Testament, the apostle Peter cited Sarah as an example of a righteous woman who trusted in God, possessed inward spiritual beauty and was submissive to her husband. In "The MERCHANT'S TALE," the priest who marries the aged knight JANUARY and young MAY urges the bride to be "lyk Sarra and Rebekke / In wysdom and in trouthe of mariage" (lines 1704–05) [like Sarah and Rebecca / In wisdom and in faithfulness of marriage]—an exhortation that was a customary part of the marriage service in the 14th century. During the Middle Ages, both women were considered biblical exemplars of faithfulness and wisdom.

Sarpedon (Sarpedoun) In classical mythology, Sarpedon was the son of Zeus and Europa, and the younger brother of MINOS of Crete. He became king of the Lycians and fought in the TROJAN WAR as an ally of the Trojans. He was slain in battle by the Greek Patroclus. Sometimes the Sarpedon who aided Troy is considered distinct from the brother of Minos, and is represented as the son of Zeus and LAODAMIA, the daughter of Bellerophon. In Chaucer's *TROILUS AND CRISEYDE*, Sarpedon is one of the warriors who fights unsuccessfully to keep ANTENOR from being taken prisoner (book 4, lines 50–56). While TROILUS awaits CRISEYDE's return from the Greek camp, he and PANDARUS make a visit to Sarpedon to help pass the time (book 5, lines 430–501). Sarpedon provides sumptuous feasts and entertainment, including the company of many beautiful ladies, but none of these things are able to make Troilus forget his sorrow or to lessen his desire for Criseyde's speedy return.

Sarra *See* SARAH.

Sarray Sarray, modern Tzarev, near Volgograd in southeastern Russia, was the capital of the Mongol Empire. Ruled by the emperor Genghis Khan, at its most extensive the empire encompassed much of the continent of Asia from the Black Sea to the Pacific. The city is the setting for "The SQUIRE's TALE" which, until it is interrupted, tells the story of a birthday party for King CAMBYUSKAN (Genghis Khan) and of the gifts he received.

Satalye *See* ATTALEIA.

Satan Satan was the name given to the devil after his fall from grace. Before that time, he was known as LUCIFER, which means "light-bearer." In "The MILLER'S TALE," ABSALOM (1) vows that the devil may take his soul unless he gets revenge for the trick played upon him by ALISON (1) and NICHOLAS (lines 3750–53). In "The MAN OF LAW'S TALE," the SULTANESS OF SYRIA is inspired by Satan to engineer the murder of her son

and his new wife's Christian attendants in order to destroy their Christian marriage (lines 365–69). He also causes a young knight of NORTHUMBERLAND to lust after CONSTANCE and, when she refuses his advances, to kill her friend HERMENGILD and make it look as if Constance committed the murder (lines 582–602). In "The FRIAR'S TALE" Satan becomes the traveling companion to a wicked summoner; when the summoner is cursed by one of the people from whom he tries to extort money, Satan carries him off to hell. In "The PRIORESS' TALE," Satan urges the Jewish people to murder the little Christian boy who walks to school through their neighborhood singing a hymn of praise to the Virgin MARY (lines 558–64). Surprisingly, Satan is mentioned only once in "The PARSON'S TALE," a sermon on penance which, is one section, vividly describes the torment of hell. The PARSON compares the transformation of Satan from an angel of light into a creature of darkness to the change that occurs in a priest who commits deadly sin (lines 894–95). In the short poem "LENVOY DE CHAUCER À BUKTON," Chaucer humorously compares marriage to the bonds of Satan (lines 9–16).

Sathan (Sathanas) *See* SATAN.

Saturn(e) (Saturnus) Saturn is mentioned in Chaucer's work both as the Roman god identified with the Greek Cronus, the father of all the gods, and as the seventh planet from Earth in our solar system (*see* SATURN [2]). According to legend, when Zeus and Saturn fought for supremacy, Saturn was defeated and fled to Latium (Italy) where he was received by the god Janus. Saturn taught the people there the art of agriculture and introduced a period of great prosperity. One day Saturn vanished from the earth. Janus built an altar to him and established the festival of Saturnalia in his honor. In "The KNIGHT'S TALE," Saturn decides the contest between the two knights PALAMON and ARCITE (1) for the love of EMILY by asking PLUTO to send a Fury from the underworld which frightens Arcite's horse (lines 2453–78). The fall Arcite suffers is fatal. In *TROILUS AND CRISEYDE*, CRISEYDE vows to return to TROILUS, asking Saturn's daughter, JUNO, to make her go mad if she does not (book 4, lines 1534–40).

Saturn(e) (2) The planet Saturn was described by PTOLEMY, whose work on astronomy was considered authoritative during the Middle Ages, as a cold and maleficent planet, characteristics which inform the god as he appears in "The KNIGHT'S TALE." Troilus seems to be referring to these aspects when he prays to VENUS to mitigate the evil influence of MARS (2) and Saturn that may have presided over his birth (book 3, line 716). According to "The Canon's Yeoman's Tale," the metal of Saturn, lead, is used in some alchemical experiments (line 828). In *The HOUSE OF FAME*, the Jewish historian

Josephus (*see* EBRAECUS, Flavius Josephus) is referred to as belonging to the "sect" of Saturn because just as Saturn is the father of all the planets, Judaism is the father of all sects (lines 1432–33). The pillar that the image of Josephus stands on is made of iron and lead (lines 1430–50). In book 3 of *TROILUS AND CRISEYDE,* it was the planet Saturn who, in conjunction with JUPITER and CANCER, caused the storm that prevented CRISEYDE from returning home from her uncle's house (lines 624–30). During the night TROILUS approached her bed and the two finally became lovers.

Sayne   *See* SEINE.

Scariot   *See* JUDAS (1).

Scedasus   A Greek whose daughter chose to kill herself rather than to live with the shame of having been raped. In the *Epistola adversus Jovinianum* (Letter against Jovinian) of Saint JEROME, she is praised for doing so. She is mentioned in "The FRANKLIN'S TALE" as one of the women whom DORIGEN remembers when she is faced with a crisis that tests her own faithfulness to her husband, ARVERAGUS (line 1428).

Scipio (Scipioun)   *See* SCIPIO AFRICANUS THE YOUNGER.

Scipio Africanus the Elder   Born in Liternum, Campania (now Patria, Italy) in 236 B.C. Scipio Africanus the Elder was a Roman general and one of the greatest soldiers of the ancient world. By his tactical reforms and strategic insight, he created an army that defeated even the great Carthaginian leader Hannibal, bringing an end to the Second Punic War and asserting Rome's influence in Spain, Africa and Greece. Scipio had a great appreciation of Greek culture and welcomed its civilizing influences, which were beginning to permeate Roman society. His Greek sympathies led him to prefer the establishment of Roman protection over direct conquest and annexation. For 10 years (210–201 B.C.) he commanded a devoted army. He was at one time hailed as king by Spanish tribes and he may have been the first Roman general to be acclaimed imperator (emperor) by his troops. However, he offered no challenge to the dominance of the Roman Senate and appeared to possess no outstanding ability in political maneuvering. Reaction against his generous foreign policy and against his encouragement of Greek culture in Roman life led to his downfall amid personal and political rivalries, but his career had proven that Rome was destined to be a Mediterranean rather than merely an Italian power.

Because of his great success as a military leader and his personal charisma, legends began to cluster around Scipio, suggesting that he enjoyed divine inspiration and protection. Some people believed that he had received a promise of help from NEPTUNE, the god of the sea, in a dream on the eve of his assault on Carthage. He was also said to have a close relationship with JUPITER and was reported to pray at that god's temple on the Capitol at night. A later story claimed that he was a son of Jupiter, and that he had appeared in his mother's bed in the form of a snake. Scipio's influence lived on into the Middle Ages and the Renaissance, as his example helped the early humanists build a bridge between the classical and Christian worlds. His dialogue with his grandson (SCIPIO AFRICANUS THE YOUNGER) in the *DREAM OF SCIPIO* expresses philosophical ideas regarding the rewards of good behavior and the punishment of self-interest that fit extremely well with the Christian worldview. Chaucer was profoundly interested in these ideas, and several of his works—*The HOUSE OF FAME, The PARLIAMENT OF FOWLS* and *TROILUS AND CRISEYDE*—show the influence of this classical text. *The Parliament of Fowls* even incorporates a summary of the *Dream,* followed by the narrator's own dream, in which Scipio Africanus the Elder appears as a guide.

Scipio Africanus the Younger   Born in Rome around 184 B.C., Scipio Africanus the Younger was the adopted grandson of SCIPIO AFRICANUS THE ELDER and, like his grandfather, achieved fame through his military exploits, most notably in the Third Punic War and the subjugation of Spain in 134–133 B.C. Although the younger Scipio contributed greatly to the maintenance and extension of Rome's power during his 20-year military career, he had many political enemies, and his leadership was often challenged. His stern conservative character led him to try to maintain traditional Roman values, which he felt were being undermined by unstable elements in society. He was also a cultured man who, like his grandfather, encouraged the blending of Greek and Roman thought, and he supported such leading intellectual figures as the poet Terence, the satirist Lucilius and the Stoic philosopher Panaetius. In this way he exerted considerable influence on the development of Latin literature. For many later Romans, especially CICERO, he was an ideal statesman, representing in his personal virtue, political leadership and cultural patronage, the golden days of the republic. This is perhaps why Cicero chose Scipio Africanus the Younger and his grandfather, Scipio the Elder, as the speakers in the dialogue that formed a part of his *Republic,* a work intended to describe the perfect state. Although the main portion of the *Republic* was lost to the Middle Ages, the part of the text that contained the dialogue was made available through a translation by fifth-century Latin writer MACROBIUS. Commonly known as the *Somnium Scipionis* (*DREAM OF SCIPIO*), this text became one of the most important classical sources that Chaucer would draw upon, substantially influencing such works as *The HOUSE OF FAME*, *The PAR-LIAMENT OF FOWLS* and *TROILUS AND CRISEYDE*.

Scipioun, Drem of   *See* DREAM OF SCIPIO.

Scithero, Marcus Tullius   *See* CICERO, MARCUS TULLIUS.

Scithia   *See* SCYTHIA.

Scogan, Henry   Henry Scogan is the addressee of one of Chaucer's short poems, the "Envoy to Scogan" (*see* "LENVOY DE CHAUCER À SCOGAN"), in which Chaucer accuses his friend, Scogan, of having committed some dreadful offense that is going to have dire consequences in heaven and on Earth. But when he reveals the nature of that offense—having given up a lover because she will not return his affections—the poem's tone suddenly emerges as playful and teasing. Although the first name of the person to whom the verses are addressed is not given in the poem, scholars believe that it is was Henry Scogan, a squire in the household of King HENRY IV and, later, tutor to the king's sons. In a moral BALLADE addressed to the young princes, Scogan quotes another of Chaucer's short poems, "GENTILESSE," in its entirety, and refers to Chaucer as his "master," suggesting that he generally took the older poet's work as a model for his own.

Scorpio (Scorpioun)   One of the 12 divisions of the zodiac, an imaginary belt in the heavens extending for about eight degrees on either side of the apparent path of the Sun and including the paths of the moon and the principal planets. The zodiac is divided into 12 equal parts, or signs, each named for a different constellation. Scorpio is the eighth sign (*see* diagram under ASTROLOGY), which in Chaucer's day, the Sun entered on October 12. The constellation of Scorpio, which is supposed to represent a scorpion, appears in the Southern Hemisphere near LIBRA and lies partly inside the MILKY WAY. Chaucer generally uses such astrological terms to indicate the approximate date of a narrative event or to show the passage of time. This is not the case with Scorpio, however, which is only mentioned in two of his works, *The HOUSE OF FAME* and the *TREATISE ON THE ASTROLABE*. In the latter, which explains the use of an instrument designed for studying the heavens, he discusses its characteristics and position in the sky (part II, division 3, lines 56–58 and part II, division 28, line 28). In *The House of Fame,* the EAGLE who ferries Chaucer through the heavens pauses to point out some stellar landmarks, including the Milky Way. He then tells the story of how PHAETON, when he drove the chariot of the sun through the sky, became frightened when he saw the constellation of Scorpio, and lost control of the chariot, which careered through the sky scorching the atmosphere and the earth (lines 936–56).

Scot   Scot is the name of two different horses in Chaucer's work. The first is the dappled gray horse ridden by the REEVE who is described in the GENERAL PROLOGUE TO *THE CANTERBURY TALES* (lines 615–16). The second is the horse cursed by its rider in "The FRIAR'S TALE" (lines 1543–44).

Scriveyne, Adam   *See* ADAM SCRIVEYNE.

Scrope, Sir Richard   *See* SCROPE-GROSVENOR TRIAL.

Scrope-Grosvenor trial   The Scrope-Grosvenor case involved a dispute between two families over the right to bear a particular coat of arms. The heraldic appellation for the device in question was "azure bend," which basically means a simple design of a gold stripe on an azure background. The suit was brought to trial in 1385 by Sir Richard Scrope, who had held the offices of treasurer and chancellor under RICHARD II, against Sir Robert Grosvenor. The suit was tried in the High Court of Chivalry, where such matters were taken quite seriously. Although the Grosvenor family could trace their title back to the Norman Conquest in 1066, while the Scrope family had only obtained the rank of nobility in the last decade of the previous century, Scrope's prominent position in the royal household helped him to win the case after five years of hearings and debate; some of the sessions were attended by the king himself.

Chaucer gave a deposition in the early days of the case on October 15, 1386, and his testimony provides the strongest evidence we have about the date of his birth. It identifies him as "Geoffrey Chaucer, esquire, forty and some years of age and armed for twenty-seven years." The "forty and some years" may have been an educated guess made by the royal clerk, but the statement that Chaucer had borne arms for 27 years provides a stronger clue. This, in conjunction with other evidence providing an approximate date for the time at which Chaucer first took up arms (the first time he went on a military campaign), suggests that he was probably born no later than in the early months of 1343, and possibly a year or two before.

Scylla   In classical mythology, Scylla was the daughter of King NISUS of Megara. When the city of Megara was besieged by King MINOS of Crete, Scylla fell in love with Minos while watching him from behind the city walls. Scylla's father had a purple lock of hair growing upon his head which magically protected him from usurpation and death. To prove her love for Minos, Scylla cut off the lock of hair. Instead of showing gratitude for her behavior, Minos rejected Scylla, and she either swam along behind his ship as it sailed away, or was bound beneath it and dragged along under the water. As punishment for her crime against her father, Scylla was changed into a lark while her father was transformed into a bird of prey who would seek to kill her. The story of Scylla and Minos is related briefly in Chaucer's LEGEND OF GOOD WOMEN, at the beginning of the tale of ARIADNE (lines 1900–21) Her story is also depicted on the walls of Venus's temple in *The* PARLIAMENT OF FOWLS (line 292).

Scythia   An ancient region in southeastern Europe, centered around the northern coast of the Black Sea. In "The KNIGHT'S TALE," Scythia is named as the land where the AMAZONS live, which is also called FEMENYE (line 867). THESEUS of ATHENS is on his way back from having conquered the warrior women of Scythia when he engages in a conflict with CREON of THEBES and takes prisoner the two knights, PALAMON and ARCITE (1), who become the protagonists of the tale. The same incident is referred to at the beginning of the unfinished poem ANELIDA AND ARCITE, which likewise uses the history of the famous siege of Thebes (*see* SEVEN AGAINST THEBES) to set the stage for events that will be narrated in the poem (line 37).

Second Nun, the   The Second Nun is presumably the nun who is mentioned in the GENERAL PROLOGUE TO THE CANTERBURY TALES as a member of the PRIORESS' household. She is not described in the prologue, but she does participate in the tale-telling contest. The subject of "The SECOND NUN'S TALE" is the life of Saint CECILIA, an early Christian martyr.

"Second Nun's Tale, The"   "The Second Nun's Tale" tells the life story of Saint CECILIA who, in popular tradition, became known as the patron saint of music and art.

SUMMARY

Unlike most of the other Canterbury tales, "The Second Nun's Tale" begins with no introductory words between the Host, Harry BAILLY, and the teller, but commences rather abruptly, following the epilogue to "The NUN'S PRIEST'S TALE." The SECOND NUN speaks first of the vice of idleness and the harm that it does, making humanity more vulnerable to Satan and temptation. To keep herself safe from idleness, the Second Nun has made a translation of the life of Saint CECILIA. This explanation of her tale's provenance is followed by an invocation to the Virgin MARY, praising the Blessed Mother of God for her service to mankind and asking for her protection and assistance. The tale itself is preceded by an explanatory etymology, based on Latin, of Cecilia's name. *Cecilia* is variously interpreted to mean "heaven's lily," "lack of blindness" and "the heaven of people," all of which relate to her character and deeds.

The life of Saint Cecilia opens with a brief summary of her origins: She is the offspring of Roman nobility,

Artist's rendering of the Second Nun, from the Ellesmere Manuscript of The Canterbury Tales. *The Second Nun is mentioned but not described in the General Prologue, so the artist had complete liberty in creating her portrait. Unfortunately, his inspiration seems to have deserted him. This is one of the least interesting of all the Ellesmere portraits.*

yet has been, from birth, brought up in the Christian faith. She has also, all her life, prayed that God will allow her to remain a virgin. Nevertheless the time comes when she is to be married, to a young man named VALERIAN. On their wedding night she tells him that an angel watches over her constantly. If Valerian touches her, or tries to make love to her, the angel will kill him immediately. Therefore, she explains, it would be best if her husband would willingly agree to love her chastely. Valerian responds that he will believe her only if he is able to see the angel. But if the angel turns out to be another man, he will slay them both. Cecilia then explains that he may only see the angel if he believes in Christ and takes the sacrament of baptism. She sends Valerian to Pope URBAN, who is in hiding lest he be executed by the Roman government. After joining Urban, Valerian sees a vision of an old man (probably Saint PAUL) in white who reads from a book of golden letters. Valerian affirms his belief and is baptized.

When he returns home he is able to see Cecilia's angel, who presents the two of them with two crowns made of roses entwined with lilies. The flowers are from Paradise and will never rot or lose their sweetness, and no one who is not chaste and free from sin will be able to see them. Because Valerian assented so quickly to his wife's good counsel, the angel grants him a boon. Valerian asks that his brother, TIBURTIUS (Tiburce), whom he loves more than anyone else in the world, should also be able to experience God's grace. Tiburtius appears shortly thereafter and is able to smell the fragrant blossoms of their crowns, even though he cannot see them. The odor has such an effect on him that he mentions it to his brother, who explains its source. Cecilia then explains the source of their Christian faith, showing Tiburtius the vanity of believing in pagan idols. Thus instructed, Tiburtius visits Pope Urban to receive baptism. After receiving the sacrament, Tiburtius joins the ranks of those who are able to see the angel.

After a time, Valerian and Tiburtius are arrested and brought before ALMACHIUS, a Roman prefect, who questions them about their faith and commands them to either perform a sacrifice to JUPITER or lose their heads. One of the Roman officers, MAXIMUS, takes pity on them and gains permission to take the brothers home with him for the night. Tiburtius and Valerian spend the night teaching and preaching to their host and other Roman officers, who all give up their false faith to believe in the Christian God. During the night Cecilia comes, bringing priests who baptize the group all together.

In the morning the two prisoners are called to perform a sacrifice to the pagan gods. When they refuse, they are beheaded. Maximus, who saw their souls rise up to heaven when they died, through his preaching converts many other people to Christianity until Almachius has him beaten to death. Learning that Cecilia buried Maximus' body, Almachius sends some officers to arrest her, but they all return, converted to Christianity by Cecilia's teaching.

When the woman is finally brought before him, Almachius questions her and then demands that she either perform a sacrifice or renounce Christianity. Cecilia refuses. Unable to make her change her mind, Almachius commands some men to take her home and burn her to death in a cauldron of fire. When the flames are unable to harm her, he orders someone to cut her head off. After three strokes, her head remains attached to her shoulders. The man cannot strike her again, we are told, because there is a law forbidding a fourth stroke. He leaves her there, and some of the Christian people who live around her dress her wounds and attend her. She talks to them until she dies, preaching and disposing of her worldly goods, and asking that her house be converted into a church. Pope Urban consecrates the house as the first church of Saint Cecilia.

COMMENTARY

The Second Nun's story of the Christian martyr Saint Cecilia clearly belongs to the genre of saints' lives,

which was a popular form in the early medieval period. Popular as the tale may have been during its time, however, it has not found a great deal of favor with modern readers, at least not until very recently when a few scholars have pointed out that it is the best surviving example of a saint's life in Middle English, and that it relates to several other of the Canterbury tales in a pleasingly complex manner. The source for most of the tale is a version of Cecilia's life included in the *Legenda aurea* ("Golden Legend") of Jacobus de Voragine, which Chaucer, following the Nun's avowal, translates fairly closely, although he does abbreviate his source now and then. He breaks away from this source around line 345, in the midst of relating Tiburtius' conversion, and for the rest of the nun's tale draws upon a different version, probably one descended from a longer Latin "legend" of Cecilia. The invocation to Mary which serves as a prologue to the tale comes directly from DANTE's *Paradiso*, where it is spoken by Saint BERNARD of Clairvaux.

As a literary genre, saint's lives in general tend to concentrate on the miraculous aspects of a particular saint's personal history. There is little dramatic tension in such stories because of the certainty that although horrible things will happen, usually in the form of torture administered to the saint, a person's perfect faith guarantees that he or she will come through it spiritually unscathed, to be especially honored by God in heaven following the death of the body. This story of Cecilia's life neatly fits the pattern. There are four miracles, beginning with the presence of an angel who can only be seen by believers in Christ. When Valerian turns away from the pagan gods and embraces Christianity, another miracle occurs, with the flower garlands presented to the couple by the angel. The third, and greatest, occurs in the attempt to burn Cecilia, who, held in a cauldron over a fire, does not even sweat. She is much more vulnerable to knife attack, yet still survives for three days after having her throat cut.

Aside from her Christian faith, the virtues that cause Cecilia to become a saint are those alluded to in the explanation of her name. These virtues also have a symbolic relationship to the miracles associated with her. The first etymology referred to above, the one that takes her name to mean "heaven's lily," suggests the virtue of purity, of which the lily was a popular Christian symbol. The crown of flowers given by the angel contains lilies and also roses, the symbol of martyrdom. Likewise, the fire that will not burn her suggests the fire of lust to which she has ever been immune. The second etymology, "lack of blindness," relates to the clear-sightedness of her faith. Whenever she confronts someone who believes in the pagan gods, she very rationally calls attention to the fact that idols are merely stones, both deaf and dumb, whereas the God she serves is a living spirit, one whose messenger she, in token of her faith, is able to see and converse with. Those she converts likewise have their blindness lifted. When Tiburtius asks Valerian whether the sweet odor that surrounds them is a dream, his brother responds, "In dremes . . . han we be / Unto this tyme, brother myn, ywis. / But now at erst in trouthe oure dwellyng is." (lines 262–64) [In dreams have we been until now, my brother, indeed. But now for the first time we dwell in the truth]. The third etymology, "the heaven of people," suggests her diligence in standing up for what she believes and in converting other people. Her final act, to request that her house be made into a church, shows that this work will continue even after she is dead.

Structurally, "The Second Nun's Tale" is divided into three parts: the invocation to Mary, the etymological explanation of Cecilia's name and the story of her life. This tripartite structure is echoed by a number of other triplets in both the narrative structure of the "life" and its descriptive details. The invocation commemorates the mercy, goodness and pity of the Virgin as Maid, Mother and Daughter of Christ, who rules over the "trine compas" [threefold universe] of the earth, heavens and the sea. Although many people are converted through Cecilia's preaching and example, three of these conversions (of Valerian, Tiburtius and Maximus) are particularized. When Tiburtius asks Cecilia to explain the paradox of the Trinity, she offers the three mental faculties of man: memory, imagination and intellect, all existing within a single person, as an analogy for the Trinity, in which one divinity contains three persons. When the executioner tries to behead Cecilia, it takes three strokes, following which she survives for three days. Structural devices that include a symbolic dimension are common features of medieval saints' lives.

Seine A river in northern France that flows northwest through PARIS (2) and into the English Channel. In "The FRANKLIN'S TALE," the magician hired by AURELIUS agrees to remove all the rocks from the sea that extends from GIRONDE River to the Seine (lines 1221–22). DORIGEN, the married woman with whom Aurelius is infatuated, has promised to become his lover if he can accomplish this feat. In Chaucer's translation of the ROMAN DE LA ROSE, the dreamer compares the Seine to the stream that leads him to the Garden of MIRTH (line 118).

Seint Thomas, Wateryng of *See* WATERING OF SAINT THOMAS.

Seint-Denys A town north of Paris, of which it is now a suburb. It is the setting of "The SHIPMAN'S TALE," which tells the story of a merchant and his wife who are duped by a deceitful monk who appears to be their friend.

Seintes Legende of Cupide *See* SAINT'S LEGEND OF CUPID.

Seint-Jame *See* JAMES OF COMPOSTELLA, SAINT.

Semiramus (Semyrame; Semyramis; Semyramus) An Assyrian queen of the late eighth–early ninth century B.C. She ruled the country from 810–805 B.C. following the death of her husband, King NINUS (whose tomb is mentioned in *The LEGEND OF GOOD WOMEN* as the meeting place of PYRAMUS and THISBE). During her reign she wore trousers to hide her gender from her troops, whom she led in a successful military campaign against Ethiopia. She was also known to have had many lovers, an aspect of her character that earned her a negative reputation during the medieval period. In his *De claris mulieribus* ("On famous women"), BOCCACCIO says that she tainted all her other accomplishments by giving herself to so many men. Semiramus is mentioned several times in Chaucer's work, not always in a negative context. In *The PARLIAMENT OF FOWLS*, she is depicted on the walls of the TEMPLE OF VENUS, where she is referred to as one of those who died for love (line 288). In *The Legend of Good Women*, she is credited with having built and fortified the city of BABYLON (lines 706–09). But in "The MAN OF LAW'S TALE," the SULTANESS OF SYRIA, who kills her son, is referred to as a second Semiramus (lines 358–59). Semiramus did not kill her son but, according to Boccaccio, became his lover.

Seneca (Senec; Senek; Senekke) Seneca, whose full name was Lucius Annaeus Seneca, was one of three eminent disciples of the philosophy of Stoicism who lived and taught in ROME in the two centuries following the rule of the emperor AUGUSTUS. Born in 4 B.C., Seneca had become an orator by the time of CALIGULA's accession. In A.D. 41 he was banished to the island of Corsica on charges of adultery, but was recalled in 49 to be a tutor to the young NERO, whose minister he would later become. When he could no longer agree with the young emperor's policies, Seneca retired from political service. But he was not allowed to live out the rest of his life in peace. In 65, named in a conspiracy against the emperor, he was commanded to commit suicide, which he did by cutting open some veins and bleeding to death in a bath. Seneca's writings enjoyed an outstanding reputation among scholars during the Middle Ages, at least partly because the morality of his essays displayed a close kinship with Christian morality.

It seems likely that Chaucer's knowledge of Seneca's work derived from other sources in which it was quoted—and not, perhaps, always accurately. Many of the sayings attributed to Seneca in Chaucer's poetry are actually taken from other works in which Seneca was quoted, and a number of them do not derive from the Roman orator at all. Most of the quotations attributed to Seneca in "The TALE OF MELIBEE," for example, derive from other Roman writers.

Some references that appear to be authentic are as follows. In "The WIFE OF BATH'S TALE," the LOATHLY HAG refers to Seneca's attitude toward poverty as she tutors her young husband in the true meaning of gentility (lines 1184). In "The SUMMONER'S TALE," the corrupt friar tells anecdotes illustrating the dangers of anger (lines 2019, 2043–73 and 2079–88), both from Seneca's *De ira* ("On anger"). In "The MERCHANT'S TALE, the aged knight JANUARY quotes Seneca's comment about the value of a humble wife (lines 1375–76); and in "The PARDONER'S TALE," the narrator uses Seneca's comparison between a man who is drunk and one who is insane—finding little difference between the two—to support his condemnation of drunkenness (lines 492–97). The manner of Seneca's death is mentioned twice in Chaucer's work: in the *BOECE,* Chaucer's translation of BOETHIUS' *Consolation of Philosophy* (Book Three, Prosa 5, lines 53–60), and in the life of Nero included in "The MONK'S TALE" (lines 2495–2518).

Senecciens   The followers of the Roman philosopher SENECA are referred to as Senecciens in the *BOECE,* Chaucer's translation of BOETHIUS' *Consolation of Philosophy* (Book One, Prosa 3, line 57).

Senior   In "The CANON'S YEOMAN'S TALE," *Senior* is the title that Chaucer gives to an alchemical treatise attributed to an Arabian scholar of the 10th century, Muhammad ibn Umail al-Tamimi. The CANON'S YEOMAN reports a conversation between PLATO and one of his disciples as, he claims, it is written in this work. In this dialogue, the disciple asks his master for the secret of the Philosopher's Stone, whose virtue was to turn base metals into gold. Plato refuses the information on grounds that Christ does not wish it to be communicated openly among men (lines 1448–71).

According to John Reidy's notes on the tale in *The RIVERSIDE CHAUCER,* the passage described here is probably based on a passage in a Latin translation of an Arabic commentary on an alchemical poem which, in its translation, bears the title "Senioris Zadith fil Hamuelis Tabula Chimica" ("The Chemical Table of Senior Zadith, Son of Hamuel"), whence Chaucer's reference to *Senior* undoubtedly derives.

Septe   *Septe* is the name by which the narrator of "The MAN OF LAW'S TALE" refers to a ridge of seven mountain peaks (*sept* is French for "seven") that stand opposite GIBRALTAR in what was formerly Spanish Morocco. When CONSTANCE, the heroine of this tale, is cast adrift by the SULTANESS OF SYRIA, she sails across the Mediterranean, between Jubaltre (Gibraltar) and Septe (line 946) and into the Atlantic Ocean.

Septemtryones   *Septemtryones* is the name given to the constellation Ursa Minor, or the Little Bear, in the

BOECE, Chaucer's translation of BOETHIUS' *Consolation of Philosophy* (Book Two, Metrum 6, line 21).

Serapion   Serapion is mentioned in Chaucer's GENERAL PROLOGUE TO *THE CANTERBURY TALES* as one of the medical authorities whose teachings the DOCTOR OF PHYSIC had studied; the name may refer to one of three men who wrote on medical topics. It could be the Alexandrian Serapion, who in the second century B.C. propounded the use of empirical methods in the study of medicine; the ninth-century Christian of Damascus, Serapion the Elder, whose works were translated into Latin and thus made available to western European scholars of the Middle Ages; or the Arab known as Serapion the Younger, who is believed to have written the popular *Liber medicamentis simplicibus* in the 12th century.

Sergeant of the Law, the   The Sergeant of the Law's portrait follows that of the CLERK in the GENERAL PROLOGUE TO *The CANTERBURY TALES.* He tells "THE MAN OF LAW'S TALE." His title, sergeant, indicates that he belongs to the most prestigious and powerful rank of lawyers in Chaucer's time. Three things are emphasized in this man's portrait: his professional activities, such as sitting as a judge at assizes; his discretion and dignity, which make him appear wise; and finally, his

Artist's rendering of the Sergeant of the Law, from the Ellesmere Manuscript of The Canterbury Tales. *The coif on his head denotes his profession and rank as a judge.*

wealth, which has earned him a reputation as a buyer of property. Scholars have debated over whether this portrait contains elements of satire. The strongest hint appears in the lines which state that "Nowher so bisy a man as he ther nas, / And yet he semed bisier than he was" (lines 321–22) [Nowhere was there a man as busy as he was, and yet he seemed busier than he was]. Jill MANN, in *Chaucer and Medieval Estates Satire,* points out that Chaucer omits traditional censures of greed or dishonesty which would have been known to him from depictions of the legal profession in the work of John GOWER and William LANGLAND. The Sergeant's unostentatious clothing also creates a favorable impression of the man, especially when he is compared to some of the more heavily satirized pilgrims whose dress inappropriately corresponds to their rank or profession. Chaucer himself may have studied law, and he certainly had firsthand experience with lawyers of the sergeant's rank arising from his involvement in various types of litigation, including his arrest in 1388 on a charge of debt. When the Sergeant is invited to participate in the tale-telling contest, the Host, Harry BAILLY, addresses him as "Sire Man of Lawe," which was evidently an acceptable form of address for one of his rank. The tale that he tells is the story of the long-suffering CONSTANCE, the emperor of Rome's daughter whose life is an exemplary fable of the virtues of submission to God's divine plan. Thematically, it is somewhat similar to "The CLERK'S TALE," concerning patient GRISELDA.

Seven against Thebes In classical mythology, the Seven against Thebes is the name often given to the conflict that occurred when POLYNICES, one of the sons of OEDIPUS, gathered together a force of mighty Greek warriors to help him reclaim the throne that his brother, ETEOCLES, refused to surrender even though they had previously agreed to take turns governing THEBES. The force that Polynices raised to support his efforts included the following six heroes who, with himself, served as leaders of his army: ADRASTUS, TYDEUS, PARTHENOPAEUS, CAPANEUS, HIPPOMEDON and AMPHIARAUS. On the Theban side they were opposed by Eteocles, Melanippus, Polyphontes, Megareus, Hyperbius, Lasthenes and Menoecus. The war lasted for some seven years without decided successes for either side. Finally, to bring the conflict to a conclusion, it was agreed that the brothers in whose interest the war was being fought should come together in single combat. They fought and killed one another, fulfilling a curse uttered against them by their father, Oedipus, when they drove him out of Thebes. Instead of dispersing after this event, the two armies continued to fight, and the battle ultimately concluded with the defeat of Polynices' forces. Adrastus was the only one of the seven warriors fighting on his side who escaped alive. Although Chaucer does not adapt the events of

the Seven against Thebes into a major narrative work, it is a mythological story that seems often to have been in the back of Chaucer's mind. The closing events of the conflict set the stage for the opening of "The KNIGHT'S TALE," as THESEUS, king of ATHENS, comes upon a group of grieving women who demand his assistance in forcing CREON to let them bury their dead. (Creon was Eteocles' uncle and the governor of Thebes following his death.) When Creon refuses, Theseus attacks the city and in the course of that conflict takes prisoner two Theban knights, PALAMON and ARCITE (1), who become the central protagonists of the tale. The siege of Thebes also looms in the background of the unfinished *ANELIDA AND ARCITE,* as we learn, at the beginning of that poem, that ANELIDA, the queen of ARMENIA, is being held captive by Creon following the battle with Polynices. Finally, in *TROILUS AND CRISEYDE,* the story of the siege is summarized (lines 1457–1519) by the prophetess CASSANDRA as she prepares to tell her brother TROILUS that the reason CRISEYDE has not returned to Troy is because she has fallen for DIOMEDE, son of Tydeus, one of the Greek heroes at Thebes.

Seyne *See* SEINE.

Seys *See* CEYX.

Shame In the *ROMAUNT OF THE ROSE,* Chaucer's translation of the French *ROMAN DE LA ROSE,* CUPID, known in this text as the God of Love, has two bows and two sets of arrows. One of the bows is made of wood that is knotty, foul and black. The other is elegant, smooth and long, proportional and without blemish. Its surface is decorated with geometric designs and portraits of ladies and young men. In addition to the bows there are 10 arrows. Five of the arrows are excellently made and tipped with pure gold points, and each of them has a name. The first, and fairest, is called Beauty; the second, Simplicity; the third, Franchise (generosity of spirit); the fourth, Company (companionship); and the fifth, Fair-Semblaunt (fair-seeming). Fair-Semblaunt is the least hurtful arrow of all because, although it can make a large wound, the wound will nevertheless heal quickly. These arrows belong to the elegant, well-proportioned bow. The other five arrows are described as being "black as the fiend of hell," and they belong to the foul, crooked bow. The first of these is called Pride; the second, Villainy; the third, Shame; the fourth, Wanhope (despair); and the last is New-Thought. The function of the arrows belonging to the crooked bow are as obstacles, standing in the way of love to those who are shot with them.

Shapur The most famous of the Sassanid kings of PERSIA, Shapur I reigned from A.D. 241 to 272. He frequently made raids into the eastern provinces of the

Roman Empire and captured one of the emperors, Valerian, in 260. In the story of Queen ZENOBIA of Palmyra that appears in "The MONK'S TALE," the narrator notes that Zenobia and her husband, ODENATHUS, defeated Shapur (line 2320).

Sheen(e)   A royal residence belonging to the kings of England, located in the county of Surrey. In *The LEGEND OF GOOD WOMEN,* Queen ALCESTIS commands Chaucer to write a book taking the lives of good women as his subject matter, and when he is finished, to present it to the queen (Queen ANNE OF BOHEMIA) at ELTHAM or at Sheene (prologue F, line 496–97). Sheen was supposedly the queen's favorite residence, and after she died RICHARD II had the palace at least partially demolished so that it would not remind him of his loss. The rest was destroyed by fire in 1499. It was later rebuilt by Henry VII, who changed its name to Richmond to reflect his own title, earl of Richmond.

Sheffield (Sheffeld)   Now a large metropolitan area, located in north-central England in the county of YORKSHIRE, in Chaucer's day Sheffield was a small town. In "The REEVE'S TALE," SIMKIN the miller wears a Sheffield "thwitel," an obscure word which probably means "knife," concealed in his hose (line 3933), always ready for a fight. Until recently, Sheffield remained famous for its steel.

Shipman, the   The Shipman's portrait follows that of the COOK in the GENERAL PROLOGUE to *The CANTERBURY TALES.* Like the MERCHANT, the Shipman appears to be engaged in trade, though as an employee rather than a manager. His modern-day equivalent would be a sailor on a commercial vessel, although various hints regarding his character suggest a certain roguishness reminiscent of an era when the threat of piracy was still real. The strongest of these hints is the reference to his sending those he fought home by water (i.e., tossing them overboard in a fight), which is typically interpreted as a defense of his ship's cargo. Still, he is not above sneaking cups of wine during return voyages from the French region of BORDEAUX. In spite of this, he seems to be a valued member of his crew, singled out for his navigational skills. Because shipmen are rarely found in other examples of medieval estates satire, some scholars have argued that this portrait is not meant to be satirical, discounting the mild criticism implied by the reference to his filching wine. On the other hand, "The SHIPMAN'S TALE," concerning the double-dealing monk, Sir John (*see* JOHN THE MONK), who superbly swindles his rich merchant friend, suggests a fairly contemptuous attitude toward members of the profession that provided him with his employment. Looking back at the portrait after having read the tale lends a darker coloring to the activities mentioned in the latter.

Artist's rendering of the Shipman, from the Ellesmere Manuscript of The Canterbury Tales. *The Shipman is bearded, clothed in a dark gown and wears a dagger slung under his arm (the point can just be seen sticking out behind). Compare this to his description in the General Prologue.*

"Shipman's Tale, The"   Like the MILLER, the REEVE and the MERCHANT, the SHIPMAN tells a ribald story about a deceived husband whose wife's unfaithfulness occurs within the context of a trick or practical joke.

SUMMARY

Once there was a rich merchant who lived at SEINT-DENYS, a small town north of Paris. He had a wife who was very beautiful but who loved festive gatherings and all other social occasions and for that reason, spent a great deal of money on clothing and other expenses associated with entertainment. This merchant has a friend, John, who is a monk (*see* JOHN THE MONK). The merchant and John have been friends for so long that they call each other cousin and pretend to be related. John visits the merchant often; the merchant's wife and all other members of the household are very fond of him.

On the eve of his departure to BRUGES to conduct some business, the merchant invites John for a visit at his home. John arrives with gifts of Malmsey and Italian wine, and a fowl for supper. On the third day of his visit, while the merchant is busy conducting an inventory of the year's profits and losses, the monk is approached by the merchant's wife in the garden. The wife seems depressed but brightens considerably as the monk confesses to being in love with her. After telling John what a stingy man her husband is, the wife begs him for a loan of 100 francs, offering to lie with him one entire night in exchange. John promises to bring the money while her husband is away in FLAN-DERS. The wife leaves him and summons the merchant to dinner. Annoyed at being called away from his business, the merchant rebukes his wife, telling her how important it is for him to be constantly at work to improve his fortune, and urging her to be frugal with their household expenses. After dinner, the monk speaks alone with the merchant, asking for a loan of 100 francs to purchase some animals. The merchant very readily grants the loan, but also reminds John that to maintain good credit he should pay it back as soon as he is able.

The following day the merchant leaves for Bruges, where he eagerly pursues his business, taking no time out for recreation. Meanwhile the monk returns to the merchant's house and gives the wife the same 100 francs he borrowed from her husband, but without revealing the money's source. The wife keeps her end of the bargain and spends the night with the monk. The next morning he departs, with no one in the household any the wiser regarding his relationship with the wife. Soon after this the merchant travels to PARIS (2), again on business, and while there pays a visit to the monk. He does not ask the monk for repayment of his loan; nevertheless, the monk asserts that he has already given the money back—to the merchant's wife, while the merchant was out of town.

With his business at last successfully concluded, the merchant returns home to celebrate with his wife. They make love all night and again the following morning. When his wife begins to tease him, saying he has had enough, the merchant reveals that he is a little angry with her for neglecting to tell him about the return of the money he had loaned to the monk. At this, the wife becomes incensed. Admitting that John gave her a sum of money while the merchant was out of town, she says she thought it was a gift to her in honor of the good cheer and hospitality that he has received in their home. She promises to repay her husband, then says that she is poor and may have to pay him in bed. When the merchant realizes the hopelessness of his situation, he forgives his wife, again telling her that she must, in future, be less of a spendthrift.

COMMENTARY

Unlike the other stories in *The CANTERBURY TALES*, "The Shipman's Tale" exhibits at most a tenuous relationship between the tale and its teller. The primary reason

behind this phenomenon is that the tale seems to have been originally intended for another teller, most likely the WIFE OF BATH. Several lines near the beginning of the tale suggest that the teller is a woman. Speaking of a husband's obligation to clothe and properly array his wife, the narrator uses the first person plural pronoun "us," instead of "them": "The sely housbonde, algate he moot paye / He moot us clothe, and he moot us arraye" (lines 1201–02) [The innocent husband, never-theless he must clothe us and give us things to wear]. Additionally, several lines appearing later in the text repeat the Wife of Bath's definition of a good husband as a man who is brave, wise, rich, generous, obedient to his wife and talented in the bedroom. After coming up with a different tale for the Wife of Bath, Chaucer may have decided to give this one to the Shipman because one of the characters, the merchant, like a shipman, travels a lot; no stronger explanation has been offered.

"The Shipman's Tale" is based on a folktale motif, that of the lover's gift regained. It belongs to the genre of the FABLIAU, a type of story that originated in France and that typically features members of the middle class engaged in deceitful behavior with sex as the motive. The story most likely to have been Chaucer's source, because of its similarity in plot and characterization, is found in BOCCACCIO's *DECAMERON* and concerns a rich merchant whose wife spends a lot of money. The man who falls in love with her, however, is a soldier rather than a monk. When the soldier asks the wife to grant her love to him, she agrees on condition that he give her a large sum of money. The soldier borrows the money from her husband and, like Chaucer's monk, later tells the husband that he has repaid it to the wife. Chaucer's decision to change the profession of this character from soldier to monk is in keeping with the vein of clerical satire that runs throughout *The Canterbury Tales*.

Because "The Shipman's Tale" is a fabliau, it is useful to compare it to other fabliaux within *The Canterbury Tales* such as "The MILLER'S TALE," "The REEVE'S TALE" and "The MERCHANT'S TALE." In "The Miller's Tale" and "The Merchant's Tale," the motives of the characters who deceive the husband are exclusively sexual, while in the tales told by the REEVE and the Shipman there are other grounds—those of revenge and profit, respectively. The demonstration of additional motives like this, because they are antecedent to the sexual one, tends to give unpleasant connotations to the sex that takes place in these tales. For example, the merchant's wife in the Shipman's narrative agrees to have sex with the monk not because she is in love with or even lusts after him, but in exchange for money, reducing the interaction to an act of prostitution. Similarly, the two young men who have sexual intercourse with the miller's wife and daughter in "The Reeve's Tale" act purely out of their desire for revenge against the miller.

Despite the apparent violence of such a motive, the act that they perform is welcomed by the two women, and so ultimately is nonviolent in nature. The damage done is to the miller, and most particularly to his pride. The relationships between NICHOLAS and ALISON in "The Miller's Tale," and between DAMIAN and MAY in "The Merchant's Tale," seem, in contrast, more lighthearted and even wholesome because they arise wholly from sexual motives. The genre of the fabliau is represented more than any other genre in *The Canterbury Tales,* yet the characters in these tales exhibit a variety of motives and behaviors, suggesting that not only was Chaucer simply fond of telling a bawdy story, but that he was using the stories to investigate variations on the theme of romantic or sexual love that appears in most of his poetry (*see The* PARLIAMENT OF FOWLS, TROILUS AND CRISEYDE, ANELIDA AND ARCITE, "The KNIGHT'S TALE," "The FRANKLYN'S TALE," "The CLERK'S TALE" and "The WIFE OF BATH'S TALE").

Considered apart from the rest of the Canterbury tales, "The Shipman's Tale" reveals a preoccupation with themes that are material and spiritual as well as emotional. Superficially, the merchant, with his absorption in affairs of business, would appear to be a man completely enmeshed in the material world, while the monk, given his profession, ought to be more concerned with matters of the spirit. The merchant's innocence and generosity, his genuine affection for both the monk and his wife, the patient tolerance with which he responds to the wife's imprudent spending and his honest success in business together create the image of a complex and sympathetic character who deserves better treatment than that given to him by his wife and his dearest friend. The monk, in contrast, and despite his spiritual avocation, comes across as something of a sensualist. He never visits the merchant without bringing gifts of food and wine. He is also generous to the servants, which initially would seem to correspond to the merchant's generosity; but in retrospect, when the monk's lust for his host's wife has been revealed, this suggests that he may simply have been trying to buy the servants' goodwill. Evidently he is successful, for even when he spends the night with the merchant's wife, none of the servants notice, as the text explicitly informs us.

The paradoxical nature of the two men's characters relative to their professions gives the tale a decidedly ironic tone, one that is enhanced further by Chaucer's frequent use of words and phrases that carry a double meaning. The most often-used is *cozenage* (cosynage). Its surface meaning refers to the relationship between the monk and the merchant, who, because they were born in the same village, have claimed kinship with each other. The word *cozenage* also meant to act duplicitously for one's own advantage, and applies very neatly to the monk's behavior, whereby he uses his cosynage

(relationship) with the merchant to cozen (trick) him. The monk claims to need a loan from the merchant to buy "certein beestes," when he actually means to buy a woman's body, and the merchant responds that he would give not only his gold but his property ("chaffare") as well, a kind of ironic invitation for the monk to sleep with his wife. Finally, at the climax of the story, there is a sudden shower of wit and punning in the wife's last speech. First she tells her husband she thought that the monk gave her the money for "cosynage," meaning for the sake of their relationship, but again, the word also contains the other meaning—in order for her to trick her husband. Then she reminds him that he has slacker debtors than herself, playing on the double association of the word *debt* in Middle English, where it could mean either the sexual debt to a marriage partner or a financial obligation. Last, she tells him to score her debt upon her "taille," meaning her account ("tally") and her "tail" (I suppose the modern equivalent would be "ass"), and that he shall have her pretty body "to wedde," meaning that he shall enjoy it as a marriage partner, and that it shall stand as a pledge for her monetary debt.

"The Shipman's Tale" is rarely assigned reading in college-level courses; scholars have typically viewed it as a superficial story not requiring a great deal of consideration. But, although it may not provide as engrossing an object of study as some of Chaucer's other works, the evidence presented here suggests that it does deserve a reading, concerned as it is with another of Chaucer's abiding themes—that of appearances versus reality, a theme that this tale presents in an entertaining and thought-provoking manner.

Shirley, John (1366?–1456)   The scribe for many of the works of Chaucer and for Chaucer's contemporary, John LYDGATE. His attribution of particular works to Chaucer has been especially important for determining the authorship of some of the shorter poems, including the "COMPLAINT UNTO PITY," the "COMPLAINT TO HIS LADY," the "COMPLAINT OF MARS," the "COMPLAINT OF VENUS," "CHAUCER'S WORDS UNTO ADAM, HIS OWNE SCRIVEYN," "TRUTH" and "LAK OF STEDFASTNESSE." Shirley is reputed to have traveled widely, and he translated a number of French and Latin works into English, including an important chronicle (written in Latin) that recorded the events surrounding the death of King James I of Scotland.

Sibille   *Sibille* is another name by which CASSANDRA, TROILUS' prophetess sister, is called in book 5 of *TROILUS AND CRISEYDE* (line 1450). The name apparently refers to her ability to see into the future.

Sibyl(e)   Term that refers to any of the priestesses of APOLLO. Drawing from VIRGIL's *Aeneid,* Chaucer includes the Trojan hero AENEAS' descent into the underworld under the guidance of a Sibyl among the scenes depicted in the TEMPLE OF VENUS in *The HOUSE OF FAME*.

Sichaeus   The first husband of DIDO, the queen of CARTHAGE who was loved and betrayed by AENEAS. Sichaeus was a prince of Phoenicia. When his brother had him murdered in order to seize his wealth, the ghost of Sichaeus appeared to Dido. Receiving this warning, she fled to Africa, where she founded Carthage. Chaucer refers to Sichaeus ("Sytheo") as Dido's deceased husband in *The LEGEND OF GOOD WOMEN* (line 1005).

Sicily   A large island off the coast of southern Italy; for much of its history, it has maintained an independent existence. In the *BOECE*, Chaucer's translation of BOETHIUS' *Consolation of Philosophy*, LADY PHILOSOPHY uses the example of a "kyng of Sysile" [king of Sicily] who reminded himself of the fearful responsibilities of his position by keeping a naked sword hanging over the head of his friend Damocles (Book Three, Prosa 5, lines 20–29). The Damoclean sword became proverbial for a constantly looming threat.

Sidyngborne   *See* SITTINGBOURNE.

Signifer   In book five of *TROILUS AND CRISEYDE*, the narrator states that the "Signifer" used its bright candles (stars) to light CRISEYDE's way to bed after an evening spent with DIOMEDE (lines 1020–21). Signifer, or "Sign Bearer," is another name for the belt of stars extending across the heavens, more familiarly known as the zodiac (*see* ASTROLOGY).

Silla   *See* SCYLLA.

Simkin   A miller who is the principle character in "The REEVE'S TALE." The portrait of the miller in this tale is an obvious satirization of ROBYN (1), the teller of "The MILLER'S TALE." Simkin is proud and happy as a peacock. Like Robyn, he plays the bagpipes and has a quarrelsome temper, a feature of his personality best illustrated by the fact that he carries three knives, a long dagger (panade) in his belt, a short knife tucked into his pocket and a small jackknife concealed in his hose. The Reeve refers to him as a "market-betere," which suggests that he is fond of hanging out in town on the days when the farmers and other merchants bring their goods to sell in the market square, and that while there he often finds occasion to get into a fight. The name *Simkin* is a diminutive of *Symond* and itself has unflattering connotations, alluding to the miller's simian, or apelike, features and his reprehensible moral qualities, which include pride, drunkenness, lying and treachery.

Economically, the miller seems to be fairly well-off, having sole right to grind all the grain within a specified geographic area, a right which basically constitutes a service monopoly. SOLER HALL (King's College) at Cambridge University is located within his jurisdiction and provides him with a good deal of his business. His virtual monopoly on the grinding of grain helps to explain why the miller is able to get away with cheating his customers over and over again. They have no choice but to return to him when they need to have some grain processed into flour, and if they have accused him of stealing, he is likely to take more the next time.

Like Robyn, the miller in the GENERAL PROLOGUE of *The CANTERBURY TALES*, Simkin is proud and disdainful toward others. For this reason the "revenge" that the two students, ALAN and JOHN THE CLERK take by having sex with the miller's daughter and his wife would seem to be particularly painful.

Simkin's wife   Although never named, the wife of SIMKIN the miller is an important character in "The REEVE'S TALE." The illegitimate daughter of the local church parson, she has gone to school in a nunnery, and both she and her husband think of her as a lady. There is a great deal of irony residing in her pride over her lineage, which provides Chaucer with yet another opportunity to criticize corruption or worldliness in the church, something he does quite often in his descriptions of the clerical figures in the GENERAL PROLOGUE TO *THE CANTERBURY TALES*. His description of her is otherwise pointedly evocative, though not detailed. She is as "pert," or impudent, as a magpie, a simile that also suggests that she is a gossip or chatterbox. Another interesting comparison states that she is as "as digne as water in a dich," i.e., "as haughty as ditchwater," a proverbial expression for which the *Oxford English Dictionary* offers this definition: "stinking with pride." When her husband unties the horse belonging to JOHN THE CLERK and ALAN, the miller's wife eagerly comes forward to blame them for not tying the animal up properly. As soon as they run out to try to catch it, she participates with her husband in stealing the students's flour, baking the stolen portion into a cake. We do not encounter the wife again until the evening meal, when she joins the miller in having perhaps a bit too much to drink. When they retire to bed, her snoring accompanies her husband's and their daughter's to make a "melody" that prevents the students from sleeping. Eventually the victim of the misplaced cradle trick, she climbs into bed with John, thinking she is returning to her own bed. When the student climbs on top of her and they have sex, it is not at all clear that she knows who he is. Her reaction when she is awoken by the pair of men fighting on the floor suggests that she believes her sleeping companion to be her husband. On the other hand, her apparent enjoyment of the unaccustomed sexual activity suggests a slyer motive in her calling out for her husband when she awakes—i.e., she may simply be trying to suggest to him that she does not realize she is sharing a bed with John.

Simois The Simois (the modern Turkish Dümberek su) is a tributary of the ancient Scamander River, which flowed into the Dardanelles. In *TROILUS AND CRISEYDE*, Chaucer says, incorrectly, that it flowed through TROY. (book 4, line 1504).

Simon *See* SIMKIN.

Simon, Saint One of Christ's apostles, called Simon the Canaanite to distinguish him from Simon PETER. The name could also indicate that he was a member of a radical Jewish sect, the Zealots, who strenuously opposed Roman rule in Palestine. According to tradition, after Christ's ascension, Simon preached the Gospel in Egypt, northern Africa, Mesopotamia and Persia, where he died. In "The SUMMONER'S TALE," trying to avoid obligating himself to the corrupt friar who is trying to get money from him in exchange for hearing his confession, poor sick THOMAS (1) swears by Saint Simon that he has already been shriven that same day by his curate (lines 2094–95).

Simon Magus In the New Testament, Simon Magus is a Samaritan magician whose performances were so impressive that many Samaritans thought he was a god and followed him until Philip the evangelist persuaded them to convert to Christianity. Simon Magus was also baptized. Later, the apostles PETER and John (*see* JOHN, SAINT) visited Samaria to make sure that believers there had received the power of the Holy Spirit. When Simon saw that the Holy Spirit was bestowed by the laying on of hands, he attempted to buy this power and was rebuked and cursed by Peter for his presumption (the etymological origin of the word *Simony*, which means the buying or selling of sacred or spiritual things). Simon Magus is mentioned along with other magicians who dwell in FAME's palace in *The HOUSE OF FAME* (line 1274).

Simon the Pharisee In the New Testament, Simon the Pharisee was a man in whose house Christ ate. When a woman who was a sinner anointed Christ's feet, Simon grew upset, feeling that she should not have been allowed near the Savior. Jesus responded by saying that people like her were the very ones who needed access to him and his forgiveness. The story appears in Luke 7:36–50. In "The PARSON'S TALE," Simon's complaining is given as an example of envy that arises out of pride (line 504). The example appears in the portion of the PARSON's sermon having to do with the Seven Deadly Sins, specifically with the sin of envy.

Simplicius Gallus *See* GALLUS, SULPICIUS.

Sinai *See* HOREB.

Sinon A cousin of ULYSSES, Sinon fought in the TROJAN WAR on the side of the Greeks. When the Greeks appeared to have sailed away, he pretended to have been abandoned. Out of his supposed hatred for those who had deserted him, he told the Trojans that the giant wooden horse that the Greeks had left behind them had been intended as an offering to propitiate PALLAS Athena. It had been built so large because of the prophecy that, if it were taken inside the walls of Troy, the city would never fall to the Greeks. Thus its size was ostensibly intended to make its removal difficult. When the Trojans succeeded at dragging it into Troy, Sinon released the Greek warriors hidden within and the city was captured. Sinon's deeds at Troy are depicted on the walls of the TEMPLE OF VENUS in *The HOUSE OF FAME* (lines 151–56). In *The LEGEND OF GOOD WOMEN*, the story of Queen DIDO of CARTHAGE and her tragic love affair with the Trojan AENEAS begins with a summary of Sinon's treachery (lines 930–33). In "The NUN'S PRIEST'S TALE," Sinon is one of the famous traitors with whom RUSSELL, the fox who seizes CHAUNTICLEER, is compared (line 3228), and in "The SQUIRE'S TALE," the magical bronze horse that King CAMBYUSKAN receives for his birthday is compared to the Greek horse of Sinon, although there is no indication that this horse is to be an instrument of treachery (line 209).

Sirius The brightest star of the constellation Canis major, the Greater Dog; it is in fact the brightest star in the heavens, best observed in winter and summer. Medieval astronomers believed that Sirius displayed characteristics of extreme heat and cold, which is how the "dog days" of summer got their name. In the *BOECE*, Chaucer's translation of BOETHIUS' *Consolation of Philosophy*, Boethius notes that the corn is ready to harvest when it is scorched by Sirius (Book One, Metrum 5, lines 26–28). In Chaucer's *TREATISE ON THE ASTROLABE*, Sirius is referred to as ALHABOR, the name assigned to it by Arab astronomers (part 2, div. 3, line 47).

Sir Thopas *See* THOPAS, SIR.

Sisyphus In classical mythology, Sisyphus was the son of AEOLUS the wind god, and the king of the city of Corinth. He was known to the ancient Greeks as one of the most intelligent and crafty of men. When he attempted to thwart the plans of Zeus (JUPITER) to abduct a young woman, Zeus sent Thanatos (Death) to punish Sisyphus. Aware of what was coming, Sisyphus managed to bind Thanatos in chains, thus preventing him from doing any harm. Zeus finally freed Thanatos and gave him full control of Sisyphus, but the latter speedily crafted another plan to escape death by commanding his wife not to make the usual funeral offerings when he died. After Sisyphus' death, when PLUTO learned of his wife's neglect, he permitted Sisyphus to return to Earth to settle the matter, but once released, Sisyphus refused to return and eventually died of old age. Finally, in Hades, his clever attempts to outwit the gods caught up with him and he was condemned to the famous punishment of having to roll a great rock up a steep hill. Although he could accomplish the feat with tremendous and painful exertion, the rock always escaped and rolled to the bottom again, so that he had to repeat the task eternally. In *The BOOK OF THE DUCHESS*, the BLACK KNIGHT compares his suffering at the loss of his lady to that of Sisyphus in hell, thus suggesting that it is both eternal and futile (lines 588–90).

Sittingbourne   A town lying southeast of LONDON between ROCHESTER and CANTERBURY. Sittingbourne is one of the places mentioned in *The CANTERBURY TALES* to mark the progress of the pilgrims along the road to the shrine of Saint THOMAS À BECKET, their ultimate destination. At the conclusion of the WIFE OF BATH's prologue, the SUMMONER vows to tell two or three tales about friars before the group reaches Sittingbourne (lines 845–47). Throughout *The Canterbury Tales* there is ongoing hostility between the Summoner and the FRIAR that is most clearly expressed in their respective tales (*see* "The SUMMONER'S TALE" and "The FRIAR'S TALE").

Skeat, W. W. (1835–1912)   Walter William Skeat was one of the greatest of the 19th-century editors of Chaucer's work, as well as of many other works of Old and Middle English literature. Educated at Christ's College, Cambridge University, he first lectured in mathematics, but devoted much of his time to the study of Old English. In 1878 his career took a dramatic turn when he was appointed to the chair of Anglo-Saxon at Cambridge. His work on Chaucer includes the important book *The Chaucer Canon: With a Discussion of Works Associated with the Name of Geoffrey Chaucer* (1900), in which he argues for the establishment of Chaucer's canon by applying various tests of grammar and rhyme. Modern scholars accept his suggestions with minor variations, leaving doubt about several of the short lyric poems. Skeat's greatest accomplishments were the editions of William LANGLAND's *PIERS PLOWMAN* and of Chaucer's collected writings. The seven-volume *Complete Works of Geoffrey Chaucer,* published by Oxford's Clarendon Press from 1894 to 1897 was the first complete modern edition of Chaucer's poetry and prose based on manuscripts rather than earlier editions. Its glossary and extensive scholarly notes are still valued by contemporary scholars.

Skeat's Oxford Chaucer   *See* SKEAT, W. W.

Socrates   Born in ATHENS in 649 B.C., Socrates was one of the most important and influential philosophers to come out of ancient Greece, even though he himself wrote nothing. He is generally regarded by scholars as primarily a teacher of ethics who had no interest in abstract philosophy. He is reckoned to have been the first person to use philosophical methods in order to examine the basic assumptions underlying human behavior. Plato, who was his pupil, admits that a large part of his famous doctrine of Ideas was really of Socratic origin. Socrates' method of questioning his fellow citizens and forcing them to consider their behavior from a different point of view made him a controversial figure and aroused the anger of many prominent Athenians. Accused of corrupting the youth of Athens and of denying the gods, he was condemned to death in 399 B.C. and forced to drink a beverage made from hemlock, a poisonous evergreen. Some scholars believe that the real reason for his death was the tragic outcome of the Peloponnesian War, which Athens lost to her rival Sparta. Overwhelmed by their resentment and despair, the people may have turned against Socrates because of his association with the traitor ALCIBIADES and other aristocrats.

Socrates is mentioned several times in Chaucer's work, most often as an example of steadfastness in the face of misfortune. In *The BOOK OF THE DUCHESS*, the narrator encourages the BLACK KNIGHT to remember that Socrates was resilient to FORTUNE's attacks (lines 717–19) as he tries to help the knight overcome the sorrow he feels for the loss of his queen. In the *BOECE,* Chaucer's translation of BOETHIUS' *Consolation of Philosophy,* LADY PHILOSOPHY also uses Socrates' life and death as an example of the way to deal with Fortune's mutations (Book One, Prosa 3, lines 26–28, 29–34 and 53–59; Book One, Prosa 4, lines 157–62). "FORTUNE," a short poem dealing with the same issues, begins with an apostrophe to Socrates, who is praised as being immune to Fortune's torments (lines 17–24). In "The MAN OF LAW'S TALE," the narrator meditates on destiny, noting that the death of many famous people, including Socrates, was written in the stars before they were even born (lines 197–203). The reputation of Socrates' wife, Xantippe, as a scold was proverbial in the Middle Ages, and the WIFE OF BATH alludes to this in her prologue, when she says that Xantippe is mentioned in her fifth husband's "Book of Wicked Wives" (lines 727–32).

Soler Hall   The name given in "The REEVE'S TALE" to one of the colleges of Cambridge University. It is where the two student protagonists of the tale are studying. The official name of the college, which was later merged into Trinity College, was King's Hall. King's Hall grew out of a society of scholars founded by King

Edward II. The unofficial name *Soler Hall* may refer to the number of solars (rooms admitting sunlight) that the college contained.

Solomon In the Old Testament, Solomon was the son of DAVID, the second king of Israel. Inheriting the throne from his father, Solomon became one of Israel's most successful kings. He was responsible for building the great temple in Jerusalem and for establishing profitable trade relations with other nations. Renowned for his great wisdom, he is the supposed author of three books of the Old Testament: Proverbs, the Song of Solomon and Ecclesiastes.

Solomon is mentioned numerous times in Chaucer's work, usually (always in *The Canterbury Tales*) with reference to his exemplary wisdom, but occasionally with reference to what was considered by the Latin church fathers to be a weakness—his numerous marriages. In "The KNIGHT'S TALE," Solomon is among those men whose stories are depicted on the walls of the TEMPLE OF VENUS because of the folly they committed in the name of love (line 1942). Solomon undoubtedly appears here because of his many wives, an attribute that also gains him notice in the prologue to "The WIFE OF BATH'S TALE." The Wife uses his bigamy in a bid to justify her own multiple (but not simultaneous) marriages (line 35).

Most often Solomon is mentioned for the proverbial advice he offers in the works attributed to him. In "The MILLER'S TALE," for example, the clever student NICHOLAS claims to use some words of Solomon when he advises JOHN THE CARPENTER how to respond to his prediction concerning a second NOAH's Flood: "Werk al by conseil, and thou shalt nat rewe" (line 1350) [Do everything according to good advice, and you won't be sorry]. In "The MERCHANT'S TALE," JANUARY's brother PLACEBO gives him the same advice when January decides to get married (line 1485). This advice, although commonly attributed to Solomon, actually comes from the apocryphal Book of Ecclesiasticus attributed to JESUS, SON OF SIRACH. The wisdom contained in Solomon's sayings is called upon most often (24 times, most from the Book of Proverbs) in "The TALE OF MELIBEE" as Dame PRUDENCE and her husband try to decide how he will deal with the men who have robbed him and injured his family. A number of other sayings in this tale are attributed to Solomon but actually come from other sources. "The PARSON'S TALE" also features some wisdom from Proverbs, such as the idea that the fear of God causes men to forsake their sins (line 119; cf. Proverbs 16:6). In the prologue to "The CLERK'S TALE," the Host, Harry BAILLY, invokes perhaps the most famous of Solomon's verses when he says, "Salomon seith 'every thyng hath tyme'" (line 6) [Solomon says, "Everything has a time"]. The verse echoed here appears in Ecclesiastes 3:1: "To every thing there is a season, and a time to every purpose under the heavens." A collection of wise sayings from the Book of Proverbs, the "Parables of Solomon," is one of the texts included in the WIFE OF BATH's fifth husband's "Book of Wicked Wives" ("WIFE OF BATH'S PROLOGUE," line 679). These verses include some pronouncements praising virtuous women and condemning those who reflect poorly on their husbands and families. The medieval notion that Solomon was adept in magic is alluded to in "The SQUIRE'S TALE," when those who see the magic ring given to CANACEE (1) say that they have never heard of anything like it, save the rings that were reputedly possessed by MOSES and King Solomon (lines 247–51).

Somnium Scipionis *See* DREAM OF SCIPIO.

Sophia The daughter of MELIBEE and PRUDENCE in Chaucer's "TALE OF MELIBEE." When Melibee's enemies break into his house during his absence, they beat his wife and wound his daughter with "five mortal wounds" in her feet, hands, ears, nose and mouth. When Prudence begins advising her husband upon what course of action to take in response to the attack, she mentions that Sophia may yet recover, and says that they ought to work day and night to that effect. On the level of allegory, Sophia, whose name means "wisdom," represents the wounded intelligence of Melibee, who must be schooled by his wife Prudence (who represents discretion and sound judgment) toward mending his behavior. On a literal level, it is interesting that, aside from the mention of her existence and her wounds, Sophia herself does not appear in the tale.

Soranas In the BOECE, Chaucer's translation of BOETHIUS' *Consolation of Philosophy,* Soranas refers to Soranas Barea, a Roman who served as proconsul in Asia under the emperor NERO. Soranas was already on the emperor's bad side for his demonstrations of fairness toward conquered peoples in Asia when he was accused of plotting against Nero and condemned to death. LADY PHILOSOPHY uses Soranas as an example of one who was betrayed by his friends (Book One, Prosa 3, lines 53–59).

Southwark (Southwerk) A suburb of London located south of the Thames River. In Shakespeare's day this locale became known for the entertainments that were offered there at least in part because they were prohibited within the City. These included bear baiting, cockfighting and theatrical productions. The TABARD Inn, an actual 14th-century establishment at which the pilgrims of *The CANTERBURY TALES* gathered before embarking on their pilgrimage to the shrine of Saint THOMAS À BECKET, was located in Southwark.

Spain (Spaigne; Spayne)   The country that occupies most of the Iberian peninsula in southwest Europe, Spain is mentioned several times in Chaucer's work. In the GENERAL PROLOGUE TO *THE CANTERBURY TALES*, the SHIPMAN's navigational knowledge is so extensive that he knows every creek in Britain and in Spain (lines 407–09). In "The PARDONER'S TALE," the narrator tells how innkeepers blend French wine with wines from Spain. The result is particularly intoxicating (lines 565–70). In "The MONK'S TALE," the narrator refers to PEDRO OF CASTILE as the "glorie of Spayne" (line 2375) for his noble deeds. In *The HOUSE OF FAME*, FAME's palace stands on a rock higher than any mountain peak in Spain (lines 1116–17).

Speculum historiale   *See* ESTORYAL MYROUR.

Speght, Thomas   Late 16th-century editor of Chaucer's work. *See* EDITIONS OF CHAUCER.

Squire, the   The Squire is the second pilgrim described in the GENERAL PROLOGUE TO *THE CANTERBURY TALES*. He is the son of the KNIGHT (1) and, as his father's squire, would be responsible for bearing and maintaining his father's armor, in addition to carving at his table. On the other hand, because his own military experience has been in FLANDERS and parts of northern France (ARTOIS and PICARDY), it seems unlikely that the Squire has accompanied his father to the rather exotic locations mentioned in the Knight's portrait. The Squire's youthful high spirits, his concern with fashion that is reflected in his embroidered clothing, and his courtly accomplishments such as riding, composing and singing songs, playing the flute, and dancing, together constitute a rather conventional iconographic image of the noble young lover whose characteristics are mirrored elsewhere in *The Canterbury Tales* by AURELIUS, who appears in "The FRANKLIN'S TALE." Many of the details of his portrait, such as the flowers embroidered on his clothing and the simile stating that he is "as fressh as is the month of May," are associated with springtime and recall the opening lines of the General Prologue. The Squire, like his father, attempts to tell a chivalric romance. His performance, however, is considerably less skilled, and he is courteously interrupted by the FRANKLIN.

"Squire's Tale, The"   The SQUIRE's rambling romance of CANACEE (1), the daughter of a Mongol king, is interrupted before we have a clear sense of where it might be headed. The description of the Mongol court and the magical gifts people bring to King CAMBYUSKAN's birthday party are nevertheless worthy of some attention.

SUMMARY

After a very brief introduction that consists of the Host, Harry BAILLY, asking the squire to tell a tale and the squire acquiescing, the tale begins. In SARRAY (modern Tsarev, in southeastern Russia), lives a Mongol king named Cambyuskan (Cambuskan). He is described in the typical exemplary terms of a romance hero as noble, just, wise, rich, charitable, courageous, young and strong. His wife's name is ELPHETA and they have two sons. ALGARSIF (Algarsyf) is the oldest and CAMBALO the next. They also have a daughter named Canacee whose beauty, the squire claims, he lacks skill to describe.

The plot begins with Cambyuskan announcing plans to celebrate his birthday, in the 20th anniversary of his reign, on the 15th day of March, which he refers to as the Ides of March. In the midst of this feast, a stranger comes riding into the court on a horse made of brass. He speaks to the gathering very courteously, announcing that he brings greetings and gifts from the king of Arabia and India. The first gift is the brass horse. The knight describes the features of the horse, which include the ability to carry the king wherever he wishes to go, in fair weather or foul, within the space of 24 hours. The second gift, which is intended for the king's daughter Canacee, is a magic mirror. The mirror can be used, the knight explains, to foresee disaster and to keep an eye on any young man to whom Canacee attaches her affection. The third gift, also for Canacee, is a ring that she may either wear on her finger or carry in her purse. It will enable her to both understand and speak the language of birds and to understand the healing powers of all plants. The final gift is a sword that can cut through the thickest armor. When a man is wounded by this sword, the stranger further explains, the only way in which he can be healed is by stroking the wound with the flat of the same sword.

During the next part of the banquet, those present discuss various theories regarding the sources of the gifts' powers. When this part of the feast is done, the king departs to his chamber of presence, and the celebration continues with music and dancing, drinking and eating, until everyone goes to bed. Canacee, who went to bed earlier than everyone else, is up with the dawn. While sleeping she had a dream which was prompted by the mirror. She rouses her attendants and goes for a walk in the castle grounds. She takes her ring with her and is delighted by her ability to understand what the birds are singing.

At this point, the squire digresses to say that he is now coming to the "knotte" or point of the story, speaking briefly of how important it is to do this before one's listeners have lost interest.

As she walks, Canacee comes upon a peregrine falcon perched high in a tree who cries pitifully while beating herself with her wings and tearing her breast with her beak. When Canacee asks the bird what is wrong with her, she cries even louder and falls from the tree in a faint. Canacee takes the bird into her lap. When the bird awakens, it tells her the rather lengthy story of its love affair with tercelet, a male falcon, who for a long time convinced her of his sincerity and faithfulness, but who at last betrayed her by falling in love with another bird, this time a female kite. And this is what has brought his erstwhile mate to the brink of despair.

Canacee feels great pity for the bird, so she takes it home, dresses its wounds with salves and bandages and makes a pen for it right next to her bed. On the sides of the pen she paints pictures of "false" birds, like the former lover, along with magpies to suggest the chiding they ought to receive for what they have done. (According to medieval beast lore, magpies were supposedly capable of speech, and considered voluminous chatterers.)

At this point the squire digresses again, saying that he has come to the end of this part of the story, but that he will later pick up this thread of the plot again to tell how, through the mediation of the king's son Cambalo, the falcon was reunited with her lover. But first, he says, he is going to tell of many battles and adventures involving Cambyuskan and his two sons. He is only two lines into the next part of his recital, however, when the FRANKLIN interrupts him. Although the Franklin's words consist of nothing but praise for the Squire's storytelling abilities, it seems likely that he is simply trying, without being rude, to bring an end to a tale that is beginning to seem more like an ordeal than an entertainment. The Host interrupts the Franklin to demand that he now take his turn in the storytelling.

COMMENTARY

"The Squire's Tale" belongs to the genre of chivalric romance. Like other stories in this genre, it features members of the nobility as its characters and deals with marvelous adventures and matters of love. No single source survives for this tale, but it appears that, for the first part, Chaucer may have drawn upon two 13th-century French romances, the *Cleomadès* of Adenet le Roi and the *Meliacin* of Girard d'Amiens, which were originally based on an Oriental story of a magic horse. Either of these texts may have provided the material for the part of the Squire's narrative that tells of the king's birthday celebration and the marvelous gifts sent by the king of Arabia and India. For the second part of the story, Chaucer seems to have drawn heavily on one of his own unfinished works, ANELIDA AND ARCITE. The situation of the lamenting falcon in "The Squire's Tale" is practically identical to that of the abandoned ANELIDA, and Chaucer even replicates some of Anelida's phras-

ing in the falcon's lengthy complaint. The only substantial difference in the characters' situation is that Anelida is human, the falcon avian. Romantic birds also feature in another of Chaucer's works, The PARLIAMENT OF FOWLS, which was written earlier in his career as an occasional poem for Saint Valentine's Day.

The Squire is the youngest member of the pilgrimage. The GENERAL PROLOGUE informs us that he is the son of the KNIGHT (1), with whom, as a squire, he is in training. He is described as a very romantic young man with curly hair who pays a lot of attention to his looks and who is preoccupied with the courtly attainments of dancing, singing, riding and storytelling. The tale he tells belongs to the same genre as his father's story of EMILY, PALAMON and ARCITE (1), but is much less accomplished in style, characterization and plot. If Chaucer's aim was, as has been deduced from the variety of genres that appear in The CANTERBURY TALES, to give at least one example of every genre that existed in his day, then "The Squire's Tale" may be considered an example of the episodic or interlaced romance which was so popular in France, its most famous example being the vast, sprawling prose *Lancelot*. This idea is supported by the Squire's promise to return to the falcon's story following his recital of the adventures of Cambyuskan and Algarsif. Needless to say, it would be very difficult to include an entire romance of this sort in a group of tales like The Canterbury Tales, since such works were themselves groups of tales.

There has been some debate over whether Chaucer intended "The Squire's Tale" as a parody of chivalric romance, but given the much more deliberate and obvious silliness of his Sir THOPAS, it seems more likely that he was simply attempting to suit the nature of the tale to its teller. In the General Prologue, the Squire comes off not only as young, but as somewhat immature and superficial. Thus, it seems suitable that the story he tells should also be marked by those characteristics.

Perhaps the most pervasive indication of the narrator's superficiality is his preoccupation with rhetorical devices. At every available opportunity, he launches into *amplificatio,* a rhetorical device which consists of extended, elaborately detailed description. For example, every reference to time comes in the form of astronomical periphrasis—a long circumlocution using the position of the planets on the zodiac to denote the time. The Squire's descriptions nearly always tend toward the superlative, which is typical of chivalric romance but which, in the Squire's unpracticed hands, sometimes achieves a comic effect.

On the other hand, in contrast to these extended forays into loquaciousness, the Squire often finds himself at a loss for words. When it comes to describing Canacee, for instance, he says "But for to telle yow al hir beautee, / It lyth nat in my tonge, n'yn my konnyng" (lines 34–35) [For to tell you all of her beauty, / It lies not in my speaking-ability, nor in my knowledge]. Likewise, when it is time to describe the dancing at Cambyuskan's birthday feast, he asks who is able to describe such a scene and answers, "No man but Launcelot, and he is deed" (i.e., dead; line 287). Indeed, many such omissions come not from a lack of willingness to describe the matter, but from a lack of knowledge and/or experience, as the Squire admits when attempting to describe the last part of the feasting, where there were "deyntees mo than been in my knowyng" (line 301) [More dainties than exist in my experience]. He is, however, like many enthusiastic young students, more than willing to share what he does know, and this seems the likely reason for the extended astronomical descriptions and for the bits of "scientific" and other types of learning that appear. He also has a young person's sense of humor, and is not above making a pun when he excuses himself from speaking the exact same words as the strange knight who entered the court on Cambyuskan's birthday: "Al be that I kan nat sowne his stile, / Ne kan nat clymben over so heigh a style" (lines 105–06) [Since I cannot mimic his style, / Nor can I climb over so high a stile], "stile" being a Middle (and Modern) English word denoting steps for climbing over a fence or wall.

Another telling mark of the Squire's immaturity as an artist appears in the tale's lack of narrative cohesion. The link between the two parts of the narrative, the first describing a feast and four marvelous gifts, the second concerned with a bird's complaint of a lost love, is tenuous at best. The king's daughter Canacee, who receives the magic ring and mirror in the first part, and who is able, through the ring's power, to understand the bird in the second part, forms the only link between the tale's two halves. The tale's unfinished state provides one argument against judging it on this basis. Still, the Squire's forecast of what he intends to tell next, stories of the battles and other adventures of King Cambyuskan and his son Algarsif, then returning to the resolution of the bird's story later, seems a less than adequate promise that the narrative structure of the finished product would be coherent, especially considering its state thus far. The number of smaller discontinuities in the tale, such as Canacee's holding out her skirt to catch the falcon in case it should fall, followed by its crashing to the ground some 30 lines later with no mention of why or how Canacee failed to catch it, further undermine the tale's artistic integrity.

Of historical interest is the probability that the name "Cambyuskan" was derived from the Latinized version of the name of the Mongol emperor "Genghis Khan," although Walter SKEAT has argued that the narrator's description of Cambyuskan better suits the grandson of Genghis, Kublai Khan, whose court was visited by the explorer Marco Polo and who became the inspiration for Samuel Coleridge's famous poem, "Kubla Khan."

Statius (Stace) Publius Papinius Statius was a Roman epic poet of the first century A.D. who wrote in the tradition of VIRGIL. His *Thebaid,* a Latin epic in 12 books, relates the story of the conflict between POLYNICES and ETEOCLES, the two sons of OEDIPUS whose struggle for the Theban throne ended with both of them dead. The Italian poet BOCCACCIO drew on the *Thebaid* for *Il FILOSTRATO,* which was in turn Chaucer's source for his *TROILUS AND CRISEYDE.* The *Thebaid* was not translated into English until 1648, but Statius' work was widely studied by medieval readers of Latin. The major events of the work are summarized by CASSANDRA in book 5 of *Troilus and Criseyde* (lines 1485–1510). At the end of *Troilus and Criseyde,* Chaucer directs his book to go and follow in the footsteps of Virgil, OVID, HOMER, LUCAN and Statius ("Stace"), paying tribute to its classical heritage (book 5, lines 1786–92). Chaucer hints at the ultimate origin of "The KNIGHT'S TALE" within that narrative when he directs those readers who would like to learn more about EMILY's prayers and sacrifices to DIANA to look in "Stace of Thebes" (lines 2294–95). Lines 22–42 of the fragment ANELIDA AND ARCITE are a paraphrase of some lines from the *Thebaid* and constitute the same series of events with which "The Knight's Tale" opens (i.e., Theseus' homecoming from the Scythian wars, in which he has conquered the AMAZONS). In *The HOUSE OF FAME,* Statius' image stands on a pillar of iron (the metal symbolizing MARS (1), the god of war), where he bears up the fame of THEBES and of "cruel Achilles" (lines 1456–63). In addition to the *Thebaid* and several minor works, Statius also wrote an unfinished epic, the *Achilleid,* about the life of the Greek hero ACHILLES.

Steward A very minor character in "The MAN OF LAW'S TALE." When CONSTANCE's rudderless ship comes to rest on the sand below the castle where this man is steward, he sneaks aboard at night and attempts to rape Constance. As she struggles against him he falls overboard and drowns. Like all of the people who attack or plot against Constance in this tale, the steward is a pagan.

Stilboun In "The PARDONER'S TALE," Stilboun is the Greek ambassador sent by the Lacedaemonians (Spartans) to the city of CORINTH for the purpose of forging an alliance between the two city-states. He changes his mind when he finds so many of the Corinthians engaged in gambling. The anecdote forms part of the PARDONER's disquisition on the tavern vices of gambling, gluttony and swearing. It has been suggested that Stilboun is actually Chilon of Sparta, a philosopher of the sixth century who was known as one of the seven wise men of Greece.

Stix   *See* STYX.

Stoics (Stoyciens)   Followers of the philosopher Zeno, who founded the philosophical school of thought known as stoicism around 300 B.C. Stoicism taught that the cosmos is an ordered whole in which all contradictions are resolved for the ultimate good. Evil, therefore, is relative. The particular misfortunes which fall to individuals are seen as necessary to the final perfection of the universe, and everything that happens is determined according to a rational purpose. The destiny of an individual is predetermined, and he can only accept his fate or rebel against it. By accepting fate and submitting to the order of the universe in the knowledge that that order is good, human beings may attain to the highest happiness, which consists of a tranquil mind untainted by bitterness toward events, which anyway are beyond one's control. In the *BOECE*, Chaucer's translation of BOETHIUS' *Consolation of Philosophy*, LADY PHILOSOPHY mentions the Stoics several times in her dialogue with Boethius. The attitude that she wishes him to adopt toward the vicissitudes of FORTUNE is similar to that of Zeno and his followers.

Stratford atte Bowe (Stratford at Bow)   A town about three miles from London in Chaucer's day. It now lies in Middlesex county in the metropolitan borough of Poplar in the Limehouse district. In the description of the PRIORESS that appears in the GENERAL PROLOGUE TO *THE CANTERBURY TALES*, we are told that she speaks very elegant French, though her accent is "after the scole of Stratford atte Bowe" (line 125) [in the style of the school of Stratford at Bow] rather than Parisian. The reference may indicate that the Prioress was a member of the Benedictine nunnery of Saint Leonard's, which was located there.

Strode, Ralph (fl. 1350–1400)   A scholastic philosopher and logician, Ralph Strode was Chaucer's contemporary. Educated at Merton College, Oxford, he became a fellow there around 1360. John WYCLIFFE was also there at this time, and an antagonistic debate developed between the two men because Strode opposed Wycliffe's doctrine of predestination. Two of Strode's philosophical treatises, both in Latin, survive. He was also known to have composed some love lyrics. Strode moved to London in November, 1373, when he was elected Common Pleader (a legal position) for the City of London. Some scholars believe that Strode and Chaucer were friends, because Chaucer dedicated *TROILUS AND CRISEYDE* to Strode and another writer, John GOWER, trusting that they would, if need be, correct any errors found within (book 5, lines 1856–62). Chaucer and Strode also both served as guarantors for a rich London draper who was having

legal problems over his acquisition of some estates in Essex. This latter incident suggests that the men were at least acquainted.

Strother   The northern English town from which the two students in "The REEVE'S TALE" come (line 4014). Although no such town exists today, it could have been a small village that has since disappeared. According to Douglas GRAY's notes to "The Reeve's Tale" in *The RIVERSIDE CHAUCER*, the name means "a place overgrown with brushwood." Gray also refers to a "Lange Strother" recorded in the 13th century, which could have been the location of which Chaucer was thinking. Or he could have just chosen the name because of its rustic associations, since, in Chaucer's day, people from the north of England were typically considered to be uncouth bumpkins by those living in the more urban and urbane south, near the metropolis of London.

Studies in the Age of Chaucer   The yearbook of the New Chaucer Society, which publishes articles and reviews on Chaucer, his contemporaries and the historical, religious, intellectual and literary background of their works. Although most of the articles are on Chaucer, the reviews cover books on other authors and topics. The yearbook also publishes an annual "Annotated Chaucer Bibliography."

Stymphalis (Stymphalides)   According to legend, Stymphalis was a virgin who was wooed by Aristoclides of Orchomenos. When the tyrant murdered her father, Stymphalis took refuge in the temple of DIANA, where Aristoclides stabbed her to death as she clung to the altar. In "The FRANKLIN'S TALE," Stymphalis is one of the virtuous women whose example DORIGEN considers when she is debating whether to break her promise to the squire AURELIUS or to be unfaithful to her husband (lines 1387–94). Dorigen had previously promised to become Aurelius' lover if he could remove some rocks lining the coast of BRITTANY.

Styx   In classical mythology, Styx is the chief river that flowed in Hades, or the realm of the dead (the underworld). The river was considered sacred to the gods, whose most binding oaths might be given in the name of the Styx. For the taking of such an oath, Iris, JUNO's messenger, would bring water from the stream, and the god who was to swear would pour it out. If the swearer broke such an oath, he would fall and lie as if dead for one year. The Styx is mentioned once in Chaucer's work, in book five of *TROILUS AND CRISEYDE* when CRISEYDE swears that if she does not return from the Greek camp to be with her lover, may she be sent by the gods to dwell eternally in Styx, which she calls the "put" [pit] of hell (line 1540).

Suetonius Gaius Suetonius Tranquilus, commonly known as Suetonius, was a Roman imperial secretary under the emperor Trajan in the second century A.D. His principal surviving work is *De vita Caesarum* ("The Lives of the Caesars"). The narrator of "The MONK'S TALE" claims that Suetonius is the source for his tale of NERO (lines 2463–65), but source studies have revealed that Chaucer actually drew upon BOCCACCIO's *De casibus virorum illustrium* (Concerning the misfortunes of famous men) and BOETHIUS' *Consolation of Philosophy*.

Sulpicius Gallus *See* GALLUS, SULPICIUS.

Sultan of Syria In "The MAN OF LAW'S TALE," the Sultan of Syria is the pagan ruler who agrees to convert to Christianity in order to marry CONSTANCE, the daughter of the Roman emperor and the heroine of the tale. When he takes his bride home to his kingdom, he and all of Constance's attendants are murdered at the instigation of the Sultan's mother, who was angry because he had forsaken the religion of Islam. (*See* SULTANESS OF SYRIA.)

Sultaness of Syria Mother of the SULTAN OF SYRIA in "The MAN OF LAW'S TALE." The Sultaness of Syria is the first of two mothers-in-law who take a dislike to their son's choice of a mate because that mate is Christian. When the Sultan leaves SYRIA to travel to ROME, where he bargains for the hand of CONSTANCE, the daughter of the emperor of Rome, his mother, in consultation with her counselors, plots revenge against her son for his betrayal of their Muslim religion. Shortly after the Sultan returns to Syria, the Sultaness invites him, his new bride and the retinue of Christian bishops, lords, ladies and knights who accompany her, to a banquet, where every Christian but Constance is slaughtered. She, the only survivor, is put out to sea in a rudderless ship with all of her belongings and an ample stock of provisions. When Constance's father, the emperor of Rome, learns what the Sultaness has done, he sends an army which destroys her and all of those who participated in her scheme.

Summoner, the The Summoner's portrait follows that of the REEVE in the GENERAL PROLOGUE TO *THE CANTERBURY TALES*. The title of this man's profession indicates his employment as a server of summonses for an ecclesiastical court. Despite the nature of his duties, the position was a nonclerical one and so did not require entering the priesthood of the Catholic Church. The most striking feature of this man's portrait is his physical appearance, particularly his skin which is described as fire-red, pimpled ("saucefleem"), and infected with something called "scall" (probably alopicia) that has caused hair loss from his eyebrows and beard. These details of his description are dramatically emphasized by further reference to the "whelkes white" (pustules) and "knobbes" (swellings) on his cheeks. The causes of these eruptions are likewise hinted at in the text when we are told he loves to eat garlic, onions and leeks and to drink strong red wine, all of which were considered to aggravate conditions such as his. These physical characteristics also, according to the medieval pseudoscience of PHYSIOGNOMY, suggest that he is lecherous, a hint that is at least partially confirmed by his willingness to excuse this vice in others, provided they give him a suitable bribe, and by the information that he has the young girls of his diocese in his control because he knows all of their secrets. What he does with that power is left to the imagination. Further indication of the man's moral corruption resides in his attitude that money is all that is needed to buy a clear conscience and a clean soul, and that therefore no one ought to fear excommunication as long as he can pay. The Summoner's companionship with the PARDONER, in light of the Pardoner's description, has led some commentators to speculate that a homosexual relationship exists between the two. The final details of the Summoner's portrait—the garland or wreath he wears upon his head and the shield he has fashioned for himself from a loaf of bread—suggest a frivolity that only increases the portrait's grotesqueness. In the tale-telling contest, the Summoner clashes with the FRIAR, whose tale paints a damning portrait of the Summoner's occupation. The Summoner's tale requites that performance with an equally damning portrayal of a friar. The antagonism between the two could be explained by the fact that they might both be competing for the same sources of income if the Summoner were visiting people within the district where the Friar had his license to beg.

"Summoner's Tale, The" "The Summoner's Tale" features a vengeful attack on the FRIAR, whose tale, immediately preceding this one, attacked a summoner.

SUMMARY

In a brief anecdote, the SUMMONER's prologue tells the story of a friar who was taken by an angel to visit hell in a vision. Walking about the infernal pit, the man remarks upon the apparent absence of friars there, assuming it to be because of their close relationship with God. The angel corrects this misconception by taking him down to the region of hell where Satan's giant buttocks reside and commanding the devil to lift his tail. There under Satan's tail is a veritable nest of friars, swarming in and out of Satan's anus like bees swarming in and out of a hive.

The mood of "The Summoner's Tale" is similar to that of his prologue, though the story is considerably

Artist's rendering of the Summoner, from the Ellesmere Manuscript of The Canterbury Tales. *The illustrator portrays the "scalled browes," and "piled berd" described in the General Prologue, but neglects to include the garland that he wears on his head or the buckler made of cake. He carries a summons in his extended hand.*

more developed. As it opens we are introduced to John, a mendicant friar of Holderness in Yorkshire. JOHN THE FRIAR is licensed as a limiter, like the Friar in the GENERAL PROLOGUE OF *THE CANTERBURY TALES*. This means that he has a license to beg within the boundaries of a certain geographical area. Such boundaries were established so that there would not be too many friars begging in the same location. This was important because, unlike other clergy, friars depended entirely upon charity for their income. Friar John is also like the Friar in the General Prologue in that he is licensed to preach, a privilege he exploits both inside and outside local pulpits. In the first part of the tale, we are given an inside view of how he uses his status and position to get money. One of his methods is to offer to sing 30 requiem masses ("trentals") in one day, instead of in 30 days (at the rate of one each day), as was the accustomed practice. Since the purpose of these masses was to help the soul of a departed person gain release from purgatory, the friar argues that he can effect that release in a much shorter time. The fees collected from the performance of these and other ecclesiastical functions, such as the hearing of confession, helped the fri-

ars to make a living. Friars also begged for food, drink, clothing and other goods. This friar, in particular, carries about a pair of ivory tablets whereon he writes the names of people who give him money or other goods, promising to pray for them. But, as the narrator informs us, as soon as he is out of sight of the people whose names he has written down, he wipes his tablets clean and starts anew, never having intended to keep his word. At this point, the actual Friar who is a member of the pilgrimage interrupts the tale to accuse the Summoner of lying, but the Host, Harry BAILLY, intervenes, demanding that the man be allowed to finish his tale.

The Summoner resumes by describing Friar John's interaction with a sick man named THOMAS (1) who has in the past donated money to the friar's convent. Thomas first asks the friar why he has been away for so long. The friar answers by saying that he has been praying for Thomas' salvation. Thomas' wife appears and greets the friar, whose reaction—to embrace her and chirp like a sparrow—hints at lechery, particularly because of the sparrow's iconographic association with lust. The wife then complains of her husband's bad mood, his "ire," and asks the friar to chide him for it. When the wife reveals that one of her children has died since the friar last visited, he avows a kind of divine knowledge of that event, professing to have seen the child ascend to heaven in a vision.

After she leaves the two men alone, John embarks on a kind of paean to himself, extolling the virtues, such as cleanness from sin and fasting, that cause a friar's prayers to be more acceptable to Christ than the prayers of others, and comparing himself to MOSES, who fasted 40 days before receiving the Ten Commandments, and to Aaron, who would abstain from wine before going into the Jewish temple to pray for the sins of his people. His catalogue of those virtues belonging to friars includes poverty, chastity, charity, humility, abstinence, fasting, mercy, purity and a willingness to be persecuted for righteousness. A number of these virtues are treated ironically at various moments in the tale. When Thomas interrupts the friar's speech to say that he has already given so much of his money to various friars that he has none left, Friar John tells him that he has erred in dividing his money up among different groups; he should, instead, have given it all to Friar John.

The next part of the friar's sermonizing serves to berate Thomas for his anger. John uses three tales to illustrate the dangers of anger. The first tells of two knights who ride out of town together. When only one of them returns, he is accused of murdering his companion and sentenced to death by an angry judge. The condemned knight is taken away by a third knight, who is commanded to execute him; but before the sentence can be carried out, the missing knight returns to town. The three knights go back to the judge, who now condemns all three of them: the first because he has already been judged dead, the second because he killed the first and the third because he failed to carry out orders. The next tale tells the story of CAMBYSES, a king of Persia who was notorious for his bad temper. When one of Cambyses' counselors suggests that it is not fitting for a king to drink so much because he will lose his wits and control over his body, the king goes to extreme lengths to prove his counselor wrong. Drinking more than he ever has before, Cambyses commands that the counselor's son be brought before him, and shoots him to death with a bow and arrow, thereby illustrating that he still has control over his will and his body. The third story tells of the Persian commander CYRUS THE GREAT, who delayed the movement of his troops for half a year so that he could disperse a river in whose waters a sacred horse had been drowned.

Immediately following these stories about the dangers of anger, the friar asks Thomas to make his confession and be shriven. Thomas refuses, saying that he has already made his confession to the local curate. John accepts this; but instead of leaving, he begins an extended plea for Thomas to donate some money to assist with the building of his order's cloister. Thomas, who is extremely angry by this time, pretends to be calm and answers that he will give such a donation as he is able, provided John agrees to divide it equally among all the brethren in his convent. John eagerly accepts his terms. Thomas then directs John to put his hand beneath the bedcovers and to grope down by his buttocks, where he will find something that Thomas has hidden there. As soon as Thomas feels John's hand move near his "tuwel" (anus), he farts loudly and forcefully.

Infuriated by this insult, Friar John angrily departs and immediately seeks out the lord of the village to complain of what Thomas has done. Comically, however, it appears that what has upset John the most is that Thomas commanded him to do what cannot be done, i.e., divide his gift into equal parts to be shared with all his brethren. There follows some discussion of the nature of a fart, its savor and reverberation, and the apparent difficulty of solving this problem of division. The lord's squire, who is serving as carver at the table, overhears the conversation and proposes that he can solve the problem, in exchange for new clothing. The lord agrees to the exchange and the squire, JANKIN (2), suggests that the lord acquire a cartwheel with 12 spokes, corresponding to the number of brethren, besides John, in the convent. After turning the wheel upon its side and positioning the 12 friars at the outer ends of the 12 spokes, kneeling down with their noses against the wheel, Thomas should be stationed in the middle, atop the hub, and Friar John directly below him, beneath the hub. Then, according to Jankin, when Thomas farts, a 12th part of the sound and smell should travel along each spoke, reaching the nose and ears of each friar. By sitting directly beneath Thomas, Friar John, the worthiest and most deserving of all the friars, shall be served first and best.

COMMENTARY

The description of the Summoner in the General Prologue is one of the darkest psychological portraits to appear in Chaucer's work, and commentators nearly always refer to it when discussing "The Summoner's Tale," using it to justify readings of the tale that seem unjustifiably dark. The obvious discomfort that some scholars have felt when writing about this tale arises from its subject matter. Not only does it deal with assholes and farting, but the prologue and ending of the tale focus on these matters with an unflinching zeal for investigation, a scrutiny that is almost scientific, particularly in the squire's deadpan solution to the division of a fart into 12 parts. And there is certainly no more vivid image anywhere in Chaucer's work than that of the devil's anus with the friars swarming in and out of it like bees swarming in and out of a hive.

Like the MILLER's, the REEVE's and the Friar's tales that have come before it, "The Summoner's Tale" has requital as its motive, and like the first two in this series, it is a FABLIAU, the medieval equivalent of a humorous, off-color story. The tale has no known sources, but the motif of the worthless gift was not uncommon in the Middle Ages, though Chaucer was unique in making the gift a fart. The ingenuity of this choice becomes apparent when we realize how utterly appropriate the gift is to its recipient, whose preaching consists of nothing more than hot air and noise.

Compared to the depiction of the summoner in "The FRIAR's TALE," the portrait of Friar John is subtle caricature. The only instance in which the teller actually confirms the friar's outright dishonesty is at the beginning, when we are told about the ivory tablets whereon he writes the names of people for whom he promises to pray in return for their gifts to him, but which he erases as soon as he leaves their dwellings. In contrast, when he tells the sick Thomas that he has been praying for his salvation the entire two weeks since his last visit, or when he describes his vision of Thomas' child ascending to heaven, it is left to the reader to determine whether or not he is telling the truth. Other aspects of his character lead us to determine, as does poor Thomas, that he is not.

At one point the friar lists the characteristics of his order. They are poverty, chastity, charity, humility, abstinence, mercy and the willingness to be persecuted in a just cause. In the course of the tale, Friar John violates each and every one of these requirements. His greed violates the vow of poverty. The lustful feelings he evidently has for Thomas' wife violate the vow of chastity, which, in the accepted religious thought of the time, precluded sinful desires as well as deeds. His unwillingness to have Thomas share his wealth with other friars and members of the regular clergy shows a lack of charity. He violates his vow of humility by proudly proclaiming how much more acceptable to God are his own prayers than are those of ordinary (secular) people, and his pretense at abstinence is belied by the gluttony evident in his request for a meal of capon (chicken) liver and a roasted pig's head. The quality of mercy is sadly lacking in his spiritual and emotional response to Thomas' prevailing "ire" or anger. Rather than trying to find out what is troubling the man, who is sick enough to be bedridden, Friar John simply berates him with a sermon that gives several highly irrelevant examples of how ire can bring grief to those who are its victims. At the very least, he ought to have chosen stories which would illustrate how anger is dangerous to the person experiencing that emotion. Furthermore, even though Thomas has told John that he is broke, John continues to beg for money. Finally, Friar John's unwillingness to suffer in a just cause is illustrated by his readiness to try a great many manipulative tactics to get money out of a man who is himself in obvious distress, both physically and economically. Rather than trying to offer comfort to this man without trying to get money out of him, he persecutes the poor man until that man, unwilling to be victimized any longer, and perhaps seeing no other way to get rid of the importunate friar, gives him the only gift that he has.

Surreye   *See* SYRIA.

Susanna (Susanne)   Susanna, the heroine of the apocryphal Book of Susanna, was accused of adultery by some lecherous Elders but was defended by the prophet DANIEL. When her innocence was clearly established, her accusers were put to death. In "The MAN OF LAW'S TALE," CONSTANCE prays to God, who saved Susanna from false blame, when she is accused of having killed HERMENGILD, the woman who provided her with lodging when she landed in Northumberland (lines 639–40). In "The PARSON'S TALE," Susanna is mentioned as an example of one who suffered great sorrow and pain when others bore false witness against her (line 797).

Sweet-Looking   In the ROMAUNT OF THE ROSE, Chaucer's translation of the French ROMAN DE LA ROSE, Sweet-Looking is an allegorical character who serves as squire to the god of love (CUPID), carrying his two bows and two sheaths of arrows as the god dances in the Garden of MIRTH.

Swetonius (Swetoun)   *See* SUETONIUS.

Swynford, Katherine   Katherine Swynford was a favored mistress of JOHN OF GAUNT, one of the sons of King EDWARD III and England's most powerful nobleman during the reign of his nephew RICHARD II. Katherine was originally the daughter of Sir Paon de Roet of Hainault. If Philippa CHAUCER, Geoffrey's wife, was, as many scholars believe, originally Philippa de Roet, the two women were sisters. Katherine married a knight, Sir Hugh de Swynford, who was one of Gaunt's retainers, and when she was widowed became first John of Gaunt's mistress and later his third wife. She and Gaunt had four children, who were legitimized after their marriage.

Symkyn   *See* SIMKIN.

Symmachus (Symacus)   Aurelius Memmius Symmachus was the father-in-law of BOETHIUS, author of the *Consolation of Philosophy,* which Chaucer translated under the title BOECE. He served as Roman consul in 485 under Odoacer. Like his son-in-law, Symmachus was to fall under suspicion of plotting against the government of King THEODORIC. He was executed soon after Boethius. In the *Boece,* LADY PHILOSOPHY, pointing out to Boethius all the many things he has had to be thankful for, refers to Symmachus as a man of wisdom and virtue (Book two, Prosa 4, lines 25–29).

Symond   *See* SIMKIN.

Symoun, Seint   *See* SIMON, SAINT.

Symplicius Gallus   *See* GALLUS, SULPICIUS.

Synay   *Synay* is Chaucer's spelling of *Sinai* (*see* HOREB).

Synon (Synoun)   *See* SINON.

Syria   In ancient times, the term *Syria* denoted a region at the eastern end of the Mediterranean, bordered by Egypt and Arabia to the south and west, and by Mesopotamia to the north. It forms part of the setting for "The MAN OF LAW'S TALE," in which the heroine of the tale, the Roman emperor's daughter CONSTANCE, embarks upon a long series of adventures following her marriage to the SULTAN OF SYRIA, a Muslim prince who converted to Christianity in order to marry her.

Syrius   *See* SIRIUS.

Sysile   *See* SICILY.

Sytheo   *See* SICHAEUS.

Sytho, stream of   The stream of Sytho is the name Chaucer gives to the Sea of Thrace in the story of PHYL-LIS and DEMOPHON in his *LEGEND OF GOOD WOMEN*. After promising to marry Phyllis, Demophon sails home for ATHENS, saying that he goes to prepare for their wedding day. Phyllis waits for him patiently, but the stream of Sytho does not carry him back (line 2508), and she eventually commits suicide.

T

Tabard The inn where Chaucer claims to have met the pilgrims whose stories as they traveled together he recorded in *The CANTERBURY TALES*. Records show that an inn of this name actually existed in 14th-century SOUTHWARK (a district on the south bank of the Thames, opposite the City of LONDON). The inn's name derives from its sign, which would either have borne a picture of, or been shaped like, a tabard, a sleeveless smock embroidered with armorial symbols.

Tagus The Tagus (Spanish, *Tajo*) River flows west across central Spain and Portugal, emptying into the Atlantic through a broad estuary. In Book Three, Metrum 10 of the *BOECE* (Chaucer's translation of BOETHIUS' *Consolation of Philosophy*), LADY PHILOSOPHY mentions the Tagus along with several other rivers; she informs the narrator that all of the riches these rivers could bring him would only cloud his mind rather than clear it, by encouraging an attachment to worldly goods. The image of the rivers' running water causing the mind to be troubled rather than cleared plays ingeniously on the common symbolic association between running water and cleanliness or clarity, to illustrate the point that, in man's limited perception, things are not always what they seem.

tail-rhyme A stanza form containing among longer lines two or more short lines which, although they are separated from each other by some of the long lines, rhyme. They appear in the middle and at the end of a stanza, marking its division into two or more parts and serving as "tails" to those parts. The form is derived from French verse where it had the name *rime couée*, which translates precisely into the English name, tail-rhyme. Chaucer's metrical romance, "The TALE OF SIR THOPAS," is written in tail-rhyme stanzas in which the longer lines have four metrical feet (stressed units) and the shorter ones, three. The effect of this combination is to give the poem a kind of galloping pace which emphasizes the tale's silliness, as can be appreciated by reading the following stanza aloud:

> Sire Thopas wax a doghty swayne;
> Whit was his face as paynedemayn,
> His lippes rede as rose;
> His rode is lyke scarlet in grayn,

> And I yow telle in good certayn
> He hadde a semely nose.

> [Sir Thopas grew a doughty swain;
> His face as white as fine white bread,
> His lips as red as rose;
> His cheeks the color of rich scarlet cloth,
> And I tell you for certain sure
> He had a lovely nose.]
>
> (lines 724–29)

It is believed that Chaucer intended "The Tale of Sir Thopas" to serve as a parody of metrical romances, which were quite popular in England during the latter part of the 14th century.

Tajo *See* TAGUS.

Talbot One of the dogs owned by the poor widow in "The NUN'S PRIEST'S TALE." It and two others join in the chase after RUSSELL, the sly fox who has seized the widow's rooster, CHAUNTICLEER.

"Tale of Melibee, The" The pilgrim Chaucer tells two tales on the road to CANTERBURY. The "Tale of Melibee" is his second. "Melibee" and "The PARSON'S TALE" are the only Canterbury tales written in prose.

SUMMARY

A young, well-to-do man named MELIBEE has a wife named PRUDENCE and a daughter named SOPHIA. One day, while he is absent from home, some of his enemies break into his house. They beat his wife and assault his daughter, giving her "five mortal wounds," in five different places—in her feet, hands, ears, nose and mouth. After giving Melibee some time to grieve, Prudence counsels him not to indulge in excessive grief over what has happened but to call a council of various types of people, including physicians, lawyers, longtime friends, friends who used to be enemies and others to help him decide how he should respond to the attack upon his wife and daughter. He receives conflicting advice, but decides to follow that which urges him to seek vengeance through warring against his foes.

Prudence asks him to reconsider and to listen to what she has to say about the matter, but first she has to convince him that he will not be foolish to consider the advice of a woman. She succeeds by way of reason and examples. When he has agreed to hear her arguments, she begins by explaining the principles of wise decision-making and the importance of being able to distinguish between good and bad counselors and advice. This done, she specifically analyzes the mistakes Melibee has made in coming to his decision, mistakes that arise from listening to people who either do not have enough experience to advise him well, or to those who do not have his best interests at heart. All of her arguments are supported by sayings from either biblical authors or philosophers.

When Prudence has finished explaining her husband's mistaken response to the crisis, she expounds upon the true causes of his misfortune, which she believes to be sent by God to counteract the general trend of Melibee's life, which has of late been to put too much value on worldly possessions, the "sweet temporeel richesses, and delices and honours of this world" (line 1410). Next Prudence argues the superiority of patience over vengeance. When Melibee resists her argument on the basis of his own wealth and power, which will help him to overcome his enemies, she advises the careful use of his wealth, concern for his reputation and a healthy distrust of the chances of battle. Finally, she overrides his objections to a peaceful settlement, and Melibee agrees to seek reconciliation with his enemies. Having brought her husband to this decision, Prudence now seeks out his enemies so that she can persuade them that they have done wrong and that they should seek forgiveness for their crime. They listen to her arguments and agree to meet with her husband. Following the meeting, in which his enemies admit their wrongdoing and submit themselves to Melibee's judgment, he experiences yet another urge to punish them, this time by confiscating their property and sending them into exile. Prudence intervenes once again and persuades him to forgive them so that, when the time comes, God will forgive Melibee his trespasses instead of giving him the punishment he deserves.

COMMENTARY

"The Tale of Melibee" is a close translation of the French writer Renaud de Louens' *Livre de Melibée et de Dame Prudence*. This text, which appeared around 1336, was itself a translation of a Latin work, the *Liber consolationis et consilii*, composed by ALBERTANO OF BRESCIA in 1246. Albertano, a judge, wrote the treatise as a collection of advice for his sons. It was immensely popular in its day because it brought together such a large number of wise sayings, or "sentences," as Chaucer (and other Middle English writers) call them. Many of the sayings derive from biblical authors such as SOLOMON; JESUS; SON OF SIRACH (the supposed author of Ecclesiastes);

Saint PAUL; and Saint JAMES. Others are taken from classical authors like Tullius (CICERO), DIONYSIUS CATO, SENECA and OVID. Medieval authors such as PETRUS ALPHONSUS are occasionally represented, as are the church fathers, of whom CASSIODORUS is most frequently cited.

When Renaud de Louens translated the *Liber consolationis et consilii* from Latin into French, he cut out a lot of material and added substantial passages of his own. Chaucer's translation of Renaud's work is very close to the French, even to the point of paraphrase. In style, however, it presents quite a contrast. As Helen COOPER remarks in her commentary on *The Canterbury Tales*, "The first thing that strikes the reader of Melibee is the clogged prose style" (p. 321). She further notes that a comparison with the French original only strengthens this impression. Indeed, the most frustrating part of reading "The Tale of Melibee" must, for any reader, be the seemingly endless repetition, not only of form (argumentative point followed by wise sayings in support), but of mere words, as synonyms flesh out line after line yet add no additional meaning. In comparison with "The TALE OF SIR THOPAS," these words and phrases do not even have the excuse of existing to make the rhyme or meter come out right, since Melibee's tale is rendered in prose rather than poetry. Neither can the gaucheness of the style be considered accidental, considering the careful craftsmanship Chaucer exhibits elsewhere. A number of scholars have determined that the overly elaborate style of "Melibee" must be parody, yet few are willing to admit that the tale in its entirety, given its serious subject matter and its length, should be read as either a joke or as a caricature of the type of wisdom literature it represents. Indeed, those who have argued for taking it seriously cite evidence that the work is typical for its time, reminding us of the occasional difficulties we must encounter in trying to appreciate the idiosyncracies of taste in the art and literature of the Middle Ages. If "The Tale of Melibee" seems to us tedious or silly, we would do well to step back and take a look at popular titles on the shelves of our own bookstores where we find such wisdom-literature descendants as *The Quotable Woman, A Father's Book of Wisdom, Life's Little Instruction Book, The Tao of Pooh* and *Voices of Struggle, Voices of Pride: Quotations of Great African Americans.*

Still, even if books like *Le Livre de Melibée* were taken seriously in their day, we are left with the fact that Chaucer translated his source in such a way as to multiply its difficulties, if only by rendering it in language both lackluster and repetitive. This makes it impossible to entirely dismiss the idea that the work is at some level parodical. Why would Chaucer want to parody this form? As a further way of making fun of himself, a continuation of the spoofing that began in "Sir Thopas"? To show how he was such an accomplished a storyteller that he could take one of the most popular literary forms of his century and turn it into something so boring that it put his listeners to sleep? The answers to these questions are veiled in mystery, and since Chaucer himself is unavailable to answer them, they are likely to remain so. Even if the work is a parody of the wisdom-book form, it nevertheless contains much sound advice directed toward persons in positions of political power.

With this in mind, some scholars have argued that Chaucer made the translation as a political tract, the kind of book of advice to princes that became even more popular in the later Middle Ages and early Renaissance. Attempts to link it to a specific political event have not been successful, yet the thrust of the argument, that reconciliation is superior to war in most cases, would have been applicable to a number of occasions during Chaucer's lifetime, particularly regarding England's tempestuous relationship with France. As late as 1360, when Chaucer would have been 17 years old, perhaps already in service to the king, EDWARD III still laid claim to the crown of France. (This claim was renounced in 1361 under the terms of the Treaty of Bretigny, which nevertheless gave the English king sovereignty over Gascony, Poitou, Ponthieu and Calais.)

Like "The Tale of Sir Thopas," "Melibee" lacks the type of overt linkages with other tales supplied by conflict or interaction among the pilgrims. Chaucer is the only pilgrim whose profession goes unmentioned. Never does he provide an answer to the Host's question, "What man artow?" and the subject matter of his tales does little to guide our powers of deduction. The actual details of his life show him to be a merchant, civil servant and poet, but these seem to have little relationship to the portrait of the man given in the prologue to "Sir Thopas." "Melibee" does however display a concern with themes that appear elsewhere in *The Canterbury Tales,* such as the idea that FORTUNE should be mistrusted ("The KNIGHT'S TALE" and "The MONK'S TALE"), that patience is an important virtue ("The CLERK'S TALE" and "The FRANKLIN'S TALE"), and that covetousness is the root of all harm ("The PARDONER'S TALE").

But perhaps the most important theme that links this tale to the rest is that of the Woman Question. Whether or not a man can trust the counsel or judgment of a woman is an issue that comes up over and over again, in "The WIFE OF BATH"s PROLOGUE and "The WIFE OF BATH'S TALE," in "The Franklin's Tale" of JANUARY and MAY and in "The NUN'S PRIEST'S TALE." All answer the question differently, some showing support for the antifeminist tradition, some supporting the opposite, profeminist side of the debate.

"Tale of Sir Thopas, The"   The rollicking romance of Sir THOPAS (Topaz) is the pilgrim Chaucer's first attempt at tale-telling on the road to CANTERBURY.

SUMMARY

Seeing that his companions have been stunned into silence by the pathos of "The PRIORESS' TALE," the Host, Harry BAILLY, approaches Chaucer, himself a member of the group, asking who he is and making some comments upon his appearance and demeanor. Before Chaucer has a chance to respond, however, the Host goes on to request that he take his turn at story-telling, and that he tell a tale of mirth. Chaucer replies that he will tell the only tale he knows, one he learned in a rhyme long ago.

Part I
A knight named Sir THOPAS once lived in a town of FLANDERS. He was a brave and handsome knight, as is described in a long catalogue of conventional and clichéd phrases. He is good at hunting, archery, and (unconventionally) wrestling. One day he rides out into the forest and falls into a fit of love-longing, sprung from a dream he has had in which an elf-queen was his lover. Vowing to find the lover of his dream, he rides until he enters the country of Fairy where he is confronted by a giant named OLIPHAUNT. Thopas cannot fight with Oliphaunt because he does not have his armor, but promises that he shall return the following day, with his armor, and slay the giant. The giant attacks Thopas as he retreats, throwing stones at him from a sling. Thopas escapes through the grace of God.

Part II
Thopas returns home to his "merry men" and asks his minstrels and jesters to regale him with tales while he eats and puts on his armor. A comical description of the meal and of his arming follows.

Part III
Sir Thopas' return to the forest is heralded by a recitation of the names of other heroes of English romance, HORNE CHILD, YPOTIS (the child hero of a pious legend), Sir LIBEAUX Desconsus ("The Fair Unknown"), Sir BEVIS of Hampton and GUY OF WARWICK. Before Chaucer can get any further than to tell us that Thopas, like any knight adventurous, sleeps out in the wild rather than in a house, the Host interrupts him, referring to his tale as "drasty" (crappy, awful) and commending it to the devil as not worth a "toord" (turd). The Host then asks him to tell something else, perhaps something in prose, and Chaucer responds that he will do so gladly, embarking upon the moral and virtuous "Tale of MELIBEE."

COMMENTARY

Composed in galloping lines of TAIL-RHYME, "The Tale of Sir Thopas" is unanimously considered to be an elaborate parody of the most popular literary form of Chaucer's day, the metrical romance. By having his own persona tell the silliest, most awful tale of the Canterbury group, the author also seems to be poking a bit of fun at his literary genius. Like most of the other tales, "Sir Thopas" has no exact source but contains striking similarities to several Middle English metrical romances. Verbal echoes of *Guy of Warwick, Bevis of Hampton* and *Horn Childe,* all in the 14th-century Auchinleck Manuscript, appear throughout "Sir Thopas." The poet also seems to have adapted some lines from *Lybeaus Desconus, Sir Launfal, Perceval of Gales, Sir Eglamour* and *Thomas of Erceldoune.* Most of the heroes of these romances are mentioned by name within the poem as exemplars to whom Sir Thopas may be compared.

Structurally the poem is divided into three "fits," and the modern definition of this noun (a sudden, uncontrollable attack) aptly describes the content of the stanzas, which are full of action leading nowhere. Although the plot of "Sir Thopas" contains many of the themes and motifs traditional to medieval romance, it does so in a way that parodies the form through merciless exaggeration and antithesis. In keeping with the convention that romances were typically set in either a faraway place or time, Thopas was born in the "far country" of Flanders, which of course is not far away at all unless one is out of western Europe. His face is as white as white bread, and his lips are red as roses, details that suggest a commonplace femininity rather than robust masculinity. Like other knights adventurous, he enjoys hunting and other contests which allow him to demonstrate his strength, but he excels at wrestling, a sport more suited to someone like ROBYN (1), the MILLER, than a man of his class and station. When Thopas calls for storytelling during his arming, he oddly enough asks for romances "of popes and of cardinals" rather than of knights and ladies, and the actual arming begins at the very beginning, with his underwear ("breech and shirt"). The poetry of the tale is equally bad. In straining after mechanically perfect meter, the narrator readily chops off final *e* (as in "entent" and "plas"). He also makes frequent use of silly rhyme tags, phrases that have no meaning but are included to make the rhyme and meter of the lines come out right. Similarly, while helping to flesh out the rhyme, unusual dialect language and incorrect usage obscure the words' meaning. Finally, it should be remembered that, although this particular tale pokes fun at the genre of romance, showing everything that could possibly go wrong with a form that had become absurdly stylized and bound to convention, Chaucer also chose that form for the first tale in the Canterbury group, and one that many readers consider his most serious and beautiful, "The KNIGHT'S TALE."

Tantalus (Tantale) In classical mythology, Tantalus was a son of Jove (JUPITER) who became king of Lydia. He achieved great power and wealth and was invited to the councils and banquets of the gods. He betrayed their kindness, however, by revealing their secrets and

by stealing nectar and ambrosia, which he gave to his mortal friends. When he cut his son, Pelops, into pieces which he offered to the gods to test their powers, they recognized the boy and restored him to life. To punish Tantalus, Jove suspended above his head a stone which was likely to fall at any moment. In Hades, he was condemned to stand in water but suffer eternal thirst: whenever he bowed his head to drink it, it would flow away. Likewise, branches full of fruit hung over his head, always just out of his reach. In *The BOOK OF THE DUCHESS,* the BLACK KNIGHT claims that since the loss of his queen, he suffers more than Tantalus (line 709). In *TROILUS AND CRISEYDE,* PANDARUS swears that if anything untoward would happen to CRISEYDE for accepting his dinner invitation, he should suffer in hell with Tantalus (book 3, lines 589–93). In the *BOECE,* when LADY PHILOSOPHY tells the story of ORPHEUS' descent into the underworld and the music he performed there. She says that all of its denizens forgot their suffering, including Tantalus, who despised the stream for which he had thirsted so long (Book Three, Metrum 12, lines 38–40).

Tapestry Maker, the (Tapycer) One of a group of tradesmen mentioned, but not described individually, in the GENERAL PROLOGUE to *The CANTERBURY TALES.* His title indicates that he is engaged in the profession of weaving tapestries; these could range in size from small pieces used to adorn a piece of clothing to large wall hangings used for decorative and insulation purposes in medieval houses and castles. The others in his group include a Weaver ("Webbe"), a Dyer of cloth ("Dyere"), a Carpenter and a Haberdasher. These five men are all wearing the same type of uniform, indicating their membership in one of the medieval trade guilds, the forerunner of modern-day trade unions. The guilds set standards for the quality of the goods produced, regulated holidays and hours of work and fixed prices and wages to some extent. Certain details of Chaucer's portrait of the Guildsmen, such as their silver- (rather than brass-) mounted knives, might suggest either prosperity or pretentiousness, depending upon whether or not one judges the portraits to contain elements of satire. Those scholars who argue against finding satire in their description note that Chaucer provided his Guildsmen with none of the traditional mercantile vices such as fraud, usury and avarice. None of the five Guildsmen tells a tale on the pilgrimage to CANTERBURY.

Tapycer *See* TAPESTRY MAKER.

Tarbe *See* THARBE.

Tarquinius (Tarquinus the yonge; Tarquinius Sextus; Tarquyn; Tarquyny) Tarquinius Sextus was the son of TARQUINIUS SUPERBUS, and the cousin of Lucretia's (*see* LUCRECE) husband, COLLATINUS. According to the Roman writer Livy, the two men, Tarquinius and

Collatinus, were stationed together at the siege of Ardea. During a lull in the fighting, Collatinus boasted that his wife was both beautiful and virtuous, and he took a group of officers to spy on her to prove it. Just a glimpse of Lucretia caused Tarquinius to become inflamed with desire for her. He returned to the house in secret and threatened to kill Lucretia if she would not become his lover. Then he raped her. The next day, after telling her husband and father what had happened, Lucretia committed suicide. The story of Tarquinius and Lucretia is narrated in Chaucer's LEGEND OF GOOD WOMEN (lines 1680–1885). In "*The FRANKLIN'S TALE*," Lucretia is one of the virtuous women DORIGEN recalls when she is faced with the decision of whether to keep her promise to the squire AURELIUS or to remain faithful to her husband (lines 1405–08).

Tarquinus Superbus   The Tarquinus mentioned as the last king of ROME at the beginning of the story of LUCRECE in Chaucer's *LEGEND OF GOOD WOMEN* (line 1682) is Tarquinius Superbus, who ruled from 534–510 B.C. His son, TARQUINIUS SEXTUS, raped Lucretia (Lucrece), the wife of the king's nephew and his own cousin, COLLATINUS. Lucretia committed suicide. When the people of Rome learned what had happened, Tarquinius and his son were driven out of Rome.

Tarsia (Tars)   In "The KNIGHT'S TALE," the noble EMETREUS, king of India, who comes to support ARCITE (1) in the battle for EMILY's hand in marriage, wears a surcoat ("cote-armure") made of cloth from Tarsia (line 2160), a city in Chinese Turkestan known for its export of fine silk.

Tartary(e)   Region in present-day southern Russia. SARRAY (Tsarev) in Tartarye is the exotic setting of "The Squire's Tale." In the Middle Ages, *Tartary* (or *Tatary*) was the name given to those regions in eastern Europe and central and western Asia which fell under the control of invading Mongolian and Turkic tribes. CAMBYUSKAN, the king in whose court the events of "The Squire's Tale" take place, was a Mongolian conqueror. Tartary is also mentioned in *The BOOK OF THE DUCHESS* by the BLACK KNIGHT, who says that his beloved lady was not one of those disdainful women who send their lovers off to perform impossible deeds in faraway places like PRUSSIA, ALEXANDRIA or Tartary (line 1024).

Tatlock, John S. P. (1876–1948)   A prolific medieval scholar, J. S. P. Tatlock taught at the University of Michigan, Stanford University and the University of California at Los Angeles. Among his numerous contributions to Chaucer scholarship, the most outstanding is certainly *A Concordance to the Complete Works of Geoffrey Chaucer and to the Romaunt of the Rose* (1927; rptd. 1963), coauthored with Arthur G. Kennedy. This huge book

provides an alphabetical list of all but the most common words (such as *and, but, his*) in all of Chaucer's works with the exception of the *TREATISE ON THE ASTROLABE*. Each entry mentions every occurrence of a word in the body of Chaucer's work, with quotation of the whole line for each instance, including the citation of line numbers. Although it is based on the outdated Globe edition of Chaucer's works published in 1913, this remains a standard reference for those who do not yet have access to the new computer-generated concordance edited by Akio Oizumi (*see* CONCORDANCES TO CHAUCER). Tatlock also wrote *The Development and Chronology of Chaucer's Works* (1907; rptd. 1963), which used various kinds of internal (textual) and external evidence in the attempt to establish a chronology for most of Chaucer's writings. This was the earliest serious effort to do so. His last book, *The Mind and Art of Chaucer* (1950; rptd. 1966) emphasizes the impact of Chaucer's personality upon his literary creations, also considering his political, intellectual and social environment.

Taurus (Taur; Tawr)   One of the 12 divisions of the zodiac, an imaginary belt in the heavens extending for about eight degrees on either side of the apparent path of the Sun and including the paths of the Moon and the principal planets. The zodiac is divided into 12 equal parts, or signs, each named for a different constellation. Taurus is the second sign (*see* diagram under ASTROLOGY), which, in Chaucer's day, the Sun entered around April 12. The constellation of Taurus, which is supposed to represent a bull, appears in the Northern Hemisphere sky between ARIES and GEMINI, near ORION. Chaucer most often uses such astrological terms to indicate the approximate date of a narrative event, to show the passage of time or to show their influence over people and events. An example of the latter appears in the WIFE OF BATH's prologue, when she says that she was born when Taurus was in the ascendant (lines 609–13), something that, according to W. C. CURRY's *Chaucer and the Medieval Sciences*, helps to explain her appearance. Chaucer's use of Taurus as a time marker occurs in "The MERCHANT'S TALE," when the narrator notes that the aged JANUARY and young MAY are married as the Moon passes from the second degree of Taurus into CANCER (lines 1885–89). Similarly, in "The NUN'S PRIEST'S TALE," CHAUNTICLEER crows when the Sun is 21 degrees in the sign of Taurus (lines 3187–97). In his *TREATISE ON THE ASTROLABE*, Chaucer notes that Taurus controls the neck and throat of those born under the sign (part 1, division 21, line 74) and describes its position in the sky (part 2, division six, line 16).

Telephus   According to classical mythology, Telephus was a son of HERCULES who became, through his adopted father, king of Mysia. When the Greeks landed in Mysia on their way to the TROJAN WAR, a battle ensued in which Telephus was wounded by the spear of ACHILLES. Informed by the oracle at DELPHI that his wound could only be healed by the man who made it, Telephus disguised himself as a beggar and followed the Greeks. Achilles agreed to the cure after CALKAS advised him that without the help of a son of Hercules, Troy could not be taken. In "The SQUIRE'S TALE," the magic sword that King CAMBYUSKAN receives for his birthday reminds people of Achilles' spear, because it also has the ability to hurt and to heal (lines 236–42).

Temple of Love   *See* TEMPLE OF VENUS.

Temple of Venus   The Temple of Venus, or Temple of Love, is a recurring image in Chaucer's poetry. In *The HOUSE OF FAME*, when the narrator begins telling the story of the marvelous dream that he has had, he first describes visiting a temple made of glass filled with golden images set on pedestals or in jewel-adorned niches. He perceives that it is a temple of VENUS, the goddess of love, because he sees her there, floating naked on the sea, accompanied by doves and her son CUPID. Also within the temple, he finds a brass tablet upon which is engraved the story of AENEAS, the Trojan adventurer who, after surviving the fall of TROY, sailed to Italy, where he founded the city that was to become the capital of the Roman Empire. On the way to this glorious destiny, Aeneas landed on the coast of northern Africa, where he was received by DIDO, queen of CARTHAGE, who fell in love with him and became his mistress. Dido's love for Aeneas and his betrayal of her are the focus of the story related on the brass tablet.

The temple's appearance in the dream and the poem would seem to stem from the narrator's preoccupation with the theme of love. He has, as the EAGLE who carries him to FAME's palace informs us, hitherto devoted his creative energies to writing about love. His efforts thus far have not been particularly successful, at least not in gaining him the reward of love. The purpose of his visit to Fame is to give him other types of material to write about. Ironically, once there, his attention is never fully engaged until, in the HOUSE OF RUMOR, he approaches a corner of the hall where men speak of love tidings and anxiously await the approach of a man of great authority.

Another Temple of Venus appears in *The PARLIAMENT OF FOWLS*, also within the context of a dream. This temple is located in a garden similar to the Garden of MIRTH in the *ROMAUNT OF THE ROSE*. Its walls are made of brass rather than glass and it stands supported by huge pillars of jasper, its doors flanked by allegorical representations of Peace and Patience, two attributes necessary for the successful practice of love. Inside the temple the dreamer sees Venus and other gods associated with her, such as BACCHUS, the god of wine, and PRIAPUS, the god of gardens and fertility. One wall is lined with broken bows betokening mortals who tried to remain faithful to DIANA, goddess of the moon and virginity. The state of the bows indicates their failure to remain chaste. Others are painted with the stories of those who, like Dido, TROILUS and THISBE, died for love. The appearance of the temple in this poem is again related to the theme of love, which is played out in the rest of the poem as the dreamer reenters the garden and finds the goddess NATURE helping the birds choose their mates. Yet another Temple of Venus appears in "The KNIGHT'S TALE," where it is one of three (the others are dedicated to Diana and MARS [1]) set within the walls of the arena where PALAMON and ARCITE (1) will do battle to determine which of them shall marry EMILY. This temple, which consists of an altar and oratory, is located in the eastward portion of the wall surrounding the battle arena. The narrator does not reveal what kind of material it is made of, but states that the walls are painted with a portrait of Venus almost identical to the one that appears in *The House of Fame*, along with representations of love's torments, and allegorical figures, such as Hope, Desire, Foolhardiness, Beauty and Youth, who serve as Venus' attendants. This Temple of Venus is taken directly from BOCCACCIO's *TESEIDA*, which was Chaucer's source for "The Knight's Tale." Of the three works discussed here, this tale may have been the last to be written; but there is evidence that Chaucer had read the *Teseida* much earlier (and probably penned an earlier version of "The Knight's Tale" also), which means that the Italian poem was probably the source of the temple's description in all three works.

tercel eagles   Tercel, i.e., male, eagles appear in several of Chaucer's works, most notably in *The PARLIAMENT OF FOWLS*, which centers on a debate between three tercel eagles who all wish to be mated with the same beautiful "formel" (female) eagle. For details of the characteristics and behavior of these competitors, *see* the Summary and Commentary sections of the entry on *The Parliament of Fowls*.

Tereus   In classical mythology, Tereus was the son of MARS (1) who became king of Phocis or THRACE. PANDION, king of ATHENS, gave Tereus his daughter PROCNE in marriage. When Procne asked to see her sister, Philomela, Pandion, despite of misgivings, let her depart in Tereus' keeping. But Tereus did not take Philomela to Procne. Instead, seized by uncontrollable desire for her, he took her to some woods in Thrace, where he raped her and cut out her tongue to keep her from telling anyone. Then he shut her away in another dwelling to keep her from contacting Procne. Philomela communicated her plight to her sister by weaving the story of her rape into a tapestry. The women avenged themselves on Tereus by killing his son Itys and feeding him to his father. When Tereus discovered what they had done, he tried to kill the two women, but the gods intervened, changing all three of them into birds. Procne became a swallow; Philomela, a nightingale; and Tereus, a hawk. In another version, Philomela became the swallow and Procne, the nightingale. The story of these three is narrated in Chaucer's *LEGEND OF GOOD WOMEN* (lines 2228–2393).

Termagant (Termagaunt) In various medieval romances, *Termagant* is the name of an idol worshipped by the Saracens (Muslims), though there is no basis for this in historical fact. In "The TALE OF SIR THOPAS," the giant whom Sir THOPAS encounters as he rides forth on his adventures swears by Termagant that he will slay Thopas' steed with a mace unless Thopas leaves his lands immediately (lines 810–13).

Tertullian (Tertulan) Quintus Septimus Florens Tertullian, born in the first century A.D., was the son of a centurion who served in Africa. After converting to Christianity he wrote a number of treatises on the conduct of a Christian life. He continues to be regarded as the greatest Christian writer in the west before Saint AUGUSTINE. One of his treatises, *De monogamia* ("On Monogamy"), claims that all marriages after the first constitute adultery. When the WIFE OF BATH says that her fifth husband's "Book of Wicked Wives" contains something by Tertullian, she may well be referring to this tract, which would reflect negatively on her own marital history (Wife of Bath's Prologue, line 676).

Tesbee   *See* THISBE.

Teseida   The *Teseida* was the poem by the Italian writer BOCCACCIO which served as the primary source for Chaucer's "KNIGHT'S TALE." It is actually an abbreviated title for the following: *Il Teseida delle nozze d'Emelia* ("The Story of Theseus concerning the Nuptials of Emily"), written around 1339–41. Chaucer probably obtained a manuscript of the poem during one of his trips to Italy. For a discussion of the relationship between the two works, *see* the Commentary section of the entry on "The Knight's Tale."

Tessalie (Tessaly)   *See* THESSALY.

Teuta   Teuta was the wife of an Illyrian king who, on her husband's death in 231 B.C., assumed the throne. She came into conflict with Rome when she refused to punish Illyrian pirates who had attacked some Roman merchants before her reign. The conflict escalated into war which ended in 228, when Teuta sued for peace and was stripped of most of her dominions. Teuta was remembered for her chastity as well as her strong rule. In "The FRANKLIN'S TALE," Teuta is one of the women DORIGEN thinks of when she is faced with the question of whether to become the lover of the squire AURELIUS, or to remain faithful to her husband (lines 1453–54). She is faced with this dilemma because she had rashly promised to give in to Aurelius if he could remove some rocks from the coast of BRITTANY, a seemingly impossible task.

Tewnes   *See* TUNIS.

Tharbe   In *TROILUS AND CRISEYDE*, Tharbe is one of CRISEYDE's nieces. She accompanies Criseyde during a walk in her garden while ANTIGONE sings a love song that causes Criseyde to have second thoughts about having accepted TROILUS' attentions (book 2, lines 813–25). Tharbe also accompanies Criseyde to DIPHOBUS' house when she has dinner there (book 2, lines 1562–63). She does not appear in BOCCACCIO's *Il FILOSTRATO* or any other known sources of the story, so Chaucer probably invented the character.

Thebes   Two cities of the ancient world bore the name Thebes. The one most often mentioned in Chaucer's work was the chief city of Boetia in east-central Greece. The city looms large in Greek mythology as the home of OEDIPUS, the Theban king who had unknowingly killed his father and married his mother. Oedipus was driven out of the city by his two sons, POLYNICES and ETEOCLES, who initially agreed to take turns governing the city. However, Eteocles violated that agreement by refusing to surrender the throne when his time was up, and Polynices raised an army and invaded. This conflict became known as the SEVEN AGAINST THEBES and is frequently alluded to in Chaucer's poetry, particularly in *TROILUS AND CRISEYDE*. In "The KNIGHT'S TALE," Thebes is the home of the two knights, PALAMON and ARCITE (1), who are taken prisoner after THESEUS of ATHENS attacks the city on his way home from his war with the AMAZONS.

Another city named Thebes was the ancient capital city of Upper Egypt (modern Luxor or Karnak). In "The Knight's Tale," Palamon escapes from prison by giving his jailer some wine spiced with opium from this city (lines 1470–72).

Thelophus   *See* TELEPHUS.

Theodamus   *See* THIODAMUS.

Theodora   The wife of ALGARSIF in "The SQUIRE'S TALE." The SQUIRE promises, at the end of the tale, to tell the story of how Algarsif won Theodora for his wife, but he is interrupted by the FRANKLIN and never resumes his narrative.

Theodoric (Theodorik) (ca. 454–526) The Ostrogothic king who conquered the Italian peninsula in 493 A.D. Theodoric ruled for 33 years, and some scholars believe, gave Italy a more enlightened rule that it had known under many of the Caesars. A patron of learning and an enforcer of religious toleration, he fostered agriculture and commerce and directed the repair of public buildings and roads. But in the final years of his life he grew suspicious of those around him and accused some of his faithful subordinates, including BOETHIUS, of plotting with the Roman aristocracy to overthrow him. Boethius wrote his *De consolatione philosophiae* (*Consolation of Philosophy*), which Chaucer translated as *BOECE*, after having been accused and forced into exile by Theodoric. Although Boethius does not mention Theodoric by name in his work, Chaucer includes in his translation two glosses (comments on the text), both of which state instances in which Boethius opposed Theodoric's policies when those policies were unjust. On one occasion (Book One, Prosa 4, lines 72–84) he canceled Theodoric's restrictions on the sale of grain during a year of famine, and on another (Book Three, Prosa 4, lines 23–26) he refused to serve as a colleague with DECORAT, a man he knew to be an informer.

Theophrastus (Theophraste) The supposed Greek author of the *Liber aureolus de nuptiis* ("The Golden Book of Marriage"), a work abstracted in the *Epistola adversus Jovinianum* ("Letter against Jovinianum") of Saint JEROME. "Valerye and Theophraste" is the name by which the WIFE OF BATH's fifth husband calls his "Book of Wicked Wives," a collection of antifeminist writings from which he reads to her each evening (Wife of Bath's Prologue, line 671). At the beginning of "The MERCHANT'S TALE," the narrator states that a wife ought to gladly serve her husband, but he notes that Theophrastus and some other clerks do not believe that this will happen (lines 1293–94). Considering the MERCHANT's own experience of marriage, which he discusses in his prologue, his ensuing comment that Theophrastus must be a liar should be taken ironically.

Thesbe(e) *See* THISBE.

Theseus The greatest king and hero of ATHENS, Theseus was the son of King Aegeas, for whom the Aegean Sea was named. Theseus achieved early fame by destroying a number of notorious bandits who plagued travelers in Greece. His most famous feat was to kill the MINOTAUR, the legendary half-man, half-bull monster who lived in the Labyrinth beneath the island of Crete. Theseus accomplished this with the help of MINOS' daughter ARIADNE, who told him how to use a ball of thread to find his way back out of the Labyrinth. Theseus promised to marry her for saving his life, but

abandoned her on his way back home. His second wife was the queen of the AMAZONS, HIPPOLYTA, with whom he had a son named Hippolytus. Like HERCULES and ULYSSES, two other outstanding Greek heroes, Theseus had many adventures. He sailed with JASON and the Argonauts to find the Golden Fleece and took part in the great Calydonian Boar Hunt, where he saved the life of his rash friend, Pirithous. When the latter announced his plan to kidnap Persephone, the queen of Hades, Theseus, not to be outdone, first kidnapped the famously beautiful daughter of Leda and Zeus (JUPITER), Helen, and then joined his friend in his descent to the underworld. When they arrived, PLUTO tricked the two men into sitting down in the Chair of Forgetfulness, but Theseus was eventually rescued by Hercules. For his third wife Theseus chose Ariadne's sister PHAEDRA, a decision he would live to regret. Because Theseus' son Hippolytus despised love, Aphrodite (VENUS) caused Phaedra to fall madly in love with him. Driven to despair by her emotions, Phaedra committed suicide but condemned the man she loved by leaving a note which claimed that he had raped her. Believing what she had written, Theseus cursed his son, who was shortly afterward killed in an accident caused by Poseidon, lord of the sea. Although he was banished from Athens and died in exile, Theseus was later recognized as the greatest ruler of that city primarily because, shortly after ascending the throne, he had abolished the monarchy and established a democracy, retaining for himself the role of commander-in-chief.

The heyday of his government in Athens forms the backdrop for the action of "The KNIGHT'S TALE" in which he is "duke" of Athens and the symbolic representative of stable and authorized government. The tale begins with the story of Theseus' battle against the Amazons, famous women warriors of SCYTHIA, whom he defeats and tames and whose leader, Hippolyta, he takes to be his own wife. His function as the representative of authorized power is suggested by his role in chastising CREON, duke of THEBES, for refusing to allow the burial of certain warriors who had been slain in battle. This function is confirmed later by his intervention in the private combat of PALAMON and ARCITE (1). By transforming their struggle into the ritual conflict of tournament, Theseus brings reason and restraint into the picture and convinces the two knights to agree to end the fighting when one or the other is captured rather than killed. His long speech at the end of "The Knights's Tale" is a meditation on the philosophical ideas of BOETHIUS contained in the *Consolation of Philosophy*. The speech argues for the recognition of a stable destinal order in the universe that subsumes the apparent fickleness of FORTUNE. Its practical effect is to convince Palamon and EMILY that they should cease grieving over Arcite, who, after all, died in honor and glory, and marry each other. A darker side of Theseus' political wisdom may be discerned in his use of the marriage of Emily to Palamon as a means of securing Thebes' obeisance to Athens. Theseus also appears as the faithless lover of ANELIDA in Chaucer's *ANELIDA AND ARCITE*, and the story of his abandonment of Ariadne appears in *The LEGEND OF GOOD WOMEN* (lines 1886–2227).

Thesiphone One of the Furies. Also known as Tisiphone. (*See* ERINYES.)

Thessaly An ancient region of eastern Greece, between the Pindus Mountains and the Aegean Sea. In the life of JULIUS CAESAR that appears in "The MONK'S TALE," the narrator mentions Thessaly as the place where Caesar overtook and fought POMPEY, with whom he had formerly shared power during the period of the first triumvirate (lines 2678–86). Thessaly is also the kingdom that the Greek adventurer JASON ought to have inherited from his father, AESON, whose throne was usurped by his brother, PELIAS. When Jason grew up and went to reassert his father's claim, Pelias sent him on his famous quest for the Golden Fleece. The story of Jason and the two women he betrayed, HYPSIPYLE and MEDEA, is narrated in Chaucer's *LEGEND OF GOOD WOMEN* (lines 1368–1679).

Thetis In classical mythology, Thetis was a Nereid, or sea nymph, who became the mother of the famous warrior ACHILLES. PELIAS, one of the men sailing on the expedition with JASON and the Argonauts, fell in love with her while she was guiding the Argonauts safely through some of the perils that they encountered at sea. The Centaur CHIRON told him that to win her he had to hold her tight, even though she would assume many forms, until she would promise to marry him. Pelias was successful and the two were married. When Achilles was born, Thetis dipped him into the river STYX to make his body invulnerable to mortal weapons, but the heel by which she held him remained vulnerable and would later receive a mortal wound. This story is the source of the proverbial "Achilles' heel." Thetis is mentioned in Chaucer's *LEGEND OF GOOD WOMEN*, where she rescues DEMOPHON from drowning, casting him upon a beach in Thrace (line 2422).

Thimotheum *See* TIMOTHY, SAINT.

Thiodamus In classical mythology, Thiodamas was a famous prophet who encouraged the troops at the siege of Thebes with invocations followed by the blasting of trumpets. In "The MERCHANT'S TALE," the trumpet music that announces each of the courses at JANUARY's wedding feast is described as being clearer than that played by Thiodamus. In *The HOUSE OF FAME*,

Thiodamus appears with other musicians in Fame's palace (line 1246).

Thisbe In classical mythology, Thisbe was the ill-fated lover of PYRAMUS, revered as one of the most beautiful young men of the ancient world. The two young people lived in ancient BABYLON, on estates with adjoining properties. They fell in love but their parents forbade them to marry. Deciding to elope, the two arranged to slip away from their homes in the dark of night. They planned to meet at the tomb of King NINUS. Thisbe arrived first but a hungry lioness frightened her into taking refuge in a cave. She dropped her cloak, which the animal attacked with bloody claws. When Pyramus arrived and found the cloak, but not Thisbe, he assumed the worst and stabbed himself. When Thisbe returned and found her lover dead, she also committed suicide. Thisbe is mentioned as one of the martyrs in the TEMPLE OF VENUS in Chaucer's *PARLIAMENT OF FOWLS* (line 289). She is mentioned briefly in "The MERCHANT'S TALE," where the narrator remarks that in the case of MAY and DAMIAN, love will find a way, just as it did for Pyramus and Thisbe (lines 2125–28). A complete version of the story of Pyramus and his lover is told in *The LEGEND OF GOOD WOMEN* (lines 706–923). The introduction to "The MAN OF LAW'S TALE" notes that the story of Thisbe appears among Chaucer's works (line 63).

Thoas In classical mythology, Thoas was the son of Dionysus and ARIADNE who became king of Lemnos. When the women of Lemnos conspired to kill all the men on the island, Thoas escaped through the assistance of his daughter HYPSIPYLE. After concealing him in Dionysus' shrine, she later conducted him, disguised as a statue of the god, to the coast, from where a ship carried him to safety. Thoas is mentioned in the story of Hypsipyle and JASON that appears in Chaucer's *LEGEND OF GOOD WOMEN* (lines 1465–68).

Thobie *See* TOBIAS.

Tholome *See* PTOLEMY.

Thomas (1) The man who gives the worthless gift to JOHN THE FRIAR in "The SUMMONER'S TALE." Thomas has given money to various friars all his life but never seen any good come of it. Furthermore, John has been negligent in visiting Thomas during a time of illness which included the death of his young child. For these reasons, when John importunately begs the bedridden Thomas for money, the latter bestows upon him a gift that is both worthless and insulting—a fart.

Thomas (2) In the prologue to "The MONK'S TALE," Thomas is one of the names the Host, Harry BAILLY, mentions when he guesses at the MONK's first name (line 1930). The man's name is actually PIERS, and the Host correctly uses this name to address him in the prologue to "The NUN'S PRIEST'S TALE" (line 2792).

Thomas à Becket, Saint   Thomas à Becket was born around 1118 into a middle-class family in London. After receiving a good education, he entered into service in the household of Theobald, the archbishop of Canterbury. After being employed by Theobald on missions to Rome, his emerging talent for diplomatic service caused Henry II, when newly crowned, to appoint him to the powerful office of chancellor (chief administrator) of the realm, a post in which he performed admirably from 1154 to 1162. Contemporary reports reveal the personality of a courtier—he dressed handsomely, was fond of hunting and other courtly entertainments, and soon became the constant companion of the king. During this period he was instrumental in supporting the interests of the king against those of the church whenever the two came into conflict, which is one reason why Henry advocated his appointment to the archbishopric of Canterbury following Theobald's death. But instead of continuing to favor the interests of the Crown, Becket's attitudes and policies suddenly and drastically changed. Upon his appointment in 1162, he devoted himself to preserving and advancing the interests of the church, even when they brought him into conflict with the king. It was his unbending and often ostentatious resistance to the king's wishes which eventually led to his murder, before the altar of Canterbury cathedral, by four of the king's knights who, according to tradition, were responding to the king's despairing cry, "Will no one rid me of this troublesome priest?" This murder of the head of the church in England, at the supposed instigation of the English king, sent shock waves throughout western Europe. Although attempts were made to suppress the rumors of miracles that grew up surrounding his memory, Thomas was canonized in 1173, three years after his death. He was especially associated with miracles of healing, an association that is noted in the GENERAL PROLOGUE of *The CANTERBURY TALES* when the narrator states that English pilgrims often journey to CANTERBURY in the spring to pay homage to the "hooly blisful martir" who "hem hath holpen whan that they were seeke" (lines 17–18). In the Middle Ages, the cult of Saint Thomas grew and prospered until visits to the shrine of Canterbury became the most popular of English pilgrimages. Perhaps this is why Chaucer chose it as the occasion for the tale-telling contest that provides the framework for his *Canterbury Tales*.

Thomas of India (Ynde)   The man whom Chaucer refers to as Thomas of India was one of the 12 apostles of Jesus. Thomas is probably most well known for his inability to believe that Jesus had risen from the dead until he had touched the holes made by the nails in Christ's palms. For that reason he earned the name "doubting Thomas." Thomas appears three times in the Gospel of John (*see* JOHN, SAINT), but is absent from the other three Gospels, excepting lists of the 12. Later in his life, Thomas was known for spreading the Gospel to parts of Parthia and PERSIA. In later tradition, he also went to India, where he was martyred.

In "The SUMMONER'S TALE," the corrupt monk directs poor sick THOMAS (1) to read the life of Saint Thomas of India to learn about the importance of building churches (line 1980). The monk is hinting that he needs Thomas to make a contribution so that he and his brothers may build a church. He may also be attempting to suggest some relationship between the skepticism of his audience and that formerly expressed by the saint. In the prologue to "The MERCHANT'S TALE," the MERCHANT swears by Saint Thomas of India that "we wedded men lyven in sorwe and care" (lines 1228–30) [we wedded men live in sorrow and care]. There is no particular reason why he should name this particular saint in this instance.

Thomas of Kent, Saint   *See* THOMAS À BECKETT, SAINT.

Thomas of Woodstock (d. 1397)   Thomas of Woodstock, the duke of Gloucester, was the youngest son of King EDWARD III. Thomas was in his early 30s when RICHARD II, Edward's grandson, began to arouse serious opposition among the nobility with some of the favors he bestowed upon his friends. In the absence of JOHN OF GAUNT, Edward's oldest living son, who had managed to keep peace between Richard and the magnates for a long while, but was now living in France, Woodstock organized an opposition party. In 1386, at the urging of this group of men, Parliament demanded and obtained the removal of one of Richard's friends, Michael de la Pole, from the chancellorship, then impeached him and condemned him to prison. Following this event a council, known as the Commission of Government, was set up to advise the young king. It was led by Gloucester, by now Richard's most hated uncle. When Richard challenged their authority the following year by restoring de la Pole, an explosion followed in which the advisory council accused Richard and his followers of treason before Parliament. Since this council was made up of the most powerful magnates in England, Richard could only give way. Because of their alliance with Richard some of Chaucer's friends and acquaintances were executed in the "Merciless Parliament" of 1388. Among those who lost their lives was the poet Thomas USK.

After this blow-up, relations between Richard and Woodstock remained peaceful, at least on the surface, for nearly 10 years. But in 1397 Richard suddenly lashed out at his foes, having Woodstock and others who had opposed him arrested and accused in Parliament just as they had done to the king's friends in 1388. Two of the most powerful, the earl of Arundel and the earl of Warwick, were, respectively, executed and banished. Woodstock was murdered in prison shortly after his arrest.

Chaucer would have been a firsthand witness to many of these happenings because he was a member of Parliament in 1386. Unfortunately there exists no record of his thoughts or reactions to these events. Whatever they were, after this 1397 meeting of Parliament, a number of minor officials were dismissed from the government. Since Chaucer's service as Controller of Customs ended this same year, it is assumed that either he was dismissed as part of the political shake-up that was taking place, or he resigned to avoid being dismissed.

Thomas of Ynde   *See* THOMAS OF INDIA.

Thopas, Sir   The remarkably silly and inconsequential "hero" of Chaucer's "TALE OF SIR THOPAS," one of the two Canterbury tales supposedly told by the poet himself. Like the typical romance hero, Thopas is a knight and a gentleman of an attractive appearance, though the similes used to describe his features make his beauty sound more feminine than masculine. His activities include hawking, archery and the rather less knightly accomplishment of being a good wrestler. Known for his chastity, he causes great pain and love-longing among the young women of his acquaintance. Because of a dream he has had, Thopas is determined to find and fall in love with an elf-queen. He is in search of his fantasy woman when he encounters a giant named OLIPHAUNT, but is unable to fight the giant because he has left his armor at home. He has returned home, fetched his armor, and rides forth once more to meet the giant when the Host, Harry BAILLY, interrupts the story, pronouncing it "not worth a turd."

Thorus   In *The LEGEND OF GOOD WOMEN*, Chaucer lists Thorus with NEPTUNE, Thetis and TRITON, sea deities who rescue DEMOPHON after his ship is destroyed on the way home from the TROJAN WAR (lines 2421–23). It is assumed that Chaucer intended the name to represent another god of the sea but none by this name is known to have existed in classical mythology.

Thrace   An ancient region in the eastern Balkan peninsula of Greece. The modern region of Thrace is divided between Greece and Turkey. Thrace is mentioned several times in Chaucer's poetry. In "The KNIGHT'S TALE," the temple of Mars (1) that THESEUS has constructed as part of the arena where PALAMON and ARCITE (1) are to fight for the hand of EMILY is compared to the great temple of Mars in Thrace (line 1972). PHYLLIS, who was betrayed by DEMOPHON, was the daughter of the king of Thrace. Her story is recounted briefly in *The HOUSE OF FAME* (lines 388–96), where her situation is compared to that of DIDO, queen of CARTHAGE, who was similarly betrayed by AENEAS. A longer version appears in *The LEGEND OF GOOD WOMEN* (lines 2394–2561). TEREUS, the man who married PROCNE and raped her sister PHILOMELA, was also king of Thrace. Their story is likewise narrated in *The Legend of Good Women* (lines 2228–2393). Thrace is also the home of AEOLUS, the god of wind, according to *The House of Fame* (lines 1571–72).

Thymalao   *See* TIMOLAUS.

Thymeo   *See* PLATO.

Thymothee   *See* TIMOTHEUS.

Tiber   River in central Italy that flows from the Apennine Mountains south through Rome, emptying into the Tyrrhenian Sea. In "The MONK'S TALE," the narrator states that the emperor NERO made a pastime of fishing in the Tiber River with nets made of gold (lines 2475–76).

Tiburtius (Tiburce)   Brother-in-law to CECILIA in "The SECOND NUN'S TALE." Tiburtius was converted to Christianity by his brother, VALERIAN, who was married to Cecilia. Both brothers were martyred after being arrested by Roman authorities and refusing to sacrifice to the pagan gods of Rome. It is interesting to note that they were not required to renounce being Christians, an option later presented to Cecilia, but simply required to honor the Roman gods, in keeping with the Roman policy of accepting the religious practices of conquered nations, provided the people of those nations honored the Roman gods in addition to their own.

Ticius   *See* TITYUS.

Tigris   River in the ancient region of Mesopotamia. *See* EUPHRATES for a discussion of the reference to this river that appears in the *BOECE*, Chaucer's translation of BOETHIUS' *Consolation of Philosophy*.

Timaeus   *See* PLATO.

Timolaus   The son of Queen ZENOBIA of PALMYRA and her husband Odenathus. The story of Zenobia's rise and fall is told in Chaucer's "MONK'S TALE" (lines 2247–2374). Following the Italian writer BOCCACCIO's version of the story, Chaucer supplies the detail that Zenobia dressed her two sons after the manner of kings (lines 2343–45).

Timotheus   Syrian general who was defeated by JUDAS MACCABEUS in the conflict between the Jews and KING ANTIOCHUS (1) of SYRIA. His role in the conflict is mentioned in the story of Antiochus that appears in "The MONK'S TALE" (lines 2591–98). The source of the story is the apocryphal book of 2 Maccabees, which was included in the Vulgate (Latin) Bible of Chaucer's time.

Timothy, Saint   One of the apostle PAUL's disciples. With Paul he was the coauthor of the Epistles (Letters) to the Thessalonians, the second Epistles to the Corinthians, and the Epistles to the Philippians, Colossians and Philemon, all of which appear in the New Testament. Two of Paul's epistles are addressed to Timothy. They are primarily concerned with instructing Timothy on how to establish sound doctrine in the churches that he ministered to. According to the historian Eusebius, Timothy was the first bishop of Ephesus. Paul's Epistles to Timothy are mentioned in the prologue to "The PARSON'S TALE" when the PARSON refuses to tell a story or fable because of Paul's warnings to Timothy regarding the dangers of such stories (line 32).

Tiresias   In classical mythology, Tiresias was a blind Theban seer who gained his powers in a bizarre fashion. Once when walking on MOUNT CITHAERON he encountered two snakes embracing and struck them with his walking staff. He was immediately changed into a woman. Seven years later he had a similar experience and was changed back into a man. Because he had experience as both a man and a woman, Zeus asked him to settle a dispute with Hera over whether men or women enjoyed love more. When Tiresias supported Zeus' opinion that women did, Hera punished him with blindness, a condition Zeus attempted to alleviate by giving him the gift of prophecy as well. Other stories give alternate reasons for his blindness, but this is the most interesting. Tiresias is best known to modern readers for his role in Sophocles' *Oedipus Rex*, in which he helps OEDIPUS discover his fate and later prophesizes the death of CREON and the destruction of THEBES. In the *BOECE*, BOETHIUS refers to Tiresias' powers as "japeworthi" [trickery] (Book Five, Prosa 13, line 134).

Tisbe   *See* THISBE.

Tisiphone   *See* ERINYES.

Titan   The name given to the Sun by OVID in his *Metamorphoses*. Chaucer uses this name for the Sun in *TROILUS AND CRISEYDE* when TROILUS, after spending the night with CRISEYDE for the first time, chides Titan for allowing the dawn to come so soon (book three, line 1464).

Titus (Livius)   *See* LIVY.

Tityus   In classical mythology, Tityus was a giant son of Gaea (Earth). He was killed and condemned to eternal suffering in Hades because of an attack he made against Latona, the mother of APOLLO and DIANA. His punishment in the underworld was to lie stretched out over the pit of hell while vultures forever fed on his liver. In *TROILUS AND CRISEYDE*, PANDARUS says that even if TROILUS suffers as much as Tityus, he ought to tell his friend the source of his woe and perhaps, in doing so, relieve it (book 1, lines 785–91). In the *BOECE*, Chaucer's translation of BOETHIUS' *Consolation of Philosophy*, LADY PHILOSOPHY tells the story of how the vultures who gnawed at Tityus' liver were so enthralled by the music of ORPHEUS that they ceased to torment the giant while Orpheus played (Book Three, Metrum 12, line 42).

Tlemcen   Rendered as "Tramyssene" in *The RIVERSIDE CHAUCER*, Tlemcen, near Morocco in northern Africa, is one of the places which the KNIGHT (1), who is described in the GENERAL PROLOGUE to *The CANTERBURY TALES*, has visited on military campaign (line 62).

"To Rosemounde"   One of the shortest poems attributed to Chaucer.

SUMMARY

"To Rosemounde" consists of only three stanzas. The first praises the qualities of its addressee, referring to her as the shrine of all beauty and noting the merriment with which she dances, which, the poet claims, is like a healing salve to the wound in his heart. The second stanza notes that despite the tears she causes him to weep, he will never become despondent, because of the joy afforded him by the sound of her voice. It is enough that he should love her, even if she does not return his affection. In the last stanza the lover humorously compares himself in love to a pike boiled in galantine (a pickling sauce made of brown bread, vinegar, salt and pepper), and then, more nobly, to TRISTRAM (Tristan), one of the famous lovers of Arthurian romance. Returning to the food metaphor, he announces that his love will never grow cold, that he will burn forever in amorous delight.

COMMENTARY

"To Rosemounde" exists in only one manuscript. The poem was discovered by W. W. SKEAT, who attributed it to Chaucer and gave it the present title. In the manuscript, it follows Chaucer's *TROILUS AND CRISEYDE,* and both are followed by the words *Chaucer* and *Tregentil.* Skeat believed that *Tregentil* was the name of the scribe, but it could also be a tribute (French "trés gentil" = English "very noble") to the poem's author. The BALLADE form in which it is written (not to be confused with the English ballad) was one of the most popular of the artificial French verse forms. Although the form varied somewhat, it most frequently employed three eight-line stanzas with the rhyme scheme *ababbcbc*, which is the exact pattern Chaucer followed here. Other earmarks of the ballade form to which Chaucer adhered were the single-line refrain that recurred regularly at the end of each stanza ("Thogh he to me ne do no daliaunce") and the use of only three rhymes in the entire poem, occurring at the same position in each stanza and with no rhyme-word repeated except in the refrain. One perennial question that readers of this poem have raised is whether or not Rosemounde was a real person; the answer to that, based on current knowledge, is *no*. The name *Rosemunde*, which means "Rose of the World," was fairly common in verse. As with most of the other short poems attributed to Chaucer, the date of composition for "To Rosemounde" is uncertain.

Toas   In classical mythology, Toas was the king of Aetolia who fought on the side of the Greeks in the TROJAN WAR. Captured by the Trojans, he was later traded for ANTENOR, who had been taken by the Greeks. In *TROILUS AND CRISEYDE*, the Trojans exchange Toas and CRISEYDE for Antenor (book 4, lines 1333–39). This separation of TROILUS and Criseyde signals the beginning of Troilus' tragic fate.

Tobias   The Book of Tobit is an apocryphal book of the Bible that was included in the Vulgate (Latin) Bible of Chaucer's day. The book tells the story of Tobit, a Jew who was taken in captivity to NINEVAH after the defeat of Israel by the Assyrians in 722 B.C. He was blinded when the droppings of a swallow fell into his eyes. Tobit's son, Tobias, married a devout Jewish woman, Sara, whom he saved from a demon by the assistance of the angel Raphael. In "The TALE OF MELIBEE," Dame PRUDENCE quotes from the Book of Tobit when she reminds her husband of how Tobit taught his son to bless God at all times and to always look to him for counsel in everything (line 1118). In "The PARSON'S TALE," in the section of his sermon dealing with the sin of lechery, the PARSON notes that in the Book of Tobit, the angel Raphael told Tobit that the devil has power over people who, even though they are married, enjoy the pleasures of the flesh (lines 905–06).

Tolletanes   In "The FRANKLIN'S TALE," the magician hired by AURELIUS consults his "tables Tolletanes" [tables of Toledo] in order to determine when will be the most propitious time to perform the "natural magic" that will cause some rocks lining the coast of BRITTANY to magically disappear beneath the waters (line 1273). The tables referred to here were astrological tables corrected for a specific latitude (that of Toledo in Spain). Aurelius wants the magician to perform this feat because DORIGEN, the married lady with whom he is infatuated, has promised to become his lover if he can effect the rocks' removal.

Topas, Sir   *See* THOPAS, SIR.

Trace   *See* THRACE.

Tramyssene   *See* TLEMCEN.

Treatise on the Astrolabe, A   The only scientific text that Chaucer is known to have written, the *Treatise on the Astrolabe* explains the construction and use of this astronomer's tool.

SUMMARY

A Treatise on the Astrolabe opens with Chaucer addressing his little son, Lewis (*see* CHAUCER, LEWIS), for whom he was writing the text. He first acknowledges his son's interest and ability regarding scientific study, then notes that it has been the special request of Lewis to be taught to use the astrolabe. For that reason he has given Lewis an astrolabe and embarked upon the composition of the treatise that is to follow. It will be divided into five parts and rendered in plainest English so that Lewis may the more easily understand it. The theory contained within, however, will be taken from

This simplified drawing of a rete is similar to one that appears in the Rawlinson manuscript of the Treatise. *The rete was cut out of flattened metal to fit over the primary metal disk of the astrolabe (the "mother"), where it was held in place by a pin inserted through a central hole. The plate is inscribed with the zodiac circle marked out in graduations of two degrees.*

the work of old astrologers, authorities on the subject. The first part of the treatise will contain a description of the instrument and all its parts. The second part will teach Lewis how to use the instrument that he has been given. Only these two parts are extant in the surviving manuscripts. The third part was intended to contain tables of longitudes and latitudes for the fixed stars, tables of the declinations of the Sun, tables of longitudes for cities and towns and various other information taken from the astronomical tables of John Somer, a Franciscan friar and astronomer, and Nicholas of Lynn, a Carmelite friar at Oxford. The fourth and fifth parts of the treatise were then to deal with astronomical and astrological (the two were considered a single science during the medieval period) theory.

COMMENTARY

Despite the fact that Chaucer was writing for a 10-year-old boy, most modern readers encounter more difficulty reading his *Treatise on the Astrolabe* than any other text he wrote, for two reasons. First of all, with the astrolabe no longer in existence (it was long ago replaced as a navigational tool by the sextant), many modern readers do not even know what it is; secondly, Chaucer's text was written for someone in possession of two things most modern readers do not have: an astrolabe and a personal instructor (perhaps Chaucer, but probably a tutor) to provide assistance should the need arise. The two surviving parts of the text are particularly geared toward becoming familiar with the instrument by handling it and are impossible to understand without a more extensive and intimate knowledge of the astrolabe than can be provided here. For that reason, those sections are not summarized above; the interested reader should consult Chaucer's own text, expertly edited by John Reidy, in the Riverside edition of Chaucer's work. Reidy's explanatory notes provide some assistance in comprehending Chaucer's detailed instructions. The word *astrolabe* derives from the Greek and means "star-catcher." There were three types—linear, planispheric and spherical—with the most common being the planispheric, the type which Chaucer refers to. The primary function of the planispheric astrolabe was to enable astronomers to calculate the position of the Sun and other stars with respect to both the horizon and the meridian. It was not until the mid-15th century, however, that astrolabes were adopted by mariners and used in navigation. The principle parts of the instrument were a base plate ("mater," which Chaucer translates into English as "mother") with a network of lines representing celestial coordinates; an open-pattern disk called the *rete,* which provided a map of the stars and which rotated on the mater around a central pin corresponding to the north celestial pole; and a straight rule called the *alidade,* which was used for sighting objects in the sky. Chaucer's *Treatise on the Astrolabe* earns a notable place in literary and scientific

history by being the oldest text written in English about an elaborate scientific instrument.

For Further Reading: A translation and partial edition of the *Treatise on the Astrolabe* appears in R. T. Gunther's *Chaucer and Messahalla on the Astrolabe* (1929), which reproduces 62 illustrations that accompany one of the manuscripts of the work. It also includes a translation of Messahalla's *Astrolabe,* which may have been one of Chaucer's sources. The view that Chaucer's *Treatise* was largely translated from sources is challenged by Carol Lipson in "'I N'am But a Lewd Compilator': Chaucer's *Treatise on the Astrolabe* as Translation" (*Neuphilologische Mitteilungen,* 1984), who argues that it is mostly Chaucer's own composition. A portion of J. A. W. BENNETT's *Chaucer at Oxford and Cambridge* (1974) examines the records of the library at Merton College, Oxford University, to determine what resources related to the *Treatise* were available in Chaucer's day. Readers interested in a discussion of Chaucer's prose style should consult Margaret Schlauch's essay "The Art of Chaucer's Prose" (in *Chaucer and Chaucerians: Critical Studies in Middle English Literature,* 1966), which considers the BOECE and "The Tale of MELIBEE" as well as the *Treatise on the Astrolabe.*

Triguilla   In the BOECE, Chaucer's translation of BOETHIUS' *Consolation of Philosophy,* Triguilla ("Trygwille") is described as a person who, like Boethius, served under THEODORIC. Boethius criticizes Triguilla and a man named CONIGASTUS for using their influence to oppress the poor, and tells LADY PHILOSOPHY that he denounced them both (Book One, Prosa 4, lines 57–61). Aside from this comment, no other historical evidence of this man's life exists.

Trismegistus, Hermes   *See* HERMES TRISMEGISTUS.

Tristram (Tristam; Tristan)   Heroic character who was a central figure in the popular medieval romance of *Tristram* (or *Tristan*) *and Isolde* (also spelled *Isoude* and *Iseult*). Three early versions of the Tristram story survive: one French, one Welsh and one German, all of them penned in the 12th century. The version of the romance most often read today was written by Gottfried von Strassburg early in the 13th century. The son of Blanchefleur of Cornwall and Rivalen of Lyonesse (a legendary island country), Tristram was born in BRITTANY shortly after his father's death. It was because of her loss that the widow Blanchefleur named him Tristram, which meant "child of sadness." Tristram grew to manhood at the court of his uncle, King Mark of Cornwall; he was handsome, an accomplished musician and the bravest of knights. When Mark decided to marry, he sent his nephew to Ireland to fetch Isolde, whom he intended to make his wife. During their voyage back to Cornwall, Tristram and ISOLDE unwittingly drank a love potion that Isolde's mother had prepared for her daughter and King

Mark, and fell hopelessly in love. Even though circumstances demanded that she be married to Mark, the two continued their famous love affair, always having to circumvent Mark's suspicions and jealousy, until Tristram's tragic death. Tristram is mentioned in *The PARLIAMENT OF FOWLS* as one of those who died for love. His story is portrayed on the walls of the TEMPLE OF VENUS (lines 290–94). Also, the narrator of the BALLADE "TO ROSEMOUNDE" refers to himself as "trewe Tristram the secounde" (line 20) [true Tristram the second]. In his *Passion and Society* (1934), the French literary theorist Denis de Rougement (1906–85) claimed that Tristram was the prototype of the courtly lover and cites repeated references to him in courtly love lyrics such as Chaucer's.

Triton   In classical mythology, Triton was a son of the sea god NEPTUNE. He was depicted as a man to the hips,

Triton, the son of Neptune, who rescues Demophon from drowning in the sea.

but in place of legs he had a single or double fish tail. He sometimes carried a trident, which he could use to raise rocks from the sea to make islands, and a conch, which he used to create winds upon the surface of the sea. In *The HOUSE OF FAME*, Triton is called upon to accompany AEOLUS to Fame's palace, carrying his two trumpets, which are named "Sklaundre" (Slander) and "Clere Laude" (Pure Praise) (lines 1583–1605). In *The LEGEND OF GOOD WOMEN*, Triton is one of the sea deities who rescues DEMOPHON, causing him to be washed up on the shore of RHODOPE, where he meets PHYLLIS (lines 2417–24).

Trivet, Nicholas (ca. 1258–1334)   An English Dominican who studied at Oxford and Paris, Nicholas Trivet wrote commentaries on a number of classical texts, including one on BOETHIUS' *Consolation of Philosophy* which provided numerous glosses (explanatory passages) that Chaucer used in his own translation of *The Consolation*, entitled BOECE. Modern editions of the *Boece* usually set these glosses in italics and/or parentheses. Trivet is best remembered, however, as historian. His *Anglo-Norman Chronicle*, claiming to recount the history of the world from the Creation to 1285, was Chaucer's source for the story of CONSTANCE in "The MAN OF LAW'S TALE." The title of this work derives from the language in which it was written, ANGLO-NORMAN, a French dialect that had been spoken in England since the invasion of William the Conqueror in 1066.

Troilus   The hero of Chaucer's longest single poem, *TROILUS AND CRISEYDE*. That famous conflict between the Greeks and the Trojans known as the TROJAN WAR forms the backdrop of the poem and often intersects with the lives of the two lovers. Troilus is the son of King PRIAM, the ruler of TROY, and his wife, HECUBA. One of Troy's most powerful warriors, he is described at the beginning of the poem as one who scorns the emotion of love. When his comrades in arms succumb to the attractions of some young women, he is the first to torment them for their supposed foolishness, proud that he has never been prey to such weakness. But then one day, at a festival in the PALLADIUM, he sees the beautiful young widow CRISEYDE. He is immediately stricken with an infatuation that grows and grows until it threatens his ability to function. Finally persuaded by his friend PANDARUS to reveal the source of his woe, he begins taking steps to woo the lady. She resists at first, but her determination to remain independent is slowly broken down through the combination of Troilus' persistence and Pandarus' manipulations. The two finally become lovers, enjoy a brief period of (mostly sexual) bliss and are then separated when Criseyde is given to the Greek host in exchange for a Trojan warrior. She promises Troilus that nothing can prevent her returning to him within a short time, but when she fails to appear,

Troilus despairs and then falls in battle, killed by the Greek warrior ACHILLES.

Chaucer did not invent the character of Troilus but took him from the Italian poet BOCCACCIO's *Il FILOSTRATO* (The one overcome by love), which was his major source for *Troilus and Criseyde*. The character did not originate with Boccaccio, either, but can be traced back to the *De excidio Troiae historia* ("History of the Fall of Troy") of DARES Phrygius, who mentions the bravery of Troilus but says nothing about a love affair. BENOÎT DE SAINT MAURE's *Roman de Troie* ("Romance of Troy"), composed in the latter part of the 12th century, describes a love affair between Troilus and a woman named Briseida who, like Criseyde, betrayed her lover. Boccaccio seems to be the one who changed the lover's name to Criseyde, also adding the process of Troilus ("Troilo" in Boccaccio) falling in love with and wooing her. Chaucer developed the story further by increasing the psychological depth and complexity of the characters so that what happens to them seems the result of character traits as much as external events. In the case of Troilus, the reticence he displays in pursuing Criseyde (at one point Pandarus actually has to throw him into Criseyde's bed) helps to explain his later failure to prevent her being given to the Greeks. Although reflective, emotional and shy around women, he is at the same time a brave and effective warrior. Chaucer successfully combines all of these traits to give us a character both complex and realistic. Those readers who have criticized him for being weak seem to have focused on certain aspects of his character without considering the total effect.

Troilus and Criseyde Chaucer's longest single poem, concerning the love affair of a Trojan prince, TROILUS, and a young widow, CRISEYDE, during the TROJAN WAR.

SUMMARY

This lengthy poem is divided into five "books." Book one begins with an introduction spoken by the narrator, who announces his intention to tell the story of Troilus, son to the king of TROY, and his misfortunes in love. He speaks here, and later in this introduction, of Troilus' "double sorrow," referring to the fact that Troilus endured two periods of intense suffering in love. The first occurred when he fell in love with Criseyde but was afraid to reveal his passion. The second followed her betrayal of him after their love had been consummated. Calling upon the Fury Thesiphone (TISIPHONE) as his muse, the narrator asks for help in composing his woeful verses. He suggests a motive for his decision to write the poem by referring to himself as the servitor of love's servants, i.e., one who serves those who serve CUPID, the god of love. In writing the poem, he hopes to bring pleasure and solace to all

lovers who read it, but he also asks that those who are happy in love remember and pray for those who, like Troilus, suffer adversity.

Following this introduction, the narrative portion of the poem begins with a brief mention of the historical situation that serves as backdrop to the poem, the Trojan War. In the midst of these events a Trojan lord named CALKAS, who is also a soothsayer, discovers by his calculations and through divine revelation that Troy will ultimately be destroyed by the Greeks. Therefore he decides to leave the city and goes out to join the Greeks, who welcome him, hoping to benefit by his knowledge of the city and its people. Meanwhile, the citizens of Troy, learning of Calkas' treachery, suggest that he and all his kin ought to be killed. Calkas has a daughter, Criseyde, whom he has left behind and who, until he had left the city, knew nothing of her father's plans. A widow with no one to turn to for help, filled with shame and fear, she approaches the king's son Ector (HECTOR) to beg for mercy, all the while protesting her innocence. The fact that she is very beautiful and that Hector is inclined to be kind serve her in good stead, and she is granted immunity from the taint of her father's treason. Thus assured of her safety, Criseyde returns to her home, where she maintains a household suited to her station and degree.

The war drags on. Sometimes the Greeks have the upper hand, sometimes the Trojans. The image of the Wheel of FORTUNE is invoked to explain the turn, and turn again, of events.

Despite the war waging outside their gates, the Trojans continue with their accustomed activities, including the observance of religious festivals such as the feast of PALLAS Athena, here called "Palladione." The time of year is spring, and the Trojans gather at the temple of Athena to observe the appropriate rites. Criseyde attends the gathering, wearing black to symbolize her status as a widow. Despite these sober garments, her beauty is matchless, like a star shining out from under a black cloud. Troilus, also in attendance at the festival, walks up and down amidst the assembly with his soldiers, watching how they react to the various women in attendance and noting any suggestion of affection so that he may goad them later. His disparaging attitude toward love, which causes him to consider himself wiser than his comrades, soon proves the man's undoing. Cupid, the god of love, perceives Troilus' attitude and quickly fits an arrow to his bow. The wound that Troilus receives, however, comes not from any invisible arrow but through his eyes when he catches sight of Criseyde. Henceforth the man who held himself highest in pride above those who loved finds himself most subject to love.

Stricken by the sight of Criseyde, Troilus watches her throughout the assembly, falling more and more deeply in love. He is careful, however, to keep his interest hidden by intentionally averting his glance from time to time. Realizing what has happened to him as he leaves the temple, he repents of his former attitude which, if his sudden passion should become known, would bring a heap of scorn down on his own head. Therefore he determines to keep his feelings secret. Following this resolution, he returns to the palace where he lives and attempts to behave as he always has, making fun of those who are in love. He is unable, however, to keep it up for very long and soon retires to his chamber, where he initially feels optimistic about the possibility of serving his lady and winning her love. With that in mind, he composes a song. In the text of the poem the song is headed by the rubric *Canticus Troili,* i.e., "Song of Troilus." Its verses philosophically explore the paradoxes of love, particularly its sweet painfulness that leaves the lover longing for more of the things, such as the sight of his lady, that cause pain.

Unmindful of everything that was important in his life before he fell in love, Troilus becomes more and more possessed by his passion. Although he continues to fight in the ongoing war, he cares little for the fate of his country, but excels in battle so that Criseyde may be impressed by his skill and bravery. Eventually his passion gets the best of him, depriving him of sleep and appetite and filling him with misery. His progression into despair makes him unable to leave his bed. As he suffers alone in his chamber, crying aloud from the emotional pain he endures, his friend PANDARUS comes in. Unperceived by Troilus, he glimpses the man's agony. Pandarus rouses Troilus from his self-absorption, and a lengthy exchange follows in which Pandarus first persuades Troilus to reveal the general cause of his grief, and eventually convinces him to disclose the name of the woman. In the course of their argument, the Wheel of Fortune image is again invoked, this time by Troilus, who bewails his fall from former happiness. Pandarus consoles him with the idea that the wheel may turn again and bring him even greater bliss by uniting him with his beloved. Obtaining Troilus' consent to act on his behalf, Pandarus promises to help Troilus win Criseyde's affection. At this point we learn that Criseyde is Pandarus' niece.

Having entrusted his problem to someone else's care, Troilus soon feels some relief from his woe, but his passion, now inspired by hope, burns even hotter. Nevertheless, before Pandarus leaves, Troilus assures his friend that his intentions are honorable, that he would never desire to bring Criseyde any harm or shame. After Pandarus has left him, Troilus no longer keeps himself isolated in his chamber, but takes to the field. His newfound hope, combined with the passion of his love, inspires him to greater and greater feats in battle. At home, he becomes the friendliest, most well-mannered and generous knight, no longer displaying any cruelty to those of his companions who are in love.

Book two opens with an invocation of CLIO, the Muse of history, which, in contrast to the narrator's invocation of the Fury Thesiphone at the outset of book one, indicates that the story will now take a happier turn. Before taking up the story, however, the narrator expresses the hope that nothing he writes here will be offensive to his readers. Should anyone take offense, he says, they should not blame him, for two reasons. First, he is merely translating the story out of Latin from another source, and secondly, he himself has no experience in love and is therefore unable to judge the story's credibility.

The narrative itself resumes with Pandarus, himself stricken by a perennial unrequited lovesickness, resorting to his own bed to nurse his sorrow. Awakening from a fitful slumber, he remembers his promise to Troilus, and goes to visit his niece, Criseyde. He finds her surrounded by female companions, listening to a maiden read the story of the siege of THEBES which includes the story of King LAIUS and his son OEDIPUS. Criseyde welcomes her uncle, and as they begin to talk together he immediately assails her sobriety by suggesting that she cast off her widow's veil, put away her book and join him in a dance to celebrate the coming of May. Criseyde is shocked by his request and reminds him that she is neither a maiden nor a young bride. Not to be deterred from his errand by this discouraging start, Pandarus immediately hints at his possession of a secret that, if he chose to reveal it, would cause his niece great amusement. Her curiosity piqued, Criseyde presses him to tell her what it is, but he refuses, saying that she is too proud, which only whets her desire the more. Instead of begging him to tell her, Criseyde veils her feelings and passes lightly onto other subjects of conversation. By chance she asks about Hector, Troilus' brother, and how he fares in the ongoing conflict. Pandarus takes the opportunity to praise Troilus as being equally important to the success of the Trojan effort, and after Criseyde expresses agreement, he announces his intention to go home. When his niece urges him to stay longer, he again baits her curiosity, saying she ought to cast off her widow's clothing and dance because a wonderful opportunity has come her way. Criseyde finally convinces her uncle that it is safe to tell her this wonderful secret.

Pandarus knows that he must proceed very carefully, and so, before he makes his full confession, pauses to confirm his devotion to his niece and to swear that he would never urge her to do something that could imperil her honor or renown. This makes Criseyde a little fearful and, most of all, feeds her curiosity to the bursting point. Seizing this opportunity, Pandarus tells her plainly that the king's son, Troilus, is in love with her—so much in love that she has the power to make him live or die. To add weight to the seriousness of his message, Pandarus vows that he, too, will die should his niece show disdain instead of mercy to the prince. Without waiting for her response, he attempts to anticipate every argument she might make against welcoming Troilus' attentions. He reaffirms the honorable nature of Troilus' love, and cautions her against wasting her youth and beauty, which will only be present for a short time. Once she has had time to consider her uncle's proposition, Criseyde's reaction is sorrow rather than joy. She tearfully reproves him for the role he has chosen to play, accusing him of endangering her honor when, as her uncle, he ought to be protecting it. Pandarus reacts strongly to her words. Swearing that both he and Troilus will soon be dead, and that their deaths will be on her hands, he makes ready to depart. Criseyde, filled with fear and uncertainty over what may happen when her uncle returns to Troilus, especially considering her own status as the daughter of a traitor, stops him from going and issues her promise that she will, so far as honor extends, be kind to Troilus. When they are accorded thus, they pass on to talk of other things. During their conversation Criseyde asks her uncle how he came to know of Troilus' affection. The version he tells her is slightly more elaborate than the one given in book one, with two episodes instead of one in which he overhears Troilus complaining of his passion. In this we have the first indication that Pandarus is not completely trustworthy, even though his lie in this case does not appear to be harmful. This visit with Criseyde also shows how much he enjoys manipulating people, and we begin to see the development of the scheming and plotting that will ultimately bring Criseyde and Troilus together.

When her uncle finally does leave, Criseyde goes to her chamber to think over what has transpired and decides that her plight is not as threatening as it seemed at first. Reflecting upon her observance of other people's behavior, she concludes that it will do her no harm to be the object of a knight's love, that accepting his devotion will not obligate her to return it. While she is meditating, she hears a commotion out in the street and goes to her window. There she sees Troilus returning from battle, all armed except for his head. Fresh, young and vigorous, his valor attested by his battered helm and shield, he rides proudly to the accompaniment of the people's cheers. Criseyde, observing, feels herself blush, thinking of the power that she has over this man's life. She begins to feel some pity for him which opens the way to further emotional involvement. Her anxiety breaks through again, however, when she considers how much she values her independence. Love could deprive her of that, and furthermore, love's course does not always run smooth, but has stormy periods. She also weighs the dangers of being a subject of gossip and, finally, the possibility that once he has won her, Troilus might fall out of love.

Unable to settle her mind, Criseyde decides to walk in the garden with her nieces, FLEXIPPE, THARBE and ANTIGONE. As they walk up and down, arm in arm, Antigone sings a hymn of praise to Love. Prompted by this introduction, Criseyde engages her niece in a dialogue which further eases her fears. When she goes to bed that night, she dreams that an eagle flies into her bedroom, tears her heart out of her breast and exchanges it with his own, all without causing her fear or pain.

In the meantime, Pandarus has returned to Troilus. He teasingly delays telling the prince how Criseyde responded to his news, but finally reveals that she has given in so far as to promise a love of friendship. Encouraged by this news, Troilus ecstatically gives thanks to VENUS, the goddess of love, and asks Pandarus when he may see his niece. Pandarus instructs him to write a letter to her, expressing his feelings in his own hand. Pandarus will then deliver the letter, at which time he suggests that Troilus should dress up in his finest attire and then ride by on the street that runs beside Criseyde's house. Pandarus says he will contrive to have his niece read the letter, and then he will go sit at a window so that she may see the man whose passionate words she has just read.

The following day, Pandarus takes the letter to his niece. At first she refuses to accept it, fearing that it may compromise her honor. Pandarus swears that it will do no such thing and stuffs it into the bosom of her dress. She does not refuse it again, but says that she will certainly write no answer, to which Pandarus humorously responds that he will write it for her, as long as she tells him what to say. After she has read the letter, Pandarus draws her to a window overlooking the street and asks how she liked it. She blushingly admits that it was good. Urged on by her uncle's persistence, she finally agrees to write a response. Within her letter, which she claims is the first she has ever written, Criseyde states plainly that she will not lead Troilus on with false promises or agree to anything more than a kind of sisterly love that she hopes may put his heart at ease. She gives the letter to her uncle, and they are again standing near the window as Troilus and 10 of his companions come riding along the street. Looking up to Criseyde's window, he salutes her and Pandarus. Again, Criseyde is impressed by his appearance, as well as by his good manners and nobility, and her resolve against loving him melts a bit more. Perceiving her reaction, Pandarus urges her to agree to meet and speak with Troilus, but Criseyde refuses, saying it is too soon to grant him such liberties, especially when her intention is to love him from afar.

Reading the letter Criseyde has written to him, Troilus does not know whether to rejoice or despair at her kind, but far from passionate, response. Eventually, he settles upon the most hopeful interpretation of her words, consoling himself with the belief that her love will grow. Pressed on by Pandarus, Troilus begins to write to Criseyde often. Sometimes the answers he receives make him happy; sometimes they fill him with sorrow. Pandarus coaches him through this trying period, encouraging him to look at its positive side, to see her resistance, for example, as a sign of a strong will that, once it has been won over to his affection, will not easily depart. Finally, Pandarus comes up with a plan for getting the two of them together, this time face to face. To this effect, Pandarus goes to see Troilus' brother Deiphebus (DEIPHOBUS), and tells him that his niece, Criseyde, is being oppressed by some men of the town who are trying to take her property away. He asks Deiphebus for his protection in this matter. The man readily assents, and then asks what should he do to help. Pandarus suggests that first of all he invite Criseyde to visit him tomorrow so that she can advise him, firsthand, of her complaints. It would also be good, he suggests, if Deiphebus had some of his brothers in attendance so that they can also help out if necessary. Deiphebus agrees. This portion of his plan accomplished, Pandarus rushes over to his niece's to tell her that a man named POLIPHETE, who has caused trouble for her before, is taking legal action against her to get possession of her property. Not knowing how to oppose his suit, she asks advice from her uncle. He tells her of the meeting he has arranged with Deiphebus and his brothers, who have sworn to act as her protectors. While they are talking, Deiphebus himself appears and invites Criseyde to dinner.

These arrangements settled, the final preparations for Pandarus' plan must be concluded. Pandarus returns to the house of Troilus, whom he encourages to attend the dinner, but, once there, to pretend that he is sick and go to bed. Troilus responds that he will hardly have to pretend, considering his state of nervous anticipation.

At the dinner, things fall out exactly as Pandarus has hoped. Troilus arrives early at his brother's house and, pleading illness, takes to bed. Deiphebus and his other guests hear Criseyde's complaint, and all present agree to take her side in the legal skirmish. When Helen (HELEN OF TROY), Deiphebus' sister-in-law, asks whether Troilus has knowledge of this matter, Pandarus suggests that if he is awake, they should bring Criseyde in to speak with him. Deiphebus, Helen and Pandarus go in to see him first and Pandarus acquaints him with Criseyde's difficulties. He then secures Troilus' permission for her to come in herself to speak with him. Then, as he and Pandarus have arranged beforehand, Troilus gives a letter to his brother and sister-in-law concerning the fate of a man who is to be executed, asking them to consider whether or not the sentence ought to be carried out. They go out to the garden, where they remain occupied by the letter's contents while

Pandarus goes back to the dining room to fetch his niece. Guiding her to the chamber where Troilus lies, he exhorts her to have pity on the man, repeating many of the arguments that he has made before. Book two closes with a glimpse of Troilus, who awaits her entry in a fever of anticipation.

Book three begins with a hymn of praise to the goddess of love, Venus, that foreshadows the blissful progress of the narrative that is soon to unfold. Enumerating the various accomplishments of this powerful goddess, the narrator asks her to come to his aid in describing the joys that lovers experience. He also invokes CALLIOPE, the Muse of epic poetry; this does not seem entirely appropriate to his subject matter, unless he wishes to emphasize the colossal proportions of the love affair that is about to ensue.

The narrative resumes with Troilus trying to plan what he is going to say when Criseyde arrives. Pandarus enters with her, and it is he who speaks first to Troilus, announcing that she who is to blame for his death has come to pay a visit. Troilus responds in the manner of one so ill that he cannot see who is there. Criseyde is so distressed by his appearance that she begs him not to suffer this way for her. She says that she has come to him for two reasons, first to thank him and then to ask for his continuing patronage. Troilus, dumbstruck by her presence and her request, can say nothing. Criseyde, realizing how deeply he is affected, is pleased to find him neither arrogant nor too self-assured. Finally Troilus begins to speak, declaring his love and asking for her mercy. Pandarus, who remains by her side, weeps and pokes at his niece, adding his own pleas for mercy. Criseyde, still unsure of Troilus' intentions, demands to know exactly what he wants. He eagerly complies, asking that she look favorably on him and allow him to be her knight. He vows to serve her to the best of his ability, promising to be true, humble, honest, discreet, patient and willing to suffer death if he should offend her in any way. Criseyde considers his request while Pandarus underlines its reasonableness. At last she consents to his terms, reiterating the condition that he must always be careful of her honor and stating that even though he is the son of a king, she will never give him sovereignty over her in love. She concludes by telling him to be joyful, that she will comfort him as best she can; she then takes him in her arms and kisses him.

Later that night, Pandarus visits Troilus at home, where he briefly recounts the service he has performed for his friend and asks that, in return, Troilus will always be discreet regarding his relationship with Criseyde. Troilus agrees to his friend's request and vows lifelong service to Pandarus in appreciation for his assistance. By way of keeping his promise, Troilus is careful to hide his joy from those he associates with on a day-to-day basis. He and Criseyde see each other whenever time and occasion permit, but they never have a chance to speak at leisure for fear of being discovered. During this time, Criseyde discovers that Troilus is able to anticipate her desires before she speaks them. He serves her so well that she begins to fall deeply in love with him. Pandarus continues to act as go-between, bearing letters when Troilus is away from home.

Pandarus begins to make arrangements for the lovers to meet privately at his house. As usual, instead of informing his niece regarding his plans, he employs a subterfuge, inviting her to dine. When she asks if Troilus will be there also, Pandarus lies, saying that he is out of town. To keep people from knowing that he will be in Criseyde's company, Troilus has in the meantime told his companions that he is going to APOLLO's temple that night to make a sacrifice and to ask for advice regarding the outcome of the war. In actuality, he arrives at Pandarus' house before Criseyde, and Pandarus hides him in a closet where he can observe the dinner without being seen. Criseyde arrives, accompanied by some of her women attendants. After they have eaten and engaged in various after-dinner entertainments such as singing and telling stories, Criseyde prepares to leave. At this point, Fortune steps in and a tremendous rainstorm begins to blow. Pandarus, delighted by this turn of events, invites his niece to spend the night. He situates her in a bedroom by herself with her ladies in an outer chamber.

Once the women are in bed, Pandarus goes to Troilus, whose closet features a trapdoor leading directly into Criseyde's bedroom. He tells Troilus to ready himself for the blissful union, but Troilus hesitates, pausing to say a long prayer to various gods in the Greek pantheon. Finally Pandarus loses patience with him and drags him into Criseyde's room. Startled by her uncle's approach, Criseyde sits up in bed and asks that she be allowed to call for company. Pandarus says to do so would be foolish. He then begins to talk of Troilus, whom he claims has just arrived in a state of great distress because of a rumor that Criseyde has fallen in love with someone else. Pandarus urges her to provide Troilus with some reassurance of her faithfulness, and Criseyde promises that she will, the very next day. Pandarus, of course, wants her to see him tonight, and finally, after assuring Criseyde that her honor will remain intact, he gets his wish. At first Criseyde is so abashed by Troilus' sudden appearance that she cannot speak. When she regains her composure, she renews her vows of love, denying the charge that she has been unfaithful and upbraiding Troilus for his jealousy. Troilus focuses only upon her anger. Telling her that he is not to blame for what is happening, he falls down in a faint. Pandarus seizes this opportunity to throw Troilus into bed with Criseyde, tearing off his outer clothing and urging his niece to assist with the man's resuscita-

tion. Criseyde, fearing that he may die, tries to rouse him by massaging his wrists and hands and kissing him, all the while exclaiming that all is forgiven. When he revives, she continues to kiss and embrace him. Pandarus, delighted with the way things seem to be proceeding, takes the candle and leaves them alone.

Finding herself unafraid of Troilus being in her bed, Criseyde decides to let him stay, but insists upon knowing who told him she was unfaithful. If he cannot tell her, she says, she will believe that he has made the story up in order to test her, which he could only have done out of malice. Knowing that he dares not be completely honest, Troilus says that he became jealous when he saw her looking at another man. Criseyde accuses him of being childish and makes him promise to cease such foolish behavior. Troilus swears never to offend her again. At this point, he suddenly seizes her in his arms. Initially, the narrator uses an image of violence to convey Criseyde's impression, suggesting that she is like the lark who has been seized by a sparrowhawk. Soon, however, she opens her heart to her lover and finds her anxiety melting away.

After experiencing the bliss of complete physical union, the lovers exchange rings. Criseyde also gives Troilus a gold and silver brooch set with a ruby shaped like a heart. Remembering the uncertainty and anxiety which characterized their courtship, the lovers contrast those events with present joy. The dawn arrives all too soon, requiring that Troilus leave to preclude any chance of their being discovered. After Troilus' departure, Pandarus comes to visit Criseyde, who scolds him for bringing Troilus to her bed, hinting that she suspects him of deception. In typical fashion, Pandarus tells her that if she blames him in anything, she may cut off his head, while at the same time giving her a hug and a kiss, using his comic behavior to dispel the atmosphere of tension.

It isn't long before the two lovers are able to meet again. Their second intimate encounter is even better than the first because they no longer feel any reluctance or anxiety about being together. Moreover, their joy, the narrator claims, is so complete that it cannot be described in words. When the dawn comes, they once again part in sorrow, but not without establishing a time for their next meeting, so that, for a time, they live in a state of nearly perpetual bliss. Troilus, whose gender and responsibilities put him continually in the public sphere, becomes even more famous for his nobility, his generosity and his skill on the battlefield.

Ever mindful of the debt he owes to his lover's uncle, from time to time Troilus finds the opportunity to speak with him, which also provides him with the chance to praise Criseyde's beauty and her character. He also continues to praise the properties of love, as is illustrated in the *Canticus Troili* ("Song of Troilus") which helps to bring book three to a conclusion. In contrast to his earlier verses in praise of love, this time Troilus speaks of it as a force that binds together otherwise contrary or disruptive forces in nature, as well as the hearts of men and women, and thus keeps the universe functioning in an orderly fashion. Book three closes with further description of how being in love has affected Troilus, reemphasizing his sympathy for other lovers.

Book four opens with confirmation of the foreboding hinted at in the farewell to the Muses at the end of book three. This is followed by the narrator's explicit statement that Fortune began to turn her face away from Troilus. The subject of this book will be the story of Criseyde's betrayal. Thus, to guide his inspiration he now calls upon the "Herynes" or ERINYES, also known as the Furies in Greek literature and mythology, to assist him. He further enlists the aid of MARS (1), the Greek god of war.

Fittingly enough, after the invocation of Mars, the narrative reopens with a return to the circumstances surrounding the romance between Troilus and Criseyde, the Trojan War. Following a battle during which the Trojans suffer the greatest losses, the Greeks ask for a declared truce so that the two sides can meet together for an exchange of prisoners. The Trojans agree and preparations ensue. Calkas, Criseyde's father, who foresaw the defeat of the Trojans and fled to the Greek side, now approaches the Greek leaders, asking that one of the Trojan prisoners be exchanged for his daughter, who remains inside the besieged city. Out of consideration for the service he has provided to the Greek side, they grant his request, and a Trojan warrior named ANTENOR, who himself will eventually betray the Trojans, is offered for the exchange.

Troilus is present at the council meeting where the exchange is proposed and agreed upon, despite Ector's disapproval. He is stunned by the news and unable to think of a solution; he only knows that he cannot speak without revealing his love affair and thus breaking his sworn promise to Criseyde. Ector is rebuked by the rest of the assembly for not wanting to give up this woman, the daughter of a traitor, in exchange for a valued warrior. Once arrangements regarding the exchange of prisoners have been concluded, the assembly adjourns. Troilus, overwhelmed by the sudden turn of events, takes to his bed where he wails and moans the hopelessness of his situation, upbraiding Fortune who has turned her back on him.

Pandarus, who also attended the assembly and is equally stunned by the news, goes to visit Troilus. For a while they cry together, which provides some consolation. Pandarus' grief is quickly spent, and it is not long before he asks Troilus to cheer up and to consider that at least he has experienced the consummation of his desire, something Pandarus has yet to enjoy. He goes on to suggest that Troilus stop mourning the loss of

Criseyde and consider taking one of the city's other fair ladies as a lover. Troilus declines his friend's advice, saying he would rather die first. Furthermore, he says to Pandarus, if he thinks such a course of action advisable, why hasn't he tried it himself rather than always fruitlessly pursuing the same unobtainable woman? Without waiting for an answer, Troilus continues with his lament, praying for death to come and take him, until Pandarus tries another argument: If Troilus loves Criseyde so much, then he should just kidnap her. Troilus claims he has already considered and rejected that solution, reminding Pandarus that the city is now at war over a similar crime, his brother PARIS' (1) kidnapping of Helen. Furthermore, he would have to defy the will of his father, PRIAM, who made the decision to surrender Criseyde in exchange for Antenor. Troilus goes on to say that he has also thought of revealing the situation to his father and asking him to rescind the order, but is afraid to do so without consulting Criseyde. Pandarus refuses to give up, urging Troilus that he must do something to help himself and stop worrying so much about other people. He also argues that Criseyde's feelings may be very different from what Troilus fears, that she could consider him a weak fool to let her go. Or, he reasons, if she doesn't want to stay with Troilus, then perhaps she doesn't love him anyway. In this way, he finally convinces Troilus at least to talk to Criseyde.

Criseyde, meanwhile, has also heard the news from the assembly, but hopes that it is just a rumor. She cares little for her father and has no wish to join him; however, her feelings for Troilus are as strong as ever. Some women who have heard the assembly's decision come to visit Criseyde to tell her the news. While they are there, Criseyde begins to cry, remembering all the joy she has experienced with Troilus and anticipating the loss that is to come. When the women try to console her, she dismisses them and goes to bed, weeping and tearing her hair. Like Troilus, she curses Fortune, and swears that she will henceforth wear black, the color of mourning, until she dies. The narrator finally breaks off, saying he records no more of her lament because he feels unable to do it justice.

Pandarus, eager to arrange a meeting between Troilus and his niece, arrives at Criseyde's house and finds her in a pitiful state. Revealing that he has just come from Troilus, Pandarus tells her that her lover wishes to see her so that together they may devise some remedy to their misfortune.

Pandarus then departs in search of Troilus, who has gone to a temple to pray to the gods to send him death since he can see no other solution to his pain. In the midst of his prayers, Troilus presents a long meditation on the role of predestination in human life. The argument Troilus makes in these lines closely follows that presented by BOETHIUS in his *Consolation of Philosophy,* although Troilus concludes fatalistically, without presenting Boethius' defense of human free will. Pandarus arrives and begins to upbraid him for wallowing in self-pity. Criseyde as yet remains in the city and may still be saved. Telling Troilus of her willingness to meet, Pandarus arranges the tryst.

When the two lovers come together they at first find themselves unable to speak, but can only cry together in sorrow and fear of what is to come. Exhausted, Criseyde cries out for Troilus to help her and faints. When Troilus is unable to arouse her, he believes that she has died. He unsheathes his sword and is about to follow her (as he thinks), when she suddenly awakens. Troilus immediately comforts her, and her spirits slowly revive. When Criseyde asks why his sword is drawn, Troilus reveals that he thought she was dead and was going to take his own life. Hearing this, Criseyde vows that if he had, she would have done the same. Realizing that dawn is on its way, they go to bed, but this fails to provide them with its accustomed solace.

In the midst of their sorrow, Criseyde tells Troilus that it is time to look beyond their present misery to see what they can do for themselves. Considering thus, she announces what appears a straightforward solution: She will leave willingly in exchange for the prisoner Antenor, but then, since there is no reason for the Greeks to hold her prisoner, she will simply return to Troy after a week or two. This she will be able to do because of the continuing truce between the two warring parties. Her optimism is boosted by the rumor that the Greeks and Trojans are on the verge of peacefully concluding their conflict. When she is done, the narrator intrudes for a moment to assure the reader that she speaks in earnest and with good intentions. Troilus feels strong misgivings about the solutions she has projected, but is temporarily able to quell his fears, at least long enough for the two to enjoy making love. Afterward, however, he reveals his fear that her plans may fail. First, he does not believe she will be able to deceive her father, a man known for his wisdom. And what if her father should desire her to marry a Greek to further his own ends? Her father may frighten her with prophecies, or she may, after spending some time in their company, discover some inclination to remain among the Greek soldiers. Therefore, he concludes, they should run away now, while they are still together, rather than take the chance of being separated. Having enough wealth between them to support themselves for the rest of their lives, he reasons, they need not fear poverty; nor would they be forced to live always among strangers, since he has many friends in other cities and countries.

Criseyde is not at all swayed by his arguments, but feels that running away will bring dishonor upon both of them by revealing their affair, and particularly upon him for deserting his people when they depend on his leadership in the Trojan army. She argues that he is too impatient and unreasonable, and reiterates her promise to return. When Troilus still insists that it would be wiser to run away, Criseyde accuses him of mistrusting her and reassures him once more of her devotion. If she did not believe she would be able to return in a short time, she swears she would kill herself here and now. Troilus pledges his faith in exchange for hers and they are reconciled, but when the dawn arrives and they part company, Troilus remains filled with foreboding.

The prologue to book five is shorter than that of the preceding books and refers immediately to the fatal destiny of the two lovers, which has been determined, the narrator claims, by Jove (JUPITER) and the three angry PARCAE (Fates). Three years have passed since Troilus first fell in love with Criseyde.

On the morning of her departure, Troilus accompanies Criseyde as she rides out of the city. DIOMEDE, a Greek warrior, comes to escort her to her father. When Troilus turns to go back to the city, Diomede grabs Criseyde's bridle. Although he is perceptive enough to see that she is in love with Troilus, he begins considering how to further his own intentions in winning her favor. First he tries to comfort her, offering to do anything within his power to ease her sorrow. He begs her to consider him as a brother, but his pledges of service soon modulate into the words of a suitor as he vows that he has never loved a lady till now and begs her to have mercy on him. Criseyde is so oppressed with sorrow that she hears little of what he is saying, but she thanks him for his efforts on her behalf and accepts his offer of friendship. When they reach the Greek camp, she is delivered to her father, who joyfully embraces her.

Meanwhile Troilus, having returned home, shuts himself up in a chamber where he curses the gods. Taking to his bed, he wallows there in pain and fury, crying out upon the loss of his lover. Finally he falls asleep, but he has horrible dreams. At dawn he sends for Pandarus. As soon as Pandarus enters his bedchamber, Troilus begins talking of plans for his funeral and the disposal of his worldly goods. He particularly desires that Pandarus should remove the ashes of his heart from the funeral pyre, put them in a golden urn and give the urn to Criseyde. Although he feels sympathy for Troilus, Pandarus seems to be growing tired of his friend's wallowing in self-pity. He criticizes Troilus for overreacting, reminding him that time will bring the cure to his present woe. What Troilus needs, he suggests, is some entertainment to help the time pass quickly. With that in mind, he urges Troilus to join him in taking advantage of the continuing truce to visit SARPEDON, the king of Licia, one of the Trojan's allies. This will get Troilus up and out of bed; if he remains there much longer, people will begin to think he is a coward, feigning sickness so that he doesn't have to fight again. Troilus consents to visit Sarpedon, where the two men are entertained with feasting, music, dancing and other festivities. Troilus, however, finds himself incapable of enjoyment. He sits by himself reading Criseyde's old letters and reliving their moments together. When they return to Troy, Troilus visits his lover's abandoned house and other places in the city that remind him of her. Back at home, he composes another song in which he personifies Criseyde as a star and himself as a ship. Having lost her, he sails blindly toward his death.

The days and nights seem to pass more and more slowly. Troilus takes to walking on the city walls, looking out on the Greek host where Criseyde is, and imagining the wind is made of her sighs. Pandarus is often with him during this period of waiting, and does his best to soothe Troilus and lighten his mood.

Back at the Greek camp, Criseyde finds herself unable to convince her father to let her return to Troy. She considers stealing away after dark but is afraid that if caught, she will be considered a spy; or even worse, that she may be apprehended by a man who will take advantage of her. She reproaches herself for not following Troilus' plan for them to run away together.

Diomede is eager to woo Criseyde, and sets various unspecified traps to catch her heart, but his efforts are frustrated by Criseyde's sadness. He can only cheer himself with the thought that to win her over despite her mourning for Troilus would make him a true conqueror.

At this point, Chaucer pauses to describe the physical characteristics of the three lovers. Diomede is described as a courageous man, possessing a stern voice and strong, stocky limbs. He is hard, impetuous and eager to perform chivalrous deeds, just like his father, Tideus. He also has a reputation for being "of tonge large" [large of tongue], which could mean that he is a braggart, or, in a more positive sense, that he is able to speak with lavish eloquence. The description of him in this section is followed by one of Criseyde, which adds little information to that which was provided in books one, two and three, aside from one very interesting detail—that her eyebrows are joined together, which would be a violation of the conventional ideal of female beauty during the 14th century. This one physical flaw is mirrored by one of character. Although she is wise, straightforward, well-educated and well-spoken, charitable, dignified, cheerful and generous as well as tenderhearted, her determination or mood ("corage") is likely to waver, a detail that prepares us for what is to come. The description of Troilus which follows that of Criseyde shows him to be tall, perfectly proportioned, young, vigorous, strong, as true as steel and as hardy as a lion. An implied comparison to Diomede is established with the statement that during the time in which

he lived, Troilus was second to no man in bravery, although his strength might well be less than that of a giant.

On the 10th day after Criseyde has come to the Greek camp, on the same day that she promised to return to Troilus, Diomede visits Calkas. He directs most of his attention to Criseyde, asking her opinion on various matters including the siege of Troy and whether or not she finds the Greeks "strange" in their manners and customs. He also asks why her father has waited so long to marry her to some worthy knight. Criseyde, not understanding his intentions, answers him as best she can. Diomede refuses to let the subject drop and begins to speculate that she is in love with some Trojan. If that is true, he states, it is a pity because not a single one of that city's inhabitants is going to escape death when the Greeks have their revenge. And he knows that the Greeks are going to win because of her father's prophecies. Therefore, she ought to forego any affection she has for the Trojans and seek among the Greeks for a more perfect love, which he, more eager to serve her than to be king of the 12 Greek nations, would be happy to provide. He again swears that she is the first woman he has ever loved and vows to serve her as heartily as he can if she will only grant him the opportunity. So movingly does he speak that Criseyde grants his request to see her again, on the condition that he leave off trying to win her love. She criticizes the disdain he expresses for the people of Troy, saying that although the Greeks are worthy, the Trojans are equally so. Finally, she explains that she is a widow and has no desire to love or wed again before she dies. She does, however, give him slight encouragement with the promise that if she should ever love a Greek, he will be the man. Diomede ignores her request not to pursue her love, and continues to beg for mercy. Later in the evening, after he has gone, Criseyde ponders what he has said. She considers his status as the son of a king, compared to the perils that await in Troy and her own lack of friends. Thus begin to grow the reasons why she will ultimately decide to stay with the Greeks.

To make a long story short (says the narrator), the next day Diomede spoke so well for himself and was so successful in comforting Criseyde that he soon took away the greatest part of her pain. Not long after this occasion, she presents him with a bay steed that had belonged to Troilus (which, according to one of Chaucer's sources, Diomede had won from Troilus, presented to Criseyde, and then requested back again when he lost his own horse). She also gives him a brooch that Troilus had given her and one of her sleeves to use as a pennon on his lance. As if to mitigate the apparent callousness of her actions, the narrator digresses at this point to tell us that Criseyde seems to have truly loved Diomede, as was later shown by the way she cared for him when Troilus wounded him in battle.

Furthermore, he says, there was never a woman who felt more woe than Criseyde when she betrayed Troilus, knowing that her name would be despised forever.

The story returns to Troilus on the evening before Criseyde's promised return. He spends a restless night and, rising with the dawn, summons Pandarus to accompany him to the city walls, where they eagerly watch all who approach. At first they imagine that every person who approaches is Criseyde, until each one draws close enough for them to realize their mistake. When she doesn't arrive in the morning hours, Troilus starts rationalizing her failure to appear, blaming it on her father. They leave their post to have a meal and then return for the afternoon watch. Despite her continuing absence, Troilus maintains his optimism, coming up with various reasons why she could have been delayed, until night comes and the gates of the city are closed. At this point, Pandarus begins to doubt his niece's intention to return, but he says nothing to his friend. On his way home, Troilus decides that he must have miscounted the days, but after one more day of watching and waiting, he gives up.

Determining that he must die, Troilus isolates and begins to starve himself. He grows so weak from lack of food and exercise that he can only walk with the aid of a crutch. When his family tries to find out what is wrong, he refuses to tell anyone the source of his pain but continues to look forward to nothing but death. During this period of mourning, Troilus dreams that he is walking in a forest, weeping over his loss of Criseyde. Walking up and down he comes upon a great boar sleeping in the sun. Criseyde lies in the boar's embrace, kissing him while he sleeps. In the morning Troilus sends for Pandarus, to whom he describes the dream along with his own opinion that it is a revelation sent by the gods to inform him of Criseyde's betrayal. Pandarus cautions him against such hasty interpretation and provides an alternative reading, suggesting that the boar represents Criseyde's old father, Calkas. He then urges Troilus to write to Criseyde, expressing his fears and asking for an explanation of her delay. Consenting to the wisdom of this plan, Troilus composes a letter in which he describes his suffering, reminds her of her promise to return in 10 days, and notes that two months have now passed. He claims that all he currently suffers will be turned to joy as soon as she returns, but still urges her to respond, whatever the state of her feelings toward him. Upon receiving his letter, Criseyde immediately writes back, promising that she will come but professing that she is unable to tell him when. Troilus is only mildly reassured by her letter. The longer she delays, the more his suffering grows, and his might decreases as his hope wanes. He falls back into his old despair, refusing food, drink and conversation, and begins to dwell upon the dream in which Criseyde appeared in the boar's embrace. Finally, he

asks his sister CASSANDRA, who is reputed to have the gift of prophecy, to interpret it for him. Her lengthy interpretation contains the entire story of STATIUS' *Thebaid* in capsule form, which appears to be given in order to establish the genealogy of Diomede, who, she at last informs him, has become Criseyde's new lover. Troilus angrily refuses to believe her. His rage overcomes his woe and he leaves his bed to find some answers for himself.

The death of his brother Ector, slain in battle by the Greek ACHILLES, diverts Troilus from his purpose and foreshadows the coming misfortunes of the city. Troilus considers various means of locating Criseyde in the Greek camp, including disguising himself as a pilgrim and going to search for her himself, but then he considers what would happen if he were recognized and captured. He continues writing to her and eventually receives another letter. She again promises to return, but still refuses to say when. She also hints that she is annoyed by his impatience and by some rumors she has heard. The rumors suggest that he has revealed their love affair and would deceive her regarding his true intentions. But it does not matter, she says, for she cannot believe that he would be anything but noble and true. Finally, she asks that whatever may happen, she may always have his good word and friendship.

Troilus is troubled by the letter, which seems to him strange and a harbinger of change. Nevertheless he still clings to the hope that she will return until one day when Diomede's torn tunic is paraded through the streets as a token of Deiphebus' victory in battle that day. On the collar of that tunic Troilus sees the brooch he gave Criseyde to keep in remembrance of him on the day that she left the city. Now certain of her disloyalty, he sends for Pandarus and tells him what he has seen. Pandarus curses his niece, hoping that death will soon take her. Troilus, however, finds that he cannot stop loving her, in spite of everything. Unable to come up with any other remedy, he vows to seek death in battle.

Troilus reenters the war, fighting relentlessly and always seeking Diomede. They meet on many occasions and exchange blows, but none proves fatal. At this point the narrator takes a brief detour from his story to say that if the reader desires to hear more about Troilus' prowess in battle, he should consult DARES, the supposed author of an ancient history of the Trojan War. As for the narrator's treatment of Criseyde, he asks his female readers not to be angry with him over Criseyde's faults, since he did not invent them himself but merely repeated what others have written. It would give him great joy, he says, if they so desire, to write about PENELOPE or the good ALCESTIS. These several stanzas are followed by an envoy, a kind of formal launching of his book to take its place in the world of poetry.

The narrative resumes with the report of Troilus' death at the hands of Achilles. Following his death, Troilus' spirit leaves his body and flies up to the eighth sphere (*see* PTOLEMY), where he can look down and observe the wandering stars (planets) and hear the music created by the movement of the spheres. Looking down at the earth from such a great height, he observes the smallness of the planet and begins to despise the wretchedness of human vanity, laughing at the sorrow of those who weep for his death. The final stanzas of the poem offer to apply a Christian coloring to the pagan story, admonishing young people to give their love to God rather than to someone who can betray them. Troilus' fate is considered as an example of how the pagan gods have rewarded those who worship them. Chaucer dedicates the poem to John GOWER ("moral Gower") and Ralph STRODE ("philosophical Strode"), asking that they provide any corrections that may be desirable, and to Christ, whom he beseeches to grant him mercy and protection.

COMMENTARY

Troilus and Criseyde is the longest single poem that Chaucer wrote. Its exact date of composition is unknown, but a number of convincing arguments have been made for assigning it to the decade of the 1380s. It must have been written before 1388, since Thomas USK, who died in that year, drew upon it to write his own *Testament of Love*. Because the philosophical dimension of Chaucer's *Troilus* derives from Boethius' *Consolation of Philosophy,* a number of scholars believe that Chaucer was working on his translation of Boethius (BOECE) at or around the same time. "The KNIGHT'S TALE," the first to be told on the pilgrimage to CANTERBURY, is also heavily influenced by Boethius.

The "historical" event that serves as backdrop to the action of Chaucer's poem is the Trojan War. The history of this ancient war was a popular topic among medieval authors, most of whom treated the entire story from beginning to end. Benoît de Sainte-Maure, a French writer of the 12th century, was the first to describe the love affair between Troilus and Criseyde, but in his work it is imbedded within a long chronicle-style narrative called the *Roman de Troie* ("Romance of Troy"). Not until the Italian writer BOCCACCIO came along and composed *Il FILOSTRATO* did an author focus exclusively on the lovers' relationship against the backdrop of the war. Boccaccio's poem appeared in the late 1330s and constitutes the major source of Chaucer's work, despite the latter's claim to have taken the story from a fictitious author named LOLLIUS. The tight focus of both Chaucer's and Boccaccio's narratives allowed them to emphasize the examination of human motive and behavior, particularly that belonging to the realm of the emotions.

The changes Chaucer made to Boccaccio's text consisted primarily of expanding some portions and contracting or eliminating others. The overall effect of his changes is a shift in emphasis from the personal to the philosophical, while retaining the Italian author's concern with the emotional lives of his characters. So while Boccaccio identifies himself with Troiolo (the counterpart of Chaucer's Troilus) and claims to have suffered a similar betrayal at the hands of a beautiful but faithless young lady, Chaucer's narrator is sympathetic to Troilus from the standpoint of an uninvolved observer. Quite early in the poem, Chaucer's narrator admits that he has no personal experience of love. Be that as it may, love is without a doubt the poem's dominant theme, and when philosophical reflections or notions of tragedy enter into the story, they do so within the context of that theme.

Chaucer's interest in love as a literary theme was already well established by the time he wrote *Troilus and Criseyde.* It was a principal topic of concern in *The BOOK OF THE DUCHESS* and *The PARLIAMENT OF FOWLS.* And in book two of *The HOUSE OF FAME,* the EAGLE who has been sent to transport the narrator, "Geffrey," to his destination informs him that this experience has been sent by Jove to reward him for his previously unrewarded service to Cupid, the god of love. It is not, moreover, any vague notion of romantic love that informs Chaucer's treatment of this theme, but a complex literary tradition ultimately derived from the French troubadours and trouvères of the 11th and 12th centuries. In literary criticism that tradition has come to be known as COURTLY LOVE, and its influence provides an explanation for the assumptions and rules of behavior that characterize the affair between Chaucer's Trojan lovers.

The book *De Arte Honeste Amandi* ("The Art of Loving Decently"), written by Andreas Capellanus in the 12th century and based on the writings of OVID in the *Ars Amatoria* ("The Art of Love"), provides a means of understanding the abstract principles and laws underlying the courtly system. One basic principle of this system is the idea that courtly love is sensual and erotic. Andreas defines love as a passion arising from the observance of beauty in the opposite sex. The goal of this passion is sexual fulfillment. In keeping with this idea, nearly three-fifth's of Chaucer's *Troilus* is devoted to a minutely detailed description of the lovers' developing desire with its culmination in the moment of sexual union. Another important principle of the courtly love system requires that the lady who is the object of the man's affections be difficult to obtain. This difficulty must furthermore arise primarily from her own will rather than from external obstacles. Criseyde's initial reaction to Troilus and the subsequent difficulty he encounters in winning her fulfills this requirement. One final feature of courtly love relevant here is the necessity for secrecy. Sometimes this necessity arose from the fact that one or other of the lovers was married to someone else. In this case, the need for secrecy arises from Criseyde's desire to remain autonomous (i.e., unmarried) and her fear that her reputation would suffer should it be known that she has a lover. She frequently mentions her dread of becoming the subject of gossip. Andreas notes that a divulged love rarely lasts, an idea that also seems to inform Criseyde's reluctance to go public with the affair. One positive effect of courtly love was to exalt and ennoble those who practiced it. This is clearly seen in the behavior of Troilus, who, under the influence of his passion for Criseyde, becomes even more generous, affable and valorous on the battlefield than he has been before. Conversely, the most grievous fault that could be committed by a lover was inconstancy, otherwise known as betrayal. Criseyde, of course, is guilty of this crime, and when Troilus discovers her guilt, his doom is sealed. A full discussion of the role that courtly love plays in the poem may be found in Thomas Kirby's *Chaucer's Troilus: A Study in Courtly Love* (1940).

Woven into the conventions of courtly love that inform this poem is a philosophical dimension that derives from the medieval conception of tragedy as arising from the vicissitudes of Fortune (in contrast to classical and Shakespearean tragedy, in which character is the determining factor). It was this conception of tragedy that Boethius wrestled with in the *Consolation of Philosophy*. Chaucer's use of Boethian philosophy in *Troilus and Criseyde* has its most dramatic impact at the end of the poem, when, after describing the journey of Troilus' spirit up into the heavens, the narrator condemns every aspect of the morality upon which the poem's characters have acted, directing his young readers to repudiate the vanity of earthly, physical love in favor of loving Christ. A number of critics have regarded this palinode as a flaw because of the way that it contradicts the apparent meaning of everything that has gone before. And it does, without a doubt, seriously undermine a sympathetic reading of the lovers' plight and their suffering. In this light, the ending seems disjunctive. But if the entire poem is understood to reflect the philosophical views of Boethius, the case is altered and the ending seems to follow quite naturally from what has gone before.

The *Consolation*'s primary concern is to explore how mankind may cope with the vicissitudes of Fortune. The most important argument made by LADY PHILOSOPHY within Boethius' text is that a human being may avoid the suffering that attends the deprivation of worldly attainments by refusing to become overly attached to such attainments. These "false goods" (things that appear to be good but that can actually become a source of vice and misery) are power, dignities and fame. Boethius does not include romantic love

among the false goods, and perhaps Chaucer, in providing his Troilus with a Boethian coloring, sees himself filling a gap. JEAN DE MEUN, coauthor of the *ROMAN DE LA ROSE,* a text that also influenced Chaucer's thinking, mentions that lovers invite the caprice of Fortune just as much as ambitious men, and Chaucer does emphasize, over and over, the role that Fortune plays in the lovers' tragedy, a role of which both lovers are painfully aware.

Near the beginning of the poem, although Cupid shoots the arrow that wounds Troilus with the sight of Criseyde's beauty, Troilus immediately blames Fortune, not the god of Love, for his plight. Comparing his former happiness to his present torment, he tells Pandarus, "Fortune is my fo; / Ne al the men that riden konne or go / May of hire cruel whiel the harm withstonde; / For as hire list she pleyeth with free and bonde" (book 1, lines 837–40) [Fortune is my enemy; / Not a single one of all mankind / May withstand the cruel torment of her wheel; / For just as she desires, she plays with both freemen and slaves]. Pandarus does not deny that Fortune is involved, but he does suggests a different perspective on her involvement. First he reminds Troilus that everyone suffers, from time to time, the changes of Fortune; then he suggests that Troilus look forward to her wheel's next revolution, which will certainly bring him joy. When Troilus does finally win Criseyde's heart, however, he seems to forget the role of Fortune, addressing his thanks and hymns of praise to Venus, Cupid and HYMEN, those gods who have assisted him, he believes, in gaining his desire. For the time being, Troilus forgets about Fortune, but the narrator steps in to remind us that she is still there. The prologue to book four opens with these words: "But al to litel, weylaway the whyle, / Lasteth swich joie, ythonked be Fortune, / That semeth trewest whan she wol bygyle / That she hem hent and blent, traitour comune!" (lines 1–5) [But all too little, alas the while, / Lasts such joy, thanks to Fortune, / Who seems most true when she wishes to beguile / Those whom she seizes and blinds, like a common traitor!]. The stanza following this one specifically notes that the next revolution of Fortune's wheel will bring Troilus down and set Diomede up in his place. Upon hearing the news that Criseyde will be given to the Greeks in exchange for the Trojan Antenor, and himself unable to discover a remedy for their plight, Troilus does indeed put the blame on Fortune. His meditation on the idea of predestination, derived directly from Boethius, concludes that he will lose Criseyde no matter what action he takes, but Troilus' argument significantly breaks off before presenting Boethius' defense of free will.

From the moment that he saw Criseyde in Athena's temple, Troilus has considered himself a victim of forces beyond his control. Criseyde, on the other hand, while acknowledging the inescapable pressures and consequences of external events, consistently exercises her will in making choices. Although she finds Troilus attractive, it is still necessary, for her, to make a conscious decision that she will accept his devotion and service. And even though she is tricked into the nocturnal meeting that leads to their sexual union, when Troilus embraces her with sudden passion, saying, "O swete, as evere mot I gon, / Now be ye kaught; now is ther but we tweyne!" (book 3, lines 1206–07) [O sweet, as I may ever thrive, / Now are you caught; now that there is none but us two (here)!], she informs him that "Ne hadde I er now, my swete herte deere, / Ben yolde, ywis, I were now nought heere!" (book 3, lines 1210–11) [If I had not before now, my dear sweet heart, / Already yielded, indeed, I would not be here now!]. She may have little control over the events that force her removal to the Greek camp, but she exercises her will both in choosing to go and in deciding against returning to Troy, in the latter instance weighing the difficulty and dangers involved against the security she feels under the protection of her father and Diomede. Troilus finally stops blaming Fortune when he sees the brooch he gave Criseyde adorning Diomede's tunic, but the narrator reminds us of her continuing presence when he notes that despite the two men's efforts, Fortune would allow neither Diomede nor Troilus to die by the other's hand.

Troilus' inability to acknowledge the force of human free will seems to have two important functions. First, it informs his own behavior, providing an explanation for his otherwise incomprehensible reluctance to take action on his own behalf in matters of love, a reluctance that shows up all the more strikingly in comparison with Diomede's decisiveness and self-determination. Yet while Diomede, Criseyde and Pandarus are all more capable of acting on their own behalf than is Troilus, their attitudes and behavior are at best practical and opportunist, in contrast to the idealism which makes Troilus the most noble and admirable of the group. What ultimately defeats him is not his inability to act, which as often arises from his desire not to hurt or offend someone as it does from a fear of being hurt or from his fatalism, but the limitations of his philosophical perspective. Having established himself so firmly as a worshipper of the god of love, when his religion fails him he can see no other alternative but death. Without Lady Philosophy to instruct him, with no gods to turn to but those of the pagan pantheon, he can go no further, at least not until after he has died and can compare the felicity of heaven to the wretched vanity of blind lust such as he experienced while on Earth. The philosophy of this poem has been examined in a number of critical texts. One of the most thorough and concise is Donald HOWARD's "The Philosophies in Chaucer's Troilus," in *The Wisdom of Poetry: Essays in Early English Literature* (1982).

Bringing his final commentary on the lives of Troilus and Criseyde to a close, the narrator exclaims, "Lo here, of payens corsed olde rites! / Lo here, what alle hire goddes may availle! / Lo here, thise wrecched worldes appetites! / Lo here, the fyn and guerdoun for travaille / Of Jove, Appollo, of Mars, of swich rascaille!" (book 5, lines 1849–53) [Lo here, of pagans' cursed rites! / Lo here, what all their gods may do! / Lo here, these wretched worldly appetites! / Lo here, the result and reward for one's effort / Given by Jove, Apollo, Mars, and other such worthless rabble]. With these words, the narrator appears to denounce not only the inadequacy of Troilus, but of the entire pagan worldview, which helps to explain why those characters who do possess the qualities Troilus lacks, particularly that of exercising free will, have other flaws that seem designed to undermine their appeal to a Christian audience. The typical hero of courtly romance would be a knight both virtuous and capable of exercising his will. The heroes and heroine of Chaucer's *Troilus* possess either one trait or the other, and as a result seem incomplete in spite of their additional beauties and/or attainments.

Interestingly, many early readers of the poem—Chaucer's contemporaries and those belonging to the centuries immediately following—seem to have understood the tragedy of the lovers quite differently. Troilus, as indicated above, was seen as weak, pitiable at best, while Criseyde's name became associated with absolute faithlessness and prostitution. The two best-known treatments of the story in the late medieval and Renaissance periods seem to follow this pattern. Robert HENRYSON's *Testament of Cresseid* takes up where Chaucer's poem leaves off, punishing Criseyde for deserting Troilus by having Diomede desert her in turn, after which she contracts leprosy. (In the Middle Ages this disease was considered a sexual one.) Compared to Henryson's moralizing treatment of the story, in which Troilus is still heroic, Shakespeare's *History of Troilus and Cressida* takes a satirical tone with all of the characters. Cressida is a flirtatious slut; Troilus, a self-absorbed man who mistakes lust for love; and Pandarus is little more than a pander (a word that derives from his name), one who procures a woman for another man to have sex with. Interestingly, the play was originally (in the quarto edition) grouped with the comedies, which in itself indicates Shakespeare's decidedly different take on the story. Generally speaking, the play looks at a number of ideas, including romantic love, heroic action and man's ability to reason, submitting them to unrelenting scrutiny and finding that men's actions rarely live up to their lofty words. Whether this conclusion has anything in common with what Chaucer was trying to communicate is up to the reader to decide.

For Further Reading: One of the most informative books on *Troilus and Criseyde* is *The European Tragedy of Troilus* (ed. Piero Boitani, 1989), which considers other treatments of the story, including Chaucer's source, Boccaccio's *Filostrato*. It also features an essay by Jill MANN comparing Shakespeare's treatment of Criseyde to Chaucer's, one by Derek BREWER on comedy and tragedy in the poem and a discussion of the poem's philosophical background. Another collection, *Essays on Troilus and Criseyde* (ed. Mary Salu, 1979), contains commentary on textual history, realism, paganism and rhetorical aspects of the poem, as well as a "Criseydan" reading of the poem which attempts to analyze the events of books one through three through the eyes of the female protagonist.

Trojan War   The Trojan War forms the historical backdrop for one of Chaucer's most famous poems, *TROILUS AND CRISEYDE*. For many years this war was thought to have been a fictional occurrence, existing only in the imagination of such writers as HOMER and VIRGIL. Archeological digs organized by Heinrich Schliemann in the late 19th century have provided surprising evidence that the war may have indeed taken place, although we have no existing written record of them apart from the literary ones. According to those accounts, this war was fought over the love of a woman, the famous HELEN OF TROY. Reported in legend to have been the most beautiful woman of ancient Greece, Helen, who was married to the Greek MENELAUS, was kidnapped by PARIS (1), a prince of the city of TROY. The Greeks attacked Troy not only to retrieve Helen, but also to avenge their honor which had been violated by Paris' behavior. The lengthy war which followed, and which led to the fall of Trojan civilization, was the subject of the classical Greek epic the *Iliad*. Versions of the story that circulated during the medieval period include Latin versions by DARES the Phrygian and DICTYS of Crete, along with BENOÎT DE SAINT MAURE's French *Roman de Troie* (Romance of Troy). The Trojan War was a popular subject in Chaucer's day, at least partly because the Trojans were believed to have brought classical culture to western Europe when they migrated to Italy after the fall of Troy. Chaucer's *Troilus and Criseyde* is a love story set in Troy during the siege of the Greeks, which ended when the Trojans accepted the Greeks' gift of a large wooden horse. The horse was filled with Greek soldiers, who, once the people of Troy had gone to sleep for the night, left their hiding place and easily overcame the city's resistance.

Trophee   In "The MONK'S TALE," the MONK's life of HERCULES refers to a writer named Trophee as a source for the story about Hercules setting up pillars at either boundary of the world to hold up the sky (lines 2117–18). The identity of this source remains uncertain, though Lyman KITTREDGE suggested that the Latin noun *tropaea*, or *trophea*, which could mean "pillars," may have been misunderstood as the name of a book or an author.

Trotula   Trotula di Ruggiero, also known simply as Trota, was a woman who practiced and taught medicine at Salerno, Italy, in the 12th century. She is believed to have written a handbook of general medical care, which was lost. Around 1200, however, three medical treatises appeared which circulated under the name of Trotula, all of which concentrate on the subjects of gynecology and obstetrics. These three texts, none of which was actually written by Trotula, exhibit a negative view of women and the female body that was typical of the Middle Ages. As a matter of fact, what little we do know of Trotula's practice shows that her approach to women's medicine was far more sympathetic and enlightened than that of her male contemporaries. For example, unlike most physicians of her day, she did not prescribe phlebotomy (bleeding) for such disorders as excessive menstruation. The WIFE OF BATH says that Trotula (i.e., one of the antifeminist treatises attributed to her) appears in the "Book of Wicked Wives" from which her fifth husband used to read aloud (line 677). The apparent purpose of this entertainment was to mortify the Wife's pride in being female.

Troy (Troye)   An ancient city that was situated near the Dardanelles in what is now Turkey. For centuries it was thought to have been a mythical city, existing only in ancient Greek and Roman literature. In the 19th century it was excavated by the German millionaire adventurer Heinrich Schliemann. Excavations revealed that there had been nine distinct settlements on the site, including the realm of King PRIAM that was engaged in the TROJAN WAR. The Trojan War forms the background for Chaucer's poem *TROILUS AND CRISEYDE*, and is alluded to in many of his other works, including *The BOOK OF THE DUCHESS*, *The HOUSE OF FAME*, the story of AENEAS and DIDO as related in *The LEGEND OF GOOD WOMEN* and a number of stories told in *The CANTERBURY TALES*.

Trumpington (Trumpyngton)   A village near the town of CAMBRIDGE in England. In "The REEVE'S TALE," some students who are attending Cambridge University travel to Trumpington to oversee the grinding of some grain for their college by the miller who lives in this village. Douglas GRAY's notes to the tale in *The RIVERSIDE CHAUCER* suggest that Chaucer's accurate description of the place and its location could have derived from local knowledge imparted by Sir Roger of Trumpington, a knight who served in King EDWARD III's household and who was responsible for the last of the annuities granted by the king to Philippa CHAUCER.

"Truth" One of the short poems attributed to Chaucer, "Truth" is written in the French BALLADE form with three stanzas of seven lines each (the most common ballade stanza was eight lines, but there were variations); a rhyme scheme of *ababbcc* with the same three rhymes repeated in all three stanzas; and a concluding envoy (a conventionalized stanza appearing at the close and usually addressed to a prince or some other important person). Each of the stanzas and the envoy concludes with the same one-line refrain, "And trouthe thee shal delivere, it is no drede" [And truth shall set you free, without a doubt], which could be seen as an echo of the words of Saint John the Evangelist: "Ye shall know the truth and the truth shall make you free." The poem's primary inspiration, however, was the work of Italian writer and philosopher BOETHIUS, whose *Consolation of Philosophy* contains similar advice for preserving the tranquility of the soul in an unstable and unpredictable world. In some of the manuscripts the poem is labeled "Balade de Bon Conseyl" ("Ballade of Good Counsel"), and the advice it offers urges the reader to preserve his own integrity by avoiding the "prees" (the ambitious crowd of people at the royal court) and exercising self-control rather than letting other people rule him. He is further instructed to accept what fate brings him with humility, rather than struggling against it. The final exhortation, to let his spirit lead him to his true home which is not on Earth, but in heaven, comes directly from LADY PHILOSOPHY's advice to Boethius in the *Consolation*. The envoy addressing someone named VACHE appears in only one of the manuscripts; nevertheless, it has aroused much speculation about the identity of the addressee, who has been tentatively identified as Sir Philip la Vache, who occupied positions in the king's household during the reigns of EDWARD III, RICHARD II and HENRY IV. The poem's early popularity is attested to by the fact that it survives in 22 manuscripts, plus two early printed editions by William CAXTON and William Thynne. Of all Chaucer's other works, only *The CANTERBURY TALES* and *A TREATISE ON THE ASTROLABE* are preserved in more manuscripts than "Truth." Like most of Chaucer's short poems, the date of composition is uncertain. Although the scribe John SHIRLEY includes a note in his transcription of the poem saying that "Truth" was a poem Chaucer wrote on his deathbed, the late date of composition implied by this statement has no other support and has not been generally accepted.

Trygwille *See* TRIGUILLA.

Tubal *See* AURORA (2).

Tullius *See* CICERO, MARCUS TULLIUS.

Tullius Hostillius A legendary king of Rome who supposedly ruled from 673 to 642 B.C. The LOATHLY HAG in "The WIFE OF BATH'S TALE" cites Tullius Hostillius as an example of a man who rose from poverty to nobility and wealth, as she argues against the idea that being poor is inherently ignoble (lines 1165–70). According to the Roman historian VALERIUS Maximus, this legendary king started out as a herdsman but rose to become the third king of Rome and, in his old age, enjoyed great honors and dignities.

Tully *See* CICERO, MARCUS TULLIUS.

Tunis A town in northern Africa near ancient CARTHAGE. In *The BOOK OF THE DUCHESS*, the narrator dreams that he wakes up in a beautiful chamber to hear the birds sing "so mery a soun, so swete entewnes, / That certes, for the toun of Tewnes / I nolde but I had herd hem synge" (lines 309–11) [so merry a sound, such sweet tunes, / That certainly, not even for the town of Tunis / Would I have given up hearing them sing]. Since "Tewnes" rhymes with "entewnes," the town was probably chosen for that reason and not because of its riches or other features.

Turkey (Turkye) In Chaucer's day, Turkey comprised the present-day part of Turkey that is in Asia Minor, an area that mostly fell under the rule of Ottoman and Seljuk Turks. In the GENERAL PROLOGUE TO *THE CANTERBURY TALES*, we are told that the KNIGHT (1) has been on military campaign in Turkey, fighting alongside the lord of "Palatye" (Balat) against another pagan king (lines 64–66). In *The BOOK OF THE DUCHESS*, the BLACK KNIGHT tells the dreamer-narrator that the lady with whom he was in love would never do silly, frivolous things like demand that her suitors should travel to faraway lands, like Turkey, ALEXANDRIA and other exotic locations or perform impossible deeds to prove their love for her (lines 1015–32).

Turnus According to classical mythology, Turnus was king of the Rutuli in the region of Ardea in Latium (modern Italy). LAVINIA, the daughter of King LATINUS, had been promised to Turnus in marriage, but Latinus reneged on his vow and gave his daughter to the Trojan AENEAS because of a prophecy that their children would become the founders of a great nation. The outraged Turnus declared war on the Trojans and was successful for a time, but eventually he was killed by Aeneas, bringing the conflict to an end. In "The KNIGHT'S TALE," Turnus is depicted on the walls of the TEMPLE OF VENUS along with others who died for love (line 1945). In "The MAN OF LAW'S TALE," the narrator notes that the fate of all men, including Turnus, was written in the stars before they were even born (lines 190–203). In

The HOUSE OF FAME, the death of Turnus is portrayed on the brass tablet which relates the story of how Aeneas established himself in Italy (line 457).

Tuve, Rosemond (1903–1964)   American scholar, perhaps best remembered for her innovative and brilliant critical work on the literature of the English Renaissance. Tuve received her Ph.D. from Bryn Mawr and went on to teach at Connecticut College for most of her career, although she obtained visiting lectureships at the University of Minnesota, Harvard and Princeton. The year before her death she joined the faculty of the University of Pennsylvania. Tuve's most significant work relevant to Chaucer studies is the book *Seasons and Months: Studies in a Tradition of Middle English Poetry* (1933). In the part of the book devoted to Chaucer, Tuve traces the poet's use of seasonal description back to the ancient Greeks and forward to the end of the Middle English period. Perhaps the only surprise in what seems a cut-and-dried description of straight-line influence is the realization that the famous April description that opens the GENERAL PROLOGUE TO *THE CANTERBURY TALES* reflects Chaucer's development of a long tradition, one that, until Tuve's work, had not been explained or catalogued. A later article, "Spring in Chaucer and Before Him" (*Modern Language Notes,* 1937) expands further on the lineage of these opening lines.

Tybre   *See* TIBER.

Tydeus   In classical mythology, Tydeus was the king of CALYDON and Periboea who, because of some crime he committed (perhaps killing his own brother), was exiled from his home. He was taken in by ADRASTUS, the king of ARGOS, who gave him his daughter, Deipyle, in marriage. Their son, DIOMEDE, became a hero in the TROJAN WAR. Tydeus accompanied Adrastus on the expedition of the SEVEN AGAINST THEBES and was killed in battle. His death at THEBES is mentioned in *ANELIDA AND ARCITE* (line 57). In *TROILUS AND CRISEYDE,* CASSANDRA includes him in her summary of the Theban conflict which she gives as a prelude to telling TROILUS that CRISEYDE has betrayed him with Tydeus' son, Diomede (book 5, lines 1480–1515). The latter is her interpretation of a dream that Troilus had in which he saw Criseyde embraced by a boar. Diomede's ancestor, MELEAGER, participated in the famous hunt of the Calydonian boar.

Tyle   *See* ULTIMA THULE.

Tyler, Wat   The leader of a group of peasants, artisans, craftsmen and yeoman from the county of Kent who converged on London in the PEASANTS' REVOLT OF 1381.

Almost nothing is known of Tyler outside his participation in the revolt. Donald HOWARD's biography of Chaucer suggests that he may have been a skilled worker—an artisan, or a former soldier, or even the rebellious younger son of a respectable and propertied Kentish family. What is certain is that he was a powerful orator and a determined leader, who is likely to have been responsible for the ideology of the revolt—the belief that the nobility was responsible for many of the ills the peasantry suffered in society, and that King RICHARD II, if he could be freed from the influence of these magnates, would take their side and see justice done.

To bring an end to the revolt, Tyler insisted upon, and was granted, a meeting with the king which took place at Smithfield near the Tower of London, just north of the city wall. At this meeting he informed the king of the peasants' grievances and demands, which included the abolition of villeinage (whereby peasants were legally bound to the land and unable to leave) and the revolutionary concept that there should be no lord in the land save the king, and no bishop save the archbishop of Canterbury. The lands of the wealthy nobility and clergy, he argued, should be confiscated and divided among the peasantry. Richard initially declared that all their demands would be met, but then an argument arose between Tyler and the mayor of London, who accompanied the king, and Tyler was suddenly pulled off his horse and killed. When the peasants appeared on the verge of riot, the king rode forward and shouted that he would be their captain. He then led them away from the city and ordered them to disperse, which they immediately did, believing, perhaps, that all their aims had been accomplished, or perhaps just at a loss for what to do without the guidance of their former leader. Within a month the king's promises were rescinded, the peasants were punished and the revolt had come to nothing.

typology   A method of literary interpretation that early Christian theologians applied to the Old Testament. According to this method, certain motifs, people and events belonging to the period of history before the birth of Christ could be understood as "types" or "figures" foreshadowing the life of the Savior. The tree of knowledge from which Adam and Eve ate the forbidden fruit, for example, was considered a type or forerunner of the cross upon which Christ was crucified. By the time Chaucer was writing, a complicated system of typology had been created which divided the meaning of anything in the Old Testament into four levels: the literal; the allegorical (referring to the New Testament or the church); the moral or tropological (referring to the fate of the individual soul); and the anagogical (referring to universal history and eschatology). The city of JERUSALEM, for example, allegorically symbolized the church; tropologically, the soul of the individual Christian; and anagogically, the heavenly city of God, the New Jerusalem spoken of in Revelation. This system of interpretation has often been applied to literary works written during the medieval period, with varying degrees of success. Some medieval scholars, such as D. W. ROBERTSON in his *Preface to Chaucer,* have argued for interpreting Chaucer's poetry using typology. Reading *The CANTERBURY TALES* as an allegory of the soul's pilgrimage to heaven is a good example of such an interpretation.

Tyre   A seaport in southwestern Lebanon, on the Mediterranean Sea. In ancient times it was the center of Phoenician culture and known for its cloth, which was dyed a brilliant purple derived from shellfish. This dye is mentioned in the *BOECE,* Chaucer's translation of BOETHIUS' *Consolation of Philosophy.* In Book Two, Metrum 5, LADY PHILOSOPHY describes the "first age" of man, a time when human beings coexisted peacefully without building cities or even tilling the soil, but by simply gathering the fruits of the earth. The dye manufactured in Tyre and used to make beautiful clothing is referred to as one of the luxurious trappings of modern civilization which, the implication is, we could easily do without (lines 10–15). In Book Three, Metrum 4, LADY PHILOSOPHY describes the emperor NERO appareled with white pearls and the beautiful purple of Tyre, both signifying his royalty and magnificence, in spite of which he was still hated by the Roman people (lines 1–8).

Tyrene   *Tyrene* is the name that Chaucer uses in the *BOECE,* his translation of BOETHIUS' *Consolation of Philosophy,* to refer to the Tyrrhenian, or Tuscan, Sea off the coast of Italy. LADY PHILOSOPHY tells Boethius that just as men do not look for gold in the trees or for diamonds on the vine, or seek deer in the Tyrhene waters, they also ought to know better than to seek on Earth the Sovereign God who properly lies in heaven (Book Three, Metrum 8, lines 1–24).

Tyresie   *See* TIRESIAS.

Tyrie (Tyro)   *See* TYRE.

Tytus   *See* DICTYS CRETENSIS.

Tzarev   *See* SARRAY.

U

Ugolino of Pisa Ugolino della Gherardesca, also known as Ugolino of Pisa, conspired with his grandson, and later with the archbishop of Pisa, to sieze control of the Italian city of PISA in 1288. In 1299 he was arrested by the citizens of Pisa on charges of betraying the city's interests and thrown into prison, together with his two sons and grandsons. They all died of starvation. The story of Ugolino's death appears in Chaucer's "MONK'S TALE," where it is told with considerable emphasis on the pathetic suffering of the children (lines 2407–62). This account of the tale is based primarily on DANTE's *Inferno,* where Ugolino appears in the lowest circle of hell because he was a traitor to his country. The emotional power of Chaucer's rendition has led many critics to proclaim it the finest of the 17 tragedies narrated by the MONK.

Ulixes *See* ULYSSES.

Ultima Thule (Thule) A legendary island thought to exist to the west and north of Britain. In the *BOECE,* Chaucer's translation of BOETHIUS' *CONSOLATION OF PHILOSOPHY,* LADY PHILOSOPHY tells Boethius that even if a man was lord over all lands from India in the east to Thule ("Tyle") in the west, his power would count for nothing if he were unable to control his lust (Book Three, Metrum 5, lines 1–11).

Ulysses In classical mythology, Ulysses (also known as Odysseus) was the son of Laertes, king of Ithaca. After succeeding to the throne of Ithaca, Ulysses became one of the suitors of Helen (HELEN OF TROY), acclaimed as the most beautiful woman in the world. It was he who proposed the idea that the suitors allow Helen the freedom to make her choice with the promise that the claim of whoever she chose would henceforth be defended by all of the other men who had wanted to marry her. Helen chose another man, MENELAUS, for her husband, and Ulysses married the prudent PENELOPE. Together they had one child, Telemachus; but despite his happiness, Ulysses was unable to remain aloof from the affairs of Helen. When she was kidnapped by PARIS (1) of TROY, Menelaus invoked the suitors' promise to raise a fighting force to attack the Trojans. At first Ulysses feigned madness to avoid taking part in the expedition, but eventually he agreed to participate and brought 12 vessels of fighting men. In addition to being a successful warrior, he was most highly valued for his ability to formulate strategy and for his eloquent and persuasive speaking ability, which helped settle differences among the Greeks. He was also responsible for finding ACHILLES, the warrior without whose presence the Greeks could not have won the war, and bringing him to Troy. Another crucial feat he performed was to steal the statue of PALLAS Athena from the PALLADIUM in Troy; a prophecy insisted that the city could never be taken as long as the statue remained intact. Finally, he was said to have planned the stratagem of the wooden horse by which Troy was invaded, and to have led the band of warriors who were hidden inside its body. His 10-year return trip from the Trojan conflict formed the subject of HOMER's *Odyssey,* one of the earliest and greatest epic poems.

His adventures are too lengthy to narrate here, but his encounter with the sorceress CIRCE is recounted by LADY PHILOSOPHY in the *BOECE,* Chaucer's translation of BOETHIUS' *Consolation of Philosophy.* She says that Ulysses' men were transformed by Circe into a boar, a lion, a tiger and a wolf. (Homer only mentions pigs.) When Lady Philosophy describes the transformation of Ulysses' men into different animals, she points out that Circe's power over those men was negligible compared to the power of vice, because while Circe transformed their appearance, their hearts and minds remained human. Those who are corrupted by vice, though they look the same on the outside, are destroyed within (Book Four, Metrum 3, lines 1–47). Ulysses is not mentioned in Chaucer's *TROILUS AND CRISEYDE,* in spite of the important role he played in the TROJAN WAR.

Urban Pope and martyr of the third century. Urban appears briefly in "The SECOND NUN'S TALE," where he receives the confessions and performs the baptisms of VALERIAN and TIBURTIUS, who are sent to him by CECILIA, the heroine of the tale. Urban died a martyr in A.D. 230, and virtually anything else that is known about him comes from the Life of Saint Cecilia, which itself is considered of doubtful authenticity.

Ursa *Ursa* and *Bere* (Bear) are the names by which LADY PHILOSOPHY refers to the constellation Ursa Major, Latin for "Great Bear," in the *BOECE,* Chaucer's translation of BOETHIUS' *Consolation of Philosophy*. The most conspicuous constellation in the northern sky (it contains the Big Dipper), Ursa Major never dips below the horizon. Lady Philosophy uses its stability in the skies as an example of how the stars abide peacefully by the rules of the universe (Book Four, Metrum 6, lines 1–18).

Usk, Thomas   A contemporary of Chaucer's who served as private secretary to John of Northampton, mayor of London after the PEASANTS' REVOLT OF 1381, and then as undersheriff of London. After becoming closely identified with those citizens who supported the interests of the king against those of the nobility, Usk became a victim of the political shake-up that occurred between King RICHARD II and his magnates, and was executed by order of the "Merciless Parliament" of 1388. Accused of treason, Usk was hanged, cut down while still alive and then beheaded. During his imprisonment prior to his death, Usk wrote an allegorical debate poem called "The Testament of Love," which borrows heavily from Chaucer's TROILUS AND CRISEYDE and from his BOECE (a Middle English translation of the *Consolation of Philosophy* by BOETHIUS). The latter seems to have provided Usk with the form for his work and was itself written while Boethius was in exile for supposed political crimes. Much of Usk's poem, which features a debate between the narrator and "Lady Love," seems aimed at exculpating Usk from the plots and intrigues with which he had been associated during the reign of King Richard. Some 19th-century editors believed that the "Testament" was written by Chaucer because of its borrowings. It was printed in the appendix to W. W. SKEAT's edition of Chaucer, titled *Chaucerian and Other Pieces* (1897).

V

Vache The man whom Chaucer addresses as "Vache" in the envoy of the short poem "TRUTH" is probably Sir Philip de la Vache, who married the daughter of one of Chaucer's closest friends, Sir Lewis Clifford. The poem advises its addressee to avoid conflict and striving, but to trust in steadfastness and truth to deliver him from present trouble. The final stanza, the envoy, speaks directly to Vache and advises him further to seek assistance from God as an escape from "thyn old wrecchednesse" (line 22) [thine old wretchedness]. Edith RICKERT originally made the argument for interpreting "vache" as a personal name instead of assigning the word its French meaning of "cow." Laila Gross' notes to the poem in *The RIVERSIDE CHAUCER* suggest that the poem may date from a period when Vache was in disfavor with the government, between 1386 and 1389. He regained his position in 1390 and was made a Knight of the Garter (*see* Order of the GARTER) in 1399. Rickert also suggested that Vache may have been the model for the FRANKLIN in the GENERAL PROLOGUE TO *THE CANTERBURY TALES* because of his reputation for generous hospitality.

Valence A town on the Rhone River near Lyon, France. In *The PARLIAMENT OF FOWLS*, the narrator observes the goddess VENUS in her temple (*see* TEMPLE OF VENUS) wearing nothing but a "subtyl coverchef of Valence" (line 272) [thin swatch of cloth from Valence]. A textile center in the Middle Ages, Valence remains competitive in the manufacture of fine cloth to this day.

Valentine, Saint (Valentyne) There are three Saint Valentines whose deaths are commemorated on February 14. The first is believed to have been a Roman priest of the third century who, with Saint Marius and his family, assisted the Christian martyrs during the persecution which occurred under the Roman emperor Claudius II. He was beheaded for his faith around A.D. 270. The second was a bishop of Terni in Italy who suffered martyrdom during the same persecution of Christians two or three years later. The third was Valentine of Rhetie, a seventh-century itinerant bishop. There was originally no connection between any of these saints and the celebration of love that has come to be associated with February 14. In fact, some schol-

ars believe that the tradition of Saint Valentine as the patron of lovers may have originated with Chaucer, since there is no strong evidence of a prior popular cult, or of another relationship between these or any other Saint Valentines (there are traditionally about seven—the exact number is uncertain) and the subject of erotic love. The association may have come about serendipitously because February 14 falls just after a traditional date for the beginning of spring. So it would seem that Chaucer began this literary and social tradition when he wrote, in *The PARLIAMENT OF FOWLS*, that the events of his dream took place "on Seynt Valentynes day, / Whan every foul cometh there to chese his make" (lines 309–10) [on Saint Valentine's day, / When every bird comes there to choose its mate]. Another reference to the saint appears in "The COMPLAINT OF MARS," which, according to the narrator, is sung by a bird on Saint Valentine's Day (lines 13–14). In *The LEGEND OF GOOD WOMEN*, the narrator notes that the birds all sing to Saint Valentine on the first day of May, which is also, here, considered the first day of spring (prologue F, lines 108–46). In CHAUCER'S RETRACTION, which appears at the end of "The PARSON'S TALE" in *The CANTERBURY TALES*, the poet mentions *The Parliament of Fowls*, referring to it as "The book of Seint Valentynes day of the Parlement of Briddes" (line 1086).

Valeria In "The FRANKLIN'S TALE," Valeria is one of the virtuous women whose example DORIGEN would like to follow when she must choose between keeping her promise to the squire AURELIUS or remaining faithful to her marriage vows (line 1456). Valeria is mentioned by Saint JEROME in his *Epistola adversus Jovinianum* ("Letter against Jovinianum") as a woman who refused to remarry after the death of her husband, Servius.

Valerian Husband of CECILIA in "The SECOND NUN'S TALE. Valerian is a pagan Roman who, after displaying some skepticism regarding his wife's reasons for wanting to remain chaste (she has told him that the angel who guards her will kill him if he attempts to have intercourse with her), agrees to become baptized as a Christian and to honor his wife's wish to remain a virgin. After his baptism, Valerian does indeed see the angel, who bestows upon him and his wife wreaths of lilies and roses to signify their spiritual sweetness and sanctity. Valerian asks for and receives God's help in converting his brother TIBURTIUS (Tiburce). Soon afterward, both men are questioned and imprisoned by the Roman prefect, who, when they refuse to sacrifice to the pagan gods, condemns them to death.

Valerie In the prologue to "The WIFE OF BATH'S TALE," "Valerye and Theophrastus" is the name by which the Wife refers to her husband's "Book of Wicked Wives" (line 671), from which he reads to her every night until she cannot stand it anymore and burns some of the book's pages. "Valerie" is actually an abbreviation for the title of an antifeminist treatise, "Dissuasio Valerii ad Rufinum philosophum ne uxorem ducat" ("Valerie's advice to the philosopher Rufino against taking a wife") by Walter Map, a 12th-century Welshman. Containing many details and examples of the trials and tribulations of the married man, its presence in JANKIN (1)'s anthology is unsurprising. During the Middle Ages some scholars believed the treatise to have been written by the Roman historian VALERIUS Maximus, who was the source for two other stories of reprobate women mentioned in the Wife's prologue. The treatise also contained examples of virtuous wives, which must be what the god of love (CUPID) is referring to in *The LEGEND OF GOOD WOMEN* when he directs Chaucer's attention to works by writers like "Valerye" that tell stories of "clene maydenes" and "trewe wyves" (prologue G, lines 280–82) [clean maidens and true wives].

Valerius Valerius Maximus, whom Chaucer refers to simply as "Valerius," was a Roman historian of the first century A.D. In addition to his historical writings, he created a handbook of rhetoric titled *Factorum dictorumque memorabilium libri novem* ("Nine books of memorable deeds and sayings"), which consisted primarily of stories with a moral or philosophical point. The WIFE OF BATH's prologue mentions two stories found in this collection. The first is that of METELLIUS, who beat his wife for drinking wine (lines 460–62). The other tells about Sulpicius (Simplicius) GALLUS, who divorced his wife for appearing bareheaded in the street (lines 643–46). Within "The WIFE OF BATH'S TALE" proper, Dame Alice also mentions Valerius' story of TULLIUS HOSTILLIUS, the king of Rome who began life as a pauper (lines 1165–67). In "The MONK'S TALE," the narrator mentions the Roman author as one of his sources for the life of JULIUS CAESAR (line 2720).

Venice Venice, the seaport in northern Italy that is built upon more than 100 small islands in the Lagoon of Venice, is mentioned twice in Chaucer's poetry. In *The HOUSE OF FAME,* the narrator says that the walls, floors and roof of FAME's palace are all plated in gold half a foot thick and "as fyn as ducat in Venyse" (lines 1342–48) [as fine as a ducat in Venice]. A ducat was a gold coin so named because it bore the image of a duke. The city is also mentioned in the prologue to "The CLERK'S TALE" (line 51), where the narrator describes the geography of the PIEDMONT region of Italy which forms the setting for his tale of patient GRISELDA.

Venus The Roman goddess of love, Venus, is mentioned more often in Chaucer's work than any other mythological figure. Originally a goddess of gardens, identified with the productivity of nature, she became identified with the Greek Aphrodite, taking on all of Aphrodite's myths and attributes, in addition to possessing a plentiful supply of her own. Her parentage was uncertain. According to some traditions she was the daughter of Jove (JUPITER). In other stories of her origin, SATURN was her father, and she was born of the foam from his severed testicles after his son, Jupiter, cut them off and threw them into the sea. In "The KNIGHT'S TALE" (lines 2438–82), Chaucer represents her as the daughter of Saturn. At any rate, her birth from the waves was a common image in medieval art and literature. Chaucer uses it in his descriptions of the TEMPLE OF VENUS in both "The Knight's Tale" (lines 1955–58) and *The HOUSE OF FAME* (lines 131–39). In Roman tradition, Venus was the mother of AENEAS by ANCHISES, which made her, by extension, the mother of the Roman people. She plays an important role in the *AENEID,* assisting Aeneas and his followers on their long and adventurous voyages from Troy to Latium, saving them from the wrath of JUNO. Venus was married to VULCAN, the god of fire and blacksmiths, but she had many lovers, including MARS (1), the god of war, by whom she was CUPID's mother. In the Middle Ages, Venus had two aspects or faces, which are reflected by the two inscriptions on the gates leading into the GARDEN OF LOVE in *The PARLIAMENT OF FOWLS.* One of the gates speaks of love as a blissful place of grace and healing influences; the other describes it as a barren and sorrowful prison (lines 127–40). As this example illustrates, the two faces of Venus corresponded to the two possible experiences of love. The goddess also possessed a dual nature, comprising both charitable love and physical love, or lust. Although she is mentioned many times throughout Chaucer's work, Venus plays her most prominent role in "The Knight's Tale" where PALAMON prays to her to help him win the hand of EMILY. A number of characters in Chaucer's poetry are dominated by Venus, including the WIFE OF BATH (*see* her prologue, lines 609–10), the squires DAMIAN ("The MERCHANT'S TALE") and AURELIUS ("The FRANKLIN'S TALE"), the rooster CHAUNTICLEER ("The NUN'S PRIEST'S TALE"), the aged knight JANUARY ("The MERCHANT'S TALE"), and TROILUS as well as Palamon. In "The COM-

PLAINT OF MARS," Venus appears as both goddess and planet as the poet uses the movements of the planets as a vehicle for describing how APOLLO (Phoebus) caught Venus and Mars embracing.

Vergil *See* VIRGIL.

Verona (Verone) The ancient city of Verona, located in northern Italy, is mentioned once in Chaucer's work, in the *BOECE*, Chaucer's translation of BOETHIUS' *Consolation of Philosophy*. As Boethius narrates the trials that he has endured under the rule of THEODORIC the Ostrogoth, he mentions an occasion that occurred in the city of Verona when the king accused the entire Senate of plotting against him, and Boethius imperiled his own safety by defending the Senate. Verona was one of the alternate cities in which Theodoric held court. His main palace, at which he conducted most of his affairs, was in RAVENNA.

Vesulus, Mount *See* MONTE VISO.

Vesuvius A famous volcano in southern Italy, on the Bay of Naples. Its eruption in A.D. 79 destroyed Pompeii and Herculaneum. Vesuvius is mentioned in the *BOECE*, Chaucer's translation of BOETHIUS' *Consolation of Philosophy*. In Book One, Metrum 4, LADY PHILOSOPHY tells Boethius that if a man is virtuous, steadfast and exercises self-control, he will not be moved by either a raging sea or the smoking fire and brimstone of Vesuvius (lines 1–12).

Via Appia *See* APPIAN WAY.

Vincent The man whom Chaucer refers to as Vincent in prologue G of his *LEGEND OF GOOD WOMEN* was Vincent of Beauvais, the 13th-century Dominican who authored *Speculum naturale, historiale, doctrinale,* a huge compendium of all knowledge supposed to be in existence at the time. It contained works by PLATO, Pliny and ISIDORE OF SEVILLE, and dealt with natural history, the history of civilization, theology and art and the history of learning. The LOATHLY HAG in "The WIFE OF BATH'S TALE" quotes from the *Speculum historiale* when she lectures her young husband on the benefits of poverty, saying that it encourages industry and improves wisdom (lines 1195–98). In prologue G of *The Legend of Good Women*, the god of love mentions the "Estoryal Myrour" (*Speculum historial*) as a source of stories about good and faithful women (line 307).

Virgil Virgil, full name Publius Vergilius Maro, is generally acknowledged to be the greatest Roman poet. Born October 15, 70 B.C., near Mantua, Italy, he is best known for his epic the *AENEID*, which he began writing around 29 B.C. and never completed. Virgil was the son of a prosperous Roman farmer and received a thorough education. Although his own life was relatively untouched by civil disturbances that rocked Italy during his lifetime, that turbulence did find its way into his poetry, as did the sense of stability that followed the rise of OCTAVIAN to power in 31–30 B.C. Virgil became a member of the emperor's court circle and was patronized by the imperial minister Maecenas, one of the most famous supporters of the arts in imperial Rome. Virgil's first major work was a collection of 10 pastoral poems called *Eclogues*. These poems, which are often read as a visionary prophecy of the tranquility that he would see imposed in the final years of his life, under the reign of AUGUSTUS, enjoyed considerable popularity during the Middle Ages. His *Georgics* provides the recipe for a Golden Age in the form of practical goals such as the repopulation of rural Italy and the rehabilitation of its agriculture. The 12 completed books of the *Aeneid* celebrate the founding of Rome by AENEAS of TROY and the Roman unification of the world by Augustus.

Virgil's poetry was studied extensively during the medieval period. Several writers composed commentaries and interpretations of his work, which easily lent itself to the medieval penchant for moral philosophy that made PLATO so popular among Christian scholars. The *Aeneid* also provided material that could be readily adapted to the romance form. In the 12th century, a Norman poet composed a romance called *Eneas*, based on the adventures of Aeneas, which was almost immediately imitated by a Flemish poet in a German version of the story. Out of all the material he found in the *Aeneid*, Chaucer seems to have been most fascinated by the story of Aeneas and DIDO, queen of CARTHAGE, which he relates twice, first in *The HOUSE OF FAME* (lines 219–382), then in an even longer version in *The LEGEND OF GOOD WOMEN* (lines 924–1367). Twice Chaucer refers to Virgil as an authority on the torments of hell. In "The FRIAR'S TALE," the devil tells the corrupt summoner that, once he has experienced hell, he will be more of an authority on the subject than either Virgil or DANTE (lines 1517–20); and in *The HOUSE OF FAME*, the narrator states that whoever wants to learn about hell should read Virgil, Claudian or Dante (lines 445–50). An image of the Roman poet actually appears in FAME's palace, standing on a pillar made of tin and iron where he supports the fame of Troy (lines 1481–85) through his poetry. Finally, at the end of *TROILUS AND CRISEYDE*, the narrator bids his little tragedy to follow in the footsteps of five classical poets, the first of whom is Virgil (lines 1786–92), thus indicating his own wish to take his place as a poet of their standing, one whose work would be remembered and honored throughout history.

Virginia The daughter of VIRGINIUS in "The PHYSICIAN'S TALE." Virginia is chaste, beautiful and a model daughter in every way; nevertheless, and through no fault of her own, she suffers a terrible fate when the false judge APIUS exploits his judicial power to gain possession of her with the intention of raping her. Virginius' father, determined that his daughter should lose her life rather than her honor, beheads his daughter only moments before a crowd of townspeople come to his aid, emphasizing the senseless nature of her death. The story of Virginia also appears in John GOWER's CONFESSIO AMANTIS and in ROMAN DE LA ROSE.

Virginius   The father of VIRGINIA in "The PHYSICIAN'S TALE." When the false judge APIUS secures means to rape Virginia, her father decides to execute his daughter rather than allow her to suffer such shame. Some scholars have used Virginius' Roman (pagan) status to excuse or rationalize his behavior toward his daughter, citing the Roman obsession with honor; yet the story's Christian framework seems to overshadow its pagan setting. This, together with the fact that a large group of citizens comes to help Virginius immediately after his daughter's death, suggests that he may have acted too hastily.

Virgo   One of the 12 divisions of the zodiac, an imaginary belt in the heavens extending for about eight degrees on either side of the apparent path of the sun and including the paths of the moon and the principal planets. The zodiac is divided into 12 equal parts, or signs, each named for a different constellation. Virgo is the sixth sign (*see* diagram under ASTROLOGY), which, in Chaucer's day, the Sun entered on August 12. The constellation of Virgo, which is supposed to represent a virgin, appears in the Northern Hemisphere between LEO and LIBRA. Chaucer uses such astrological terms most often to indicate the approximate date of a narrative event or to show the passage of time. This is not the case with Virgo, however, which is only mentioned in his *TREATISE ON THE ASTROLABE*, where he describes its position in the sky (part 2, division 6, lines 17–18) and its influence over the other astrological signs (part 2, division 28, line 37).

Viscounte, Barnabo   *See* VISCONTI, BERNABÒ.

Visconti, Bernabò   Bernabò Visconti, with his brother Galeazzo, ruled the Italian province of Lombardy during Chaucer's lifetime. His niece, Violante, married the English prince Lionel, duke of Clarence, in whose household Chaucer served, and Chaucer himself was later involved in marriage negotiations between King RICHARD II and Bernabò for the hand of Bernabò's daughter Catherine in 1378. One of the most powerful and ostentatious of Italian rulers, Bernabò was constantly provoking the anger of the papacy by proclaiming himself the head of the church in Milan and was

known, on one occasion, to force some Vatican emissaries to eat the official papal document of excommunication they had brought him. He also possessed an extensive library and may have given Chaucer copies of BOCCACCIO's *FILOSTRATO* and *TESEIDA*, which provided Chaucer with the source material for his *TROILUS AND CRISEYDE* and for "The KNIGHT's TALE." This seems likely because Bernabò was known for displaying great generosity when it came to gifts, and Chaucer began working on *Troilus* and possibly "The Knight's Tale" shortly after his trip to Milan in 1378. Bernabò fell from power in 1385 when he was captured by his nephew, Gian Galeazzo. In December of the same year he died suddenly in prison, possibly having been poisoned. He is one of the four contemporary rulers whose biography Chaucer included as one of the tragedies in "The MONK's TALE." In that portrait Chaucer refers to him as the "God of delit and scourge of Lumbardye" (line 2400) [God of delight and scourge of Lombardy], describing his downfall as yet another example of a man who possessed great power and was then brought low by the turning of FORTUNE's wheel.

Visconti, Galeazzo   Galeazzo Visconti, with his brother Bernabò, ruled the Italian province of Lombardy during Chaucer's lifetime. In 1368 his daughter Violante married the English prince Lionel, duke of Clarence, under whom Chaucer had served during the war with France.

Visevus   *See* VESUVIUS.

Vitulon   *See* WITELO.

Vulcan (Vulcano; Vulcanus)   In classical mythology, Vulcan was the Roman god of fire and of blacksmiths who was invoked to keep fire from home and city. Vulcan was lame, the result of having been thrown down from Mount Olympus. In some versions of the legend he was thrown by JUNO because he was so ugly. In others, Jove (JUPITER) threw him down because he sided with Juno in an argument. Vulcan was married to VENUS, the goddess of love, who betrayed him with many lovers. When he discovered that she was having an affair with MARS (1), he forged a golden net to trap the two lovers together. Then, after they had been caught, he called the other gods to witness their embarrassment. In "The KNIGHT's TALE," PALAMON addresses Venus as the spouse of Vulcan when he prays to her to grant him success in the battle for EMILY's hand in marriage (line 2222). His opponent, ARCITE (1), mentions Vulcan in his prayer to Mars, comparing his own situation to that of Mars, caught in Vulcan's net (lines 2383–91). In *The HOUSE OF FAME*, Vulcan appears as a golden image in the TEMPLE OF VENUS (lines 119–39).

W

Wade According to Jacqueline de Weever's *Chaucer Dictionary,* Wade is a figure from Norse legend. The son of a king and a sea woman, Wade was a giant who became the father of Weyland, whom he took to some dwarves to be educated as a smith. He made arrangements to return for the boy one year later, but Weyland displayed such talent and skill that the dwarves decided to kill his father and keep him for themselves. The dwarves murdered Wade in a landslide, but Weyland discovered their treachery and killed them, escaping from their country in a marvelous boat that he made himself. In "The MERCHANT'S TALE," the aged knight JANUARY says that he does not want to marry a woman nearer his own age because older women are crafty like Wade's boat (lines 1421–24). De Weever suggests that "Wade" has come to be substituted for "Weyland," who escaped from the dwarves in his magical boat. Another reference to Wade appears in *TROILUS AND CRISEYDE* when PANDARUS tells the story of Wade after CRISEYDE has dinner at his house (book 3, lines 610–15).

Wales Wales, the division of the United Kingdom that occupies a hilly region to the west of central England, and that, like Scotland, has maintained a distinct identity apart from the rest of Great Britain, is mentioned once in Chaucer's work. In "The MAN OF LAW'S TALE," the narrator relates that NORTHUMBERLAND, the part of England where CONSTANCE lands after drifting through the Mediterranean and out into the ocean, is now pagan. The Christians who were there before the pagan invasion have all fled to Wales, he says (lines 541–46). Since the historical framework provided by Nicholas TRIVET places the tale's (fictional) events at the end of the sixth and beginning of the seventh centuries, the narrator could be referring to the Anglo-Saxon invasions which occurred around that period and which did indeed see some of Britain's Christian inhabitants fleeing toward the western parts of the island (and even south to BRITTANY), where they eventually settled.

Wallachia (Walakye) A region in eastern Europe, south of the Transylvanian Alps, and since 1859 part of Romania. According to F. P. MAGOUN, in Chaucer's day Wallachia was an independent Romanic-speaking kingdom which under Vladislav Bassarab (1364–74) accepted Hungarian lordship. In *The BOOK OF THE DUCHESS,* the BLACK KNIGHT says that his lady was too noble and generous to play games with her suitors, sending them on impossible quests to faraway places like Wallachia, ALEXANDRIA and TURKEY (lines 1024–32).

Walter The Marquis of SALUZZO, who marries GRISELDA in "The CLERK'S TALE." The CLERK's description of Walter at the beginning of his tale portrays a young man of considerable fine qualities whose ability to rule is appreciated by his subjects. Walter behaves as a good governor in every way save one—he remains unmarried, which disturbs his people because they would like for him to provide them with an heir that would prevent the succession from passing to a stranger in the event of Walter's death. Although marriage is not something that Walter particularly relishes, he agrees to marry, but unconventionally chooses a peasant girl, rather than a member of his own class, as his bride. The reason given for his choice is that Griselda posseses a rare combination of virtue and beauty. Griselda soon proves that his choice was a wise one by governing with wisdom and virtue while Walter is away from home; nevertheless, Walter decides that he must test her faith and the vow she made when they were married that she would let him rule her in all things. After a series of deprivations that ultimately strip Griselda of all that she gained through becoming Walter's wife, including their two children, the sadistic Walter finally decides that he need test his wife no longer. He restores her to her position and reunites her with her children. Some readers have seen this tale as an allegory of the Christian soul's relationship to God, expressing the idea that the Christian must submit to God in all things in order to gain salvation.

Walys *See* WALES.

Ware A town in England, Ware is mentioned in the GENERAL PROLOGUE TO *THE CANTERBURY TALES* to define one limit of the territory in which the PARDONER has jurisdiction. It is also home to Roger Hogge, the COOK who participates in the tale-telling. According to F. P. MAGOUN'S *CHAUCER GAZETTEER,* there are three Wares that Chaucer could have had in mind. The most likely would be "Ware on the Lea" in Hertfordshire, which in the 14th century was the site of a Franciscan monastery. There are also two hamlets of this name, one near Sandwich in Kent and one by Kingsteignton in the county of Devonshire. After concluding that it is impossible to determine which one Chaucer meant, Magoun suggests that the one in Hertfordshire makes the most sense, at least in the case of the Pardoner, presumably because it seems probable that he would choose a well-known location to define geographical boundaries.

Watering of Saint Thomas   A spring or brook named for Saint THOMAS À BECKET, located about two miles south of London on the Old Kent Road to CANTERBURY. It is the first of the geographical markers used by Chaucer in *The CANTERBURY TALES* to indicate the passage of time and to provide an element of realism to the pilgrimage that provides the framework for the tales. The place is mentioned in the GENERAL PROLOGUE, where the poet notes that the Host, Harry BAILLY, called for the tale-telling to begin when they had reached this landmark (lines 825–31).

Watling Street (Watlyng Strete)   *See* MILKY WAY.

Watte   This name is a diminutive of *Walter*. In the GENERAL PROLOGUE to *The CANTERBURY TALES,* the narrator says that the SUMMONER, after hearing Latin spoken in court all day, can speak it himself, even though he doesn't know what the words mean. He is thus like a jay, who can squawk "Watte" as well as the pope can (lines 642–43).

Weaver, the   One of a group of tradesmen mentioned, but not described individually, in the GENERAL PROLOGUE to *The CANTERBURY TALES*. His title ("Webbe") indicates that he is a weaver of cloth (a profession also practiced by another pilgrim, the WIFE OF BATH). The others in his group include a Carpenter, Haberdasher Dyer of cloth ("Dyere") and a Tapestry maker ("Tapycer"). These five men are all wearing the same type of uniform, which indicates their membership in one of the medieval trade guilds, the forerunner of modern-day trade unions. The guilds set standards for the quality of the goods produced, regulated holidays and hours of work, and fixed prices and wages to some extent. Certain details of Chaucer's portrait of the Guildsmen, such as their silver- (rather than brass) mounted knives, might suggest either prosperity or pretentiousness, depending upon whether or not one judges the portraits to contain elements of satire. Those scholars who argue against finding satire in their description note that Chaucer provided his Guildsmen with none of the traditional mercantile vices such as fraud, usury and avarice. None of the Guildsmen tells a tale on the pilgrimage to CANTERBURY.

Webbe   *See* WEAVER.

Wetherbee, Winthrop III (1938–1989)   Chaucer scholar. Wetherbee received his Ph.D. from the University of California at Berkeley and taught at Cornell University and the University of Chicago. He contributed two important books to contemporary Chaucer criticism. The first is *Chaucer and the Poets: An Essay on Troilus and Criseyde* (1984), which interprets this poem as Chaucer's response to previous poetry, especially classical poetry such as DANTE's *Divine Comedy.* Wetherbee argues that through the experience of TROILUS, the narrator of *TROILUS AND CRISEYDE* rejects the idea of medieval courtly love in favor of a more profound Boethian (*see* BOETHIUS) philosophy. In a later book, *Geoffrey Chaucer: The Canterbury Tales* (1989), Wetherbee sees *The CANTERBURY TALES* as a fundamental break with Chaucer's earlier poetry. Rather than introducing a "courtly idyll" or spiritual quest, this work's opening movement engages directly with the reality of life in the 14th century. Wetherbee puzzles over the fact that while the work itself was popular, it was not widely imitated, nor did other authors take the opportunity to supply the missing tales (finishing or elaborating upon finished works being common during the medieval period). This was the result, Wetherbee believes, of the 15th-century audience's inability to appreciate Chaucer's realism and comic irony.

Wheel of Fortune   *See* FORTUNE.

White, Lady   *See* LADY WHITE.

Wicked Tongue   One of the allegorical figures in Fragment B of the Middle English translation of the *ROMAN DE LA ROSE.* After finding his way into the rose garden where grows the beautiful rose with which he has fallen in love, the dreamer-narrator of the poem finds his efforts to possess the rose opposed by a host of foes, including Wicked Tongue ("malicious gossip"). With the help of VENUS he succeeds in getting a kiss, but then JEALOUSY drives him out of the garden and imprisons the rosebud and BIALACOIL ("fair welcome") in a strong fortress. In the opinion of most scholars, this portion of the poem was written by someone other than Chaucer.

Wife of Bath, the   The Wife of Bath's portrait follows that of the Physician (*see* DOCTOR OF PHYSIC) in the GENERAL PROLOGUE TO *THE CANTERBURY TALES.* Like the PRIORESS, this "good Wife" has attracted a great deal of critical attention, partly because of the controversy that arises over interpreting her character. According to some scholars, she is a caricature of a strong and independent woman, the nightmarish personification of the same antifeminist literary tradition that she attempts to adapt to her own uses. Others see her as a positive representation of independent womanhood, a kind of protofeminist making the best life that she can for herself in a repressive, male-dominated society. Both of these evaluations are based upon the way the Wife is represented in her prologue and tale, but her description in the General Prologue does contain some satiric elements, hinting at qualities like pride, wrath and envy (she becomes enraged when other women go before her to present their church offering) and lust (she has had five husbands, in addition to other "company" in youth), although none of these details is as damning as those found in the portraits of the corrupt clerics such as the MONK or FRIAR. And some details of her description are positive, like the narrator's praise of her clothmaking ability, and the description of her face, which is fair and ruddy-hued. Her sanguine complexion (*see* HUMORS), in addition to her evident enjoyment of social occasions, indicates a good-natured gregariousness. Her clothing and the horse that she rides suggest prosperity. The outline provided by these details is substantially fleshed out by information contained in the prologue to her tale and throughout the tale itself. And whether our ultimate reaction to her is one of attraction or repulsion or something in-between, one thing is certain: We know more about her than we do about any of the other pilgrims.

"Wife of Bath"'s prologue The prologue to "The WIFE OF BATH'S TALE" is so long and full of details about the teller's life that it is almost a tale unto itself.

SUMMARY

The WIFE OF BATH begins by saying that she is going to speak of the woe that is in marriage. What follows is a lengthy dissertation on the particular woes of her particular marriages, which total five in number. The Wife, or woman (as the word "wife" could also mean in Middle English) of Bath claims to have had three good husbands and two bad ones. She first collectively describes her experience with the three good husbands, who were all much older than she. In order to "rule" them and have her own way (live her own life without any interference from them), she employed an ingenious ruse, accusing them of all kinds of bad behavior, from drunkenness to keeping a mistress, before they had any chance to criticize her own behavior. This way, the husbands were so busy defending themselves, and so happy to have peace after a long argument, that they never dared to start a quarrel with her regarding their own suspicions. She furthermore refused to have sex with them until they gave her control of their property. By these means, she suggests that marriage is a battle of the sexes and that one way to win that battle is through deceit and trickery.

The Wife's fourth and fifth husbands were younger men and much more difficult for her to control. The fourth she married while they were both young, and he had a mistress, for which she paid him back by becoming another man's. The fifth, JANKIN (1) (Janekyn), is the only one given a name, and he seems to be the one who held the greatest sway over her affections. He is 20 (half her age) and does not appear to love her nearly as much as she loves him; perhaps he even married her for her property. Every night, she tells us, he used to read to her from a book of wicked women, and he often beat her. One evening, though, she got so fed up with his reading to her about the evils of women that she ripped three pages out of his book and tossed them in the fire, at the same time knocking him from his chair. He responded by striking her on the head. She fell to the floor and appeared to be unconscious. Jankin was so frightened by this episode that when she regained her senses, he apologized and promised never to hit her again. Finally, she concludes, they were able to work things out and get along, but only after he gave her sovereignty over their house and land, and over himself, the latter being symbolized by his burning the book that brought them to blows.

COMMENTARY

"The Wife of Bath"'s prologue is one of the most commented-upon pieces to come from the pen of Chaucer. The Wife is notable for the apparent ease with which she speaks of personal matters, and especially of her sexual activities and appetite. While she purports to be describing the "woes of marriage," the obvious delight she takes in expounding on the problem of whether or not remarriage is permissible under God's law, and in outlining the many ingenious ways that she has found to subvert the idea that husbands should rule their wives, suggests that the woes arguably belong to her husbands rather than herself. In depicting the Wife's behavior and characteristics, Chaucer draws heavily on an antifeminist tradition which had roots in classical literature and went on to blossom quite healthily in the medieval climate, in which women were considered to have been cursed by God ever since EVE offered ADAM the forbidden fruit in Eden. Some of the specific writers whose work he drew upon are Eustache DESCHAMPS, Saint JEROME, Walter MAP and JEAN DE MEUN. Chaucer's Wife of Bath exhibits many of the stereotypical traits attributed to women by these authors. Notably, she talks too much, is too independent and flirtatious, has too large a sexual appetite and gossips.

On the other hand, she is a much more complex and sympathetic character than those depicted within the antifeminist literature, as is shown by the favorable reception she has been given by many readers. What is perhaps most appealing about her is her ingenuousness, the sense that she is, despite her deceit and trickery, an affectionate and somewhat intelligent woman who is simply trying to make the best of a bad situation. During the Middle Ages and, really, up until the 18th century, European women had very few choices when it came to maintaining a livelihood for themselves. A woman could marry, enter the church as a novitiate, weave cloth for a very modest income or become a prostitute. Whenever a woman inherited land or a business because her husband or father died without a male heir, she immediately became prey to fortune-hunting opportunists who would attempt to pressure her into marriage in order to gain control of her property. The Wife of Bath hints at this practice when she announces that her old husbands should not be master of both "my body and my good," and she goes on to explain how she would withhold the one (her body) until she got possession of the other (her goods). The sex, she says, was something she endured to have access to her property. Such a marital arrangement suggests that prostitution was not the exclusive practice of unmarried women who offered their bodies to various men in exchange for goods, but that a limited form of prostitution could exist within, and even form the actual contractual basis of, legal marriage. Early critics of Chaucer, and some even as recent as D. W. ROBERTSON, take a rather harsh moral view of the Wife of Bath and her concept of love and marriage, arguing that, motivated by the desire for sex and property, she reduces both to their basest ingredients. In this respect the Wife's prologue has much in common with the themes of "The SHIPMAN'S TALE."

"Wife of Bath's Tale, The" The Wife of Bath tells the story of a rapist, who, to save his life, must travel the world to find out what women desire most.

SUMMARY

"The Wife of Bath's Tale" opens with a traditional romance beginning, looking back to the days of King ARTHUR, when elves used to dance in the meadows. This prelude veers quickly into social satire when the Wife explains that the elves have been banished by "limytours" (limiters were holy friars licensed to beg in a limited area) who now thickly populate the countryside and pose no other threat to women travelers save that of rape. The tale itself begins with a story of rape, that of a maiden by one of King Arthur's knights. As punishment for his crime, the knight (see KNIGHT [3]) is sentenced to death. Arthur's queen and other ladies of the court beg the king to spare the knight's life, and Arthur gives the knight into their keeping, granting them the power to decide his fate. The queen decides to pose the knight a question: What thing is it that women most desire? If he can give the correct answer,

he may go free. If not, his original sentence will be carried out. Since he has no immediate response, she gives him a year and a day to seek and learn the answer, after which he must return to court and meet his fate.

During his year of grace, the knight searches high and low for the answer to this question, and receives many suggestions from the women he encounters. Some say women love riches and wealth; some, that they love honor; some say pleasure is most important; some say beautiful clothes; and some, having good sex with a variety of partners ("oftetyme to be wydwe and wedde"). Others say their greatest pleasure has come from being flattered, and some that they like best to be free to do as they please without being criticized. Finally, there are some who claim they take great delight in being thought stable, steadfast and discrete, though, as the Wife of Bath exclaims, these qualities are completely alien to woman's nature. At this point, the Wife departs briefly from the narrative of the knight to tell the story of King MIDAS, whose wife couldn't keep a secret, in order to illustrate the point that women cannot be discrete or keep a promise.

Returning to the story of the knight, the Wife tells us that for a long time the knight was unable to discover the correct answer to the queen's question. On his way back to Arthur's court to admit his defeat, he spies some ladies dancing in the woods. When he rides toward them, they vanish, but there remains sitting upon the grass an old and ugly woman. She rises and speaks to him, asking what is the matter. When he tells her the question that he must answer or else lose his life, she responds that she can help him—but first he must promise to do whatever she asks in return. The knight gives his word, and the woman accompanies him to court.

When the day comes that he must appear before the queen, the knight announces that what women most desire is to have sovereignty and dominion over their husbands as well as their lovers. No woman at the court is willing to deny the truth of this answer, so the knight wins back his life. But now he is obliged to keep the promise he made to the LOATHLY HAG, to honor whatever request she makes of him. When she asks him to marry her, though, he begs her to ask for something else, to take all of his property but to let his body go. She refuses, and so they are married. On their wedding night, the young man tosses and turns, unable to sleep. When he tells his wife the causes of his distress, that she is lowly born, old and ugly, she delivers a lecture on the true nature of gentility and the value and wisdom of old age, followed by the suggestion that she can, at least, do something about her looks. She asks the knight if he would rather that she be old and ugly and a good and faithful wife, or young, beautiful and unfaithful. The knight considers, and at last tells her that she may decide which alternative would be the most pleasing and honorable for both of them. His choice is rewarded by her swearing that she will be both—young and beautiful, *and* faithful, because he is willing to turn the decision over to her and so to grant her sovereignty. Seeing that she has indeed become beautiful, the knight embraces and kisses his wife and from that time forward, "she obeyed hym in every thyng / That myghte doon hym plesance or likyng. / And thus they lyve unto hir lyves ende / In parfit joye" (lines 1255–58) [she obeyed him in everything / That might bring him pleasure or be to his liking. / And thus they live until their lives' end / In perfect joy]. This conclusion is immediately qualified by the Wife of Bath's comment, "and Jhesu Crist us sende / Housbondes meke, yonge, and fressh abedde, / And grace t'overbyde hem that we wedde" (lines 1258–60) [and may Jesus Christ send us / Husbands who are meek, young, and eager in bed, / And the grace to rule them that we wed].

COMMENTARY

"The Wife of Bath's Tale" belongs to the genre of chivalric romance which was popular in medieval Europe from the 12th century onward. Typically set in the legendary realm of King Arthur, these tales describe the fairy-tale-like adventures of knights and ladies and other members of the feudal aristocracy. Ideologically, these tales were founded upon the ideals of loyalty, honor and COURTLY LOVE. The plot of the romance often derived from some conflict or problem arising out of sexual attraction between a man and a woman.

Although it was composed around the same time as "The WIFE OF BATH'S PROLOGUE," and seems by its subject matter to perfectly correspond to the concerns and preoccupations of its teller, "The Wife of Bath's Tale" may not have been the tale Chaucer originally intended to have the wife tell. Variant manuscripts of the epilogue to "The MAN OF LAW'S TALE" suggest that when the tale of the knight and the loathly lady was written, Chaucer had not yet decided who was to tell it. This, together with evidence that "The SHIPMAN'S TALE" was originally intended for a female teller, have led various scholars to argue that in an earlier stage of The CANTERBURY TALES' composition, the SHIPMAN told "The Wife of Bath's Tale," and the Wife of Bath told the FABLIAU ultimately assigned to the Shipman. Larry Benson's explanatory and textual notes to The RIVERSIDE CHAUCER provide more detailed information on this topic.

Because the tale of the loathly old hag who is transformed into a beautiful young woman is so widespread, and because no exact analogue to Chaucer's version of the story exists, it is impossible to trace Chaucer's tale to any one source. However, there is evidence that he knew and may have drawn upon "The Tale of Sir Florent," which appears in John GOWER's CONFESSIO

AMANTIS. The Arthurian setting may have been suggested by two other analogues, *The Marriage of Sir Gawain* and *The Wedding of Sir Gawain and Dame Ragnell*. What is unique to Chaucer's tale is the nature of the choice the hero must make: whether to have a wife who is ugly and faithful, or one who is beautiful and unfaithful. The usual formula asks the knight to choose whether the wife will be fair by day and foul at night, or vice-versa, so that he must choose between private pleasure and social esteem. Whether intentional or not, this change again foregrounds the antifeminist philosophy which has been a source of considerable grief in the life of the Wife of Bath and which theorized that all beautiful women were likely to be unfaithful.

Another change that Chaucer made, and one which enhances the artistry of the tale, is that there is more than a single transformation. The loathly hag's physical transformation is actually triggered by the young knight's spiritual one, when he listens to and accepts her definition of *gentilesse* as gentleness, kindness and honor, rather than the social class into which one is born. His own transformation is signaled by his willingness to leave the decision (as to whether she will be ugly and faithful or beautiful and faithless) up to her, indicating a profound change from the heedless desire to have his own way that led him to commit the crime of rape.

Some critics have seen this tale as an example of wish fulfillment on the Wife's behalf, an extension of her desire to dominate the men in her life. The closing lines of the tale contradict such an interpretation, showing that once the knight has shown his willingness to behave with true *gentilesse,* the hag not only transforms into a beautiful lady who will also remain faithful, but she "obeyed hym in every thyng / That myghte doon hym plesance or likyng" (lines 1255–56). Furthermore, the Wife herself, once Jankin ceases abusing her and indicates his willingness to be ruled by her, is "to hym as kynde / As any wyf from Denmark unto Ynde, / And also trewe, and so was he to me" (lines 823–25) [to him as kind / As any wife from Denmark unto India, / And also faithful, and so was he to me], showing that it isn't really sovereignty over her husband but rather a pledge of mutual love and service that led to this satisfying relationship.

Wilkin (Wilkyn) This name is a diminutive of William. The WIFE OF BATH uses the name to speak of one of her aged husbands in the prologue to her tale (line 432).

William, King The king William mentioned in the SERGEANT OF THE LAW's portrait in the GENERAL PROLOGUE TO THE CANTERBURY TALES is William the Conqueror, the Norman duke who successfully invaded England in 1066, defeating the Anglo-Saxon forces led by King Harold. The battle is considered a turning point in English history because it ended the period of Anglo-Saxon supremacy and paved the way for the establishment of a nation-state under William's successors. It was the last successful invasion of the country to date. In Chaucer's description of the Sergeant of the Law (the highest rank of lawyer), he says that the man has committed to memory all the cases and judgments made in England since the time of William (lines 323–24).

Wimsatt, James I(rving) (1927–   )   A Duke University Ph.D. who has taught at a number of universities, Wimsatt rose to the rank of Professor of English at the University of Texas at Austin. He has written a number of articles and several books on Chaucer, including *Chaucer and the Poems of "Ch" in University of Pennsylvania Manuscript French 15* (1982), which features an edited portion of the above-named manuscript containing the 15 French love poems signed "Ch" and believed by some scholars to have been written by Chaucer. Wimsatt suggests that if they were not actually written by Chaucer, the poems do exhibit the "poetic mode" of his early career. Although the latter work filled an important gap in Chaucer studies, Wimsatt is perhaps better known for *Chaucer and the French Love Poets: The Literary Background of the Book of the Duchess* (1968). Here Wimsatt traces the development of French courtly love poetry from GUILLAUME DE LORRIS' portion of the 13th-century ROMAN DE LA ROSE to Chaucer's day, concentrating specifically on the way it influenced Chaucer's BOOK OF THE DUCHESS. Wimsatt also shows how four love poems by GUILLAUME DE MACHAUT served as sources or models for different parts of Chaucer's poem, while FROISSART's *Paradys d'amours* ("Paradise of Love") provided the inspiration for the DREAM VISION with which it opens.

Wirdes   Name for the Fates derived from the Anglo-Saxon *wyrd*, the ancestor of Modern English *weird*. See PARCAE.

Witelo   A 13th-century Polish scientist and scholar, Witelo translated from Arabic an important treatise on perspective and optics which contains information about the uses of concave mirrors. In "The SQUIRE'S TALE," King CAMBYUSKAN receives a magic mirror that has the ability to reveal, like a crystal ball, any trouble looming in the future, and to distinguish the king's true friends from his foes. The people attending the birthday feast believe that the mirror's powers might be explained by the work of an authority on optics such as Witelo (lines 228–35).

"Womanly Noblesse"   One of the short poems unequivocally attributed to Chaucer in its one surviving manuscript, "Womanly Noblesse" has nevertheless not been completely accepted as authentic. Loosely following the French BALLADE form, this three-stanza poem develops what was an entirely conventional theme at the time of its composition—the lover's plea for pity based on the devotion and obedience he has demonstrated to his beloved. The poem then concludes with an envoy, a conventionalized stanza of the ballade form in which the poet addresses his lady, asking her to accept this evidence of his worship. Although Chaucer departs from the ballade form by omitting the refrain and increasing the number of stanza lines from eight to nine, he otherwise increases the difficulty of the form by using only two rhymes (-*aunce* and -*esse*), rather than three, throughout all three stanzas. As with the other short poems, the date of composition for "Womanly Noblesse" is uncertain.

Woodstock, Thomas of   *See* THOMAS OF WOODSTOCK.

Wretched Engendering of Mankind, Of the (Of the Wrecched Engendrynge of Mankynde   *See* OF THE WRETCHED ENGENDERING OF MANKIND.

Wycliffe, John   The Oxford theologian John Wycliffe was Chaucer's contemporary. Trained as a scholastic, Wycliffe lectured and wrote on logic during the early part of his career. As a royal chaplain, he became acquainted with JOHN OF GAUNT and got involved in national politics when he supported (probably at Gaunt's instigation) Parliament's rejection of Pope Urban V's claim to suzerainty over England. Wycliffe gave the official defense of Parliament's position. Later, when Wycliffe supported Gaunt against Parliament and was condemned by a group of bishops for doing so, Gaunt came to his defense with four doctors of divinity. Toward the end of his life, Wycliffe became more and more radical in his opposition to the Catholic Church, launching an attack on the church which anticipated many of the charges made by Martin Luther and John Calvin. Wycliffe denounced the immorality of the clergy, condemned indulgences and the temporal power of the church, argued for marriage among the clergy, and insisted upon the supreme authority of the Bible as the source of belief. He also denied transubstantiation, the idea that the bread and wine of the Eucharist actually become the body and blood of Christ during the Mass. Beginning in 1378, there were repeated attempts to condemn him as a heretic. Many of his followers, who were known as LOLLARDS, were executed in the early years of the 15th century. Chaucer does not mention Wycliffe by name in his work, but he was certainly aware of his ideas and influence. In the epilogue to "The MAN OF LAW'S TALE," the Host (Harry BAILLY) makes a joke about the PARSON being a "Lollere" (line 1173) because of his opposition to swearing. The Parson's condemnation of fables and his decision to preach instead of telling a tale at the end of *The CANTERBURY TALES,* also suggest that the portrait of this man was influenced by Wycliffe.

X

Xantippe (Xantippa)   *See* SOCRATES.

Xristus   *Xristus* is the name Chaucer uses for Christ in the short poem, "An ABC" to the Virgin. In this poem where each stanza begins with a different, successive letter of the alphabet, *Xristus* begins the stanza for the letter *X*. In the Greek alphabet, *X* (the letter *chi*) is the first symbol of the word for Christ. This is where we get our abbreviation for Christmas: Xmas.

Y

Yarbas *See* IARBUS.

Ycarus *See* ICARUS.

Yeoman, the The Yeoman appears third in the GENERAL PROLOGUE TO *THE CANTERBURY TALES*. He is a member of the KNIGHT (1)'s household and his occupational name, yeoman, indicates that he is a freeborn servant (i.e., that he serves the Knight voluntarily in exchange for some kind of compensation). In a feudal household, his rank places him immediately below a squire. The placing of his portrait following that of the SQUIRE would appear to preserve this hierarchical order. We are given many details about the Yeoman's appearance, all of which correspond to his function as a forester whose main responsibility was to prevent the poaching of wild game on his lord's estate. He would also preside over hunting expeditions, a role that is hinted at in the description of him as being skilled in "wodecraft," i.e., the ceremonies of the hunt. His green coat and hood, in addition to the bow, arrows and knife that he has brought on the pilgrimage, suggest that he may accompany the Knight for the purpose of providing food during the journey. Although the Yeoman's portrait consists almost entirely of external details, some of those, such as the description of his arrows which are "bright and kene" and "drouped noght with fetheres lowe" (did not fall short from being in a poor condition) and his "myghty bowe" (mighty bow) clearly suggest that he is exemplary of his type. Despite the Host's plan for all the pilgrims to participate in the taletelling contest on their way to CANTERBURY, the Yeoman does not.

Ymeneus *See* HYMEN.

Yole *See* IOLE.

Yorkshire A traditional county of northern England. Originally comprised of three "ridings" ("thirds"), the county was formally abolished in the early 1970s and replaced by four administrative units: North Yorkshire, South Yorkshire, West Yorkshire and Humberside. Chaucer's "SUMMONER'S TALE" is set in the town of HOLDERNESSE, which lay in the southeast corner of the county.

Youth One of the allegorical figures who appears in *The ROMAUNT OF THE ROSE*, Chaucer's translation of the French *ROMAN DE LA ROSE*. After the dreamer has gained entry to the GARDEN OF LOVE, he observes the garden's owner, Lord MIRTH, dancing with a group of attendants. These attendants have names like Beauty, RICHESSE (Riches) and IDLENESS, all characteristics or circumstances that encourage the pursuit of love. Youth is described as a young girl not yet 12 years of age, who dances in the company of Idleness. Wild, flighty and somewhat foolish, she intends no harm but is simply being true to her nature. Youth is accompanied by a young lover who strives to kiss her whenever he can. Like two young doves, neither of them is ashamed to be kissing in public (lines 1281–1302).

Ypermnestra *See* HYPERMNESTRA.

Ypocras *See* HIPPOCRATES.

Ypolita *See* HIPPOLYTA.

Ypomedoun *See* HIPPOMEDON.

Ypotis The hero of a Middle English verse legend in which the Roman emperor Hadrian receives instruction in the Christian religion from a pious child. Chaucer mentions Ypotis in a catalogue of heroes that appears in his "TALE OF SIR THOPAS." The reference to this pious hero is perhaps included to mirror THOPAS' evident confusion over the proper subject matter of romance, as revealed when he calls for his minstrels to sing romances "of popes and of cardinales."

Ypres In Chaucer's day, Ypres, the town that is currently located in Belgium, was part of the country of FLANDERS. In the portrait of the WIFE OF BATH that appears in the GENERAL PROLOGUE TO *THE CANTERBURY TALES*, we are told that she is as accomplished at making cloth (which would involve spinning thread and then weaving it on a loom) as anyone in Ypres or GHENT (lines 447–48), both of which were famous for their textiles in the Middle Ages. In his notes to *The Canterbury Tales by Geoffrey Chaucer* (1928), John MANLY suggests that Chaucer's praise of the Wife's weaving may be ironical, since weavers from Bath and surrounding areas in western England were not held in good repute during the latter part of the 14th century. As evidence, he cites a statute of Richard II stating that some of their cloth was so bad as to endanger the lives of English merchants who traded abroad.

Ysaye   *See* ISAIAH.

Ysidis   *See* ISIS.

Ysidre, Saint   *See* ISIDORE OF SEVILLE.

Ysoude   *See* ISOLDE.

Ytaille (Ytayle)   *See* ITALY.

Ytakus   *See* ULYSSES.

Yves, Saint   *See* IVES, SAINT.

Z

Zacharie (Zakarie) *See* ZECHARIAH.

Zanzis *See* ZEUXIS.

Zechariah In the Bible, Zechariah is an Old Testament prophet who may also have been a priest. A leader in the restoration of the nation of Israel following the period known as the Babylonian Captivity, Zechariah is credited with having written the Old Testament book that bears his name. Many scholars describe this book as the most Messianic of the Old Testament because it contains eight specific references to the coming Messiah in its brief 14 chapters. In "The PARSON'S TALE," the narrator refers to a quote from Zechariah in which God says that He will confound the horses of those who are enemies of the nation of Israel (Zechariah 10:5). The PARSON uses the quote in the part of his sermon having to do with the sin of pride, describing those who take great pride in owning many horses which they adorn with intricate harness and saddles. These, according to the Parson, are the men whom God will strike down (lines 431–34). In the short poem, "An ABC" to the Virgin, Chaucer uses *Zechariah* as the first word of the last stanza to preserve the organizational scheme of the poem, which has each stanza beginning with a successive letter of the alphabet. Here he says that Zechariah referred to the Virgin (Saint MARY) as an open well that could wash the guilt from the souls of the sinful (lines 177–78). The reference is to Zechariah 13:1, where Mary is not mentioned specifically, but the verse does describe a fountain opened from the house (genealogical line) of DAVID, wherein all the inhabitants of Jerusalem may be cleansed from sin. Mary was, according to Christian tradition, descended from David.

Zeno *See* STOICS.

Zenobia A queen of Palmyra, a city in the desert just east of Syria, in the third century A.D. Chaucer tells the story of her life in "The MONK'S TALE" (lines 2247–2374). "The Monk's Tale" is actually a series of tales, or brief biographies, each of which is intended to serve as an example of someone who achieved much but was then brought low by the turning of FORTUNE's wheel. Zenobia is the only woman whose life appears in the series, and her tale is considered one of the best. Chaucer's source for his account of Zenobia's life was BOCCACCIO's *De claris mulieribus* (Of virtuous women).

Zephyrus (Zepherus; Zephirus) In classical mythology, Zephyrus was the name of the west wind. He was the son of AURORA (1), goddess of the dawn, and AEOLUS, the chief god of the winds. Known in both ancient and modern literature as a gentle, balmy wind (hence our word *zephyr*), he wafted VENUS to shore after her birth in the waves of the sea. Chaucer refers to the west wind by this name in the famous first lines of *The Canterbury Tales:* "Whan that Aprill with his shoures soote / The droghte of March hath perced to the roote, / And bathed every veyne in swich licour / Of which vertue engendred is the flour; / Whan Zepirus eek with his sweete breeth / Inspired hath in every holt and heeth / The tendre croppes, . . ." [When April with its sweet showers / Has pierced the drought of March to the root, / And bathed every vein (of every leaf) in such liquor / Of which virtue the flower is engendered; / When Zephirus also with his sweet breath / Has inspired in every grove and field / The tender shoots. . . .]. In *TROILUS AND CRISEYDE,* this gentle wind heralds a more somber event, encouraging the green leaves to sprout just as TROILUS must say goodbye to CRISEYDE as she departs for the Greek camp (book 5, lines 10–14). The narrator of *The BOOK OF THE DUCHESS* dreams of a forest so full of springtime bloom that both FLORA and Zephyrus seem to have made their home there (lines 397–404). Similarly, in *The LEGEND OF GOOD WOMEN,* Prologue F, Zephyrus and Flora are credited with giving the flowers their sweet scent (line 171). In the story of HYPERMNESTRA that appears in the same work, Hypermnestra quivers like a branch shaken by Zephyrus when she observes her sleeping husband and remembers her father's command that she must kill him (lines 2680–89).

Zeuxis An Athenian painter who flourished in the fourth century B.C. and whose method of portraying feminine beauty was noted by CICERO. In "The PHYSICIAN'S TALE," NATURE says that neither the great sculptor, APPELLES, nor "Zanzis" (Zeuxis) could create a woman as beautiful as VIRGINIA, the heroine of the tale (lines 15–18). In *TROILUS AND CRISEYDE,* PANDARUS encourages TROILUS to seek a new love to help him forget about CRISEYDE, saying "The newe love out chaceth ofte the olde" (book 4, lines 415) [The new love often chases out the old]. The quote is attributed to Zeuxis but probably derives from OVID's *Remedia amoris* ("Remedy of love").

APPENDIX I

Characters and Historical Figures Mentioned or Quoted in Chaucer

The following names are spelled as they appear in the main entries for each character. Alternate Middle English spellings may be looked up in the text where they appear alphabetically. Each is cross-referenced to the name as it appears in the main entry.

Abigail

Abradate

Abraham

Absalom (1)

Absalom (2)

Achates

Achelous

Achilles

Achitophel

Actaeon

Adam

Adam Scriveyne

Admetus

Adonis

Adrastus

Aegeus

Aegidius, Saint (*see* GILES, SAINT)

Aegyptus

Aeneas

Aeolus

Aesculapius

Aeson

Aesop

Agamemnon

Agaton

Aglauros

Ahasuerus

Alain de Lille

Alan

Albertano of Brescia

Albon, Daun

Albyn

Alcibiades

Alcmena

Alcyone

Alecto

Alexander the Great

Algus

Alhazen

Alison (1)

Alison (2)

Alla

Almachius

Ambrose, Saint

Amphiaraus

Amphion

Anaxagoras

Anchises

Androgeus

Andromache

Anelida

Anne

Anne, Saint

Anselm, Saint

Antaeus

Antenor

Antichrist

Antigone

Antilochus

Antiochus (1)

Antiochus (2)

Antoninus, Marus Aurelius

Antony, Marc

Apius

Apollo

Appelles

Appollonius

Arcite (1)

Arcite (2)

Argus (1)

Argus (2) (*See* ALGUS)

Argus (3)

Argyve

Ariadne

Aries

Aristoclides

Aristotle

Arnaldus of Villanova (Arnold of the New Town)

Arrius

Artemesia

Arthur

Arveragus

Arzachel

Ascalaphus

Ascanius

Atalanta

Athamas

Atiteris

Atlas' daughters

Atropos

Attalus Philometor

Attila

Augustine, Saint

Augustus Caesar

Aurelian

Aurelius

Aurora

Averröes

Avicenna

Bacchus

Bailly, Harry

Ball, John

Basil, Saint

Basilius

Bayard

Becket, Saint Thomas à

Belial

Belinous

Bellona

Belshazzar

Benedict, Saint

Bernard

Bernard, Saint

Bevis

Bialacoil

Biblis

Bilia

Black Knight

Blanche of Lancaster (Lady White)

Boethius

Boreas

Bradwardine, Thomas

Briseis

Brok

Brutus, Marcus Junius

Brutus Cassius

Bukton

Burnel the Asse, Daun

Busiris

Cacus

Cadmus

Cain

Caligula

Calkas

Calliope

Callisto

Calypso

Cambalo

Cambyses

Cambyuskan

Campaneus

Canaanite Woman

Canacee (1)

Canacee (2)

Candace

Canon's Yeoman

Caracalla, Marcus Aurelius
   Antonius

Cassandra

Cassiodorus

Castor

Cato the Censor

Cato the Orator

Catullus

Caurus

Cecilia, Saint

Cenwulf's son

Cerberus

Ceres

Ceyx

Charybdis

Chaucer, Lewis

Chaunticleer

Chichevache

Chiron

Cicero, Marcus Tullius

Cilenius (*See* MERCURY)

Cipris (*See* VENUS)

Circe

Citherea

Clare, Saint

Claudianus, Claudius

Claudius (1) (Marcus Aurelius
   Claudius)

Claudius (2)

Clemence

Cleopatra

Clerk, the

Clio

Clytemnestra

Collatinus, Lucius Tarquinius

Colle (1) (Colle Tregetour)

Colle (2)

Constable of Northumberland

Constance

Constantinus the African

Cook, the

Corybantes (*See* CYBELE)

Corynne

Crassus, Marcus Licinius

Creon

Creusa

Criseyde (Criseyda)

Crisippus

Croesus

Crow

Cupid

Cuthbert, Saint

Cybele

Cynthea (Cynthia) (*See* DIANA)

Cyprian

Cyrus the Great

Daedalus

Damascien

Damasus I, Pope

Damian

Danaus

Daniel

Dante Alighieri

Daphne

Dares Phrygius

Darius (1) (the Mede)

Darius (2) (Darius III, King of Persia)

Daunger

David

Decorat

Deianira

Deiphobus

Delilah

Demetrius

Demophon

Demotion's daughter

Denis, Saint

Diana

Dictys Cretensis

Dido

Diogenes

Diomede

Diomedes

Dionysius Cato

Dioscorides

Dives

Doctor of Physic

Donegild

Dorigen

Dread

Dun

Dunstan, Saint

Dyer, the

Eagle, the

Echo

Eclympasteyr

Edward, Saint

Egyptian Mary (*See* MARY THE EGYPTIAN, SAINT)

Eglantine, Madame (*See* PRIORESS)

Elcanor

Eli

Eliachim

Eligius, Saint

Elijah

Elisha

Elpheta

Emetreus

Emily

Emperor of Rome

Enoch

Epicurus

Erinyes, the

Esther

Eteocles

Euclid

Euripides

Europa

Eurydice

Evander

Eve

Ezekiel

Fabricius, Gaius Luscinus

Fair Welcome (*See* BIALACOIL)

False-Seeming

Fame

Flexippe

Flora

Fortune

Franklin, the

Friar, the

Gabriel

Galatea

Galen

Gallienus, Publicus Licinius Egnatius

Gallus, Sulpicius

Ganelon

Ganymede

Gaudentius

Gawain

Geffrey

Geoffrey of Monmouth

Geoffrey of Vinsauf

Gerland

Germanicus

Gervaise

Gilbertus Anglicus

Giles, Saint

Gille

Glascurion

Goliath

Goodelief

Gower, John

Gregory, Saint

Grisel

Griselda

Guido delle Colonne

Guillaume de Lorris

Guillaume de Machaut

Guy of Warwick

Haberdasher, the

Haly

Ham

Hannibal

Hasdrubal's wife

Hector

Hecuba

Helen, Saint

Helen of Troy

Heloise

Hercules

Heremianus

Hermengild

Hermes Ballenus (*See* BELINOUS)

Hermes Trismegistus

Hermione

Hero

Herse

Hippocrates

Hippolyta

Hippomedon

Hogge, Roger (*see* COOK)

Holofernes

Homer

Horaste

Host (*See* BAILLY, Harry)

Huberd

Hugh of Lincoln

Huwe, Sir

Hydra

Hymen

Hypermnestra

Hypsipyle

Iarbus

Ibn-Serabi (*See* SERAPION)

Icarus

Idleness

Innocent III, Pope

Iole

Isaac

Isaiah

Isidore of Seville

Isis

Isolde

Ives, Saint

Ixion

Jack Straw

James, Saint (1)

James of Compostella, Saint

Janicula

Jankin (1)

Jankin (2)

January

Janus

Jason

Jealousy

Jean de Meun

Jepthah

Jeremiah

Jerome, Saint

Jesus, son of Sirach

Jesus Christ

Joab

Job

John, Saint

John Chrysostom, Saint

John of Gaddesden

John the Baptist

John the Carpenter

John the Clerk

John the Friar

John the Monk

Jonah

Jonathan

Joseph

Joseph, Saint

Jovinian

Judas

Judas Maccabeus

Judith

Judocus, Saint

Julian, Saint

Julius Caesar

Julius Canius

Juno

Jupiter

Justinus

Juvenal

Kenelm, Saint

Knight, the (1)

Knight (2)

Knight (3)

Laban

Lachesis

Lady Philosophy

Lady White

Laius

Lamech

Lancelot

Laodamia

Laomedon

Latinus

Latona (*See* DIANA)

Latumeus

Lavinia

Lazar

Lazarus

Leander

Lemuel

Leonard, Saint

Lignano, Giovanni da

Limote

Livia

Livy

Lollius

Longinus

Lot

Lucan

Lucifer

Lucilia (Lucia)

Lucrece

Luke, Saint

Lybeaux, Sir

Lycurgus

Lyvia (*See* LIVIA)

Mabely

Macrobius

Madrian

Maeon

Malkyn (1)

Malkyn (2)

Manciple, the

Marcia (*See* MARSYAS)

Marcia Cato

Marcian (*See* MARTIANUS CAPELLA)

Mark, Saint

Mars (1)

Martianus Capella

Martin of Tours, Saint

Mary, Saint

Mary the Egyptian, Saint

Mary Magdalene, Saint

Masinissa

Matthew, Saint

Mauricius

Maurus, Saint

Maximus

May

Medea

Megaera (*See* ERINYES)

Meleager

Melibee

Menelaus

Merchant, the (1)

Merchant, the (2)

Merchant's Wife, the

Mercury (1)

Metellius

Micah

Midas

Miller, the

Minerva

Minos

Minotaur

Mirth

Misenus

Mnestheus

Mohammed

Monk

Mordecai

Morpheus

Moses

Myrrah

Narcissus

Nature, Dame

Nebuchadnezzar

Neot, Saint

Neptune

Nero

Nessus

Nicanor

Niceratus' wife

Nicholas

Nicholas, Saint

Nicholas of Lynn

Nimrod

Ninus

Niobe

Nisus

Noah

Nonius

Nothus

Nun's Priest

Octavian, Gaius Julius Caesar

Odenathus

Oedipus

Oenone

Old Age

Oliphaunt, Sir

Oliver

Opilio

Orion

Orpheus

Oswald (*See* REEVE, THE)

Oton de Grandson

Ovid

Palamon

Palinurus

Pallas

Pamphilus

Pan

Pandarus

Pandion

Papinian

Parcae

Pardoner, the

Paris (1)

Parmenides

Parson, the

Parthenopaeus

Pasiphae

Paul, Saint

Pedro of Castile

Pegasus

Pelias

Penelope

Peneus

Pepin

Perceval

Perkin Revelour

Perotheus

Perrers, Alice

Pertelote

Peter, Saint

Petrarch, Frances

Petrus Alphonse

Phaedra

Phaeton

Phanie

Pharaoh

Phebuseo

Phidon

Philip

Philippa of Hainault

Philoctetes

Philomela

Philostrate

Phitonissa

Phoebus (*See* APOLLO)

Phyllis

Pierides

Pierre de Lusignan

Piers, Daun

Placebo

Plato

Pleyndamour

Plowman, the

Pluto

Poliphete

Polixena

Pollux (*See* CASTOR)

Polydamus

Polyhymnia

Polymnestor

Polynices

Polyphemus

Pompey the Great

Portia

Priam

Priapus

Priest

Prioress, the

Procne

Proserpina

Protesilaus

Prudence

Pseustis

Ptolemy

Pygmalion

Pyramus

Pyrrhus

Pythagoras

Python

Quirinus

Rachel

Ralph (*See* RAUF)

Raphael

Rauf

Raven

Reason

Rebecca

Reeve, the

Regulus

Reynard

Rhazes

Rhodogune

Rifeo

Robyn (1)

Robyn (2)

Robyn (3)

Roland

Romulus

Ronyon

Rosemounde

Rufus

Russell

Samaritan

Samson

Samuel

Sarah

Sarpedon

Satan

Saturn

Scedasus

Scipio Africanus the Elder

Scipio Africanus the Younger

Scogan, Henry

Scot

Scriveyne, Adam (*See* ADAM SCRIVEYNE)

Scylla

Semiramus

Seneca

Serapion

Sergeant of the Law

Shame

Shapur

Shipman, the

Sibyl

Sichaeus

Simkin

Simkin's wife

Simon, Saint

Simon Magus

Simon the Pharisee

Simplicius Gallus (*See* GALLUS SIM-
PLICIUS)

Sinon

Sisyphus

Socrates

Solomon

Sophia

Soranas

Squire, the

Statius

Steward

Stilboun

Strode, Ralph

Stymphalis

Suetonius

Sultan of Syria

Sultaness of Syria

Summoner, the

Susanna

Sweet-Looking

Symmachus

Symond

Talbot

Tantalus

Tapestry-Maker

Tarquinus

Tarquinus the Younger

Telephus

tercel eagles

Tereus

Termagant

Tertullian

Teuta

Tharbe

Theodora

Theodoric

Theophrastus

Theseus

Thetis

Thiodamus

Thisbe

Thoas

Thomas (1)

Thomas (2)

Thomas à Becket, Saint

Thomas of India, Saint

Thopas, Sir

Thorus

Tiburtius

Timothy, Saint

Tiresias

Tisiphone (*See* ERINYES)

Titan

Titus

Tityus

Triguilla

Tristram

Triton

Troilus

Trophee

Trotula

Tubal (*See* AURORA)

Tullius Hostillius

Turnus

Tydeus

Tyler, Wat

Ugolino of Pisa

Ulysses

Urban

Vache

Valentine, Saint

Valeria

Valerian

Valerius

Venus

Vincent

Virgil

Virginia

Virginius

Visconti, Bernabo

Vulcan

Wade

Walter

Weaver, the

Wicked Tongue

Wife of Bath

Wilkin

William, King

Witelo

Xantippe (*See* SOCRATES)

Yeoman, the

Youth

Ypotis

Zechariah

Zenobia

Zeuxis

APPENDIX II

Places Mentioned in Chaucer

Achemenye

Aegina

Africa

Albion

Alcathoe

Aldgate

Alexandria

Apennines, the

Appian Way

Arabia

Aragon

Arcadia

Ardea

Argos

Armenia

Armorika

Arras

Artois

Asia

Athens

Ayash

Babylon

Bath

Bawdeswell

Belle, the

Belmarin

Berwick

Bethulia

Blee

Bobbe-up-and-down

Boghton under Blee

Bologna

Bordeaux

Boulogne

Britain

Brittany

Bromeholm

Bruges

Burgundy

Calydon

Cambridge

Campania

Cana

Canterbury

Cape Finisterre

Cartegena

Carthage

Catalonia

Caucasus

Chaldea

Cheapside

Cirra

Cithaeron, Mount (*See* Mount Cithaeron)

Colchis

Cologne

Corinth

Crete

Cyprus

Dardanus, yate (gate) of

Dartmouth

Delphi

Denmark

Deptford

Domus Dedaly

Dunmowe

Eltham

Elysium

Engelond

Essex

Euphrates

Euripus

Femenye

Ferrara

Fish Street

Flanders

Florence

France

Frisia

Galgopheye

Galicie

Galilee

Gaza

Ghent

Gibraltar

Gobi Desert

Gotland

Granada

Great Sea

Greece

Greenwich

Gysen

Hailes Abbey

Helicon, Mount

Hermus

Holdernesse

Horeb

House of Rumor

Hull

Ilion

India

Indus

Inns of Court

Israel

Italy

Jaconites

Jerusalem

Kara-Nor

Kayrudd

Kent

Lacedaemon

Lavinium

Lemnos

Lepe

Lethe

Libya

Lincoln

Lithuania

Lombardy

London

Lorraine

Lydia

Macedonia

Marmarica

Mediterranean Sea

Mercia

Messene

Middleburgh

Milan, Milayne

Milesie

Milky Way

Mount Cithaeron

Monte Viso

Morocco

Neritos, Mount

Newgate Prison

Ninevah

Norfolk

Northumberland

Occian

Oise

Orkneys

Orleans

Orwell

Osney

Oxford

Padua

Palathia

Palmyra

Panik

Paris (2)

Parnassus

Patmos

Pavia

Penmarch

Persia

Phlegethon

Picardy

Piedmont

Pisa

Po

Poets' Corner

Poperinghe

Portugal

Prussia

Ravenna

Red Sea

Rennes

Rhodope

Rochester

Rome

Rouncivale

Russia

Saint Paul's Cathedral

Saluzzo

Sarray

Scythia

Seine

Seint-Denys

Septe

Seyne

Sheen

Sheffield

Sicily

Simois

Sinai (*See* HOREB)

Sittingbourne

Soler Hall

Southwark

Spain

Stratford atte Bowe

Strother

Styx

Syria

Sytho, stream of

Tabard

Tagus

Tarsia

Tartary

Thebes

Thessaly

Thrace

Tiber

Tigris

Tlemcen

Troy

Trumpington

Tunis

Turkey

Tyre

Tyrene

Tzarev (*See* SARRAY)

Valence

Venice

Verona

Vesulus, Mount (*See* MONTE VISO)

Via Appia (*See* APPIAN WAY)

Vesuvius

Wallachia

Wales

Ware

Watling Street (*See* MILKY WAY)

Watering of St. Thomas

Yorkshire

Ypres

APPENDIX III

Chronology of Chaucer's Life with Significant Historical and Literary Events

1327–77
Reign of King Edward III

Early 1340s
Geoffrey Chaucer born in London, England, to John and Agnes Chaucer. John was a vintner (wine merchant) by profession.

1348–49
The Black Death (Bubonic Plague) ravages London.

1357
Around the age of 14, Geoffrey Chaucer becomes a page in the household of Elizabeth, countess of Ulster, and her husband Lionel, the second son of Edward III. This marks the beginning of his career as a courtier.

1359–60
Chaucer serves as a soldier in the retinue of Lionel at the siege of Reims (one of the battles of the Hundred Years' War between England and France). He is taken prisoner and released on ransom. He later returns to France to participate in peace negotiations.

1360
The Treaty of Brétigny establishes peace with France.

1361
Another outbreak of plague in London.

1360–65
Not much is known about Chaucer's life during this period. It is believed that he continued to serve in the household of Prince Lionel. Chaucer may also have studied law at the Inns of Court in preparation for his later service to the crown as a diplomat.

1365/6
Chaucer marries Philippa, daughter of Paon de Roet. Philippa serves in the household of Edward III's queen, also named Philippa. Chaucer may, at this point, be serving as an esquire in the household of Edward III.

1366
John Chaucer dies; Agnes remarries.

Feb.–May, 1366
Chaucer participates in a diplomatic mission to Spain.

Jan. 1367
Richard of Bordeaux, who later becomes Richard II, is born. He is the son of Edward the Black Prince, Edward III's first son.

June 1367
Chaucer granted an annuity of 20 marks as an esquire in the household of Edward III.

1367
Thomas Chaucer, the first son of Geoffrey and Philippa, is born. Chaucer makes two diplomatic journeys to Milan, Italy.

Late 1360s
Chaucer has begun his translation of the *Roman de la Rose.*

1368
Blanche, duchess of Lancaster (wife to John of Gaunt) dies. Chaucer writes *The Book of the Duchess* within one year of her death.

Aug. 1369
Queen Philippa dies.

1369
England's war with France resumes.

1370
Chaucer travels to the Continent, possibly on a diplomatic mission concerning the war with France.

1372
Philippa Chaucer receives an annuity of £10 from John of Gaunt, duke of Lancaster, the third son of Edward III.

Dec. 1372–May 1373
Chaucer travels to Genoa and Florence, Italy, to participate in trade negotiations and diplomatic corre-

spondence. His poetry will be heavily influenced by his encounters with the work of Italian writers such as Dante, Petrarch and Boccaccio.

1374

Edward III grants Chaucer a pitcher of wine a day for life and a lifetime lease, rent-free, for a house situated above Aldgate, one of the gates in London's city wall. This same year Chaucer is also appointed to the office of Controller of Customs (export taxes) on wools, hides and skins for the port of London, and receives a lifetime annuity of £10 from John of Gaunt.

June 1376

Edward the Black Prince, Edward III's heir, dies.

1376–77

Chaucer travels to France on several occasions, serving on commissions to negotiate for peace. A deputy is appointed to fulfill his duties in the customs.

June 1377

Edward III dies.

1377–99

Reign of King Richard II.

Late 1370s

Chaucer composes *Anelida and Arcite* (unfinished).

Mar.–Apr. 1378

King Richard confirms Chaucer's annuities and offices. The pitcher of wine a day is converted to an annuity of 20 marks.

May–Sept. 1378

Chaucer travels to Italy on diplomatic business. *The House of Fame* probably completed by this time.

May 1380

Chaucer released by Cecily Champaign from any legal action regarding her "raptus" (could mean "rape" or "abduction").

1380

Chaucer's son Lewis is born. *The Parliament of Fowls,* probably written for the occasion of King Richard's engagement to Anne of Bohemia, is completed during the year-long negotiations preceding the official engagement on May 3, 1381. Chaucer may also have been working on "Palamon and Arcite," which was to become "The Knight's Tale" of *The Canterbury Tales.*

June 1381

The Peasants' Revolt.

1381

Chaucer's mother, Agnes, dies.

Early 1380s

Chaucer probably begins working on *Troilus and Criseyde,* his longest single poem, in addition to embarking on his translation of Boethius' *Consolation of Philosophy.*

Jan. 1382

Richard II marries Anne of Bohemia.

1382

Chaucer is appointed Controller of Petty Customs on wine and other merchandise in the port of London, in addition to the position he already held as controller of wool, hides and skins.

1385

Chaucer is appointed justice of the peace in Kent and moves to Greenwich, southeast of London.

Oct. 1386

Chaucer testifies in the Scrope-Grosvenor trial, which incidentally provides us with information regarding his age.

Oct.–Nov. 1386

Chaucer elected Member of Parliament for Kent and serves at one session, the "Wonderful Parliament" where the political opposition launches its attempts to curb the king's power.

Oct.–Dec. 1386

Chaucer gives up his lease on the house over Aldgate and resigns from the customs. He has probably begun work on *The Legend of Good Women* and *The Canterbury Tales.*

1387

Philippa Chaucer dies.

1388

Some of Chaucer's friends and acquaintances are executed by order of the "Merciless Parliament" because of their partisan activities on behalf of King Richard, whose power is on the wane.

1389

Richard II declares himself independent of the protectorship and takes on the full powers of kingship. He appoints Chaucer as Clerk of the King's Works, an important administrative office.

1390

Chaucer is assigned a royal commission for the repair of walls and ditches after a flood. Twice this year he is robbed of public funds by highwaymen.

1391

Chaucer resigns from his post as Clerk of the King's Works. Chaucer writes the *Treatise on the Astrolabe* for his 11 year-old son Lewis, and continues working on *The Canterbury Tales.*

1394

Queen Anne dies. Chaucer is granted an annuity of £20 by King Richard.

1395/6

Chaucer is given a costly gown by Henry, earl of Derby, who will soon become King Henry IV.

1396

In the short poem, "Envoy to Bukton," Chaucer indicates a disparaging attitude toward marriage.

Dec. 1397

Chaucer receives a royal grant of a tun (a large cask) of wine per year.

Feb. 1399

John of Gaunt dies.

Sept. 1399

Richard II deposed; Henry IV succeeds him.

1399–1413

Reign of King Henry IV.

Dec. 1399

Chaucer takes a long-term lease on a house near Westminster Abbey in London. His poem "The Complaint of Chaucer to His Purse," addressed to Henry IV, suggests that his financial situation is not good. Within a short time, Henry IV renews payment of Chaucer's annuities, increasing them by 40 marks.

1400

Chaucer dies and is buried in Westminster Abbey. He is later moved to the portion of the abbey now known as Poets' Corner.

APPENDIX IV

List of Works by Chaucer

**Major Works
(in approximate chronological order;
exact dates of composition are,
in many cases, unknown):**

The Romaunt of the Rose

The Book of the Duchess

The House of Fame

Anelida and Arcite (unfinished)

The Parliament of Fowls

Boece

Troilus and Criseyde

The Legend of Good Women

A Treatise on the Astrolabe

The Canterbury Tales (listed in the order in which
they appear in the Ellesmere Manuscript)

The General Prologue

"The Knight's Tale"

"The Miller's Tale"

"The Reeve's Tale"

"The Cook's Tale"

"The Man of Law's Tale"

"The Wife of Bath's Tale"

"The Friar's Tale"

"The Summoner's Tale"

"The Clerk's Tale"

"The Merchant's Tale"

"The Squire's Tale"

"The Franklin's Tale"

"The Physician's Tale"

"The Pardoner's Tale"

"The Shipman's Tale"

"The Prioress' Tale"

"The Tale of Sir Thopas"

"The Tale of Melibee"

"The Monk's Tale"

"The Nun's Priest's Tale"

"The Second Nun's Tale"

"The Canon's Yeoman's Tale"

"The Manciple's Tale"

"The Parson's Tale"

Chaucer's Retraction

**The Short Poems
(in approximate chronological order):**

"An ABC"

"The Complaint unto Pity"

"A Complaint to His Lady"

"The Complaint of Mars"

"The Complaint of Venus"

"To Rosemounde"

"Womanly Noblesse"

"Chaucer's Words unto Adam, His Own Scriveyn"

"The Former Age"

"Fortune"

"Truth"

"Gentilesse"

"Lak of Stedfastnesse"

"Lenvoy de Chaucer à Scogan"

"Lenvoy de Chaucer à Bukton"

"The Complaint of Chaucer to His Purse"

"Proverbs"

Poems of Uncertain Authorship
(probably Chaucer's):

"Against Women Unconstant"

"Complaynt d'Amours"

"Merciless Beauty"

"A Balade of Complaint"

APPENDIX V

The Canterbury Highway

Although it is uncertain that Chaucer himself ever made the 56-mile pilgrimage to Canterbury, he would have been familiar with the route because of his departures from Dover (see map) en route to the European continent.

The General Prologue and the links among the individual stories within *The Canterbury Tales* allude to the passing of time and mention the pilgrims' approach to certain towns, suggesting that a single day passes as the pilgrims travel and tell their stories. It would in fact have been next to impossible to make the journey in one day (without galloping headlong on a horse), but would actually have taken three to five days one way. Some scholars, including J. S. P. Tatlock, Charles Owen and F. J. Furnivall, go into great detail listing the spe-cific route, alternative routes, distances between towns and the availability of overnight accommodations. The work of such scholars is fascinating and makes it quite easy for modern-day pilgrims to retrace the steps of Chaucer's group, but it also seems important to keep in mind that *The Canterbury Tales* is an unfinished story of a fictional journey. No one knows how many tales there would have been or what order they ultimately would have taken had Chaucer been able to finish and polish the work. Perhaps he was not so concerned with the actual timetable of the journey but was using the single-day idea to help unify his innovative framing device of the pilgrimage, which has often been seen as a metaphor for the journey of life, with its ultimate desti-nation the New Jerusalem.

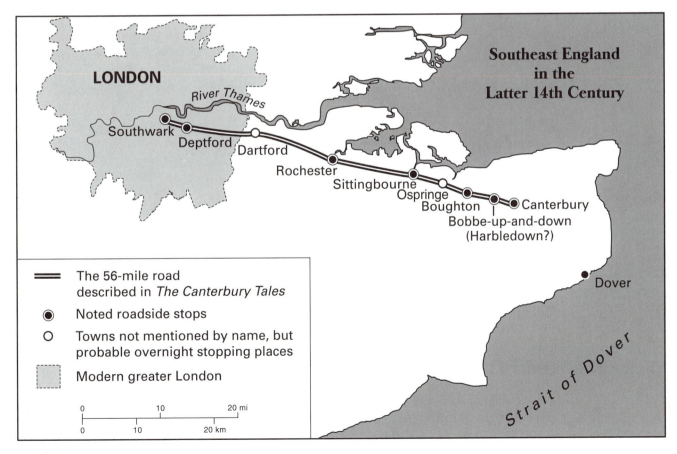

413

FOR FURTHER READING

The following bibliography is not meant to be complete in any sense. There are a number of books (yes, whole books!) devoted to cataloging what has been written by and about Chaucer over the last 500-plus years. The list presented here is intended primarily as a starting place for those who wish to pursue more in-depth study of the poet and his work. To limit potential reader frustration, I have only listed works that would be likely to appear in a well-stocked city or college library. Many of the works listed have their own bibliographies. *The Riverside Chaucer*, in addition to its other merits, features a selection of critical studies including works from the late 19th century up to 1987. Internet sources have also been listed. Regarding the following bibliographical entries, an asterisk preceding the author's name indicates the existence of a separate entry for that author.

Editions of the Complete Works
(*See also* EDITIONS OF CHAUCER'S WORK)

*Benson, Larry, ed. *The Riverside Chaucer*. Boston: Houghton Mifflin Co., 1987.

*Fisher, John H. *The Complete Poetry and Prose of Geoffrey Chaucer*. New York: Holt, Rinehart and Winston, 1989.

Dictionaries

De Weever, Jacqueline. *Chaucer Name Dictionary*. New York and London: Garland Publishing 1996.

*Davis, Norman, et al. *A Chaucer Glossary*. Oxford: Clarendon Press, 1979.

*Magoun, Francis P., Jr. *A Chaucer Gazeteer*. Chicago: University of Chicago Press, 1961.

Ross, Thomas. *Chaucer's Bawdy*. New York: E. P. Dutton, 1972.

Scott, A. F. *Who's Who in Chaucer*. New York: Taplinger Publishing, 1974.

*Tatlock, John S. P. and Arthur Kennedy. *Concordance to the Complete Works of Chaucer and to the "Romaunt of the Rose."* Gloucester, Mass: Peter Smith, 1963.

Translations and Adaptations

(Note: As of this writing, there are no available single translations of *The Book of the Duchess, The House of Fame,* or *The Parliament of Fowls.*)

The Canterbury Tales

Becker, Ronald and Eugene Crook, trans. *The Canterbury Tales Translated into Modern English*. Palatka, Fla.: Hodge and Braddock, 1993.

Coghill, Neville, trans. *The Canterbury Tales*. Harmondsworth, U.K.: Penguin Books, 1977.

Murphey, Michael, ed. *The Canterbury Tales: The General Prologue and Twelve Major Tales in Modern Spelling*. Lanham, Md.: University Presses of America, 1991.

Wright, David, trans. *The Canterbury Tales: A Verse Translation*. New York: Oxford University Press, 1985.

Collections

Morrison, Theodore, ed. and trans. *The Portable Chaucer*. New York: Viking, 1975.

*Tatlock, J. S. P. and Percy MacKaye, trans. and eds. *The Complete Poetical Works of Geoffrey Chaucer*. New York: Macmillan, 1940. (Note: This edition is so expurgated that the bawdy tales do not make much sense. I have included it here because it is one of the very few available texts to feature translations of *The House of Fame, The Book of the Duchess* and *The Parliament of Fowls.*)

Troilus and Criseyde

Coghill, Neville, trans. *Troilus and Criseyde*. Harmondsworth, U.K.: Penguin, 1971.

The Legend of Good Women

McMillan, Ann, trans. *The Legend of Good Women*. Houston: Rice University Press, 1987.

Adaptations for Children

Cohen, Barbara, trans. *The Canterbury Tales; Selected, Translated and Adapted by Barbara Cohen*. New York: Lothrop, Lee and Shepard Books, 1988.

Darton, F. J. Harvey. *The Story of the Canterbury Pilgrims, Retold from Chaucer and Others*. Philadelphia: J. B. Lippincott [n.d.].

Farjeon, Eleanor, trans. *Tales from Chaucer*. London: Oxford University Press, 1959.

Serraillier, Ian. *The Road to Canterbury: Tales from Chaucer, Retold by Ian Serraillier.* Harmondsworth, U.K.: Kestrel Books, 1979.

Biographical Works
(see also CHAUCER, BIOGRAPHIES OF)

*Brewer, Derek. *Chaucer.* 3rd Rev. Ed. London: Longman Press, 1973.

Chaucer Life Records. Edited by Martin M. Crow and Clair C. Olson. Oxford: Clarendon Press, 1966.

Gardner, John. *The Life and Times of Chaucer.* New York: Knopf, 1977.

*Howard, Donald. *Chaucer: His Life, His Works, His World.* New York: E. P. Dutton, 1987.

*Pearsall, Derek. *The Life of Geoffrey Chaucer.* Oxford: Blackwell, 1992.

General Studies

Aers, David. *Chaucer.* Brighton: Harvester Press, 1986.

*Bowden, Muriel. *A Reader's Guide to Geoffrey Chaucer.* New York: Farrar, Straus and Giroux, 1964.

*Brewer, Derek. *An Introduction to Chaucer.* London: Longman, 1984.

Coghill, Neville. *The Poet Chaucer.* 2nd ed. London: Oxford University Press, 1967.

Coulton, G. G. *Chaucer and His England.* London: Methuen and Co., 1963.

*Donaldson, E. Talbot. *Speaking of Chaucer.* Durham, N.C.: Labyrinth Press, 1983 [ca. 1977].

Halliday, F. E. *Chaucer and His World.* London: Thames and Hudson, 1968.

Howard, Edwin J. *Geoffrey Chaucer.* New York: Twayne, 1964.

Hussey, S. S. *Chaucer: An Introduction.* 2nd ed. London: Methuen, 1981.

Kane, George. *Chaucer.* New York: Oxford University Press, 1984.

*Kean, P. M. *Chaucer and the Making of English Poetry.* Abridged 1 vol. ed. London: Routledge and Kegan Paul, 1982.

*Kittredge, George Lyman. *Chaucer and His Poetry.* Cambridge, Mass.: Harvard University Press, 1915. Rpt., 1970.

Knight, Stephen. *Geoffrey Chaucer.* Oxford: Blackwell, 1986.

Lawlor, John. *Chaucer.* London: Hutchinson University Library, 1968.

Loomis, Roger Sherman. *A Mirror of Chaucer's World.* Princeton: Princeton University Press, 1965.

*Payne, Robert O. *The Key of Remembrance: A Study of Chaucer's Poetics.* New Haven: Yale University Press, 1963.

Robertson, D. W., Jr. *A Preface to Chaucer: Studies in Medieval Perspective.* Princeton: Princeton University Press, 1962.

*Rowland, Beryl, ed. *Companion to Chaucer Studies.* Rev. ed. New York: Oxford University Press, 1979.

Contemporary Social Conditions

Aers, David. *Chaucer, Langland, and the Creative Imagination.* London: Routledge and Kegan Paul, 1980.

Bennett, H. S. *Chaucer and the Fifteenth Century.* Oxford: Clarendon Press, 1947.

*Brewer, Derek. *Chaucer and His World.* New York: Dodd, Mead and Co., 1978.

Coulton, G. G. *Chaucer and His England.* 8th ed. London: Methuen and Col, 1963.

Hussey, Maurice. *Chaucer's World: A Pictorial Companion.* London: Cambridge University Press, 1967.

*Rickert, Edith, comp. *Chaucer's World.* Ed. Clair C. Olson and Martin M. Crow. New York: Columbia University Press, 1948.

Web Sites

Chaucerian Cookery—*http://www.labs.net/dmccormick/ccookery.htm* This web site features information on Chaucer's life and the food of his time, with recipes that correspond to his poetry.

Chaucernet—*http://dcwww.mediasvcs.smv.edu/chaucer/chaunet.index.html* This homepage serves as a forum for on-line discussions of Chaucer. It is intended for all who have an interest in Chaucer or questions about the poet and his works.

On-line Chaucer Bibliography—*http://galaxy.einet.net/hytelnet/FUL068.html* This web site currently includes materials from the Annotated Chaucer Bibliography published in *Studies in the Age of Chaucer* 15 (1993). *Studies in the Age of Chaucer* is the bulletin of the New Chaucer Society. The on-line bibliography will be expanded and updated to include all bibliographies published in the bulletin, covering the years 1975 forward.

On-line Medieval Texts: Chaucer—*http://www.english.udel.edu/bgastle/etexts.html* This web site features on-line texts of The Canterbury Tales, Book of the Duchess and Troilus and Criseyde.

Studies in the Age of Chaucer: The Yearbook of the New Chaucer Society—*http://ncs.rutgers.edu/sac.html* This home page provides excellent links to various Chaucer home pages, Chaucernet, Chaucer texts on-line, and additional general resources related to the poet and his work.

INDEX